W9-BLE-133

THE OXFORD-DUDEN PICTORIAL FRENCH-ENGLISH DICTIONARY

THE OXFORD-DUDEN PICTORIAL FRENCH-ENGLISH DICTIONARY

CLARENDON PRESS · OXFORD

Oxford University Press, Walton Street, Oxford OX2 6DP

Oxford New York Toronto
Delhi Bombay Calcutta Madras Karachi
Petaling Jaya Singapore Hong Kong Tokyo
Nairobi Dar es Salaam Cape Town
Melbourne Auckland

and associated companies in
Berlin Ibadan

Published in the United States
by Oxford University Press, New York

First published 1983
Reprinted 1984, 1986, 1988

Limp edition first published 1988

British Library Cataloguing in Publication Data

The Oxford-Duden pictorial French-English dictionary.
1. French language—Dictionaries—English
2. English language—Dictionaries—French
443'.21 PC2640
ISBN 0-19-864153-2
ISBN 0-19-869154-8 Limp

Library of Congress Cataloging in Publication Data

Main entry under title:

The Oxford-Duden pictorial French-English dictionary.
Includes index.
1. French language—Glossaries, vocabularies, etc.
2. English language—Glossaries, vocabularies, etc.
3. Picture dictionaries, French 4. Picture dictionaries, English. I. Moskowitz, Daniel
II. Pheby, John
PC2680.093 1983 443'.21 83-4262

ISBN 0-19-864153-2 (Oxford University Press)
ISBN 0-19-869154-8 Limp

French text edited by Daniel Moskowitz, with the assistance of Florence Herbulot, Ina Jacoub, Michel Jacoub, Andréas Kunert, Henri Moskowitz, Christian Nugue

English text edited by John Pheby, with the assistance of Roland Breitsprecher, Michael Clark, Judith Cunningham, Derek Jordan, and Werner Scholze-Stubenrecht

Illustrations by Jochen Schmidt
Printed in Hong Kong

Foreword

This French-English pictorial dictionary is based on the third, completely revised edition of the German *Bildwörterbuch* published as Volume 3 of the ten-volume *Duden* series of monolingual German dictionaries. The French text was produced by staff members at the École Supérieure d'Interprètes et de Traducteurs de l'Université de la Sorbonne Nouvelle (Paris III), with the assistance of various technical experts and numerous technicians and craftsmen in France. The English text was produced by the Oxford University Press Dictionary Department, with the assistance of numerous British companies, institutions, and technical experts.

There are certain kinds of information which can be conveyed more readily and clearly by pictures than by descriptions and explanations, and an illustration will support the simple translation by helping the reader to visualize the object denoted by a given word. This applies both to technical vocabulary sought by the layman and to everyday objects foreign to the general user.

Each double page contains a plate illustrating the vocabulary of a whole subject, together with the exact French names and their correct English equivalents. The arrangement of the text and the presence of alphabetical indexes in French and English allow the dictionary to be used either way: as a French-English or an English-French dictionary. This, together with the wide range of vocabulary, which includes a large proportion of specialized words and technical terms, makes the Oxford-Duden Pictorial Dictionary an indispensable supplement to any French-English or English-French dictionary.

Préface

Le dictionnaire en images français-anglais est établi à partir du Bildwörterbuch allemand, qui constitue le volume 3 de la collection Duden de dictionnaires allemands en 10 volumes. La version française a été établie par des enseignants de l'École Supérieure d'Interprètes et Traducteurs de l'Université de la Sorbonne Nouvelle (Paris III), avec la collaboration de quelques spécialistes et l'assistance de nombreux techniciens et artisans français. La version anglaise a été établie par le Département Lexicographique de l'Oxford University Press, avec la collaboration de nombreux experts et services de spécialistes anglais.

Des images transmettent certaines informations plus facilement et plus rapidement que des explications et descriptions. Une image permet souvent d'identifier bien plus facilement l'objet désigné par un mot donné qu'une définition de ce mot, aussi précise soit-elle.

Chaque double page comprend une planche illustrant le vocabulaire d'un domaine complet, avec les noms anglais précis et leurs équivalents français. L'articulation thématique évite la recherche fastidieuse des divers termes en fournissant sur une seule double page toute l'information relative à un domaine complet. La présentation du texte et la présence d'un index par langue permettent d'utiliser le présent dictionnaire comme dictionnaire anglais-français à double entrée.

Cette conception et le fait que le thésaurus comprend une forte proportion de termes spécialisés ou techniques font de ce dictionnaire le complément indispensable de tout dictionnaire anglais-français ou français-anglais.

Abbreviations used in the English text

Am.	American usage	*m.*	male (animal)
c.	castrated (animal)	*poet.*	poetic
coll.	colloquial	*sg.*	singular
f.	female (animal)	*sim.*	similar
form.	formerly	*y.*	young (animal)
joc.	jocular		

Abréviations utilisées dans le texte français

anal.	analogue	*f.*	féminin
égal.	également	*fam.*	familier
ELF	expression ou terme figurant dans un arrêté pris en application du décret n°72-19 du 7 janvier 1972 relatif à l'enrichissement de la langue française	*m.*	masculin
		var.	variétés

Table des matières

Les nombres arabes sont les numéros de planche

Contents

The arabic numerals are the numbers of the pictures

Table des matières

Table des matières

Contents

Table des matières

Contents

Table des matières

Contents

1-8 modèles *m* atomiques
– *atom models*
1 le modèle de l'atome *m* d'hydrogène *m* (H)
– *model of the hydrogen (H) atom*
2 le noyau atomique, un proton
– *atomic nucleus, a proton*
3 l'électron *m*
– *electron*
4 le spin de l'électron *m*
– *electron spin*
5 le modèle de l'atome *m* d'hélium *m* (He)
– *model of the helium (He) atom*
6 l'orbite *f* de l'électron *m*
– *electron shell*
7 le principe de Pauli
– *Pauli exclusion principle (exclusion principle, Pauli principle)*
8 les orbites *f* stationnaires de l'atome *m* de Na (atome de sodium *m*)
– *complete electron shell of the Na atom (sodium atom)*
9-14 structures *f* des molécules *f* (structures *f* cristallines)
– ***molecular structures** (lattice structures)*
9 le cristal de chlorure *m* de sodium *m*
– *crystal of sodium chloride (of common salt)*
10 l'ion *m* chlorure
– *chlorine ion*
11 l'ion *m* sodium
– *sodium ion*
12 le cristal de cristobalite *f*
– *crystal of cristobalite*
13 l'atome *m* d'oxygène *m*
– *oxygen atom*
14 l'atome *m* de silicium *m*
– *silicon atom*
15 les niveaux *m* d'énergie *f* (sauts *m* quantiques possibles) de l'atome *m* d'hydrogène *m*
– ***energy levels** (possible quantum jumps) of the hydrogen atom*
16 le noyau atomique (le proton)
– *atomic nucleus (proton)*
17 l'électron *m*
– *electron*
18 l'état *m* fondamental
– *ground state level*
19 l'état *m* excité
– *excited state*
20-25 les sauts *m* quantiques
– *quantum jumps* *(quantum transitions)*
20 la série de Lyman
– *Lyman series*
21 la série de Balmer
– *Balmer series*
22 la série de Paschen
– *Paschen series*
23 la série de Brackett
– *Brackett series*
24 la série de Pfund
– *Pfund series*
25 l'électron *m* libre
– *free electron*
26 le modèle atomique de Bohr-Sommerfeld de l'atome *m* d'H
– *Bohr-Sommerfeld model of the H atom*
27 les niveaux *m* énergétiques de l'électron *m*
– *energy levels of the electron*
28 la désintégration spontanée d'une matière radioactive
– ***spontaneous decay** of radioactive material*
29 le noyau atomique
– *atomic nucleus*
30-31 le rayonnement alpha (α, la particule alpha, le noyau d'hélium *m*)
– *alpha particle (α, alpha radiation, helium nucleus)*
30 le neutron
– *neutron*
31 le proton
– *proton*
32 le rayonnement béta (β, la particule béta, l'électron *m*)
– *beta particle (β, beta radiation, electron)*
33 le rayonnement gamma (γ, un rayonnement Roentgen dur)
– *gamma radiation (γ, a hard X-radiation)*
34 la fission nucléaire
– *nuclear fission*
35 le noyau atomique lourd
– *heavy atomic nucleus*
36 le bombardement neutronique
– *neutron bombardment*
37-38 les fragments *m* de fission *f*
– *fission fragments*
39 le neutron libéré
– *released neutron*
40 le rayonnement gamma (γ)
– *gamma radiation (γ)*
41 la réaction en chaîne *f*
– *chain reaction*
42 le neutron qui désintègre le noyau
– *incident neutron*
43 le noyau avant la fission
– *nucleus prior to fission*
44 le fragment de fission *f*
– *fission fragment*
45 le neutron libéré
– *released neutron*
46 la nouvelle fission nucléaire
– *repeated fission*
47 le fragment de fission *f*
– *fission fragment*
48 la réaction en chaîne *f* contrôlée dans un réacteur atomique
– *controlled chain reaction in a nuclear reactor*
49 le noyau atomique d'un élément fissile
– *atomic nucleus of a fissionable element*
50 le bombardement par un neutron
– *neutron bombardment*
51 le fragment de fission *f* (le nouveau noyau atomique)
– *fission fragment (new atomic nucleus)*
52 le neutron libéré
– *released neutron*
53 les neutrons *m* absorbés
– *absorbed neutrons*
54 le modérateur, une couche de ralentissement *m* en graphite *m*
– *moderator, a retarding layer of graphite*
55 la dissipation de chaleur *f* (la production d'énergie *f*)
– *extraction of heat (production of energy)*
56 le rayonnement Roentgen (les rayons X)
– *X-radiation*
57 le caisson de réacteur *m* en béton *m* et plomb *m*
– *concrete and lead shield*
58 la chambre à bulles *f* pour visualisation *f* des trajectoires *f* de particules *f* ionisantes à haute énergie *f*
– ***bubble chamber** for showing the tracks of high-energy ionizing particles*
59 la source lumineuse
– *light source*
60 l'appareil *m* photographique
– *camera*
61 le réservoir d'expansion *f*
– *expansion line*
62 la marche des rayons *m* lumineux
– *path of light rays*
63 l'électro-aimant *m*
– *magnet*
64 l'entrée *f* du rayonnement *m*
– *beam entry point*
65 le miroir
– *reflector*
66 la chambre
– *chamber*

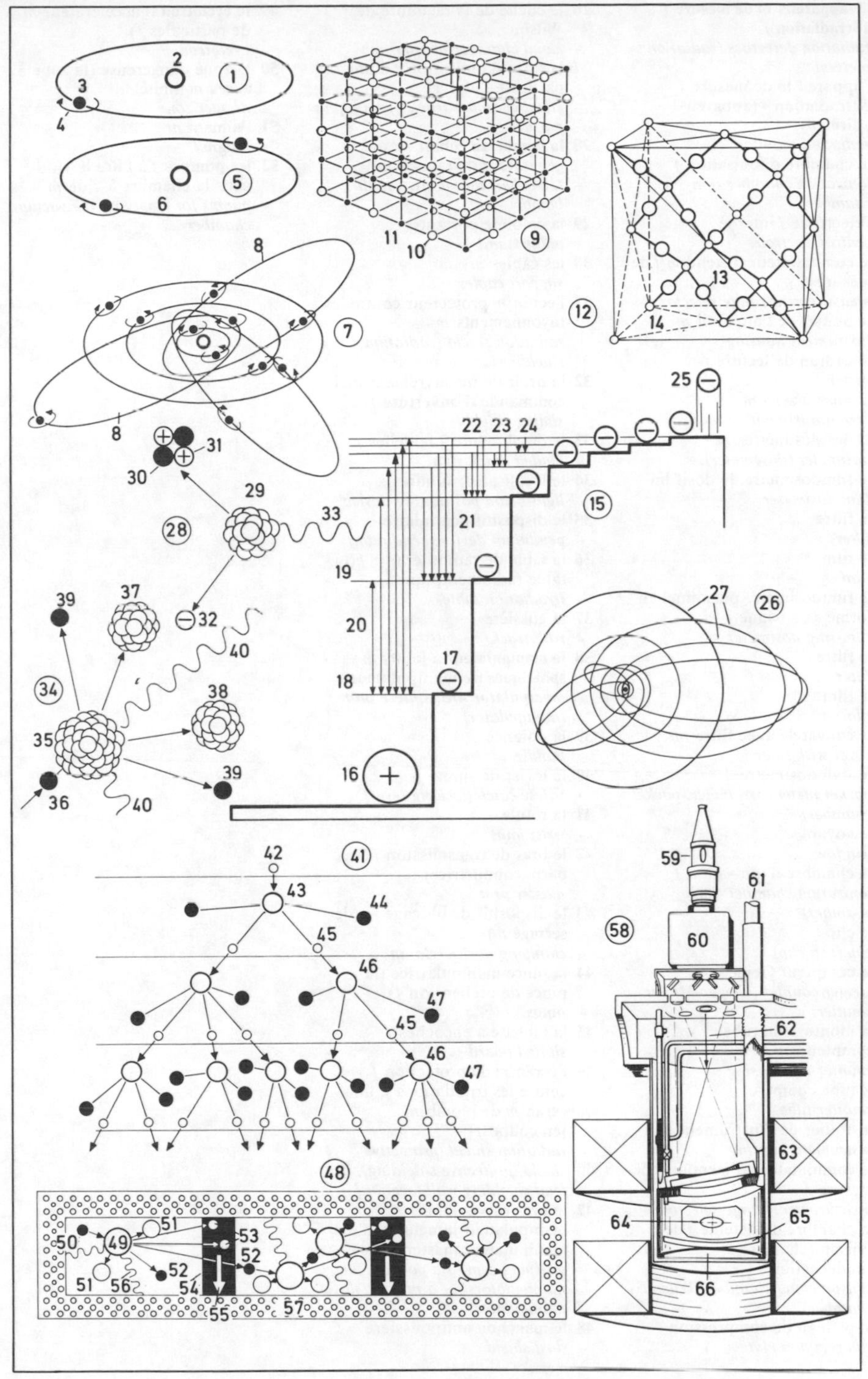
1
2
3
4
5
6
7
8
9
10
11
12
13
14
15
16
17
18
19
20
21
22
23
24
25
26
27
28
29
30
31
32
33
34
35
36
37
38
39
40
41
42
43
44
45
46
47
48
49
50
51
52
53
54
55
56
57
58
59
60
61
62
63
64
65
66

1-23 appareils *m* **de mesure** *f* **d'irradiation** *f*
– ***radiation detectors*** *(radiation meters)*
1 l'appareil *m* de mesure *f* d'irradiation *f* (appareil «direct»)
– *radiation monitor*
2 la chambre d'ionisation *f*
– *ionization chamber (ion chamber)*
3 l'électrode *f* interne
– *central electrode*
4 le commutateur d'étendue *f* de mesure *f*
– *measurement range selector*
5 le boîtier de l'appareil *m*
– *instrument housing*
6 le cadran de lecture *f*
– *meter*
7 la mise à zéro *m*
– *zero adjustment*
8-23 les dosimètres *m*
– *dosimeter (dosemeter)*
8 le filmdosimètre, le dosifilm
– *film dosimeter*
9 le filtre
– *filter*
10 le film
– *film*
11 le filmdosimètre personnel en forme *f* de bague *f*
– *film-ring dosimeter*
12 le filtre
– *filter*
13 le film
– *film*
14 le couvercle avec filtre *m*
– *cover with filter*
15 le stylodosimètre
– *pocket meter (pen meter, pocket chamber)*
16 le voyant
– *window*
17 la chambre d'ionisation *f*
– *ionization chamber (ion chamber)*
18 le clip
– *clip (pen clip)*
19 le compteur Geiger
– *Geiger counter (Geiger-Müller counter)*
20 la monture du tube compteur *m*
– *counter tube casing*
21 le tube compteur
– *counter tube*
22 le boîtier de l'instrument *m*
– *instrument housing*
23 le commutateur d'étendue *f* de mesure *f*
– *measurement range selector*
24 la chambre de détente *f* de Wilson (chambre à condensation *f*)
– *Wilson cloud chamber (Wilson chamber)*
25 le plateau de compression *f*
– *compression plate*
26 le cliché de la chambre de Wilson
– *cloud chamber photograph*
27 la trace d'ionisation *f* d'une particule *f* alpha
– *cloud chamber track of an alpha particle*
28 la bombe au cobalt *m*, un générateur de rayons *m*
– ***telecobalt unit*** (coll. *cobalt bomb)*
29 la colonne portante
– *pillar stand*
30 les câbles *m*
– *support cables*
31 l'écran *m* protecteur contre les rayonnements *m*
– *radiation shield (radiation shielding)*
32 le tiroir de recouvrement *m*, la commande d'ouverture *f*
– *sliding shield*
33 le diaphragme à lamelles *f*
– *bladed diaphragm*
34 le localisateur lumineux
– *light-beam positioning device*
35 le dispositif pendulaire
– *pendulum device (pendulum)*
36 la table de radiothérapie *f* (la table radiothérapique)
– *irradiation table*
37 la glissière
– *rail (track)*
38 le manipulateur à joints *m* **sphériques** (le manipulateur)
– ***manipulator with sphere unit*** *(manipulator)*
39 la poignée
– *handle*
40 le levier de sûreté *f*
– *safety catch (locking lever)*
41 la rotule
– *wrist joint*
42 le bras de transmission *f* (la barre conductrice)
– *master arm*
43 le dispositif de blocage *m* (de serrage *m*)
– *clamping device (clamp)*
44 la pince manipulatrice (la pince de préhension *f*)
– *tongs*
45 la tablette à encoches *f*
– *slotted board*
46 l'écran *m* de protection *f* contre les irradiations *f*, un écran *m* de plomb *m* [en coupe *f*]
– *radiation shield (protective shield, protective shielding), a lead shielding wall [section]*
47 le bras-robot d'un manipulateur jumelé *m* (d'un manipulateur master-slave)
– *grasping arm of a pair of manipulators (of a master/slave manipulator)*
48 le manchon antipoussière
– *dust shield*
49 le cyclotron (l'accélérateur *m* de particules *f*)
– ***cyclotron***
50 la zone dangereuse (la zone à accès *m* limité)
– *danger zone*
51 l'aimant *m*
– *magnet*
52 les pompes *f* à faire le vide dans la chambre à vide *m*
– *pumps for emptying the vacuum chamber*

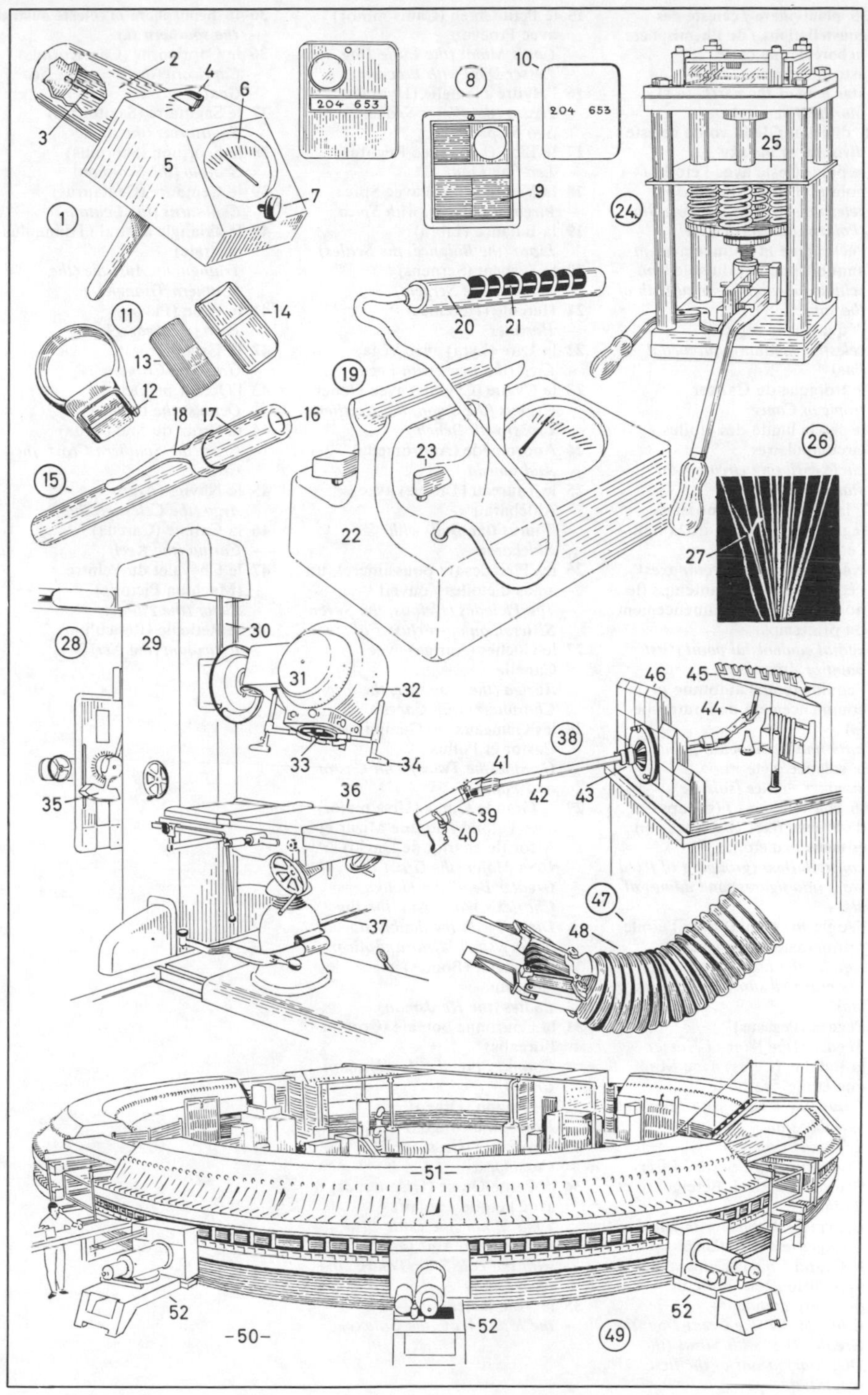
1
2
3
4
5
6
7
204 653
8
10.
204 653
9
11
12
13
14
15
16
17
18
19
20
21
22
23
24
25
26
27
28
29
30
31
32
33
34
35
36
37
38
39
40
41
42
43
44
45
46
47
48
49
50
51
52
52
52

1-35 planisphère *f* céleste des constellations *f* de l'hémisphère *m* boréal, une carte astronomique
– ***star map of the northern sky*** *(northern hemisphere)*
1-8 division *f* de la voûte céleste
– *divisions of the sky*
1 le pôle céleste avec l'étoile *f* polaire (l'étoile du nord *m*)
– *celestial pole with the Pole Star (Polaris, the North Star)*
2 l'écliptique *m* (mouvement *m* annuel apparent du soleil *m*)
– *ecliptic (apparent annual path of the sun)*
3 l'équateur *m* céleste
– *celestial equator (equinoctial line)*
4 le tropique du Cancer
– *tropic of Cancer*
5 le cercle limite des étoiles *f* circumpolaires
– *circle enclosing circumpolar stars*
6-7 les points *m* équinoxiaux (égalité *f* du jour et de la nuit, l'équinoxe *m*)
– *equinoctial points (equinoxes)*
6 l'équinoxe *m* du printemps (le point vernal, le commencement du printemps)
– *vernal equinoctial point (first point of Aries)*
7 l'équinoxe *m* d'automne *m* (le commencement de l'automne *m*)
– *autumnal equinoctial point*
8 le solstice d'été *m*
– *summer solstice (solstice)*
9-48 constellations *f* (groupes *m* d'étoiles *f* fixes et d'astres *m*) **et noms** *m* d'étoiles *f*
– ***constellations*** *(grouping of fixed stars into figures)* ***and names of stars***
9 l'Aigle *m* (Aquila) avec l'étoile *f* principale Altaïr (Atair)
– *Aquila (the Eagle) with Altair the principal star (the brightest star)*
10 Pégase (Pegasus)
– *Pegasus (the Winged Horse)*
11 la Baleine (Cetus) avec Mira, une étoile *f* variable
– *Cetus (the Whale) with Mira, a variable star*
12 Eridan (Eridanus)
– *Eridamus (the Celestial River)*
13 Orion avec Rigel, Bételgeuse et Bellatrix
– *Orion (the Hunter) with Rigel, Betelgeuse and Bellatrix*
14 le Grand Chien (Canis major) avec Sirius, une étoile de première grandeur
– *Canis Major (the Great Dog, the Greater Dog) with Sirius (the Dog Star), a star of the first magnitude*
15 le Petit Chien (Canis minor) avec Procyon
– *Canis Minor (the Little Dog, the Lesser Dog) with Procyon*
16 l'Hydre *f* femelle (Hydra)
– *Hydra (the Water Snake, the Sea Serpent)*
17 le Lion (Leo) avec Regulus
– *Leo (the Lion)*
18 la Vierge (Virgo) avec Spica
– *Virgo (the Virgin) with Spica*
19 la Balance (Libra)
– *Libra (the Balance, the Scales)*
20 le Serpent (Serpens)
– *Serpens (the Serpent)*
21 Hercule (Hercules)
– *Hercules*
22 la Lyre (Lyra) avec Véga
– *Lyra (the Lyre) with Vega*
23 le Cygne (Cygnus) avec Deneb
– *Cygnus (the Swan, the Northern Cross) with Deneb*
24 Andromède (Andromeda)
– *Andromeda*
25 le Taureau (Taurus) avec Aldébaran
– *Taurus (the Bull) with Aldebaran*
26 les Pléiades (la poussinière), un amas d'étoiles *f* ouvert
– *The Pleiades (Pleiads, the Seven Sisters), an open cluster of stars*
27 le Cocher (Auriga) avec Capella
– *Auriga (the Wagoner, the Charioteer) with Capella*
28 les Gémeaux *m* (Gemini) avec Castor et Pollux
– *Gemini (the Twins) with Castor and Pollux*
29 la Grande Ourse (Ursa major) avec l'étoile *f* double Mizar et Alcor (le chariot de David)
– *Ursa Major (the Great Bear, the Greater Bear, the Plough, Charles's Wain,* Am. *the Big Dipper) with the double star (binary star) Mizar and Alcor*
30 le Bouvier (Boötes) avec Arcturus
– *Boötes (the Herdsman)*
31 la Couronne boréale (Corona Borealis)
– *Corona Borealis (the Northern Crown)*
32 le Dragon (Drago)
– *Draco (the Dragon)*
33 Cassiopée (Cassiopeia)
– *Cassiopeia*
34 la Petite Ourse (Ursa minor) avec l'étoile *f* polaire
– *Ursa Minor (the Little Bear, Lesser Bear,* Am. *Little Dipper) with the Pole Star (Polaris, the North Star)*
35 la Voie lactée
– *the Milky Way (the Galaxy)*
36-48 hémisphère *m* **céleste austral**
– ***the southern sky***
36 le Capricorne (Capricornus)
– *Capricorn (the Goat, the Sea Goat)*
37 le Sagittaire (Sagittarius)
– *Sagittarius (the Archer)*
38 le Scorpion (Scorpius)
– *Scorpio (the Scorpion)*
39 le Centaure (Centaurus)
– *Centaurus (the Centaur)*
40 le Triangle austral (Triangulus australe)
– *Triangulum Australe (the Southern Triangle)*
41 le Paon (Pavo)
– *Pavo (the Peacock)*
42 la Grue (Grus)
– *Grus (the Crane)*
43 l'Octant *m* (Octans)
– *Octans (the Octant)*
44 la Croix du Sud (Crux)
– *Crux (the Southern Cross, the Cross)*
45 le Navire (Argo)
– *Argo (the Celestial Ship)*
46 la Carène (Carena)
– *Carina (the Keel)*
47 le Chevalet du Peintre (Machina Pictoris)
– *Pictor (the Painter)*
48 le Réticule (Reticulum)
– *Reticulum (the Net)*

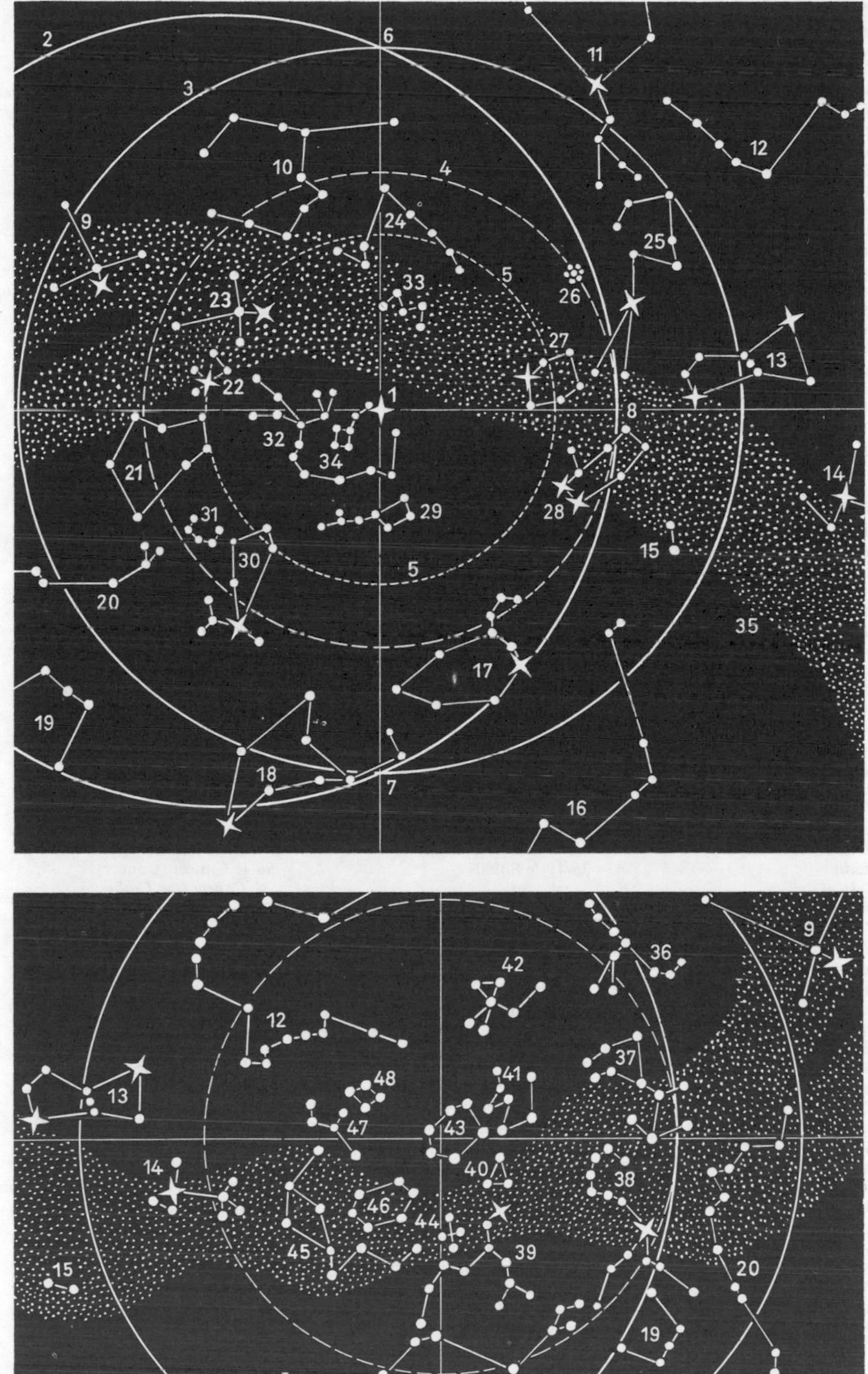
2
6
3
11
12
10
4
9
24
25
5
33
26
23
27
13
22
1
8
32
34
21
14
28
29
31
15
30
5
20
35
17
19
18
7
16
9
36
42
12
37
41
48
13
47
43
14
40
38
46
44
45
39
15
20
19

1-9 la Lune
– *the moon*
1 l'orbite *f* lunaire (la révolution de la lune autour de la terre)
– *moon's path (moon's orbit round the earth)*
2-7 les phases *f* de la Lune
– *lunar phases (moon's phases, lunation)*
2 la nouvelle Lune
– *new moon*
3 le croissant de Lune *f* (la Lune croissante)
– *crescent (crescent moon, waxing moon)*
4 le premier quartier
– *half-moon (first quarter)*
5 la pleine Lune
– *full moon*
6 le dernier quartier
– *half-moon (last quarter, third quarter)*
7 le croissant de Lune *f* (la Lune décroissante)
– *crescent (crescent moon, waning moon)*
8 la Terre (le globe terrestre)
– *the earth (terrestrial globe)*
9 la direction des rayons *m* solaires
– *direction of the sun's rays*
10-21 le mouvement apparent du Soleil au début des saisons *f*
– *apparent path of the sun at the beginning of the seasons*
10 l'axe *m* du monde (la ligne des pôles *m*)
– *celestial axis*
11 le Zénith
– *zenith*
12 l'horizon *m*
– *horizontal plane*
13 le nadir
– *nadir*
14 l'est *m*
– *east point*
15 l'ouest *m*
– *west point*
16 le nord
– *north point*
17 le sud
– *south point*
18 le mouvement apparent du Soleil le 21 décembre *m*
– *apparent path of the sun on 21 December*
19 le mouvement apparent du Soleil le 21 mars *m* et le 23 septembre *m*
– *apparent path of the sun on 21 March and 23 September*
20 le mouvement apparent du Soleil le 21 juin *m*
– *apparent path of the sun on 21 June*
21 la zone limite du crépuscule
– *border of the twilight area*
22-28 les mouvements *m* de rotation *f* de l'axe *m* de la Terre
– *rotary motions of the earth's axis*
22 l'axe *m* de l'écliptique *m*
– *axis of the ecliptic*
23 la sphère céleste
– *celestial sphere*
24 l'orbite *f* du pôle *m* céleste (précession *f* et nutation *f*)
– *path of the celestial pole (precession and nutation)*
25 l'axe *m* instantané de rotation *f*
– *instantaneous axis of rotation*
26 le pôle céleste
– *celestial pole*
27 l'axe *m* moyen de rotation *f*
– *mean axis of rotation*
28 la polhodie
– *polhode*
29-35 l'éclipse *f* de Soleil *m* et l'éclipse *f* de Lune *f* [échelle *f* non respectée]
– *solar and lunar eclipse [not to scale]*
29 le Soleil
– *the sun*
30 la Terre
– *the earth*
31 la Lune
– *the moon*
32 l'éclipse *f* de Soleil *m*
– *solar eclipse*
33 l'éclipse *f* totale
– *area of the earth in which the eclipse appears total*
34-35 l'éclipse *f* de Lune *f*
– *lunar eclipse*
34 la pénombre
– *penumbra (partial shadow)*
35 l'ombre *f*
– *umbra (total shadow)*
36-41 le Soleil
– *the sun*
36 le disque solaire
– *solar disc (disk) (solar globe, solar sphere)*
37 les taches *f* solaires
– *sunspots*
38 tourbillons *m* au voisinage des taches *f* solaires
– *cyclones in the area of sunspots*
39 la couronne solaire observable lors d'une éclipse totale de Soleil *m* ou avec des instruments *m* spéciaux
– *corona (solar corona), observable during total solar eclipse or by means of special instruments*
40 les protubérances *f*
– *prominences (solar prominences)*
41 le bord du disque lunaire lors d'une éclipse totale de Soleil *m*
– *moon's limb during a total solar eclipse*
42-52 les planètes *f* (le système planétaire, le système solaire) [échelle non respectée] et les symboles *m* des planètes *f*
– *planets (planetary system, solar system) [not to scale] and planet symbols*
42 le Soleil
– *the sun*
43 Mercure
– *Mercury*
44 Vénus
– *Venus*
45 la Terre et la Lune, un satellite
– *Earth, with the moon, a satellite*
46 Mars avec deux satellites *m*
– *Mars, with two moons (satellites)*
47 les astéroïdes *m*
– *asteroids (minor planets)*
48 Jupiter avec 14 satellites *m*
– *Jupiter, with 14 moons (satellites)*
49 Saturne avec 10 satellites *m*
– *Saturn, with 10 moons (satellites)*
50 Uranus avec cinq satellites *m*
– *Uranus, with five moons (satellites)*
51 Neptune avec deux satellites *m*
– *Neptune, with two moons (satellites)*
52 Pluton
– *Pluto*
53-64 les signes *m* du Zodiaque
– *signs of the zodiac (zodiacal signs)*
53 le Bélier (Aries)
– *Aries (the Ram)*
54 le Taureau (Taurus)
– *Taurus (the Bull)*
55 les Gémeaux *m* (Gemini)
– *Gemini (the Twins)*
56 le Cancer (Cancer)
– *Cancer (the Crab)*
57 le Lion (Leo)
– *Leo (the Lion)*
58 la Vierge (Virgo)
– *Virgo (the Virgin)*
59 la Balance (Libra)
– *Libra (the Balance, the Scales)*
60 le Scorpion (Scorpius)
– *Scorpio (the Scorpion)*
61 le Sagittaire (Sagittarius)
– *Sagittarius (the Archer)*
62 le Capricorne (Capricornus)
– *Capricorn (the Goat, the Sea Goat)*
63 le Verseau (Aquarius)
– *Aquarius (the Water Carrier, the Water Bearer)*
64 les Poissons *m* (Pisces)
– *Pisces (the Fish)*

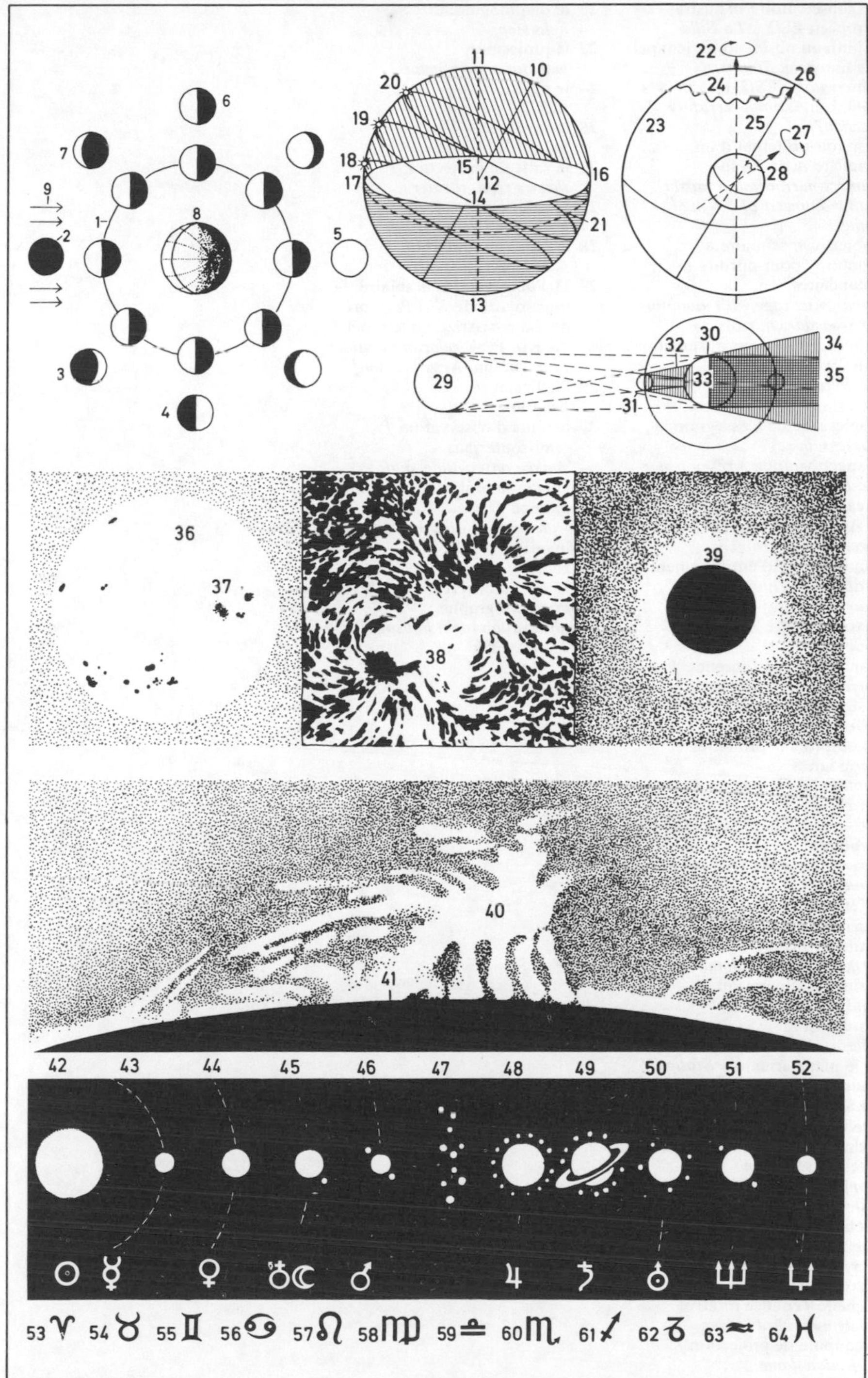
1
2
3
4
5
6
7
8
9
10
11
12
13
14
15
16
17
18
19
20
21
22
23
24
25
26
27
28
29
30
31
32
33
34
35
36
37
38
39
40
41
42
43
44
45
46
47
48
49
50
51
52
53 ♈
54 ♉
55 ♊
56 ♋
57 ♌
58 ♍
59 ♎
60 ♏
61 ♐
62 ♑
63 ♒
64 ♓

1-16 l'observatoire *m* austral européen ESO à *La Silla* (Chili), un observatoire [coupe]
- *the European Southern Observatory (ESO) on* Cerro la Silla, Chile, *an observatory [section]*

1 le miroir principal d'un diamètre *m* de 3,6 m
- *primary mirror (main mirror) with a diameter of 3.6 m (144 inches)*

2 l'objectif *m* primaire avec monture *f* pour miroirs *m* secondaires
- *prime focus cage with mounting for secondary mirrors*

3 le miroir plan pour observation *f* en foyer *m* coudé
- *flat mirror for the coudé ray path*

4 le télescope de Cassegrain
- *Cassegrain cage*

5 le spectrographe à réseau *m*
- *grating spectrograph*

6 la caméra électronique (d'André Lallemand)
- *spectrographic camera*

7 le mécanisme d'entraînement *m* de l'axe *m* horaire
- *hour axis drive*

8 l'axe *m* horaire
- *hour axis*

9 la monture «en fourche» *f*
- *horseshoe mounting*

10 le support hydraulique
- *hydrostatic bearing*

11 les objectifs *m* primaires et secondaires
- *primary and secondary focusing devices*

12 le toit en coupole *f* (la coupole pivotante)
- *observatory dome (revolving dome)*

13 la fente d'observation *f*
- *observation opening*

14 la trappe mobile
- *vertically movable dome shutter*

15 le rideau, le paravent
- *wind screen*

16 le sidérostat
- *siderostat*

17-28 le planétarium de *Stuttgart* [coupe *f*]
- *the* Stuttgart *Planetarium [section]*

17 l'administration *f*, les ateliers *m* et les entrepôts *m*
- *administration, workshop, and store area*

18 la charpente métallique
- *steel scaffold*

19 la pyramide de verre *m*
- *glass pyramid*

20 l'échelle *f* coudée rotative
- *revolving arched ladder*

21 la coupole de projection *f*
- *projection dome*

22 le diaphragme
- *light stop*

23 le projecteur
- *planetarium projector*

24 le puits
- *well*

25 le foyer
- *foyer*

26 la salle de projection *f*
- *theatre* (Am. *theater)*

27 la cabine de projection *f*
- *projection booth*

28 le pilier de fondation *f*
- *foundation pile*

29-33 l'observatoire *m* solaire, la tour solaire de *Kitt Peak* près de *Tucson* (Arizona) [coupe]
- *the* Kitt Peak *solar observatory near* Tucson, Ariz. *[section]*

29 l'héliostat *m*
- *heliostat*

30 le puits d'observation *f* semi-souterrain
- *sunken observation shaft*

31 l'écran *m* protecteur refroidi par eau *f*
- *water-cooled windshield*

32 le miroir concave
- *concave mirror*

33 la salle d'observation *f* abritant le spectrographe
- *observation room housing the spectrograph*

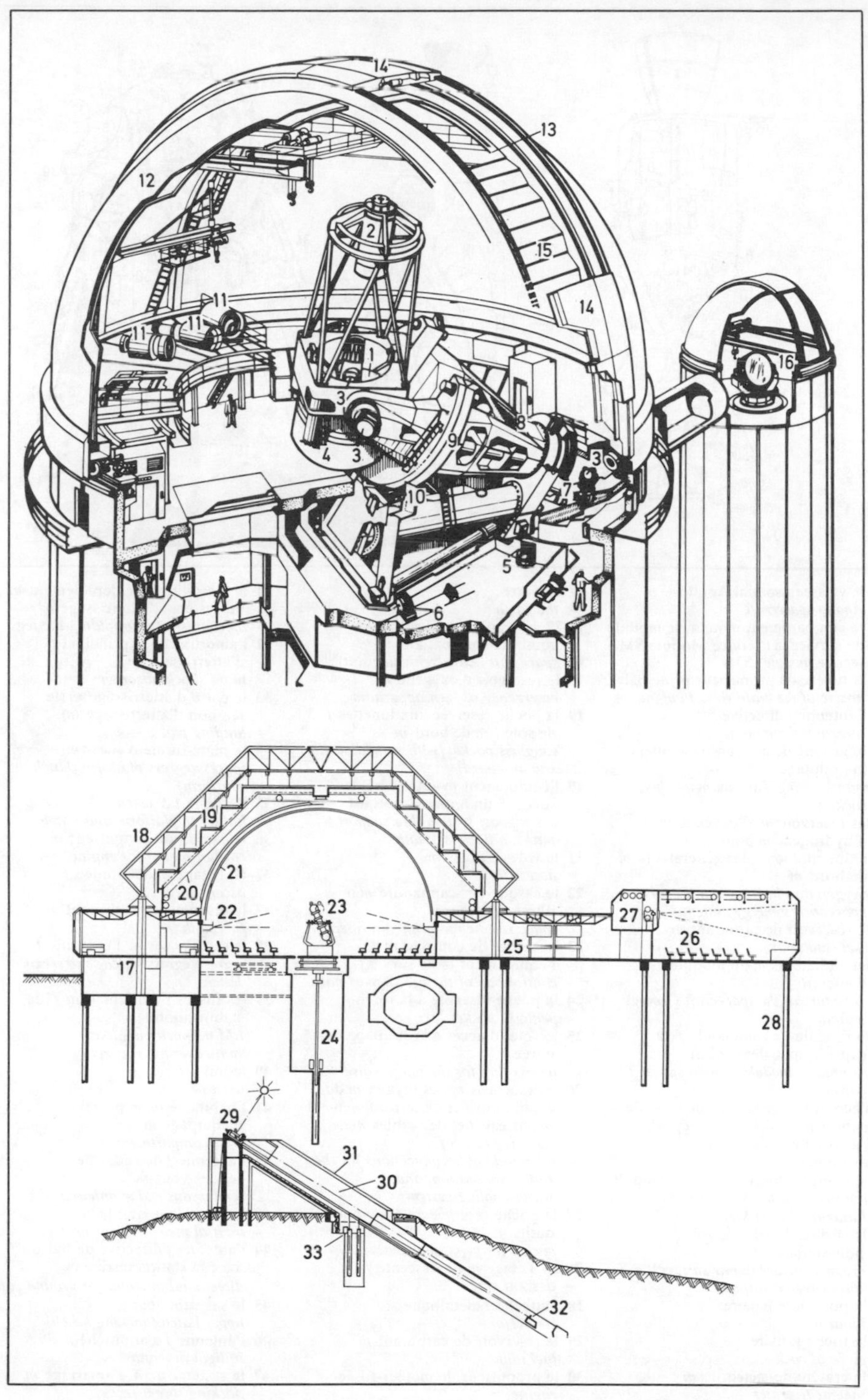
14
13
12
2
15
11
11
11
14
16
1
3
8
9
4
3
3
7
10
5
6
19
18
21
20
22
23
27
26
25
17
24
28
29
31
30
33
32

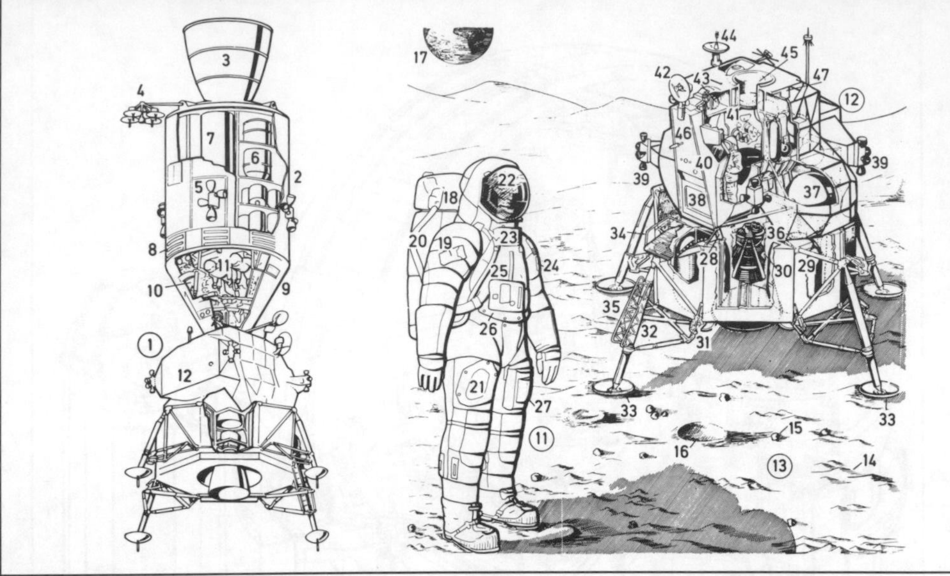

1 le vaisseau spatial Apollo
– *Apollo spacecraft*

2 le compartiment moteur, le module de service *m* (Service Module SM)
– *service module (SM)*

3 la tuyère du propulseur principal
– *nozzle of the main rocket engine*

4 l'antenne *f* directive
– *directional antenna*

5 le groupe de moteurs *m* verniers (de pilotage *m*)
– *manoeuvring* (Am. *maneuvering) rockets*

6 les réservoirs *m* d'oxygène *m* et d'hydrogène *m* pour l'alimentation *f* des générateurs *m* de bord *m*
– *oxygen and hydrogen tanks for the spacecraft's energy system*

7 le réservoir de carburant *m*
– *fuel tank*

8 les radiateurs *m* du module d'énergie *f*
– *radiators of the spacecraft's energy system*

9 le module de commande *f* (la capsule spatiale Apollo)
– *command module (Apollo space capsule)*

10 l'écoutille *f* de la capsule spatiale
– *entry hatch of the space capsule*

11 l'astronaute *m*
– *astronaut*

12 le compartiment lunaire, le module lunaire (Lunar Module LM)
– *lunar module (LM)*

13 la surface lunaire, le sol poussiéreux
– *moon's surface (lunar surface), a dust-covered surface*

14 la poussière lunaire
– *lunar dust*

15 la roche lunaire
– *piece of rock*

16 le cratère de météorite *m*
– *meteorite crater*

17 la Terre
– *the earth*

18-27 le scaphandre spatial, la combinaison spatiale
– *space suit (extra-vehicular suit)*

18 le réservoir d'oxygène *m*
– *emergency oxygen apparatus*

19 la poche réservée aux lunettes *f* de soleil *m* de bord *m*
– *sunglass pocket [with sunglasses for use on board]*

20 l'équipement *m* autonome de survie *f*, un appareil portatif
– *life support system (life support pack), a backpack unit*

21 le volet d'accès *m*
– *access flap*

22 le casque de scaphandre *m* à filtres *m* solaires
– *space suit helmet with sun filters*

23 le boîtier de contrôle *m* de l'équipement *m* de survie *f*
– *control box of the life support pack*

24 la poche réservée à la torche
– *penlight pocket*

25 le volet d'accès à la soupape de purge *f*
– *access flap for the purge valve*

26 les raccords *m* des tuyaux *m* de ventilation *f* et de refroidissement *m* par eau *f* et des câbles *m* de liaison *f* radio *f*
– *tube and cable connections for the radio, ventilation, and water-cooling systems*

27 la poche réservée aux crayons *m*, outils *m*, etc.
– *pocket for pens, tools, etc.*

28-36 l'étage *m* de descente *f*
– *descent stage*

28 l'attache *f* métallique
– *connector*

29 le réservoir de carburant *m*
– *fuel tank*

30 le propulseur, le moteur-fusée
– *engine*

31 le mécanisme de déploiement *m* du système d'atterrissage *m*
– *mechanism for unfolding the legs*

32 l'amortisseur *m* principal d'atterrissage *m*
– *main shock absorber*

33 le patin d'atterrissage *m* (le tampon d'atterrissage *m*)
– *landing pad*

34 la plate-forme d'accès *m*
– *ingress/egress platform (hatch platform)*

35 l'échelle *f* d'accès *m*
– *ladder to platform and hatch*

36 le cardan du propulseur *m*
– *cardan mount for engine*

37-47 l'étage *m* de montée *f*
– *ascent stage*

37 le réservoir de carburant *m*
– *fuel tank*

38 le sas d'accès *m*, l'écoutille *f*
– *ingress/egress hatch (entry/exit hatch)*

39 les fusées *f* d'orientation *f* (de stabilisation *f*)
– *LM manoeuvring* (Am. *maneuvering) rockets*

40 le hublot
– *window*

41 l'habitacle *m*, le poste d'équipage *m*
– *crew compartment*

42 l'antenne *f* du radar de rendez-vous *m*
– *rendezvous radar antenna*

43 la centrale inertielle
– *inertial measurement unit*

44 l'antenne *f* directive de liaison *f* avec la station terrienne
– *directional antenna for ground control*

45 le sas supérieur
– *upper hatch (docking hatch)*

46 l'antenne *f* d'approche *f*
– *inflight antenna*

47 le système actif d'amarrage *m*
– *docking target recess*

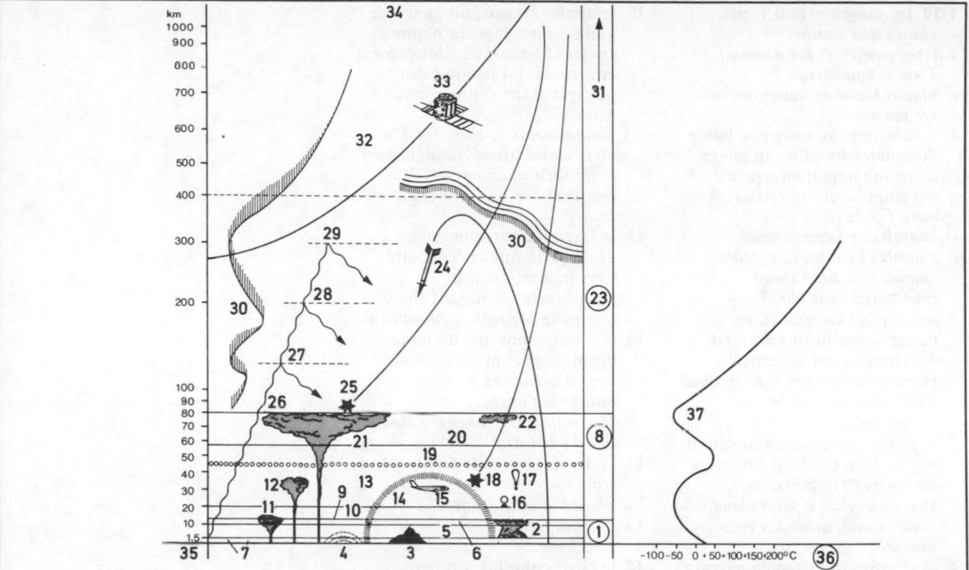

1 la troposphère
– ***the troposphere***
2 les nuages *m* orageux
– *thunderclouds*
3 la plus haute montagne du monde, le *Mont Everest* [8882 m]
– *the highest mountain,* Mount Everest *[8,882m]*
4 l'arc-en-ciel *m*
– *rainbow*
5 le niveau des courants-jets *m* (jets-streams *m*)
– *jet stream level*
6 le niveau zéro (inversion *f* des mouvements *m* verticaux de l'air *m*)
– *zero level (inversion of vertical air movement)*
7 la couche de surface *f*
– *ground layer (surface boundary layer)*
8 la stratosphère
– ***the stratosphere***
9 la tropopause
– *tropopause*
10 la couche de séparation *f* (couche *f* à faibles mouvements *m* de l'air *m*)
– *separating layer (layer of weaker air movement)*
11 explosion *f* d'une bombe atomique
– *atomic explosion*
12 explosion *f* d'une bombe à hydrogène *m*
– *hydrogen bomb explosion*
13 la couche d'ozone *m*
– *ozone layer*
14 la propagation des ondes *f* sonores
– *range of sound wave propagation*
15 l'avion *m* stratosphérique
– *stratosphere aircraft*
16 le ballon avec équipage *m*
– *manned balloon*
17 le ballon sonde
– *sounding balloon*
18 le météore
– *meteor*
19 la limite supérieure de la couche d'ozone *m*
– *upper limit of ozone layer*
20 la couche D (la région D)
– *zero level*
21 l'éruption *f* du Krakatoa
– *eruption of Krakatoa*
22 les nuages *m* lumineux
– *luminous clouds (noctilucent clouds)*
23 l'ionosphère *f*
– ***the ionosphere***
24 le domaine d'exploration *f* par fusées *f*
– *range of research rockets*
25 l'étoile *f* filante
– *shooting star*
26 les ondes *f* courtes (hautes fréquences *f*)
– *short wave (high frequency)*
27 la couche E (la région E)
– *E-layer (Heaviside-Kennelly Layer)*
28 la couche F_1 (la région F_1)
– *F_1-layer*
29 la couche F_2 (la région F_2)
– *F_2-layer*
30 l'aurore *f* boréale
– *aurora (polar light)*
31 l'exosphère *f*
– ***the exosphere***
32 la couche atomique
– *atom layer*
33 le domaine d'exploration *f* par satellite *m*
– *range of satellite sounding*
34 le passage vers l'espace *m* interstellaire
– *fringe region*
35 l'échelle *f* des altitudes *f*
– *altitude scale*
36 l'échelle *f* des températures *f*
– *temperature scale (thermometric scale)*
37 la courbe des températures *f*
– *temperature graph*

1-19 les nuages *m* et le temps
– *clouds and weather*
1-4 les nuages *m* des masses *f* d'air *m* homogènes
– *clouds found in homogeneous air masses*
1 le cumulus, un nuage en boule *f* (cumulus humilis, un nuage de beau temps), un nuage à développement *m* vertical, à base *f* plate
– *cumulus (woolpack cloud, cumulus humilis, fair-weather cumulus), a heap cloud (flat-based heap cloud)*
2 le cumulus congestus, un nuage cumuliforme à grand développement *m* vertical
– *cumulus congestus, a heap cloud with more marked vertical development*
3 le strato-cumulus, un nuage en nappe *f* (en banc *m*), composé de masses *f* importantes
– *stratocumulus, a layer cloud (sheet cloud) arranged in heavy masses*
4 le stratus, un nuage en nappe *f* épaisse et uniforme, un brouillard élevé au-dessus du sol
– *stratus (high fog), a thick, uniform layer cloud (sheet cloud)*
5-12 les nuages *m* de front *m* chaud
– *clouds found at warm fronts*
5 le front chaud
– *warm front*
6 le cirrus, un nuage de cristaux *m* de glace *f*, d'altitude *f* élevée ou très élevée, composé de filaments *m* fins aux formes *f* variables
– *cirrus, a high to very high ice-crystal cloud, thin and assuming a wide variety of forms*
7 le cirro-stratus, un nuage de cristaux *m* de glace *f* en voile *m*
– *cirrostratus, an ice-crystal cloud veil*
8 l'altostratus *m*, un nuage en nappe *f* d'altitude *f* moyenne
– *altostratus, a layer cloud (sheet cloud) of medium height*
9 l'altostratus precipitans, un nuage en nappe *f* avec des précipitations *f* à la partie supérieure
– *altostratus praecipitans, a layer cloud (sheet cloud) with precipitation in its upper parts*
10 le nimbo-stratus, un nuage de pluie *f*, un nuage en nappe *f* épaisse à grand développement *m* vertical qui produit des précipitations *f*, pluie *f* ou neige *f*
– *nimbostratus, a rain cloud, a layer cloud (sheet cloud) of very large vertical extent which produces precipitation (rain or snow)*
11 le fracto-stratus, un nuage déchiqueté qui se rencontre sous le nimbostratus
– *fractostratus, a ragged cloud occurring beneath nimbostratus*
12 le fracto-cumulus, un nuage déchiqueté comme 11, mais avec des formes *f* bourgeonnantes
– *fractocumulus, a ragged cloud like 11 but with billowing shapes*
13-17 les nuages *m* de front *m* froid
– *clouds at cold fronts*
13 le front froid
– *cold front*
14 le cirro-cumulus, un petit nuage en forme *f* de bille *f*
– *cirrocumulus, thin fleecy cloud in the form of globular masses;* covering the sky: *mackerel sky*
15 l'altocumulus, un nuage en forme *f* de boule *f* qui donne un ciel pommelé
– *altocumulus, a cloud in the form of large globular masses*
16 l'altocumulus *m* castellanus et l'altocumulus *m* floccus, formes *f* dérivées de 15
– *altocumulus castellanus and altocumulus floccus, species of 15*
17 le cumulo-nimbus, un nuage à très grand développement *m* vertical, à sommet *m* en enclume *f*; il se classe dans la catégorie 1-4 en cas d'ouragan *m* tropical
– *cumulonimbus, a heap cloud of very large vertical extent, to be classified under 1-4 in the case of tropical storms*
18-19 les différentes sortes *f* de précipitations *f*
– *types of precipitation*
18 la chute de pluie *f* ou de neige *f* sur une vaste région, des précipitations *f* de caractère *m* uniforme
– *steady rain or snow covering a large area, precipitation of uniform intensity*
19 l'averse *f*, des précipitations *f* intermittentes
– *shower, scattered precipitation*

flèche noire = air froid
black arrow = cold air
flèche blanche = air chaud
white arrow = warm air

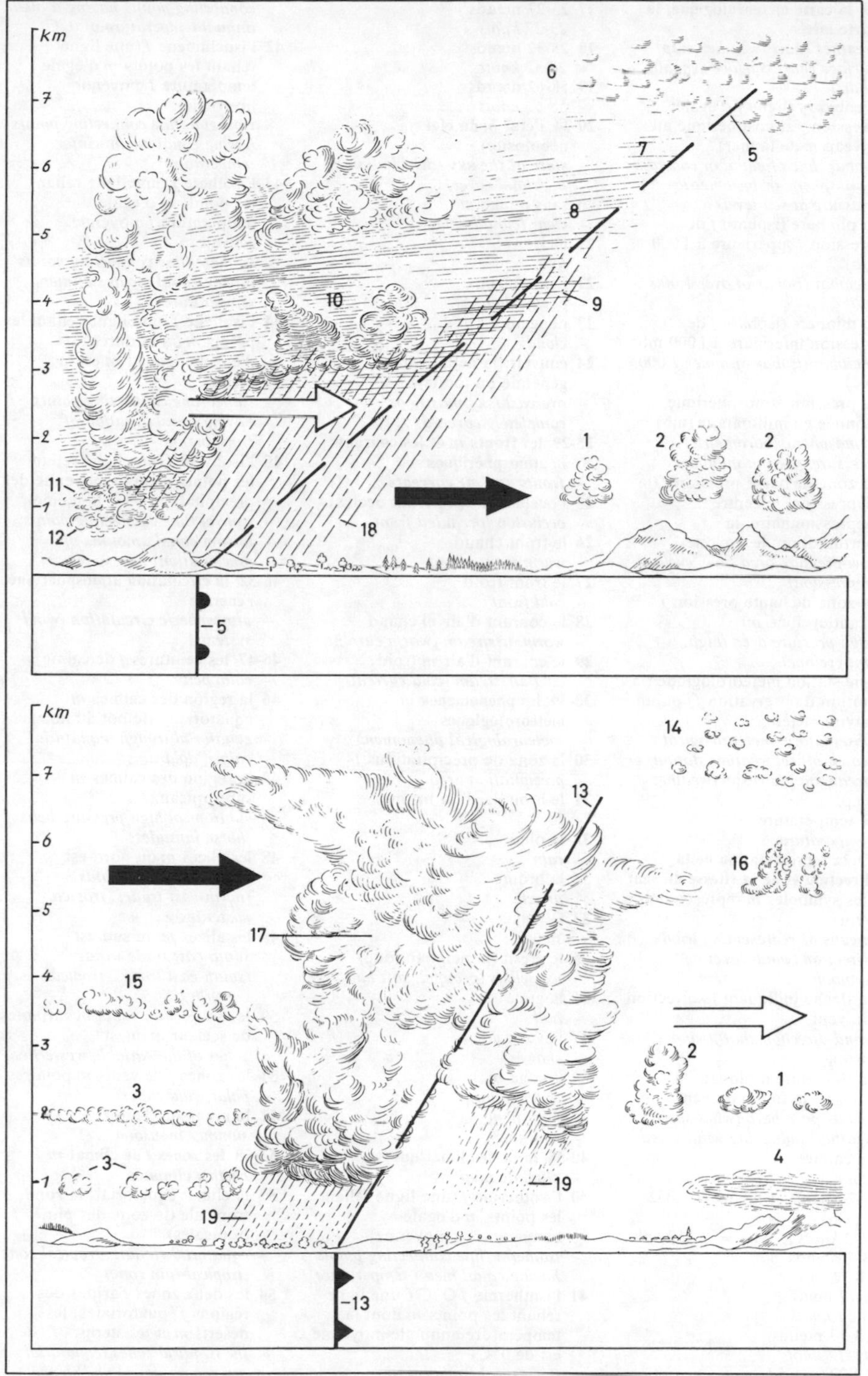
km
7
6
5
4
3
2
1
6
7
5
8
10
9
1
2
2
11
12
18
5
km
7
6
5
4
3
2
1
14
13
16
17
15
2
3
1
3
4
19
19
13

1-39 la carte météorologique, la carte météo
– ***weather chart*** *(weather map, surface chart, surface synoptic chart)*
1 l'isobare *f* (ligne *f* d'égale pression *f* atmosphérique au niveau *m* de la mer)
– *isobar (line of equal or constant atmospheric or barometric pressure at sea level)*
2 la pliobare (isobare *f* de pression *f* supérieure à 1 000 mb)
– *pleiobar (isobar of over 1,000 mb)*
3 la miobare (isobare *f* de pression inférieure à 1 000 mb)
– *meiobar (isobar of under 1,000 mb)*
4 la pression atmosphérique donnée en millibars *m* (mb)
– *atmospheric (barometric) pressure given in millibars*
5 la zone de basse pression *f* (la dépression, le centre dépressionnaire, la perturbation, le cyclone)
– *low-pressure area (low, cyclone, depression)*
6 la zone de haute pression *f* (l'anticyclone *m*)
– *high-pressure area (high, anticyclone)*
7 une station météorologique (la station d'observation *f*) ou un navire météo
– *observatory (meteorological watch office, weather station) or ocean station vessel (weather ship)*
8 la température
– *temperature*
9-19 la représentation de la direction et de la vitesse du vent (les symboles *m* représentant le vent)
– ***means of representing wind direction*** *(wind-direction symbols)*
9 la flèche indiquant la direction du vent
– *wind-direction shaft (wind arrow)*
10 la barbelure indiquant la vitesse (la force) du vent
– *wind-speed barb (wind-speed feather) indicating wind speed*
11 le calme
– *calm*
12 1-2 nœuds (1 nœud = 1,852 km/h)
– *1-2 knots (1 knot = 1.852 kph)*
13 3-7 nœuds
– *3-7 knots*
14 8-12 nœuds
– *8-12 knots*
15 13-17 nœuds
– *13-17 knots*
16 18-22 nœuds
– *18-22 knots*
17 23-27 nœuds
– *23-27 knots*
18 28-32 nœuds
– *28-32 knots*
19 58-62 nœuds
– *58-62 knots*
20-24 l'état *m* du ciel (la nébulosité)
– ***state of the sky*** *(distribution of the cloud cover)*
20 sans nuage *m*
– *clear (cloudless)*
21 clair
– *fair*
22 peu nuageux
– *partly cloudy*
23 nuageux
– *cloudy*
24 couvert (la nébulosité est générale ou totale)
– *overcast (sky mostly or completely covered)*
25-29 les fronts *m* et les courants *m* atmosphériques
– ***fronts and air currents***
25 l'occlusion *f* (un front occlus)
– *occlusion (occluded front)*
26 le front chaud
– *warm front*
27 le front froid
– *cold front*
28 le courant d'air *m* chaud
– *warm airstream (warm current)*
29 le courant d'air *m* froid
– *cold airstream (cold current)*
30-39 les phénomènes *m* météorologiques
– ***meteorological phenomena***
30 la zone de précipitations *f*
– *precipitation area*
31 le brouillard (la brume)
– *fog*
32 la pluie
– *rain*
33 la bruine
– *drizzle*
34 la neige
– *snow*
35 le grésil (la neige fondue)
– *ice pellets (graupel, soft hail)*
36 la grêle
– *hail*
37 l'averse *f*
– *shower*
38 l'orage *m*
– *thunderstorm*
39 l'éclair *m*
– *lightning*
40-58 la carte climatique
– ***climatic map***
40 l'isotherme *f* (une ligne reliant les points *m* d'égale température *f* moyenne)
– *isotherm (line connecting points having equal mean temperature)*
41 l'isotherme *f* 0 °C (une ligne reliant les points *m* dont la température annuelle moyenne est de 0 °C)
– *0 °C (zero) isotherm (line connecting points having a mean annual temperature of 0 °C)*
42 l'isochimène *f* (une ligne reliant les points *m* d'égale température *f* moyenne hivernale)
– *isocheim (line connecting points having equal mean winter temperature)*
43 l'isothère *f* (une ligne reliant les points *m* d'égale température *f* moyenne estivale)
– *isothere (line connecting points having equal mean summer temperature)*
44 l'isohélie *f* (une ligne reliant les points *m* où la durée d'ensoleillement *m* est la même)
– *isohel (line connecting points having equal duration of sunshine)*
45 l'isohyète *f* (une ligne reliant les points *m* où la moyenne des précipitations *f* est la même)
– *isohyet (line connecting points having equal amounts of precipitation)*
46-52 la circulation atmosphérique générale
– ***atmospheric circulation*** *(wind systems)*
46-47 les ceintures *f* de calme *m*
– *calm belts*
46 la région des calmes *m* équatoriaux (le pot au noir)
– *equatorial trough (equatorial calms, doldrums)*
47 la région des calmes *m* subtropicaux
– *subtropical high-pressure belts (horse latitudes)*
48 les alizés *m* du nord-est
– *north-east trade winds (north-east trades, tropical easterlies)*
49 les alizés *m* du sud-est
– *south-east trade winds (south-east trades, tropical easterlies)*
50 les zones *f* de vents *m* variables de secteur *m* ouest
– *zones of the variable westerlies*
51 les zones *f* de vents *m* polaires
– *polar wind zones*
52 la mousson d'été *f*
– *summer monsoon*
53-58 les zones *f* de climat *m*
– ***earth's climates***
53 le climat équatorial: la zone tropicale (la zone des pluies *f* tropicales)
– *equatorial climate: tropical zone (tropical rain zone)*
54 les deux zones *f* arides des régions *f* équatoriales: les déserts *m* et les steppes *f*
– *the two arid zones (equatorial dry zones): desert and steppe zones*

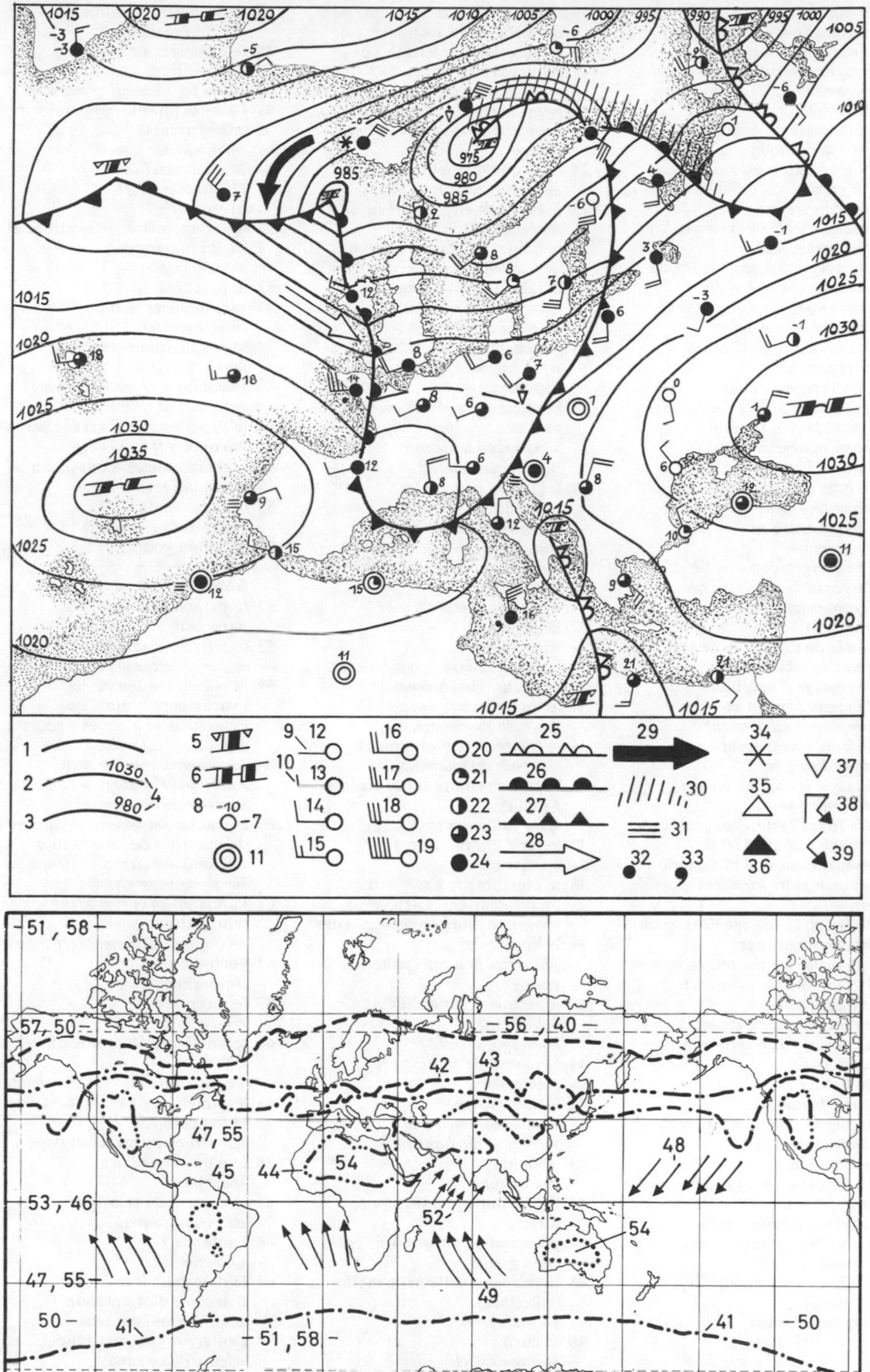

1015
1020
1010
1005
1000
995
990
985
980
975
1025
1030
1035
1 2 3 4 5 6 7 8 9 10 11 12 13 14 15 16 17 18 19 20 21 22 23 24 25 26 27 28 29 30 31 32 33 34 35 36 37 38 39
51, 58
57, 50
56, 40
42
43
47, 55
45
44
54
48
53, 46
52
49
50
41

1 le baromètre à mercure *m*, un baromètre à siphon *m*, un baromètre à liquide *m*
– *mercury barometer, a siphon barometer, a liquid-column barometer*
2 la colonne de mercure *m*
– *mercury column*
3 la graduation en millibars *m* (la graduation en millimètres *m* de mercure *m*)
– *millibar scale (millimetre,* Am. *millimeter, scale)*
4 le barographe, un baromètre enregistreur anéroïde
– *barograph, a self-registering aneroid barometer*
5 le tambour (le cylindre) enregistreur
– *drum (recording drum)*
6 la série de boîtes *f* anéroïdes (les capsules *f* anéroïdes)
– *bank of aneroid capsules (aneroid boxes)*
7 le bras portant le style
– *recording arm*
8 l'hygromètre *m*
– *hygrograph*
9 le fil hygroscopique (le faisceau de cheveux *m*)
– *hygrometer element (hair element)*
10 la vis de réglage *m* de lecture *f*
– *reading adjustment*
11 le réglage d'amplitude *f* de l'enregistrement *m*
– *amplitude adjustment*
12 le bras enregistreur
– *recording arm*
13 le style (la plume encrée)
– *recording pen*
14 les roues *f* interchangeables (roues *f* amovibles) du mouvement *m* d'horlogerie *f*
– *change gears for the clockwork drive*
15 le levier de dégagement *m* du bras enregistreur
– *off switch for the recording arm*
16 le tambour (le cylindre) enregistreur
– *drum (recording drum)*
17 l'échelle *f* de temps *m*
– *time scale*
18 le boîtier
– *case (housing)*
19 le thermomètre enregistreur (le thermographe)
– *thermograph*
20 le tambour (le cylindre) enregistreur
– *drum (recording drum)*
21 l'aiguille *f* enregistreuse
– *recording arm*
22 l'élément *m* sensible (le capteur)
– *sensing element*
23 le pyrhéliomètre à disque *m* d'argent *m*, un instrument de mesure *f* de l'intensité *f* des radiations *f* solaires
– *silver-disc (silver-disk) pyrheliometer, an instrument for measuring the sun's radiant energy*
24 le disque d'argent *m*
– *silver disc (disk)*
25 le thermomètre de précision *f*
– *thermometer*
26 le boîtier isolant en bois *m*
– *wooden insulating casing*
27 le tube à diaphragmes *m*
– *tube with diaphragm (diaphragmed tube)*
28 l'anémomètre *m*
– *wind gauge (*Am. *gage) (anemometer)*
29 l'indicateur *m* de vitesse *f* du vent *m*
– *wind-speed indicator (wind-speed meter)*
30 les tiges *f* portant les coupelles *f*
– *cross arms with hemispherical cups*
31 l'indicateur *m* de direction *f* du vent *m*
– *wind-direction indicator*
32 la girouette
– *wind vane*
33 le psychomètre à aspiration *f*
– *aspiration psychrometer*
34 le thermomètre «sec»
– *dry bulb thermometer*
35 le thermomètre «humide»
– *wet bulb thermometer*
36 l'écran *m* contre les radiations *f* solaires
– *solar radiation shielding*
37 le tube d'aspiration *f*
– *suction tube*
38 le pluviomètre enregistreur, totalisateur-enregistreur
– *recording rain gauge (*Am. *gage)*
39 le boîtier
– *protective housing (protective casing)*
40 le récipient collecteur (le collecteur)
– *collecting vessel*
41 le rebord de protection *f*
– *rain cover*
42 le mécanisme d'enregistrement *m*
– *recording mechanism*
43 le siphon
– *siphon tube*
44 le pluviomètre à lecture *f* directe
– *precipitation gauge (*Am. *gage) (rain gauge)*
45 le récipient collecteur *m* (le collecteur)
– *collecting vessel*
46 la cuve
– *storage vessel*
47 l'éprouvette *f* graduée
– *measuring glass*
48 le dispositif de mesure *f* nivométrique
– *insert for measuring snowfall*
49 l'abri *m* pour les appareils *m* enregistreurs
– *thermometer screen (thermometer shelter)*
50 l'hygromètre *m*
– *hygrograph*
51 le thermomètre enregistreur *m* (le thermographe)
– *thermograph*
52 le psychromètre
– *psychrometer (wet and dry bulb thermometer)*
53-54 les thermomètres *m* à maximum *m* et à minimum *m*
– *thermometers for measuring extremes of temperature*
53 le thermomètre à maximum *m*
– *maximum thermometer*
54 le thermomètre à minimum *m*
– *minimum thermometer*
55 la radiosonde
– *radiosonde assembly*
56 le ballon gonflé à l'hydrogène *m*
– *hydrogen balloon*
57 le parachute
– *parachute*
58 le réflecteur radar haubané
– *radar reflector with spacing lines*
59 le boîtier contenant les instruments *m* ainsi que l'émetteur *m* à ondes *f* courtes et l'antenne *f* radio
– *instrument housing with radiosonde (a short-wave transmitter) and antenna*
60 le transmissomètre, un appareil de mesure *f* de la visibilité
– *transmissometer, an instrument for measuring visibility*
61 l'appareil *m* enregistreur (enregistreur *m*)
– *recording instrument (recorder)*
62 l'émetteur *m*
– *transmitter*
63 le récepteur
– *receiver*
64 le satellite météorologique (ITOS)
– *weather satellite (ITOS satellite)*
65 les volets *m* de régulation *f* de la température
– *temperature regulation flaps*
66 le panneau solaire
– *solar panel*
67 la caméra de télévision *f*
– *television camera*
68 l'antenne *f*
– *antenna*
69 le détecteur solaire (le détecteur d'orientation *f*)
– *solar sensor (sun sensor)*
70 l'antenne *f* télémétrique
– *telemetry antenna*
71 le radiomètre
– *radiometer*

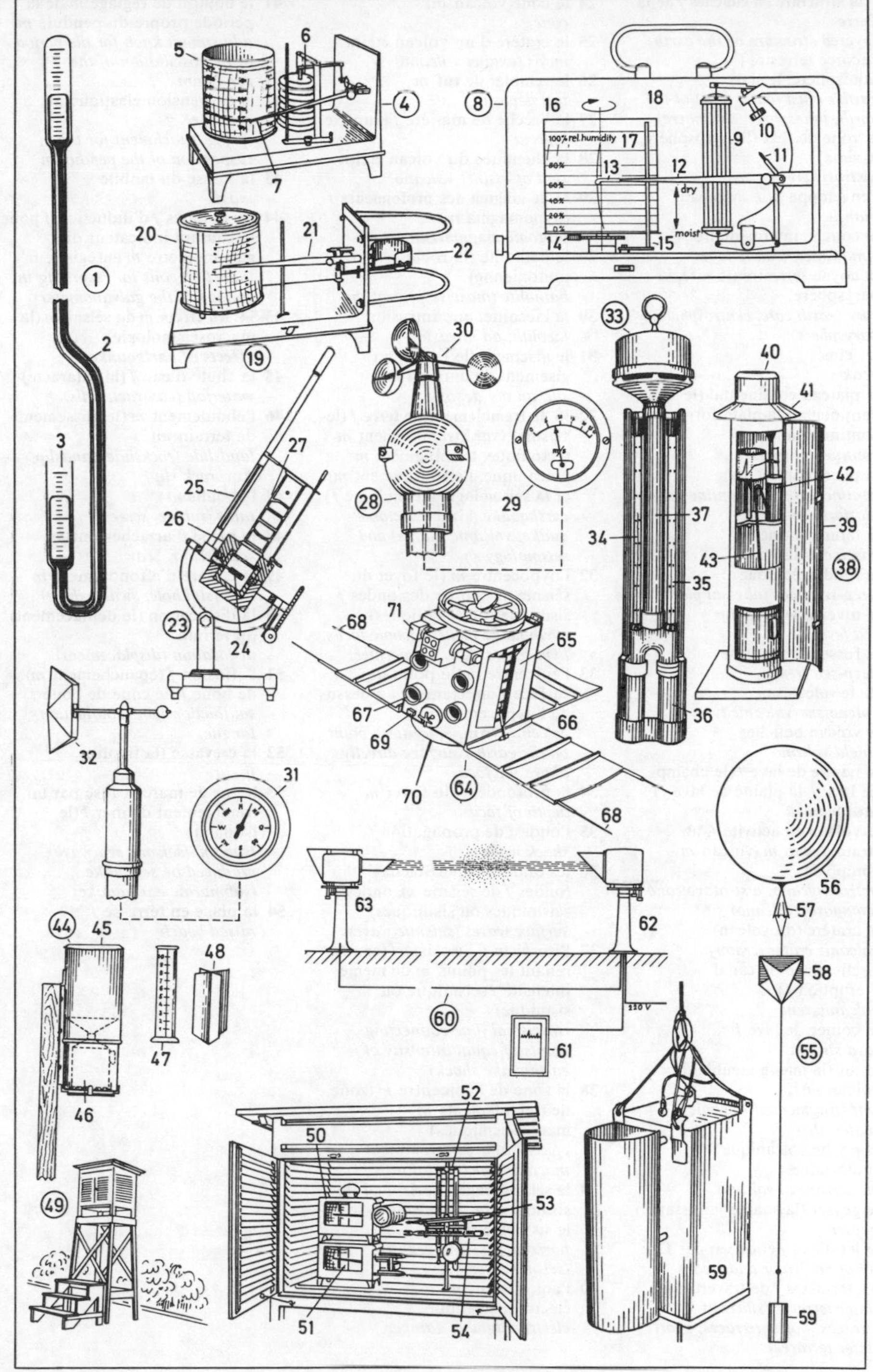
100% rel. humidity
80%
60%
40%
20%
0%
dry
moist
220 V

1-5 la structure en couches *f* de la Terre
– ***layered structure of the earth***
1 l'écorce terrestre (la lithosphère, le sial)
– *earth's crust (outer crust of the earth, lithosphere, oxysphere)*
2 la zone de flux (la pyrosphère, le sima)
– *hydrosphere*
3 l'enveloppe *f* (le manteau)
– *mantle*
4 la couche intermédiaire
– *sima (intermediate layer)*
5 le noyau terrestre (le nifé, la barysphère)
– *core (earth core, centrosphere, barysphere)*
6 les cimes *f*
– *peak*
7 le plateau continental (le socle continental, la plate-forme continentale)
– *continental mass*
8 la pente continentale
– *continental shelf (continental platform, shelf)*
9 le talus continental
– *continental slope*
10 le fond océanique
– *deep-sea floor (abyssal plane)*
11 le niveau de la mer
– *sea level*
12 la fosse sous-marine
– *deep-sea trench*
13-28 le volcanisme
– ***volcanism*** *(vulcanicity)*
13 le volcan bouclier
– *shield volcano*
14 la nappe de lave *f* (le champ de lave *f*, la plaine de lave *f*)
– *lava plateau*
15 le volcan en activité *f*, un stratovolcan *m* (volcan *m* composé)
– *active volcano, a stratovolcano (composite volcano)*
16 le cratère (du volcan)
– *volcanic crater (crater)*
17 la cheminée (le canal d'éruption *f*)
– *volcanic vent*
18 la coulée de lave *f*
– *lava stream*
19 le tuf (la masse meuble du volcan *m*)
– *tuff (fragmented volcanic material)*
20 la poche volcanique souterraine
– *subterranean volcano*
21 le geyser (la source jaillissante)
– *geyser*
22 le jet d'eau *f* et de vapeur *f*
– *jet of hot water and steam*
23 les terrasses *f* de travertin *m*
– *sinter terraces (siliceous sinter terraces, fiorite terraces, pearl sinter terraces)*
24 le cône(volcan *m*)
– *cone*
25 le cratère d'un volcan éteint
– *maar (extinct volcano)*
26 le remblai de tuf *m*
– *tuff deposit*
27 la brèche de matière *f* éruptive
– *breccia*
28 la cheminée du volcan éteint
– *vent of extinct volcano*
29-31 le magma des profondeurs *f* (hypomagma *m*)
– ***plutonic magmatism***
29 le batholite (la roche plutonienne)
– *batholite (massive protrusion)*
30 la laccolite, une intrusion
– *lacolith, an intrusion*
31 le gisement (le filon), un gisement de minerai *m*
– *sill, an ore deposit*
32-38 le tremblement de terre *f* (le séisme) (*var.:* tremblement *m* tectonique, tremblement *m* volcanique, l'effondrement *m*) **et la séismologie** (sismologie *f*)
– ***earthquake*** (kinds: *tectonic quake, volcanic quake)* ***and seismology***
32 l'hypocentre *m* (le foyer du séisme, la source des ondes *f* sismiques ou séismiques)
– *earthquake focus (seismic focus, hypocentre,* Am. *hypocenter)*
33 l'épicentre *m* (le point de surface *f* directement au-dessus de l'hypocentre *m*)
– *epicentre (*Am. *epicenter), point on the earth's surface directly above the focus*
34 la profondeur du foyer *m*
– *depth of focus*
35 l'onde *f* de propagation *f*
– *shock wave*
36 les ondes *f* superficielles (ondes *f* de séisme *m*, ondes *f* séismiques ou sismiques)
– *surface waves (seismic waves)*
37 l'isoséiste *f*, l'isosiste *f* (courbe reliant les points *m* de même intensité *f* séismique ou sismique)
– *isoseismal (line connecting points of equal intensity of earthquake shock)*
38 la zone de l'épicentre *m* (zone de tremblements *m* macroséismiques)
– *epicentral area (area of macroseismic vibration)*
39 le séismographe horizontal (le sismographe, le séismomètre, le sismomètre)
– ***horizontal seismograph*** *(seismometer)*
40 l'amortisseur *m* électromagnétique
– *electromagnetic damper*
41 le bouton de réglage *m* de la période propre du pendule *m*
– *adjustment knob for the period of free oscillation of the pendulum*
42 la suspension élastique du pendule
– *spring attachment for the suspension of the pendulum*
43 la masse du mobile
– *mass*
44 les bobines *f* d'induction *f* pour le courant indicateur du galvanomètre *m* enregistreur
– *induction coils for recording the voltage of the galvanometer*
45-54 les effets *m* du séisme *m* (la macroséismologie)
– ***effects of earthquakes***
45 la chute d'eau *f* (la cataracte)
– *waterfall (cataract, falls)*
46 l'éboulement *m* (le glissement de terrain *m*)
– *landslide (rockslide, landslip,* Am. *rock slip)*
47 l'éboulis *m*
– *talus (rubble, scree)*
48 la niche d'arrachement *m*
– *scar (scaur, scaw)*
49 le cratère d'effondrement *m*
– *sink (sinkhole, swallowhole)*
50 la dislocation (le déplacement) du terrain
– *dislocation (displacement)*
51 l'effusion *f* (épanchement *m*) de boue *f* (le cône de boue *f*)
– *solifluction lobe (solifluction tongue)*
52 la crevasse (la fissure)
– *fissure*
53 le raz de marée causé par un tremblement de mer *f* (le tsunami)
– *tsunami (seismic sea wave) produced by seaquake (submarine earthquake)*
54 la plage en terrasse *f*
– *raised beach*

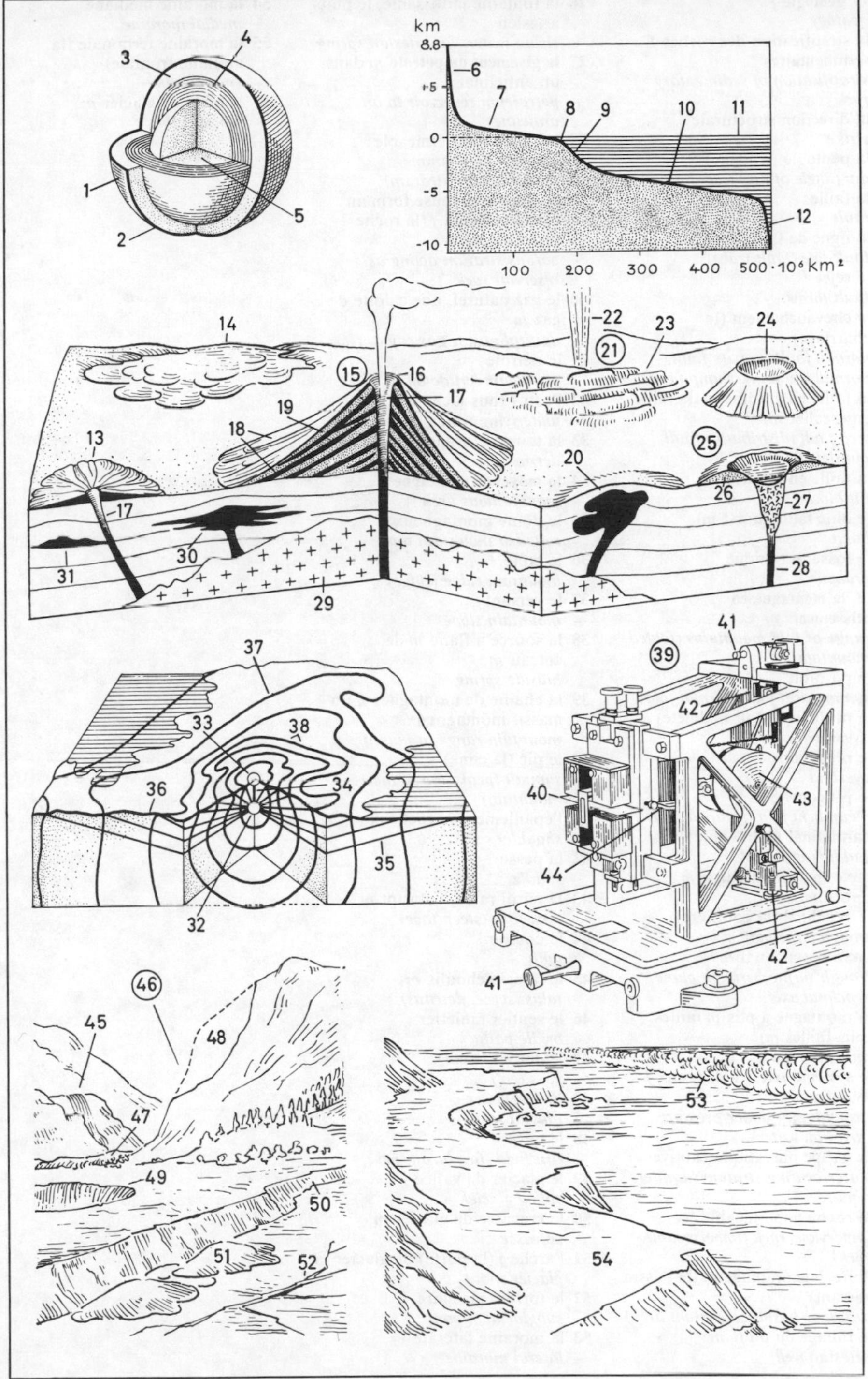
km
8.8
+5
0
-5
-10
100
200
300
400
500 · 10⁶ km²
1
2
3
4
5
6
7
8
9
10
11
12
13
14
15
16
17
18
19
20
21
22
23
24
25
26
27
28
29
30
31
32
33
34
35
36
37
38
39
40
41
42
43
44
45
46
47
48
49
50
51
52
53
54

1-33 géologie *f*
– ***geology***
1 la stratification des roches *f* sédimentaires
– *stratification of sedimentary rock*
2 la direction structurale
– *strike*
3 la pente (le pendage)
– *dip (angle of dip, true dip)*
4 la faille
– *fault*
5 la ligne de faille *f*
– *fault line (fault trace)*
6 le rejet
– *fault throw*
7 le chevauchement (le charriage)
– *normal fault (gravity fault, normal slip fault, slump fault)*
8 la faille en gradins *m* (la faille en escalier *m*)
– *step fault (distributive fault, multiple fault)*
9 la faille en pupitre *m*
– *tilt block*
10 le bloc faillé (horst *m*)
– *horst*
11 le fossé tectonique
– *graben*
12-20 la montagne en plissements *m*
– ***range of fold mountains*** *(folded mountains)*
12 le pli droit
– *symmetrical fold (normal fold)*
13 le pli oblique (pli *m* déjeté)
– *asymmetrical fold*
14 le pli déversé
– *overfold*
15 le pli couché
– *recumbent fold (reclined fold)*
16 l'anticlinal *m* (la voûte)
– *saddle (anticline)*
17 l'axe *m* de l'anticlinal *m*
– *anticlinal axis*
18 le synclinal (la gouttière)
– *trough (syncline)*
19 l'axe *m* synclinal *m*
– *trough surface (trough plane, synclinal axis)*
20 la montagne à plis *m* faillés (plis-failles *m*)
– *anticlinorium*
21 le système artésien des eaux *f* **souterraines**
– ***groundwater under pressure*** *(artesian water)*
22 la nappe phréatique captive
– *water-bearing stratum (aquifer, aquafer)*
23 la roche imperméable
– *impervious rock (impermeable rock)*
24 l'aire *f* de drainage *m* (le bassin versant)
– *drainage basin (catchment area)*
25 le tubage du puits *m*
– *artesian well*
26 la fontaine jaillissante, le puits artésien
– *rising water, an artesian spring*
27 **le gisement de pétrole** *m* dans un anticlinal
– ***petroleum reservoir*** *in an anticline*
28 la couche imperméable
– *impervious stratum (impermeable stratum)*
29 la couche poreuse formant roche-magasin *f* (la roche réservoir *m*)
– *porous stratum acting as reservoir rock*
30 le gaz naturel, une calotte de gaz *m*
– *natural gas, a gas cap*
31 le pétrole
– *petroleum (crude oil)*
32 l'eau *f* sous-jacente
– *underlying water*
33 la tour de forage *m* (derrick *m*)
– *derrick*
34 la moyenne montagne
– ***mountainous area***
35 le dôme montagneux
– *rounded mountain top*
36 la crête
– *mountain ridge (ridge)*
37 le versant
– *mountain slope*
38 la source à flanc *m* de coteau *m*
– *hillside spring*
39 la chaîne de montagnes *f*, un massif montagneux
– *mountain range, a massif*
40 le pic (la cime)
– *summit (peak, top of the mountain)*
41 l'épaulement *m* rocheux
– *shoulder*
42 la passe
– *saddle*
43 la paroi raide, l'abrupt *m*
– *rock face (steep face)*
44 le couloir
– *gully*
45 le talus d'éboulis *m*
– *talus (scree, detritus)*
46 le sentier muletier
– *bridle path*
47 le défilé (le col)
– *pass (col)*
48-56 le glacier
– ***glacial ice***
48 le névé
– *firn field (firn basin, nevé)*
49 le glacier de vallée *f*
– *valley glacier*
50 la crevasse de glacier *m*
– *crevasse*
51 l'arche *f* (la porte) de glacier *m*
– *glacier snout*
52 le torrent glaciaire
– *subglacial stream*
53 la moraine latérale
– *lateral moraine*
54 la moraine médiane
– *medial moraine*
55 la moraine terminale (la moraine frontale)
– *end moraine*
56 la table de glacier *m*
– *glacier table*

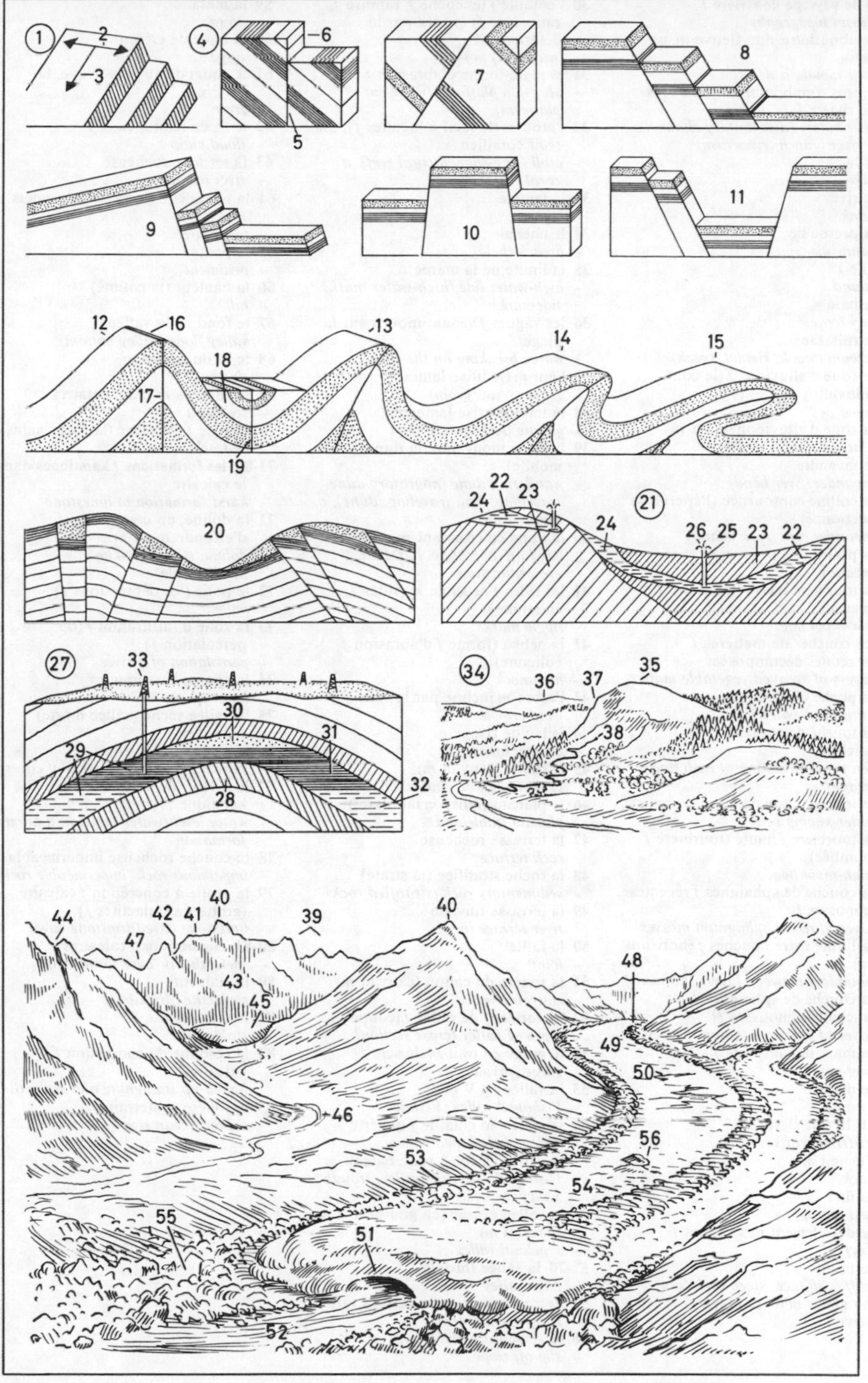
1
2
3
4
5
6
7
8
9
10
11
12
13
14
15
16
17
18
19
20
21
22
23
24
25
26
27
28
29
30
31
32
33
34
35
36
37
38
39
40
41
42
43
44
45
46
47
48
49
50
51
52
53
54
55
56

1-13 le paysage de rivière *f*
– ***fluvial topography***
1 l'embouchure *f* du fleuve *m*, un delta
– *river mouth, a delta*
2 le bras d'embouchure *f*, un bras de rivière *f*
– *distributary (distributary channel), a river branch (river arm)*
3 le lac
– *lake*
4 la rive
– *bank*
5 la presqu'île
– *peninsula (spit)*
6 l'île *f*
– *island*
7 la baie
– *bay (cove)*
8 le ruisseau
– *stream (brook, rivulet, creek)*
9 le cône d'alluvions *f* (le cône alluvial)
– *levee*
10 la zone d'alluvionnement *m*
– *alluvial plain*
11 le méandre
– *meander (river bend)*
12 la colline contournée (l'éperon *m* sectionné)
– *meander core (rock island)*
13 la prairie
– *meadow*
14 la tourbière basse (tourbière *f* plate)
– *low-moor bog*
15 les couches de matières *f* végétales décomposées
– *layers of decayed vegetable matter*
16 la poche d'eau *f*
– *entrapped water*
17 la tourbe de roseaux *m* de laiches *f*
– *fen peat [consisting of rush and sedge]*
18 la tourbe d'aunaie *f*
– *alder-swamp peat*
19 la tourbière *f* haute (tourbière *f* bombée)
– *high-moor bog*
20 la couche de sphaignes *f* récentes [mousses *f*]
– *layer of recent sphagnum mosses*
21 la limite entre couches *f* (horizons *m*)
– *boundary between layers (horizons)*
22 la couche de sphaignes *f* anciennes [mousses *f*]
– *layer of older sphagnum mosses*
23 la mare de tourbière *f*
– *bog pool*
24 le marais
– *swamp*
25-31 la côte élevée
– ***cliffline*** *(cliffs)*
25 l'écueil *m*
– *rock*
26 la mer
– *sea (ocean)*
27 le déferlement des vagues *f*
– *surf*
28 la falaise
– *cliff (cliff face, steep rock face)*
29 les galets *m* de la plage
– *scree*
30 l'entaille *f* (encoche *f*, rainure *f*, cannelure *f*) érodée par le déferlement
– *[wave-cut] notch*
31 la plate-forme d'abrasion *f*
– *abrasion platform (wave-cut platform)*
32 l'atoll *m* (le récif à lagunes *f*), un récif corallien
– *atoll (ring-shaped coral reef), a coral reef*
33 la lagune
– *lagoon*
34 le chenal
– *breach (hole)*
35 la limite de la marée
– *high-water line (high-water mark, tidemark)*
36 les vagues *f* venant mourir sur la plage
– *waves breaking on the shore*
37 l'épi *m* (le brise-lames)
– *groyne* (Am. *groin)*
38 la tête de brise-lames *m*
– *groyne* (Am. *groin) head*
39 la dune mouvante (la dune mobile)
– *wandering dune (migratory dune, travelling,* Am. *traveling, dune), a dune*
40 la dune en croissant *m*
– *barchan (barchane, barkhan, crescentic dune)*
41 les rides *f* de sable *m* (rides *f* éoliennes)
– *ripple marks*
42 la nebka (forme *f* d'abrasion *f* éolienne)
– *hummock*
43 l'arbre *m* incliné par le vent
– *wind cripple*
44 le lac de rivage *m*
– *coastal lake*
45 **le cañon** (canyon *m*)
– ***canyon*** *(cañon, coulee)*
46 le plateau (relief *m* tabulaire)
– *plateau (tableland)*
47 la terrasse rocheuse
– *rock terrace*
48 la roche stratifiée (la strate)
– *sedimentary rock (stratified rock)*
49 la terrasse fluviale
– *river terrace (bed)*
50 la faille
– *joint*
51 la rivière du cañon (canyon *m*)
– *canyon river*
52-56 formes ***f*** **de vallée** *f* [coupe *f*]
– ***types of valley*** *[cross section]*
52 la gorge en trait *m* de scie *f*
– *gorge (ravine)*
53 la vallée en V *m*
– *V-shaped valley (V-valley)*
54 la vallée en entaille *f* ouverte
– *widened V-shaped valley*
55 la vallée en fond *m* de bateau *m*
– *U-shaped valley (U-valley, trough valley)*
56 la vallée évasée (en gouttière *f*, en berceau *m*)
– *synclinal valley*
57-70 la vallée fluviale
– ***river valley***
57 l'escarpement *m* (le versant raide)
– *scarp (escarpment)*
58 le versant de glissement *m*
– *slip-off slope*
59 la mesa
– *mesa*
60 la ligne de crête *f*
– *ridge*
61 le cours d'eau *f* (le fleuve, la rivière)
– *river*
62 le lit de hautes eaux *f*
– *flood plain*
63 la terrasse rocheuse
– *river terrace*
64 la banquette (terrasse *f* de galets *m*)
– *terracette*
65 la pente
– *pediment*
66 la hauteur (la colline)
– *hill*
67 le fond de la vallée
– *valley floor (valley bottom)*
68 le lit du fleuve *m*
– *riverbed*
69 les dépôts *m* sédimentaires
– *sediment*
70 l'assise *f* rocheuse (la roche saine)
– *bedrock*
71-83 les formations ***f*** **karstiques** dans le calcaire
– ***karst formation*** *in limestone*
71 la doline, un cratère d'effondrement *m*
– *dolina, a sink (sinkhole, swallowhole)*
72 le poljé (les dépressions *f*)
– *polje*
73 la zone d'infiltration *f* (de percolation *f*)
– *percolation of a river*
74 la source karstique
– *karst spring*
75 la vallée sèche (vallée morte)
– *dry valley*
76 le réseau de cavernes *f*
– *system of caverns (system of caves)*
77 le niveau de la nappe d'eau *f* karstique
– *water level (water table) in a karst formation*
78 la couche rocheuse imperméable
– *impervious rock (impermeable rock)*
79 la grotte à concrétion *f* calcaire (grotte *f* à stalactites *f*)
– *limestone cave (dripstone cave)*
80-81 concrétions *f* calcaires
– *speleothems (cave formations)*
80 la stalactite
– *stalactite (dripstone)*
81 la stalagmite
– *stalagmite*
82 la colonne de concrétion *f* calcaire
– *linked-up stalagmite and stalactite*
83 la rivière souterraine
– *subterranean river*

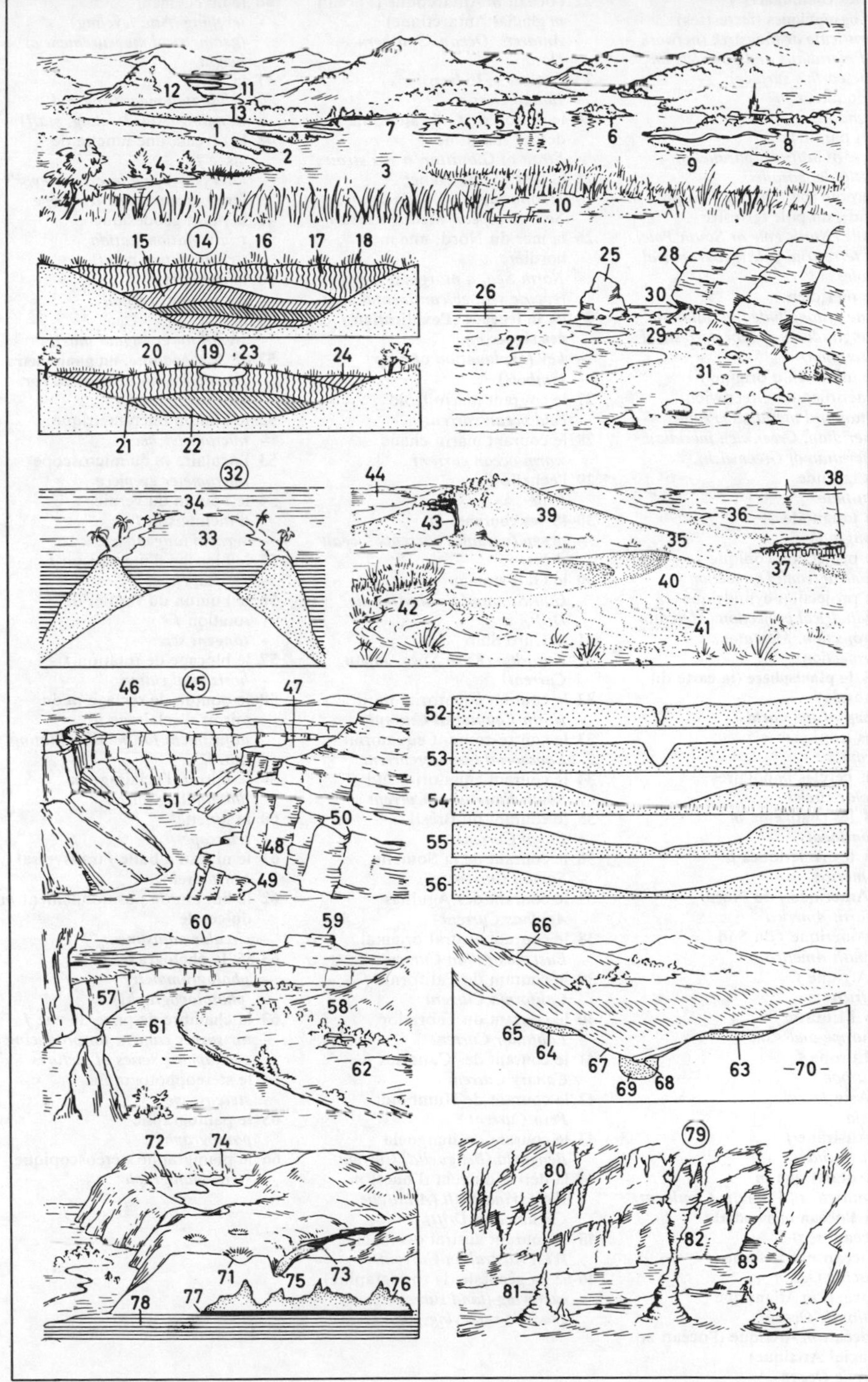
1
2
3
4
5
6
7
8
9
10
11
12
13
14
15
16
17
18
19
20
21
22
23
24
25
26
27
28
29
30
31
32
33
34
35
36
37
38
39
40
41
42
43
44
45
46
47
48
49
50
51
52
53
54
55
56
57
58
59
60
61
62
63
64
65
66
67
68
69
70
71
72
73
74
75
76
77
78
79
80
81
82
83

1-7 les coordonnées *f* **géographiques** (terrestres)
– ***graticule of the earth*** *(network of meridians and parallels on the earth's surface)*
1 l'équateur *m*
– *equator*
2 un parallèle
– *line of latitude (parallel of latitude, parallel)*
3 le pôle (pôle *m* nord ou pôle *m* sud), un pôle terrestre
– *pole (North Pole or South Pole), a terrestrial pole (geographical pole)*
4 le méridien
– *line of longitude (meridian of longitude, meridian, terrestrial meridian)*
5 le méridien d'origine *f* (méridien de Greenwich)
– *Standard meridian (Prime meridian, Greenwich meridian, meridian of Greenwich)*
6 la latitude
– *latitude*
7 la longitude
– *longitude*
8 la projection conique
– *conical (conic) projection*
9 la projection cylindrique
– *cylindrical projection (Mercator projection, Mercator's projection)*
10-45 le planisphère (la carte du monde)
– ***map of the world***
10 les tropiques *m*
– *tropics*
11 les cercles *m* polaires
– *polar circles*
12-18 les continents *m*
– ***continents***
12-13 les Amériques *f*
– *America*
12 l'Amérique *f* du Nord
– *North America*
13 l'Amérique *f* du Sud
– *South America*
14 l'Afrique *f*
– *Africa*
15-16 l'Eurasie *f*
– *Europe and Asia*
15 l'Europe *f*
– *Europe*
16 l'Asie *f*
– *Asia*
17 l'Australie *f*
– *Australia*
18 l'Antarctique *m*
– *Antarctica (Antarctic Continent)*
19-26 l'océan *m* **mondial**
– ***ocean*** *(sea)*
19 l'océan *m* Pacifique
– *Pacific Ocean*
20 l'océan *m* Atlantique
– *Atlantic Ocean*
21 l'océan *m* Arctique (l'océan *m* glacial Arctique)
– *Arctic Ocean*
22 l'océan *m* Antarctique (l'océan *m* glacial Antarctique)
– *Antarctic Ocean (Southern Ocean)*
23 l'océan *m* Indien
– *Indian Ocean*
24 le détroit de Gilbraltar, un détroit maritime
– *Strait of Gibraltar, a sea strait*
25 la mer Méditerranée
– *Mediterranean (Mediterranean Sea, European Mediterranean)*
26 la mer du Nord, une mer bordière
– *North Sea, a marginal sea (epeiric sea, epicontinental sea)*
27-29 la légende (l'explication *f* **des signes** *m*)
– ***key (explanation of map symbols)***
27 le courant marin froid
– *cold ocean current*
28 le courant marin chaud
– *warm ocean current*
29 l'échelle *f*
– *scale*
30-45 les courants *m*
– ***ocean (oceanic) currents*** *(ocean drifts)*
30 le Gulf stream
– *Gulf Stream (North Atlantic Drift)*
31 le Kuro Shio
– *Kuroshio (Kuro Siwo, Japan Current)*
32 le courant équatorial nord
– *North Equatorial Current*
33 le contre-courant équatorial
– *Equatorial Countercurrent*
34 le courant équatorial sud
– *South Equatorial Current*
35 le courant du Brésil
– *Brazil Current*
36 le courant de la Somalie
– *Somali Current*
37 le courant des Agulhas
– *Agulhas Current*
38 le courant austral oriental
– *East Australian Current*
39 le courant de Californie *f*
– *California Current*
40 le courant du Labrador
– *Labrador Current*
41 le courant des Canaries *f*
– *Canary Current*
42 le courant de Humboldt
– *Peru Current*
43 le courant de Benguela
– *Benguela (Benguella) Current*
44 la dérive du vent d'ouest *m*
– *West Wind Drift (Antarctic Circumpolar Drift)*
45 le courant austral occidental
– *West Australian Current*
46-62 la géodésie (la topographie)
– ***surveying*** *(land surveying, geodetic surveying, geodesy)*
46 le nivellement
– *levelling (*Am. *leveling) (geometrical measurement of height)*
47 la mire
– *graduated measuring rod (levelling,* Am. *leveling, staff)*
48 le niveau, une lunette de visée *f*
– *level (surveying level, surveyor's level), a surveyor's telescope*
49 le point géodésique
– *triangulation station (triangulation point)*
50 le chevalet
– *supporting scaffold*
51 le mât
– *signal tower (signal mast)*
52-62 le théodolite, un goniomètre
– ***theodolite, an instrument for measuring angles***
52 le bouton micrométrique
– *micrometer head*
53 l'oculaire *m* du microscope
– *micrometer eyepiece*
54 le bouton du vernier d'inclinaison *f*
– *vertical tangent screw*
55 le blocage d'inclinaison *f*
– *vertical clamp*
56 le bouton du vernier de rotation *f*
– *tangent screw*
57 le blocage de rotation *f*
– *horizontal clamp*
58 le bouton de réglage *m* du miroir d'éclairage *m*
– *adjustment for the illuminating mirror*
59 le miroir d'éclairage *m*
– *illuminating mirror*
60 la lunette
– *telescope*
61 le niveau à bulle *f* transversal
– *spirit level*
62 le bouton de positionnement *m* du cercle
– *circular adjustment*
63-66 la photogrammétrie
– ***photogrammetry*** *(phototopography)*
63 la chambre de prise de vue *f*
– *air survey camera for producing overlapping series of pictures*
64 le stéréophotographe
– *stereoscope*
65 le pantographe
– *pantograph*
66 le planigraphe stéréoscopique
– *stereoplanigraph*

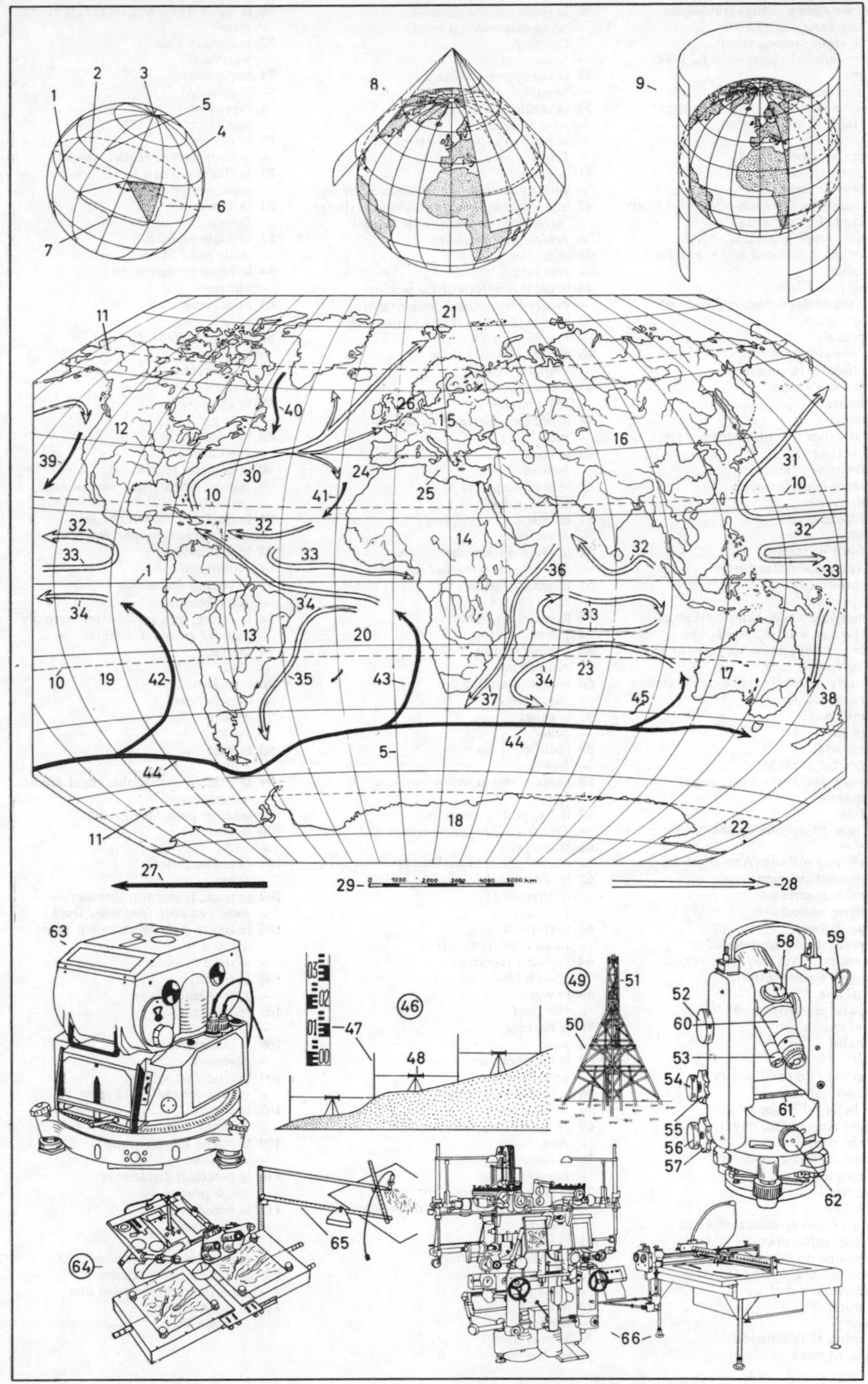

1-114 les signes *m* **topographiques** d'une carte au 1/25 000
– ***map signs*** *(map symbols, conventional signs) on a 1:25 000 map*
1 le bois de conifères *m*
– *coniferous wood (coniferous trees)*
2 la clairière
– *clearing*
3 la maison forestière
– *forestry office*
4 le bois de feuillus *m*
– *deciduous wood (non-coniferous trees)*
5 la lande (la garrigue)
– *heath (rough grassland, rough pasture, heath and moor, bracken)*
6 le sable
– *sand (sand hills)*
7 l'élyme *m* des sables *m* (l'oyat *m*)
– *beach grass*
8 le phare
– *lighthouse*
9 la laisse de basse mer *f*
– *mean low water*
10 la balise
– *beacon*
11 les courbes *f* de profondeur *f* (les isobathes *f*)
– *submarine contours*
12 le ferry-boat (le bac)
– *train ferry*
13 le bateau-phare
– *lightship*
14 la forêt mixte
– *mixed wood (mixed trees)*
15 les broussailles *f*
– *brushwood*
16 l'autoroute *f* avec rampe *f* d'accès *m*
– *motorway with slip road* (Am. *freeway with on-ramp, freeway with acceleration lane)*
17 la route nationale (la route de grande circulation *f*)
– *trunk road*
18 la prairie
– *grassland*
19 la prairie humide
– *marshy grassland*
20 le marais
– *marsh*
21 la ligne principale de chemin de fer *m*
– *main line railway* (Am. *trunk line)*
22 le passage inférieur
– *road over railway*
23 la ligne secondaire
– *branch line*
24 le poste de cantonnement *m*
– *signal box* (Am. *switch tower)*
25 la ligne à voie *f* étroite
– *local line*
26 le passage à niveau *m*
– *level crossing*
27 la halte
– *halt*
28 le groupe de pavillons *m*
– *residential area*
29 l'échelle *f* d'étiage *m*
– *water gauge* (Am. *gage)*
30 le chemin vicinal
– *good, metalled road*
31 le moulin à vent *m*
– *windmill*
32 la saline
– *thorn house (graduation house, salina, salt-works)*
33 le pylône de T.S.F. *f*
– *broadcasting station (wireless or television mast)*
34 la mine
– *mine*
35 la mine abandonnée
– *disused mine*
36 la route départementale
– *secondary road (B road)*
37 l'usine *f*
– *works*
38 la cheminée d'usine *f*
– *chimney*
39 la clôture en fil de fer *m*
– *wire fence*
40 le passage supérieur (le pont)
– *bridge over railway*
41 la gare
– *railway station* (Am. *railroad station)*
42 le passage supérieur du chemin de fer *m* (le pont de chemin de fer *m*)
– *bridge under railway*
43 le sentier
– *footpath*
44 le passage inférieur du sentier
– *bridge for footpath under railway*
45 la voie (le cours d'eau *f*) navigable
– *navigable river*
46 le pont de bateaux *m*
– *pontoon bridge*
47 le bac à voitures *f*
– *vehicle ferry*
48 la jetée en pierres *f* (le môle)
– *mole*
49 le fanal
– *beacon*
50 le pont en pierre *f*
– *stone bridge*
51 la ville
– *town (city)*
52 la place du marché
– *market place (market square)*
53 la grande église
– *large church*
54 le bâtiment public
– *public building*
55 le pont routier
– *road bridge*
56 le pont métallique
– *iron bridge*
57 le canal
– *canal*
58 l'écluse *f* à sas *m*
– *lock*
59 l'appontement *m*
– *jetty*
60 le bac pour piétons *m*
– *foot ferry (foot passenger ferry)*
61 la chapelle
– *chapel (church) without tower or spire*
62 les courbes *f* de niveau *m* (les isohypses *f*)
– *contours*
63 le couvent
– *monastery (convent)*
64 l'église *f* repère *m*
– *church landmark*
65 la vigne
– *vineyard*
66 le barrage
– *weir*
67 le téléphérique
– *aerial ropeway*
68 la tour d'observation *f*
– *view point*
69 l'écluse *f* de refoulement *m*
– *dam*
70 le tunnel
– *tunnel*
71 le point géodésique
– *triangulation station (triangulation point)*
72 la ruine
– *remains of a building*
73 l'éolienne *f*
– *wind pump*
74 le fort
– *fortress*
75 le bras mort
– *ox-bow lake*
76 le cours d'eau *f*, le fleuve, la rivière
– *river*
77 le moulin à eau *f*
– *watermill*
78 la passerelle
– *footbridge*
79 l'étang *m*
– *pond*
80 le ruisseau
– *stream (brook, rivulet, creek)*
81 le château d'eau *f*
– *water tower*
82 la source
– *spring*
83 la route principale
– *main road (A road)*
84 la route en déblai *m*
– *cutting*
85 la caverne
– *cave*
86 le four à chaux *f*
– *lime kiln*
87 la carrière
– *quarry*
88 la glaisière
– *clay pit*
89 la briqueterie
– *brickworks*
90 la desserte ferroviaire
– *narrow-gauge* (Am. *narrow gage) railway*
91 le quai de chargement *m*
– *goods depot (freight depot)*
92 le monument
– *monument*
93 le champ de bataille *f*
– *site of battle*
94 la ferme, une exploitation agricole
– *country estate, a demesne*
95 le mur
– *wall*
96 le château
– *stately home*
97 le parc
– *park*
98 la haie
– *hedge*
99 le chemin carrossable régulièrement entretenu
– *poor or unmetalled road*
100 le puits
– *well*
101 la ferme isolée
– *farm*
102 la piste, le chemin forestier
– *unfenced path (unfenced track)*
103 la limite d'arrondissement *m*, de canton *m*
– *district boundary*
104 le remblai
– *embankment*
105 le village
– *village*
106 le cimetière
– *cemetery*
107 l'église *f* du village
– *church (chapel) with spire*
108 le verger
– *orchard*
109 la borne kilométrique
– *milestone*
110 le poteau indicateur *m*
– *guide post*
111 la pépinière
– *tree nursery*
112 la laie
– *ride (aisle, lane, section line)*
113 la ligne à haute tension *f*
– *electricity transmission line*
114 la houblonnière
– *hop garden*

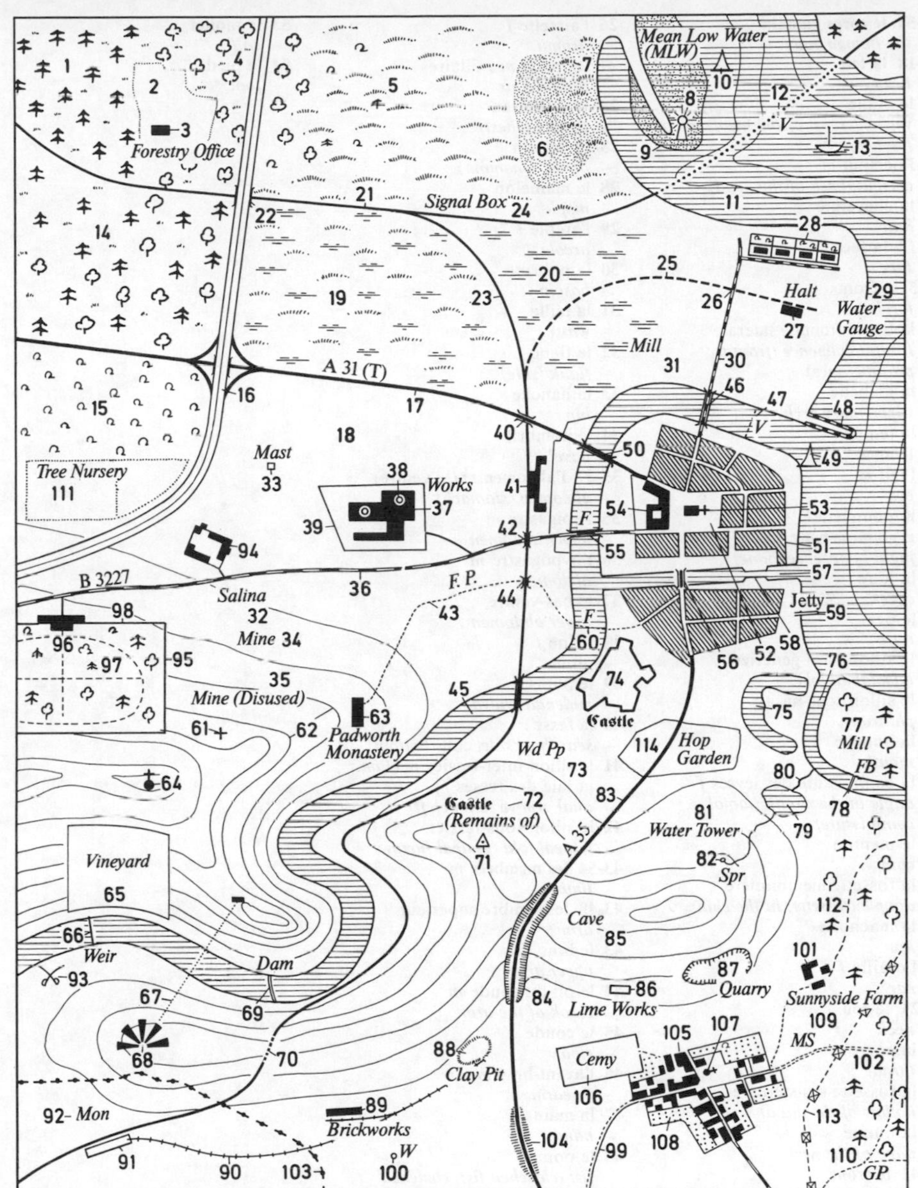
Mean Low Water (MLW)
Forestry Office
Signal Box
Halt
Water Gauge
Mill
A 31 (T)
Mast
Works
Tree Nursery
B 3227
Salina
Mine
Mine (Disused)
F. P.
Jetty
Castle
Padworth Monastery
Hop Garden
Wd Pp
Castle (Remains of)
Water Tower
Spr
Vineyard
Weir
Dam
Cave
Quarry
Lime Works
Sunnyside Farm
MS
Cemy
Clay Pit
Brickworks
Mon
GP
FB

1-54 le corps humain
– ***the human body***
1-18 la tête
– ***head***
1 le crâne
– *vertex (crown of the head, top of the head)*
2 l'occiput *m*
– *occiput (back of the head)*
3 la chevelure
– *hair*
4-17 la face
– ***face***
4-5 le front
– *forehead*
4 la bosse frontale latérale
– *frontal eminence (frontal protuberance)*
5 la glabelle
– *superciliary arch*
6 la tempe
– *temple*
7 l'œil *m*
– *eye*
8 la pommette
– *zygomatic bone (malar bone, jugal bone, cheekbone)*
9 la joue
– *cheek*
10 le nez
– *nose*
11 le sillon naso-génerien
– *nasolabial fold*
12 le sillon sous-nasal
– *philtrum*
13 la bouche
– *mouth*
14 la commissure des lèvres *f*
– *angle of the mouth (labial commissure)*
15 le menton
– *chin*
16 la fossette mentonnière
– *dimple (fossette) in the chin*
17 la mâchoire
– *jaw*
18 l'oreille *f*
– *ear*
19-21 le cou
– ***neck***
19 la gorge
– *throat*
20 la fossette sus-sternale
– *hollow of the throat*
21 la nuque
– *nape of the neck*
22-41 le tronc
– ***trunk***
22-25 le dos
– ***back***
22 l'épaule *f*
– *shoulder*
23 l'omoplate *f*
– *shoulderblade (scapula)*
24 les lombes *m* (la région lombaire)
– *loins*
25 les fosses *f* lombaires
– *small of the back*
26 l'aisselle *f*
– *armpit*
27 les poils *m* axillaires
– *armpit hair*
28-30 le thorax
– ***thorax** (chest)*
28-29 le sein
– *breast (mamma)*
28 le mamelon
– *nipple*
29 l'aréole *f*
– *areola*
30 la poitrine
– *bosom*
31 la taille
– *waist*
32 le flanc
– *flank (side)*
33 la hanche
– *hip*
34 le nombril
– *navel*
35-37 l'abdomen *m* (le ventre)
– ***abdomen** (stomach)*
35 l'épigastre *m*
– *upper abdomen*
36 l'hypogastre *m*
– *abdomen*
37 le bas-ventre
– *lower abdomen*
38 l'aine *f*
– *groin*
39 le pubis
– *pudenda (vulva)*
40 la fesse
– *seat (backside,* coll. *bottom)*
41 le sillon inter-fessier *m* (*fam.:* la raie des fesses *f*)
– *anal groove (anal cleft)*
42 le sillon sous-fessier
– *gluteal fold (gluteal furrow)*
43-54 les membres *m*
– ***limbs***
43-48 le membre supérieur
– *arm*
43 le bras
– *upper arm*
44 le pli du coude *m*
– *crook of the arm*
45 le coude
– *elbow*
46 l'avant-bras *m*
– *forearm*
47 la main
– *hand*
48 le poing
– *fist (clenched fist, clenched hand)*
49-54 le membre inférieur
– ***leg***
49 la cuisse
– *thigh*
50 le genou
– *knee*
51 le creux poplité
– *popliteal space*
52 la jambe
– *shank*
53 le mollet
– *calf*
54 le pied
– *foot*

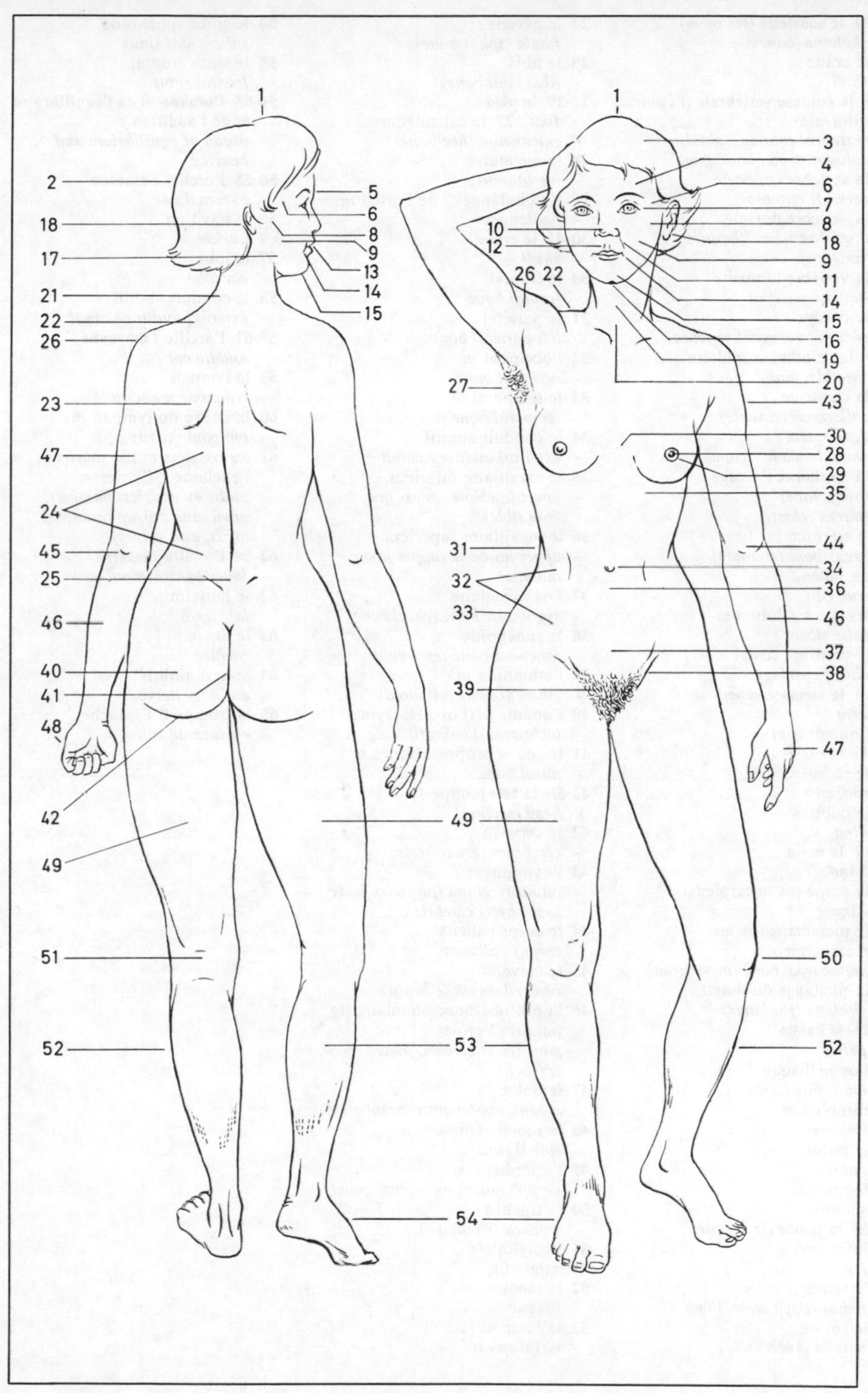
1
2
18
17
21
22
26
23
47
24
45
25
46
40
41
48
42
49
51
52
5
6
8
9
13
14
15
10
12
26 22
27
31
32
33
39
49
53
54
1
3
4
6
7
8
18
9
11
14
15
16
19
20
43
30
28
29
35
44
34
36
46
37
38
47
50
52

1-29 le squelette (les os *m*)
– ***skeleton** (bones)*
1 le crâne
– *skull*
2-5 la colonne vertébrale (l'épine *f* dorsale)
– ***vertebral column** (spinal column, spine, backbone)*
2 la vertèbre cervicale
– *cervical vertebra*
3 la vertèbre dorsale
– *dorsal vertebra (thoracic vertebra)*
4 la vertèbre lombaire
– *lumbar vertebra*
5 le coccyx
– *coccyx (coccygeal vertebra)*
6-7 la ceinture scapulaire
– *shoulder girdle*
6 la clavicule
– *collarbone (clavicle)*
7 l'omoplate *f*
– *shoulderblade (scapula)*
8-11 le thorax (la cage thoracique)
– ***thorax** (chest)*
8 le sternum
– *breastbone (sternum)*
9 les côtes *f*
– *true ribs*
10 les côtes *f* flottantes
– *false ribs*
11 le cartilage costal
– *costal cartilage*
12-14 le membre supérieur
– ***arm***
12 l'humérus *m*
– *humerus*
13 le radius
– *radius*
14 le cubitus
– *ulna*
15-17 la main
– ***hand***
15 le carpe (os *m* carpiens)
– *carpus*
16 le métacarpe (os *m* métacarpiens)
– *metacarpal bone (metacarpal)*
17 la phalange du doigt
– *phalanx (phalange)*
18-21 le bassin
– ***pelvis***
18 l'os *m* iliaque
– *ilium (hip bone)*
19 l'ischion *m*
– *ischium*
20 le pubis
– *pubis*
21 le sacrum
– *sacrum*
22-25 la jambe (le membre inférieur)
– ***leg***
22 le fémur
– *femur (thigh bone, thigh)*
23 la rotule
– *patella (kneecap)*
24 le péroné
– *fibula (splint bone)*
25 le tibia
– *tibia (shinbone)*
26-29 le pied
– ***foot*** **27** le calcanéum
– *calcaneum (heelbone)*
28 le métatarse
– *metatarsus*
29 les phalanges *f* de l'orteil *m*
– *phalanges*
30-41 le crâne
– ***skull***
30 le frontal
– *frontal bone*
31 le pariétal
– *left parietal bone*
32 l'occipital *m*
– *occipital bone*
33 le temporal
– *temporal bone*
34 le conduit auditif
– *external auditory canal*
35 le maxillaire inférieur
– *lower jawbone (lower jaw, mandible)*
36 le maxillaire supérieur
– *upper jawbone (upper jaw, maxilla)*
37 l'os *m* malaire
– *zygomatic bone (cheekbone)*
38 le sphénoïde
– *sphenoid bone (sphenoid)*
39 l'ethmoïde *m*
– *ethmoid bone (ethmoid)*
40 l'unguis *m* (l'os *m* lacrymal)
– *lachrimal (lacrimal) bone*
41 les os *m* propres du nez *m*
– *nasal bone*
42-55 la tête [coupe *f*]
– ***head** [section]*
42 le cerveau
– *cerebrum (great brain)*
43 l'hypophyse *f*
– *pituitary gland (pituitary body, hypophysis cerebri)*
44 le corps calleux
– *corpus callosum*
45 le cervelet
– *cerebellum (little brain)*
46 la protubérance annulaire (le pont de Varole)
– *pons (pons cerebri, pons cerebelli)*
47 le bulbe
– *medulla oblongata (brain-stem)*
48 la moelle épinière
– *spinal cord*
49 l'œsophage *m*
– *oesophagus (esophagus, gullet)*
50 la trachée
– *trachea (windpipe)*
51 l'épiglotte *f*
– *epiglottis*
52 la langue
– *tongue*
53 la fosse nasale
– *nasal cavity*
54 le sinus sphénoïde
– *sphenoidal sinus*
55 le sinus frontal
– *frontal sinus*
56-65 l'organe *m* **de l'équilibre** *m* **et de l'audition** *f*
– ***organ of equilibrium and hearing***
56-58 l'oreille *f* **externe**
– ***external ear***
56 le pavillon
– *auricle*
57 le lobe
– *ear lobe*
58 le conduit auditif
– *external auditory canal*
59-61 l'oreille *f* **moyenne**
– ***middle ear***
59 le tympan
– *tympanic membrane*
60 la caisse du tympan *m*
– *tympanic cavity*
61 les osselets *m* : le marteau, l'enclume *f*, l'étrier *m*
– *auditory ossicles: hammer, anvil, and stirrup (malleus, incus, and stapes)*
62-64 l'oreille *f* **interne**
– ***inner ear** (internal ear)*
62 le labyrinthe
– *labyrinth*
63 le limaçon
– *cochlea*
64 le nerf auditif
– *auditory nerve*
65 la trompe d'Eustache
– *eustachian tube*

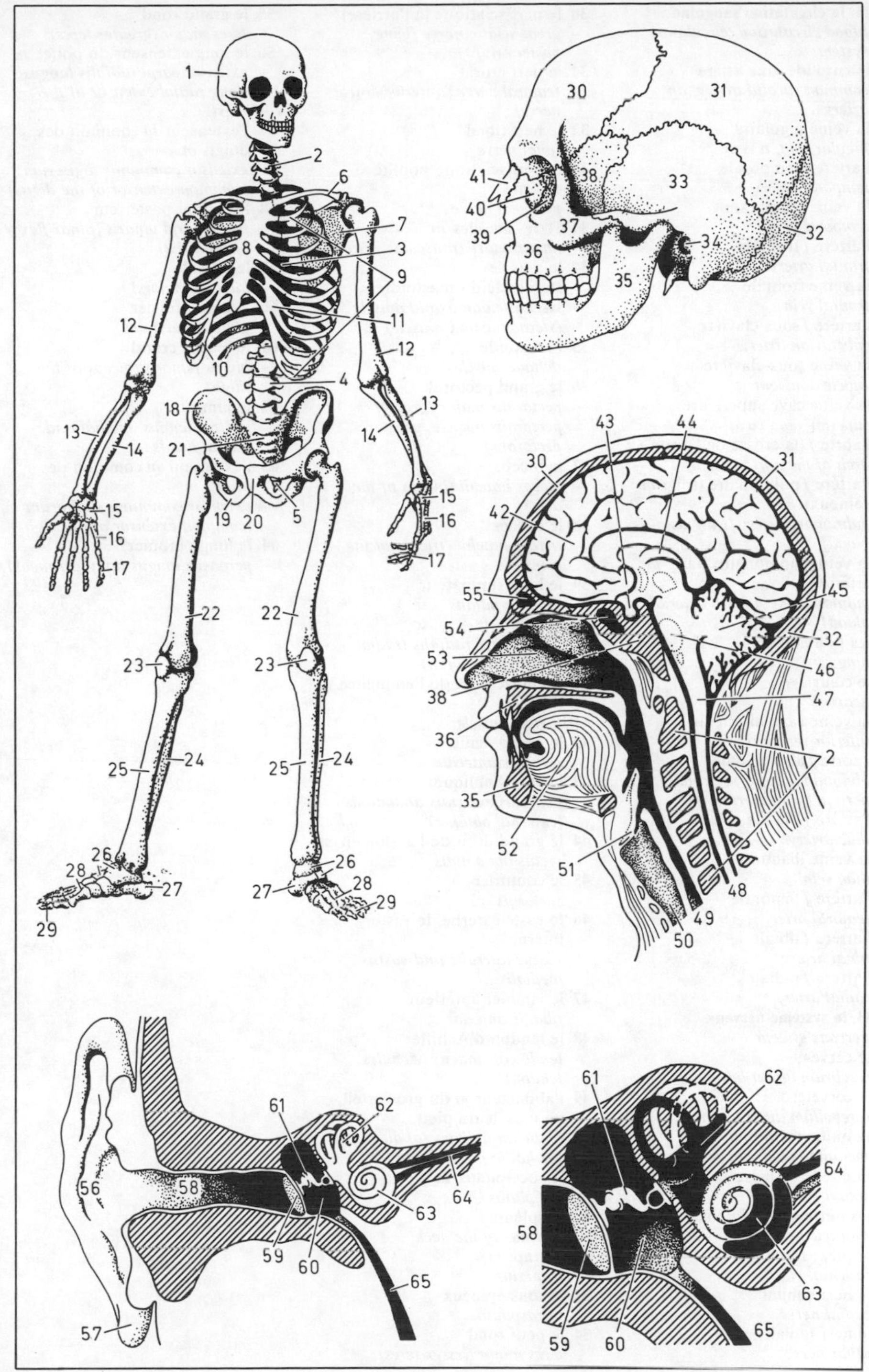
1
2
6
7
3
8
9
11
12
10
4
18
13
14
21
19
20
5
15
16
17
22
23
24
25
26
28
27
29
30
31
41
38
33
40
37
39
36
34
32
35
43
44
42
55
54
53
45
46
47
2
36
35
52
51
48
49
50
56
58
61
62
64
63
59
60
65
57

1-21 la circulation sanguine
– ***blood circulation*** *(circulatory system)*
1 la carotide, une artère
– *common carotid artery, an artery*
2 la veine jugulaire
– *jugular vein, a vein*
3 l'artère *f* temporale
– *temporal artery*
4 la veine temporale
– *temporal vein*
5 l'artère *f* frontale
– *frontal artery*
6 la veine frontale
– *frontal vein*
7 l'artère *f* sous-clavière
– *subclavian artery*
8 la veine sous-clavière
– *subclavian vein*
9 la veine cave supérieure
– *superior vena cava*
10 l'aorte *f* (la crosse de l'aorte *f*)
– *arch of the aorta (aorta)*
11 l'artère *f* pulmonaire (sang *m* veineux)
– *pulmonary artery [with venous blood]*
12 la veine pulmonaire (sang *m* artériel)
– *pulmonary vein [with arterial blood]*
13 les poumons *m*
– *lungs*
14 le cœur
– *heart*
15 la veine cave inférieure
– *inferior vena cava*
16 l'aorte *f* abdominale
– *abdominal aorta (descending portion of the aorta)*
17 l'artère *f* iliaque
– *iliac artery*
18 la veine iliaque
– *iliac vein*
19 l'artère *f* fémorale
– *femoral artery*
20 l'artère *f* tibiale
– *tibial artery*
21 l'artère *f* radiale
– *radial artery*
22-33 le système nerveux
– ***nervous system***
22 le cerveau
– *cerebrum (great brain)*
23 le cervelet
– *cerebellum (little brain)*
24 le bulbe rachidien
– *medulla oblongata (brain-stem)*
25 la mœlle épinière
– *spinal cord*
26 les nerfs *m* rachidiens
– *thoracic nerves*
27 le plexus brachial
– *brachial plexus*
28 le nerf cubital
– *radial nerve*
29 le nerf radial
– *ulnar nerve*
30 le nerf sciatique [à l'arrière]
– *great sciatic nerve [lying posteriorly]*
31 le nerf crural
– *femoral nerve (anterior crural nerve)*
32 le nerf tibial
– *tibial nerve*
33 le nerf sciatique poplité externe
– *peroneal nerve*
34-64 les muscles *m*
– ***musculature*** *(muscular system)*
34 le muscle sterno-cléido-mastoïdien
– *sternocleidomastoid muscle (sternomastoid muscle)*
35 le deltoïde
– *deltoid muscle*
36 le grand pectoral
– *pectoralis major (greater pectoralis muscle, greater pectoralis)*
37 le biceps
– *biceps brachii (biceps of the arm)*
38 le triceps
– *triceps brachii (triceps of the arm)*
39 le long supinateur
– *brachioradialis*
40 le palmaire
– *flexor carpi radialis (radial flexor of the wrist)*
41 les muscles *m* de l'éminence *f* thénar
– *thenar muscle*
42 le grand dentelé
– *serratus anterior*
43 le grand oblique
– *obliquus externus abdominis (external oblique)*
44 le grand droit de l'abdomen *m*
– *rectus abdominis*
45 le couturier
– *sartorius*
46 le vaste externe, le vaste interne
– *vastus lateralis and vastus medialis*
47 le jambier antérieur
– *tibialis anterior*
48 le tendon d'Achille
– *tendo calcanaeus (Achilles' tendon)*
49 l'abducteur *m* du gros orteil, un muscle du pied
– *abductor hallucis (abductor of the hallux), a foot muscle*
50 les occipitaux *m*
– *occipitalis*
51 le splénius
– *splenius of the neck*
52 le trapèze
– *trapezius*
53 le sous-épineux
– *infraspinatus*
54 le petit rond
– *teres minor (lesser teres)*
55 le grand rond
– *teres major (greater teres)*
56 le long extenseur du pouce *m*
– *extensor carpi radialis longus (long radial extensor of the wrist)*
57 l'extenseur *m* commun des doigts *m*
– *extensor communis digitorum (common extensor of the digits)*
58 le cubital postérieur
– *flexor carpi ulnaris (ulnar flexor of the wrist)*
59 le dorsal
– *latissimus dorsi*
60 le grand fessier
– *gluteus maximus*
61 le biceps crural
– *biceps femoris (biceps of the thigh)*
62 le jumeau
– *gastrocnemius, medial and lateral heads*
63 l'extenseur *m* commun des orteils *m*
– *extensor communis digitorum (common extensor of the digits)*
64 le long péronier
– *peroneus longus (long peroneus)*

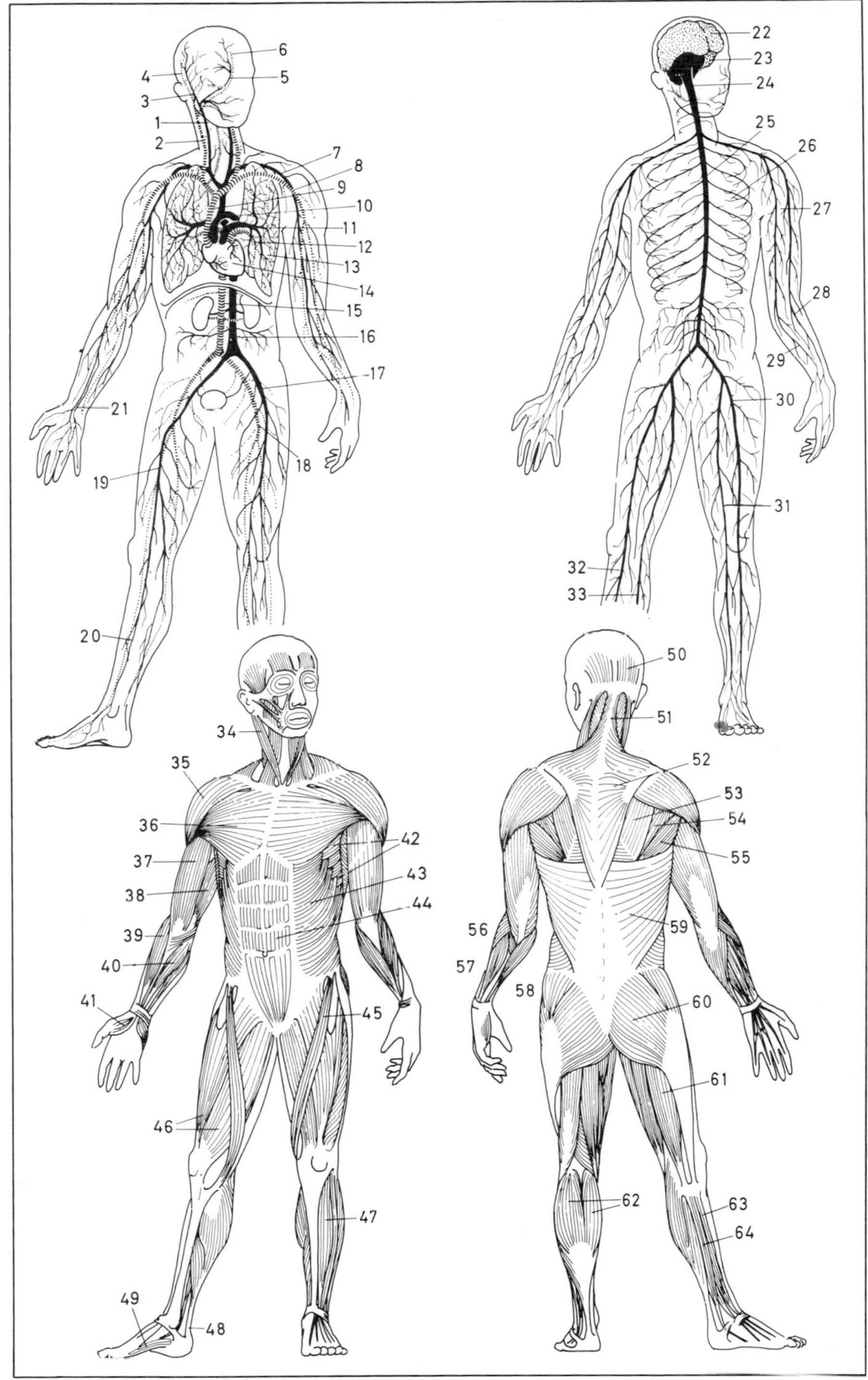
1
2
3
4
5
6
7
8
9
10
11
12
13
14
15
16
17
18
19
20
21
22
23
24
25
26
27
28
29
30
31
32
33
34
35
36
37
38
39
40
41
42
43
44
45
46
47
48
49
50
51
52
53
54
55
56
57
58
59
60
61
62
63
64

1-13 la tête et le cou
– *head and neck*
1 le sterno-cléido-mastoïdien
– *sternocleidomastoid muscle (sternomastoid muscle)*
2 le muscle occipital
– *occipitalis*
3 le muscle temporal
– *temporalis (temporal, temporal muscle)*
4 le muscle frontal
– *occipito frontalis (frontalis)*
5 l'orbiculaire *m* des paupières *f*
– *orbicularis oculi*
6 les muscles *m* zygomatiques
– *muscles of facial expression*
7 le masséter
– *masseter*
8 l'orbiculaire *m* des lèvres *f*
– *orbicularis oris*
9 la glande parotide
– *parotid gland*
10 le glanglion lymphatique
– *lymph node (submandibular lymph gland)*
11 la glande sous-maxillaire
– *submandibular gland (submaxillary gland)*
12 le peaucier du cou
– *muscles of the neck*
13 la pomme d'Adam [chez l'homme *m* seulement]
– *Adam's apple (laryngeal prominence) [in men only]*
14-37 la bouche et le pharynx
– *mouth and throat*
14 la lèvre supérieure
– *upper lip*
15 la gencive
– *gum*
16-18 la denture
– *teeth* *(set of teeth)*
16 les incisives *f*
– *incisors*
17 la canine
– *canine tooth (canine)*
18 les molaires *f*
– *premolar (bicuspid) and molar teeth (premolars and molars)*
19 la commissure des lèvres *f*
– *angle of the mouth (labial commissure)*
20 le palais
– *hard palate*
21 le voile du palais
– *soft palate (velum palati, velum)*
22 la luette
– *uvula*
23 l'amygdale *f*
– *palatine tonsil (tonsil)*
24 le pharynx
– *pharyngeal opening (pharynx, throat)*
25 la lèvre
– *tongue*
26 la lèvre inférieure
– *lower lip*
27 la mâchoire supérieure
– *upper jaw (maxilla)*
28-37 la dent
– *tooth*
28 la coiffe de la racine
– *periodontal membrane (periodontium, pericementum)*
29 le cément
– *cement (dental cementum, crusta petrosa)*
30 l'émail *m*
– *enamel*
31 l'ivoire *m*
– *dentine (dentin)*
32 la pulpe dentaire
– *dental pulp (tooth pulp, pulp)*
33 les nerfs *m* et les vaisseaux *m* sanguins
– *nerves and blood vessels*
34 l'incisive *f*
– *incisor*
35 la molaire
– *molar tooth (molar)*
36 la racine
– *root (fang)*
37 la couronne
– *crown*
38-51 l'œil *m*
– *eye*
38 le sourcil
– *eyebrow (supercilium)*
39 la paupière supérieure
– *upper eyelid (upper palpebra)*
40 la paupière inférieure
– *lower eyelid (lower palpebra)*
41 le cil
– *eyelash (cilium)*
42 l'iris *m*
– *iris*
43 la pupille
– *pupil*
44 les muscles *m* oculo-moteurs
– *eye muscles (ocular muscles)*
45 le globe oculaire
– *eyeball*
46 le corps vitré
– *vitreous body*
47 la cornée
– *cornea*
48 le cristallin
– *lens*
49 la rétine
– *retina*
50 la papille
– *blind spot*
51 le nerf optique
– *optic nerve*
52-63 le pied
– *foot*
52 le gros orteil
– *big toe (great toe, first toe, hallux, digitus I)*
53 le deuxième orteil
– *second toe (digitus II)*
54 le troisième orteil
– *third toe (digitus III)*
55 le quatrième orteil
– *fourth toe (digitus IV)*
56 le petit orteil
– *little toe (digitus minimus, digitus V)*
57 l'ongle *m* de l'orteil *m*
– *toenail*
58 l'éminence *f* de l'articulation *f* métatarso- phalangienne
– *ball of the foot*
59 la malléole externe
– *lateral malleolus (external malleolus, outer malleolus, malleolus fibulae)*
60 la malléole interne
– *medial malleolus (internal malleolus, inner malleolus, malleolus tibulae, malleolus medialis)*
61 le dos du pied
– *instep (medial longitudinal arch, dorsum of the foot, dorsum pedis)*
62 la plante du pied
– *sole of the foot*
63 le talon
– *heel*
64-83 la main
– *hand*
64 le pouce
– *thumb (pollex, digitus I)*
65 l'index *m*
– *index finger (forefinger, second finger, digitus II)*
66 le majeur
– *middle finger (third finger, digitus medius, digitus III)*
67 l'annulaire *m*
– *ring finger (fourth finger, digitus anularis, digitus IV)*
68 l'auriculaire *m*
– *little finger (fifth finger, digitus minimus, digitus V)*
69 le bord radial de la main
– *radial side of the hand*
70 le bord cubital de la main
– *ulnar side of the hand*
71 la paume
– *palm of the hand (palma manus)*
72-74 les lignes *f* de la main
– *lines of the hand*
72 la ligne de vie *f*
– *life line (line of life)*
73 la ligne de tête *f*
– *head line (line of the head)*
74 la ligne de cœur *m*
– *heart line (line of the heart)*
75 l'éminence *f* thénar
– *ball of the thumb (thenar eminence)*
76 le poignet
– *wrist (carpus)*
77 la phalange
– *phalanx (phalange)*
78 la pulpe de la phalangette
– *finger pad*
79 le bout du doigt
– *fingertip*
80 l'ongle du doigt
– *fingernail (nail)*
81 la lunule
– *lunule (lunula) of the nail*
82 le nœud de l'articulation *f* métacarpo-phalangienne
– *knuckle*
83 le dos de la main
– *back of the hand (dorsum of the hand, dorsum manus)*

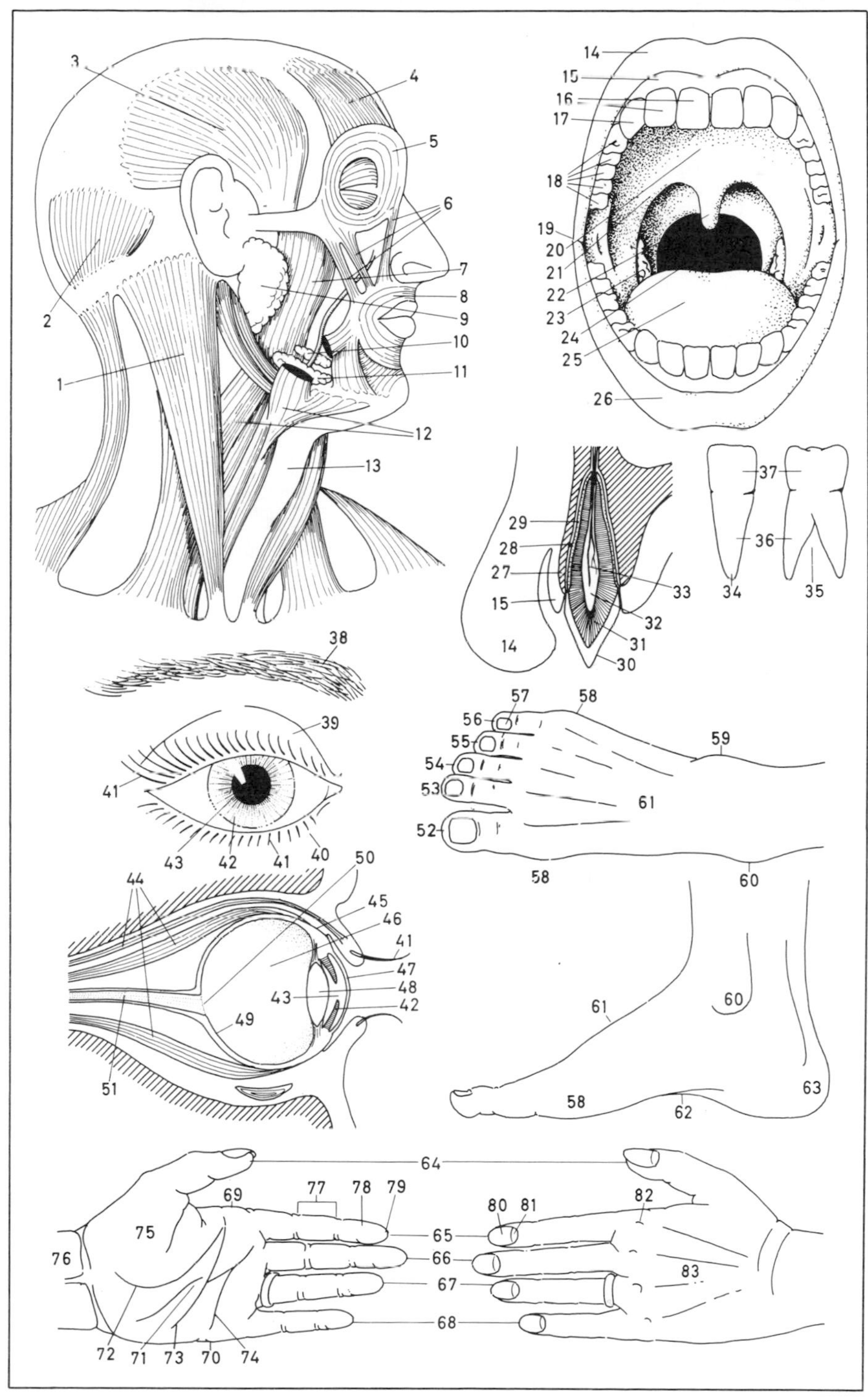
1
2
3
4
5
6
7
8
9
10
11
12
13
14
15
16
17
18
19
20
21
22
23
24
25
26
27
28
29
30
31
32
33
34
35
36
37
38
39
40
41
42
43
44
45
46
47
48
49
50
51
52
53
54
55
56
57
58
59
60
61
62
63
64
65
66
67
68
69
70
71
72
73
74
75
76
77
78
79
80
81
82
83

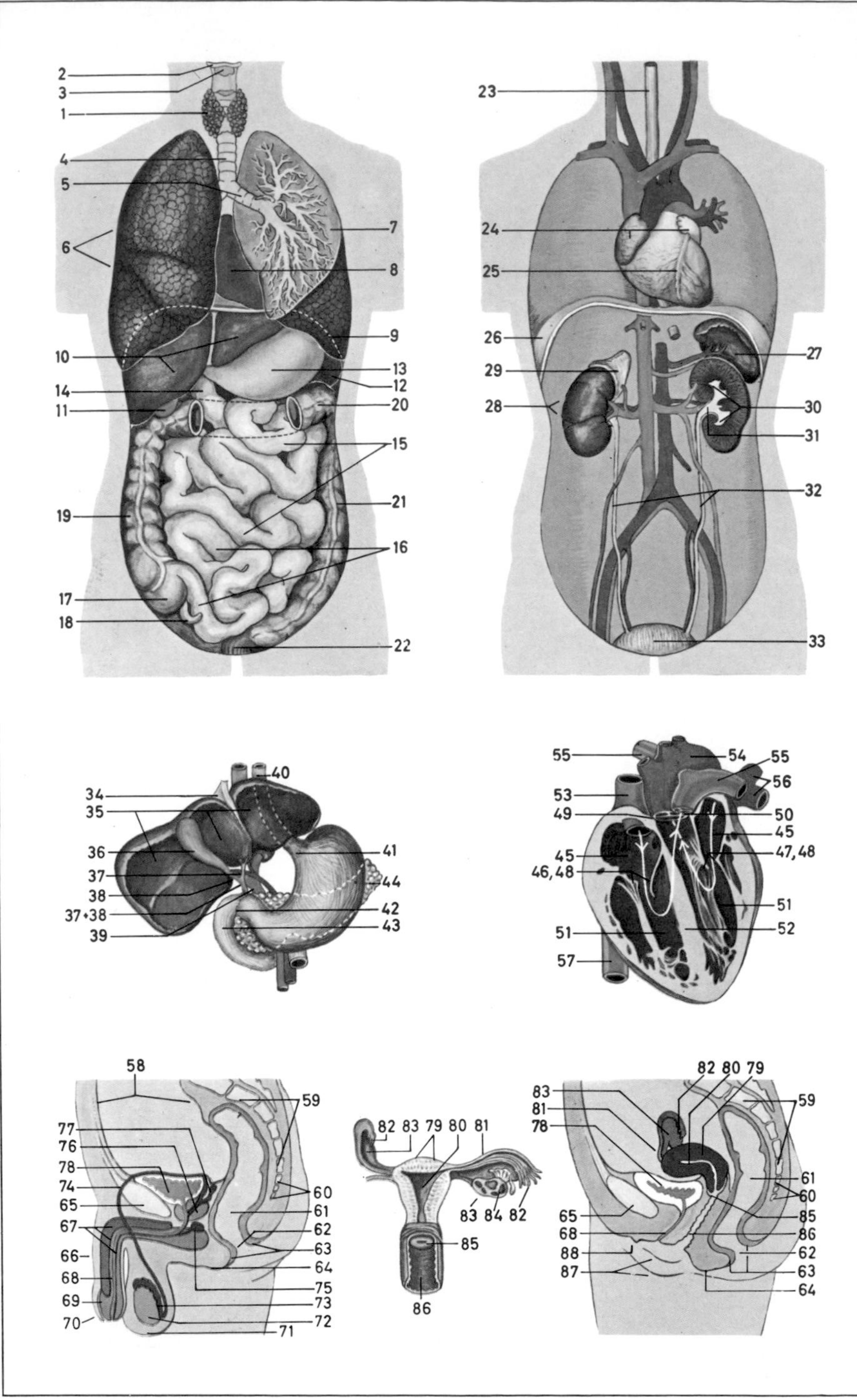
2
3
1
4
5
6
7
8
9
10
13
12
14
11
20
15
19
21
16
17
18
22
23
24
25
26
27
29
28
30
31
32
33
40
34
35
36
37
38
37+38
39
41
44
42
43
55
54
55
56
53
49
50
45
45
47,48
46,48
51
51
52
57
58
59
77
76
78
74
65
67
66
68
69
70
60
61
62
63
64
75
73
72
71
82
83
79
80
81
83
84
82
85
86
82
80
79
83
81
78
59
61
60
65
85
68
86
88
62
87
63
64

1-57 les organes *m* internes [vus de face]
– ***internal organs*** *[front view]*
1 le corps thyroïde
– *thyroid gland*
2-3 le larynx
– *larynx*
2 l'os *m* hyoïde
– *hyoid bone (hyoid)*
3 le cartilage thyroïde
– *thyroid cartilage*
4 la trachée
– *trachea (windpipe)*
5 les bronches *f*
– *bronchus*
6-7 les poumons *m*
– *lung*
6 le poumon droit
– *right lung*
7 le lobe supérieur du poumon [coupe *f*]
– *upper pulmonary lobe (upper lobe of the lung) [section]*
8 le cœur
– *heart*
9 le diaphragme
– *diaphragm*
10 le foie
– *liver*
11 la vésicule biliaire
– *gall bladder*
12 la rate
– *spleen*
13 l'estomac *m*
– *stomach*
14-22 l'intestin *m*
– ***intestines*** *(bowel)*
14-16 l'intestin *m* grêle
– ***small intestine*** *(intestinum tenue)*
14 le duodénum
– *duodenum*
15 le jéjunum
– *jejunum*
16 l'iléon *m*
– *ileum*
17-22 le gros intestin
– ***large intestine*** *(intestinum crassum)*
17 le cæcum
– *caecum (cecum)*
18 l'appendice *m*
– *appendix (vermiform appendix)*
19 le côlon ascendant
– *ascending colon*
20 le côlon transverse
– *transverse colon*
21 le côlon descendant
– *descending colon*
22 le rectum
– *rectum*
23 l'œsophage *m*
– *oesophagus (esophagus, gullet)*
24-25 le cœur
– *heart*
24 l'oreillette *f*
– *auricle*
25 le sillon inter-ventriculaire antérieur
– *anterior longitudinal cardiac sulcus*
26 le diaphragme
– *diaphragm*
27 la rate
– *spleen*
28 le rein droit
– *right kidney*
29 la capsule surrénale
– *suprarenal gland*

30-31 le rein gauche [coupe longitudinale]
– *left kidney [longitudinal section]*
30 le calice
– *calyx (renal calyx)*
31 le bassinet
– *renal pelvis*
32 l'uretère *m*
– *ureter*
33 la vessie
– *bladder*
34-35 le foie [rabattu]
– *liver [from behind]*
34 le hile du foie
– *falciform ligament of the liver*
35 le lobe du foie
– *lobe of the liver*
36 la vésicule biliaire
– *gall bladder*
37-38 le canal cholédoque
– *common bile duct*
37 le canal hépatique
– *hepatic duct (common hepatic duct)*
38 le canal cystique
– *cystic duct*
39 la veine porte
– *portal vein (hepatic portal vein)*
40 l'œsophage *m*
– *oesophagus (esophagus, gullet)*
41-42 l'estomac *m*
– *stomach*
41 le cardia
– *cardiac orifice*
42 le pylore
– *pylorus*
43 le duodénum
– *duodenum*
44 le pancréas
– *pancreas*
45-57 le cœur [coupe longitudinale]
– ***heart*** *[longitudinal section]*
45 l'oreillette *f*
– *atrium*
46-47 les valvules *f* cardiaques
– *valves of the heart*
46 la valvule tricuspide
– *tricuspid valve (right atrioventricular valve)*
47 la valvule mitrale
– *bicuspid valve (mitral valve, left atrioventricular valve)*
48 la valvule
– *cusp*
49 la valvule sigmoïde de l'aorte *f*
– *aortic valve*
50 la valvule sigmoïde de l'artère *f* pulmonaire
– *pulmonary valve*
51 le ventricule
– *ventricle*
52 la cloison interventriculaire
– *ventricular septum (interventricular septum)*
53 la veine cave supérieure
– *superior vena cava*
54 l'aorte *f*
– *aorta*
55 l'artère *f* pulmonaire
– *pulmonary artery*
56 les veines *f* pulmonaires
– *pulmonary vein*
57 la veine cave inférieure
– *inferior vena cava*
58 le péritoine
– *peritoneum*
59 le sacrum
– *sacrum*

60 le coccyx
– *coccyx (coccygeal vertebra)*
61 le rectum
– *rectum*
62 l'anus *m*
– *anus*
63 le sphincter anal
– *anal sphincter*
64 le périnée
– *perineum*
65 la symphyse pubienne
– *pubic symphysis (symphysis pubis)*
66-77 les organes *m* génitaux masculins [coupe longitudinale]
– ***male sex organs*** *[longitudinal section]*
66 la verge
– *penis*
67 le tissu érectile
– *corpus cavernosum and spongiosum of the penis (erectile tissue of the penis)*
68 l'urètre *m*
– *urethra*
69 le gland
– *glans penis*
70 le prépuce
– *prepuce (foreskin)*
71 le scrotum
– *scrotum*
72 le testicule droit
– *right testicle (testis)*
73 l'épididyme *m*
– *epididymis*
74 le conduit séminal
– *spermatic duct (vas deferens)*
75 la glande de Cowper
– *Cowper's gland (bulbourethral gland)*
76 la prostate
– *prostate (prostate gland)*
77 la vésicule séminale
– *seminal vesicle*
78 la vessie
– *bladder*
79-88 les organes *m* génitaux féminins [coupe longitudinale]
– ***female sex organs*** *[longitudinal section]*
79 l'utérus *m*
– *uterus (matrix, womb)*
80 la cavité utérine
– *cavity of the uterus*
81 l'oviducte *m*
– *fallopian tube (uterine tube, oviduct)*
82 les franges *f* de la trompe
– *fimbria (fimbriated extremity)*
83 l'ovaire *m*
– *ovary*
84 le follicule et l'ovule *m*
– *follicle with ovum (egg)*
85 le col de l'utérus *m* (le museau de tanche *f*)
– *os uteri externum*
86 le vagin
– *vagina*
87 les lèvres *f*
– *lip of the pudendum (lip of the vulva)*
88 le clitoris
– *clitoris*

1-13 pansements *m* **d'urgence** *f*
– ***emergency bandages***
1 le pansement du bras *m*
– *arm bandage*
2 l'écharpe *f* utilisée pour soutenir le bras
– *triangular cloth used as a sling (an arm sling)*
3 la fronde de la tête
– *head bandage (capeline)*
4 le paquet de pansements *m*
– *first aid kit*
5 le pansement adhésif
– *first aid dressing*
6 la gaze stérile
– *sterile gauze dressing*
7 le sparadrap
– *adhesive plaster (sticking plaster)*
8 la blessure
– *wound*
9 la bande de gaze *f* (la gaze)
– *bandage*
10 les attelles *f* pour la fixation d'un membre brisé
– *emergency splint for a broken limb (fractured limb)*
11 la jambe cassée
– *fractured leg (broken leg)*
12 l'attelle *f* (la gouttière, l'éclisse *f*)
– *splint*
13 le coussinet (secourisme *m*)
– *headrest*
14-17 soins *m* **en cas** *m* **d'hémorragie** *f* (compression *f* d'un vaisseau sanguin)
– ***measures for stanching the blood flow*** *(tying up of, ligature of, a blood vessel)*
14 les points *m* de compression *f* des artères *f*
– *pressure points of the arteries*
15 la pose d'un garrot à la cuisse
– *emergency tourniquet on the thigh*
16 la canne utilisée pour serrer le garrot
– *walking stick used as a screw*
17 le garrot
– *compression bandage*
18-23 le sauvetage et le transport d'un blessé
– ***rescue and transport of an injured person***
18 transport *m* d'un blessé de la route
– *Rautek grip (for rescue of victim of a car accident)*
19 le secouriste
– *helper*
20 le blessé sans connaissance *f* (la victime d'un accident)
– *injured person (casualty)*
21 la chaise à porteur *m* (secourisme *m*)
– *chair grip*
22 la torchette
– *carrying grip*
23 le brancard fait de bâtons *m* et d'une veste
– *emergency stretcher of sticks and a jacket*
24-27 disposition *f* d'un blessé inanimé et respiration *f* artificielle (la réanimation)
– ***positioning of an unconscious person and artificial respiration*** *(resuscitation)*
24 la position latérale de sécurité *f*
– *coma position*
25 la personne inanimée
– *unconscious person*
26 le bouche-à-bouche; *var.*: le bouche-à-nez
– *mouth-to-mouth resuscitation* (variation: *mouth-to-nose resuscitation)*
27 le réanimateur électrique, un appareil de réanimation *f*, un appareil respiratoire
– *resuscitator (respiratory apparatus, resuscitation apparatus), a respirator (artificial breathing device)*
28-33 secours *m* **en cas** *m* **de rupture** *f* **d'une couche de glace** *f*
– ***methods of rescue in ice accidents***
28 la personne tombée à l'eau *f* à travers la glace
– *person who has fallen through the ice*
29 le sauveteur
– *rescuer*
30 la corde
– *rope*
31 la table (ou un autre moyen de secours *m*)
– *table (or similar device)*
32 l'échelle *f*
– *ladder*
33 l'auto-sauvetage *m*
– *self-rescue*
34-38 secours *m* **aux noyés** *m*
– ***rescue of a drowning person***
34 le dégagement de l'étreinte *f*
– *method of release (release grip, release) to free rescuer from the clutch of a drowning person*
35 le noyé
– *drowning person*
36 le sauveteur
– *lifesaver*
37 la prise axillaire, une prise pour le transport du noyé
– *chest grip, a towing grip*
38 la prise par les hanches *f*
– *tired swimmer grip (hip grip)*

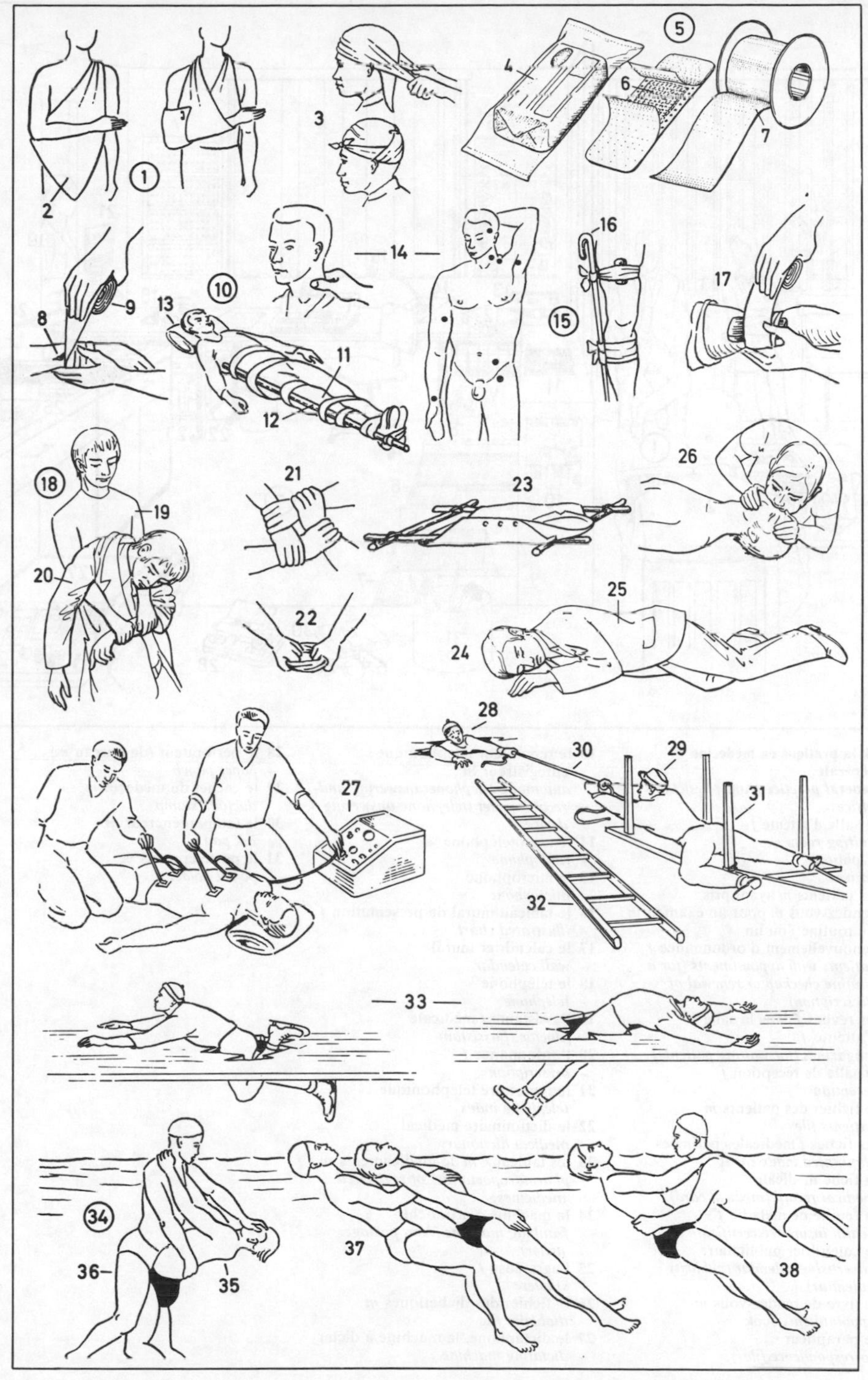
1
2
3
4
5
6
7
8
9
10
11
12
13
14
15
16
17
18
19
20
21
22
23
24
25
26
27
28
29
30
31
32
33
34
35
36
37
38

1-74 la pratique en médecine *f* **générale**
– ***general practice*** (Am. *physician's office)*
1 la salle d'attente *f*
– ***waiting room***
2 le patient
– *patient*
3 les patients *m* ayant pris rendez-vous *m* pour un examen *m* de routine *f* ou un renouvellement d'ordonnance *f*
– *patients with appointments (for a routine checkup or renewal of prescription)*
4 les revues *f* dans la salle d'attente *f*
– *magazines [for waiting patients]*
5 la salle de réception *f*
– *reception*
6 le fichier des patients *m*
– *patients file*
7 les fiches *f* médicales périmées
– *eliminated index cards*
8 la fiche médicale
– *medical record (medical card)*
9 la feuille de maladie *f*
– *health insurance certificate*
10 le calendrier publicitaire
– *advertising calendar (publicity calendar)*
11 le livre de rendez-vous *m*
– *appointments book*
12 le parapheur
– *correspondence file*
13 le répondeur téléphonique enregistreur *m*
– *automatic telephone answering and recording set (telephone answering device)*
14 le radiotéléphone
– *radiophone*
15 le microphone
– *microphone*
16 le tableau mural de présentation *f*
– *illustrated chart*
17 le calendrier mural
– *wall calendar*
18 le téléphone
– *telephone*
19 l'assistante *f* médicale
– *[doctor's] assistant*
20 l'ordonnance *f*
– *prescription*
21 le répertoire téléphonique
– *telephone index*
22 le dictionnaire médical
– *medical dictionary*
23 les tableaux *m* de médicaments *m*
– *pharmacopoeia (list of registered medicines)*
24 la machine à affranchir
– *franking machine* (Am. *postage meter)*
25 l'agrafeuse *f*
– *stapler*
26 le fichier des diabétiques *m*
– *diabetics file*
27 le dictaphone, la machine à dicter
– *dictating machine*
28 le perforateur (de bureau *m*)
– *paper punch*
29 le cachet du médecin *m*
– *doctor's stamp*
30 le tampon encreur *m*
– *ink pad*
31 le porte-crayons *m*
– *pencil holder*

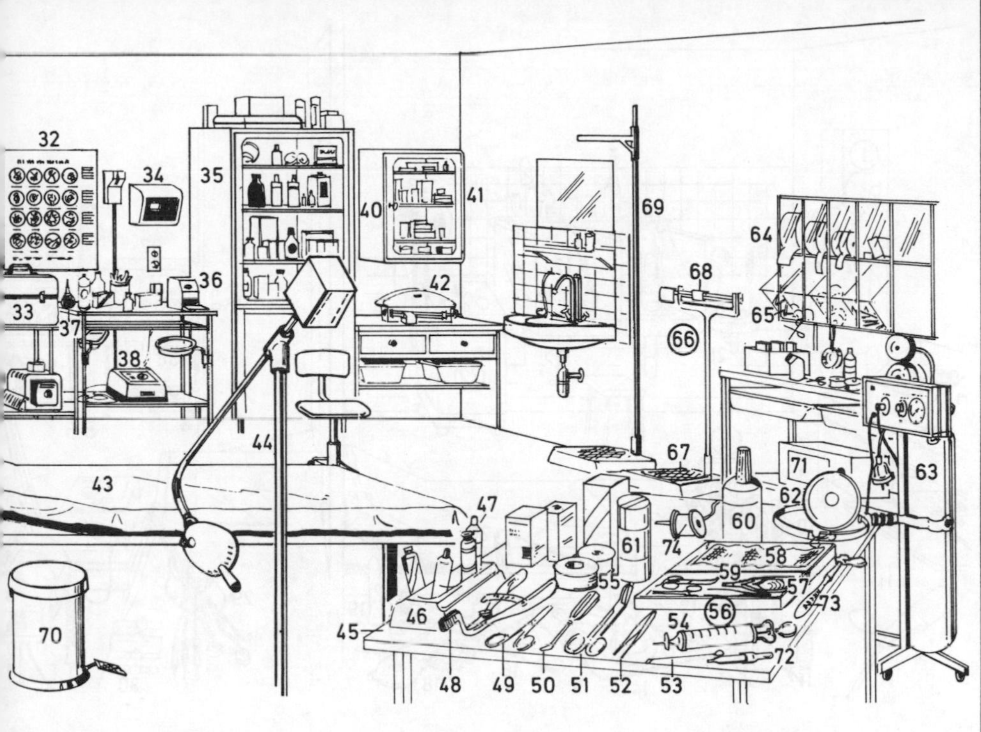

32-74 la salle de soins *m*
– ***surgery***
32 le tableau d'acuité *f* visuelle
– *chart of eyegrounds*
33 la serviette médicale
– *doctor's bag (doctor's case)*
34 l'interphone *m*
– *intercom*
35 l'armoire *f* à pharmacie *f*
– *medicine cupboard*
36 le distributeur de coton *m*
– *swab dispenser*
37 l'insufflateur*m* (la poire de Politzer)
– *inflator (Politzer bag)*
38 l'électrotome *m*
– *electrotome*
39 le stérilisateur à vapeur *f*
– *steam sterilizer*
40 l'armoire *f* murale
– *cabinet*
41 les échantillons *m* médicaux
– *medicine samples (from the pharmaceutical industry)*
42 le pèse-bébé
– *baby scales*
43 la table d'examen *m*
– *examination couch*
44 la lampe à faisceau *m* dirigé
– *directional lamp*
45 la table de pansements *m*
– *instrument table*
46 le porte-tubes
– *tube holder*
47 le tube de pommade *f*
– *tube of ointment*
48-50 les instruments *m* **de petite chirurgie** *f*
– ***instruments for minor surgery***
48 l'ouvre-bouche *m*
– *mouth gag*
49 la pince Kocher
– *Kocher's forceps*
50 la curette
– *scoop (curette)*
51 les ciseaux *m* courbes
– *angled scissors*
52 la pince
– *forceps*
53 la sonde béquille
– *olive-pointed (bulb-headed) probe*
54 la seringue vésicale
– *syringe for irrigations of the ear or bladder*
55 le sparadrap
– *adhesive plaster (sticking plaster)*
56 le matériel de suture *f*
– *surgical suture material*
57 une aiguille courbe à sutures *f*
– *curved surgical needle*
58 la gaze stérile
– *sterile gauze*
59 la pince porte-aiguille *m*
– *needle holder*
60 la pissette de désinfection *f* cutanée
– *spray for disinfecting the skin*
61 le porte-fils
– *thread container*
62 l'ophtalmoscope *m*
– *ophthalmoscope*
63 l'appareil *m* de cryothérapie *f*
– *freezer for cryosurgery*
64 le distributeur de sparadrap *m* et de petites pièces *f*
– *dispenser for plasters and small pieces of equipment*
65 les aiguilles *f* et les seringues *f* à usage *m* unique
– *disposable hypodermic needles and syringes*
66 le balance médicale, une balance à curseur *m*
– *scales, sliding-weight scales*
67 le plateau de balance *f*
– *weighing platform*
68 le curseur de balance *f*
– *sliding weight (jockey)*
69 la toise
– *height gauge (*Am.* gage)*
70 le seau à pansements *m*
– *waste bin (*Am.* trash bin)*
71 le stérilisateur à air *m* chaud
– *hot-air sterilizer*
72 la pipette
– *pipette*
73 le marteau à réflexes *m*
– *percussor*
74 l'otoscope *m*
– *aural speculum (auriscope, aural syringe)*

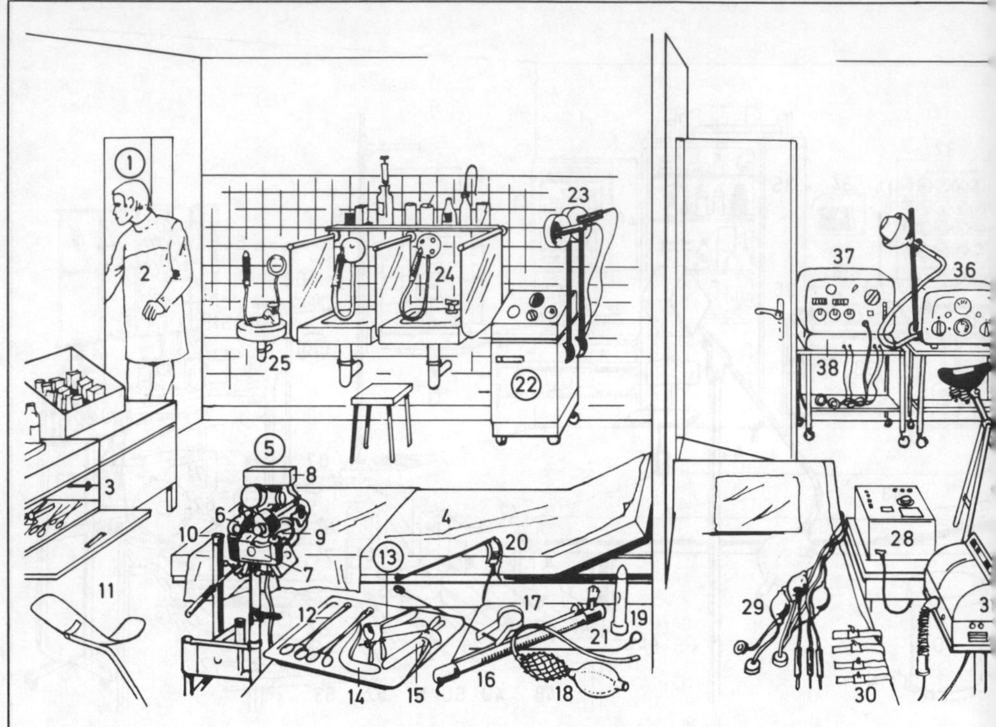

1 le cabinet de consultation *f*
– *consulting room*
2 le médecin de médecine *f* générale (le généraliste)
– *general practitioner*
3-21 instruments *m* d'examen *m* gynécologique ou proctologique
– ***instruments for gynecological and proctological examinations***
3 le réchauffage des instruments *m* à la température du corps
– *warming the instruments up to body temperature*
4 la table d'examen *m*
– *examination couch*
5 le colposcope
– *colposcope*
6 le binoculaire
– *binocular eyepiece*
7 l'appareil *m* pour photos *m* de petit format *m*
– *miniature camera*
8 la source de lumière *f* froide
– *cold light source*
9 le déclencheur
– *cable release*
10 le tube de fixation *f* de l'étrier *m*
– *bracket for the leg support*
11 l'étrier
– *leg support (leg holder)*
12 la pince à pansements *m*
– *holding forceps (sponge holder)*
13 le spéculum [vaginal]
– *vaginal speculum*
14 la branche inférieure du spéculum *m*
– *lower blade of the vaginal speculum*
15 la boucle de platine *m* (pour frottis *m*)
– *platinum loop (for smears)*
16 le rectoscope
– *rectoscope*
17 la pince à biopsie *f* pour le rectoscope
– *biopsy forceps used with the rectoscope (proctoscope)*
18 l'insufflateur *m* d'air *m* pour le rectoscope
– *insufflator for proctoscopy (rectoscopy)*
19 l'anuscope *m*
– *proctoscope (rectal speculum)*
20 le fibroscope urinaire
– *urethroscope*
21 la sonde de guidage *m* pour l'anuscope *m*
– *guide for inserting the proctoscope*
22 l'appareil *m* de diathermie *f* (appareil *m* à ondes *f* courtes)
– *diathermy unit (short-wave therapy apparatus)*
23 le radiateur de diathermie *f*
– *radiator*
24 l'inhalateur *m*
– *inhaling apparatus (inhalator)*
25 le crachoir
– *basin (for sputum)*
26-31 l'ergométrie *f*
– ***ergometry***
26 le cycloergomètre
– *bicycle ergometer*
27 le moniteur (l'écran *m* de visualisation *f* de l'électrocardiogramme *m* et de la fréquence cardiaque et respiratoire pendant l'effort *m*)
– *monitor (visual display of the ECG and of pulse and respiratory rates when performing work)*
28 l'électrocardiographe *m*
– *ECG (electrocardiograph)*
29 les électrodes *f* à ventouse *f* (pour les dérivations *f* précordiales)
– *suction electrodes*
30 les électrodes *f* à sangles *f* pour les dérivations *f* standards
– *strap-on electrodes for the limbs*
31 le spiromètre (pour la mesure des fonctions *f* respiratoires)
– *spirometer (for measuring respiratory functions)*
32 la mesure de la pression sanguine
– *measuring the blood pressure*
33 le tensiomètre (le sphygmomanomètre)
– *sphygmomanometer*
34 le brassard
– *inflatable cuff*
35 le stéthoscope
– *stethoscope*

36 l'appareil *m* de traitement *m* par hyperfréquences *f*
– *microwave treatment unit*
37 l'appareil *m* de faradisation *f* (application *f* de courants *m* à basse fréquence *f* avec diverses formes *f* d'impulsions *f*)
– *faradization unit (application of low-frequency currents with different pulse shapes)*
38 l'appareil *m* d'accord *m* automatique
– *automatic tuner*
39 l'appareil *m* de traitement *m* par ondes *f* courtes à monode *f*
– *short-wave therapy apparatus*
40 le chronomicromètre
– *timer*
41-59 le laboratoire
– ***laboratory***
41 la laborantine
– *medical laboratory technician*
42 le portoir de tubes *m* capillaires pour la détermination de la vitesse de sédimentation *f*
– *capillary tube stand for blood sedimentation*
43 l'éprouvette *f*
– *measuring cylinder*
44 la pipette automatique
– *automatic pipette*
45 le haricot (médecine *f*)
– *kidney dish*
46 l'électrocardiographe *m* portatif pour les urgences *f*
– *portable ECG machine for emergency use*
47 le titrimètre automatique
– *automatic pipetting device*
48 le bain-marie *m* thermostatique
– *constant temperature water bath*
49 le robinet avec trompe *f* à eau *f*
– *tap with water jet pump*
50 la cuve à coloration *f* (pour la coloration des frottis *m* sanguins, des sédiments *m* et des frottis *m*)
– *staining dish (for staining blood smears, sediments and other smears)*
51 le microscope binoculaire
– *binocular research microscope*
52 le portoir à pipettes *f* pour la photométrie
– *pipette stand for photometry*
53 le calculateur-analyseur de photométrie *f*
– *computer and analyser for photometry*
54 le photomètre
– *photometer*
55 l'enregistreur *m* potentiométrique
– *potentiometric recorder*
56 le poste transformateur *m*
– *transforming section*
57 la verrerie et le matériel de laboratoire *m*
– *laboratory apparatus (laboratory equipment)*
58 le tableau des éléments *m* figurés urinaires
– *urine sediment chart*
59 la centrifugeuse
– *centrifuge*

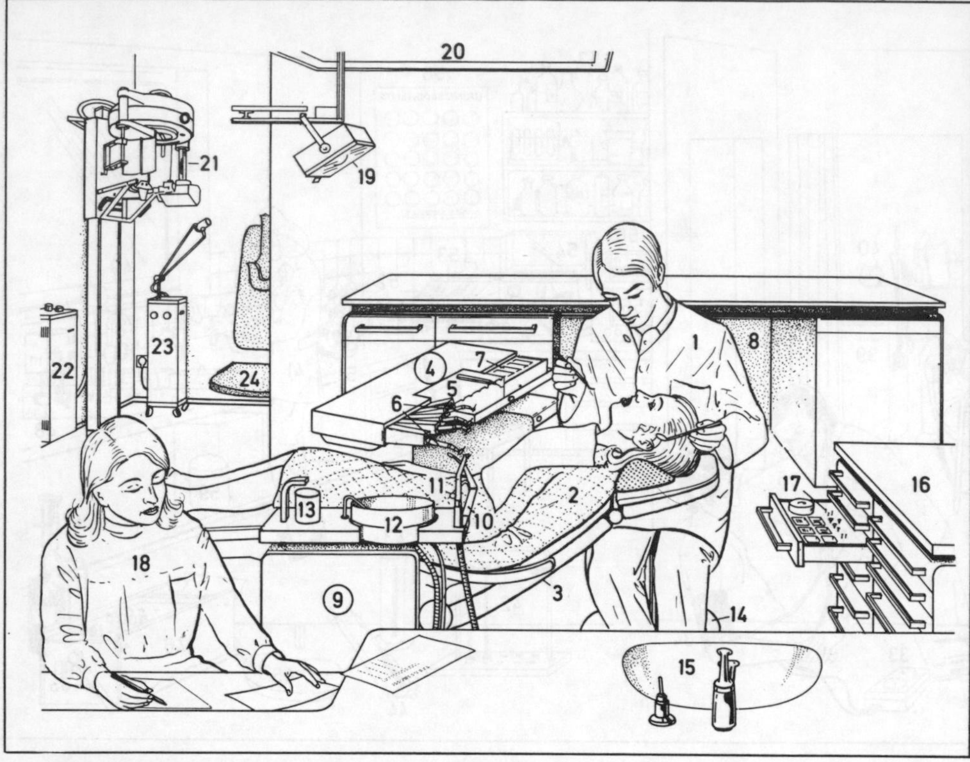

1 le dentiste (le chirurgien dentiste)
– *dentist (dental surgeon)*
2 le patient
– *patient*
3 le fauteuil de dentiste *m*
– *dentist's chair*
4 la tablette porte-instrumentation *m*
– *dental instruments*
5 le plateau à instruments *m*
– *instrument tray*
6 les fraises *f* avec diverses pièces-à-main *f*
– *drills with different handpieces*
7 le casier à médicaments *m*
– *medicine case*
8 le bloc de rangement *m* de la tablette porte-instrumentation *m*
– *storage unit (for dental instruments)*
9 le bloc de l'assistante *f*
– *assistant's unit*
10 l'insufflateur *m* multifonctionnel (d'eau *f* froide ou chaude, de spray *m* ou d'air *m*)
– *multi-purpose syringe (for cold and warm water, spray or air)*
11 la pompe à salive *f*
– *suction apparatus*
12 le crachoir
– *basin*
13 le gobelet à remplissage *m* automatique
– *water glass, filled automatically*
14 le tabouret de dentiste *m*
– *stool*
15 le lavabo
– *washbasin*
16 le meuble à instrumentation *f*
– *instrument cabinet*
17 le tiroir à fraises *f*
– *drawer for drills*
18 l'assistante *f* du dentiste *m*
– *dentist's assistant*
19 la lampe de dentiste *m*
– *dentist's lamp*
20 le plafonnier
– *ceiling light*
21 l'appareil *m* de radiographie *f* pour clichés *m* panoramiques
– *X-ray apparatus for panoramic pictures*
22 le générateur de rayons *m* X
– *X-ray generator*
23 l'appareil *m* à hyperfréquences *f*, un appareil d'irradiation *f*
– *microwave treatment unit, a radiation unit*
24 le siège
– *seat*

25 la prothèse dentaire (le dentier, l'appareil *m* dentaire)
– *denture (set of false teeth)*
26 le bridge
– *bridge (dental bridge)*
27 le chicot retaillé
– *prepared stump of the tooth*
28 la couronne; *var.:* la couronne en or *m*, la jaquette
– *crown (*kinds: *gold crown, jacket crown)*
29 la dent en porcelaine *f*
– *porcelain tooth (porcelain pontic)*
30 l'obturation *f*; *anc.:* le plombage
– *filling*
31 la dent à pivot *m* (la couronne à pivot *m*)
– *post crown*
32 la face
– *facing*
33 la couronne
– *diaphragm*
34 le pivot
– *post*
35 le disque en carborundum *m*
– *carborundum disc (disk)*
36 la meule en corindon *m*
– *grinding wheel*
37 fraises *f* pour cavités *f*
– *burs*
38 la fraise flamme *f*
– *flame-shaped finishing bur*
39 fraises *f* fissures *f*
– *fissure burs*
40 la fraise diamantée
– *diamond point*
41 le miroir à bouche *f*
– *mouth mirror*
42 la lampe à bouche *f*
– *mouth lamp*
43 le thermocautère (le cautère)
– *cautery*
44 l'électrode *f* en platine *m* iridié
– *platinum-iridium electrode*
45 instruments *m* à nettoyer les dents *f*
– *tooth scalers*
46 la sonde
– *probe*
47 le davier
– *extraction forceps*
48 l'élévateur *m*
– *tooth-root elevator*
49 le ciseau à os *m*
– *bone chisel*
50 la spatule
– *spatula*
51 le mélangeur de produit *m* d'obturation *f*
– *mixer for filling material*
52 la minuterie synchrone
– *synchronous timer*
53 la seringue hypodermique pour anesthésie *f* locale (anesthésie *f* du nerf)
– *hypodermic syringe for injection of local anaesthetic*
54 l'aiguille *f* hypodermique
– *hypodermic needle*
55 la pince porte-matrice *m*
– *matrix holder*
56 le porte-empreinte
– *impression tray*
57 la lampe à alcool *m*
– *spirit lamp*

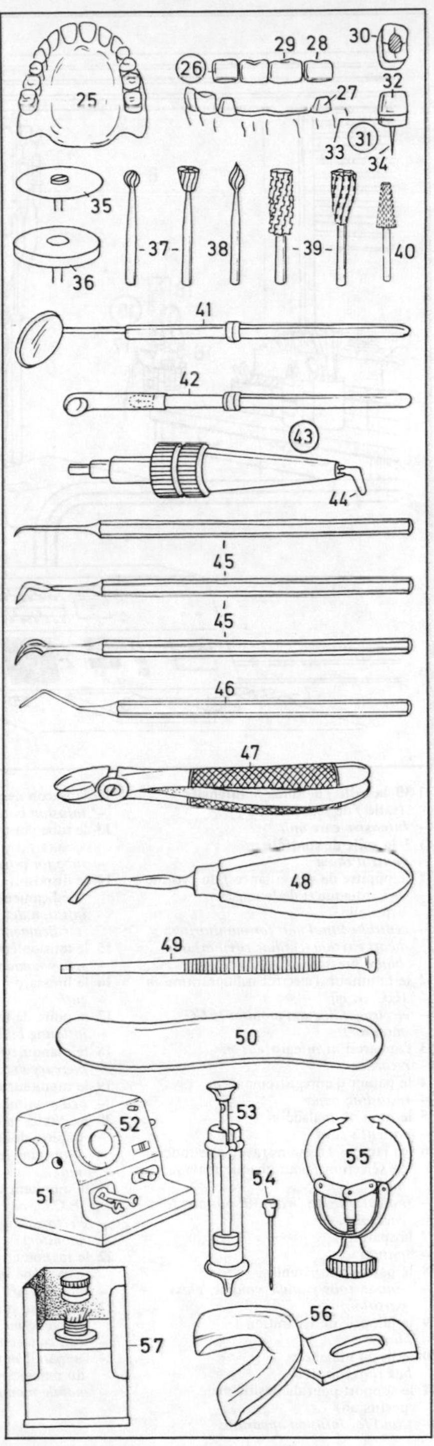

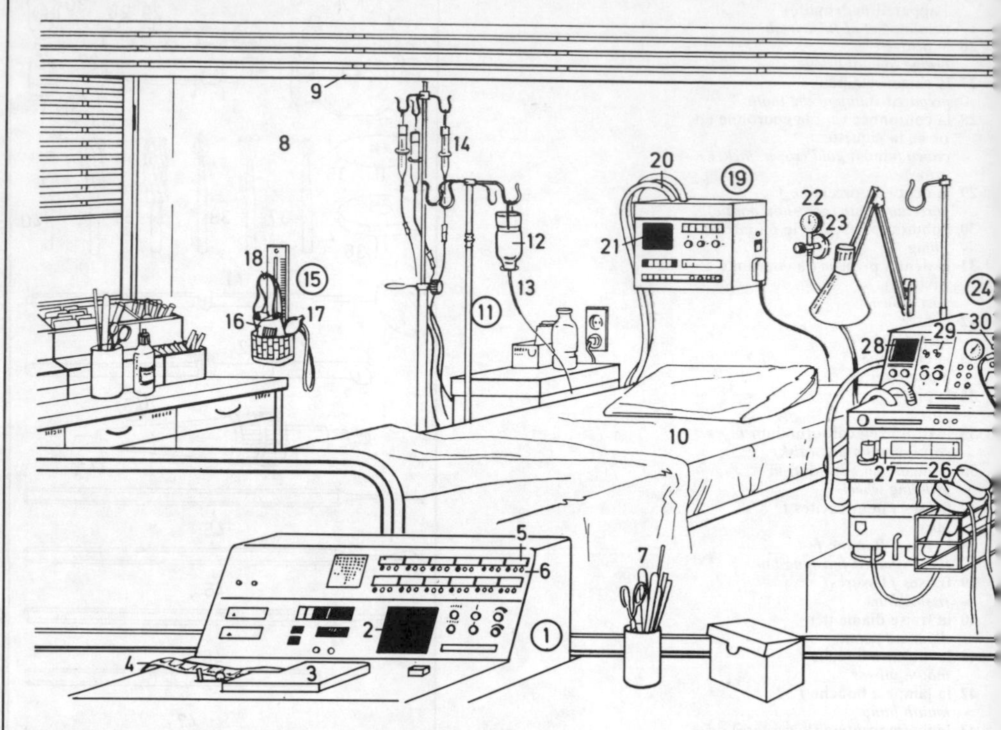

1-30 la salle *f* de soins *m* intensifs (salle *f* de réanimation *f*)
– ***intensive care unit***

1-9 la salle de contrôle *m*
– ***control room***

1 le pupitre de surveillance *f* du rythme *m* cardiaque et de la tension artérielle
– *central control unit for monitoring heart rhythm (cardiac rhythm) and blood pressure*

2 le moniteur d'électrocardiogramme *m* [E.C.G. *m*]
– *electrocardiogram monitor (ECG monitor)*

3 l'appareil *m* enregistreur *m*
– *recorder*

4 le papier d'enregistrement *m*
– *recording paper*

5 le nom du malade *m*
– *patient's card*

6 les lampes *f* témoins (avec une touche de sélection *f* pour chaque malade *m*)
– *indicator lights (with call buttons for each patient)*

7 la spatule
– *spatula*

8 la paroi transparente
– *window (observation window, glass partition)*

9 la jalousie de séparation *f*
– *blind*

10 le lit du malade *m*
– *bed (hospital bed)*

11 le support pour dispositif *m* de perfusion *f*
– *stand for infusion apparatus*

12 le flacon de perfusion *f*
– *infusion bottle*

13 le tube pour perfusion *f* goutte à goutte *f*
– *tube for intravenous drips*

14 le dispositif de perfusion *f* pour médicaments *m* hydrosolubles
– *infusion device for water-soluble medicaments*

15 le tensiomètre
– *sphygmomanometer*

16 le brassard
– *cuff*

17 la poire de tensiomètre *m*
– *inflating bulb*

18 le manomètre à mercure *m*
– *mercury manometer*

19 le moniteur de lit *m*
– *bed monitor*

20 les câbles *m* de connexion *f* au pupitre de surveillance *f*
– *connecting lead to the central control unit*

21 le moniteur d'électrocardiogramme *m* [E.C.G. *m*]
– *electrocardiogram monitor (ECG monitor)*

22 le manomètre de distribution *f* d'oxygène *m*
– *manometer for the oxygen supply*

23 le raccord mural de masque *m* à oxygène *m*
– *wall connection for oxygen treatment*

24 l'appareil *m* mobile de surveillance *f* du malade *m*
– *mobile monitoring unit*

25 le câble d'électrode *f* de stimulateur *m* cardiaque temporaire
– *electrode lead to the short-term pacemaker*

26 les électrodes *f* de défibrillation *f*
– *electrodes for shock treatment*

27 l'électrocardiographe *m*
– *ECG recording unit*

28 le moniteur d'électrocardiogramme *m* [E.C.G. *m*]
– *electrocardiogram monitor (ECG monitor)*

29 les boutons *m* de réglage *m* du moniteur
– *control switches and knobs (controls) for adjusting the monitor*

30 les boutons *m* de commande *f* du stimulateur cardiaque
– *control buttons for the pacemaker unit*

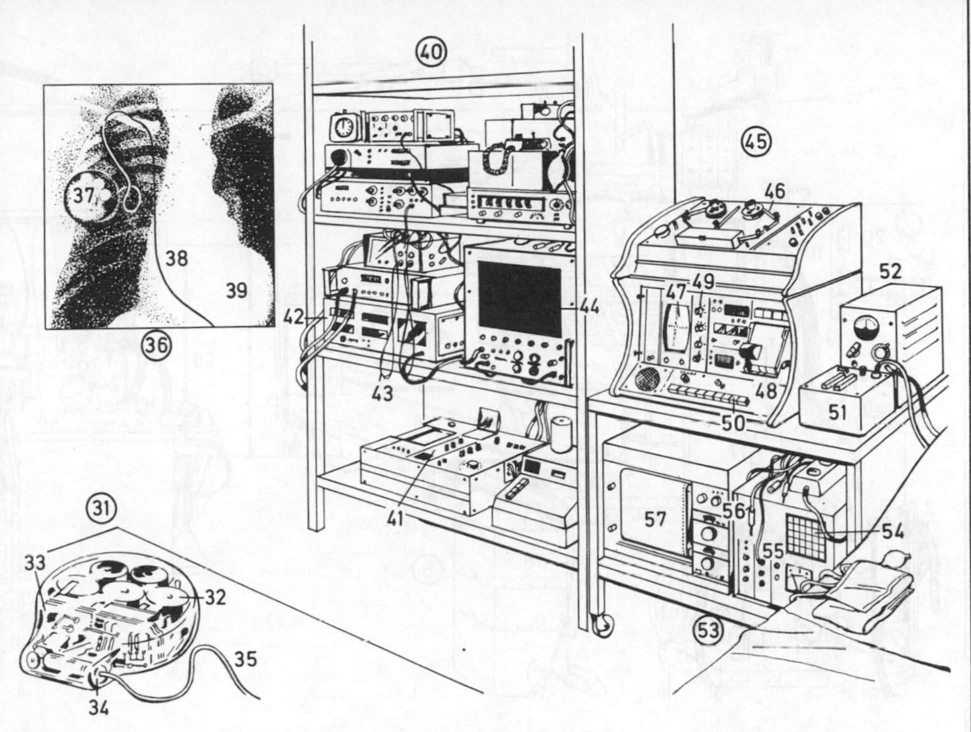

31 le stimulateur cardiaque
– ***pacemaker** (cardiac pacemaker)*
32 la batterie à mercure *m*
– *mercury battery*
33 le générateur d'impulsions *f* programmable
– *programmed impulse generator*
34 la sortie d'électrode *f*
– *electrode exit point*
35 l'électrode *f*
– *electrode*
36 l'implantation *f* du stimulateur *m* cardiaque
– *implantation of the pacemaker*
37 le stimulateur cardiaque intracorporel
– *internal cardiac pacemaker (internal pacemaker, pacemaker)*
38 l'électrode *f* poussée par cathétérisme *m* intraveineux
– *electrode inserted through the vein*
39 la silhouette cardiaque vue aux rayons X *m*
– *cardiac silhouette on the X-ray*
40 l'installation *f* de contrôle *m* du stimulateur cardiaque
– ***pacemaker control unit***
41 l'électrocardiographe *m*
– *electrocardiograph (ECG recorder)*
42 le mesureur d'impulsions *f*
– *automatic impulse meter*
43 le câble de connexion *f* du patient *m* (câble *m* E.C.G.)
– *ECG lead to the patient*
44 le moniteur pour contrôle *m* visuel des impulsions *f* du stimulateur
– *monitor unit for visual monitoring of the pacemaker impulses*
45 l'analyseur *m* d'E.C.G. *m* de longue durée *f*
– *long-term ECG analyser*
46 la bande magnétique d'enregistrement *m* des impulsions *f* de l'E.C.G. *m* analysé
– *magnetic tape for recording the ECG impulses during analysis*
47 le moniteur de contrôle de l'E.C.G. *m*
– *ECG monitor*
48 l'analyse *f* automatique du rythme de l'E.C.G. *m* sur papier *m*
– *automatic analysis on paper of the ECG rhythm*
49 le bouton d'ajustement *m* de l'amplitude *f* de l'E.C.G. *m*
– *control knob for the ECG amplitude*
50 le clavier de sélection *f* du programme d'analyse *f* de l'E.C.G. *m*
– *program selector switches for the ECG analysis*
51 le chargeur des batteries *f* du stimulateur du patient
– *charger for the pacemaker batteries*
52 le contrôleur de batteries *f*
– *battery tester*
53 le manomètre du cathétère cardiaque droit
– *pressure gauge (Am. gage) for the right cardiac catheter*
54 le moniteur de contrôle *m* de courbes *f*
– *trace monitor*
55 l'indicateur *m* de pression *f*
– *pressure indicator*
56 le câble de connexion *f* à l'enregistreur *m* à bande *f*
– *connecting lead to the paper recorder*
57 l'enregistreur *m* à bande *f* des courbes *f* de pression *f*
– *paper recorder for pressure traces*

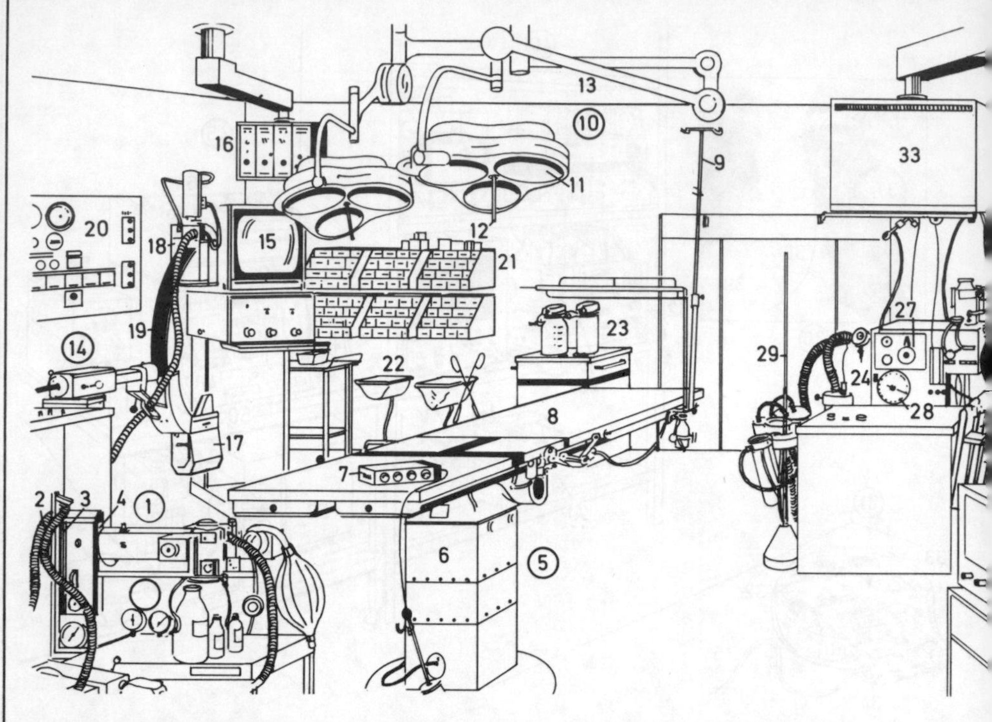

1-54 le service de chirurgie *f*
– ***surgical unit***
1-33 la salle d'opération *f*
– ***operating theatre*** (Am. *theater)*
1 l'appareil *m* d'anesthésie *f*
– *anaesthesia and breathing apparatus (respiratory machine)*
2 le tube *m* d'inhalation *f*
– *inhalers (inhaling tubes)*
3 le débitmètre de gaz *m* hilarant (le protoxyde d'azote *m*)
– *flowmeter for nitrous oxide*
4 le débitmètre d'oxygène *m*
– *oxygen flow meter*
5 la table d'opération *f* sur socle *m*
– *pedestal operating table*
6 le socle de table *f*
– *table pedestal*
7 l'appareil *m* de commande *f*
– *control device (control unit)*
8 la table d'opération *f* articulée
– *adjustable top of the operating table*
9 le support de perfusion *f*
– *stand for intravenous drips*
10 le dispositif pivotant d'éclairage *m* sans ombre *f* portée
– *swivel-mounted shadow-free operating lamp*
11 la lampe
– *individual lamp*
12 la poignée
– *handle*
13 le bras orientable
– *swivel arm*
14 l'appareil *m* mobile de radiologie *f*
– *mobile fluoroscope*
15 le moniteur du convertisseur *m* d'image *f*
– *monitor of the image converter*
16 le moniteur [face *f* arrière]
– *monitor [back]*
17 le tube
– *tube*
18 le convertisseur d'image *f*
– *image converter*
19 le bâti en C *m*
– *C-shaped frame*
20 le tableau de commande *f* du conditionnement d'air *m*
– *control panel for the air-conditioning*
21 le matériel de sutures *f*
– *surgical suture material*
22 le seau à pansements *m*
– *mobile waste tray*
23 la boîte de compresses *f* non stériles
– *containers for unsterile (unsterilized) pads*
24 le respirateur artificiel
– *anaesthesia and respiratory apparatus*
25 la poche de contrôle *m* de la respiration
– *respirator*
26 le réservoir de fluothane *m* (halothane *m*)
– *fluothane container (halothane container)*
27 le bouton de réglage *m* de la ventilation
– *ventilation control knob*
28 le tableau d'enregistrement *m* avec indicateur *m* du volume respiratoire
– *indicator with pointer for respiratory volume*
29 le statif avec tubes *m* d'inhalation *f* et manomètre *m*
– *stand with inhalers (inhaling tubes) and pressure gauges (*Am. *gages)*
30 le porte-cathétères
– *catheter holder*
31 le cathètère sous emballage *m* stérile
– *catheter in sterile packing*

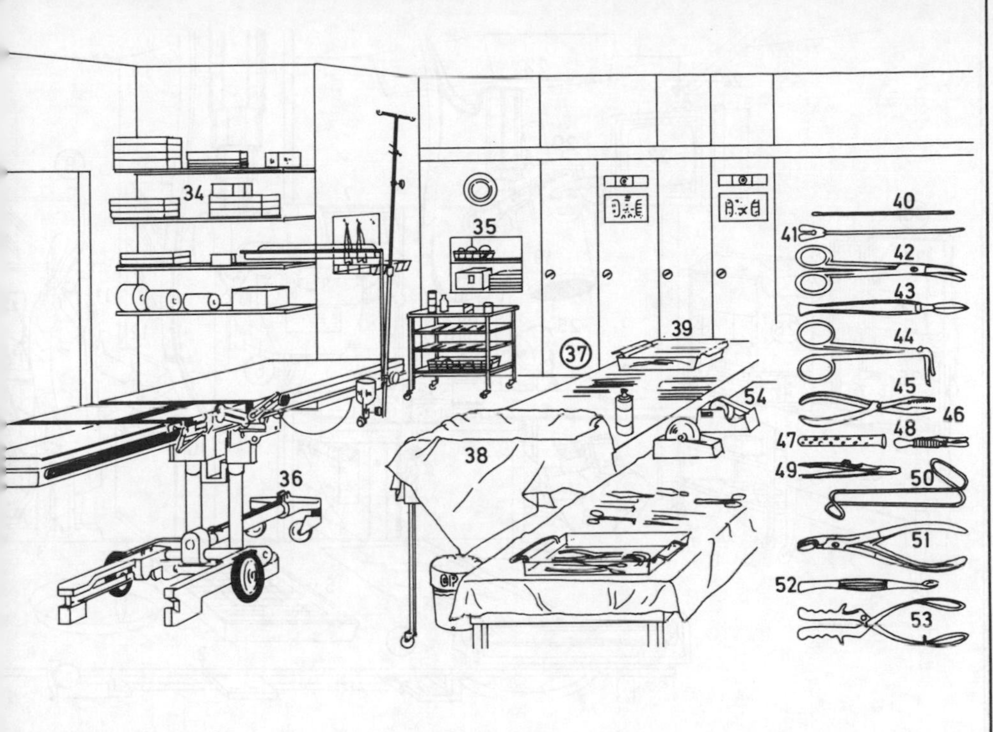

32 le sphygmographe (l'enregistreur *m* d'impulsions *f*)
– *sphygmograph*
33 le moniteur
– *monitor*
34-54 la salle de préparation *f* et de stérilisation *f*
– ***preparation and sterilization room***
34 les pansements *m*
– *dressing material*
35 le petit stérilisateur
– *small sterilizer*
36 le chariot de la table d'opération *f*
– *carriage of the operating table*
37 la table d'instruments *m* mobile
– *mobile instrument table*
38 le champ stérile
– *sterile cloth*
39 le plateau à instruments *m*
– *instrument tray*
40-53 les instruments *m* chirurgicaux
– ***surgical instruments***
40 la sonde à boule *f* olivaire
– *olive-pointed (bulb-headed) probe*
41 la sonde cannelée
– *hollow probe*
42 les ciseaux *m* courbes
– *curved scissors*
43 le bistouri
– *scalpel (surgical knife)*
44 la pince à ligature *f*
– *ligature-holding forceps*
45 la pince à séquestre *m*
– *sequestrum forceps*
46 la branche de pince *f*
– *jaw*
47 le drain
– *drainage tube*
48 le tourniquet
– *surgeon's tourniquet*
49 la pince hémostatique
– *artery forceps*
50 l'écarteur *m* en fil *m*
– *blunt hook*
51 la pince-gouge
– *bone nippers (bone-cutting forceps)*
52 la curette pour le curetage *m*
– *scoop (curette) for erasion (curettage)*
53 le forceps
– *obstetrical forceps*
54 le rouleau de sparadrap *m*
– *roll of plaster*

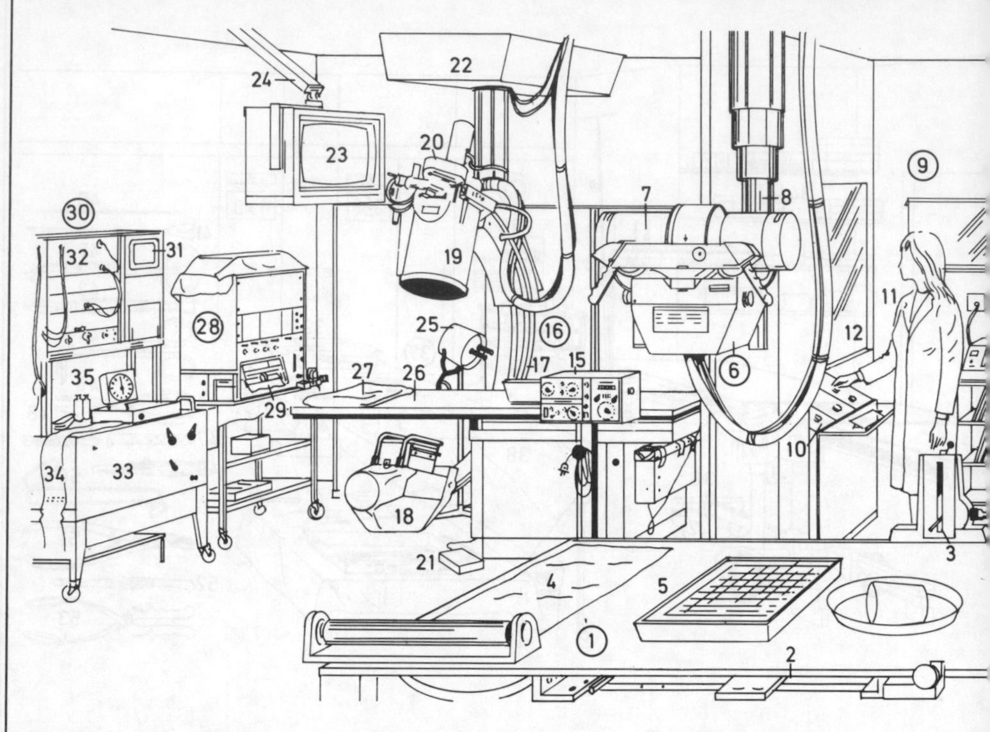

1-35 le service de radiologie ***f***
– ***X-ray unit***

1 la table d'examen *m* radiologique
– *X-ray examination table*

2 le support de cassettes *f* X
– *support for X-ray cassettes*

3 le réglage vertical du faisceau central pour clichés *m* latéraux
– *height adjustment of the central beam for lateral views*

4 la compresse pour radiographie *f* des reins *m* et des voies *f* biliaires (urographie *f* et cholecystographie *f*)
– *compress for pyelography and cholecystography*

5 le plateau d'instruments *m*
– *instrument basin*

6 l'équipement *m* à rayons *m* X pour urétéro-pyélographie *f*
– *X-ray apparatus for pyelograms*

7 le tube à rayons *m* X
– *X-ray tube*

8 le support télescopique du tube à rayons *m* X
– *telescopic X-ray support*

9 la salle de commande *f* de radiographie *f*
– *central X-ray control unit*

10 le pupitre de commande *f*
– *control panel (control desk)*

11 l'assistante *f* radiographe (la manipulatrice)
– *radiographer (X-ray technician)*

12 la fenêtre donnant sur la salle d'angiographie *f*
– *window to the angiography room*

13 l'oxymètre *m*
– *oxymeter*

14 les cassettes *f* pour urographie *f*
– *pyelogram cassettes*

15 l'appareil *m* pour injection *f* de produits *m* de contraste *m*
– *contrast medium injector*

16 l'amplificateur *m* de brillance *f*
– *X-ray image intensifier*

17 le bâti en C *m* (bâti *m* en col *m* de cygne *m*)
– *C-shaped frame*

18 la tête de radiographie *f* avec le tube à rayons *m* X
– *X-ray head with X-ray tube*

19 le convertisseur d'image *f* avec le tube convertisseur *m*
– *image converter with converter tube*

20 la caméra
– *film camera*

21 l'interrupteur *m* à pédale *f*
– *foot switch*

22 le support mobile
– *mobile mounting*

23 le moniteur (écran *m* de contrôle *m*)
– *monitor*

24 le bras pivotant du moniteur
– *swivel-mounted monitor support*

25 la lampe sans ombre *f* portée
– *operating lamp*

26 la table d'angiographie *f*
– *angiographic examination table*

27 l'oreiller *m*
– *pillow*

28 l'enregistreur *m* à huit canaux *m*
– *eight-channel recorder*

29 le papier d'enregistrement *m*
– *recording paper*

30 le poste de mesure *f* pour cathétérisme *m* cardiaque
– *catheter gauge (Am. gage) unit for catheterization of the heart*

31 le moniteur à six canaux *m* pour courbes *f* de tension *f* et E.C.G. *m*
– *six-channel monitor for pressure graphs and ECG*

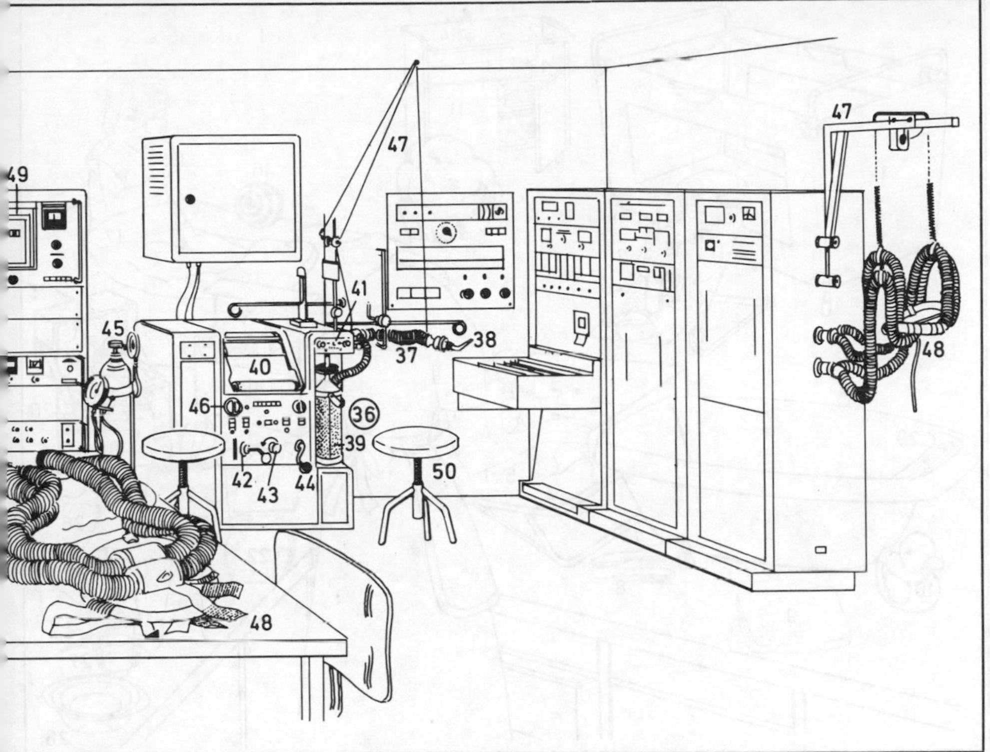

32 les tiroirs *m* de transducteur *m* de pression *f*
– *slide-in units of the pressure transducer*

33 l'unité *f* de développement *m* avec révélateur *m* pour enregistrement *m* photographique
– *paper recorder unit with developer for photographic recording*

34 le papier d'enregistrement *m*
– *recording paper*

35 le chronomètre
– *timer*

36-50 la spirométrie
– ***spirometry***

36 le spirographe pour l'exploration *f* fonctionnelle respiratoire
– *spirograph for pulmonary function tests*

37 le tube respiratoire
– *breathing tube*

38 l'embout *m* buccal
– *mouthpiece*

39 l'absorbeur *m* à chaux *f* sodée
– *soda-lime absorber*

40 le papier d'enregistrement *m*
– *recording paper*

41 la régulation d'alimentation *f* en gaz *m*
control knobs for gas supply

42 le stabilisateur de O_2 *m*
– *O_2-stabilizer*

43 le robinet d'étranglement *m* (étrangleur *m*)
– *throttle valve*

44 le branchement de l'absorbeur *m*
– *absorber attachment*

45 la bouteille d'oxygène *m*
– *oxygen cylinder*

46 l'alimentation *f* en eau *f*
– *water supply*

47 le support de tube *m* flexible
– *tube support*

48 le masque
– *mask*

49 le poste de mesure *f* de la consommation de CO_2 *m*
– *CO_2 consumption meter*

50 le tabouret du patient *m*
– *stool for the patient*

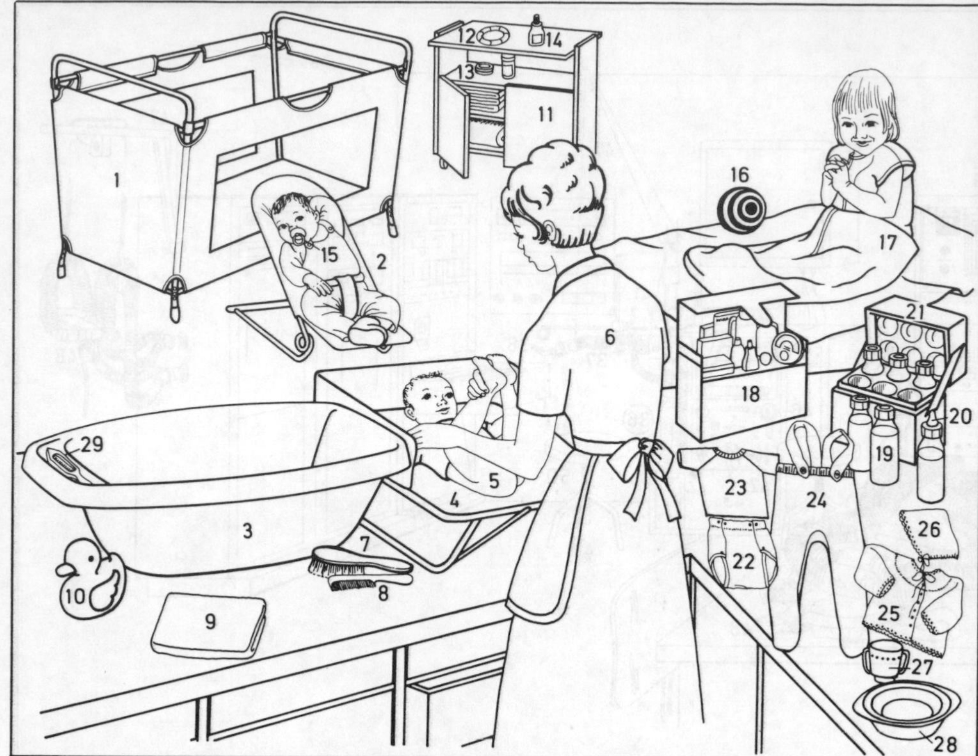

1 le lit d'enfant à roulettes *f*
– *collapsible cot*
2 siège de détente *f* (le siège de repos *m*)
– *bouncing cradle*
3 la baignoire
– *baby bath*
4 le support à langer
– *changing top*
5 le nourrisson (le bébé)
– *baby (new-born baby)*
6 la mère
– *mother*
7 la brosse à cheveux *m*
– *hairbrush*
8 le peigne
– *comb*
9 la serviette
– *hand towel*
10 le jouet flottant
– *toy duck*
11 la commode à layette *f*
– *changing unit*
12 l'anneau *m* de dentition *f*
– *teething ring*
13 la boîte de crème *f*
– *cream jar*
14 la boîte de talc *m*
– *box of baby powder*
15 la sucette
– *dummy*
16 la balle
– *ball*
17 le nid douillet (le nid d'ange *m*)
– *sleeping bag*
18 la mallette pour nécessaire *m* de bébé *m*
– *layette box*
19 le biberon
– *feeding bottle*
20 la tétine
– *teat*
21 la mallette à biberons *m*
– *bottle warmer*
22 la couche-culotte jetable
– *rubber baby pants for disposable nappies* (Am. *diapers*)
23 la brassière américaine
– *vest*
24 la culotte pantin
– *leggings*
25 la brassière
– *baby's jacket*
26 le bonnet
– *hood*
27 la tasse pour enfant *m*
– *baby's cup*
28 l'assiette *f* à bouillie *f*, une assiette *f* chauffante
– *baby's plate, a stay-warm plate*
29 le thermomètre
– *thermometer*

30 le berceau, un berceau en osier *m*
– *bassinet, a wicker pram*
31 la garniture de berceau *m*
– *set of bassinet covers*
32 le baldaquin *m*
– *canopy*
33 la chaise haute, une chaise pliante
– *baby's high chair, a folding chair*
34 le landeau à vision *f* panoramique
– *pram (baby-carriage) [with windows]*
35 la capote repliable
– *folding hood*
36 la fenêtre
– *window*
37 la poussette
– *pushchair (Am. stroller)*
38 la chancelière
– *foot-muff (Am. foot-bag)*
39 le parc pliant
– *play pen*
40 le plancher du parc *m*
– *floor of the play pen*
41 le jeu de construction *f*
– *building blocks (building bricks)*
42 le petit enfant
– *small child*
43 le bavoir
– *bib*
44 le hochet
– *rattle (baby's rattle)*
45 les chaussures *f* d'enfant *m*
– *bootees*
46 l'ours *m* en peluche *f*
– *teddy bear*
47 le pot
– *potty (baby's pot)*
48 la nacelle porte-bébé
– *carrycot*
49 la fenêtre
– *window*
50 les poignées *f*
– *handles*

1-12 la layette
– ***baby clothes***
1 l'ensemble *m* de promenade *f*
– *pram suit*
2 le bonnet
– *hood*
3 le paletot
– *pram jacket (matinée coat)*
4 le pompon
– *pompon (bobble)*
5 les chaussons *m*
– *bootees*
6 la chemise
– *sleeveless vest*
7 la brassière américaine
– *envelope-neck vest*
8 la brassière croisante
– *wrapover vest*
9 la brassière de tricot *m*
– *baby's jacket*
10 la culotte ouvrante
– *rubber baby pants*
11 la grenouillère
– *playsuit*
12 le deux-pièces pour bébé *m*
– *two-piece suit*
13-30 les vêtements *m* des petits *m*
– ***infants' wear***
13 la robe d'été *m*, une robe à bretelles *f*
– *child's sundress, a pinafore dress*
14 la manche volantée
– *frilled shoulder strap*
15 l'empiècement *m* à smocks *m*
– *shirred top*
16 le chapeau de soleil *m*
– *sun hat*
17 la combinaison en jersey *m*
– *one-piece jersey suit*
18 la fermeture à glissière *f* devant
– *front zip*
19 la salopette
– *catsuit (playsuit)*
20 l'application *f*
– *motif (appliqué)*
21 la barboteuse
– *romper*
22 la combinaison-short
– *playsuit (romper suit)*
23 le pyjama
– *coverall (sleeper and strampler)*
24 le peignoir de bain *m*
– *dressing gown (bath robe)*
25 la culotte courte
– *children's shorts*
26 les bretelles *f*
– *braces* (Am. *suspenders)*
27 le T-shirt (le tee-shirt)
– *children's T-shirt*
28 la robe de tricot *m*
– *jersey dress (knitted dress)*
29 la broderie
– *embroidery*
30 les socquettes *f*
– *children's ankle socks*
31-47 les vêtements *m* d'écolier *m*
– ***school children's wear***
31 l'imperméable *m*, le loden
– *raincoat (loden coat)*
32 la culotte de peau *f*
– *leather shorts (lederhosen)*
33 le bouton en corne *f* de cerf *m*
– *staghorn button*
34 les bretelles *f* de cuir *m*
– *braces* (Am. *suspenders)*
35 le pont
– *flap*
36 la robe paysanne *f*
– *girl's dirndl*
37 le lacet, un laçage décoratif
– *cross lacing*
38 la combinaison de ski *m* (combinaison *f* matelassée)
– *snow suit (quilted suit)*
39 la surpiqûre
– *quilt stitching (quilting)*
40 la salopette
– *dungarees (bib and brace)*
41 le jumper
– *bib skirt (bib top pinafore)*
42 le collant
– *tights*
43 le sweat-shirt en éponge velours*m*
– *sweater (jumper)*
44 le blouson imitation *f* fourrure *f*
– *pile jacket*
45 le pantalon à sous-pieds *m*
– *leggings*
46 la jupe
– *girl's skirt*
47 le pull-over
– *child's jumper*
48-68 les vêtements *m* junior *m*
– ***teenagers' clothes***
48 la marinière
– *girl's overblouse (overtop)*
49 le pantalon fillette *f*
– *slacks*
50 le deux-pièces fillette *f*
– *girl's skirt suit*
51 la veste
– *jacket*
52 la jupe
– *skirt*
53 les mi-bas *m*
– *knee-length socks*
54 le manteau fillette *f*
– *girl's coat*
55 la ceinture
– *tie belt*
56 le sac à bandoulière *f*
– *girl's bag*
57 le bonnet de laine *f*
– *woollen* (Am. *woolen) hat*
58 le chemisier
– *girl's blouse*
59 la jupe-culotte
– *culottes*
60 le pantalon
– *boy's trousers*
61 la chemise
– *boy's shirt*
62 l'anorak *m*
– *anorak*
63 les poches *f* coupées
– *inset pockets*
64 le cordon de serrage *m* de la capuche
– *hood drawstring (drawstring)*
65 le bord-côtes tricot *m*
– *knitted welt*
66 le parka
– *parka coat (parka)*
67 la ceinture coulissante
– *drawstring (draw cord)*
68 les poches *f* plaquées
– *patch pockets*

1
2
3
4
5
6
7
8
9
10
11
12
13
14
15
16
17
18
19
20
21
22
23
24
25
26
27
28
29
30
31
32
33
34
35
36
37
38
39
40
41
42
43
44
45
46
47
48
49
50
51
52
53
54
55
56
57
58
59
60
61
62
63
64
65
66
67
68

30 Vêtements pour dames I (vêtements d'hiver)

1 la veste de vison *m*
– *mink jacket*
2 le pull-over à col *m* roulé
– *cowl neck jumper*
3 le col-boule
– *cowl collar*
4 la marinière de tricot *m*
– *knitted overtop*
5 le col marin
– *turndown collar*
6 la manche à revers *m*
– *turn-up (turnover) sleeve*
7 le sous-pull
– *polo neck jumper*
8 la robe-jumper
– *pinafore dress*
9 le chemisier
– *blouse with revers collar*
10 la robe-chemisier, une robe entièrement boutonnée
– *shirt-waister dress, a button-through dress*
11 la ceinture
– *belt*
12 la robe d'hiver *m*
– *winter dress*
13 le passepoil
– *piping*
14 la manchette
– *cuff*
15 la manche longue
– *long sleeve*
16 le gilet matelassé
– *quilted waistcoat*
17 la surpiqûre
– *quilt stitching (quilting)*
18 la garniture de cuir *m*
– *leather trimming*
19 le pantalon long d'hiver *m*
– *winter slacks*
20 le pull-over rayé
– *striped polo jumper*
21 la salopette
– *boiler suit (dungarees, bib and brace)*
22 la poche plaquée
– *patch pocket*
23 la poche de poitrine *f*
– *front pocket*
24 la bavette
– *bib*
25 la robe portefeuille
– *wrapover dress (wrap-around dress)*
26 le polo
– *shirt*
27 la robe folklore *m*
– *peasant-style dress*
28 le galon fleuri
– *floral braid*
29 la tunique
– *tunic (tunic top, tunic dress)*
30 le poignet
– *ribbed cuff*
31 les surpiqûres décoratives
– *quilted design*
32 la jupe plissée
– *pleated skirt*
33 le deux-pièces tricot *m*
– *two-piece knitted dress*
34 le décolleté bateau *m*
– *boat neck, a neckline*
35 le revers de manche *f*
– *turn-up*
36 la manche kimono *m*
– *kimono sleeve*
37 le dessin jacquard
– *knitted design*
38 le blouson
– *lumber-jacket*
39 le point torsade *f*
– *cable pattern*
40 la chemise
– *shirt-blouse*
41 la fermeture à brides *f*
– *loop fastening*
42 la broderie
– *embroidery*
43 le col officier *m*
– *stand-up collar*
44 le pantalon bouffant
– *cossack trousers*
45 le deux-pièces tunique *f*
– *two-piece combination (shirt top and long skirt)*
46 le nœud
– *tie (bow)*
47 l'empiècement *m*
– *decorative facing*
48 la fente de la manche
– *cuff slit*
49 la fente de côté*m*
– *side slit*
50 la chasuble
– *tabard*
51 la jupe fendue sur le côté
– *inverted pleat skirt*
52 le pli Dior
– *godet*
53 la robe du soir *m*
– *evening gown*
54 la manche pagode *f* plissée
– *pleated bell sleeve*
55 la blouse de cocktail *m*
– *party blouse*
56 la jupe de cocktail *m*
– *party skirt*
57 le costume pantalon *m*
– *trouser suit (slack suit)*
58 la veste en daim *m*
– *suede jacket*
59 la garniture de fourrure *f*
– *fur trimming*
60 le manteau de fourrure *f* (astrakan *m*, breitschwanz *m*, vison *m*, zibeline *f*)
– *fur coat (*kinds: *Persian lamb, broadtail, mink, sable)*
61 le manteau d'hiver *m* (le manteau e drap *m*)
– *winter coat (cloth coat)*
62 le poignet de fourrure *f*
– *fur cuff (fur-trimmed cuff)*
63 le col de fourrure *f*
– *fur collar (fur-trimmed collar)*
64 le loden
– *loden coat*
65 la pèlerine
– *cape*
66 les boutons *m* olive *f*
– *toggle fastenings*
67 la jupe en loden *m*
– *loden skirt*
68 le manteau-cape
– *poncho-style coat*
69 la capuche
– *hood*

1
2
3
4
5
6
7
8
9
10
11
12
13
14
15
16
17
18
19
20
21
22
23
24
25
26
27
28
29
30
31
32
33
34
35
36
37
38
39
40
41
42
43
44
45
46
47
48
49
50
51
52
53
54
55
56
57
58
59
60
61
62
63
64
65
66
67
68
69

31 Vêtements pour dames II (vêtements d'été)

1 le costume tailleur *m* (le tailleur)
– *skirt suit*
2 la veste de tailleur *m*
– *jacket*
3 la jupe de tailleur *m*
– *skirt*
4 la poche coupée
– *inset pocket*
5 la surpiqûre
– *decorative stitching*
6 l'ensemble *m* robe *f*
– *dress and jacket combination*
7 le passepoil
– *piping*
8 la robe à bretelles *f*
– *pinafore dress*
9 la robe d'été *m*
– *summer dress*
10 la ceinture
– *belt*
11 le deux-pièces
– *two-piece dress*
12 la boucle de ceinture *f*
– *belt buckle*
13 la jupe portefeuille *m*
– *wrapover (wrap-around) skirt*
14 la ligne tube *m*
– *pencil silhouette*
15 les boutons *m* d'épaule *f*
– *shoulder buttons*
16 les manches *f* chauve-souris *f*
– *batwing sleeve*
17 la robe housse *f*
– *overdress*
18 l'empiècement *m* kimono *m*
– *kimono yoke*
19 la ceinture nouée
– *tie belt*
20 le manteau d'été *m*
– *summer coat*
21 le capuchon amovible
– *detachable hood*
22 le chemisier manches *f* courtes
– *summer blouse*
23 le col
– *lapel*
24 la jupe
– *skirt*
25 le pli de devant
– *front pleat*
26 la robe paysanne *f*
– *dirndl (dirndl dress)*
27 la manche ballon *m*
– *puffed sleeve*
28 le collier folklore *m*
– *dirndl necklace*
29 la blouse paysanne *f*
– *dirndl blouse*
30 le corselet
– *bodice*
31 le tablier paysanne *f*
– *dirndl apron*
32 la garniture de dentelle *f* (la dentelle, dentelle *f* de coton *m*)
– *lace trimming (lace), cotton lace*
33 le tablier à volants *m*
– *frilled apron*
34 le volant
– *frill*
35 la tunique
– *smock overall*
36 la robe d'intérieur *m*
– *house frock (house dress)*
37 la veste de popeline *f*
– *poplin jacket*
38 le T-shirt (le tee-shirt)
– *T-shirt*
39 le short
– *ladies' shorts*
40 le revers
– *trouser turn-up*
41 la ceinture
– *waistband*
42 le blouson
– *bomber jacket*
43 le bord-côtes élastique
– *stretch welt*
44 le bermuda
– *Bermuda shorts*
45 la surpiqûre
– *saddle stitching*
46 le col à volants *m*
– *frill collar*
47 le nœud
– *knot*
48 la jupe-culotte
– *culotte*
49 le twin-set
– *twin set*
50 la veste tricot *m*
– *cardigan*
51 le pull-over
– *sweater*
52 le pantalon d'été *m*
– *summer (lightweight) slacks*
53 la combinaison de mécanicien *m*
– *jumpsuit*
54 le revers de manche *f*
– *turn-up*
55 la fermeture à glissière *f*
– *zip*
56 la poche plaquée
– *patch pocket*
57 le gavroche
– *scarf (neckerchief)*
58 le deux-pièces jeans
– *denim suit*
59 la veste jeans
– *denim waistcoat*
60 le jeans (blue jeans)
– *jeans (denims)*
61 la tunique
– *overblouse*
62 la manche retroussée
– *turned-up sleeve*
63 la ceinture élastique
– *stretch belt*
64 le T-shirt dos *m* nu (le tee-shirt dos *m* nu)
– *halter top*
65 la tunique tricot *m*
– *knitted overtop*
66 la ceinture coulissée
– *drawstring waist*
67 le pull-over d'été *m*
– *short-sleeved jumper*
68 le décolleté en V
– *V-neck (vee-neck)*
69 le col rabattu
– *turndown collar*
70 le bord-côtes
– *knitted welt*
71 le châle (le châle triangulaire)
– *shawl*

1
2
3
4
5
6
7
8
9
10
11
12
13
14
15
16
17
18
19
20
21
22
23
24
25
26
27
28
29
30
31
32
33
34
35
36
37
38
39
40
41
42
43
44
45
46
47
48
49
50
51
52
53
54
55
56
57
58
59
60
61
62
63
64
65
66
67
68
69
70
71

1-15 les sous-vêtements *m* **féminins**, lingerie *f*
– ***ladies' underwear*** *(ladies' underclothes, lingerie)*
1 le soutien-gorge
– *brassière (bra)*
2 le panty
– *pantie-girdle*
3 la gaine-culotte
– *pantie-corselette*
4 le bustier
– *longline brassière (longline bra)*
5 la gaine
– *stretch girdle*
6 la jarretelle
– *suspender*
7 la chemise américaine
– *vest*
8 le boxer
– *pantie briefs*
9 le mi-bas
– *ladies' knee-high stocking*
10 la culotte à jambes *f*
– *long-legged (long leg) panties*
11 le collant pied *m* nu
– *long pants*
12 le collant
– *tights (pantie-hose)*
13 le fond de robe *f*
– *slip*
14 le jupon
– *waist slip*
15 le slip
– *bikini briefs*
16-21 les vêtements *m* **de nuit** *f* **féminins**
– ***ladies' nightwear***
16 la chemise de nuit *f*
– *nightdress (nightgown, nightie)*
17 le pyjama
– *pyjamas* (Am. *pajamas)*
18 le haut de pyjama *m*
– *pyjama top*
19 le pantalon de pyjama *m*
– *pyjama trousers*
20 le peignoir ou robe *f* d'intérieur *m*
– *housecoat*
21 le bloomer ou pyjama-short
– *vest and shorts set [for leisure wear and as nightwear]*
22-29 les sous-vêtements *m* **masculins**
– ***men's underwear*** *(men's underclothes)*
22 le maillot de corps *m* filet *m*
– *string vest*
23 le slip filet *m*
– *string briefs*
24 la doublure de braguette *f*
– *front panel*
25 le maillot de corps *m*
– *sleeveless vest*
26 le slip
– *briefs*
27 le boxer
– *trunks*
28 le gilet de corps *m* à manches *f* courtes (T-shirt *m*, tee-shirt *m*)
– *short-sleeved vest*
29 le caleçon long
– *long johns*
30 les bretelles *f*
– *braces* (Am. *suspenders)*
31 la pince de bretelles *f*
– *braces clip*
32-34 chaussettes *f*
– ***men's socks***
32 mi-bas *m*
– *knee-length sock*
33 la bande élastique
– *elasticated top*
34 mi-chaussettes *f*
– *long sock*
35-37 les vêtements *m* **de nuit** *f* **pour hommes** *m*
– ***men's nightwear***
35 la robe de chambre *f*
– *dressing gown*
36 le pyjama droit
– *pyjamas* (Am. *pajamas)*
37 la veste de nuit *f*
– *nightshirt*
38-47 chemises *f* **d'homme** *m*
– ***men's shirts***
38 la chemise sport *m*
– *casual shirt*
39 la ceinture
– *belt*
40 le foulard
– *cravat*
41 la cravate
– *tie*
42 le nœud de la cravate
– *knot*
43 la chemise de smoking *m*
– *dress shirt*
44 le plastron plissé
– *frill (frill front)*
45 la manchette
– *cuff*
46 le bouton de manchette *f*
– *cuff link*
47 le nœud papillon *m*
– *bow-tie*

1
2
3
4
5
6
7
8
9
10
11
12
13
14
15
16
17
18
19
20
21
22
23
24
25
26
27
28
29
30
31
32
33
34
35
36
37
38
39
40
41
42
43
44
45
46
47

1-67 la mode masculine
– ***men's fashion***
1 le complet droit
– *single-breasted suit, a men's suit*
2 la veste
– *jacket*
3 le pantalon
– *suit trousers*
4 le gilet
– *waistcoat (vest)*
5 le revers
– *lapel*
6 la jambe de pantalon *m* avec pli *m*
– *trouser leg with crease*
7 le smoking, une tenue de soirée *f*
– *dinner dress, an evening suit*
8 le revers de soie *f*
– *silk lapel*
9 la poche de poitrine *f*
– *breast pocket*
10 la pochette
– *dress handkerchief*
11 le nœud papillon *m*
– *bow-tie*
12 la poche extérieure
– *side pocket*
13 l'habit *m*, un vêtement de cérémonie *f*
– *tailcoat (tails), evening dress*
14 la basque
– *coat-tail*
15 le gilet d'habit *m* blanc
– *white waistcoat (vest)*
16 le nœud papillon *m* blanc
– *white bow-tie*
17 le costume de week-end *m*
– *casual suit*
18 le rabat de poche *f*
– *pocket flap*
19 l'empiècement *m*
– *front yoke*
20 le costume jeans
– *denim suit*
21 la veste jeans
– *denim jacket*
22 le jeans (blue-jeans)
– *jeans (denims)*
23 la ceinture
– *waistband*
24 le costume de plage *f*
– *beach suit*
25 le short
– *shorts*
26 la saharienne
– *short-sleeved jacket*
27 le survêtement
– *tracksuit*
28 le blouson de survêtement *m* avec fermeture *f* à glissière *f*
– *tracksuit top with zip*
29 le pantalon de survêtement *m*
– *tracksuit bottoms*
30 la veste tricot *m*
– *cardigan*
31 le col en tricot *m*
– *knitted collar*
32 le pull-over d'été *m* pour hommes *m*
– *men's short-sleeved pullover (men's short-sleeved sweater)*
33 la chemisette
– *short-sleeved shirt*
34 le bouton de chemise *f*
– *shirt button*
35 le revers de manche *f*
– *turn-up*
36 le polo
– *knitted shirt*
37 la chemise de sport *m*
– *casual shirt*
38 la poche plaquée
– *patch pocket*
39 la veste sport *m*
– *casual jacket*
40 le pantalon de varappe *f*
– *knee-breeches*
41 le bas de jambe *f*
– *knee strap*
42 le mi-bas
– *knee-length sock*
43 la veste de cuir *m*
– *leather jacket*
44 la salopette
– *bib and brace overalls*
45 les bretelles *f* réglables
– *adjustable braces* (Am. *suspenders)*
46 la poche de poitrine *f*
– *front pocket*
47 la poche de pantalon *m*
– *trouser pocket*
48 la braguette
– *fly*
49 la poche à mètre *m*
– *rule pocket*
50 la chemise à carreaux *m*
– *check shirt*
51 le pull-over d'homme *m*
– *men's pullover*
52 le pull-over de ski *m*
– *heavy pullover*
53 le gilet de tricot *m*
– *knitted waistcoat (vest)*
54 le blazer
– *blazer*
55 le bouton du veston
– *jacket button*
56 la blouse de travail *m* (la blouse blanche)
– *overall*
57 le trench-coat
– *trenchcoat*
58 le col
– *coat collar*
59 la ceinture
– *coat belt*
60 le manteau (de demi-saison *f*) en popeline *f* [*en France:* un imperméable]
– *poplin coat*
61 la poche
– *coat pocket*
62 le boutonnage sous patte *f*
– *fly front*
63 le caban
– *car coat*
64 le bouton
– *coat button*
65 le foulard
– *scarf*
66 le manteau de drap *m*
– *cloth coat*
67 le gant
– *glove*

1
2
3
4
5
6
7
8
9
10
11
12
13
14
15
16
17
18
19
20
21
22
23
24
25
26
27
28
29
30
31
32
33
34
35
36
37
38
39
40
41
42
43
44
45
46
47
48
49
50
51
52
53
54
55
56
57
58
59
60
61
62
63
64
65
66
67

1-25 coupes *f* de barbe *m* et coiffures *f* masculines
– ***men's beards and hairstyles*** *(haircuts)*
1 les cheveux *m* longs
– *long hair worn loose*
2 la perruque longue bouclée (perruque Louis XIV); ne couvrant que le haut de la tête: le toupet
– *allonge periwig (full-bottomed wig), a wig;* shorter and smoother: *bob wig, toupet*
3 les boucles *f*
– *curls*
4 la perruque à bourse *f*
– *bag wig (purse wig)*
5 la perruque à la Cadogan
– *pigtail wig*
6 le catogan (le cadogan)
– *queue (pigtail)*
7 le nœud de perruque *f*
– *bow (ribbon)*
8 la moustache
– *handlebars (handlebar moustache,* Am. *mustache)*
9 la raie de milieu *m*
– *centre* (Am. *center) parting*
10 la barbe en pointe (le bouc)
– *goatee (goatee beard), chintuft*
11 la coupe en brosse *f* (cheveux *m* en brosse *f*)
– *closely-cropped head of hair (crew cut)*
12 les favoris *m*
– *whiskers*
13 l'impériale *f*
– *Vandyke beard (stiletto beard, bodkin beard), with waxed moustache* (Am. *mustache)*
14 la raie de côté
– *side parting*
15 la barbe longue
– *full beard (circular beard, round beard)*
16 la barbe carrée
– *tile beard*
17 la mouche
– *shadow*
18 la coiffure bouclée
– *head of curly hair*
19 la moustache en brosse *f*
– *military moustache* (Am. *mustache) (English-style moustache)*
20 la tête chauve
– *partly bald head*
21 la calvitie
– *bald patch*
22 la calvitie totale
– *bald head*
23 la barbe de trois jours *m*
– *stubble beard (stubble, short beard bristles)*
24 les pattes *f*
– *side-whiskers (sideboards, sideburns)*
25 le visage rasé
– *clean shave*
26 la coiffure afro (pour hommes *m* et femmes *f*)
– *Afro look (for men and women)*

27-38 coiffures de dame *f*
– ***ladies' hairstyles*** *(coiffures, women's and girls' hairstyles)*
27 la queue de cheval *m*
– *ponytail*
28 la coiffure à chignon *m*
– *swept-back hair (swept-up hair, pinned-up hair)*
29 le chignon
– *bun (chignon)*
30 les nattes *f*
– *plaits (bunches)*
31 la coiffure en diadème *m*
– *chaplet hairstyle (Gretchen style)*
32 le diadème
– *chaplet (coiled plaits)*
33 la coiffure bouclée
– *curled hair*
34 la coiffure à la garçonne
– *shingle (shingled hair, bobbed hair)*
35 la coiffure à frange *f*
– *pageboy style*
36 la frange
– *fringe* (Am. *bangs)*
37 la coiffure à macarons *m*
– *earphones*
38 le macaron
– *earphone (coiled plait)*

1
2
3
4
5
6
7
9
14
11
13
12
8
10
15
16
18
17
19
26
22
20
21
24
25
23
28
30
32
29
27
31
35
34
37
36
33
38

1-21 les chapeaux ***m*****, les bonnets** ***m*** **et les casquettes** ***f*** **de dame** ***f***
– ***ladies' hats and caps***
1 la modiste lors de la confection d'un chapeau
– *milliner making a hat*
2 la forme
– *hood*
3 le moule
– *block*
4 les différentes parures *f*
– *decorative pieces*
5 le sombrero
– *sombrero*
6 le chapeau à plumes *f* en mohair *m*
– *mohair hat with feathers*
7 le chapeau orné d'un bouquet *m*
– *model hat with fancy appliqué*
8 la casquette de toile *f*
– *linen cap (jockey cap)*
9 le bonnet de grosse laine *f*
– *hat made of thick candlewick yarn*
10 le bonnet tricoté
– *woollen (*Am.* woolen) hat (knitted hat)*
11 le bonnet en tissu *m* mohair*m*
– *mohair hat*
12 le chapeau à plumes *f*
– *cloche with feathers*
13 le chapeau d'homme *m* en fibre *f* de sisal *m* avec ruban *m* de reps *m*
– *large men's hat made of sisal with corded ribbon*
14 le chapeau d'homme *m* avec ruban *m* décoratif
– *trilby-style hat with fancy ribbon*
15 le chapeau de feutre *m* de poil *m*
– *soft felt hat*
16 le panama
– *Panama hat with scarf*
17 la casquette de vison *m*
– *peaked mink cap*
18 le chapeau de vison *m*
– *mink hat*
19 le bonnet (en fourrure *f*) de renard *m* avec dessus *m* en cuir *m*
– *fox hat with leather top*
20 le bonnet de vison *m*
– *mink cap*
21 le chapeau florentin
– *slouch hat trimmed with flowers*

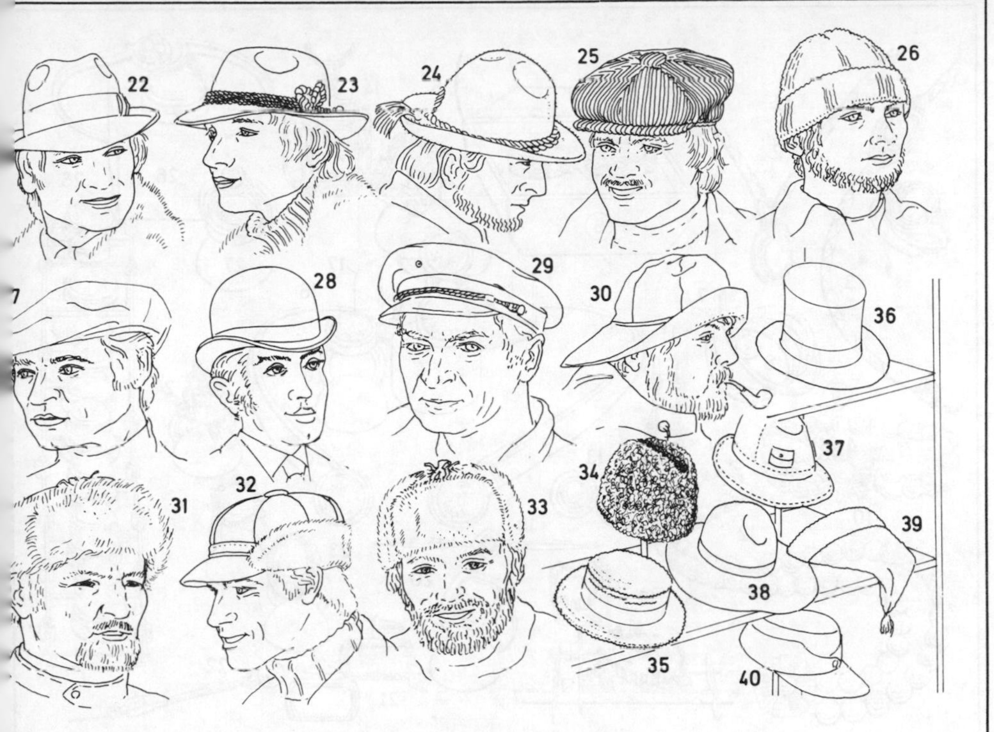

22-40 les chapeaux *m*, **les casquettes** *f* **et les bonnets** *m* **d'homme** *m*
– ***men's hats and caps***
22 le chapeau de feutre *m*
– *trilby hat (trilby)*
23 le chapeau loden
– *loden hat (Alpine hat)*
24 le chapeau de feutre *m* de poil *m* rèche avec houppe *f*
– *felt hat with tassels (Tyrolean hat, Tyrolese hat)*
25 la casquette de velours *m*
– *corduroy cap*
26 le bonnet de laine *f*
– *woollen* (Am. *woolen) hat*
27 le béret basque
– *beret*
28 le chapeau melon
– *bowler hat*
29 la casquette de marin *m* avec visière *f*
– *peaked cap (yachting cap)*
30 le suroît
– *sou'wester (southwester)*
31 la toque de fourrure *f* (de renard *m*) avec couvre-oreilles *m*
– *fox cap with earflaps*
32 la casquette de cuir *m* avec couvre-oreilles *m* de fourrure *f*
– *leather cap with fur flaps*
33 le bonnet de musc *m*
– *musquash cap*
34 la toque de fourrure *f*, une toque d'astrakan *m*, une toque de cosaque *m*
– *astrakhan cap, a real or imitation astrakhan cap*
35 le chapeau de paille *f* (le canotier)
– *boater*
36 le chapeau haut de forme *f* (le haut-de-forme) de taffetas *m*; *à ressorts m:* le chapeau claque (le gibus)
– *(grey,* Am. *gray, or black) top hat made of silk taffeta;* collapsible: *crush hat (opera hat, claque)*
37 le chapeau d'été *m* en tissu *m* avec pochette *f*
– *sun hat (lightweight hat) made of cloth with small patch pocket*
38 le chapeau mou à larges bords *m* (le chapeau d'artiste *m*)
– *wide-brimmed hat*
39 le bonnet à pointe *f* (le bonnet de ski *m*)
– *toboggan cap (skiing cap, ski cap)*
40 la casquette
– *workman's cap*

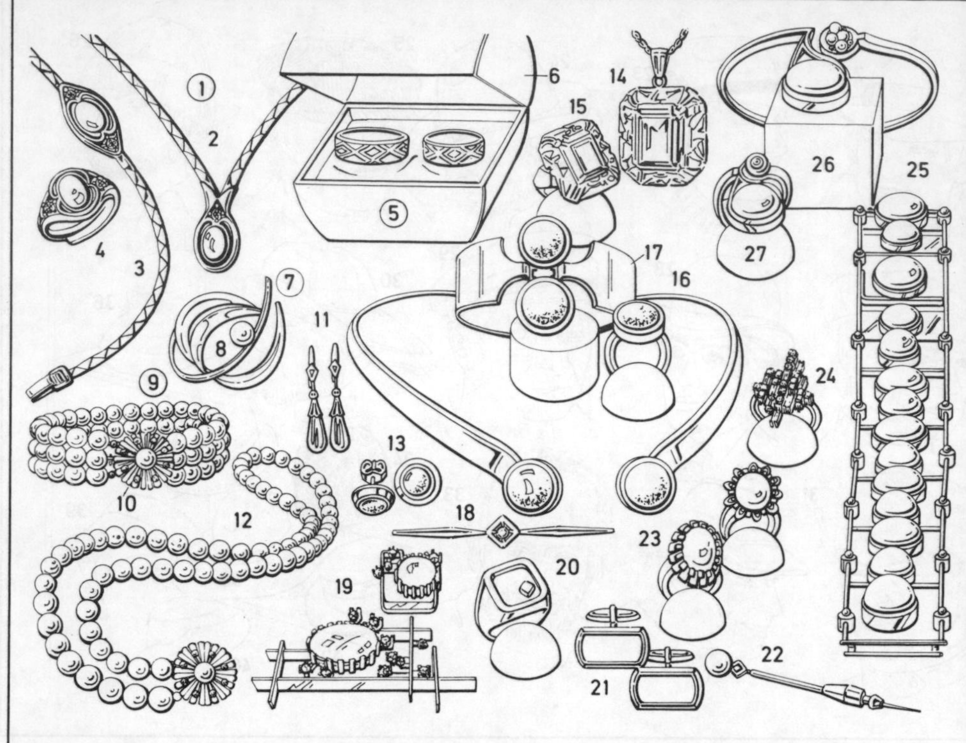

1 la parure
– *set of jewellery (Am. jewelry)*
2 le collier
– *necklace*
3 le bracelet
– *bracelet*
4 la bague
– *ring*
5 l'alliance *f*
– *wedding rings*
6 l'écrin *m* à alliances *f*
– *wedding ring box*
7 la broche
– *brooch, a pearl brooch*
8 la perle
– *pearl*
9 le bracelet en perles *f* de culture *f*
– *cultured pearl bracelet*
10 le fermoir, un fermoir en or *m* blanc
– *clasp, a white gold clasp*
11 le pendant d'oreille *f*
– *pendant earrings (drop earrings)*
12 le collier en perles *f* de culture *f*
– *cultured pearl necklace*
13 les boucles *f* d'oreille *f*
– *earrings*
14 le pendentif en pierres *f* fines (pierres *f* précieuses)
– *gemstone pendant*
15 la bague en pierres *f* fines (pierres *f* précieuses)
– *gemstone ring*
16 le tour de cou *m*
– *choker (collar, neckband)*
17 le bracelet rigide
– *bangle*
18 la barrette avec brillant *m*
– *diamond pin*
19 la broche moderne
– *modern-style brooches*
20 la bague d'homme *m* (la chevalière)
– *man's ring*
21 les boutons *m* de manchette *f*
– *cuff links*
22 l'épingle *f* de cravate *f*
– *tiepin*
23 la bague perle *f* entourage *m* brillants *m*
– *diamond ring with pearl*
24 la bague brillants *m* moderne
– *modern-style diamond ring*
25 le bracelet en pierres *f* fines (pierres *f* précieuses)
– *gemstone bracelet*
26 le bracelet rigide asymétrique
– *asymmetrical bangle*
27 la bague asymétrique
– *asymmetrical ring*
28 le collier d'ivoire *m*
– *ivory necklace*
29 la rose en ivoire *m* taillé
– *ivory rose*
30 la broche en ivoire *m*
– *ivory brooch*
31 le coffret à bijoux *m*
– *jewel box (jewel case)*
32 le collier de perles *f*
– *pearl necklace*
33 la montre bijou *m*
– *bracelet watch*
34 le collier de corail *m* véritable
– *coral necklace*
35 les breloques *f*
– *charms*
36 la chaîne avec pièces *f*
– *coin bracelet*
37 la pièce d'or *m*
– *gold coin*
38 l'entourage *m* de la pièce
– *coin setting*
39 le maillon de la chaîne
– *link*
40 la chevalière à monogramme *m*
– *signet ring*
41 la gravure (le monogramme)
– *engraving (monogram)*
42-86 les différentes tailles *f* de pierres *f*
– *cuts and forms*
42-71 pierres *f* taillées à facettes *f*
– *faceted stones*
42-43 taille *f* ronde normale à facettes *f*
– *standard round cut*
44 la taille brillant *m*
– *brilliant cut*
45 la taille rose *f*
– *rose cut*
46 la table plate
– *flat table*
47 la table bombée
– *table en cabochon*

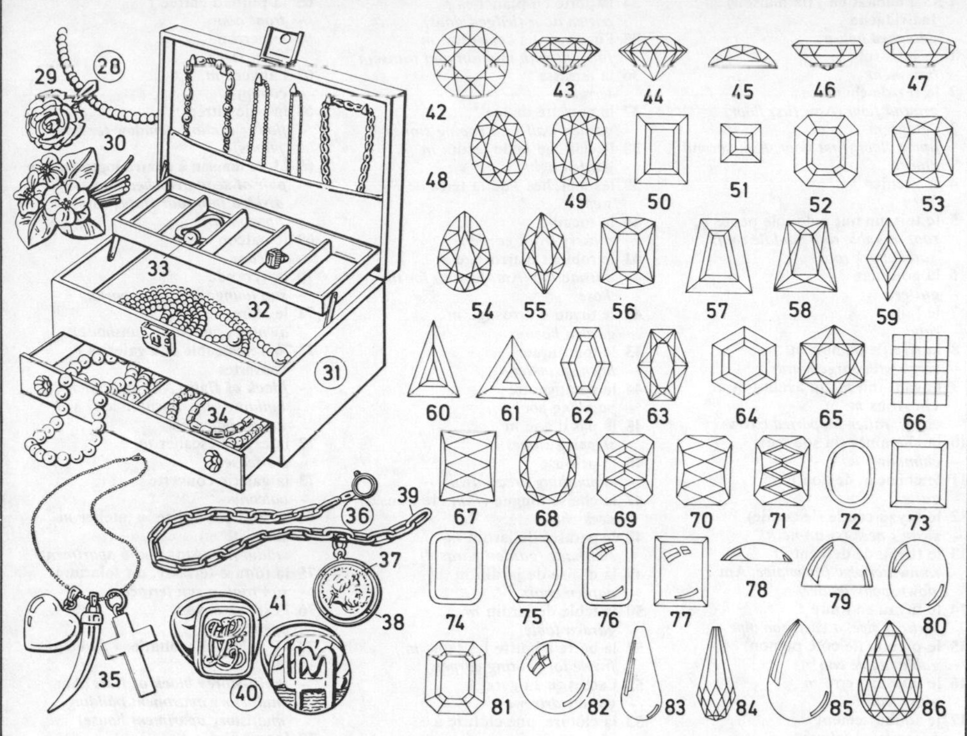

48 la taille ovale normale
– *standard cut*
49 la taille ancienne (la taille anglaise)
– *standard antique cut*
50 la taille rectangle *m* à angles *m* vifs
– *rectangular step-cut*
51 la taille carré *m* à angles *m* vifs
– *square step-cut*
52 la taille rectangle *m* à pans *m* coupés (octogonale, taille *f* émeraude *f*)
– *octagonal step-cut*
53 la taille octogonale à facettes *f* croisées
– *octagonal cross-cut*
54 la taille poire *f*
– *standard pear-shape (pendeloque)*
55 la navette
– *marquise (navette)*
56 le coussin
– *standard barrel-shape*
57 la taille trapèze *m* à angles *m* vifs
– *trapezium step-cut*
58 la taille trapèze *m* à facettes *f* croisées
– *trapezium cross-cut*
59 la taille losange *m* à angles *m* vifs
– *rhombus step-cut*
60-61 le triangle à angles *m* vifs
– *triangular step-cut*
62 le six-pans à angles *m* vifs
– *hexagonal step-cut*
63 le six-pans à facettes *f* croisées
– *oval hexagonal cross-cut*
64 l'hexagone *m* à angles *m* vifs
– *round hexagonal step-cut*
65 l'hexagone *m* à facettes *f* croisées
– *round hexagonal cross-cut*
66 la taille en damiers *m*
– *chequer-board cut*
67 la taille en triangles *m*
– *triangle cut*
68-71 tailles *f* fantaisie
– *fancy cuts*
72-77 pierres *f* pour écussons *m*
– *ring gemstones*
72 la table plate ovale
– *oval flat table*
73 la table plate rectangulaire
– *rectangular flat table*
74 la table plate rectangulaire à angles *m* ronds
– *octagonal flat table*
75 la table plate tonneau *m*
– *barrel-shape*
76 la table bombée à l'ancienne (à angles *m* ronds)
– *antique table en cabochon*
77 la table bombée rectangulaire à angles *m* vifs
– *rectangular table en cabochon*
78-81 les cabochons *m*
– *cabochons*
78 le cabochon rond
– *round cabochon (simple cabochon)*
79 le cabochon pain *m* de sucre *m*
– *high dome (high cabochon)*
80 le cabochon ovale
– *oval cabochon*
81 le cabochon octogonal
– *octagonal cabochon*
82-86 boules *f* et pampilles *f*
– *spheres and pear-shapes*
82 la boule lisse
– *plain sphere*
83 la pampille lisse
– *plain pear-shape*
84 la pampille à facettes *f*
– *faceted pear-shape*
85 la goutte lisse
– *plain drop*
86 la goutte à briolet *m*
– *faceted briolette*

1-53 l'habitation *f* (la maison) **individuelle**
– ***detached house***
1 le sous-sol
– *basement*
2 le rez-de-chaussée
– *ground floor* (Am. *first floor)*
3 l'étage *m*
– *upper floor (first floor,* Am. *second floor)*
4 le grenier
– *loft*
5 le toit, un toit à double pente *f*
– *roof, a gable roof (saddle roof, saddleback roof)*
6 la gouttière
– *gutter*
7 le faîte
– *ridge*
8 la rive de pignon *m*
– *verge with bargeboards*
9 l'avant-toit *m*, un avant-toit à chevrons *m*
– *eaves, rafter-supported eaves*
10 la cheminée (la souche)
– *chimney*
11 le chéneau de gouttière
– *gutter*
12 le tuyau coudé (le coude)
– *swan's neck (swan-neck)*
13 le tuyau de descente *f*
– *rainwater pipe (downpipe,* Am. *downspout, leader)*
14 le tuyau en fonte *f*
– *vertical pipe, a cast-iron pipe*
15 le pignon (le côté pignon)
– *gable (gable end)*
16 le mur en verre *m*
– *glass wall*
17 le soubassement
– *base course (plinth)*
18 la loggia
– *balcony*
19 la balustrade
– *parapet*
20 la jardinière
– *flower box*
21 la porte de la loggia à deux battants *m*
– *French window (French windows) opening on to the balcony*
22 la fenêtre à deux vantaux *m*
– *double casement window*
23 la fenêtre à un vantail *m*
– *single casement window*
24 l'appui *m* (l'allège *f*) de fenêtre
window breast with window sill
25 le linteau
– *lintel (window head)*
26 l'embrasure *f*
– *reveal*
27 le soupirail
– *cellar window (basement window)*
28 le volet roulant (le store à enroulement)
– *rolling shutter*
29 le bras de projection *f* du store
– *rolling shutter frame*
30 les persiennes *f* (les contrevents *m*, les volets *m*)
– *window shutter (folding shutter)*
31 l'arrêt *m* de persienne *f*
– *shutter catch*
32 le garage et le débarras
– *garage with tool shed*
33 l'espalier *m*
– *espalier*
34 la porte en planches *f*
– *batten door (ledged door)*
35 l'imposte *f* à croisillon *m*
– *fanlight with mullion and transom*
36 la terrasse
– *terrace*
37 la murette dallée
– *garden wall with coping stones*
38 l'éclairage *m* de jardin *m*
– *garden light*
39 les marches *f* de la terrasse *f*
– *steps*
40 la rocaille
– *rockery (rock garden)*
41 le robinet d'arrosage *m*
– *outside tap* (Am. *faucet) for the hose*
42 le tuyau d'arrosage *m*
– *garden hose*
43 le tourniquet
– *lawn sprinkler*
44 la pataugeoire
– *paddling pool*
45 le pas d'âne *m*
– *stepping stones*
46 la pelouse
– *sunbathing area (lawn)*
47 la chaise longue (*fam.:* le transat)
– *deck-chair*
48 le parasol de jardin *m*
– *sunshade (garden parasol)*
49 la chaise de jardin *m*
– *garden chair*
50 la table de jardin *m*
– *garden table*
51 la barre à battre les tapis *m*
– *frame for beating carpets*
52 l'accès *m* au garage
– *garage driveway*
53 la clôture, une clôture à claire-voie *f*
– *fence, a wooden fence*
54-57 le lotissement résidentiel
– ***housing estate*** *(housing development)*
54 la maison de lotissement *m*
– *house on a housing estate (on a housing development)*
55 le toit en appentis *m*
– *pent roof (penthouse roof)*
56 la lucarne sur toit *m* en appentis *m* (chatière *f*)
– *dormer (dormer window)*
57 le jardin particulier
– *garden*
58-63 la maison en bandes *f*, décalée
– ***terraced house*** *[one of a row of terraced houses],* ***stepped***
58 la jardinet
– *front garden*
59 la haie vive
– *hedge*
60 le trottoir
– *pavement* (Am. *sidewalk, walkway)*
61 la rue
– *street (road)*
62 le lampadaire (*autrefois:* le réverbère, le bec de gaz *m*)
– *street lamp (street light)*
63 la corbeille à papier *m*
– *litter bin* (Am. *litter basket)*
64-68 la maison à deux logements *m*
– ***house divided into two flats*** (Am. *house divided into two apartments, duplex house)*
64 le toit en croupe *f*
– *hip (hipped) roof*
65 la porte d'entrée *f*
– *front door*
66 le perron
– *front steps*
67 l'auvent *m*
– *canopy*
68 la baie vitrée
– *flower window (window for house plants)*
69-71 la maison à quatre logements *m*
– ***pair of semi-detached houses divided into four flats*** (Am. *apartments)*
69 le balcon
– *balcony*
70 la véranda
– *sun lounge* (Am. *sun parlor)*
71 le store
– *awning (sun blind, sunshade)*
72-76 l'immeuble *m* à galeries *f* couvertes
– ***block of flats*** (Am. *apartment building, apartment house) with access balconies*
72 la cage d'escalier *m*
– *staircase*
73 la galerie couverte
– *balcony*
74 le studio d'artiste *m* (atelier *m* d'artiste *m*)
– *studio flat* (Am. *studio apartment)*
75 la toiture-terrasse, un solarium
– *sun roof, a sun terrace*
76 l'espace *m* vert
– *open space*
77-81 le bloc d'habitations *f* à étages *m*
– ***multi-storey block of flats*** (Am. *multistory apartment building, multistory apartment house)*
77 le toit plat
– *flat roof*
78 le toit en appentis *m*
– *pent roof (shed roof, lean-to roof)*
79 le garage
– *garage*
80 la pergola
– *pergola*
81 la fenêtre de l'escalier *m*
– *staircase window*
82 la tour d'habitation *f*
– *high-rise block of flats* (Am. *high-rise apartment building, high-rise apartment house)*
83 l'attique *m*, l'étage *m* hors-toit
– *penthouse*
84-86 la résidence secondaire, une maison en bois *m*
– ***weekend house****, a timber house*
84 le mur de planches *f*
– *horizontal boarding*
85 le soubassement en pierres *f* de taille *f*
– *natural stone base course (natural stone plinth)*
86 la baie vitrée
– *strip windows (ribbon windows)*

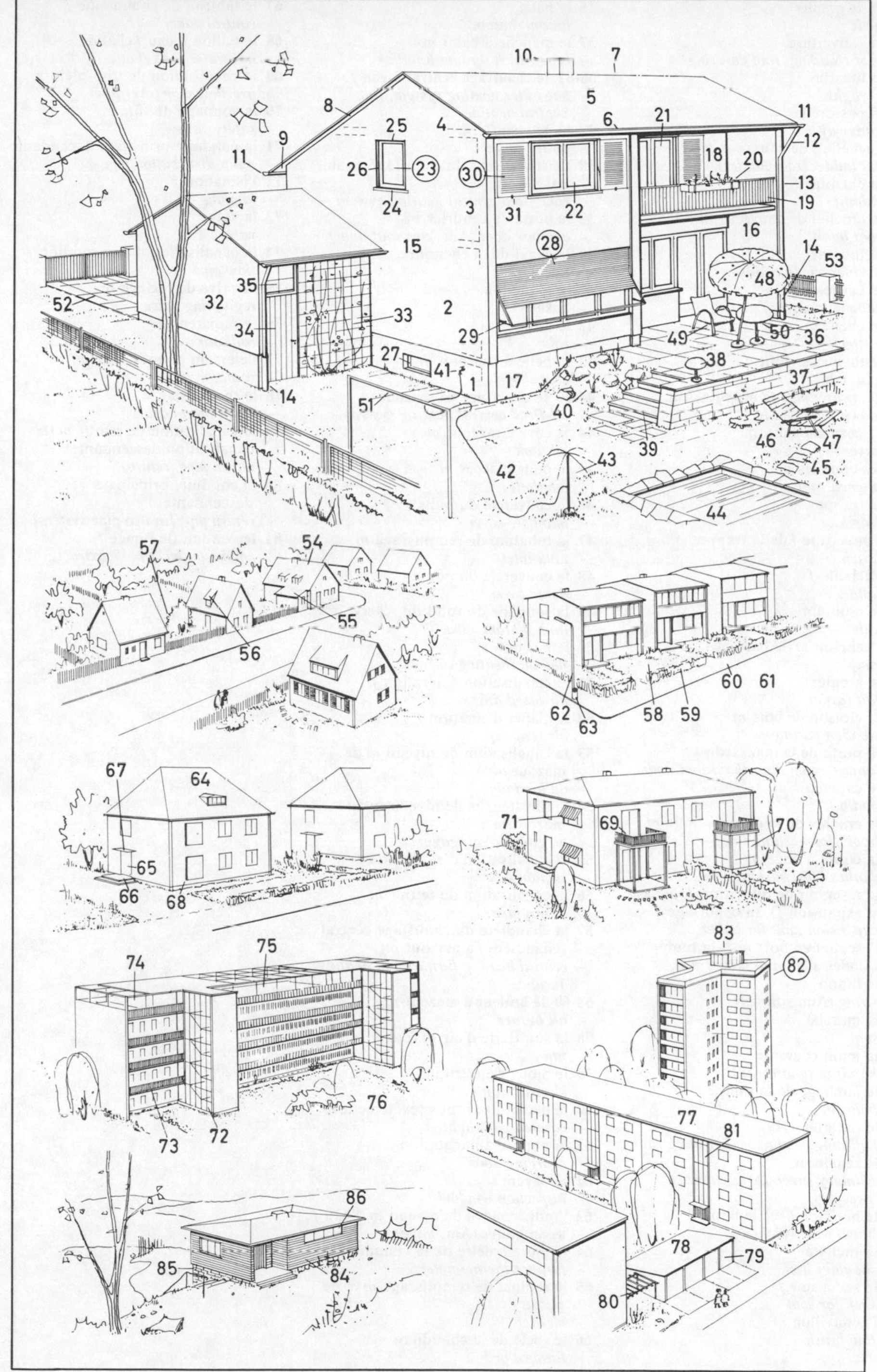
10
7
8
25
4
5
6
21
11
12
9
26
23
30
18
20
13
11
24
3
31
22
19
16
15
28
14
53
48
35
32
52
34
33
2
29
49
50
36
27
41
1
17
38
37
51
14
40
39
46
47
45
43
42
44
57
54
55
56
60
61
58
59
62
63
67
64
65
66
68
71
69
70
83
82
75
74
76
73
72
77
81
86
85
84
78
79
80

1-29 le grenier
– ***attic***
1 la couverture
– *roof cladding (roof covering)*
2 la lucarne
– *skylight*
3 la passerelle
– *gangway*
4 l'échelle *f* de couvreur *m*
– *cat ladder (roof ladder)*
5 la cheminée
– *chimney*
6 le crochet de couvreur *m*
– *roof hook*
7 la lucarne
– *dormer window (dormer)*
8 le garde-neige
– *snow guard (roof guard)*
9 le chéneau
– *gutter*
10 le tuyau de chute *f* d'eau *f* pluviale
– *rainwater pipe (downpipe,* Am. *downspout, leader)*
11 la corniche du toit
– *eaves*
12 les combles *m*
– *pitched roof*
13 la trappe
– *trapdoor*
14 l'ouverture *f* de la trappe
– *hatch*
15 l'échelle *f*
– *ladder*
16 le montant
– *stile*
17 l'échelon *m* (le barreau)
– *rung*
18 le grenier
– *loft (attic)*
19 la cloison de bois *m*
– *wooden partition*
20 la porte de la mansarde
– *lumber room door (boxroom door)*
21 le cadenas
– *padlock*
22 le crochet de la corde à linge *m*
– *hook [for washing line]*
23 la corde à linge *m*
– *clothes line (washing line)*
24 le réservoir de dilatation *f* (le vase d'expansion *f*) du chauffage
– *expansion tank for boiler*
25 l'escalier en bois *m* et la rampe
– *wooden steps and balustrade*
26 le limon
– *string (*Am. *stringer)*
27 la marche
– *step*
28 la main courante
– *handrail (guard rail)*
29 le jambage de la rampe
– *baluster*
30 le paratonnerre
– *lightning conductor (lightning rod)*
31 le ramoneur
– ***chimney sweep*** *(*Am. *chimney sweeper)*
32 le hérisson avec le boulet
– *brush with weight*
33 la raclette
– *shoulder iron*
34 le sac à suie *f*
– *sack for soot*
35 l'écouvillon *m*
– *flue brush*
36 le balai
– *broom (besom)*
37 le manche à balai *m*
– *broomstick (broom handle)*
38-81 le chauffage central à eau *f*
– ***hot-water heating system****, full central heating*
38-43 la chaufferie
– ***boiler room***
38 l'installation *f* de chauffage *m* au coke
– *coke-fired central heating system*
39 la porte de cendrier *m*
– *ash box door (*Am. *cleanout door)*
40 le canal de la cheminée
– *flueblock*
41 le pique-feu
– *poker*
42 le râble
– *rake*
43 la pelle à charbon *m*
– *coal shovel*
44-60 le chauffage au mazout *m*
– ***oil-fired central heating system***
44 la cuve à mazout *m*
– *oil tank*
45 le puits d'accès *m*
– *manhole*
46 le couvercle du puits
– *manhole cover*
47 la tubulure de remplissage *m*
– *tank inlet*
48 le couvercle du dôme
– *dome cover*
49 la soupape du fond du réservoir
– *tank bottom valve*
50 le mazout
– *fuel oil (heating oil)*
51 la canalisation d'aération *f*
– *air-bleed duct*
52 le clapet d'aération *f*
– *air vent cap*
53 la canalisation de niveau *m* de mazout *m*
– *oil level pipe*
54 l'indicateur *m* de niveau *m* du mazout *m*
– *oil gauge (*Am. *gage)*
55 la canalisation d'aspiration *f*
– *suction pipe*
56 la canalisation de retour *m*
– *return pipe*
57 la chaudière du chauffage central (chaudière *f* à mazout *m*)
– *central heating furnace (oil heating furnace)*
58-60 le brûleur à mazout *m*
– ***oil burner***
58 la soufflerie d'air *m* frais
– *fan*
59 le moteur électrique
– *electric motor*
60 le bec brûleur sous revêtement *m*
– *covered pilot light*
61 la porte d'alimentation *f*
– *charging door*
62 le voyant
– *inspection window*
63 l'indicateur *m* de niveau *m* d'eau *f*
– *water gauge (*Am. *gage)*
64 le thermomètre de la chaudière
– *furnace thermometer*
65 le robinet de remplissage *m* et de purge *f*
– *bleeder*
66 le socle de la chaudière
– *furnace bed*
67 le tableau de commande *f*
– *control panel*
68 le ballon d'eau *f* chaude
– *hot water tank (boiler)*
69 la canalisation de trop-plein *m*
– *overflow pipe (overflow)*
70 la soupape de sûreté *f*
– *safety valve*
71 la conduite principale ascendante
– *main distribution pipe*
72 l'isolation *f*
– *lagging*
73 la valve
– *valve*
74 la canalisation d'alimentation *f*
– *flow pipe*
75 la valve de réglage *m*
– *regulating valve*
76 le radiateur
– *radiator*
77 l'élément de radiateur *m*
– *radiator rib*
78 le thermostat
– *room thermostat*
79 la canalisation de retour *m* (la canalisation descendante)
– *return pipe (return)*
80 la conduite principale descendante
– *return pipe [in two-pipe system]*
81 le conduit de fumée *f*
– *smoke outlet (smoke extract)*

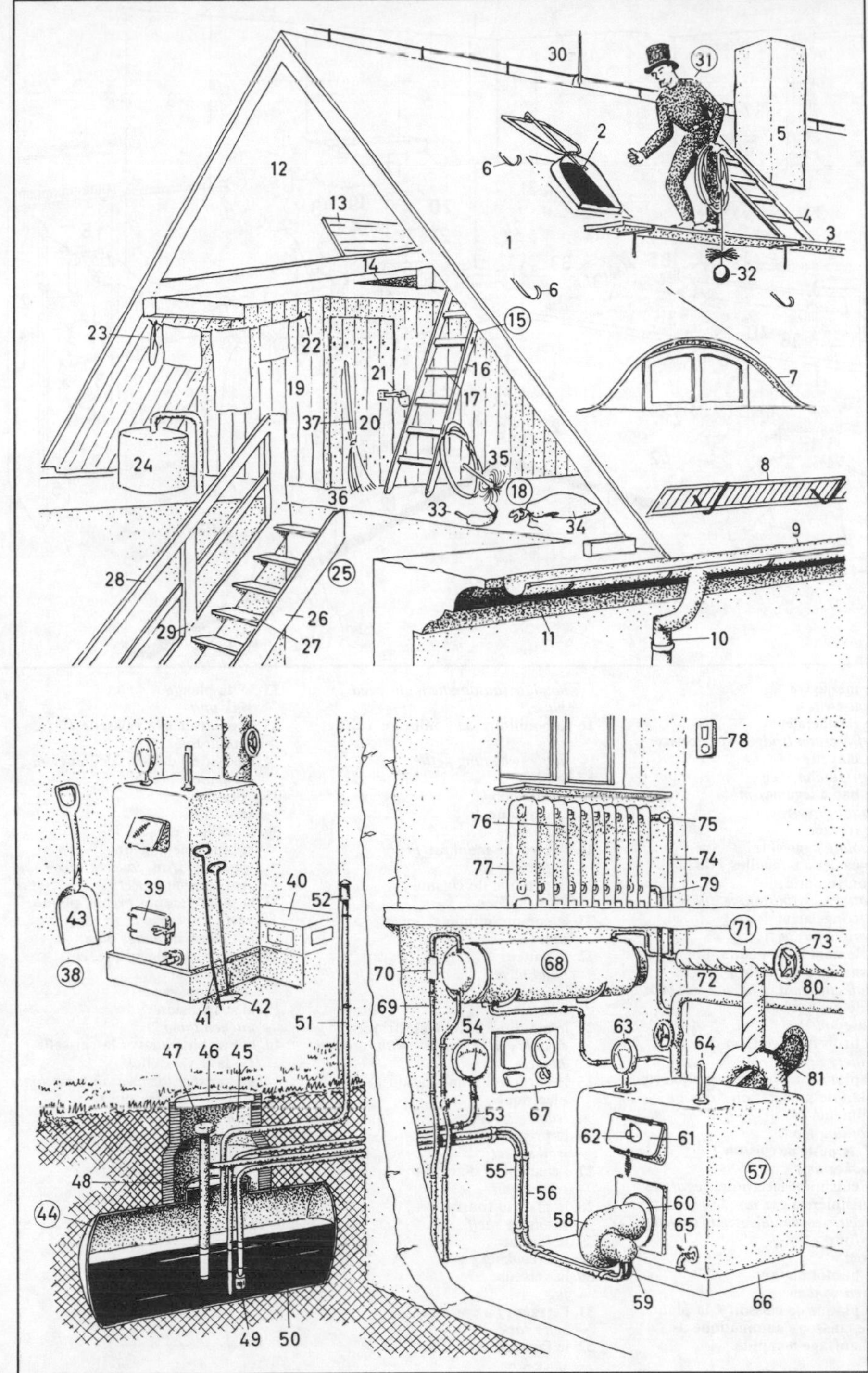
1
2
3
4
5
6
7
8
9
10
11
12
13
14
15
16
17
18
19
20
21
22
23
24
25
26
27
28
29
30
31
32
33
34
35
36
37
38
39
40
41
42
43
44
45
46
47
48
49
50
51
52
53
54
55
56
57
58
59
60
61
62
63
64
65
66
67
68
69
70
71
72
73
74
75
76
77
78
79
80
81

1 la ménagère
– *housewife*
2 le refrigérateur
– *refrigerator (fridge,* Am. *icebox)*
3 la clayette
– *refrigerator shelf*
4 le bac à légumes *m*
– *salad drawer*
5 le freezer
– *cooling aggregate*
6 le casier à bouteilles *f* de la contre-porte
– *bottle rack (in storage door)*
7 le congélateur
– *upright freezer*
8 l'élément *m* suspendu, une armoire à vaisselle *f*
– *wall cupboard, a kitchen cupboard*
9 l'élément *m* bas
– *base unit*
10 le tiroir à couverts *m*
– *cutlery drawer*
11 le plan de travail *m* principal (le plan de préparation *f* des aliments *m*)
– *working top*
12-17 le poste de cuisson *f*
– ***cooker unit***
12 la cuisinière électrique (*égal.:* la cuisinière à gaz *m*)
– *electric cooker* (also: *gas cooker)*
13 le four
– *oven*
14 le hublot du four
– *oven window*
15 la plaque de cuisson *f*, la plaque de cuisson *f* automatique à chauffage *m* rapide
– *hotplate (automatic high-speed plate)*
16 la bouilloire, la bouilloire à sifflet *m*
– *kettle (whistling kettle)*
17 la hotte
– *cooker hood*
18 la manique
– *pot holder*
19 l'accroche-manique *m*
– *pot holder rack*
20 la pendule de cuisine *f*
– *kitchen clock*
21 le compte-minutes
– *timer*
22 le batteur
– *hand mixer*
23 le fouet
– *whisk*
24 le moulin à café *m* électrique
– *electric coffee grinder (with rotating blades)*
25 le cordon d'alimentation *f* électrique
– *lead*
26 la prise murale
– *wall socket*
27 l'élément *m* d'angle *m*
– *corner unit*
28 le plateau tournant
– *revolving shelf*
29 le faitout
– *pot (cooking pot)*
30 la verseuse
– *jug*
31 l'étagère *f* à épices *f*
– *spice rack*
32 le flacon à épices *f*
– *spice jar*
33-36 la plonge
– ***sink unit***
33 l'égouttoir *m* à vaisselle *f*
– *dish drainer*
34 l'assiette *f* de petit déjeuner *m*
– *tea plate*
35 l'évier *m*
– *sink*
36 le robinet d'eau *f*, le robinet-mélangeur
– *water tap* (Am. *faucet) (mixer tap,* Am. *mixing faucet)*
37 la plante en pot *m*, une plante verte
– *pot plant, a foliage plant*
38 la cafetière électrique, le percolateur
– *coffee maker*
39 la suspension
– *kitchen lamp*
40 la machine à laver la vaisselle *f* (le lave-vaisselle)
– *dishwasher (dishwashing machine)*
41 le panier à vaisselle *f*
– *dish rack*
42 l'assiette *f*
– *dinner plate*
43 la chaise de cuisine *f*
– *kitchen chair*
44 la table de cuisine *f*
– *kitchen table*

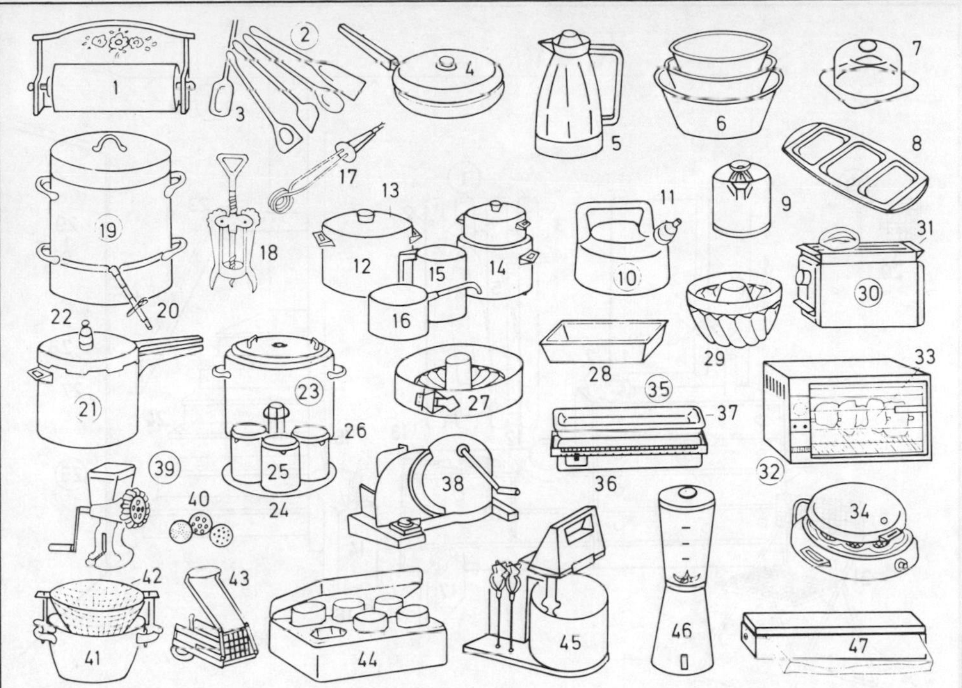

1 le distributeur de papier *m* ménage *m*
– *general-purpose roll holder with kitchen roll (paper towels)*
2 le jeu d'ustensiles *m* en bois *m*
– *set of wooden spoons*
3 la cuillère en bois *m*
– *mixing spoon*
4 la sauteuse
– *frying pan*
5 la verseuse isolante
– *Thermos jug*
6 saladiers *m*
– *set of bowls*
7 la cloche à fromages *m*
– *cheese dish with glass cover*
8 le plat à hors d'œuvre *m* (le plat à compartiments *m*)
– *three-compartment dish*
9 le presse-agrumes
– *lemon squeezer*
10 la bouilloire à sifflet *m*
– *whistling kettle*
11 le sifflet à vapeur *f*
– *whistle*
12-16 le jeu de casseroles *f*
– ***pan set***
12 le faitout
– *pot (cooking pot)*
13 le couvercle
– *lid*
14 la cocotte
– *casserole dish*
15 le pot à lait *m*
– *milk pot*
16 la casserole
– *saucepan*
17 le thermo-plongeur
– *immersion heater*
18 le tire-bouchon à levier *m*
– *corkscrew [with levers]*
19 l'extracteur *m* de jus *m* [inconnu en France]
– *juice extractor*
20 la pince à tube *m*
– *tube clamp (tube clip)*
21 la marmite à pression *f*
– *pressure cooker*
22 la soupape de sécurité *f*
– *pressure valve*
23 le stérilisateur
– *fruit preserver*
24 le porte-bocaux
– *removable rack*
25 le bocal
– *preserving jar*
26 le joint de couvercle *m* (rondelle *f*)
– *rubber ring*
27 le moule démontable
– *spring form*
28 le moule à cake *m*
– *cake tin*
29 le moule à kouglof *m*
– *cake tin*
30 le grille-pain
– *toaster*
31 le support pour petits pains *m*
– *rack for rolls*
32 la rôtissoire
– *rotisserie*
33 la broche
– *spit*
34 le gaufrier électrique
– *electric waffle iron*
35 la balance de ménage *m*
– *sliding-weight scales*
36 le poids-curseur
– *sliding weight*
37 le plateau
– *scale pan*
38 la machine à découper
– *food slicer*
39 le hachoir à viande *f*
– *mincer (Am. meat chopper)*
40 les grilles *f*
– *blades*
41 la friteuse
– *chip pan*
42 le panier de la friteuse *f*
– *basket*
43 le coupe-frites
– *potato chipper*
44 la yaourtière
– *yoghurt maker*
45 le robot de cuisine *f*
– *mixer*
46 le mixer
– *blender*
47 le soude-sacs
– *bag sealer*

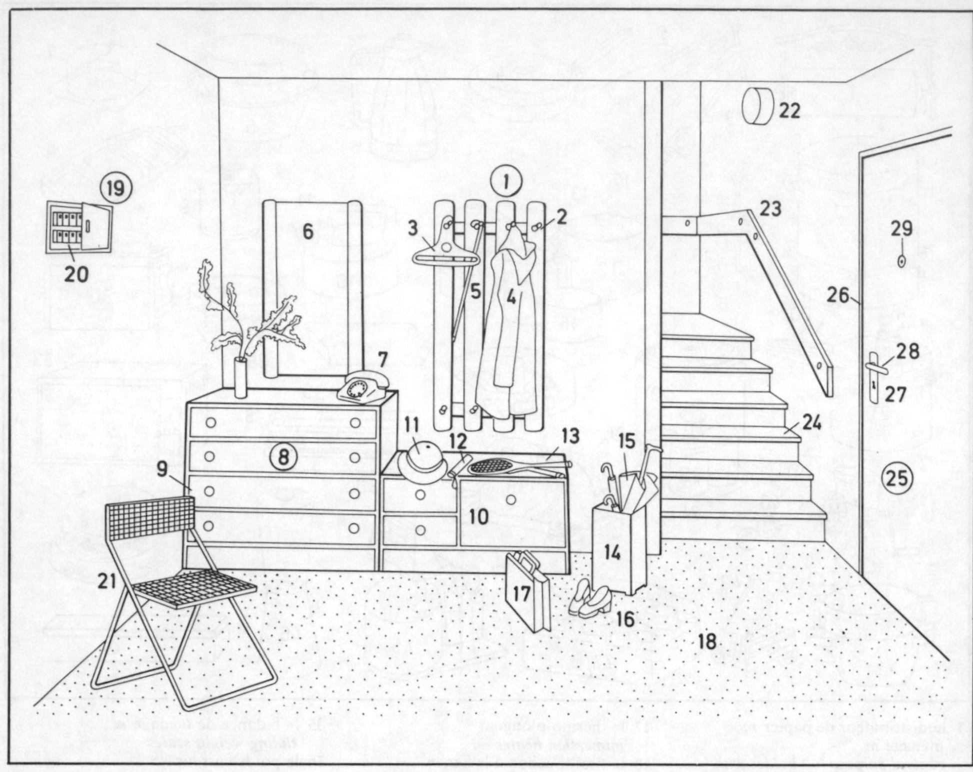

1-29 l'entrée *f* (le vestibule, le couloir)
– ***hall*** *(entrance hall)*
1 le porte-manteaux
– *coat rack*
2 la patère
– *coat hook*
3 le cintre à vêtements *m*
– *coat hanger*
4 la cape imperméable
– *rain cape*
5 la canne
– *walking stick*
6 la glace
– *hall mirror*
7 le téléphone
– *telephone*
8 l'armoire *f* à chaussures *f* fourre-tout
– *chest of drawers for shoes, etc.*
9 le tiroir
– *drawer*
10 le banc
– *seat*
11 le chapeau de dame *f*
– *ladies' hat*
12 le parapluie pliant
– *telescopic umbrella*
13 les raquettes *f* de tennis *m*
– *tennis rackets (tennis racquets)*
14 le porte-parapluies
– *umbrella stand*
15 le parapluie
– *umbrella*
16 les chaussures *f*
– *shoes*
17 le porte-documents (l'attaché-case *m*)
– *briefcase*
18 la moquette
– *fitted carpet*
19 le coffret électrique
– *fuse box*
20 le disjoncteur
– *miniature circuit breaker*
21 la chaise en tube *m* métallique
– *tubular steel chair*
22 l'applique *f* d'éclairage *m* de l'escalier *m*
– *stair light*
23 la main-courante
– *handrail*
24 la marche
– *step*
25 la porte d'entrée *f*
– *front door*
26 le chambranle
– *door frame*
27 la serrure
– *door lock*
28 le bec-de-cane *f*
– *door handle*
29 le judas
– *spyhole*

1 le meuble à éléments *m*
– *wall units*
2 le casier *m*
– *side wall*
3 le rayonnage de bibliothèque *f*
– *bookshelf*
4 la rangée de livres *m*
– *row of books*
5 l'élément *m* vitrine *f*
– *display cabinet unit*
6 l'élément bas
– *cupboard base unit*
7 l'élément *m* armoire *f*
– *cupboard unit*
8 le téléviseur
– *television set (TV set)*
9 la chaîne haute-fidélité *f* (hi-fi)
– *stereo system (stereo equipment)*
10 le baffle
– *speaker (loudspeaker)*
11 le râtelier à pipes *f*
– *pipe rack*
12 la pipe
– *pipe*
13 la mappemonde
– *globe*
14 la bouilloire en laiton *m*
– *brass kettle*
15 la longue-vue
– *telescope*
16 la pendule de cheminée *f*
– *mantle clock*
17 le buste
– *bust*
18 l'encyclopédie *f* en plusieurs volumes *m*
– *encyclopaedia [in several volumes]*
19 l'élément en épi *m*
– *room divider*
20 le bar
– *drinks cupboard*
21-26 le salon tapissier
– ***upholstered suite*** *(seating group)*
21 le fauteuil
– *armchair*
22 l'accoudoir *m*
– *arm*
23 le coussin de siège *m*
– *seat cushion (cushion)*
24 le canapé
– *settee*
25 le dossier
– *back cushion*
26 le fauteuil d'angle *m*
– *[round] corner section*
27 le coussin
– *scatter cushion*
28 la table basse
– *coffee table*
29 le cendrier
– *ashtray*
30 le plateau
– *tray*
31 la bouteille de whisky *m* (le flacon à whisky *m*)
– *whisky (whiskey) bottle*
32 le siphon
– *soda water bottle (soda bottle)*
33-34 le coin repas *m*
– ***dining set***
33 la table
– *dining table*
34 la chaise
– *chair*
35 le panneau de voilage *m*
– *net curtain*
36 les plantes *f* d'appartement *m*
– *indoor plants (houseplants)*

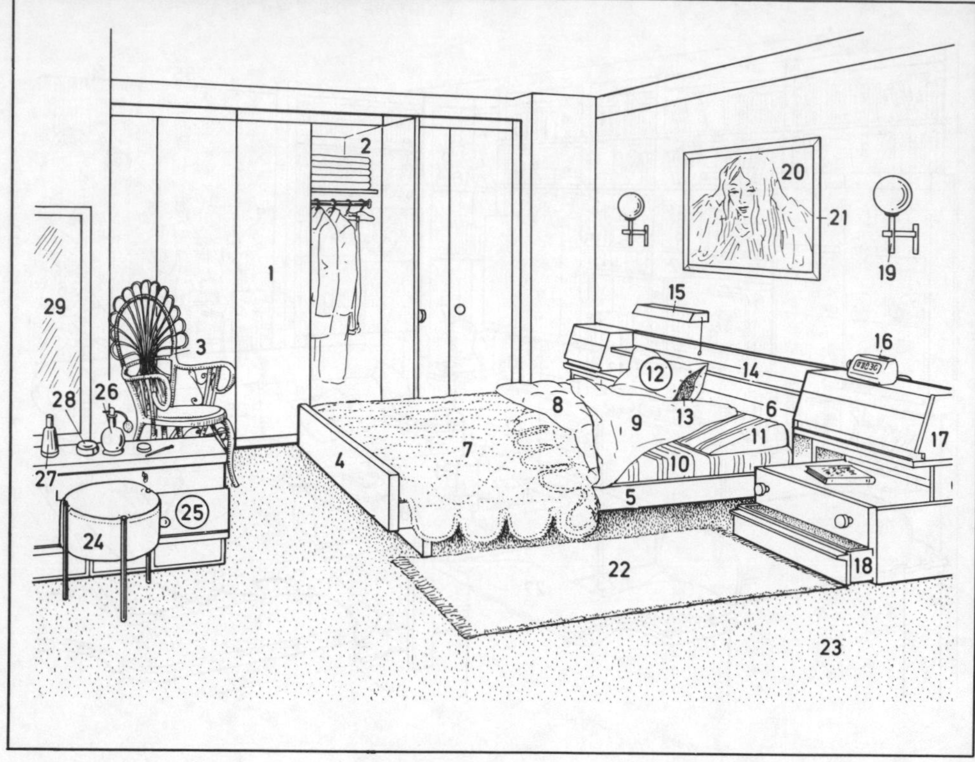

1 l'armoire *f* de chambre *f* à coucher, une armoire haute
– *wardrobe* (Am. *clothes closet)*

2 l'étagère *f* à linge *m*
– *linen shelf*

3 le fauteuil en rotin *m*
– *cane chair*

4-13 le lit deux personnes *f* (le lit à la française)
– ***double bed*** *(*sim.: *double divan)*

4-6 le lit
– ***bedstead***

4 le pied du lit (le dosseret de pied *m*)
– *foot of the bed*

5 le bois de lit *m*
– *bed frame*

6 la tête du lit (le dosseret de tête *f*)
– *headboard*

7 le dessus de lit *m*
– *bedspread*

8 la couverture, une couverture piquée
– *duvet, a quilted duvet*

9 le drap, un drap de lin *m*
– *sheet, a linen sheet*

10 le matelas, un matelas de mousse *f* recouvert de coutil *m*
– *mattress, a foam mattress with drill tick*

11 le traversin *[ici: type allemand]*
– *[wedge-shaped] bolster*

12-13 l'oreiller *m*
– *pillow*

12 la taie d'oreiller *m*
– *pillowcase (pillowslip)*

13 l'oreiller *m*
– *tick*

14 l'étagère *f* bibliothèque *f*
– *bookshelf [attached to the headboard]*

15 la lampe de chevet *m*
– *reading lamp*

16 le réveil électrique
– *electric alarm clock*

17 le meuble de chevet *m*
– *bedside cabinet*

18 le tiroir
– *drawer*

19 l'applique *f* d'éclairage *m*
– *bedroom lamp*

20 le tableau
– *picture*

21 le cadre
– *picture frame*

22 la descente de lit *m*
– *bedside rug*

23 la moquette
– *fitted carpet*

24 le tabouret de coiffeuse *f*
– *dressing stool*

25 la coiffeuse
– *dressing table*

26 le vaporisateur à parfum *m*
– *perfume spray*

27 le flacon de parfum *m*
– *perfume bottle*

28 le poudrier
– *powder box*

29 la glace de coiffeuse *f*
– *dressing-table mirror (mirror)*

1-11 le coin repas *m*
– ***dining set***
1 la table
– *dining table*
2 le pied de table *f*
– *table leg*
3 le plateau de table *f*
– *table top*
4 le set de table *f*
– *place mat*
5 le couvert
– *place (place setting, cover)*
6 l'assiette *f* creuse
– *soup plate (deep plate)*
7 l'assiette *f* plate
– *dinner plate*
8 la soupière
– *soup tureen*
9 le verre à vin *m*
– *wineglass*
10 la chaise
– *dining chair*
11 l'assise *f*
– *seat*
12 la suspension
– *lamp (pendant lamp)*
13 les doubles rideaux *m*
– *curtains*
14 le panneau de voilage *m*
– *net curtain*
15 la boîte à rideaux *m*
– *curtain rail*
16 le tapis
– *carpet*
17 l'élément *m* suspendu
– *wall unit*
18 la porte vitrée
– *glass door*
19 la tablette
– *shelf*
20 le buffet bas
– *sideboard*
21 le tiroir à couverts *m*
– *cutlery drawer*
22 le tiroir à linge *m* de table *f*
– *linen drawer*
23 l'embase *f*
– *base*
24 le plateau rond
– *round tray*
25 la plante en pot *m*
– *pot plant*
26 l'armoire *f* à vaisselle *f*, la vitrine
– *china cabinet (display cabinet)*
27 le service à café *m*
– *coffee set (coffee service)*
28 la cafetière
– *coffee pot*
29 la tasse à café *m*
– *coffee cup*
30 la soucoupe
– *saucer*
31 le crémier
– *milk jug*
32 le sucrier
– *sugar bowl*
33 le service de table *f*
– *dinner set (dinner service)*

1 la table de la salle à manger
– *dining table*
2 la nappe, une nappe damassée
– *tablecloth, a damask cloth*
3-12 le couvert *[pour une personne]*
– ***place*** *(place setting, cover)*
3 l'assiette *f* de présentation*f*
– *bottom plate*
4 l'assiette *f* plate
– *dinner plate*
5 l'assiette *f* creuse
– *deep plate (soup plate)*
6 l'assiette *f* à dessert *m*
– *dessert plate (dessert bowl)*
7 le couvert
– *knife and fork*
8 le couvert à poisson *m*
– *fish knife and fork*
9 la serviette de table *f*
– *serviette (napkin, table napkin)*
10 le rond de serviette *f*
– *serviette ring (napkin ring)*
11 le porte-couteau *m*
– *knife rest*
12 les verres *m* à vin *m*
– *wineglasses*
13 le carton de table *f*
– *place card*
14 la louche
– *soup ladle*
15 la soupière
– *soup tureen (tureen)*
16 le chandelier *m* de table *f*
– *candelabra*
17 la saucière
– *sauceboat (gravy boat)*
18 la cuiller à sauce *f*
– *sauce ladle (gravy ladle)*
19 la décoration de table *f*
– *table decoration*
20 la corbeille à pain *m*
– *bread basket*
21 le petit pain *m*
– *roll*
22 la tranche de pain *m*
– *slice of bread*
23 le saladier
– *salad bowl*
24 le couvert à salade *f*
– *salad servers*
25 le légumier
– *vegetable dish*
26 le plat à rôti *m*
– *meat plate* (Am. *meat platter)*
27 le rôti
– *roast meat (roast)*
28 le compotier
– *fruit dish*
29 la coupe à compote *f*
– *fruit bowl*
30 la compote
– *fruit (stewed fruit)*
31 le légumier
– *potato dish*
32 la desserte roulante
– *serving trolley*
33 le plat de légumes *m*
– *vegetable plate* (Am. *vegetable platter)*
34 le toast
– *toast*
35 le plateau à fromages *m*
– *cheeseboard*
36 le beurrier
– *butter dish*
37 la tartine
– *open sandwich*
38 la garniture de la tartine
– *filling*
39 le sandwich
– *sandwich*
40 la coupe à fruits *m*
– *fruit bowl*
41 les amandes *f* (*égal.*: les chips *f*, les cacahuètes *f*)
– *almonds* (also: *potato crisps, peanuts)*
42 l'huilier *m*
– *oil and vinegar bottle*
43 le ketchup (la sauce anglaise)
– *ketchup (catchup, catsup)*
44 le dressoir
– *sideboard*
45 le chauffe-plats électrique
– *electric hotplate*
46 le tire-bouchon
– *corkscrew*
47 le décapsuleur (l'ouvre-bouteille *m*)
– *crown cork bottle-opener (crown cork opener), a bottle-opener*
48 le carafon à liqueur *f*
– *liqueur decanter*
49 le casse-noix
– *nutcrackers (nutcracker)*

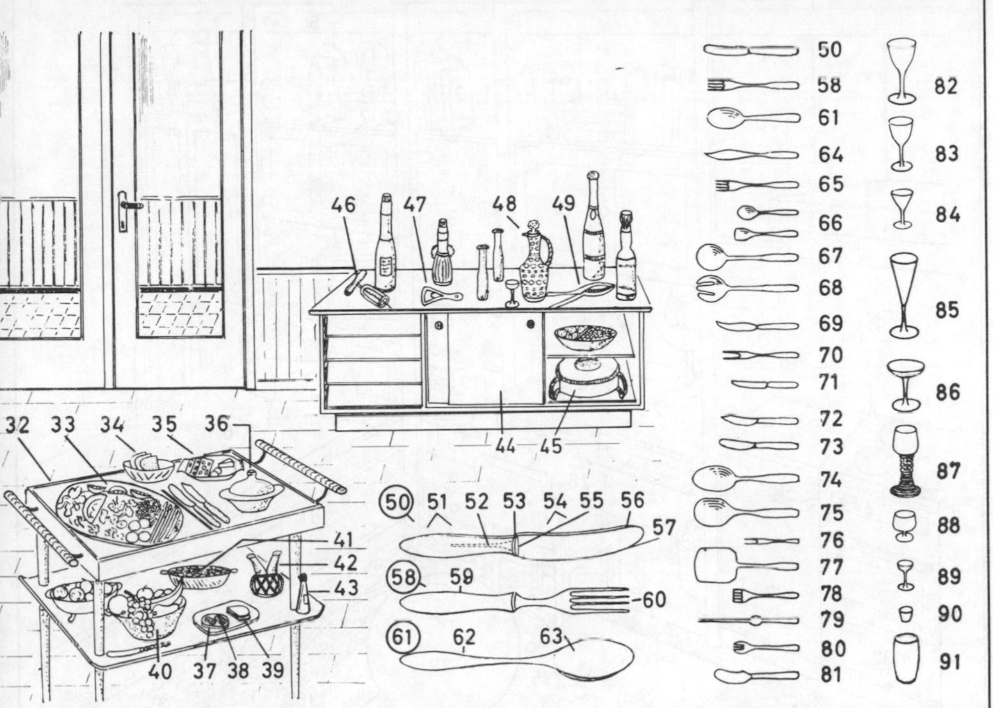

50 le couteau
– *knife*
51 le manche
handle
52 la soie
– *tang (tongue)*
53 la virole
– *ferrule*
54 la lame
– *blade*
55 la mitre
– *bolster*
56 le dos
– *back*
57 le tranchant
– *edge (cutting edge)*
58 la fourchette
– *fork*
59 le manche
– *handle*
60 la dent
– *prong (tang, tine)*
61 la cuiller à soupe
– *spoon (dessert spoon, soup spoon)*
62 le manche
– *handle*
63 le cuilleron
– *bowl*
64 le couteau à poisson *m*
– *fish knife*
65 la fourchette à poisson *m*
– *fish fork*
66 la cuiller à entremets *m*
– *dessert spoon (fruit spoon)*
67 la cuiller à salade *f*
– *salad spoon*
68 la fourchette à salade *f*
– *salad fork*
69-70 le couvert à servir
carving set (serving cutlery)
69 le couteau à servir
– *carving knife*
70 la grande fourchette (fourchette *f* à servir)
– *serving fork*
71 le couteau à fruits *m*
fruit knife
72 le couteau à fromage *m*
– *cheese knife*
73 le couteau à beurre *m*
– *butter knife*
74 la cuiller à légumes *m*, une cuiller à servir
– *vegetable spoon, a serving spoon*
75 la cuiller à pommes de terre *f*
– *potato server (serving spoon for potatoes)*
76 la fourchette à sandwich *m*
– *cocktail fork*
77 la pelle à asperges *f*
– *asparagus server (asparagus slice)*
78 la fourchette à sardines *f*
– *sardine server*
79 la fourchette à homards *m*
– *lobster fork*
80 la fourchette à huîtres *f*
– *oyster fork*
81 le couteau à caviar *m*
– *caviare knife*
82 le verre à vin *m* blanc
– *white wine glass*
83 le verre à vin *m* rouge
– *red wine glass*
84 le verre à madère *m*
– *sherry glass (madeira glass)*
85-86 les verres à champagne *m*
– *champagne glasses*
85 la flûte
– *tapered glass*
86 la coupe
– *champagne glass, a crystal glass*
87 le verre à vin *m* du Rhin
– *rummer*
88 le verre ballon
– *brandy glass*
89 le verre à liqueur *f*
– *liqueur glass*
90 le verre à eau-de-vie *f*
– *spirit glass*
91 le verre à bière *f*
– *beer glass*

1 le mural
– *wall units (shelf units)*
2 l'élément *m* armoire *f*
– *wardrobe door (*Am. *clothes closet door)*
3 le recueil
body
4 le casier
– *side wall*
5 la corniche
– *trim*
6 l'élément *m* deux portes *f*
– *two-door cupboard unit*
7 l'étagère *f* à livres *m* (la niche de vitrine *f*)
– *bookshelf unit (bookcase unit) [with glass door]*
8 les livres *m*
– books
9 la vitrine
– *display cabinet*
10 les fichiers *m*
– *card index boxes*
11 le tiroir
– *drawer*
12 la bonbonnière
– *decorative biscuit tin*
13 l'animal *m* en tissu *m*
– *soft toy animal*
14 le téléviseur
– *television set (TV set)*
15 les disques *m*
– *records (discs)*
16 le lit encastrable
– *bed unit*
17 le coussin
– *scatter cushion*
18 le tiroir de lit *m*
– *bed unit drawer*
19 le casier de lit *m*
– *bed unit shelf*
20 les journaux *m*
– *magazines*
21 la niche secrétaire *m*
– *desk unit (writing unit)*
22 le secrétaire
– *desk*
23 le sous-main
– *desk mat (blotter)*
24 la lampe de table *f*
– *table lamp*
25 le panier à papier *m* (la corbeille à papier *m*)
– *wastepaper basket*
26 le tiroir du secrétaire
– *desk drawer*
27 le fauteuil de bureau *m*
– *desk chair*
28 l'accoudoir *m*
– *arm*
29 le mur cuisine (les éléments *m* de cuisine *f*)
– *kitchen unit*
30 l'élément *m* haut
– *wall cupboard*
31 la hotte
– *cooker hood*
32 la cuisinière électrique
– *electric cooker*
33 le réfrigérateur
– *refrigerator (fridge,* Am. *icebox)*
34 la table
– *dining table*
35 le tapis de table *f*
– *table runner*
36 le tapis d'Orient *m*
– *oriental carpet*
37 le lampadaire
– *standard lamp*

1 le lit d'enfant *m*, des lits *m* superposés
– *children's bed, a bunk-bed*
2 le tiroir de rangement *m*
– *storage box*
3 le matelas
– *mattress*
4 l'oreiller *m*
– *pillow*
5 l'échelle
– *ladder*
6 l'éléphant *m* d'étoffe *f* (de chiffon *m*)
– *soft toy elephant, a cuddly toy animal*
7 le chien d'étoffe *f* (de chiffon *m*)
– *soft toy dog*
8 le pouf
– *cushion*
9 la poupée-mannequin
– *fashion doll*
10 la voiture de poupée *f*
– *doll's pram*
11 la poupée
– *sleeping doll*
12 le baldaquin
– *canopy*
13 le tableau noir
– *blackboard*
14 le boulier
– *counting beads*
15 le cheval en peluche *f* à bascule *f* et à roulettes *f*
– *toy horse for rocking and pulling*
16 les patins-bascules *m*
– *rockers*
17 le livre d'enfant *m*
– *children's book*
18 le coffret de jeux *m*
– *compendium of games*
19 le jeu des petits chevaux *m* [*équivalent français*]
– *ludo*
20 l'échiquier *m*
– *chessboard*
21 l'armoire *f* de chambre *f* d'enfant *m*
– *children's cupboard*
22 le tiroir à linge *m*
– *linen drawer*
23 l'abattant *m* secrétaire *m*
– *drop-flap writing surface*
24 le cahier
– *notebook (exercise book)*
25 les livres de classe *f*
– *school books*
26 le crayon (*égal.:* le crayon de couleur *f*, le crayon-feutre, le crayon à bille *f*, le stylo à bille *f*)
– *pencil (also: crayon, felt tip pen, ballpoint pen)*
27 l'épicerie *f*
– *toy shop*
28 le comptoir
– *counter*
29 l'étagère *f* à épices *f*
– *spice rack*
30 la vitrine
– *display*
31 les bonbons *m* assortis
– *assortment of sweets* (Am. *candies*)
32 le cornet à bonbons *m*
– *bag of sweets* (Am. *candies*)
33 la balance
– *scales*
34 la caisse
– *cash register*
35 le téléphone-jouet
– *toy telephone*
36 les casiers *m* à marchandises *f*
– *shop shelves (goods shelves)*
37 le train en bois *m*
– *wooden train set*
38 le camion-benne, une voiture-jouet
– *dump truck, a toy lorry (toy truck)*
39 la grue
– *tower crane*
40 la bétonnière
– *concrete mixer*
41 le grand chien en peluche *f*
– *large soft toy dog*
42 le cornet à dés *m*
– *dice cup*

1-20 l'éducation *f* préscolaire
– ***pre-school education*** *(nursery education)*

1 la jardinière d'enfants *m*
– *nursery teacher*

2 l'enfant *m*
– *nursery child*

3 le travail manuel
– *handicraft*

4 la colle
– *glue*

5 l'aquarelle *f*
– *watercolour* (Am. *watercolor*) *painting*

6 la boîte de peintures *f*
– *paintbox*

7 le pinceau pour l'aquarelle *f*
– *paintbrush*

8 le verre d'eau *f*
– *glass of water*

9 le puzzle
– *jigsaw puzzle (puzzle)*

10 la pièce de puzzle *m*
– *jigsaw puzzle piece*

11 les crayons *m* de couleur *f* (crayons *m* gras)
– *coloured* (Am. *colored*) *pencils (wax crayons)*

12 la pâte à modeler
– *modelling* (Am. *modeling*) *clay (plasticine)*

13 les sujets *m* modelés
– *clay figures (plasticine figures)*

14 la planche à modeler
– *modelling* (Am. *modeling*) *board*

15 la craie (le bâton de craie *f*)
– *chalk (blackboard chalk)*

16 le tableau
– *blackboard*

17 les cubes *m* de boulier *m*
– *counting blocks*

18 le marqueur
– *felt pen (felt tip pen)*

19 le jeu de reconnaissance *f* des formes *f*
– *shapes game*

20 le groupe de joueurs *m*
– *group of players*

21-32 les jouets *m*
– ***toys***

21 le jeu de cubes *m*
– *building and filling cubes*

22 le jeu de constructions *f* mobiles
– *construction set*

23 les livres *m* d'image *f*
– *children's books*

24 le berceau de poupée *f*, un berceau d'osier *m*
– *doll's pram, a wicker pram*

25 le baigneur
– *baby doll*

26 le baldaquin
– *canopy*

27 le jeu de constructions *f* en bois *m*
– *building bricks (building blocks)*

28 la construction en bois *m*
– *wooden model building*

29 le train jouet
– *wooden train set*

30 l'ours *m* à bascule *f*
– *rocking teddy bear*

31 la poussette de poupée *f*
– *doll's pushchair*

32 la poupée mannequin
– *fashion doll*

33 l'enfant *m* d'âge *m* préscolaire
– *child of nursery school age*

34 le vestiaire
– *cloakroom*

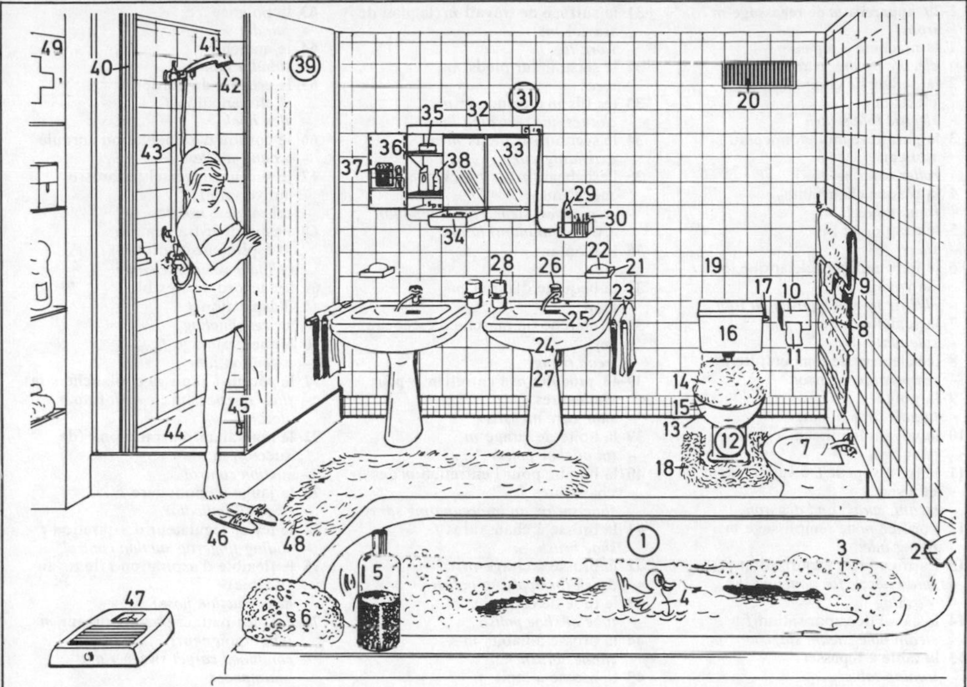

1 la baignoire
– *bath*

2 le robinet mélangeur
– *mixer tap (*Am. *mixing faucet) for hot and cold water*

3 le bain moussant
– *foam bath (bubble bath)*

4 le canard de caoutchouc *m*
– *toy duck*

5 les sels de bain *m*
– *bath salts*

6 l'éponge de toilette *f*
– *bath sponge (sponge)*

7 le bidet
– *bidet*

8 le porte-serviettes
towel rail

9 la serviette-éponge
– *terry towel*

10 le distributeur de papier *m* hygiénique
– *toilet roll holder (*Am. *bathroom tissue holder)*

11 le papier hygiénique
– *toilet paper (*coll. *loo paper,* Am. *bathroom tissue), a roll of crepe paper*

12 les cabinets *m* (le W.C., les W.C. *m*)
– *toilet (lavatory, W.C.,* coll. *loo)*

13 la cuvette de cabinet *m*
– *toilet pan (toilet bowl)*

14 l'abattant *m* de cuvette *f* avec dessus *m* en éponge *f*
– *toilet lid with terry cover*

15 la lunette
– *toilet seat*

16 la chasse d'eau *f*
– *cistern*

17 le levier de la chasse d'eau *f*
– *flushing lever*

18 le contour de cuvette *f*
– *pedestal mat*

19 le carreau
– *tile*

20 la bouche d'aération *f*
– *ventilator (extraction vent)*

21 le porte-savon
– *soap dish*

22 le savon
– *soap*

23 la serviette
– *hand towel*

24 le lavabo
– *washbasin*

25 le trop-plein
– *overflow*

26 le robinet d'eau *f* froide-eau *f* chaude
– *hot and cold water tap*

27 la console
– *washbasin pedestal with trap (anti-syphon trap)*

28 la verre à dents *f* (le gobelet à dents *f*)
– *tooth glass (tooth mug)*

29 la brosse à dents *f* électrique
– *electric toothbrush*

30 les brosses *f* de rechange
– *detachable brush heads*

31 l'armoire *f* de toilette *f* à miroirs *m*
– *mirrored bathroom cabinet*

32 le tube fluorescent
– *fluorescent lamp*

33 le miroir
– *mirror*

34 le tiroir
– *drawer*

35 le poudrier
– *powder box*

36 l'eau *f* dentifrice
– *mouthwash*

37 le rasoir électrique
– *electric shaver*

38 la lotion de rasage *m* (l'after-shave *m*, la lotion d'après-rasage *m*)
– *aftershave lotion*

39 la cabine de douche *f*
– *shower cubicle*

40 le rideau de douche *f*
– *shower curtain*

41 la douchette réglable
– *adjustable shower head*

42 le pommeau de la douche
– *shower nozzle*

43 le rail de réglage *m*
– *shower adjustment rail*

44 le récepteur de douche *f*
– *shower base*

45 l'écoulement *m* (le trop-plein)
– *waste pipe (overflow)*

46 la pantoufle de bain *m*
bathroom mule

47 le pèse-personne
– *bathroom scales*

48 le tapis de bain *m*
– *bath mat*

49 la pharmacie de ménage *m*
– *medicine cabinet*

1-20 appareils *m* **de repassage** *m*
– ***irons***
1 la machine à repasser
– *electric ironing machine*
2 la pédale de commande *f* électrique
– *electric foot switch*
3 la garniture molletonnée du rouleau
– *roller covering*
4 la plaque chauffante
– *ironing head*
5 le drap de lit *m*
– *sheet*
6 le fer à repasser électrique (le fer de voyage *m*)
– *electric iron, a lightweight iron*
7 la semelle du fer
– *sole-plate*
8 le sélecteur de température *f*
– *temperature selector*
9 la poignée
– *handle (iron handle)*
10 le voyant lumineux
– *pilot light*
11 le fer à vapeur *f*, à vaporisateur *m* et à sec
– *steam, spray, and dry iron*
12 l'orifice *m* de remplissage *m*
– *filling inlet*
13 l'orifice *m* de vaporisation *f*
– *spray nozzle for damping the washing*
14 le canal de vaporisation *f*
– *steam hole (steam slit)*
15 la table à repasser
– *ironing table*
16 le plateau de la table à repasser
– *ironing board (ironing surface)*
17 la garniture de plateau *m*
– *ironing-board cover*
18 le repose-fer
– *iron well*
19 le piètement en aluminium *m*
– *aluminium* (Am. *aluminum) frame*
20 la jeannette
– *sleeve board*
21 le coffre à linge *m*
– *linen bin*
22 le linge sale
– *dirty linen*
23-34 appareils *m* **de lavage** *m* **et de séchage** *m*
– ***washing machines and driers***
23 la machine à laver (la machine à laver automatique, ..le lave-linge)
– *washing machine (automatic washing machine)*
24 le tambour laveur
– *washing drum*
25 le verrouillage de sécurité *f* de la porte
– *safety latch (safety catch)*
26 le sélecteur de programme *m*
– *program selector control*
27 le bac à produits *m* lessiviels (avec compartiments *m* multiples)
– *front soap dispenser [with several compartments]*
28 le sèche-linge électrique à air *m* pulsé
– *tumble drier*
29 le panier de séchage *m*
– *drum*
30 la porte frontale avec les fentes *f* d'aération *f*
– *front door with ventilation slits*
31 la surface de travail *m* (le plan de travail *m*)
– *work top*
32 le séchoir sur pieds *m*
– *airer*
33 les fils *m* d'étendage *m*
– *clothes line (washing line)*
34 le séchoir sur pieds *m* en X
– *extending airer*
35 l'escabeau *m* (le marchepied) métallique
– *stepladder (steps), an aluminium* (Am. *aluminum) ladder*
36 le montant
– *stile*
37 la béquille d'appui *m*
– *prop*
38 la marche (la marche d'escabeau *m*)
– *tread (rung)*
39-43 produits *m* **d'entretien** *m* **pour chaussures** *f*
– ***shoe care utensils***
39 la boîte de cirage *m*
– *tin of shoe polish*
40 la bombe pour l'entretien *m* des chaussures *f*
– *shoe spray, an impregnating spray*
41 la brosse à chaussures *f*
– *shoe brush*
42 la brosse à cirage *m*
– *brush for applying polish*
43 le tube de cirage *m*
– *tube of shoe polish*
44 la brosse à habits *m*
– *clothes brush*
45 la brosse à tapis *m*
– *carpet brush*
46 le balai
– *broom*
47 les soies *f* du balai
– *bristles*
48 la monture du balai
– *broom head*
49 le manche du balai
– *broomstick (broom handle)*
50 le filetage
– *screw thread*
51 la brosse à vaisselle *f*
– *washing-up brush*
52 la pelle à poussière *f*
– *pan (dust pan)*
53-86 l'entretien *m* **des sols** *m*
– ***floor and carpet cleaning***
53 la balayette
– *brush*
54 le seau
– *bucket (pail)*
55 la serpillière (la wassingue)
– *floor cloth (cleaning rag)*
56 la brosse à récurer
– *scrubbing brush*
57 le balai mécanique
– *carpet sweeper*
58 l'aspirateur *m* balai *m*
– *upright vacuum cleaner*
59 le levier de commutation *f* (le sélecteur de position *f*)
– *changeover switch*
60 la rotule de suceur *m*
– *swivel head*
61 l'indicateur *m* de remplissage *m* (la jauge de poussière *f*)
– *bag-full indicator*
62 le logement du sac à poussière *f*
– *dust bag container*
63 la poignée
– *handle*
64 le manche
– *tubular handle*
65 le crochet du cordon d'alimentation *f*
– *flex hook*
66 le cordon d'alimentation enroulé
– *wound-up flex*
67 le suceur universel (la brosse universelle)
– *all-purpose nozzle*
68 l'aspirateur-traîneau *m* (l'aspirateur-chariot *m*)
– *cylinder vacuum cleaner*
69 le raccord du flexible d'aspiration *f*
– *swivel coupling*
70 le tube rallonge *f*
– *extension tube*
71 le suceur à tapis *m* et planchers *m*
– *floor nozzle (*sim.: *carpet beater nozzle)*
72 le régulateur d'aspiration *f* (de succion *f*)
– *suction control*
73 la jauge de poussière *f*
– *bag-full indicator*
74 le levier régulateur d'aspiration *f*
– *sliding fingertip suction control*
75 le flexible d'aspiration *f* (le tuyau flexible)
– *hose (suction hose)*
76 l'aspiro-batteur-shampooineur *m* (shampoigneur)
– *combined carpet sweeper and shampooer*
77 le cordon électrique
– *electric lead (flex)*
78 la prise de courant *m*
– *plug socket*
79 le raccord de l'aspiro-batteur *m*, de la shampooineuse (shampoigneuse), de la brosse aspirante
– *carpet beater head (*sim.: *shampooing head, brush head)*
80 l'aspirateur *m* universel
– *all-purpose vacuum cleaner (dry and wet operation)*
81 la roulette orientable
– *castor*
82 le bloc moteur
– *motor unit*
83 le verrouillage du couvercle
– *lid clip*
84 le flexible d'aspiration *f* des grosses pièces *f*
– *coarse dirt hose*
85 l'accessoire *m* spécial pour grosses pièces *f*
– *special accessory (special attachment) for coarse dirt*
86 la cuve à poussière *f*
– *dust container*
87 le chariot à provisions *f* (le caddie)
– *shopper (shopping trolley)*

1
2
3
4
5
6
7
8
9
10
11
12
13
14
15
16
17
18
19
20
21
22
23
24
25
26
27
28
29
30
31
32
33
34
35
36
37
38
39
40
41
42
43
44
45
46
47
48
49
50
51
52
53
54
55
56
57
58
59
60
61
62
63
64
65
66
67
68
69
70
71
72
73
74
75
76
77
78
79
80
81
82
83
84
85
86
87

1-35 le jardin d'agrément *m*
– ***flower garden***
1 la pergola
– *pergola*
2 la chaise longue (*fam.:* le transat)
– *deck-chair*
3 le balai à feuilles *f* (le balai à gazon *m*)
– *lawn rake (wire-tooth rake)*
4 le râteau
– *garden rake*
5 la vigne vierge, une plante grimpante
– *Virginia creeper (American ivy, woodbine), a climbing plant (climber, creeper)*
6 la rocaille
– *rockery (rock garden)*
7 les plantes de rocaille *f*; *var.:* le poivre de muraille *f*, la joubarbe, la dryade, l'aubrietia *f*
– *rock plants;* varieties: *stonecrop (wall pepper), houseleek, dryas, aubretia*
8 le gynérium (l'herbe *f* des pampas *f*)
– *pampas grass*
9 la haie vive
– *garden hedge*
10 l'épicéa *m* (*ici:* Picea pungens glauca)
– *blue spruce*
11 les hortensias *m*
– *hydrangeas*
12 le chêne
– *oak (oak tree)*
13 le bouleau
– *birch (birch tree)*
14 l'allée *f* de jardin *m*
– *garden path*
15 la bordure de l'allée *f*
– *edging*
16 la pièce d'eau *f* (le bassin)
– *garden pond*
17 le rebord dallé
– *flagstone (stone slab)*
18 le nénuphar
– *water lily*
19 les bégonias *m* tubéreux
– *tuberous begonias*
20 les dahlias *m*
– *dahlias*
21 l'arrosoir *m*
– *watering can* (Am. *sprinkling can)*
22 la démarieuse
– *weeding hoe*
23 le lupin polyphylle
– *lupin*
24 les marguerites *f*
– *marguerites (oxeye daisies, white oxeye daisies)*
25 la rose à haute tige *f*
– *standard rose*
26 la gerbéra
– *gerbera*
27 l'iris *m*
– *iris*
28 les glaïeuls
– *gladioli*
29 les chrysanthèmes *m*
– *chrysanthemums*
30 le coquelicot *m*
– *poppy*
31 la sarrette (la serratula)
– *blazing star*
32 la gueule-de-loup (le muflier des jardins)
– *snapdragon (antirrhinum)*
33 le gazon
– *lawn*
34 la dent-de-lion
– *dandelion*
35 le tournesol (l'hélianthe *m*)
– *sunflower*

1-32 le jardinet (le jardin potager et fruitier)
– ***allotment*** *(fruit and vegetable garden)*
1 la palmette candélabre, un arbre en espalier *m*
– *quadruple cordon, a wall espalier*
2 l'arbre *m* taillé en cordon *m*
– *vertical cordon*
3 la cabane à outils *m*
– *tool shed (garden shed)*
4 la tonne à eau *f* de pluie *f*
– *water butt (water barrel)*
5 la plante volubile
– *climbing plant (climber, creeper, rambler)*
6 le tas de terreau *m* (le tas de compost *m*)
– *compost heap*
7 le tournesol (l'hélianthe *m*)
– *sunflower*
8 l'échelle *f* de jardin *m*
– *garden ladder (ladder)*
9 la plantule, l'arbrisseau *m*
– *perennial (flowering perennial)*
10 la clôture en lattis *m* (clôture *f* à claire-voie *f*)
– *garden fence (paling fence, paling)*
11 l'arbuste *m* à baies *f* à haute tige *f*
– *standard berry tree*
12 le rosier grimpant sur arceau *m* en espalier *m*
– *climbing rose (rambling rose) on the trellis arch*
13 le rosier en buisson *m* (rosier *m* nain)
– *bush rose (standard rose tree)*
14 la gloriette (la tonnelle)
– *summerhouse (garden house)*
15 le lampion (la lanterne vénitienne)
– *Chinese lantern (paper lantern)*
16 l'arbre taillé en pyramide, la pyramide horizontale, un arbre en espalier *m* détaché
– *pyramid tree (pyramidal tree, pyramid), a free-standing espalier*
17 le cordon horizontal à deux bras *m*, un arbre en espalier *m* mural
– *double horizontal cordon*
18 la plate-bande, un parterre de fleurs *f* en bordure *f*
– *flower bed, a border*
19 l'arbuste à baies *f* (le groseillier à maquereau *m*, le groseillier)
– *berry bush (gooseberry bush, currant bush)*
20 la bordure de ciment *m*
– *concrete edging*
21 le rosier à haute tige *f* (le rosier, la rose à haute tige *f*)
– *standard rose (standard rose tree)*
22 la planche de plantes *f* vivaces
– *border with perennials*
23 l'allée de jardin *m*
– *garden path*
24 le jardinier amateur (le jardinier du dimanche)
– *allotment holder*
25 la planche d'asperges *f*
– *asparagus patch (asparagus bed)*
26 la planche de légumes *m*
– *vegetable patch (vegetable plot)*
27 l'épouvantail *m*
– *scarecrow*
28 les haricots *m* à rames *f*, une rame de haricots *m*
– *runner bean* (Am. *scarlet runner), a bean plant on poles (bean poles)*
29 le cordon horizontal simple
– *horizontal cordon*
30 l'arbre *m* fruitier à haute tige *f*
– *standard fruit tree*
31 le tuteur
– *tree stake*
32 la haie vive
– *hedge*

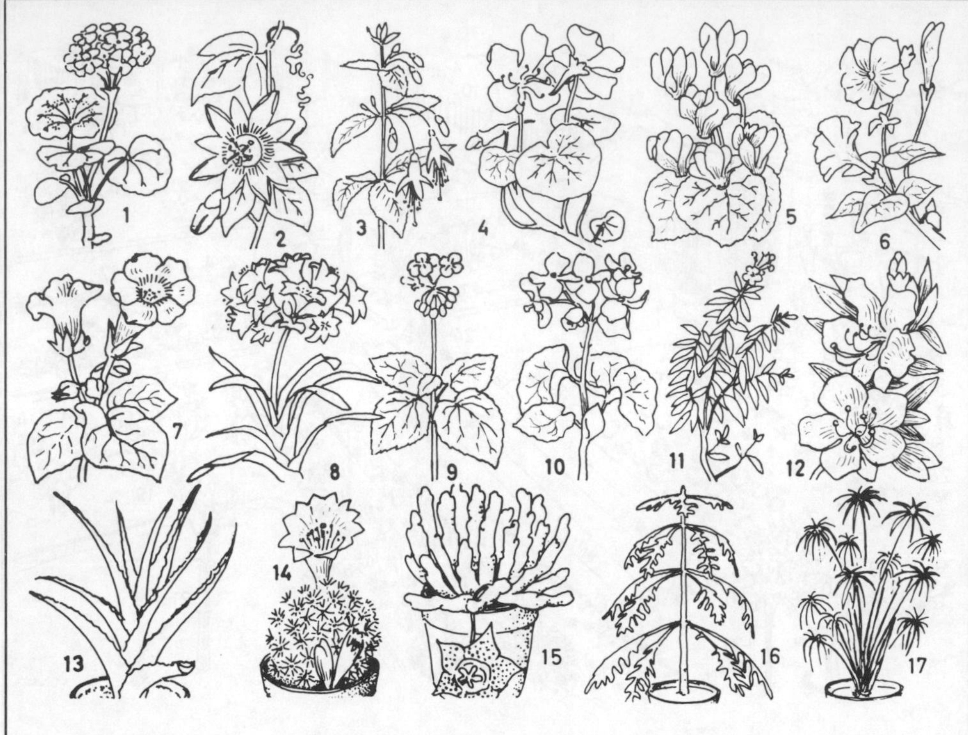

1 le pélargonium (le géranium), une géraniacée
– *pelargonium (crane's bill), a geranium*
2 la passiflore (la fleur de la Passion), une pariétale
– *passion flower (Passiflora), a climbing plant (climber, creeper)*
3 le fuchsia, une œnothéracée
– *fuchsia, an anagraceous plant*
4 la capucine, une tropéolée
– *nasturtium (Indian cress, tropaeolum)*
5 le cyclamen, une primulacée
– *cyclamen, a primulaceous herb*
6 le pétunia, une solanacée
– *petunia, a solanaceous herb*
7 la gloxinie, une gesnériacée
– *gloxinia (Sinningia), a gesneriaceous plant*
8 la clivie, une amaryllidacée
– *Clivia minata, an amaryllis (narcissus)*
9 le tilleul nain (le sparmannia), une tiliacée
– *African hemp (Sparmannia), a tiliaceous plant, a linden plant*
10 le bégonia, une bégoniacée
– *begonia*
11 le myrte, une myrtacée
– *myrtle (common myrtle, Myrtus)*
12 l'azalée *f*, une éricacée
– *azalea, an ericaceous plant*
13 l'aloès *m*, une liliacée
– *aloe, a liliaceous plant*
14 l'échinocactus *m* (le coussin de belle-mère *f*)
– *globe thistle (Echinops)*
15 le stapélia (la stapélie), une asclépiadacée
– *stapelia (carrion flower), an asclepiadaceous plant*
16 l'araucaria *m*, un conifère
– *Norfolk Island Pine (an araucaria, grown as an ornamental)*
17 le souchet (le cypérus), une cypéracée
– *galingale, a cyperacious plant of the sedge family*

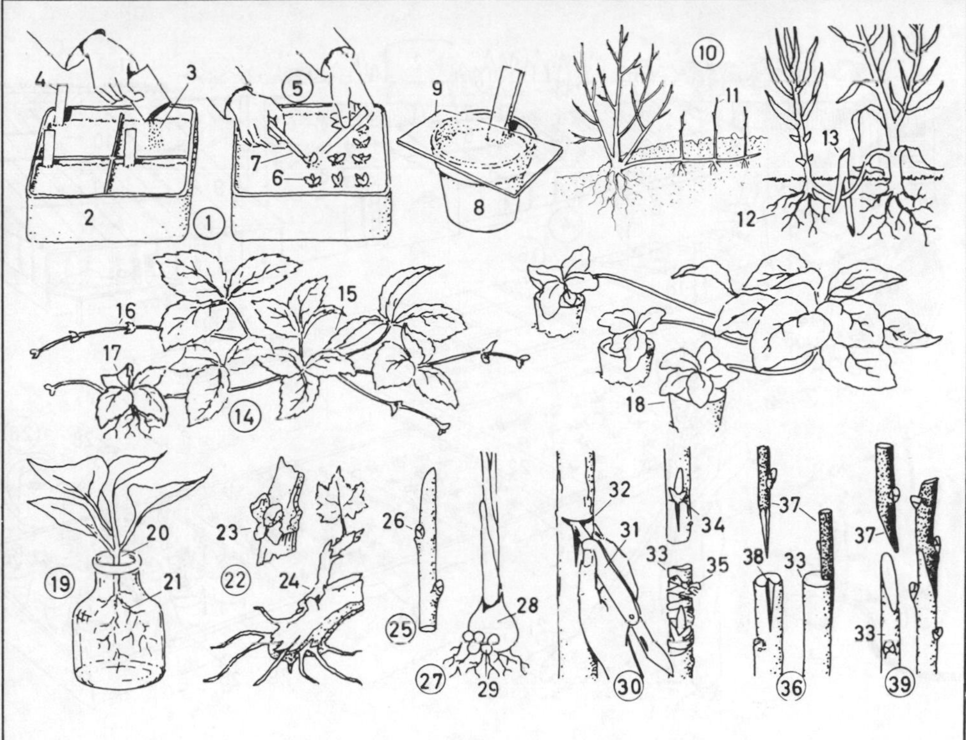

1 l'ensemencement *m*
– *seed sowing (sowing)*
2 la terrine à semis *m*
– *seed pan*
3 la graine (la semence)
– *seed*
4 l'étiquette *f*
– *label*
5 le repiquage
– *pricking out (pricking off, transplanting)*
6 le plant
– *seedling (seedling plant)*
7 le plantoir
– *dibber (dibble)*
8 le pot à fleurs *f*, un pot à semis *m*
– *flower pot (pot)*
9 la plaque de verre *m*
– *sheet of glass*
10 le marcottage en archet *m* (le couchage simple)
– *propagation by layering*
11 la marcotte *f*
– *layer*
12 la marcotte enracinée
– *layer with roots*
13 l'épingle *f* de fixation *f*
– *forked stick used for fastening*
14 le marcottage par stolons *m*
– *propagation by runners*
15 la plante mère *f*
– *parent (parent plant)*
16 le stolon (le jet, le rejet)
– *runner*
17 la plantule enracinée
– *small rooted leaf cluster*
18 le marcottage en pot *m*
– *setting in pots*
19 le bouturage dans l'eau
– *cutting in water*
20 la bouture
– *cutting (slip, set)*
21 la racine
– *root*
22 le bouturage de la vigne par boutures *f* d'œil *m* (boutures *f* anglaises)
– *bud cutting on vine tendril*
23 la bouture d'œil *m*, un bouton
– *scion bud, a bud*
24 le plant de bouture *f*
– *sprouting (shooting) cutting*
25 la bouture ligneuse
– *stem cutting (hardwood cutting)*
26 le bourgeon
– *bud*
27 la multiplication par caïeux *m*
– *propagation by bulbils (brood bud bulblets)*
28 le bulbe
– *old bulb*
29 le caïeu (le cayeu)
– *bulbil (brood bud bulblet)*
30-39 la greffe (ente *f*)
– ***grafting** (graftage)*
30 la greffe en écusson *m* par œil *m* levé
– *budding (shield budding)*
31 le greffoir
– *budding knife*
32 l'incision *f* en T
– *T-cut*
33 le sujet
– *support (stock, rootstock)*
34 le greffon mis en place *f*
– *inserted scion bud*
35 la ligature de raphia *m*
– *raffia layer (bast layer)*
36 la greffe en fente *f*
– *side grafting*
37 le greffon
– *scion (shoot)*
38 l'incision *f* en coin *m*
– *wedge-shaped notch*
39 la greffe à l'anglaise
– *splice graft (splice grafting)*

55 Horticulture et culture maraîchère

1-51 l'entreprise *f* **de production** *f* **horticole et maraîchère** (l'exploitation *f* d'un jardin de rapport *m*)
– ***market garden*** (Am. *truck garden, truck farm)*

1 la remise à outils *m*
– *tool shed*

2 le réservoir surélevé
– *water tower (water tank)*

3 la pépinière
– *market garden (*Am. *truck garden, truck farm), a tree nursery*

4 la serre chaude (la forcerie)
– *hothouse (forcing house, warm house)*

5 le toit vitré
– *glass roof*

6 le paillasson (la claie)
– *[roll of] matting (straw matting, reed matting, shading)*

7 la chaufferie (la salle de chauffe *f*)
– *boiler room (boiler house)*

8 le tube de chauffage *m* (la conduite à haute pression *f*)
– *heating pipe (pressure pipe)*

9 la planche de recouvrement *m*
– *shading panel (shutter)*

10-11 l'aération *f*
– *ventilators (vents)*

10 la fenêtre d'aération *f* (le panneau à tabatière *f*)
– *ventilation window (window vent, hinged ventilator)*

11 le panneau d'aération *f* coulissant
– *ridge vent*

12 la table à empoter
– *potting table (potting bench)*

13 le crible à béquille *f* (le crible à terreau *m*)
– *riddle (sieve, garden sieve, upright sieve)*

14 la pelle à terreau *m*
– *garden shovel (shovel)*

15 le tas de terre *f* (le compost, la terre végétale)
– *heap of earth (composted earth, prepared earth, garden mould,* Am. *mold)*

16 la couche chaude
– *hotbed (forcing bed, heated frame)*

17 le châssis de couche *f*
– *hotbed vent (frame vent)*

18 la cale d'aération *f* (l'aération *f* à crémaillère *f*)
– *vent prop*

19 l'arroseur rotatif (le tourniquet)
– *sprinkler (sprinkling device)*

20 le jardinier (l'horticulteur *m*, le maraîcher)
– *gardener (nursery gardener, grower, commercial grower)*

21 le cultivateur à main *f*
– *cultivator(hand cultivator, grubber)*

22 la passerelle
– *plank*

23 les jeunes plants *m* repiqués
– *pricked-out seedlings(pricked-off seedlings)*

24 les fleurs *f* précoces(fleurs *f* forcées)
– *forced flowers [forcing]*

25 les plantes *f* en pots *m*
– *potted plants(plants in pots, pot plants)*

26 l'arrosoir *m* à anse *f*
– *watering can (*Am. *sprinkling can)*

27 l'anse *f*
– *handle*

28 la pomme d'arrosoir *m*
– *rose*

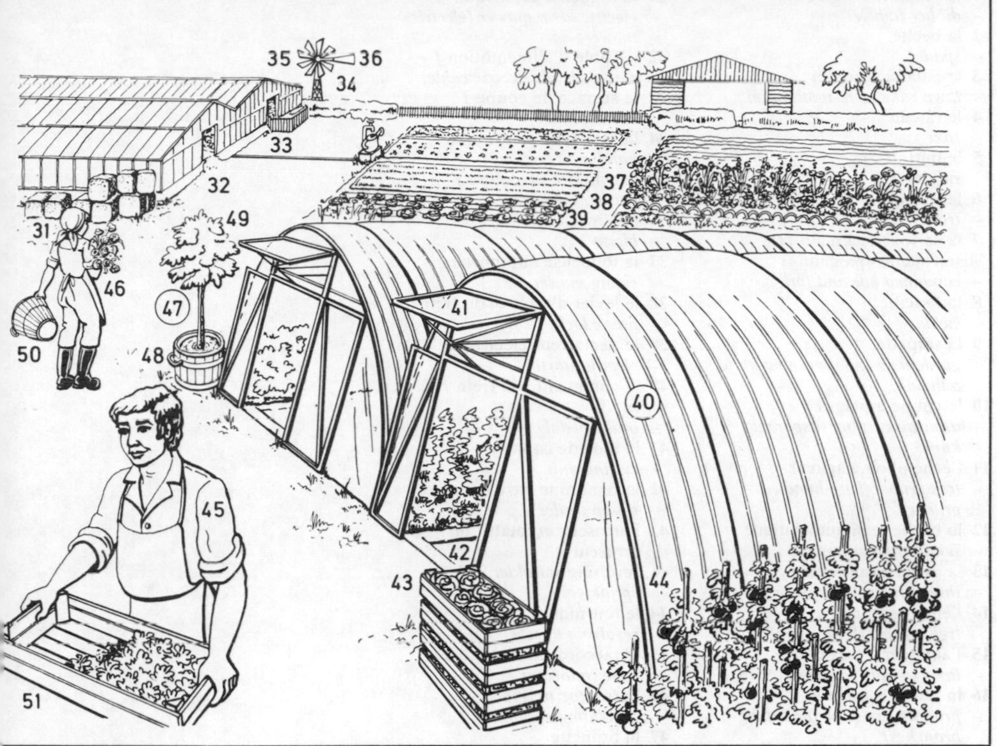

29 le bac à eau *f*
– *water tank*
30 le tuyau d'eau *f*
– *water pipe*
31 la balle de tourbe *f*
– *bale of peat*
32 la serre chaude
– *warm house(heated greenhouse)*
33 la serre froide
– *cold house(unheated greenhouse)*
34 l'éolienne *f*
– *wind pump;* sim.: *wind generator (aerogenerator)*
35 la roue à ailettes *f* (à aubes *f*, à palettes *f*)
– *wind wheel*
36 l'empennage *m*
– *wind vane*
37 la plate-bande, une planche de fleurs *f*
– *shrub bed, a flower bed*
38 la bordure d'arceaux *m*
– *hoop edging*
39 la planche de légumes *m*
– *vegetable plot*
40 l'abri-serre *m* (le tunnel plastique)
– *plastic tunnel (polythene greenhouse)*
41 le vasistas
– *ventilation flap*
42 l'allée centrale *f*
– *central path*
43 les cageots *m* de légumes *m*
– *vegetable crate*
44 le plant de tomates *f*
– *tomato plant*
45 l'aide-jardinier *m*
– *nursery hand*
46 l'aide-jardinier *f*
– *nursery hand*
47 la plante en baquet *m*
– *tub plant*
48 le baquet à plante *f*
– *tub*
49 le jeune plant d'oranger *m*
– *orange tree*
50 le panier en fil *m* métallique
– *wire basket*
51 la boîte portoir de semis *m*
– *seedling box*

1 le plantoir à crosse *f*
– *dibber (dibble)*
2 la bêche
– *spade*
3 le balai à gazon *m*
– *lawn rake (wire-tooth rake)*
4 le râteau
– *rake*
5 le buttoir
– *ridging hoe*
6 le transplantoir
– *trowel*
7 la serfouette à main *f* (la serfouette «piochon»)
– *combined hoe and fork*
8 la faucille
– *sickle*
9 la serpette
– *gardener's knife (pruning knife, billhook)*
10 le coupe-asperges
– *asparagus cutter (asparagus knife)*
11 l'échenilloir élagueur
– *tree pruner (long-handled pruner)*
12 la bêche semi-automatique
– *semi-automatic spade*
13 la griffe à trois dents *f*
– *three-pronged cultivator*
14 l'émoussoir *m*
– *tree scraper (bark scraper)*
15 l'aérateur à gazon *m*
– *lawn aerator (aerator)*
16 la scie d'élagage *m*
– *pruning saw (saw for cutting branches)*
17 le taille-haies autonome
– *battery-operated hedge trimmer*
18 la motobineuse
– *motor cultivator*
19 la perceuse à main *f*
– *electric drill*
20 la transmission
– *gear*
21 les deux jeux *m* de fraises *f*
– *cultivator attachment*
22 le cueille-fruits
– *fruit picker*
23 la brosse-émoussoir
– *tree brush (bark brush)*
24 le pulvérisateur à insecticide *m*
– *sprayer for pest control*
25 la lance d'aspersion *f*
– *lance*
26 l'enrouleur *m* mobile
– *hose reel (reel and carrying cart)*
27 le tuyau d'arrosage *m*
– *garden hose*
28 la tondeuse à moteur *m*
– *motor lawn mower (motor mower)*
29 le bac récupérateur (bac *m* à herbe *f*)
– *grassbox*
30 le moteur à deux temps *m*
– *two-stroke motor*
31 la tondeuse électrique
– *electric lawn mower (electric mower)*
32 le câble d'alimentation *f*
– *electric lead (electric cable)*
33 la surface de coupe *f*
– *cutting unit*
34 la tondeuse mécanique
– *hand mower*
35 le cylindre de coupe *f*
– *cutting cylinder*
36 la lame
– *blade*
37 la tondeuse autoportée
– *riding mower*
38 le levier d'arrêt *m* du frein
– *brake lock*
39 le démarreur électrique
– *electric starter*
40 la commande de frein *m* à pied *m*
– *brake pedal*
41 le bloc de coupe *f*
– *cutting unit*
42 la remorque basculante
– *tip-up trailer*
43 l'arroseur *m* rotatif, un arroseur
– *revolving sprinkler, a lawn sprinkler*
44 le tourniquet
– *revolving nozzle*
45 le raccord fileté du tuyau
– *hose connector*
46 l'arroseur *m* fixe
– *oscillating sprinkler*
47 la brouette
– *wheelbarrow*
48 la cisaille à gazon *m*
– *grass shears*
49 la cisaille à haies *f*
– *hedge shears*
50 le sécateur
– *secateurs (pruning shears)*

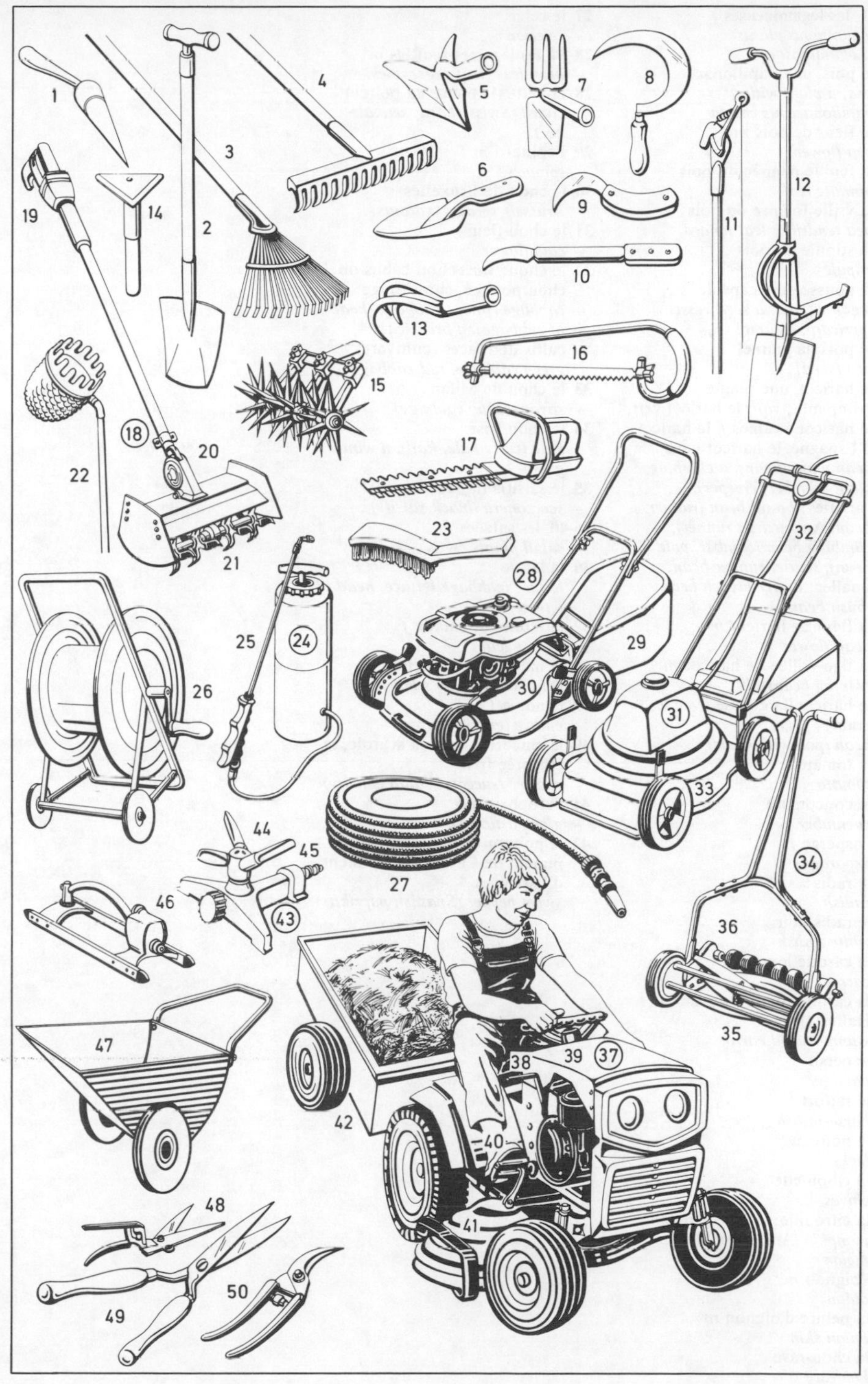
1
2
3
4
5
6
7
8
9
10
11
12
13
14
15
16
17
18
19
20
21
22
23
24
25
26
27
28
29
30
31
32
33
34
35
36
37
38
39
40
41
42
43
44
45
46
47
48
49
50

1-11 les légumineuses *f*
- *leguminous plants (Leguminosae)*

1 le pois, une papilionacée
- *pea, a plant with a papilionaceous corola*

2 la fleur de pois *m*
- *pea flower*

3 la feuille pennée du pois
- *pinnate leaf*

4 la vrille foliaire du pois
- *pea tendril, a leaf tendril*

5 la stipule du pois
- *stipule*

6 la gousse, une capsule
- *legume (pod), a seed vessel (pericarp, legume)*

7 le pois [la graine]
- *pea [seed]*

8 le haricot, une plante grimpante; *var.:* le haricot vert, le haricot à rames *f*, le haricot d'Espagne, le haricot nain
- *bean plant (bean), a climbing plant (climber, creeper);* varieties: *broad bean (runner bean,* Am. *scarlet runner), climbing bean (climber, pole bean), scarlet runner bean;* smaller: *dwarf French bean (bush bean)*

9 la fleur de haricot *m*
- *bean flower*

10 la tige vrillée de haricot *m*
- *twining beanstalk*

11 le haricot [la gousse avec les graines *f*]
- *bean [pod with seeds]*

12 la tomate
- *tomato*

13 le concombre
- *cucumber*

14 l'asperge *f*
- *asparagus*

15 le radis
- *radish*

16 le radis noir
- *white radish*

17 la carotte longue
- *carrot*

18 la carotte ronde (le grelot des Halles *f*)
- *stump-rooted carrot*

19 le persil
- *parsley*

20 le raifort
- *horse-radish*

21 le poireau
- *leeks*

22 la ciboulette
- *chives*

23 la citrouille; *anal.:* le melon
- *pumpkin* (Am. *squash);* sim.: *melon*

24 l'oignon *m*
- *onion*

25 la pelure d'oignon *m*
- *onion skin*

26 le chou-rave
- *kohlrabi*

27 le céleri
- *celeriac*

28-34 les légumes-feuilles *m*
- ***brassicas*** *(leaf vegetables)*

28 la bette (la blette, la poirée)
- *chard (Swiss chard, seakale beet)*

29 l'épinard *m*
- *spinach*

30 le chou de Bruxelles
- *Brussels sprouts (sprouts)*

31 le chou-fleur
- *cauliflower*

32 le chou; *var.:* chou cabus ou chou pommé, chou rouge
- *cabbage (round cabbage, head of cabbage), a brassica;* cultivated races (cultivars): *green cabbage, red cabbage*

33 le chou de Milan
- *savoy (savoy cabbage)*

34 le chou frisé
- *kale (curly kale, kail), a winter green*

35 le salsifis (la scorsonère)
- *scorzonera (black salsify)*

36-40 les salades *f*
- ***salad plants***

36 la laitue
- *lettuce (cabbage lettuce, head of lettuce)*

37 la feuille de salade *f*
- *lettuce leaf*

38 la mâche (la doucette)
- *corn salad (lamb's lettuce)*

39 l'endive *f*
- *endive (endive leaves)*

40 la chicorée; *var.:* la scarole, la chicorée frisée
- *chicory (succory, salad chicory)*

41 l'artichaut *m*
- *globe artichoke*

42 le poivron (le piment, le piment de Cayenne, le piment d'Espagne)
- *sweet pepper (Spanish paprika)*

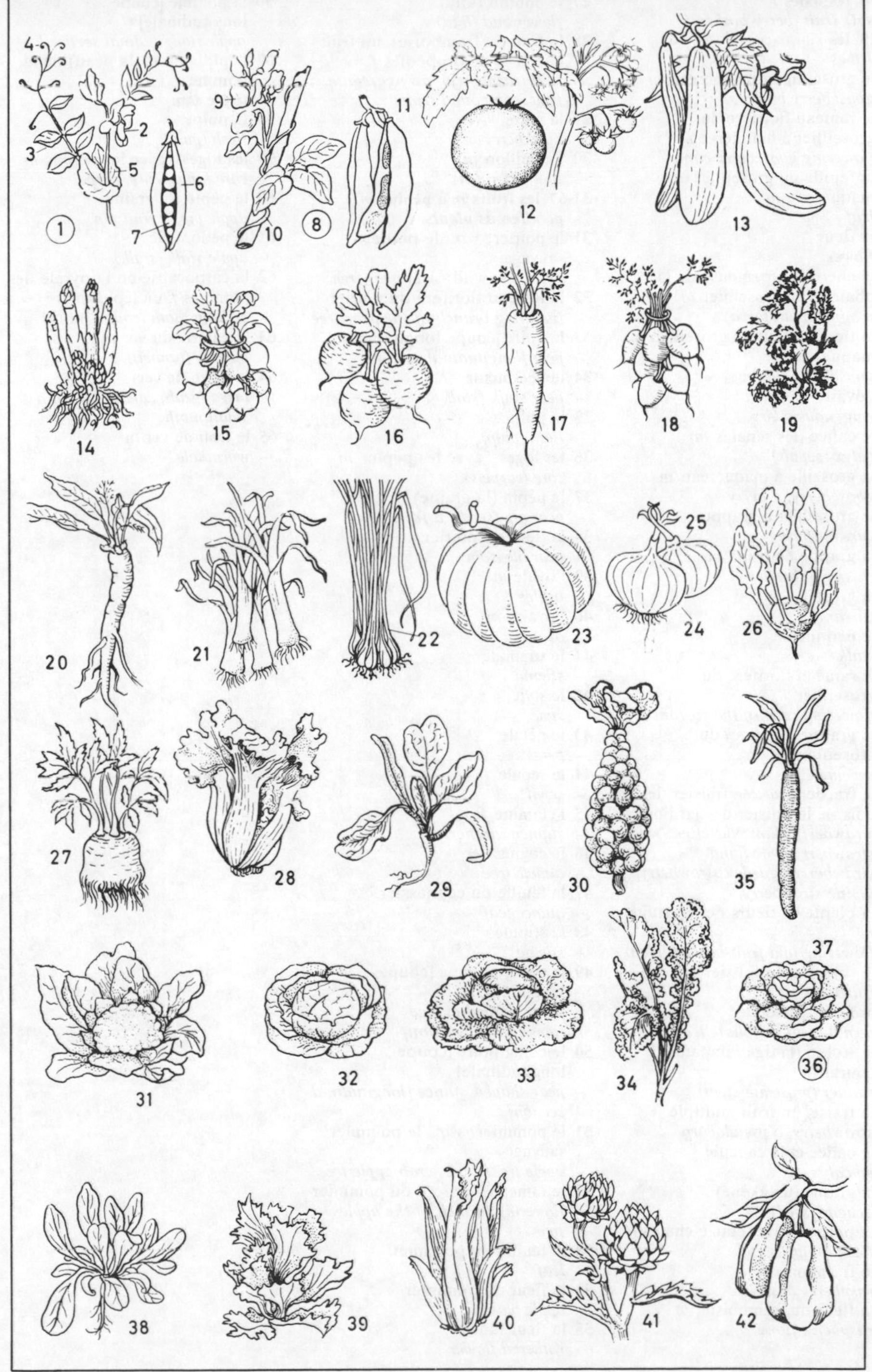
4
2
3
5
6
1
7
9
10
8
11
12
13
14
15
16
17
18
19
20
21
22
23
25
24
26
27
28
29
30
35
37
31
32
33
34
36
38
39
40
41
42

1-30 les baies *f*
– ***soft fruit*** *(berry bushes)*
1-15 les ribésiacées *f*
– ***Ribes***
1 le groseillier à maquereau *m*
– *gooseberry bush*
2 le rameau florifère du groseillier à maquereau *m*
– *flowering gooseberry cane*
3 la feuille du groseillier à maquereau *m*
– *leaf*
4 la fleur
– *flower*
5 la chenille arpenteuse de la phalène du groseillier *m*
– *magpie moth larva*
6 la fleur [détail] du groseillier à maquereau *m*
– *gooseberry flower*
7 l'ovaire *m* infère
– *epigynous ovary*
8 le calice (les sépales *m*)
– *calyx (sepals)*
9 la groseille à maquereau *m*
– *gooseberry, a berry*
10 le groseillier à grappe
– *currant bush*
11 la grappe de fruits *m*
– *cluster of berries*
12 la groseille
– *currant*
13 le pédoncule
– *stalk*
14 le rameau florifère du groseillier
– *flowering cane of the currant*
15 la grappe à fleurs *f* du groseillier
– *raceme*
16 le fraisier; *var.:* le fraisier des bois *m*, le fraisier des jardins *m*
– *strawberry plant;* varieties: *wild strawberry (woodland strawberry), garden strawberry, alpine strawberry*
17 la plante en fleurs *f* et en fruits *m*
– *flowering and fruit-bearing plant*
18 le rhizome du fraisier
– *rhizome*
19 la feuille trifoliée
– *ternate leaf (trifoliate leaf)*
20 le stolon (la tige rampante, le courant)
– *runner (prostrate stem)*
21 la fraise, un fruit multiple
– *strawberry, a pseudocarp*
22 le calice et le calicule
– *epicalyx*
23 la graine (un akène)
– *achene (seed)*
24 la pulpe (le réceptacle charnu)
– *flesh (pulp)*
25 le framboisier
– *raspberry bush*
26 la fleur du framboisier
– *raspberry flower*
27 le bouton floral
– *flower bud (bud)*
28 le fruit (la framboise), un fruit composé de drupéoles *f*
– *fruit (raspberry), an aggregate fruit (compound fruit)*
29 la mûre
– *blackberry*
30 l'aiguillon *m*
– *thorny tendril*
31-61 les fruits *m* **à pépins** *m*
– ***pomiferous plants***
31 le poirier; *var.:* le poirier sauvage
– *pear tree;* wild: *wild pear tree*
32 le rameau florifère du poirier
– *flowering branch of the pear tree*
33 la poire [coupe longitudinale]
– *pear [longitudinal section]*
34 le pédoncule
– *pear stalk (stalk)*
35 la pulpe
– *flesh (pulp)*
36 les loges *f* avec les pépins *m*
– *core (carpels)*
37 le pépin (la graine)
– *pear pip (seed), a fruit pip*
38 la fleur du poirier
– *pear blossom*
39 l'ovule *m*
– *ovules*
40 l'ovaire *m*
– *ovary*
41 le stigmate
– *stigma*
42 le style
– *style*
43 le pétale
– *petal*
44 le sépale
– *sepal*
45 l'étamine *f*
– *stamen (anther)*
46 le cognassier
– *quince tree*
47 la feuille du cognassier
– *quince leaf*
48 la stipule
– *stipule*
49 le coing pomme [coupe longitudinale]
– *apple-shaped quince [longitudinal section]*
50 le coing poire [coupe longitudinale]
– *pear-shaped quince [longitudinal section]*
51 le pommier; *var.:* le pommier sauvage
– *apple tree;* wild: *crab apple tree*
52 le rameau florifère du pommier
– *flowering branch of the apple tree*
53 la feuille du pommier
– *leaf*
54 la fleur du pommier
– *apple blossom*
55 la fleur fanée
– *withered flower*
56 la pomme [coupe longitudinale]
– *apple [longitudinal section]*
57 l'épiderme *m* (la peau) de la pomme
– *apple skin*
58 la pulpe
– *flesh (pulp)*
59 les loges *f* avec les pépins *m*
– *core (apple core, carpels)*
60 le pépin (la graine)
– *apple pip, a fruit pip*
61 le pédoncule
– *apple stalk (stalk)*
62 la carpocapse ou la pyrale des pommes *f*, un lépidoptère
– *codling moth (codlin moth)*
63 la galerie du ver *m*
– *burrow (tunnel)*
64 la larve (le ver)
– *larva (grub, caterpillar) of a small moth*
65 le trou de ver *m*
– *wormhole*

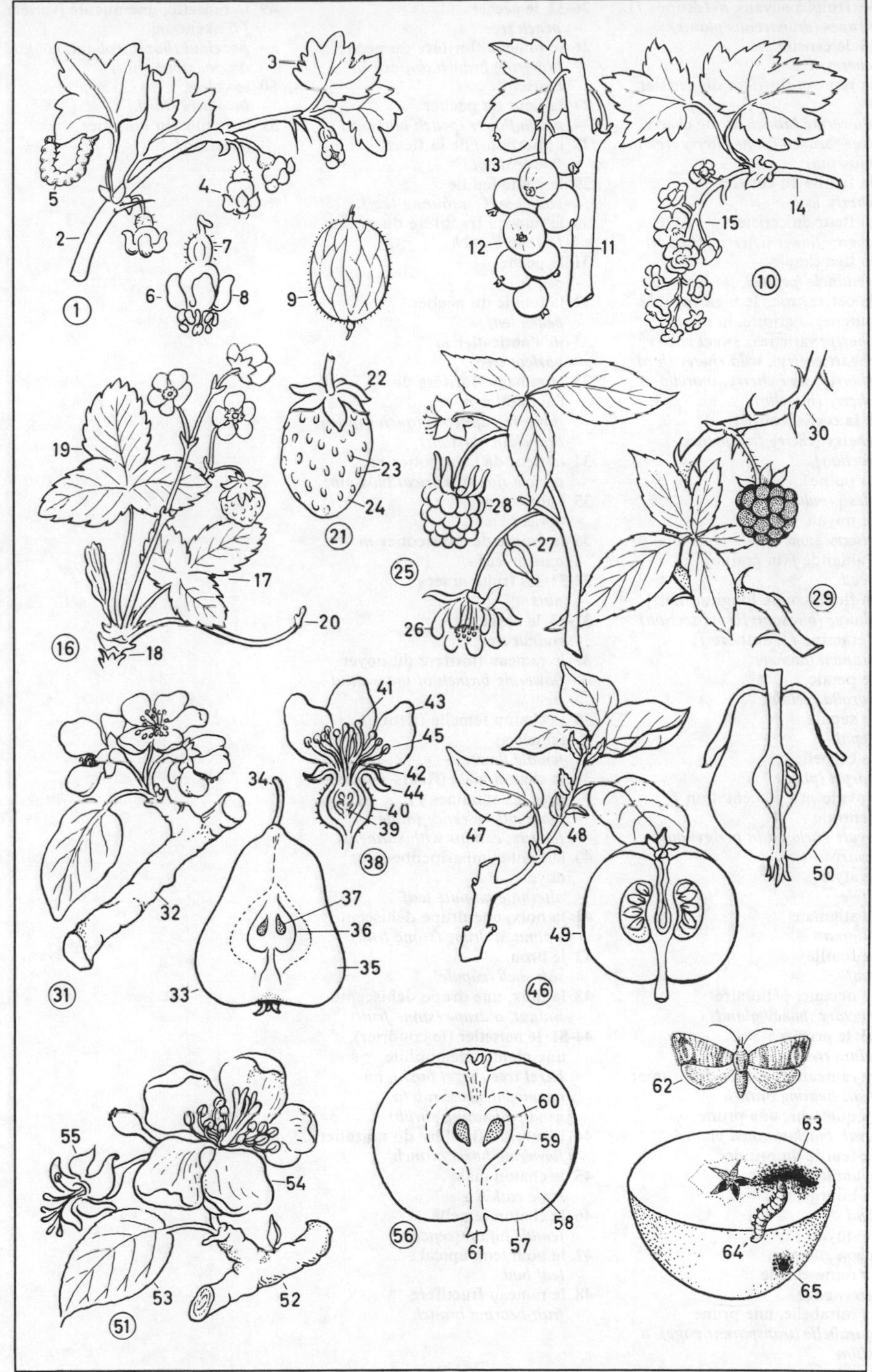
1
2
3
4
5
6
7
8
9
10
11
12
13
14
15
16
17
18
19
20
21
22
23
24
25
26
27
28
29
30
31
32
33
34
35
36
37
38
39
40
41
42
43
44
45
46
47
48
49
50
51
52
53
54
55
56
57
58
59
60
61
62
63
64
65

1-36 fruits à noyaux *m* (drupes *f*)
- ***drupes*** *(drupaceous plants)*

1-18 le cerisier
- ***cherry tree***

1 le rameau florifère du cerisier *m*
- *flowering branch of the cherry tree (branch of the cherry tree in blossom)*

2 la feuille du cerisier
- *cherry leaf*

3 la fleur du cerisier
- *cherry flower (cherry blossom)*

4 la tige florale
- *peduncle (pedicel, flower stalk)*

5 la cerise; *var.:* le bigarreau, la guigne, la griotte, la merise
- *cherry;* varieties: *sweet cherry (heart cherry), wild cherry (bird cherry), sour cherry, morello cherry (morello)*

6-8 la cerise [coupe]
- ***cherry*** *(cherry fruit) [cross section]*

6 la pulpe
- *flesh (pulp)*

7 le noyau
- *cherry stone*

8 l'amande *f* (la graine)
- *seed*

9 la fleur [coupe longitudinale]
- *flower (blossom) [cross section]*

10 l'étamine *f* (l'anthère *f*)
- *stamen (anther)*

11 le pétale
- *corolla (petals)*

12 le sépale
- *sepal*

13 le carpelle
- *carpel (pistil)*

14 l'ovule *m* à placentation *f* centrale
- *ovule enclosed in perigynous ovary*

15 le style
- *style*

16 le stigmate
- *stigma*

17 la feuille
- *leaf*

18 le nectaire pétiolaire
- *nectary (honey gland)*

19-23 le prunier
- ***plum tree***

19 le rameau fructifère du prunier
- *fruit-bearing branch*

20 la quetsche, une prune
- *oval, black-skinned plum*

21 la feuille du prunier
- *plum leaf*

22 le bourgeon
- *bud*

23 le noyau
- *plum stone*

24 la reine-claude
- *greengage*

25 la mirabelle, une prune
- *mirabelle (transparent gage), a plum*

26-32 le pêcher
- ***peach tree***

26 le rameau florifère du pêcher
- *flowering branch (branch in blossom)*

27 la fleur du pêcher
- *peach flower (peach blossom)*

28 l'insertion *f* de la fleur
- *flower shoot*

29 la jeune feuille
- *young leaf (sprouting leaf)*

30 le rameau fructifère du pêcher
- *fruiting branch*

31 la pêche
- *peach*

32 la feuille du pêcher
- *peach leaf*

33-36 l'abricotier *m*
- ***apricot tree***

33 le rameau florifère de l'abricotier *m*
- *flowering apricot branch (apricot branch in blossom)*

34 la fleur de l'abricotier *m*
- *apricot flower (apricot blossom)*

35 l'abricot *m*
- *apricot*

36 la feuille de l'abricotier *m*
- *apricot leaf*

37-51 les fruits *m* **secs**
- ***nuts***

37-43 le noyer
- ***walnut tree***

37 le rameau florifère du noyer
- *flowering branch of the walnut tree*

38 le chaton femelle (fleurs *f* femelles)
- *female flower*

39 le chaton mâle (fleurs *f* mâles avec les étamines *f*)
- *male inflorescence (male flowers, catkins with stamens)*

40 la feuille imparipennée du noyer
- *alternate pinnate leaf*

41 la noix, une drupe déhiscente
- *walnut, a drupe (stone fruit)*

42 le brou
- *soft shell (cupule)*

43 la noix, une drupe déhiscente
- *walnut, a drupe (stone fruit)*

44-51 le noisetier (le coudrier), une plante anémophile
- ***hazel tree*** *(hazel bush), an anemophilous shrub (a wind-pollinating shrub)*

44 le rameau florifère du noisetier
- *flowering hazel branch*

45 le chaton mâle
- *male catkin*

46 le chaton femelle
- *female inflorescence*

47 le bourgeon apical
- *leaf bud*

48 le rameau fructifère
- *fruit-bearing branch*

49 la noisette, une nucule [variété *f* d'akène *m*]
- *hazelnut (hazel, cobnut, cob), a drupe (stone fruit)*

50 le calice
- *involucre (husk)*

51 la feuille du noisetier
- *hazel leaf*

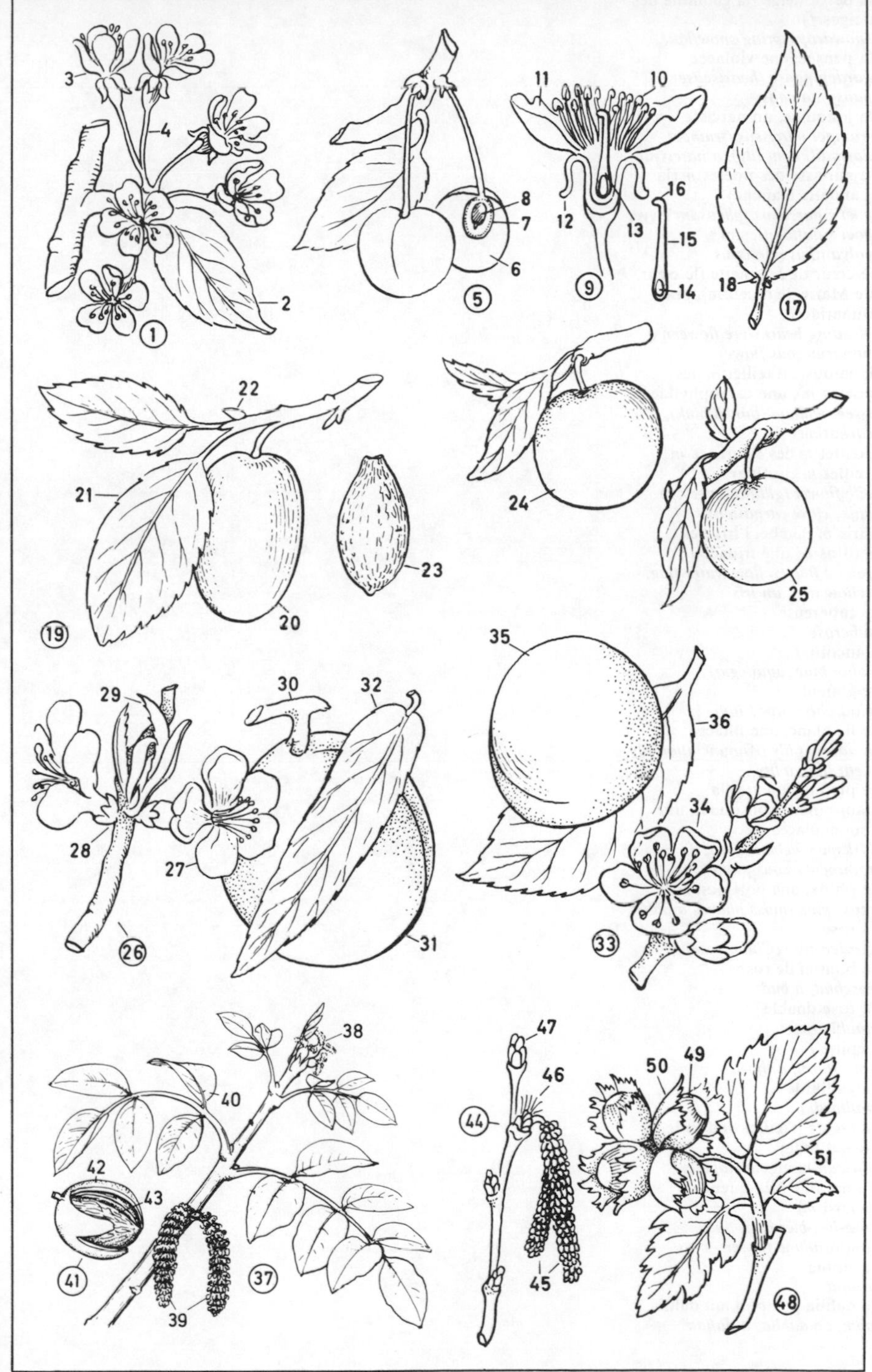
3
4
2
1
8
7
6
5
11
10
16
12
13
15
9
14
18
17
22
21
23
20
19
24
25
35
36
29
30
32
28
27
26
31
34
33
38
40
42
43
41
39
37
47
46
44
45
50
49
51
48

1 le perce-neige (la galanthe des neiges *f*)
– *snowdrop (spring snowflake)*
2 la pensée, une violacée
– *garden pansy (heartsease pansy), a pansy*
3 la jonquille, un narcisse
– *trumpet narcissus (trumpet daffodil, Lent lily), a narcissus*
4 le narcisse des poètes *m* (la jeannette blanche)
– *poet's narcissus (pheasant's eye, poet's daffodil);* sim.: *polyanthus narcissus*
5 le cœur de Jeannette (le cœur de Marie, le dicentra), une fumariacée
– *bleeding heart (lyre flower), a fumariaceous flower*
6 la jalousie (l'œillet *m* des poètes *m*), une caryophyllacée
– *sweet william (bunch pink), a carnation*
7 l'œillet *m* des fleuristes *m* (œillet *m* giroflée)
– *gillyflower (gilliflower, clove pink, clove carnation)*
8 l'iris *m* flambe, l'iris des jardins *m*, une iridacée
– *yellow flag (yellow water flag, yellow iris), an iris*
9 la tubéreuse
– *tuberose*
10 l'ancolie *f*
– *columbine (aquilegia)*
11 le glaïeul
– *gladiolus (sword lily)*
12 le lis blanc, une liliacée
– *Madonna lily (Annunciation lily, Lent lily), a lily*
13 le pied d'alouette (la dauphinelle consoude), une renonculacée
– *larkspur (delphinium), a ranunculaceous plant*
14 le phlox, une polémoniacée
– *moss pink (moss phlox), a phlox*
15 la rose
– *garden rose (China rose)*
16 le bouton de rose
– *rosebud, a bud*
17 la rose double
– *double rose*
18 l'épine *f*
– *rose thorn, a thorn*
19 la gaillarde
– *gaillardia*
20 la tagète (l'œillet *m* d'Inde, la rose d'Inde)
– *African marigold (tagetes)*
21 l'amarante *f* (la queue de renard *m*)
– *love-lies-bleeding, an amaranthine flower*
22 le zinnia
– *zinnia*
23 le dahlia pompon, un dahlia
– *pompon dahlia, a dahlia*

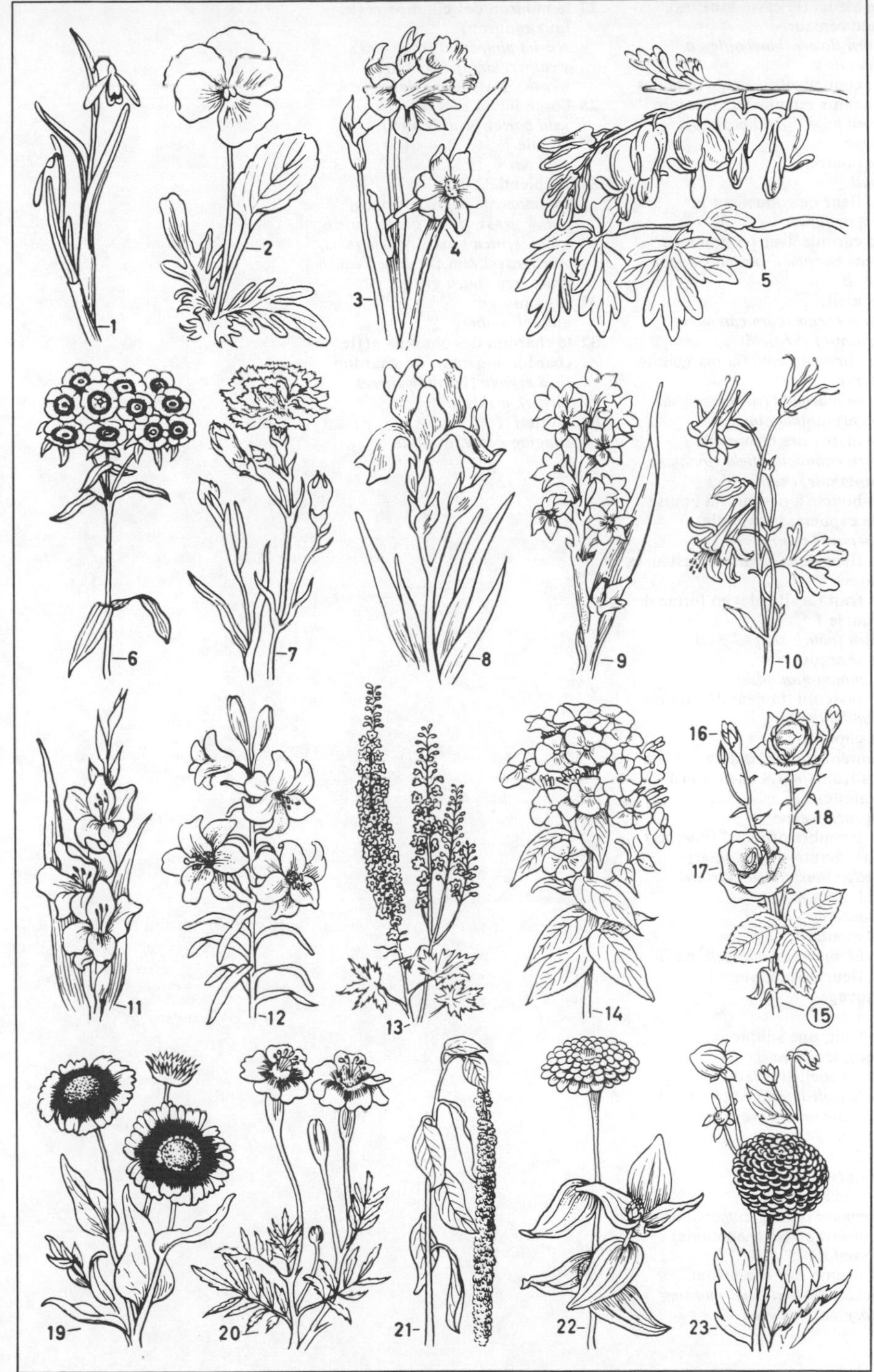
1
2
3
4
5
6
7
8
9
10
11
12
13
14
15
16
17
18
19
20
21
22
23

1 le bleuet (le casse-lunettes), une centaurée
– *corn flower (bluebottle), a centaury*
2 le coquelicot (le coquelicot des champs *m*), une papavéracée
– *corn poppy (field poppy), a poppy*
3 le bouton
– *bud*
4 la fleur de coquelicot *m*
– *poppy flower*
5 la capsule avec les graines *f*
– *seed capsule containing poppy seeds*
6 la nielle
– *corn cockle (corn campion, crown-of-the-field)*
7 le chrysanthème (la marguerite dorée)
– *corn marigold (field marigold), a chrysanthemum*
8 la matricaire camomille
– *corn camomile (field camomile, camomile, chamomile)*
9 la bourse à pasteur (la bourse de capucin, la capselle)
– *shepherd's purse*
10 la fleur de la bourse à pasteur
– *flower*
11 le fruit (la silicule) en forme de bourse *f*
– *fruit (pouch-shaped pod)*
12 le séneçon
– *common groundsel*
13 le pissenlit (la dent de lion *m*)
– *dandelion*
14 le capitule
– *flower head (capitulum)*
15 les fruits *m* (les akènes *m* à aigrettes *f*)
– *infructescence*
16 le sisymbre officinal (l'herbe *f* aux chantres *m*, le vélar)
– *hedge mustard, a mustard*
17 l'alysson *m*
– *stonecrop*
18 la moutarde sauvage
– *wild mustard (charlock, runch)*
19 la fleur de la moutarde sauvage
– *flower*
20 le fruit, une silique
– *fruit, a siliqua (pod)*
21 la ravenelle (le radis sauvage)
– *wild radish (jointed charlock)*
22 la fleur de la ravenelle
– *flower*
23 le fruit, une silique
– *fruit (siliqua, pod)*
24 l'arroche *f* hastée
– *common orache (common orach)*
25 l'ansérine *f* (le chénopode)
– *goosefoot*
26 le liseron des champs *m*
– *field bindweed (wild morning glory), a bindweed*
27 le mouron des champs *m* (le faux mouron)
– *scarlet pimpernel (shepherd's weatherglass, poor man's weatherglass, eye-bright)*
28 l'orge *m* des rats *m*
– *wild barley (wall barley)*
29 l'ivraie *f*
– *wild oat*
30 le chiendent
– *common couch grass (couch, quack grass, quick grass, quitch grass, scutch grass, twitch grass, witchgrass);* sim.: *bearded couch grass, sea couch grass*
31 le galinsoge
– *gallant soldier*
32 le chardon des champs *m* (le chardon argenté), un chardon
– *field eryngo (Watling Street thistle), a thistle*
33 l'ortie *f*
– *stinging nettle, a nettle*

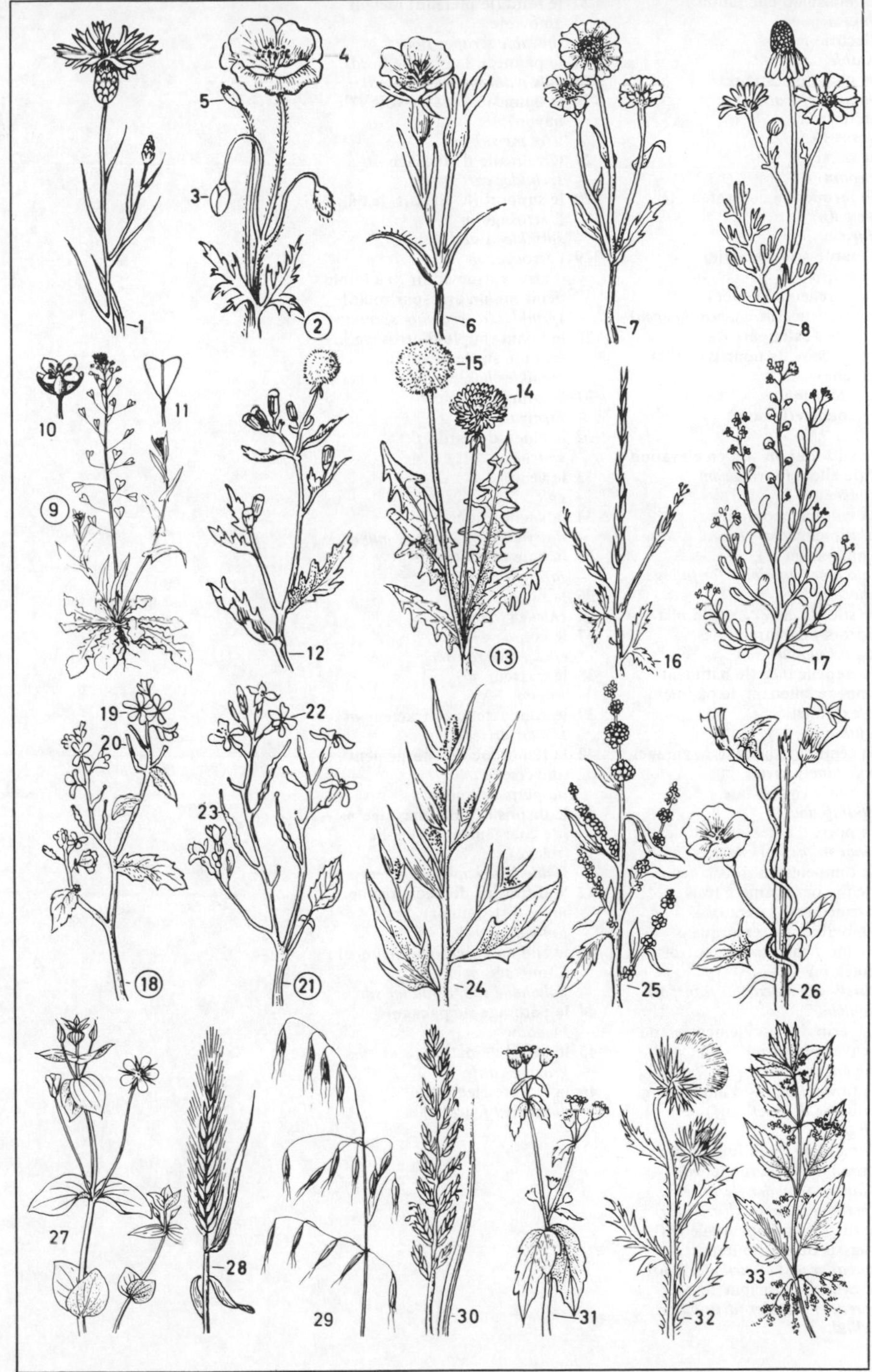
1
2
3
4
5
6
7
8
9
10
11
12
13
14
15
16
17
18
19
20
21
22
23
24
25
26
27
28
29
30
31
32
33

1 la maison d'habitation *f*
- *house*
2 l'écurie *f*
- *stable*
3 le chat domestique
- *house cat (cat)*
4 la fermière
- *farmer's wife*
5 le balai
- *broom*
6 le fermier (le cultivateur, le paysan)
- *farmer*
7 l'étable *f* (la vacherie)
- *cowshed*
8 la porcherie (la soue)
- *pigsty (sty,* Am. *pigpen, hogpen)*
9 l'auge *f* extérieure (la mangeoire, le nourrisseur, la crèche)
- *outdoor trough*
10 le cochon (le porc)
- *pig*
11 le silo-tour ou silo en élévation *f* (le silo à fourrage *m*)
- *fodder silo*
12 la colonne montante d'alimentation *f* (de chargement *m*)
- *silo pipe (standpipe for filling the silo)*
13 le silo (la cuve) à purin *m* à parois *f* imputrescibles
- *liquid manure silo*
14 la dépendance (le bâtiment annexe, attenant, le bâtiment d'exploitation *f*)
- *outhouse*
15 la remise (le hangar, le garage)
- *machinery shed*
16 la porte coulissante
- *sliding door*
17 la porte d'accès *m* à l'atelier *m*
- *door to the workshop*
18 le tombereau à trois côtés *m* (la benne basculante à trois panneaux *m* latéraux amovibles, la remorque à benne *f* basculante des trois côtés *m*)
- *three-way tip-cart, a transport vehicle*
19 le vérin de basculement *m* (de renversement *m*)
- *tipping cylinder*
20 le timon (le bras d'attelage *m*, la barre de traction *f*)
- *shafts*
21 l'épandeur *m* de fumier *m* (le distributeur de fumier *m*)
- *manure spreader (fertilizer spreader, manure distributor)*
22 le dispositif d'épandage *m* (le châssis du distributeur)
- *spreader unit (distributor unit)*
23 le cylindre distributeur
- *spreader cylinder (distributor cylinder)*
24 le fond (le plateau) racleur amovible
- *movable scraper floor*
25 le panneau latéral (le bord)
- *side planking (side board)*
26 le panneau à claire-voie *f* (le hayon)
- *wire mesh front*
27 le véhicule d'arrosage *m*
- *sprinkler cart*
28 le support (le châssis, le bâti) d'arrosage *m*
- *sprinkler stand*
29 l'arroseur *m* (l'arroseur-dévidoir *m* à faible débit *m*), un arroseur rotatif
- *sprinkler, a revolving sprinkler*
30 le tuyau souple d'arrosage *m* enroulé sur le dévidoir
- *sprinkler hoses*
31 la cour de ferme *f*
- *farmyard*
32 le chien de garde *f*
- *watchdog*
33 le veau
- *calf*
34 la vache laitière
- *dairy cow (milch-cow, milker)*
35 la haie de clôture *f*
- *farmyard hedge*
36 la poule
- *chicken (hen)*
37 le coq
- *cock* (Am. *rooster)*
38 le tracteur
- *tractor*
39 le conducteur de tracteur *m*
- *tractor driver*
40 la remorque de chargement *m* universelle
- *all-purpose trailer*
41 le dispositif de ramassage *m* (de chargement *m*) replié (relevé)
- *[folded] pickup attachment*
42 le dispositif de déchargement *m* (le distributeur)
- *unloading unit*
43 le silo en polythène *m*, un silo à fourrage *m*
- *polythene silo, a fodder silo*
44 le pâturage (le pacage)
- *meadow*
45 le bétail de pâturage *m*
- *grazing cattle*
46 la clôture électrique
- *electrified fence*

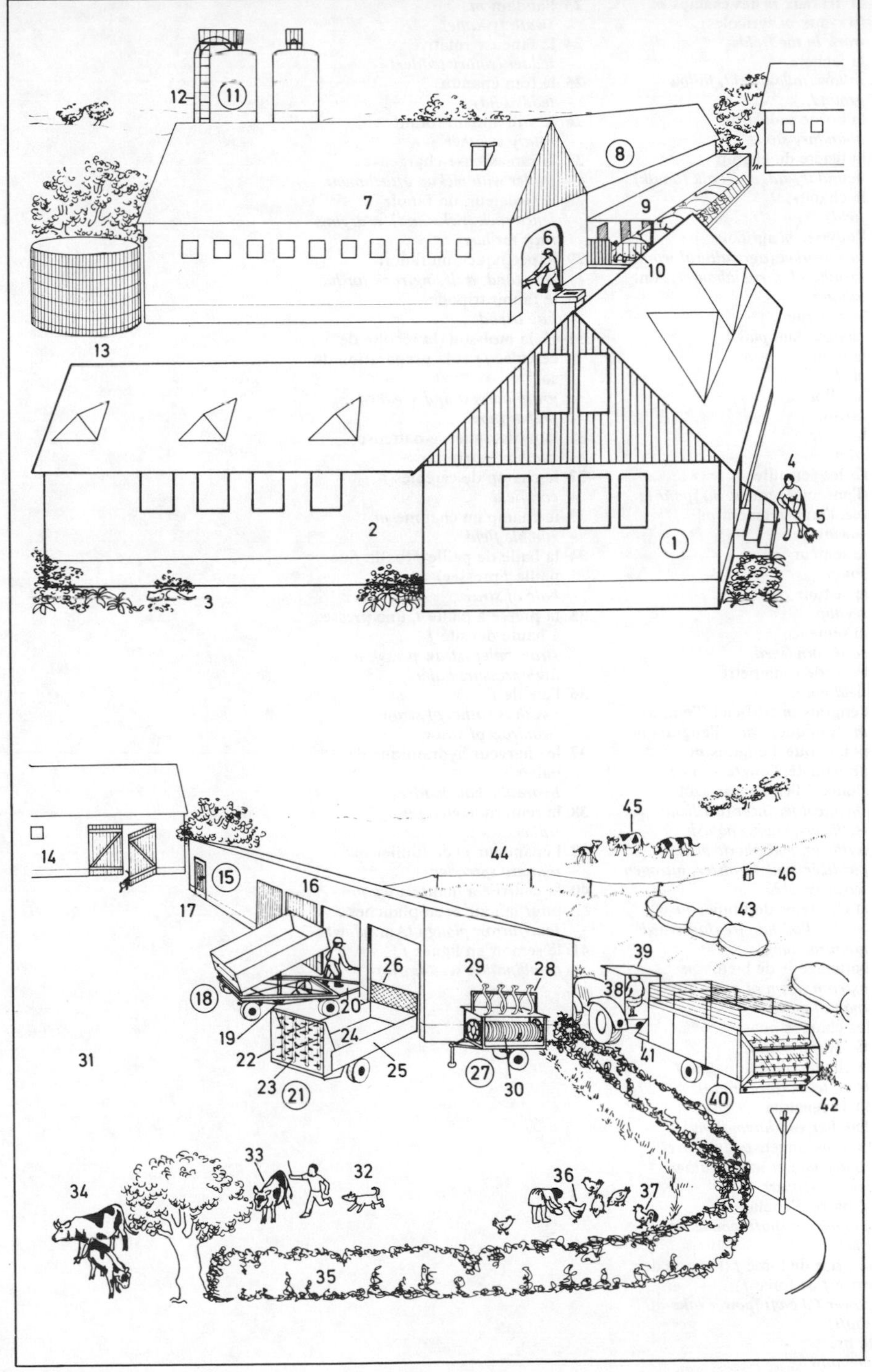
1
2
3
4
5
6
7
8
9
10
11
12
13
14
15
16
17
18
19
20
21
22
23
24
25
26
27
28
29
30
31
32
33
34
35
36
37
38
39
40
41
42
43
44
45
46

1-41 travaux *m* **des champs** *m* (travaux *m* agricoles)
– ***work in the fields***
1 la jachère
– *fallow (fallow field, fallow ground)*
2 la borne cadastrale
– *boundary stone*
3 la lisière du champ
– *boundary ridge, a balk (baulk)*
4 le champ
– *field*
5 l'ouvrier *m* agricole
– *farmworker (agricultural worker farmhand, farm labourer,* Am. *laborer)*
6 la charrue
– *plough (*Am. *plow)*
7 la motte
– *clod*
8 le sillon
– *furrow*
9 la pierre
– *stone*
10-12 les semailles *f* (l'ensemencement *m*) [*pour le blé:* l'emblavement *m*]
– *sowing*
10 le semeur
– *sower*
11 le semoir
– *seedlip*
12 la semence
– *seed corn (seed)*
13 le garde champêtre
– *field guard*
14 l'engrais *m* artificiel (l'engrais *m* chimique); *var.:* l'engrais *m* potassique, l'engrais *m* phosphaté, l'engrais *m* de chaux *f*, l'engrais *m* azoté
– *chemical fertilizer (artificial fertilizer);* kinds: *potash fertilizer, phosphoric acid fertilizer, lime fertilizer, nitrogen fertilizer*
15 la charretée de fumier *m*
– *cartload of manure (farmyard manure, dung)*
16 l'attelage *m* de bœufs *m*
– *oxteam (team of oxen,* Am. *span of oxen)*
17 les champs *m*
– *fields (farmland)*
18 le chemin de campagne *f*
– *farm track (farm road)*
19-30 la fenaison
– ***hay harvest*** *(haymaking)*
19 la moissonneuse-javeleuse
– *rotary mower with swather (swath reaper)*
20 la barre d'attelage *m*
– *connecting shaft (connecting rod)*
21 la prise de force *f* (l'axe *m* de prise *f* de force *f*)
– *power take-off (power take-off shaft)*
22 le pré
– *meadow*
23 l'andain *m*
– *swath (swathe)*
24 la faneuse rotative
– *tedder (rotary tedder)*
25 le foin épandu
– *tedded hay*
26 le vire-andain rotatif
– *rotary swather*
27 la ramasseuse-chargeuse
– *trailer with pickup attachment*
28 le siccateur, un fanoir
– *fence rack (rickstand), a drying rack for hay*
29 le perroquet, un fanoir
– *rickstand, a drying rack for hay*
30 le fanoir tripode
– *hay tripod*
31-41 la moisson (la récolte de céréales *f*) et la préparation du sol
– *grain harvest and seedbed preparation*
31 la moissonneuse-batteuse
– *combine harvester*
32 le champ de céréales *f*
– *cornfield*
33 le champ en chaume *m*
– *stubble field*
34 la balle de paille *f* (balle *f* de paille *f* pressée)
– *bale of straw*
35 la presse à paille *f*, une presse à haute densité *f*
– *straw baler (straw press), a high-pressure baler*
36 l'éteule *f*
– *swath (swathe) of straw (windrow of straw)*
37 le chargeur hydraulique de balles *f*
– *hydraulic bale loader*
38 la remorque chargée
– *trailer*
39 l'épandeur *m* de fumier *m*
– *manure spreader*
40 la charrue à quatre socs *m* pour labour *m* en planches *f*
– *four-furrow plough (*Am. *plow)*
41 le semoir en lignes *f*
– *combination seed-harrow*

1
2
3
4
5
6
7
8
9
10
11
12
13
14
15
16
17
18
19
20
21
22
23
24
25
26
27
28
29
30
31
32
33
34
35
36
37
38
39
40
41

1-33 la moissonneuse-batteuse
– ***combine harvester*** *(combine)*
1 le diviseur de chaumes *m*
– *divider*
2 le releveur d'épis *m*
– *grain lifter*
3 la barre de coupe *f*
– *cutter bar*
4 *ELF:* le rabatteur (le pick-up)
– *pickup reel, a spring-tine reel*
5 le mécanisme de commande *f* (du releveur *m*)
– *reel gearing*
6 le dispositif d'amenée *f*
– *auger*
7 le tablier élévateur
– *chain and slat elevator*
8 le verin (commandant la hauteur de la barre de coupe *f*)
– *hydraulic cylinder for adjusting the cutting unit*
9 le dispositif d'élimination *f* de cailloux *m*
– *stone catcher (stone trap)*
10 l'ébarbeur *m*
– *awner*
11 la grille-panier
– *concave*
12 le batteur
– *threshing drum (drum)*
13 le tambour de guidage *m* de la paille
– *revolving beater [for freeing straw from the drum and preparing it for the shakers]*
14 le secoueur de paille *f*
– *straw shaker (strawwalker)*
15 la buse de tuyère *f* d'aspiration *f*
– *fan for compressed-air winnowing*
16 la table de préparation *f*
– *preparation level*
17 le crible de menues pailles *f*
– *louvred-type sieve*
18 la rallonge du crible *m*
– *sieve extension*
19 un crible plus fin
– *shoe sieve (reciprocating sieve)*
20 une vis sans fin *f* [pour amener le grain dans la trémie]
– *grain auger*
21 la vis sans fin *f* vers l'ébarbeur *m*
– *tailings auger*
22 l'évacuation *f* des barbes *f* et de l'enveloppe *f*
– *tailings outlet*
23 la trémie
– *grain tank*
24 la vis d'alimentation *f* de la trémie
– *grain tank auger*
25 les vis *f* d'alimentation *f* du vidage de la trémie
– *augers feeding to the grain tank unloader*
26 le conduit de vidage *m* [de la trémie]
– *grain unloader spout*
27 l'ouverture *f* de contrôle *m* [du remplissage de la trémie]
– *observation ports for checking tank contents*
28 le moteur Diesel six cylindres *m*
– *six-cylinder diesel engine*
29 la pompe hydraulique avec réservoir *m* d'huile *f*
– *hydraulic pump with oil reservoir*
30 l'arbre *m* de transmission *f*
– *driving axle gearing*
31 le pneu (d'une roue *f* motrice)
– *driving wheel tyre* (Am. *tire)*
32 le pneu (d'une roue *f* directrice)
– *rubber-tyred* (Am. *rubber-tired) wheel on the steering axle*
33 le poste de conduite *f*
– *driver's position*
34-39 l'ensileuse *f* à maïs *m* automotrice
– ***self-propelled forage harvester*** *(self-propelled field chopper)*
34 le tambour de coupe *f*
– *cutting drum (chopper drum)*
35 le bec à maïs *m*
– *corn head*
36 la cabine du conducteur
– *cab (driver's cab)*
37 le tuyau d'éjection *f*
– *swivel-mounted spout (discharge pipe)*
38 le pot d'échappement *m*
– *exhaust*
39 une roue arrière directrice
– *rear-wheel steering system*
40-45 l'andaineur *m* rotatif
– ***rotary swather***
40 l'arbre *m* de transmission *f* à cardan *m*
– *cardan shaft*
41 la roue
– *running wheel*
42 les dents *f* à ressort *m*
– *double spring tine*
43 la manivelle
– *crank*
44 le râteau
– *swath rake*
45 le trois-points
– *three-point linkage*
46-58 le roto-faneur
– ***rotary tedder***
46 le tracteur
– *tractor*
47 la barre à trous *m*
– *draw bar*
48 l'arbre *m* de transmission *f* à cardan *m*
– *cardan shaft*
49 la prise de force *f*
– *power take-off (power take-off shaft)*
50 le mécanisme
– *gearing (gears)*
51 le châssis
– *frame bar*
52 le plateau tournant
– *rotating head*
53 la tige-support des dents *f*
– *tine bar*
54 les dents *f* à ressort *m*
– *double spring tine*
55 la bride de protection *f*
– *guard rail*
56 la roue
– *running wheel*
57 la manivelle de réglage *m* de la hauteur
– *height adjustment crank*
58 le réglage des roues *f*
– *wheel adjustment*
59-84 l'arracheur-chargeur *m* de pommes de terre *f*
– ***potato harvester***
59 les leviers *m* de commande *f*
– *control levers for the lifters of the digger and the hopper and for adjusting the shaft*
60 l'anneau *m* d'attelage *m* [réglable en hauteur *f*]
– *adjustable hitch*
61 la barre d'attelage *m*
– *drawbar*
62 la béquille [de la barre d'attelage *m*]
– *drawbar support*
63 le branchement de la prise de force *f*
– *cardan shaft connection*
64 le cylindre compresseur
– *press roller*
65 le mécanisme du système hydraulique
– *gearing (gears) for the hydraulic system*
66 le coutre en disque *m* (le coutre circulaire)
– *disc (disk) coulter* (Am. *colter) (rolling coulter)*
67 le soc à trois lames *f*
– *three-bladed share*
68 le mécanisme de commande *f* du coutre en disque *m*
– *disc (disk) coulter* (Am. *colter) drive*
69 le crible élévateur
– *open-web elevator*
70 le dispositif de secousses *f* [du crible *m* élévateur]
– *agitator*
71 le démultiplicateur à plusieurs vitesses *f*
– *multi-step reduction gearing*
72 le chargeur
– *feeder*
73 l'arracheur *m* d'herbes *f* (le rotor à ailettes *f*)
– *haulm stripper (flail rotor)*
74 la roue élévatrice
– *rotary elevating drum*
75 le séparateur oscillant
– *mechanical tumbling separator*
76 le transporteur d'herbes *f* avec arracheurs *m* souples
– *haulm conveyor with flexible haulm strippers*
77 le dispositif de secousses *f* [du transporteur *m* d'herbes *f*]
– *haulm conveyor agitator*
78 le mécanisme de commande *f* à courroie *f* trapézoïdale
– *haulm conveyor drive with V-belt*
79 la courroie cloutée en caoutchouc *m* pour la séparation des tiges *f*, des mottes *f* de terre *f* et des cailloux *m*
– *studded rubber belt for sorting vines, clods and stones*
80 le convoyeur d'impuretés *f*
– *trash conveyor*
81 la table de visite *f* et de triage *m*
– *sorting table*
82 les rouleaux *m* à disques *m* en caoutchouc *m* assurant le premier tri
– *rubber-disc (rubber-disk) rollers for presorting*
83 la bande de déchargement *m*
– *discharge conveyor*
84 la trémie à fond *m* mouvant
– *endless-floor hopper*
85-96 l'arracheur de betteraves *f* (une arracheuse-décolleteuse-chargeuse de betteraves *f*)
– ***beet harvester***
85 la décolleteuse
– *topper*
86 la roue directrice
– *feeler*
87 le couteau de décolletage *m*
– *topping knife*
88 la roue d'appui *m* avec ajustement *m* de la profondeur
– *feeler support wheel with depth adjustment*
89 le décrotteur de betteraves *f*
– *beet cleaner*
90 l'élévateur *m* de fanes *f*
– *haulm elevator*
91 la pompe hydraulique
– *hydraulic pump*
92 le réservoir à air *m* comprimé
– *compressed-air reservoir*
93 le réservoir d'huile *f*
– *oil tank (oil reservoir)*
94 le dispositif de réglage *m* de tension *f* de l'élévateur *m* de betteraves *f*
– *tensioning device for the beet elevator*
95 l'élévateur *m* de betteraves *f*
– *beet elevator belt*
96 la trémie
– *beet hopper*

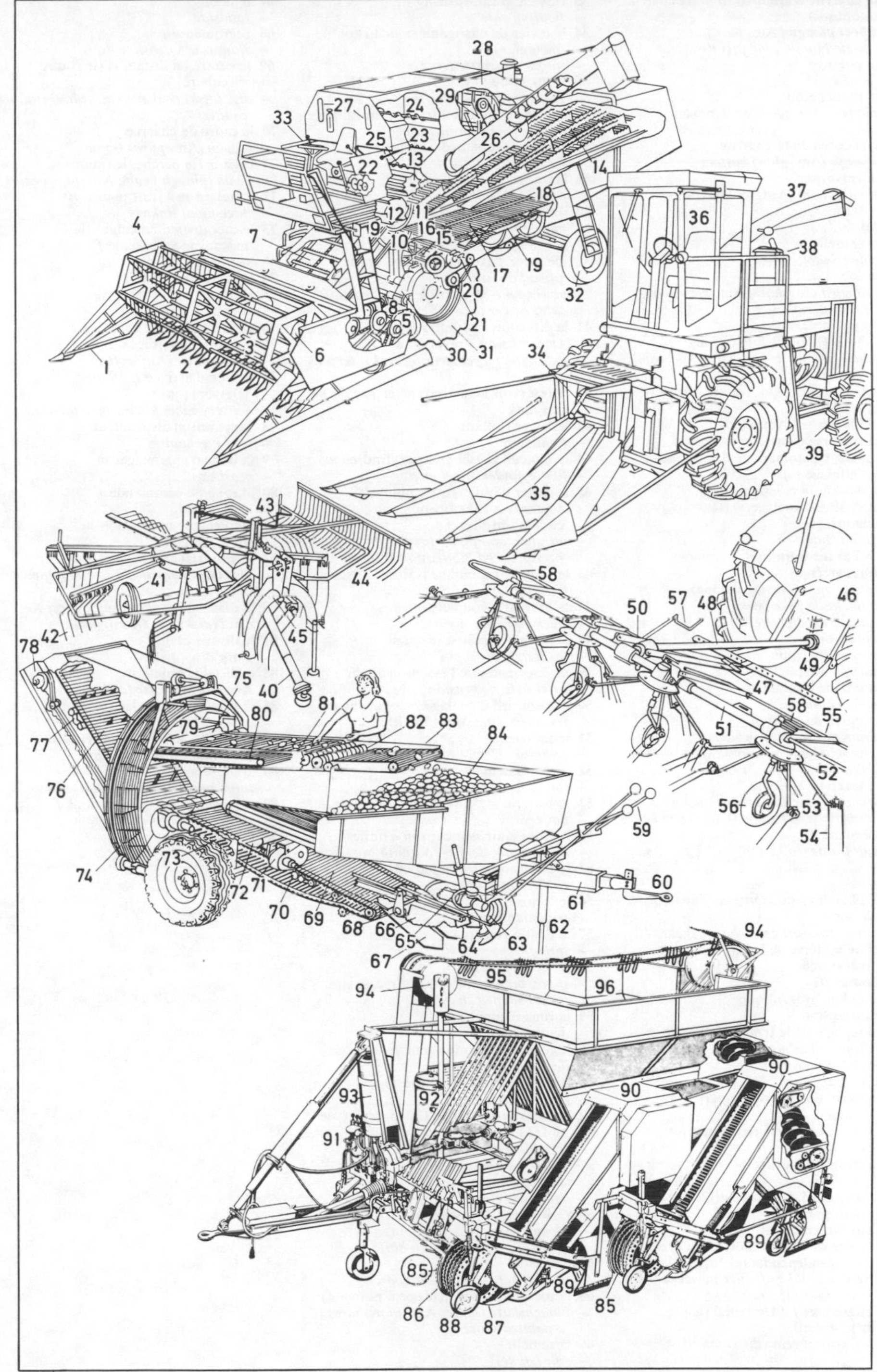
1
2
3
4
5
6
7
8
9
10
11
12
13
14
15
16
17
18
19
20
21
22
23
24
25
26
27
28
29
30
31
32
33
34
35
36
37
38
39
40
41
42
43
44
45
46
47
48
49
50
51
52
53
54
55
56
57
58
59
60
61
62
63
64
65
66
67
68
69
70
71
72
73
74
75
76
77
78
79
80
81
82
83
84
85
86
87
88
89
90
91
92
93
94
95
96

1 **la charrue à avant-train** *m* (la charrue monosoc)
– ***wheel plough*** *(*Am. *plow), a single-bottom plough* [form.]
2 la poignée
– *handle*
3 le mancheron
– *plough (*Am. *plow) stilt (plough handle)*
4-8 le corps de la charrue
– ***plough (*Am. *plow) bottom***
4 le versoir
– *mouldboard (*Am. *moldboard)*
5 le talon
– *landside*
6 la semelle
– *sole (slade)*
7 le soc
– *ploughshare (share,* Am. *plowshare)*
8 l'étançon *m*
– *frog (frame)*
9 l'age *m* (la perche, le timon)
– *beam (plough beam,* Am. *plowbeam)*
10 le coutre
– *knife coulter (*Am. *colter), a coulter*
11 la rasette
– *skim coulter (*Am. *colter)*
12 la traverse d'attelage *m* pour le guidage automatique des chaînes *f* (d'attelage *m*)
– *guide-chain crossbar*
13 la chaîne d'attelage *m* (la chaîne-guide)
– *guide chain*
14-19 l'avant-train *m*
– ***forecarriage***
14 l'étrier *m* (la travée, le joug)
– *adjustable yoke (yoke)*
15 la roue de support *m*
– *land wheel*
16 la roue de sillon *m*
– *furrow wheel*
17 la chaîne de traction *f*
– *hake chain*
18 la barre de traction *f*
– *draught beam (drawbar)*
19 le crochet de traction *f*
– *hake*
20 le tracteur agricole
– ***tractor*** *(general-purpose tractor)*
21 le cadre de la cabine (l'arceau *m* de sécurité *f*)
– *cab frame (roll bar)*
22 le siège
– *seat*
23 le changement de vitesse *f* de la prise de force *f*
– *power take-off gear-change (gearshift)*
24-29 le système de levage *m* **hydraulique**
– ***power lift***
24 le bélier hydraulique
– *ram piston*
25 le réglage de la tringle de levage *m*
– *lifting rod adjustment*
26 le cadre de remorque *f*
– *drawbar frame*
27 la barre conductrice supérieure
– *top link*
28 la barre conductrice inférieure
– *lower link*
29 la tringle de levage *m*
– *lifting rod*
30 le dispositif d'attelage *m* [de la remorque]
– *drawbar coupling*
31 la prise de force *f* moteur (la prise de force *f* indépendante)
– *live power take-off (live power take-off shaft, take-off shaft)*
32 l'engrenage *f* différentiel (le différentiel)
– *differential gear (differential)*
33 l'essieu *m* full-floating
– *floating axle*
34 le levier de changement *m* du couple moteur *m*
– *torque converter lever*
35 le levier de vitesse *f*
– *gear-change (gearshift)*
36 la transmission à vitesses *f* multiples
– *multi-speed transmission*
37 l'embrayage *m* hydraulique
– *fluid clutch (fluid drive)*
38 la transmission de prise *f* de force *f*
– *power take-off gear*
39 l'embrayage *m* principal
– *main clutch*
40 le changement de vitesse *f* de la prise de force *f* avec embrayage *m* (de prise *f* de force *f*)
– *power take-off gear-change (gearshift) with power take-off clutch*
41 la direction hydraulique avec transmission *f* réversible
– *hydraulic power steering and reversing gears*
42 le réservoir de carburant *m* [gazole *m*]
– *fuel tank*
43 le levier flottant
– *float lever*
44 le moteur Diesel quatre cylindres *m*
– *four-cylinder diesel engine*
45 le carter d'huile *f* avec pompe *f* assurant la lubrification par circulation *f* forcée
– *oil sump and pump for the pressure-feed lubrication system*
46 le réservoir d'huile *f* fraîche
– *fresh oil tank*
47 la barre d'accouplement *m*
– *track rod (*Am. *tie rod)*
48 le pivot de l'essieu *m* avant
– *front axle pivot pin*
49 la suspension de l'essieu *m* avant
– *front axle suspension*
50 le dispositif d'attelage *m* à l'avant *m*
– *front coupling (front hitch)*
51 le radiateur
– *radiator*
52 le ventilateur
– *fan*
53 la batterie
– *battery*
54 le filtre à air *m* à bain *m* d'huile *f*
– *oil bath air cleaner (oil bath air filter)*
55 le cultivateur (le canadien)
– ***cultivator*** *(grubber)*
56 le cadre
– *sectional frame*
57 la dent à ressort *m*
– *spring tine*
58 le soc de charrue *f*
– *share, a diamond-shaped share;* sim.: *chisel-shaped share*
59 la roue d'appui *m*
– *depth wheel*
60 le réglage de profondeur *f*
– *depth adjustment*
61 le dispositif d'accrochage *m*
– *coupling (hitch)*
62 la charrue réversible (la charrue type *m* 1/2 tour)
– ***reversible plough*** *(*Am. *plow), a mounted plough*
63 la roue d'appui *m*
– *depth wheel*
64-67 le corps de la charrue
– ***plough*** *(*Am. *plow) bottom, a general-purpose plough bottom*
64 le versoir
– *mouldboard (*Am. *moldboard)*
65 le soc de charrue *f* (le soc à pointe *f*)
– *ploughshare (share,* Am. *plowshare), a pointed share*
66 la semelle
– *sole (slade)*
67 le talon
– *landside*
68 l'écrouteuse *f*
– *skim coulter (*Am. *colter)*
69 le coutre en disque *m* (le coutre circulaire)
– *disc (disk) coulter (*Am. *colter) (rolling coulter)*
70 le cadre de charrue *f*
– *plough (*Am. *plow) frame*
71 l'age *m* (la perche, le timon)
– *beam (plough beam,* Am. *plowbeam)*
72 l'attelage *m* à trois points *m*
– *three-point linkage*
73 le mécanisme basculant (le mécanisme à bascule *f*)
– *swivel mechanism*
74 le semoir en ligne *f*
– ***drill***
75 la boîte à semence *f*
– *seed hopper*
76 le coutre rayonneux
– *drill coulter (*Am. *colter)*
77 le tube d'arrivée *f*, un tube télescopique
– *delivery tube; a telescopic tube*
78 l'appareil *m* distributeur
– *feed mechanism*
79 la boîte d'engrenages *m*
– *gearbox*
80 la roue de commande *f*
– *drive wheel*
81 l'indicateur *m* de sillon *m*
– *track indicator*
82 le pulvériseur à disques *m*
– ***disc (disk) harrow,*** *a semimounted implement*
83 la disposition des disques *m* en X
– *discs (disks) in X-configuration*
84 le disque plein
– *plain disc (disk)*
85 le disque crénelé
– *serrated-edge disc (disk)*
86 le dispositif d'attelage *m* rapide
– *quick hitch*
87 l'attelage *m* **herse-émotteuse** *f*
– ***combination seed-harrow***
88 la herse à trois sections *f*
– *three-section spike-tooth harrow*
89 l'émotteuse *f* à trois sections *f*
– *three-section rotary harrow*
90 le bâti fixe
– *frame*

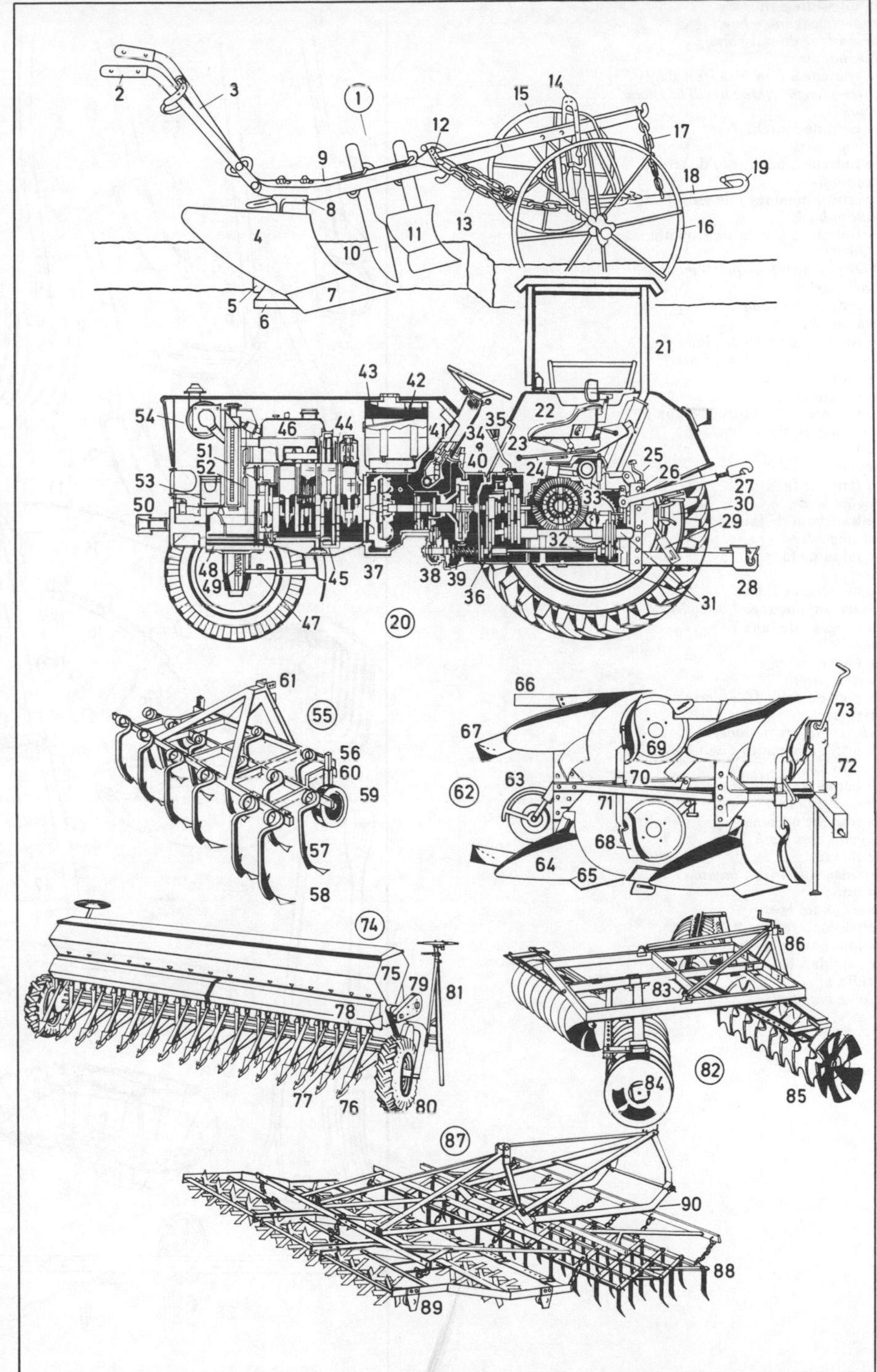
1
2
3
4
5
6
7
8
9
10
11
12
13
14
15
16
17
18
19
20
21
22
23
24
25
26
27
28
29
30
31
32
33
34
35
36
37
38
39
40
41
42
43
44
45
46
47
48
49
50
51
52
53
54
55
56
57
58
59
60
61
62
63
64
65
66
67
68
69
70
71
72
73
74
75
76
77
78
79
80
81
82
83
84
85
86
87
88
89
90

1 la ratissoire à tirer
– *draw hoe (garden hoe)*
2 le manche de ratissoire *f*
– *hoe handle*
3 la fourche à foin *m*, à trois dents *f*
– *three-pronged (three-tined) hay fork (fork)*
4 la dent de fourche *f*
– *prong (tine)*
5 la fourche à pommes *f* de terre *f*
– *potato fork*
6 le croc à pommes *f* de terre *f*
– *potato hook*
7 la fourche à fumier *m*, à quatre dents *f*
– *four-pronged (four-tined) manure fork (fork)*
8 le croc à fumier *m*
– *manure hoe*
9 le marteau à battre les faux *f*
– *whetting hammer [for scythes]*
10 la panne de marteau *m*
– *peen (pane)*
11 l'enclumette *f* à battre les faux *f*
– *whetting anvil [for scythes]*
12 la faux
– *scythe*
13 la lame de faux *f*
– *scythe blade*
14 le tranchant de faux *f*
– *cutting edge*
15 le talon de faux *f*
– *heel*
16 le manche de faux *f*
– *snath (snathe, snead, sneath)*
17 la poignée de faux *f*
– *handle*
18 le couvre-lame
– *scythe sheath*
19 la pierre à faux *f* (la pierre à aiguiser)
– *whetstone (scythestone)*
20 la griffe à pommes *f* de terre *f*
– *potato rake*
21 le panier à plants *m*
– *potato planter*
22 la fourche à bêcher
– *digging fork (fork)*
23 le râteau
– *wooden rake (rake, hayrake)*
24 la houe
– *hoe (potato hoe)*
25 le panier à récolte *f*
– *potato basket, a wire basket*
26 le semoir à bras *m*, un semoir à trèfle *m*
– *clover broadcaster*

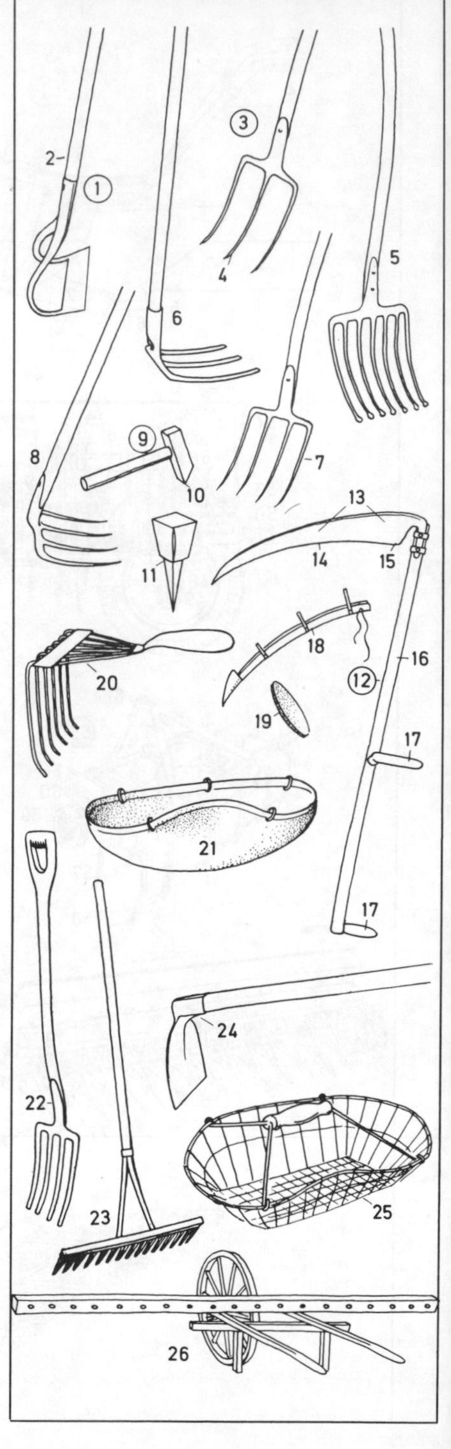

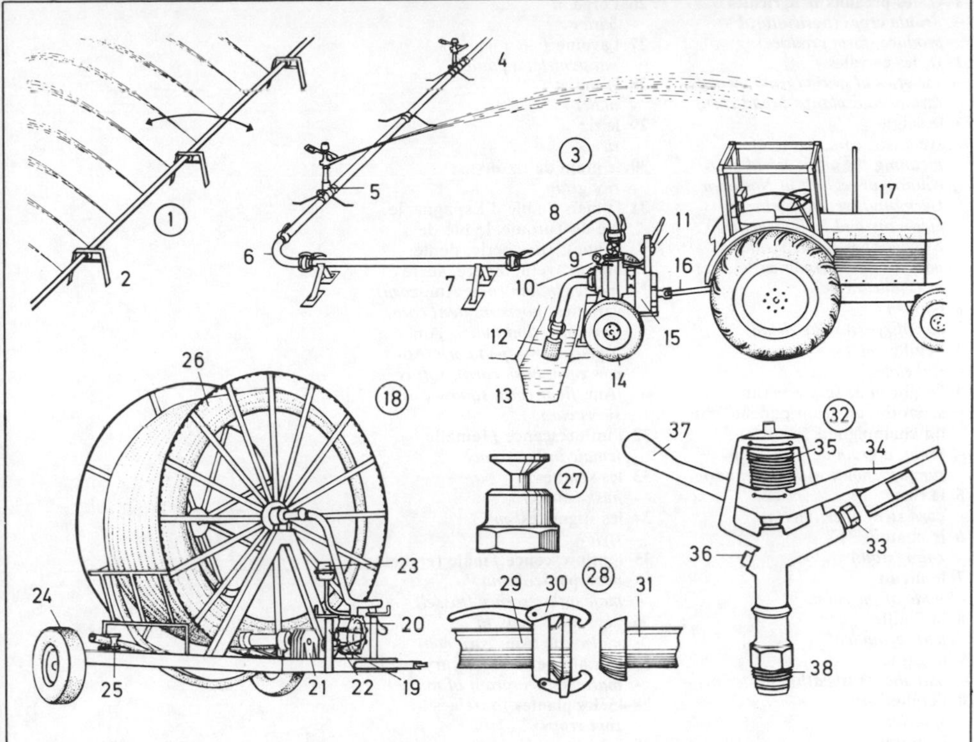

1 la rampe d'arrosage *m* oscillante
– *oscillating spray line*
2 l'étrier *m* support
– *stand (steel chair)*
3 le dispositif d'arrosage *m* mobile
– *portable irrigation system*
4 l'arroseur *m* rotatif
– *revolving sprinkler*
5 le raccord de tuyau *m*
– *standpipe coupler*
6 le coude à cardan *m*
– *elbow with cardan joint (cardan coupling)*
7 le support de tuyau *m*
– *pipe support (trestle)*
8 le coude de raccordement *m* de pompe *f*
– *pump connection*
9 la tubulure de refoulement *m*
– *delivery valve*
10 le manomètre
– *pressure gauge* (Am. *gage*) *(manometer)*
11 la pompe d'évacuation *f*
– *centrifugal evacuating pump*
12 la crépine d'aspiration *f*
– *basket strainer*
13 la rigole d'arrosage *m*
– *channel*
14 le châssis de la pompe commandée par la prise de force *f* du tracteur
– *chassis of the p.t.o.-driven pump (power take-off-driven pump)*
15 la pompe commandée par la prise de force *f* du tracteur
– *p.t.o.-driven (power take-off-driven) pump*
16 l'arbre articulé (l'arbre *m* à cardan *m*)
– *cardan shaft*
17 le tracteur
– *tractor*
18 l'arroseur *m* pour grandes surfaces *f*
– *long-range irrigation unit*
19 la tubulure d'entraînement *m*
– *drive connection*
20 la turbine
– *turbine*
21 le réducteur
– *gearing (gears)*
22 la béquille ajustable
– *adjustable support*
23 la pompe d'évacuation *f*
– *centrifugal evacuating pump*
24 la roue portante
– *wheel*
25 le guide-tuyau
– *pipe support*
26 le tuyau en polyester *m*
– *polyester pipe*
27 la buse d'arrosage *m*
– *sprinkler nozzle*
28 le tuyau à raccord *m* instantané avec joint *m* à cardan *m*
– *quick-fitting pipe connection with cardan joint*
29 la pièce mâle de raccord *m* instantané
– *M-cardan*
30 l'accouplement *m*
– *clamp*
31 la pièce femelle de raccord *m* instantané
– *V-cardan*
32 l'arroseur *m* circulaire
– *revolving sprinkler, a field sprinkler*
33 la buse
– *nozzle*
34 le levier oscillant
– *breaker*
35 le ressort de levier *m* oscillant
– *breaker spring*
36 le bouchon
– *stopper*
37 le contrepoids
– *counterweight*
38 le filetage
– *thread*

1-47 les produits *m* agricoles
– ***arable crops*** *(agricultural produce, farm produce)*
1-37 les céréales *f*
– ***varieties of grain*** *(grain, cereals, farinaceous plants, bread-corn)*
1 le seigle
– *rye (*also: *corn, 'corn' often meaning the main cereal of a country or region; in Northern Germany: rye; in Southern Germany and Italy: wheat; in Sweden: barley; in Scotland: oats; in North America: maize; in China: rice)*
2 l'épi *m*
– *ear of rye, a spike (head)*
3 l'épillet *m*
– *spikelet*
4 l'ergot *m* de seigle *m* (un sclérote), un grain parasité par un champignon
– *ergot, a grain deformed by fungus [shown with mycelium]*
5 la tige
– *corn stem after tillering*
6 le chaume
– *culm (stalk)*
7 le nœud
– *node of the culm*
8 la feuille
– *leaf (grain leaf)*
9 la gaine
– *leaf sheath (sheath)*
10 l'épillet *m*
– *spikelet*
11 la glume
– *glume*
12 l'arête *f*
– *awn (beard, arista)*
13 le caryopse
– *seed (grain, kernel, farinaceous grain)*
14 le grain germé
– *embryo plant*
15 le grain
– *seed*
16 le germe
– *embryo*
17 la racine
– *root*
18 la radicelle
– *root hair*
19 la feuille de blé *m*
– *grain leaf*
20 le limbe
– *leaf blade (blade, lamina)*
21 la gaine
– *leaf sheath*
22 la ligule
– *ligule (ligula)*
23 le blé
– *wheat*
24 l'épeautre *m*
– *spelt*
25 le caryopse, le grain de blé *m*; *non mûri:* le grain vert pour potage *m*
– *seed;* unripe: *green spelt, a soup vegetable*
26 l'orge *m*
– *barley*
27 l'avoine *f*
– *oat panicle, a panicle*
28 le millet
– *millet*
29 le riz
– *rice*
30 le grain de riz *m*
– *rice grain*
31 le maïs (le blé d'Espagne, le blé de Turquie, le blé de l'Inde); *var.:* perlé, denté, vitreux, vêtu, tendre, sucré
– *maize (Indian corn,* Am. *corn);* varieties: *popcorn, dent corn, flint corn (flint maize,* Am. *Yankee corn), pod corn (*Am. *cow corn, husk corn), soft corn (*Am. *flour corn, squaw corn), sweet corn*
32 l'inflorescence *f* femelle
– *female inflorescence*
33 les spathes *f*
– *husk (shuck)*
34 les stigmates *m*
– *style*
35 l'inflorescence *f* mâle (épillets *m* en panicule *m*)
– *male inflorescence (tassel)*
36 l'épi *m* de maïs *m*
– *maize cob (*Am. *corn cob)*
37 le grain de maïs (le caryopse)
– *maize kernel (grain of maize)*
38-45 les plantes *f* sarclées
– ***root crops***
38 la pomme de terre, un tubercule [*forme:* ronde, ovale, allongée, réniforme; *couleur:* blanche, jaune, rouge, violette]
– *potato plant (potato), a tuberous plant;* varieties: *round, round-oval (pear-shaped), flat-oval, long, kidney-shaped potato;* according to colour: *white (*Am. *Irish), yellow, red, purple potato*
39 le plant (le tubercule germé)
– *seed potato (seed tuber)*
40 la pomme de terre (le tubercule)
– *potato tuber (potato, tuber)*
41 la feuille
– *potato top (potato haulm)*
42 la fleur
– *flower*
43 la baie non comestible (la baie de pomme *f* de terre)
– *poisonous potato berry (potato apple)*
44 la betterave sucrière
– *sugar beet, a beet*
45 la racine charnue
– *root (beet)*
46 le collet de betterave *f*
– *beet top*
47 la feuille de betterave *f*
– *beet leaf*

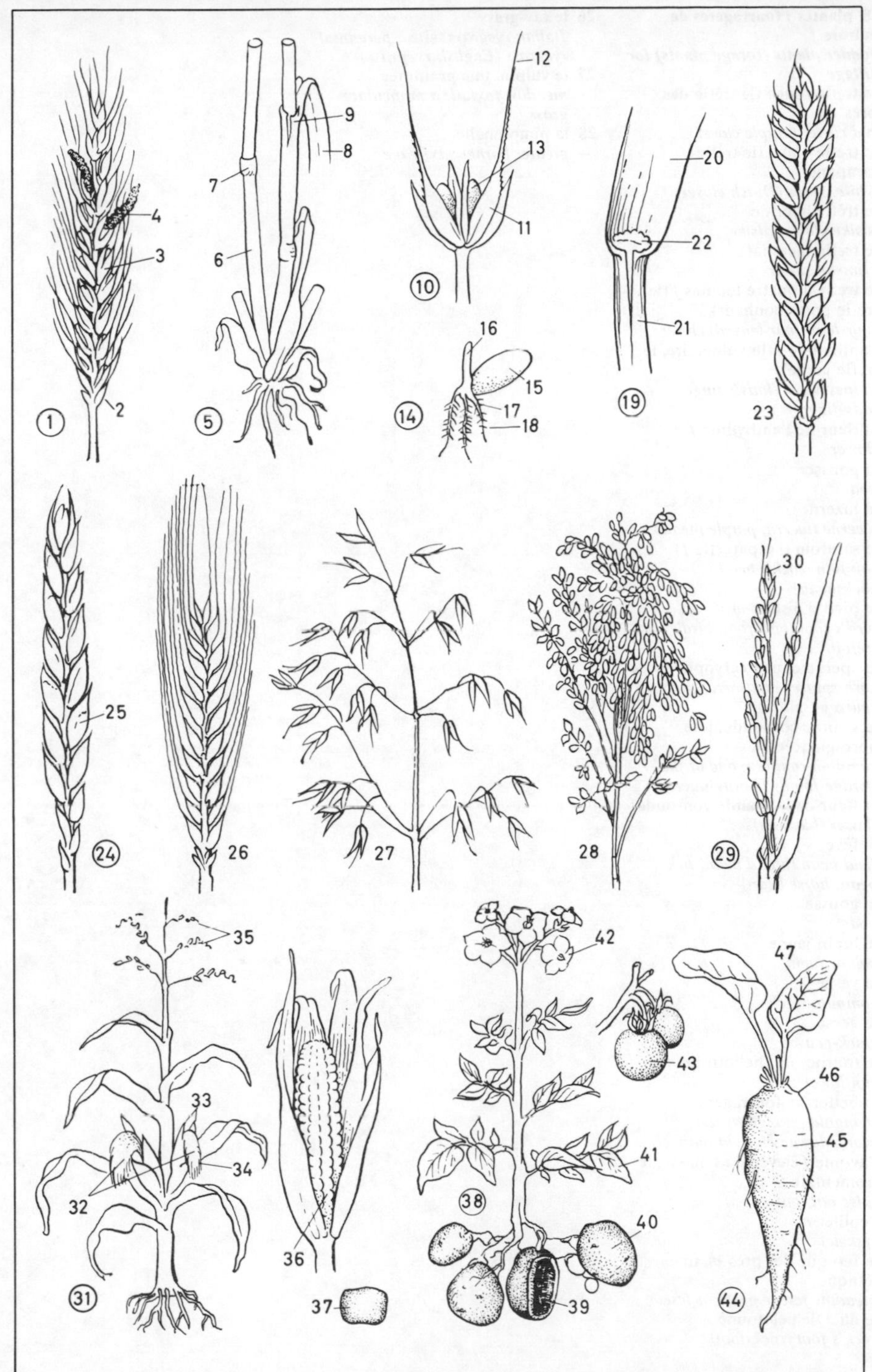
1
2
3
4
5
6
7
8
9
10
11
12
13
14
15
16
17
18
19
20
21
22
23
24
25
26
27
28
29
30
31
32
33
34
35
36
37
38
39
40
41
42
43
44
45
46
47

1-28 plantes *f* fourragères de culture *f*
– ***fodder plants (forage plants) for tillage***

1 le trèfle rouge (le trèfle des prés *m*)
– *red clover (purple clover)*

2 le trèfle blanc (le trèfle rampant)
– *white clover (Dutch clover)*

3 le trèfle hybride
– *alsike clover (alsike)*

4 le trèfle incarnat
– *crimson clover*

5 le trèfle à quatre feuilles *f* (le trèfle porte-bonheur)
– *four-leaf (four-leaved) clover*

6 l'anthyllide *f* (la vulnéraire, le trèfle jaune)
– *kidney vetch (lady's finger, lady-finger)*

7 la fleur de l'anthyllide *f*
– *flower*

8 la gousse
– *pod*

9 la luzerne
– *lucerne (lucern, purple medick)*

10 le sainfoin (l'esparcette *f*)
– *sainfoin (cock's head, cockshead)*

11 le pied d'oiseau *m*
– *bird's foot (bird-foot, bird's foot trefoil)*

12 la spergule, une caryophyllacée
– *corn spurrey (spurrey, spurry), a spurrey (spurry)*

13 la grande consoude, une borraginacée
– *common comfrey, one of the borage family (Boraginaceae)*

14 la fleur de la grande consoude
– *flower (blossom)*

15 la fève
– *field bean (broad bean, tick bean, horse bean)*

16 la gousse
– *pod*

17 le lupin jaune
– *yellow lupin*

18 la vesce
– *common vetch*

19 la gesse
– *chick-pea*

20 le tournesol (l'héliotrope *m*)
– *sunflower*

21 la betterave fourragère
– *mangold (mangelwurzel, mangoldwurzel, field mangel)*

22 l'avoine *f* élevée (la fenasse, le fromental)
– *false oat (oat-grass)*

23 l'épillet *m*
– *spikelet*

24 la fétuque des prés *m*, une fétuque
– *meadow fescue grass, a fescue*

25 le dactyle pelotonné
– *cock's foot (cocksfoot)*

26 le ray-grass
– *Italian ryegrass;* sim.: *perennial ryegrass (English ryegrass)*

27 le vulpin, une graminée
– *meadow foxtail, a paniculate grass*

28 la pimprenelle
– *greater burnet saxifrage*

1
2
3
4
5
6
7
8
9
10
11
12
13
14
15
16
17
18
19
20
21
22
23
24
25
26
27
28

1 le bouledogue
– *bulldog*
2 l'oreille pendante
– *ear, a rose-ear*
3 la gueule (le museau)
– *muzzle*
4 le nez (le mufle)
– *nose*
5 le membre antérieur (la patte avant)
– *foreleg*
6 le pied (antérieur)
– *forepaw*
7 le membre postérieur (la patte arrière)
– *hind leg*
8 le pied (postérieur)
– *hind paw*
9 le carlin
– *pug (pug dog)*
10 le boxer
– *boxer*
11 le garrot
– *withers*
12 la queue du chien, une queue coupée
– *tail, a docked tail*
13 le collier de chien *m*
– *collar*
14 le dogue danois
– *Great Dane*
15 le fox-terrier (le fox à poil *m* dur, le fox)
– *wire-haired fox terrier*
16 le bull-terrier
– *bull terrier*
17 le terrier écossais
– *Scottish terrier*
18 le bedlington (le bedlington-terrier)
– *Bedlington terrier*
19 le pékinois
– *Pekinese (Pekingese, Pekinese dog, Pekingese dog)*
20 le grand spitz (le loulou)
– *spitz (Pomeranian)*
21 le chow-chow
– *chow (chow-chow)*
22 le chien esquimau
– *husky*
23 le lévrier afghan
– *Afghan (Afghan hound)*
24 le greyhound, un chien courant
– *greyhound (*Am. *grayhound), a courser*
25 le berger allemand, un chien d'utilité *f*, un chien de garde *f* et de compagnie *f*
– *Alsatian (German sheepdog,* Am. *German shepherd), a police dog, watch dog, and guide dog*
26 les babines *f*
– *flews (chaps)*
27 le doberman
– *Dobermann terrier*

28-31 le nécessaire pour chiens *m*
- ***dog's outfit***

28 la brosse à chien *m*
- *dog brush*

29 l'étrille *f*
- *dog comb*

30 la laisse
- *lead (dog lead, leash);* for hunting: *leash*

31 la muselière
- *muzzle*

32 l'écuelle *f*
- *feeding bowl (dog bowl)*

33 l'os *m*
- *bone*

34 le terre-neuve
- *Newfoundland dog*

35 le schnauzer
- *schnauzer*

36 le caniche (*plus petit:* le caniche nain)
- *poodle;* sim. and smaller: *pygmy (pigmy) poodle*

37 le saint-bernard
- *St. Bernard (St. Bernard dog)*

38 le cocker spaniel
- *cocker spaniel*

39 le teckel (basset) à poil *m* ras, le basset allemand
- *dachshund, a terrier*

40 le braque allemand
- *German pointer*

41 le setter anglais, un chien d'arrêt *m*
- *English setter*

42 le braque
- *trackhound*

43 le pointer, un chien d'arrêt *m*
- *pointer, a trackhound*

1-6 l'équitation *f* (la haute école)
– ***equitation*** *(high school riding, haute école)*
1 le piaffer
– *piaffe*
2 le pas
– *walk*
3 le passage (le pas espagnol)
– *passage*
4 la levade (la pesade)
– *levade (pesade)*
5 la cabriole
– *capriole*
6 la courbette
– *courbette (curvet)*
7-25 **le harnais** (le harnachement)
– ***harness***
7-13 la bride (le filet, le bridon)
– *bridle*
7-11 **le harnachement de tête** *f*
– ***headstall*** *(headpiece, halter)*
7 la muserole
– *noseband*
8 le montant
– *cheek piece (cheek strap)*
9 le frontal
– *browband (front band)*
10 la têtière
– *crownpiece*
11 la sous-gorge
– *throatlatch (throatlash)*
12 la gourmette
– *curb chain*
13 le mors
– *curb bit*
14 le boucleteau d'attelle *f*
– *hasp (hook) of the hame (*Am. *drag hook)*
15 le collier
– *pointed collar, a collar*
16 l'ornement *m* du collier (la cocarde)
– *trappings (side trappings)*
17 la sellette (la dossière)
– *saddle-pad*
18 la sous-ventrière (la sangle)
– *girth*
19 le mantelet
– *backband*
20 la chaîne de flèche *f*
– *shaft chain (pole chain)*
21 le timon (la flèche)
– *pole*
22 le trait
– *trace*
23 la fausse sous-ventrière
– *second girth (emergency girth)*
24 le trait
– *trace*
25 la rêne (la guide)
– *reins (*Am. *lines)*
26-36 **le harnachement de poitrail** *m*
– ***breast harness***
26 l'œillère *f*
– *blinker (*Am. *blinder, winker)*
27 la chaînette
– *breast collar ring*
28 le poitrail
– *breast collar (Dutch collar)*
29 les bras du dessus-de-cou
– *fork*
30 le dessus-de-cou
– *neck strap*
31 le mantelet
– *saddle-pad*
32 le surdos
– *loin strap*
33 la rêne (la guide)
– *reins (rein,* Am. *line)*
34 la croupière
– *crupper (crupper-strap)*
35 le trait
– *trace*
36 la sous-ventrière
– *girth (belly-band)*
37-49 **les selles** *f*
– ***saddles***
37-44 **la selle de cavalerie** *f* (selle d'armes *f*)
– ***stock saddle*** (Am. *western saddle)*
37 le siège
– *saddle seat*
38 le pommeau (l'arçon *m* avant)
– *pommel horn (horn)*
39 le troussequin (l'arçon *m* arrière)
– *cantle*
40 le quartier
– *flap* (Am. *fender)*
41 la matelassure
– *bar*
42 l'étrivière *f*
– *stirrup leather*
43 l'étrier *m*
– *stirrup (stirrup iron)*
44 la couverture de selle *f*
– *blanket*
45-49 **la selle anglaise** (selle de chasse *f*)
– ***English saddle*** *(cavalry saddle)*
45 le siège
– *seat*
46 le pommeau
– *cantle*
47 le quartier
– *flap*
48 le faux quartier
– *roll (knee roll)*
49 le troussequin
– *pad*
50-51 **les éperons** *m*
– ***spurs***
50 l'éperon *m* à mollette
– *box spur (screwed jack spur)*
51 l'éperon *m* à la chevalière
– *strapped jack spur*
52 le mors
– *curb bit*
53 le mors de force *f*
– *gag bit (gag)*
54 l'étrille *f*
– *currycomb*
55 la brosse de pansage *m*
– *horse brush (body brush, dandy brush)*

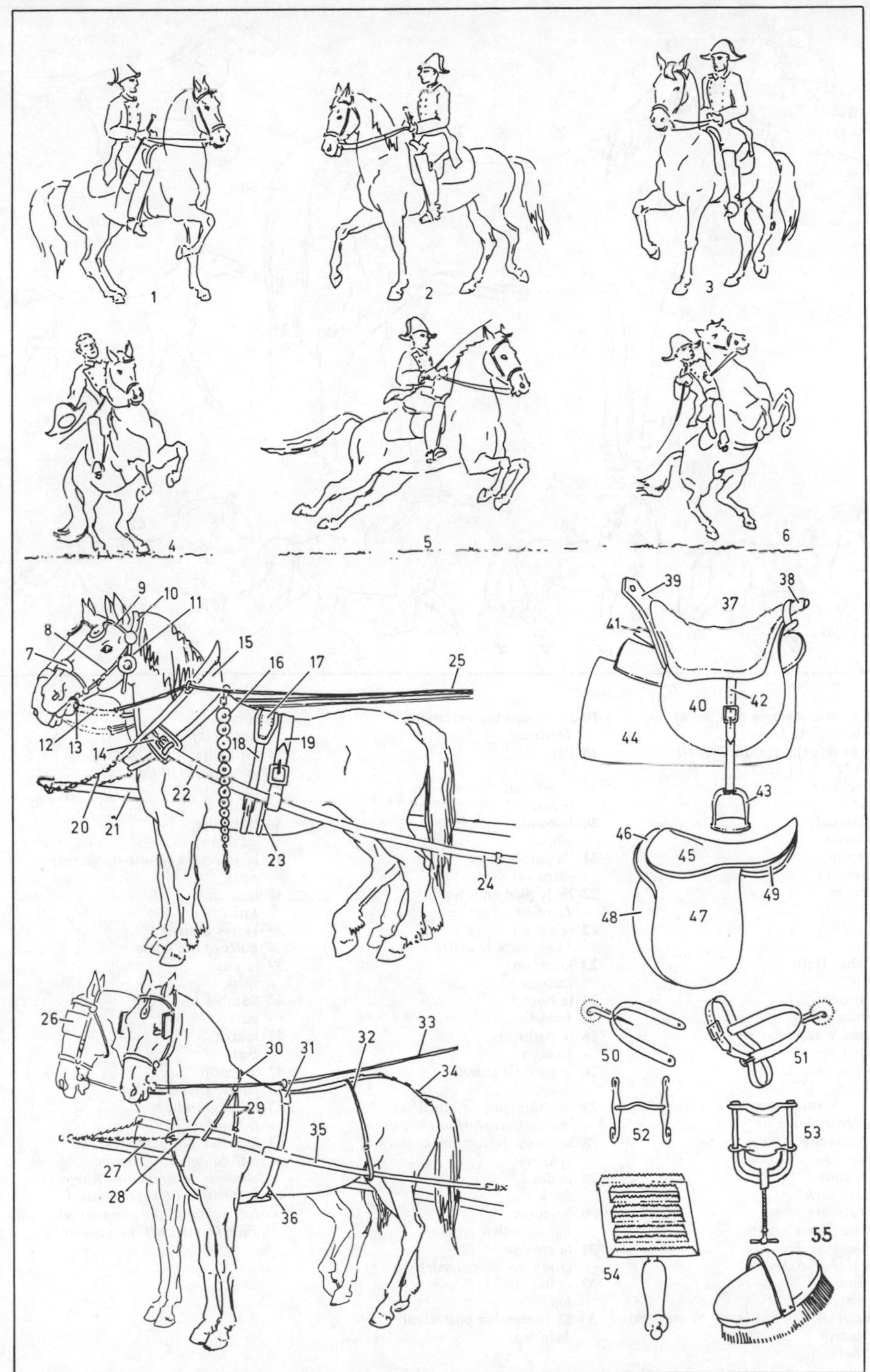
1
2
3
4
5
6
7
8
9
10
11
12
13
14
15
16
17
18
19
20
21
22
23
24
25
26
27
28
29
30
31
32
33
34
35
36
37
38
39
40
41
42
43
44
45
46
47
48
49
50
51
52
53
54
55

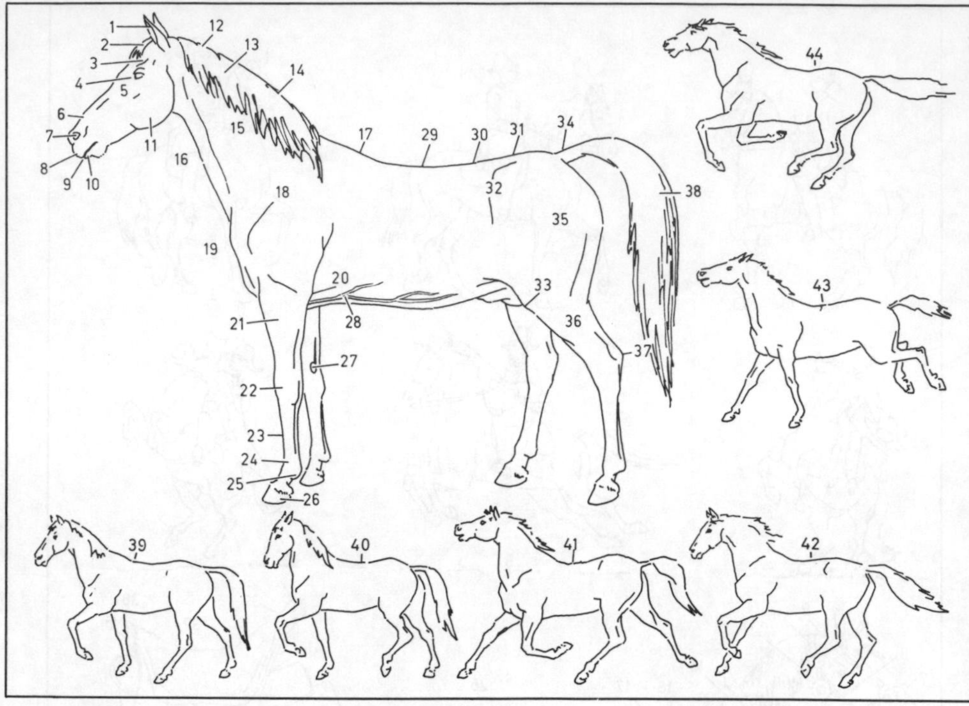

1-38 la morphologie du cheval
– ***points*** *of the horse*
1-11 la tête (la tête du cheval)
– ***head*** *(horse's head)*
1 l'oreille *f*
– *ear*
2 le toupet
– *forelock*
3 le front
– *forehead*
4 l'œil *m*
– *eye*
5 la face
– *face*
6 le chanfrein
– *nose*
7 le naseau
– *nostril*
8 la lèvre supérieure
– *upper lip*
9 la bouche
– *mouth*
10 la lèvre inférieure
– *underlip (lower lip)*
11 la ganache
– *lower jaw*
12 la nuque
– *crest (neck)*
13 la crinière
– *mane (horse's mane)*
14 l'encolure *f*
– *crest (horse's crest)*
15 *le cou*
16 la gorge
– *throat* (Am. *throatlatch, throatlash)*
17 le garrot
– *withers*
18-27 le membre antérieur
– ***forehand***
18 l'épaule *f*
– *shoulder*
19 le poitrail
– *breast*
20 le coude
– *elbow*
21 l'avant-bras *m*
– *forearm*
22-26 le pied antérieur
– ***forefoot***
22 le genou
– *knee (carpus, wrist)*
23 le canon
– *cannon*
24 le boulet
– *fetlock*
25 le paturon
– *pastern*
26 le pied (le sabot)
– *hoof*
27 la châtaigne, un durillon
– *chestnut (castor), a callosity*
28 la veine thoracique externe
– *spur vein*
29 le dos
– *back*
30 les reins
– *loins (lumbar region)*
31 la croupe
– *croup (rump, crupper)*
32 la hanche
– *hip*
33-37 le membre postérieur
– ***hind leg***
33 le grasset
– *stifle (stifle joint)*
34 l'attache *f* de la queue
– *root (dock) of the tail*
35 la cuisse
– *haunch*
36 la jambe
– *gaskin*
37 le jarret (la pointe du jarret)
– *hock*
38 la queue
– *tail*
39-44 les allures *f*
– ***gaits*** *of the horse*
39 le pas
– *walk*
40 l'amble *m*
– *pace*
41 le trot
– *trot*
42 le galop
– *canter (hand gallop)*
43-44 le grand galop
– *full gallop*
43 le poser des antérieurs *m*
– *full gallop at the moment of descent on to the two forefeet*
44 la période de suspension *f*
– *full gallop at the moment when all four feet are off the ground*

Abréviations: *m.* = mâle; *ch.* = châtré; *f.* = femelle; *p.* = le petit
Abbreviations: m. = *male;* c. = *castrated;* f. = *female;* y. = *young*

1-2 le gros bétail
– *cattle*

1 le boviné, une bête à cornes *f*, un ruminant; *m.* le taureau; *ch.* le bœuf; *f.* la vache; *p.* le veau
– *cow, a bovine animal, a horned animal, a ruminant;* m. *bull;* c. *ox;* f. *cow;* y. *calf*

2 le cheval; *m.* l'étalon *m* (cheval entier); *ch.* le hongre; *f.* la jument; *p.* le poulain (la pouliche)
– *horse;* m. *stallion;* c. *gelding;* f. *mare;* y. *foal*

3 l'âne *m*; *f.* l'ânesse *f*
– *donkey*

4 le bât
– *pack saddle (carrying saddle)*

5 la charge
– *pack (load)*

6 la queue
– *tufted tail*

7 la touffe de crins *m*
– *tuft*

8 le mulet (le croisement d'un âne et d'une jument)
– *mule, a cross between a male donkey and a mare*

9 le cochon, le porc, un suidé artiodactyle; *m.* le verrat; *f.* la truie; *p.* le goret (le porcelet, le cochon de lait *m*)
– *pig, a cloven-hoofed animal;* m. *boar;* f. *sow;* y. *piglet*

10 le groin
– *pig's snout (snout)*

11 l'oreille *f*
– *pig's ear*

12 la queue en tire-bouchon *m*
– *curly tail*

13 le mouton; *m.* le bélier; *ch.* le mouton; *f.* la brebis; *p.* l'agneau *m*
– *sheep;* m. *ram;* c. *wether;* f. *ewe;* y. *lamb*

14 la chèvre; *m.* le bouc; *p.* le chevreau, la chevrette
– *goat*

15 la barbiche
– *goat's beard*

16 le chien, un chien de berger *m*; *f.* la chienne; *p.* le chiot
– *dog, a Leonberger;* m. *dog;* f. *bitch;* y. *pup (puppy, whelp)*

17 le chat, un chat angora; *m.* le matou; *f.* la chatte; *p.* le chaton
– *cat, an Angora cat (Persian cat);* m. *tom (tom cat)*

18-36 la basse-cour
– ***small domestic animals***

18 le lapin; *m.* le bouquin; *f.* la lapine; *p.* le lapereau
– *rabbit;* m. *buck;* f. *doe*

19-36 la volaille
– ***poultry (domestic fowl)***

19-26 le poulet
– ***chicken***

19 la poule
– *hen*

20 le jabot
– *crop (craw)*

21 le coq; *ch.* le chapon
– *cock* (Am. *rooster);* c. *capon*

22 la crête
– *cockscomb (comb, crest)*

23 l'oreillon *m*
– *lap*

24 le barbillon
– *wattle (gill, dewlap)*

25 les faucilles *f* de la queue
– *falcate (falcated) tail*

26 l'ergot *m*
– *spur*

27 la pintade; *p.* le pintadeau
– *guinea fowl*

28 le dindon; *f.* la dinde; *p.* le dindonneau
– *turkey;* m. *turkey cock (gobbler);* f. *turkey hen*

29 la roue
– *fan tail*

30 le paon; *f.* la paonne
– *peacock*

31 la plume de paon *m*
– *peacock's feather*

32 l'ocelle *f*
– *eye (ocellus)*

33 le pigeon; *f.* la pigeonne; *p.* le pigeonneau
– *pigeon;* m. *cock pigeon*

34 l'oie; *m.* le jars; *p.* l'oison *m*
– *goose;* m. *gander;* y. *gosling*

35 le canard; *f.* la cane; *p.* le caneton
– *duck;* m. *drake;* y. *duckling*

36 la palmure
– *web (palmations) of webbed foot (palmate foot)*

1-27 l'élevage *m* avicole
– ***poultry farming (intensive poultry management)***
1-17 l'élevage *m* sur litière *f*
– ***straw yard (strawed yard) system***
1 la poussinière
– *fold unit for growing stock (chick unit)*
2 le poussin
– *chick*
3 l'éleveuse *f* artificielle
– *brooder (hover)*
4 la mangeoire
– *adjustable feeding trough*
5 le poulailler d'élevage *m*
– *pullet fold unit*
6 l'abreuvoir *m*
– *drinking trough*
7 le tuyau d'eau *f*
– *water pipe*
8 la litière
– *litter*
9 le poulet
– *pullet*
10 le ventilateur
– *ventilator*
11-17 l'élevage *m* de poulets *m*
– ***broiler rearing** (rearing of broiler chickens)*
11 le poulailler
– *chicken run (*Am. *fowl run)*
12 le poulet (la poulette)
– *broiler chicken (broiler)*
13 la mangeoire automatique
– *mechanical feeder (self-feeder, feed dispenser)*
14 la chaîne d'alimentation *f*
– *chain*
15 la goulotte d'alimentation *f*
– *feed supply pipe*
16 l'abreuvoir *m* automatique
– *mechanical drinking bowl (mechanical drinker)*
17 le ventilateur
– *ventilator*
18 la batterie de ponte *f*
– *battery system (cage system)*
19 la cage supérieure
– *battery (laying battery)*
20 la cage inférieure
– *tiered cage (battery cage, stepped cage)*
21 la mangeoire
– *feeding trough*
22 la bande transporteuse de récolte *f* des œufs *m*
– *egg collection by conveyor*
23-27 le système automatique d'alimentation *m* et d'enlèvement *m* des déjections *f*
– ***mechanical feeding and dunging** (manure removal, droppings removal)*
23 l'alimentation *f* automatique pour la batterie
– *rapid feeding system for battery feeding (mechanical feeder)*
24 le silo
– *feed hopper*
25 la bande transporteuse d'alimentation *f* des mangeoires *f*
– *endless-chain feed conveyor (chain feeder)*
26 l'alimentation *f* en eau *f*
– *water pipe (liquid feed pipe)*
27 la bande transporteuse d'enlèvement *m* des déjections *f*
– *dunging chain (dunging conveyor)*
28 l'armoire *f* d'incubation *f* et d'éclosion *f*
– *[cabinet type] setting and hatching machine*
29 le ventilateur de la chambre d'incubation *f*
– *ventilation drum [for the setting compartment]*
30 l'éclosoir *m*
– *hatching compartment (hatcher)*
31 le chariot de métal *m* portant les casiers *m* à œufs *m*
– *metal trolley for hatching trays*
32 le casier à œufs *m*
– *hatching tray*
33 le moteur du ventilateur
– *ventilation drum motor*
34-53 la production d'œufs *m*
– ***egg production***
34 le système de récolte *f* des œufs *m*
– *egg collection system (egg collection)*
35 la bande transporteuse
– *multi-tier transport*
36 la table de calibrage *m*
– *collection by pivoted fingers*
37 le moteur d'entraînement *m*
– *drive motor*
38 la trieuse
– *sorting machine*
39 le chariot de transport *m*
– *conveyor trolley*
40 l'écran *m* de mirage *m*
– *fluorescent screen*
41 le système de transport *m* à dépression *f*
– *suction apparatus (suction box) for transporting eggs*
42 l'étagère *f* pour les plateaux *m* à œufs *m* pleins ou vides
– *shelf for empty and full egg boxes*
43 la pesée
– *egg weighers*
44 le calibrage
– *grading*
45 le plateau à œufs *m*
– *egg box*
46 l'emballeuse *f* automatique
– *fully automatic egg-packing machine*
47 l'installation *f* de mirage *m*
– *radioscope box*
48 la table de mirage *m*
– *radioscope table*
49-51 le système d'alimentation *f*
– *feeder*
49 le transporteur à dépression *f*
– *suction transporter*
50 le tuyau souple à vide *m*
– *vacuum line*
51 la table d'alimentation *f*
– *supply table*
52 la trieuse-calibreuse automatique
– *automatic counting and grading*
53 le distributeur de boîtes *f*
– *packing box dispenser*
54 la bague
– *leg ring*
55 la marque d'aile *f*
– *wing tally (identification tally)*
56 la poule naine
– *bantam*
57 la poule pondeuse
– *laying hen*
58 l'œuf *m* de poule *f*
– *hen's egg (egg)*
59 la coquille, l'enveloppe *f* de l'œuf *m*
– *eggshell, an egg integument*
60 la membrane coquillère
– *shell membrane*
61 la chambre à air *m*
– *air space*
62 le blanc de l'œuf *m* (l'albumen *m*)
– *white [of the egg] (albumen)*
63 la chalaze
– *chalaza (*Am. *treadle)*
64 la membrane vitelline
– *vitelline membrane (yolk sac)*
65 le blastoderme
– *blastodisc (germinal disc, cock's tread, cock's treadle)*
66 la cicatricule (le disque germinatif)
– *germinal vesicle*
67 le blastocœle (la cavité de segmentation *f*)
– *white*
68 le jaune (le vitellus)
– *yolk*

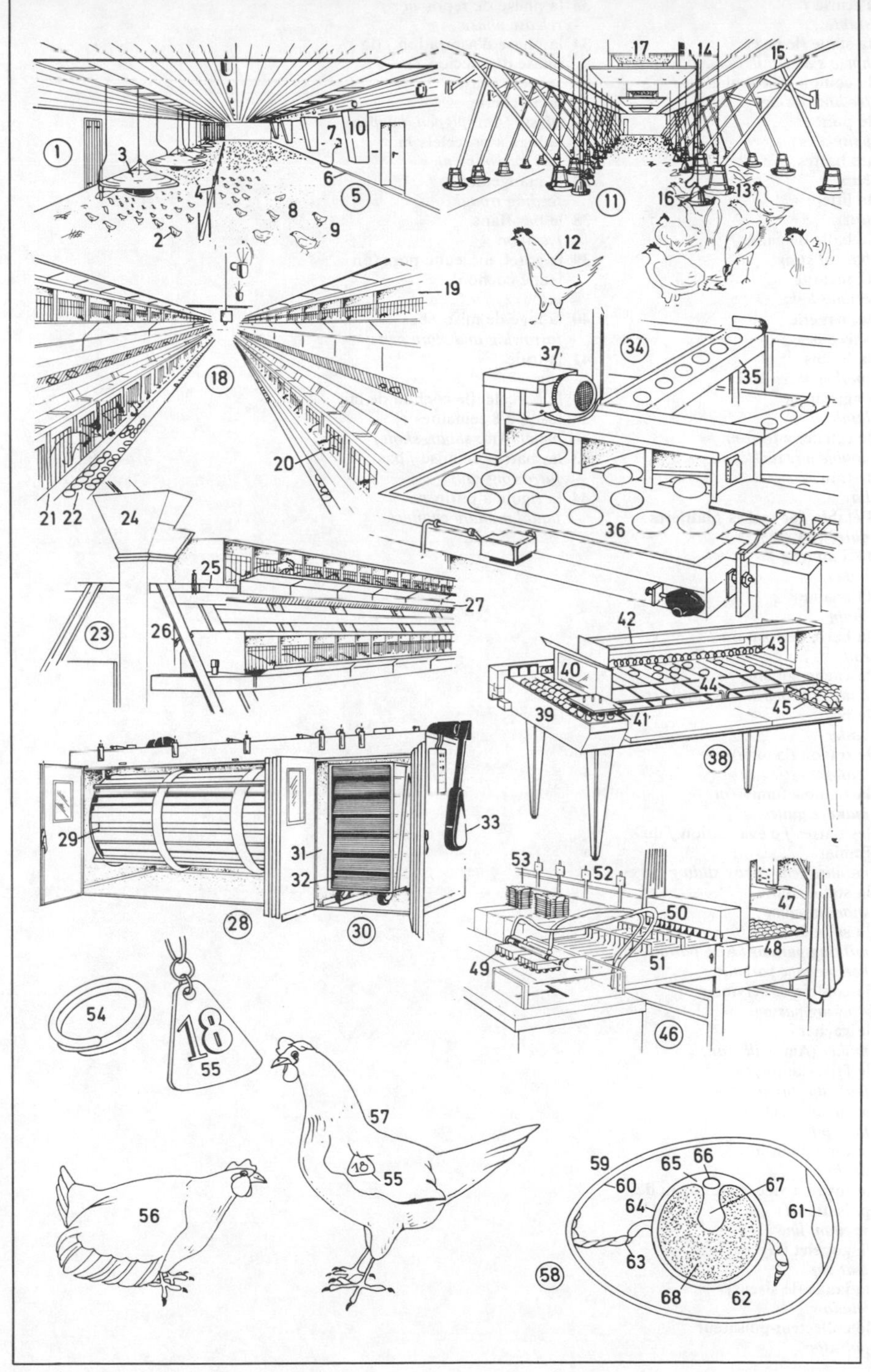
1
2
3
4
5
6
7
8
9
10
11
12
13
14
15
16
17
18
19
20
21
22
23
24
25
26
27
28
29
30
31
32
33
34
35
36
37
38
39
40
41
42
43
44
45
46
47
48
49
50
51
52
53
54
18
55
56
57
58
59
60
61
62
63
64
65
66
67
68

1 l'écurie *f*
– ***stable***
2 la stalle (le box)
– *horse stall (stall, horse box, box)*
3 le couloir de circulation *f*
– *feeding passage*
4 le poney
– *pony*
5 les barres *f*
– *bars*
6 la litière
– *litter*
7 la balle de paille *f*
– *bale of straw*
8 la lucarne
– *ceiling light*
9 la bergerie
– ***sheep pen***
10 la brebis
– *mother sheep (ewe)*
11 l'agneau *m*
– *lamb*
12 le râtelier à foin *m*
– *double hay rack*
13 le foin
– *hay*
14 l'étable *f* **de vaches** *f* **laitières**
– ***dairy cow shed***
15-16 l'attache *f*
– *tether*
15 la chaîne
– *chain*
16 la barre de fixation *f*
– *rail*
17 la vache laitière
– *dairy cow (milch-cow, milker)*
18 le pis
– *udder*
19 le trayon (la tette)
– *teat*
20 la rigole à fumier *m*
– *manure gutter*
21 les barres *f* d'évacuation *f* du fumier
– *manure removal by sliding bars*
22 la stalle courte
– *short standing*
23 la salle de traite *f*
– ***milking parlour*** *(*Am. *parlor), a herringbone parlour*
24 le couloir de service *m*
– *working passage*
25 le vacher
– *milker (*Am. *milkman)*
26 le faisceau trayeur
– *teat cup cluster*
27 le tuyau à lait *m*
– *milk pipe*
28 le tube d'air *m*
– *air line*
29 le tuyau à vide *m* (le tuyau de pulsation *f*)
– *vacuum line*
30 le gobelet trayeur
– *teat cup*
31 la jauge (le viseur)
– *window*
32 le collecteur-pulsateur
– *pulsator*
33 la phase de repos *m*
– *release phase*
34 la phase d'aspiration *f* (la phase de succion *f*)
– *squeeze phase*
35 la porcherie
– ***pigsty*** *(*Am. *pigpen, hogpen)*
36 la loge à porcelets *m*
– *pen for young pigs*
37 la mangeoire
– *feeding trough*
38 le bas-flanc
– *partition*
39 le goret, un jeune porc (un jeune cochon)
– *pig*
40 la loge de mise *f* bas
– *farrowing and store pen*
41 la truie
– *sow*
42 le porcelet [le cochon de lait jusqu'à 8 semaines *f*]
– *piglet (*Am. *shoat, shote)*
43 les barres de mise *f* bas
– *farrowing rails*
44 la rigole à purin *m*
– *liquid manure channel*

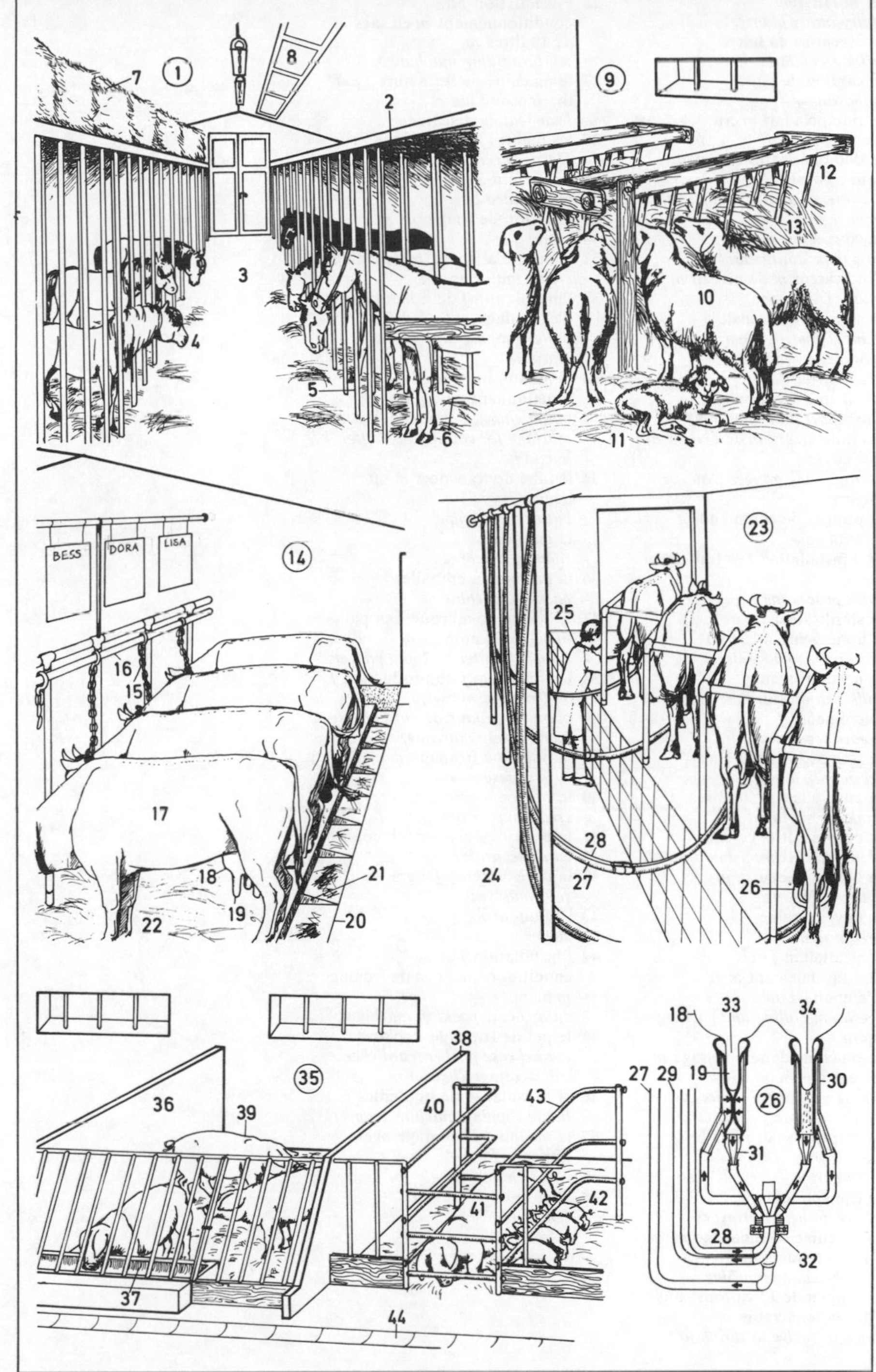
BESS
DORA
LISA
1
2
3
4
5
6
7
8
9
10
11
12
13
14
15
16
17
18
19
20
21
22
23
24
25
26
27
28
29
30
31
32
33
34
35
36
37
38
39
40
41
42
43
44

1-48 la laiterie
– ***dairy*** *(dairy plant)*
1 la réception du lait
– ***milk reception***
2 le camion de lait *m*
– *milk tanker*
3 la pompe à lait *m* cru
– *raw milk pump*
4 le débitmètre, un compteur à roues *f* ovales
– *flowmeter, an oval (elliptical) gear meter*
5 la cuve à lait *m* cru
– *raw milk storage tank*
6 l'indicateur *m* de niveau *m*
– *gauge (*Am. *gage)*
7 la salle de commande *f*
– ***central control room***
8 le tableau synoptique
– *chart of the dairy*
9 le schéma fonctionnel
– *flow chart (flow diagram)*
10 les indicateurs *m* de niveau *m* des cuves *f*
– *storage tank gauges (*Am. *gages)*
11 le pupitre de commande *f*
– *control panel*
12-48 l'installation *f* de traitement *m*
– ***milk processing area***
12 le stérilisateur (l'homogénéisateur *m*)
– *sterilizer (homogenizer)*
13 le pasteurisateur
– *milk heater;* sim.: *cream heater*
14 l'écrémeuse *f*
– *cream separator*
15 les cuves *f* à lait *m* frais
– *fresh milk tanks*
16 la cuve à lait *m* stérilisé
– *tank for sterilized milk*
17 la cuve à lait *m* écrémé
– *skim milk (skimmed milk) tank*
18 la cuve à babeurre *m*
– *buttermilk tank*
19 la cuve à crème *f*
– *cream tank*
20 l'installation *f* de conditionnement *m* et d'emballage *m*
– *fresh milk filling and packing plant*
21 la machine de remplissage *m* de cartons *m* de lait *m*
– *filling machine for milk cartons;* sim.: *milk tub filler*
22 le carton de lait *m* (la brique de lait *m*)
– *milk carton*
23 le transporteur
– *conveyor belt (conveyor)*
24 la machine d'emballage *m* sous film *m* rétractable
– *shrink-sealing machine*
25 le paquet de 12 cartons sous film *m* rétractable
– *pack of twelve in shrink foil*
26 l'installation *f* de conditionnement *m* en sacs *m* de 10 litres *m*
– *ten-litre filling machine*
27 la machine de fermeture *f* par thermosoudage *m*
– *heat-sealing machine*
28 les feuilles *f* de plastique *m*
– *plastic sheets*
29 le sac fermé
– *heat-sealed bag*
30 le carton de transport *m*
– *crate*
31 la cuve d'affinage *m* de crème *f*
– *cream maturing vat*
32 l'installation *f* de moulage *m* et d'emballage *m* du beurre
– *butter shaping and packing machine*
33 la baratte industrielle fonctionnant en continu *m*
– *butter churn, a creamery butter machine for continuous butter making*
34 le tube de transport *m* du beurre
– *butter supply pipe*
35 la mouleuse
– *shaping machine*
36 la machine à emballer
– *packing machine*
37 le beurre de marque *f* en pains *m* de 250 grammes *m*
– *branded butter in 250 g packets*
38 l'installation *f* de production *f* de fromage *m* blanc
– *plant for producing curd cheese (curd cheese machine)*
39 la pompe à fromage *m* blanc
– *curd cheese pump*
40 la pompe à crème *f*
– *cream supply pump*
41 la centrifugeuse à caillebotte *f*
– *curds separator*
42 la cuve à crème *f* aigre
– *sour milk vat*
43 l'agitateur *m*
– *stirrer*
44 l'installation *f* de conditionnement *m* de fromage *m* blanc
– *curd cheese packing machine*
45 le pot de fromage *m* blanc
– *curd cheese packet (curd cheese;* sim.: *cottage cheese)*
46 la capsuleuse de bouteilles *f*
– *bottle-capping machine (capper)*
47 la machine à fromage *m* en tranches *f*
– *cheese machine*
48 la cuve de présure *f*
– *rennet vat*

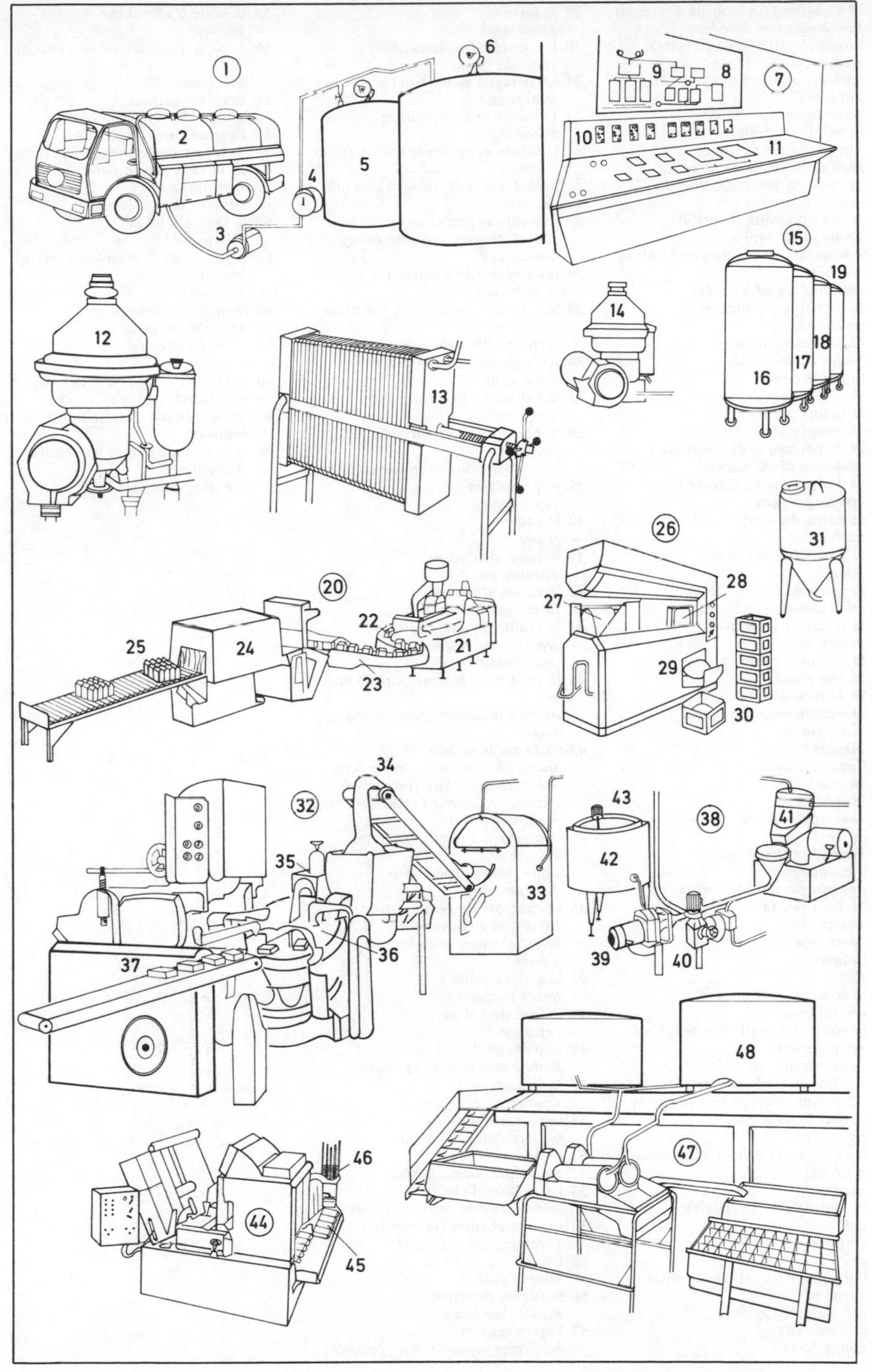
1
2
3
4
5
6
7
8
9
10
11
12
13
14
15
16
17
18
19
20
21
22
23
24
25
26
27
28
29
30
31
32
33
34
35
36
37
38
39
40
41
42
43
44
45
46
47
48

1-25 l'abeille *f* (la mouche à miel *m*)
– ***bee*** *(honey-bee, hive-bee)*
1 l'ouvrière *f* (l'abeille *f* neutre)
– *worker (worker bee)*
2 les trois ocelles *f* (les yeux *m* simples)
– *three simple eyes (ocelli)*
3 la pelote de pollen *m* (la culotte) sur les pattes *f* arrière
– *load of pollen on the hind leg*
4 la reine (la reproductrice)
– *queen (queen bee)*
5 le faux-bourdon (le mâle)
– *drone (male bee)*
6-9 la patte postérieure gauche d'une ouvrière
– ***left hind leg of a worker***
6 la corbeille à pollen *m*
– *pollen basket*
7 la brosse à pollen *m*
– *pollen comb (brush)*
8 la griffe double
– *double claw*
9 la pelote adhésive
– *suctorial pad*
10-19 l'abdomen *m* **de l'ouvrière** *f*
– ***abdomen of the worker***
10-14 l'organe *m* **de défense** *f*
– ***stinging organs***
10 la barbe du dard
– *barb*
11 le dard (l'aiguillon *m*)
– *sting*
12 la gaine de l'aiguillon *m*
– *sting sheath*
13 le réservoir à venin *m*
– *poison sac*
14 la glande à venin *m*
– *poison gland*
15-19 le tube digestif
– ***stomachic-intestinal canal***
15 l'intestin *m*
– *intestine*
16 l'estomac *m*
– *stomach*
17 le sphincter
– *contractile muscle*
18 le jabot
– *honey bag (honey sac)*
19 l'œsophage *m*
– *oesophagus (esophagus, gullet)*
20-24 l'œil *m* **à facettes** *f* (œil *m* composé)
– ***compound eye***
20 la facette
– *facet*
21 le cône cristallin
– *crystal cone*
22 la zone sensorielle (les cellules *f* rétiniennes)
– *light-sensitive section*
23 la fibre du nerf optique
– *fibre* (Am. *fiber*) *of the optic nerve*
24 le nerf optique
– *optic nerve*
25 les écailles *f* de cire (les plaques *f* cirières)
– *wax scale*
26-30 l'alvéole *m* (la cellule)
– ***cell***
26 l'œuf *m*
– *egg*
27 l'alvéole *m* (la cellule) contenant l'œuf *m*
– *cell with the egg in it*
28 la jeune larve *f*
– *young larva*
29 la larve
– *larva (grub)*
30 la nymphe (la chrysalide)
– *chrysalis (pupa)*
31-43 le rayon de miel *m* (le gâteau)
– ***honeycomb***
31 l'alvéole *m* à couvain *m*
– *brood cell*
32 l'alvéole *m* operculé contenant la nymphe
– *sealed (capped) cell with chrysalis (pupa)*
33 l'alvéole *m* à miel *m* operculé
– *sealed (capped) cell with honey (honey cell)*
34 les alvéoles *m* d'ouvrières *f*
– *worker cells*
35 les alvéoles *m* de stockage *m* de pollen *m*
– *storage cells, with pollen*
36 les alvéoles *m* de mâles *m*
– *drone cells*
37 la cellule de la reine
– *queen cell*
38 la nouvelle reine sortant de sa cellule
– *queen emerging from her cell*
39 l'opercule *m*
– *cap (capping)*
40 le cadre
– *frame*
41 la pièce d'écart *m*
– *distance piece*
42 le rayon artificiel
– *[artificial] honeycomb*
43 la feuille de cire *f* gaufrée
– *septum (foundation, comb foundation)*
44 la cage pour le transport de la reine
– *queen's travelling* (Am. *traveling*) *box*
45-50 la ruche en bois *m*
– ***frame hive*** *(movable-frame hive, movable-comb hive [into which frames are inserted from the rear], a beehive (hive))*
45 le magasin à miel *m* avec les rayons *m*
– *super (honey super) with honeycombs*
46 la chambre de ponte *f* avec les rayons *m* à couvain *m*
– *brood chamber with breeding combs*
47 la grille à reine *f*
– *queen-excluder*
48 le trou de vol *m*
– *entrance*
49 la planche de vol *m*
– *flight board (alighting board)*
50 la fenêtre
– *window*
51 le rucher d'autrefois
– *old-fashioned bee shed*
52 la ruche en paille *f*
– *straw hive (skep), a hive*
53 l'essaim *m* d'abeilles *f*
– *swarm (swarm cluster) of bees*
54 le gobe-abeilles (le cueille-essaim)
– *swarming net (bag net)*
55 le croc
– *hooked pole*
56 le rucher moderne
– *apiary (bee house)*
57 l'apiculteur *m*
– *beekeeper (apiarist,* Am. *beeman)*
58 le voile d'apiculteur *m*
– *bee veil*
59 la pipe d'apiculteur *m* (l'enfumoir *m*)
– *bee smoker*
60 le rayon naturel
– *natural honeycomb*
61 l'extracteur *m* centrifuge
– *honey extractor (honey separator)*
62-63 le miel extrait par centrifugation *f*
– *strained honey (honey)*
62 le seau à miel *m*
– *honey pail*
63 le pot de miel *m* en verre *m* (le bocal)
– *honey jar*
64 le miel en rayon *m*
– *honey in the comb*
65 le rat de cave *f*
– *wax taper*
66 la chandelle de cire *f* (la bougie)
– *wax candle*
67 le bloc de cire *f* d'abeilles *f*
– *beeswax*
68 la pommade contre les piqûres d'abeilles *f*
– *bee sting ointment*

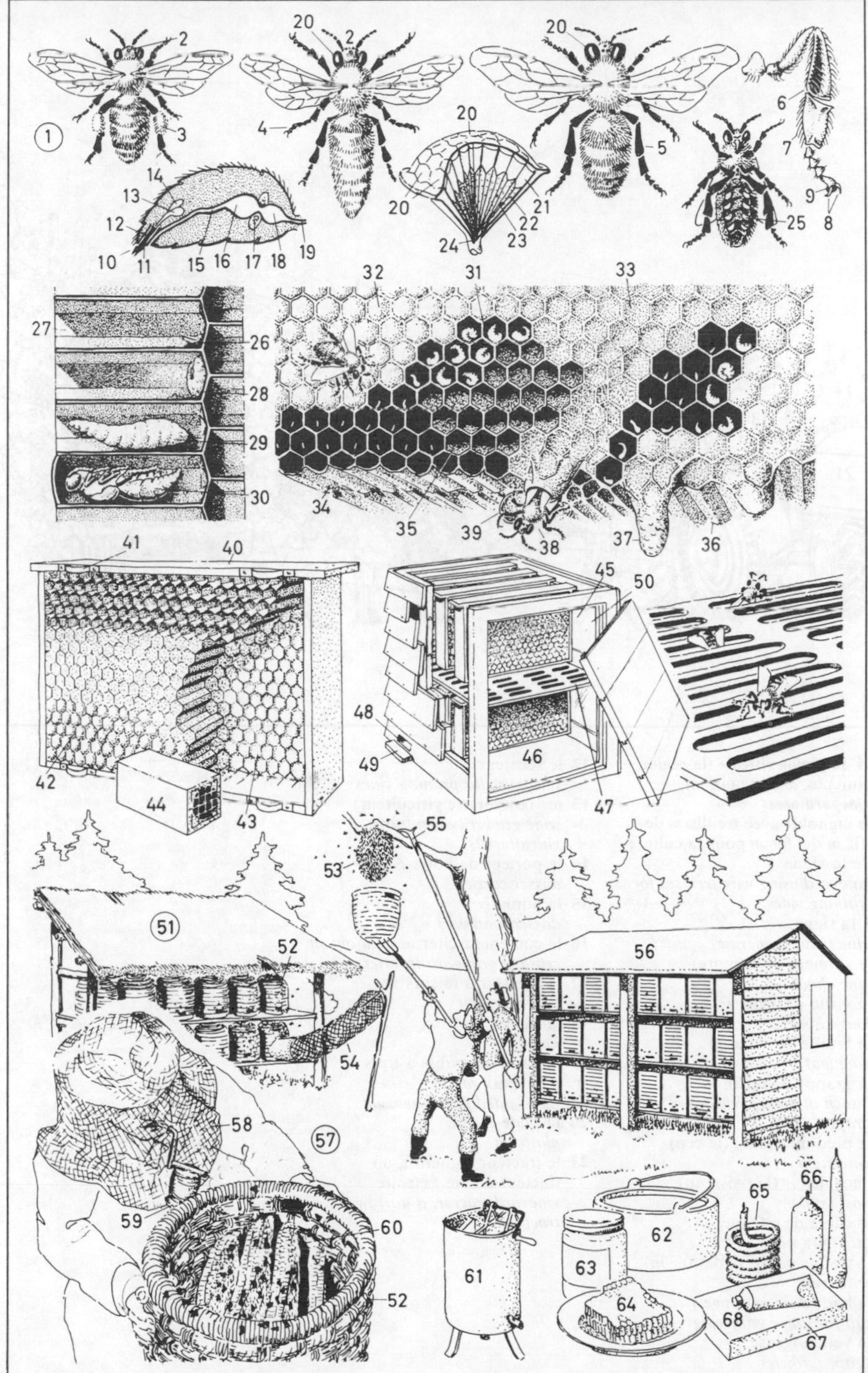
1
2
3
4
5
6
7
8
9
10
11
12
13
14
15
16
17
18
19
20
21
22
23
24
25
26
27
28
29
30
31
32
33
34
35
36
37
38
39
40
41
42
43
44
45
46
47
48
49
50
51
52
53
54
55
56
57
58
59
60
61
62
63
64
65
66
67
68

1-21 la région viticole (la région vinicole, les coteaux *m*)
– ***vineyard area***
1 le vignoble avec treillis *m* de (fil *m* de) fer *m* pour la culture de la vigne
– *vineyard using wire trellises for training vines*
2-9 la vigne
– ***vine*** (Am. *grapevine)*
2 le sarment (le pampre)
– *vine shoot*
3 la vrille de vigne *f*
– *long shoot*
4 la feuille de vigne *f*
– *vine leaf*
5 la grappe de raisin *m*
– *bunch of grapes (cluster of grapes)*
6 le pied de vigne *f* (le cep)
– *vine stem*
7 l'échalas *m* (le paisseau)
– *post (stake)*
8 le câble de retenue *f*
– *guy (guy wire)*
9 le treillis de (fil *m* de) fer *m*
– *wire trellis*
10 le baquet à vendange *f*
– *tub for grape gathering*
11 la vendangeuse
– *grape gatherer*
12 le sécateur
– *secateurs for pruning vines*
13 le vigneron (le viticulteur)
– *wine grower (viniculturist, viticulturist)*
14 le porteur de hotte *f*
– *dosser carrier*
15 la hotte
– *dosser (pannier)*
16 le conteneur-citerne de moût *m*
– *crushed grape transporter*
17 le pressoir à raisins *m*
– *grape crusher*
18 la trémie
– *hopper*
19 la paroi amovible à trois panneaux *m*
– *three-sided flap extension*
20 la plate-forme
– *platform*
21 le tracteur vigneron, un tracteur à voie *f* étroite
– *vineyard tractor, a narrow-track tractor*

1-22 la cave à vin *m* (le cellier)
– ***wine cellar*** *(wine vault)*
1 la voûte
– *vault*
2 le tonneau sur chantier *m* (le fût)
– *wine cask*
3 la cuve à vin *m*, une cuve en béton *m*
– *wine vat, a concrete vat*
4 la cuve en acier *m* spécial (*égal.:* la cuve en matière *f* plastique)
– *stainless steel vat (*also: *vat made of synthetic material)*
5 l'agitateur *m* à hélice *f*
– *propeller-type high-speed mixer*
6 l'hélice *f*
– *propeller mixer*
7 la pompe centrifuge
– *centrifugal pump*
8 le filtre à sédiments *m* en acier *m* spécial
– *stainless steel sediment filter*
9 l'embouteilleuse *f* circulaire semi-automatique
– *semi-automatic circular bottling machine*
10 le presse-bouteilles semi-automatique (la machine à boucher les bouteilles *f*)
– *semi-automatic corking machine*
11 le casier à bouteilles *f*
– *bottle rack*
12 le caviste
– *cellarer's assistant*
13 le panier à bouteilles *f*
– *bottle basket*
14 la bouteille à vin *m*
– *wine bottle*
15 le pichet à vin *m*
– *wine jug*
16 la dégustation de vin *m*
– *wine tasting*
17 le maître de chai *m*
– *head cellarman*
18 le dégustateur
– *cellarman*
19 le verre à vin *m*
– *wineglass*
20 l'appareil *m* d'examen *m* rapide
– *inspection apparatus [for spot-checking samples]*
21 le pressoir horizontal
– *horizontal wine press*
22 l'humidificateur *m*
– *humidifier*

1-19 parasites *m* **des fruits** *m*
– ***fruit pests***
1 le bombyx disparate (le zigzag, le spongieux)
– *gipsy (gypsy) moth*
2 la ponte des œufs *m*
– *batch (cluster) of eggs*
3 la chenille
– *caterpillar*
4 la nymphe
– *chrysalis (pupa)*
5 l'hyponomeute *f* du pommier, un tinéidé
– *small ermine moth, an ermine moth*
6 la larve
– *larva (grub)*
7 le cocon, le réseau de soie *f*
– *tent*
8 la chenille squelettisant la feuille
– *caterpillar skeletonizing a leaf*
9 la pyrale des pommes *f* (le carpocapse)
– *fruit surface eating tortrix moth (summer fruit tortrix moth)*
10 l'anthonome *m* du pommier
– *appleblossom weevil, a weevil*
11 le bouton floral desséché après attaque *f* du parasite, «le clou de girofle *m*»
– *punctured, withered flower (blossom)*
12 le trou de ponte *f*
– *hole for laying eggs*
13 le bombyx à livrée *f*
– *lackey moth*
14 la chenille
– *caterpillar*
15 les œufs *m*
– *eggs*
16 la phalène (l'hibernie *f* défeuillante), un géométridé
– *winter moth, a geometrid*
17 la chenille
– *caterpillar*
18 la mouche des cerises *f* [Rhagoletis cerasi], une mouche à fruits *m*
– *cherry fruit fly, a borer*
19 la larve (l'asticot *m*)
– *larva (grub, maggot)*
20-27 parasites *m* **de la vigne**
– ***vine pests***
20 le mildiou de la vigne *f* (le faux oïdium), un champignon qui provoque la chute des feuilles *f*
– *downy mildew, a mildew, a disease causing leaf drop*
21 le grain desséché (le mildiou de la grappe)
– *grape affected with downy mildew*
22 la tordeuse de la grappe, la pyrale de la vigne
– *grape-berry moth*
23 la chenille de la 1ère génération
– *first-generation larva of the grape-berry moth (*Am. *grape worm)*
24 la chenille de la 2ème génération
– *second-generation larva of the grape-berry moth (*Am. *grape worm)*
25 la nymphe (la pupe)
– *chrysalis (pupa)*
26 le puceron des racines *f* de la vigne, un phylloxera, un aphidé
– *root louse, a grape phylloxera*
27 les nodosités *f* des radicelles *f*, les radicelles *f* galeuses (boursouflées)
– *root gall (knotty swelling of the root, nodosity, tuberosity)*
28 le cul brun, le cul doré
– *brown-tail moth*
29 la chenille
– *caterpillar*
30 la ponte des œufs *m*
– *batch (cluster) of eggs*
31 le nid de feuilles *f* (le nid d'hibernation *f*)
– *hibernation cocoon*
32 le puceron lanigère ou lanifère, un aphidé
– *woolly apple aphid (American blight), an aphid*
33 la prolifération consécutive à la piqûre du puceron
– *gall caused by the woolly apple aphid*
34 la colonie de pucerons *m*
– *woolly apple aphid colony*
35 le pou de San-José, une cochenille
– *San-José scale, a scale insect (scale louse)*
36 les larves *f* mâles allongées et les larves *f* femelles arrondies
– *larvae (grubs) [*male *elongated,* female *round]*
37-55 parasites *m* **des cultures** *f*
– ***field pests***
37 le taupin des moissons *f*, un élatéridé
– *click beetle, a snapping beetle (*Am. *snapping bug)*
38 le ver fil *m* de fer, une larve du taupin
– *wireworm, larva of the click beetle*
39 l'altise *f* des crucifères *f* (la puce de terre *f*, le tiquet)
– *flea beetle*
40 la cécidomyie destructive (la mouche de Hesse), un diptère gallicole
– *Hessian fly, a gall midge (gall gnat)*
41 la larve
– *larva (grub)*
42 la noctuelle des céréales *f*, un noctuidé
– *turnip moth, an earth moth*
43 la nymphe
– *chrysalis (pupa)*
44 la chenille de la noctuelle, l'agrotis *m*
– *cutworm, a caterpillar*
45 le silphe opaque de la betterave
– *beet carrion beetle*
46 la larve
– *larva (grub)*
47 la piéride du chou
– *large cabbage white butterfly*
48 la chenille de la piéride du chou
– *caterpillar of the small cabbage white butterfly*
49 le charançon, un curculionidé
– *brown leaf-eating weevil, a weevil*
50 le trou du charançon
– *feeding site*
51 l'anguillule *f* de la betterave, un nématode
– *sugar beet eelworm, a nematode (a threadworm, hairworm)*
52 le doryphore
– *Colorado beetle (potato beetle)*
53 la larve prête à la nymphose
– *mature larva (grub)*
54 la jeune larve
– *young larva (grub)*
55 les œufs *m*
– *eggs*

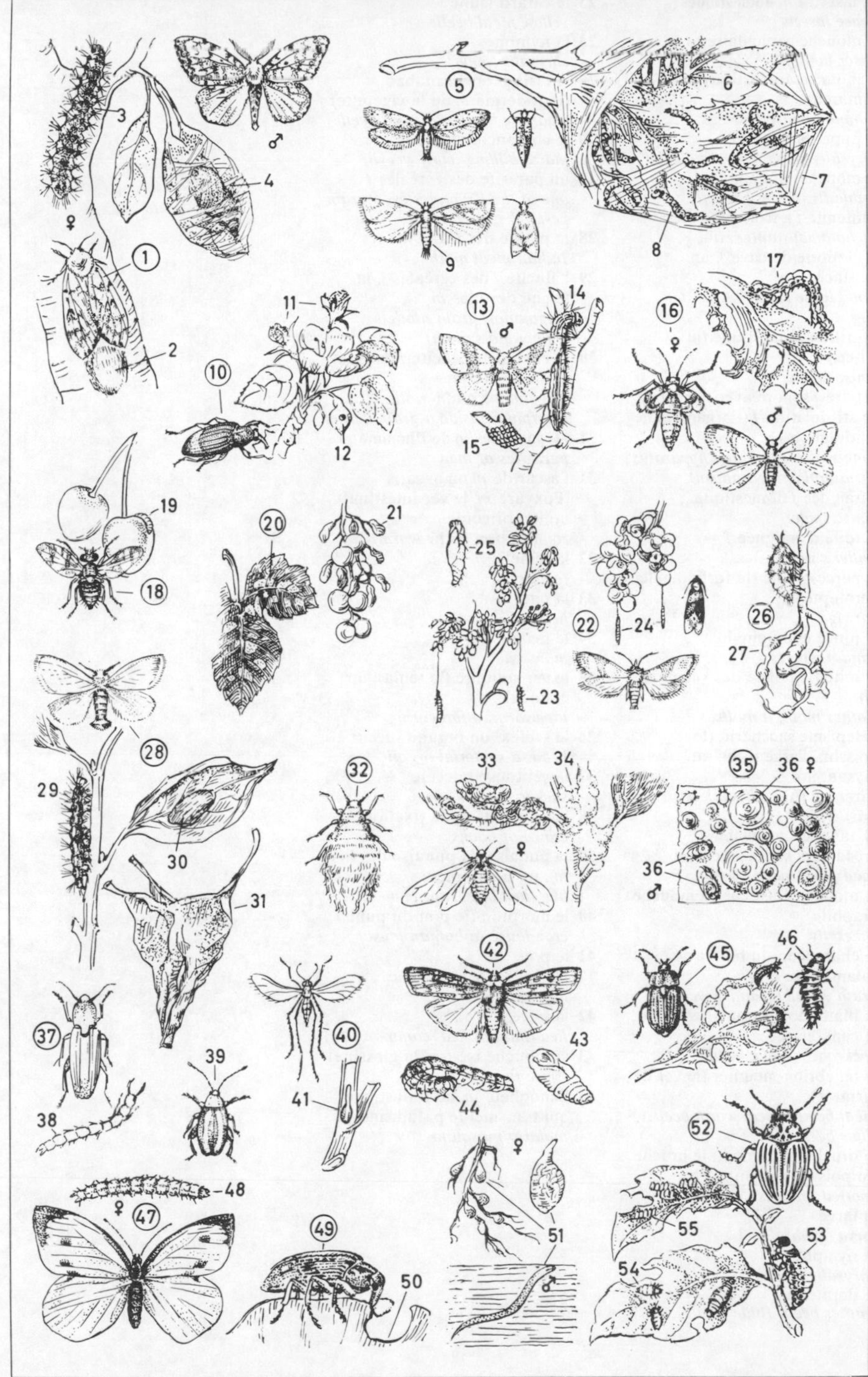
1
2
3
4
♀
♂
5
6
7
8
9
10
11
12
13
14
15
16
17
18
19
20
21
22
23
24
25
26
27
28
29
30
31
32
33
34
35
36 ♀
36 ♂
37
38
39
40
41
42
43
44
45
46
47
48
49
50
51
52
53
54
55

81 Insectes domestiques, prédateurs et parasites

1-14 insectes *m* domestiques
– ***house insects***
1 la mouche caniculaire
– *lesser housefly*
2 la mouche domestique ou commune
– *common housefly*
3 la pupe (la nymphe)
– *chrysalis (pupa, coarctate pupa)*
4 la mouche piqueuse
– *stable fly (biting housefly)*
5 l'antenne *f* à trois branches *f*
– *trichotomous antenna*
6 le cloporte de cave *f*, un crustacé
– *wood louse (slater,* Am. *sow bug)*
7 le grillon domestique (le cri-cri)
– *house cricket*
8 l'élytre *f* sonore avec nervure *f* de stridulation *f* (l'organe *m* de stridulation *f*)
– *wing with stridulating apparatus (stridulating mechanism)*
9 l'araignée *f* domestique
– *house spider*
10 la toile d'araignée *f*
– *spider's web*
11 le perce-oreille (la forficule, le dermoptère)
– *earwig*
12 la pince abdominale
– *caudal pincers*
13 la mite (la teigne des vêtements *m*)
– *clothes moth, a moth*
14 le lépisme saccharin (le poisson d'argent *m*), un thysanoure
– *silverfish (*Am. *slicker), a bristletail*

15-30 insectes *m* nuisibles, prédateurs *m* des stocks *m*
– ***food pests*** *(pests to stores)*
15 la mouche à asticot, la mouche piophile
– *cheesefly*
16 le charançon du blé (la calandre du blé)
– *grain weevil (granary weevil)*
17 la blatte domestique (le cafard, le cancrelat)
– *cockroach (black beetle)*
18 le ténébrion-meunier (le ver de farine *f*)
– *meal beetle (meal worm beetle, flour beetle)*
19 le bruche du haricot, le bruche du pois (le cusson)
– *spotted bruchus*
20 la larve
– *larva (grub)*
21 la nymphe
– *chrysalis (pupa)*
22 le dermeste
– *leather beetle (hide beetle)*
23 le cafard jaune
– *yellow meal beetle*
24 la nymphe
– *chrysalis (pupa)*
25 le lasioderme du tabac (lasioderme *m* de la cigarette)
– *cigarette beetle (tobacco beetle)*
26 le charançon du maïs
– *maize billbug (corn weevil)*
27 un parasite des céréales *f*
– *one of the Cryptolestes, a grain pest*
28 la pyrale des fruits *m* secs
– *Indian meal moth*
29 l'alucite *f* des céréales *f*, la teigne des blés *m*
– *Angoumois grain moth (Angoumois moth)*
30 la chenille d'alucite *f* dans le grain de blé *m*
– *Angoumois grain moth caterpillar inside a grain kernel*

31-42 parasites *m* de l'homme *m*
– ***parasites of man***
31 l'ascaride *m* ou ascaris (l'oxyure *m*, le ver intestinal), un lombricoïde
– *round worm (maw worm)*
32 la femelle
– *female*
33 la tête
– *head*
34 le mâle
– *male*
35 le ver solitaire (le ténia), un cestode
– *tapeworm, a flatworm*
36 le scolex, un organe suceur
– *head, a suctorial organ*
37 la ventouse buccale
– *sucker*
38 les crochets *m* de fixation *f*
– *crown of hooks*
39 la punaise (la punaise des lits *m*), un hétéroptère
– *bug (bed bug,* Am. *chinch)*
40 le morpion (le pou du pubis)
– *crab louse (a human louse)*
41 le pou
– *clothes louse (body louse, a human louse)*
42 la puce
– *flea (human flea, common flea)*
43 la mouche tsé-tsé (la glossine)
– *tsetse fly*
44 l'anophèle *m*, un moustique qui transmet le paludisme
– *malaria mosquito*

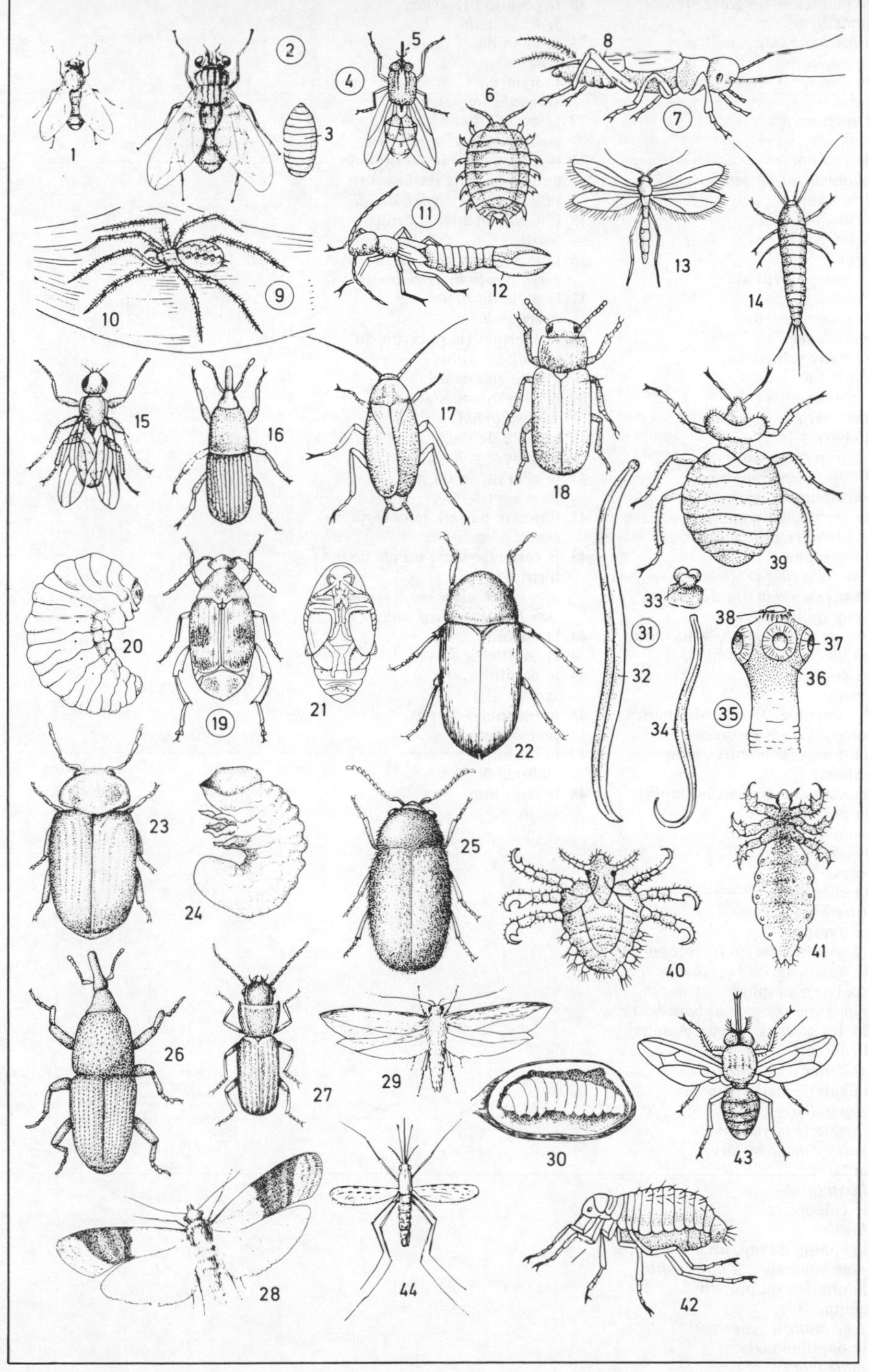
1
2
3
4
5
6
7
8
9
10
11
12
13
14
15
16
17
18
19
20
21
22
23
24
25
26
27
28
29
30
31
32
33
34
35
36
37
38
39
40
41
42
43
44

1 le hanneton, un coléoptère lamellicorné
– *cockchafer (May bug), a lamellicorn*
2 la tête
– *head*
3 l'antenne *f*
– *antenna (feeler)*
4 le prothorax (le corselet)
– *thoracic shield (prothorax)*
5 l'écusson *m*
– *scutellum*
6-8 les pattes *f*
– *legs*
6 la patte antérieure
– *front leg*
7 la patte médiane
– *middle leg*
8 la patte postérieure
– *back leg*
9 l'abdomen *m*
– *abdomen*
10 l'élytre *f*
– *elytron (wing case)*
11 l'aile *f* membraneuse
– *membranous wing*
12 le ver blanc (le man), une larve
– *cockchafer grub, a larva*
13 la nymphe
– *chrysalis (pupa)*
14 la processionnaire du chêne, un papillon nocturne
– *processionary moth, a nocturnal moth (night-flying moth)*
15 le papillon
– *moth*
16 les chenilles *f* processionnaires
– *caterpillars in procession*
17 la nonne (le bombyx moine, le moine)
– *nun moth (black arches moth)*
18 le papillon
– *moth*
19 les œufs *m*
– *eggs*
20 la chenille
– *caterpillar*
21 la nymphe
– *chrysalis (pupa) in its cocoon*
22 la bostryche de l'épicéa (le scolyte), un ipidé
– *typographer beetle, a bark beetle*
23-24 les galeries *f* creusées sous l'écorce *f*
– *galleries under the bark*
23 la galerie maternelle
– *egg gallery*
24 la galerie larvaire
– *gallery made by larva*
25 la larve
– *larva (grub)*
26 le coléoptère
– *beetle*
27 le sphinx du pin, un sphingidé
– *pine hawkmoth, a hawkmoth*
28 le phalène du pin, un géométridé
– *pine moth, a geometrid*
29 le papillon mâle
– *male moth*
30 le papillon femelle
– *female moth*
31 la chenille
– *caterpillar*
32 la nymphe
– *chrysalis (pupa)*
33 le cynips du chêne
– *oak-gall wasp, a gall wasp*
34 la gale du chêne (la noix de galle *f*, la galle du Levant)
– *oak gall (oak apple), a gall*
35 l'insecte *m* ailé, le cynips
– *wasp*
36 la larve dans son nid *m*
– *larva (grub) in its chamber*
37 la galle du hêtre
– *beech gall*
38 le chermès (le puceron du sapin), un aphidé
– *spruce-gall aphid*
39 le puceron au stade ailé
– *winged aphid*
40 la galle de l'ananas *m*
– *pineapple gall*
41 le charançon du pin
– *pine weevil*
42 l'insecte parfait, le coléoptère
– *beetle (weevil)*
43 la tordeuse verte du chêne, un tortricidé
– *green oak roller moth (green oak tortrix), a leaf roller*
44 la chenille
– *caterpillar*
45 le papillon
– *moth*
46 la noctuelle du pin
– *pine beauty*
47 la chenille
– *caterpillar*
48 le papillon
– *moth*

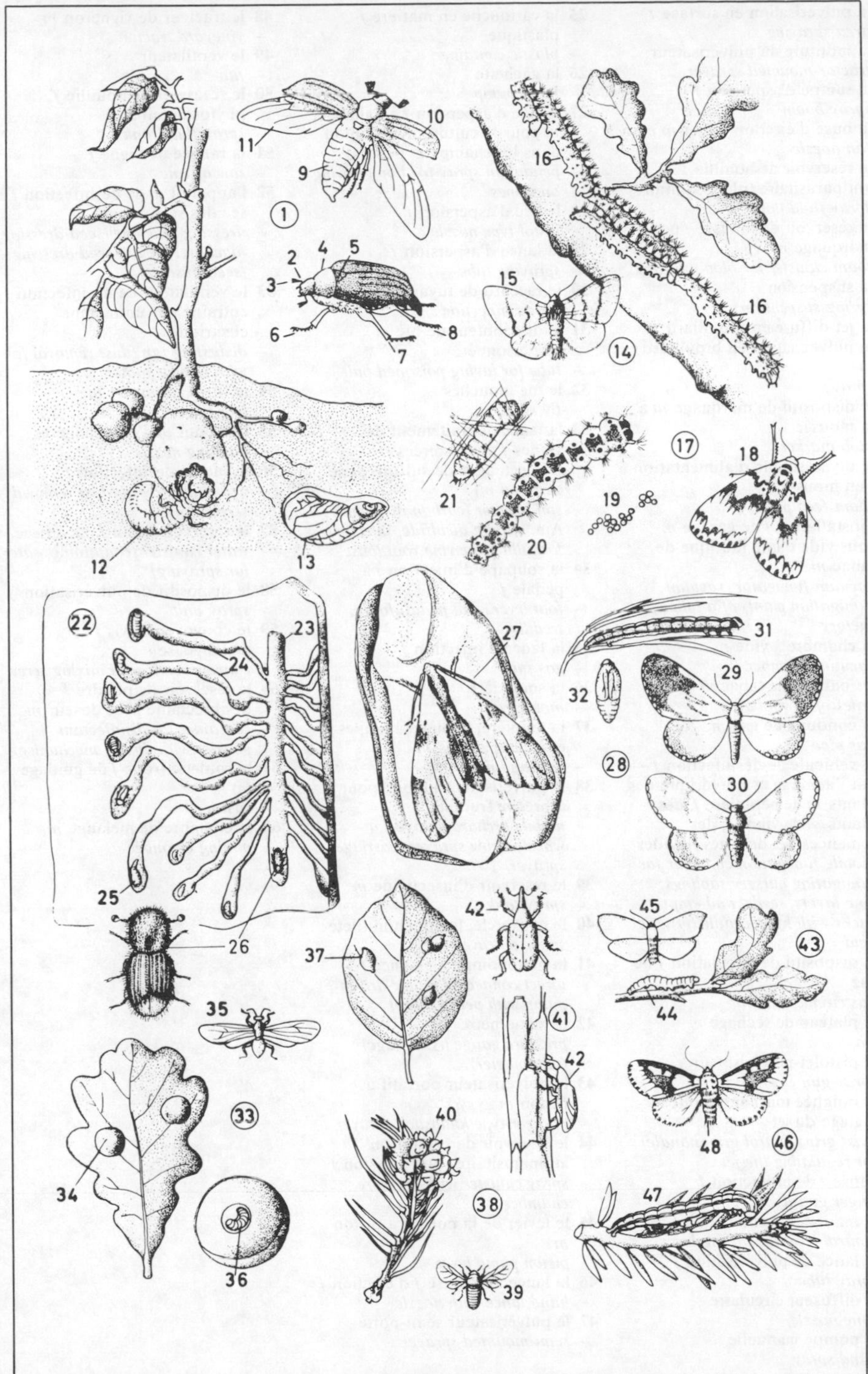
1
2
3
4
5
6
7
8
9
10
11
12
13
14
15
16
17
18
19
20
21
22
23
24
25
26
27
28
29
30
31
32
33
34
35
36
37
38
39
40
41
42
43
44
45
46
47
48

1 la pulvérisation en surface *f*
– *area spraying*
2 la monture du pulvérisateur
– *tractor-mounted sprayer*
3 la rampe d'aspersion *f*
– *spray boom*
4 la buse d'éjection *f* à jet *m* plan
– *fan nozzle*
5 le réservoir de bouillie *f* antiparasitaire (phytosanitaire)
– *spray fluid tank*
6 le réservoir de mousse *f* pour marquage *m*
– *foam canister for blob marking*
7 la suspension
– *spring suspension*
8 le jet diffusé en brouillard *m*, la pulvérisation en brouillard *m*
– *spray*
9 le dispositif de marquage *m* à la mousse
– *blob marker*
10 le tuyau souple d'alimentation *f* en mousse *f*
– *foam feed pipe*
11 l'installation *f* de gazage *m* sous vide d'une fabrique de tabac *m*
– *vacuum fumigator (vacuum fumigation plant) of a tobacco factory*
12 la chambre à vide *m*
– *vacuum chamber*
13 les balles *f* de tabac *m* brut
– *bales of raw tobacco*
14 la conduite de gaz *m*
– *gas pipe*
15 le véhicule de désinfection *f* par l'acide *m* cyanhydrique des plants *m* de pépinière *f*, des plants *m* de vigne *f*, des semences *f* et des sacs *m* vides
– *mobile fumigation chamber for fumigating nursery saplings, vine layers, seeds, and empty sacks with hydrocyanic (prussic) acid*
16 le dispositif de circulation *f* du gaz
– *gas circulation unit*
17 le plateau de séchage *m*
– *tray*
18 le pistolet-pulvérisateur
– *spray gun*
19 la poignée tournante pour le réglage du jet
– *twist grip (control grip, handle) for regulating the jet*
20 l'anse *f* de protection *f*
– *finger guard*
21 la manette de commande*f*
– *control lever (operating lever)*
22 la lance de pulvérisation *f*
– *spray tube*
23 le diffuseur circulaire
– *cone nozzle*
24 la pompe manuelle
– *hand spray*
25 la cartouche en matière *f* plastique
– *plastic container*
26 la gâchette
– *hand pump*
27 la tige d'aspersion *f* à balancier *m* pour la culture du houblon dans les champs *m* pentus
– *pendulum spray for hop growing on slopes*
28 le bec d'aspersion *f*
– *pistol-type nozzle*
29 la lance d'aspersion *f*
– *spraying tube*
30 le raccord de tuyau *m*
– *hose connection*
31 le distributeur de blé *m* empoisonné
– *tube for laying poisoned bait*
32 le tue-mouches
– *fly swat*
33 la lance de traitement des vignes *f* phylloxérées (l'injecteur *m* de sulfure *m* de carbone *m*)
– *soil injector (carbon disulphide,* Am. *carbon disulfide, injector) for killing the vine root louse*
34 la soupape d'injection *f* à pédale *f*
– *foot lever (foot pedal, foot treadle)*
35 la lance d'injection *f*
– *gas tube*
36 la souricière
– *mousetrap*
37 la taupière, le piège à taupes *f* et à campagnols *m*
– *vole and mole trap*
38 le pulvérisateur mobile pour arbres *m* fruitiers
– *mobile orchard sprayer, a wheelbarrow sprayer (carriage sprayer)*
39 le réservoir d'insecticide *m*
– *spray tank*
40 le couvercle, le bouchon fileté
– *screw-on cover*
41 la motopompe à essence *f*
– *direct-connected motor-driven pump with petrol motor*
42 le manomètre
– *pressure gauge (*Am. *gage) (manometer)*
43 le pulvérisateur portatif à piston *m*
– *plunger-type knapsack sprayer*
44 le réservoir de produit *m* antiparasitaire sous pression *f*
– *spray canister with pressure chamber*
45 le levier de la pompe à piston *m*
– *piston pump lever*
46 la lance avec buse *f* d'éjection *f*
– *hand lance with nozzle*
47 le pulvérisateur semi-porté
– *semi-mounted sprayer*
48 le tracteur de vigneron *m*
– *vineyard tractor*
49 le ventilateur
– *fan*
50 le réservoir de bouillie *f* phytosanitaire
– *spray fluid tank*
51 la rangée de vigne *f*
– *row of vines*
52 l'appareil *m* de désinfection *f* à sec des semences *f*
– *dressing machine (seed-dressing machine) for dry-seed dressing (seed dusting)*
53 le ventilateur de désinfection *f* entraîné par un moteur électrique
– *dedusting fan (dust removal fan) with electric motor*
54 le filtre à manche *m*
– *bag filter*
55 l'embout *m* d'ensachage *m*
– *bagging nozzle*
56 le sac de désinfection *f*
– *dedusting screen (dust removal screen)*
57 le réservoir d'eau *f* pulvérisée
– *water canister [containing water for spraying]*
58 le dispositif de pulvérisation *f*
– *spray unit*
59 le convoyeur à vis *f* mélangeuse
– *conveyor unit with mixing screw*
60 le réservoir de poudre *f* désinfectante avec doseur *m*
– *container for disinfectant powder with dosing mechanism*
61 la roulette (roue *f* de guidage *m*)
– *castor*
62 la chambre de mélange *m*
– *mixing chamber*

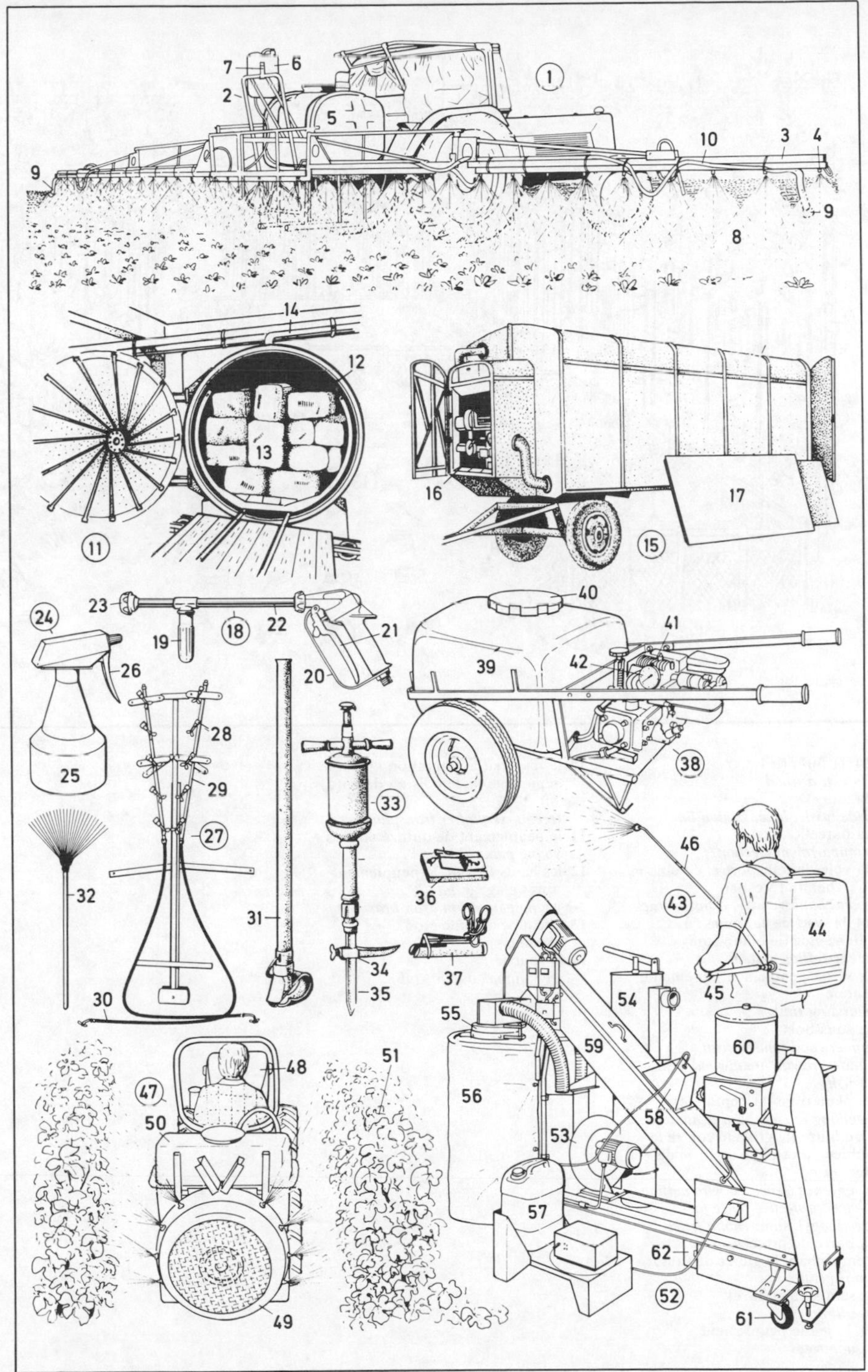
1
2
3
4
5
6
7
8
9
9
10
11
12
13
14
15
16
17
18
19
20
21
22
23
24
25
26
27
28
29
30
31
32
33
34
35
36
37
38
39
40
41
42
43
44
45
46
47
48
49
50
51
52
53
54
55
56
57
58
59
60
61
62

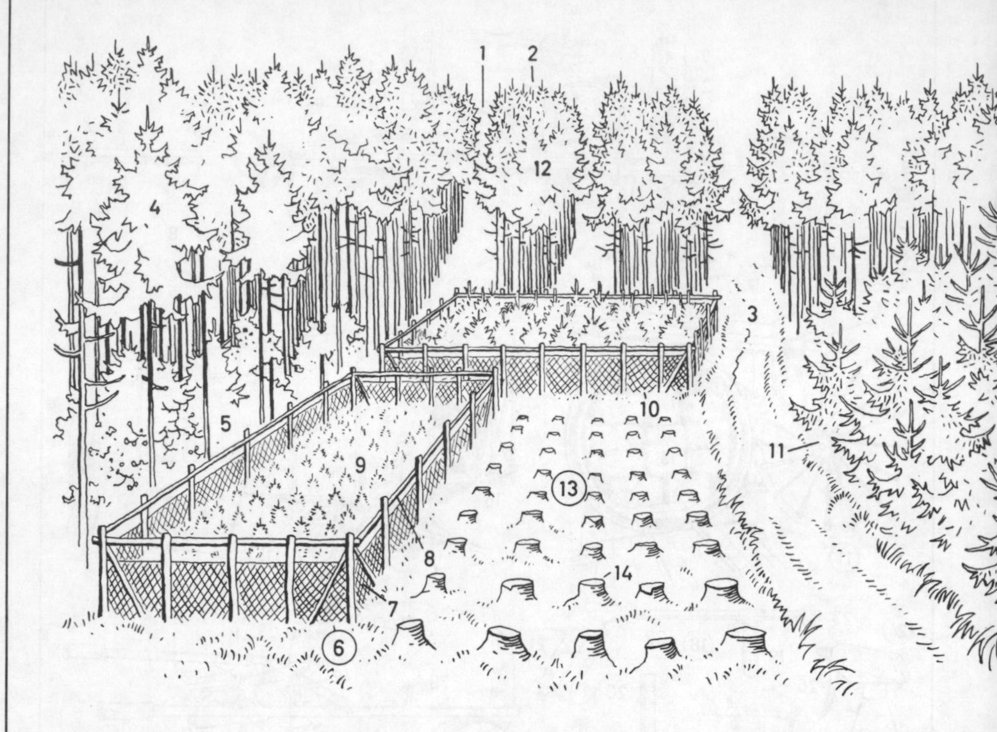

1-34 la forêt (le bois)
– ***forest,** a wood*
1 la laie
– *ride (aisle, lane, section line)*
2 la parcelle
– *compartment (section)*
3 la voie de transport *m* de bois *m*, un chemin forestier
– *wood haulage way, a forest track*
4-14 le système de coupe *f* **à blanc-étoc** (le blanc-étoc)
– ***clear-felling system***
4 le vieux peuplement, une haute futaie
– *standing timber*
5 le sous-bois
– *underwood (underbrush, undergrowth, brushwood,* Am. *brush)*
6 la plantation (la pépinière)
– *seedling nursery, a tree nursery*
7 la clôture (le grillage contre le gibier), un treillis de fil *m* de fer *m*
– *deer fence (fence), a wire netting fence (protective fence for seedlings);* sim.: *rabbit fence*
8 la barre de protection *f* (empêchant le gibier de sauter)
– *guard rail*
9 le semiš (la culture)
– *seedlings*
10-11 le jeune peuplement
– *young trees*
10 la réserve (la plantation après repiquage *m*, le bois en défen(d)s *m*)
– *tree nursery after transplanting*
11 le peuplement de quinze années *f*
– *young plantation*
12 les hauts fûts *m* (le peuplement après élagage *m*)
– *young plantation after brashing*
13 la coupe à blanc-étoc
– *clearing*
14 la souche
– *tree stump (stump, stub)*

15-37 la coupe en exploitation *f*
– ***wood cutting*** *(timber cutting, tree felling,* Am. *lumbering)*

15 les troncs *m* empilés
– *timber skidded to the stack (stacked timber,* Am. *yarded timber)*

16 le stère de bois *m* empilé, un mètre cube de bois *m*
– *stack of logs, one cubic metre (*Am. *meter) of wood*

17 le pieu
– *post (stake)*

18 l'ouvrier *m* forestier tournant une bille
– *forest labourer (woodsman,* Am. *logger, lumberer, lumberjack, lumberman, timberjack) turning (*Am. *canting) timber*

19 le tronc (la bille, le long bois)
– *bole (tree trunk, trunk, stem)*

20 le chef de chantier *m* en train de numéroter
– *feller numbering the logs*

21 le pied à coulisse *f* en acier *m*
– *steel tree calliper (caliper)*

22 la tronçonneuse (en train de couper un tronc)
– *power saw (motor saw) cutting a bole*

23 le casque de protection *f* avec visière *f* et protection *f* acoustique
– *safety helmet with visor and ear pieces*

24 les cernes *m* (couches *f* annuelles, anneaux *m*, cercles *m* annuels)
– *annual rings*

25 le vérin de fixation *f*
– *hydraulic felling wedge*

26 les vêtements *m* protecteurs [chemise *f* orange, pantalon *m* vert]
– *protective clothing [orange top, green trousers]*

27 l'abattage *m* avec une tronçonneuse *f*
– *felling with a power saw (motor saw)*

28 l'entaille *f* (l'encoche *m*)
– *undercut (notch, throat, gullet, mouth, sink, kerf, birdsmouth)*

29 le trait de scie *f*
– *back cut*

30 la poche avec coin *m* (d'abattage *m*)
– *sheath holding felling wedge*

31 le tronçon de bois *m*
– *log*

32 la scie de dégagement *m* pour couper le sous-bois et les mauvaises herbes *f*
– *free-cutting saw for removing underwood and weeds*

33 la scie circulaire (ou couteau *m* frappeur) adaptable
– *circular saw (or activated blade) attachment*

34 le moteur
– *power unit (motor)*

35 le bidon d'huile *f* adhérente pour chaînes *f* à scier
– *canister of viscous oil for the saw chain*

36 le bidon d'essence *f*
– *petrol canister (*Am. *gasoline canister)*

37 l'abattage *m* du menu bois (l'éclaircissage *m*)
– *felling of small timber (of small-sized thinnings) (thinning)*

1 la hache
– *axe* (Am. *ax)*
2 le tranchant
– *edge (cutting edge)*
3 le manche
– *handle (helve)*
4 le coin (à abattre) avec insert *m* en bois *m* et anneau *m*
– *felling wedge (falling wedge) with wood insert and ring*
5 le merlin de bûcheron *m* (la hache pour fendre le bois)
– *riving hammer (cleaving hammer, splitting hammer)*
6 le pic, un tourne-billes
– *lifting hook*
7 le tourne-billes (le crochet à grumes *f*)
– *cant hook*
8 le décortiqueur
– *barking iron (bark spud)*
9 le coin de fixation *f* avec crochet à grumes *f*
– *peavy*
10 le compas forestier
– *slide calliper (caliper) (calliper square)*
11 la serpe (pour couper et élaguer)
– *billhook, a knife for lopping*
12 le marteau numéroteur rotatif
– *revolving die hammer (marking hammer, marking iron,* Am. *marker)*
13 la tronçonneuse
– *power saw (motor saw)*
14 la chaîne à scier
– *saw chain*
15 le frein de sécurité *f* (pour la chaîne à scier) avec protège-mains *m*
– *safety brake for the saw chain, with finger guard*
16 le guide-chaîne
– *saw guide*
17 le blocage de l'accélérateur *m*
– *accelerator lock*
18 la machine à émonder
– *snedding machine (trimming machine,* Am. *knotting machine, limbing machine)*
19 les cylindres *m* d'avancement *m*
– *feed rolls*
20 la lame articulée
– *flexible blade*
21 le vérin hydraulique
– *hydraulic arm*
22 l'outil *m* de tranchage *m* des pointes *f*
– *trimming blade*
23 l'écorçage *m* des grumes *f*
– *debarking (barking, bark stripping) of boles*
24 le cylindre d'avancement *m*
– *feed roller*
25 le rotor à lames *f*
– *cylinder trimmer*
26 la lame rotative
– *rotary cutter*
27 le tracteur forestier (pour le transport de bois *m* en forêt *f*)
– *short-haul skidder*
28 la grue de chargement *m*
– *loading crane*
29 le grappin à bois *m*
– *log grips*
30 le rancher
– *post*
31 la direction pivotante (la direction par châssis *m* articulé)
– *Ackermann steering system*
32 la pile de grumes *f*
– *log dump*
33 le tronc numéroté
– *number (identification number)*
34 le skidder
– *skidder*
35 la plaque frontale
– *front blade (front plate)*
36 la cabine avec arceau *m* de sécurité *f*
– *crush-proof safety bonnet (*Am. *safety hood)*
37 la direction pivotante (la direction par châssis *m* articulé)
– *Ackermann steering system*
38 le treuil à câble *m*
– *cable winch*
39 le rouleau de guidage *m* du câble
– *cable drum*
40 la plaque arrière
– *rear blade (rear plate)*
41 les grumes *f* soulevées
– *boles with butt ends held off the ground*
42 le transport routier des grumes *f*
– *haulage of timber by road*
43 le véhicule tracteur
– *tractor (tractor unit)*
44 la grue de chargement *m*
– *loading crane*
45 la béquille hydraulique
– *hydraulic jack*
46 le treuil à câble *m*
– *cable winch*
47 le rancher
– *post*
48 la sellette d'accouplement *m* articulée
– *bolster plate*
49 la remorque
– *rear bed (rear bunk)*

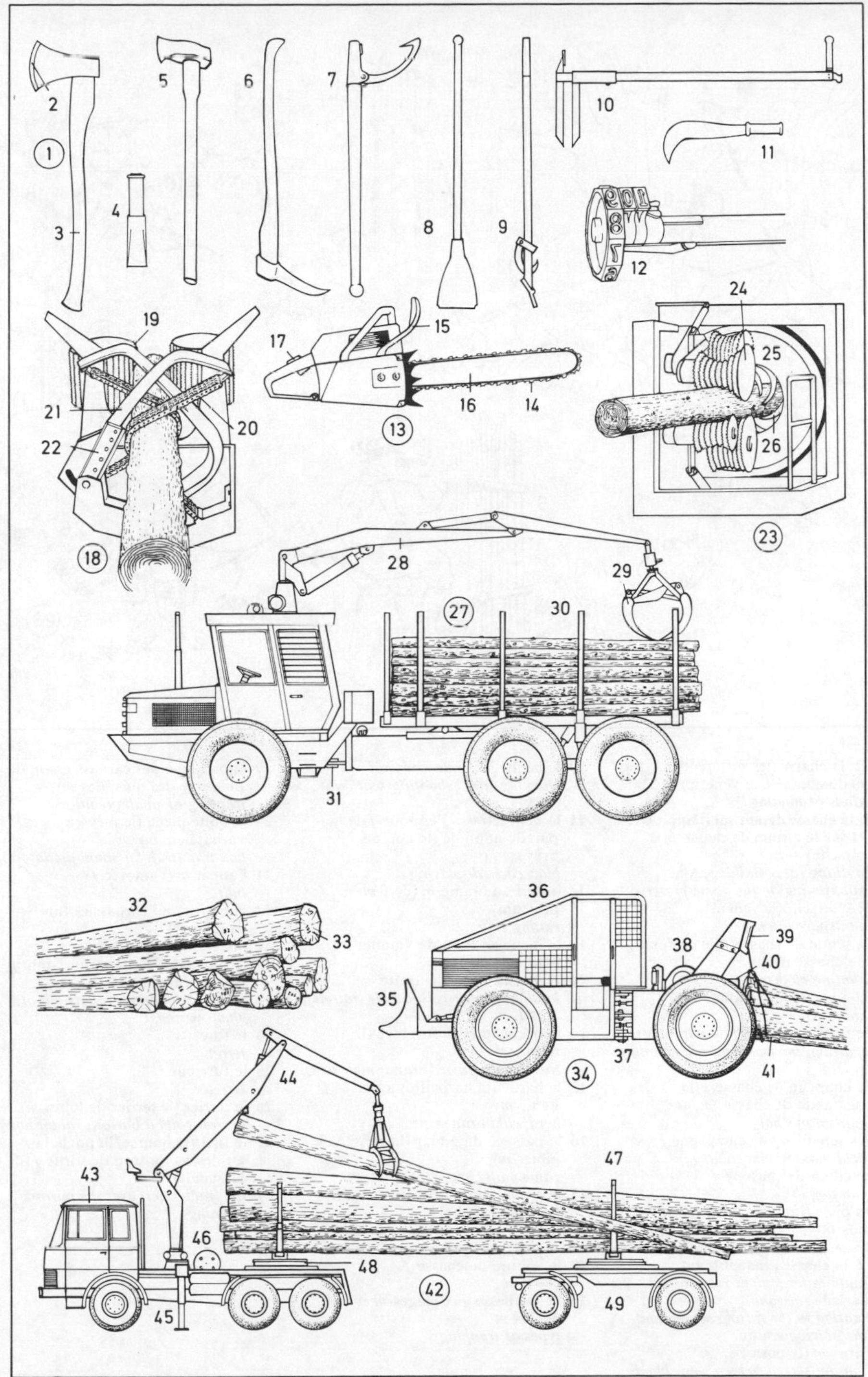
1
2
3
4
5
6
7
8
9
10
11
12
13
14
15
16
17
18
19
20
21
22
23
24
25
26
27
28
29
30
31
32
33
34
35
36
37
38
39
40
41
42
43
44
45
46
47
48
49

1-52 la chasse (les différents modes *m* de chasse *f*, la vénerie)
– ***kinds of hunting***
1-8 la chasse devant soi (l'approche *f*) **sur le terrain de chasse** *f* (la pirsche)
– ***stalking*** *(deer stalking,* Am. *stillhunting) in the game preserve*
1 le chasseur (le veneur)
– *huntsman (hunter)*
2 la tenue de chasse *f* (le costume de chasseur *m*)
– *hunting clothes*
3 la gibecière (la carnassière)
– *knapsack*
4 le fusil de chasse *f* (la carabine)
– *sporting gun (sporting rifle, hunting rifle)*
5 le chapeau de chasse *f* (la casquette de chasse *f*)
– *huntsman's hat*
6 les jumelles *f* de campagne *f*
– *field glasses, binoculars*
7 le chien de chasse *f*
– *gun dog*
8 la piste (la trace, l'empreinte *f* de pas *m*)
– *track (trail, hoofprints)*
9-12 la chasse pendant le rut *(mammifères m)* **et pendant la pariade** *(oiseaux)*
– ***hunting in the rutting season and the pairing season***
9 l'abri *m* (le poste)
– *hunting screen (screen,* Am. *blind)*
10 la canne-siège de chasse *f*
– *shooting stick (shooting seat, seat stick)*
11 le petit tétras à l'époque *f* de la parade nuptiale (le coq de bruyère *f*)
– *blackcock, displaying*
12 le cerf au brame *m* (cerf *m* bramant)
– *rutting stag*
13 la biche en train de viander
– *hind, grazing*
14-17 l'affût *m* **à la murette**
– ***hunting from a raised hide*** *(raised stand)*
14 l'observatoire *m* surélevé (le mirador)
– *raised hide (raised stand, high seat)*
15 la harde (la harpaille) à portée *f* de tir *m*
– *herd within range*
16 le passage du gibier (la passée de gibier *m*)
– *game path* (Am. *runway)*
17 le chevreuil (le brocard) touché à l'épaule et achevé
– *roebuck, hit in the shoulder and killed by a finishing shot*
18 la voiture de chasse *f*
– *phaeton*
19-27 la chasse aux pièges *m* **et aux engins** *m*
– ***types of trapping***
19 le piégeage des carnassiers *m* (le piégeage des nuisibles *m*)
– *trapping of small predators*
20 la boîte-piège (le piège à carnassiers *m*)
– *box trap (trap for small predators)*
21 l'appât *m* (l'amorce *f*)
– *bait*
22 la martre, un carnassier (un prédateur)
– *marten, a small predator*
23 le furetage (la chasse au lapin *m* avec le furet)
– *ferreting (hunting rabbits out of their warrens)*
24 le furet
– *ferret*
25 le fureteur
– *ferreter*
26 le terrier (le terrier de lapin *m*)
– *burrow (rabbit burrow, rabbit hole)*
27 le filet (la bourse, la poche) au-dessus du trou de sortie *f* (de la gueule)
– *net (rabbit net) over the burrow opening*

28 le ratelier à fourrage *m* pour l'hiver *m*
– *feeding place for game (winter feeding place)*
29 le braconnier
– *poacher*
30 la petite carabine
– *carbine, a short rifle*
31 courre le sanglier (la traque au sanglier)
– *boar hunt*
32 le cochon (le sanglier, la laie)
– *wild sow (sow, wild boar)*
33 le chien dressé à la chasse du sanglier (le chien de meute; *plusieurs:* la meute)
– *boarhound (hound, hunting dog;* collectively: *pack, pack of hounds)*
34-39 la battue (la chasse en rond *m*, la chasse au chaudron *m*)
– ***beating** (driving, hare hunting)*
34 la mise en joue
– *aiming position*
35 le lièvre (le roussin, l'oreillard *m*, le couard), un gibier à poil *m*
– *hare, furred game (ground game)*
36 le rapport du gibier
– *retrieving*
37 le rabatteur
– *beater*
38 le tableau de chasse *f*
– *bag (kill)*
39 la voiture à gibier *m*
– *cart for carrying game*
40 la chasse au gibier d'eau *f* (chasse à la sauvagine, chasse au canard)
– *waterfowling (wildfowling, duck shooting,* Am. *duck hunting)*
41 le vol (le passage) de canards *m* sauvages, le gibier à plumes *f*
– *flight of wild ducks, winged game*
42-46 la chasse au faucon (la fauconnerie)
– ***falconry** (hawking)*
42 le fauconnier
– *falconer*
43 le pât, un morceau de viande *f*
– *reward, a piece of meat*
44 le chaperon du faucon
– *falcon's hood*
45 la longe (la courroie)
– *jess*
46 un faucon mâle (le tiercelet) fondant sur un héron
– *falcon, a hawk, a male hawk (tiercel) swooping (stooping) on a heron*
47-52 la chasse en hutte *f* (l'affût *m* au grand duc)
– ***shooting from a butt***
47 l'arbrisseau *m* de pose *f* des becs *m* droits
– *tree to which birds are lured*
48 le grand duc, un oiseau-appât, l'appelant *m*
– *eagle owl, a decoy bird (decoy)*
49 le piquet (le perchoir)
– *perch*
50 l'oiseau *m* attiré, une corneille
– *decoyed bird, a crow*
51 la hutte (hutte *f* d'affût *m*)
– *butt for shooting crows or eagle owls*
52 la meurtrière (le créneau, la guignette) * In der Jägersprache auch Waidwerk, Waidmann, Waidsack
– *gun slit*

87 Armes de chasse, matériel de chasse

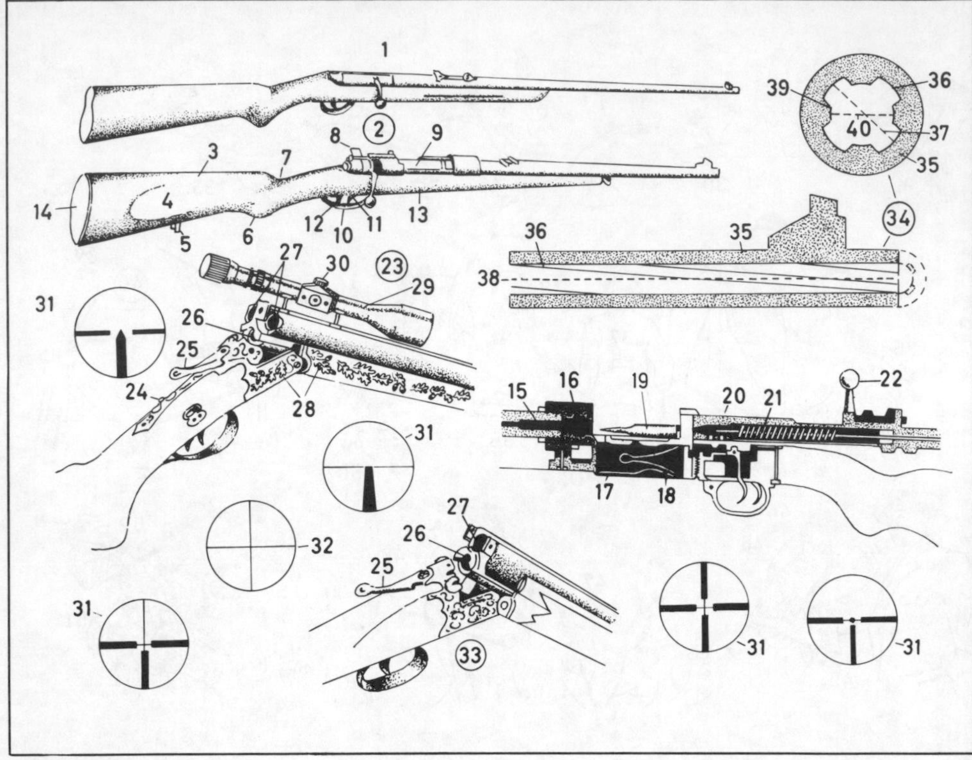

1-40 armes *f* **sportives** (fusils *m* de chasse *f*)
– ***sporting guns*** *(sporting rifles, hunting rifles)*
1 la carabine à un coup
– *single-loader (single-loading rifle)*
2 la carabine à répétition *f* automatique, une arme à feu *m* portative, une arme à plusieurs coups *m* (fusil *m* à magasin *m*)
– *repeating rifle, a small-arm (fire-arm), a repeater (magazine rifle, magazine repeater)*
3 la crosse
– *butt*
4 la joue (face *f* gauche)
– *cheek [on the left side]*
5 le porte-bretelle
– *sling ring*
6 la poignée de pistolet *m*
– *pistol grip*
7 le col de la crosse
– *small of the butt*
8 la sûreté (le verrou de sûreté *f*)
– *safety catch*
9 la culasse
– *lock*
10 le pontet
– *trigger guard*
11 la gâchette
– *second set trigger (firing trigger)*
12 la détente
– *hair trigger (set trigger)*
13 le fût
– *foregrip*
14 la plaque de couche *f* de la poignée
– *butt plate*
15 le chargeur
– *cartridge chamber*
16 la boîte de culasse *f*
– *receiver*
17 le magasin de cartouches *f*
– *magazine*
18 le ressort d'apport *m*
– *magazine spring*
19 la munition
– *ammunition (cartridge)*
20 la culasse mobile
– *chamber*
21 le percuteur
– *firing pin (striker)*
22 le levier d'armement *m*
– *bolt handle (bolt lever)*
23 le drilling (la carabine superposée à trois canons *m*), un fusil à détente *f* automatique
– *triple-barrelled (triple-barreled) rifle, a self-cocking gun*
24 la sûreté à glissière *f*
– *reversing catch (*in various guns: *safety catch)*
25 le levier de verrouillage *m*
– *sliding safety catch*
26 le canon à âme *f* rayée
– *rifle barrel (rifled barrel)*
27 le canon lisse (le canon à plombs *m*)
– *smooth-bore barrel*
28 la gravure décorative
– *chasing*
29 la lunette de visée *f*
– *telescopic sight (riflescope, telescope sight)*
30 les vis *f* micrométriques de reglage *m* de visée *f*
– *graticule adjuster screws*
31-32 le viseur
– *graticule (sight graticule)*
31 différents systèmes *m* de visée *f*
– *various graticule systems*
32 le réticule à fourchette *f*
– *cross wires (*Am. *cross hairs)*
33 le fusil à deux canons *m* superposés (le fusil à canon *m* double)
– *over-and-under shotgun*
34 le canon rayé
– *rifled gun barrel*
35 le tube (la paroi) du canon
– *barrel casing*
36 la rayure
– *rifling*
37 le calibre des rayures *f*
– *rifling calibre (*Am. *caliber)*
38 l'axe *m* de l'âme *f*
– *bore axis*
39 la paroi intérieure du canon
– *land*
40 le calibre du fusil
– *calibre (bore diameter,* Am. *caliber)*

41-48 accessoires *m* de chasse *f*
– ***hunting equipment***
41 le coutelas
– *double-edged hunting knife*
42 le poignard (le couteau de chasse *f*)
– *[single-edged] hunting knife*
43-47 appeaux *m* (appelants *m*) pour attirer le gibier
– ***calls for luring game (for calling game)***
43 l'appeau *m* pour le chevreuil
– *roe call*
44 l'appeau *m* pour le lièvre
– *hare call*
45 l'appeau *m* pour la caille
– *quail call*
46 l'appeau *m* pour le cerf
– *stag call*
47 l'appeau *m* pour la perdrix
– *partridge call*
48 le piège «col de cygne», un piège à mâchoires *f*
– *bow trap (bow gin), a jaw trap*
49 la cartouche à plombs *m*
– *small-shot cartridge*
50 la douille en carton *m*
– *cardboard case*
51 la charge de plombs *m*
– *small-shot charge*
52 la bourre
– *felt wad*
53 la poudre sans fumée *f* (poudre noire)
– *smokeless powder (*different kind: *black powder)*
54 la cartouche
– *cartridge*
55 la balle pleine
– *full-jacketed cartridge*
56 la balle à tête de plomb *m*
– *soft-lead core*
57 la charge de poudre *f*
– *powder charge*
58 le culot
– *detonator cap*
59 l'amorce *f*
– *percussion cap*
60 la trompe (le cor de chasse *f*)
– *hunting horn*
61-64 les instruments *m* de nettoyage *m*
– *rifle cleaning kit*
61 la baguette de nettoyage *m*
– *cleaning rod*
62 l'écouvillon *m* (la brosse)
– *cleaning brush*
63 l'étoupe *f*
– *cleaning tow*
64 le cordon
– *pull-through (*Am. *pull-thru)*
65 le viseur
– *sights*
66 le cran de mire *f*
– *notch (sighting notch)*
67 la planche de hausse *f*
– *back sight leaf*
68 la graduation
– *sight scale division*
69 le curseur (le coulisseau)
– *back sight slide*
70 la butée
– *notch [to hold the spring]*
71 le guidon
– *front sight (foresight)*
72 le sommet du guidon
– *bead*
73 la balistique
– ***ballistics***
74 l'horizontale *f* de l'ouverture *f*
– *azimuth*
75 l'angle *m* au niveau
– *angle of departure*
76 l'angle d'élévation *f*
– *angle of elevation*
77 la flèche
– *apex (zenith)*
78 l'angle *m* de chute *f*
– *angle of descent*
79 la courbe balistique (la trajectoire)
– *ballistic curve*

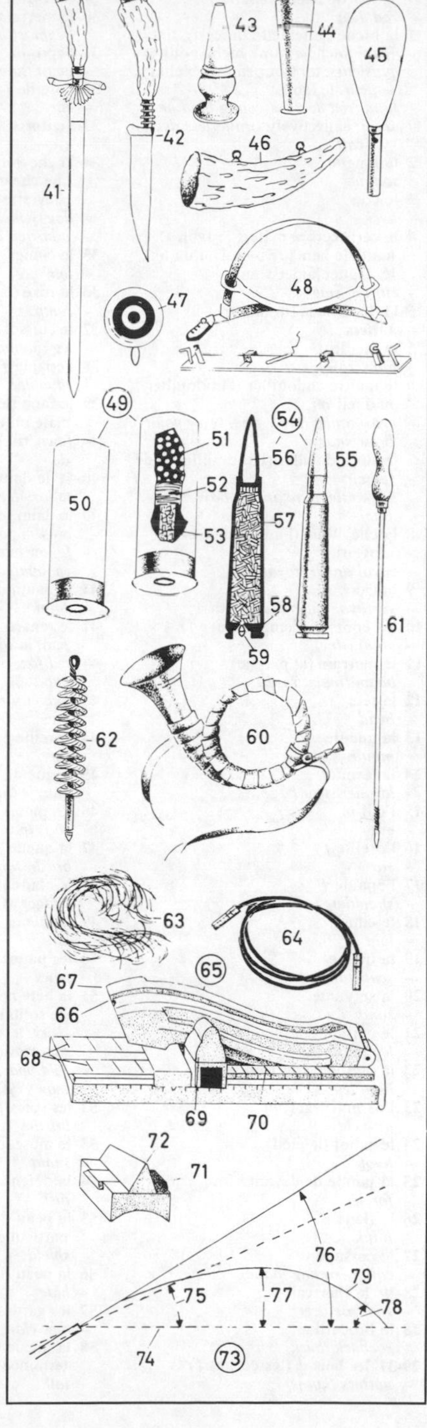

1-27 le gros gibier (grand gibier, gibier de haute vénerie *f*)
– ***red deer***
1 la biche (la femelle du cerf), une jeune biche ou une biche adulte; *plusieurs:* un troupeau de biches; *le petit:* le faon
– *hind (red deer), a young hind or a dam;* collectively: *antlerless deer,* (y.) *calf*
2 la langue
– *tongue*
3 le cou
– *neck*
4 le cerf (cerf *m* mâle); le faon mâle, le hère [de 6 mois à un an], le daguet [à deux ans]
– *rutting stag*
5-11 les bois *m* (la ramure)
– ***antlers***
5 la meule
– *burr (rose)*
6 le maître-andouiller (l'andouiller *m* d'œil *m*)
– *brow antler (brow tine, brow point, brow snag)*
7 le surandouiller (l'andouiller *m* de fer *m*)
– *bez antler (bay antler, bay, bez tine)*
8 la chevillure (l'andouiller *m* moyen)
– *royal antler (royal, tray)*
9 la trochure
– *surroyal antlers (surroyals)*
10 les épois *m* d'empaumure *f*
– *point (tine)*
11 le merrain (la perche)
– *beam (main trunk)*
12 la tête
– *head*
13 la gueule
– *mouth*
14 le larmier
– *larmier (tear bag)*
15 l'œil *m*
– *eye*
16 l'oreille *f*
– *ear*
17 l'épaule *f*
– *shoulder*
18 le cimier
– *loin*
19 la queue
– *scut (tail)*
20 la serviette
– *rump*
21 le cuissot
– *leg (haunch)*
22 la jambe de derrière *m*
– *hind leg*
23 l'os *m* (l'ergot *m*)
– *dew claw*
24 le sabot (le pied)
– *hoof*
25 la jambe de devant
– *foreleg*
26 le flanc
– *flank*
27 le corsage
– *collar (rutting mane)*
28-39 le chevreuil
– ***roe*** *(roe deer)*
28 le brocard
– *roebuck (buck)*
29-31 les bois *m* (les cornes *f*)
– ***antlers*** *(horns)*
29 la meule
– *burr (rose)*
30 le merrain avec les perlures *f*
– *beam with pearls*
31 l'époi *m*
– *point (tine)*
32 l'oreille *f*
– *ear*
33 l'œil*m*
– *eye*
34 la chevrette (le chevreuil femelle), une chevrette vierge ou une chevrette adulte
– *doe (female roe), a female fawn or a barren doe*
35 le cimier
– *loin*
36 la roze (la serviette)
– *rump*
37 le cuissot
– *leg (haunch)*
38 l'épaule *f*
– *shoulder*
39 le faon (le chevrillard), un faon mâle ou un faon femelle
– *fawn,* (m.) *young buck,* (f.) *young doe*
40-41 le daim
– *fallow deer*
40 le daim (daim mâle), un cervidé à bois *m* palmés, *fem.* la daine
– *fallow buck, a buck with palmate (palmated) antlers,* (f.) *doe*
41 la paumure (la palmature)
– *palm*
42 le renard roux (renard commun); *fem.* la renarde
– *red fox,* (m.) *dog,* (f.) *vixen,* (y.) *cub*
43 les yeux *m*
– *eyes*
44 l'oreille *f*
– *ear*
45 la gueule
– *muzzle (mouth)*
46 les pattes *f*
– *pads (paws)*
47 la queue
– *brush (tail)*
48 le blaireau
– *badger,* (f.) *sow*
49 la queue
– *tail*
50 les pattes *f*
– *paws*
51 la bête noire; *ici:* le sanglier mâle (le solitaire); *fem.* la laie; *tous les deux:* le sanglier; *le petit:* le marcassin
– *wild boar,* (m.) *boar,* (f.) *wild sow (sow),* (y.) *young boar*
52 les soies *f*
– *bristles*
53 le museau (le boutoir, le groin)
– *snout*
54 la défense
– *tusk*
55 la peau de l'épaule *f*, une peau particulièrement épaisse
– *shield*
56 la peau (le cuir)
– *hide*
57 les gardes *m* (les ergots *m*)
– *dew claw*
58 la queue en tire-bouchon *m* terminée par un panache
– *tail*
59 le lièvre de plaine *f* (l'oreillard *m*); *fem.* la hase
– *hare,* (m.) *buck,* (f.) *doe*
60 l'œil *m*
– *eye*
61 l'oreille *f*
– *ear*
62 la queue
– *scut (tail)*
63 la patte de derrière *m*
– *hind leg*
64 la patte de devant *m*
– *foreleg*
65 le lapin
– *rabbit*
66 le petit coq de bruyère *f* (le petit tétras, le tétras-lyre, le coq des bouleaux *m*)
– *blackcock*
67 la queue (la lyre)
– *tail*
68 les pennes *f* rectrices (les faucilles *f*)
– *falcate (falcated) feathers*
69 la gélinotte des bois *m* (la poule des bois *m*, la poule des coudriers *m*)
– *hazel grouse (hazel hen)*
70 la perdrix
– *partridge*
71 le fer à cheval *m*
– *horseshoe (horseshoe marking)*
72 le grand tétras (le grand coq de bruyère *f*)
– *wood grouse (capercaillie)*
73 la barbe (barbe de plumes *f*)
– *beard*
74 la tache blanche
– *axillary marking*
75 la queue en éventail *m*
– *tail (fan)*
76 les pennes *f* rémiges
– *wing (pinion)*
77 le faisan, *fem.* la faisane (le coq faisan, la poule faisane)
– *common pheasant, a pheasant,* (m.) *cock pheasant (pheasant cock),* (f.) *hen pheasant (pheasant hen)*
78 l'aigrette *f*
– *plumicorn (feathered ear, ear tuft, ear, horn)*
79 l'aile *f*
– *wing*
80 la queue
– *tail*
81 la patte
– *leg*
82 l'ergot *m*
– *spur*
83 la bécasse
– *snipe*
84 le bec
– *bill (beak)*

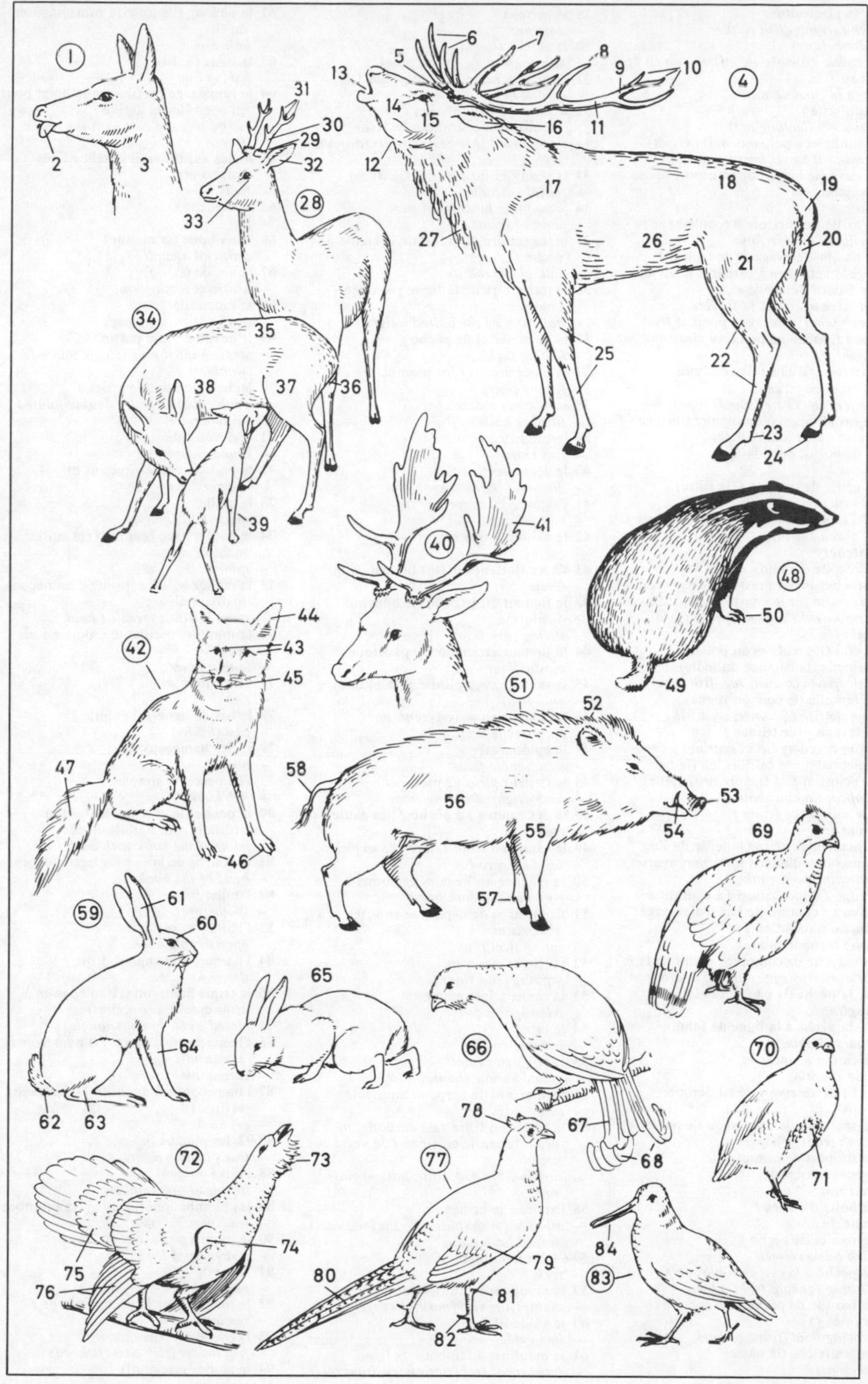
1
2
3
4
5
6
7
8
9
10
11
12
13
14
15
16
17
18
19
20
21
22
23
24
25
26
27
28
29
30
31
32
33
34
35
36
37
38
39
40
41
42
43
44
45
46
47
48
49
50
51
52
53
54
55
56
57
58
59
60
61
62
63
64
65
66
67
68
69
70
71
72
73
74
75
76
77
78
79
80
81
82
83
84

1-19 la pisciculture
– ***fish farming*** *(fish culture, pisciculture)*
1 la caisse grillagée (le châssis) au fil de l'eau *f*
– *cage in running water*
2 l'épuisette *f*
– *hand net (landing net)*
3 le tonnelet à poissons *m* (le vivier)
– *semi-oval barrel for transporting fish*
4 la cuve (le bidon) de transport *m* des poissons *m*
– *vat*
5 la grille de la rigole d'écoulement *m*
– *trellis in the overflow*
6 le bassin d'élevage *m* de truites *f*; *égal.*: l'étang *m* à carpes *f*, le vivier, le bassin d'élevage *m*, de grossissement *m*, la frayère
– *trout pond;* sim.: *carp pond, a fry pond, fattening pond, or cleansing pond*
7 l'arrivée *f* d'eau *f* (la conduite d'amenée *f* d'eau)
– *water inlet (water supply pipe)*
8 la canalisation d'écoulement *m* d'eau *f*
– *water outlet (outlet pipe)*
9 le dispositif de vidange *f*
– *monk*
10 la grille de retenue *f* (le filtre)
– *screen*
11-19 l'établissement *m* de pisciculture *f* (l'alevinage *m*)
– ***hatchery***
11 la récolte des œufs *m* (du frai) de brochet *m* par pressions *f* légères des doigts *m* sur le ventre du poisson
– *stripping the spawning pike (seed pike)*
12 le frai (les œufs *m* du poisson femelle, la laitance du mâle)
– *fish spawn (spawn, roe, fish eggs)*
13 la femelle (le poisson rogué)
– *female fish (spawner, seed fish)*
14 l'élevage *m* de truites *f*
– *trout breeding (trout rearing)*
15 l'incubateur *m* californien (le bac d'éclosion *f*, la frayère artificielle)
– *Californian incubator*
16 les œufs *m* de truite *f*
– *trout fry*
17 l'incubateur *m* (la bouteille de Zug, une bouteille sans fond *m* renversée)
– *hatching jar for pike*
18 l'auge *f* d'incubation *f* à courant *m* d'eau *f* continu (le bac d'alevinage *m*, de stabulation *f*)
– *long incubation tank*
19 la clayette de comptage *m* des œufs *m*
– *Brandstetter egg-counting board*
20-94 la pêche (la pêche à la ligne)
– ***angling***
20-31 la pêche à la ligne de fond *m*
– ***coarse fishing***
20 la canne à lancer *m*
– *line shooting*
21 le fil de réserve *f* (le fil déroulé)
– *coils*
22 le morceau de tissu *m* ou de papier *m*
– *cloth (rag) or paper*
23 le support de cannes *f* (le repose-cannes)
– *rod rest*
24 la boîte d'esches *f*
– *bait tin*
25 le panier de pêche *f*
– *fish basket (creel)*
26 la pêche à la carpe en barque *f*
– *fishing for carp from a boat*
27 la barque de pêche *f* (le canot à rames *f*)
– *rowing boat (fishing boat)*
28 la bourriche (la nasse)
– *keep net*
29 le carrelet
– *drop net*
30 la perche (la gaffe)
– *pole (punt pole, quant pole)*
31 l'épervier *m* (le filet de pêche *f*)
– *casting net*
32 le lancer à deux mains *f* avec moulinet *m* à tambour *m* fixe
– *two-handed side cast with fixed-spool reel*
33 la position initiale (de départ *m*)
– *initial position*
34 le point de lancement *m*
– *point of release*
35 la trajectoire du scion de la canne à pêche *f*
– *path of the rod tip*
36 la trajectoire de la ligne plombée amorcée
– *trajectory of the baited weight*
37-94 le matériel de pêche *f*
– ***fishing tackle***
37 la pince à serrer les plombs *m*
– *fishing pliers*
38 le couteau à découper
– *filleting knife*
39 le couteau à écailler
– *fish knife*
40 le dégorgeoir
– *disgorger (hook disgorger)*
41 l'aiguille *f* à amorcer
– *bait needle*
42 le baillon à brochet *m*
– *gag*
43-48 les flotteurs *m* (les bouchons *m*)
– ***floats***
43 le flotteur en liège *m* (le bouchon) fusiforme
– *sliding cork float*
44 le flotteur en matière *f* plastique
– *plastic float*
45 le flotteur avec plume *f* (la plume)
– *quill float*
46 le flotteur en polystyrène *m*
– *polystyrene float*
47 le buldo oval
– *oval bubble float*
48 le flotteur-glisseur plombé
– *lead-weighted sliding float*
49-58 les cannes *f* à pêche *f* (les gaules *f*)
– ***rods***
49 la canne en fibre *f* de verre *m* plein
– *solid glass rod*
50 la poignée en liège *m* aggloméré
– *cork handle (cork butt)*
51 l'anneau *m* de départ *m* en acier *m* à ressorts *m*
– *spring-steel ring*
52 la tête de scion *m*
– *top ring (end ring)*
53 la canne télescopique
– *telescopic rod*
54 le brin
– *rod section*
55 la poignée gainée
– *bound handle (bound butt)*
56 l'anneau *m* de corps *m* amovible
– *ring*
57 la canne en fibre *f* de carbone *m*; *égal.*: la canne en fibre *f* de verre *m* creux
– *carbon-fibre rod;* sim.: *hollow glass rod*
58 l'anneau *m* bridge
– *all-round ring (butt ring for long cast), a steel bridge ring*
59-64 les moulinets *m*
– ***reels***
59 le moulinet à multiplication *f*
– *multiplying reel (multiplier reel)*
60 le guide-fil
– *line guide*
61 le moulinet à tambour *m* fixe
– *fixed-spool reel (stationary-drum reel)*
62 le pick-up (l'anse *f* de ramassage *m* du fil)
– *bale arm*
63 la ligne (le fil)
– *fishing line*
64 le ramassage du fil avec le doigt pour en contrôler la dérive
– *controlling the cast with the index finger*
65-76 les appâts *m* (les esches *f*, les leurres *m*)
– ***baits***
65 la mouche
– *fly*
66 la nymphe (la manne)
– *artificial nymph*
67 le ver de terre *f*
– *artificial earthworm*
68 la sauterelle
– *artificial grasshopper*
69 le devon en une partie
– *single-jointed plug (single-jointed wobbler)*
70 le devon en deux parties *f*
– *double-jointed plug (double-jointed wobbler)*
71 le devon sphérique
– *round wobbler*
72 le poisson cuiller imitant un vif
– *wiggler*
73 la cuiller
– *spoon bait (spoon)*
74 la cuiller avec écailles *f* (la cuiller tachetée)
– *spinner*
75 la cuiller écaillée munie d'hameçons *m* dissimulés
– *spinner with concealed hook*
76 la monture oscillante à poisson *m* mort
– *long spinner*
77 l'émerillon *m*
– *swivel*
78 le bas de ligne *f* (l'empile *f*)
– *cast (leader)*
79-87 les hameçons *m*
– ***hooks***
79 l'hameçon *m* simple
– *fish hook*
80 la pointe (le crochet, le dard) à ardillon *m* (à barbillon *m*)
– *point of the hook with barb*
81 la courbe de la tige (la tige courbée)
– *bend of the hook*
82 l'œillet *m*
– *spade (eye)*
83 l'hameçon *m* double
– *open double hook*
84 l'hameçon *m* anglais droit
– *limerick*
85 le triple hameçon (l'hameçon *m* à trois crochets *m* scellés)
– *closed treble hook (triangle)*
86 l'hameçon *m* à carpe *f* (l'hameçon *m* à cran *m*)
– *carp hook*
87 l'hameçon *m* à anguille *f* (l'hameçon *m* droit)
– *eel hook*
88-92 les plombs *m*
– ***leads*** *(lead weights)*
88 l'olive *f*
– *oval lead (oval sinker)*
89 les plombs sphériques *m* (la plombée)
– *lead shot*
90 le plomb piriforme
– *pear-shaped lead*
91 la sonde
– *plummet*
92 le plomb pour la pêche en mer *f*
– *sea lead*
93 l'échelle *f* à poissons *m*
– *fish ladder (fish pass, fish way)*
94 le guideau (le gord)
– *stake net*

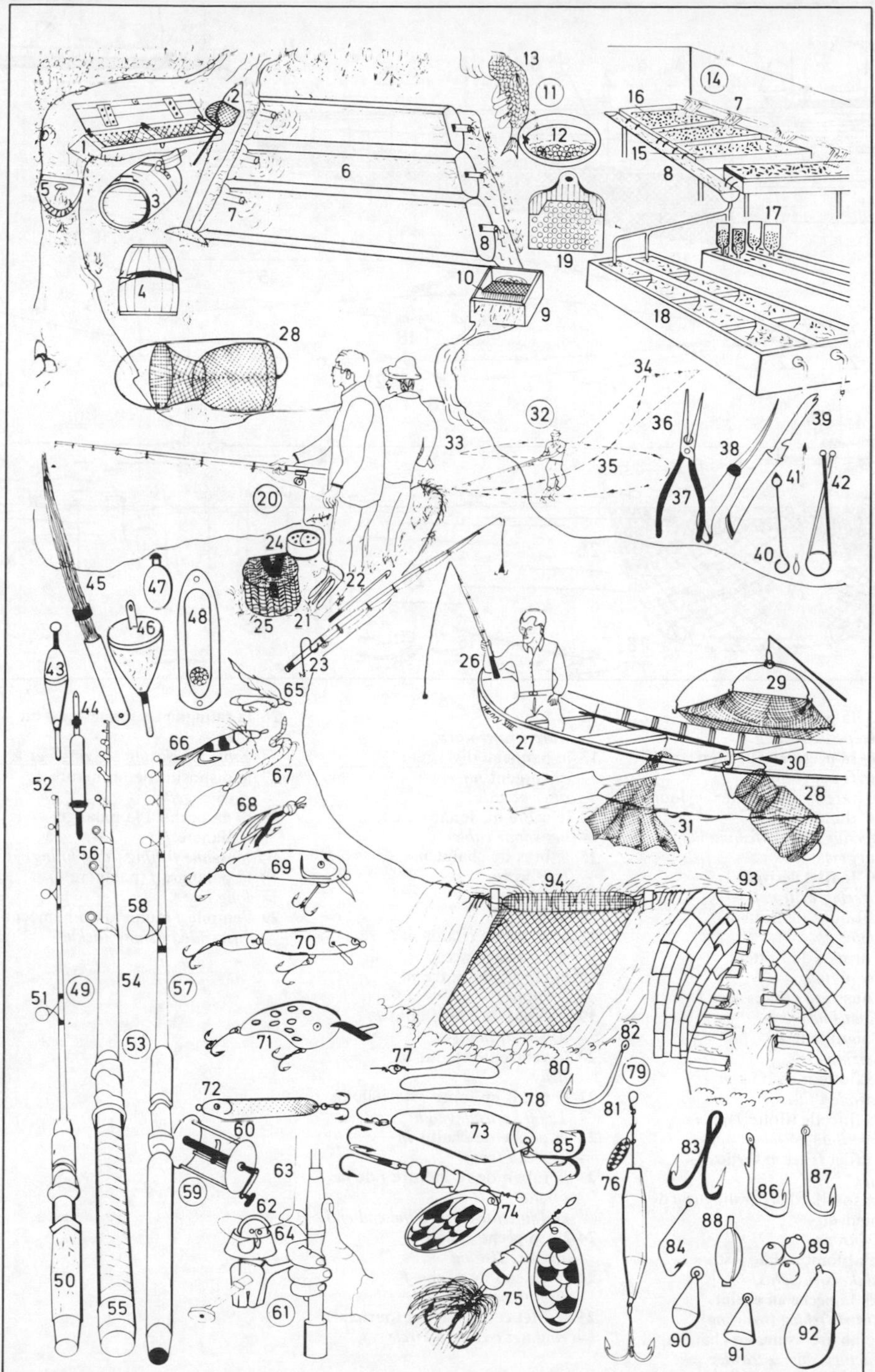

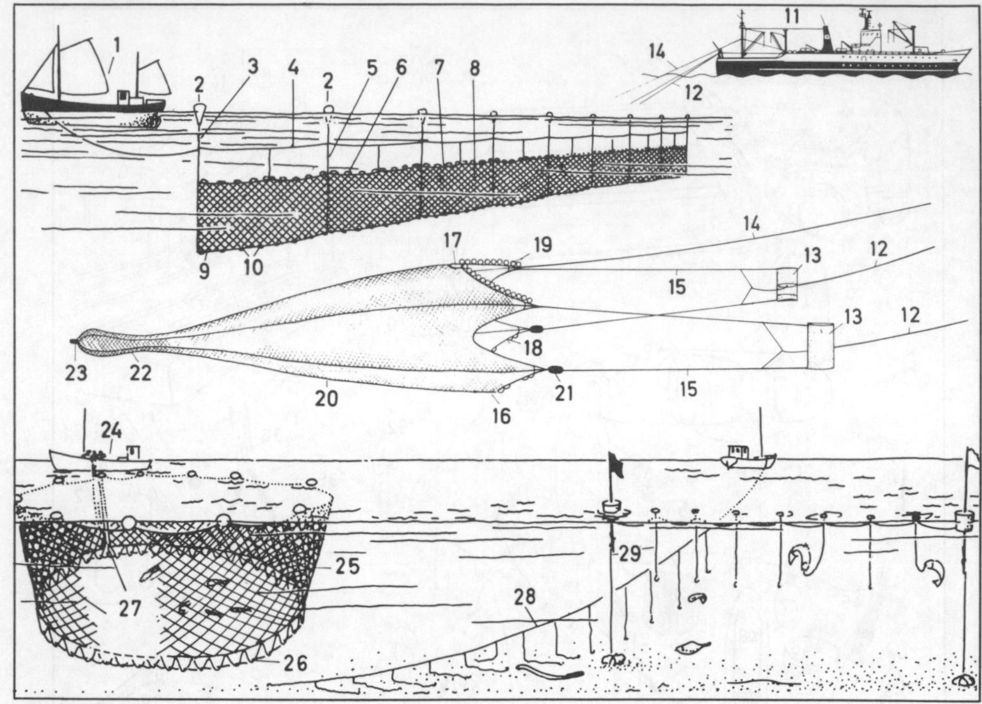

1-23 la pêche hauturière
– ***deep-sea fishing***
1-10 la pêche au filet dérivant
– ***drift net fishing***
1 le harenguier (drifter *m*, lougre *m*, dundee *m*)
– *herring lugger (fishing lugger, lugger)*
2-10 le filet dérivant
– ***herring drift net***
2 la bouée (le flotteur)
– *buoy*
3 l'orin *m* du flotteur
– *buoy rope*
4 l'aussière *f* (haussière *f*)
– *float line*
5 l'aiguillette *f*
– *seizing*
6 le flotteur en bois *m*
– *wooden float*
7 la fincelle (flotte *f*)
– *headline*
8 le filet (filet *m* vertical)
– *net*
9 la souillardière (ralingue *f* de pied *m*)
– *footrope*
10 les plombs *m* de lest *m*
– *sinkers (weights)*
11-23 la pêche au chalut
– ***trawl fishing*** *(trawling)*
11 le navire usine, un chalutier
– *factory ship, a trawler*
12 la fune
– *warp (trawl warp)*
13 le panneau divergent (divergent *m*)
– *otter boards*
14 le câble du sonar de chalut *m*
– *net sonar cable*
15 le bras de chalut *m*
– *wire warp*
16 l'aile *f*
– *wing*
17 le sonar de chalut *m*
– *net sonar device*
18 la corde de ventre *m*
– *footrope*
19 les sphères *f* de chalut *m*
– *spherical floats*
20 le ventre de chalut *m*
– *belly*
21 le poids en fonte *f* de 1800 kg
– *1,800 kg iron weight*
22 la poche de chalut *m*
– *cod end (cod)*
23 le ruban de fermeture *f* de la poche
– *cod line for closing the cod end*
24-29 la pêche côtière
– ***inshore fishing***
24 le bateau de pêche *f*
– *fishing boat*
25 le filet cernant (filet tournant)
– *ring net cast in a circle*
26 la ralingue de fermeture *f* du filet
– *cable for closing the ring net*
27 le dispositif de fermeture *f*
– *closing gear*
28-29 la pêche à la palangre (palancre *f*)
– *long-line fishing (long-lining)*
28 la palangre *f* (palancre *f*)
– *long line*
29 l'empile *f* munie d'un hameçon
– *suspended fishing tackle*

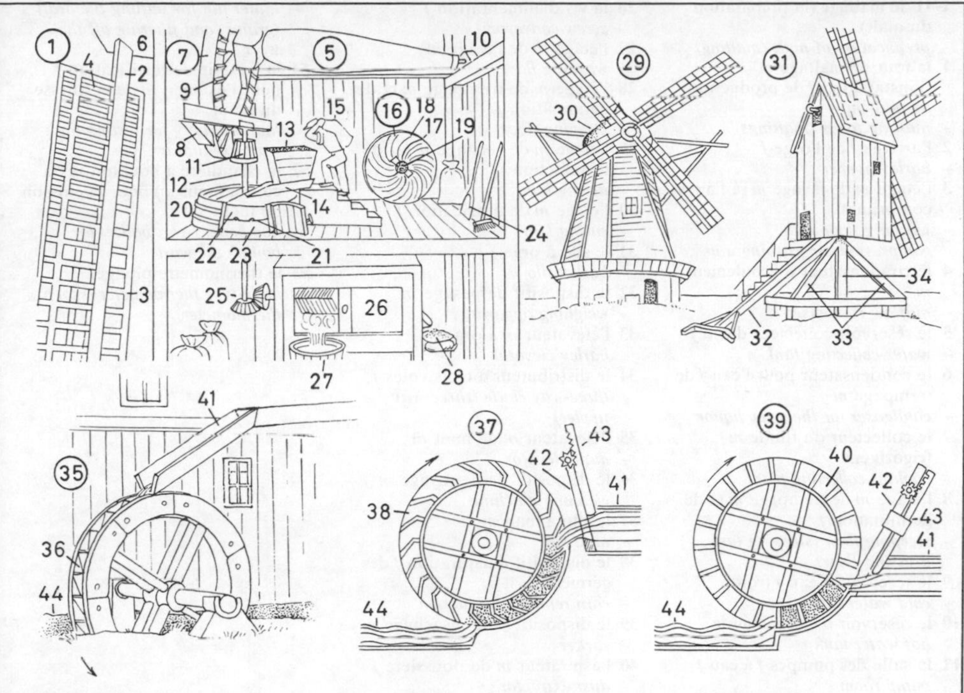

1-34 le moulin à vent *m*
– ***windmill***
1 l'aile *f* du moulin à vent *m* (le volant du moulin à vent *m*)
– *windmill vane (windmill sail, windmill arm)*
2 le bras du volant
– *stock (middling, back, radius)*
3 la lamelle (le cadre)
– *frame*
4 le volet
– *shutter*
5 l'arbre *m* (entraîné par les ailes *f*)
– *wind shaft (sail axle)*
6 la tête de l'aile *f*
– *sail top*
7 la roue à dents *f* de bois *m*
– *brake wheel*
8 le frein de la roue
– *brake*
9 l'alluchon *m* (la dent de bois *m*)
– *wooden cog*
10 la crapaudine (le palier)
– *pivot bearing (step bearing)*
11 l'engrenage *m* du moulin à vent *m*
– *wallower*
12 le gros fer
– *mill spindle*
13 la trémie
– *hopper*
14 le sabot de la trémie
– *shoe (trough, spout)*
15 le meunier
– *miller*
16 la meule
– *millstone*
17 la rainure
– *furrow (flute)*
18 le tranchant
– *master furrow*
19 l'œillard *m* de meule *f*
– *eye*
20 la cuve (la caisse des meules *f*)
– *hurst (millstone casing)*
21 la paire de meules *f*
– *set of stones (millstones)*
22 la meule courante (la meule supérieure)
– *runner (upper millstone)*
23 la meule dormante (la meule gisante)
– *bed stone (lower stone, bedder)*
24 la pelle en bois *m*
– *wooden shovel*
25 l'engrenage *m* conique (l'engrenage *m* d'angle *m*)
– *bevel gear (bevel gearing)*
26 le crible rond (le sas)
– *bolter (sifter)*
27 le baquet en bois *m*
– *wooden tub (wooden tun)*
28 la farine
– *flour*
29 le moulin (à vent *m*) hollandais
– *smock windmill (Dutch windmill)*
30 la calotte pivotante du moulin
– *rotating (revolving) windmill cap*
31 le moulin sur pile *f*
– *post windmill (German windmill)*
32 la queue du moulin
– *tailpole (pole)*
33 le pied sur pile *f*
– *base*
34 le pivot central
– *post*

35-44 le moulin à eau *f* (le moulin hydraulique)
– ***watermill***
35 la roue à augets *m* (la roue à godets *m*) mue en dessus, une roue de moulin *m*, une roue hydraulique
– *overshot mill wheel (high-breast mill wheel), a mill wheel (waterwheel)*
36 l'auget *m* (le godet)
– *bucket (cavity)*
37 la roue hydraulique mue dans le milieu
– *middleshot mill wheel (breast mill wheel)*
38 l'aube *f* courbée
– *curved vane*
39 la roue hydraulique mue en dessous
– *undershot mill wheel*
40 l'aube *f* droite (l'aube *f* rectiligne)
– *flat vane*
41 le bief d'amont *m*
– *headrace (discharge flume)*
42 le batardeau de moulin *m*
– *mill weir*
43 le déversoir
– *overfall (water overfall)*
44 le bief du moulin (le bief d'aval *m*)
– *millstream (millrace,* Am. *raceway)*

1-41 le maltage (la préparation du malt)
– ***preparation of malt** (malting)*
1 la tour de maltage *m* (l'installation *f* de production *f* de malt *m*)
– *malting tower (maltings)*
2 l'arrivée *f* de l'orge *f*
– *barley hopper*
3 l'étage *m* de lavage *m* (à l'air *m* comprimé)
– *washing floor with compressed-air washing unit*
4 le condensateur d'écoulement *m*
– *outflow condenser*
5 le réservoir-collecteur d'eau *f*
– *water-collecting tank*
6 le condensateur pour l'eau *f* de trempage *m*
– *condenser for the steep liquor*
7 le collecteur du fluide *m* frigorigène
– *coolant-collecting plant*
8 l'étage *m* de trempage *m* et de germination *f*
– *steeping floor (steeping tank, dressing floor)*
9 le réservoir d'eau *f* froide
– *cold water tank*
10 le réservoir d'eau *f* chaude
– *hot water tank*
11 la salle des pompes *f* à eau *f*
– *pump room*
12 l'installation *f* pneumatique
– *pneumatic plant*
13 l'installation *f* hydraulique
– *hydraulic plant*
14 la cheminée d'aération *f*
– *ventilation shaft (air inlet and outlet)*
15 le ventilateur
– *exhaust fan*
16-18 les étages *m* de touraille *f* (le séchoir de malt *m*)
– ***kilning floors***
16 l'étage *m* de séchage *m* (et de torréfaction *f*)
– *drying floor*
17 le ventilateur de touraillage *m*
– *burner ventilator*
18 l'étage *m* de dessication *f*
– *curing floor*
19 le conduit d'évacuation *f* du séchoir *m*
– *outlet duct from the kiln*
20 la trémie de malt *m*
– *finished malt collecting hopper*
21 le poste de transformateurs *m*
– *transformer station*
22 les compresseurs frigorifiques
– *cooling compressors*
23 le malt vert (l'orge *f* germante)
– *green malt (germinated barley)*
24 le système de touraille *f* rotatif
– *turner (plough)*
25 le poste de commande *f* avec tableau *m* synoptique
– *central control room with flow diagram*
26 la vis d'alimentation *f*
– *screw conveyor*
27 l'étage *m* de lavage *m*
– *washing floor*
28 l'étage *m* de trempage *m* et de germination *f*
– *steeping floor*
29 l'étage *m* de séchage *m* (et de torréfaction *f*)
– *drying kiln*
30 l'étage *m* de dessication *f*
– *curing kiln*
31 le silo à orge *f*
– *barley silo*
32 le dispositif de pesage *m*
– *weighing apparatus*
33 l'élévateur *m* à orge *f*
– *barley elevator*
34 le distributeur à trois voies *f*
– *three-way chute (three-way tippler)*
35 l'élévateur *m* de malt *m*
– *malt elevator*
36 le dispositif de nettoyage *m*
– *cleaning machine*
37 le silo à malt *m*
– *malt silo*
38 le dispositif d'aspiration *f* des germes *m*
– *corn removal by suction*
39 le dispositif *m* d'ensachage *m*
– *sacker*
40 l'aspirateur *m* de poussière *f*
– *dust extractor*
41 la réception de l'orge *f*
– *barley reception*
42-53 la cuisson dans la salle de brassage *m*
– ***mashing process in the mashhouse***
42 l'hydrateur *m* pour le mélange de farine *f* et d'eau *f*
– *premasher (converter) for mixing grist and water*
43 le macérateur pour l'empâtage *m* de la farine
– *mash tub (mash tun) for mashing the malt*
44 la cuve-matière (la chaudière) pour la cuisson de la trempe
– *mash copper (mash tun,* Am. *mash kettle) for boiling the mash*
45 la calotte (le dôme) de la cuve
– *dome of the tun*
46 l'agitateur *m*
– *propeller (paddle)*
47 la porte coulissante
– *sliding door*
48 la conduite d'amenée *f* d'eau *f*
– *water (liquor) supply pipe*
49 le brasseur (le maître-brasseur, le chef-brasseur)
– *brewer (master brewer, masher)*
50 la cuve de clarification *f* pour laisser se déposer la drêche (les résidus *m*) et pour filtrer le moût
– *lauter tun for settling the draff (grains) and filtering off the wort*
51 la batterie de rectification *f* pour l'examen *m* de la finesse du moût
– *lauter battery for testing the wort for quality*
52 la chaudière à houblon *m* (la cuve à moût *m*) pour la cuisson du moût
– *hop boiler (wort boiler) for boiling the wort*
53 le thermomètre plongeur
– *ladle-type thermometer (scoop thermometer)*

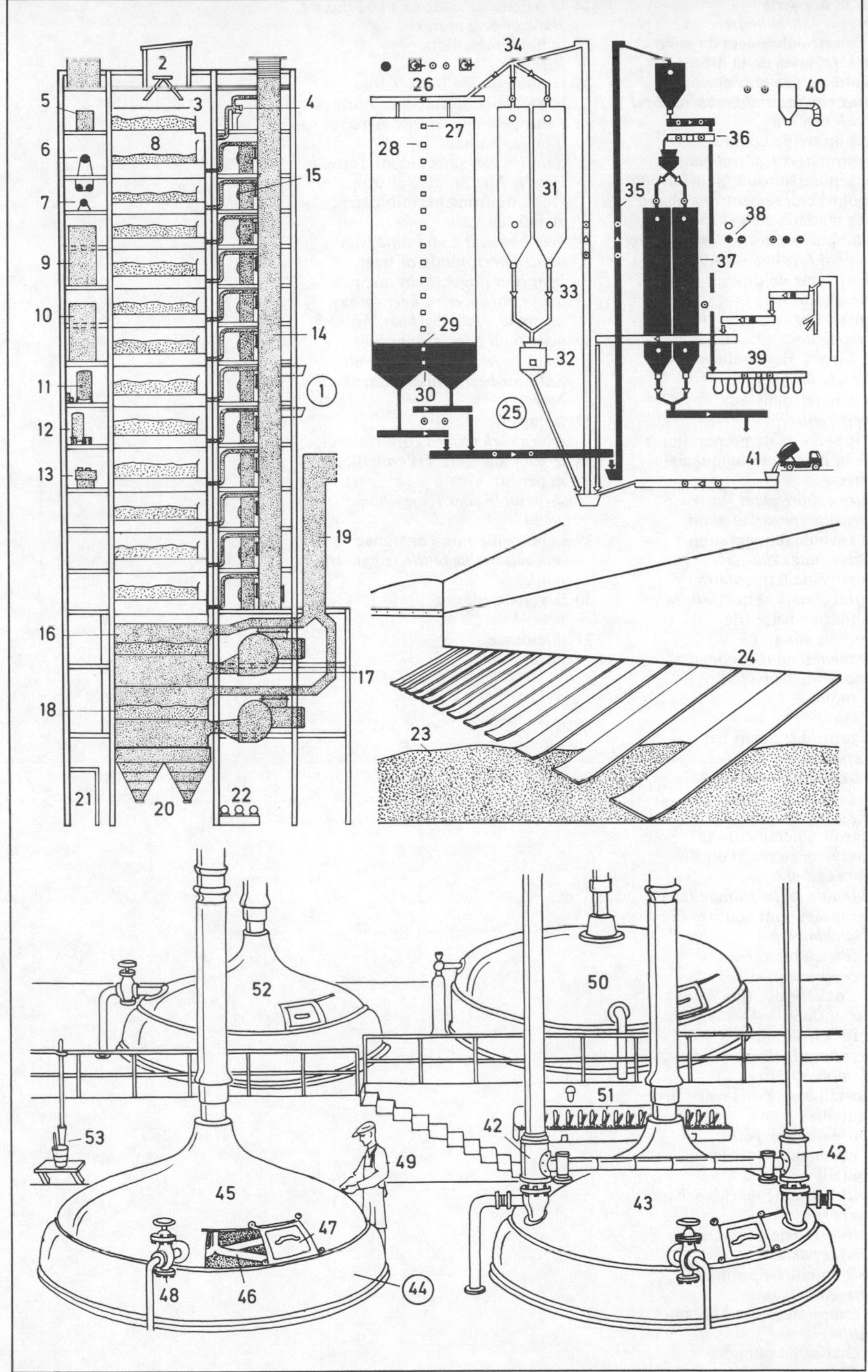
1
2
3
4
5
6
7
8
9
10
11
12
13
14
15
16
17
18
19
20
21
22
23
24
25
26
27
28
29
30
31
32
33
34
35
36
37
38
39
40
41
42
43
44
45
46
47
48
49
50
51
52
53

1-31 la brasserie
– ***brewery*** *(brewhouse)*
1-5 le refroidissement du moût et la séparation de la drêche (les matières *f* en suspension *f*)
– ***wort cooling and break removal*** *(trub removal)*
1 le pupitre de commande *f*
– *control desk (control panel)*
2 le séparateur du type whirlpool (pour l'enlèvement *m* à chaud des matières *f* en suspension *f*)
– *whirlpool separator for removing the hot break (hot trub)*
3 le système de dosage *m* du kieselguhr *m*
– *measuring vessel for the kieselguhr*
4 le filtre à kieselguhr *m*
– *kieselguhr filter*
5 le bac refroidisseur
– *wort cooler*
6 l'appareil *m* de préparation *f* de la levure biologiquement pure
– *pure culture plant for yeast (yeast propagation plant)*
7 la cave de fermentation *f*
– *fermenting cellar*
8 la cuve de fermentation *f*
– *fermentation vessel (fermenter)*
9 le thermomètre (de fermentation *f*)
– *fermentation thermometer (mash thermometer)*
10 le moût
– *mash*
11 le refroidissement par serpentin *m*
– *refrigeration system*
12 la cave de stockage *m*
– *lager cellar*
13 le trou d'homme (le sas) pour l'accès *m* au réservoir de stockage *m*
– *manhole to the storage tank*
14 le robinet pour soutirer la bière
– *broaching tap*
15 le filtre à bière *f*
– *beer filter*
16 le stockage des fûts *m*
– *barrel store*
17 le fût en aluminium *m*
– *beer barrel, an aluminium* (Am. *aluminum) barrel*
18 l'installation *f* de lavage *m* des bouteilles *f*
– *bottle-washing plant*
19 la machine à laver les bouteilles *f*
– *bottle-washing machine (bottle washer)*
20 l'armoire *f* de commande *f*
– *control panel*
21 les bouteilles *f* propres
– *cleaned bottles*
22 le remplissage des bouteilles *f*
– *bottling*
23 le chariot élévateur
– *forklift truck (fork truck, forklift)*
24 la palette de cartons *m* de bière *f*
– *stack of beer crates*
25 la boîte métallique
– *beer can*
26 la bouteille de bière *f*, une bouteille conforme aux normes *f* européennes; *sortes de bière:* blonde, brune, Pils, munichoise, sans alcool, forte, Porter, Ale, Stout, Salvator, Gose, de froment, faiblement alcoolisée
– *beer bottle, a Eurobottle with bottled beer;* kinds of beer: *light beer (lager, light ale, pale ale or bitter), dark beer (brown ale, mild), Pilsener beer, Munich beer, malt beer, strong beer (bock beer), porter, ale, stout, Salvator beer, wheat beer, small beer*
27 la capsule
– *crown cork (crown cork closure)*
28 le pack de bière *f* (l'emballage *m* perdu)
– *disposable pack (carry-home pack)*
29 la bouteille non consignée
– *non-returnable bottle (single-trip bottle)*
30 le verre à bière *f*
– *beer glass*
31 la mousse
– *head*

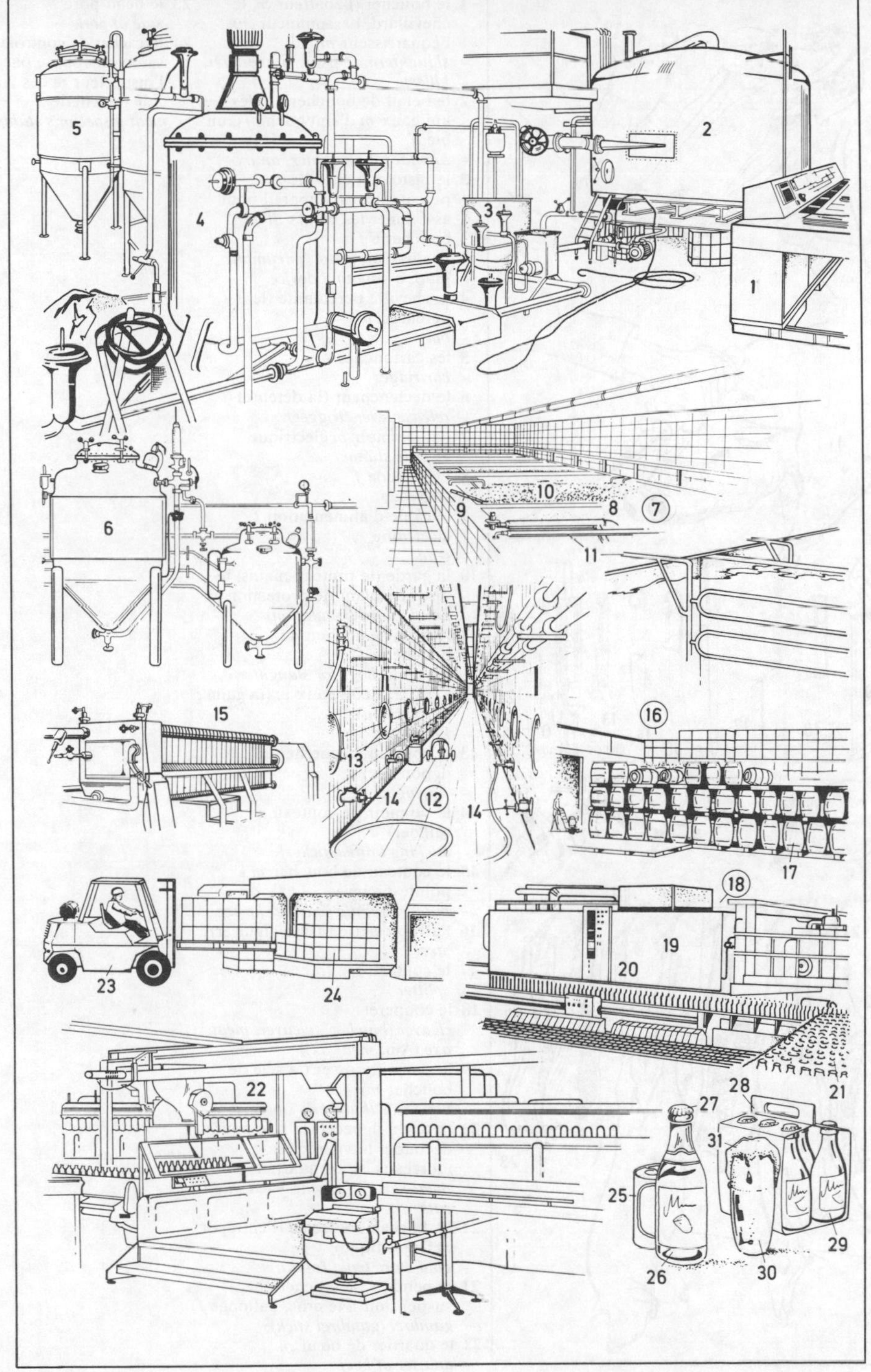
1
2
3
4
5
6
7
8
9
10
11
12
13
14
14
15
16
17
18
19
20
21
22
23
24
25
26
27
28
29
30
31

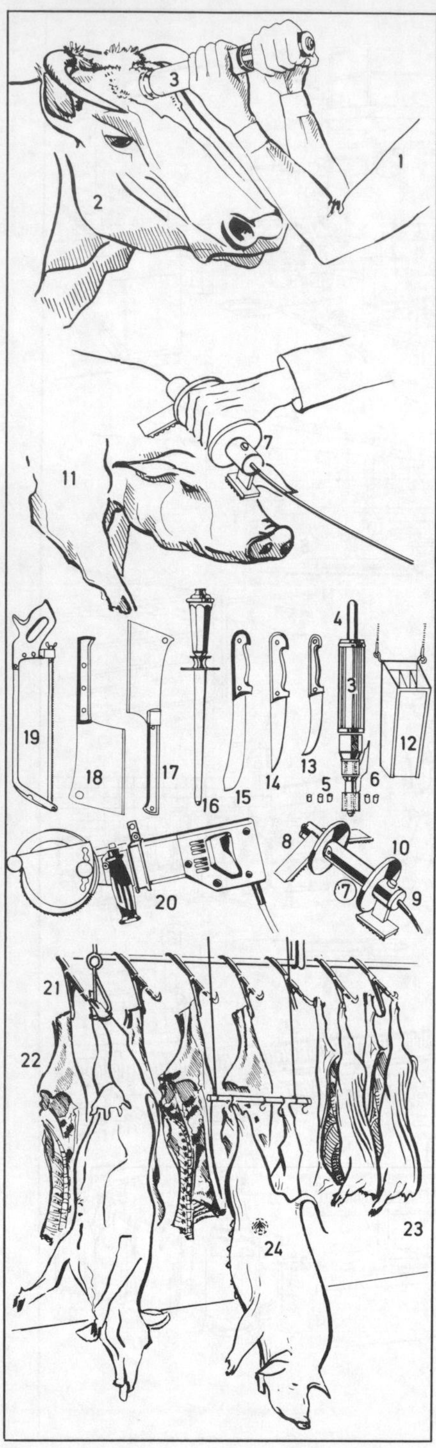

1 le boucher (l'abatteur *m*, le chevillard, l'assommeur *m*, l'équarrisseur *m*)
– *slaughterman (*Am. *slaughterer, killer)*

2 le bétail de boucherie *f* (les animaux *m* d'embouche *f*), un bœuf
– *animal for slaughter, an ox*

3 le pistolet à cheville *f* percutante, un appareil pour assommer les bœufs *m* de boucherie *f*
– *captive-bolt pistol (pneumatic gun), a stunning device*

4 la cheville percutante (le percuteur)
– *bolt*

5 les cartouches *f*
– *cartridges*

6 le déclencheur (la détente)
– *release lever (trigger)*

7 l'assommoir *m* électrique
– *electric stunner*

8 l'électrode *f*
– *electrode*

9 le câble d'alimentation *f* électrique
– *lead*

10 la garde (le protège-mains, le disque isolant de protection *f*)
– *hand guard (insulation)*

11 le porc (le cochon de boucherie *f*)
– *pig (*Am. *hog) for slaughter*

12 l'étui *m* à couteaux *m* (la gaine, le fourreau)
– *knife case*

13 le couteau à écorcher (à dépouiller)
– *flaying knife*

14 le saignoir (le couteau à saigner)
– *sticking knife (sticker)*

15 le couteau de boucher *m* à pointe *f* relevée
– *butcher's knife (butcher knife)*

16 l'affiloir *m* (le fusil à aiguiser)
– *steel*

17 le couteau-fendoir
– *splitter*

18 le couperet
– *cleaver (butcher's cleaver, meat axe (*Am. *meat ax))*

19 la scie à désosser (la scie de boucher *m*)
– *bone saw (butcher's saw)*

20 la scie à dépecer (la scie pour découper la viande en morceaux *m*, en quartiers *m*)
– *meat saw for sawing meat into cuts*

21-24 la chambre froide (l'entrepôt *m* frigorifique)
– ***cold store*** *(cold room)*

21 le pendoir (le crochet de suspension *f*, le croc, l'allonge *f*)
– *gambrel (gambrel stick)*

22 le quartier de bœuf *m*
– *quarter of beef*

23 le demi-porc
– *side of pork*

24 le cachet de contrôle *m* sanitaire apposé par l'inspecteur *m* des viandes *f* de boucherie *f*
– *meat inspector's stamp*

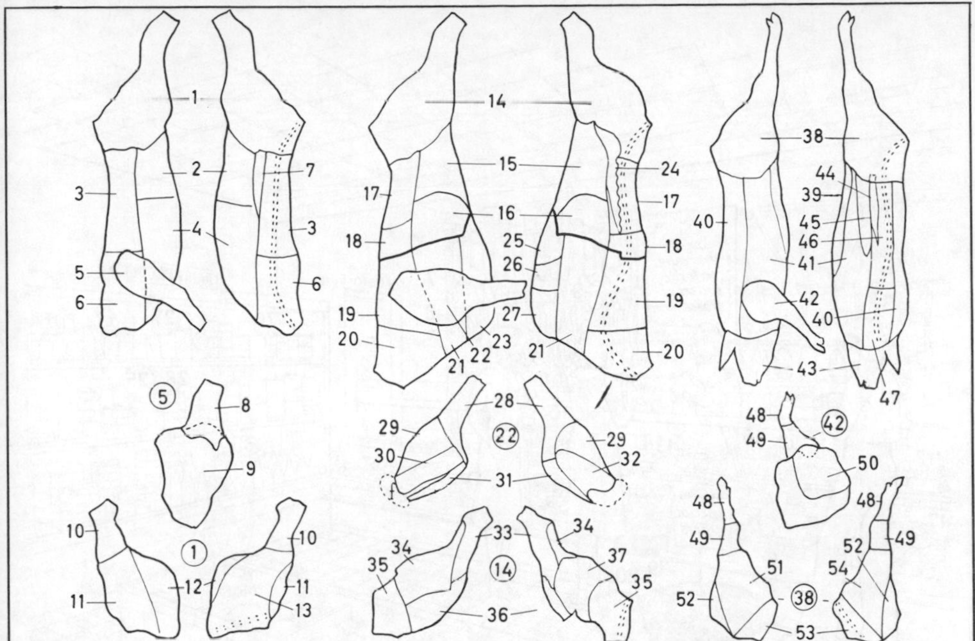

à gauche: la viande;
à droite: les os *m*
left: meat side
right: bone side

1-13 le veau
– animal: ***calf;*** meat: ***veal***
1 le cuisseau avec le jarret de derrière *m*
– *leg with hind knuckle*
2 le flanchet
– *flank*
3 la longe avec les côtes *f* de veau *m*
– *loin and rib*
4 la poitrine de veau *m* (le tendron)
– *breast (breast of veal)*
5 l'épaule *f* avec le jarret (avec les côtes *f* découvertes)
– *neck with scrag (scrag end)*
7 le filet de veau *m*
– *best end of loin (of loin of veal)*
8 le jarret de devant *m*
– *fore knuckle*
9 l'épaule *f* de veau *m*
– *shoulder*
10 le jarret de derrière *m*
– *hind knuckle*
11 la sous-noix
– *roasting round (oyster round)*
12 la noix pâtissière
– *cutlet for frying or braising*
13 le quasi
– *undercut (fillet)*

14-37 le bœuf
– animal: ***ox;*** meat: ***beef***
14 la cuisse avec la jambe (le jarret, le trumeau) de derrière *m*
– *round with rump and shank*
15-16 les flanchets *m*
– *flank*
15 le flanchet
– *thick flank*
16 le tendron
– *thin flank*
17 l'aloyau *m*
– *sirloin*
18 l'entrecôte *f* (la côte première, la côte couverte à la noix)
– *prime rib (fore ribs, prime fore rib)*
19 la surlonge (les basses côtes *f*, le paleron)
– *middle rib and chuck*
20 le collier
– *neck*
21 le plat de côtes *f* découvert
– *flat rib*
22 l'épaule *f* avec la jambe (le jarret, le trumeau) de devant *m*
– *leg of mutton piece (bladebone) with shin*
23 la poitrine de bœuf *m*
– *brisket (brisket of beef)*
24 le filet de bœuf *m*
– *fillet (fillet of beef)*
25 la poitrine (morceau *m* arrière, le tendron)
– *hind brisket*
26 la poitrine (morceau *m* intermédiaire, le tendron)
– *middle brisket*
27 la poitrine proprement dite (le poitrail)
– *breastbone*
28 la jambe (le jarret) de devant *m* (la crosse, le trumeau)
– *shin*
29 la macreuse
– *leg of mutton piece*
30 le paleron
– *part of bladebone*
31 le plat de côtes *f*
– *part of top rib*
32 le jumeau
– *part of bladebone*
33 le gîte-gîte
– *shank*
34 le gîte à la noix
– *silverside*
35 la culotte (le cimier de bœuf *m*)
– *rump*
36 la tranche grasse
– *thick flank*
37 le tende de tranche *f*
– *top side*

38-54 le porc
– animal: ***pig;*** meat: ***pork***
38 le jambon avec le jambonneau et le pied
– *leg with knuckle and trotter*
39 le ventre
– *ventral part of the belly*
40 le lard dorsal (la bardière, la longe)
– *back fat*
41 la poitrine de porc *m*
– *belly*
42 l'épaule *f* avec le jambonneau et le pied
– *bladebone with knuckle and trotter*
43 la tête de porc *m*
– *head (pig's head)*
44 le filet de porc *m*
– *fillet (fillet of pork)*
45 la panne de porc *m*
– *leaf fat (pork flare)*
46 la côtelette de porc *m*
– *loin (pork loin)*
47 l'échine de porc *m*
– *spare rib*
48 le pied de porc *m*
– *trotter*
49 le jambonneau
– *knuckle*
50 la palette
– *butt*
51 le jambon de manche *m*
– *fore end (ham)*
52 la noix de jambon *m*
– *round end for boiling*
53 la pointe de filet *m*
– *fat end*
54 le jambon démangé
– *gammon steak*

1-30 la boucherie-charcuterie
– *butcher's shop*
1-4 les morceaux *m* **de viande** *f*
– *meat*
1 le jambon à l'os *m*
ham on the bone
2 la flèche de lard *m* (le quartier de lard *m*, la tranche de bacon *m*)
– *flitch of bacon*
3 la viande séchée (la viande fumée)
– *smoked meat*
4 le morceau de filet *m*
– *piece of loin (piece of sirloin)*
5 le saindoux (l'axonge *f*)
– *lard*
6-11 les saucisses *f* **(la charcuterie)**
– *sausages*
6 l'étiquette *f* de prix *m*
– *price label*
7 la mortadelle
– *mortadella*
8 la petite saucisse à bouillir; *sortes f:* la saucisse de Vienne, la saucisse de Francfort, la saucisse de Strasbourg
– *scalded sausage;* kinds: *Vienna sausage (Wiener), Frankfurter sausage (Frankfurter)*
9 le fromage de tête *f*
– *collared pork* (Am. *headcheese)*
10 la saucisse longue en anneau *m* (la saucisse de Lyon)
– *ring of [Lyoner] sausage*
11 la saucisse à griller
– *pork sausages*; also *beef sausages*
12 la vitrine réfrigérante
– *cold shelves*
13 la salade de viande *f*
– *meat salad (diced meat salad)*
14 la viande froide en tranches *f* (la charcuterie en tranches *f*)
– *cold meats (Am. cold cuts)*
15 le pâté (la terrine)
– *pâté*
16 la viande hachée (le hachis)
– *mince (mincemeat, minced meat)*
17 le jambonneau
– *knuckle of pork*
18 la corbeille d'offres *f* spéciales (de promotions *f*)
– *basket for special offers*
19 la liste des prix *m* de promotion *f*
– *price list for special offers*
20 le produit en promotion *f*
– *special offer*
21 le congélateur
– *freezer*
22 le rôti préemballé
– *pre-packed joints*
23 le plat préparé (cuisiné) surgelé (congelé)
– *deep-frozen ready-to-eat meal*
24 le poulet
– *chicken*
25 les conserves *f* (les conserves *f* longue durée *f*; *avec date f limite de vente f:* semi-conserves f)
– *canned food*
26 la boîte de conserve *f*
– *can*
27 la boîte de conserve *f* de légumes *m*
– *canned vegetables*
28 la boîte de conserve *f* de poisson *m*
– *canned fish*
29 le bocal de sauce *f* remoulade
salad cream
30 les boissons *f* rafraîchissantes (désaltérantes)
– *soft drinks*

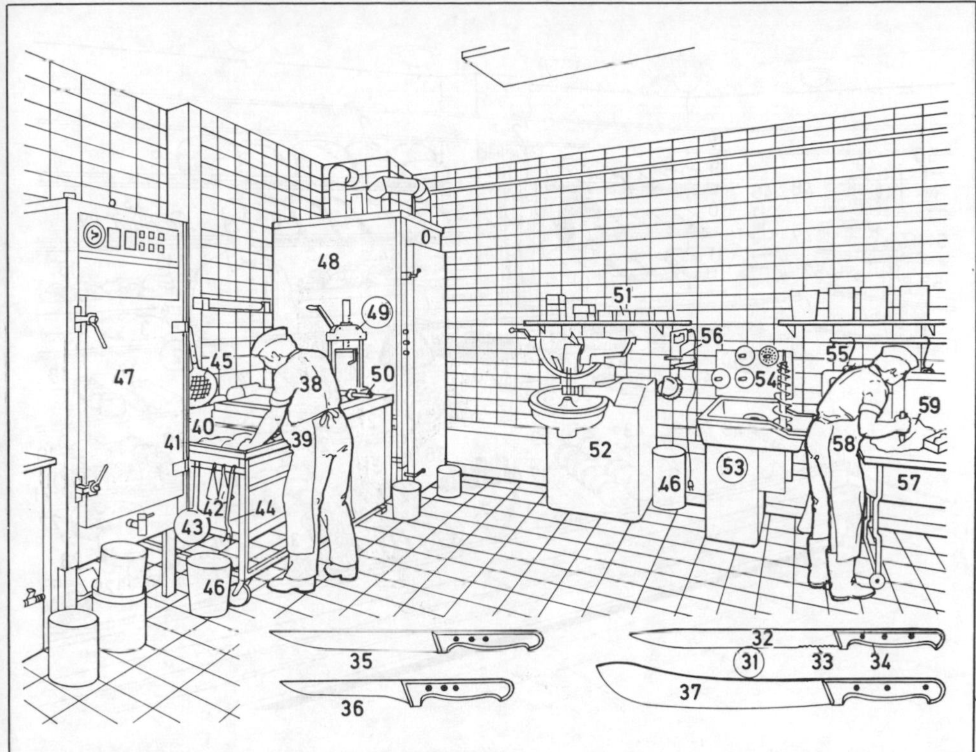

31-59 la cuisine (l'office *f ou m*) **de la charcuterie** (le lieu de préparation *f* des saucisses *f*)
– ***kitchen for making sausages***

31-37 les couteaux *m* **de boucher** *m*
– ***butcher's knives***

31 le couteau à découper
– *slicer*

32 la lame de couteau *m*
– *knife blade*

33 la denture du couteau
– *saw teeth*

34 le manche du couteau
– *knife handle*

35 le couteau à viande *f* (le couteau à dépecer)
– *carver (carving knife)*

36 le couteau à désosser
– *boning knife*

37 le couteau à pointe *f* relevée
– *butcher's knife (butcher knife)*

38 le boucher (le maître boucher)
– *butcher (master butcher)*

39 le tablier de cuisine *f*
– *butcher's apron*

40 le pétrin à viande *f* (la cuve de malaxage *m*, de pétrissage *m*)
– *meat-mixing trough*

41 la chair à saucisse *f* (le hachis, la farce)
– *sausage meat*

42 le racloir
– *scraper*

43 l'écumoire *m*
– *skimmer*

44 la fourchette à chair *f* à saucisse *f*
– *sausage fork*

45 la passoire
– *scalding colander*

46 la boîte à déchets *m* (la poubelle, la boîte à ordures *f*)
– *waste bin (Am. trash bin)*

47 le réchaud-buffet (le fourneau) avec dispositif *m* de production *f* de vapeur *f* ou d'air *m* chaud pour la cuisson à l'étuvée (à l'étouffée *f*)
– *cooker, for cooking with steam or hot air*

48 le fumoir
– *smoke house*

49 la machine à remplir les boyaux *m* à saucisses *f*
– *sausage filler (sausage stuffer)*

50 le tube d'alimentation *f* (l'entonnoir *m* de remplissage *m*)
– *feed pipe (supply pipe)*

51 les bocaux *m* de légumes *m*
– *containers for vegetables*

52 la machine à préparer la chair à saucisse *f*
– *mincing machine for sausage meat*

53 le hachoir (le hache-viande)
– *mincing machine (meat mincer, mincer,* Am. *meat grinder)*

54 les plaques *f* de fond *m* à trous *m* (les grilles *f* avec couteau *m* hacheur)
– *plates (steel plates)*

55 le tendoir (l'esse *f*, l'allonge *f*, le croc à viande *f*)
– *meathook (butcher's hook)*

56 la scie à désosser (la scie de boucher *m*)
– *bone saw*

57 l'étal *m*
– *chopping board*

58 le garçon (le commis) boucher découpant la viande
– *butcher, cutting meat*

59 le morceau de viande *f*
– *piece of meat*

1-54 la boulangerie (la boulangerie-pâtisserie)
– ***baker's shop***
1 la vendeuse
– *shop assistant (*Am. *salesgirl, saleslady)*
2 le pain
– *bread (loaf of bread, loaf)*
3 la mie
– *crumb*
4 la croûte
– *crust (bread crust)*
5 le croûton
– *crust (*Am. *heel)*
6-12 sortes *f* **de pains** *m*
– ***kinds of bread*** *(breads)*
6 le pain rond (la miche, la boule, le pain de campagne *f*, le pain boulot), un pain bis
– *round loaf, a wheat and rye bread*
7 la petite boule
– *small round loaf*
8 le pain long, un pain de seigle *m*
– *long loaf (bloomer), a wheat and rye bread*
9 le pain blanc
– *white loaf*
10 le pain moulé (le pain de munition *f*), un pain complet
– *pan loaf, a wholemeal rye bread*
11 le stolle de Dresde (le gâteau de Noël)
– *yeast bread (*Am. *stollen)*
12 le pain blanc français (la baguette, la flûte)
– *French loaf (baguette, French stick)*
13-16 petits pains *m*
– ***rolls***
13 le petit pain chapelet
– *brown roll*
14 le petit pain de froment *m* (le petit pain blanc fendu, *égal.:* le petit pain au sel, le petit pain au pavot, au cumin)
– *white roll*
15 le petit pain double
– *finger roll*
16 le petit pain au seigle
– *rye-bread roll*
17-47 la pâtisserie (les gâteaux *m*)
– ***cakes*** *(confectionery)*
17 le cornet feuilleté à la crème
– *cream roll*
18 le vol-au-vent (la bouchée), un gâteau en pâte *f* feuilletée
– *vol-au-vent, a puff pastry (*Am. *puff paste)*
19 le biscuit roulé (le roulé)
– *Swiss roll (*Am. *jelly roll)*
20 la tartelette
– *tartlet*
21 la tranche de gâteau *m* à la crème
– *slice of cream cake*
22-24 gâteaux *m* **à la crème** (flans *m*) et tartes *f* aux fruits *m*
– ***flans*** *(*Am. *pies) and gateaux (torten)*
22 la tarte aux fruits *m* (*var.:* tarte aux fraises *f*, tarte aux cerises *f* (clafoutis *m*), tarte aux groseilles *f* à maquereau, tarte aux pêches *f*, tarte à la rhubarbe)
– *fruit flan (*kinds: *strawberry flan, cherry flan, gooseberry flan, peach flan, rhubarb flan)*
23 le gâteau au fromage
– *cheesecake*
24 le gâteau à la crème (*égal.:* flan *m*; *var.:* le gâteau garni de crème *f* au beurre, le clafoutis de la Forêt-Noire)
– *cream cake (*Am. *cream pie) (*kinds: *butter-cream cake, Black Forest gateau)*
25 le plat à gâteau *m*
– *cake plate*
26 la meringue
– *meringue*
27 le chou à la crème
– *cream puff*
28 la crème fouettée (la crème Chantilly)
– *whipped cream*
29 la boule de Berlin (le «Krapfen», le beignet viennois, le beignet soufflé)
– *doughnut (*Am. *bismarck)*
30 le palmier
– *Danish pastry*
31 le bâtonnet salé (*égal.:* le bâtonnet au cumin)
– *saltstick (saltzstange) (*also: *caraway roll, caraway stick)*
32 le croissant
– *croissant (crescent roll,* Am. *crescent)*
33 le kouglof ou kugelhof
– *ring cake (gugelhupf)*
34 le gâteau moulé nappé (enrobé) de chocolat *m*
– *slab cake with chocolate icing*
35 le biscuit saupoudré de rognures *f* de pâte *f*
– *oatcake*
36 la profiterole au chocolat (le nègre en chemise *f*)
– *marshmallow*

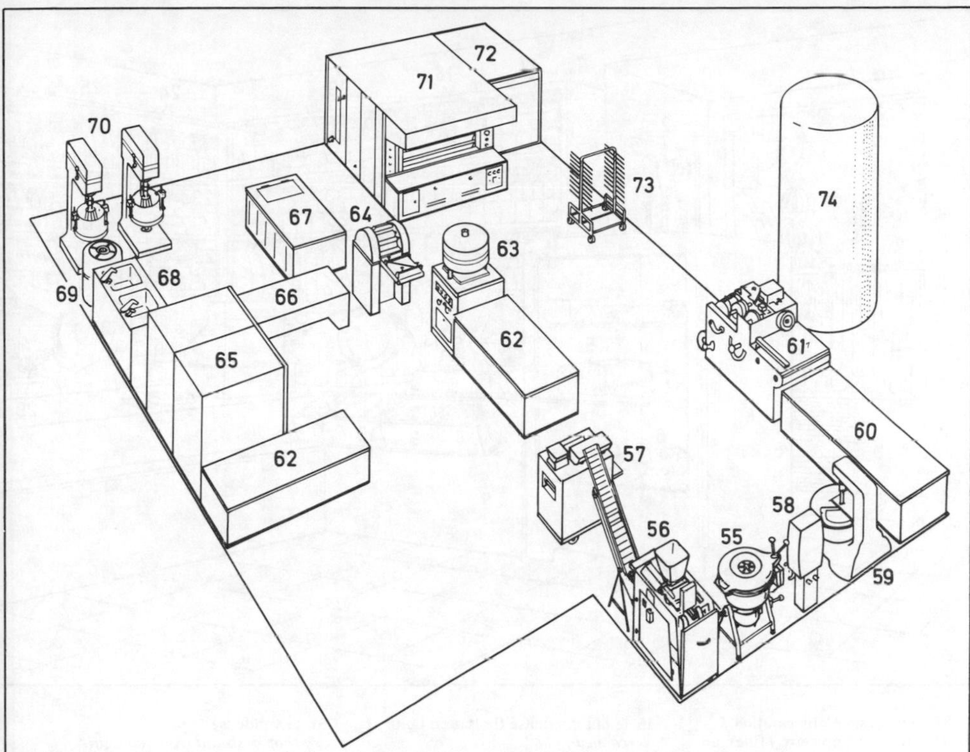

37 le macaron
– *coconut macaroon*
38 l'escargot (le petit pain aux raisins *m*)
– *pastry whirl*
39 le gâteau américain
– *iced bun*
40 le pain de mie *f*
– *sweet bread*
41 la tresse
– *plaited bun (plait)*
42 la couronne de Francfort
– *iced sponge*
43 le gâteau en tranches *f* (*var.:* le gâteau garni de rognures *f* de pâte *f*, le gâteau couvert de sucre *m* glace, le gâteau aux quetsches)
– *slices* (kinds: *cream slices, apple slices, plum slices)*
44 le bretzel
– *pretzel*
45 la gaufre
– *wafer (*Am. *waffle)*
46 le gâteau monté (la pièce montée)
– *tree cake (baumkuchen)*
47 le fond de tarte *f* (l'abaisse *f*)
– *flan case*
48-50 pains *m* préemballés
– ***wrapped bread***
48 le pain complet (*égal.:* le pain aux germes *m* de blé *m*)
– *wholemeal bread (*also: *wheatgerm bread)*
49 le pain noir de Westphalie (le «Pumpernickel»)
– *pumpernickel (wholemeal rye bread)*
50 le pain croustillant (la galette suédoise)
– *crispbread*
51 le pain d'épice(s) *f*
*gingerbread (*Am. *lebkuchen)*
52 la farine (*var.:* la farine de froment *m* (de blé *m*), la farine de seigle *m*)
– *flour (*kinds: *wheat flour, rye flour)*
53 le levain (la levure de boulanger *m*)
– *yeast (baker's yeast)*
54 la biscotte
– *rusks (French toast)*
55-74 le fournil
– ***bakery** (bakehouse)*
55 le pétrin (la pétrisseuse)
– *kneading machine (dough mixer)*
56-57 l'unité *f* de fabrication *f* du pain
– ***bread unit***
56 la machine à découper la pâte (le découpe-pâte)
– *divider*
57 l'unité *f* de façonnage *m* (de mise *f* en forme *f*)
– *moulder (*Am. *molder)*
58 l'appareil *m* de mélange *m* et de dosage *m* de l'eau *f* et de la farine
– *premixer*
59 le malaxeur (le batteur, le mélangeur, le mixeur)
– *dough mixer*
60 la table de travail *m*
– *workbench*
61 l'unité *f* de fabrication *f* des petits pains *m*
– *roll unit*
62 la table de travail *m*
– *workbench*
63 la machine à découper et à façonner la pâte
– *divider and rounder (rounding machine)*
64 la machine à façonner les croissants *m*
– *crescent-forming machine*
65 le congélateur (le freezer)
– *freezers*
66 la friteuse (la bassine à friture *f*)
– *baking oven*
67-70 l'unité *f* de fabrication *f* de pâtisserie *f*
– ***confectionery unit***
67 la table de refroidissement *m*
– *cooling table*
68 l'évier *m*
– *sink*
69 le réchaud
– *boiler*
70 le batteur-mélangeur
– *whipping unit [with beater]*
71 le four à étages *m* (le four de boulanger *m*)
– *reel oven (oven)*
72 la chambre de fermentation *f* (de levage *m* de la pâte)
– *fermentation room*
73 le chariot de la chambre de fermentation *f*
– *fermentation trolley*
74 le silo à farine *f*
– *flour silo*

1-87 le magasin d'alimentation *f* (l'épicerie *f*, l'épicerie *f* fine), un magasin de détail *m*
– ***grocer's shop*** *(grocer's, delicatessen shop,* Am. *grocery store, delicatessen store), a retail shop (*Am. *retail store)*

1 l'étalage *m*
– *window display*

2 l'affiche *f* publicitaire
– *poster (advertisement)*

3 la vitrine réfrigérée
– *cold shelves*

4 la charcuterie
– *sausages*

5 le fromage
– *cheese*

6 le poulet à rôtir
– *roasting chicken (broiler)*

7 la poularde
– *poulard, a fattened hen*

8-11 les produits *m* **pour la pâtisserie**
– ***baking ingredients***

8 les raisins *m* secs
– *raisins;* sim.: *sultanas*

9 les raisins *m* de Corinthe
– *currants*

10 le citronnat (le citron confit)
– *candied lemon peel*

11 l'orangeat (l'orange *f* confite)
– *candied orange peel*

12 la balance automatique
– *computing scale, a rapid scale*

13 le vendeur
– *shop assistant (*Am. *salesclerk)*

14 les rayonnages *m*
– *goods shelves (shelves)*

15-20 les conserves *f*
– ***canned food***

15 le lait condensé (le lait en boîte *f*)
– *canned milk*

16 les fruits *m* en conserve *f*
– *canned fruit (cans of fruit)*

17 les légumes *m* en conserve *f*
– *canned vegetables*

18 le jus de fruits *m*
– *fruit juice*

19 les sardines *f* à l'huile *f*, une conserve de poisson *m*
– *sardines in oil, a can of fish*

20 la viande en conserve *f*
– *canned meat (cans of meat)*

21 la margarine
– *margarine*

22 le beurre
– *butter*

23 la graisse végétale
– *coconut oil, a vegetable oil*

24 l'huile *f* (*var.:* huile *f* de table *f*, d'olives *f*, de tournesol *m*, de germes *m* de blé *m*, d'arachides *f*)
– *oil;* kinds: *salad oil, olive oil, sunflower oil, wheatgerm oil, ground-nut oil*

25 le vinaigre
– *vinegar*

26 le potage en tablettes *f* (en cubes *m*)
– *stock cube*

27 le consommé en cubes *m*
– *bouillon cube*

28 la moutarde
– *mustard*

29 le cornichon au vinaigre *m*
– *gherkin (pickled gherkin)*

30 l'arôme *m* pour potages *m*
– *soup seasoning*

31 la vendeuse
– *shop assistant (*Am. *salesgirl, saleslady)*

32-34 les pâtes *f* **alimentaires**
– ***pastas***

32 les spaghetti *m*
– *spaghetti*

33 les macaroni *m*
– *macaroni*

34 les nouilles *f*
– *noodles*

35-39 produits *m* **alimentaires**
– ***cereal products***

35 l'orge *m* perlé
– *pearl barley*

36 la semoule
– *semolina*

37 les flocons *m* d'avoine *f*
– *rolled oats (porridge oats, oats)*

38 le riz
– *rice*

39 le tapioca
– *sago*

40 le sel
– *salt*

41 le commerçant, un commerçant-détaillant
– *grocer (*Am. *groceryman), a shopkeeper (tradesman, retailer,* Am. *storekeeper)*

42 les câpres *f*
– *capers*

43 la cliente
– *customer*

44 la fiche de caisse *f*
– *receipt (sales check)*

45 le sac à provisions *f*
– *shopping bag*

46-49 les matériaux *m* **d'emballage** *m*
– ***wrapping material***
46 le papier d'emballage *m*
– *wrapping paper*
47 le ruban adhésif
– *adhesive tape*
48 le sac en papier *m*
– *paper bag*
49 le cornet
– *cone-shaped paper bag*
50 l'entremets *m* en sachet *m*
– *blancmange powder*
51 la configure
– *whole-fruit jam (preserve)*
52 la marmelade
– *jam*
53-55 le sucre
– ***sugar***
53 le sucre en morceaux *m*
– *cube sugar*
54 le sucre en poudre *f*
– *icing sugar* (Am. *confectioner's sugar)*
55 le sucre cristallisé
– *refined sugar in crystals*
56-59 les spiritueux *m*
– ***spirits***
56 l'alcool *m* de grains *m*
– *whisky (whiskey)*
57 le rhum
– *rum*
58 la liqueur
– *liqueur*
59 le cognac
– *brandy (cognac)*
60-64 vins *m* **en bouteilles** *f*
– ***wine** in bottles (bottled wine)*
60 le vin blanc
– *white wine*
61 le chianti
– *Chianti*
62 le vermouth
– *vermouth*
63 le vin mousseux (le mousseux)
– *sparkling wine*
64 le vin rouge
– *red wine*
65-68 les stimulants *m*
– ***tea, coffee, etc.***
65 le café (café en grains *m*)
– *coffee (pure coffee)*
66 le cacao
– *cocoa*
67 la variété de café *m*
– *coffee*
68 le thé en sachets *m*
– *tea bag*
69 le moulin à café *m* électrique
– *electric coffee grinder*
70 le torréfacteur
– *coffee roaster*
71 le tambour de torréfaction *f*
– *roasting drum*
72 la pelle de prélèvement *m*
– *sample scoop*
73 le tableau des prix *m* du jour *m*
– *price list*
74 le congélateur
– *freezer*
75-86 la confiserie
– ***confectionery*** (Am. *candies)*
75 le bonbon
– *sweet* (Am. *candy)*
76 les bonbons acidulés
– *drops*
77 les caramels *m*
– *toffees*
78 la tablette de chocolat *m*
– *bar of chocolate*
79 la boîte de chocolats *m*
– *chocolate box*
80 un chocolat (une crotte de chocolat *m*)
– *chocolate, a sweet*
81 le nougat
– *nougat*
82 la pâte d'amandes *f*
– *marzipan*
83 la bouchée à la liqueur
– *chocolate liqueur*
84 la langue de chat *m*
– *cat's tongue*
85 la nougatine
– *croquant*
86 les truffes *f* au chocolat
– *truffle*
87 l'eau *f* de table *f* (l'eau *f* minérale, l'eau *f* gazeuse)
– *soda water*

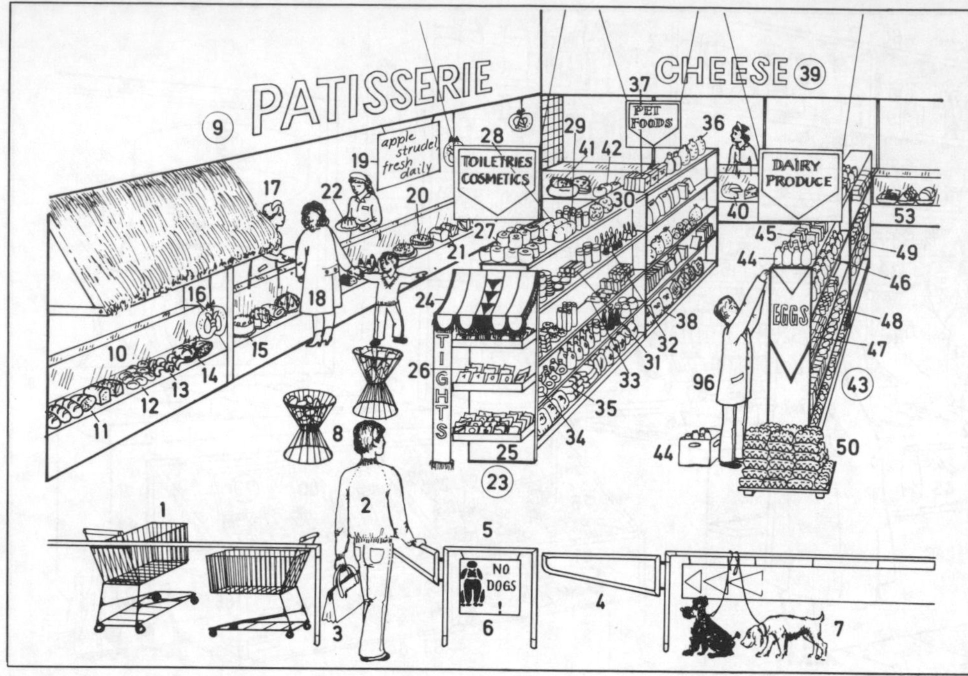

1-95 le supermarché, un magasin d'alimentation *f* libre service *m*
– ***supermarket,*** *a self-service food store*

1 le caddie
– *shopping trolley*

2 le client (l'acheteur *m*)
– *customer*

3 le sac à provisions *f*
– *shopping bag*

4 le portillon d'entrée *f*
– *entrance to the sales area*

5 la barrière
– *barrier*

6 le panneau interdisant l'entrée *f* des chiens *m*
– *sign (notice) banning dogs*

7 les chiens *m* attachés
– *dogs tied by their leads*

8 la corbeille de présentation *f*
– *basket*

9 le rayon boulangerie-pâtisserie *f*
– ***bread and cake counter*** *(bread counter, cake counter)*

10 la vitrine
– *display counter for bread and cakes*

11 les variétés *f* de pain *m*
– *kinds of bread (breads)*

12 les petits pains *m*
– *rolls*

13 les croissants *m*
– *croissants (crescent rolls,* Am. *crescents)*

14 le pain de campagne *f*
– *round loaf*

15 le gâteau
– *gateau*

16 le bretzel [inconnu en France sous forme de grand pain]
– *pretzel*

17 la vendeuse
– *shop assistant (*Am. *salesgirl, saleslady)*

18 la cliente (l'acheteuse *f*)
– *customer*

19 le panonceau pour offres *f* spéciales
– *sign listing goods*

20 la tarte aux fruits *m*
– *fruit flan*

21 le cake
– *slab cake*

22 le kouglof ou kugelhof
– *ring cake*

23 la gondole de produits *m* **de beauté** *f* (une gondole, une étagère)
– ***cosmetics gondola,*** *a gondola (sales shelves)*

24 le baldaquin
– *canopy*

25 le présentoir à bas *m*
– *hosiery shelf*

26 le sachet de bas *m*
– *stockings (nylons)*

27-35 cosmétiques*m*
– ***toiletries*** *(cosmetics)*

27 le pot de crème *f* (*var.:* crème *f* hydratante, crème *f* de jour *m*, crème *f* de nuit *f*, crème *f* pour les mains *f*)
– *jar of cream (*kinds: *moisturising cream, day cream, night-care cream, hand cream)*

28 le paquet de coton *m* hydrophile
– *packet of cotton wool*

29 la boîte de poudre *f*
– *talcum powder*

30 le paquet de cotons *m* à démaquiller
– *packet of cotton wool balls*

31 le tube de pâte *f* dentifrice
– *toothpaste*

32 le vernis à ongles *m*
– *nail varnish (nail polish)*

33 le tube de crème *f*
– *shaving cream*

34 les sels *m* de bain *m*
– *bath salts*

35 articles *m* d'hygiène *f*
– *sanitary articles*

36-37 aliments *m* pour animaux *m*
– *pet foods*

36 l'aliment *m* complet pour chiens *m*
– *complete dog food*

37 le biscuit de chien *m*
– *packet of dog biscuits*

38 la sciure pour chat *m*
– *bag of cat litter*

39 le rayon fromages *m*
– ***cheese counter***

40 la meule de fromage *m*
– *whole cheese*

41 le fromage suisse (Emmental) à trous *m*
– *Swiss cheese (Emmental cheese) with holes*

42 le fromage de Hollande (Edam), un fromage en boule *f*
– *Edam cheese, a round cheese*

43 la gondole des produits *m* laitiers
– *gondola for dairy products*

44 le lait longue conservation *f*
– *long-life milk*; also: *pasteurized milk, homogenized milk*

45 le lait en briques *f* carton *m*
– *milk*

46 la crème
– *cream*

47 le beurre
– *butter*
48 la margarine
– *margarine*
49 le fromage en boîte *f*
– *box of cheeses*
50 les œufs en boîte *f*
– *box of eggs*
51 le rayon boucherie *f*
– ***fresh meat counter*** *(meat counter)*
52 le jambon de pays *m*
– *ham on the bone*
53 les viandes *f*
– *meat (meat products)*
54 les saucissons *m*
– *sausages*
55 la saucisse
– *ring of pork sausage*
56 le boudin
– *ring of blood sausage*
57 le congélateur
– *freezer*
58-61 les produits *m* **surgelés**
– ***frozen food***
58 la poularde
– *poulard*
59 la cuisse de dinde *f*
– *turkey leg (drumstick)*
60 la poule
– *boiling fowl*
61 les légumes *m* surgelés
– *frozen vegetables*
62 la gondole des produits *m* **pâtissiers et alimentaires**
– ***gondola for baking ingredients and cereal products***
63 la farine de blé *m*
– *wheat flour*
64 le pain de sucre *m*
– *sugar loaf*
65 le paquet de pâtes *f* à potage *m*
– *packet of noodles [for soup]*
66 l'huile *f*
– *salad oil*
67 le paquet d'épices *f*
– *packet of spice*
68 le café
– *coffee*
69 le paquet de thé *m*
– *packet of tea*
70 le café soluble (café instantané)
– *instant coffee*
71 la gondole des boissons *f*
– ***drinks gondola***
72 le pack de bière *f*
– *beer crate (crate of beer)*
73 la bière en boîtes *f*
– *canned beer*
74 la bouteille de jus *m* de fruits *m*
– *bottle of fruit juice*
75 le jus de fruits *m* en boîte *f*
– *canned fruit juice*
76 la bouteille de vin *m*
– *bottle of wine*
77 la bouteille de chianti *m*
– *bottle of Chianti*
78 la bouteille de vin *m* mousseux
– *bottle of champagne*
79 la sortie de secours *m*
– *emergency exit*
80 le rayon légumes *m* **et fruits** *m*
– ***fruit and vegetable counter***
81 le cageot de légumes *m*
– *vegetable basket*
82 les tomates *f*
– *tomatoes*
83 les concombres *m*
– *cucumbers*
84 le chou-fleur
– *cauliflower*
85 l'ananas *m*
– *pineapple*
86 les pommes *f*
– *apples*
87 les poires *f*
– *pears*
88 la balance
– *scales for weighing fruit*
89 les raisins *m*
– *grapes (bunches of grapes)*
90 les bananes *f*
– *bananas*
91 la boîte de conserves *f*
– *can*
92 la caisse
– ***checkout***
93 la caisse enregistreuse
– *cash register*
94 la caissière
– *cashier*
95 la chaîne
– *chain*

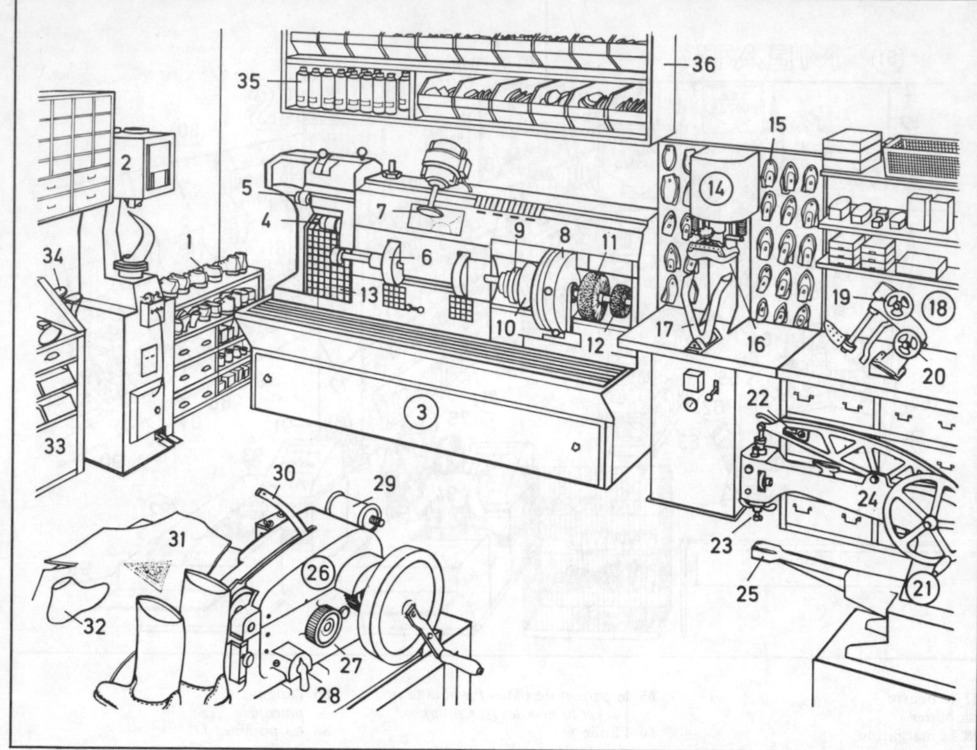

1-68 l'atelier *m* de cordonnier *m* (la cordonnerie)
– *shoemaker's workshop (bootmaker's workshop)*
1 les chaussures *f* réparées (ressemelées)
– *finished (repaired) shoes*
2 la machine à piquer (à ressemeler)
– *auto-soling machine*
3 la machine de finissage *m*
– *finishing machine*
4 la fraise à talon *m*
– *heel trimmer*
5 les fraises *f* de rechange *m*
– *sole trimmer*
6 la meule
– *scouring wheel*
7 le disque de ponçage *m*
– *naum keag*
8 l'organe *m* d'entraînement *m*
– *drive unit (drive wheel)*
9 le poussoir
– *iron*
10 le disque de polissage *m* en toile *f* de coton *m* (la meule à polir, le polissoir)
– *buffing wheel*
11 la brosse à polir
– *polishing brush*
12 la brosse de crin *m*
– *horsehair brush*
13 la grille d'aspiration *f*
– *extractor grid*
14 la presse à monter les semelles *f* automatique
– *automatic sole press*
15 les moules *m* (les accessoires *m* de presse *f*)
– *press attachment*
16 le coussinet amortisseur (le patin amortisseur)
– *pad*
17 le pied presseur (le socle, l'enclume *f*)
– *press bar*
18 la machine à élargir les chaussures *f*
– *stretching machine*
19 le dispositif de réglage *m* de la largeur
– *width adjustment*
20 le dispositif de réglage *m* de la longueur
– *length adjustment*
21 la machine à coudre
– *stitching machine*
22 le dispositif de réglage *m* de la tension du fil
– *power regulator (power control)*
23 la barre à aiguille *f* (le presseur)
– *foot*
24 le volant
– *handwheel*
25 le pied-de-biche
– *arm*
26 la machine à piquer (à monter les semelles *f*)
– *sole stitcher (sole-stitching machine)*
27 le relève-presseur (le dispositif de levage *m*)
– *foot bar lever*
28 la manette d'avancement *m*
– *feed adjustment (feed setting)*
29 la bobine (la canette, le dévidoir)
– *bobbin (cotton bobbin)*
30 le guide-fil
– *thread guide (yarn guide)*
31 le cuir à semelle *f*
– *sole leather*
32 la forme (l'embauchoir *m*)
– *[wooden] last*
33 la table de travail *m* (l'établi *m*)
– *workbench*
34 la forme métallique (l'embauchoir *m* en fer *m*)
– *last*
35 le pulvérisateur de teinture *f*
– *dye spray*
36 l'étagère *f* de rangement *m* du matériel de cordonnier *m* (des crépins *m*, du saint-crépin)
– *shelves for materials*

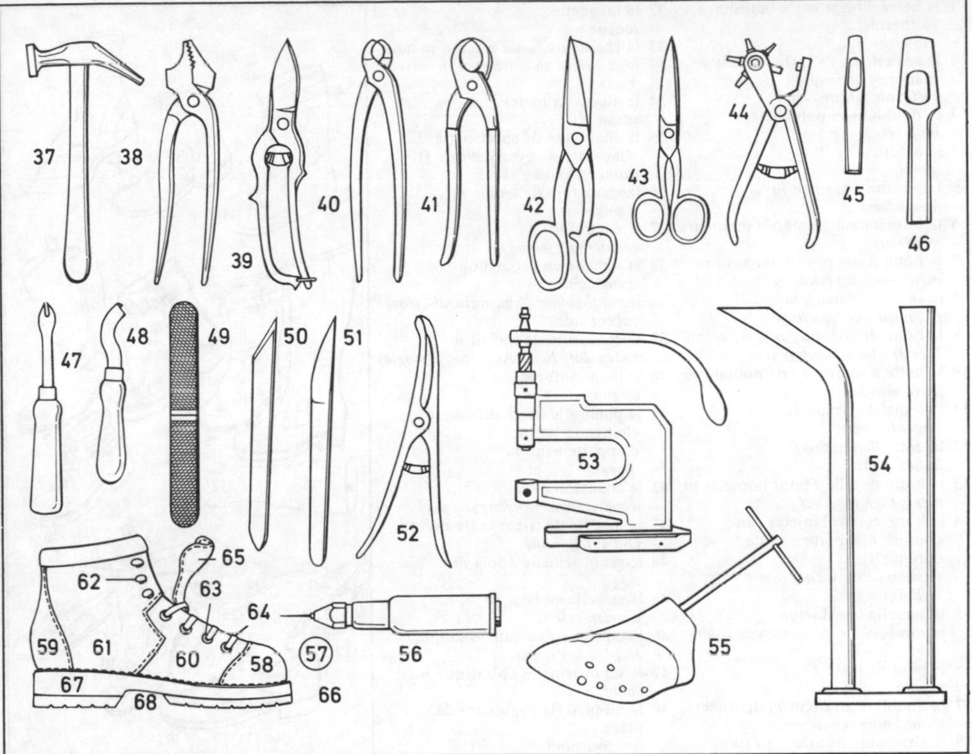

37 le marteau de cordonnier *m*
– *shoemaker's hammer*
38 la pince multiprise
– *shoemaker's pliers (welt pincers)*
39 la cisaille articulée
– *sole-leather shears*
40 les tenailles *f* russes
– *small pincers (nippers)*
41 les grosses tenailles *f*
– *large pincers (nippers)*
42 les grands ciseaux *m* pour couper les empeignes *f*
– *upper-leather shears*
43 les ciseaux *m* de lingère *f*
– *scissors*
44 l'emporte-pièce *m* «revolver» (la pince emporte-pièce *m* à barillet *m* de six tubes *m*)
– *revolving punch (rotary punch)*
45 l'emporte-pièce *m*
– *punch*
46 l'emporte-pièce *m* à poignée *f*
– *punch with handle*
47 le tire-clous (le pied-de-biche)
– *nail puller*
48 le tranchet à faire les bords *m* (le buis)
– *welt cutter*
49 la râpe de cordonnier
– *shoemaker's rasp*
50 le couteau de cordonnier *m*
– *cobbler's knife (shoemaker's knife)*
51 le tranchet
– *skiving knife (skife knife, paring knife)*
52 la pince à bout *m* renforcé
– *toecap remover*
53 la machine à poser les œillets *m*, les crochets *m* et les boutons-pression *m*
– *eyelet, hook, and press-stud setter*
54 l'enclume *f* (le socle de travail *m* à formes *f* métalliques)
– *stand with iron lasts*
55 l'embauchoir *m* tendeur
– *width-setting tree*
56 la poignée à poincon *m*
– *nail grip*
57 la chaussure montante (la chaussure de marche *f*)
– *boot*
58 le bout dur (renforcé, bombé)
– *toecap*
59 le contrefort
– *counter*
60 l'empeigne *f* (la claque)
– *vamp*
61 le quartier de tige *f*
– *quarter*
62 le crochet
– *hook*
63 l'œillet *m*
– *eyelet*
64 le lacet
– *lace (shoelace, bootlace)*
65 la languette (le soufflet lorsque cousue des deux côtés *m*)
– *tongue*
66 la semelle
– *sole*
67 le talon
– *heel*
68 la cambrure
– *shank (waist)*

1 la botte d'hiver *m* (le bottillon isotherme)
– *winter boot*
2 la semelle en PVC (la semelle en matière *f* plastique)
– *PVC sole (plastic sole)*
3 la doublure en peluche *f*
– *high-pile lining*
4 le nylon
– *nylon*
5 la bottine d'homme *m*
– *men's boot*
6 la fermeture à glissière *f* intérieure
– *inside zip*
7 la botte haute pour hommes *m*
– *men's high leg boot*
8 la semelle plateau *m*
– *platform sole (platform)*
9 la botte de cow-boy *m*
– *Western boot (cowboy boot)*
10 la botte à fourrure *f* de poulain *m*
– *pony-skin boot*
11 la semelle surmoulée
– *cemented sole*
12 la botte de femme *f*
– *ladies' boot*
13 la botte de ville *f* pour hommes *m*
– *men's high leg boot*
14 la botte en PVC injecté sans couture *f* (la botte à toute épreuve *f*)
– *seamless PVC waterproof wellington boot*
15 la semelle translucide
– *natural-colour* (Am. *natural-color*) *sole*
16 le bout de botte *f*
– *toecap*
17 la doublure en tricot *m* (tricotée)
– *tricot lining (knitwear lining)*
18 la chaussure de marche *f* (la chaussure montante, le botillon)
– *hiking boot*
19 la semelle profilée à crampons *m* (à crans *m*, à crantage *m* antidérapant)
– *grip sole*
20 le haut de tige *f* rembourré (matelassé)
– *padded collar*
21 les lacets *m* (le laçage)
– *tie fastening (lace fastening)*
22 la mule de bain *m*
– *open-toe mule*
23 l'empeigne *f* en tissu *m* éponge
– *terry upper*
24 la semelle extérieure
– *polo outsole*
25 la mule (la pantoufle)
– *mule*
26 l'empeigne *f* en velours *m* côtelé
– *corduroy upper*
27 le soulier de bal *m* (le haut-talon, le soulier à brides *f*, décolleté)
– *evening sandal (sandal court shoe)*
28 le talon aiguille *f*
– *high heel (stiletto heel)*
29 l'escarpin *m*
– *court shoe* (Am. *pump*)
30 le mocassin
– *moccasin*
31 la chaussure basse (la chaussure de ville *f*, le soulier à lacets *m*, le derby)
– *shoe, a tie shoe (laced shoe, Oxford shoe,* Am. *Oxford)*
32 la languette
– *tongue*
33 la chaussure basse à talon *m* haut
– *high-heeled shoe (shoe with raised heel)*
34 le mocassin loafer
– *casual*
35 la chaussure de sport *m* (la chaussure de gymnastique *f*)
– *trainer (training shoe)*
36 la chaussure de tennis *m*
– *tennis shoe*
37 le contrefort
– *counter (stiffening)*
38 la semelle en caoutchouc *m* translucide
– *natural-colour* (Am. *natural-color*) *rubber sole*
39 la chaussure de travail *m*
– *heavy-duty boot* (Am. *stogy, stogie*)
40 le bout renforcé
– *toecap*
41 la pantoufle (le chausson, la chaussure légère, d'appartement *m*)
– *slipper*
42 le chausson en laine *f*
– *woollen* (Am. *woolen*) *slip sock*
43 le modèle de tricot *m* (le point)
– *knit stitch (knit)*
44 le sabot semelle *f* bois *m*
– *clog*
45 la semelle en bois *m*
– *wooden sole*
46 l'empeigne *f* en cuir *m* souple
– *soft-leather upper*
47 le sabot semelle *f* plastique *m*
– *sabot*
48 le nu-pied (la chaussure de plage *f*)
– *toe post sandal*
49 la sandalette
– *ladies' sandal*
50 la semelle orthopédique intérieure
– *surgical footbed (sock)*
51 la sandale
– *sandal*
52 la boucle
– *shoe buckle (buckle)*
53 le soulier à bride *f* à talon *m* haut
– *sling-back court shoe* (Am. *sling pump*)
54 l'escarpin *m* en toile *f* (l'espadrille *f*)
– *fabric court shoe*
55 la semelle compensée
– *wedge heel*
56 la chaussure de marche *f* pour enfants *m*
– *baby's first walking boot*

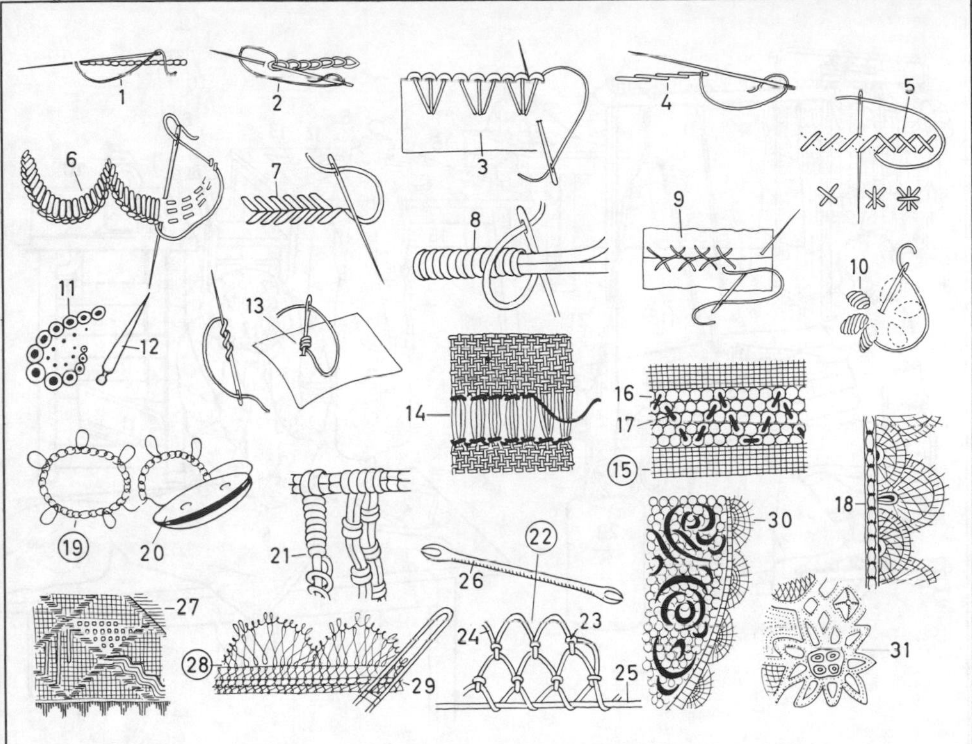

1 le point de piqûre *f*
– *backstitch seam*
2 le point de chaînette *f*
– *chain stitch*
3 le point de fantaisie *f*
– *ornamental stitch*
4 le point de tige *f*
– *stem stitch*
5 le point de croix *f*
– *cross stitch*
6 le point de feston *m*
– *buttonhole stitch (button stitch)*
7 le point d'épine *f*
– *fishbone stitch*
8 le point de bourdon *m* (le point de cordonnet *m*)
– *overcast stitch*
9 le point de chausson *m*
– *herringbone stitch (Russian stitch, Russian cross stitch)*
10 le plumetis
– *satin stitch (flat stitch)*
11 la broderie anglaise
– *eyelet embroidery (broderie anglaise)*
12 le poinçon
– *stiletto*
13 le point d'arme *f*
– *French knot (French dot, knotted stitch, twisted knot stitch)*
14 les jours *m*
– *hem stitch work*
15 la broderie sur tulle *m*
– *tulle work (tulle lace)*
16 le fond de tulle *m*
– *tulle background (net background)*
17 le point de reprise *f*
– *darning stitch*
18 la dentelle aux fuseaux *m* (*var.:* dentelle de Valenciennes, dentelle de Bruxelles)
– *pillow lace (bobbin lace, bone lace);* kinds: *Valenciennes, Brussels lace*
19 la frivolité
– *tatting*
20 la navette
– *tatting shuttle (shuttle)*
21 le macramé
– *knotted work (macramé)*
22 le filet
– *filet (netting)*
23 la maille (le nœud)
– *netting loop*
24 le fil à filet *m*
– *netting thread*
25 le moule
– *mesh pin (mesh gauge)*
26 la navette
– *netting needle*
27 la broderie sur filet *m*
– *open work*
28 la dentelle à la fourche
– *gimping (hairpin work)*
29 la fourche
– *gimping needle (hairpin)*
30 la dentelle à l'aiguille *f* (*var.:* dentelle reticella, point *m* de Venise, point *m* d'Alençon, avec fil métallique: filigrane *m*)
– *needlepoint lace (point lace, needlepoint);* kinds: *reticella lace, Venetian lace, Alençon lace;* sim. *with metal thread: filigree work*
31 la dentelle Renaissance
– *braid embroidery (braid work)*

1-27 l'atelier *m* **de tailleur** *m* **pour dames** *f*
- ***dressmaker's workroom***

1 le tailleur pour dames *f*
- *dressmaker*

2 le mètre ruban, un centimètre
- *tape measure (measuring tape), a metre* (Am. *meter) tape measure*

3 les ciseaux *m* de coupe *f* (les ciseaux *m* de tailleur *m*)
- *cutting shears*

4 la table de coupe *f*
- *cutting table*

5 la robe modèle *m*
- *model dress*

6 le mannequin de tailleur *m*
- *dressmaker's model (dressmaker's dummy, dress form)*

7 le manteau modèle *m*
- *model coat*

8 la machine à coudre de tailleur *m*
- *sewing machine*

9 le moteur d'entraînement *m*
- *drive motor*

10 la courroie de transmission *f*
- *drive belt*

11 la pédale
- *treadle*

12 le fil à coudre, une bobine de fil *m*
- *sewing machine cotton (sewing machine thread) [on bobbin]*

13 l'équerre *f* de patronnage *m*
- *cutting template*

14 l'extra-fort *m* (l'extrafort *m*)
- *seam binding*

15 la boîte de boutons *m*
- *button box*

16 la chute de tissu *m*
- *remnant*

17 le portemanteau mobile
- *movable clothes rack*

18 la table de repassage *m*
- *hand-iron press*

19 la repasseuse
- *presser (ironer)*

20 le fer à vapeur *f*
- *steam iron*

21 le tuyau d'arrivée *f* d'eau *f*
- *water feed pipe*

22 le réservoir d'eau *f*
- *water container*

23 le plan de repassage *m* inclinable
- *adjustable-tilt ironing surface*

24 le portique de guidage *m* du fer à repasser
- *lift device for the iron*

25 le bac d'aspiration *f* de vapeur *f*
- *steam extractor*

26 la pédale d'aspiration *f*
- *foot switch controlling steam extraction*

27 le non-tissé repassé
- *pressed non-woven woollen* (Am. *woolen) fabric*

1-32 l'atelier *m* **de tailleur** *m* **pour hommes** *m*
– ***tailor's workroom***
1 le miroir triple
– *triple mirror*
2 les coupes *f* de tissu *m*
– *lengths of material*
3 le tissu pour costumes *m*
– *suiting*
4 le journal de mode *f* (la revue de mode *f*)
– *fashion journal (fashion magazine)*
5 le cendrier
– *ashtray*
6 le catalogue de mode *f*
– *fashion catalogue*
7 la table de travail *m*
– *workbench*
8 l'étagère *f* murale
– *wall shelves (wall shelf unit)*
9 la bobine de fil *m* à coudre
– *cotton reel*
10 les fusettes *f* de soie *f* à coudre
– *small reels of sewing silk*
11 les ciseaux *m* de tailleur *m*
– *hand shears*
12 la machine à coudre mixte, électrique et à pédale *f*
– *combined electric and treadle sewing machine*
13 la pédale
– *treadle*
14 le protège-jupe
– *dress guard*
15 le volant
– *band wheel*
16 le bobinage de canette *f*
– *bobbin thread*
17 la table de machine *f* à coudre
– *sewing machine table*
18 le tiroir de machine *f* à coudre
– *sewing machine drawer*
19 l'extra-fort *m* (l'extrafort *m*)
– *seam binding*
20 la pelote à épingles *f*
– *pincushion*
21 le marquage à la craie
– *marking out*
22 le tailleur pour hommes *m*
– *tailor*
23 la forme de tailleur *m*
– *shaping pad*
24 la craie tailleur *m*
– *tailor's chalk (French chalk)*
25 la pièce
– *workpiece*
26 la table de repassage *m* à la vapeur
– *steam press (steam pressing unit)*
27 le bras pivotant
– *swivel arm*
28 la jeannette
– *pressing cushion (pressing pad)*
29 le fer à repasser
– *iron*
30 la moufle de repassage *m*
– *hand-ironing pad*
31 la brosse à habits *m*
– *clothes brush*
32 la pattemouille
– *pressing cloth*

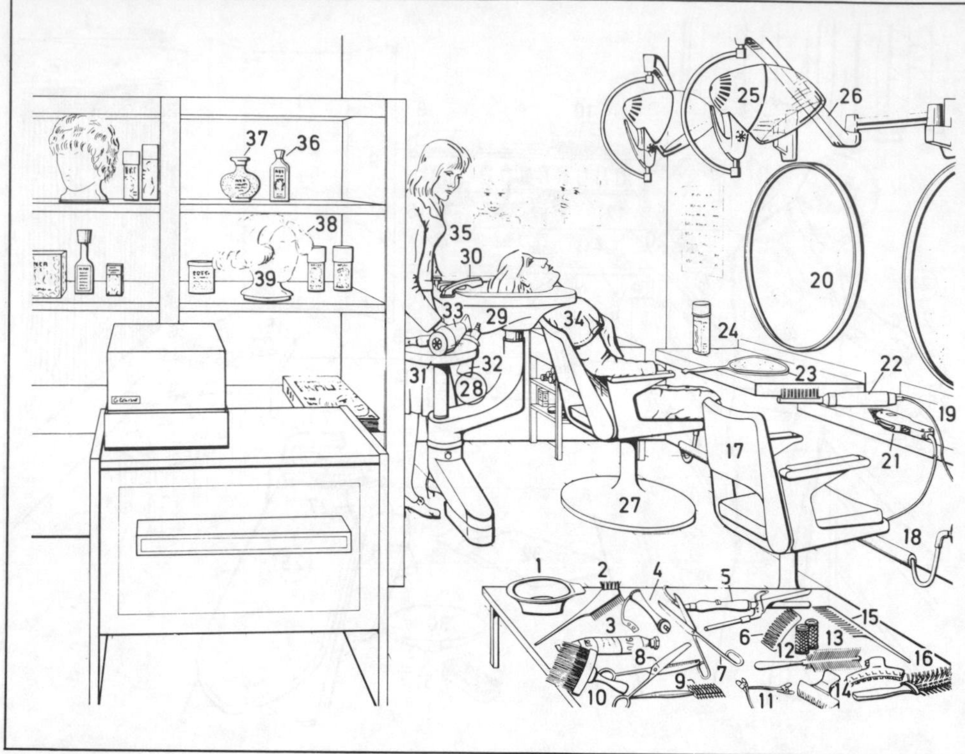

1-39 le salon de coiffure *f* **pour dames** *f* (l'institut *m* de beauté *f*)
- ***ladies' hairdressing salon and beauty salon*** (Am. *beauty parlor, beauty shop)*

1-16 ustensiles *m* **de coiffure** *f*
- ***hairdresser's tools***

1 la cuvette contenant l'agent *m* de décoloration *f* (le produit décolorant)
- *bowl containing bleach*

2 la brosse à démêler les cheveux *m*
- *detangling brush*

3 le tube d'agent *m* de décoloration *f* (de produit *m* décolorant)
- *bleach tube*

4 le rouleau à mise *f* en plis *m* utilisé lors de la teinture des cheveux *m*
- *curler [used in dyeing]*

5 le fer à friser
- *curling tongs (curling iron)*

6 le peigne de parure *f* (le peigne à chignon *m*)
- *comb (back comb, side comb)*

7 les grands ciseaux *m* de coiffeur *m* (les ciseaux *m* de coupe *f*)
- *haircutting scissors*

8 les ciseaux *m* à effiler (à désépaissir)
- *thinning scissors (*Am. *thinning shears)*

9 le rasoir effileur (le rasoir à désépaissir)
- *thinning razor*

10 le blaireau
- *hairbrush*

11 la pince à cheveux *m* (la barrette)
- *hair clip*

12 le bigoudi (le rouleau à mise *f* en plis *m*)
- *roller*

13 la brosse à boucler les cheveux *m* (la brosse à cheveux *m* radiale)
- *curl brush*

14 la pince à boucle *f* de cheveux *m*
- *curl clip*

15 le démêloir (le gros peigne)
- *dressing comb*

16 la brosse à cheveux *m* en soies *f* dures
- *stiff-bristle brush*

17 le fauteuil de coiffeur *m* réglable (ajustable)
- *adjustable hairdresser's chair*

18 le repose-pieds
- *footrest*

19 la coiffeuse (la table-coiffeuse)
- *dressing table*

20 le miroir mural (à supports *m* muraux) du salon de coiffure *f*
- *salon mirror (mirror)*

21 la tondeuse
- *electric clippers*

22 le peigne soufflant (le peigne chauffant, à jet *m* d'air *m* chaud, le peigne sèche-cheveux)
- *warm-air comb*

23 le miroir à main *f*
- *hand mirror (hand glass)*

24 la laque pour cheveux *m* (le fixatif)
- *hair spray (hair-fixing spray)*

25 le casque sèche-cheveux (le séchoir), un casque à bras *m* support orientable (adaptable, pivotant)
- *drier, a swivel-mounted drier*

26 le bras support orientable (adaptable, pivotant)
- *swivel arm of the drier*

27 l'assise (le socle) du fauteuil
- *round base*

28 le lavabo pour le lavage des cheveux *m*
- *shampoo unit*

29 la cuvette de lavabo *m* (la cuvette lave-cheveux)
- *shampoo basin*

30 la douche à main *f*
- *hand spray (shampoo spray)*

31 la table porte-objets (la desserte)
- *service tray*

32 la bouteille de shampooing *m*
- *shampoo bottle*

33 le sèche-cheveux
- *hair drier (hand hair drier, hand-held hair drier)*

34 le peignoir
- *cape (gown)*

35 la coiffeuse
- *hairdresser*

36 le flacon de parfum *m*
- *perfume bottle*

37 le flacon d'eau *f* de toilette *f*
- *bottle of toilet water*

38 la perruque (le postiche, les cheveux *m* postiches)
- *wig*

39 la tête à perruque *f* (le porte-perruque)
- *wig block*

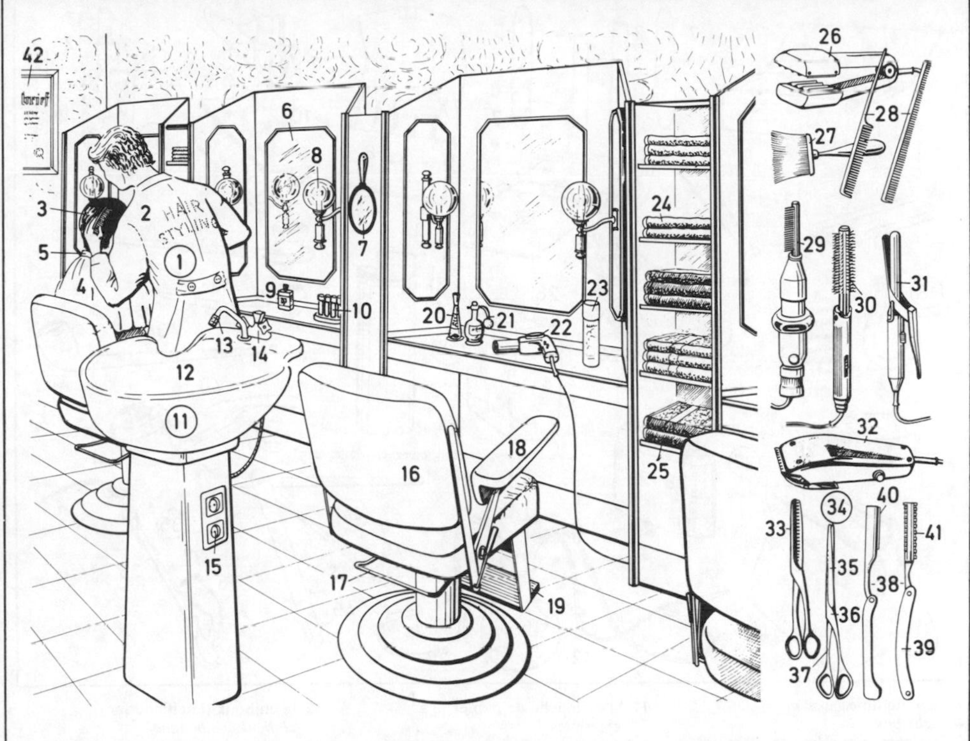

1-42 le salon de coiffure *f* pour hommes *m*
– *men's salon (men's hairdressing salon, barber's shop,* Am. *barbershop)*
1 le coiffeur (le maître-coiffeur)
– *hairdresser (barber)*
2 la blouse de coiffeur *m*
– *overalls (hairdresser's overalls)*
3 la coupe de cheveux *m* (la coiffure)
– *hairstyle (haircut)*
4 le peignoir
– *cape (gown)*
5 le col de papier *m*
– *paper towel*
6 le miroir mural (à supports *m* muraux) du salon de coiffure *f*
– *salon mirror (mirror)*
7 le miroir à main *f*
– *hand mirror (hand glass)*
8 l'applique *f* murale (la lampe d'éclairage *m*)
– *light*
9 l'eau *f* de toilette *f*
– *toilet water*
10 la lotion capillaire (le tonique, la lotion revitalisante)
– *hair tonic*
11 le lavabo pour le lavage des cheveux *m*
– *shampoo unit*
12 la cuvette de lavabo *m* (la cuvette lave-cheveux)
– *shampoo basin*
13 la douche à main *f*
– *hand spray (shampoo spray)*
14 la robinetterie mélangeuse (les robinets *m* mélangeurs, le mélangeur, le mitigeur)
– *mixer tap (*Am. *mixing faucet)*
15 les prises *f* de sèche-cheveux *m*
– *sockets, e.g. for hair drier*
16 le fauteuil de coiffeur *m* réglable (ajustable)
– *adjustable hairdresser's chair (barber's chair)*
17 la barre (l'arceau *m*) de réglage *m*
– *height-adjuster bar (height adjuster)*
18 l'accoudoir *m* (le bras du fauteuil)
– *armrest*
19 le repose-pieds
– *footrest*
20 le shampooing
– *shampoo*
21 le vaporisateur de parfum *m*
– *perfume spray*
22 le sèche-cheveux
– *hair drier (hand hair drier, hand-held hair drier)*
23 l'atomiseur *m* (la bombe) de fixatif *m* pour cheveux *m*
– *setting lotion in a spray can*
24 les serviettes *f* de toilette *f* pour sécher les cheveux *m*
– *hand towels for drying hair*
25 les petites serviettes *f* pour compresses *f* faciales
– *towels for face compresses*
26 le fer à crêper les cheveux *m*
– *crimping iron*
27 le blaireau
– *neck brush*
28 le peigne de coiffeur *m* (le peigne fin, le démêloir)
– *dressing comb*
29 le peigne à jet *m* d'air *m* chaud (le peigne soufflant, le peigne sèche-cheveux)
– *warm-air comb*
30 la brosse à jet *m* d'air *m* chaud (la brosse chauffante)
– *warm-air brush*
31 le fer à friser (le fer à coiffer)
– *curling tongs (hair curler, curling iron)*
32 la tondeuse électrique
– *electric clippers*
33 les ciseaux *m* à effiler (à désépaissir)
– *thinning scissors (*Am. *thinning shears)*
34 les grands ciseaux *m* de coiffeur *m*, *égal.:* les ciseaux *m* «sculpteurs» *m*
– *haircutting scissors;* sim.: *styling scissors*
35 la lame (le tranchant) des ciseaux *m*
– *scissor-blade*
36 le pivot (l'entablure *f*, l'articulation *f*)
– *pivot*
37 la branche
– *handle*
38 le rasoir à main *f*
– *open razor (straight razor)*
39 le manche
– *razor handle*
40 le tranchant (le fil) du rasoir
– *edge (cutting edge, razor's edge, razor's cutting edge)*
41 le rasoir effileur (le rasoir à désépaissir)
– *thinning razor*
42 le brevet de maîtrise *f* (le diplôme de maître-coiffeur *m*)
– *diploma*

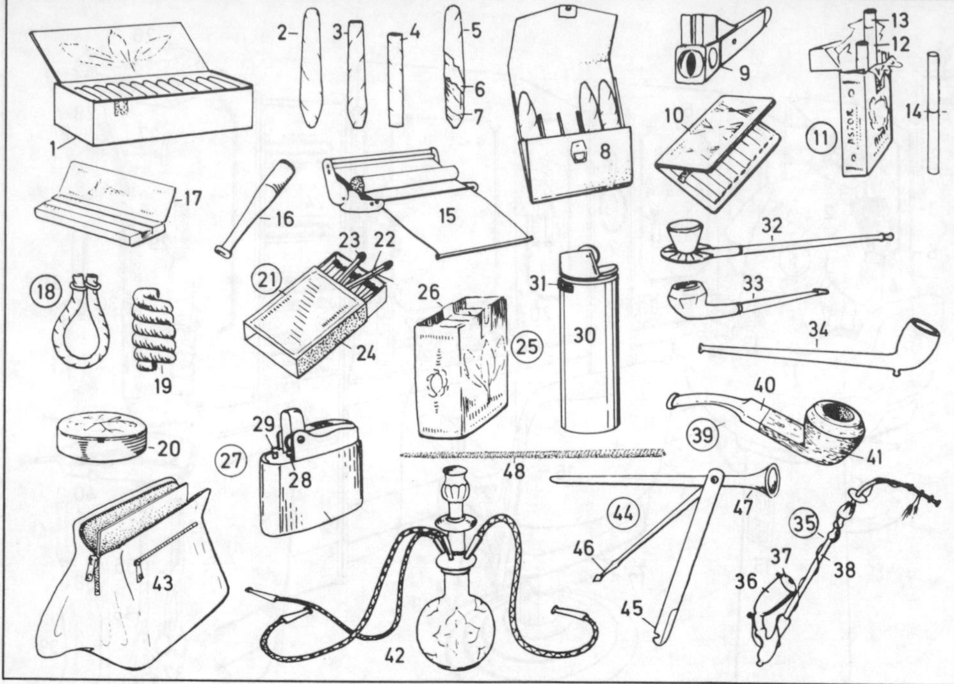

1 la boîte de cigares *m*
– *cigar box*
2 le cigare; *var.:* Havane, Brésil, Sumatra
– *cigar;* kinds: *Havana cigar (Havana), Brazilian cigar, Sumatra cigar*
3 le cigarillo
– *cigarillo*
4 le bout coupé
– *cheroot*
5 la cape (la robe)
– *wrapper*
6 la sous-cape (la première enveloppe)
– *binder*
7 la tripe (l'intérieur *m*)
– *filler*
8 l'étui *m* à cigares *m* (le porte-cigares)
– *cigar case*
9 le coupe-cigares
– *cigar cutter*
10 l'étui *m* à cigarettes *f* (le porte-cigarettes)
– *cigarette case*
11 le paquet de cigarettes *f*
– *cigarette packet* (Am. *pack)*
12 la cigarette, une cigarette-filtre
– *cigarette, a filter-tipped cigarette*
13 le bout; *var.:* le bout-liège, le bout doré
– *cigarette tip;* kinds: *cork tip, gold tip*
14 la cigarette à bouquin *m*
– *Russian cigarette*
15 la rouleuse
– *cigarette roller*
16 le fume-cigarettes
– *cigarette holder*
17 la cartouche de papier *m* à cigarettes *f*
– *packet of cigarette papers*
18 le tabac roulé (le rôle)
– *pigtail (twist of tobacco)*
19 le tabac à chiquer; *un fragment:* la chique
– *chewing tobacco;* a piece: *plug (quid, chew)*
20 la tabatière [contenant le tabac à priser]
– *snuff box, containing snuff*
21 la boîte d'allumettes *f*
– *matchbox*
22 l'allumette *f*
– *match*
23 le bout soufré (la tête soufrée)
– *head (match head)*
24 le frottoir
– *striking surface*
25 le paquet de tabac *m*; *var.:* la coupe fine (le scaferlati), le caporal, la coupe marine
– *packet of tobacco;* kinds: *fine cut, shag, navy plug*
26 la vignette fiscale
– *revenue stamp*
27 le briquet à essence *f*
– *petrol cigarette lighter (petrol lighter)*
28 la pierre à briquet *m*
– *flint*
29 la mèche
– *wick*
30 le briquet à gaz *m*, un briquet à jeter
– *gas cigarette lighter (gas lighter), a disposable lighter*
31 la molette de réglage *m* de la flamme
– *flame regulator*
32 le chibouk (la chibouque)
– *chibonk (chibonque)*
33 la pipe courte
– *short pipe*
34 la pipe en terre *f*
– *clay pipe (Dutch pipe)*
35 la pipe longue
– *long pipe*
36 le fourneau de pipe *f*
– *pipe bowl (bowl)*
37 le couvercle de pipe *f*
– *bowl lid*
38 le tuyau de pipe *f*
– *pipe stem (stem)*
39 la pipe de bruyère*f*
– *briar pipe*
40 l'embout *m*
– *mouthpiece*
41 le veinage (obtenu par sablage ou polissage de la racine de bruyère *f)*
– *sand-blast finished or polished briar grain*
42 le narguilé (ou narghilé), une pipe à eau *f*
– *hookah (narghile, narghileh), a water pipe*
43 la blague à tabac *m*
– *tobacco pouch*
44 le nécessaire du fumeur de pipe *f*
– *smoker's companion*
45 le coupe-carbone
– *pipe scraper*
46 le bourre-pipe
– *pipe cleaner*
47 le cure-pipe
– *tobacco presser*
48 le nettoie-pipe
– *pipe cleaner*

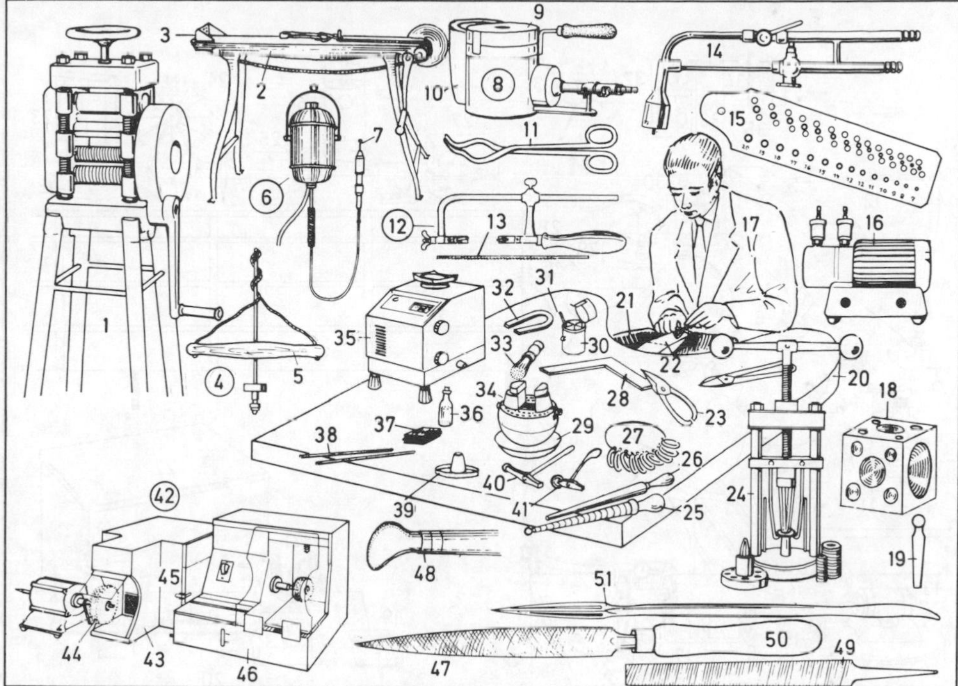

1 le laminoir pour fil *m* et plané *m*
– *wire and sheet roller*
2 le banc à étirer
– *drawbench (drawing bench)*
3 le fil (fil *m* d'or *m* ou d'argent *m*)
– *wire (gold or silver wire)*
4 le drille
– *archimedes drill (drill)*
5 la poignée
– *crossbar*
6 la perceuse électrique
– *suspended (pendant) electric drilling machine*
7 la pièce à main *f* avec fraise *f*
– *spherical cutter (cherry)*
8 le four de fonte *f*
– *melting pot*
9 le couvercle
– *fireclay top*
10 le creuset en graphite *m*
– *graphite crucible*
11 la pince de fondeur *m*
– *crucible tongs*
12 la scie de bijoutier *m*
– *piercing saw (jig saw)*
13 la lame de scie *f* de bijoutier *m*
– *piercing saw blade*
14 le chalumeau
– *soldering gun*
15 la filière
– *thread tapper*
16 le compresseur
– *blast burner (blast lamp) for soldering*
17 le bijoutier, l'orfèvre *m*
– *goldsmith*
18 le dé à cambrer
– *swage block*
19 la bouterolle
– *punch*
20 l'établi *m*
– *workbench (bench)*
21 la peau
– *bench apron*
22 la cheville
– *needle file*
23 la cisaille
– *metal shears*
24 le balancier pour anneaux *m*
– *wedding ring sizing machine*
25 le triboulet métrique
– *ring gauge (Am. gage)*
26 le triboulet
– *ring-rounding tool*
27 l'annelier *m*
– *ring gauge (Am. gage)*
28 l'équerre *f*
– *steel set-square*
29 le coussin d'orfèvre *m*
– *leather pad*
30 la boîte à poinçons *m*
– *box of punches*
31 le poinçon
– *punch*
32 l'aimant *m*
– *magnet*
33 la brosse d'orfèvre *m*
– *bench brush*
34 la boule de graveur *m*
– *engraving ball (joint vice, clamp)*
35 le trébuchet, une balance de précision *f*
– *gold and silver balance (assay balance), a precision balance*
36 le fondant
– *soldering flux (flux)*
37 le charbon [la plaque de charbon *m* de bois *m*]
– *charcoal block*
38 la soudure (la baguette d'apport *m*)
– *stick of solder*
39 le borax
– *soldering borax*
40 le marteau à façonner
– *shaping hammer*
41 le marteau à ciseler
– *chasing (enchasing) hammer*
42 le tour à polir
– *polishing and burnishing machine*
43 l'aspirateur *m* de table *f*
– *dust exhauster (vacuum cleaner)*
44 la brosse à polir
– *polishing wheel*
45 la boîte d'aspiration *f*
– *dust collector (dust catcher)*
46 la machine à polir en milieu *m* humide
– *buffing machine*
47 la lime queue *f* de rat *m* (la queue-de-rat)
– *round file*
48 le brunissoir
– *bloodstone (haematite, hematite)*
49 la lime plate
– *flat file*
50 le manche de lime *f*
– *file handle*
51 le grattoir
– *polishing iron (burnisher)*

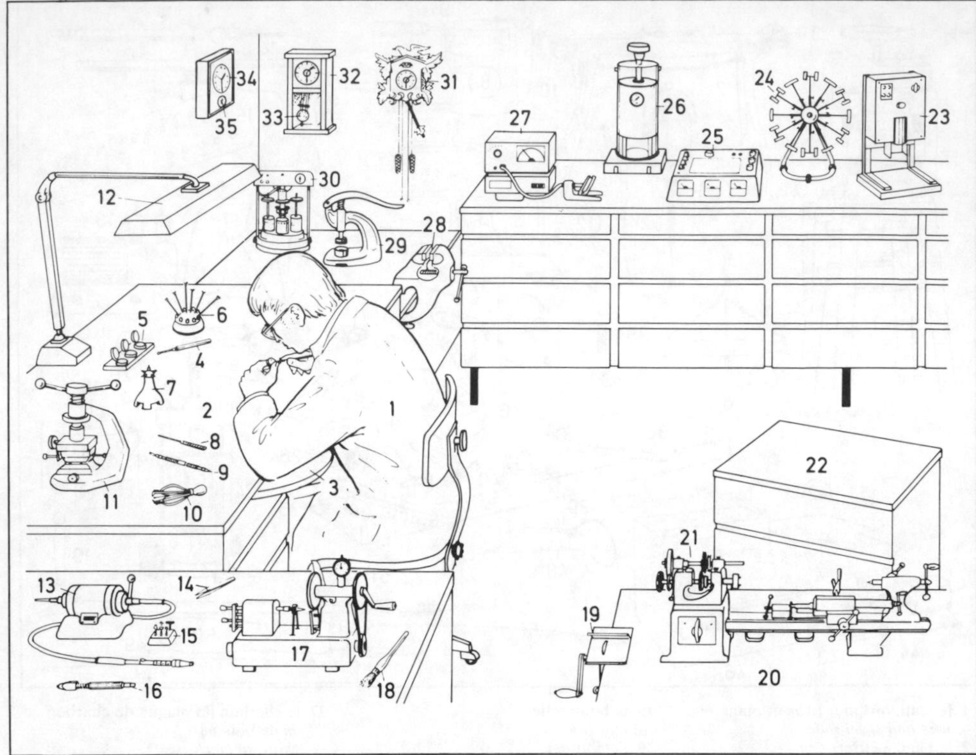

1 l'horloger *m*
– *watchmaker;* also: *clockmaker*
2 l'établi *m*
– *workbench*
3 le repose-bras
– *armrest*
4 le pique-huile
– *oiler*
5 l'huilier *m* pour montres *f*
– *oil stand*
6 le jeu de tournevis *m*
– *set of screwdrivers*
7 l'enclume *f* à aiguilles *f*
– *clockmaker's anvil*
8 l'alésoir *m*, l'équarrissoir *m*
– *broach, a reamer*
9 l'outil *m* à poser et enlever les barrettes *f* à ressorts *m*
– *spring pin tool*
10 l'outil *m* presto pour enlever les aiguilles *f* de montre-bracelet *f*
– *hand-removing tool*
11 la potence à ouvrir et fermer les boîtes *f* de montre *f* étanche
– *watchglass-fitting tool*
12 la lampe d'établi *m*
– *workbench lamp, a multi-purpose lamp*
13 le moteur multi-usage
– *multi-purpose motor*
14 les brucelles *f*
– *tweezers*
15 les meules *f*
– *polishing machine attachments*
16 le mandrin à main *f*
– *pin vice (pin holder)*
17 le tour à pivoter pour rouler, polir, arrondir et raccourcir les pivots *m*
– *burnisher, for burnishing, polishing, and shortening of spindles*
18 le pinceau
– *dust brush*
19 la cisaille pour bracelets *m* métalliques
– *cutter for metal watch straps*
20 le tour d'horloger *m* (le tour de précision *f*)
– *precision bench lathe (watchmaker's lathe)*
21 le renvoi à courroie *f* trapézoïdale
– *drive-belt gear*
22 la layette de rangement *m* des pièces *f* de rechange *m*
– *workshop trolley for spare parts*
23 l'appareil *m* de nettoyage *m* par ultrasons *m*
– *ultrasonic cleaner*
24 l'appareil *m* rotatif à contrôler les montres *f* automatiques
– *rotating watch-testing machine for automatic watches*
25 le pupitre de mesure *f* pour contrôle *m* de composants électroniques
– *watch-timing machine for electronic components*
26 l'appareil *m* à contrôler l'étanchéité *f* des montres *f*
– *testing device for waterproof watches*
27 le chronocomparateur
– *electronic timing machine*
28 l'étau *m*
– *vice* (Am. *vise)*
29 la potence de pose *f* des verres *m* armés (verres *m* à bague *f* de tension *f)*
– *watchglass-fitting tool for armoured* (Am. *armored) glasses*
30 la machine automatique de nettoyage *m* traditionnel
– *[automatic] cleaning machine for conventional cleaning*
31 le coucou (une horloge à coucou *m* de la Forêt-Noire)
– *cuckoo clock (Black Forest clock)*
32 la pendule murale (l'horloge *f* de paroi *f*, le régulateur)
– *wall clock (regulator)*
33 le pendule à gril (le pendule de Harrison, le pendule compensateur *m)*
– *compensation pendulum*
34 la pendule de cuisine *f*
– *kitchen clock*
35 le compte-minutes (le minuteur)
– *timer*

1 la montre-bracelet (la montre) électronique
- *electronic wristwatch*

2 l'affichage *m* numérique, un affichage à diodes électroluminescentes (LED); *égal.:* un affichage à cristaux *m* liquides
- *digital readout, a light-emitting diode (LED) readout;* also: *liquid crystal readout*

3 le poussoir heures-minutes *f*
- *hour and minute button*

4 le poussoir date-secondes *f*
- *date and second button*

5 le bracelet
- *strap (watch strap)*

6 le principe du diapason (le principe de la montre à diapason *m*)
- *tuning fork principle (principle of the tuning fork watch)*

7 la source d'électricité (une pile bouton)
- *power source (battery cell)*

8 le circuit électronique
- *transformer*

9 le diapason (l'élément *m* vibrant)
- *tuning fork element (oscillating element)*

10 la roue à rochet *m*
- *wheel ratchet*

11 le rouage de montre *f*
- *wheels*

12 l'aiguille *f* des minutes *f*
- *minute hand*

13 l'aiguille *f* des heures *f*
- *hour hand*

14 le principe de la montre à quartz *m* électronique
- *principle of the electronic quartz watch*

15 le quartz (le quartz vibrant)
- *quartz*

16 la division de fréquence *f* (circuits *m* intégrés)
- *integrated circuit*

17 le moteur pas-à-pas
- *oscillation counter*

18 le décodeur
- *decoder*

19 le réveil (le réveil-matin)
- *calendar clock (alarm clock)*

20 l'affichage *m* numérique à chiffres *m* pivotants
- *digital display with flip-over numerals*

21 l'affichage *m* des secondes *f*
- *second indicator*

22 le bouton d'arrêt *m*
- *stop button*

23 la molette de réglage *m*
- *forward and backward wind knob*

24 l'horloge *f* (la pendule de parquet *m*)
- *grandfather clock*

25 le cadran
- *face*

26 le coffre (le cabinet d'une horloge de parquet *m*)
- *clock case*

27 la pendule
- *pendulum*

28 le poids de sonnerie *f*
- *striking weight*

29 le poids moteur
- *time weight*

30 le cadran solaire
- *sundial*

31 le sablier
- *hourglass (egg timer)*

32-43 la vue éclatée d'une montre-bracelet automatique (la montre à remontage *m* automatique)
- ***components of an automatic watch*** *(automatic wristwatch)*

32 la masse oscillante (le volant, le rotor) de remontoir *m* automatique
- *weight (rotor)*

33 la pierre d'horlogerie *f*, un rubis synthétique
- *stone (jewel, jewelled bearing), a synthetic ruby*

34 le cliquet de remontage *m*
- *click*

35 la roue à cliquet *m* de remontage *m*
- *click wheel*

36 le mouvement d'horlogerie *f*
- *clockwork (clockwork mechanism)*

37 la platine
- *bottom train plate*

38 le barillet
- *spring barrel*

39 le balancier
- *balance wheel*

40 la roue d'échappement *m*
- *escape wheel*

41 la roue de couronne *f*
- *crown wheel*

42 la couronne de remontoir *m*
- *winding crown*

43 le mécanisme moteur *m*
- *drive mechanism*

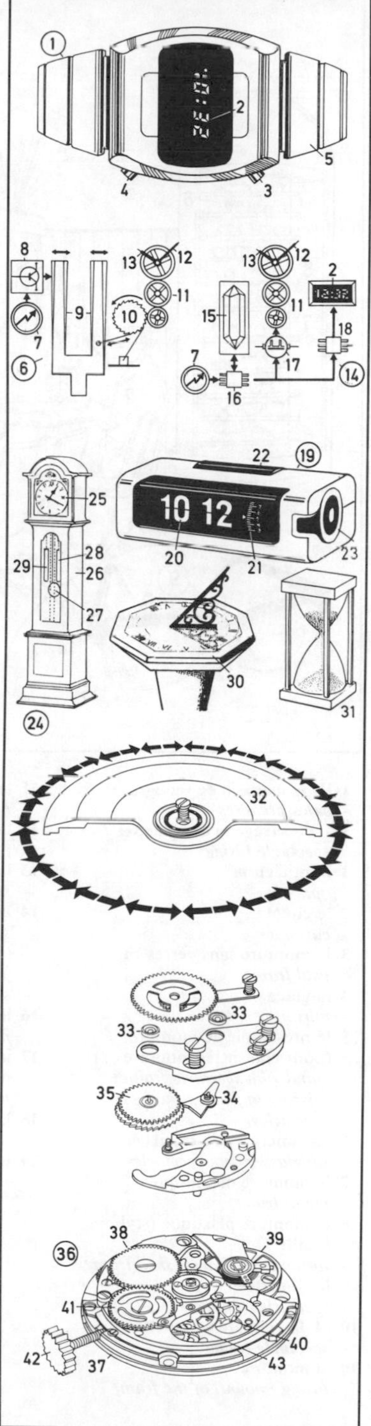

1-19 le magasin de vente *f*
– ***sales premises***
1-4 l'essayage *m* **des lunettes** *f*
– ***spectacle fitting***
1 l'opticien *m*
– *optician*
2 le client
– *customer*
3 la monture sans verres *m*
– *trial frame*
4 la glace
– *mirror*
5 le présentoir de montures *f* (pour choisir les montures *f*)
– *stand with spectacle frames (display of frames, range of spectacles)*
6 les lunettes *f* de soleil *m*
– *sunglasses (sun spectacles)*
7 la monture métallique
– *metal frame*
8 la monture plastique (style *m* écaille *f*)
– *tortoiseshell frame (shell frame)*
9 les lunettes *f*
– *spectacles (glasses)*
10-14 la monture de lunettes *f*
– ***spectacle frame***
10 la monture
– *fitting (mount) of the frame*
11 le pont
– *bridge*
12 la plaquette
– *pad bridge*
13 la branche
– *side*
14 la charnière
– *side joint*
15 le verre de lunettes *f*, un verre à double foyer *m* (bifocal)
– *spectacle lens, a bifocal lens*
16 le miroir à main *f*
– *hand mirror (hand glass)*
17 une paire de jumelles *f* (les jumelles)
– *binoculars*
18 la longue-vue
– *monocular telescope (tube)*
19 le microscope
– *microscope*

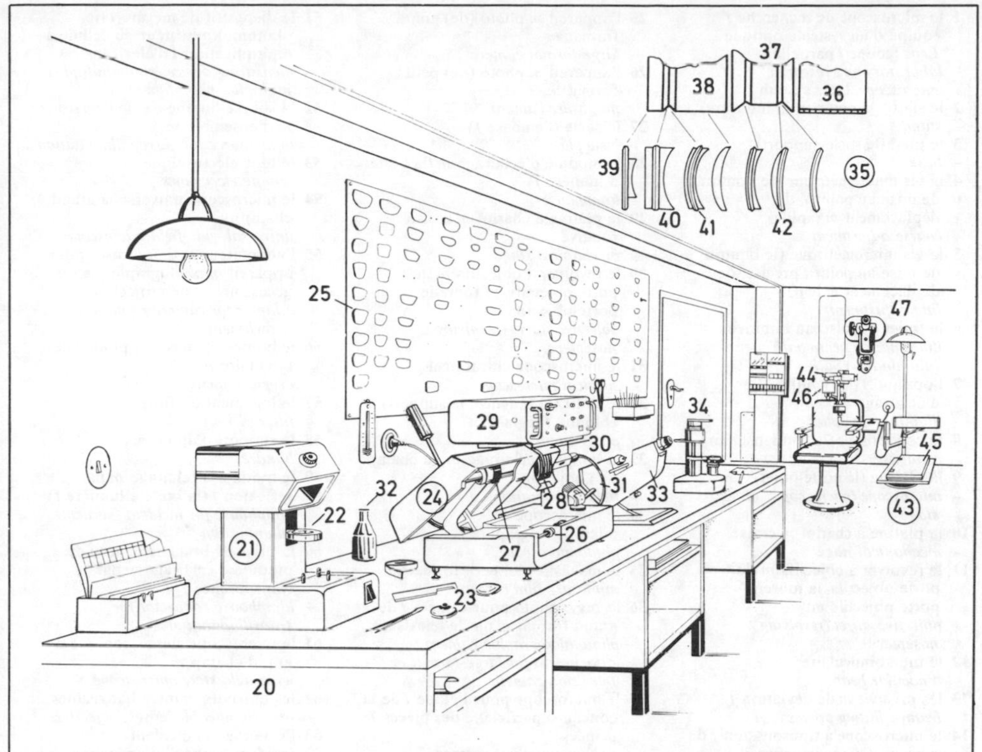

20-47 l'atelier *m* d'opticien *m*
– ***optician's workshop***

20 la table de travail *m*
– *workbench*

21 le focomètre universel (pour centrer le verre par rapport à l'œil *m*)
– *universal centring (centering) apparatus*

22 le support de centrage *m*
– *centring (centering) suction holder*

23 la ventouse de centrage *m*
– *sucker*

24 l'appareil *m* automatique pour le façonnage des verres *m* de lunettes *f*
– *edging machine*

25 le tableau de calibres *m* pour le travail automatique
– *formers for the lens edging machine*

26 le calibre monté sur l'appareil *m*
– *inserted former*

27 la copie verre *m* à verre *m*
– *rotating printer*

28 le jeu de meules *f*
– *abrasive wheel combination*

29 l'appareil *m* de commande *f*
– *control unit*

30 le mécanisme
– *machine part*

31 l'arrivée *f* d'eau *f* de refroidissement *m*
– *cooling water pipe*

32 le liquide de dégraissage *m*, un produit de nettoyage *m*
– *cleaning fluid*

33 le fronto-focomètre
– *focimeter (vertex refractionometer)*

34 l'appareil *m* à centrer et à ventouser
– *metal-blocking device*

35 le jeu de meules *f* pour façonner le verre
– *abrasive wheel combination and forms of edging*

36 la meule de dégrossissage *m*
– *roughing wheel for preliminary surfacing*

37 la meule de finition *f* pour biseautage *m* des verres *m* positifs et négatifs
– *fining lap for positive and negative lens surfaces*

38 la meule de finition *f* pour biseautage *m* des verres *m* spéciaux ou plats à facette *f*
– *fining lap for special and flat lenses*

39 le verre plan-concave *m* avec facette *f* plate
– *plano-concave lens with a flat surface*

40 le verre plan-concave *m* avec facette *f* spéciale
– *plano-concave lens with a special surface*

41 le verre concave-convexe avec facette *f* spéciale
– *concave and convex lens with a special surface*

42 le verre concave-convexe avec facette *f* négative
– *convex and concave lens with a special surface*

43 l'équipement *m* ophtalmologique
– *ophthalmic test stand*

44 l'ophtalmomètre *m* et le réfractomètre
– *phoropter with ophthalmometer and optometer (refractometer)*

45 la boîte d'essai *m* de verres *m*
– *trial lens case*

46 le support de projection *f* de lettres *f*
– *collimator*

47 le projecteur
– *acuity projector*

1 le microscope de recherche *f* équipé d'un système optique *Leitz* [coupe *f* partielle]
– *laboratory and research microscope,* Leitz system
2 le statif (la potence, la monture)
– *stand*
3 le pied (le socle-support)
– *base*
4 la vis macrométrique (le bouton de mise au point *f,* de déplacement *m* rapide)
– *coarse adjustment*
5 la vis micrométrique (le bouton de mise au point *f* précise, de déplacement *m* lent)
– *fine adjustment*
6 le trajet du faisceau lumineux
– *illumination beam path (illumination path)*
7 l'optique *f* (les lentilles *f*) d'éclairage *m*
– *illumination optics*
8 le condenseur (le condensateur)
– *condenser*
9 la platine (le porte-objet)
– *microscope (microscopic, object) stage*
10 la platine à chariot *m* croisé
– *mechanical stage*
11 le revolver à objectifs *m* (le porte-objectifs, la tourelle porte-objectifs *m*)
– *objective turret (revolving nosepiece)*
12 le tube binoculaire
– *binocular head*
13 les prismes *m* de déviation *f*
– *beam-splitting prisms*
14 le microscope à transmission *f* de type *m Zeiss* avec appareil photographique et polariseur *m* (le microscope polarisant de microphotographie *f*)
– *transmitted-light microscope with camera and polarizer,* Zeiss system
15 le socle-support de la platine (le module porte-platine)
– *stage base*
16 le curseur (le coulisseau) du diaphragme d'ouverture *f*
– *aperture-stop slide*
17 la platine rotative universelle
– *universal stage*
18 le (module) porte-objectifs *m*
– *lens panel*
19 le module d'observation *f*
– *polarizing filter*
20 la chambre photographique
– *camera*
21 l'écran *m* de mise au point *f*
– *focusing screen*
22 la pièce de fixation *f* des tubes *m* de discussion *f*
– *discussion tube arrangement*
23 le microscope de métallographie *f* à grand champ *m,* un microscope à lumière *f* réfléchie (à éclairage *m* incident)
– *wide-field metallurgical microscope, a reflected-light microscope (microscope for reflected light)*
24 le (verre) dépoli de projection *f*
– *matt screen (ground glass screen, projection screen)*
25 l'appareil *m* photo (de) grand format *m*
– *large-format camera*
26 l'appareil *m* photo (de) petit format *m*
– *miniature camera*
27 le socle (l'embase *f*)
– *base plate*
28 le module d'éclairage *m* (la boîte à lumière *f*)
– *lamphouse*
29 la platine à chariot *m* croisé rotative
– *mechanical stage*
30 le revolver à objectifs *m* (le porte-objectifs, la tourelle porte-objectifs *m*)
– *objective turret (revolving nosepiece)*
31 le microscope chirurgical
– *surgical microscope*
32 le statif (la potence, le support) à colonne *f* réglable
– *pillar stand*
33 la lampe d'éclairage *m* du champ de l'objet *m*
– *field illumination*
34 le microscope de microphotographie *f*
– *photomicroscope*
35 le magasin (de) petit format *m*
– *miniature film cassette*
36 la prise photo pour caméra *f* de grand format *m* ou de télévision *f*
– *photomicrographic camera attachment for large-format or television camera*
37 le microscope pour l'étude *f* de la couche superficielle des pièces *f* usinées
– *surface-finish microscope*
38 le tube à coupes *f* optiques
– *light section tube*
39 la crémaillère
– *rack and pinion*
40 le microscope stéréoscopique équipé d'un zoom à grand champ *m*
– *zoom stereomicroscope*
41 le zoom (l'objectif *m* à focale *f* variable)
– *zoom lens*
42 le compteur de poussières *f* micrométrique
– *dust counter*
43 la chambre de mesure *f*
– *measurement chamber*
44 la sortie des données *f*
– *data output*
45 la sortie analogique
– *analogue* (Am. *analog*) *output*
46 le sélecteur des zones *f* de mesure *f* (des plages *f* d'étude *f*)
– *measurement range selector*
47 l'affichage *m* numérique
– *digital display (digital readout)*
48 le réfractomètre à immersion *f* de contrôle *m* alimentaire
– *dipping refractometer for examining food*
49 le microscope à photomètre *m*
– *microscopic photometer*
50 la source lumineuse du photomètre (la cellule photo-électrique)
– *photometric light source*
51 le dispositif de mesure *f* (le photomultiplicateur ou cellule à multiplication *f* d'électrons *m*)
– *measuring device (photomultiplier, multiplier phototube)*
52 la source lumineuse de l'éclairage *m* d'ensemble *m*
– *light source for survey illumination*
53 le bloc électronique
– *remote electronics*
54 le microscope universel à grand champ *m*
– *universal wide-field microscope*
55 l'adaptateur *m* (le raccord) pour appareil *m* photographique ou accessoire *m* de projection *f*
– *adapter for camera or projector attachment*
56 le bouton de mise au point *f* de l'oculaire *m*
– *eyepiece focusing knob*
57 le logement du filtre
– *filter pick-up*
58 le support d'appui *m*
– *handrest*
59 le module d'éclairage *m* par reflexion *f* (la boîte à lumière *f*)
– *lamphouse for incident (vertical) illumination*
60 la prise de branchement *m* du module d'éclairage *m* par transparence *f*
– *lamphouse connector for transillumination*
61 le microscope stéréoscopique à grand champ *m*
– *wide-field stereomicroscope*
62 les objectifs *m* interchangeables
– *interchangeable lenses (objectives)*
63 l'éclairage *m* incident
– *incident (vertical) illumination (incident top lighting)*
64 l'appareil *m* photo de microscope *m* entièrement automatique, un appareil photographique à adaptateur *m*
– *fully automatic microscope camera, a camera with photomicro mount adapter*
65 le magasin du film photographique
– *film cassette*
66 le condenseur universel du microscope de recherche *f*
– *universal condenser for research microscope 1*
67 la chambre métrique universelle de photogrammétrie *f* (le photothéodolite)
– *universal-type measuring machine for photogrammetry (phototheodolite)*
68 l'appareil *m* de photogrammétrie *f*
– *photogrammetric camera*
69 le niveau à moteur *m,* un niveau à compensateur *m*
– *motor-driven level, a compensator level*
70 le tachéomètre électro-optique
– *electro-optical distance-measuring instrument*
71 l'appareil *m* de stéréométrie *f*
– *stereometric camera*
72 le bras de support *m* horizontal
– *horizontal base*
73 le théodolite universel
– *one-second theodolite*

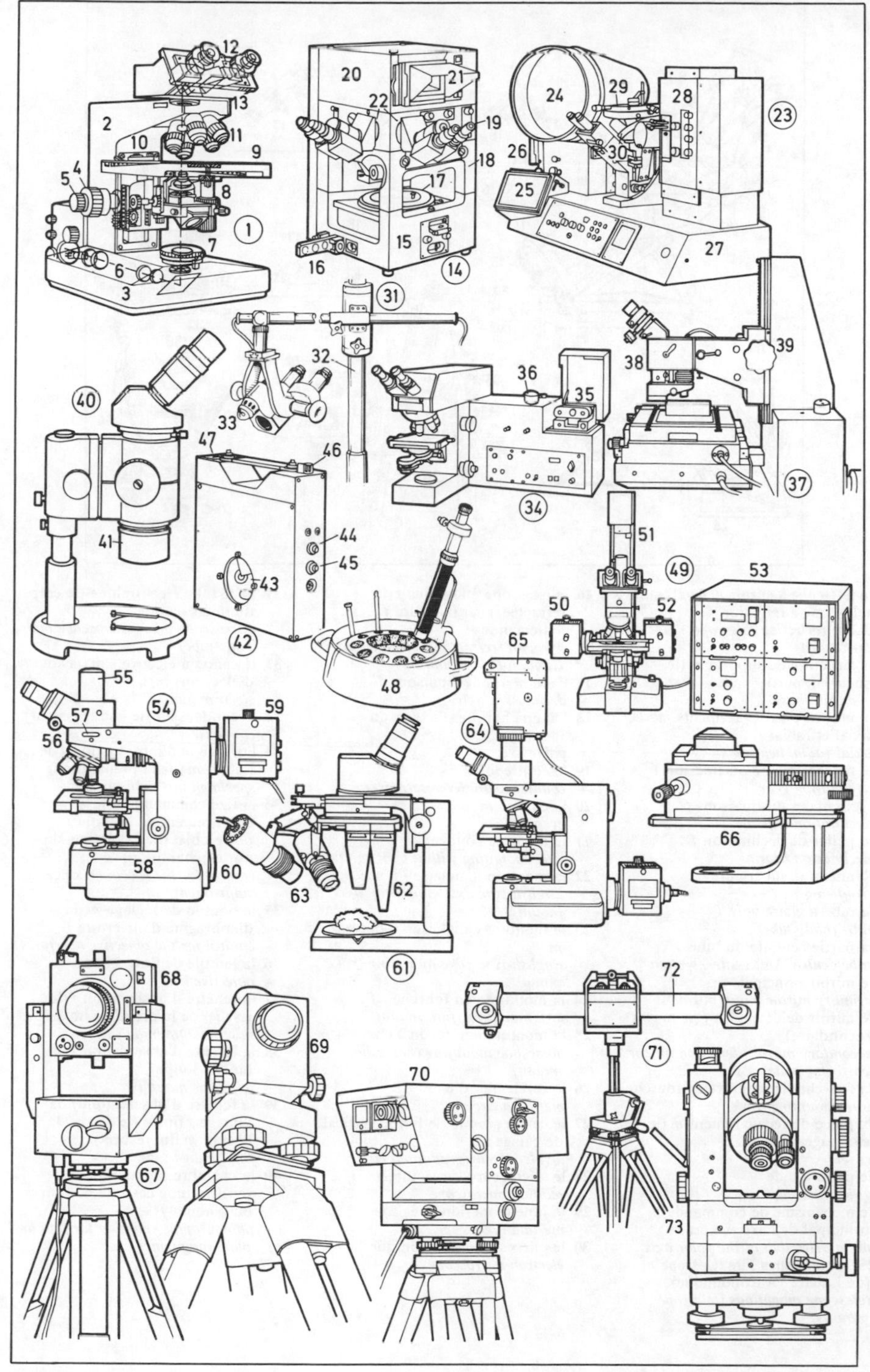
1
2
3
4
5
6
7
8
9
10
11
12
13
14
15
16
17
18
19
20
21
22
23
24
25
26
27
28
29
30
31
32
33
34
35
36
37
38
39
40
41
42
43
44
45
46
47
48
49
50
51
52
53
54
55
56
57
58
59
60
61
62
63
64
65
66
67
68
69
70
71
72
73

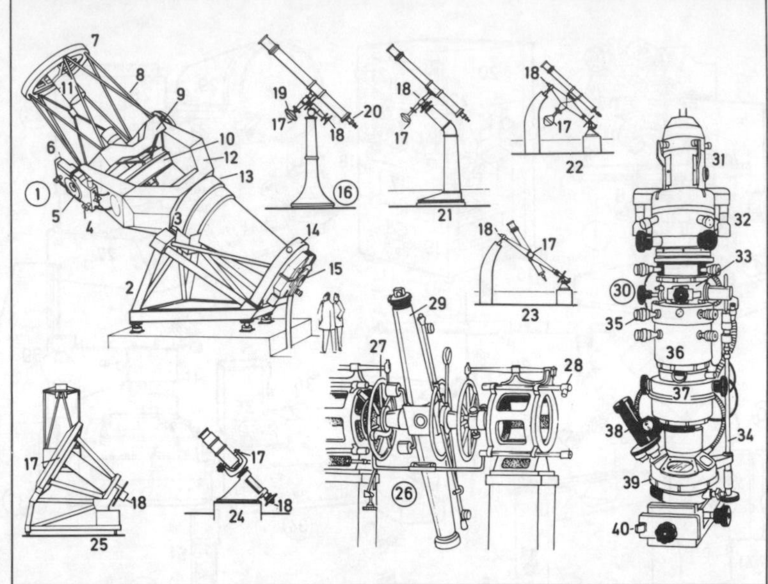

1 le télescope à miroir *m* **de 2,2 m** (le télescope à reflexion *f*)
– ***2.2 m reflecting telescope*** *(reflector)*
2 la structure de support *m* (le socle-support)
– *pedestal (base)*
3 la monture à déplacements *m* axial et radial
– *axial-radial bearing*
4 le mécanisme de déclinaison *f*
– *declination gear*
5 l'axe *m* des déclinaisons *f*
– *declination axis*
6 le palier de déclinaison *f*
– *declination bearing*
7 l'anneau *m* supérieur
– *front ring*
8 le tube à claire-voie *f*
– *tube (body tube)*
9 la partie centrale du tube
– *tube centre (*Am. *center) section*
10 le miroir principal
– *primary mirror (main mirror)*
11 le miroir de déviation *f* (le miroir secondaire)
– *secondary mirror (deviation mirror, corrector plate)*
12 la fourche (la monture en fourche *f*)
– *fork mounting (fork)*
13 la pièce de recouvrement *m* (le carénage, la chape)
– *cover*
14 le palier-guide
– *guide bearing*
15 le mécanisme de commande *f* principal de l'axe *m* horaire
– *main drive unit of the polar axis*
16-25 les montures *f* **de télescope** *m* (de lunette *f* astronomique)
– ***telescope mountings*** *(telescope mounts)*
16 le télescope à lentilles *f* (le réfracteur) sur monture *f* «allemande»
– *refractor (refracting telescope) on a German-type mounting*
17 l'axe *m* des déclinaisons *f*
– *declination axis*
18 l'axe *m* horaire (l'axe *m* du monde)
– *polar axis*
19 le contrepoids
– *counterweight (counterpoise)*
20 l'oculaire *m*
– *eyepiece*
21 la monture coudée
– *knee mounting with a bent column*
22 la monture «anglaise» à axe *m*
– *English-type axis mounting (axis mount)*
23 la monture «anglaise» à berceau *m*
– *English-type yoke mounting (yoke mount)*
24 la monture «en fourche» *f*
– *fork mounting (fork mount)*
25 la monture «en fer *m* à cheval» *m*
– *horseshoe mounting (horseshoe mount)*
26 le cercle méridien
– *meridian circle*
27 le cercle gradué (le limbe vertical de calage *m*)
– *divided circle (graduated circle)*
28 le microscope de lecture *f*
– *reading microscope*
29 la lunette méridienne
– *meridian telescope*
30 le microscope électronique
– *electron microscope*
31-39 le tube électronique (le corps du microscope)
– *microscope tube (microscope body, body tube)*
31 le canon à électrons *m* (la source d'électrons *m*)
– *electron gun*
32 le condenseur (le condensateur)
– *condensers*
33 l'orifice *m* d'introduction *f* de l'objet *m* (de la préparation)
– *specimen insertion air lock*
34 la tige commandant le déplacement de la grille porte-objet (de la platine, du porte-échantillon)
– *control for the specimen stage adjustment*
35 le bouton de réglage *m* du diaphragme d'ouverture *f*
– *control for the objective apertures*
36 la lentille de l'objectif *m*
– *objective lens*
37 la fenêtre d'observation *f* (le viseur) de la première image
– *intermediate image screen*
38 la lunette d'observation *f* (la lunette-loupe)
– *telescope magnifier*
39 la fenêtre d'observation *f* de l'image *f* finale (le viseur de l'écran *m* fluorescent)
– *final image tube*
40 la chambre photographique recevant une cassette de film *m* ou plaques *f*
– *photographic chamber for film and plate magazines*

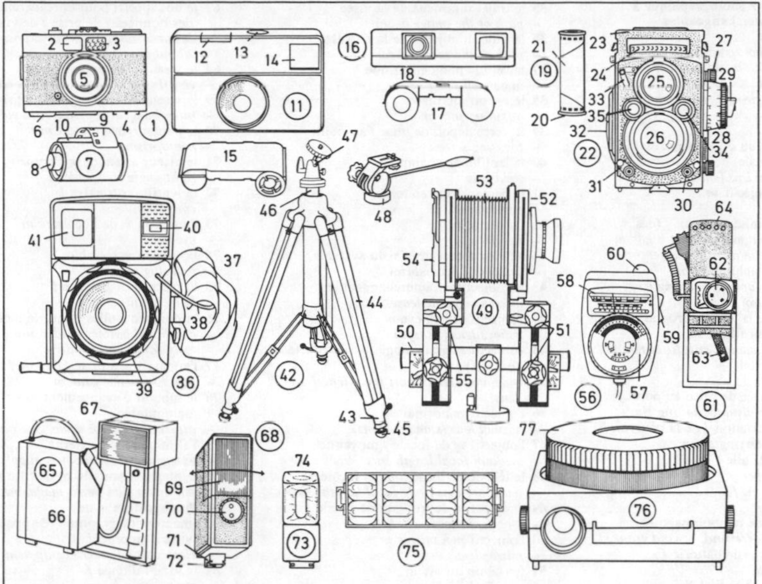

1 l'appareil *m* photographique petit format *m* (le 24 x 36)
- *miniature camera (35 mm camera)*

2 la fenêtre du viseur
- *viewfinder eyepiece*

3 la fenêtre du posemètre (de la cellule)
- *meter cell*

4 la griffe de fixation *f* d'accessoires *m*
- *accessory shoe*

5 l'objectif *m* rentrant
- *flush lens*

6 la manivelle de rembobinage *m*
- *rewind handle (rewind, rewind crank)*

7 la cartouche de pellicule *f* petit format *m* 135
- *miniature film cassette (135 film cassette, 35 mm cassette)*

8 la bobine de pellicule *f*
- *film spool*

9 la pellicule avec l'amorce *f* de chargement *m*
- *film with leader*

10 la fente de la cartouche
- *cassette slit (cassette exit slot)*

11 l'appareil *m* photographique à cassettes *f*
- *cartridge-loading camera*

12 le bouton de déclenchement *m*
- *shutter release (shutter release button)*

13 la fixation du cube à éclairs *m* (du flash-cube)
- *flash cube contact*

14 le viseur carré
- *rectangular viewfinder*

15 la cassette de pellicule *f* format *m* 126 (la cassette Instamatic)
- *126 cartridge (instamatic cartridge)*

16 l'appareil *m* photographique de poche *f*
- *pocket camera (subminiature camera)*

17 la cassette très petit format *m* 110
- *110 cartridge (subminiature cartridge)*

18 la fenêtre de lecture *f* du numéro
- *film window*

19 la pellicule en rouleau *m* 120
- *120 rollfilm*

20 la bobine
- *rollfilm spool*

21 le papier de protection *f*
- *backing paper*

22 l'appareil *m* photographique reflex *m* à deux objectifs *m*
- *twin-lens reflex camera*

23 le viseur à capuchon *m*
- *folding viewfinder hood (focusing hood)*

24 la fenêtre du posemètre (de la cellule)
- *meter cell*

25 l'objectif *m* de visée *f*
- *viewing lens*

26 l'objectif *m* de prise *f* de vue *f*
- *object lens*

27 le bouton de l'axe *m* de bobine *f*
- *spool knob*

28 le bouton de mise *f* au point (de réglage *m* de la distance)
- *distance setting (focus setting)*

29 la commande du posemètre *m* couplé (de la cellule couplée)
- *exposure meter using needle-matching system*

30 la prise de flash *m*
- *flash contact*

31 le bouton de déclenchement *m*
- *shutter release*

32 la manivelle d'avancement *m* du film (manivelle d'armement *m*)
- *film transport (film advance, film wind)*

33 le commutateur du flash
- *flash switch*

34 le bouton de réglage *m* du diaphragme (de l'ouverture *f*)
- *aperture-setting control*

35 le bouton de réglage *m* du temps de pose *f*
- *shutter speed control*

36 l'appareil *m* de reportage *m* grand format *m*
- *large-format hand camera (press camera)*

37 la poignée
- *grip (handgrip)*

38 le déclencheur souple
- *cable release*

39 la bague moletée de mise *f* au point (de réglage *m* de la distance)
- *distance-setting ring (focusing ring)*

40 la fenêtre du télémètre
- *rangefinder window*

41 le viseur multiformat
- *multiple-frame viewfinder (universal viewfinder)*

42 le pied tubulaire (à trois branches *f*)
- *tripod*

43 la semelle du pied
- *tripod leg*

44 la branche du pied
- *tubular leg*

45 l'embout *m* en caoutchouc *m*
- *rubber foot*

46 la colonne centrale
- *central column*

47 la rotule
- *ball and socket head*

48 la tête cinéma *m* (la tête 3 D)
- *cine camera pan and tilt head*

49 la chambre grand format *m* à soufflet *m*
- *large-format folding camera*

50 le banc d'optique *f*
- *optical bench*

51 la noix de réglage *m* frontale
- *standard adjustment*

52 la platine d'objectif *m*
- *lens standard*

53 le soufflet
- *bellows*

54 le dos de la chambre
- *camera back*

55 la noix de réglage *m* arrière
- *back standard adjustment*

56 le posemètre
- *hand-held exposure meter (exposure meter)*

57 le calculateur du posemètre
- *calculator dial*

58 les échelles *f* avec l'aiguille *f* de mesure *f*
- *scales (indicator scales) with indicator needle (pointer)*

59 le commutateur de sensibilité *f*
- *range switch (high/low range selector)*

60 la calotte diffusante pour mesure *f* en lumière *f* incidente
- *diffuser for incident light measurement*

61 le châssis à posemètre *m*
- *probe exposure meter for large-format cameras*

62 l'appareil *m* de mesure *f*
- *meter*

63 la cellule (la sonde)
- *probe*

64 le volet du châssis
- *dark slide*

65 le flash à accumulateur *m* séparé
- *battery-portable electronic flash (battery-portable electronic flash unit)*

66 l'accumulateur *m* (la batterie)
- *powerpack unit (battery)*

67 la lampe flash *m*
- *flash head*

68 le flash compact
- *single-unit electronic flash (flashgun)*

69 le réflecteur orientable
- *swivel-mounted reflector*

70 la photodiode
- *photodiode*

71 le sabot de fixation *f*
- *foot*

72 le contact central
- *hot-shoe contact*

73 le flash à cubes *m*
- *flash cube unit*

74 le flashcube
- *flash cube*

75 la barrette flash *m* (AGFA)
- *flash bar (AGFA)*

76 le projecteur pour diapositives *f*
- *slide projector*

77 le carrousel
- *rotary magazine*

1-105 l'appareil *m* photographique à objectifs *m* interchangeables
– *system camera*
1 l'appareil *m* photographique petit format *m* reflex *m*, appareil *m* mono-objectif
– *miniature single-lens reflex camera*
2 le boîtier
– *camera body*
3-8 l'objectif *m*, un objectif normal (de focale *f* normale)
– *lens, a normal lens (standard lens)*
3 le barillet d'objectif *m*
– *lens barrel*
4 l'échelle *f* de mise au point *f* (des distances *f*) en mètres *m* et pieds *m*
– *distance scale in metres and feet*
5 la bague de diaphragme *m*
– *aperture ring (aperture-setting ring, aperture control ring)*
6 la monture de la lentille frontale avec fixation *f* pour filtres *m*
– *front element mount with filter mount*
7 la lentille frontale
– *front element*
8 la bague moletée de mise au point *f*
– *focusing ring (distance-setting ring)*
9 l'œillet *m* de fixation *f* de la courroie
– *ring for the carrying strap*
10 le logement de pile *f*
– *battery chamber*
11 le bouchon à vis *f*
– *screw-in cover*
12 la manivelle de rembobinage *m*
– *rewind handle (rewind, rewind crank)*
13 l'interrupteur *m* de batterie *f*
– *battery switch*
14 la prise de flash *m* F et X
– *flash socket for F and X contact*
15 le levier d'armement *m* du déclencheur à retardement *m*
– *self-time lever (setting lever for the self-timer, setting lever for the delayed-action release)*
16 le levier d'avancement *m* de la pellicule
– *single-stroke film advance lever*
17 le compteur de vues *f*
– *exposure counter (frame counter)*
18 le bouton de déclenchement *m*
– *shutter release (shutter release button)*
19 le bouton de réglage *m* des temps de pose *m* (des vitesses *f*)
– *shutter speed setting knob (shutter speed control)*
20 la griffe à accessoires *m*
– *accessory shoe*
21 le contact central pour flash *m*
– *hot-shoe flash contact*
22 la fenêtre (l'oculaire *m*) du viseur avec lentille *f* correctrice
– *viewfinder eyepiece with correcting lens*
23 le dos de l'appareil *m*
– *camera back*
24 le presse-film
– *pressure plate*
25 la griffe d'entraînement *m* de pellicule *f* du système de chargement *m* rapide
– *take-up spool of the rapid-loading system*
26 les pignons *m* d'entraînement *m* de la pellicule
– *transport sprocket*
27 le débrayage de rembobinage *m*
– *rewind release button (reversing clutch)*
28 la fenêtre de prise *f* de vue *f*
– *film window*
29 l'entraînement *m* de rembobinage *m*
– *rewind cam*
30 l'écrou *m* du pied
– *tripod socket (tripod bush)*
31 le système reflex
– *reflex system (mirror reflex system)*
32 l'objectif *m*
– *lens*
33 le miroir reflex
– *reflex mirror*
34 la fenêtre de prise *f* de vue *f*
– *film window*
35 le trajet lumineux de la visée
– *path of the image beam*
36 le trajet lumineux de la mesure
– *path of the sample beam*
37 la cellule photoélectrique
– *meter cell*
38 le miroir auxiliaire
– *auxiliary mirror*
39 le verre dépoli de mise *f* au point
– *focusing screen*
40 la lentille de champ *m*
– *field lens*
41 le pentaprisme en toit *m*
– *pentaprism*
42 l'oculaire *m*
– *eyepiece*
43-105 les accessoires *m* du système
– *system of accessories*
43 les objectifs *m* interchangeables
– *interchangeable lenses*
44 l'objectif *m* fish-eye *m*
– *fisheye lens (fisheye)*
45 l'objectif *m* grand angle *m* (de courte focale *f*)
– *wide-angle lens (short focal length lens)*
46 l'objectif *m* normal
– *normal lens (standard lens)*
47 l'objectif *m* de focale *f* moyenne
– *medium focal length lens*
48 le télé-objectif (de longue focale *f*)
– *telephoto lens (long focal length lens)*
49 l'objectif *m* de très grande focale *f*
– *long-focus lens*
50 l'objectif *m* à miroir *m*
– *mirror lens*
51 le champ du viseur
– *viewfinder image*
52 l'indicateur *m* de commande *f* manuelle
– *signal to switch to manual control*
53 l'anneau *m* dépoli
– *matt collar (ground glass collar)*
54 la grille de microprismes *m*
– *microprism collar*
55 le stigmomètre (le prisme de mesure *f*)
– *split-image rangefinder (focusing wedges)*
56 l'échelle *f* des diaphragmes *m*
– *aperture scale*
57 l'aiguille *f* du posemètre *m*
– *exposure meter needle*
58-66 les verres *m* de visée *f* interchangeables
– *interchangeable focusing screens*
58 le verre dépoli à microprismes *m*
– *all-matt screen (ground glass screen) with microprism spot*
59 le verre dépoli à stigmomètre *m*
– *all-matt screen (ground glass screen) with microprism spot and split-image rangefinder*
60 le verre dépoli sans accessoire *m* de mise *f* au point
– *all-matt screen (ground glass screen) without focusing aids*
61 le verre dépoli à quadrillage *m*
– *matt screen (ground glass screen) with reticule*
62 l'anneau *m* de microprismes *m* pour objectifs *m* de grande ouverture *f*
– *microprism spot for lenses with a large aperture*
63 l'anneau *m* de microprismes *m* pour objectifs *m* d'ouverture *f* à partir de 1/3,5
– *microprism spot for lenses with an aperture of f = 1 : 3.5 or larger*
64 la lentille de Fresnel avec anneau *m* dépoli et stigmomètre *m*
– *Fresnel lens with matt collar (ground glass collar) and split-image rangefinder*
65 le verre dépoli avec zone *f* centrale à grain *m* fin et réticule *m* gradué
– *all-matt screen (ground glass screen) with finely matted central spot and graduated markings*
66 le verre dépoli avec zone *f* centrale claire et double réticule *m*
– *matt screen (ground glass screen) with clear spot and double cross hairs*
67 le dos spécial pour enregistrement *m* des données *f* de prise *f* de vue *f*
– *data recording back for exposing data about shots*
68 le viseur à capuchon *m*
– *viewfinder hood (focusing hood)*
69 le viseur interchangeable à prisme *m*
– *interchangeable pentaprism viewfinder*
70 le pentaprisme en toit *m*
– *pentaprism*
71 le viseur à renvoi *m* d'angle *m*
– *right-angle viewfinder*
72 la lentille corrective
– *correction lens*
73 l'œilleton *m* de l'oculaire *m*
– *eyecup*
74 l'oculaire *m* réglable
– *focusing telescope*
75 le raccord de batterie *f*
– *battery unit*
76 la poignée à piles *f* pour le moteur
– *combined battery holder and control grip for the motor drive*
77 l'appareil *m* à prise *f* de vue *f* rapide
– *rapid-sequence camera*
78 le moteur d'avancement *m* démontable
– *attachable motor drive*
79 l'alimentation *f* externe
– *external (outside) power supply*
80 le magasin pour 10 m de film *m*
– *ten meter film back (magazine back)*
81-98 dispositifs *m* de macrophotographie *f* (de prise *f* de vues *f* rapprochées)
– *close-up and macro equipment*
81 le tube rallonge *f*
– *extension tube*
82 la bague d'adaptation *f*
– *adapter ring*
83 la bague d'inversion *f*
– *reversing ring*
84 l'objectif *m* en position *f* inversée
– *lens in retrofocus position*
85 le soufflet
– *bellows unit (extension bellows, close-up bellows attachment)*
86 la glissière de réglage *m*
– *focusing stage*
87 l'adaptateur *m* pour reproduction *f* de diapositives *f*
– *slide-copying attachment*
88 le porte-diapositive
– *slide-copying adapter*
89 le dispositif de microphotographie *f*
– *micro attachment (photomicroscope adapter)*
90 le pied de reproduction *f*
– *copying stand (copy stand, copypod)*
91 les branches *f* du pied
– *spider legs*
92 le support de reproduction *f*
– *copying stand (copy stand)*
93 le bras du support
– *arm of the copying stand (copy stand)*
94 le pied de macrophotographie *f*
– *macrophoto stand*
95 les platines *f* interchangeables pour le pied de macrophotographie *f*
– *stage plates for the macrophoto stand*
96 la rondelle
– *insertable disc (disk)*
97 le réflecteur Lieberkühn
– *Lieberkühn reflector*
98 la platine à coordonnées *f*
– *mechanical stage*
99 le pied de table *f*
– *table tripod (table-top tripod)*
100 la poignée crosse *f*
– *rifle grip*
101 le déclencheur souple
– *cable release*
102 le déclencheur souple double
– *double cable release*
103 le sac d'appareil *m* (le sac tout-prêt)
– *camera case (ever-ready case)*
104 l'étui *m* d'objectif *m*
– *lens case*
105 le sac d'objectif *m* en cuir *m* souple
– *soft-leather lens pouch*

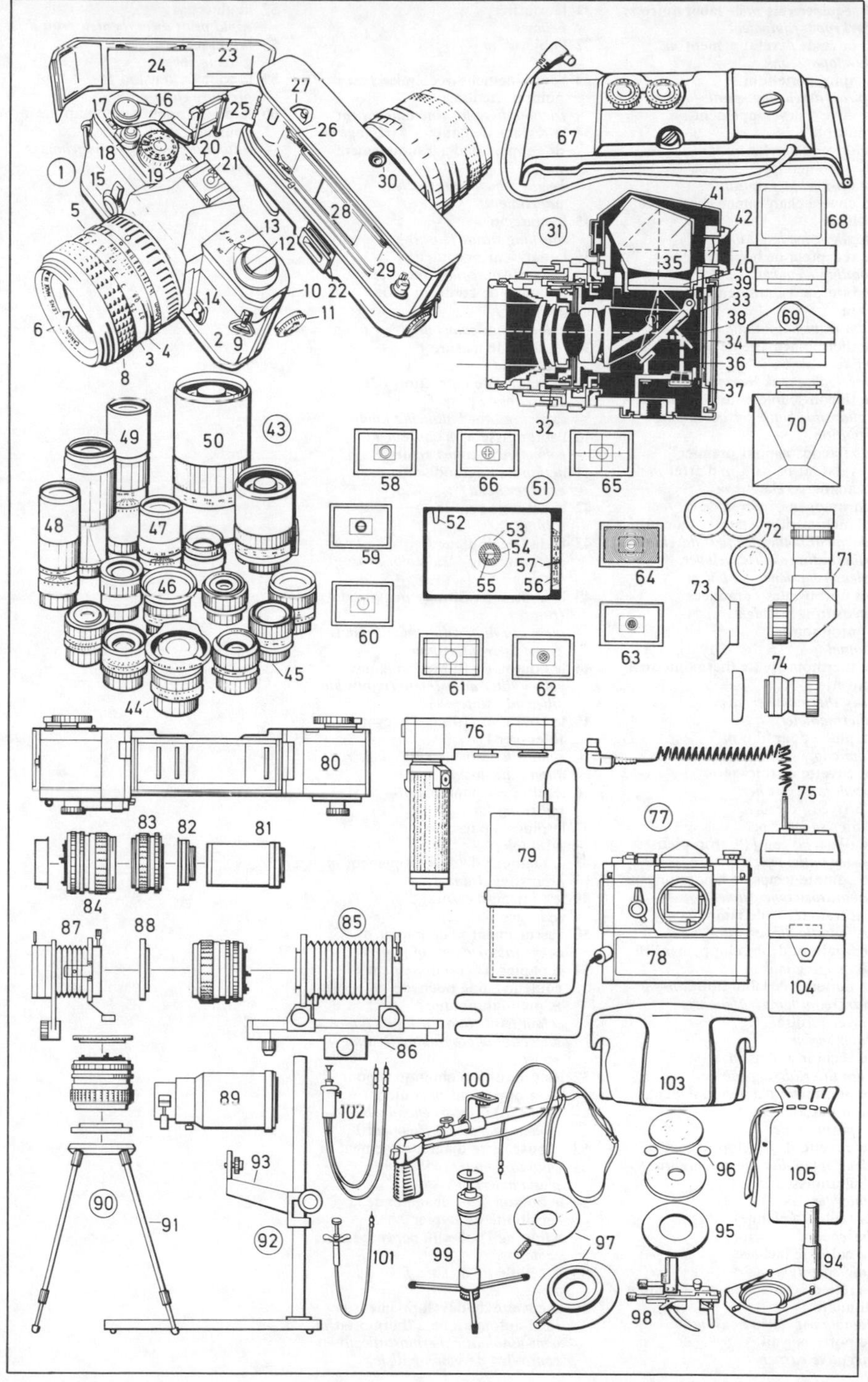
1
2
3
4
5
6
7
8
9
10
11
12
13
14
15
16
17
18
19
20
21
22
23
24
25
26
27
28
29
30
31
32
33
34
35
36
37
38
39
40
41
42
43
44
45
46
47
48
49
50
51
52
53
54
55
56
57
58
59
60
61
62
63
64
65
66
67
68
69
70
71
72
73
74
75
76
77
78
79
80
81
82
83
84
85
86
87
88
89
90
91
92
93
94
95
96
97
98
99
100
101
102
103
104
105

1-60 équipements *m* **de laboratoire** *m*
– ***darkroom equipment***
1 la cuve de développement *m*
– *developing tank*
2 la spire porte-film *m*
– *spiral (developing spiral, tank reel)*
3 la cuve à développement *m* multiple
– *multi-unit developing tank*
4 la spire multiple
– *multi-unit tank spiral*
5 la cuve à chargement *m* en plein jour *m*
– *daylight-loading tank*
6 le récepteur de bobine *f*
– *loading chamber*
7 le bouton d'entraînement *m* du film
– *film transport handle*
8 le thermomètre de développement *m*
– *developing tank thermometer*
9 le flacon souple pour révélateur *m*
– *collapsible bottle for developing solution*
10 les flacons *m* pour premier révélateur *m*, bain *m* d'arrêt *m* tannant, révélateur *m* chromogène, bain *m* de blanchiment *m*, stabilisateur *m*
– *chemical bottles for first developer, stop bath, colour developer, bleach-hardener, stabilizer*
11 les éprouvettes *f* graduées
– *measuring cylinders*
12 l'entonnoir *m*
– *funnel*
13 le thermomètre (le thermomètre à cuvette *f*)
– *tray thermometer (dish thermometer)*
14 la pince pour film *m*
– *film clip*
15 la cuvette de rinçage *m*
– *wash tank (washer)*
16 l'arrivée *f* d'eau *f*
– *water supply pipe*
17 le départ d'eau *f* (le trop-plein)
– *water outlet pipe*
18 le compte-temps de laboratoire *m*
– *laboratory timer (timer)*
19 l'entraîneur *m* de tambour *m*
– *automatic film agitator*
20 le tambour de développement *m*
– *developing tank*
21 la lanterne de laboratoire *m*
– *darkroom lamp (safelight)*
22 le verre filtre
– *filter screen*
23 le séchoir à films *m*
– *film drier (drying cabinet)*
24 le posemètre d'agrandissement *m* à minuterie *f*
– *exposure timer*
25 la cuvette de développement *m*
– *developing dish (developing tray)*
26 l'agrandisseur *m*
– *enlarger*
27 la table (la platine)
– *baseboard*
28 la colonne inclinée
– *angled column*
29 la tête d'éclairement *m* (la boîte à lumière *f*)
– *lamphouse (lamp housing)*
30 le porte-négatif
– *negative carrier*
31 le soufflet
– *bellows*
32 l'objectif *m*
– *lens*
33 l'entraînement *m* de mise *f* au point à friction *f*
– *friction drive for fine adjustment*
34 le réglage de hauteur *f* (réglage *m* de rapport *m* d'agrandissement *m*)
– *height adjustment (scale adjustment)*
35 le margeur
– *masking frame (easel)*
36 l'analyseur *m* couleur *f*
– *colour* (Am. *color) analyser*
37 la lampe de contrôle *m* de couleur *f*
– *colour* (Am. *color) analyser lamp*
38 le câble de mesure *f*
– *probe lead*
39 le bouton de correction *f* de temps *m* de pose *f*
– *exposure time balancing knob*
40 l'agrandisseur *m* couleur *f*
– *colour* (Am. *color) enlarger*
41 la tête de l'agrandisseur *m*
– *enlarger head*
42 la colonne profilée
– *column*
43-45 la tête couleur *f*
– *colour-mixing* (Am. *color-mixing) knob*
43 le bouton de filtrage *m* magenta (pourpre)
– *magenta filter adjustment (minus green filter adjustment)*
44 le bouton de filtrage *m* jaune
– *yellow filter adjustment (minus blue filter adjustment)*
45 le bouton de filtrage *m* cyan (bleu-vert)
– *cyan filter adjustment (minus red filter adjustment)*
46 le filtre escamotable
– *red swing filter*
47 la pince à papier *m*
– *print tongs*
48 le tambour de développement *m*
– *processing drum*
49 le rouleau d'essorage *m*
– *squeegee*
50 l'assortiment *m* de papier *m*
– *range (assortment) of papers*
51 le papier d'agrandissement *m* couleur *f*, une pochette de papier *m* photographique
– *colour* (Am. *color) printing paper, a packet of photographic printing paper*
52 les produits *m* chimiques pour développement *m* couleur
– *colour* (Am. *color) chemicals (colour processing chemicals)*
53 le posemètre d'agrandissement *m*
– *enlarging meter (enlarging photometer)*
54 le bouton d'affichage *m* de la sensibilité du papier
– *adjusting knob with paper speed scale*
55 la cellule de mesure *f*
– *probe*
56 la cuvette de développement *m* semi-automatique à thermostat *m*
– *semi-automatic thermostatically controlled developing dish*
57 la glaceuse
– *rapid print drier (heated print drier)*
58 la plaque polie
– *glazing sheet*
59 la toile de tension *f*
– *pressure cloth*
60 la développeuse automatique à rouleaux *m*
– *automatic processor (machine processor)*

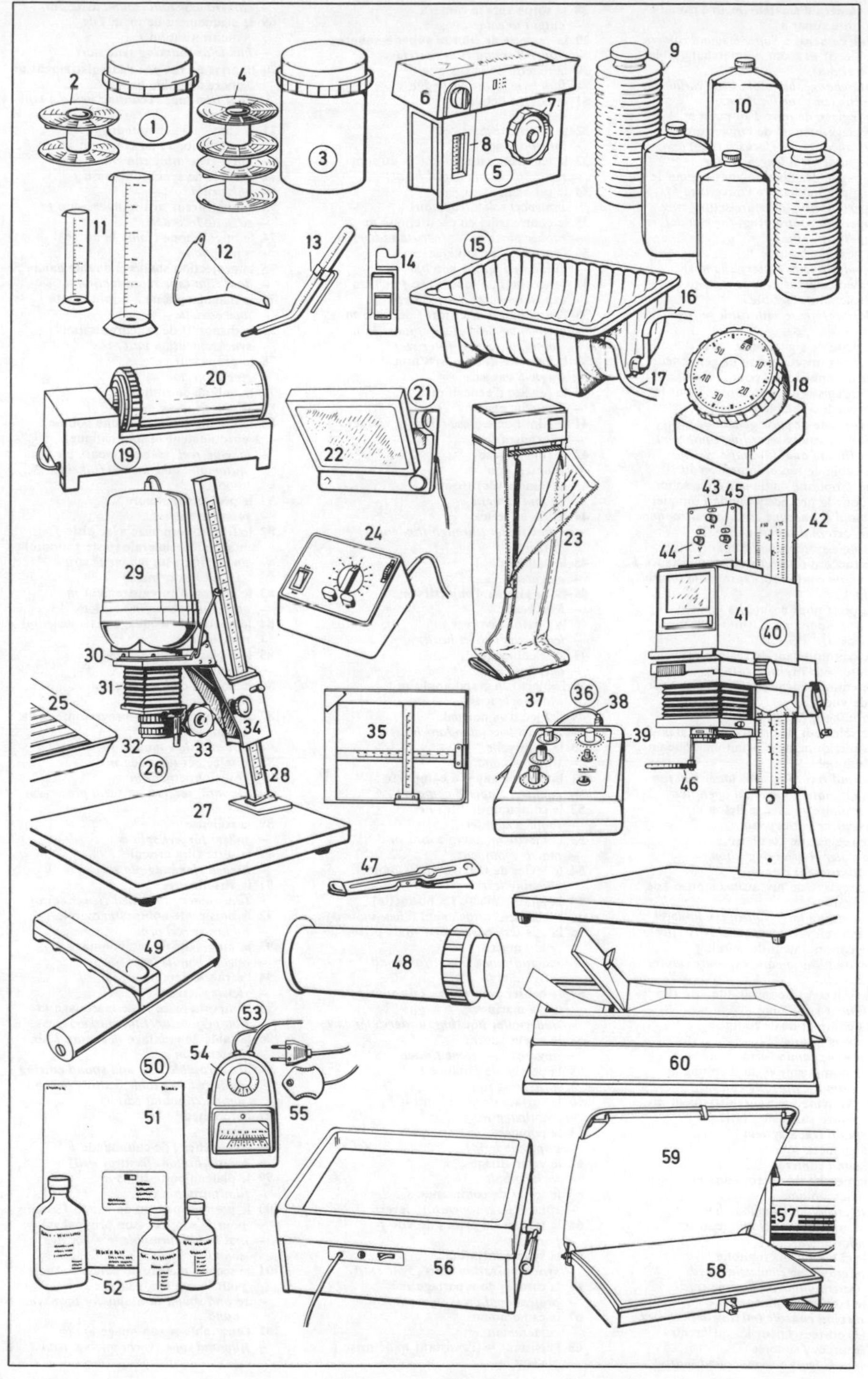
1
2
3
4
5
6
7
8
9
10
11
12
13
14
15
16
17
18
19
20
21
22
23
24
25
26
27
28
29
30
31
32
33
34
35
36
37
38
39
40
41
42
43
44
45
46
47
48
49
50
51
52
53
54
55
56
57
58
59
60

1 **la caméra d'amateur** *m*, une caméra sonore super 8
– ***cine camera***, *a Super-8 sound camera*
2 l'objectif *m* zoom *m* interchangeable (le zoom)
– *interchangeable zoom lens (variable focus lens, varifocal lens)*
3 le réglage de mise *f* au point et le réglage manuel de l'ouverture *f*
– *distance setting (focus setting) and manual focal length setting*
4 la bague des diaphragmes *m* pour le réglage manuel de l'ouverture *f*
– *aperture ring (aperture-setting ring, aperture control ring) for manual aperture setting*
5 la poignée batterie *f*
– *handgrip with battery chamber*
6 le déclencheur avec le raccord du déclencheur souple
– *shutter release with cable release socket*
7 la prise de signal *m* de synchronisation *f* ou de générateur *m* d'impulsions *f* pour l'enregistrement *m* sonore [pour le procédé à double bande *f*]
– *pilot tone or pulse generator socket for the sound recording equipment (with the dual film-tape system)*
8 le câble de raccordement *m* du microphone ou de la source sonore [pour le procédé à bande *f* unique]
– *sound connecting cord for microphone or external sound source (in single-system recording)*
9 le raccord du déclencheur à distance *f*
– *remote control socket (remote control jack)*
10 la prise pour écouteurs *m*
– *headphone socket* (sim.: *earphone socket)*
11 le commutateur de réglage *m*
– *autofocus override switch*
12 le commutateur de vitesse *f* de prise *f* de vue *f*
– *filming speed selector*
13 le sélecteur de prise *f* de son *m* pour fonctionnement *m* automatique ou manuel
– *sound recording selector switch for automatic or manual operation*
14 l'oculaire *m* avec œilleton *m*
– *eyepiece with eyecup*
15 le réglage de l'oculaire *m*
– *diopter control ring (dioptric adjustment ring)*
16 le réglage de niveau *m* de prise *f* de son *m*
– *recording level control (audio level control, recording sensitivity selector)*
17 le commutateur de cellule *f*
– *manual/automatic exposure control switch*
18 le sélecteur de sensibilité *f* du film
– *film speed setting*
19 la commande de zoom *m* automatique
– *power zooming arrangement*
20 l'automatisme *m* du diaphragme
– *automatic aperture control*
21 **le système pour enregistrement** *m* **sonore sur piste** *f* **latérale**
– ***sound track system***
22 la caméra sonore
– *sound camera*
23 la perche de microphone *m* télescopique
– *telescopic microphone boom*
24 le microphone (*fam.:* le micro)
– *microphone*
25 le câble du microphone
– *microphone connecting lead (microphone connecting cord)*
26 **le boîtier de mixage** *m*
– ***mixing console*** *(mixing desk, mixer)*
27 les entrées *f* pour les différentes sources *f* sonores
– *inputs from various sound sources*
28 la sortie vers la caméra
– *output to camera*
29 **la cassette de film** *m* **super 8 sonore**
– ***Super-8 sound film cartridge***
30 la fenêtre de la cassette
– *film gate of the cartridge*
31 la bobine débitrice
– *feed spool*
32 la bobine réceptrice
– *take-up spool*
33 la tête d'enregistrement *m* du son
– *recording head (sound head)*
34 le cabestan
– *transport roller (capstan)*
35 le contre-galet en caoutchouc *m*
– *rubber pinch roller (capstan idler)*
36 l'encoche *f* de guidage *m*
– *guide step (guide notch)*
37 l'encoche *f* de sensibilité *f* de film *m*
– *exposure meter control step*
38 l'encoche *f* d'insertion *f* de filtre *m*
– *conversion filter step (colour,* Am. *color, conversion filter step)*
39 **la cassette de film** *m* **8 mm**
– ***single-8 cassette***
40 la fenêtre d'exposition *f*
– *film gate opening*
41 le film non exposé (film *m* vierge)
– *unexposed film*
42 le film exposé
– *exposed film*
43 **la caméra (de) 16 mm**
– ***16 mm camera***
44 le viseur reflex
– *reflex finder (through-the-lens reflex finder)*
45 le magasin
– *magazine*
46-49 **la platine d'objectifs** *m*
– ***lens head***
46 la platine revolver *m*
– *lens turret (turret head)*
47 le téléobjectif
– *telephoto lens*
48 l'objectif *m* grand angle *m*
– *wide-angle lens*
49 l'objectif *m* normal
– *normal lens (standard lens)*
50 la manivelle
– *winding handle*
51 **la caméra super 8 compacte**
– ***compact Super-8 camera***
52 le compteur de film *m*
– *footage counter*
53 l'objectif *m* macro-zoom *m*
– *macro zoom lens*
54 le levier de réglage *m* du zoom
– *zooming lever*
55 la lentille macro (la bonnette)
– *macro lens attachment (close-up lens)*
56 la glissière porte-objet *m* de prise *f* de vue *f* macro
– *macro frame (mount for small originals)*
57 **le boîtier pour prises** *f* **de vues** *f* **sous-marines**
– ***underwater housing*** *(underwater case)*
58 le viseur sportif
– *direct-vision frame finder*
59 la perche de distance *f*
– *measuring rod*
60 la surface de stabilisation *f*
– *stabilizing wing*
61 la poignée
– *grip (handgrip)*
62 le verrouillage
– *locking bolt*
63 le levier de commande *f*
– *control lever (operating lever)*
64 la fenêtre de prise *f* de vue *f*
– *porthole*
65 **la synchronisation**
– ***synchronization start*** *(sync start)*
66 la caméra de reportage *m*
– *professional press-type camera*
67 le cameraman
– *cameraman*
68 l'assistant *m* (l'assistant *m* de prise *f* de son *m*)
– *camera assistant (sound assistant)*
69 le claquement de main *f* de synchronisation *f*
– *handclap marking sync start*
70 **la prise de vue** *f* **et l'enregistrement** *m* **sonore à double bande** *f*
– ***dual film-tape recording using a tape recorder***
71 la caméra à générateur *m* d'impulsions *f* de synchronisation *f*
– *pulse-generating camera*
72 le câble de synchronisation *f*
– *pulse cable*
73 l'enregistreur *m* à mini-cassette *f*
– *cassette recorder*
74 le microphone (*fam.:* le micro)
– *microphone*
75 **la projection sonore à double bande** *f*
– ***dual film-tape reproduction***
76 le magnétophone à mini-cassette *f*
– *tape cassette*
77 le dispositif de synchronisation *f*
– *synchronization unit*
78 le projecteur
– *cine projector*
79 la bobine de film *m*
– *film feed spool*
80 la bobine réceptrice (une bobine à enroulement *m* automatique)
– *take-up reel (take-up spool), an automatic take-up reel (take-up spool)*
81 **le projecteur sonore**
– ***sound projector***
82 le film sonore pisté avec piste *f* magnétique latérale (piste *f* sonore)
– *sound film with magnetic stripe (sound track, track)*
83 le bouton d'enregistrement *m*
– *automatic-threading button*
84 le bouton de truquage *m* (trucage *m*)
– *trick button*
85 le réglage de niveau *m*
– *volume control*
86 le bouton d'effacement *m*
– *reset button*
87 le commutateur de programme *m* de truquage *m*
– *fast and slow motion switch*
88 le sélecteur de mode *m* de fonctionnement *m*
– *forward, reverse, and still projection switch*
89 la colleuse
– *splicer for wet splices*
90 le serre-film articulé
– *hinged clamping plate*
91 **la visionneuse**
– ***film viewer*** *(animated viewer editor)*
92 le bras porte-bobines *m* mobile
– *foldaway reel arm*
93 la manivelle de rembobinage *m*
– *rewind handle (rewinder)*
94 l'écran *m* dépoli
– *viewing screen*
95 l'emporte-pièce *m* de marquage *m*
– *film perforator (film marker)*
96 **la table de montage** *m* **sonore à six plateaux** *m*
– ***six-turntable film and sound cutting table*** *(editing table, cutting bench, animated sound editor)*
97 le moniteur
– *monitor*
98 les touches *f* de commande *f*
– *control buttons (control well)*
99 le plateau porte-films *m*
– *film turntable*
100 le premier plateau de bande *f* sonore pour le son live (son original *m*)
– *first sound turntable, e.g. for live sound*
101 le second plateau de bande *f* sonore pour le son secondaire
– *second sound turntable for post-sync sound*
102 l'ensemble *m* son-image *m*
– *film and tape synchronizing head*

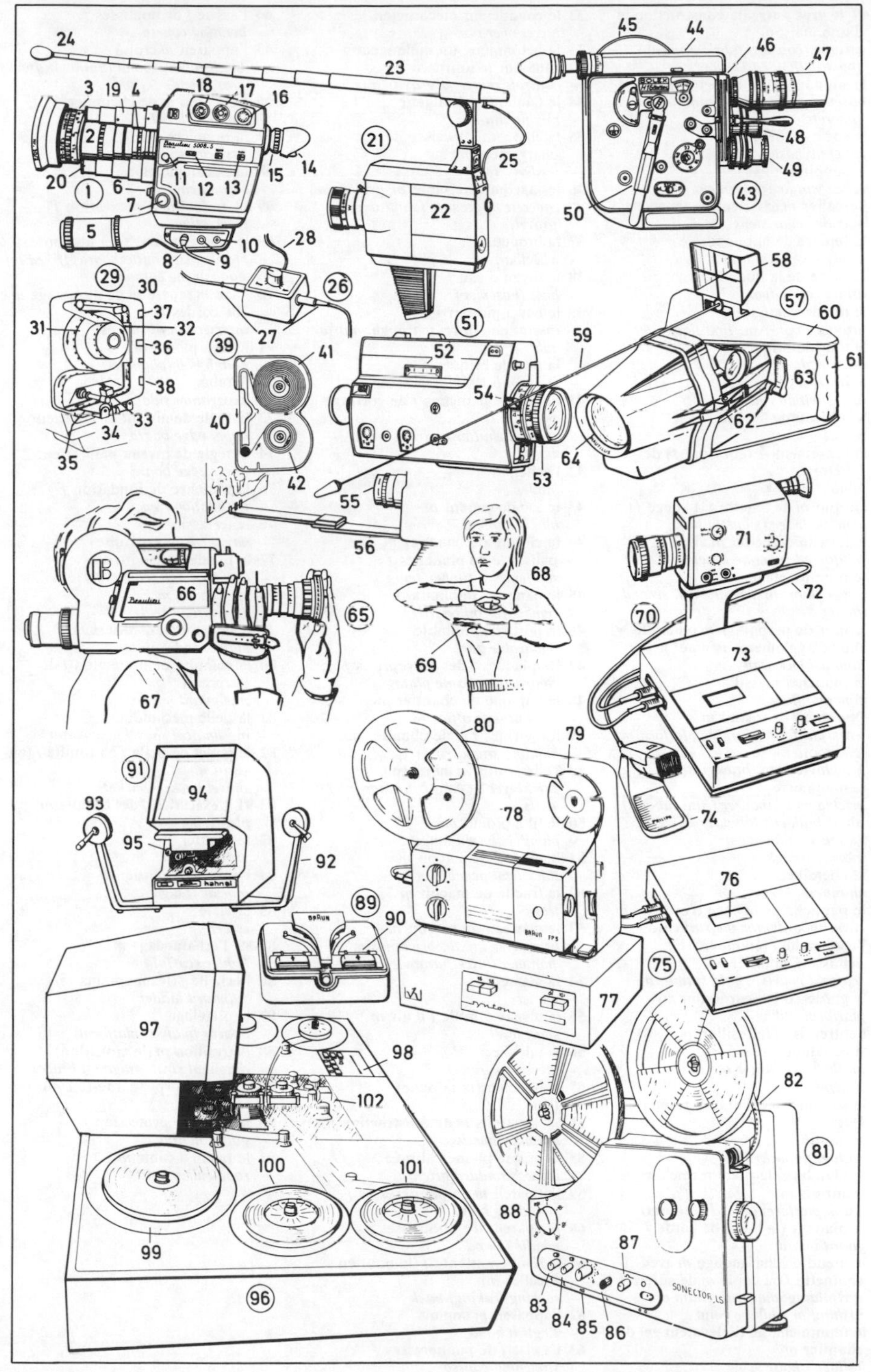
1 2 3 4 5 6 7 8 9 10 11 12 13 14 15 16 17 18 19 20
21 22 23 24 25 26 27 28 29 30 31 32 33 34 35 36 37 38 39 40
41 42 43 44 45 46 47 48 49 50 51 52 53 54 55 56 57 58 59 60
61 62 63 64 65 66 67 68 69 70 71 72 73 74 75 76 77 78 79 80
81 82 83 84 85 86 87 88 89 90 91 92 93 94 95 96 97 98 99 100 101 102
Beaulieu 5008.S
Beaulieu
BOLEX
hahnel
BRAUN
BRAUN FP5
PHILIPS
SONECTOR LS

1-49 le gros œuvre [la construction d'une maison]
– ***carcase*** *(carcass, fabric) [house construction, carcassing]*
1 le soubassement en béton *m* damé
– *basement of tamped (rammed) concrete*
2 le socle de béton *m*
– *concrete base course*
3 le soupirail
– *cellar window (basement window)*
4 l'escalier *m* extérieur de la cave
– *outside cellar steps*
5 la fenêtre de la buanderie
– *utility room window*
6 la porte de la buanderie
– *utility room door*
7 le rez-de-chaussée
– *ground floor* (Am. *first floor)*
8 le mur de briques *f*
– *brick wall*
9 le linteau de fenêtre *f*
– *lintel (window head)*
10 le tableau de fenêtre *f*
– *reveal*
11 l'ébrasement *m* (ébrasure *f*) de fenêtre *f*
– *jamb*
12 l'appui *m* de fenêtre *f* (l'allège *f*)
– *window ledge (window sill)*
13 le linteau de béton *m* armé
– *reinforced concrete lintel*
14 le premier étage
– *upper floor (first floor,* Am. *second floor)*
15 le mur de parpaings *m* creux (le mur d'agglomérés *m* creux)
– *hollow-block wall*
16 le plancher massif
– *concrete floor*
17 l'estrade *f* de travail *m*
– *work platform (working platform)*
18 le maçon
– *bricklayer* (Am. *brickmason)*
19 le manœuvre
– *bricklayer's labourer* (Am. *laborer);* also: *builder's labourer*
20 l'auge *f* à mortier *m*
– *mortar trough*
21 la cheminée
– *chimney*
22 le panneau de la cage d'escalier *m*
– *cover (boards) for the staircase*
23 l'écoperche *f* (étamperche *f*, échasse *f*, pointier *m*)
– *scaffold pole (scaffold standard)*
24 le garde-corps (garde-fou *m*)
– *platform railing*
25 l'entretoise *f* (étrésillon *m*) d'échafaudage *m*
– *angle brace (angle tie) in the scaffold*
26 le sommier d'échafaudage *m*
– *ledger*
27 le boulin
– *putlog (putlock)*
28 le platelage (la plate-forme de madriers *m*)
– *plank platform (board platform)*
29 la planche (la latte) de garde *f*
– *guard board*
30 le nœud d'échafaudage *m* avec chaînette *f* ou câble *m* de sûreté *f*
– *scaffolding joint with chain or lashing or whip or bond*
31 le monte-charge (l'élévateur *m*) de chantier *m*
– *builder's hoist*
32 le conducteur mécanicien
– *mixer operator*
33 la bétonnière, un mélangeur à tambour *m* tournant
– *concrete mixer, a gravity mixer*
34 le tambour mélangeur
– *mixing drum*
35 le chargeur (la caisse de chargement *m*)
– *feeder skip*
36 les agrégats *m* [sable *m*, gravier *m*]
– *concrete aggregate [sand and gravel]*
37 la brouette
– *wheelbarrow*
38 le tuyau d'eau *f*
– *hose (hosepipe)*
39 le bac à mortier *m*
– *mortar pan (mortar trough, mortar tub)*
40 la pile de briques *f*
– *stack of bricks*
41 la pile de planches *f* de coffrage *m*
– *stacked shutter boards (lining boards)*
42 l'échelle *f*
– *ladder*
43 le sac de ciment *m*
– *bag of cement*
44 la clôture du chantier *m*, une palissade de planches *f*
– *site fence, a timber fence*
45 le panneau publicitaire
– *signboard (billboard)*
46 la porte démontable
– *removable gate*
47 les plaques *f* des entreprises *f*
– *contractors' name plates*
48 la baraque de chantier *m*
– *site hut (site office)*
49 les latrines *f pl* de chantier *m*
– *building site latrine*
50-57 les outils *m* du maçon
– ***bricklayer's*** (Am. *brickmason's)* ***tools***
50 le fil à plomb *m*
– *plumb bob (plummet)*
51 le crayon de maçon *m*
– *thick lead pencil*
52 la truelle de maçon *m*
– *trowel*
53 le marteau de maçon *m*
– *bricklayer's* (Am. *brickmason's) hammer (brick hammer)*
54 la massette
– *mallet*
55 le niveau à bulle *f* d'air *m*
– *spirit level*
56 la taloche
– *laying-on trowel*
57 le bouclier (la taloche)
– *float*
58-68 appareils *m* de construction *f*
– ***masonry bonds***
58 la brique pleine calibrée
– *brick (standard brick)*
59 l'appareil *m* en panneresses *f*
– *stretching bond*
60 l'appareil *m* en boutisses *f*
– *heading bond*
61 le bout en attente *f* (le bout en escalier *m*)
– *racking (raking) back*
62 l'appareil *m* anglais
– *English bond*
63 l'assise *f* de panneresses *f*
– *stretching course*
64 l'assise *f* de boutisses *f*
– *heading course*
65 l'appareil *m* croisé
– *English cross bond (Saint Andrew's cross bond)*
66 l'appareil *m* de cheminée *f*
– *chimney bond*
67 la première assise
– *first course*
68 la deuxième assise
– *second course*
69-82 la fouille (l'excavation *f*)
– ***excavation***
69 le chevalet pour tirer au cordeau
– *profile* (Am. *batterboard) [fixed on edge at the corner]*
70 l'axe *m* repère *m* de piquetage *m* (de cordes *f*)
– *intersection of strings*
71 le fil à plomb *m*
– *plumb bob (plummet)*
72 le talus
– *excavation side*
73 la règle de niveau *m* supérieur
– *upper edge board*
74 la règle de niveau *m* inférieur
– *lower edge board*
75 la tranchée de fondation *f*
– *foundation trench*
76 le terrassier
– *navvy (* Am. *excavator)*
77 la bande transporteuse
– *conveyor belt (conveyor)*
78 les déblais *m*
– *excavated earth*
79 le chemin en madriers *m*
– *plank roadway*
80 la ceinture de protection *f* de l'arbre *m*
– *tree guard*
81 la pelle mécanique
– *mechanical shovel (excavator)*
82 le godet de pelle *f* en fouille *f* (en rétro *m*)
– *shovel bucket (bucket)*
83-91 l'exécution *f* des enduits *m*
– ***plastering***
83 le plâtrier
– *plasterer*
84 l'auge *m* à mortier *m*
– *mortar trough*
85 la claie
– *screen*
86-89 l'échafaudage *m*
– ***ladder scaffold***
86 l'échelle *f* (les montants *m*)
– *standard ladder*
87 le platelage
– *boards (planks, platform)*
88 l'étrésillon *m* (le croisillon)
– *diagonal strut (diagonal brace)*
89 le garde-corps (garde-fou *m*)
– *railing*
90 la grille de protection *f*
– *guard netting*
91 le palan à câble *m*
– *rope-pulley hoist*

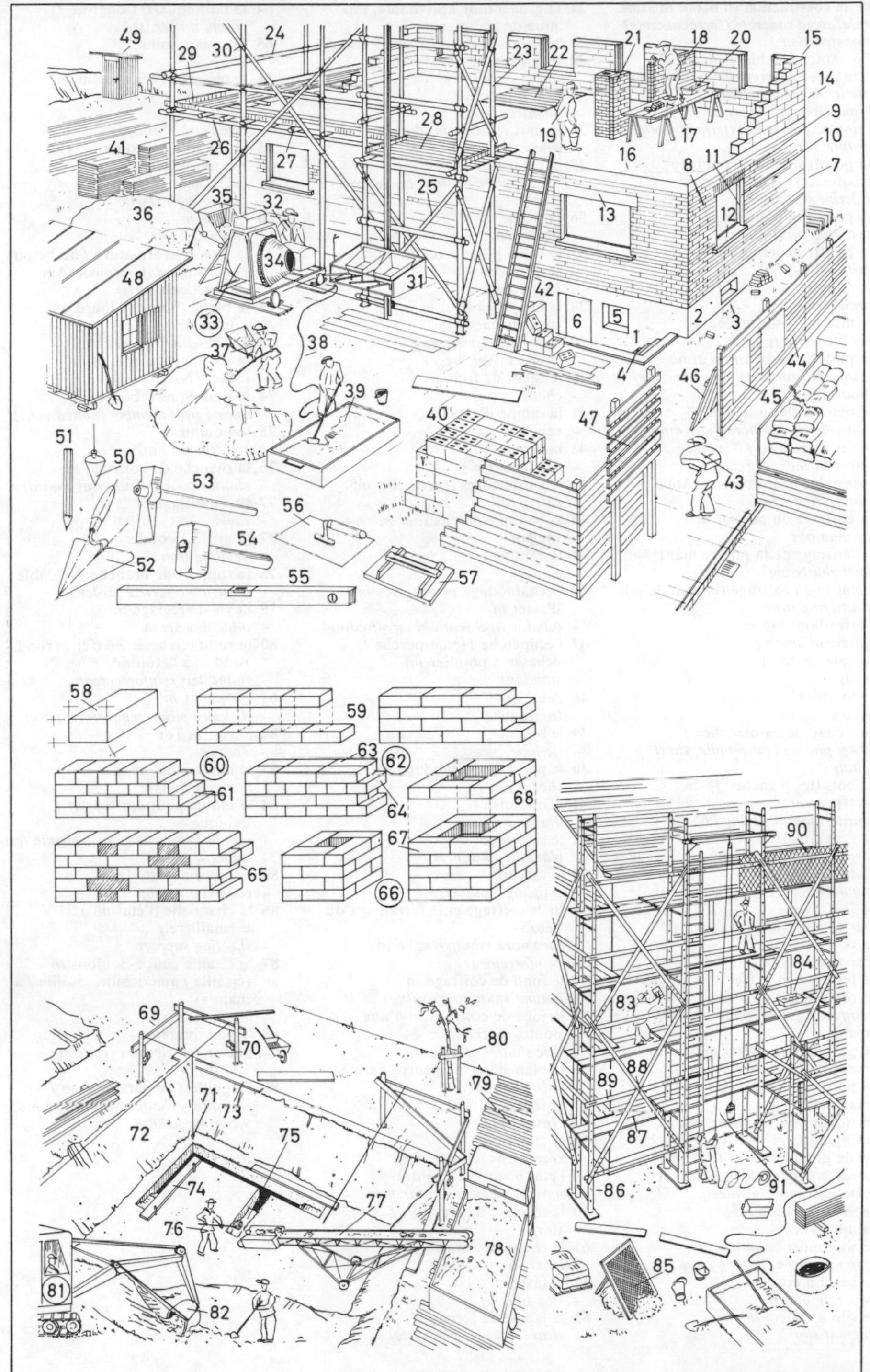

1
2
3
4
5
6
7
8
9
10
11
12
13
14
15
16
17
18
19
20
21
22
23
24
25
26
27
28
29
30
31
32
33
34
35
36
37
38
39
40
41
42
43
44
45
46
47
48
49
50
51
52
53
54
55
56
57
58
59
60
61
62
63
64
65
66
67
68
69
70
71
72
73
74
75
76
77
78
79
80
81
82
83
84
85
86
87
88
89
90
91

1-89 la construction en béton *m* armé
– *reinforced concrete (ferroconcrete) construction*
1 l'ossature *f* en béton *m* armé
– *reinforced concrete (ferroconcrete) skeleton construction*
2 l'encadrement *m* en béton *m* armé
– *reinforced concrete (ferroconcrete) frame*
3 la poutre de rive *f* (poutre *f* maîtresse)
– *inferior purlin*
4 la panne en béton *m*
– *concrete purlin*
5 la poutre maîtresse
– *ceiling joist*
6 le gousset
– *arch (flank)*
7 le mur en béton *m* coulé
– *rubble concrete wall*
8 le plafond en béton *m* armé
– *reinforced concrete (ferroconcrete) floor*
9 le bétonneur au lissage *m*
– *concreter (concretor), flattening out*
10 le fer de reprise *f* (fer *m* de raccord *m*)
– *projecting reinforcement (*Am. *connection rebars)*
11 le coffrage du poteau *m*
– *column box*
12 le coffrage de la poutre maîtresse
– *joist shuttering*
13 l'étai *m* du coffrage (la chandelle)
– *shuttering strut*
14 l'étrésillonnage *m*
– *diagonal bracing*
15 la cale (le coin)
– *wedge*
16 le madrier
– *board*
17 le rideau de palplanches *f*
– *sheet pile wall (sheet pile, sheet piling)*
18 le bois (les planches *f*) de coffrage *m*
– *shutter boards (lining boards)*
19 la scie circulaire
– *circular saw (buzz saw)*
20 la table à couder
– *bending table*
21 le ferrailleur
– *bar bender (steel bender)*
22 la cisaille à main *f*
– *hand steel shears*
23 le fer à béton *m* (fer *m* d'armature *f*, rond *m* à béton *m*)
– *reinforcing steel (reinforcement rods)*
24 le parpaing en béton *m* de ponce *f*
– *pumice concrete hollow block*
25 la palissade, une cloison de planches *f*
– *partition wall, a timber wall*
26 les agrégats *m* [gravier *m* et sable *m* de granulométrie *f* variable]
– *concrete aggregate [gravel and sand of various grades]*
27 la voie de la grue
– *crane track*
28 le wagonnet basculant
– *tipping wagon (tipping truck)*
29 la bétonnière
– *concrete mixer*
30 le silo à ciment *m*
– *cement silo*
31 la grue à tour *f* pivotante, une grue de chantier *m*
– *tower crane (tower slewing crane)*
32 le châssis de translation *f*
– *bogie (*Am. *truck)*
33 le contrepoids
– *counterweight*
34 la tour (pylône *m*) de grue *f*
– *tower*
35 la cabine du grutier *m*
– *crane driver's cabin (crane driver's cage)*
36 la flèche
– *jib (boom)*
37 le câble porteur (câble *m* de transport *m*)
– *bearer cable*
38 la benne à béton *m*
– *concrete bucket*
39 la voie de traverses *f*
– *sleepers (*Am. *ties)*
40 le sabot de frein *m*
– *chock*
41 la rampe d'accès *m*
– *ramp*
42 la brouette
– *wheelbarrow*
43 le garde-corps (garde-fou *m*)
– *safety rail*
44 la baraque de chantier *m*
– *site hut*
45 la cantine
– *canteen*
46 l'échafaudage *m* en tubes *m* d'acier *m*
– *tubular steel scaffold (scaffolding)*
47 l'écoperche *f* (étamperche *f*, échasse *f*, pointier *m*)
– *standard*
48 la moise
– *ledger tube*
49 le boulin
– *tie tube*
50 le patin d'échafaudage *m*
– *shoe*
51 l'entretoise *f*
– *diagonal brace*
52 le platelage
– *planking (platform)*
53 le raccord
– *coupling (coupler)*
54-76 le coffrage et le ferraillage du béton
– ***formwork*** *(shuttering) and reinforcement*
54 le fond de coffrage *m*
– *bottom shuttering (lining)*
55 la joue de coffrage *m* d'une poutre de rive *f*
– *side shutter of a purlin*
56 le plancher avec poutre *f* armée
– *cut-in bottom*
57 la solive
– *cross beam*
58 le crampon
– *cramp iron (cramp, dog)*
59 l'étai *m*, un étai frontal
– *upright member, a standard*
60 la traverse de jonction *f*
– *strap*
61 le chapeau d'étaiement *m*
– *cross piece*
62 la fasce
– *stop fillet*
63 la jambe de force *f*
– *strut (brace, angle brace)*
64 le bois équarri (longrine *f*)
– *frame timber (yoke)*
65 le couvre-joint
– *strap*
66 le tasseau d'écartement *m*
– *reinforcement binding*
67 l'entretoise *f*
– *cross strut (strut)*
68 le ferraillage (armature *f*)
– *reinforcement*
69 le fer *m* de répartition *f*
– *distribution steel*
70 l'étrier *m*
– *stirrup*
71 la crosse (d'armature *f* du béton)
– *projecting reinforcement (*Am. *connection rebars)*
72 le béton (béton *m* lourd ou compact)
– *concrete (heavy concrete)*
73 le coffrage du poteau *m*
– *column box*
74 le bois équarri boulonné
– *bolted frame timber (bolted yoke)*
75 le boulon
– *nut (thumb nut)*
76 la planche de coffrage *m*
– *shutter board (shuttering board)*
77-89 l'outillage *m*
– *tools*
77 la griffe à couder
– *bending iron*
78 le support de branche *f* réglable
– *adjustable service girder*
79 la vis de réglage *m*
– *adjusting screw*
80 le rond (en acier *m*) (fer *m* rond, rond *m* á béton *m*)
– *round bar reinforcement*
81 l'écarteur *m*
– *distance piece (separator, spacer)*
82 l'acier *m* Tor
– *Torsteel*
83 la dame à béton *m*
– *concrete tamper*
84 le moule pour éprouvette *f* cubique
– *mould (*Am. *mold) for concrete test cubes*
85 la pince à ferrailler
– *concreter's tongs*
86 la chandelle (l'étai *m*) à crémaillère *f*
– *sheeting support*
87 la cisaille coupe-boulons *m* (cisaille *f* américaine, cisaille *f* à main *f*)
– *hand shears*
88 le pervibrateur
– *immersion vibrator (concrete vibrator)*
89 l'aiguille *f* de pervibration *f*
– *vibrating cylinder (vibrating head, vibrating poker)*

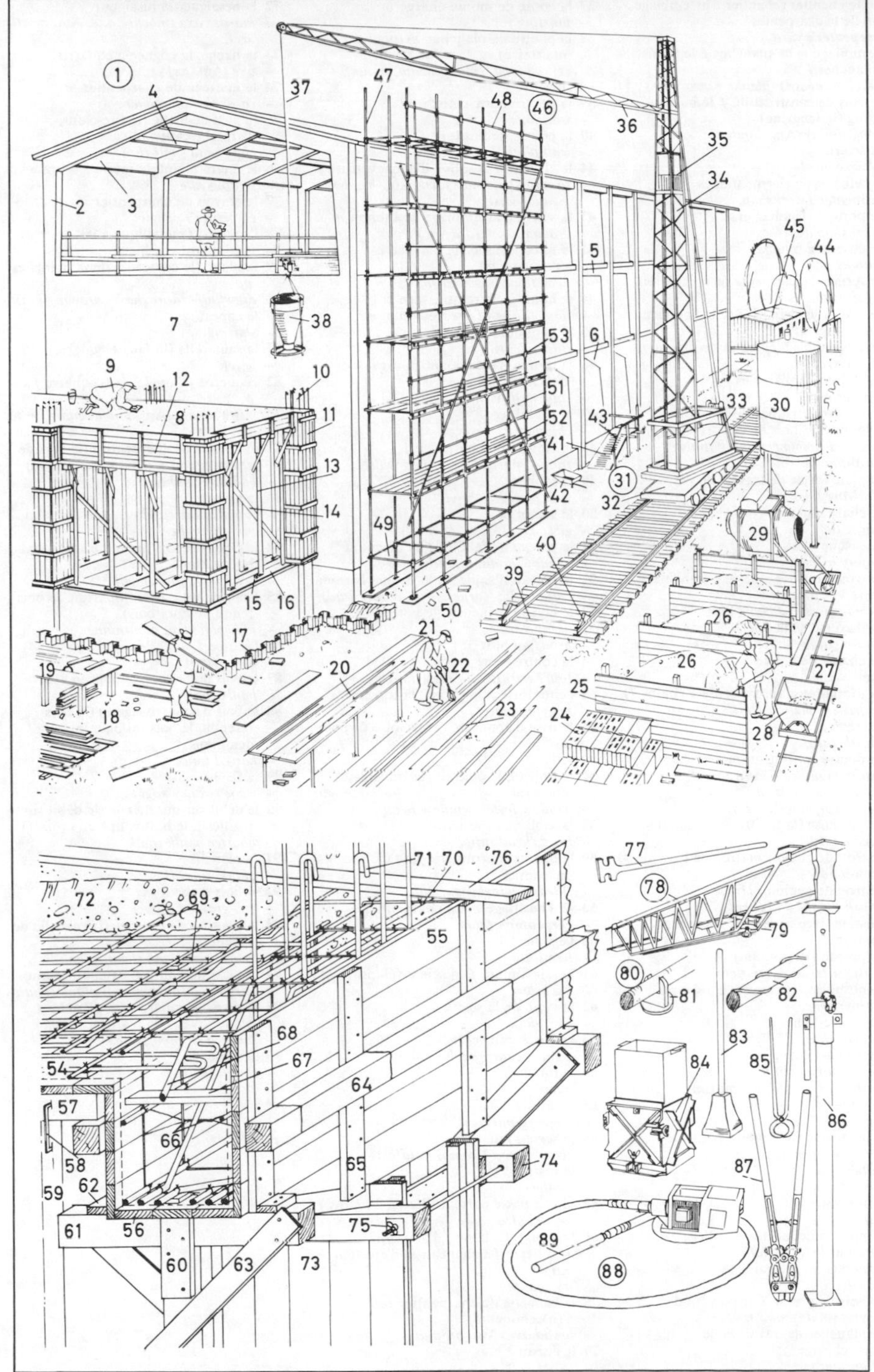
1
2
3
4
5
6
7
8
9
10
11
12
13
14
15
16
17
18
19
20
21
22
23
24
25
26
27
28
29
30
31
32
33
34
35
36
37
38
39
40
41
42
43
44
45
46
47
48
49
50
51
52
53
54
55
56
57
58
59
60
61
62
63
64
65
66
67
68
69
70
71
72
73
74
75
76
77
78
79
80
81
82
83
84
85
86
87
88
89

1-59 le chantier (chantier d'assemblage *m* de la charpente)
– ***carpenter's yard***
1 l'empilage *m* de planches *f*, le tas de planches *f*
– *stack of boards (planks)*
2 le bois de construction *f*, le bois de long (la longrine)
– *long timber (*Am. *lumber)*
3 la scierie
– *sawing shed*
4 l'atelier *m* de charpentier *m*
– *carpenter's workshop*
5 la porte de l'atelier *m*
– *workshop door*
6 le chariot à bras *m*
– *handcart*
7 la ferme (la charpente de comble *m*)
– *roof truss*
8 le mât de faîtage *m* avec le bouquet de faîtage *m*
– *tree [used for topping out ceremony], with wreath*
9 la cloison de planches *f*
– *timber wall*
10 le bois équarri (bois avivé, bois d'œuvre *m*, bois de construction *f*)
– *squared timber (building timber, scantlings)*
11 la plate-forme de travail *m*
– *drawing floor*
12 le charpentier
– *carpenter*
13 le casque
– *safety helmet*
14 la tronçonneuse, une scie à chaîne *f*, une scie articulée
– *cross-cut saw, a chain saw*
15 la traverse de la scie
– *chain guide*
16 la chaîne de la scie
– *saw chain*
17 la mortaiseuse (la fraiseuse à chaîne *f*)
– *mortiser (chain cutter)*
18 le tréteau
– *trestle (horse)*
19 la poutre sur tréteau *m*
– *beam mounted on a trestle*
20 la caisse à outils *m*
– *set of carpenter's tools*
21 la perceuse (la foreuse électrique)
– *electric drill*
22 le trou de goujon *m* (trou de cheville *f*)
– *dowel hole*
23 le trou de goujon *m* tracé
– *mark for the dowel hole*
24 l'assemblage *m* de bois *m* équarri
– *beams*
25 le poteau (le montant)
– *post (stile, stud, quarter)*
26 l'entretoise *f*, la moise, la traverse
– *corner brace*
27 la contre-fiche
– *brace (strut)*
28 le soubassement
– *base course (plinth)*
29 le mur de la maison (mur *m* extérieur)
– *house wall (wall)*
30 l'ouverture *f* de fenêtre *f*, la baie
– *window opening*
31 le tableau
– *reveal*
32 l'embrasure *f*
– *jamb*
33 l'appui *m* de fenêtre *f* (l'allège *f*)
– *window ledge (window sill)*
34 l'ancrage *m*, le chaînage
– *cornice*
35 le bois de grume *f*, le bois rond
– *roundwood (round timber)*
36 le plancher de travail *m*, le planchéiage
– *floorboards*
37 la corde de monte-charge *m*
– *hoisting rope*
38 la poutre de plancher *m* (poutre *f* maîtresse)
– *ceiling joist (ceiling beam, main beam)*
39 la poutre porte-cloison *m*
– *wall joist*
40 la poutre de bordure *f*
– *wall plate*
41 le chevêtre, la solive d'enchevêtrure *f*
– *trimmer (trimmer joist,* Am. *header, header joist)*
42 la solive d'assemblage *m* à tenon *m*
– *dragon beam (dragon piece)*
43 le faux plafond (le plafond à entrevous *m*)
– *false floor (inserted floor)*
44 le hourdis, le remplissage
– *floor filling of breeze, loam, etc.*
45 la lambourde
– *fillet (cleat)*
46 la trémie d'escalier *m*, la cage d'escalier *m*
– *stair well (well)*
47 la cheminée
– *chimney*
48 la cloison en charpente *f*
– *framed partition (framed wall)*
49 la sablière
– *wall plate*
50 le sommier
– *girt*
51 le poteau de fenêtre *f*, le dormant
– *window jamb, a jamb*
52 le poteau d'angle *m*, le poteau cornier
– *corner stile (corner strut, corner stud)*
53 le poteau principal, le poteau de refend *m*
– *principal post*
54 la contre-fiche
– *brace (strut) with skew notch*
55 l'entretoise *f*, la moise, la traverse
– *nogging piece*
56 la lisse d'appui *m*, l'entretoise d'appui *m*
– *sill rail*
57 le linteau, le poitrail (la traverse dormante)
– *window lintel (window head)*
58 la sablière supérieure
– *head (head rail)*
59 le pan de maçonnerie *f*, la cloison maçonnée
– *filled-in panel (bay, pan)*

60-82 l'outillage *m* du charpentier
– ***carpenter's tools***
60 l'égoïne *f*
– *hand saw*
61 la scie à main *f*, la scie à refendre
– *bucksaw*
62 la lame de la scie
– *saw blade*
63 la scie à guichet *m*
– *compass saw (keyhole saw)*
64 le rabot
– *plane*
65 la tarière
– *auger (gimlet)*
66 le serre-joint
– *screw clamp (cramp, holdfast)*
67 le maillet
– *mallet*
68 la scie passe-partout dite «à 2 mains *f*»
– *two-handed saw*
69 l'équerre *f* à lame *f* d'acier *m* (l'équerre *f* à chapeau *m* d'ajusteur *m*)
– *try square*
70 la hachette de charpentier *m*, l'(h)erminette *f*
– *broad axe (*Am. *broadax)*
71 le ciseau à bois *m*
– *chisel*
72 la besaïgue (la bisaïgue)
– *mortise axe (mortice axe,* Am. *mortise ax)*
73 la hache, la cognée à équarrir
– *axe (*Am. *ax)*
74 le marteau de charpentier *m*
– *carpenter's hammer*
75 le pied-de-biche (le tire-clous, l'arrache-clous *m*)
– *claw head (nail claw)*
76 le mètre pliant, le mètre à 5 branches *f*
– *folding rule*
77 le crayon de charpentier *m*
– *carpenter's pencil*
78 l'équerre *f* métallique à 90°
– *iron square*
79 la plane (le couteau à deux manches *m*)
– *drawknife (drawshave, drawing knife)*
80 le copeau
– *shaving*
81 la sauterelle (la fausse équerre)
– *bevel*
82 l'équerre *f* d'onglet *m* (l'équerre *f* à 45°)
– *mitre square (*Am. *miter square, miter angle)*

83-96 le bois de charpente *f* (le bois de construction *f*, le bois d'œuvre *m*)
– ***building timber***
83 la grume
– *round trunk (undressed timber,* Am. *rough lumber)*
84 le cœur du bois *m* (le duramen, le bois parfait)
– *heartwood (duramen)*
85 l'aubier *m* (le bois imparfait, le bois fendu, le faux bois)
– *sapwood (sap, alburnum)*
86 l'écorce *f*
– *bark (rind)*
87 le bois de brin *m*, le bois en état *m*
– *baulk (balk)*
88 le bois d'équarrissage *m* (le bois refendu, le bois mi-plat, le demi-bois)
– *halved timber*
89 la flache
– *wane (waney edge)*
90 le débit sur quartier *m* (le débit sur mailles *f*, le bois coupé en croix *f*)
– *quarter baulk (balk)*
91 la planche
– *plank (board)*
92 le bois de bout *m*
– *end-grained timber*
93 la planche de cœur *m* (la planche de moelle *f*)
– *heartwood plank (heart plank)*
94 la planche non équarrie, en grume *f*
– *unsquared (untrimmed) plank (board)*
95 la planche équarrie (la planche à arêtes vives *f*, la planche avivée)
– *squared (trimmed) board*
96 la dosse
– *slab (offcut)*

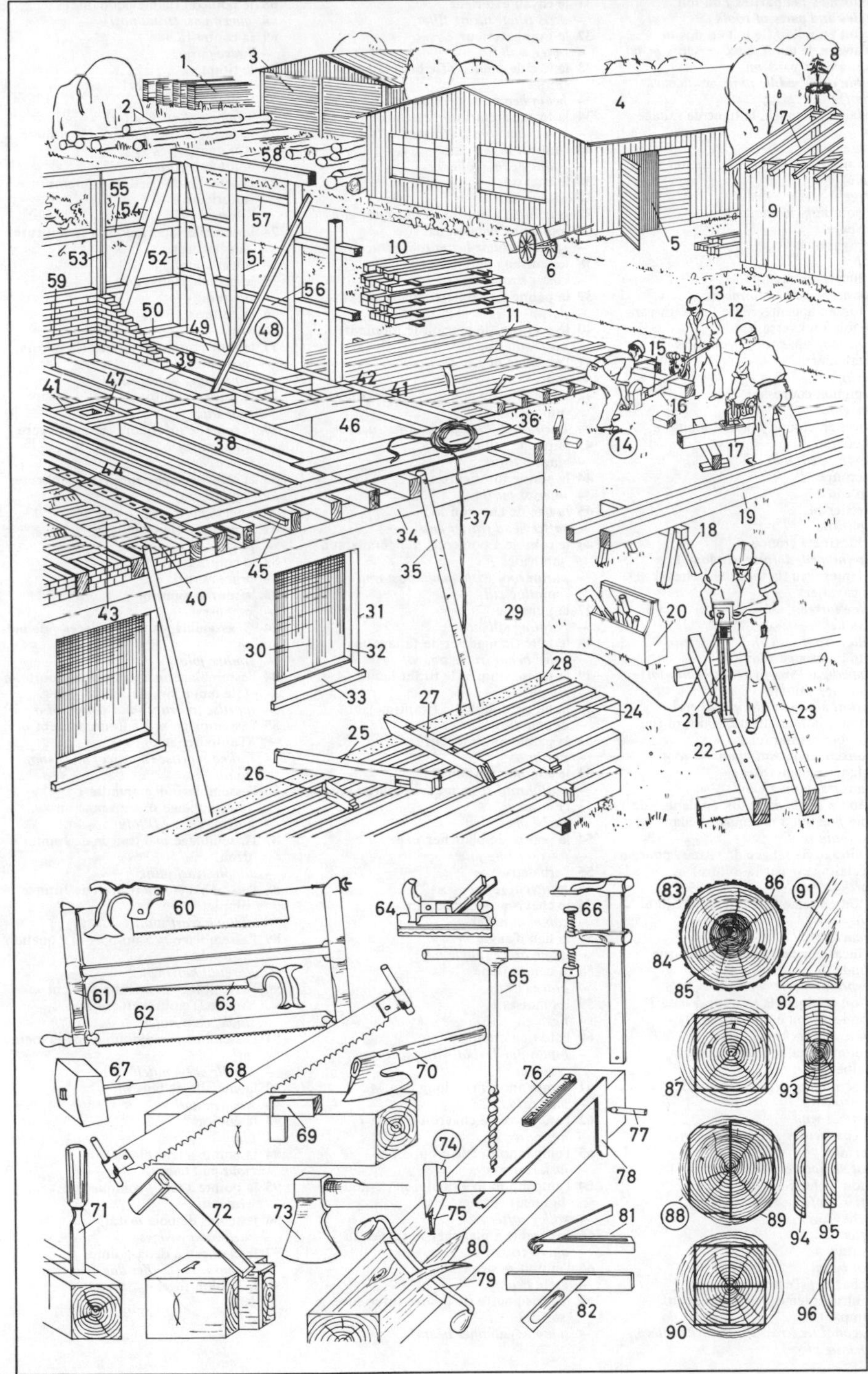
1
2
3
4
5
6
7
8
9
10
11
12
13
14
15
16
17
18
19
20
21
22
23
24
25
26
27
28
29
30
31
32
33
34
35
36
37
38
39
40
41
42
43
44
45
46
47
48
49
50
51
52
53
54
55
56
57
58
59
60
61
62
63
64
65
66
67
68
69
70
71
72
73
74
75
76
77
78
79
80
81
82
83
84
85
86
87
88
89
90
91
92
93
94
95
96

1-26 formes *f* et parties *f* du toit
– ***styles and parts of roofs***
1 le toit en selle *f* (le toit en dos *m* d'âne *m*, le toit à deux versants *m*, le toit à deux pans *m*)
– *gable roof (saddle roof, saddleback roof)*
2 le faîte, le faîtage, la ligne de faîtage *m*
– *ridge*
3 l'avant-toit *m* (le dessous de toit *m*, la rive)
– *verge*
4 la gouttière (le chéneau)
– *eaves*
5 le pignon
– *gable*
6 la lucarne rampante
– *dormer window (dormer)*
7 le toit en appentis *m* (le toit à un pan, le toit à un versant)
– *pent roof (shed roof, lean-to roof)*
8 la tabatière
– *skylight*
9 le pignon coupe-feu
– *fire gable*
10 le toit en croupe *f* (le toit à quatre arêtiers *m*)
– *hip (hipped) roof*
11 la croupe
– *hip end*
12 l'arêtier *m*
– *hip (arris)*
13 la lucarne à croupe *f*
– *hip (hipped) dormer window*
14 le lanterneau (la tourelle à cheval *m*, le cavalier)
– *ridge turret*
15 la noue
– *valley (roof valley)*
16 le toit à croupe *f* faîtière
– *hipped-gable roof (jerkin head roof)*
17 la croupe faîtière
– *partial-hip (partial-hipped) end*
18 le toit à la Mansart ou Mansard (le comble mansardé)
– *mansard roof* (Am. *gambrel roof)*
19 la fenêtre mansardée
– *mansard dormer window*
20 le toit à sheds *m* (le toit en dents *f* de scie *f*, le toit à redents ou redans *m*)
– *sawtooth roof*
21 le vitrage (la rangée de vitres *f* pour l'éclairage *m* par la toiture)
– *north light*
22 le toit en tente *f* (le toit en pavillon *m*)
– *broach roof*
23 la lucarne à tabatière *f* (la lucarne ronde, la chatière)
– *eyebrow*
24 le toit conique (la tourelle à base *f* ronde, le toit en poivrière *f*)
– *conical broach roof*
25 le dôme à bulbe *f* (la coupole bulbeuse)
– *imperial dome (imperial roof)*
26 la girouette
– *weather vane*

27-83 charpentes *f* de combles *m* (fermes *f*)
– ***roof structures of timber***
27 le toit à chevrons *m*
– *rafter roof*
28 le chevron
– *rafter*
29 l'entrait *m*
– *roof beam*
30 l'écharpe *f* (l'entretoise *f* de contreventement *m*, le poinçon rampant)
– *diagonal tie (cross tie, sprocket piece, cocking piece)*
31 le coyau extérieur
– *arris fillet (tilting fillet)*
32 le mur extérieur
– *outer wall*
33 la tête de poutre *f* (le bout d'entrait *m*)
– *beam head*
34 la ferme à entrait *m* retroussé
– *collar beam roof (trussed-rafter roof)*
35 l'entrait *m* retroussé
– *collar beam (collar)*
36 le chevron
– *rafter*
37 le comble à entrait *m* retroussé et à poinçons *m* latéraux
– *strutted collar beam roof structure*
38 les entraits *m* retroussés
– *collar beams*
39 la panne (la sablière supérieure)
– *purlin*
40 le poinçon (le poteau, le montant)
– *post (stile, stud)*
41 l'aisselier *m*
– *brace*
42 le comble à panne *f* et à poinçon *m* unique
– *unstrutted (king pin) roof structure*
43 la panne faîtière
– *ridge purlin*
44 la panne inférieure
– *inferior purlin*
45 la tête de chevron *m*
– *rafter head (rafter end)*
46 le comble à poinçons *m* latéraux et à jambettes *f*
– *purlin roof with queen post and pointing sill*
47 la jambette
– *pointing sill*
48 le faîte (le madrier de faîtage *m*)
– *ridge beam (ridge board)*
49 la moise simple (le tirant haut)
– *simple tie*
50 la moise double (le tirant moisé)
– *double tie*
51 la panne intermédiaire
– *purlin*
52 le comble polygonal
– *purlin roof structure with queen post*
53 l'entrait *m*
– *tie beam*
54 la poutre de plancher *m*
– *joist (ceiling joist)*
55 l'arbalétrier *m*
– *principal rafter*
56 le chevron intermédiaire
– *common rafter*
57 le lien d'angle *m*
– *angle brace (angle tie)*
58 la contre-fiche
– *brace (strut)*
59 les moises *f*
– *ties*
60 le toit en croupe *f*
– *hip (hipped) roof with purlin roof structure*
61 l'empannon *m* de long pan *m*
– *jack rafter*
62 l'arêtier *m* (le chevron d'arête *f*)
– *hip rafter*
63 l'empannon *m* de croupe *f*
– *jack rafter*
64 l'empannon *m* à noulet *m* (le noulet, la noue)
– *valley rafter*
65 le comble à plancher *m* suspendu
– *queen truss*
66 l'entrait *m* suspendu
– *main beam*
67 la sous-poutre (la poutre inférieure, le soffite)
– *summer (summer beam)*
68 le poinçon (la clé pendante)
– *queen post (truss post)*
69 la contre-fiche
– *brace (strut)*
70 le tirant
– *collar beam (collar)*
71 le chevêtre
– *trimmer* (Am. *header)*
72 la ferme à âme *f* pleine (le comble sur chandelles *f*)
– *solid-web girder*
73 la semelle inférieure (la membrure inférieure)
– *lower chord*
74 la semelle supérieure (la membrure supérieure)
– *upper chord*
75 le planchéiage (l'âme *f*)
– *boarding*
76 la panne
– *purlin*
77 le mur porteur extérieur (la paroi portante)
– *supporting outer wall*
78 la ferme à treillis *m*
– *roof truss*
79 la semelle inférieure (la membrure inférieure)
– *lower chord*
80 la semelle supérieure (la membrure supérieure)
– *upper chord*
81 le poinçon (la chandelle)
– *post*
82 la contre-fiche
– *brace (strut)*
83 le mur d'appui *m*
– *support*

84-98 assemblages *m* des pièces *f* de bois *m*
– ***timber joints***
84 l'assemblage *m* à tenon *m* et mortaise *f* (le tenon simple)
– *mortise (mortice) and tenon joint*
85 l'assemblage *m* à enfourchement *m* (l'enfourchement *m*)
– *forked mortise (mortice) and tenon joint*
86 l'assemblage *m* à entaille *f* (l'assemblage *m* à mi-bois *m*)
– *halving (halved) joint*
87 l'assemblage *m* à trait *m* de Jupiter droit
– *simple scarf joint*
88 l'assemblage *m* à trait *m* de Jupiter simple
– *oblique scarf joint*
89 l'assemblage *m* à mi-bois *m* à queue *f* d'aronde *f*
– *dovetail halving*
90 l'assemblage *m* à embrèvement *m* simple (l'embrèvement *m*)
– *single skew notch*
91 l'assemblage *m* à double épaulement *m*
– *double skew notch*
92 la cheville de bois *m*
– *wooden nail*
93 le goujon
– *pin*
94 la pointe à tête *f* large
– *clout nail (clout)*
95 la pointe à tête *f* conique
– *wire nail*
96 les coins de bois *m* dur
– *hardwood wedges*
97 le clameau à deux pointes *f*
– *cramp iron (timber dog, dog)*
98 le boulon fileté
– *bolt*

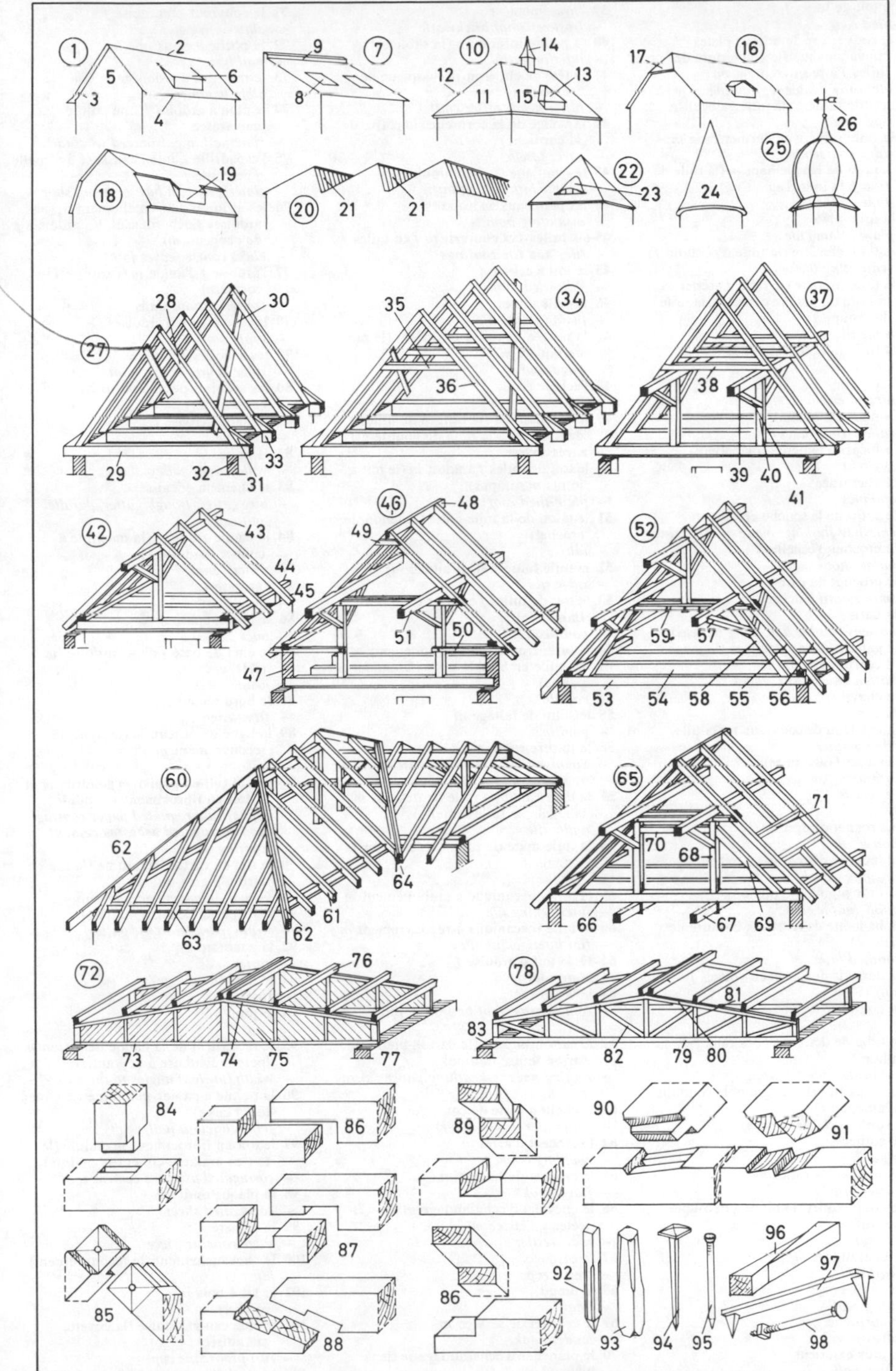
1
2
3
4
5
6
7
8
9
10
11
12
13
14
15
16
17
18
19
20
21
21
22
23
24
25
26
27
28
29
30
31
32
33
34
35
36
37
38
39
40
41
42
43
44
45
46
47
48
49
50
51
52
53
54
55
56
57
58
59
60
61
62
62
63
64
65
66
67
68
69
70
71
72
73
74
75
76
77
78
79
80
81
82
83
84
85
86
86
87
88
89
90
91
92
93
94
95
96
97
98

1 le toit de tuiles *f*
– *tiled roof*
2 la couverture de tuiles *f* plates chevauchantes (la couverture de tuiles *f* à recouvrement *m*)
– *plain-tile double-lap roofing*
3 la tuile faîtière (la tuile galbée)
– *ridge tile*
4 la tuile faîtière de dernier rang *m*
– *ridge course tile*
5 la tuile de batellement *m* (la tuile de rive *f*, la tuile d'égout *m*)
– *under-ridge tile*
6 la tuile plate
– *plain (plane) tile*
7 la tuile chatière (la tuile d'aération *f*)
– *ventilating tile*
8 la tuile arêtière (la tuile d'arêtier *m*, la tuile de faîte *m* cornière, la tuile de croupe *f*)
– *ridge tile*
9 la tuile faîtière d'about *m*
– *hip tile*
10 la croupe
– *hipped end*
11 la noue (le noulet)
– *valley (roof valley)*
12 la lucarne faîtière (la tabatière)
– *skylight*
13 la cheminée
– *chimney*
14 le solin de la souche en zinc *m*
– *chimney flashing, made of sheet zinc*
15 le crochet d'échelle *f*
– *ladder hook*
16 le crochet du pare-neige
– *snow guard bracket*
17 le lattis
– *battens (slating and tiling battens)*
18 le gabarit d'écartement *m* (la jauge d'écartement *m*)
– *batten gauge (*Am. *gage)*
19 le chevron
– *rafter*
20 le marteau de couvreur *m* (la tille)
– *tile hammer*
21 l'assette *f* (asseau *m*)
– *lath axe (*Am. *ax)*
22 l'auget *m*
– *hod*
23 le crochet d'auget *m*
– *hod hook*
24 la lucarne d'accès *m* au toit *m*
– *opening (hatch)*
25 le mur pignon (le pignon)
– *gable (gable end)*
26 la baguette de rive *f* (la bordure de rive *f*)
– *toothed lath*
27 le dessous de toit *m* en voliges *f*
– *soffit*
28 la gouttière (le chéneau)
– *gutter*
29 le tube de descente *f* des eaux *f* de pluie *f*
– *rainwater pipe (downpipe)*
30 la naissance (le moignon, la conduite d'amenée *f*)
– *swan's neck (swan-neck)*
31 le collier
– *pipe clip*
32 le crochet (la patte)
– *gutter bracket*
33 le coupe-tuiles (la pince à découper les tuiles *f*)
– *tile cutter*
34 l'échafaudage *m*
– *scaffold*
35 le garde-corps
– *safety wall*
36 la corniche
– *eaves*
37 le mur extérieur
– *outer wall*
38 l'enduit *m* extérieur
– *exterior rendering*
39 l'arasement *m*
– *frost-resistant brickwork*
40 la panne inférieure (la sablière)
– *inferior purlin*
41 la tête de chevron *m* (la queue de vache *f*)
– *rafter head (rafter end)*
42 la volige de la corniche (le coffre de la corniche)
– *eaves fascia*
43 la chanlatte (la latte double)
– *double lath (tilting lath)*
44 les panneaux *m* isolants
– *insulating boards*

45-60 tuiles *f* et couverture *f* en tuiles *f*
– *tiles and tile roofings*

45 le toit à éclisse *f*
– *split-tiled roof*
46 la tuile plate
– *plain (plane) tile*
47 la rangée de tuiles *f* faîtières (le rang de faîtage *m*)
– *ridge course*
48 l'éclisse *f*
– *slip*
49 le batellement (la rangée de tuiles *f* débordeuses, le rang de gouttière *f*)
– *eaves course*
50 le toit de tuiles *f* à talon *m* (le toit à joints *m* rompus)
– *plain-tiled roof*
51 le talon de la tuile plate (le tenon, le crochet)
– *nib*
52 la tuile faîtière (l'enfaîteau *m*)
– *ridge tile*
53 le toit de tuiles *f* creuses (la toiture flamande)
– *pantiled roof*
54 la tuile creuse sans emboîtement *m* (la tuile en S *m*, la tuile flamande, la panne)
– *pantile*
55 le solin de faîtage *m*
– *pointing*
56 la toiture romaine
– *Spanish-tiled roof (*Am. *mission-tiled roof)*
57 la tuile canal (la tuile de dessous *m*, la tégole, la tuile femelle)
– *under tile*
58 la tuile mâle (la tuile de dessus *m*, la «canali»)
– *over tile*
59 la tuile mécanique à emboîtement *m*
– *interlocking tile*
60 la tuile mécanique à recouvrement *m*
– *flat interlocking tile*

61-89 le toit d'ardoise *f*
– *slate roof*

61 le voligeage
– *roof boards (roof boarding, roof sheathing)*
62 le carton bitumé (le carton-pierre, le carton feutre bitumé)
– *roofing paper (sheathing paper);* also: *roofing felt (*Am. *rag felt)*
63 l'échelle *f* plate de couvreur *m*
– *cat ladder (roof ladder)*
64 le crochet d'arrêt *m*
– *coupling hook*
65 le crochet de faîtage *m*
– *ridge hook*
66 le chevalet d'échafaudage *m* (le tréteau, l'étrier *m*)
– *roof trestle*
67 le cordage
– *trestle rope*
68 le nœud
– *knot*
69 le crochet de service *m*
– *ladder hook*
70 le plancher d'échafaudage *m* (le plateau)
– *scaffold board*
71 le couvreur en ardoise *f*
– *slater*
72 la poche à clous *m*
– *nail bag*
73 le marteau d'ardoisier *m*
– *slate hammer*
74 le clou à ardoise *f*, une pointe galvanisée
– *slate nail, a galvanized wire nail*
75 l'espadrille *f*, une chaussure à semelle *f* de corde *f*
– *slater's shoe, a bast or hemp shoe*
76 les ardoises *f* de batellement *m* (les ardoises *f* débordeuses, les ardoises *f* de chéneau *m*)
– *eaves course (eaves joint)*
77 l'ardoise *f* d'angle *m* (l'ardoise *f* cornière)
– *corner bottom slate*
78 la couverture d'ardoises *f*
– *roof course*
79 les ardoises *f* faîtières
– *ridge course (ridge joint)*
80 les ardoises de pignon *m*
– *gable slate*
81 la ligne de base *f*
– *tail line*
82 la noue
– *valley (roof valley)*
83 le chéneau encaissé
– *box gutter (trough gutter, parallel gutter)*
84 le coupe-ardoises (la machine à couper l'ardoise *f*)
– *slater's iron*
85 l'ardoise *f*
– *slate*
86 le bord apparent
– *back*
87 le chef de base *f* d'une ardoise (la tête)
– *head*
88 le bord recouvert
– *front edge*
89 la ligne de pureau *m* (la ligne de recouvrement *m*)
– *tail*

90-103 le toit en papier *m* goudronné et le toit en fibrociment *m* ondulé
– *asphalt-impregnated paper roofing and corrugated asbestos cement roofing*

90 le toit en carton *m* bitumé (le toit en carton-pierre *m*)
– *asphalt-impregnated paper roof*
91 le lé [parallèle à la gouttière]
– *width [parallel to the gutter]*
92 la gouttière
– *gutter*
93 le faîte (le faîtage)
– *ridge*
94 le joint
– *join*
95 le lé vertical de la bande de carton *m* [perpendiculaire à la gouttière]
– *width [at right angles to the gutter]*
96 la pointe à papier *m* bitumé (le clou à tête *f* large)
– *felt nail (clout nail)*
97 le toit en fibrociment *m* ondulé (le toit en amiante-ciment *m* ondulé)
– *corrugated asbestos cement roof*
98 la plaque ondulée
– *corrugated sheet*
99 la faîtière
– *ridge capping piece*
100 le chevauchement (le recouvrement)
– *lap*
101 la vis à bois *m*
– *wood screw*
102 le chapeau galvanisé (la cuvette galvanisée)
– *rust-proof zinc cup*
103 la rondelle en plomb *m*
– *lead washer*

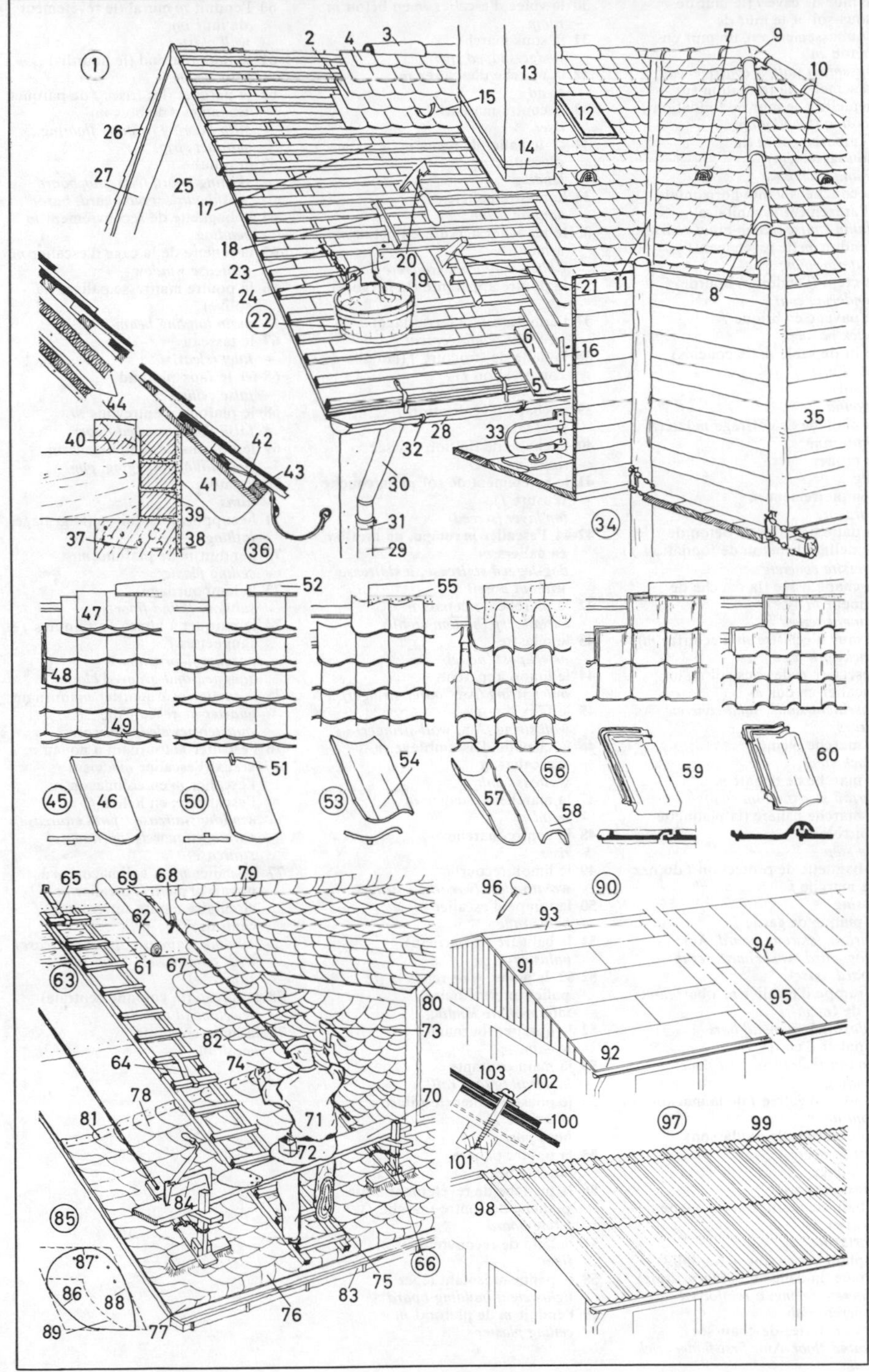
1
2
3
4
5
6
7
8
9
10
11
12
13
14
15
16
17
18
19
20
21
22
23
24
25
26
27
28
29
30
31
32
33
34
35
36
37
38
39
40
41
42
43
44
45
46
47
48
49
50
51
52
53
54
55
56
57
58
59
60
61
62
63
64
65
66
67
68
69
70
71
72
73
74
75
76
77
78
79
80
81
82
83
84
85
86
87
88
89
90
91
92
93
94
95
96
97
98
99
100
101
102
103

1 le mur de cave *f* (le mur de sous-sol *m*, le mur de soubassement *m*), un mur en béton *m*
– *basement wall, a concrete wall*
2 la semelle (la fondation sur semelle *f*, le mur de fondation *f*)
– *footing (foundation)*
3 l'embasement *m* (le soubassement)
– *foundation base*
4 la couche isolante horizontale (l'arasement *m* sanitaire)
– *damp course (damp-proof course)*
5 l'enduit *m* (le revêtement)
– *waterproofing*
6 le crépi (l'enduit *m* hourdé)
– *rendering coat*
7 le pavage en brique *f*
– *brick paving*
8 le lit de sable *m* (le couchis)
– *sand bed*
9 le sol
– *ground*
10 la planche de coffrage *m* latéral
– *shuttering*
11 le piquet
– *peg*
12 l'empierrement *m*
– *hardcore*
13 la dalle béton *m* (le béton de semelle *f*, le béton de fondation *f*)
– *oversite concrete*
14 la chape lissée (la couche de ciment *m* lissé)
– *cement screed*
15 le mur d'échiffre *m* (l'échiffre *m*)
– *brickwork base*
16 l'escalier *m* de sous-sol *m*, un escalier en dur *m*
– *basement stairs, solid concrete stairs*
17 la marche pleine
– *block step*
18 la marche de départ *m*
– *curtail step (bottom step)*
19 la marche palière (la plaquette d'arrivée *f*)
– *top step*
20 la baguette de protection *f* du nez de marche *f*
– *nosing*
21 la plaque de garde *f*
– *skirting (skirting board,* Am. *mopboard, washboard, scrub board, base)*
22 la rampe d'escalier *m* à barreaux *m* de fer *m*
– *balustrade of metal bars*
23 le palier d'entrée *f*
– *ground-floor (*Am. *first-floor) landing*
24 la porte d'entrée *f* de la maison
– *front door*
25 le décrottoir (le paillasson)
– *foot scraper*
26 le dallage
– *flagstone paving*
27 le bain de mortier *m* (la chape de mortier *m*)
– *mortar bed*
28 le plancher en dur *m* (la dalle armée, la dalle en béton *m* armé)
– *concrete ceiling, a reinforced concrete slab*
29 le mur du rez-de-chaussée
– *ground-floor (*Am. *first-floor) brick wall*
30 la volée d'escalier *m* en béton *m*
– *ramp*
31 la sous-marche
– *wedge-shaped step*
32 la marche d'escalier *m*
– *tread*
33 la contre-marche
– *riser*
34-41 le palier de repos *m* (le palier d'escalier *m*)
– ***landing***
34 la poutre palière
– *landing beam*
35 le plancher nervuré en béton *m* armé
– *ribbed reinforced concrete floor*
36 la poutre apparente (la nervure)
– *rib*
37 l'armature *f* (le ferraillage)
– *steel-bar reinforcement*
38 la dalle de structure *f* (la dalle de compression *f*)
– *subfloor (blind floor)*
39 la chape d'égalisation *f*
– *level layer*
40 la chape de finition *f* lissée
– *finishing layer*
41 le revêtement de sol *m* (la couche d'usure *f*)
– *top layer (screed)*
42-44 l'escalier *m* rompu, un escalier en paliers *m*
– ***dog-legged staircase, a staircase without a well***
42 la marche de départ *m*
– *curtail step (bottom step)*
43 le pilastre
– *newel post (newel)*
44 le limon apparent
– *outer string (*Am. *outer stringer)*
45 le faux limon
– *wall string (*Am. *wall stringer)*
46 la cheville d'assemblage *m* d'escalier *m*
– *staircase bolt*
47 la marche d'escalier *m*
– *tread*
48 la contre-marche
– *riser*
49 le limon recourbé
– *wreath piece (wreathed string)*
50 la rampe d'escalier *m*
– *balustrade*
51 le balustre (le barreau)
– *baluster*
52-62 le palier *m* de repos *m* (le palier intermédiaire)
– ***intermediate landing***
52 le quartier tournant
– *wreath*
53 la main courante
– *handrail (guard rail)*
54 le pilastre palier (le pilastre d'arrivée *f*)
– *head post*
55 la poutre palière
– *landing beam*
56 la planche de revêtement *m* (la planche de contre-marche *f*)
– *lining board*
57 la latte de recouvrement *m*
– *fillet*
58 le panneau isolant léger
– *lightweight building board*
59 l'enduit *m* de plafond *m*
– *ceiling plaster*
60 l'enduit *m* mural (le revêtement de mur *m*)
– *wall plaster*
61 le faux plafond (le hourdis)
– *false ceiling*
62 le parquet (les frises *f* de parquet, les lames *f* de bois *m*)
– *strip flooring (overlay flooring, parquet strip)*
63 la plinthe
– *skirting board (*Am. *mopboard, washboard, scrub board, base)*
64 la baguette de recouvrement *m*
– *beading*
65 la fenêtre de la cage d'escalier *m*
– *staircase window*
66 la poutre maîtresse palière (la solive)
– *main landing beam*
67 le tasseau
– *fillet (cleat)*
68-69 le faux plafond
– *false ceiling*
68 le plafond à entrevous *m*
– *false floor (inserted floor)*
69 le hourdis de remplissage *m*
– *floor filling (plugging, pug)*
70 le lattis
– *laths*
71 le support d'enduit *m* (le grillage)
– *lathing*
72 l'enduit *m* de plafond *m*
– *ceiling plaster*
73 le lambourdage
– *subfloor (blind floor)*
74 le parquet à lames *f* à rainures *f* et languettes *f*
– *parquet floor with tongued-and-grooved blocks*
75 l'escalier *m* à quartier *m* tournant
– *quarter-newelled (*Am. *quarter-neweled) staircase*
76 l'escalier *m* tournant à noyau *m* creux (l'escalier *m* à vis *f*, l'escalier *m* en colimaçon *m*, l'escalier *m* en hélice *f*)
– *winding staircase (spiral staircase) with open newels (open-newel staircase)*
77 l'escalier *m* en colimaçon *m* à noyau *m* plein (l'escalier *m* circulaire monté sur colonne *f* centrale)
– *winding staircase (spiral staircase) with solid newels (solid-newel staircase)*
78 le noyau (la colonne centrale)
– *newel (solid newel)*
79 la main courante
– *handrail*

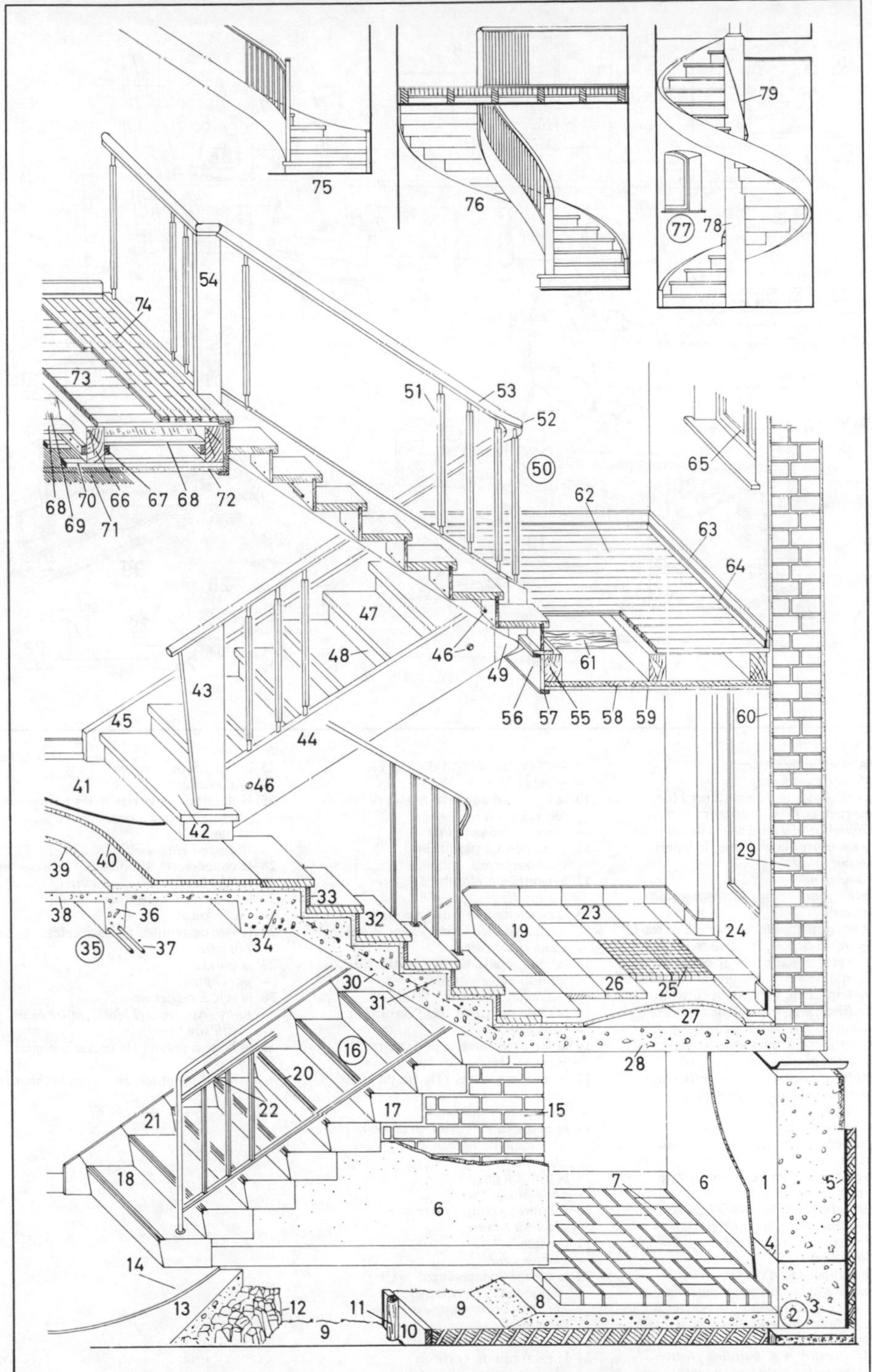

75
76
79
77
78
54
74
73
51
53
52
50
65
68
70
66
67
68
72
69
71
62
63
64
47
48
46
49
61
43
56
57
55
58
59
60
45
44
41
46
42
39
40
29
38
33
36
34
32
35
37
19
23
24
30
31
26
25
27
28
16
20
22
17
15
21
18
6
7
6
1
5
4
14
13
12
11
10
9
9
8
2
3

1 l'atelier *m* de vitrier *m*
– *glazier's workshop*
2 les modèles *m* de moulures *f* (de baguettes *f*) pour encadrement *m*
– *frame wood samples (frame samples)*
3 la moulure (la baguette, le listel)
– *frame wood*
4 l'onglet *m*
– *mitre joint (mitre,* Am. *miter joint, miter)*
5 le verre plat; *var.:* le verre à vitres *f*, le verre dépoli, le verre mousseline *f*, le verre à glace *f*, la glace (le verre épais), le verre opaque, le verre type *m* triplex (le verre de sécurité *f* feuilleté), le verre armé (le verre de sécurité *f*, le verre *sécurit*)
– *sheet glass;* kinds: *window glass, frosted glass, patterned glass, crystal plate glass, thick glass, milk glass, laminated glass (safety glass, shatterproof glass)*
6 le verre coulé; *var.:* le verre cathédrale, le verre de décoration *f*, le verre brut (le verre non poli), le verre en cul *m* de bouteille *f*, le verre armé, le verre strié
– *cast glass;* kinds: *stained glass, ornamental glass, raw glass, bull's-eye glass, wired glass, line glass (lined glass)*
7 l'estampeuse *f* d'onglets *m*
– *mitring* (Am. *mitering) machine*
8 le vitrier; *catégories f:* le vitrier de bâtiment *m*, l'encadreur *m*, le maître verrier
– *glassworker* (e.g. *building glazier, glazier, decorative glass worker)*
9 le chevalet portatif du vitrier
– *glass holder*
10 le morceau de verre *m* (les débris *m* de verre *m*)
– *piece of broken glass*
11 le marteau à plomb *m*
– *lead hammer*
12 le couteau à plomb *m*
– *lead knife*
13 la baguette à rainure *f* pour le sertissage des vitres *f* avec du plomb
– *came (lead came)*
14 la fenêtre aux vitres *f* serties au plomb *m* (le vitrail)
– *leaded light*
15 la table de travail *m* (l'établi *m*)
– *workbench*
16 la vitre (le carreau de fenêtre *f*)
– *pane of glass*
17 le mastic à vitres *f* (le lut de vitrier *m*)
– *putty*
18 le marteau de vitrier *m* à bec *m* plat et à manche *m* mince
– *glazier's hammer*
19 la pince à gruger
– *glass pliers*
20 l'équerre *f* coupe-verre *m*
– *glazier's square*
21 la règle
– *glazier's rule*
22 le compas coupe-verre *m* (le coupe-verre circulaire)
– *glazier's beam compass*
23 l'attache *f*
– *eyelet*
24 le morceau de verre *m*
– *glazing sprig*
25-26 les coupe-verre *m*
– *glass cutters*
25 le diamant de vitrier *m* (la pointe de diamamt *m*), un coupe-verre à diamant *m*
– *diamond glass cutter*
26 le coupe-verre à molettes *f* en acier *m*
– *steel-wheel (steel) glass cutter*
27 le couteau à mastiquer
– *putty knife*
28 la tige de pointes *f* détachables
– *pin wire*
29 la pointe
– *panel pin*
30 la scie à onglet *m*
– *mitre* (Am. *miter) block (mitre box) [with saw]*
31 la boîte à recaler (la presse à onglet *m*)
– *mitre* (Am. *miter) shoot (mitre board)*

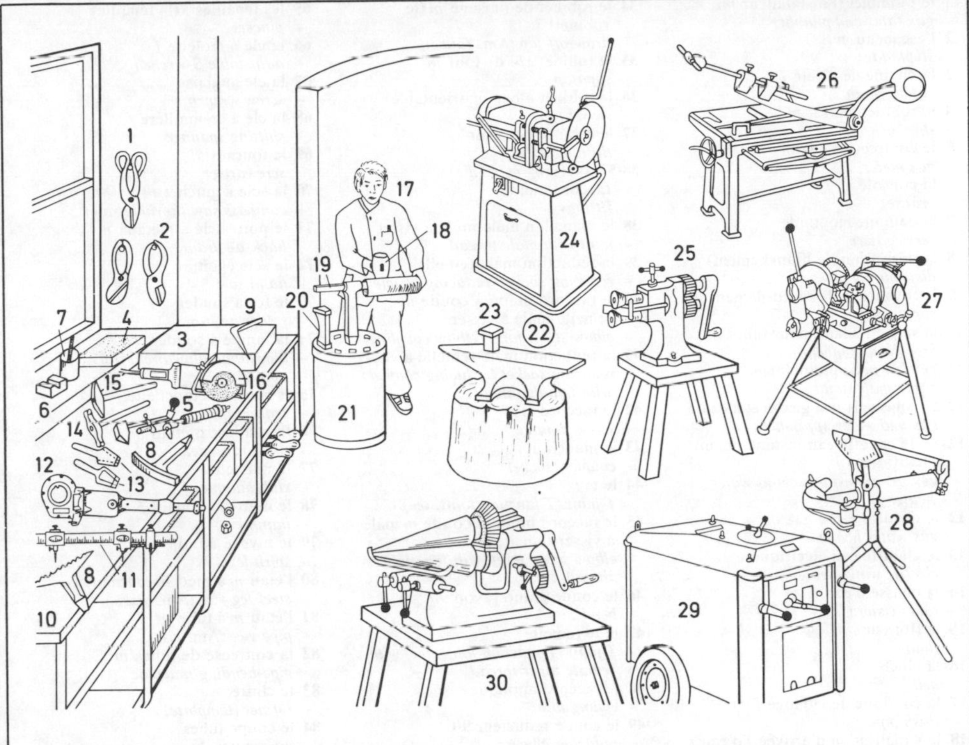

1 la cisaille
– *metal shears (tinner's snips,* Am. *tinner's shears)*
2 la cisaille à chantourner
– *elbow snips (angle shears)*
3 la plaque à dresser (le marbre à dresser)
– *gib*
4 la plaque à planer
– *lapping plate*
5-7 le chalumeau à propane *m*
– *propane soldering apparatus*
5 le fer à souder à propane *m*, un fer à souder à marteau *m*
– *propane soldering iron, a hatchet iron*
6 la pierre à souder, une pierre ammoniacale
– *soldering stone, a sal-ammoniac block*
7 l'esprit *m* de sel *m* (le décapant)
– *soldering fluid (flux)*
8 le bigorneau pour façonnage *m* de bourrelets *m* (moulures *f*)
– *beading iron for forming reinforcement beading*
9 l'alésoir *m* coudé, un alésoir
– *angled reamer*
10 l'établi *m*
– *workbench (bench)*
11 le trusquin
– *beam compass (trammel,* Am. *beam trammel)*
12 la filière électrique
– *electric hand die*
13 l'emporte-pièce *m*
– *hollow punch*
14 le marteau à bigorner
– *chamfering hammer*
15 le marteau à pointes *f*
– *beading swage (beading hammer)*
16 la tronçonneuse à meule *f*
– *abrasive-wheel cutting-off machine*
17 le ferblantier
– *plumber*
18 le maillet
– *mallet*
19 la bigorne
– *mandrel*
20 le tasseau
– *socket (tinner's socket)*
21 le billot
– *block*
22 l'enclume *f*
– *anvil*
23 le tas
– *stake*
24 la scie circulaire
– *circular saw (buzz saw)*
25 la machine à moulurer, border et sertir
– *flanging, swaging, and wiring machine*
26 la cisaille-guillotine
– *sheet shears (guillotine)*
27 la machine à fileter
– *screw-cutting machine (thread-cutting machine, die stocks)*
28 la machine à cintrer les tubes *m*
– *pipe-bending machine (bending machine, pipe bender)*
29 le transformateur de soudage *m*
– *welding transformer*
30 la machine à cintrer pour le façonnage des entonnoirs *m*
– *bending machine (rounding machine) for shaping funnels*

1 le plombier (l'installateur *m*)
– *gas fitter and plumber*
2 l'escabeau *m*
– *stepladder*
3 la chaîne de sûreté *f*
– *safety chain*
4 le robinet d'arrêt *m*
– *stopcock*
5 le compteur à gaz *m*
– *gas meter*
6 la console
– *bracket*
7 la colonne montante
– *service riser*
8 la dérivation (le branchement)
– *distributing pipe*
9 la tuyauterie de raccordement *m*
– *supply pipe*
10 la scie circulaire pour tubes *m*
– *pipe-cutting machine*
11 l'établi *m* de plombier *m*
– *pipe repair stand*
12-25 appareils *m* à gaz *m* et à eau *f*
– ***gas and water appliances***
12-13 le chauffe-eau instantané, un chauffe-eau
– *geyser, an instantaneous water heater*
12 le chauffe-eau à gaz *m*
– *gas water heater*
13 le chauffe-eau électrique
– *electric water heater*
14 la chasse d'eau *f*
– *toilet cistern*
15 le flotteur
– *float*
16 la cloche
– *bell*
17 la conduite de vidange *f*
– *flush pipe*
18 la canalisation d'arrivée *f* d'eau *f*
– *water inlet*
19 le levier de manœuvre *f*
– *flushing lever (lever)*
20 le radiateur
– *radiator*
21 l'élément *m* de radiateur *m*
– *radiator rib*
22 le système à deux tuyaux *m*
– *two-pipe system*
23 la conduite de départ *m*
– *flow pipe*
24 la conduite de retour *m*
– *return pipe*
25 le radiateur à gaz *m*
– *gas heater*
26-37 la robinetterie
– ***plumbing fixtures***
26 le siphon
– *trap (anti-syphon trap)*
27 le robinet mélangeur
– *mixer tap* (Am. *mixing faucet) for washbasins*
28 le robinet d'eau *f* chaude
– *hot tap*
29 le robinet d'eau *f* froide
– *cold tap*
30 la douchette
– *extendible shower attachment*
31 le robinet de lavabo *m*
– *water tap (pillar tap) for washbasins*
32 la tige de robinet *m*
– *spindle top*
33 la tête de robinet *m*
– *shield*
34 le robinet de puisage *m* (le robinet)
– *draw-off tap* (Am. *faucet)*
35 le robinet 1/4 de tour *m*
– *supatap*
36 le robinet à bec *m* orientable
– *swivel tap*
37 le robinet-poussoir
– *flushing valve*
38-52 raccords *m* [*ELF:* la raccorderie]
– ***fittings***
38 le mamelon mâle-mâle à visser
– *joint with male thread*
39 la réduction mâle-femelle
– *reducing socket (reducing coupler)*
40 le raccord union à coude *m* femelle-mâle à visser
– *elbow screw joint (elbow coupling)*
41 la réduction mâle-femelle à visser
– *reducing socket (reducing coupler) with female thread*
42 le raccord vissé
– *screw joint*
43 le manchon
– *coupler (socket)*
44 le té
– *T-joint (T-junction joint, tee)*
45 le raccord union à coude *m* mâle à visser-femelle à visser
– *elbow screw joint with female thread*
46 le coude grand rayon 90°
– *bend*
47 le té femelle
– *T-joint (T-junction joint, tee) with female taper thread*
48 le raccord applique
– *ceiling joint*
49 le coude réducteur 90°
– *reducing elbow*
50 la croix
– *cross*
51 le coude 90° femelle-mâle à visser
– *elbow joint with male thread*
52 le coude 90°
– *elbow joint*
53-57 attaches *f* de tubes *m*
– ***pipe supports***
53 le collier à contrepartie *f* et embase *f* plate
– *saddle clip*
54 le collier à contrepartie *f* et embase *f* taraudée
– *spacing bracket*
55 la patte à vis *f*
– *plug*
56 colliers *m* simples
– *pipe clips*
57 le pontet
– *two-piece spacing clip*
58-86 outillage *m* de plombier *m*
– ***plumber's tools, gas fitter's tools***
58 la pince à gaz *m*
– *gas pliers*
59 la clé serre-tubes *m*
– *footprints*
60 la pince universelle
– *combination cutting pliers*
61 la pince multiprise
– *pipe wrench*
62 la pince plate
– *flat-nose pliers*
63 l'outil *m* à emboîture *f*
– *nipple key*
64 la pince à écrous *m*
– *round-nose pliers*
65 les tenailles *f* (la tenaille)
– *pincers*
66 la clé à molette *f*
– *adjustable S-wrench*
67 la clé anglaise
– *screw wrench*
68 la clé à crémaillère *f*
– *shifting spanner*
69 le tournevis
– *screwdriver*
70 la scie à guichet *m*
– *compass saw (keyhole saw)*
71 le porte-scie à métaux *m*
– *hacksaw frame*
72 la scie égoïne
– *hand saw*
73 le fer à souder
– *soldering iron*
74 la lampe à souder
– *blowlamp (blowtorch) [for soldering]*
75 le ruban d'étanchéité *f*
– *sealing tape*
76 la soudure d'étain *m*
– *tin-lead solder*
77 la massette
– *club hammer*
78 le marteau à main *f*
– *hammer*
79 le niveau à bulle *f*
– *spirit level*
80 l'étau *m* à pied *m* tournant
– *steel-leg vice* (Am. *vise)*
81 l'étau *m* à tube *m*
– *pipe vice* (Am. *vise)*
82 la cintreuse de tubes *m*
– *pipe-bending machine*
83 le cintre
– *former (template)*
84 le coupe-tubes
– *pipe cutter*
85 la filière à main *f*
– *hand die*
86 la machine à fileter
– *screw-cutting machine (thread-cutting machine)*

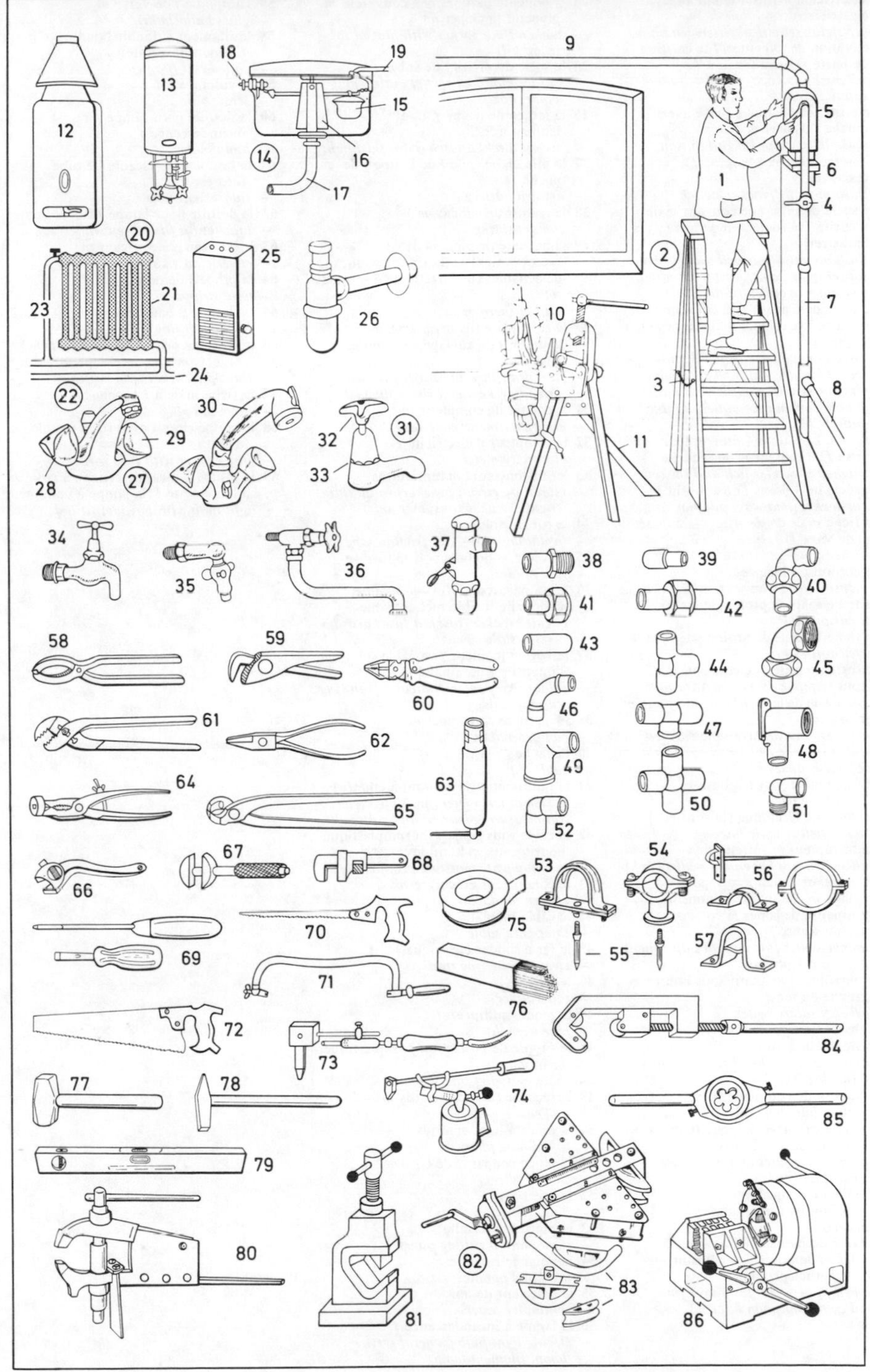
1
2
3
4
5
6
7
8
9
10
11
12
13
14
15
16
17
18
19
20
21
22
23
24
25
26
27
28
29
30
31
32
33
34
35
36
37
38
39
40
41
42
43
44
45
46
47
48
49
50
51
52
53
54
55
56
57
58
59
60
61
62
63
64
65
66
67
68
69
70
71
72
73
74
75
76
77
78
79
80
81
82
83
84
85
86

1 l'électricien *m* (installateur *m* électricien)
– *electrician (electrical fitter, wireman)*
2 le bouton de sonnette *f* (de carillon *m* de porte *f*) basse tension *f*
– *bell push (doorbell) for low-voltage safety current*
3 le poste téléphonique privé avec touche *f* d'appel *m*
– *house telephone with call button*
4 l'interrupteur *m* à bascule *f* à encastrer
– *[flush-mounted] rocker switch*
5 le socle de prise *f* de courant *m* de sécurité *f* (à contact *m* de terre *f*) [à encastrer]
– *[flush-mounted] earthed socket (wall socket, plug point,* Am. *wall outlet, convenience outlet, outlet)*
6 le socle de 2 prises *f* de courant *m* de sécurité *f* (à contact *m* de terre *f*) [en saillie *f*]
– *[surface-mounted] earthed double socket (double wall socket, double plug point,* Am. *double wall outlet, double convenience outlet, double outlet)*
7 le socle 2 postes *m* (interrupteur *m* et prise *f* de courant *m* de sécurité *f*)
– *switched socket (switch and socket)*
8 le socle de 4 prises *f* de courant *m*
– *four-socket (four-way) adapter*
9 la fiche mâle de sécurité *f* (à contact *m* de terre *f*)
– *earthed plug*
10 le cordon prolongateur *m*
– *extension lead* (Am. *extension cord)*
11 la fiche mâle de prolongateur *m*
– *extension plug*
12 la fiche femelle de prolongateur *m*
– *extension socket*
13 le socle de prise *f* de courant *m* 3 P [pour triphasé *m*] avec neutre *m* et contact *m* de terre *f*, pour montage *m* en saillie *f*
– *surface-mounted three-pole earthed socket [for three-phase circuit] with neutral conductor*
14 la fiche mâle pour triphasé *m*
– *three-phase plug*
15 la sonnerie électrique (le ronfleur)
– *electric bell (electric buzzer)*
16 l'interrupteur *m* à tirette *f*
– *pull-switch (cord-operated wall switch)*
17 le variateur de lumière *f* [pour réglage *m* continu de l'intensité *f* lumineuse de lames *f* à incandescence *f*]
– *dimmer switch [for smooth adjustment of lamp brightness]*
18 l'interrupteur *m* rotatif sous boîtier *m* étanche en fonte *f*
– *drill-cast rotary switch*
19 le disjoncteur miniature (le disjoncteur à visser)
– *miniature circuit breaker (screw-in circuit breaker, fuse)*
20 le bouton de réarmement *m*
– *resetting button*
21 la vis de calibrage *m* [pour fusibles *m* et disjoncteurs *m* à visser]
– *set screw [for fuses and miniature circuit breakers]*
22 la boîte de parquet *m*
– *underfloor mounting (underfloor sockets)*
23 la boîte de parquet *m* pivotante à socles *m* de prises *f* de courant *m* force *f* et téléphonique
– *hinged floor socket for power lines and communication lines*
24 la boîte de parquet *m* à couvercle *m* pivotant (à clapet *m*)
– *sunken floor socket with hinged lid (snap lid)*
25 le socle de prises *f* de sol *m*
– *surface-mounted socket outlet (plug point) box*
26 la lampe de poche *f*, une lampe-torche
– *pocket torch, a torch* (Am. *flashlight)*
27 la pile sèche (pile *f* de lampe *f* de poche *f*)
– *dry cell battery*
28 le ressort de contact *m*
– *contact spring*
29 la barrette de plots *m* de raccordement *m* thermoplastiques détachables (la barrette de dominos *m*)
– *strip of thermoplastic connectors*
30 le ruban tire-fils *m* en acier *m* à goupille *f* de guidage *m* et œillet *m* rivé
– *steel draw-in wire (draw wire) with threading key, and ring attached*
31 le coffret de compteur *m*
– *electricity meter cupboard*
32 le compteur d'électricité *f*
– *electricity meter*
33 les disjoncteurs *m* miniatures
– *miniature circuit breakers (miniature circuit breaker consumer unit)*
34 le ruban isolant
– *insulating tape* (Am. *friction tape)*
35 l'alvéole *m* de bouchon *m* fusible
– *fuse holder*
36 le coupe-circuit à fusible *m*, une cartouche fusible rechargeable
– *circuit breaker (fuse), a fuse cartridge with fusible element*
37 le voyant [couleur *f* variable selon l'intensité *f* nominale]
– *colour* (Am. *color) indicator [showing current rating]*
38-39 la pièce de contact *m*
– *contact maker*
40 l'attache *f* plastique
– *cable clip*
41 le multimètre (le voltampèremètre)
– *universal test meter (multiple meter for measuring current and voltage)*
42 le câble sous gaine *f* thermoplastique pour locaux *m* humides
– *thermoplastic moisture-proof cable*
43 le conducteur en cuivre *m*
– *copper conductor*
44 le câble méplat
– *three-core cable*
45 le fer à souder électrique
– *electric soldering iron*
46 le tournevis
– *screwdriver*
47 la pince multiprise *f*
– *pipe wrench*
48 le casque de protection *f* en plastique *m* antichoc
– *shock-resisting safety helmet*
49 la sacoche (le sac) à outils *m*
– *tool case*
50 la pince à becs *m* ronds
– *round-nose pliers*
51 la pince coupante de côté *m*
– *cutting pliers*
52 la scie bocfil
– *junior hacksaw*
53 la pince universelle
– *combination cutting pliers*
54 la poignée isolante
– *insulated handle*
55 le détecteur de tension *f*
– *continuity tester*
56 la lampe à incandescence *f*
– *electric light bulb (general service lamp, filament lamp)*
57 l'ampoule *f* de verre *m*
– *glass bulb (bulb)*
58 le filament à double boudinage *m* (le filament bispiralé)
– *coiled-coil filament*
59 le culot à vis *f*
– *screw base*
60 la douille pour lampe *f* à incandescence *f*
– *lampholder*
61 la lampe fluorescente (le tube fluorescent)
– *fluorescent tube*
62 la douille pour lampe *f* fluorescente
– *bracket for fluorescent tubes*
63 le couteau d'électricien *m*
– *electrician's knife*
64 la pince à dénuder
– *wire strippers*
65 la douille à baïonnette *f*
– *bayonet fitting*
66 le socle de prise *f* de courant *m* à 3 contacts *m* avec interrupteur *m*
– *three-pin socket with switch*
67 la fiche mâle à 3 broches *f*
– *three-pin plug*
68 le coupe-circuit avec fil *m* fusible (le fusible)
– *fuse carrier with fuse wire*
69 la lampe à incandescence *f* à culot *m* à baïonnette *f* (la lampe à baïonnette *f*)
– *light bulb with bayonet fitting*

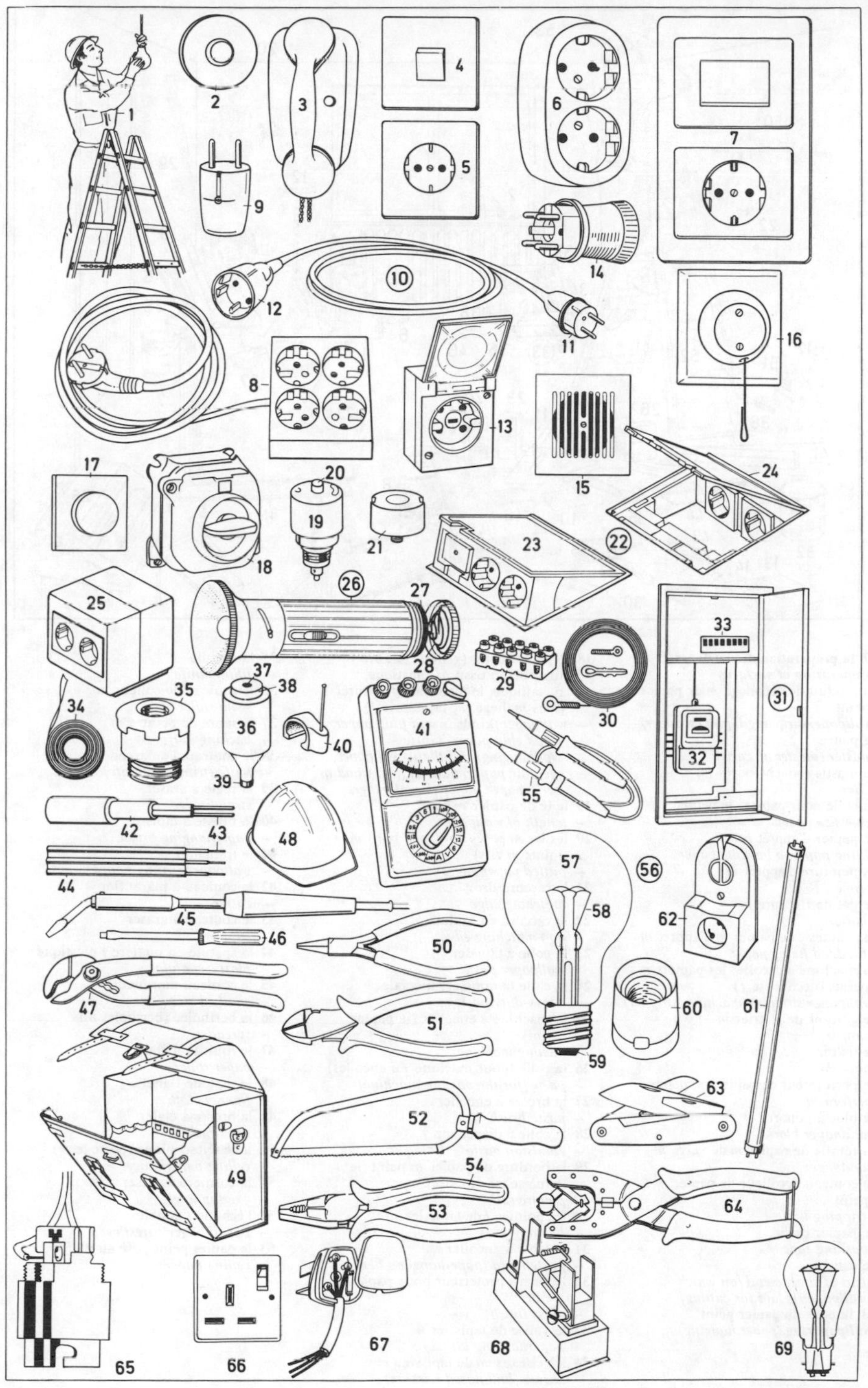
1
2
3
4
5
6
7
8
9
10
11
12
13
14
15
16
17
18
19
20
21
22
23
24
25
26
27
28
29
30
31
32
33
34
35
36
37
38
39
40
41
42
43
44
45
46
47
48
49
50
51
52
53
54
55
56
57
58
59
60
61
62
63
64
65
66
67
68
69

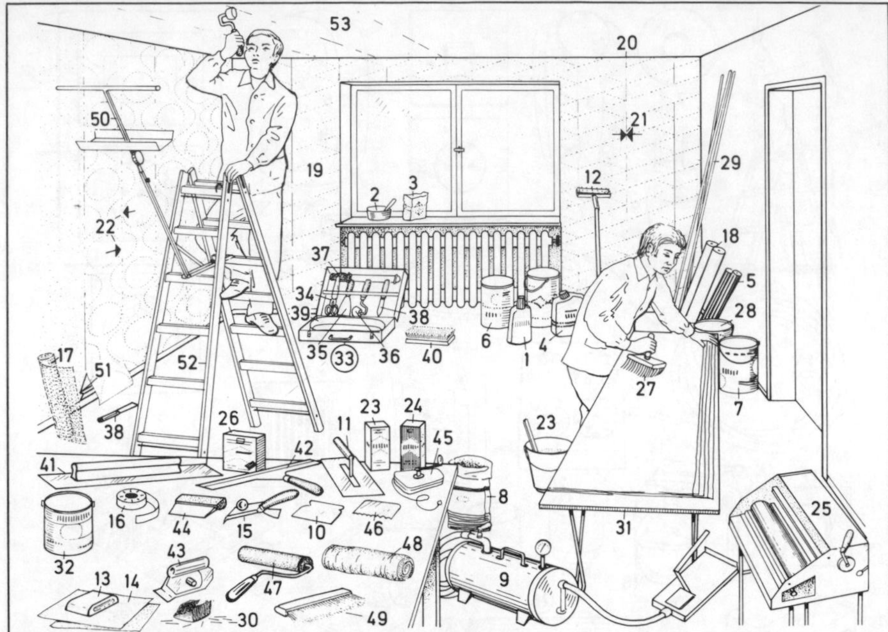

1-17 la préparation des surfaces *f*
– ***preparation of surfaces***
1 le produit de décollage *m* de papier *m* peint
– *wallpaper-stripping liquid (stripper)*
2 le plâtre
– *plaster (plaster of Paris)*
3 le mastic (bouche-pores *m*)
– *filler*
4 la colle pour papiers *m* peints
– *glue size (size)*
5 le papier d'apprêt *m*
– *lining paper, a backing paper*
6 la peinture d'apprêt *m*
– *primer*
7 le pot de fluorure *m*
– *fluate*
8 les chutes *f* de papier *m* d'apprêt *m*
– *shredded lining paper*
9 la machine à décoller les papiers *m* peints (décolleuse *f*)
– *wallpaper-stripping machine (stripper)*
10 le grattoir de plâtrier *m*
– *scraper*
11 le lissoir
– *smoother*
12 le perforateur de papiers *m* peints
– *perforator*
13 le bloc à poncer
– *sandpaper block*
14 la feuille de papier *m* de verre *m*
– *sandpaper*
15 le couteau décolleur de papier *m* peint
– *stripping knife*
16 le papier cache
– *masking tape*
17 le calicot
– *strip of sheet metal [on which wallpaper is laid for cutting]*
18-53 la pose du papier peint
– ***wallpapering*** *(paper hanging)*
18 le papier peint (*genres:* tenture *f* ingrain, en tissu *m*, plastique, métallique, le matériau *m* naturel [bois *m*, liège *m*], tapisserie *f*)
– *wallpaper (*kinds: *wood pulp paper, wood chip paper, fabric wallhangings, synthetic wallpaper, metallic paper, natural (*e.g. *wood or cork) paper, tapestry wallpaper)*
19 le lé de papier *m* peint
– *length of wallpaper*
20 les lés *m* posés bord *m* à bord *m* (à joints *m* vifs)
– *butted paper edges*
21 le raccord droit
– *matching edge*
22 le raccord en sautoir *m*
– *non-matching edge*
23 la colle à tapisser
– *wallpaper paste*
24 la colle (à tapisser) spéciale
– *heavy-duty paste*
25 la machine à encoller (le papier peint)
– *pasting machine*
26 la colle (pour machine *f* à encoller)
– *paste [for the pasting machine]*
27 la brosse à encoller
– *paste brush*
28 la colle à dispersion *f*
– *emulsion paste*
29 la bordure de papier *m* peint (la cimaise ou cymaise)
– *picture rail*
30 les pointes *f* de tapissier *m*
– *beading pins*
31 la table à encoller
– *pasteboard (paperhanger's bench)*
32 le vernis protecteur pour papier *m* peint
– *gloss finish*
33 la valise de tapissier *m*
– *paperhanging kit*
34 les ciseaux *m* de tapissier *m*
– *shears (bull-nosed scissors)*
35 la spatule
– *filling knife*
36 le rouleau de colleur *m*
– *seam roller*
37 le sabre de peintre *m*
– *hacking knife*
38 le couteau à émarger
– *knife (trimming knife)*
39 la règle à araser
– *straightedge*
40 la brosse à tapisser
– *paperhanging brush*
41 le tranchoir
– *wallpaper-cutting board*
42 le couteau à maraufler
– *cutter*
43 le couteau à araser
– *trimmer*
44 la spatule en matière *f* plastique
– *plastic spatula*
45 le cordeau marqueur
– *chalked string*
46 la bertholée (bertholet *m*)
– *spreader*
47 le rouleau à étaler
– *paper roller*
48 le tissu de flanelle *f*
– *flannel cloth*
49 la brosse à étaler
– *dry brush*
50 le té télescopique (porte-lé *m*)
– *ceiling paperhanger*
51 la cornière à araser
– *overlap angle*
52 l'échelle *f* double
– *paperhanger's trestles*
53 le papier peint posé au plafond
– *ceiling paper*

1 la peintre
– ***painting***
2 le peintre (en bâtiment *m*)
– *painter*
3 la brosse à badigeonner
– *paintbrush*
4 la peinture à dispersion *f*
– *emulsion paint (emulsion)*
5 l'échelle *f* pliante (triquet *m*)
– *stepladder*
6 la boîte de peinture *f*
– *can (tin) of paint*
7-8 les pots *m* de peinture *f*
– *cans (tins) of paint*
7 le pot à poignée *f* fixe
– *can (tin) with fixed handle*
8 le pot à anse *f*
– *paint kettle*
9 le camion (de peinture *f*)
– *drum of paint*
10 le seau de peinture *f*
– *paint bucket*
11 le rouleau à peindre
– *paint roller*
12 la grille essoreuse
– *grill [for removing excess paint from the roller]*
13 le rouleau à pochoir *m*
– *stippling roller*
14 le laquage
– ***varnishing***
15 le soubassement peint à l'huile *f*
– *oil-painted dado*
16 le bidon de diluant *m*
– *canister for thinner*
17 le pinceau plat
– *flat brush for larger surfaces (flat wall brush)*
18 la brosse à encoller
– *stippler*
19 le pinceau rond
– *fitch*
20 le pinceau à rechampir
– *cutting-in brush*
21 le pinceau pour radiateurs *m*
– *radiator brush (flay brush)*
22 la spatule de peintre *m*
– *paint scraper*
23 le couteau étendeur
– *scraper*
24 le couteau à mastiquer (spatule *f* de vitrier *m*)
– *putty knife*
25 le papier de verre *m*
– *sandpaper*
26 le bloc à poncer
– *sandpaper block*
27 le balai
– *floor brush*
28 le ponçage et la peinture au pistolet *m*
– ***sanding and spraying***
29 la ponceuse
– *grinder*
30 la ponceuse vibrante
– *sander*
31 le réservoir d'air *m*
– *pressure pot*
32 le pistolet à peinture *f*
– *spray gun*
33 le compresseur
– *compressor (air compressor)*
34 l'appareil *m* de remplissage *m* en eau *f* de radiateurs *m*, etc..
– *flow coating machine for flow coating radiators, etc.*
35 le pistolet à peinture *f* à main *f*
– *hand spray*
36 l'équipement *m* pour peinture *f* sans air *m*
– *airless spray unit*
37 le pistolet à peinture *f* sans air *m*
– *airless spray gun*
38 la coupe consistométrique pour mesurer la viscosité (viscosimètre *m* pour peinture *f*)
– *efflux viscometer*
39 le compte-secondes
– *seconds timer*
40 le marquage et la dorure
– ***lettering and gilding***
41 le pinceau à lettres *f*
– *lettering brush (signwriting brush, pencil)*
42 la roulette à calquer
– *tracing wheel*
43 le couteau-pochoir
– *stencil knife*
44 l'huile *f* d'applique *f*
– *oil gold size*
45 l'or *m* d'applique *f* (or *m* en feuilles *f*) (feuille *f* d'or *m*)
– *gold leaf*
46 la peinture au trait *m*
– *outline drawing*
47 le bâton de peinture *f*
– *mahlstick*
48 le ponçage du dessin *m*
– *pouncing*
49 le sac de ponçage *m*
– *pounce bag*
50 le coussin à or *m*
– *gilder's cushion*
51 le couteau à or *m*
– *gilder's knife*
52 la prise de la feuille d'or *m*
– *sizing gold leaf*
53 le remplissage des lettres *f* avec de la peinture
– *filling in the letters with stipple paint*
54 le pinceau à dorer
– *gilder's mop*

130 Tonnellerie et construction de réservoirs
Cooper and Tank Construction Engineer

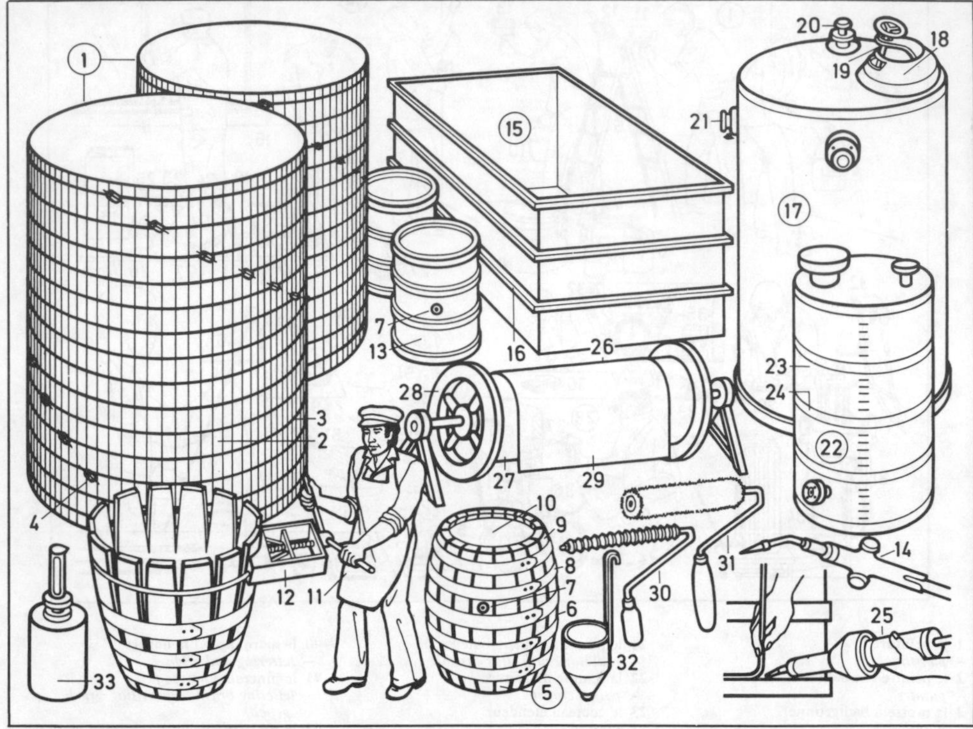

1-33 la tonnellerie et la construction de réservoirs *m*
– ***cooper's and tank construction engineer's workshops***
1 la cuve
– *tank*
2 la claie circulaire à lamelles *f* en bois *m* et à ferrures *f*
– *circumference made of staves (staved circumference)*
3 le cercle métallique
– *iron rod*
4 le tendeur
– *turnbuckle*
5 le tonneau (le fût, la futaille, la barrique)
– *barrel (cask)*
6 le corps du tonneau (la bouge, la panse)
– *body of barrel (of cask)*
7 la bonde
– *bunghole*
8 le cercle (le cerceau)
– *band (hoop) of barrel*
9 la douve
– *barrel stave*
10 le fond du tonneau (le couvercle)
– *barrelhead (heading)*
11 le tonnelier
– *cooper*
12 l'appareil *m* de cerclage *m*
– *trusser*
13 le bidon (le fût métallique cerclé)
– *drum*
14 le chalumeau oxyacétylénique
– *gas welding torch*
15 le bac de teinture *f* en matière *f* thermoplastique
– *staining vat, made of thermoplastics*
16 le raidisseur profilé
– *iron reinforcing bands*
17 le réservoir de stockage *m* (la citerne) en résine *f* polyester armée de fibres *f* de verre *m*
– *storage container, made of glass fibre (*Am. *glass fiber) reinforced polyester resin*
18 le trou d'homme *m* (l'orifice *m* de nettoiement *m*)
– *manhole*
19 le couvercle à tige *f*
– *manhole cover with handwheel*
20 le raccord à brides *f*
– *flange mount*
21 l'obturateur *m*
– *flange-type stopcock*
22 le réservoir gradué
– *measuring tank*
23 la paroi
– *shell (circumference)*
24 la frette
– *shrink ring*
25 le pistolet à air *m* chaud
– *hot-air gun*
26 le tube en résine *f* synthétique armée de fibres *f* de verre *m*
– *roller made of glass fibre (*Am. *glass fiber) reinforced synthetic resin*
27 le cylindre
– *cylinder*
28 la flasque de support *m* du cylindre
– *flange*
29 le tissu de fibres *f* de verre *m*
– *glass cloth*
30 le cylindre cannelé
– *grooved roller*
31 le rouleau en peau *f* de mouton *m*
– *lambskin roller*
32 le viscosimètre (la louche, le gobelet doseur)
– *ladle for testing viscosity*
33 le doseur de durcisseur *m*
– *measuring vessel for hardener*

1-25 l'atelier *m* **de pelleterie** *f*
– ***furrier's workroom***
1 le pelletier (le fourreur)
– *furrier*
2 le pulvérisateur (le pistolet à vapeur *f*)
– *steam spray gun*
3 le fer (à repasser) à vapeur *f*
– *steam iron*
4 la batteuse
– *beating machine*
5 la machine à découper pour allonger les fourrures *f*
– *cutting machine for letting out furskins*
6 la fourrure non découpée
– *uncut furskin*
7 la fourrure découpée en lanières *f*
– *let-out strips (let-out sections)*
8 la pelletière (la couturière)
– *fur worker*
9 la machine à coudre les fourrures *f*
– *fur-sewing machine*
10 le ventilateur
– *blower for letting out*
11-21 fourrures *f*
– *furskins*
11 la fourrure de vison *m*
– *mink skin*
12 le côté poil *m* (la fourrure)
– *fur side*
13 le côté cuir *m* (la peau)
– *leather side*
14 la fourrure découpée
– *cut furskin*
15 la fourrure de lynx *m* avant découpe *f* et allongement *m*
– *lynx skin before letting out*
16 la fourrure de lynx *m* allongée
– *let-out lynx skin*
17 le côté poil *m* (la fourrure)
– *fur side*
18 le côté cuir *m* (la peau)
– *leather side*
19 la fourrure de vison *m* allongée
– *let-out mink skin*
20 la fourrure de lynx *m* assemblée
– *lynx fur, sewn together (sewn)*
21 la fourrure d'astrakan *m* (de Breitschwanz *m*, de mouton *m* de Perse *f*)
– *broadtail*
22 la pointe de pelletier *m*
– *fur marker*
23 la pelletière
– *fur worker*
24 le manteau de vison *m*
– *mink coat*
25 le manteau d'ocelot *m*
– *ocelot coat*

1-73 l'atelier *m* **de menuisier** *m* (la menuiserie)
– ***joiner's workshop***
1-28 les outils *m* **de menuisier** *m*
– ***joiner's tools***
1 la râpe à bois *m*
– *wood rasp*
2 la lime à bois *m*
– *wood file*
3 la scie à guichet *m*
– *compass saw (keyhole saw)*
4 le manche de la scie à guichet *m* (la poignée ouverte)
– *saw handle*
5 le maillet plat (le maillet à tête *f* rectangulaire)
– *[square-headed] mallet*
6 l'équerre *f* de menuisier *m*
– *try square*
7-11 l'outillage *m* **à creuser**
– ***chisels***
7 le ciseau biseauté (le ciseau de menuisier *m*)
– *bevelled-edge chisel (chisel)*
8 le bédane à bois *m* (le bec d'âne *m*)
– *mortise (mortice) chisel*
9 la gouge
– *gouge*
10 le manche
– *handle*
11 le ciseau biseauté à brides *f* (le ciseau à bords *m* biseautés)
– *framing chisel (cant chisel)*
12 le chauffe-colle à bain-marie *m*
– *glue pot in water bath*
13 le pot de colle *f* forte (de colle *f* en tablettes *f*, à base *f* de gélatine *f*, de «colle de Lyon»)
– *glue pot (glue well), an insert for joiner's glue*
14 le serre-joint à coller (le sergent)
– *handscrew*
15-28 l'outillage *m* **à façonner** (les rabots *m* à main *f*)
– ***planes***
15 le rabot plat (à recaler)
– *smoothing plane*
16 le riflard (le rabot à dégrossir, la demi-varlope)
– *jack plane*
17 le rabot à dents *f* (le rabot denté)
– *toothing plane*
18 la poignée (le nez, la corne, le pommeau du rabot)
– *handle (toat)*
19 le coin
– *wedge*
20 le fer
– *plane iron (cutter)*
21 la lumière
– *mouth*
22 la semelle (le talon)
– *sole*
23 la joue
– *side*
24 le fût
– *stock (body)*
25 le guillaume
– *rebate (rabbet) plane*
26 la guimbarde
– *router plane (old woman's tooth)*
27 la wabstringue
– *spokeshave*
28 le rabot cintré
– *compass plane*

29-37 l'établi *m* **de menuisier** *m*
– ***woodworker's bench***
29 le pied de l'établi *m*
– *foot*
30 la presse d'établi *m*
– *front vice* (Am. *vise)*
31 le bloc de serrage *m* (la mâchoire, le mors mobile)
– *vice* (Am. *vise) handle*
32 la vis de presse *f*
– *vice* (Am. *vise) screw*
33 le mors (la mâchoire) fixe
– *jaw*
34 le plateau d'établi *m*
– *bench top*
35 le râtelier
– *well*
36 la griffe d'établi *m*
– *bench stop (bench holdfast)*
37 la presse arrière de l'établi *m* (la presse parisienne)
– *tail vice* (Am. *vise)*
38 le menuisier (l'ébéniste *m*)
– *cabinet maker (joiner)*
39 la varlope (le rabot long)
– *trying plane*
40 les copeaux *m*
– *shavings*
41 la vis à bois *m*
– *wood screw*
42 le tourne-à-gauche
– *saw set*
43 la boîte à coupes *f* (la boîte à onglets *m*)
– *mitre* (Am. *miter) box*
44 l'égoïne *f*, une scie à dosseret *m* (la scie d'encadreur *m*)
– *tenon saw*
45 la raboteuse (la machine à tirer d'épaisseur *f*)
– *thicknesser (thicknessing machine)*
46 la table de rabotage *m* mobile avec les rouleaux *m* entraîneurs
– *thicknessing table with rollers*
47 l'écran *m* antiprojection *f*
– *kick-back guard*
48 le capot d'évacuation *f* des copeaux *m*
– *chip-extractor opening*
49 la mortaiseuse à chaîne *f*
– *chain mortising machine (chain mortiser)*
50 la chaîne à mortaiser (dentée, articulée) sans fin *f*
– *endless mortising chain*
51 le volant de serrage *m* du bois
– *clamp (work clamp)*
52 la perceuse à dénoder
– *knot hole moulding* (Am. *molding) machine*
53 la fraise à dénoder
– *knot hole cutter*
54 les mandrins *m* à serrage *m* rapide
– *quick-action chuck*
55 le levier à main *f* (la manette)
– *hand lever*
56 le levier de débrayage *m*
– *change-gear handle*
57 la scie circulaire pour mise *f* au format et délignage *m*
– *sizing and edging machine*
58 l'interrupteur *m* principal (le bouton de commande *f*)
– *main switch*
59 la lame de scie *f* circulaire
– *circular-saw (buzz saw) blade*

60 le volant de réglage *m* en hauteur *f*
– *height (rise and fall) adjustment wheel*
61 la glissière prismatique (en V *m* renversé)
– *V-way*
62 la table porte-pièce amovible
– *framing table*
63 la potence
– *extension arm (arm)*
64 la table de délignage *m*
– *trimming table*
65 le guide d'onglet *m*
– *fence*
66 le volant de réglage *m* du guide
– *fence adjustment handle*
67 le levier de serrage *m*(de blocage *m*)
– *clamp lever*
68 la scie circulaire pour exécuter les plates-bandes *f* des panneaux *m*
– *board-sawing machine*
69 le moteur coulissant
– *swivel motor*
70 le dispositif de fixation *f* des panneaux *m*
– *board support*
71 le chariot de scie *f*
– *saw carriage*
72 la pédale de levage *m* des galets *m* transporteurs
– *pedal for raising the transport rollers*
73 le panneau de lamellé *m* collé
– *block board*

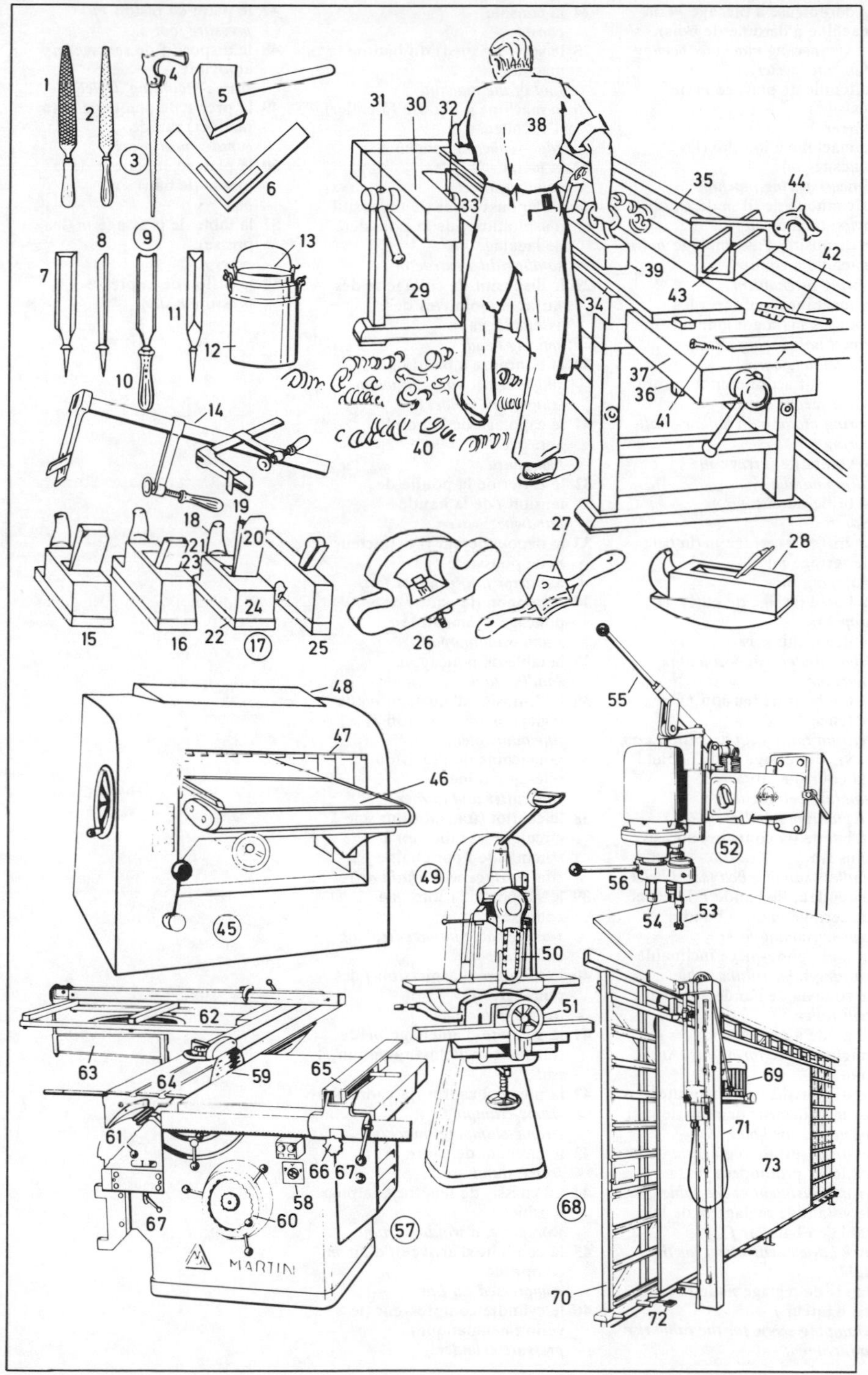
1
2
3
4
5
6
7
8
9
10
11
12
13
14
15
16
17
18
19
20
21
22
23
24
25
26
27
28
29
30
31
32
33
34
35
36
37
38
39
40
41
42
43
44
45
46
47
48
49
50
51
52
53
54
55
56
57
58
59
60
61
62
63
64
65
66
67
68
69
70
71
72
73
MARTIN

1 la dérouleuse à placage *m* (la machine à dérouler le bois)
- *veneer-peeling machine (peeling machine, peeler)*
2 la feuille de placage *m* (le placage)
- *veneer*
3 la machine à joindre (les placages *m*)
- *veneer-splicing machine*
4 la cannette de fil *m* de nylon *m*
- *nylon-thread cop*
5 le dispositif d'assemblage *m* (la machine à coudre)
- *sewing mechanism*
6 la machine à enfoncer les goujons *m* (la goujonneuse)
- *dowel hole boring machine (dowel hole borer)*
7 le moteur actionnant un arbre porte-mèche creux
- *boring motor with hollow-shaft boring bit*
8 le volant de serrage *m*
- *clamp handle*
9 la bride de serrage *m*
- *clamp*
10 la griffe de serrage *m* (la cale de serrage *m*)
- *clamping shoe*
11 la butée (la tige de butée *f*)
- *stop bar*
12 la dégauchisseuse
- *edge sander (edge-sanding machine)*
13 le tambour de tension *f* à potence *f*
- *tension roller with extension arm*
14 la vis de réglage *m* de la bande (la courroie) abrasive
- *sanding belt regulator (regulating handle)*
15 la bande (la courroie) abrasive sans fin *f*
- *endless sanding belt (sand belt)*
16 le tendeur de bande *f* (le levier de serrage *m* de la bande)
- *belt-tensioning lever*
17 la table porte-pièce inclinable
- *canting table (tilting table)*
18 le rouleau de bande *f* abrasive
- *belt roller*
19 le guide à onglets *m*
- *angling fence for mitres (*Am. *miters)*
20 le dépoussiéreur (l'aspirateur *m*, le collecteur de poussière *f*)
- *opening dust hood*
21 le dispositif de réglage *m* de la table en profondeur *f*
- *rise adjustment of the table*
22 le volant de réglage *m* de la table en hauteur *f*
- *rise adjustment wheel for the table*
23 la vis de réglage *m* de la table en hauteur *f*
- *clamping screw for the table rise adjustment*
24 la console
- *console*
25 le socle (le pied) du bâti de la machine
- *foot of the machine*
26 la machine à joindre (à coller) (l'encolleuse *f*)
- *edge-veneering machine*
27 la meule
- *sanding wheel*
28 le dépoussiéreur (le dispositif d'aspiration *f* de la poussière de meulage *m*)
- *sanding dust extractor*
29 le dispositif de collage *m* des surfaces *f* jointives des assemblages *m*
- *splicing head*
30 la ponceuse à bande *f*
- *single-belt sanding machine (single-belt sander)*
31 le capotage de la bande abrasive
- *belt guard*
32 le carter de la poulie de tension *f* de la bande
- *bandwheel cover*
33 le dépoussiéreur (l'extracteur *m* de poussière *f*)
- *extractor fan (exhaust fan)*
34 le tampon (le patin) de ponçage *m* amovible
- *frame-sanding pad*
35 la table de ponçage *m*
- *sanding table*
36 le dispositif d'ajustage *m* (de réglage *m* de précision *f*)
- *fine adjustment*
37 la machine de précision *f* à scier et à rainer
- *fine cutter and jointer*
38 le chariot (transportant scie *f* circulaire et rabot *m*) à commande *f* par chaîne *f*
- *saw carriage with chain drive*
39 le support de câble *m* à coulisse *f*
- *trailing cable hanger (trailing cable support)*
40 la tubulure d'aspiration *f* des poussières *f*
- *air extractor pipe*
41 la glissière d'amenage *m* (de transport *m*, de manutention *f*)
- *rail*
42 la presse à cadrer (la cadreuse)
- *frame-cramping (frame-clamping) machine*
43 le montant de cadre *m*
- *frame stand*
44 un châssis de fenêtre *f*, la pièce à usiner
- *workpiece, a window frame*
45 la conduite d'arrivée *f* d'air *m* comprimé
- *compressed-air line*
46 le cylindre compresseur (le vérin pneumatique)
- *pressure cylinder*
47 le patin de piston *m*
- *pressure foot*
48 le dispositif de serrage *m* amovible
- *frame-mounting device*
49 la presse de plaquage *m* (à plaquer) rapide
- *rapid-veneer press*
50 le plateau supérieur de la presse (le bâti)
- *bed*
51 la table de pressage *m* (la presse)
- *press*
52 le piston de la presse
- *pressure piston*

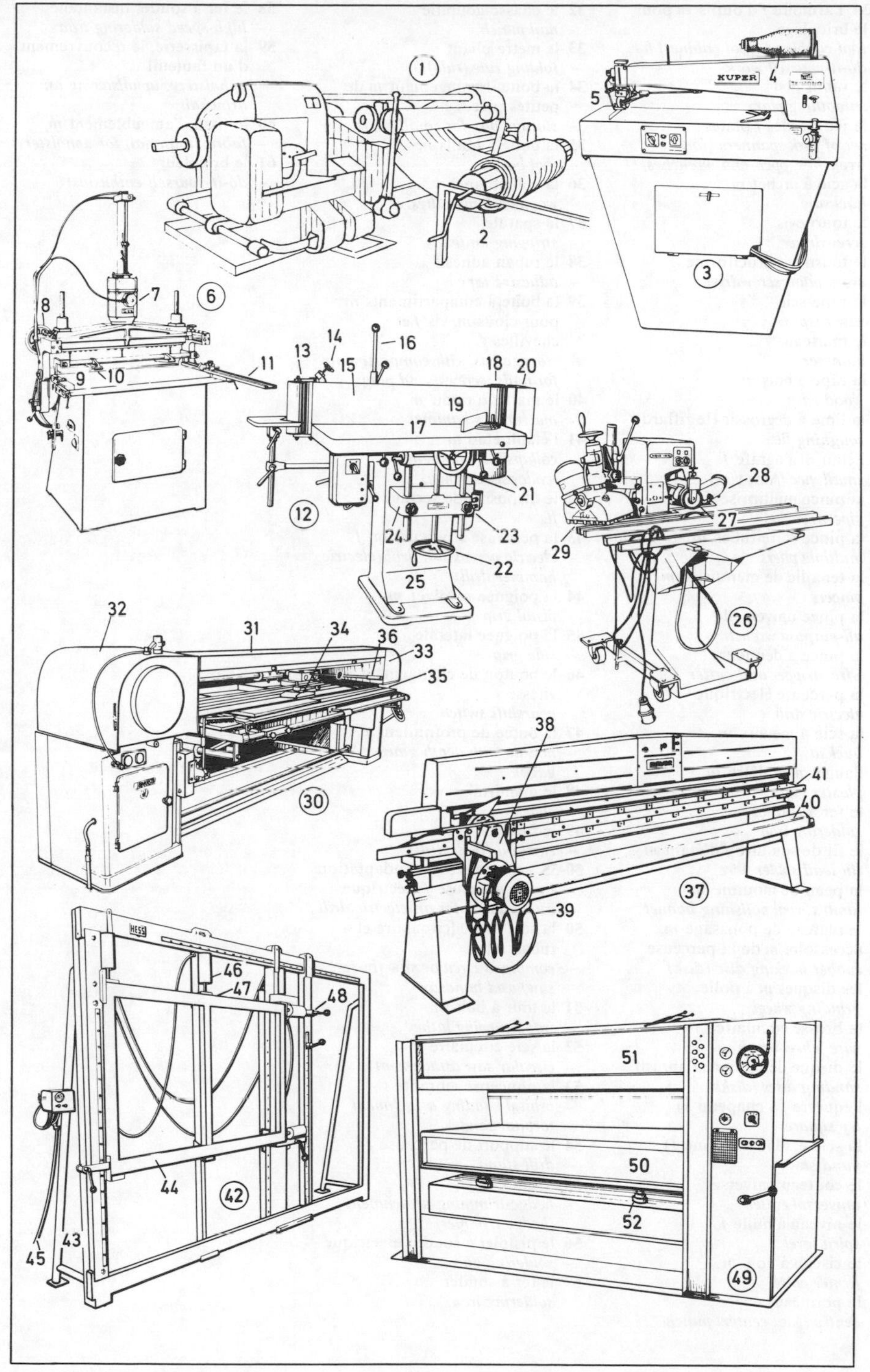
KUPER
HESS
1
2
3
4
5
6
7
8
9
10
11
12
13
14
15
16
17
18
19
20
21
22
23
24
25
26
27
28
29
30
31
32
33
34
35
36
37
38
39
40
41
42
43
44
45
46
47
48
49
50
51
52

1-34 l'armoire *f* d'outils *m* pour le bricolage
– *tool cupboard (tool cabinet) for do-it-yourself work*
1 le rabot plat
– *smoothing plane*
2 le jeu de clés *f* plates
– *set of fork spanners (fork wrenches, open-end wrenches)*
3 la scie à archet *m*
– *hacksaw*
4 le tournevis
– *screwdriver*
5 le tournevis cruciforme
– *cross-point screwdriver*
6 la râpe-scie
– *saw rasp*
7 le marteau
– *hammer*
8 la râpe à bois *m*
– *wood rasp*
9 la lime à dégrossir (le riflard)
– *roughing file*
10 l'étau *m* à agrafe *f*
– *small vice* (Am. *vise)*
11 la pince multiprise *f*
– *pipe wrench*
12 la pince serre-tubes *m*
– *multiple pliers*
13 la tenaille de menuisier *m*
– *pincers*
14 la pince universelle
– *all-purpose wrench*
15 la pince à dénuder
– *wire stripper and cutter*
16 la perceuse électrique
– *electric drill*
17 la scie à métaux *m*
– *hacksaw*
18 l'auget *m* à plâtre *m*
– *plaster cup*
19 le fer à souder
– *soldering iron*
20 le fil de soudure *f* d'étain *m*
– *tin-lead solder wire*
21 la peau de mouton *m*
– *lamb's wool polishing bonnet*
22 le plateau de polissage *m*, accessoire *m* de la perceuse
– *rubber backing disc (disk)*
23 les disques *m* à polir
– *grinding wheel*
24 la brosse circulaire
– *wire wheel brush*
25 le disque de papier *m* abrasif
– *sanding discs (disks)*
26 l'équerre *f* à chapeau *m*
– *try square*
27 la scie égoïne (l'égoïne *f*)
– *hand saw*
28 le couteau universel
– *universal cutter*
29 le niveau à bulle *f*
– *spirit level*
30 le ciseau à bois *m*
– *firmer chisel*
31 le pointeau
– *centre* (Am. *center) punch*
32 le chasse-goupille
– *nail punch*
33 le mètre pliant
– *folding rule (rule)*
34 la boîte de rangement *m* de petites pièces *f*
– *storage box for small parts*
35 la boîte à outils *m*
– *tool box*
36 la colle blanche
– *woodworking adhesive*
37 la spatule
– *stripping knife*
38 le ruban adhésif
– *adhesive tape*
39 la boîte à compartiments *m* pour clous *m*, vis *f* et chevilles *f*
– *storage box with compartments for nails, screws, and plugs*
40 le marteau rivoir *m*
– *machinist's hammer*
41 l'établi étau *m*
– *collapsible workbench (collapsible bench)*
42 le dispositif de serrage *m*
– *jig*
43 la perceuse à percussion *f*
– *electric percussion drill (electric hammer drill)*
44 la poignée revolver *m*
– *pistol grip*
45 la poignée latérale
– *side grip*
46 le bouton de changement *m* de vitesse *f*
– *gearshift switch*
47 la butée de profondeur *f*
– *handle with depth gauge* (Am. *gage)*
48 le mandrin
– *chuck*
49 le foret
– *twist bit (twist drill)*
50-55 accessoires *m* et adaptations *f* pour perceuse *f* électrique
– *attachments for an electric drill*
50 la scie mixte [circulaire et à ruban *m*]
– *combined circular saw (buzz saw) and bandsaw*
51 le tour à bois *m*
– *wood-turning lathe*
52 la scie circulaire
– *circular saw attachment*
53 la ponceuse vibrante
– *orbital sanding attachment (orbital sander)*
54 le support de perceuse *f*
– *drill stand*
55 le taille-haies
– *hedge-trimming attachment (hedge trimmer)*
56 le pistolet à souder électrique
– *soldering gun*
57 le fer à souder
– *soldering iron*
58 le fer à souder instantané
– *high-speed soldering iron*
59 la tapisserie, le recouvrement d'un fauteuil
– *upholstery, upholstering an armchair*
60 le tissu d'ameublement *m*
– *fabric (material) for upholstery*
61 le bricoleur
– *do-it-yourself enthusiast*

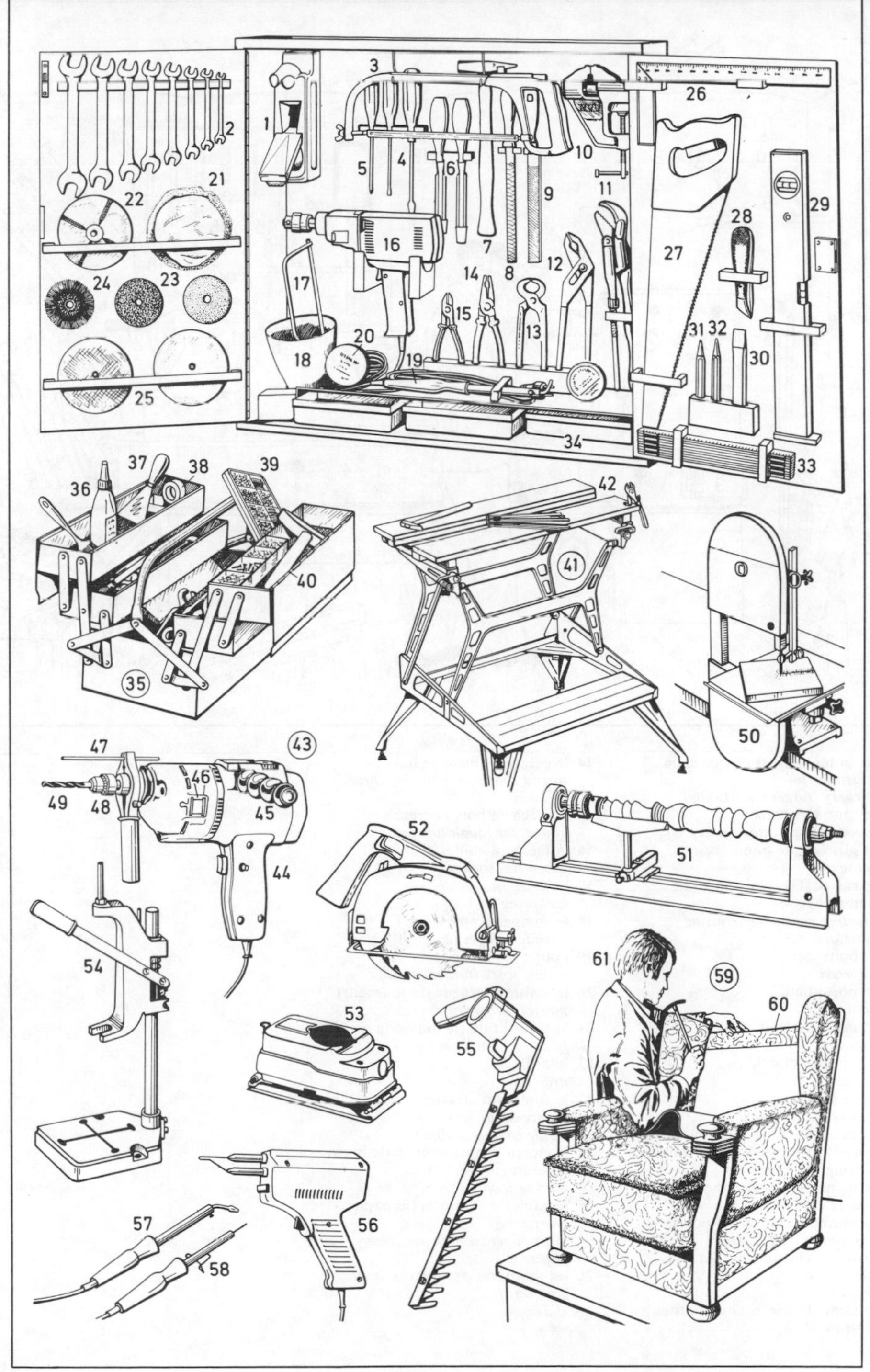
1
2
3
4
5
6
7
8
9
10
11
12
13
14
15
16
17
18
19
20
21
22
23
24
25
26
27
28
29
30
31
32
33
34
35
36
37
38
39
40
41
42
43
44
45
46
47
48
49
50
51
52
53
54
55
56
57
58
59
60
61

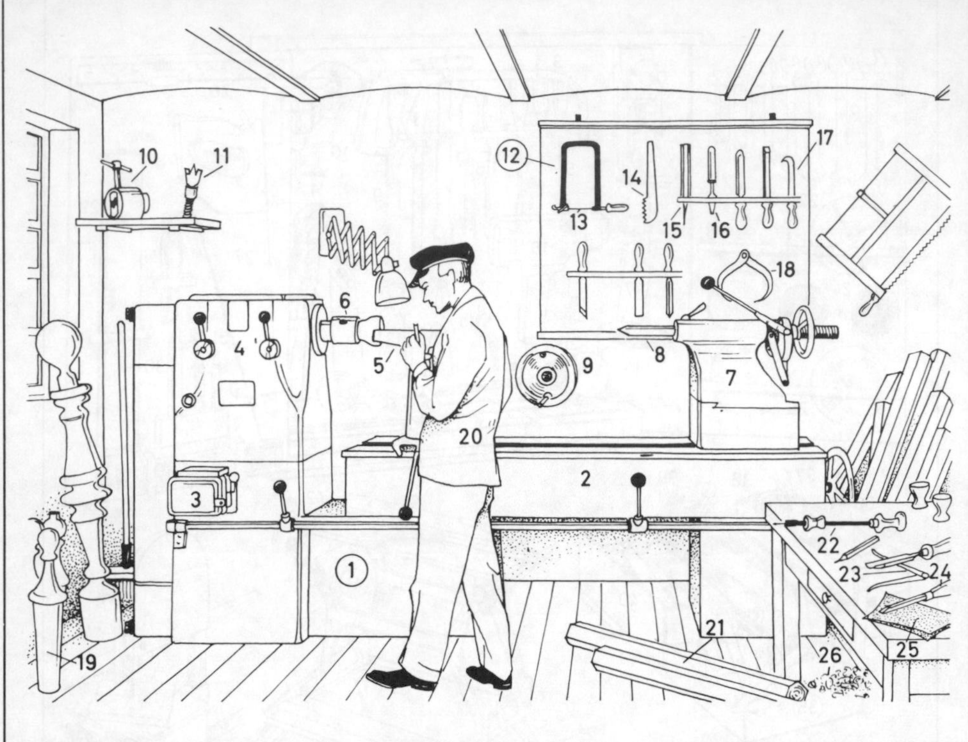

1-26 la tournerie (l'atelier *m* de tourneur *m*)
– ***turnery** (turner's workshop)*

1 le tour à dégauchir
– *wood-turning lathe (lathe)*

2 la glissière du banc
– *lathe bed*

3 le rhéostat (la résistance) de démarrage *m*
– *starting resistance (starting resistor)*

4 la boîte de vitesses *f*
– *gearbox*

5 le porte-outil
– *tool rest*

6 le mandrin creux
– *chuck*

7 la poupée mobile
– *tailstock*

8 la pointe vive
– *centre (*Am. *center)*

9 la poulie à corde *f*, une poulie à gorge *f* et toc *m* d'entraînement *m*
– *driving plate with pin*

10 le mandrin à deux mors *m*
– *two-jaw chuck*

11 la mèche à bois *m* à 3 pointes *f*
– *live centre (*Am. *center)*

12 la scie à chantourner (la scie à découper)
– *fretsaw*

13 la lame de scie *f*à chantourner
– *fretsaw blade*

14 le peigne à fileter le bois
– *thread chaser, for cutting threads in wood*

15 la mèche à bois *m* creuse
– *gouge, for rough turning*

16 la mèche à cuiller *f*
– *spoon bit (shell bit)*

17 l'alésoir *m*
– *hollowing tool*

18 le compas d'épaisseur *f*
– *outside calliper (caliper)*

19 l'objet *m* tourné
– *turned work (turned wood)*

20 le maître-tourneur (le tourneur)
– *master turner (turner)*

21 la pièce brute (le bois non usiné)
– *[piece of] rough wood*

22 la drille
– *drill*

23 le compas d'alésage *m* (le maître-à-danser)
– *inside calliper (caliper)*

24 le ciseau de tourneur *m* (le burin de tourneur *m*)
– *parting tool*

25 le papier de verre *m* (le papier émeri)
– *glass paper (sandpaper, emery paper)*

26 les tournures *f* (copeaux *m* de bois *m*)
– *shavings*

1-40 la vannerie
– ***basket making*** *(basketry, basketwork)*
1-4 points *m* **de tressage** *m* (modes *m* d'entrelacement *m*)
– ***weaves*** *(strokes)*
1 le tressage en torsade *f* (en fleur *f* de lys *m*)
– *randing*
2 le tressage à brin *m* perdu (devant 2 derrière 1)
– *rib randing*
3 le tressage en crocane *f* simple
– *oblique randing*
4 l'ouvrage *m* tressé (l'ouvrage *m* de vannerie *f*)
– *randing, a piece of wickerwork (screen work)*
5 le brin de clôture *f*
– *weaver*
6 le montant
– *stake*
7 la planche de travail *m*
– *workboard;* also: *lapboard*
8 la traverse
– *screw block*
9 le trou de fixation *f* de la traverse
– *hole for holding the block*
10 le chevalet
– *stand*
11 le panier en copeaux *m*
– *chip basket (spale basket)*
12 le copeau (l'éclat *m* de bois *m*)
– *chip (spale)*
13 le bac de trempage *m*
– *soaking tub*
14 les verges *f* d'osier *m* (les brins *m*, la botte)
– *willow stakes (osier stakes)*
15 les baguettes *f* d'osier *m*
– *willow rods (osier rods)*
16 la corbeille, un ouvrage de vannerie *f*
– *basket, a piece of wickerwork (basketwork)*
17 la bordure
– *border*
18 la clôture
– *woven side*
19 la base (le fond) en forme *f* d'étoile *f*
– *round base*
20 la clôture de fond *m*
– *woven base*
21 la croisée de fond *m* (les bâtons *m* de croisée *f* ligaturés)
– *slath*
22-24 le travail sur monture *f* (sur bâti *m*)
– ***covering a frame***
22 la monture (le bâti)
– *frame*
23 l'éclisse *f* (le brin dépassant du pied de la monture)
– *end*
24 la canne (la baguette garnissant le fond d'un fauteuil)
– *rib*
25 la charpente (les montants *m*)
– *upsett*
26 les graminées *f*; *var.:* sparte *m*, alfa *m*
– *grass;* kinds: *esparto grass, alfalfa grass*
27 le roseau
– *rush (bulrush, reed mace)*
28 le jonc (la lanière de jonc *m*)
– *reed*
29 le raphia
– *raffia (bast)*
30 la paille
– *straw*
31 le bambou
– *bamboo cane*
32 le rotin ou rotang
– *rattan (ratan) chair cane*
33 le vannier
– *basket maker*
34 le fer à cintrer
– *bending tool*
35 le fendoir
– *cutting point (bodkin)*
36 la batte
– *rapping iron*
37 les tenailles *f*
– *pincers*
38 l'épluchoir *m*
– *picking knife*
39 le rabot
– *shave*
40 la scie à archet *m dite* «violon» *m*
– *hacksaw*

1-8 la forge et le feu de forge *f*
– ***hearth (forge) with blacksmith's fire***
1 la forge
– *hearth (forge)*
2 la pelle à feu *m*
– *shovel (slice)*
3 l'arrosoir *m*
– *swab*
4 l'attisoir *m* (le tisonnier)
– *rake*
5 le ringard
– *poker*
6 l'arrivée *f* d'air *m*
– *blast pipe (tue iron)*
7 la hotte
– *chimney (cowl, hood)*
8 le bac de trempe *f*
– *water trough (quenching trough, bosh)*
9 le marteau-pilon pneumatique
– *power hammer*
10 la masse tombante
– *ram (tup)*
11-16 l'enclume *f*
– ***anvil***
11 l'enclume *f*
– *anvil*
12 la bigorne conique
– *flat beak (beck, bick)*
13 la bigorne pyramidale
– *round beak (beck, bick)*
14 la table auxiliaire
– *auxiliary table*
15 le patin
– *foot*
16 le refouloir
– *upsetting block*
17 l'affûteuse *f*
– *swage block*
18 l'affûteuse *f*
– *tool-grinding machine (tool grinder)*
19 la meule d'affûtage *m*
– *grinding wheel*
20 la moufle
– *block and tackle*
21 l'établi *m*
– *workbench (bench)*
22-39 outils *m* **de forgeron** *m*
– ***blacksmith's tools***
22 le marteau à frapper devant
– *sledge hammer*
23 le marteau à main *f* (le marteau de forgeron *m*)
– *blacksmith's hand hammer*
24 les tenailles *f* droites
– *flat tongs*
25 les tenailles *f* à coquilles *f* rondes
– *round tongs*
26 les parties *f* du marteau
– *parts of the hammer*
27 la panne
– *peen (pane, pein)*
28 la table
– *face*
29 l'œil *m*
– *eye*
30 le manche
– *haft*
31 l'angrois *m*
– *cotter punch*
32 le tranchet (le tranchet d'enclume *f*)
– *hardy (hardie)*
33 la masse à pans *m*
– *set hammer*
34 la tranche à chaud *m*
– *sett (set, sate)*
35 le marteau à planer
– *flat-face hammer (flatter)*
36 le marteau à poinçon *m*
– *round punch*
37 les tenailles *f* angulaires
– *angle tongs*
38 la tranche à froid *m*
– *blacksmith's chisel (scaling hammer, chipping hammer)*
39 le fer à cintrer
– *moving iron (bending iron)*

Forgeron II (machinisme agricole) 138
Blacksmith (Smith) II (Farm vehicle Engineering)

1 l'installation *f* à air *m* comprimé
– *compressed-air system*
2 le moteur électrique
– *electric motor*
3 le compresseur
– *compressor*
4 le réservoir d'air *m* comprimé
– *compressed-air tank*
5 la canalisation d'air *m* comprimé
– *compressed-air line*
6 le tournevis à frapper pneumatique (le tournevis à percussion *f* pneumatique)
– *percussion screwdriver*
7 le touret (l'affûteuse *f* d'atelier *m*)
– *pedestal grinding machine (floor grinding machine)*
8 la meule
– *grinding wheel*
9 le carter de protection *f*
– *guard*
10 la remorque
– *trailer*
11 le tambour de frein *m*
– *brake drum*
12 la mâchoire de frein *m*
– *brake shoe*
13 la garniture de frein *m*
– *brake lining*
14 la valise de contrôle *m*
– *testing kit*
15 le manomètre
– *pressure gauge* (Am. *gage)*
16 le banc d'essai *m* des freins *m*, un banc d'essai *m* de frein *m* à rouleaux *m*
– *brake-testing equipment, a rolling road*
17 la fosse
– *pit*
18 le rouleau de freinage *m*
– *braking roller*
19 l'enregistreur *m*
– *meter (recording meter)*
20 le tour de précision *f* pour freins *m* de tambour *m*
– *precision lathe for brake drums*
21 la roue de camion *m*
– *lorry wheel*
22 la perceuse (verticale à colonne *f*)
– *boring mill*
23 la scie rapide, une scie alternative
– *power saw, a hacksaw (power hacksaw)*
24 l'étau *m*
– *vice* (Am. *vise)*
25 le bâti de scie *f*
– *saw frame*
26 la canalisation de réfrigérant *m*
– *coolant supply pipe*
27 la riveteuse (la riveuse)
– *riveting machine*
28 le châssis de remorque *f* en construction *f*
– *trailer frame (chassis) under construction*
29 le poste de soudage *m* en atmosphère *f* inerte
– *inert-gas welding equipment*
30 le redresseur
– *rectifier*
31 l'appareil *m* de commande *f* (le contrôleur)
– *control unit*
32 la bouteille de CO_2 *m*
– *CO_2 cylinder*
33 l'enclume *f*
– *anvil*
34 la forge avec le feu de forge *f*
– *hearth (forge) with blacksmith's fire*
35 le chariot de soudage *m* autogène
– *trolley for gas cylinders*
36 le véhicule en réparation *f*, un tracteur
– *vehicle under repair, a tractor*

139 Forgeage libre et estampage

1 le four poussant continu à sole *f* à grille *f* pour le réchauffage de ronds *m*
– *continuous furnace with grid hearth for annealing of round stock*
2 la porte de déchargement *m*
– *discharge opening (discharge door)*
3 les brûleurs à gaz *m*
– *gas burners*
4 la porte de chargement *m*
– *charging door*
5 le marteau-pilon à contre-frappe *f*
– *counterblow hammer*
6 la masse supérieure
– *upper ram*
7 la masse inférieure
– *lower ram*
8 le guidage de la masse mobile
– *ram guide*
9 l'entraînement *m* électrique
– *hydraulic drive*
10 les jambages *m*, les montants *m*
– *column*
11 le pilon d'estampage *m* à faible course *f*
– *short-stroke drop hammer*
12 la masse de pilon *m*, le marteau de pilon *m*
– *ram (tup)*
13 la matrice supérieure
– *upper die block*
14 la matrice inférieure
– *lower die block*
15 l'entraînement *m* hydraulique
– *hydraulic drive*
16 le bâti de pilon *m*
– *frame*
17 la chabotte (l'enclume *f*)
– *anvil*
18 la presse d'estampage *m* et de calibrage *m*
– *forging and sizing press*
19 le montant de presse *f*
– *standard*
20 la table de presse *f*
– *table*
21 l'embrayage *m* à disques *m*
– *disc (disk) clutch*
22 la canalisation d'air *m* comprimé
– *compressed-air pipe*
23 l'électrovalve *f*
– *solenoid valve*
24 le marteau-pilon autocompresseur
– *air-lift gravity hammer (air-lift drop hammer)*
25 le moteur d'entraînement *m*
– *drive motor*
26 la masse de pilon *m*
– *hammer (tup)*
27 la pédale de commande *f*
– *foot control (foot pedal)*
28 la pièce forgée (ébauchée) au marteau-pilon
– *preshaped (blocked) workpiece*
29 la tête de guidage *m* de la masse
– *hammer guide*
30 le cylindre de marteau *m*
– *hammer cylinder*
31 la chabotte
– *anvil*
32 le manipulateur pour déplacer la pièce forgée en frappe *f* libre
– *mechanical manipulator to move the workpiece in hammer forging*
33 les tenailles
– *dogs*
34 le contrepoids
– *counterweight*
35 la presse à forger hydraulique
– *hydraulic forging press*
36 l'ensemble *m* hydraulique coiffant la presse
– *crown*
37 la traverse principale
– *cross head*
38 la matrice supérieure
– *upper die block*
39 la matrice inférieure
– *lower die block*
40 la chabotte
– *anvil*
41 le piston hydraulique
– *hydraulic piston*
42 les colonnes *f* de guidage *m*
– *pillar guide*
43 le retourneur
– *rollover device*
44 la chaîne de palan *m*
– *burden chain (chain sling)*
45 le crochet de palan *m*
– *crane hook*
46 la pièce forgée
– *workpiece*
47 le four de forge *f* à gaz *m*
– *gas furnace (gas-fired furnace)*
48 le brûleur à gaz *m*
– *gas burner*
49 l'ouverture *f* de chargement *m*
– *charging opening*
50 le rideau de chaînes *f*
– *chain curtain*
51 la porte levante
– *vertical-lift door*
52 la conduite d'air *m* chaud
– *hot-air duct*
53 le réchauffeur d'air *m*
– *air preheater*
54 l'alimentation *f* en gaz *m*
– *gas pipe*
55 le dispositif de levage *m* de la porte
– *electric door-lifting mechanism*
56 le rideau d'air *m*
– *air blast*

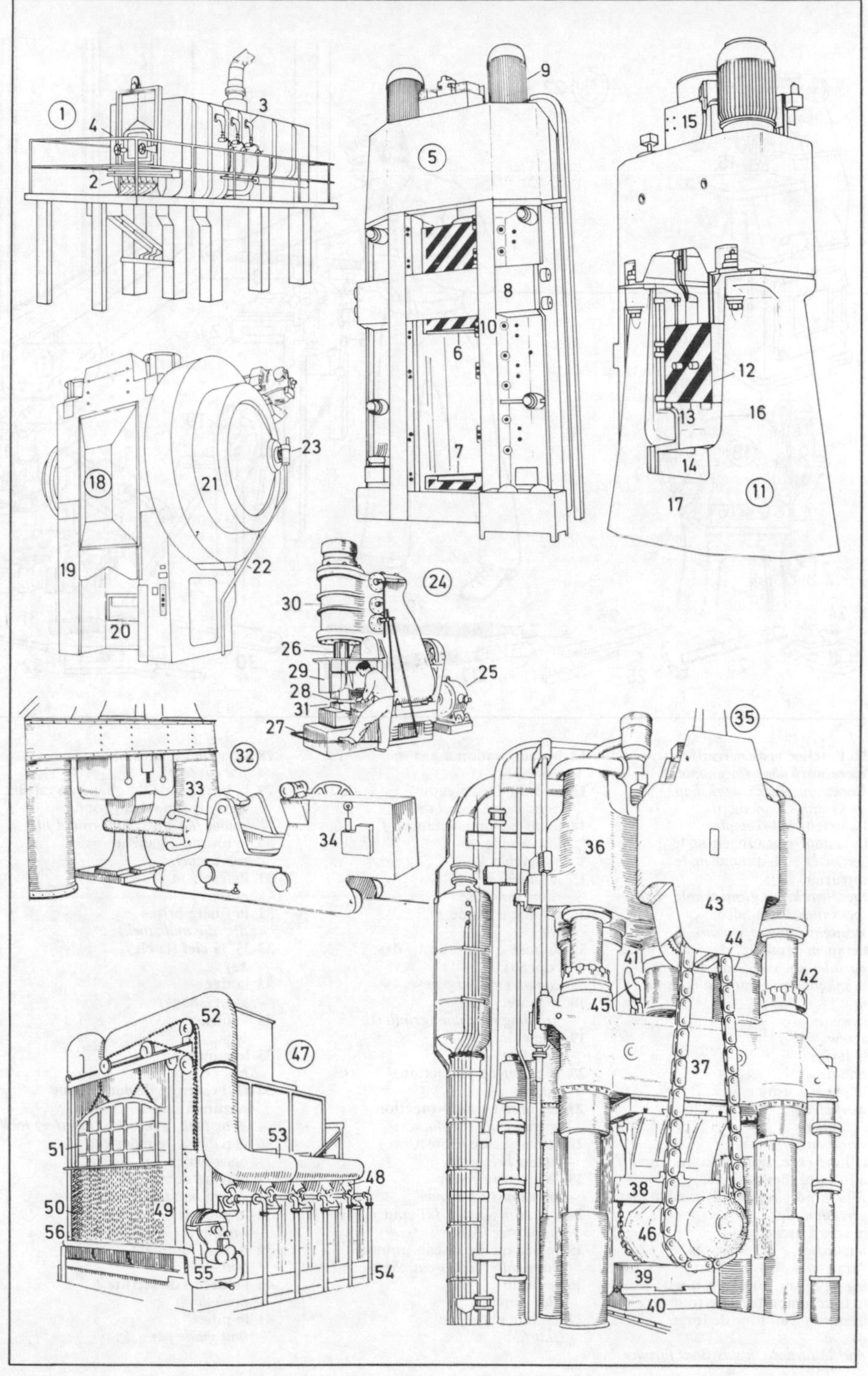

1
2
3
4
5
6
7
8
9
10
11
12
13
14
15
16
17
18
19
20
21
22
23
24
25
26
27
28
29
30
31
32
33
34
35
36
37
38
39
40
41
42
43
44
45
46
47
48
49
50
51
52
53
54
55
56

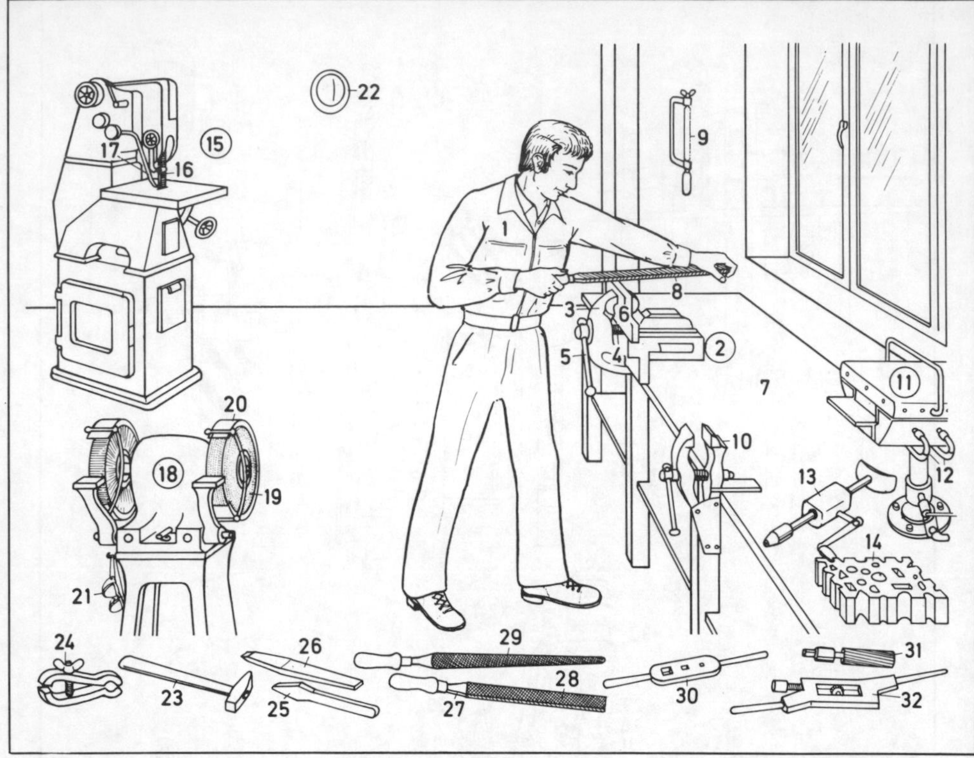

1-22 l'atelier *m* du serrurier
– ***metalwork shop*** *(mechanic's workshop, fitter's workshop, locksmith's workshop)*
1 l'ajusteur *m* (*exemples:* l'ajusteur-mécanicien *m*, le serrurier en bâtiment *m*, le serrurier)
– *metalworker (*e.g. *mechanic, fitter, locksmith;* form. also: *wrought-iron craftsman)*
2 l'étau *m* parallèle
– *parallel-jaw vice (*Am. *vise)*
3 la mâchoire (le mors d'étau *m*)
– *jaw*
4 la vis
– *screw*
5 le levier
– *handle*
6 la pièce à usiner
– *workpiece*
7 l'établi *m*
– *workbench (bench)*
8 la lime (*var.:* lime *f* bâtarde, lime *f* mi-douce, lime *f* douce)
– *files (*kinds: *rough file, smooth file, precision file)*
9 la scie à archet *m*
– *hacksaw*
10 l'étau *m* à pied *m*
– *leg vice (*Am. *vise), a spring vice*
11 le four à moufle *m* (le four de trempe *f*), un four de forge *f* à gaz *m*
– *muffle furnace, a gas-fired furnace*
12 la canalisation à gaz *m*
– *gas pipe*
13 la drille (la chignole)
– *hand brace (hand drill)*
14 le tas-étampe, l'étampe *f* universelle
– *swage block*
15 la limeuse
– *filing machine*
16 la lime à bande *f*
– *file*
17 la buse d'aspiration *f* des copeaux *m*
– *compressed-air pipe*
18 le touret
– *grinding machine (grinder)*
19 la meule
– *grinding wheel*
20 le carter de protection *f*
– *guard*
21 les lunettes de protection *f*
– *goggles (safety glasses)*
22 le casque de protection *f*
– *safety helmet*
23 le marteau-rivoir
– *machinist's hammer*
24 l'étau *m* à main *f* (l'étau *m* à vis *f*)
– *hand vice (*Am. *vise)*
25 le bédane (le ciseau pointu)
– *cape chisel (cross-cut chisel)*
26 le burin
– *flat chisel*
27 la lime plate
– *flat file*
28 la taille de lime *f*
– *file cut (cut)*
29 la lime ronde, la queue de rat *m*; *égal.:* la lime demi-ronde
– *round file (*also: *half-round file)*
30 le tourne-à-gauche
– *tap wrench*
31 l'alésoir *m*
– *reamer*
32 la filière brisée
– *die (die and stock)*
33-35 la clef (la clé)
– ***key***
33 la tige
– *stem (shank)*
34 l'anneau *m*
– *bow*
35 le panneton
– *bit*
36-43 la serrure de porte *f*, une serrure à larder
– ***door lock, a mortise (mortice) lock***
36 le palâtre (le palastre)
– *back plate*
37 le pêne demi-tour *m*
– *spring bolt (latch bolt)*
38 la gâchette
– *tumbler*
39 le pêne dormant
– *bolt*
40 l'entrée *f* de serrure *f*
– *keyhole*
41 le pilier
– *bolt guide pin*

42 le ressort de gâchette *f*
– *tumbler spring*
43 le fouillot
– *follower, with square hole*
44 la serrure cylindrique (serrure *f* de sûreté *f*)
– *cylinder lock (safety lock)*
45 le cylindre
– *cylinder (plug)*
46 le ressort
– *spring*
47 la goupille
– *pin*
48 la clé de sûreté *f*, une clé plate
– *safety key, a flat key*
49 la paumelle double
– *lift-off hinge*
50 la paumelle à équerre *f*
– *hook-and-ride band*
51 la penture droite
– *strap hinge*
52 le pied à coulisse *f*
– *vernier calliper (caliper) gauge (*Am. *gage)*
53 le calibre à lames *f*, la jauge d'épaisseur *f*
– *feeler gauge (*Am. *gage)*
54 le calibre de profondeur *f*, le pied de profondeur *f*
– *vernier depth gauge (*Am. *gage)*
55 le vernier
– *vernier*
56 la règle de vérification *f*
– *straightedge*
57 l'équerre *f* de précision *f*
– *square*
58 le vilebrequin
– *breast drill*
59 le foret américain, la mèche hélicoïdale
– *twist bit (twist drill)*
60 le taraud
– *screw tap (tap)*
61 les coussinets-peignes *m* de filière *f*
– *halves of a screw die*
62 le tournevis
– *screwdriver*
63 le grattoir; *égal.:* le grattoir triangulaire
– *scraper (*also: *pointed triangle scraper)*
64 le pointeau
– *centre (*Am. *center) punch*
65 le chasse-goupille
– *round punch*
66 la pince plate
– *flat-nose pliers*
67 la pince coupante en bout *m*
– *detachable-jaw cut nippers*
68 la pince à gaz *m*
– *gas pliers*
69 la tenaille de menuisier *m*
– *pincers*

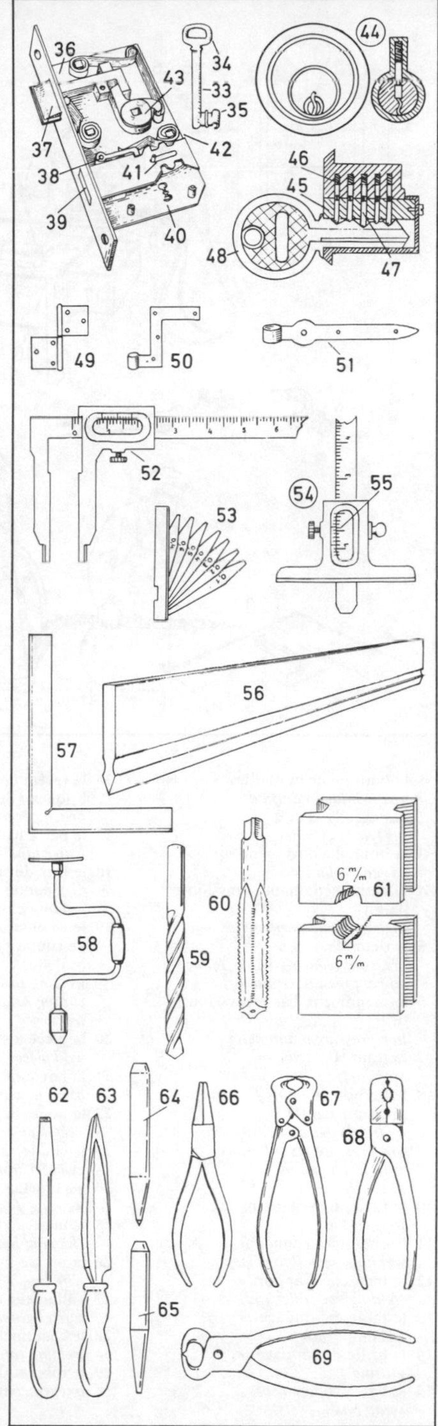

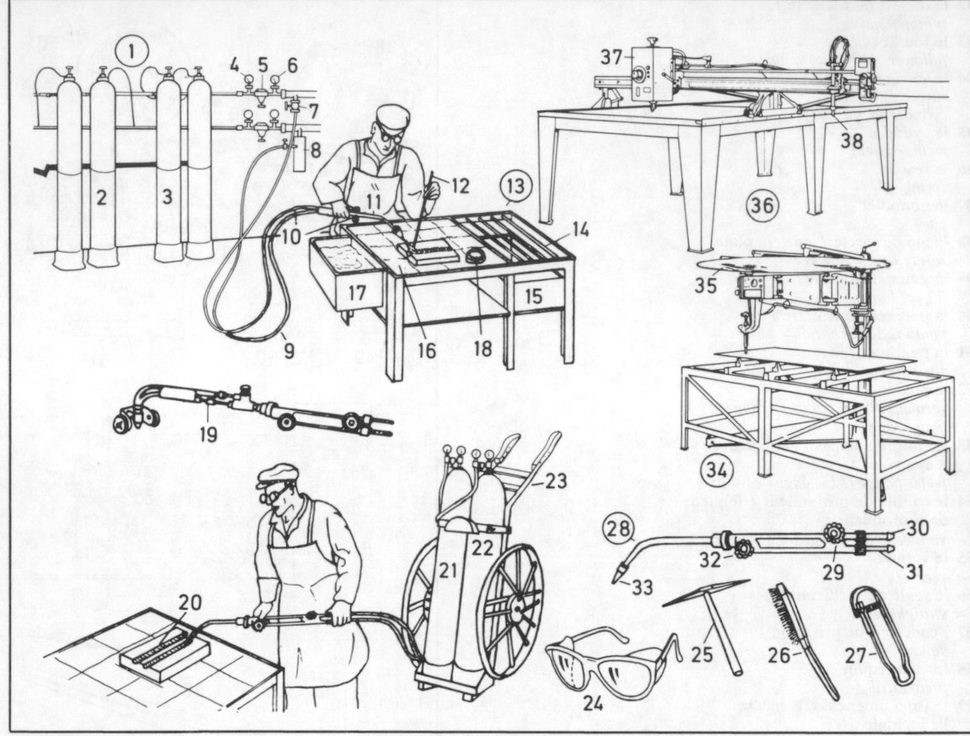

1 la batterie de bouteilles *f*
– *gas cylinder manifold*
2 la bouteille d'acétylène *m*
– *acetylene cylinder*
3 la bouteille d'oxygène *m*
– *oxygen cylinder*
4 le manomètre haute pression *f* [H.P.]
– *high-pressure manometer*
5 le détendeur
– *pressure-reducing valve (reducing valve, pressure regulator)*
6 le manomètre basse pression *f* [B.P.]
– *low-pressure manometer*
7 le robinet d'arrêt *m*
– *stopcock*
8 le barboteur à eau *f* basse pression *f* [B.P.]
– *hydraulic back-pressure valve for low-pressure installations*
9 le tuyau à gaz *m*
– *gas hose*
10 le tuyau à oxygène *m*
– *oxygen hose*
11 le chalumeau soudeur
– *welding torch (blowpipe)*
12 la baguette d'apport *m*
– *welding rod (filler rod)*
13 la table de soudage *m*
– *welding bench*
14 la grille de coupage *m*
– *grating*
15 le bac à chutes *f*
– *scrap box*
16 le revêtement de table *f* en briques *f* de chamotte *f*
– *bench covering of chamotte slabs*
17 le bac à eau *f*
– *water tank*
18 le flux de soudage *m* (la pâte décapante)
– *welding paste (flux)*
19 le chalumeau équipé d'une buse de coupe *f* et d'un guide à roulettes *f*
– *welding torch (blowpipe) with cutting attachment and guide tractor*
20 la pièce à souder
– *workpiece*
21 la bouteille d'oxygène *m*
– *oxygen cylinder*
22 la bouteille d'acétylène *m*
– *acetylene cylinder*
23 le chariot à bouteilles *f*
– *cylinder trolley*
24 les lunettes *f* de soudeur *m*
– *welding goggles*
25 le marteau à piquer
– *chipping hammer*
26 la brosse métallique
– *wire brush*
27 l'allumeur *m* de chalumeau *m*
– *torch lighter (blowpipe lighter)*
28 le chalumeau soudeur
– *welding torch (blowpipe)*
29 le robinet d'oxygène *m*
– *oxygen control*
30 le raccord d'oxygène *m*
– *oxygen connection*
31 le raccord de gaz *m* combustible
– *gas connection (acetylene connection)*
32 le robinet de gaz *m* combustible
– *gas control (acetylene control)*
33 la buse de chalumeau *m* soudeur
– *welding nozzle*
34 la machine d'oxycoupage *m*
– *cutting machine*
35 le gabarit circulaire
– *circular template*
36 la machine d'oxycoupage *m* universelle
– *universal cutting machine*
37 la tête de commande *f*
– *tracing head*
38 la buse de chalumeau *m* coupeur
– *cutting nozzle*

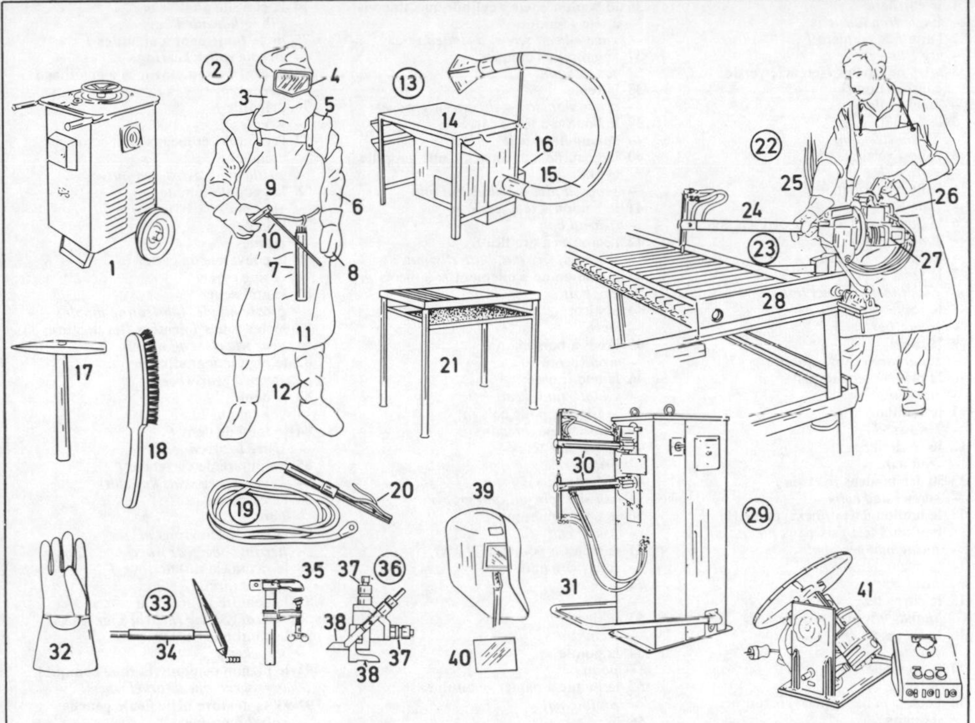

1 le transformateur de soudage *m*
– *welding transformer*
2 le soudeur à l'arc *m*
– *arc welder*
3 la coiffe de soudeur *m*
– *arc welding helmet*
4 le verre protecteur relevable
– *flip-up window*
5 l'épaulière *f* (le coltin)
– *shoulder guard*
6 le brassard de protection *f*
– *protective sleeve*
7 l'étui *m* à électrodes *f*
– *electrode case*
8 la moufle de soudeur *m* à trois doigts *m*
– *three-fingered welding glove*
9 le porte-électrode
– *electrode holder*
10 l'électrode *f*
– *electrode*
11 le tablier de cuir *m*
– *leather apron*
12 la guêtre de protection *f*
– *shin guard*
13 la table de soudage *m* à aspiration *f*
– *welding table with fume extraction equipment*
14 le plateau de table *f* à aspiration *f*
– *table top*
15 le tuyau d'aspiration *f* pivotant
– *movable extractor duct*
16 la tubulure d'évacuation *f* d'air *m*
– *extractor support*
17 le marteau à piquer
– *chipping hammer*
18 la brosse métallique
– *wire brush*
19 le câble de soudage *m*
– *welding lead*
20 le porte-électrode
– *electrode holder*
21 la table de soudage *m*
– *welding bench*
22 le soudage par points *m*
– *spot welding*
23 la pince à souder
– *spot welding electrode holder*
24 le bras porte-électrode *m*
– *electrode arm*
25 l'amenée *f* de courant *m* (le câble d'alimentation *f*)
– *power supply (lead)*
26 le vérin de pression *f* d'électrode *f*
– *electrode-pressure cylinder*
27 le transformateur de soudage *m*
– *welding transformer*
28 la pièce à souder
– *workpiece*
29 la machine à souder par points *m* commandée par pédale *f*
– *foot-operated spot welder*
30 les branches *f* de soudage *m*
– *welder electrode arms*
31 la pédale commandant la pression d'électrode *f*
– *foot pedal for welding pressure adjustment*
32 le gant de soudeur *m* à cinq doigts *m*
– *five-fingered welding glove*
33 le chalumeau de soudage *m* à l'arc *m* en atmosphère *f* protégée (le chalumeau à gaz *m* inerte)
– *inert-gas torch for inert-gas welding (gas-shielded arc welding)*
34 l'alimentation *f* en gaz *m* inerte
– *inert-gas (shielding-gas) supply*
35 la pince de mise *f* à la terre (la pince de masse *f*)
– *work clamp (earthing clamp)*
36 le calibre de joint *m* d'angle *m*
– *fillet gauge (Am. gage) (weld gauge) [for measuring throat thickness]*
37 la vis micrométrique
– *micrometer*
38 la branche de mesure *f*
– *measuring arm*
39 la marque de soudeur *m*
– *arc welding helmet*
40 le verre de coiffe *f*
– *filter lens*
41 la petite table tournante
– *small turntable*

143 Profilés, boulons, vis et éléments de machine

1 la cornière
– *angle iron (angle)*
2 l'aile *f* de cornière *f*
– *leg (flange)*
3-7 les poutrelles *f* [en acier *m* de construction *f*]
– ***steel girders***
3 le fer à T
– *T-iron (tee-iron)*
4 l'aile *f* verticale
– *vertical leg*
5 l'aile *f* horizontale
– *flange*
6 la poutre en I *m* (la poutre en double T *m*)
– *H-girder (H-beam)*
7 le fer à U *m*
– *E-channel (channel iron)*
8 le rond
– *round bar*
9 le carré
– *square iron* (Am. *square stock)*
10 le plat (le produit plat)
– *flat bar*
11 le feuillard
– *strip steel*
12 le fil de fer *m*
– *iron wire*
13-50 les boulons *m* **et vis** *f*
– ***screws and bolts***
13 le boulon à tête *f* hexagonale (le boulon à tête *f* six-pans *m*)
– *hexagonal-head bolt*
14 la tête
– *head*
15 le corps lisse
– *shank*
16 le filetage
– *thread*
17 la rondelle
– *washer*
18 l'écrou *m* hexagonal (l'écrou *m* six-pans *m*)
– *hexagonal nut*
19 la goupille fendue
– *split pin*
20 le bout rond
– *rounded end*
21 le surplat (la largeur sur pans *m*)
– *width of head (of flats)*
22 le goujon (le prisonnier)
– *stud*
23 le bout du goujon
– *point (end)*
24 l'écrou *m* à créneaux *m* (l'écrou *m* crénelé)
– *castle nut (castellated nut)*
25 le trou de goupille *f*
– *hole for the split pin*
26 la vis à tête *f* cruciforme (la vis Phillips), une vis à tôle *f* (une vis taraudeuse, une vis Parker)
– *cross-head screw, a sheet-metal screw (self-tapping screw)*
27 la vis à tête *f* cylindrique à six-pans *m* intérieur (la vis à six-pans *m* creux)
– *hexagonal socket head screw*
28 le boulon à tête *f* fraisée
– *countersunk-head bolt*
29 l'ergot *m* de boulon *m*
– *catch*
30 le contre-écrou
– *locknut (locking nut)*
31 le téton de boulon *m*
– *bolt (pin)*
32 le boulon à embase *f*
– *collar-head bolt*
33 l'embase *f*
– *set collar (integral collar)*
34 la rondelle Grower
– *spring washer (washer)*
35 l'écrou *m* cylindrique à trous *m* percés en croix *f*, un écrou de réglage *m*
– *round nut, an adjusting nut*
36 le boulon à tête *f* cylindrique, une vis à tête *f* fendue
– *cheese-head screw, a slotted screw*
37 la goupille conique
– *tapered pin*
38 la fente
– *screw slot (screw slit, screw groove)*
39 le boulon à tête *f* carrée
– *square-head bolt*
40 la goupille à encoches *f*, une goupille cylindrique
– *grooved pin, a cylindrical pin*
41 le boulon à tête *f* en T *m*
– *T-head bolt*
42 l'écrou *m* à oreilles *f*
– *wing nut (fly nut, butterfly nut)*
43 le goujon de scellement *m* à picots *m*
– *rag bolt*
44 le picot
– *barb*
45 la vis à bois *m*
– *wood screw*
46 la tête fraisée
– *countersunk head*
47 le filetage pour bois *m*
– *wood screw thread*
48 la vis sans tête *f*
– *grub screw*
49 la fente de vis *f*
– *pin slot (pin slit, pin groove)*
50 le bout sphérique
– *round end*
51 le clou (la pointe de Paris)
– *nail (wire nail)*
52 la tête
– *head*
53 la tige
– *shank*
54 la pointe
– *point*
55 la pointe à papier *m* bitumé
– *roofing nail*
56 le rivetage
– *riveting (lap riveting)*
57-60 le rivet
– ***rivet***
57 la tête
– *set head (swage head, die head), a rivet head*
58 la tige
– *rivet shank*
59 la tête fermante
– *closing head*
60 le pas de rivetage *m*
– *pitch of rivets*
61 l'arbre *m*
– *shaft*
62 le chanfrein
– *chamfer (bevel)*
63 le tourillon
– *journal*
64 le collet
– *neck*
65 la portée
– *seat*
66 la rainure de clavetage *m*
– *keyway*
67 l'embase *f* conique
– *conical seat (cone)*
68 le filetage
– *thread*
69 le roulement à billes *f*, un roulement
– *ball bearing, an antifriction bearing*
70 la bille d'acier *m*
– *steel ball (ball)*
71 la bague extérieure
– *outer race*
72 la bague intérieure
– *inner race*
73-74 les clavettes *f*
– ***keys***
73 la clavette ordinaire (la clavette normale, la clavette noyée)
– *sunk key (feather)*
74 la clavette à talon *m*
– *gib (gib-headed key)*
75-76 le roulement à aiguilles *f*
– ***needle roller bearing***
75 la cage de roulement *m* à aiguilles *f*
– *needle cage*
76 l'aiguille *f*
– *needle*
77 l'écrou *m* à créneaux *m* (l'écrou *m* crénelé)
– *castle nut (castellated nut)*
78 la goupille fendue
– *split pin*
79 le carter
– *casing*
80 le couvercle de carter *m*
– *casing cover*
81 le graisseur
– *grease nipple (lubricating nipple)*
82-96 les roues *f* **dentées** (les dentures *f*)
– ***gear wheels, cog wheels***
82 le pignon à gradins *m*
– *stepped gear wheel*
83 la dent
– *cog (tooth)*
84 le fond de dent *f*
– *space between teeth*
85 la rainure de clavetage *f*
– *keyway (key seat, key slot)*
86 l'alésage *m*
– *bore*
87 la roue à chevrons *m*
– *herringbone gear wheel*
88 le rayon (le rai) de roue *f*
– *spokes (arms)*
89 la denture hélicoïdale
– *helical gearing (helical spur wheel)*
90 la couronne dentée
– *sprocket*
91 le pignon conique (la roue conique)
– *bevel gear wheel (bevel wheel)*
92-93 la denture hélicoïdale gauche
– ***spiral toothing***
92 le pignon
– *pinion*
93 la crémaillère circulaire
– *crown wheel*
94 l'engrenage *m* planétaire cylindrique (le train planétaire plan *m*)
– *epicyclic gear (planetary gear)*
95 la denture intérieure
– *internal toothing*
96 la denture extérieure
– *external toothing*
97-107 freins *m* **dynamométriques d'absorption** *f*
– ***absorption dynamometer***
97 le frein à mâchoires *f*
– *shoe brake (check brake, block brake)*
98 le disque de frein *m*
– *brake pulley*
99 l'arbre *m* de frein *m*
– *brake shaft (brake axle)*
100 le sabot de frein *m* (la mâchoire de frein *m*)
– *brake block (brake shoe)*
101 le tirant
– *pull rod*
102 l'électroaimant *m* desserreur de frein *m*
– *brake magnet*
103 le contrepoids de frein *m*
– *brake weight*
104 le frein à bande *f*
– *band brake*
105 la bande de frein *m*
– *brake band*
106 la garniture de frein *m*
– *brake lining*
107 la vis de réglage *m* pour un desserrage régulier
– *adjusting screw, for even application of the brake*

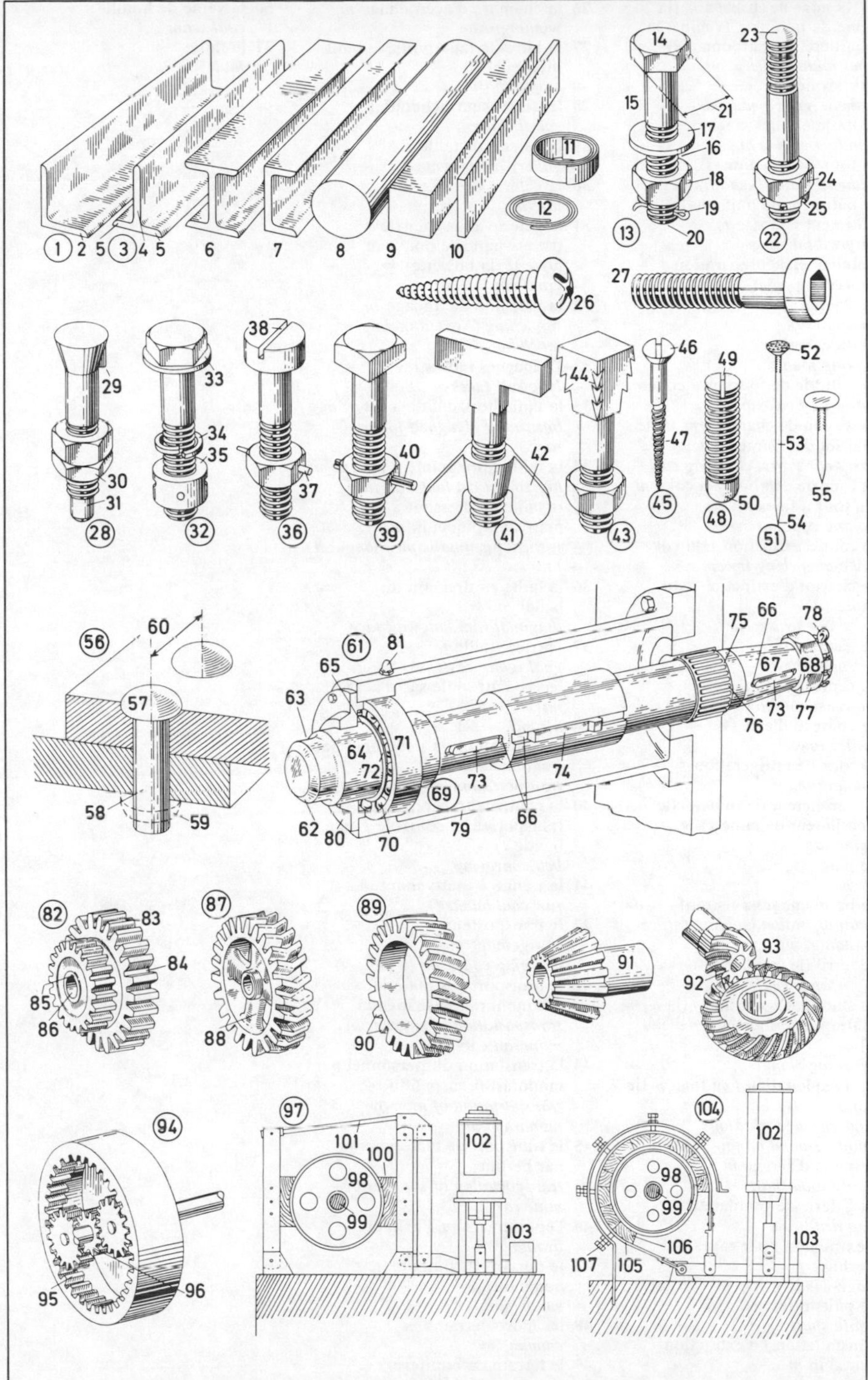
1
2
5
3
4
5
6
7
8
9
10
11
12
13
14
15
16
17
18
19
20
21
22
23
24
25
26
27
28
29
30
31
32
33
34
35
36
37
38
39
40
41
42
43
44
45
46
47
48
49
50
51
52
53
54
55
56
57
58
59
60
61
62
63
64
65
66
67
68
69
70
71
72
73
74
75
76
77
78
79
80
81
82
83
84
85
86
87
88
89
90
91
92
93
94
95
96
97
98
99
100
101
102
103
104
105
106
107

1-51 la mine de charbon *m* (la mine de houille *f*, la mine, la houillère, le charbonnage)
– ***coal mine*** *(colliery, pit)*
1 le chevalement
– *pithead gear (headgear)*
2 le bâtiment des machines *f*
– *winding engine house*
3 la tour d'extraction *f*
– *pithead frame (head frame)*
4 le bâtiment de puits *m* (le bâtiment de fosse *f*)
– *pithead building*
5 l'atelier *m* de préparation *f*
– *processing plant*
6 la scierie
– *sawmill*
7-11 la cokerie
– ***coking plant***
7 la batterie de fours *m* à coke *m*
– *battery of coke ovens*
8 le wagon de chargement *m* (le chariot de chargement *m*)
– *larry car (larry, charging car)*
9 la tour de charbon *m*à coke *m* (la tour à fines *f*)
– *coking coal tower*
10 la tour d'extinction *f* du coke
– *coke-quenching tower*
11 le chariot d'extinction *f* du coke
– *coke-quenching car*
12 le gazomètre
– *gasometer*
13 la centrale électrique
– *power plant (power station)*
14 le château d'eau *f*
– *water tower*
15 la tour de réfrigération *f*
– *cooling tower*
16 le ventilateur de puits *m* (le ventilateur de mine *f*)
– *mine fan*
17 le parc
– *depot*
18 le bâtiment administratif
– *administration building (office building, offices)*
19 le terril (le crassier)
– *tip heap (spoil heap)*
20 la station d'épuration *f* (la station de traitement *m* d'eau *f*)
– *cleaning plant*
21-51 l'exploitation *f* **au fond** *m* (le fond)
– ***underground workings*** *(underground mining)*
21 le puits d'aérage *m*
– *ventilation shaft*
22 la galerie de ventilateur *m*
– *fan drift*
23 l'extraction *f* par cages *f* à berlines *f*
– *cage-winding system with cages*
24 le puits principal
– *main shaft*
25 l'installation *f* d'extraction *f* par skip *m*
– *skip-winding system*
26 la chambre d'accrochage *m*
– *winding inset*
27 la bure (le faux puits, le puits intérieur)
– *staple shaft*
28 le descenseur hélicoïdal
– *spiral chute*
29 la galerie de taille *f*
– *gallery along seam*
30 la galerie en direction *f*
– *lateral*
31 la galerie au rocher (le travers-banc, le bouveau, la bovette, la bowette)
– *cross-cut*
32 la machine de traçage *m*
– *tunnelling (*Am. *tunneling) machine*
33-37 longues tailles *f*
– ***longwall faces***
33 la taille horizontale à rabot *m*
– *horizontal ploughed longwall face*
34 la taille horizontale à havage *m*
– *horizontal cut longwall face*
35 la taille en dressant à marteaux-piqueurs *m*
– *vertical pneumatic pick longwall face*
36 la taille en dressant au bélier *m*
– *diagonal ram longwall face*
37 l'arrière-taille *f*
– *goaf (gob, waste)*
38 le sas à air *m* (le sas d'aérage *m*)
– *air lock*
39 la translation du personnel par wagonnets *m*
– *transportation of men by cars*
40 la courroie transporteuse (le transporteur à courroie *f* ou à bande *f*)
– *belt conveying*
41 la trémie à tout-venant *m*
– *raw coal bunker*
42 le transporteur de chargement *m*
– *charging conveyor*
43 le transport des matériaux *m* par monorail *m* suspendu
– *transportation of supplies by monorail car*
44 la translation du personnel par monorail *m* suspendu
– *transportation of men by monorail car*
45 le transport de matériaux *m* par berlines *f*
– *transportation of supplies by mine car*
46 l'épuisement *m*, l'exhaure *m*
– *drainage*
47 le puisard de puits *m* (le bougnou)
– *sump (sink)*
48 les morts-terrains *m*
– *capping*
49 le terrain carbonifère
– *[layer of] coal-bearing rock*
50 la veine de houille *f*
– *coal seam*
51 la faille
– *fault*

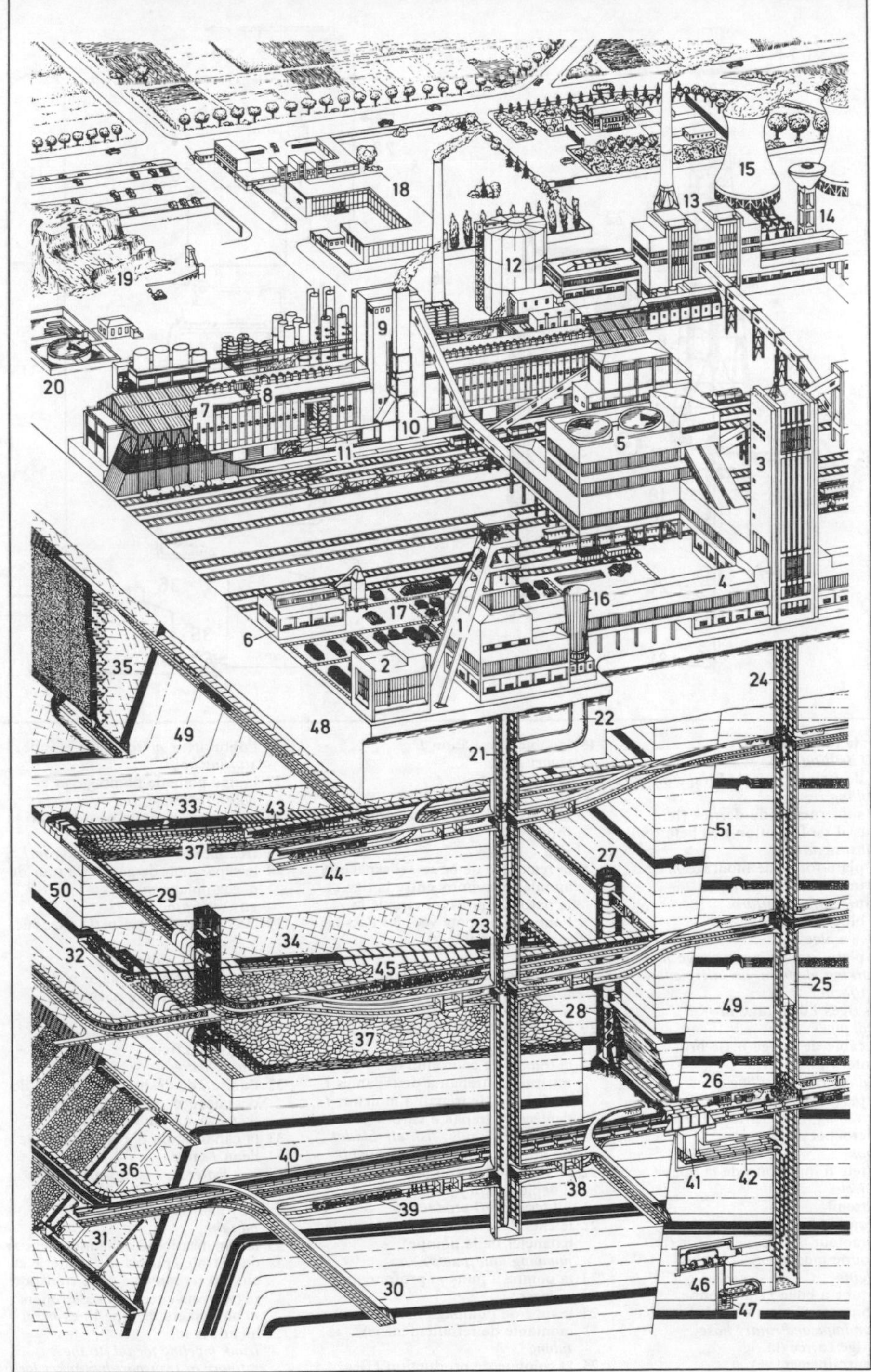
18
15
13
14
12
19
9
20
8
7
10
5
11
3
16
17
4
1
6
2
24
35
49
48
22
21
33
43
51
37
44
27
50
29
23
32
34
45
25
49
28
37
26
40
38
41
42
36
39
31
46
30
47

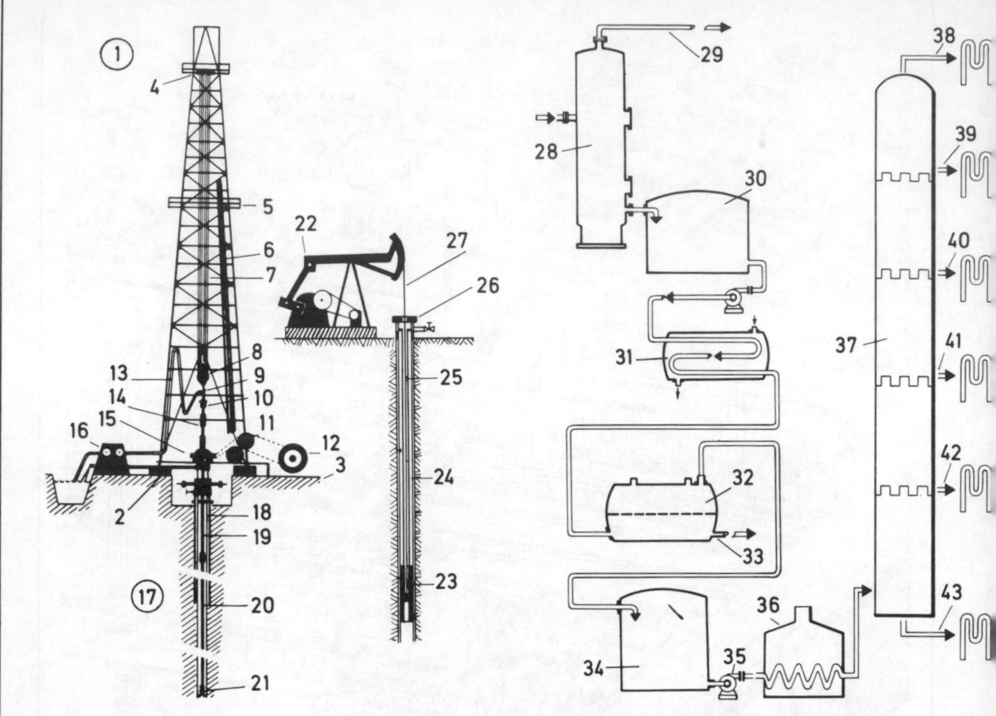

1-21 le forage pétrolier
– ***oil drilling***
1 le derrick (la tour de forage *m*)
– *drilling rig*
2 la substructure du derrick (le massif de fondation *f* en béton *m*)
– *substructure*
3 la plate-forme de montage *m* (le plancher de forage *m*)
– *crown safety platform*
4 le bloc-couronne
– *crown blocks*
5 la plate-forme d'accrochage *m*
– *working platform, an intermediate platform*
6 les tiges *f* de forage *m*
– *drill pipes*
7 le câble de forage *m* (le brin moteur *m*)
– *drilling cable (drilling line)*
8 le palan mobile (les moufles *f*)
– *travelling (*Am. *traveling) block*
9 le crochet de levage *m*
– *hook*
10 la tête d'injection *f* de la boue
– *swivel*
11 le treuil
– *draw works, a hoist*
12 le moteur d'entraînement *m* (le groupe moteur *m*)
– *engine*
13 le tube à boue *f* (la colonne montante d'injection *f* de boue *f*)
– *standpipe and rotary hose*
14 la tige carrée (la tige d'entraînement *m*)
– *kelly*
15 la table de rotation *f*
– *rotary table*
16 la pompe à boue *f*
– *slush pump (mud pump)*
17 le puits de forage *m* (le trou de forage *m*)
– *well*
18 la remontée de boue *f* (l'espace *m* annulaire compris entre la tige et la paroi du puits où circule la boue qui remonte vers les bassins *m* de décantation *f*)
– *casing*
19 le train de tiges *f* (les tiges *f* de forage *m*)
– *drilling pipe*
20 le tubage (le cuvelage)
– *tubing*
21 le trépan (la couronne de forage *m*); *var.:* le trépan à deux lames *f* ou fish tail, le trépan à molettes *f* dentées, le trépan à carotte *f*
– *drilling bit;* kinds: *fishtail (blade) bit, rock (*Am. *roller) bit, core bit*
22-27 l'extraction *f* du pétrole (l'exploitation *f* du pétrole)
– ***oil (crude oil) production***
22 le chevalement de pompage *m* (le balancier de la pompe)
– *pumping unit (pump)*
23 la pompe à puits *m* profond
– *plunger*
24 le tube de pompage *m* (la colonne montante de refoulement *m*)
– *tubing*
25 la colonne de production *f* (les tiges *f* de pompage *m*, tubing *m*)
– *sucker rods (pumping rods)*
26 l'obturateur *m* (le presse-étoupe)
– *stuffing box*
27 la tige polie de pompage *m*
– *polish (polished) rod*
28-35 le traitement du pétrole brut (l'épuration *f*) [schéma]
– ***treatment of crude oil [diagram]***
28 le séparateur de gaz *m* (la tour de dégazolinage *m*)
– *gas separator*
29 la conduite de gaz *m* (le gazoduc, le feeder)
– *gas pipe (gas outlet)*
30 le réservoir de stockage *m* du pétrole brut traité par voie *f* humide
– *wet oil tank (wash tank)*
31 le préchauffeur
– *water heater*
32 l'unité *f* de déshydratation *f* et de dessalage *m* du pétrole brut
– *water and brine separator*
33 la canalisation d'évacuation *f* de l'eau *f* salée
– *salt water pipe (salt water outlet)*
34 le réservoir de stockage *m* du pétrole brut épuré
– *oil tank*
35 la canalisation d'acheminement *m* du pétrole épuré à la raffinerie et aux divers moyens *m* de transport *m* (wagons-citernes *m*, pétroliers *m* ou tankers *m*, pipe-lines *m* ou oléoducs *m*)
– *trunk pipeline for oil [to the refinery or transport by tanker lorry (*Am. *tank truck), oil tanker, or pipeline]*

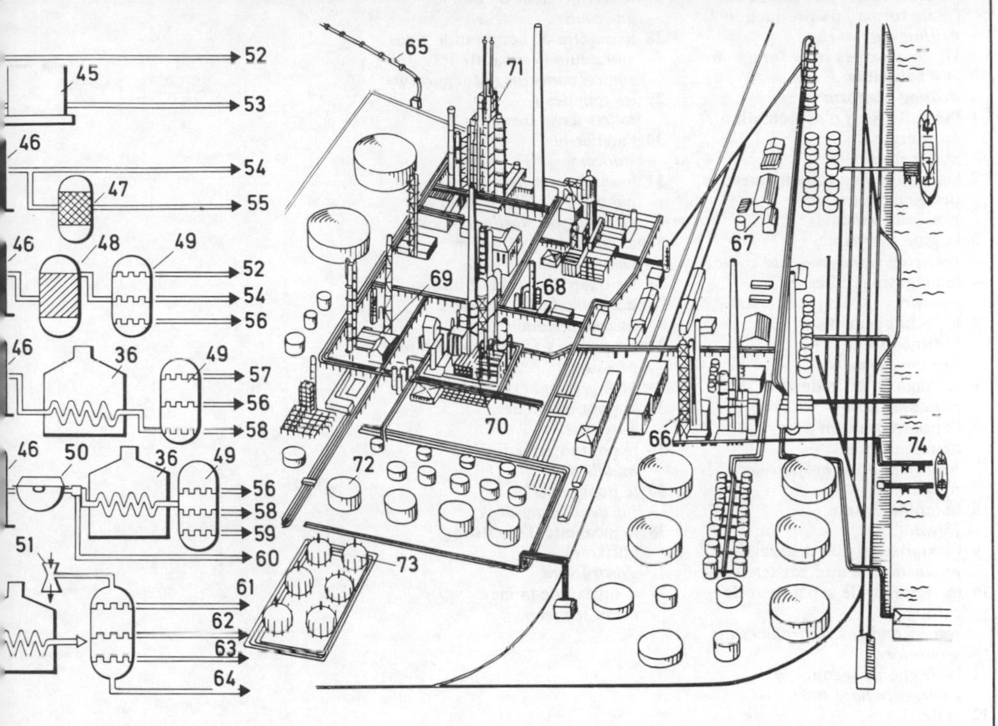

36-64 le raffinage du pétrole brut (la transformation du pétrole brut) [schéma]
– ***processing of crude oil [diagram]***
36 le four tubulaire (le pipe still)
– *oil furnace (pipe still)*
37 la tour de fractionnement *m* (la colonne de distillation *f* à plateaux *m* superposés)
– *fractionating column (distillation column) with trays*
38 les gazs *m* légers (accumulés au sommet de la colonne)
– *top gases (tops)*
39 la fraction d'essence *f* légère
– *light distillation products*
40 la fraction d'essence *f* lourde
– *heavy distillation products*
41 le pétrole lampant
– *petroleum*
42 la fraction de gas-oil *m* ou gazole *m*
– *gas oil component*
43 les résidus *m* lourds (rassemblés au fond de la colonne)
– *residue*
44 le condenseur
– *condenser (cooler)*
45 le compresseur
– *compressor*
46 l'unité *f* de désulfuration *f*
– *desulphurizing (desulphurization,* Am. *desulfurizing, desulfurization) plant*
47 l'unité *f* de reformage *m* ou reforming *m*
– *reformer (hydroformer, platformer)*
48 l'unité *f* de craquage *m* ou cracking *m* catalytique
– *catalytic cracker (cat cracker)*
49 la tour de fractionnement *m* sous vide *m*
– *distillation column*
50 l'unité *f* de déparaffinage *m*
– *de-waxing (wax separation)*
51 le dispositif de production *f* de vide *m* (le canal d'aspiration *f*)
– *vacuum equipment*
52-64 les produits *m* dérivés du pétrole
– ***oil products***
52 le gaz de chauffage *m* (le fuel-gaz)
– *fuel gas*
53 le gaz liquéfié (butane *m*, propane *m*)
– *liquefied petroleum gas (liquid gas)*
54 l'essence *f* auto *f* (le carburant)
– *regular grade petrol* (Am. *gasoline)*
55 l'essence *f* super (le supercarburant)
– *super grade petrol* (Am. *gasoline)*
56 le gazole (le diesel-oil, le carburant diesel)
– *diesel oil*
57 l'essence *f* d'aviation *f* (le carburéacteur)
– *aviation fuel*
58 le fuel-oil léger
– *light fuel oil*
59 le fuel-oil lourd (le mazout)
– *heavy fuel oil*
60 la paraffine
– *paraffin (paraffin oil, kerosene)*
61 le lubrifiant spindle (l'huile *f* légère)
– *spindle oil*
62 le lubrifiant (l'huile *f* lourde, l'huile *f* de graissage *m*)
– *lubricating oil*
63 l'huile *f* de graissage *m* pour cylindres *m*
– *cylinder oil*
64 le bitume
– *bitumen*
65-74 la raffinerie de pétrole *m*
– ***oil refinery***
65 le pipe-line (l'oléoduc *m*)
– *pipeline (oil pipeline)*
66 l'unité *f* de distillation *f*
– *distillation plants*
67 l'unité *f* de raffinage *m* d'huiles *f*
– *lubricating oil refinery*
68 l'unité *f* de désulfuration *f*
– *desulphurizing (desulphurization,* Am. *desulfurizing, desulfurization) plant*
69 la tour de dégazolinage *m* (le séparateur de gaz *m*)
– *gas-separating plant*
70 l'unité *f* de craquage *m* catalytique
– *catalytic cracking plant*
71 l'unité *f* de reformage *m* catalytique
– *catalytic reformer*
72 le réservoir de stockage *m* cylindrique
– *storage tank*
73 le réservoir de stockage *m* sphérique
– *spherical tank*
74 le port pétrolier
– *tanker terminal*

1-39 plate-forme *f* de forage *m*
(plate-forme *f* de production *f*)
– ***drilling rig (oil rig)***

1-37 les quartiers *m* de forage *m* et d'habitation *f*
– ***drilling platform***

1 l'installation *f* d'alimentation *f* en énergie *f*
– *power station*

2 les tuyaux *m* d'échappement *m* des générateurs *m*
– *generator exhausts*

3 la grue tournante
– *revolving crane (pedestal crane)*

4 le magasin à tubes *m*
– *piperack*

5 les échappements *m* des turbines *f*
– *turbine exhausts*

6 le magasin de matériaux *m*
– *materials store*

7 l'appontement *m* pour hélicoptères *m*
– *helicopter deck (heliport deck, heliport)*

8 le monte-charge
– *elevator*

9 l'installation *f* de dégazage *m*
– *production oil and gas separator*

10 le vibrateur (le séparateur de carotte *f*)
– *test oil and gas separators (test separators)*

11 la torche de secours *m*
– *emergency flare stack*

12 le derrick
– *derrick*

13 le réservoir à gazole *m*
– *diesel tank*

14 les bureaux *m*
– *office building*

15 les bacs *m* à ciment *m*
– *cement storage tanks*

16 le réservoir d'eau *f* potable
– *drinking water tank*

17 le réservoir d'eau *f* industrielle (eau *f* salée)
– *salt water tank*

18 les réservoirs *m* à carburant *m* pour hélicoptères *m*
– *jet fuel tanks*

19 les bateaux *m* de sauvetage *m*
– *lifeboats*

20 la trémie d'ascenseur *m*
– *elevator shaft*

21 le réservoir d'air *m* comprimé
– *compressed-air reservoir*

22 l'installation *f* de pompage *m*
– *pumping station*

23 le compresseur d'air *m*
– *air compressor*

24 l'installation *f* de climatisation *f*
– *air lock*

25 l'installation *f* de dessalement *m* d'eau *f* de mer *f*
– *seawater desalination plant*

26 l'installation *f* de filtrage *m* de gazole *m*
– *inlet filters for diesel fuel*

27 le réfrigérateur de gaz *m*
– *gas cooler*

28 le pupitre de commande *f* des vibrateurs *m* séparateurs
– *control panel for the separators*

29 les toilettes *f*
– *toilets (lavatories)*

30 l'atelier *m*
– *workshop*

31 le sas à furet *m*
– *pig trap [the 'pig' is used to clean the oil pipeline]*

32 le poste de contrôle *m*
– *control room*

33 les quartiers *m* d'habitation *f*
– *accommodation modules (accommodation)*

34 les pompes *f* à ciment *m* haute pression *f*
– *high-pressure cementing pumps*

35 le pont inférieur
– *lower deck*

36 le pont intermédiaire
– *middle deck*

37 le pont supérieur
– *top deck (main deck)*

38 la jacquette (l'ossature *f* portante)
– *substructure*

39 le niveau de la mer
– *mean sea level*

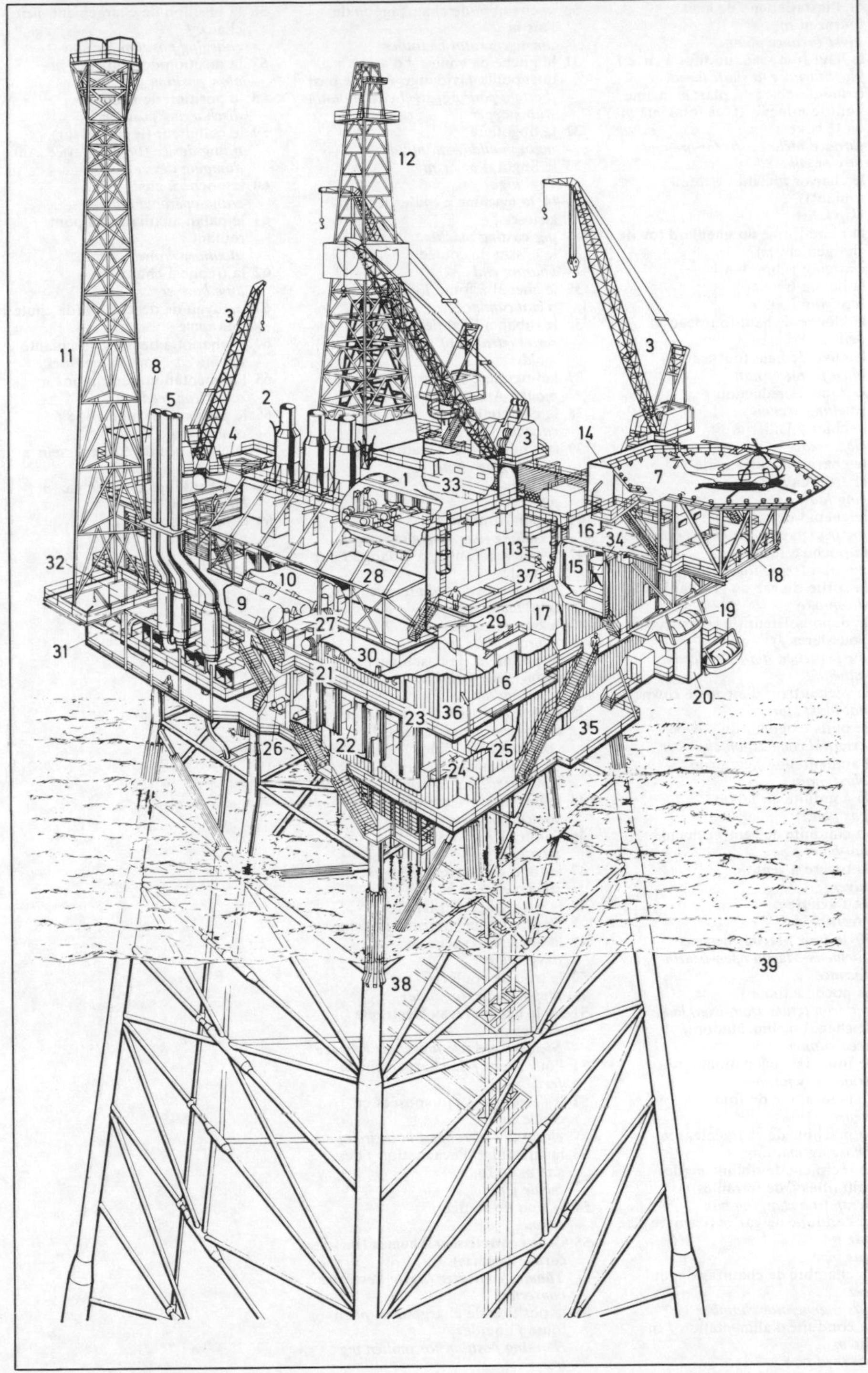
12
11
8
5
3
2
4
3
3
14
7
1
33
16
34
13
37
15
18
32
10
28
9
27
29
17
19
31
30
21
6
20
23
36
35
26
22
25
24
39
38

1-20 l'installation *f* de haut fourneau *m*
– ***blast furnace plant***
1 le haut fourneau, un four à cuve *f*
– *blast furnace, a shaft furnace*
2 le monte-charge à plan *m* incliné pour le minerai et les fondants *m* ou le coke
– *furnace incline (lift) for ore and flux or coke*
3 le chariot roulant (le treuil roulant)
– *skip hoist*
4 la plate-forme du gueulard (ou de chargement *m*)
– *charging platform*
5 la benne-trémie
– *receiving hopper*
6 la cloche de haut fourneau *m*
– *bell*
7 la cuve de haut fourneau *m*
– *blast furnace shaft*
8 la zone de réduction *f*
– *smelting section*
9 le chiot à laitier *m*
– *slag escape*
10 le chariot à laitier *m* (le chariot-cuve)
– *slag ladle*
11 le chenal de coulée *f* de la fonte
– *pig iron (crude iron, iron) runout*
12 la poche à fonte *f*
– *pig iron (crude iron, iron) ladle*
13 la sortie du gaz de gueulard *m*
– *downtake*
14 le dépoussiéreur (le collecteur de poussières *f*)
– *dust catcher, a dust-collecting machine*
15 le réchauffeur d'air *m* (le cowper)
– *hot-blast stove*
16 le puits extérieur du cowper
– *external combustion chamber*
17 l'alimentation *f* en air *m*
– *blast main*
18 la conduite de gaz *m*
– *gas pipe*
19 la conduite de vent *m* chaud
– *hot-blast pipe*
20 la tuyère à vent *m*
– *tuyère*
21-69 l'aciérie *f*
– ***steelworks***
21-30 le four Martin-Siemens
– ***Siemens-Martin open-hearth furnace***
21 la poche à fonte *f*
– *pig iron (crude iron, iron) ladle*
22 le chenal d'alimentation *f*
– *feed runner*
23 le four fixe (ou stationnaire)
– *stationary furnace*
24 le laboratoire du four
– *hearth*
25 la machine de chargement *m*
– *charging machine*
26 le récipient de riblons *m* (des mitrailles *f*, de ferrailles *f*)
– *scrap iron charging box*
27 la conduite de gaz *m* (l'arrivée *f* de gaz *m*)
– *gas pipe*
28 la chambre de chauffage *m* du gaz
– *gas regenerator chamber*
29 la conduite d'alimentation *f* en air *m*
– *air feed pipe*
30 la chambre de chauffage *m* de l'air *m*
– *air regenerator chamber*
31 la poche de coulée *f* d'acier *m* à quenouille *f* [vidange *f* par le bas]
– *[bottom-pouring] steel-casting ladle with stopper*
32 la lingotière
– *ingot mould* (Am. *mold)*
33 le lingot d'acier *m*
– *steel ingot*
34-44 la machine à couler les gueuses *f*
– ***pig-casting machine***
34 le bassin de coulée *f*
– *pouring end*
35 le chenal à fonte *f* liquide
– *metal runner*
36 le ruban à lingotières *f*
– *series (strand) of moulds* (Am. *molds)*
37 la lingotière
– *mould* (Am. *mold)*
38 la passerelle
– *catwalk*
39 la goulotte d'évacuation *f*
– *discharging chute*
40 la gueuse
– *pig*
41 le pont roulant
– *travelling* (Am. *traveling) crane*
42 la poche à fonte *f* à vidange *f* par le haut
– *top-pouring pig iron (crude iron, iron) ladle*
43 le bec de coulée *f*
– *pouring ladle lip*
44 le culbuteur (le basculeur)
– *tilting device (tipping device,* Am. *dumping device)*
45-50 le convertisseur à soufflage *m* d'oxygène *m* par le haut (le convertisseur LD)
– ***oxygen-blowing converter** (L-D converter, Linz-Donawitz converter)*
45 le bec de convertisseur *m*
– *conical converter top*
46 l'anneau *m* porteur
– *mantle*
47 le fond de convertisseur *m*
– *solid converter bottom*
48 le garnissage réfractaire
– *fireproof lining (refractory lining)*
49 la lance à oxygène *m*
– *oxygen lance*
50 le trou de coulée *f*
– *tapping hole (tap hole)*
51-54 le bas fourneau électrique Siemens
– ***Siemens electric low-shaft furnace***
51 l'ouverture *f* de chargement *m*
– *feed*
52 les électrodes *f* [disposées en cercle *m*]
– *electrodes [arranged in a circle]*
53 la circulaire d'évacuation *f* des gaz *m* du four
– *bustle pipe*
54 le trou de coulée *f*
– *runout*
55-69 le convertisseur Thomas (la cornue Thomas)
– ***Thomas converter (basic Bessemer converter)***
55 la position de chargement *m* en fonte *f* liquide
– *charging position for molten pig iron*
56 la position de chargement *m* en chaux *f*
– *charging position for lime*
57 la position de soufflage *m*
– *blow position*
58 la position de coulée *f*
– *discharging position*
59 le culbuteur (le basculeur)
– *tilting device (tipping device,* Am. *dumping device)*
60 la poche à anse *f*
– *crane-operated ladle*
61 le palan auxiliaire du pont roulant
– *auxiliary crane hoist*
62 la trémie à chaux *f*
– *lime bunker*
63 le tuyau de descente *f* (de chute *f*)
– *downpipe*
64 le chariot à benne *f* basculante
– *tipping car* (Am. *dump truck)*
65 l'alimentation *f* en riblons *m*
– *scrap iron feed*
66 le pupitre de commande *f*
– *control desk*
67 la cheminée de convertisseur *m*
– *converter chimney*
68 le tube d'injection *f* de gaz *m*
– *blast main*
69 le fond à tuyères *f*
– *wind box*

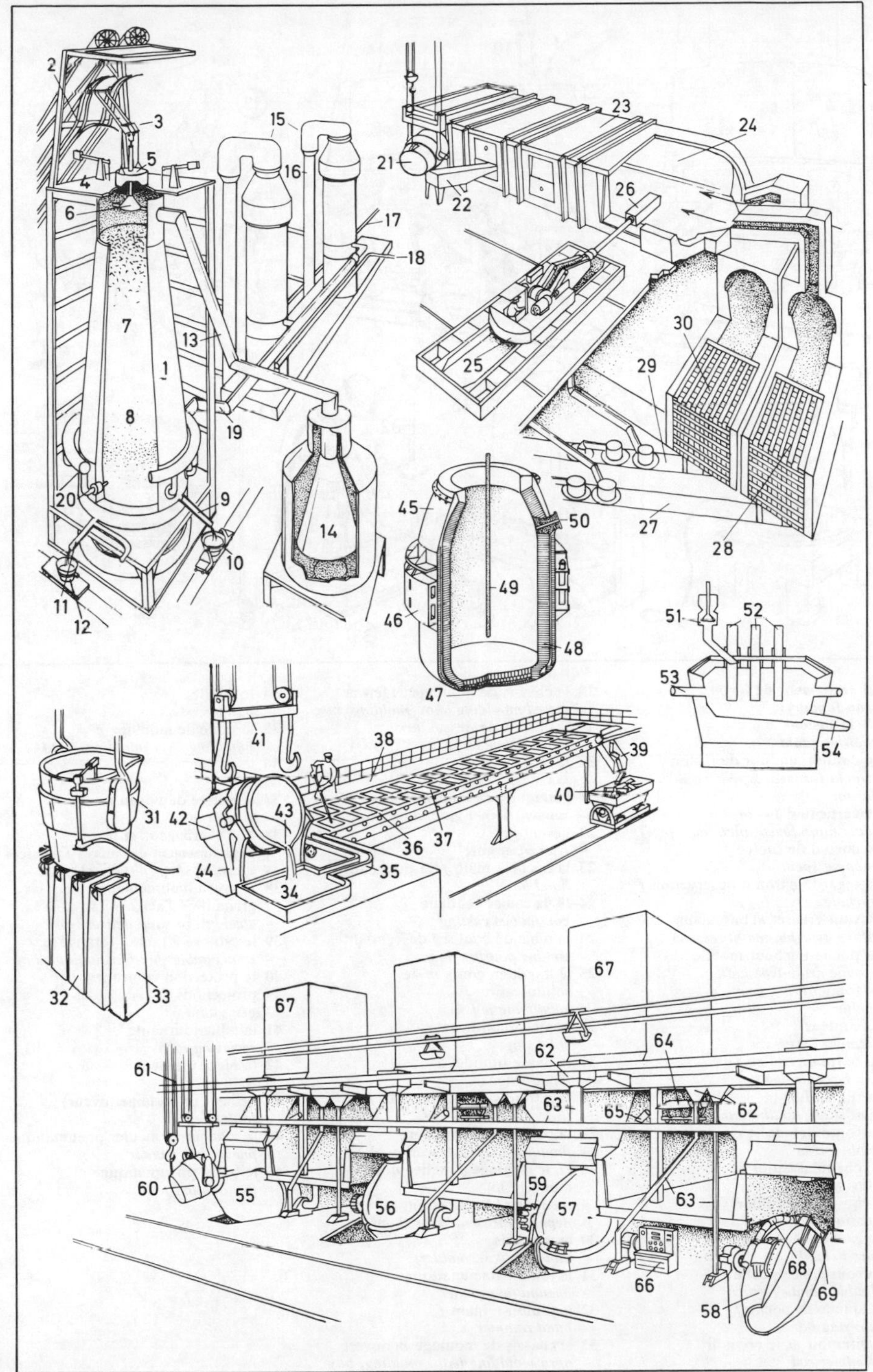
1
2
3
4
5
6
7
8
9
10
11
12
13
14
15
16
17
18
19
20
21
22
23
24
25
26
27
28
29
30
31
32
33
34
35
36
37
38
39
40
41
42
43
44
45
46
47
48
49
50
51
52
53
54
55
56
57
58
59
60
61
62
63
64
65
66
67
68
69

1-45 la fonderie de fer *m*
– ***iron foundry***
1-12 la fusion
– ***melting plant***
1 le cubilot, un four de fusion *f*
– *cupola furnace (cupola), a melting furnace*
2 le carneau d'air *m*
– *blast main (blast inlet, blast pipe)*
3 le chenal de coulée *f*
– *tapping spout*
4 le regard, le trou d'observation *f*
– *spyhole*
5 l'avant-creuset *m* basculant
– *tilting-type hot-metal receiver*
6 la poche-tambour mobile
– *mobile drum-type ladle*
7 le fondeur
– *melter*
8 le couleur
– *founder (caster)*
9 la barre de coulée *f*
– *tap bar (tapping bar)*
10 la quenouille
– *bott stick* (Am. *bot stick)*
11 la fonte liquide
– *molten iron*
12 le chenal à laitier *m*
– *slag spout*
13 l'équipe *f* de coulée *f*
– *casting team*
14 la poche à fourche *f*
– *hand shank*
15 la fourche de poche *f*
– *double handle (crutch)*
16 la queue de poche *f*
– *carrying bar*
17 l'écrémoir *m*, le crémoir
– *skimmer rod*
18 le châssis de moulage *m* fermé
– *closed moulding* (Am. *molding) box*
19 le châssis de dessus *m*
– *upper frame (cope)*
20 le châssis de dessous *m*
– *lower frame (drag)*
21 l'attaque *f* de coulée *f*
– *runner (runner gate, down-gate)*
22 l'évent *m*
– *riser (riser gate)*
23 la poche à main *f* (la pochette)
– *hand ladle*
24-29 la coulée continue
– ***continuous casting***
24 la table de coulée *f* descendante
– *sinking pouring floor*
25 le lingot en cours *m* de solidification *f*
– *solidifying pig*
26 la phase solide
– *solid stage*
27 la phase liquide
– *liquid stage*
28 le refroidissement par eau *f*
– *water-cooling system*
29 la paroi de la lingotière
– *mould* (Am. *mold) wall*
30-37 le moulage (l'atelier *m* de moulage *m*)
– ***moulding*** (Am. *molding)* ***department*** *(moulding shop)*
30 le mouleur
– *moulder* (Am. *molder)*
31 le fouloir pneumatique
– *pneumatic rammer*
32 le fouloir à main *f*
– *hand rammer*
33 le châssis de moulage *m* ouvert
– *open moulding* (Am. *molding) box*
34 le moule
– *pattern*
35 le sable de moulage *m*
– *moulding* (Am. *molding) sand*
36 le noyau
– *core*
37 la portée de noyau *m*
– *core print*
38-45 l'ébarbage *m* **et le parachèvement des pièces** *f* **moulées**
– ***cleaning shop*** *(fettling shop)*
38 le tuyau d'alimentation *f* en grenaille *f* d'acier *m* ou sable *m*
– *steel grit or sand delivery pipe*
39 le sablage à table *f* rotative
– *rotary-table shot-blasting machine*
40 la protection contre les projections *f*
– *grit guard*
41 la table tournante
– *revolving table*
42 la pièce moulée
– *casting*
43 l'ébarbeur *m* (le nettoyeur)
– *fettler*
44 la machine à meuler pneumatique
– *pneumatic grinder*
45 le burin pneumatique
– *pneumatic chisel*

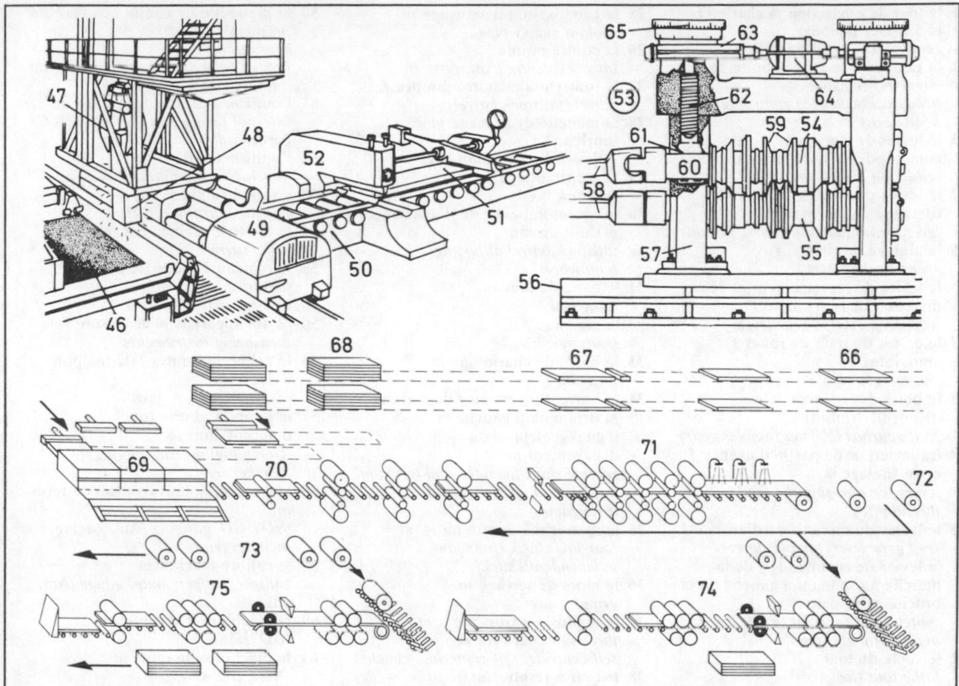

46-75 le laminoir
– ***rolling mill***
46 le four pit
– *soaking pit*
47 le pont roulant de four *m* pit, un pont à pinces *f* (le pont démouleur)
– *soaking pit crane*
48 le lingot méplat (le lingot d'acier *m* brut moulé)
– *ingot*
49 le wagonnet basculeur de lingots *m*
– *ingot tipper*
50 le train blooming (le train de rouleaux *m*)
– *blooming train (roller path)*
51 le laminé
– *workpiece*
52 la cisaille à blooms *m*
– *bloom shears*
53 la cage duo *m*
– *two-high mill*
54-55 le jeu de cylindres *m*
– ***set of rolls*** *(set of rollers)*
54 le cylindre supérieur
– *upper roll (upper roller)*
55 le cylindre inférieur
– *lower roll (lower roller)*
56-60 la cage de laminoir *m*
– ***roll stand***
56 la plaque d'assise *f*
– *base plate*
57 le montant de laminoir *m*
– *housing (frame)*
58 l'arbre *m* d'accouplement *m*
– *coupling spindle*
59 la cannelure
– *groove*
60 le palier de laminoir *m*
– *roll bearing*
61-65 le dispositif de serrage *m*
– ***adjusting equipment***
61 l'empoise *f* (la chaise) de laminoir *m*
– *chock*
62 la vis de serrage *m*
– *main screw*
63 le réducteur
– *gear*
64 le moteur
– *motor*
65 l'indicateur *m* pour réglage *m* grossier et fin
– *indicator for rough and fine adjustment*
66-75 le laminoir à feuillards *m* **d'acier** *m* (le train à bandes *f*) [schéma]
– ***continuous rolling mill train for the manufacture of strip*** *[diagram]*
66-68 le parachèvement des demi-produits *m*
– *processing of semi-finished product*
66 le demi-produit
– *semi-finished product*
67 le poste de découpage *m* autogène
– *gas cutting installation*
68 la pile de feuilles *f* finies
– *stack of finished steel sheets*
69 le four poussant
– *continuous reheating furnaces*
70 le train ébaucheur (dégrossisseur, préparateur)
– *blooming train*
71 le train finisseur
– *finishing train*
72 la bobineuse, l'enrouleuse
– *coiler*
73 le magasin de couronnes *f* de feuillard *m* pour la vente
– *collar bearing for marketing*
74 le train de cisaillage *m* 5 mm
– *5 mm shearing train*
75 le train de cisaillage *m* 10 mm
– *10 mm shearing train*

1 le tour de production *f* **à charioter et à fileter** (le tour)
– ***centre*** (Am. *center*) ***lathe***
2 la poupée fixe avec la boîte de vitesses *f* réglables
– *headstock with gear control (geared headstock)*
3 le levier de manœuvre *f* (de commande *f*) du réducteur
– *reduction drive lever*
4 le levier de filetage *m* normal, filetage *m* à pas *m* rapide
– *lever for normal and coarse threads*
5 le réglage de vitesse *f*
– *speed change lever*
6 le levier de renversement *m* de marche *f* de la vis mère *f*
– *leadscrew reverse-gear lever*
7 le carter du train de roues *f* amovibles
– *change-gear box*
8 la boîte des avances *f* (le dispositif Norton)
– *feed gearbox (Norton tumbler gear)*
9 les leviers *m* de pas *m* d'avance *f* et de filetage *m*
– *levers for changing the feed and thread pitch*
10 le levier du mécanisme d'avance *f*
– *feed gear lever (tumbler lever)*
11 le levier de commande *f* de la marche à droite ou à gauche de la broche principale
– *switch lever for right or left hand action of main spindle*
12 le socle du tour
– *lathe foot (footpiece)*
13 le volant (à main *f*) de déplacement *m* longitudinal du chariot
– *leadscrew handwheel for traversing of saddle (longitudinal movement of saddle)*
14 le levier du renversement de marche *f* du dispositif d'avance *f*
– *tumbler reverse lever*
15 la vis de commande *f* du chariot
– *feed screw*
16 le tablier du chariot
– *apron (saddle apron, carriage apron)*
17 le levier de mouvement *m* longitudinal ou transversal
– *lever for longitudinal and transverse motion*
18 la vis sans fin *f* basculante d'engagement *m* des avances *f*
– *drop (dropping) worm (feed trip, feed tripping device) for engaging feed mechanisms*
19 le levier de l'écrou *m* embrayable de vis *f* mère *f*
– *lever for engaging half nut of leadscrew (lever for clasp nut engagement)*
20 la broche
– *lathe spindle*
21 le porte-outil
– *tool post*
22 le coulisseau porte-outil (le chariot supérieur)
– *top slide (tool slide, tool rest)*
23 le coulisseau transversal (le chariot transversal)
– *cross slide*
24 le corps de chariot *m* (le traînard)
– *bed slide*
25 la canalisation d'arrosage *m*
– *coolant supply pipe*
26 la contre-pointe
– *tailstock centre* (Am. *center)*
27 le fourreau de contre-poupée *f*
– *barrel (tailstock barrel)*
28 la manette de blocage *m* du fourreau
– *tailstock barrel clamp lever*
29 la contre-poupée
– *tailstock*
30 le volant à main *f* de déplacement *m* du fourreau
– *tailstock barrel adjusting handwheel*
31 le banc de tour *m*
– *lathe bed*
32 la vis mère *f*
– *leadscrew*
33 la barre de chariotage *m*
– *feed shaft*
34 la barre d'inversion *f* de marche *f* à droite ou à gauche et d'engagement *m* ou dégagement *m*
– *reverse shaft for right and left hand motion and engaging and disengaging*
35 le mandrin à quatre mors *m*
– *four-jaw chuck (four-jaw independent chuck)*
36 le mors de serrage *m*
– *gripping jaw*
37 le mandrin à trois mors *m*
– *three-jaw chuck (three-jaw self-centring, self-centering, chuck)*
38 le tour à revolver *m* (le tour revolver)
– ***turret lathe***
39 le coulisseau transversal (le chariot transversal)
– *cross slide*
40 la tourelle revolver
– *turret*
41 le porte-outil multiple
– *combination toolholder (multiple turning head)*
42 le chariot longitudinal (le traînard)
– *top slide*
43 les croisillons *m* (le volant à croisillons *m*, le cabestan)
– *star wheel*
44 le bac à copeaux *m* et à huile *f*
– *coolant tray for collecting coolant and swarf*
45-53 les outils *m* **de tournage** *m*
– ***lathe tools***
45 l'outil *m* à plaquette *f* à jeter
– *tool bit holder (clamp tip tool) for adjustable cutting tips*
46 la plaquette à jeter en carbure *m* métallique ou céramique *f* d'oxyde *m*
– *adjustable cutting tip (clamp tip) of cemented carbide or oxide ceramic*
47 les formes *f* de plaquettes *f* à jeter en céramique *f* d'oxyde *m*
– *shapes of adjustable oxide ceramic tips*
48 l'outil *m* à plaquette *f* rapportée en carbure *m* métallique
– *lathe tool with cemented carbide cutting edge*
49 le corps d'outil *m* [de tournage *m*]
– *tool shank*
50 la plaquette de coupe *f* en carbure *m* (métallique) fixée par brasage *m*
– *brazed cemented carbide cutting tip (cutting edge)*
51 l'outil *m* à dresser les fonds *m*
– *internal facing tool (boring tool) for corner work*
52 l'outil *m* coudé
– *general-purpose lathe tool*
53 l'outil à saigner
– *parting (parting-off) tool*
54 le toc (d'entraînement *m*)
– *lathe carrier*
55 le plateau à toc *m* (le plateau d'entraînement *m*)
– *driving (driver) plate*
56-72 les appareils *m* **de mesure** *f*
– ***measuring instruments***
56 le calibre à limites *f* (le tampon lisse)
– *plug gauge* (Am. *gage)*
57 le tampon «bon» (ou d'acceptation *f*)
– *'GO' gauging* (Am. *gaging) member (end)*
58 le tampon «mauvais» (ou de refus *m*)
– *'NOT GO' gauging* (Am. *gaging) member (end)*
59 le calibre-mâchoires
– *calliper (caliper, snap) gauge* (Am. *gage)*
60 la mâchoire d'acceptation *f*
– *'GO' side*
61 la mâchoire de refus *m*
– *'NOT GO' side*
62 le palmer (le micromètre)
– *micrometer*
63 l'échelle *f* graduée
– *measuring scale*
64 le barillet
– *graduated thimble*
65 le corps de palmer *m*
– *frame*
66 la vis micrométrique
– *spindle (screwed spindle)*
67 le pied à coulisse *f*
– *vernier calliper (caliper) gauge* (Am. *gage)*
68 la jauge de profondeur *f*
– *depth gauge* (Am. *gage) attachment rule*
69 le vernier
– *vernier scale*
70 les becs *m* de mesure *f* extérieure
– *outside jaws*
71 les becs *m* de mesure *f* intérieure
– *inside jaws*
72 le calibre de profondeur *f* (le pied de profondeur *f*)
– *vernier depth gauge* (Am. *gage)*

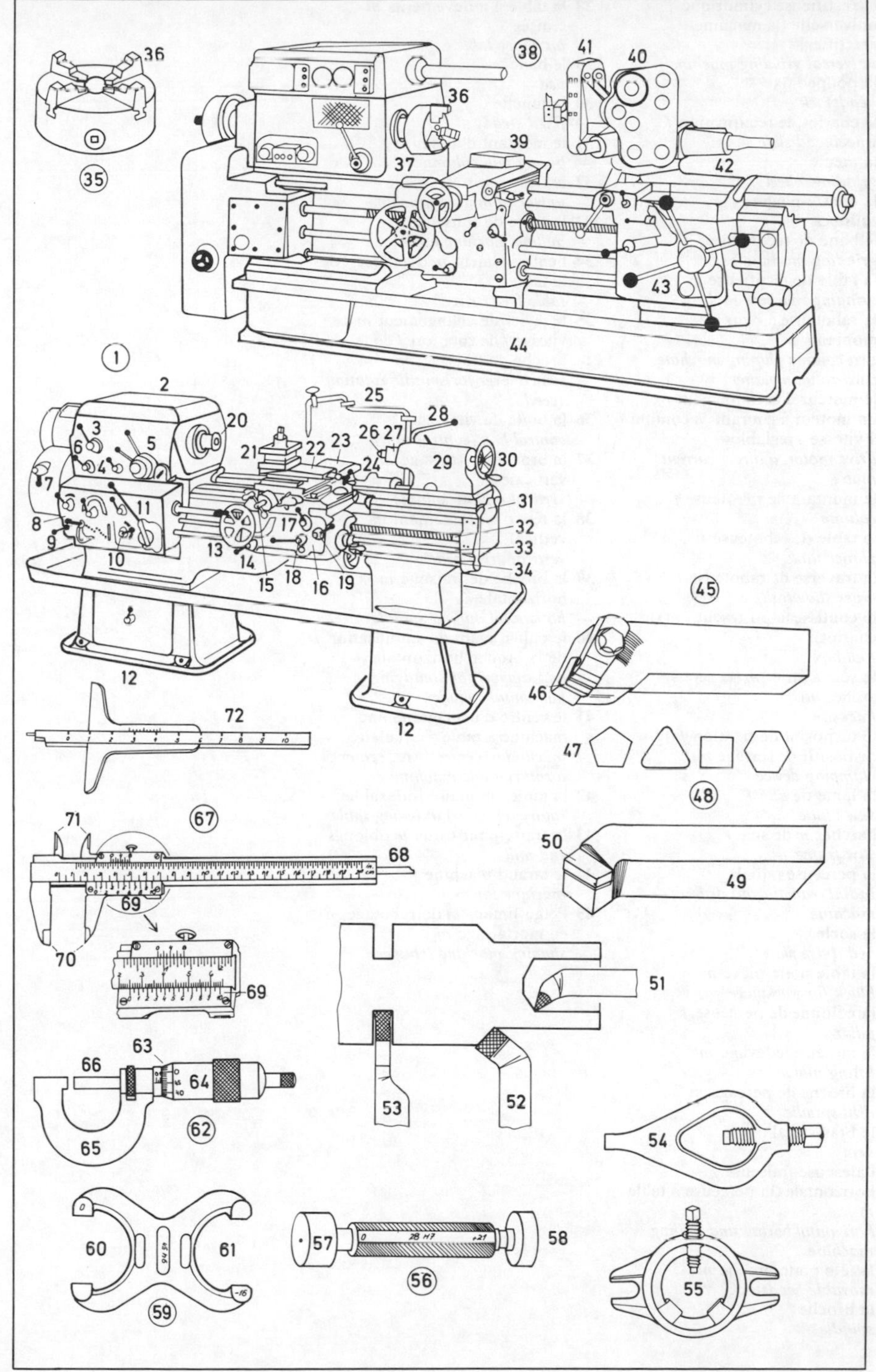

1 la rectifieuse cylindrique universelle (la machine àrectifier)
- *universal grinding machine*
2 la poupée fixe
- *headstock*
3 le chariot de rectification *f*
- *wheelhead slide*
4 la meule
- *grinding wheel*
5 la contre-poupée
- *tailstock*
6 le banc de rectifieuse *f*
- *grinding machine bed*
7 la table de rectifieuse *f*
- *grinding machine table*
8 la raboteuse à deux montants *m*
- *two-column planing machine (two-column planer)*
9 le moteur d'entraînement *m*, un moteur à courant *m* continu à vitesse *f* réglable
- *drive motor, a direct current motor*
10 le montant de raboteuse *f*
- *column*
11 la table de raboteuse *f*
- *planer table*
12 la traverse de raboteuse *f*
- *cross slide (rail)*
13 le coulisseau porte-outil *m* (le chariot)
- *tool box*
14 la scie à étrier *m* (la scie à archet *m*)
- *hacksaw*
15 le dispositif de fixation *f* (le dispositif de serrage *m*)
- *clamping device*
16 la lame de scie *f*
- *saw blade*
17 l'archet *m* de scie *f*
- *saw frame*
18 la perceuse radiale
- *radial (radial-arm) drilling machine*
19 le socle
- *bed (base plate)*
20 la table porte-pièce *m*
- *block for workpiece*
21 la colonne de perceuse *f*
- *pillar*
22 le moteur de levage *m*
- *lifting motor*
23 la broche de perçage *m*
- *drill spindle*
24 le bras radial
- *arm*
25 l'aléseuse-fraiseuse *f* horizontale (la perceuse à table *f*)
- *horizontal boring and milling machine*
26 la tête porte-broche *m*
- *movable headstock*
27 la broche
- *spindle*
28 la table à mouvements *m* croisés
- *auxiliary table*
29 le banc
- *bed*
30 la lunette
- *fixed steady*
31 le montant d'aléseuse *f*
- *boring mill column*
32 la fraiseuse universelle
- *universal milling machine*
33 la table de fraiseuse *f*
- *milling machine table*
34 l'entraînement *m* d'avance *f* de la table
- *table feed drive*
35 le levier de changement *m* de vitesse *f* de rotation *f* de la broche de fraisage *m*
- *switch lever for spindle rotation speed*
36 la boîte de vitesses *f*
- *control box (control unit)*
37 la broche de fraisage *m* verticale
- *vertical milling spindle*
38 la tête d'entraînement *m* vertical
- *vertical drive head*
39 la broche de fraisage *m* horizontale
- *horizontal milling spindle*
40 le palier avant de stabilisation *f* de la broche horizontale
- *end support for steadying horizontal spindle*
41 le centre d'usinage *m*, une machine à table *f* circulaire
- *machining centre (*Am. center*), a rotary-table machine*
42 la table circulaire indexable
- *rotary (circular) indexing table*
43 la fraise pour trous *m* oblongs
- *end mill*
44 le taraud machine *f*
- *machine tap*
45 l'étau-limeur *m* de rabotage *m* en mortaisage *m*
- *shaping machine (shaper)*

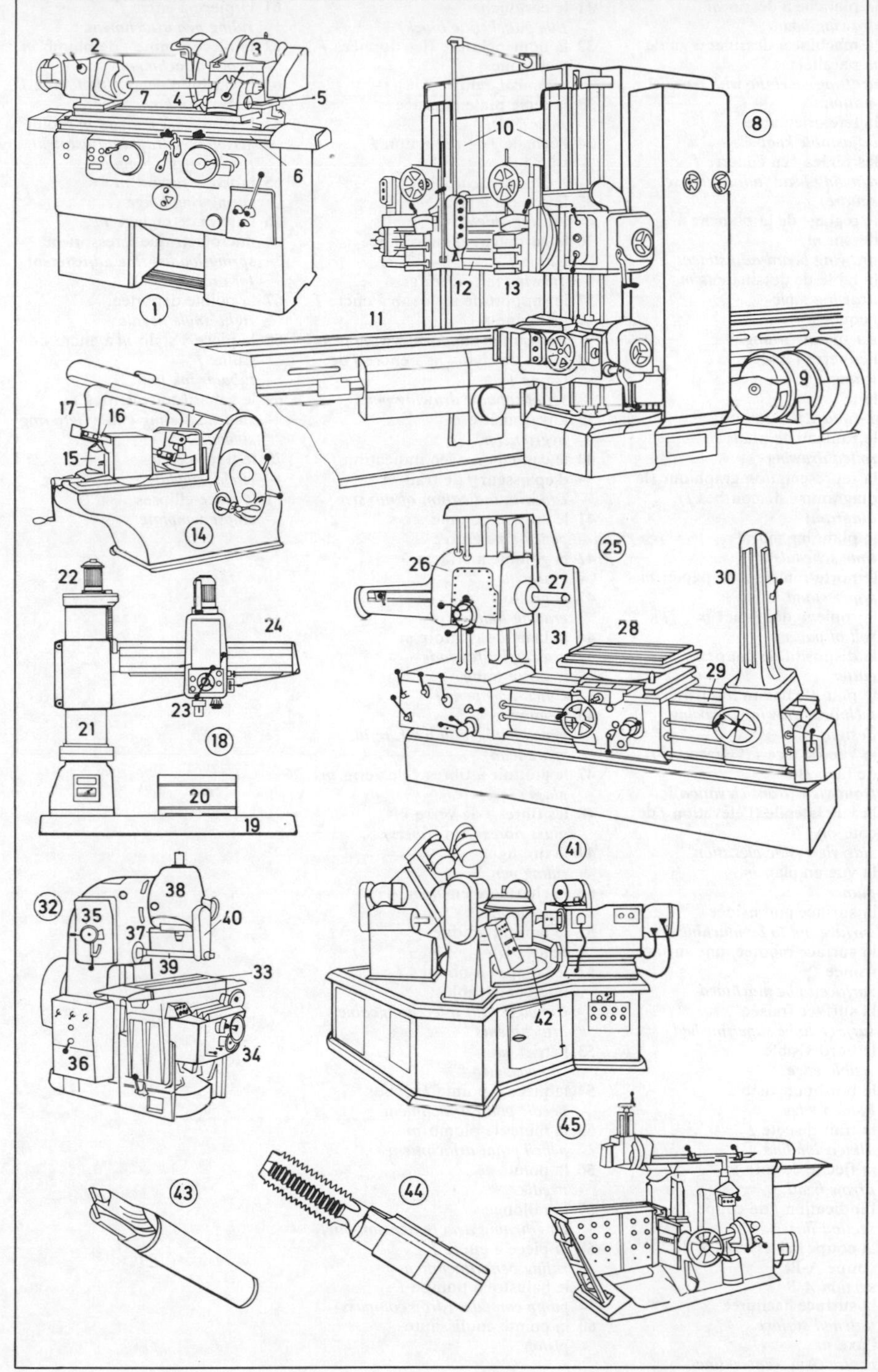
2
3
7
4
5
6
1
10
8
12
13
11
9
17
16
15
14
26
25
27
30
22
24
31
28
29
23
21
18
20
19
41
38
32
35
40
37
39
33
42
36
34
45
43
44

1 la planche à dessin *m*
– *drawing board*
2 la machine à dessiner à guide *m* parallèle
– *drafting machine with parallel motion*
3 la tête orientable
– *adjustable knob*
4 les règles *f* en équerre *f*
– *drawing head (adjustable set square)*
5 le réglage de la planche à dessin *m*
– *drawing board adjustment*
6 la table de dessinateur *m*
– *drawing table*
7 l'équerre *f*
– *set square (triangle)*
8 l'équerre *f* isocèle
– *triangle*
9 le té
– *T-square (tee-square)*
10 le rouleau de plans *m*
– *rolled drawing*
11 la représentation graphique (le diagramme de courbes *f*)
– *diagram*
12 le planning mural
– *time schedule*
13 le porte-rouleaux de papier *m*
– *paper stand*
14 le rouleau de papier *m*
– *roll of paper*
15 le dispositif de coupe *f*
– *cutter*
16 le plan (le dessin industriel)
– *technical drawing (drawing, design)*
17 la vue de face *f* (l'élévation *f* de face *f*)
– *front view (front elevation)*
18 la vue latérale (l'élévation *f* de côté *m*)
– *side view (side elevation)*
19 la vue en plan *m*
– *plan*
20 la surface non usinée
– *surface not to be machined*
21 la surface rabotée, une surface usinée
– *surface to be machined*
22 la surface fraisée
– *surface to be superfinished*
23 le bord visible
– *visible edge*
24 le bord non visible
– *hidden edge*
25 le trait de cote *f*
– *dimension line*
26 la flèche de cote *f*
– *arrow head*
27 l'indication *f* de coupe *f*
– *section line*
28 la coupe suivant A - B (la coupe A-B)
– *section A-B*
29 la surface hachurée
– *hatched surface*
30 l'axe *m*
– *centre* (Am. *center*) *line*
31 le cartouche
– *title panel (title block)*
32 la nomenclature (les données *f* techniques)
– *technical data*
33 la règle plate graduée
– *ruler (rule)*
34 l'échelle *f* de réduction *f* triangulaire
– *triangular scale*
35 le gabarit à effacer
– *erasing shield*
36 la cartouche d'encre *f* de Chine *f*
– *drawing ink cartridge*
37 le support de stylos *m* à encre *f* de Chine *f*
– *holders for tubular drawing pens*
38 le jeu de stylos *m* à encre *f* de Chine *f*
– *set of tubular drawing pens*
39 l'hygromètre *m*
– *hygrometer*
40 le capuchon avec indication *f* d'épaisseur *f* de trait *m*
– *cap with indication of nib size*
41 le crayon-gomme
– *pencil-type eraser*
42 la gomme à effacer
– *eraser*
43 le grattoir
– *erasing knife*
44 la lame de grattoir *m*
– *erasing knife blade*
45 le porte-mine
– *clutch-type pencil*
46 la mine
– *pencil lead (refill lead, refill, spare lead)*
47 le grattoir à fibres *f* de verre *m*
– *glass eraser*
48 les fibres *f* de verre *m*
– *glass fibres* (Am. *fibers)*
49 le tire-ligne
– *ruling pen*
50 la charnière en X *m*
– *cross joint*
51 le bouton gradué
– *index plate*
52 le compas à pointes *f* interchangeables
– *compass with interchangeable attachments*
53 l'étrier *m*
– *compass head*
54 la pièce à pointe *f* sèche
– *needle point attachment*
55 la mine de plomb *m*
– *pencil point attachment*
56 la pointe
– *needle*
57 la rallonge
– *lengthening arm (extension bar)*
58 la pièce à encre *f*
– *ruling pen attachment*
59 le balustre à pompe *f*
– *pump compass (drop compass)*
60 la pointe coulissante
– *piston*
61 la pièce à encre *f*
– *ruling pen attachment*
62 la pièce à mine *f* de plomb *m*
– *pencil attachment*
63 le flacon d'encre *f* de Chine *f*
– *drawing ink container*
64 le compas à réglage *m* rapide
– *spring bow (rapid adjustment, ratchet-type) compass*
65 la tête à ressort *m*
– *spring ring hinge*
66 l'arc *m* de réglage *m* micrométrique à ressort *m*
– *spring-loaded fine adjustment for arcs*
67 la pointe déportée
– *right-angle needle*
68 la pièce à stylo *m* à encre *f* de Chine *f*
– *tubular ink unit*
69 le gabarit trace-lettres *m*
– *stencil lettering guide (lettering stencil)*
70 le trace-cercles
– *circle template*
71 le trace-ellipses
– *ellipse template*

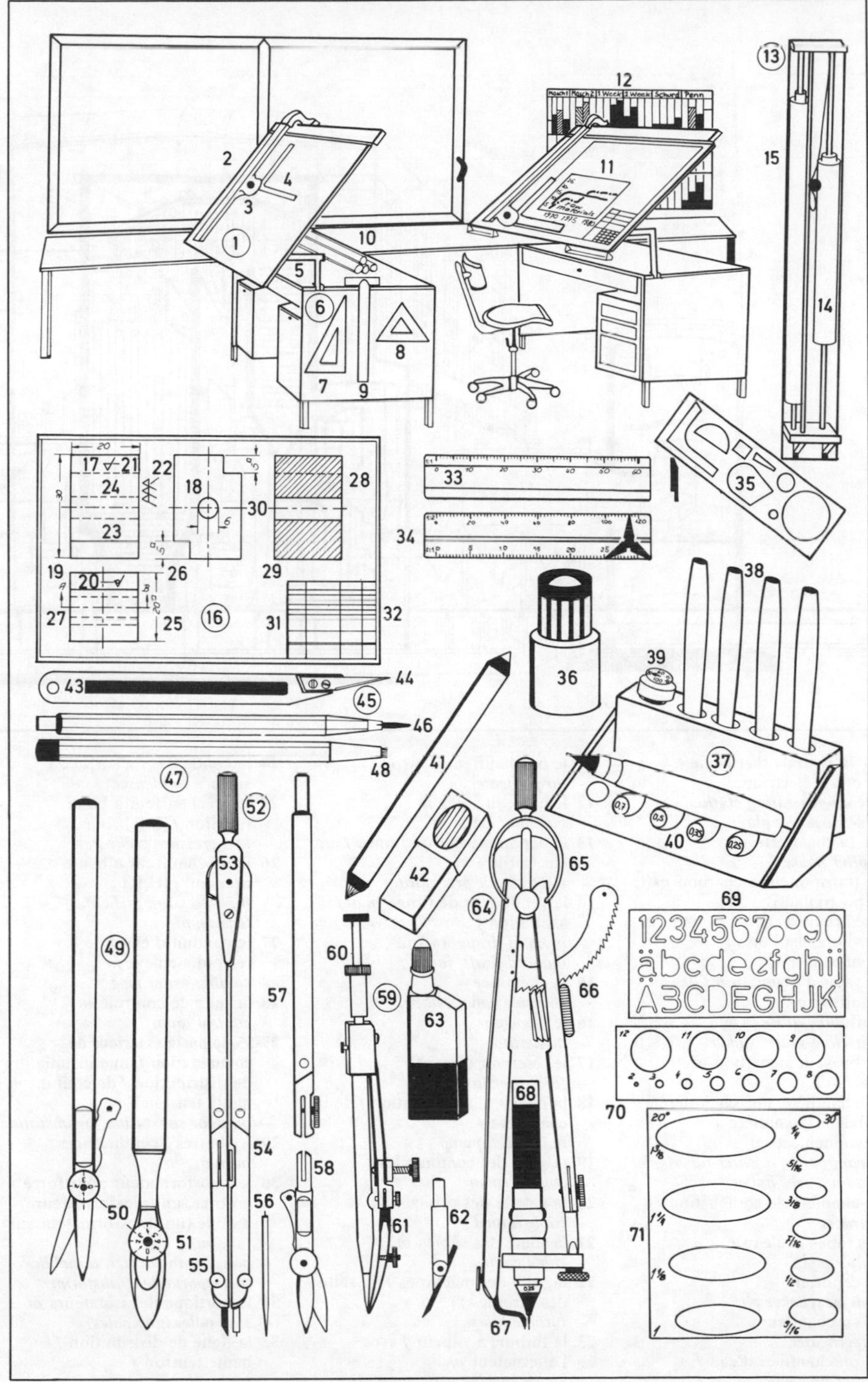

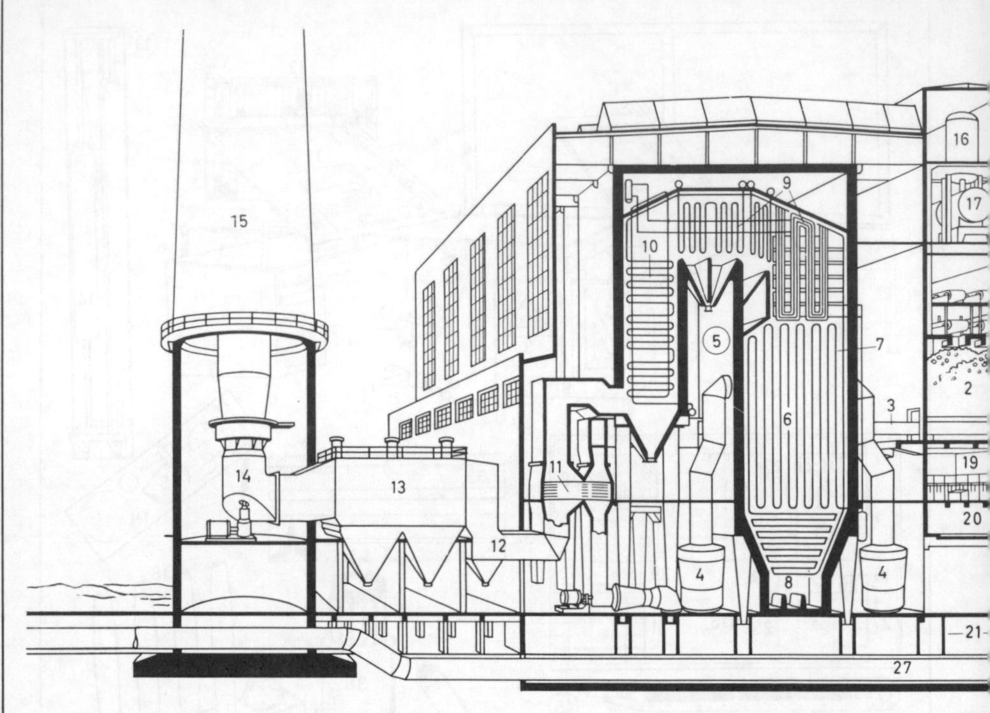

1-28 la centrale thermique *f*, une centrale électrique
– ***steam-generating station**, an electric power plant*
1-21 la chaufferie
– ***boiler house***
1 le transporteur à charbon *m* (le tapis roulant)
– *coal conveyor*
2 le silo à charbon *m*
– *coal bunker*
3 le tapis d'évacuation *f* de charbon *m*
– *travelling-grate (*Am. *traveling-grate) stoker*
4 le broyeur à charbon *m*
– *coal mill*
5 la chaudière, une chaudière à tubes *m* (chaudière à rayonnement *m*)
– *steam boiler, a water-tube boiler (radiant-type boiler)*
6 la chambre de combustion *f*
– *burners*
7 les tubes *m* d'eau *f*
– *water pipes*
8 le cendrier
– *ash pit (clinker pit)*
9 le surchauffeur
– *superheater*
10 le préchauffeur d'eau *f*
– *water preheater*
11 le préchauffeur d'air *m*
– *air preheater*
12 le carneau à gaz *m*
– *gas flue*
13 le dépoussiéreur de fumée *f*, un électrofiltre *m*
– *electrostatic precipitator*
14 le ventilateur de tirage *m* par aspiration *f*
– *induced-draught (*Am. *induced-draft) fan*
15 la cheminée
– *chimney (smokestack)*
16 le dégazeur
– *de-aerator*
17 le réservoir d'eau *f*
– *feedwater tank*
18 la pompe d'alimentation *f* de la chaudière *f*
– *boiler feed pump*
19 la salle des commandes *f*
– *control room*
20 la galerie des câbles *m*
– *cable tunnel*
21 la soute des câbles *m*
– *cable vault*
22 la salle des machines *f* (la salle des turbines *f*)
– *turbine house*
23 la turbine à vapeur *f* avec l'alternateur *m*
– *steam turbine with alternator*
24 le condenseur à surface *f*
– *surface condenser*
25 le préchauffeur à basse pression *f* [B.P.]
– *low-pressure preheater*
26 le préchauffeur à haute pression *f* [H.P.]
– *high-pressure preheater (economizer)*
27 le conduit d'eau *f* de refroidissement *m*
– *cooling water pipe*
28 la salle de contrôle *m*
– *control room*
29-35 le poste extérieur de commutation *f*, une installation de distribution *f* de courant *m* haute tension *f*
– ***outdoor substation**, a substation*
29 les barres *f* conductrices
– *busbars*
30 le transformateur pour force *f* motrice, un transformateur mobile (un transformateur sur rails *m*)
– *power transformer, a mobile (transportable) transformer*
31 le portique des isolateurs *m*
– *stay poles (guy poles)*
32 la ligne de distribution *f* à haute tension *f*
– *high-voltage transmission line*

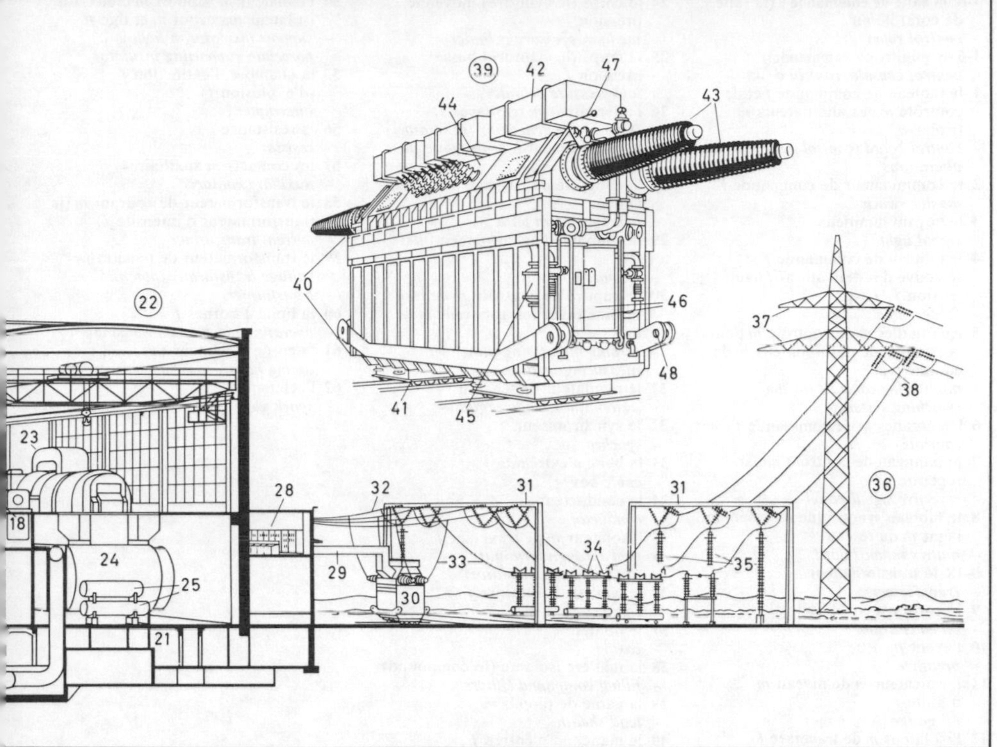

33 le câble haute tension *f*
– *high-voltage conductor*

34 le disjoncteur instantané (ultra-rapide) à air *m* comprimé, un disjoncteur
– *air-blast circuit breaker (circuit breaker)*

35 le parafoudre
– *surge diverter (*Am. *lightning arrester, arrester)*

36 le pylône (de haubanage *m*), un pylône en treillis *m*
– *overhead line support, a lattice steel tower*

37 l'entretoise *f* transversale (la traverse)
– *cross arm (traverse)*

38 l'isolateur-arrêt *m* (l'isolateur *m* d'ancrage *m*), la chaîne d'arrêt *m*
– *strain insulator*

39 le transformateur mobile (le transformateur pour force *f* motrice, le transformateur sur rails *m*)
– ***mobile (transportable) transformer*** *(power transformer, transformer)*

40 la cuve du transformateur
– *transformer tank*

41 le chariot de roulement *m* (le bogie ou boggie)
– *bogie (*Am. *truck)*

42 le conservateur d'huile *f*
– *oil conservator*

43 la traversée haute tension *f* [H.T.]
– *primary voltage terminal (primary voltage bushing)*

44 la traversée basse tension *f* [B.T.]
– *low-voltage terminals(low-voltage bushings)*

45 la pompe de circulation *f* d'huile *f*
– *oil-circulating pump*

46 le réfrigérant hydraulique d'huile *f*
– *oil cooler*

47 la corne d'éclateur *m*
– *arcing horn*

48 l'œillet *m* d'accrochage *m* pour le transport
– *transport lug*

1-8 la salle de commande *f* (la salle de contrôle *m*)
– ***control room***
1-6 le pupitre de commande *f*
– ***control console*** *(control desk)*
1 le tableau de commande *f* et de contrôle *m* des alternateurs *m* triphasés
– *control board (control panel) for the alternators*
2 le commutateur de commande *f*
– *master switch*
3 le voyant lumineux
– *signal light*
4 le tableau de commande *f* sélective des dérivations *f* haute tension *f* [H.T.]
– *feeder panel*
5 les organes *m* de contrôle *m* pour la commande des appareils *m* de couplage *m*
– *monitoring controls for the switching systems*
6 les organes *m* de commande *f*
– *controls*
7 le panneau de contrôle *m* par répétition *f*
– *revertive signal panel*
8 le tableau synoptique représentant l'état *m* du réseau
– *matrix mimic board*
9-18 le transformateur
– ***transformer***
9 le conservateur d'huile *f*
– *oil conservator*
10 l'évent *m*
– *breather*
11 l'indicateur *m* de niveau *m* d'huile *f*
– *oil gauge* (Am. *gage)*
12 l'isolateur *m* de traversée *f*
– *feed-through terminal (feed-through insulator)*
13 le changeur de prises *f* haute tension *f* [H.T.]
– *on-load tap changer*
14 la culasse
– *yoke*
15 l'enroulement *m* primaire (enroulement *m* haute tension *f*, H.T.)
– *primary winding (primary)*
16 l'enroulement *m* secondaire (enroulement basse tension *f*, B.T.)
– *secondary winding (secondary, low-voltage winding)*
17 le noyau
– *core*
18 la prise
– *tap (tapping)*
19 le couplage du transformateur
– ***transformer connection***
20 le couplage en étoile *f* (Y)
– *star connection (star network, Y-connection)*
21 le couplage en triangle *m* (le couplage delta *m*, Δ)
– *delta connection (mesh connection)*
22 le point neutre
– *neutral point*
23-30 la turbine à vapeur *f*, un groupe turbo-alternateur à vapeur *f*
– **steam turbine,** *a turbogenerator unit*
23 le corps (le cylindre) haute pression *f*
– *high-pressure cylinder*
24 le corps (le cylindre) moyenne pression *f*
– *medium-pressure cylinder*
25 le corps (le cylindre) basse pression *f*
– *low-pressure cylinder*
26 l'alternateur *m* triphasé
– *three-phase generator (generator)*
27 le refroidisseur à hydrogène *m*
– *hydrogen cooler*
28 la conduite de passage *m* de la vapeur
– *leakage steam path*
29 la soupape d'échappement *m* (le jet)
– *jet nozzle*
30 le pupitre de contrôle *m* de la turbine (avec les appareils *m* de mesure *f*)
– *turbine monitoring panel with measuring instruments*
31 le régulateur de tension *f*
– *automatic voltage regulator*
32 le synchroniseur
– *synchro*
33 la boîte d'extrémité *f*
– ***cable box***
34 le conducteur
– *conductor*
35 l'isolateur *m* de traversée *f*
– *feed-through terminal (feed-through insulator)*
36 le cône de contrainte *f*
– *core*
37 le boîtier
– *casing*
38 la matière isolante (le compound)
– *filling compound (filler)*
39 la gaine de plomb *m*
– *lead sheath*
40 le manchon d'entrée *f*
– *lead-in tube*
41 le câble
– *cable*
42 le câble à haute tension *f* pour courant triphasé *m*
– ***high voltage cable,*** *for three-phase*
43 le conducteur
– *conductor*
44 le papier métallisé
– *metallic paper (metallized paper)*
45 le bourrage
– *tracer (tracer element)*
46 le ruban huilé
– *varnished-cambric tape*
47 la gaine de plomb *m*
– *lead sheath*
48 le papier bituminé
– *asphalted paper*
49 le matelas extérieur en jute *m*
– *jute serving*
50 l'armure *f* en feuillard *m* ou fils *m* d'acier *m*
– *steel tape or steel wire armour* (Am. *armor)*
51-62 le disjoncteur instantané (ultra-rapide) à air comprimé, un disjoncteur
– ***air-blast circuit breaker,*** *a circuit breaker*
51 le réservoir d'air *m* comprimé
– *compressed-air tank*
52 la vanne-pilote
– *control valve (main operating valve)*
53 l'admission *f* d'air *m* comprimé
– *compressed-air inlet*
54 l'isolateur *m* support *m* creux, un isolateur *m* à capot *m* et tige *f*
– *support insulator, a hollow porcelain supporting insulator*
55 la chambre d'extinction *f* (d'explosion *f*)
– *interrupter*
56 la résistance
– *resistor*
57 les contacts *m* auxiliaires
– *auxiliary contacts*
58 le transformateur de courant *m* (le transformateur d'intensité *f*)
– *current transformer*
59 le transformateur de tension *f*
– *voltage transformer (potential transformer)*
60 la boîte à bornes *f*
– *operating mechanism housing*
61 la corne d'éclateur *m*
– *arcing horn*
62 l'éclateur *m*
– *spark gap*

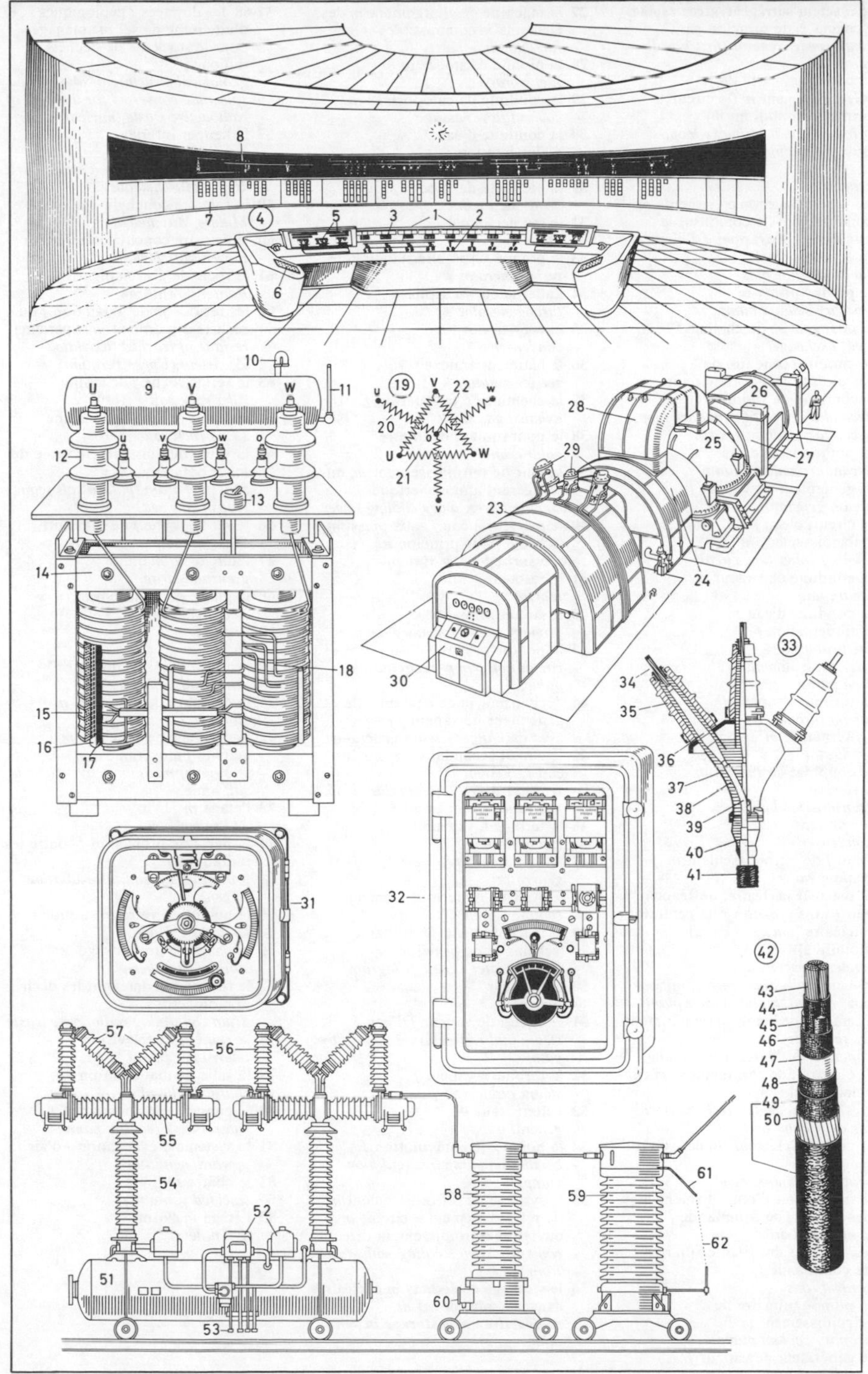

1
2
3
4
5
6
7
8
9
10
11
12
13
14
15
16
17
18
19
20
21
22
23
24
25
26
27
28
29
30
31
32
33
34
35
36
37
38
39
40
41
42
43
44
45
46
47
48
49
50
51
52
53
54
55
56
57
58
59
60
61
62
U
V
W
u
v
w
o

1 le réacteur surrégénérateur rapide [schéma *m* de principe *m*]
– ***fast-breeder reactor*** *(fast breeder) [diagram]*
2 le circuit primaire de refroidissement *m* (le circuit primaire de sodium *m*)
– *primary circuit (primary loop, primary sodium system)*
3 le réacteur
– *reactor*
4 les assemblages *m* d'éléments *m* combustibles (le combustible nucléaire, les grappes *f* d'éléments *m* combustibles)
– *fuel rods (fuel pins)*
5 la pompe primaire
– *primary sodium pump*
6 l'échangeur *m* de chaleur *f*
– *heat exchanger*
7 le circuit secondaire de refroidissement *m* (le circuit secondaire de sodium *m*)
– *secondary circuit (secondary loop, secondary sodium system)*
8 la pompe secondaire
– *secondary sodium pump*
9 le générateur de vapeur *f*
– *steam generator*
10 le circuit d'eau *f* de refroidissement *m*
– *cooling water flow circuit*
11 la conduite de vapeur *f*
– *steam line*
12 la conduite d'eau *f* d'alimentation *f*
– *feedwater line*
13 la pompe alimentaire
– *feed pump*
14 la turbine à vapeur *f*
– *steam turbine*
15 l'alternateur *m*
– *generator*
16 le couplage au réseau *m* électrique
– *transmission line*
17 le condenseur
– *condenser*
18 l'eau *f* de refroidissement *m*
– *cooling water*
19 le réacteur nucléaire, un réacteur à eau *f* sous pression *f* (la centrale nucléaire [*anc.:* la centrale atomique])
– ***nuclear reactor,*** *a pressurized-water reactor (nuclear power plant, atomic power plant)*
20 l'écran *m* de béton *m* (le bâtiment du réacteur)
– *concrete shield (reactor building)*
21 l'enceinte *f* de confinement *m* en acier *m*
– *steel containment (steel shell) with air extraction vent*
22 la cuve du réacteur (le caisson du réacteur)
– *reactor pressure vessel*
23 le mécanisme d'entraînement *m* des barres *f* de commande *f*
– *control rod drive*
24 les barres *f* absorbantes (barres *f* de commande *f*)
– *control rods*
25 la pompe primaire de refroidissement *m*
– *primary coolant pump*
26 le générateur de vapeur *f*
– *steam generator*
27 la machine de chargement *m* des éléments *m* combustibles
– *fuel-handling hoists*
28 la piscine de stockage *m*
– *fuel storage*
29 la conduite de caloporteur *m*
– *coolant flow passage*
30 la conduite d'eau *f* d'alimentation *f*
– *feedwater line*
31 la conduite de vapeur *f* vive
– *prime steam line*
32 le sas personnel
– *manway*
33 le groupe turbo-alternateur
– *turbogenerator set*
34 l'alternateur *m* triphasé
– *turbogenerator*
35 le condenseur
– *condenser*
36 le bâtiment annexe
– *service building*
37 la cheminée d'évacuation *f*
– *exhaust gas stack*
38 le pont roulant circulaire
– *polar crane*
39 la tour de refroidissement *m*, un réfrigérant atmosphérique
– *cooling tower, a dry cooling tower*
40 le réacteur à eau *f* sous pression *f* [schéma *m* de principe *m*]
– *pressurized-water system*
41 le réacteur
– *reactor*
42 le circuit primaire
– *primary circuit (primary loop)*
43 la pompe primaire
– *circulation pump (recirculation pump)*
44 l'échangeur *m* de chaleur *f* (le générateur de vapeur *f*)
– *heat exchanger (steam generator)*
45 le circuit secondaire (le circuit eau *f* - vapeur *f*)
– *secondary circuit (secondary loop, feedwater steam circuit)*
46 la turbine à vapeur *f*
– *steam turbine*
47 l'alternateur *m*
– *generator*
48 le système de refroidissement *m*
– *cooling system*
49 le réacteur à eau *f* bouillante [schéma *m* de principe *m*]
– *boiling water system [diagram]*
50 le réacteur
– *reactor*
51 le circuit de vapeur *f* d'eau *f*
– *steam and recirculation water flow paths*
52 la turbine à vapeur *f*
– *steam turbine*
53 l'alternateur *m*
– *generator*
54 la pompe de recirculation *f*
– *circulation pump (recirculation pump)*
55 le système de refroidissement *m* (le refroidissement à circuit *m* ouvert, le refroidissement direct)
– *coolant system (cooling with water from river)*
56 le stockage de déchets *m* nucléaires dans une mine de sel *m*
– ***radioactive waste storage in salt mine***
57-68 les données *f* géologiques d'une mine de sel *m* aménagée pour le stockage de déchets *m* radioactifs
– *geological structure of abandoned salt mine converted for disposal of radioactive waste (nuclear waste)*
57 le keuper inférieur
– *Lower Keuper*
58 le calcaire conchylien supérieur
– *Upper Muschelkalk*
59 le calcaire conchylien moyen
– *Middle Muschelkalk*
60 le calcaire conchylien inférieur
– *Lower Muschelkalk*
61 le socle de grès *m* bigarré
– *Bunter downthrow*
62 les résidus *m* de lixiviation *f* du zechstein (permien *m* supérieur)
– *residue of leached (lixiviated) Zechstein (Upper Permian)*
63 le sel de roche *f* de l'Aller
– *Aller rock salt*
64 le sel de roche *f* de la Leine
– *Leine rock salt*
65 la veine de Stassfurt (la veine de sel *m* potassique)
– *Stassfurt seam (potash salt seam, potash salt bed)*
66 le sel de roche *f* de Stassfurt
– *Stassfurt salt*
67 l'anhydrite *m* limite
– *grenzanhydrite*
68 la glaise de zechstein *m*
– *Zechstein shale*
69 le puits
– *shaft*
70 les installations *f* du jour
– *minehead buildings*
71 la chambre de stockage *m*
– *storage chamber*
72 le stockage des déchets *m* à activité *f* moyenne
– *storage of medium-active waste in salt mine*
73 l'étage *m* 511 m
– *511 m level*
74 la paroi de protection *f* contre les radiations *f*
– *protective screen (anti-radiation screen)*
75 le hublot en verre *m* au plomb *m*
– *lead glass window*
76 la chambre de stockage *m*
– *storage chamber*
77 le fût cerclé contenant les déchets *m* radioactifs
– *drum containing radioactive waste*
78 la caméra de télévision *f*
– *television camera*
79 la salle de manutention *f*
– *charging chamber*
80 le panneau de commande *f*
– *control desk (control panel)*
81 le système d'évacuation *f* d'air *m*
– *upward ventilator*
82 le château blindé
– *shielded container*
83 l'étage *m* 490 m
– *490 m level*

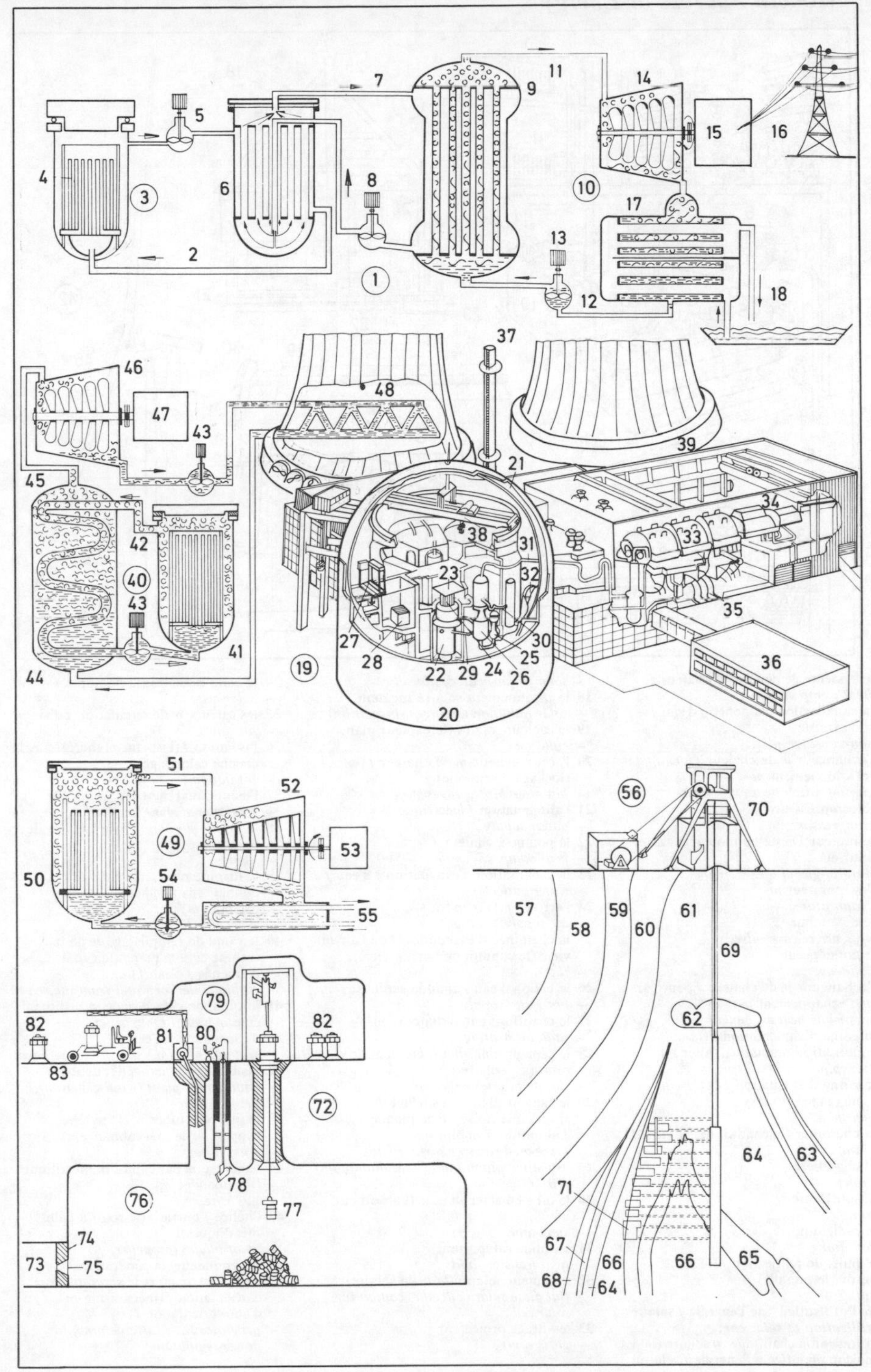
1
2
3
4
5
6
7
8
9
10
11
12
13
14
15
16
17
18
19
20
21
22
23
24
25
26
27
28
29
30
31
32
33
34
35
36
37
38
39
40
41
42
43
44
45
46
47
48
49
50
51
52
53
54
55
56
57
58
59
60
61
62
63
64
65
66
67
68
69
70
71
72
73
74
75
76
77
78
79
80
81
82
83

155 Nouvelles sources d'énergie (énergies nouvelles)
Modern Sources of Energy

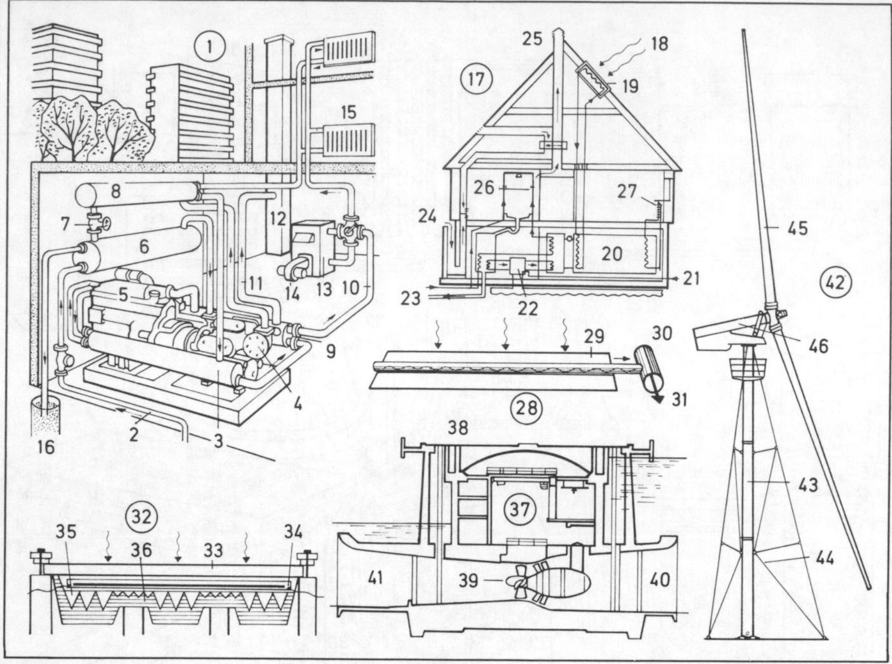

1 le système de pompe *f* à chaleur *f*
– ***heat pump system***
2 la canalisation d'amenée *f* d'eau *f* souterraine
– *source water inlet*
3 l'échangeur *m* de chaleur *f* à eau *f* de refroidissement *m*
– *cooling water heat exchanger*
4 le compresseur
– *compressor*
5 le moteur Diesel ou moteur à gaz *m* naturel
– *natural-gas or diesel engine*
6 l'évaporateur *m*
– *evaporator*
7 le détendeur
– *pressure release valve*
8 le condenseur
– *condenser*
9 l'échangeur *m* de chaleur *f* pour gaz *m* d'échappement *m*
– *waste-gas heat exchanger*
10 la gaine d'alimentation *f* (la canalisation montante, l'aller *m*)
– *flow pipe*
11 la gaine d'évacuation *f* de l'air *m* vicié (gaz *m* brûlés)
– *vent pipe*
12 la cheminée (le conduit des fumées *f*)
– *chimney*
13 la chaudière
– *boiler*
14 la soufflante
– *fan*
15 le radiateur
– *radiator*
16 le puits de réinjection *f* (le puits perdu, le puisard)
– *sink*
17-36 l'utilisation *f* de l'énergie *f* solaire
– ***utilization of solar energy***
17 la maison à chauffage *m* solaire (la maison chauffée à l'énergie *f* solaire)
– *solar (solar-heated) house*
18 le rayonnement solaire incident
– *solar radiation (sunlight, insolation)*
19 le capteur solaire (le capteur plan)
– *collector*
20 l'accumulateur *m* de chaleur *f* (le stockage thermique)
– *hot reservoir (heat reservoir)*
21 l'alimentation *f* électrique
– *power supply*
22 la pompe à chaleur *f*
– *heat pump*
23 la canalisation d'évacuation *f* d'eau *f*
– *water outlet*
24 l'arrivée *f* d'air *m* frais
– *air supply*
25 la cheminée d'évacuation *f* de l'air *m* vicié (le conduit de l'air *m* vicié)
– *flue*
26 le ballon d'eau *f* chaude sanitaire
– *hot water supply*
27 le chauffage par radiateurs *m*
– *radiator heating*
28 le capteur plan *m*, un élément de centrale *f* solaire
– *flat plate solar collector*
29 le capteur plan *m* à surface *f* absorbante noire (avec plaque *f* d'aluminium *m* bitumée)
– *blackened receiver surface with asphalted aluminium (*Am.* aluminum) foil*
30 le tube en acier *m* noir (l'absorbeur *m*)
– *steel tube*
31 le fluide caloporteur
– *heat transfer fluid*
32 le capteur solaire (la tuile solaire)
– *flat plate solar collector, containing solar cell*
33 le vitrage protecteur
– *glass cover*
34 la cellule solaire (la photopile)
– *solar cell*
35 les canaux *m* de circulation *f* d'air *m*
– *air ducts*
36 l'isolation *f* (l'isolant *m* thermique, la couche calorifuge)
– *insulation*
37 l'usine *f* marémotrice [coupe *f*]
– ***tidal power plant*** *[section]*
38 la digue de retenue *f* (le barrage de séparation *f*)
– *dam*
39 la turbine réversible (le bulbe à double sens *m*, l'hélice *f* à pales *f* orientables)
– *reversible turbine*
40 le canal de remplissage *m* de la turbine côté *m* mer *f* (le canal d'amenée *f* d'eau *f*)
– *turbine inlet for water from the sea*
41 le canal de vidage *m* de la turbine côté *m* bassin *m* (le canal d'évacuation *f* d'eau *f*)
– *turbine inlet for water from the basin*
42 l'éolienne *f* (l'aérogénérateur *m*)
– ***wind power plant*** *(wind generator, aerogenerator)*
43 le pylône à tubes *m* (le pylône support *m*, le mât tubulaire)
– *truss tower*
44 l'ancrage *m* par câbles *m* métalliques (l'haubanage *m*)
– *guy wire*
45 l'hélice *f* bipale *f* (le rotor à pales *f* métalliques)
– *rotor blades (propeller)*
46 le générateur (la génératrice, l'alternateur *m*) et le servo-moteur d'orientation *f* (mécanisme *m* d'auto-orientation *f*)
– *generator with variable pitch for power regulation*

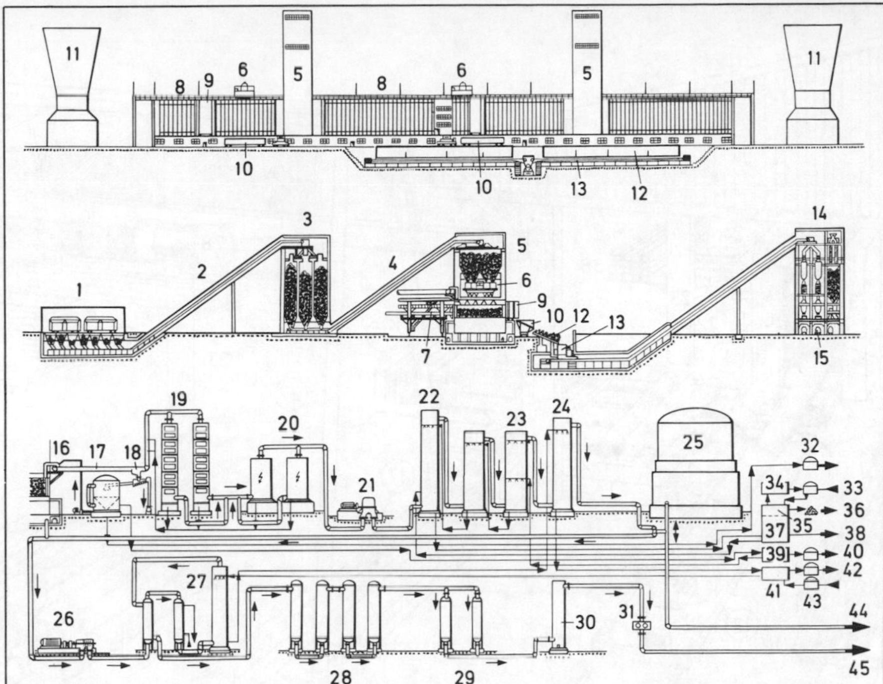

1-15 la cokerie
– ***coking plant***
1 le déchargement du charbon à coke *m* (du charbon de carbonisation *f*)
– *dumping of coking coal*
2 le transporteur à bande *f* (le transporteur à courroie *f*)
– *belt conveyor*
3 le silo de charbons *m* à coke *m*
– *service bunker*
4 le transporteur de la tour à charbon *m*
– *coal tower conveyor*
5 la tour à charbon *m*
– *coal tower*
6 le wagon de chargement *m* (le chariot de chargement *m*)
– *larry car (larry, charging car)*
7 la défourneuse à coke *m*
– *pusher ram*
8 la batterie de fours *m* à coke *m*
– *battery of coke ovens*
9 le chariot guide-coke *m*
– *coke guide*
10 le chariot d'extinction *f* (le chariot extincteur) avec locomotive *f*
– *quenching car, with engine*
11 la tour d'extinction *f* du coke
– *quenching tower*
12 la rampe de défournement *m* du coke (l'aire *f* des fours *m* à coke *m*)
– *coke loading bay (coke wharf)*
13 le transporteur de l'aire *f* des fours *m* à coke *m*
– *coke side bench*
14 l'installation *f* de criblage *m* (ou de triage *m*) du coke grossier et du coke fin (menu coke *m*)
– *screening of lump coal and culm*
15 le chargement du coke
– *coke loading*

16-45 le traitement du gaz de cokerie *f*
– ***coke-oven gas processing***
16 la sortie du gaz des fours *m* à coke *m*
– *discharge (release) of gas from the coke ovens*
17 le collecteur de gaz *m*
– *gas-collecting main*
18 l'extraction *f* du goudron
– *coal tar extraction*
19 le refroidisseur de gaz *m*
– *gas cooler*
20 l'électrofiltre *m*
– *electrostatic precipitator*
21 l'extracteur *m* de gaz *m*
– *gas extractor*
22 le laveur (le scrubber) d'acide *m* sulfhydrique (d'hydrogène *m* sulfuré)
– *hydrogen sulphide (Am. hydrogen sulfide) scrubber (hydrogen sulphide wet collector)*
23 le laveur (le scrubber) d'ammoniac *m*
– *ammonia scrubber (ammonia wet collector)*
24 le laveur (le scrubber) de benzène *m*
– *benzene (benzol) scrubber*
25 le réservoir collecteur *m* de gaz *m*
– *gas holder*
26 le compresseur de gaz *m*
– *gas compressor*
27 le débenzolage par réfrigérant *m* et échangeur *m* de chaleur *f*
– *debenzoling by cooler and heat exchanger*
28 la désulfuration du gaz comprimé
– *desulphurization (Am. desulfurization) of pressure gas*
29 le refroidissement du gaz
– *gas cooling*
30 le séchage du gaz
– *gas drying*
31 le compteur à gaz *m*
– *gas meter*
32 le réservoir de goudron *m* brut
– *crude tar tank*
33 l'alimentation *f* en acide *m* sulfurique
– *sulphuric acid (Am. sulfuric acid) supply*
34 la production d'acide *m* sulfurique
– *production of sulphuric acid (Am. sulfuric acid)*
35 la production de sulfate *m* d'ammonium *m*
– *production of ammonium sulphate (Am. ammonium sulfate)*
36 le sulfate d'ammonium *m*
– *ammonium sulphate (Am. ammonium sulfate)*
37 l'installation *f* de régénération *f* des produits *m* de lavage *m*
– *recovery plant for recovering the scrubbing agents*
38 l'évacuation *f* des eaux *f* résiduaires
– *waste water discharge*
39 la déphénolisation de l'eau *f* ammoniacale
– *phenol extraction from the gas water*
40 le réservoir de phénol *m* brut
– *crude phenol tank*
41 la production de benzène *m* brut
– *production of crude benzol (crude benzene)*
42 le réservoir de benzène *m* brut
– *crude benzol (crude benzene) tank*
43 le réservoir d'huile *f* de lavage *m*
– *scrubbing oil tank*
44 la conduite de gaz *m* basse pression *f* [B.P.]
– *low-pressure gas main*
45 la conduite de gaz *m* haute pression *f* [H.P.]
– *high-pressure gas main*

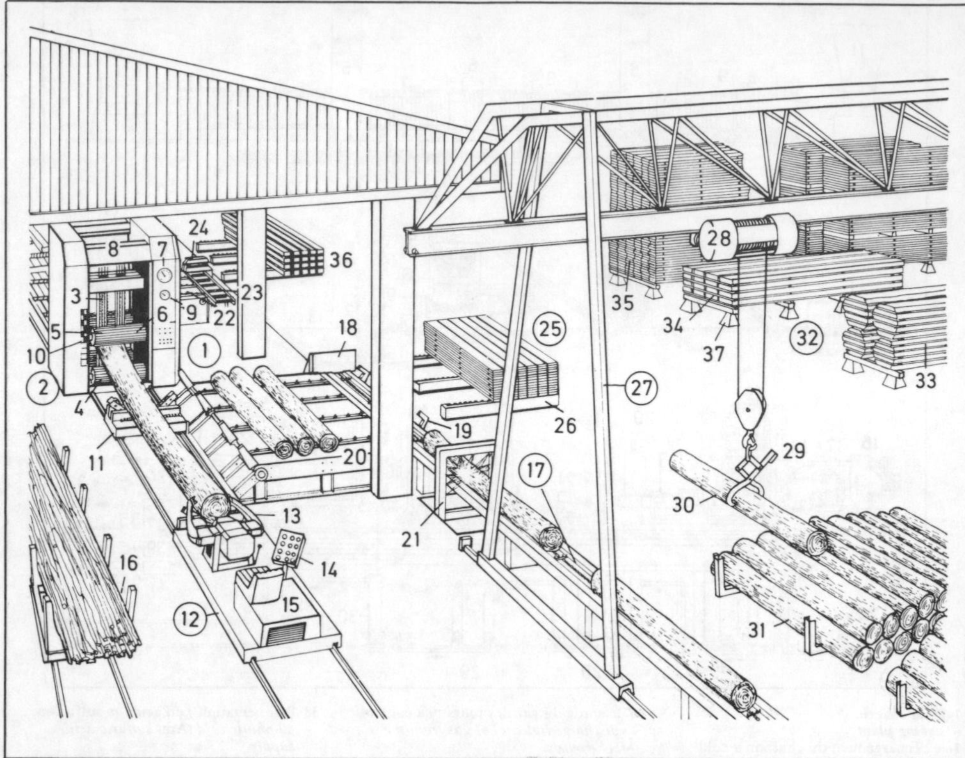

1 la scierie
– *sawmill*
2 la scie verticale (à châssis *m*) à lames *f* multiples
– *vertical frame saw (*Am. *gang mill)*
3 les lames *f* de scie *f*
– *saw blades*
4 le rouleau entraîneur cannelé
– *feed roller*
5 le rouleau guide *m* (le rouleau grimpant)
– *guide roller*
6 la cannelure
– *fluting (grooving, grooves)*
7 le manomètre de pression *f* d'huile *f* (l'indicateur *m* de pression *f* d'huile *f*)
– *oil pressure gauge (*Am. *gage)*
8 le châssis de scie *f* (le cadre porte-lames *m*)
– *saw frame*
9 l'indicateur *m* d'avance *f* de coupe *f*
– *feed indicator*
10 l'échelle *f* de hauteur *f* de coupe *f*
– *log capacity scale*
11 le chariot auxiliaire
– *auxiliary carriage*
12 le chariot de serrage *m* (à griffes *f*)
– *carriage*
13 la pince de serrage *m* (les griffes *f*)
– *log grips*
14 le boîtier de télécommande *f*
– *remote control panel*
15 le bloc moteur *m* (le système d'entraînement *m* du chariot de serrage *m*)
– *carriage motor*
16 le chariot de déchets *m* de bois *m* (planchettes *f*, éclats *m* de bois *m*, copeaux *m*)
– *truck for splinters (splints)*
17 le convoyeur de billes *f* (la chaîne d'avancement *m*)
– *endless log chain (*Am. *jack chain)*
18 la plaque de butée *f* (le butoir, le heurtoir)
– *stop plate*
19 l'éjecteur *m* de billes *f*
– *log-kicker arms*
20 le convoyeur (le transporteur) transversal
– *cross conveyor*
21 le laveur
– *washer (washing machine)*
22 le convoyeur (le transporteur) transversal de bois *m* scié à chaîne *f* sans fin *f*
– *cross chain conveyor for sawn timber*
23 le chemin de roulement *m*
– *roller table*
24 la scie de délignage *m*
– *undercut swing saw*
25 la pile de planches *f* (l'empilage *m*)
– *piling*
26 le support à rouleaux *m*
– *roller trestles*
27 la grue à portique *m*
– *gantry crane*
28 le moteur de grue *f*
– *crane motor*
29 la pince de serrage *m* orientable (le grappin)
– *pivoted log grips*
30 la grume (le bois de grume *f*, le bois rond)
– *roundwood (round timber)*
31 le dépôt de grumes *f* (le tas de grumes *f* sélectionnées)
– *log dump*
32 le parc de planches *f* (le dépôt de bois *m* débité)
– *squared timber store*
33 les plots (le sciage en plots *m* reproduisant la bille)
– *sawn logs*
34 les madriers *m*
– *planks*
35 les planches *f*
– *boards (planks)*
36 le bois équarri (les poutrelles *f*, les traverses *f*)
– *squared timber*
37 le support d'empilage *m* en ciment *m*
– *stack bearer*

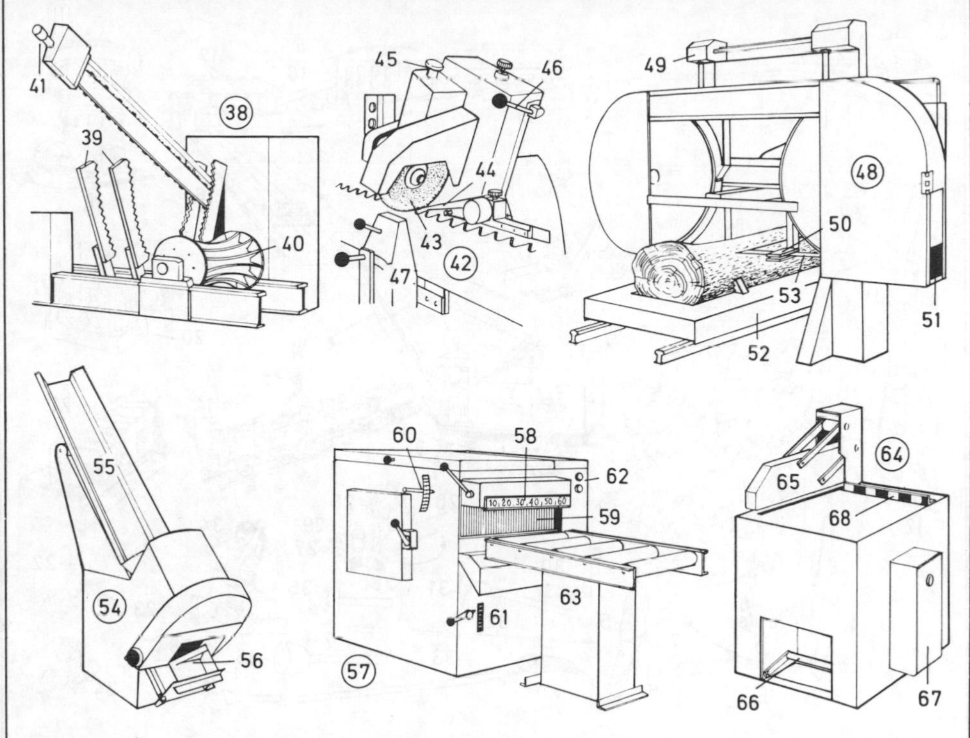

38 la tronçonneuse à chaîne *f* automatique
– *automatic cross-cut chain saw*
39 les pièces *f* d'appui *m*
– *log grips*
40 le rouleau entraîneur *m*
– *feed roller*
41 le tendeur de chaîne *f*
– *chain-tensioning device*
42 l'affûteuse *f* (la machine à affûter les lames *f* de scie *f*)
– *saw-sharpening machine*
43 la meule
– *grinding wheel (teeth grinder)*
44 le doigt d'entraînement *m*
– *feed pawl*
45 le dispositif d'ajustage *m* de la meule
– *depth adjustment for the teeth grinder*
46 le levier de débrayage *m* de l'arbre *m* porte-meule *m*
– *lifter (lever) for the grinder chuck*
47 le dispositif de serrage *m* de la lame de scie *f*
– *holding device for the saw blade*
48 la scie à ruban *m* horizontale
– *horizontal bandsaw for sawing logs*
49 le dispositif de réglage *m* de la hauteur de coupe *f*
– *height adjustment*
50 le frotteur de copeaux *m*
– *chip remover*
51 l'aspirateur de copeaux *m*
– *chip extractor*
52 le chariot transporteur
– *carriage*
53 la lame de scie *f* à ruban *m*
– *bandsaw blade*
54 la scie automatique pour le débitage du bois de chauffage *m*
– *automatic blocking saw*
55 la goulotte d'alimentation *f*
– *feed channel*
56 le bloc d'éjection *f*
– *discharge opening*
57 la scie de délignage *m* à deux lames *f*
– *twin edger (double edger)*
58 l'échelle *f* d'épaisseur *f* de débit *m*
– *breadth scale (width scale)*
59 l'écran *m* antiprotection (les lamelles *f* de protection *f*)
– *kick-back guard (plates)*
60 l'échelle *f* de hauteur *f* de trait *m*
– *height scale*
61 l'échelle *f* d'avance *f* de coupe *f*
– *in-feed scale*
62 les voyants *m* lumineux
– *indicator lamps*
63 la table porte-pièces *m*
– *feed table*
64 la tronçonneuse animée d'un mouvement de va-et-vient *m*
– *undercut swing saw*
65 le presseur automatique (avec carter *m* protecteur)
– *automatic hold-down with protective hood*
66 l'interrupteur *m* au pied
– *foot switch*
67 le bloc de distribution *f*
– *distribution board (panelboard)*
68 la butée longitudinale
– *length stop*

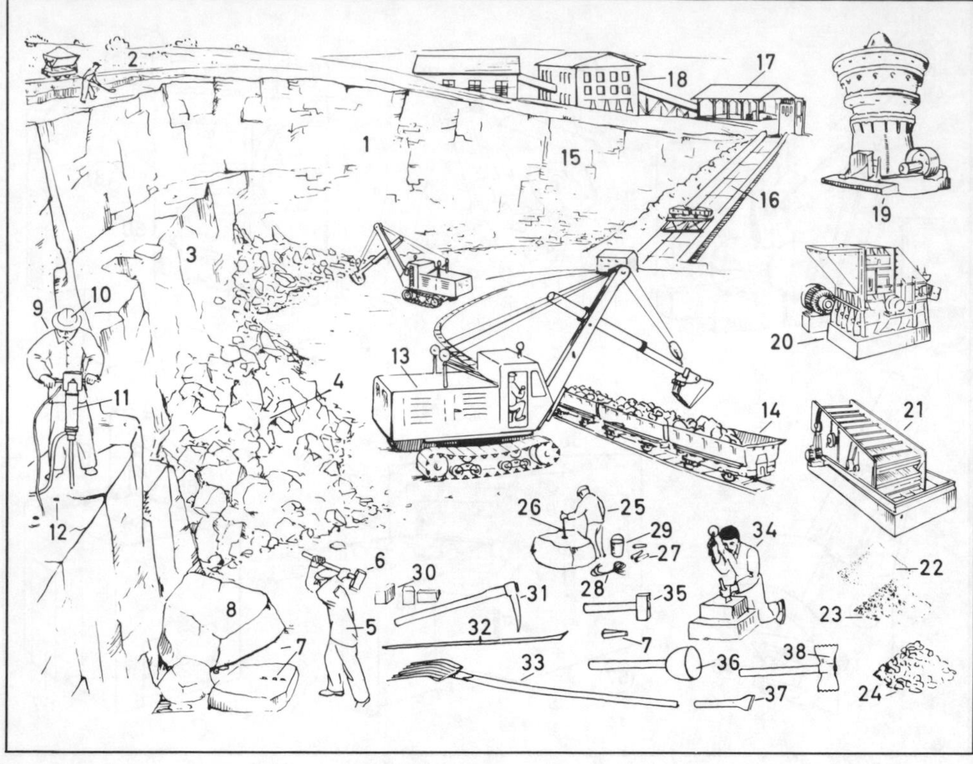

1 **la carrière,** une exploitation à ciel *m* ouvert
– ***quarry**, an open-cast working*

2 les terrains *m* morts
– *overburden*

3 la face d'abattage *m*
– *working face*

4 le déblai
– *loose rock pile (blasted rock)*

5 le carrier
– *quarryman (quarrier), a quarry worker*

6 la masse de carrier *m*
– *sledge hammer*

7 le coin
– *wedge*

8 le bloc de roche *f*
– *block of stone*

9 le foreur
– *driller*

10 le casque protecteur
– *safety helmet*

11 le marteau pneumatique (la perforatrice de roche *f*)
– *hammer drill (hard-rock drill)*

12 le trou foré
– *borehole*

13 l'excavateur *m* universel
– *universal excavator*

14 le wagonnet de grande capacité *f* (le truc)
– *large-capacity truck*

15 la paroi rocheuse
– *rock face*

16 le monte-charge incliné
– *inclined hoist*

17 le préconcasseur
– *primary crusher*

18 l'atelier *m* de concassage *m*
– *stone-crushing plant*

19 le concasseur giratoire primaire; *anal.:* le concasseur giratoire
– *coarse rotary (gyratory) crusher;* sim.: *fine rotary (gyratory) crusher*

20 le concasseur à mâchoires *f*
– *hammer crusher (impact crusher)*

21 le crible vibrant
– *vibrating screen*

22 le sable de broyage *m*
– *screenings (fine dust)*

23 le gravier de concassage *m*
– *stone chippings*

24 les pierres *f* concassées (le cailloutis)
– *crushed stone*

25 l'artificier *m*
– *shot firer*

26 la jauge
– *measuring rod*

27 la cartouche
– *blasting cartridge*

28 le cordon d'allumage *m*
– *fuse (blasting fuse)*

29 le seau de sable *m* de remplissage *m* du trou de mine *f*
– *plugging sand (stemming sand) bucket*

30 la pierre de taille *f*
– *dressed stone*

31 le pic
– *pick*

32 le levier (le pied de chèvre *f*, la pince)
– *crowbar (pinch bar)*

33 la fourche à cailloux *m*
– *fork*

34 le tailleur de pierres *f*
– *stonemason*

35-38 **les outils *m* du tailleur de pierres *f***
– ***stonemason's tools***

35 la massette
– *stonemason's hammer*

36 le tampon (la batte)
– *mallet*

37 la gradine
– *drove chisel (drove, boaster, broad chisel)*

38 le rustique
– *dressing axe* (Am. *ax)*

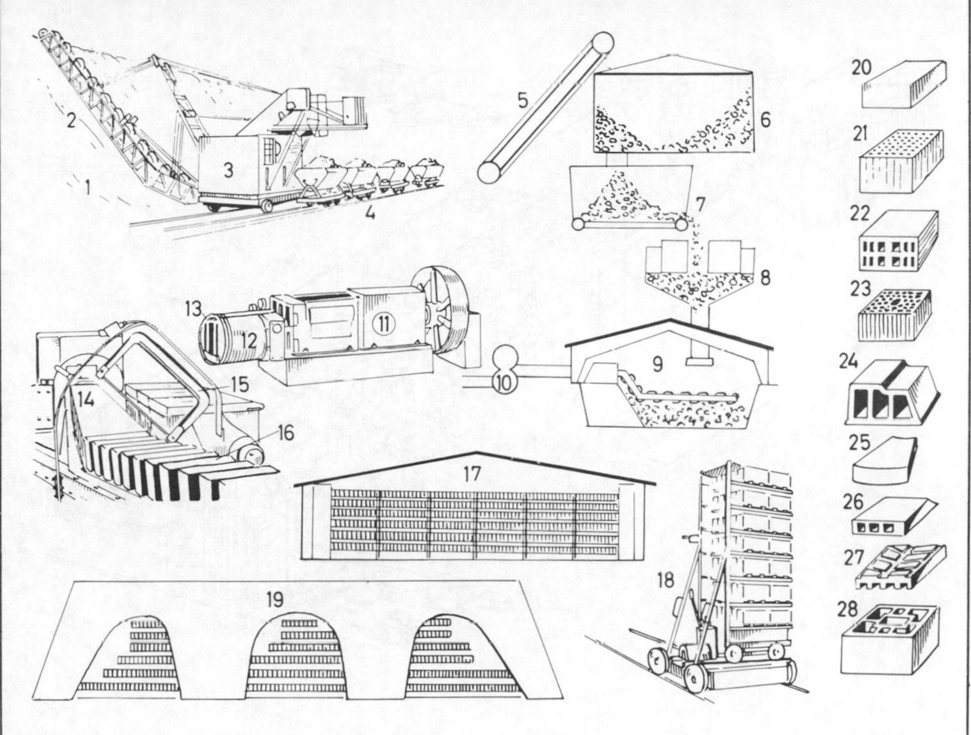

1 la glaisière (la carrière d'argile *f*)
– *clay pit*
2 la glaise, une argile brute
– *loam, an impure clay (raw clay)*
3 l'excavateur *m* de terrains *m* morts, un excavateur de grande capacité *f*
– *overburden excavator, a large-scale excavator*
4 le chemin de fer *m* à voie *f* étroite
– *narrow-gauge (Am. narrow-gage) track system*
5 le monte-charge incliné
– *inclined hoist*
6 la fosse
– *souring chambers*
7 le distributeur linéaire (distributeur *m*)
– *box feeder (feeder)*
8 le broyeur à meules *f* verticales (broyeur *m*)
– *edge runner mill (edge mill, pan grinding mill)*
9 le broyeur à cylindres *m*
– *rolling plant*
10 le mélangeur à double hélice *f*
– *double-shaft trough mixer (mixer)*
11 la mouleuse (l'étireuse *f*)
– *extrusion press (brick-pressing machine)*
12 la chambre à vide *m*
– *vacuum chamber*
13 la filière
– *die*
14 le boudin d'argile *f* (le ruban d'argile *f*)
– *clay column*
15 le coupeur (la coupeuse)
– *cutter (brick cutter)*
16 la brique crue (la brique verte)
– *unfired brick (green brick)*
17 la chambre de séchage *m*
– *drying shed*
18 le chariot élévateur *m* (chariot *m* déposeur)
– *mechanical finger car (stacker truck)*
19 le four rond (four *m* à briques *f*)
– *circular kiln (brick kiln)*
20 la brique pleine (brique *f* de mur *m*, brique *f* cuite, brique *f* de maçonnerie *f*)
– *solid brick (building brick)*
21-22 les briques *f* creuses
– *perforated bricks and hollow blocks*
21 la brique à perforation *f* verticale
– *perforated brick with vertical perforations*
22 la brique creuse tubulaire
– *hollow clay block with horizontal perforations*
23 la brique perforée en losanges *m*
– *hollow clay block with vertical perforations*
24 la brique pontée de plancher *m*
– *floor brick*
25 la brique de cheminée *f* (brique *f* radiale)
– *compass brick (radial brick, radiating brick)*
26 le hourdis
– *hollow flooring block*
27 la brique de pavement *m*
– *paving brick*
28 le boisseau
– *cellular brick [for fireplaces] (chimney brick)*

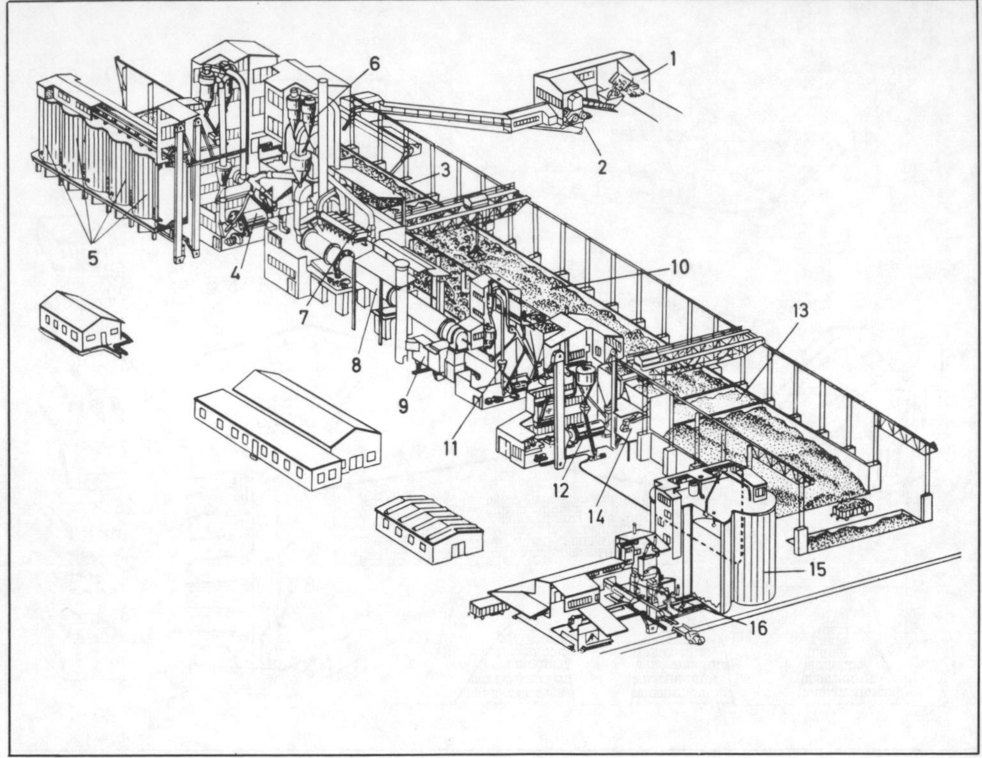

1 les matières *f* premières (calcaire *m*, argile *f* et calcaire *m* marneux)
– *raw materials (limestone, clay and, marl)*
2 le concasseur à marteaux *m*
– *hammer crusher (hammer mill)*
3 le parc de matières *f* premières
– *raw material store*
4 le broyeur de matière *f* pour broyage *m* et séchage *m* simultanés des matières *f* premières avec utilisation *f* des gaz *m* perdus de l'échangeur *m* de chaleur *f*
– *raw mill for simultaneously grinding and drying the raw materials with exhaust gas from the heat exchanger*
5 les silos *m* de farine *f* crue (silos *m* d'homogénéisation *f*)
– *raw meal silos*
6 l'échangeur *m* de chaleur *f* (l'échangeur *m* de chaleur *f* à cyclone *m*)
– *heat exchanger (cyclone heat exchanger)*
7 le dépoussiéreur (un électrofiltre pour les gaz *m* perdus de l'échangeur *m* de chaleur *f*, après leur passage *m* dans le broyeur de matière *f*)
– *dust collector (an electrostatic precipitator) for the heat exchanger exhaust from the raw mill*
8 le four rotatif
– *rotary kiln*
9 le refroidisseur de clinker *m*
– *clinker cooler*
10 le parc de clinker *m*
– *clinker store*
11 la soufflante d'air *m* primaire
– *primary air blower*
12 le broyeur de ciment *m*
– *cement-grinding mill*
13 le parc à gypse *m*
– *gypsum store*
14 le broyeur à gypse *m*
– *gypsum crusher*
15 le silo à ciment *m*
– *cement silo*
16 l'ensacheuse *f* de ciment *m* pour sacs *m* en papier *m* à valve *f*
– *cement-packing plant for paper sacks*

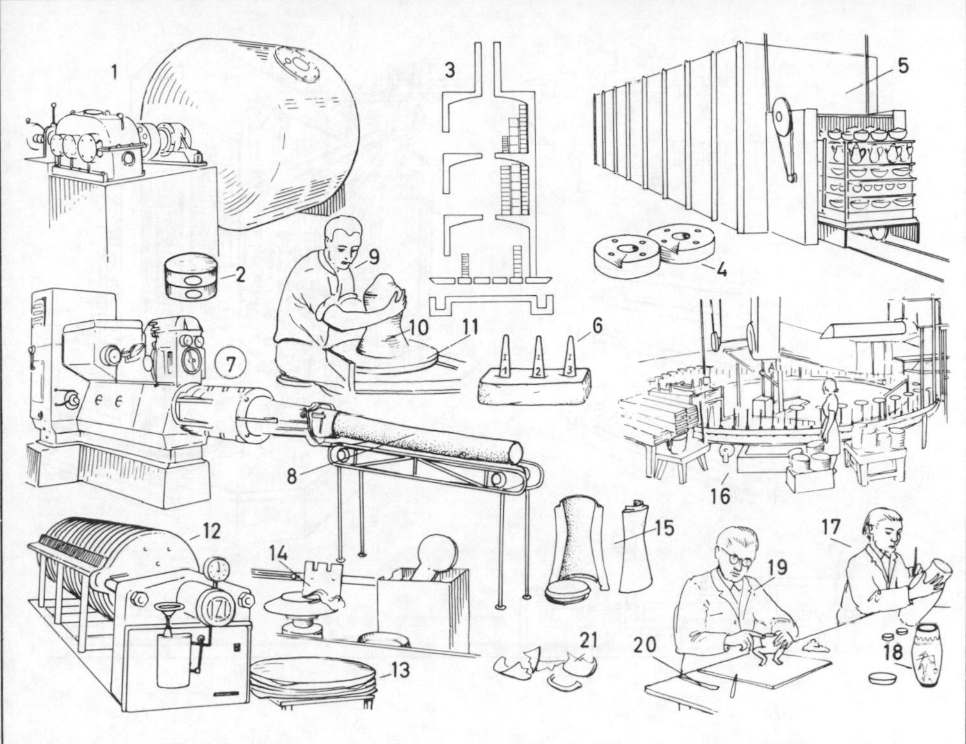

1 le broyeur tubulaire (broyeur *m* à boulets *m*) pour la préparation de la pâte par voie *f* humide
– *grinding cylinder (ball mill) for the preparation of the raw material in water*

2 les capsules *f* témoins avec une ouverture pour observation *f* de la cuisson
– *sample sagger (saggar, seggar), with aperture for observing the firing process*

3 le four rond [schéma]
– *bottle kiln (beehive kiln) [diagram]*

4 le moule de chauffe *f*
– *firing mould* (Am. *mold)*

5 le four tunnel *m*
– *tunnel kiln*

6 le cône de Seger (le cône pyrométrique) pour la mesure de températures *f* élevées
– *Seger cone (pyrometric cone,* Am. *Orton cone) for measuring high temperatures*

7 la presse à vide *m*, une presse d'extrusion *f* (produisant le colombin ou boudin *m*)
– *de-airing pug mill (de-airing pug press), an extrusion press*

8 le colombin de pâte *f* (le boudin de pâte *f*)
– *clay column*

9 le porcelainier ébauchant une pièce *f*
– *thrower throwing a ball (bat) of clay*

10 la masse d'argile *f*
– *slug of clay*

11 le tour de porcelainier *m*; *anal.:* le tour de potier *m*
– *turntable;* sim.: *potter's wheel*

12 le filtre-presse
– *filter press*

13 le gâteau de filtre-presse *m*
– *filter cake*

14 le calibrage
– *jiggering, with a profiling tool;* sim.: *jollying*

15 le moule pour la barbotine
– *plaster mould* (Am. *mold) for slip casting*

16 la machine circulaire de couverte *f*
– *turntable glazing machine*

17 le peintre sur porcelaine *f*
– *porcelain painter (china painter)*

18 le vase peint à la main
– *hand-painted vase*

19 le réparateur (le modeleur)
– *repairer*

20 la spatule de modeleur *m*
– *pallet (modelling,* Am. *modeling, tool)*

21 les débris *m* de porcelaine *f* (les tessons *m*)
– *shards (sherds, potsherds)*

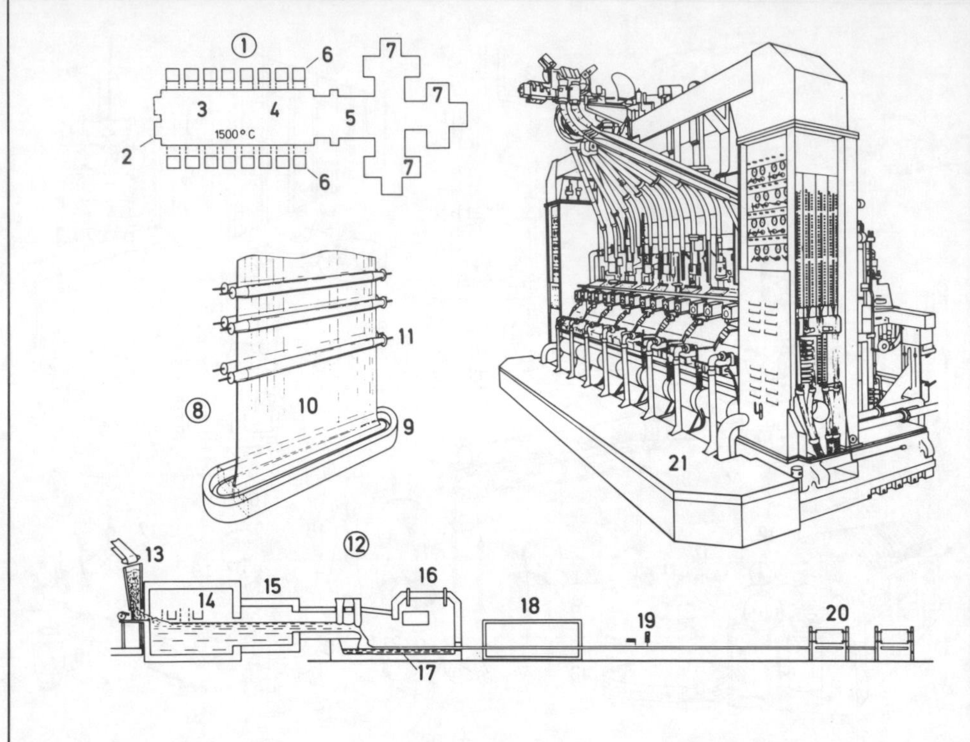

1-20 la production du verre à vitres (du verre plat)
– ***sheet glass production*** *(flat glass production)*
1 le four à verre *m* à vitres *f* Fourcault [schéma]
– *glass furnace (tank furnace) for the Fourcault process [diagram]*
2 les niches *f* d'enfournement *m* de la composition (du mélange vitrifiable)
– *filling end, for feeding in the batch (frit)*
3 le bassin de fusion *f* (le compartiment, la zone de fusion *f*)
– *melting bath*
4 le bassin d'affinage *m* (le compartiment, la zone d'affinage *m*)
– *refining bath (fining bath)*
5 l'avant-bassin *m*
– *working baths (working area)*
6 les brûleurs *m*
– *burners*
7 les étireuses *f* (les machines *f* d'étirage *m*)
– *drawing machines*
8 l'étireuse *f* Fourcault
– *Fourcault glass-drawing machine*
9 la débiteuse
– *slot*
10 la feuille de verre *m* ascendante
– *glass ribbon (ribbon of glass, sheet of glass) being drawn upwards*
11 les rouleaux *m* porteurs
– *rollers (drawing rolls)*
12 le procédé de verre *m* flotté (de verre *m* «float») [schéma]
– *float glass process*
13 le distributeur de composition *f*
– *batch (frit) feeder (funnel)*
14 le bassin de fusion *f*
– *melting bath*
15 la zone de braise *f*
– *cooling tank*
16 le bain de flottage *m* sous gaz *m* inerte
– *float bath in a protective inert-gas atmosphere*
17 l'étain *m* fondu
– *molten tin*
18 l'étenderie *f* à rouleaux *m* (la galerie de recuisson *f*)
– *annealing lehr*
19 le dispositif de coupe *f*
– *automatic cutter*
20 les empileuses *f*
– *stacking machines*
21 la machine «IS» (la machine sectionnelle), une machine de fabrication *f* du verre creux (verre *m* à bouteilles *f*)
– *IS (individual-section) machine, a bottle-making machine*

22-37 les procédés *m* **de soufflage** *m*
– ***blowing processes***
22 le procédé soufflé-soufflé
– *blow-and-blow process*
23 l'introduction *f* de la paraison
– *introduction of the gob of molten glass*
24 le perçage
– *first blowing*
25 le contre-soufflage
– *suction*
26 le transfert du moule ébaucheur au moule finisseur
– *transfer from the parison mould (Am. mold) to the blow mould (Am. mold)*
27 le réchauffage (l'uniformisation *f*)
– *reheating*
28 le soufflage (le moulage sous vide *m*)
– *blowing (suction, final shaping)*
29 la sortie du verre creux fini
– *delivery of the completed vessel*
30 le procédé pressé-soufflé
– *press-and-blow process*
31 l'introduction *f* de la paraison
– *introduction of the gob of molten glass*
32 le poinçon ébaucheur
– *plunger*
33 le pressage
– *pressing*

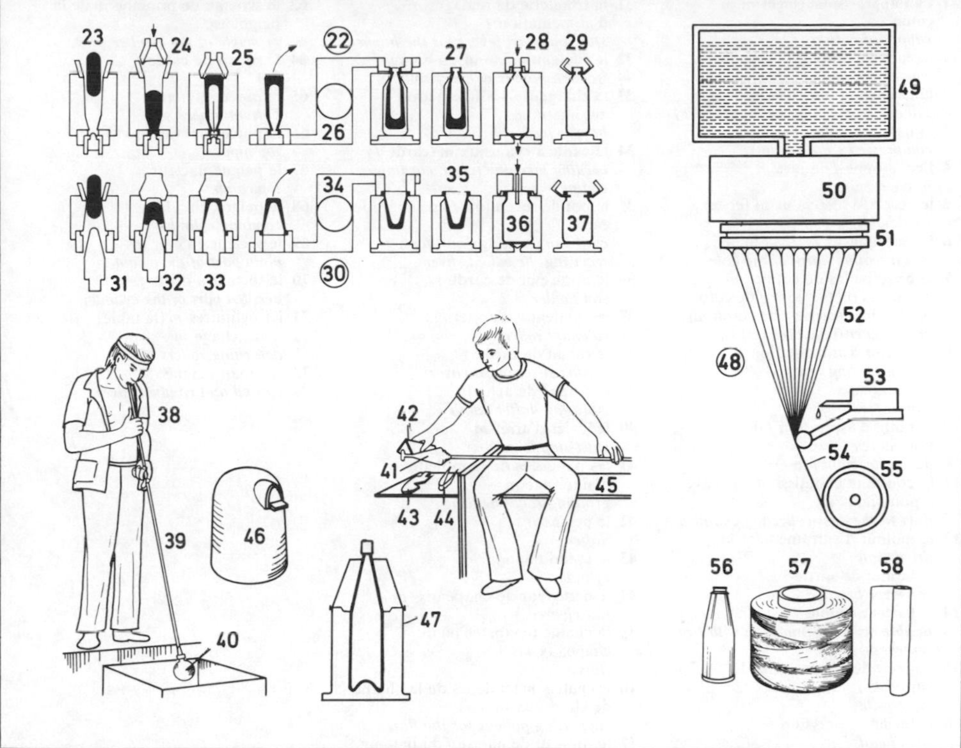

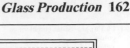

34 le transfert du moule ébaucheur au moule finisseur
– *transfer from the press mould* (Am. *mold*) *to the blow mould* (Am. *mold*)
35 le réchauffeur (l'uniformisation *f*)
– *reheating*
36 le soufflage par le vide
– *blowing (suction, final shaping)*
37 la sortie du verre creux fini
– *delivery of the completed vessel*
38-47 le travail manuel du verre creux (le soufflage à la bouche, le moulage par soufflage *m*)
– ***glassmaking*** *(glassblowing, glassblowing by hand, glass forming)*
38 le souffleur de verre *m*
– *glassmaker (glassblower)*
39 la canne du souffleur
– *blowing iron*
40 la paraison (le poste, l'ébauche *f*)
– *gob*
41 le verre à pied *m* soufflé à la bouche
– *hand-blown goblet*
42 les planchettes *f* pour formage *m* du pied de verre *m*
– *clappers for shaping the base (foot) of the goblet*
43 le calibre de verrier *m*
– *trimming tool*
44 les fers *m* à étrangler (les pinces *f* à étrangler)
– *tongs*
45 le banc de verrier *m*
– *glassmaker's chair (gaffer's chair)*
46 le pot fermé
– *covered glasshouse pot*
47 le moule pour soufflage *m* de l'ébauche *f*
– *mould (Am. mold), into which the parison is blown*
48-55 la production de verre *m* textile
– ***production of glass fibre*** (Am. *glass fiber)*
48 l'étirage *m* mécanique à travers des filières *f* (la production de fils *m* continus)
– *continuous filament process*
49 le four de fusion *f* du verre
– *glass furnace*
50 la cuve remplie de verre *m* fondu
– *bushing containing molten glass*
51 les tétons *m* de filière *f*
– *bushing tips*
52 les filaments *m* primaires de verre *m*
– *glass filaments*
53 l'ensimage *m*
– *sizing*
54 le fil (le filé) de verre *m*
– *strand (thread)*
55 la bobine
– *spool*
56-58 les produits *m* en verre *m* textile
– ***glass fibre*** (Am. *glass fiber) products*
56 le fil de silionne *f*
– *glass yarn (glass thread)*
57 le roving (le stratifil) en bobine *f*
– *sleeved glass yarn (glass thread)*
58 le feutre de verre *m*, le mat de verre *m*
– *glass wool*

1-13 l'approvisionnement *m* **en coton** *m*
– ***supply of cotton***
1 la capsule mûre du cotonnier
– *ripe cotton boll*
2 la cannette pour filés *m*
– *full cop (cop wound with weft yarn)*
3 la balle de coton *m* pressé
– *compressed cotton bale*
4 l'enveloppe *f* de jute *m*
– *jute wrapping*
5 le cerclage (cercle *m* en fer *m*)
– *steel band*
6 les marquages *m* de la balle
– *identification mark of the bale*
7 le brise-balles de cotons *m* mélangés (nettoyeuse *f* de coton *m*, dépoussiéreuse *f* de coton *m*)
– *bale opener (bale breaker)*
8 le tablier d'alimentation *f*
– *cotton-feeding brattice*
9 la chargeuse
– *cotton feed*
10 la hotte d'aspiration *f* des poussières *f*
– *dust extraction fan*
11 la conduite aboutissant à la cave à poussières *f*
– *duct to the dust-collecting chamber*
12 le moteur d'entraînement *m*
– *drive motor*
13 le tablier de sortie *f*
– *conveyor brattice*
14 le batteur double
– ***double scutcher*** *(machine with two scutchers)*
15 l'auge *f* des rouleaux *m* de nappe *f*
– *lap cradle*
16 le levier de pression *f*
– *rack head*
17 le levier de démarrage *m*
– *starting handle*
18 le volant de réglage *m* vertical du levier de pression *f*
– *handwheel, for raising and lowering the rack head*
19 la planche mobile guide-nappe *m*
– *movable lap-turner*
20 les rouleaux *m* presseurs
– *calender rollers*
21 le carter des deux tambours *m* perforés
– *cover for the perforated cylinders*
22 le canal d'aspiration *f* des poussières *f*
– *dust escape flue (dust discharge flue)*
23 les moteurs *m* d'entraînement *m*
– *drive motors (beater drive motors)*
24 l'arbre *m* d'entraînement *m* du volant batteur *m*
– *beater driving shaft*
25 le volant batteur *m* à trois règles *f*
– *three-blade beater (Kirschner beater)*
26 la grille à barreaux *m*
– *grid [for impurities to drop]*
27 le cylindre d'alimentation *f*
– *pedal roller (pedal cylinder)*
28 le levier régulateur d'alimentation *f*, un levier à pédale *f*
– *control lever for the pedal roller, a pedal lever*
29 le variateur de vitesse *f*
– *variable change-speed gear*
30 le carter des cônes *m*
– *cone drum box*
31 la tringlerie de réglages *m* d'alimentation *f*
– *stop and start levers for the hopper*
32 le rouleau presseur en bois *m*
– *wooden hopper delivery roller*
33 la chargeuse à alimentation *f* automatique
– *hopper feeder*
34 la carde à chapeaux *m* (carde *f*)
– ***carding machine*** *(card, carding engine)*
35 le pot de réception *f* du ruban de carde *f*
– *card can (carding can), for receiving the coiled sliver*
36 le porte-pot de carde *f*
– *can holder*
37 les rouleaux d'appel *m*
– *calender rollers*
38 le ruban de carde *f*
– *carded sliver (card sliver)*
39 le peigne détacheur
– *vibrating doffer comb*
40 le levier d'arrêt *m*
– *start-stop lever*
41 les paliers *m* de la molette d'aiguisage *m*
– *grinding-roller bearing*
42 le peigneur
– *doffer*
43 le grand tambour
– *cylinder*
44 le nettoyeur de chapeaux *m*
– *flat clearer*
45 la chaîne (chapelet *m*) de chapeaux *m*
– *flats*
46 les galets *m* tendeurs de la chaîne de chapeaux *m*
– *supporting pulleys for the flats*
47 le rouleau de nappe *f* du batteur
– *scutcher lap (carded lap)*
48 le guide du rouleau de nappe *f*
– *scutcher lap holder*
49 le moteur d'entraînement *m* à courroie *f* plate
– *drive motor with flat belt*
50 la poulie principale d'entraînement *m*
– *main drive pulley (fast-and-loose drive pulley)*
51 le schéma de principe *m* de la carde
– *principle of the card (of the carding engine)*
52 le cylindre d'alimentation *f*
– *fluted feed roller*
53 le briseur
– *licker-in (taker-in, licker-in roller)*
54 la grille du briseur
– *licker-in undercasing*
55 la grille du grand tambour
– *cylinder undercasing*
56 la peigneuse
– ***combing machine*** *(comber)*
57 la boîte à engrenage *m*
– *drive gearbox (driving gear)*
58 le rouleau de nappe *f* d'étirage *m*
– *laps ready for combing*
59 le serrage des rubans *m* de nappe *f*
– *calender rollers*
60 le banc d'étirage *m*
– *comber draw box*
61 le compteur
– *counter*
62 le support de ruban *m* peigné
– *coiler top*
63 le schéma de principe *m* de la peigneuse
– *principle of the comber*
64 le ruban de carde *f*
– *lap*
65 la pince inférieure
– *bottom nipper*
66 la pince supérieure
– *top nipper*
67 le peigne nacteur
– *top comb*
68 le peigne circulaire
– *combing cylinder*
69 le secteur en cuir *m*
– *plain part of the cylinder*
70 le secteur à dents *f*
– *needled part of the cylinder*
71 les cylindres *m* (la table) d'arrachage *m*
– *detaching rollers*
72 le ruban peigné
– *carded and combed sliver*

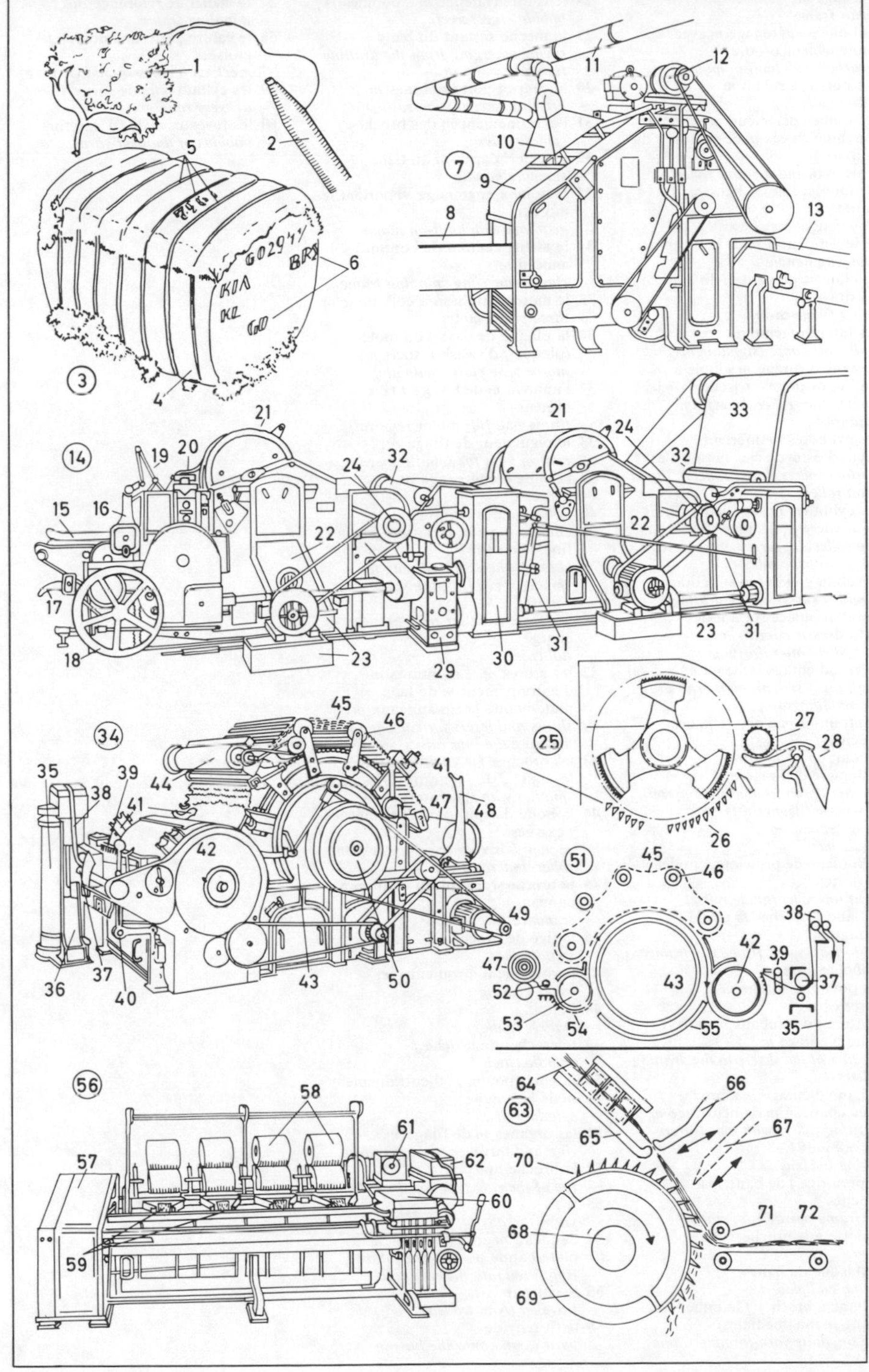
1
2
3
4
5
6
7
8
9
10
11
12
13
14
15
16
17
18
19
20
21
22
23
24
25
26
27
28
29
30
31
32
33
34
35
36
37
38
39
40
41
42
43
44
45
46
47
48
49
50
51
52
53
54
55
56
57
58
59
60
61
62
63
64
65
66
67
68
69
70
71
72

1 l'étirage *m*
– ***draw frame***
2 la boîte à engrenage *m* avec moteur *m* incorporé
– *gearbox with built-in motor*
3 les pots *m* à ruban *m*
– *sliver cans*
4 le rouleau détecteur, arrêtant la machine en cas *m* de rupture *f* du ruban
– *broken thread detector roller*
5 le doublage des rubans *m* de carde *f*
– *doubling of the slivers*
6 le levier d'arrêt *m* de la machine
– *stopping handle*
7 la planche de garde *f* du banc d'étirage *m*
– *draw frame cover*
8 les lampes *f* témoins
– *indicator lamps (signal lights)*
9 le banc d'étirage *m* simple à quatre cylindres *m* [schéma *m*]
– *simple four-roller draw frame [diagram]*
10 les cylindres *m* inférieurs (cylindres *m* d'acier *m* cannelés)
– *bottom rollers (lower rollers), fluted steel rollers*
11 les cylindres *m* supérieurs garnis de matière *f* plastique
– *top rollers (upper rollers) covered with synthetic rubber*
12 le ruban grossier avant étirage *m*
– *doubled slivers before drafting*
13 le ruban mince sortant des cylindres *m* étireurs
– *thin sliver after drafting*
14 le grand étirage [schéma *m*]
– *high-draft system (high-draft draw frame) [diagram]*
15 l'entonnoir *m* d'entrée *m* des mèches *f*
– *feeding-in of the sliver*
16 la lanière d'étirage *m*
– *leather apron (composition apron)*
17 la tringle (baguette *f*) de changement *m*
– *guide bar*
18 le rouleau de pression *f* (rouleau *m* flotteur)
– *light top roller (guide roller)*
19 le banc à broches *f* à grand étirage *m*
– *high-draft speed frame (fly frame, slubbing frame)*
20 les pots *m* d'étirage *m*
– *sliver cans*
21 l'entrée *f* des rubans *m* dans le banc d'étirage *m*
– *feeding of the slivers to the drafting rollers*
22 le banc d'étirage *m* à broches *f* avec chapeau *m* de nettoyage *m*
– *drafting rollers with top clearers*
23 les bobines *f*
– *roving bobbins*
24 l'opératrice *f* de banc *m* à broches *f*
– *fly frame operator (operative)*
25 l'ailette *f* de broche *f*
– *flyer*
26 le flasque du banc
– *frame end plate*
27 le banc à broches *f* intermédiaires (banc *m* intermédiaire)
– *intermediate yarn-forming frame*
28 le cantre (ratelier *m* à bobines *f*)
– *bobbin creel (creel)*
29 la mèche sortant du banc
– *roving emerging from the drafting rollers*
30 le chariot porte-bobines *m*
– *lifter rail (separating rail)*
31 l'entraînement *m* des broches *f*
– *spindle drive*
32 le levier d'arrêt *m* du banc
– *stopping handle*
33 la boîte à engrenage *m* portant le moteur
– *gearbox, with built-on motor*
34 **le métier continu** (le continu) **à anneau** *m*
– ***ring frame*** *(ring spinning frame)*
35 le moteur triphasé à collecteur *m*
– *three-phase motor*
36 la plaque de base *f* du moteur (plaque *f* d'assise *f*, socle *m*)
– *motor base plate (bedplate)*
37 l'anneau *m* de levage *m* du moteur
– *lifting bolt [for motor removal]*
38 le régulateur de filage *m*
– *control gear for spindle speed*
39 la boîte à engrenage *m*
– *gearbox*
40 la têtière des pignons *m* de change *m* pour variation *f* de la finesse du filé
– *change wheels for varying the spindle speed [to change the yarn count]*
41 le cantre (ratelier *m* à bobines *f*) chargé
– *full creel*
42 les arbres *m* et montants *m* d'entraînement *m* de la plate-bande porte-anneaux *m*
– *shafts and levers for raising and lowering the ring rail*
43 les broches *f* avec antimariages *m* (plaques *f* de séparation *f*)
– *spindles with separators*
44 la boîte d'aspiration *f* des mèches *f* cassées
– *suction box connected to the front roller underclearers*
45 **la broche standard** du continu à anneau *m*
– ***standard ring spindle***
46 la tige de broche *f*
– *spindle shaft*
47 le roulement à rouleaux *m*
– *roller bearing*
48 la noix
– *wharve (pulley)*
49 le crochet de broche *f*
– *spindle catch*
50 la noix (poulie *f*) d'entraînement *m* de la broche
– *spindle rail*
51 les organes *m* de filage *m*
– *ring and traveller* (Am. *traveler)*
52 la broche nue
– *top of the ring tube (of the bobbin)*
53 le fil
– *yarn (thread)*
54 l'anneau *m* encastré dans la plate-bande porte-anneaux *m*
– *ring fitted into the ring rail*
55 le curseur
– *traveller* (Am. *traveler)*
56 le fil renvidé
– *yarn wound onto the bobbin*
57 **le métier de retordage** *m*
– ***doubling frame***
58 le cantre garni de bobines *f* croisées
– *creel, with cross-wound cheeses*
59 les cylindres *m* de sortie *f*
– *delivery rollers*
60 les fuseaux *m* de fil *m* retors
– *bobbins of doubled yarn*

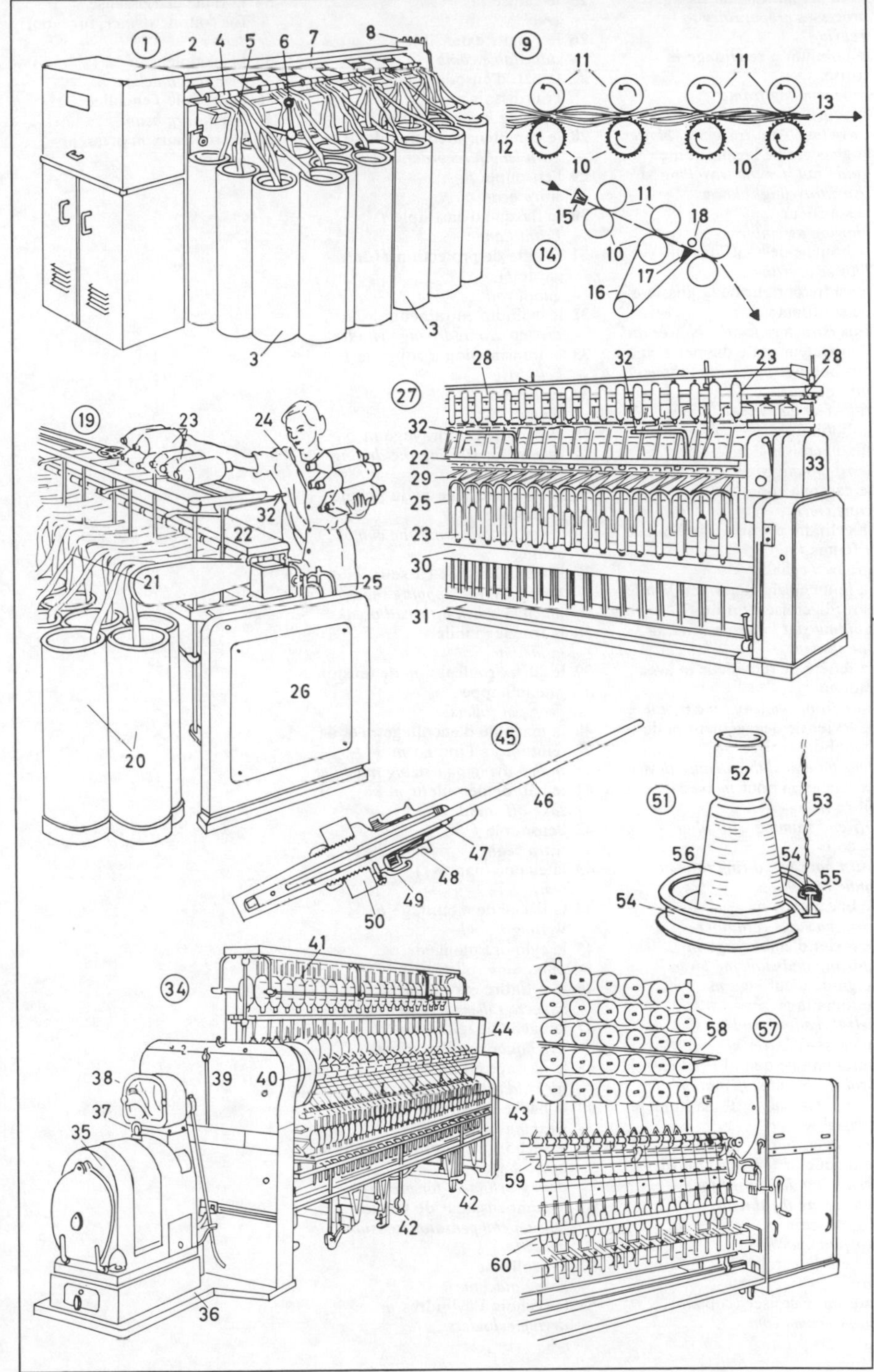
1
2
3
4
5
6
7
8
9
10
11
12
13
14
15
16
17
18
19
20
21
22
23
24
25
26
27
28
29
30
31
32
33
34
35
36
37
38
39
40
41
42
43
44
45
46
47
48
49
50
51
52
53
54
55
56
57
58
59
60

1-57 la préparation du tissage
– ***processes preparatory to weaving***
1 le bobinoir à renvidage *m* croisé
– *cone-winding frame*
2 la soufflante mobile
– *travelling* (Am. *traveling) blower*
3 la glissière de la soufflante
– *guide rail, for the travelling* (Am. *traveling) blower*
4 le souffleur
– *blowing assembly*
5 la bouche de soufflage *m*
– *blower aperture*
6 le cadre porteur de la glissière de soufflante *f*
– *superstructure for the blower rail*
7 l'indicateur *m* de diamètre *m* des bobines *f* croisées (cônes *m*)
– *full-cone indicator*
8 la bobine croisée (cône *m*) à fils *m* croisés
– *cross-wound cone*
9 le cantre à cônes *m*
– *cone creel*
10 le cylindre cannelé (tambour *m* à fentes *f*)
– *grooved cylinder*
11 la fente en zig-zag *m* (en V *m*) pour le croisement du fil
– *guiding slot for cross-winding the threads*
12 la têtière de renvideur *m* avec moteur *m*
– *side frame, housing the motor*
13 le levier de dégagement *m* de la bobine croisée
– *tension and slub-catching device*
14 la têtière en bout *m* avec filtre *m*
– *off-end framing with filter*
15 le cops
– *yarn package, a ring tube or mule cop*
16 le bac à cops *m*
– *yarn package container*
17 le levier d'embrayage *m*
– *starting and stopping lever*
18 le guide d'enfilage *m* automatique
– *self-threading guide*
19 le casse-fil [arrêt *m* automatique quand le fil casse]
– *broken thread stop motion*
20 l'épurateur *m* de fil *m*à lumière *f* réglable
– *thread clearer*
21 le disque de tension *f* du fil
– *weighting disc (disk) for tensioning the thread*
22 l'ourdissoir *m*
– *warping machine*
23 le ventilateur
– *fan*
24 la bobine croisée (cops *m*)
– *cross-wound cone*
25 le cantre
– *creel*
26 le peigne extensible
– *adjustable comb*
27 le bâti d'ensouple *f* de l'ourdissoir *m*
– *warping machine frame*
28 le compteur métrique de fil *m*
– *yarn length recorder*
29 l'ensouple *f*
– *warp beam*
30 le flasque d'ensouple *f*
– *beam flange*
31 la latte de protection *f* (de garde *f*)
– *guard rail*
32 le cylindre entraîneur
– *driving drum (driving cylinder)*
33 la transmission à courroie *f*
– *belt drive*
34 le moteur
– *motor*
35 la pédale d'embrayage *m*
– *release for starting the driving drum*
36 la vis de réglage *m* du peigne extensible
– *screw for adjusting the comb setting*
37 les lamelles *f* de casse-fil *m*
– *drop pins, for stopping the machine when a thread breaks*
38 la tringle mobile
– *guide bar*
39 les deux rouleaux *m* de tension *f* de la nappe
– *drop pin rollers*
40 la machine d'encollage *m* et de teinture *f* à l'indigo *m*
– *indigo dying and sizing machine*
41 le bâti de dérouleur *m*
– *take-off stand*
42 l'ensouple *f*
– *warp beam*
43 la chaîne (nappe *f*)
– *warp*
44 la bâche de mouillage *m*
– *wetting trough*
45 le cylindre plongeur
– *immersion roller*
46 le cylindre exprimeur
– *squeeze roller (mangle)*
47 la bâche de teinture *f*
– *dye liquor padding trough*
48 le passage à l'air *m*
– *air oxidation passage*
49 la bâche de rinçage *m*
– *washing trough*
50 le séchoir à cylindres *m* pour le préséchage
– *drying cylinders for pre-drying*
51 le compensateur de tension *f*
– *tension compensator (tension equalizer)*
52 l'encolleuse
– *sizing machine*
53 le séchoir à cylindres *m*
– *drying cylinders*
54 la rame élargisseuse
– for cotton: *stenter;* for wool: *tenter*
55 l'ensoupleuse *f*
– *beaming machine*
56 l'ensouple *f* encollée
– *sized warp beam*
57 les rouleaux *m* presseurs
– *rollers*

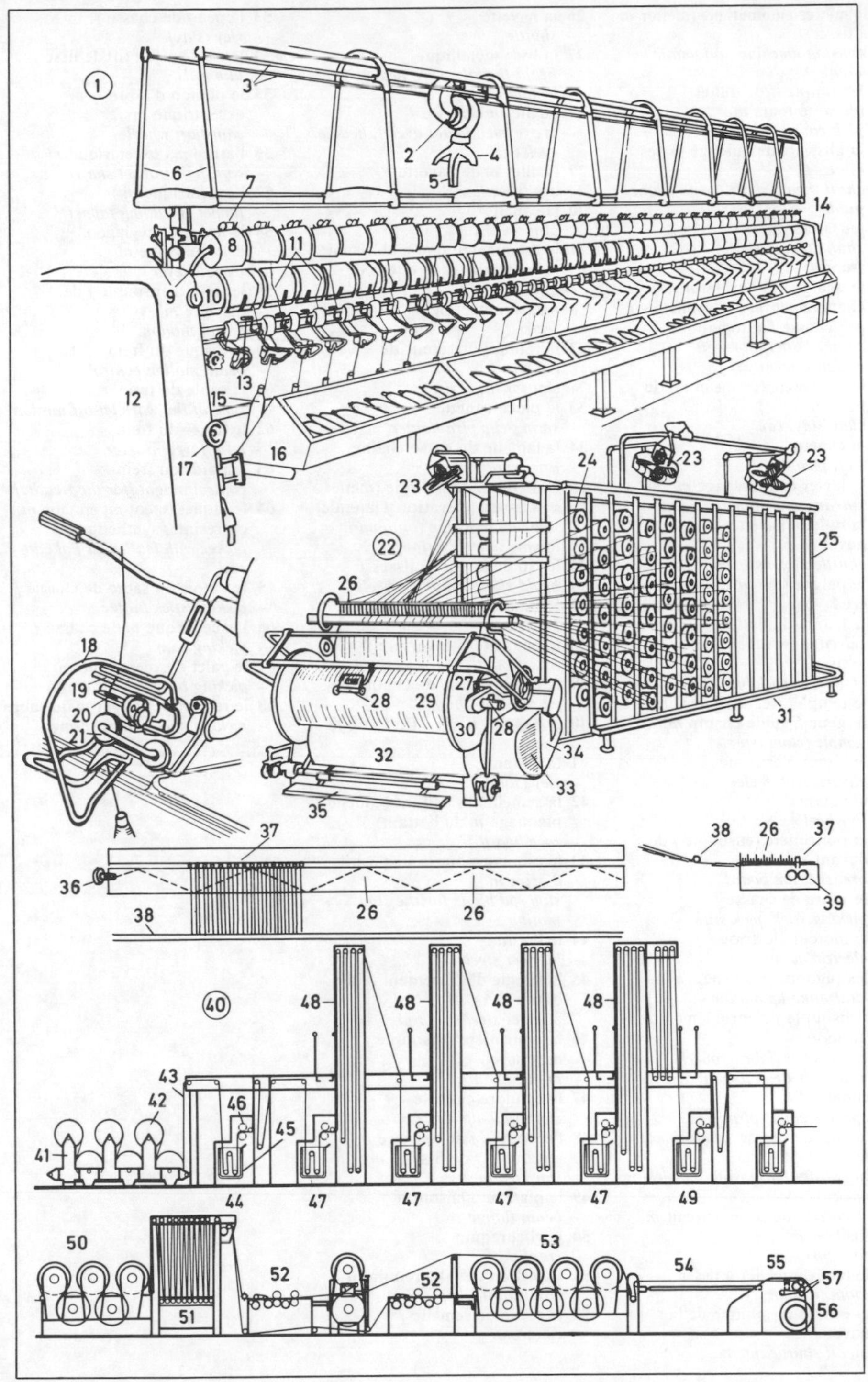
1
2
3
4
5
6
7
8
9
10
11
12
13
14
15
16
17
18
19
20
21
22
23
24
25
26
27
28
29
30
31
32
33
34
35
36
37
38
39
40
41
42
43
44
45
46
47
48
49
50
51
52
53
54
55
56
57

1 **le métier automatique** (métier *m* à tisser)
– ***weaving machine*** *(automatic loom)*
2 le compteur de duites *f* (compte-tours *m*)
– *pick counter (tachometer)*
3 la glissière de guidage *m* des lames *f*
– *shaft (heald shaft, heald frame) guide*
4 les lames *f*
– *shafts (heald shafts, heald frames)*
5 le chargeur à barillet *m* avec changement *m* des cannettes *f* par chasse *f* automatique
– *rotary battery for weft replenishment*
6 le couvercle (chapeau *m*) du battant
– *sley (slay) cap*
7 la canette
– *weft pirn*
8 le levier d'embrayage *m*
– *starting and stopping handle*
9 la boîte à navettes *f* avec ses navettes *f*
– *shuttle box, with shuttles*
10 le peigne (ros *m*)
– *reed*
11 la lisière du tissu
– *selvedge (selvage)*
12 le tissu
– *cloth (woven fabric)*
13 le templet (régulateur *m* de largeur *f*, guide-champ *m*)
– *temple (cloth temple)*
14 le tâteur électrique
– *electric weft feeler*
15 le volant
– *flywheel*
16 la poitrinière (ensouple *f* de devant *m*)
– *breast beam board*
17 le sabre de chasse *f*
– *picking stick (pick stick)*
18 le moteur électrique
– *electric motor*
19 les pignons *m* de change *m*
– *cloth take-up motion*
20 l'ensouple *f* d'enroulement *m* du tissu
– *cloth roller (fabric roller)*
21 le boîtier des tubes *m* de canette *f*
– *can for empty pirns*
22 le cuir de chasse *f* actionnant le sabre
– *lug strap, for moving the picking stick*
23 le coffret de coupe-circuit *m* fusible *m*
– *fuse box*
24 le bâti du métier à tisser
– *loom framing*
25 la pointe métallique de la navette
– *metal shuttle tip*
26 la navette
– *shuttle*
27 la lisse métallique
– *heald (heddle, wire heald, wire heddle)*
28 l'œillet *m* de lisse *f*
– *eye (eyelet, heald eyelet, heddle eyelet)*
29 l'œillet *m* de navette *f*
– *eye (shuttle eye)*
30 la canette
– *pirn*
31 le tube métallique établissant le contact avec le tâteur de navette *f*
– *metal contact sleeve for the weft feeler*
32 la rainure du tâteur de navette *f*
– *slot for the feeler*
33 le pince-canette
– *spring-clip pirn holder*
34 la lamelle du casse-chaîne
– *drop wire*
35 le métier automatique (métier *m* à tisser) [élévation *f* latérale]
– *weaving machine (automatic loom) [side elevation]*
36 les rouleaux *m* de lisses *f*
– *heald shaft guiding wheels*
37 le rouleau porte-fil *m*
– *backrest*
38 la baguette d'enverjure *f*
– *lease rods*
39 la chaîne (fil *m* de chaîne *f*)
– *warp (warp thread)*
40 le pas de chaîne *f* (la foule *f*)
– *shed*
41 le battant
– *sley (slay)*
42 la semelle du battant (couche *f*, plaquage *m* du battant)
– *race board*
43 le piqueur pour le dispositif d'arrêt *m*
– *stop rod blade for the stop motion*
44 le butoir
– *bumper steel*
45 la tringle d'effacement *m* du butoir
– *bumper steel stop rod*
46 la poitrinière (ensouple *f* de devant *m*)
– *breast beam*
47 le cylindre cannelé
– *cloth take-up roller*
48 l'ensouple *f* de derrière *m* (ensouple *f* de tissage *m*)
– *warp beam*
49 le plateau d'ensouple *f*
– *beam flange*
50 le vilebrequin
– *crankshaft*
51 le pignon de vilebrequin *m*
– *crankshaft wheel*
52 la bielle de semelle *f*
– *connector*
53 l'épée *f* de chasse *f*
– *sley (slay)*
54 le tendeur [du fil] de lisse *f*
– *lam rods*
55 le pignon d'arbre *m* à excentrique *m*
– *camshaft wheel*
56 l'arbre *m* à excentrique *m*
– *camshaft (tappet shaft)*
57 l'excentrique *m*
– *tappet (shedding tappet)*
58 le levier de réglage *m* d'excentrique *m*
– *treadle lever*
59 le frein d'ensouple *f* de derrière *m*
– *let-off motion*
60 le disque du frein
– *beam motion control*
61 le câble du frein
– *rope of the warp let-off motion*
62 le levier du frein
– *let-off weight lever*
63 le poids du frein
– *control weight [for the treadle]*
64 le taquet (tacot *m*) en cuir *m* ou résine *f* synthétique
– *picker with leather or bakelite pad*
65 le butoir du sabre de chasse *f*
– *picking stick buffer*
66 l'excentrique *m* de chasse *f*
– *picking cam*
67 le galet d'excentrique *m*
– *picking bowl*
68 le ressort de rappel *m* du sabre
– *picking stick return spring*

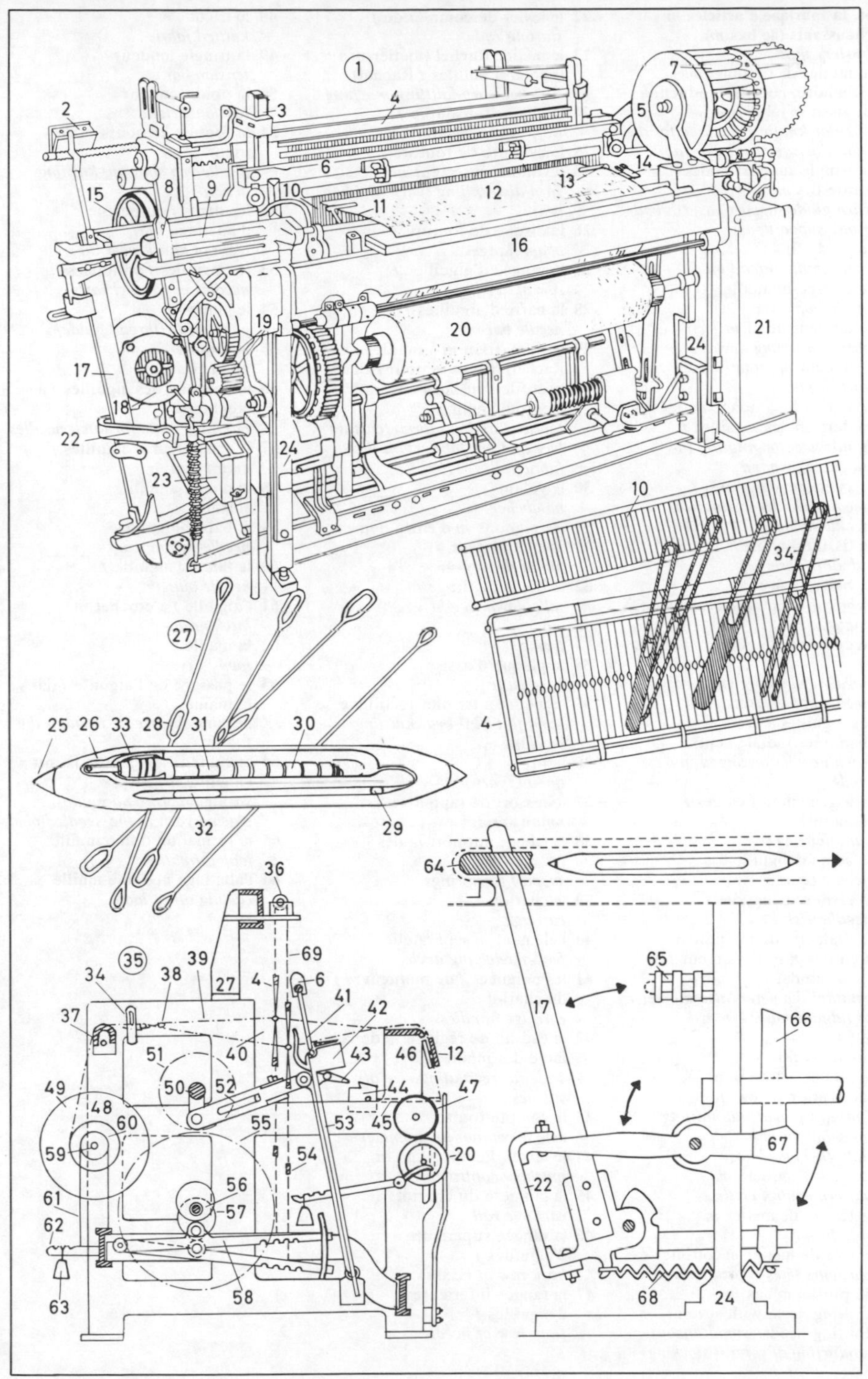

1-66 la fabrique d'articles *m* chaussants (de bas *m*)
– ***hosiery mill***
1 le métier de tricotage *m* circulaire, pour la production de tissu *m* tubulaire
– *circular knitting machine for the manufacture of tubular fabric*
2 la tringle support *m* des guide-fils *m*
– *yarn guide support post (thread guide support post)*
3 le guide-fil
– *yarn guide (thread guide)*
4 la bobine-bouteille
– *bottle bobbin*
5 le tendeur de fil *m*
– *yarn-tensioning device*
6 l'élément *m* séparateur
– *yarn feeder*
7 le volant de guidage *m* des fils *m* derrière les aiguilles *f*
– *handwheel for rotating the machine by hand*
8 le cylindre à aiguilles *f*
– *needle cylinder (cylindrical needle holder)*
9 le tissu tubulaire
– *tubular fabric*
10 le bac à tissu *m*
– *fabric drum (fabric box, fabric container)*
11 le cylindre à aiguilles *f* [coupe *f*]
– *needle cylinder (cylindrical needle holder) [section]*
12 les aiguilles à crochet *m* disposées radialement
– *latch needles arranged in a circle*
13 le logement des cames *f* d'aiguille *f*
– *cam housing*
14 la came d'aiguille f
– *needle cams*
15 la rainure d'aiguille *f*
– *needle trick*
16 le diamètre du cylindre à aiguilles *f*; *égal.:* largeur *f* du tissu tubulaire
– *cylinder diameter (also diameter of tubular fabric)*
17 le fil
– *thread (yarn)*
18 le métier cotton pour la fabrication de bas *m*
– *Cotton's patent flat knitting machine for ladies' fully-fashioned hose*
19 la chaîne modèle *m*
– *pattern control chain*
20 la têtière de métier *m*
– *side frame*
21 la tête de métier *m* cotton; *plusieurs têtes f:* production *f* de plusieurs bas *m*
– *knitting head;* with several knitting heads: *simultaneous production of several stockings*
22 le levier de commande *f*
– *starting rod*
23 le métier Rachel (métier *m* à tricoter à mailles *f* Rachel)
– *Raschel warp-knitting machine*
24 la chaîne (ensouple *f*)
– *warp (warp beam)*
25 le cylindre de fonture *f* (cylindre *m* secteur *m*)
– *yarn-distributing (yarn-dividing) beam*
26 le disque de fonture *f*
– *beam flange*
27 la rangée d'aiguilles *f*
– *row of needles*
28 la barre d'aiguilles *f*
– *needle bar*
29 le tissu (tissu *m* à mailles *f* Rachel) [tissus *m* pour rideaux *m* et filets *m*] sur l'ensouple *f* d'enroulement *m*
– *fabric (Raschel fabric) [curtain lace and net fabrics] on the fabric roll*
30 le volant
– *handwheel*
31 les pignons *m* d'entraînement *m* et le moteur
– *motor drive gear*
32 le poids de tirage *m*
– *take-down weight*
33 le bâti
– *frame*
34 la plaque d'assise *f*
– *base plate*
35 le métier à tricoter rectiligne
– *hand flat (flat-bed) knitting machine*
36 le fil
– *thread (yarn)*
37 le ressort de rappel *m*
– *return spring*
38 la tringle support *m* des ressorts *m*
– *support for springs*
39 le chariot
– *carriage*
40 l'élément *m* séparateur
– *feeder-selecting device*
41 les poignées *f* de manœuvre *f* du chariot
– *carriage handles*
42 le cadran de réglage *m* de la taille des mailles *f*
– *scale for regulating size of stitches*
43 le compte-tours
– *course counter (tachometer)*
44 le levier d'embrayage *m*
– *machine control lever*
45 la glissière du chariot
– *carriage rail*
46 la rangée supérieure d'aiguilles *f*
– *back row of needles*
47 la rangée inférieure d'aiguilles *f*
– *front row of needles*
48 le tricot
– *knitted fabric*
49 la tringle-tendeur
– *tension bar*
50 le poids tendeur
– *tension weight*
51 la fonture en cours *m* de tricotage *m*
– *needle bed showing knitting action*
52 les dents *f* du peigne d'abattage *m*
– *teeth of knock-over bit*
53 les aiguilles *f* parallèles
– *needles in parallel rows*
54 le guide-fil
– *yarn guide (thread guide)*
55 la fonture
– *needle bed*
56 le chapeau des aiguilles *f* à crochet *m*
– *retaining plate for latch needles*
57 le séparateur d'aiguilles *f*
– *guard cam*
58 le monte-aiguilles
– *sinker*
59 le baisse-aiguilles
– *needle-raising cam*
60 le talon d'aiguille *f*
– *needle butt*
61 l'aiguille *f* à crochet *m*
– *latch needle*
62 la maille
– *loop*
63 le passage de l'aiguille *f* dans la maille
– *pushing the needle through the fabric*
64 le guide-fil plaçant le fil sur l'aiguille *f*
– *yarn guide (thread guide) placing yarn in the needle hook*
65 la formation d'une maille
– *loop formation*
66 l'abattage *m* d'une maille
– *casting off of loop*

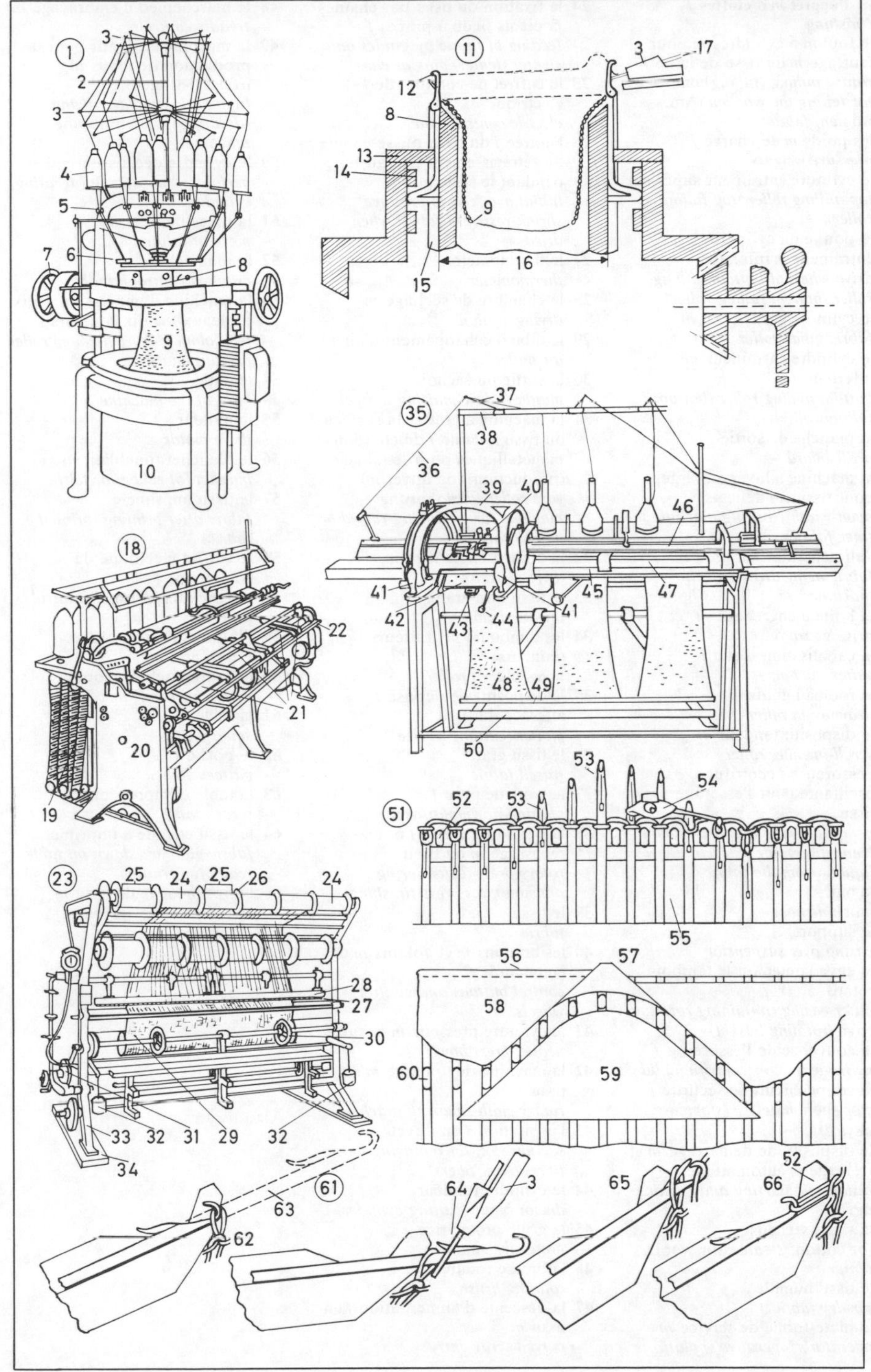
1
2
3
4
5
6
7
8
9
10
11
12
13
14
15
16
17
18
19
20
21
22
23
24
25
26
27
28
29
30
31
32
33
34
35
36
37
38
39
40
41
42
43
44
45
46
47
48
49
50
51
52
53
54
55
56
57
58
59
60
61
62
63
64
65
66

1-65 l'apprêt *m* **d'étoffes** *f*
– ***finishing***
1 le foulon à cylindres *m* pour feutrage *m* du tissu de laine *f*
– *rotary milling (fulling) machine for felting the woollen* (Am. *woolen) fabric*
2 les poids *m* de charge *f*
– *pressure weights*
3 le cylindre entraîneur supérieur
– *top milling roller (top fulling roller)*
4 la poulie du cylindre entraîneur *m* inférieur
– *drive wheel of bottom milling roller (bottom fulling roller)*
5 le cylindre guide-tissu *m*
– *fabric guide roller*
6 le cylindre entraîneur *m* inférieur
– *bottom milling roller (bottom fulling roller)*
7 la planche de sortie *f*
– *draft board*
8 la machine à laver au large, pour tissus *m* délicats
– *open-width scouring machine for finer fabrics*
9 l'alimentation *f*en tissu *m*
– *fabric being drawn off the machine*
10 la boîte à engrenage *m*
– *drive gearbox*
11 la canalisation d'eau *f*
– *water inlet pipe*
12 le rouleau-guide
– *drawing-in roller*
13 le dispositif tendeur *m*
– *scroll-opening roller*
14 l'essoreuse *f* centrifuge oscillante pour l'essorage *m* du tissu
– *pendulum-type hydro-extractor (centrifuge), for extracting liquors from the fabric*
15 le bâti
– *machine base*
16 le support
– *casing over suspension*
17 la cuve contenant le tambour rotatif
– *outer casing containing rotating cage (rotating basket)*
18 le couvercle de l'essoreuse *f*
– *hydro-extractor (centrifuge) lid*
19 le coupe-circuit de sécurité *f*
– *stop-motion device (stopping device)*
20 le dispositif de démarrage *m* et freinage *m* automatiques
– *automatic starting and braking device*
21 la rame sécheuse
– for cotton: *stenter;* for wool: *tenter*
22 le tissu humide
– *air-dry fabric*
23 la plate-forme de service *m*
– *operator's (operative's) platform*
24 la fixation du tissu par chaînes *f*à picots *m* ou à pinces *f*
– *feeding of fabric by guides onto stenter (tenter) pins or clips*
25 le coffret de commande *f* électrique
– *electric control panel*
26 l'entrée *f* du tissu plissé en vue du rétrécissement (retrait *m*) pendant le séchage
– *initial overfeed to produce shrink-resistant fabric when dried*
27 le thermomètre
– *thermometer*
28 la chambre de séchage *m*
– *drying section*
29 le tube d'échappement d'air *m*
– *air outlet*
30 la sortie du séchoir
– *plaiter (fabric-plaiting device)*
31 la machine à gratter la surface du tissu à l'aide *f* de chardons *m* métalliques pour le lainage (production *f* de duvet *m*)
– *wire-roller fabric-raising machine for producing raised or nap surface*
32 la boîte à engrenage *m*
– *drive gearbox*
33 le tissu non gratté
– *unraised cloth*
34 les tambours *m* gratteurs (laineurs)
– *wire-covered rollers*
35 le dispositif de dépose *f* alternée du tissu
– *plaiter (cuttling device)*
36 le tissu gratté
– *raised fabric*
37 le banc de pose *f*
– *plaiting-down platform*
38 la presse à cuvette *f* pour repassage *m* du tissu
– *rotary press (calendering machine), for press finishing*
39 le tissu
– *fabric*
40 les boutons *m* et volants *m* de commande *f*
– *control buttons and control wheels*
41 le cylindre presseur *m* chauffé
– *heated press bowl*
42 la machine de tondage *m* du tissu
– *rotary cloth-shearing machine*
43 l'aspiration *f* du duvet
– *suction slot, for removing loose fibres* (Am. *fibers)*
44 le cylindre tondeur
– *doctor blade (cutting cylinder)*
45 la grille protectrice
– *protective guard*
46 la brosse rotative
– *rotating brush*
47 la descente d'alimentation *f* en tissu *m*
– *curved scray entry*
48 le marchepied d'embrayage *m*
– *treadle control*
49 la machine à décatir pour la production de tissus *m* irrétrécissables
– *[non-shrinking] decatizing (decating) fabric-finishing machine*
50 le cylindre décatisseur
– *perforated decatizing (decating) cylinder*
51 la pièce de tissu *m*
– *piece of fabric*
52 la manivelle
– *cranked control handle*
53 la machine d'impression *f* aux rouleaux *m*à dix couleurs *f*
– *ten-colour* (Am. *ten-color) roller printing machine*
54 le bâti
– *base of the machine*
55 le moteur
– *drive motor*
56 le blanchet (doublier *m*)
– *blanket [of rubber or felt]*
57 le tissu imprimé
– *fabric after printing (printed fabric)*
58 le coffret électrique de commande *f*
– *electric control panel (control unit)*
59 l'impression *f* au cadre
– *screen printing*
60 le cadre-pochoir mobile
– *mobile screen frame*
61 la racle
– *squeegee*
62 le pochoir
– *pattern stencil*
63 la table d'impression *f*
– *screen table*
64 le tissu encollé à imprimer
– *fabric gummed down on table ready for printing*
65 l'imprimeur *m* de tissu *m*
– *screen printing operator (operative)*

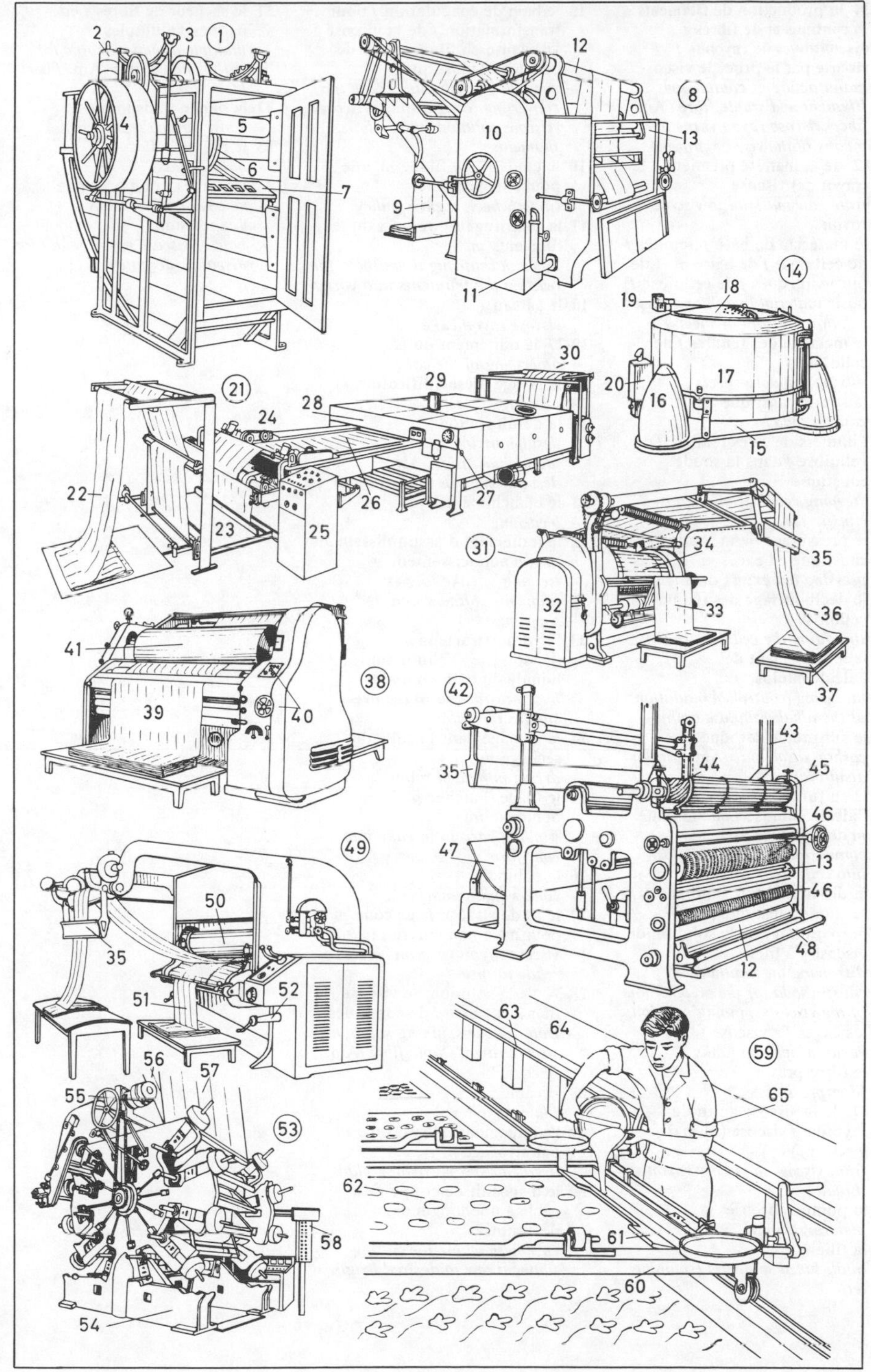
1
2
3
4
5
6
7
8
9
10
11
12
13
14
15
16
17
18
19
20
21
22
23
24
25
26
27
28
29
30
31
32
33
34
35
36
37
38
39
40
41
42
43
44
45
46
47
48
49
50
51
52
53
54
55
56
57
58
59
60
61
62
63
64
65

1-34 la production de **filaments** *m* **continus et de fibres** *f* **discontinues de rayonne** *f* **viscose** par le procédé viscose
– *manufacture of* ***continuous filament and staple fibre*** *(*Am. *fiber)* ***viscose rayon yarns*** *by means of the viscose process*

1-12 de la matière première à la (rayonne) viscose
– *from raw material to viscose rayon*

1 le matériau de base *f* [feuilles *f* de cellulose *f* de hêtre *m* et de pin *m*, plaques *f* de cellulose *f*]
– *basic material [beech and spruce cellulose in form of sheets]*

2 le mélange des feuilles *f* de cellulose *f*
– *mixing cellulose sheets*

3 la soude caustique
– *caustic soda*

4 l'immersion *f* des feuilles *f* de cellulose *f* dans la soude caustique
– *steeping cellulose sheets in caustic soda*

5 le pressurage de la soude caustique en excès *m*
– *pressing out excess caustic soda*

6 le déchiquetage des feuilles de cellulose *f*
– *shredding the cellulose sheets*

7 le mûrissement de l'alcalicellulose *f*
– *maturing (controlled oxidation) of the alkali-cellulose crumbs*

8 le sulfure de carbone *m*
– *carbon disulphide (*Am. *carbon disulfide)*

9 la sulfuration (conversion *f* de l'alcalicellulose *f* en xanthate *m* de cellulose *f*)
– *conversion of alkali-cellulose into cellulose xanthate*

10 la dissolution du xanthate dans la soude caustique pour préparation *f* de la solution de viscose *f* à filer
– *dissolving the xanthate in caustic soda for the preparation of the viscose spinning solution*

11 les caves *f* à viscose *f*
– *vacuum ripening tanks*

12 le filtre-presse
– *filter press*

13-27 de la viscose au fil de rayonne *f* viscose (fil *m* de viscose *f*)
– *from viscose to viscose rayon thread*

13 la pompe doseuse
– *metering pump*

14 la filière
– *multi-holed spinneret (spinning jet)*

15 le bain de coagulation *f* pour transformation *f* de la viscose visqueuse en filaments *m* de cellulose *f* plastiques
– *coagulating (spinning) bath for converting (coagulating) viscose (viscous solution) into solid filaments*

16 le guide-fil de filage *m*, une poulie de verre *m*
– *Godet wheel, a glass pulley*

17 la centrifugeuse réunissant les filaments *m*
– *Topham centrifugal pot (box) for twisting the filaments into yarn*

18 le gâteau
– *viscose rayon cake*

19-27 le traitement du gâteau
– *processing of the cake*

19 le lavage (désacidification *f*)
– *washing*

20 la désulfuration
– *desulphurizing (desulphurization,* Am. *desulfurizing, desulfurization)*

21 le blanchiment
– *bleaching*

22 le traitement d'assouplissement *m* et d'adoucissement *m*
– *treating of cake to give filaments softness and suppleness*

23 l'hydro-extracteur *m* (l'essoreuse *f*) éliminant le liquide du bain en excès *m*
– *hydro-extraction to remove surplus moisture*

24 le séchage dans la salle de séchage *m*
– *drying in heated room*

25 le filage (l'atelier *m* de bobinage *m*)
– *winding yarn from cake into cone form*

26 le bobinoir
– *cone-winding machine*

27 le fil de viscose *f* sur cône *m* pour mise *f* en œuvre *f* textile
– *viscose rayon yarn on cone ready for use*

28-34 de la solution de viscose *f* à filer aux fibres *f* discontinues
– *from viscose spinning solution to viscose rayon staple fibre (*Am. *fiber)*

28 le câble
– *filament tow*

29 l'équipement *m* de lavage *m* par arrosage *m*
– *overhead spray washing plant*

30 le dispositif de coupe *f* du câble à une longueur déterminée
– *cutting machine for cutting filament tow to desired length*

31 le sécheur de fibres *f* en nappes *f* multiples
– *multiple drying machine for cut-up staple fibre (*Am. *fiber) layer (lap)*

32 la bande transporteuse
– *conveyor belt (conveyor)*

33 le presse-balles
– *baling press*

34 les balles *f* de fibres *f* de viscose *f* prêtes pour l'expédition *f*
– *bale of viscose rayon ready for dispatch (despatch)*

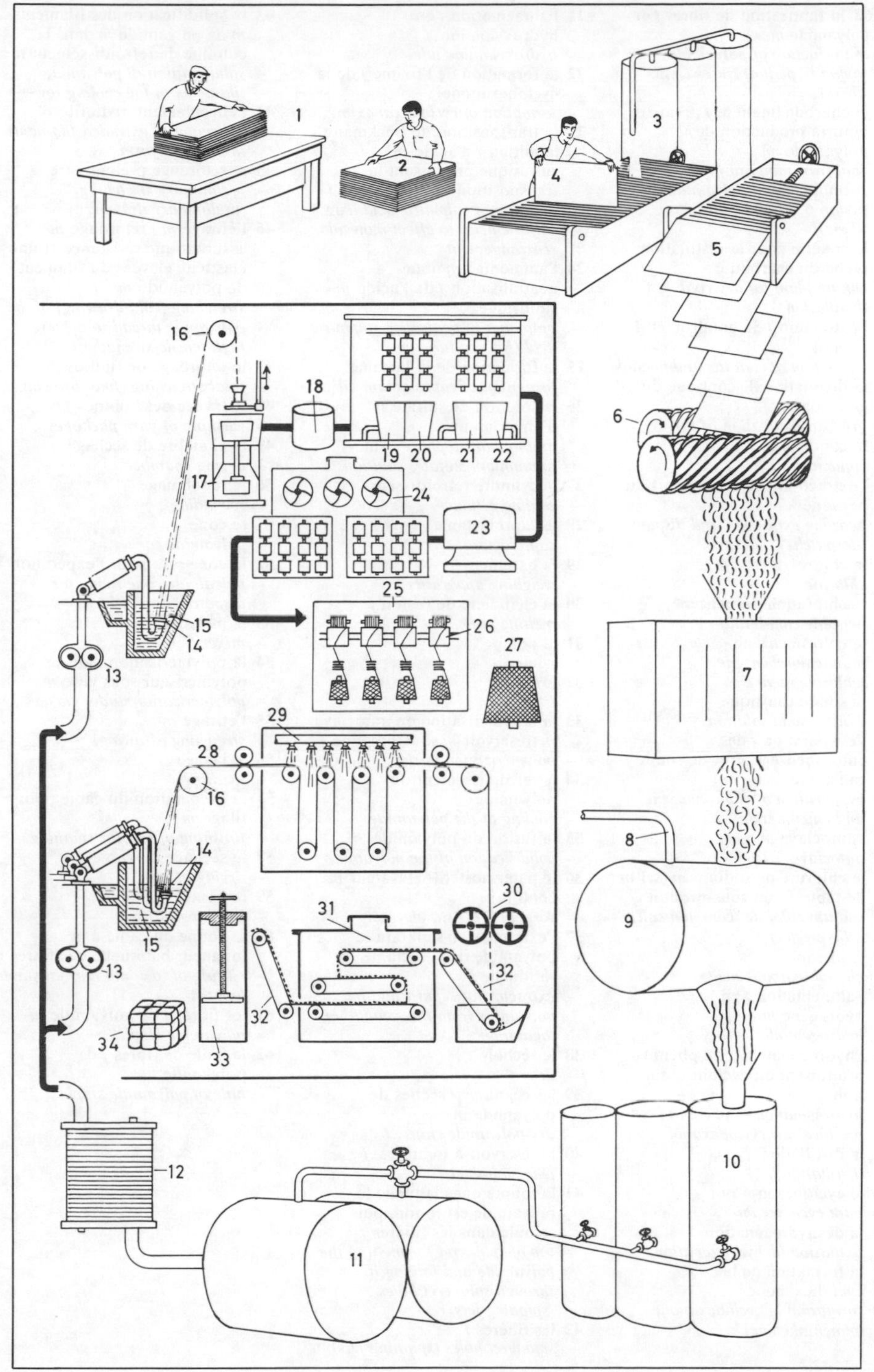
1
2
3
4
5
6
7
8
9
10
11
12
13
14
15
16
17
18
19
20
21
22
23
24
25
26
27
28
29
30
31
32
33
34

1-62 la fabrication de **fibres** *f* **de polyamide** *m*
- *manufacture of* ***polyamide*** *(nylon 6, perlon)* ***fibres*** *(*Am. *fibers)*

1 le charbon [matière *f* première pour la production de polyamide *m*]
- *coal [raw material for manufacture of polyamide (nylon 6, perlon) fibres (*Am. *fibers)]*

2 la cokerie pour la distillation sèche du charbon
- *coking plant for dry coal distillation*

3 l'extraction *f* du goudron et du phénol
- *extraction of coal tar and phenol*

4 la distillation discontinue du goudron
- *gradual distillation of tar*

5 le condenseur
- *condenser*

6 l'extraction *f* et le transport du benzène
- *benzene extraction and dispatch (despatch)*

7 le chlore
- *chlorine*

8 la chloration du benzène
- *benzene chlorination*

9 le chlorobenzène
- *monochlorobenzene (chlorobenzene)*

10 la soude caustique
- *caustic soda solution*

11 l'évaporation *f* de chlorobenzène *m* et de soude *f* caustique
- *evaporation of chlorobenzene and caustic soda*

12 l'autoclave *m*
- *autoclave*

13 le chlorure de sodium *m* (sel *m* de table *f*), un sous-produit
- *sodium chloride (common salt), a by-product*

14 le phénol
- *phenol (carbolic acid)*

15 l'alimentation *f* en hydrogène *m*
- *hydrogen inlet*

16 l'hydrogénation *f* du phénol produisant du cyclohexanol brut
- *hydrogenation of phenol to produce raw cyclohexanol*

17 la distillation
- *distillation*

18 le cyclohexanol pur
- *pure cyclohexanol*

19 la déshydrogénation
- *oxidation (dehydrogenation)*

20 la formation de la cyclohexanone
- *formation of cyclohexanone (pimehinketone)*

21 l'alimentation *f* en hydroxylamine *f*
- *hydroxylamine inlet*

22 la formation de l'oxime *f* de la cyclohexanone
- *formation of cyclohexanoxime*

23 la transposition de Beckmann [addition *f* d'acide *m* sulfurique produisant la transposition des molécules *f*]
- *addition of sulphuric acid (*Am. *sulfuric acid) to effect molecular rearrangement*

24 l'ammoniac *m* pour neutralisation *f* de l'acide *m* sulfurique
- *ammonia to neutralize sulphuric acid (*Am. *sulfuric acid)*

25 la formation de la lactame
- *formation of caprolactam oil*

26 la solution de sulfate *m* d'ammonium *m*
- *ammonium sulphate (*Am. *ammonium sulfate) solution*

27 le cylindre refroidisseur
- *cooling cylinder*

28 le caprolactame
- *caprolactam*

29 la bascule
- *weighing apparatus*

30 la chaudière de fusion *f*
- *melting pot*

31 la pompe
- *pump*

32 le filtre
- *filter*

33 la polymérisation en autoclave *m* (réservoir *m* sous pression *f*)
- *polymerization in the autoclave*

34 le refroidissement du polyamide
- *cooling of the polyamide*

35 la fusion du polyamide
- *solidification of the polyamide*

36 le pater-noster (l'élévateur *m* continu)
- *vertical lift (*Am. *elevator)*

37 l'extracteur *m* séparant le polyamide de la lactame résiduelle
- *extractor for separating the polyamide from the remaining lactam oil*

38 le séchoir
- *drier*

39 les rognures *f* sèches de polyamide *m*
- *dry polyamide chips*

40 le réservoir à rognures *f*
- *chip container*

41 la toupie dans laquelle le polyamide est fondu, puis refoulé dans les filières *f*
- *top of spinneret for melting the polyamide and forcing it through spinneret holes (spinning jets)*

42 les filières *f*
- *spinneret holes (spinning jets)*

43 la solidification des filaments *m* de polyamide *m* dans la colonne de refroidissement *m*
- *solidification of polyamide filaments in the cooling tower*

44 l'enroulement *m* du fil
- *collection of extruded filaments into thread form*

45 le retordage préliminaire
- *preliminary stretching (preliminary drawing)*

46 l'étirage *m* - retordage *m* assurant une résistance et une élasticité élevées du filament de polyamide *m*
- *stretching (cold-drawing) of the polyamide thread to achieve high tensile strength*

47 le retordage de finition *f*
- *final stretching (final drawing)*

48 le lavage des bobines *f*
- *washing of yarn packages*

49 la chambre de séchage *m*
- *drying chamber*

50 le rebobinage
- *rewinding*

51 le cône
- *polyamide cone*

52 le cône prêt pour l'expédition *f*
- *polyamide cone ready for dispatch (despatch)*

53 le mélangeur
- *mixer*

54 la polymérisation dans le polymériseur sous vide *m*
- *polymerization under vacua*

55 l'étirage *m*
- *stretching (drawing)*

56 le lavage
- *washing*

57 la préparation du câble pour filage *m*
- *finishing of tow for spinning*

58 le séchage du câble
- *drying of tow*

59 le frisage du câble
- *crimping of tow*

60 la coupe du câble à la longueur habituelle des fibres *f*
- *cutting of tow into normal staple lengths*

61 les fibres *f* de polyamide *m*
- *polyamide staple*

62 la balle de fibres *f* de polyamide *m*
- *bale of polyamide staple*

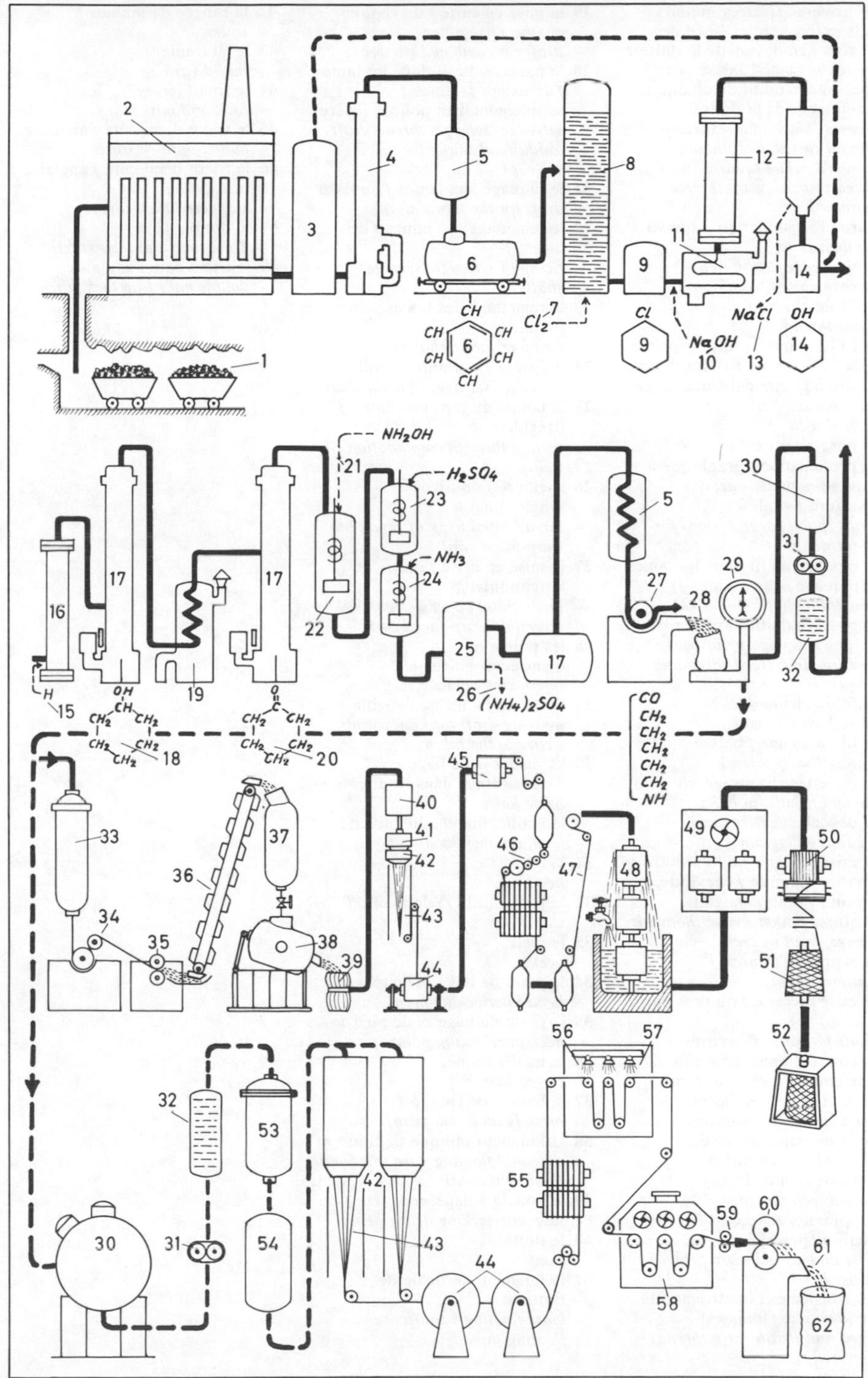
1 2 3 4 5 6 7 8 9 10 11 12 13 14 15 16 17 18 19 20 21 22 23 24 25 26 27 28 29 30 31 32 33 34 35 36 37 38 39 40 41 42 43 44 45 46 47 48 49 50 51 52 53 54 55 56 57 58 59 60 61 62
CH
CH CH
CH CH
CH
Cl2
Cl
NaOH
NaCl
OH
NH2OH
H2SO4
NH3
(NH4)2SO4
H
OH
CH
CH2 CH2
CH2 CH2
CH2
O
C
CH2 CH2
CH2 CH2
CH2
CO
CH2
CH2
CH2
CH2
CH2
NH

1-29 armures *f* [carrés *m* noirs: pris *m* (passage *m* du fil de chaîne *f* au-dessus de la duite); carrés *m* blancs: laissé *m* (passage *m* du fil de chaîne *f* au-dessous de la duite)]
- ***weaves** [black squares: warp thread raised, weft thread lowered; white squares: weft thread raised, warp thread lowered]*

1 l'armure *f* «toile» [tissu *m* vu de dessus *m*]
- *plain weave (tabby weave) [weave viewed from above]*

2 le fil de chaîne *f*
- *warp thread*

3 le fil de trame *f* (duite *f*: partie *f* du fil de trame *f* allant d'une lisière à l'autre dans une pièce de tissu *m*)
- *weft thread*

4 la mise en carte *f* [représentation *f* graphique à l'usage *m* du tisseur] de l'armure *f* «toile»
- *draft (point paper design) for plain weave*

5 le passage du fil dans les lames *f* (piquage *m* aux lames *f*)
- *threading draft*

6 le passage du fil dans le ros ou peigne (piquage *m* au ros)
- *denting draft (reed-threading draft)*

7 le fil de chaîne *f* levé
- *raised warp thread*

8 le fil de chaîne *f* baissé
- *lowered warp thread*

9 le remettage (rentrage *m*)
- *tie-up of shafts in pairs*

10 le décochement vertical
- *treadling diagram*

11 la mise en carte *f* de l'armure *f* «natté» (armure *f* cheviotte, armure *f* drap *m* anglais)
- *draft for basket weave (hopsack weave, matt weave)*

12 le rapport d'armure *f*
- *pattern repeat*

13 la mise en carte *f* du reps en trame *f*
- *draft for warp rib weave*

14 la coupe du reps en trame *f*, une coupe suivant la trame
- *section of warp rib fabric, a section through the warp*

15 le fil de trame *f* baissé
- *lowered weft thread*

16 le fil de trame *f* levé
- *raised weft thread*

17 les premier et second fils *m* de chaîne *f* [levés]
- *first and second warp threads [raised]*

18 les troisième et quatrième fils *m* de chaîne *f* [baissés]
- *third and fourth warp threads [lowered]*

19 la mise en carte *f* du reps en chaîne *f* irrégulier
- *draft for combined rib weave*

20 le passage du fil dans les lames *f* de lisière *f* (lames *f* supplémentaires pour la lisière)
- *selvedge (selvage) thread draft (additional shafts for the selvedge)*

21 le piquage aux lames *f* du tissu
- *draft for the fabric shafts*

22 le remettage des lames *f* de lisière *f*
- *tie-up of selvedge (selvage) shafts*

23 le remettage des lames *f* du tissu
- *tie-up of fabric shafts*

24 la lisière en armure *f* «toile»
- *selvedge (selvage) in plain weave*

25 la coupe du reps en chaîne *f* irrégulier
- *section through combination rib weave*

26 l'armure *f* du tricot longitudinal
- *thread interlacing of reversible warp-faced cord*

27 la mise en carte *f* du tricot longitudinal
- *draft (point paper design) for reversible warp-faced cord*

28 les points *m* d'entrecroisement *m*
- *interlacing points*

29 l'armure *f* «nid *m* d'abeille *f*»
- *weaving draft for honeycomb weave in the fabric*

30-48 modes *m* de liage *m* fondamentaux dans les tricots *m*
- ***basic knits***

30 la maille, une maille ouverte
- *loop, an open loop*

31 la tête
- *head*

32 la jambe (aile *f*) de maille *f*
- *side*

33 le pied
- *neck*

34 le point de liage *m* de tête *f*
- *head interlocking point*

35 le point de liage *m* de pied *m*
- *neck interlocking point*

36 la maille fermée
- *closed loop*

37 la boucle de charge *f*
- *mesh [with inlaid yarn]*

38 la longueur oblique de flotté *m*
- *diagonal floating yarn (diagonal floating thread)*

39 la boucle à liage *m* de tête *f*
- *loop interlocking at the head*

40 le flotté
- *float*

41 la longueur verticale de flotté *m*
- *loose floating yarn (loose floating thread)*

42 la rangée de mailles *f*
- *course*

43 le fil tramé
- *inlaid yarn*

44 le tricot jersey
- *tuck and miss stitch*

45 le tricot demi-côte *f* anglaise
- *pulled-up tuck stitch*

46 le tricot demi-côte *f* anglaise transposée
- *staggered tuck stitch*

47 le double jersey
- *2 x 2 tuck and miss stitch*

48 le tricot côte *f* anglaise
- *double pulled-up tuck stitch*

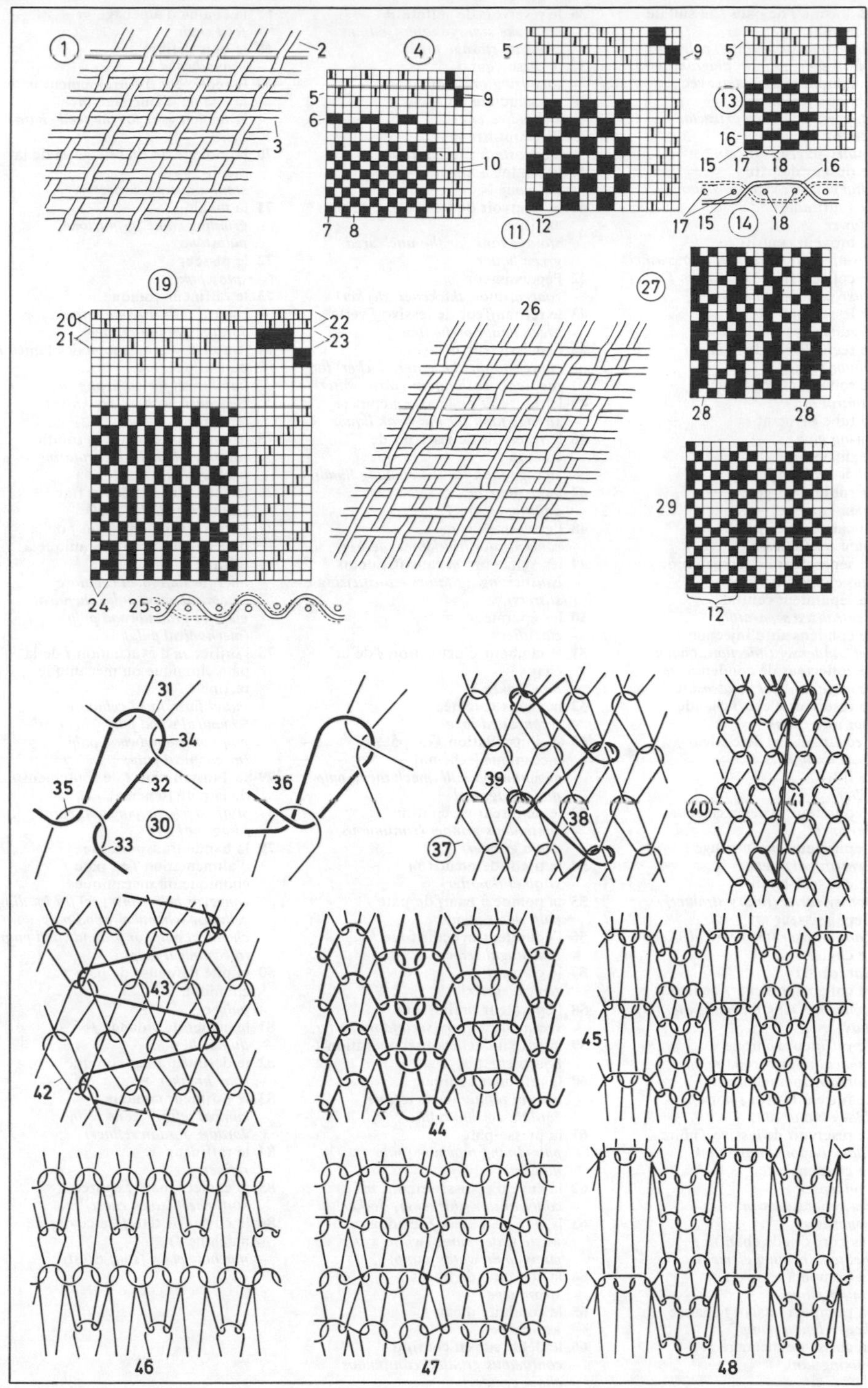

1
2
3
4
5
6
7
8
9
10
11
12
13
15
16
17
18
14
19
20
21
22
23
24
25
26
27
28
29
30
31
32
33
34
35
36
37
38
39
40
41
42
43
44
45
46
47
48

1-52 l'usine *f* de pâte *f* au sulfate [schéma]
– *sulphate* (Am. *sulfate*) *pulp mill (kraft pulp mill) [in diagram form]*
1 la coupeuse à bois *m* avec dépoussiéreur *m*
– *chippers with dust extractor*
2 l'assortisseur *m*
– *rotary screen (riffler)*
3 le doseur de pâte *f*
– *chip packer (chip distributor)*
4 la soufflante
– *blower*
5 le broyeur centrifuge
– *disintegrator (crusher, chip crusher)*
6 le collecteur de poussières *f*
– *dust-settling chamber*
7 le lessiveur
– *digester*
8 le réchauffeur de lessive *f*
– *liquor preheater*
9 le robinet distributeur
– *control tap*
10 le tube pivotant
– *swing pipe*
11 le diffuseur
– *blow tank (diffuser)*
12 le robinet purgeur
– *blow valve*
13 la caisse de diffuseur *m*
– *blow pit (diffuser)*
14 le séparateur de térébenthine *f*
– *turpentine separator*
15 le séparateur central
– *centralized separator*
16 le condenseur d'injection *f*
– *jet condenser (injection condenser)*
17 le collecteur de condensat *m*
– *storage tank for condensate*
18 le réservoir d'eau *f* chaude
– *hot water tank*
19 l'échangeur *m* de chaleur *f*
– *heat exchanger*
20 le filtre
– *filter*
21 l'épurateur *m* dégrossisseur
– *presorter*
22 l'épurateur *m* centrifuge
– *centrifugal screen*
23 le classeur rotatif
– *rotary sorter (rotary strainer)*
24 l'épaississeur *m*
– *concentrator (thickener, decker)*
25 le cuvier
– *vat (chest)*
26 le collecteur d'eau *f* de retour *m*
– *collecting tank for backwater (low box)*
27 le raffineur conique
– *conical refiner (cone refiner, Jordan, Jordan refiner)*
28 le filtre à lessive *f* noire
– *black liquor filter*
29 le réservoir de lessive *f* noire
– *black liquor storage tank*
30 le condenseur
– *condenser*
31 les séparateurs *m*
– *separators*
32 les corps *m* de chauffe *f*
– *heaters (heating elements)*
33 la pompe à lessive *f*
– *liquor pump*
34 la pompe à lessive *f* épaisse
– *heavy liquor pump*
35 la caisse de mélange *m*
– *mixing tank*
36 le réservoir de sulfate *m*
– *salt cake storage tank (sodium sulphate storage tank)*
37 le dissolveur
– *dissolving tank (dissolver)*
38 la chaudière à vapeur *f*
– *steam heater*
39 l'électrofiltre *m*
– *electrostatic precipitator*
40 la pompe à air *m*
– *air pump*
41 le réservoir de lessive *f* verte non clarifiée
– *storage tank for the uncleared green liquor*
42 l'épaississeur *m*
– *concentrator (thickener, decker)*
43 le réchauffeur de lessive *f* verte
– *green liquor preheater*
44 l'épaississeur *m* laveur
– *concentrator (thickener, decker) for the weak wash liquor (wash water)*
45 le réservoir de lessive *f* épuisée
– *storage tank for the weak liquor*
46 le réservoir de lessive *f* de cuisson *f*
– *storage tank for the cooking liquor*
47 l'agitateur *m*
– *agitator (stirrer)*
48 l'épaississeur *m*
– *concentrator (thickener, decker)*
49 les agitateurs *m* caustificateurs
– *causticizing agitators (causticizing stirrers)*
50 les épurateurs *m*
– *classifier*
51 le tambour d'extinction *f* de la chaux
– *lime slaker*
52 la chaux calcinée
– *reconverted lime*
53-65 l'installation *f* de pâte *f* mécanique [schéma]
– *groundwood mill (mechanical pulp mill) [diagram]*
53 le défibreur en continu
– *continuous grinder (continuous chain grinder)*
54 le trieur de nœuds *m*
– *strainer (knotter)*
55 la pompe à eau *f* de pâte *f*
– *pulp water pump*
56 l'épurateur *m* centrifuge
– *centrifugal screen*
57 le classeur
– *screen (sorter)*
58 l'épurateur *m* finisseur
– *secondary screen (secondary sorter)*
59 la cuve à déchets *m* d'épuration *f*
– *rejects chest*
60 le raffineur conique
– *conical refiner (cone refiner, Jordan, Jordan refiner)*
61 la presse-pâte
– *pulp-drying machine (pulp machine)*
62 la cuve d'épaississement *m*
– *concentrator (thickener, decker)*
63 la pompe à eaux *f* résiduaires
– *waste water pump (white water pump, pulp water pump)*
64 la conduite de buées *f*
– *steam pipe*
65 la conduite d'eau *f*
– *water pipe*
66 le défibreur en continu
– *continuous grinder (continuous chain grinder)*
67 la chaîne d'amenage *m*
– *feed chain*
68 le bois défibré
– *groundwood*
69 le réducteur d'entraînement *m* de la chaîne d'amenage *m*
– *reduction gear for the feed chain drive*
70 la molette de rhabillage *m* de la meule
– *stone-dressing device*
71 la meule
– *grinding stone (grindstone, pulpstone)*
72 le pisseur
– *spray pipe*
73 le raffineur conique
– *conical refiner (cone refiner, Jordan, Jordan refiner)*
74 le volant de réglage *m* des lames *f* du raffineur *m*
– *handwheel for adjusting the clearance between the knives (blades)*
75 le cône porte-lames *m* rotatif
– *rotating bladed cone (rotating bladed plug)*
76 le cône porte-lames *m* fixe
– *stationary bladed shell*
77 l'orifice *m* d'admission *f* de la pâte chimique ou mécanique à raffiner
– *inlet for unrefined cellulose (chemical wood pulp, chemical pulp) or groundwood pulp (mechanical pulp)*
78 l'orifice *m* d'évacuation *f* de la pâte chimique ou mécanique raffinée
– *outlet for refined cellulose (chemical wood pulp, chemical pulp) or groundwood pulp (mechanical pulp)*
79-86 l'installation *f* de traitement *m* de la pâte [schéma]
– *stuff (stock) preparation plant [diagram]*
79 la bande transporteuse d'alimentation *f* en pâte *f* chimique ou mécanique
– *conveyor belt (conveyor) for loading cellulose (chemical wood pulp, chemical pulp) or groundwood pulp (mechanical pulp)*
80 la pile défileuse de pâte *f* chimique
– *pulper*
81 le cuvier de vidange *f*
– *dump chest*
82 le désintégrateur conique
– *cone breaker*
83 le raffineur conique
– *conical refiner (cone refiner, Jordan, Jordan refiner)*
84 le raffineur
– *refiner*
85 le cuvier à pâte *f* épurée
– *stuff chest (stock chest)*
86 le cuvier de tête *f* (le cuvier de machine *f*)
– *machine chest (stuff chest)*

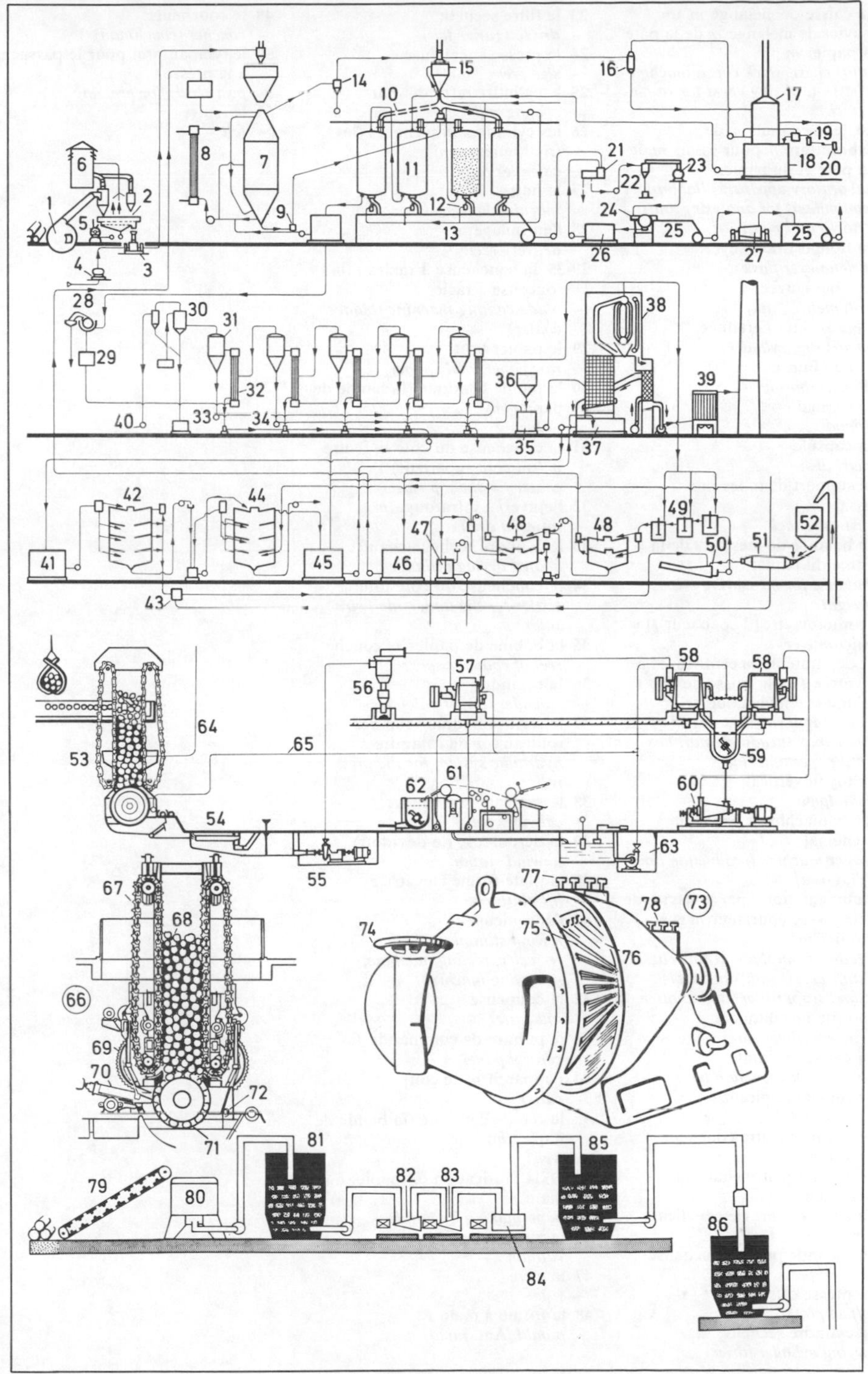
1
2
3
4
5
6
7
8
9
10
11
12
13
14
15
16
17
18
19
20
21
22
23
24
25
25
26
27
28
29
30
31
32
33
34
35
36
37
38
39
40
41
42
43
44
45
46
47
48
48
49
50
51
52
53
54
55
56
57
58
58
59
60
61
62
63
64
65
66
67
68
69
70
71
72
73
74
75
76
77
78
79
80
81
82
83
84
85
86

1 la caisse de mélange *m*, un cuvier de mélange *m* de la pâte à papier *m*
– *stuff chest (stock chest, machine chest), a mixing chest for stuff (stock)*
2-10 les appareils *m* de laboratoire *m* pour essais *m* de la pâte et du papier
– *laboratory apparatus (laboratory equipment) for analysing stuff (stock) and paper*
2 la fiole d'Erlenmeyer
– *Erlenmeyer flask*
3 la fiole jaugée
– *volumetric flask*
4 l'éprouvette *f* graduée
– *measuring cylinder*
5 le bec Bunsen
– *Bunsen burner*
6 le trépied
– *tripod*
7 la capsule
– *petri dish*
8 le support de tubes *m* à essais *m*
– *test tube rack*
9 la balance de mesure *f* de la force du papier
– *balance for measuring basis weight*
10 le micromètre [d'épaisseur *f*]
– *micrometer*
11 les épurateurs *m* centrifuges à l'entrée *f* de la caisse de tête *f* d'une machine à papier *m*
– *centrifugal cleaners ahead of the breastbox (headbox, stuff box) of a paper machine*
12 le tuyau vertical
– *standpipe*
13-28 la machine à papier *m* [schéma]
– *paper machine (production line) [diagram]*
13 l'alimentation *f* par le cuvier de tête *f* avec épurateur *m* et sablier *m*
– *feed-in from the machine chest (stuff chest) with sand table (sand trap, riffler) and knotter*
14 la toile métallique
– *wire (machine wire)*
15 la caisse aspirante
– *vacuum box (suction box)*
16 le rouleau aspirant
– *suction roll*
17 le premier feutre coucheur
– *first wet felt*
18 le second feutre coucheur
– *second wet felt*
19 la première presse coucheuse
– *first press*
20 la seconde presse coucheuse
– *second press*
21 la presse offset
– *offset press*
22 le cylindre sécheur
– *drying cylinder (drier)*
23 le filtre sécheur
– *dry felt (drier felt)*
24 la presse encolleuse
– *size press*
25 le cylindre refroidisseur
– *cooling roll*
26 les cylindres *m* sécheurs (les frictionneurs *m*)
– *calender rolls*
27 la hotte
– *machine hood*
28 l'enroulage *m*
– *delivery reel*
29-35 la coucheuse à râcles *f* (la fonceuse à râcles *f*)
– *blade coating machine (blade coater)*
29 le papier brut
– *raw paper (body paper)*
30 la feuille continue (la bande de papier *m*)
– *web*
31 la coucheuse du côté *m* feutre *m* (du côté supérieur)
– *coater for the top side*
32 l'étuve *f* à infrarouge *m*
– *infrared drier*
33 le cylindre sécheur chauffé
– *heated drying cylinder*
34 la coucheuse du côté toile
– *coater for the underside (wire side)*
35 la bobine de papier *m* couché
– *reel of coated paper*
36 la calandre
– *calender (Super-calender)*
37 le serrage hydraulique des rouleaux *m* de calandre *f*
– *hydraulic system for the press rolls*
38 le rouleau de calandre *f*
– *calender roll*
39 la dérouleuse (le dévidoir)
– *unwind station*
40 la plate-forme élévatrice
– *lift platform*
41 l'enrouleuse *f*
– *rewind station (rewinder, re-reeler, reeling machine, re-reeling machine)*
42 la coupeuse
– *roll cutter*
43 le pupitre de commande *f*
– *control panel*
44 l'appareil *m* de coupe *f*
– *cutter*
45 la feuille continue (la bande de papier *m*)
– *web*
46-51 la fabrication du papier à la main
– *papermaking by hand*
46 le puiseur
– *vatman*
47 la cuve
– *vat*
48 la forme à main *f*
– *mould (*Am. *mold)*
49 le coucheur
– *coucher (couchman)*
50 le tympan prêt pour le passage à la presse
– *post ready for pressing*
51 le feutre
– *felt*

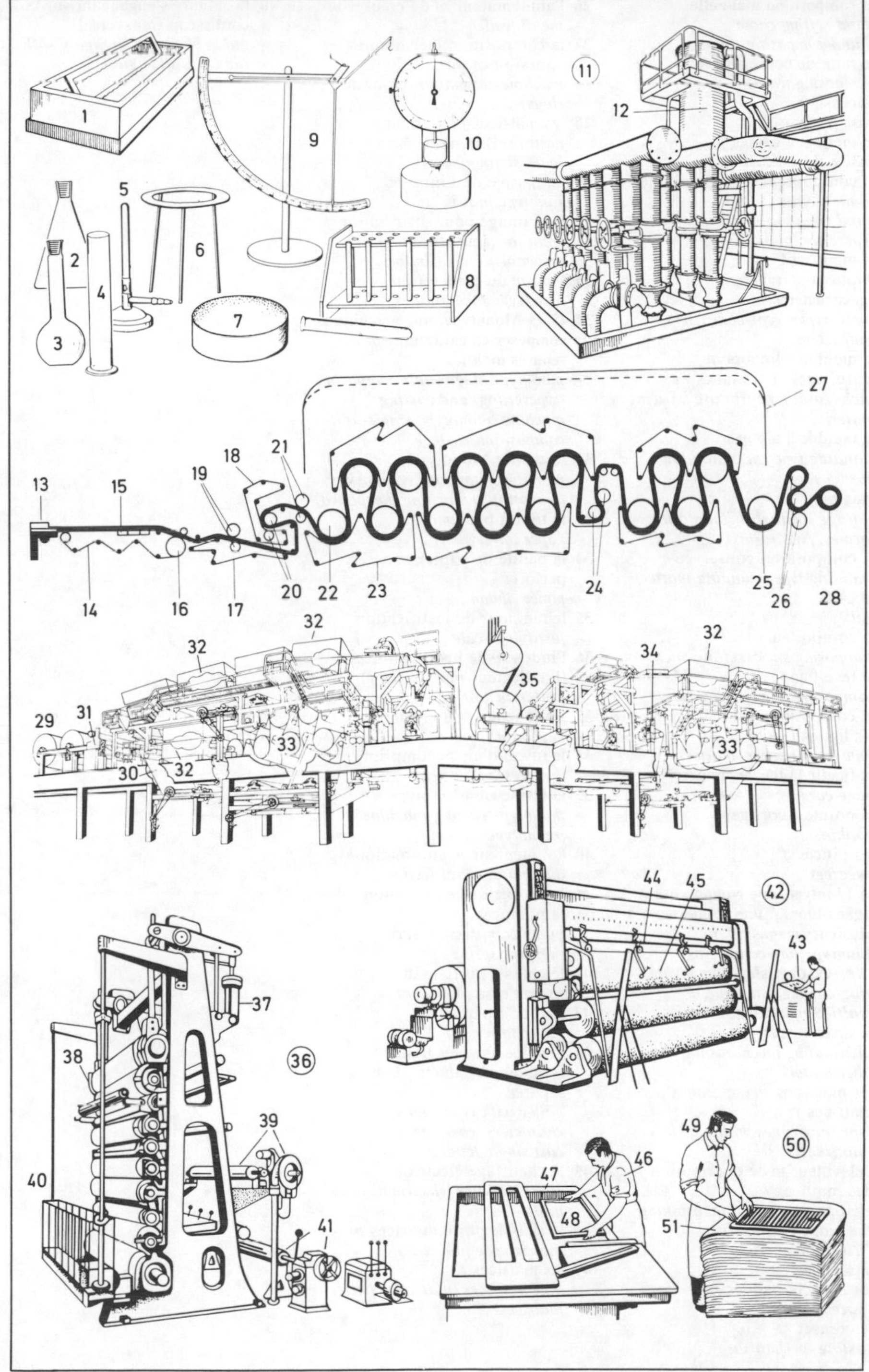
1
2
3
4
5
6
7
8
9
10
11
12
13
14
15
16
17
18
19
20
21
22
23
24
25
26
27
28
29
30
31
32
33
34
35
36
37
38
39
40
41
42
43
44
45
46
47
48
49
50
51

1 **la composition manuelle**
– ***hand-setting room*** *(hand-composing room)*
2 le rang de composition *f*
– *composing frame*
3 la casse
– *case (typecase)*
4 le meuble à casses *f*
– *case cabinet (case rack)*
5 le compositeur (le typographe, *fam.:* le typo)
– *hand compositor (compositor, typesetter, maker-up)*
6 le manuscrit
– *manuscript (typescript)*
7 les caractères *m*
– *sorts (types, type characters, characters)*
8 le meuble à lingots *m* (garnitures *f*) et blancs *m*
– *rack (case) for furniture (spacing material)*
9 le meuble à ais *m*
– *standing type rack (standing matter rack)*
10 l'ais *m*
– *storage shelf (shelf for storing formes,* Am. *forms)*
11 la composition conservée
– *standing type (standing matter)*
12 la galée
– *galley*
13 le composteur
– *composing stick (setting stick)*
14 le lève-ligne
– *composing rule (setting rule)*
15 la composition (la matière *f*, les lignes *f* de texte *m*)
– *type (type matter, matter)*
16 la ficelle [à lier les pages *f*]
– *page cord*
17 la pointe à corriger
– *bodkin*
18 les pinces *f*
– *tweezers*
19 **la Linotype, une composeuse à lignes-blocs *f*, une composeuse à plusieurs magasins *m***
– ***Linotype line-composing (line-casting, slug-composing, slug-casting) machine, a multi-magazine machine***
20 le distributeur
– *distributing mechanism (distributor)*
21 les magasins *m* contenant les matrices *f*
– *type magazines with matrices (matrixes)*
22 l'élévateur *m* de distribution *f* des matrices *f*
– *elevator carrier for distributing the matrices (matrixes)*
23 l'assembleur *m*
– *assembler*
24 les espaces-bandes *m*
– *spacebands*
25 le creuset
– *casting mechanism*
26 l'alimentateur *m* de creuset *m*
– *metal feeder*
27 la composition mécanique (les lignes-blocs *m*)
– *machine-set matter (cast lines, slugs)*
28 les matrices *f* à la main
– *matrices (matrixes) for hand-setting (sorts)*
29 la matrice de Linotype
– *Linotype matrix*
30 le crantage pour distribution *f*
– *teeth for the distributing mechanism (distributor)*
31 l'œil *m* du caractère *m*
– *face (type face, matrix)*
32-45 **la Monotype, une machine à composer en caractères *m* séparés mobiles**
– ***monotype single-unit composing*** *(typesetting)* ***and casting machine*** *(monotype single-unit composition caster)*
32 le clavier Monotype
– *monotype standard composing (typesetting) machine (keyboard)*
33 la tour à papier *m*
– *paper tower*
34 la bande de papier *m* à perforer
– *paper ribbon*
35 le tambour de justification *f*
– *justifying scale*
36 l'index *m* de justification *f* (l'indicateur *m* d'unités *f*)
– *unit indicator*
37 les touches *f* du clavier
– *keyboard*
38 le tuyau d'air *m* comprimé
– *compressed-air hose*
39 la fondeuse Monotype
– *monotype casting machine (monotype caster)*
40 l'alimenteur *m* automatique
– *automatic metal feeder*
41 le ressort de compression *f* de la pompe
– *pump compression spring (pump pressure spring)*
42 le châssis porte-matrices *m*
– *matrix case (die case)*
43 la tour à papier *m*
– *paper tower*
44 la galée avec les lignes *f* fondues en caractères *m* séparés
– *galley with types (letters, characters, cast single types, cast single letters)*
45 le chauffage électrique
– *electric heater (electric heating unit)*
46 le châssis porte-matrices *m*
– *matrix case (die case)*
47 les matrices *f*
– *type matrices (matrixes) (letter matrices)*
48 la rainure s'engageant sur le coulisseau transversal
– *guide block for engaging with the cross-slide guide*

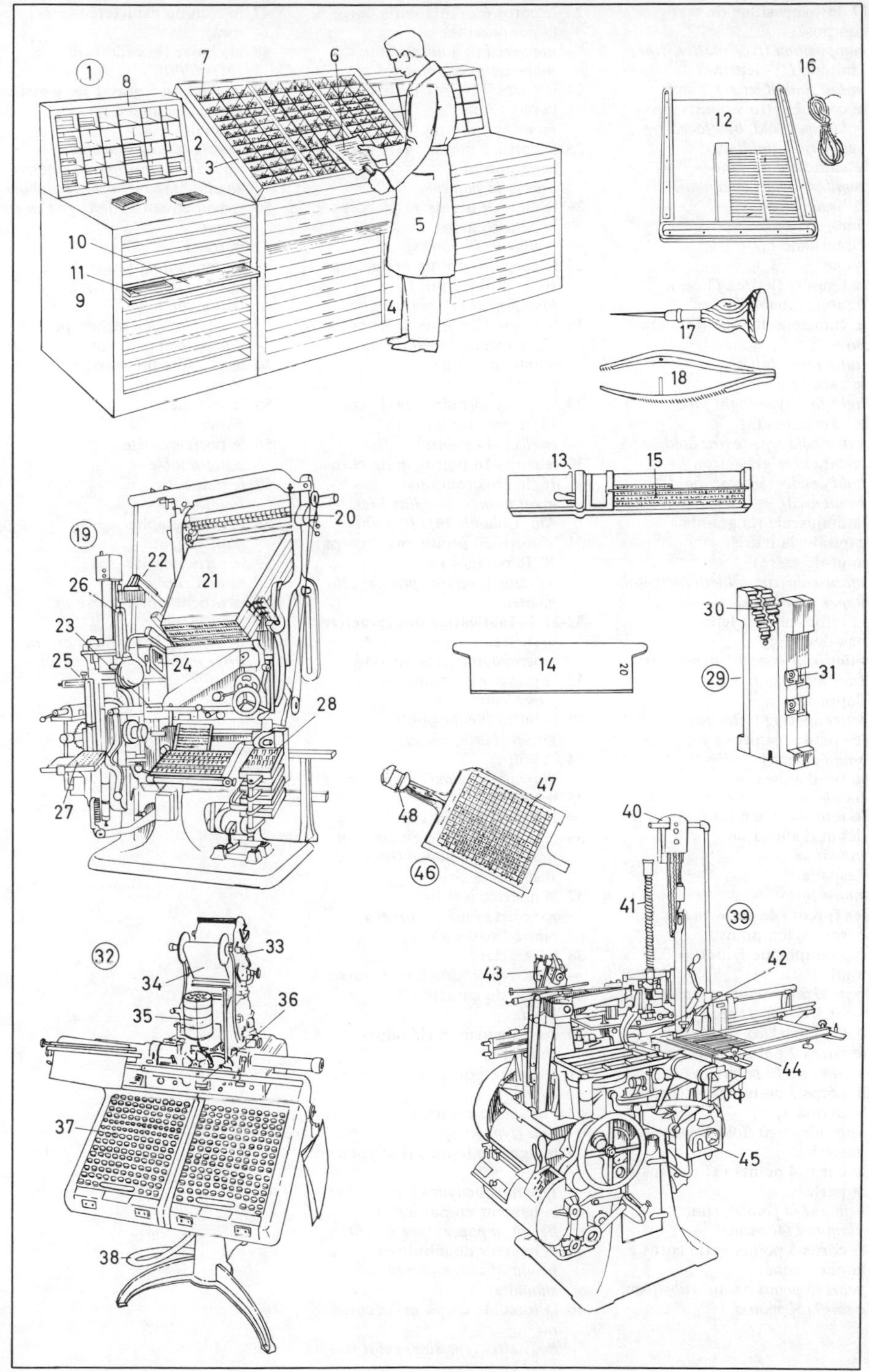
1
2
3
4
5
6
7
8
9
10
11
12
13
14
15
16
17
18
19
20
21
22
23
24
25
26
27
28
29
30
31
32
33
34
35
36
37
38
39
40
41
42
43
44
45
46
47
48

1-17 la composition (le texte composé)
– ***composition*** *(type matter, type)*
1 l'initiale *f* (la lettrine)
– *initial (initial letter)*
2 le caractère trois-quarts gras
– *bold type (bold, boldfaced type, heavy type, boldface)*
3 le caractère mi-gras
– *semibold type (semibold)*
4 la ligne
– *line*
5 l'interligne *f*
– *space*
6 la ligature (lettres *f* liées)
– *ligature (double letter)*
7 le caractère italique (l'italique *m*)
– *italic type (italics)*
8 le caractère maigre
– *light face type (light face)*
9 le caractère gras
– *extra bold type (extra bold)*
10 le caractère gras étroit
– *bold condensed type (bold condensed)*
11 la majuscule (la grande capitale, la lettre haut-de-casse)
– *majuscule (capital letter, capital, upper case letter)*
12 la minuscule (la lettre bas-de-casse)
– *minuscule (small letter, lower case letter)*
13 l'approche *f*
– *letter spacing (interspacing)*
14 les petites capitales *f*
– *small capitals*
15 la fin d'alinéa *m*
– *break*
16 le renfoncement (la rentrée, le début d'alinéa *m*)
– *indention*
17 l'espace *f*
– *space*
18 les forces *f* de corps *m* (les corps *m*) [un point typographique Didot = 0,3759 mm]
– ***type sizes*** *[one typographic point = 0.376 mm (Didot system), 0.351 mm (Pica system)]*
19 le corps 2 points *m* (le corps 2)
– *six-to-pica (2 points)*
20 le corps 3 points *m* (le corps 3, le diamant)
– *half nonpareil (four-to-pica) (3 points)*
21 le corps 4 points *m* (le corps 4, la perle)
– *brilliant (4 points);* sim.: *diamond (4½ points)*
22 le corps 5 points *m* (le corps 5, la parisienne)
– *pearl (5 points);* sim.: *ruby (*Am. *agate) (5½ points)*
23 le corps 6 points *m* (le corps 6, la nonpareille)
– *nonpareil (6 points);* sim.: *minionette (6½ points)*
24 le corps 7 points *m* (le corps 7, la mignonne)
– *minion (7 points)*
25 le corps 8 points *m* (le corps 8, la gaillarde)
– *brevier (8 points)*
26 le corps 9 points *m* (le corps 9, le petit romain)
– *bourgeois (9 points)*
27 le corps 10 points *m* (le corps 10, la philosophie)
– *long primer (10 points)*
28 le corps 12 points *m* (le corps 12, le cicéro, le douze, le Saint-Augustin)
– *pica (12 points)*
29 le corps 14 points *m* (le corps 14, le gros-texte)
– *english (14 points)*
30 le corps 16 points *m* (le corps 16, le gros romain)
– *great primer (two-line brevier,* Am. *Columbian) (16 points)*
31 le corps 20 points *m* (le corps 20, le paragon)
– *paragon (two-line primer) (20 points)*
32-37 la fabrication des caractères *m* (lettres *f*, types *m*)
– ***typefounding*** *(type casting)*
32 le graveur de poinçons *m*
– *punch cutter*
33 le burin (l'échoppe *f*)
– *graver (burin, cutter)*
34 la loupe
– *magnifying glass (magnifier)*
35 le poinçon
– *punch blank (die blank)*
36 le poinçon gravé en acier *m*
– *finished steel punch (finished steel die)*
37 la matrice justifiée
– *punched matrix (stamped matrix, strike, drive)*
38 le caractère
– ***type*** *(type character, character)*
39 la tête du caractère
– *head*
40 l'épaulement *m* (le talus)
– *shoulder*
41 le contre-poinçon
– *counter*
42 l'œil *m* du caractère
– *face (type face)*
43 la ligne de lettre *f* (l'alignement *m*)
– *type line (bodyline)*
44 la hauteur en papier *m*
– *height to paper (type height)*
45 la hauteur de moule *m*
– *height of shank (height of shoulder)*
46 la force de corps *m* (le corps *m*)
– *body size (type size, point size)*
47 le cran du caractère
– *nick*
48 la chasse (la cadrature)
– *set (width)*
49 la machine à graver les matrices *f*, une machine à graver spéciale
– ***matrix-boring machine*** *(matrix-engraving machine), a special-purpose boring machine*
50 le bâti en col *m* de cygne *m*
– *stand*
51 la fraise
– *cutter (cutting head)*
52 la table de gravure *f*
– *cutting table*
53 le chariot de pantographe *m*
– *pantograph carriage*
54 la glissière prismatique
– *V-way*
55 le modèle
– *pattern*
56 le porte-modèle
– *pattern table*
57 le palpeur
– *follower*
58 le pantographe
– *pantograph*
59 le serre-matrice
– *matrix clamp*
60 la broche porte-fraise *m*
– *cutter spindle*
61 le moteur d'entraînement *m*
– *drive motor*

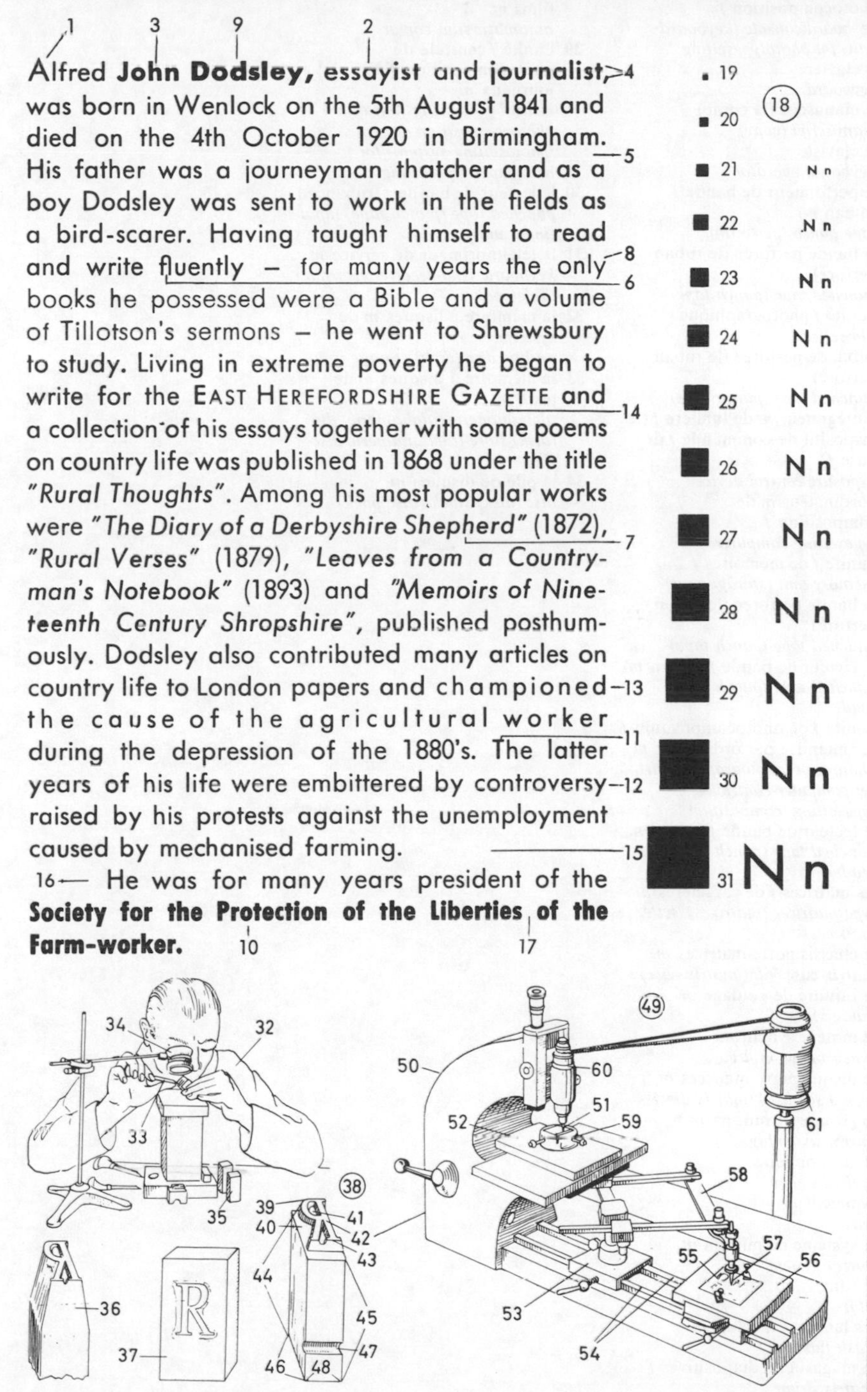
1 3 9 2
Alfred John Dodsley, essayist and journalist, 4
was born in Wenlock on the 5th August 1841 and
died on the 4th October 1920 in Birmingham.
5
His father was a journeyman thatcher and as a
boy Dodsley was sent to work in the fields as
a bird-scarer. Having taught himself to read
8
and write fluently – for many years the only
6
books he possessed were a Bible and a volume
of Tillotson's sermons – he went to Shrewsbury
to study. Living in extreme poverty he began to
write for the EAST HEREFORDSHIRE GAZETTE and
14
a collection of his essays together with some poems
on country life was published in 1868 under the title
"Rural Thoughts". Among his most popular works
were "The Diary of a Derbyshire Shepherd" (1872),
7
"Rural Verses" (1879), "Leaves from a Country-
man's Notebook" (1893) and "Memoirs of Nine-
teenth Century Shropshire", published posthum-
ously. Dodsley also contributed many articles on
country life to London papers and championed 13
the cause of the agricultural worker
11
during the depression of the 1880's. The latter
years of his life were embittered by controversy 12
raised by his protests against the unemployment
caused by mechanised farming.
15
16 He was for many years president of the
Society for the Protection of the Liberties of the
Farm-worker. 10 17
18
19
20
21 N n
22 N n
23 N n
24 N n
25 N n
26 N n
27 N n
28 N n
29 N n
30 N n
31 N n
32
33
34
35
36
37
38
39
40
41
42
43
44
45
46
47
48
R
49
50
51
52
53
54
55
56
57
58
59
60
61

176 Atelier de composition III (photocomposition)

1 l'unité *f* à clavier *m* de photocomposition *f*
– *keyboard console (keyboard unit) for phototypesetting*
2 le clavier
– *keyboard*
3 le manuscrit (la copie)
– *manuscript (copy)*
4 le claviste
– *keyboard operator*
5 le perforateur de bande *f* (ruban *m*)
– *tape punch (perforator)*
6 la bande perforée (le ruban perforé)
– *punched tape (punch tape)*
7 l'unité *f* photographique
– *filmsetter*
8 la bande perforée (le ruban perforé)
– *punched tape (punch tape)*
9 l'intégrateur *m* de lumière *f* (le dispositif de commande *f* de pose *f*)
– *exposure control device*
10 l'ordinateur *m* de composition *f*
– *typesetting computer*
11 l'unité *f* de mémoires *f*
– *memory unit (storage unit)*
12 la bande perforée (le ruban perforé)
– *punched tape (punch tape)*
13 le lecteur de bande *f* (ruban *m*)
– *punched tape (punch tape) reader*
14 l'unité *f* de photocomposition *f* commandée par ordinateur *m*
– *photo-unit (photographic unit) for computer-controlled typesetting (composition)*
15 le lecteur de bande *f* (ruban *m*)
– *punched tape (punch tape) reader*
16 les matrices *f* de caractères *m*
– *type matrices (matrixes) (letter matrices)*
17 le châssis porte-matrices *m*
– *matrix case (film matrix case)*
18 la rainure de guidage *m*
– *guide block*
19 le moteur synchrone
– *synchronous motor*
20 le disque porte-matrices *m*
– *type disc (disk) (matrix disc)*
21 le groupe de miroirs *m*
– *mirror assembly*
22 le coin optique
– *optical wedge*
23 l'objectif *m*
– *lens*
24 le système de miroirs *m*
– *mirror system*
25 le film
– *film*
26 les lampes *f* à éclats *m*
– *flash tubes*
27 le magasin de diapositives *f*
– *matrix drum*
28 le copieur automatique de films *m*
– *automatic film copier*
29 l'unité *f* centrale de photocomposition *f* de journaux *m*
– *central processing unit of a photocomposition system (photosetting system) for newspaper typesetting*
30 le lecteur de bande *f* (ruban *m*)
– *punched tape (punch tape) input (input unit)*
31 le téléimprimeur de service *m*
– *keyboard send-receive teleprinter (Teletype)*
32 la mémoire àdisques *m* du système
– *on-line disc (disk) storage unit*
33 la mémoire à disques *m* de texte *m*
– *alphanumeric (alphameric) disc (disk) store (alphanumeric disc file)*
34 la pile de disques *m*
– *disc (disk) stack (disc pack)*

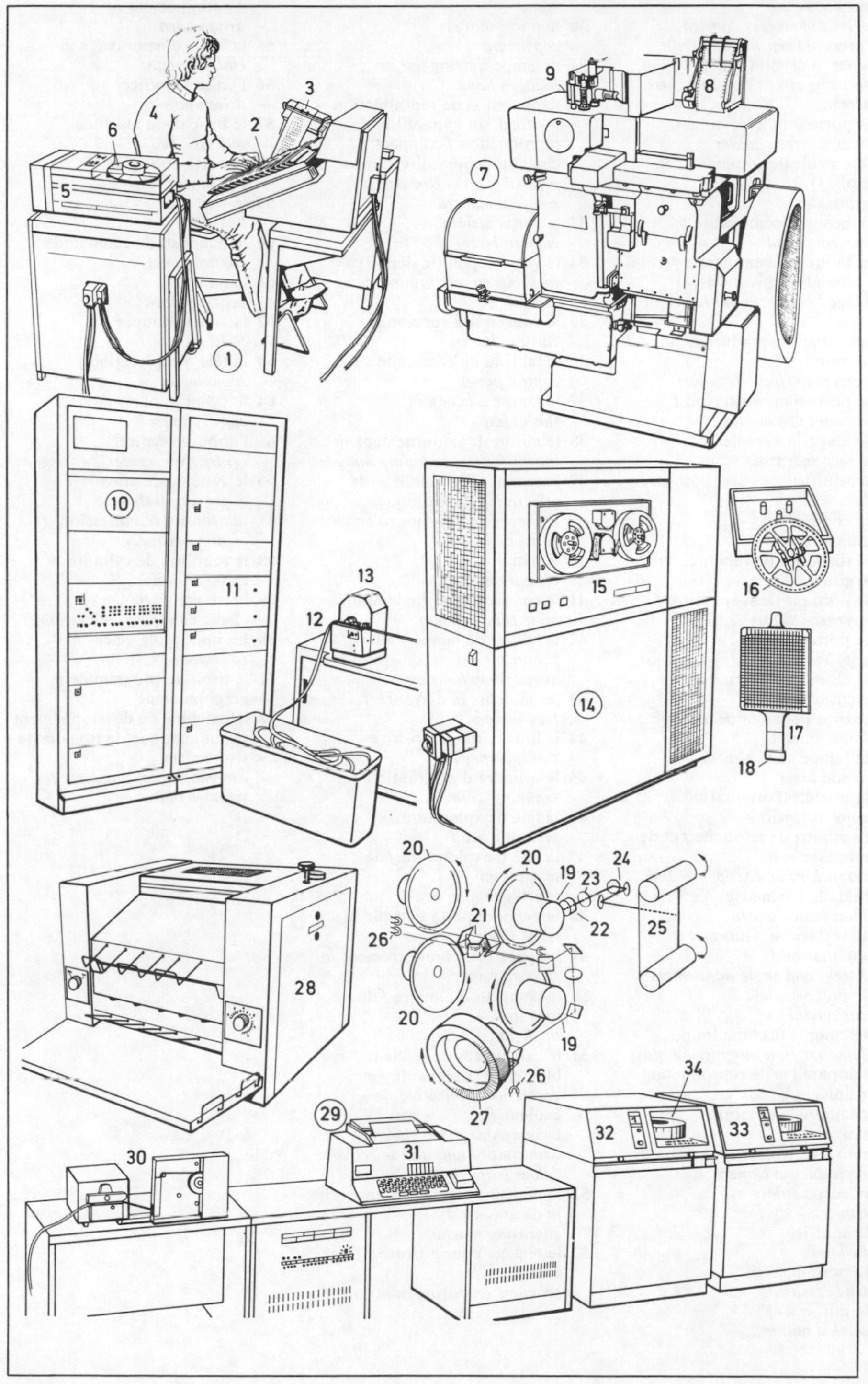
1
2
3
4
5
6
7
8
9
10
11
12
13
14
15
16
17
18
19
20
21
22
23
24
25
26
27
28
29
30
31
32
33
34

1 l'appareil *m* de reproduction *f* suspendu
– *overhead process camera (overhead copying camera)*
2 le verre dépoli (le dépoli)
– *focusing screen (ground glass screen)*
3 le porte-dépoli basculant
– *hinged screen holder*
4 le réticule (les repères *m* en croix *f*)
– *graticule*
5 le poste de commande *f*
– *control console*
6 le boîtier de commande *f* suspendu et pivotant
– *hinged bracket-mounted control panel*
7 les rubans *m* gradués de mise *f* au point
– *percentage focusing charts*
8 le porte-films à succion *f*
– *vacuum film holder*
9 le magasin à trames *f*
– *screen magazine*
10 le soufflet
– *bellows*
11 le corps avant
– *standard*
12 le dispositif de repérage *m*
– *register device*
13 le portique de suspension *f*
– *overhead gantry*
14 le porte-modèle
– *copyboard*
15 le châssis porte-modèle
– *copyholder*
16 le bras porte-lampe articulé
– *lamp bracket*
17 la lampe au xénon *m*
– *xenon lamp*
18 le modèle (l'original *m*)
– *copy (original)*
19 le pupitre de retouche *f* et de montage *m*
– *retouching and stripping desk*
20 la dalle lumineuse
– *illuminated screen*
21 le réglage en hauteur *f* et inclinaison *f*
– *height and angle adjustment*
22 le porte-modèle
– *copyboard*
23 le compte-fils, une loupe
– *linen tester, a magnifying glass*
24 l'appareil *m* de reproduction *f* universel, la chambre-laboratoire universelle
– *universal process and reproduction camera*
25 le corps arrière
– *camera body*
26 le soufflet
– *bellows*
27 le porte-objectif
– *lens carrier*
28 le miroir à 45°
– *angled mirror*
29 le montant en T *m*
– *stand*
30 le porte-modèle
– *copyboard*
31 la lampe à halogène *m*
– *halogen lamp*
32 l'appareil *m* de reproduction *f* vertical, un appareil *m* de reproduction *f* compact, la chambre-laboratoire compacte
– *vertical process camera, a compact camera*
33 le corps arrière
– *camera body*
34 le verre dépoli (le dépoli)
– *focusing screen (ground glass screen)*
35 le couvercle à succion *f*
– *vacuum back*
36 le tableau de commande *f*
– *control panel*
37 la lampe à éclats *m*
– *flash lamp*
38 le miroir de retournement *m*
– *mirror for right-reading images*
39 le scanner (l'appareil *m* de sélection *f* électronique)
– *scanner (colour,* Am. *color, correction unit)*
40 le bâti
– *base frame*
41 le compartiment de lampe *f*
– *lamp compartment*
42 le boîtier de lampe *f* au xénon *m*
– *xenon lamp housing*
43 les moteurs *m* d'avance *f*
– *feed motors*
44 le bras porte-diapositive
– *transparency arm*
45 le cylindre d'exploration *f*
– *scanning drum*
46 la tête d'exploration *f*
– *scanning head*
47 la tête d'exploration *f* de masque *m*
– *mask-scanning head*
48 le cylindre porte-masque *m*
– *mask drum*
49 l'espace *m* d'enregistrement *m*
– *recording space*
50 le chargeur à lumière *f* du jour *m*
– *daylight cassette*
51 le calculateur de couleur *f* avec bloc *m* de commande *f* et correction *f* sélective de couleur *f*
– *colour* (Am. *color) computer with control unit and selective colour correction*
52 la machine à graver (l'appareil *m* de gravure *f*)
– *engraving machine*
53 le réglage pour gravure *f* continue
– *seamless engraving adjustment*
54 l'embrayage *m* d'entraînement *m*
– *drive clutch*
55 la bride d'embrayage *m*
– *clutch flange*
56 l'unité *f* motrice
– *drive unit*
57 le banc de la machine
– *machine bed*
58 le porte-appareils
– *equipment carrier*
59 le traînard
– *bed slide*
60 le panneau de commande *f*
– *control panel*
61 le palier
– *bearing block*
62 la contre-poupée
– *tailstock*
63 la tête d'exploration *f*
– *scanning head*
64 le cylindre porte-modèle
– *copy cylinder*
65 l'appui *m* central
– *centre (*Am. *center) bearing*
66 le système de gravure *f*
– *engraving system*
67 le cylindre d'impression *f*
– *printing cylinder*
68 le tourillon de cylindre *m*
– *cylinder arm*
69 l'armoire *f* accolée
– *electronics (electronic) cabinet*
70 les unités *f* de calcul *m*
– *computers*
71 le tiroir de programme *m*
– *program input*
72 la machine de développement *m* automatique de films *m* de scanner *m*
– *automatic film processor for scanner films*

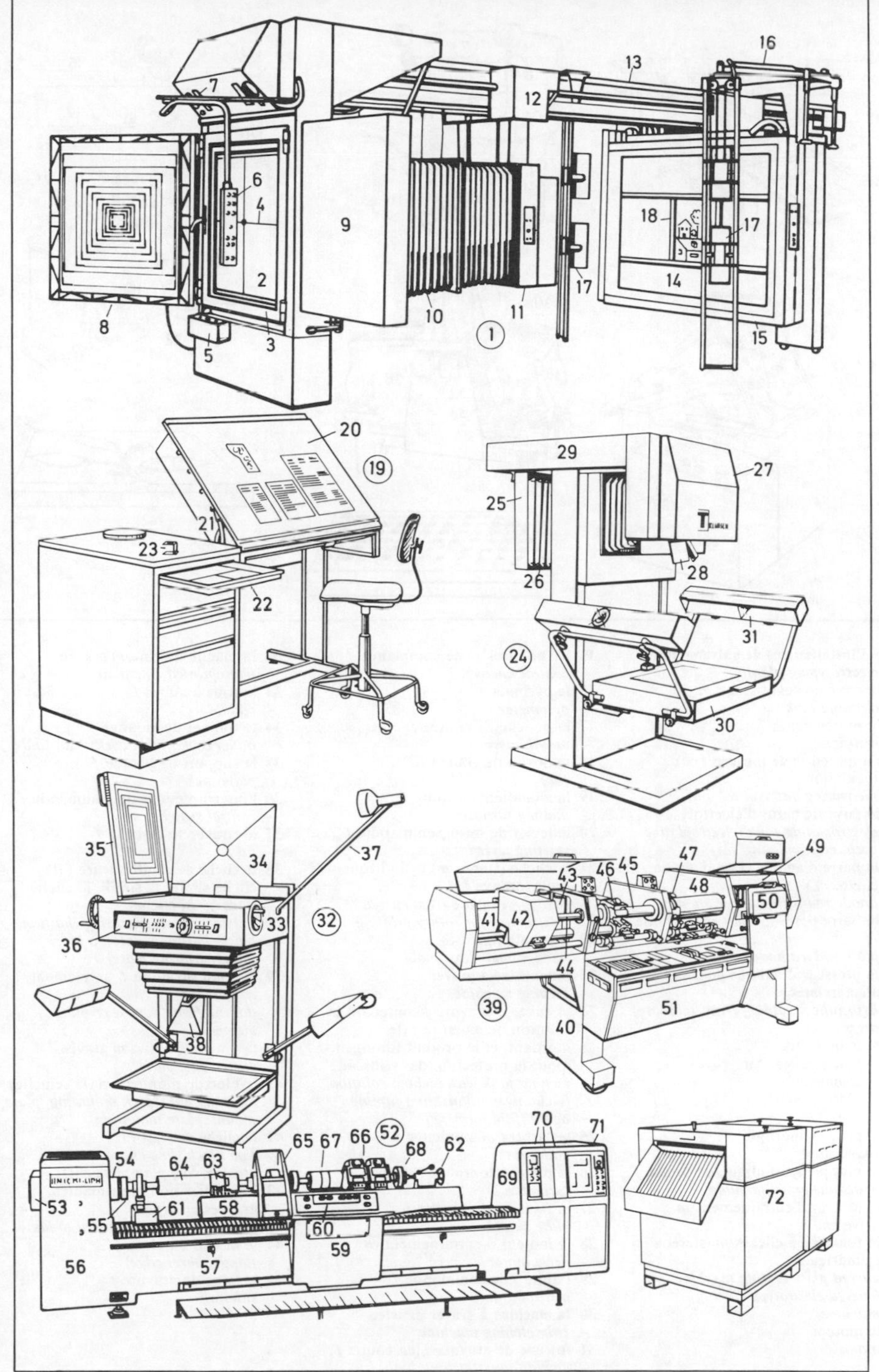
1
2
3
4
5
6
7
8
9
10
11
12
13
14
15
16
17
17
18
19
20
21
22
23
24
25
26
27
28
29
30
31
32
33
34
35
36
37
38
39
40
41
42
43
44
45
46
47
48
49
50
51
52
53
54
55
56
57
58
59
60
61
62
63
64
65
66
67
68
69
70
71
72

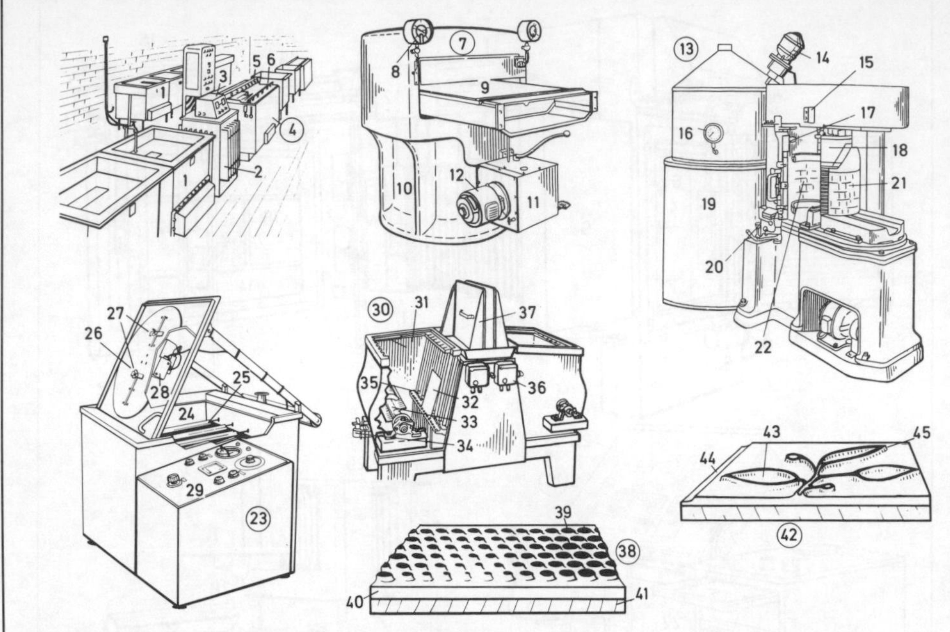

1-6 l'installation *f* **de galvanotypie** *f*
– ***electrotyping plant***
1 la cuve de dégraissage *m*
– *cleaning tank*
2 le redresseur
– *rectifier*
3 l'appareil *m* de mesure *f* et de régulation *f*
– *measuring and control unit*
4 la cuve (le bain) d'électrolyse *f*
– *electroplating tank (electroplating bath, electroplating vat)*
5 la barre d'anode *f* (anodes *f* de cuivre *m*)
– *anode rod (with copper anodes)*
6 la barre porte-moules *m* (cathode *f*)
– *plate rod (cathode)*
7 la presse hydraulique pour prise *f* **d'empreintes** *f*
– ***hydraulic moulding (***Am. *molding) press*
8 le manomètre
– *pressure gauge* (Am. *gage) (manometer)*
9 la platine inférieure de presse *f*
– *apron*
10 la base cylindrique
– *round base*
11 la pompe hydraulique de presse *f*
– *hydraulic pressure pump*
12 le moteur d'entraînement *m*
– *drive motor*
13 la fondeuse à clichés *m* (stéréos *m*) **cylindriques**
– ***curved plate casting machine*** *(curved electrotype casting machine)*
14 le moteur
– *motor*
15 les boutons *m* de commande *f*
– *control knobs*
16 le pyromètre
– *pyrometer*
17 la bouche de coulée *f*
– *mouth piece*
18 le noyau de coulée *f*
– *core*
19 la chaudière de fonte *f*
– *melting furnace*
20 le levier de mise *f* en marche *f*
– *starting lever*
21 le cliché (stéréo *m*) cylindrique pour rotative *f*
– *cast curved plate (cast curved electrotype) for rotary printing*
22 le moule fixe
– *fixed mould* (Am. *mold)*
23 la machine à graver
– ***etching machine***
24 la cuve de gravure *f* contenant la solution de morsure *f* (le mordant) et le produit filmogène [pour la protection des talus *m*]
– *etching tank with etching solution (etchant, mordant) and filming agent (film former)*
25 les arbres *m* à palettes *f*
– *paddles*
26 le plateau tournant
– *turntable*
27 la fixation de plaque *f*
– *plate clamp*
28 le moteur d'entraînement *m*
– *drive motor*
29 l'unité *f* de commande *f*
– *control unit*
30 la machine à graver jumelée
– ***twin etching machine***
31 la cuve de gravure *f* [en coupe *f*]
– *etching tank (etching bath) [in section]*
32 la plaque de zinc *m* gravée
– *photoprinted zinc plate*
33 la roue à aubes *f*
– *paddle*
34 le robinet de vidange *f*
– *outlet cock (drain cock,* Am. *faucet)*
35 le support de plaque *f*
– *plate rack*
36 l'interrupteur *m* de commande *f*
– *control switches*
37 le couvercle de cuve *f*
– *lid*
38 le cliché de similigravure *f* (le cliché simili, la simili, le cliché tramé), un cliché
– ***halftone photoengraving*** *(halftone block, halftone plate), a block (plate, printing plate)*
39 le point de simili *f*, un élément imprimant
– *dot (halftone dot), a printing element*
40 la plaque de zinc *m* gravée
– *etched zinc plate*
41 le bloc de montage *m* (la semelle)
– *block mount (block mounting, plate mount, plate mounting)*
42 le cliché de trait *m*
– ***line block*** *(line engraving, line etching, line plate, line cut)*
43 les parties non imprimantes, gravées en creux
– *non-printing, deep-etched areas*
44 le biseau du cliché
– *flange (bevel edge)*
45 le talus de gravure *f*
– *sidewall*

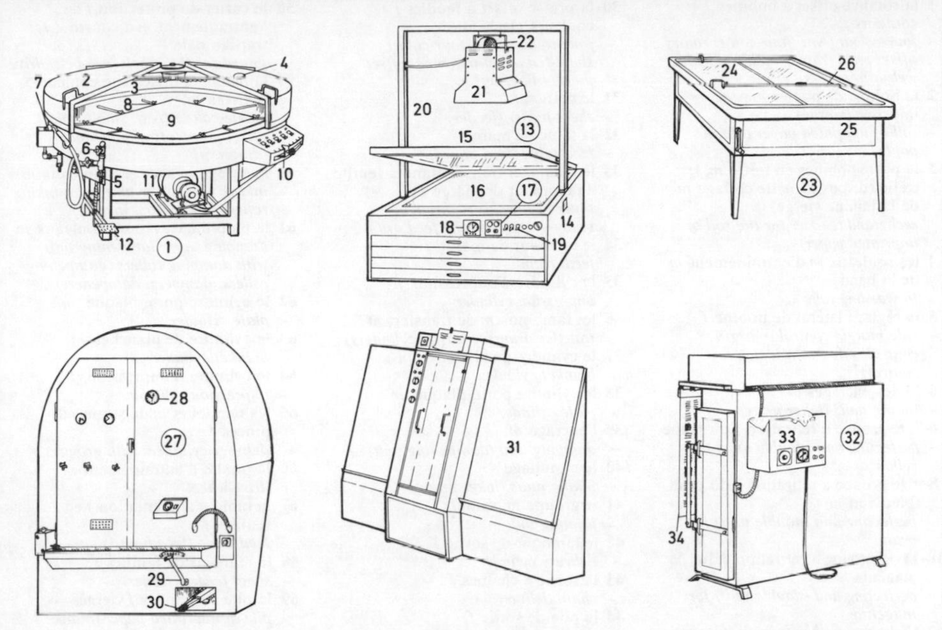

1 la tournette pour sensibiliser les plaques *f* offset
- *plate whirler (whirler, plate-coating machine) for coating offset plates*

2 le couvercle coulissant
- *sliding lid*

3 le chauffage électrique
- *electric heater*

4 le thermomètre
- *temperature gauge* (Am. *gage*)

5 le raccord d'eau *f* de rinçage *m*
- *water connection for the spray unit*

6 le rince-plaque circulaire
- *spray unit*

7 la douchette
- *hand spray*

8 les barres *f* de fixation *f* de la plaque
- *plate clamps*

9 la plaque de zinc *m* (*égal.*: plaque *f* de magnésium *m*, plaque *f* de cuivre *m*)
- *zinc plate* (also: *magnesium plate, copper plate*)

10 le pupitre de commande *f*
- *control panel*

11 le moteur d'entraînement *m*
- *drive motor*

12 la pédale de frein *m*
- *brake pedal*

13 le châssis pneumatique à copier
- *vacuum printing frame (vacuum frame, printing-down frame)*

14 le socle du châssis à copier
- *base of the vacuum printing frame (vacuum frame, printing-down frame)*

15 le couvercle vitré du châssis
- *plate glass frame*

16 la plaque offset couchée
- *coated offset plate*

17 le panneau de commande *f*
- *control panel*

18 l'intégrateur *m* de lumière *f*
- *exposure timer*

19 l'interrupteur *m* de pompe *f* à vide *m*
- *vacuum pump switches*

20 les montants *m*
- *support*

21 la lampe d'insolation *f* ponctuelle, une lampe aux halogénures *m*
- *point light exposure lamp, a quartz-halogen lamp*

22 la soufflante de lampe *f*
- *fan blower*

23 la table lumineuse de montage *m* des films *m*
- *stripping table (make-up table) for stripping films*

24 la dalle de verre *m* cristal *m*
- *crystal glass screen*

25 le caisson à lumière *f*
- *light box*

26 les règles *f* de précision *f* coulissantes
- *straightedge rules*

27 le séchoir centrifuge vertical
- *vertical plate-drying cabinet*

28 l'hygromètre *m*
- *hygrometer*

29 le réglage de vitesse *f*
- *speed control*

30 la pédale de frein *m*
- *brake pedal*

31 la machine de traitement *m* de plaques *f* présensibilisées
- *processing machine for presensitized plates*

32 le four de cuisson *f* de plaques *f* à colle-émail *f* (plaques *f* diazo)
- *burning-in oven for glue-enamel plates (diazo plates)*

33 le coffret de commande *f*
- *control box (control unit)*

34 la plaque diazo
- *diazo plate*

1 la rotative offset à bobines *f* 4 couleurs *f*
– *four-colour* (Am. *four-color) rotary offset press (rotary offset machine, web-offset press)*
2 la bobine de papier *m* non imprimé (vierge)
– *roll of unprinted paper (blank paper)*
3 le porte-bobines en trèfle *m*, le trèfle (dispositif *m* de collage *m* de la bobine vierge)
– *reel stand (carrier for the roll of unprinted paper)*
4 les rouleaux *m* d'entraînement *m* de la bande
– *forwarding rolls*
5 le réglage latéral de bobine *f*
– *side margin control (margin control, side control, side lay control)*
6-13 les encrages *m*
– *inking units (inker units)*
6-7 le groupe à retiration *f* du jaune
– *perfecting unit (double unit) for yellow*
8-9 le groupe à retiration *f* du cyan (bleu vert *m*)
– *perfecting unit (double unit) for cyan*
10-11 le groupe à retiration *f* du magenta
– *perfecting unit (double unit) for magenta*
12-13 le groupe à retiration *f* du noir
– *perfecting unit (double unit) for black*
14 le séchoir
– *drier*
15 la plieuse
– *folder (folder unit)*
16 le pupitre de commande *f*
– *control desk*
17 la feuille imprimée
– *sheet*
18 la rotative offset à bobines *f* 4 couleurs *f* [schéma]
– *four-colour* (Am. *four-color) rotary offset press (rotary offset machine, web-offset press) [diagram]*
19 le porte-bobines en trèfle *m* (le trèfle)
– *reel stand*
20 le réglage latéral de bobine *f*
– *side margin control (margin control, side control, side lay control)*
21 les rouleaux *m* d'encrage *m*
– *inking rollers (ink rollers, inkers)*
22 l'encrier *m*
– *ink duct (ink fountain)*
23 les rouleaux *m* de mouillage *m*
– *damping rollers (dampening rollers, dampers, dampeners)*
24 le cylindre de blanchet *m*
– *blanket cylinder*
25 le cylindre porte-plaque *m*
– *plate cylinder*
26 la bande (de papier *m*) mobile
– *route of the paper (of the web)*
27 le séchoir
– *drier*
28 les rouleaux *m* refroidisseurs
– *chilling rolls (cooling rollers, chill rollers)*
29 la plieuse
– *folder (folder unit)*
30 la presse offset à feuilles *f* 4 couleurs *f* [schéma]
– *four-colour* (Am. *four-color) sheet-fed offset machine (offset press) [diagram]*
31 le margeur
– *sheet feeder (feeder)*
32 la table de marge *f*
– *feed table (feed board)*
33 le balancier transmettant la feuille au tambour de marge *f*
– *route of the sheets through swing-grippers to the feed drum*
34 le tambour de marge *f*
– *feed drum*
35 le cylindre d'impression *f*
– *impression cylinder*
36 les tambours *m* de transfert *m*
– *transfer drums (transfer cylinders)*
37 le cylindre de blanchet *m*
– *blanket cylinder*
38 le cylindre porte-plaque *m*
– *plate cylinder*
39 l'encrage *m*
– *damping unit (dampening unit)*
40 le mouillage
– *inking units (inker units)*
41 le groupe imprimant
– *printing unit*
42 le tambour de sortie *f*
– *delivery cylinder*
43 la sortie à chaînes *f*
– *chain delivery*
44 la pile de sortie *f*
– *delivery pile*
45 la sortie de feuilles *f*
– *delivery unit (delivery mechanism)*
46 la machine offset une couleur (machine *f* offset)
– *single-colour* (Am. *single-color) offset press (offset machine)*
47 la pile de feuilles *f* (papier *m* pour impression *f*)
– *pile of paper (sheets, printing paper)*
48 le margeur à feuilles *f* (un margeur automatique)
– *sheet feeder (feeder), an automatic pile feeder*
49 la table de marge *f*
– *feed table (feed board)*
50 les rouleaux *m* d'encrage *m*
– *inking rollers (ink rollers, inkers)*
51 l'encrage *m*
– *inking units (inker units)*
52 les rouleaux *m* de mouillage *m*
– *damping rollers (dampening rollers, dampers, dampeners)*
53 le cylindre porte-plaque *m*, une plaque de zinc *m*
– *plate cylinder, a zinc plate*
54 le cylindre de blanchet *m*, un cylindre d'acier *m* portant un blanchet de caoutchouc *m*
– *blanket cylinder, a steel cylinder with rubber blanket*
55 la sortie à pile *f*
– *pile delivery unit for the printed sheets*
56 la barre à pinces *f*, un dispositif de pinces *f* à chaînes *f*
– *gripper bar, a chain gripper*
57 la pile de feuilles *f* imprimées
– *pile of printed paper (printed sheets)*
58 le carter de protection *f* de l'entraînement *m* à courroie *f* trapézoïdale
– *guard for the V-belt (vee-belt) drive*
59 la machine offset une couleur [schéma *m*]
– *single-colour* (Am. *single-color) offset press (offset machine) [diagram]*
60 l'encrage *m* avec ses rouleaux *m*
– *inking unit (inker unit) with inking rollers (ink rollers, inkers)*
61 le mouillage avec ses rouleaux *m*
– *damping unit (dampening unit) with damping rollers (dampening rollers, dampers, dampeners)*
62 le cylindre porte-plaque *m*
– *plate cylinder*
63 le cylindre de blanchet *m*
– *blanket cylinder*
64 le cylindre d'impression *f*
– *impression cylinder*
65 les tambours *m* de sortie *f* à pinces *f*
– *delivery cylinders with grippers*
66 la poulie d'entraînement *m*
– *drive wheel*
67 la table d'alimentation *f* en feuilles *f*
– *feed table (feed board)*
68 le margeur de feuilles *f*
– *sheet feeder (feeder)*
69 la pile de feuilles *f* vierges
– *pile of unprinted paper (blank paper, unprinted sheets, blank sheets)*
70 la machine offset de bureau *m*
– *small sheet-fed offset press*
71 l'encrage *m*
– *inking unit (inker unit)*
72 le margeur à succion *f*
– *suction feeder*
73 la sortie à pile *f*
– *pile feeder*
74 le tableau de commande *f* avec compteur *m*, manomètre *m*, régulateur *m* de débit *m* d'air *m* et interrupteur *m* de margeur *m*
– *instrument panel (control panel) with counter, pressure gauge* (Am. *gage), air regulator, and control switch for the sheet feeder (feeder)*
75 la machine offset à plat *m* (presse *f* à contre-épreuves *f* Maïländer)
– *flat-bed offset press (offset machine) (Mailänder' proofing press, proof press)*
76 l'encrage *m*
– *inking unit (inker unit)*
77 les rouleaux *m* d'encrage *m*
– *inking rollers (ink rollers, inkers)*
78 le marbre
– *bed (press bed, type bed, forme bed,* Am. *form bed)*
79 le cylindre de blanchet *m*
– *cylinder with rubber blanket*
80 le levier d'embrayage-débrayage *m* du groupe imprimant
– *starting and stopping lever for the printing unit*
81 le réglage de la pression
– *impression-setting wheel (impression-adjusting wheel)*

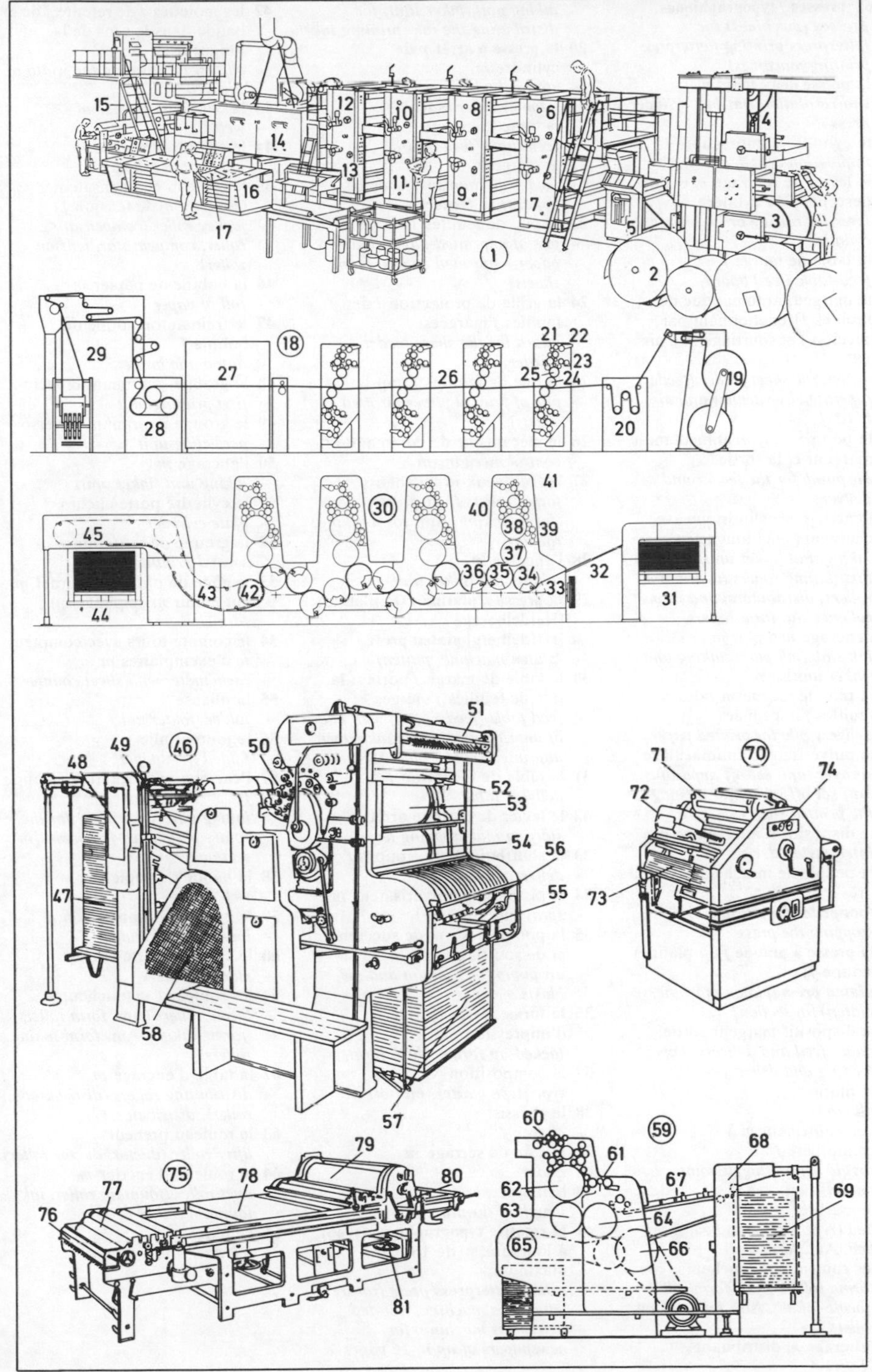
1
2
3
4
5
6
7
8
9
10
11
12
13
14
15
16
17
18
19
20
21
22
23
24
25
26
27
28
29
30
31
32
33
34
35
36
37
38
39
40
41
42
43
44
45
46
47
48
49
50
51
52
53
54
55
56
57
58
59
60
61
62
63
64
65
66
67
68
69
70
71
72
73
74
75
76
77
78
79
80
81

1-65 presses *f* **typographiques**
– ***presses (machines) for letterpress printing*** *(letterpress printing machines)*
1 la presse deux tours *m*
– ***two-revolution flat-bed cylinder press***
2 le cylindre d'impression *f*
– *impression cylinder*
3 le levier de relevage *m* et de descente *f* du cylindre
– *lever for raising or lowering the cylinder*
4 la table de marge *f*
– *feed table (feed board)*
5 le margeur automatique de feuilles *f* [fonctionnant par succion *f* et soufflage *m* d'air *m*]
– *automatic sheet feeder (feeder) [operated by vacuum and air blasts]*
6 la pompe à air *m* alimentant le margeur et la sortie
– *air pump for the feeder and delivery*
7 l'encrage *m* cylindrique avec chargeurs *m* et toucheurs *m*
– *inking unit (inker unit) with distributing rollers (distributor rollers, distributors) and forme rollers* (Am. *form rollers)*
8 l'encrage *m* à plat *m*
– *ink slab (ink plate) inking unit (inker unit)*
9 la pile de réception *f* des feuilles *f* imprimées
– *delivery pile for printed paper*
10 le pulvérisateur antimaculage
– *sprayer (anti set-off apparatus, anti set-off spray) for dusting the printed sheets*
11 le dispositif d'intercalage *m*
– *interleaving device*
12 la pédale de marche-arrêt de la presse
– *foot pedal for starting and stopping the press*
13 la presse à platine *f* (la platine) [coupe *f*]
– ***platen press*** *(platen machine, platen) [in section]*
14 le dispositif margeur-sortie
– *paper feed and delivery (paper feeding and delivery unit)*
15 la platine
– *platen*
16 l'entraînement *m* à genouillère *f*
– *toggle action (toggle-joint action)*
17 le marbre
– *bed (type bed, press bed, forme bed,* Am. *form bed)*
18 les rouleaux *m* toucheurs
– *forme rollers* (Am. *form rollers) (forme-inking,* Am. *form-inking, rollers)*
19 l'encrage *m* distribuant l'encre *f*
– *inking unit (inker unit) for distributing the ink (printing ink)*
20 la presse à arrêt *m* de cylindre *m*
– ***stop-cylinder press*** *(stop-cylinder machine)*
21 la table de marge *f*
– *feed table (feed board)*
22 le margeur
– *feeder mechanism (feeding apparatus, feeder)*
23 la pile de feuilles *f* vierges
– *pile of unprinted paper (blank paper, unprinted sheets, blank sheets)*
24 la grille de protection *f* des feuilles *f* margées
– *guard for the sheet feeder (feeder)*
25 la pile de feuilles *f* imprimées
– *pile of printed paper (printed sheets)*
26 le mécanisme de commande *f*
– *control mechanism*
27 les rouleaux *m* toucheurs
– *forme rollers* (Am. *form rollers) (forme-inking,* Am. *form-inking, rollers)*
28 l'encrage *m*
– *inking unit (inker unit)*
29 la presse à platine *f* (la platine) [Heidelberg]
– [Heidelberg] **platen press** *(platen machine, platen)*
30 la table de marge *f* portant la pile de feuilles *f* vierges
– *feed table (feed board) with pile of unprinted paper (blank paper, unprinted sheets, blank sheets)*
31 la table de réception *f*
– *delivery table*
32 le levier de marche-arrêt
– *starting and stopping lever*
33 la soufflerie de réception *f*
– *delivery blower*
34 le pistolet de pulvérisateur *m*
– *spray gun (sprayer)*
35 la pompe à air *m* de succion *f* et de soufflage *m*
– *air pump for vacuum and air blasts*
36 la forme serrée (forme *f* d'impression *f*)
– ***locked-up forme*** (Am. *form)*
37 la composition
– *type (type matter, matter)*
38 le châssis
– *chase*
39 le coin de serrage *m*
– *quoin*
40 le lingot
– *length of furniture*
41 la rotative typographique (typo) à journaux *m* de 16 pages *f* au maximum
– ***rotary letterpress press*** *(rotary letterpress machine, web-fed letterpress machine) for newspapers of up to 16 pages*
42 les molettes *f* de refente *f* de la bande dans le sens de la longueur
– *slitters for dividing the width of the web*
43 la bande de papier *m*
– *web*
44 le cylindre imprimant
– *impression cylinder*
45 le rouleau compensateur (rouleau *m* de tension *f*)
– *jockey roller (compensating roller, compensator, tension roller)*
46 la bobine de papier *m*
– *roll of paper*
47 le frein automatique de bobine *f*
– *automatic brake*
48 le groupe imprimant le recto
– *first printing unit*
49 le groupe imprimant le verso
– *perfecting unit*
50 l'encrage *m*
– *inking unit (inker unit)*
51 le cylindre porte-clichés
– *plate cylinder*
52 le groupe de retiration *f*
– *second printing unit*
53 le cône de pliage *m* (cornet *m*, entonnoir *m* de pliage *m*)
– *former*
54 le compte-tours avec compteur *m* d'exemplaires *m*
– *tachometer with sheet counter*
55 la plieuse
– *folder (folder unit)*
56 le journal plié
– *folded newspaper*
57 l'encrage *m* de rotative *f* [coupe *f*]
– ***inking unit*** *(inker unit) for the rotary press (web-fed press) [in section]*
58 la bande de papier *m*
– *web*
59 le cylindre d'impression *f*
– *impression cylinder*
60 le cylindre porte-clichés
– *plate cylinder*
61 les rouleaux *m* toucheurs
– *forme rollers* (Am. *form rollers) (forme-inking,* Am. *form-inking, rollers)*
62 la table d'encrage *m*
– *distributing rollers (distributor rollers, distributors)*
63 le rouleau preneur
– *lifter roller (ductor, ductor roller)*
64 le rouleau d'encrier *m*
– *duct roller (fountain roller, ink fountain roller)*
65 l'encrier *m*
– *ink duct (ink fountain)*

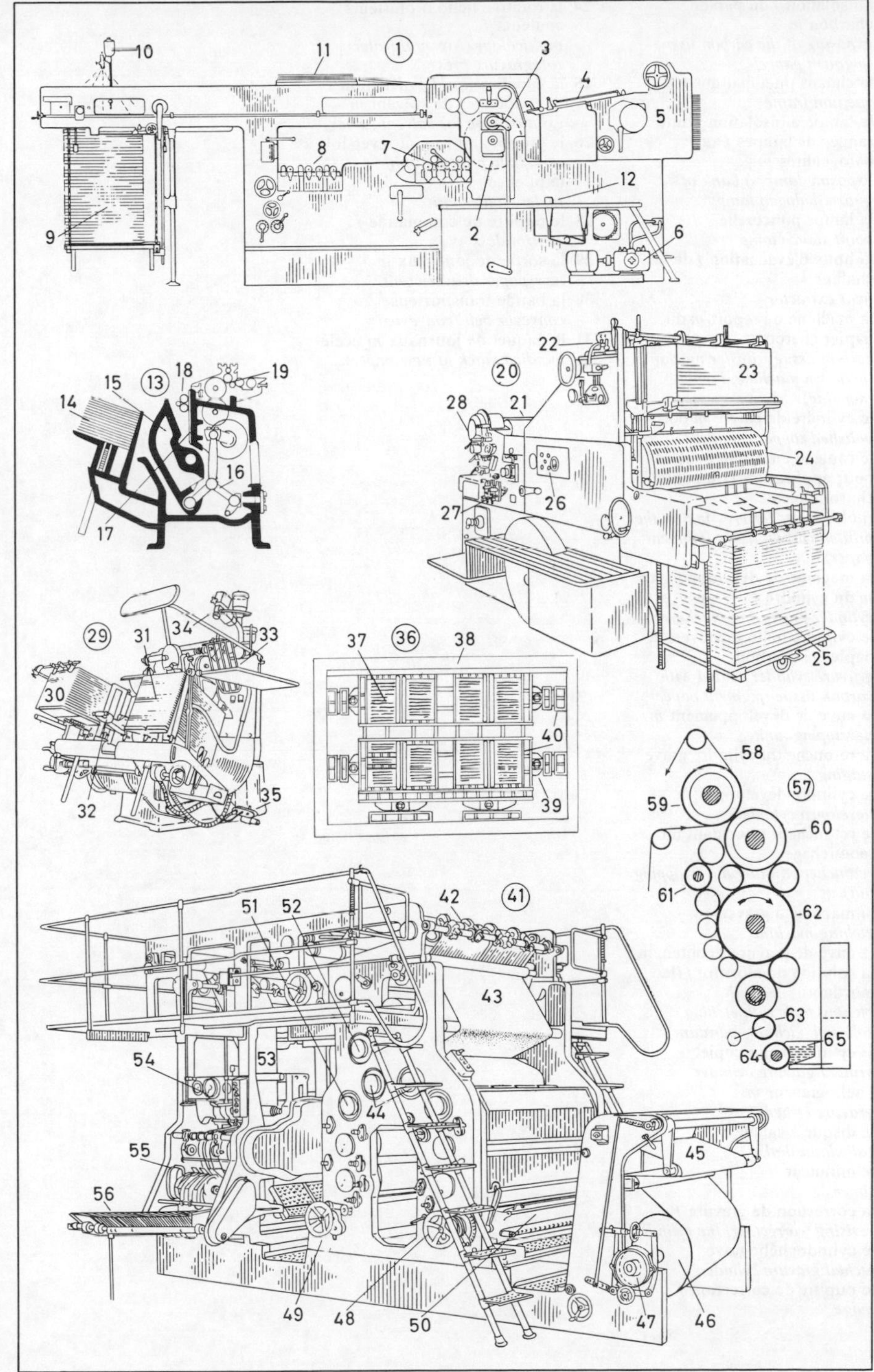
1
2
3
4
5
6
7
8
9
10
11
12
13
14
15
16
17
18
19
20
21
22
23
24
25
26
27
28
29
30
31
32
33
34
35
36
37
38
39
40
41
42
43
44
45
46
47
48
49
50
51
52
53
54
55
56
57
58
59
60
61
62
63
64
65

182 Impression en héliogravure

1 l'insolation *f* du papier charbon *m*
– *exposure of the carbon tissue (pigment paper)*
2 le châssis pneumatique
– *vacuum frame*
3 la lampe d'insolation *f*, une rangée de lampes *f* aux halogénures *m*
– *exposing lamp, a bank of quartz-halogen lamps*
4 la lampe ponctuelle
– *point source lamp*
5 la hotte d'évacuation *f* de la chaleur
– *heat extractor*
6 la machine de report *m* du papier charbon
– *carbon tissue transfer machine (laydown machine, laying machine)*
7 le cylindre de cuivre *m* poli
– *polished copper cylinder*
8 le rouleau en caoutchouc *m* pour application *f* du papier charbon insolé
– *rubber roller for pressing on the printed carbon tissue (pigment paper)*
9 la machine de développement *m* du cylindre
– *cylinder-processing machine*
10 le cylindre hélio recouvert de papier *m* charbon
– *gravure cylinder coated with carbon tissue (pigment paper)*
11 la cuve de développement *m*
– *developing tank*
12 la retouche du cylindre gravé
– *staging*
13 le cylindre développé
– *developed cylinder*
14 le retoucheur effectuant un rebouchage
– *retoucher painting out (stopping out)*
15 la machine à graver
– *etching machine*
16 la cuve de gravure *f* contenant la solution de morsure *f* (le mordant)
– *etching tank with etching solution (etchant, mordant)*
17 le cylindre hélio copié
– *printed gravure cylinder*
18 l'héliograveur *m*
– *gravure etcher*
19 le disque à calcul *m*
– *calculator dial*
20 le minuteur
– *timer*
21 la correction de gravure *f*
– *revising (correcting) the cylinder*
22 le cylindre héliogravé
– *etched gravure cylinder*
23 le pupitre de correction *f*
– *ledge*
24 la rotative hélio à plusieurs couleurs *f*
– *multicolour* (Am. *multicolor*) *rotogravure press*
25 la canalisation d'évacuation *f* des vapeurs *f* de solvant *m*
– *exhaust pipe for solvent fumes*
26 le groupe imprimant réversible
– *reversible printing unit*
27 la plieuse
– *folder (folder unit)*
28 le pupitre de commande *f*
– *control desk*
29 la sortie de journaux *m*
– *newspaper delivery unit*
30 la bande transporteuse
– *conveyor belt (conveyor)*
31 le paquet de journaux *m* ficelé
– *bundled stack of newspapers*

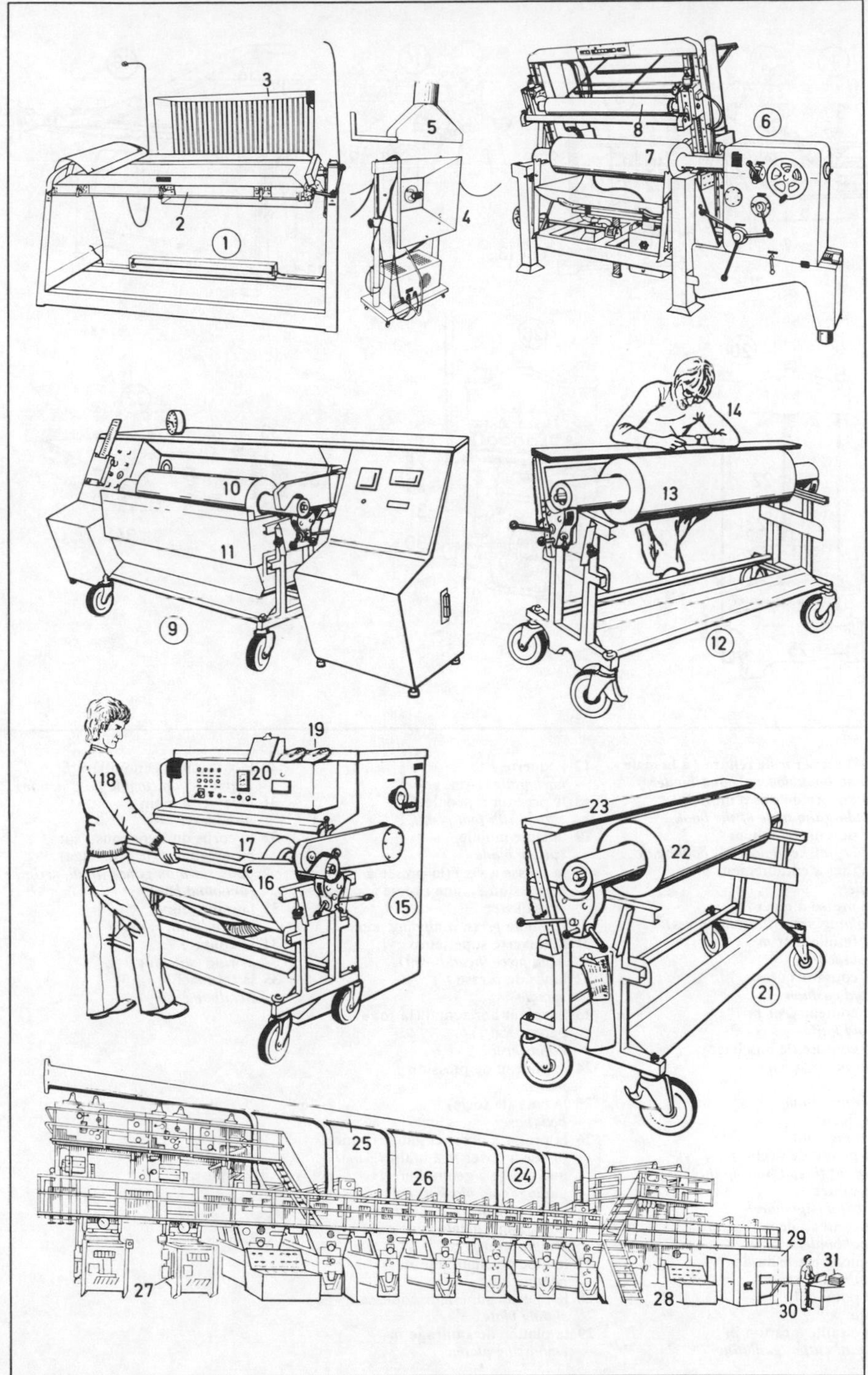
1
2
3
4
5
6
7
8
9
10
11
12
13
14
15
16
17
18
19
20
21
22
23
24
25
26
27
28
29
30
31

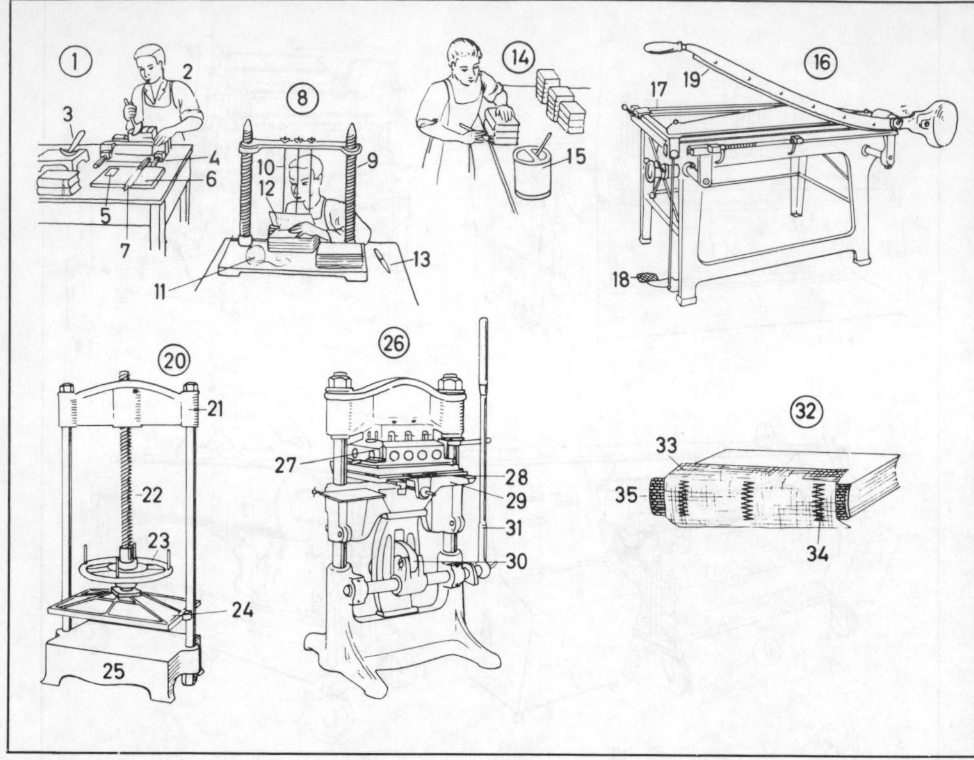

1-35 l'atelier *m* **de reliure** *f* **à la main**
– ***hand bookbindery*** *(hand bindery)*
1 la dorure du dos d'un livre
– *gilding the spine of the book*
2 le doreur, un relieur
– *gold finisher (gilder), a bookbinder*
3 le filet à encadrement *m*
– *fillet*
4 la presse à relier
– *holding press (finishing press)*
5 la feuille d'or *m*
– *gold leaf*
6 le coussin à or *m*
– *gold cushion*
7 le couteau à or *m*
– *gold knife*
8 la couture (le brochage)
– *sewing (stitching)*
9 le cousoir
– *sewing frame*
10 la ficelle
– *sewing cord*
11 la pelote de ficelle *f*
– *ball of thread (sewing thread)*
12 le cahier
– *section (signature)*
13 le couteau de relieur *m*
– *bookbinder's knife*
14 l'encollage *m* du dos
– *gluing the spine*
15 le pot à colle *f*
– *glue pot*
16 la cisaille à carton *m*
– *board cutter (guillotine)*
17 l'équerre *f*
– *back gauge (Am. gage)*
18 le pressoir à pédale *f*
– *clamp with foot pedal*
19 la lame mobile
– *cutting blade*
20 la presse à vis *f* (la presse à percussion *f*), une presse à satiner et paqueter
– *standing press, a nipping press*
21 la traverse supérieure
– *head piece (head beam)*
22 la vis de presse *f*
– *spindle*
23 le volant horizontal (la roue de percussion *f*)
– *handwheel*
24 le plateau de pression *f*
– *platen*
25 la base (le socle)
– *bed (base)*
26 la presse à dorer et gaufrer, une presse à levier *m* à main *f*; *anal.*: une presse à genouillère *f*
– *gilding (gold blocking) and embossing press, a hand-lever press;* sim.: *toggle-joint press (toggle-lever press)*
27 le bloc de chauffage *m*
– *heating box*
28 le plateau supérieur coulissant
– *sliding plate*
29 la platine de gaufrage *m*
– *embossing platen*
30 le système à genouillère *f*
– *toggle action (toggle-joint action)*
31 le levier à main *f*
– *hand lever*
32 le corps du livre cousu sur mousseline *f* (le brochage)
– *book sewn on gauze (mull, scrim) (unbound book)*
33 la mousseline
– *gauze (mull, scrim)*
34 la couture
– *sewing (stitching)*
35 la tranchefile
– *headband*

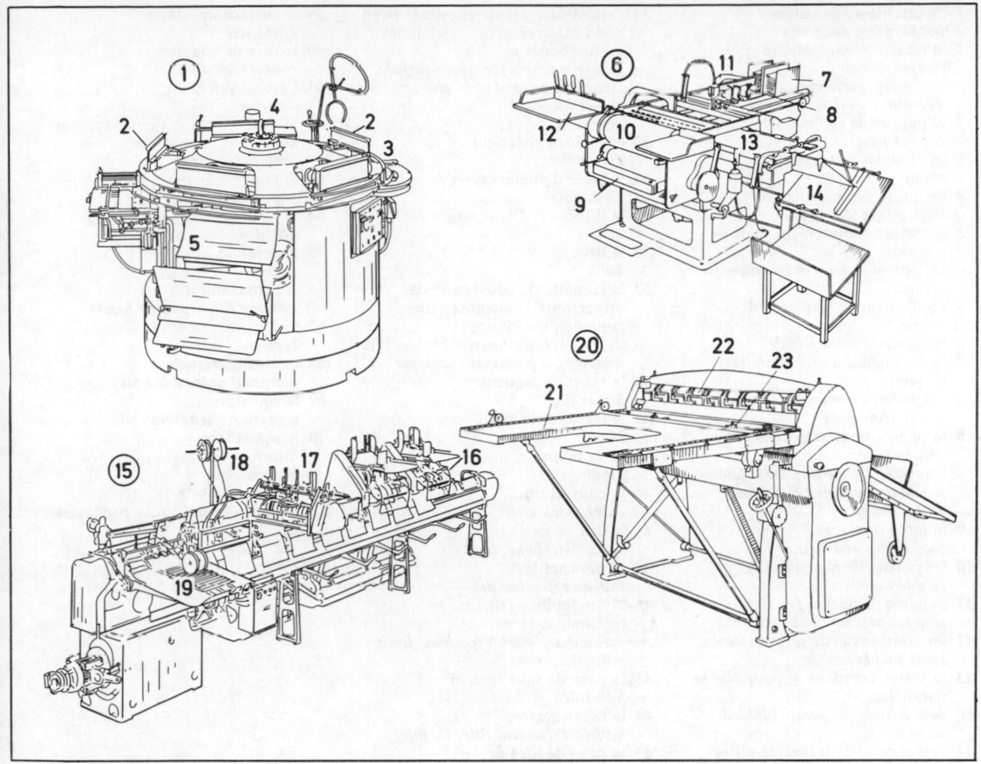

1-23 machines *f* **de reliure** *f*
– ***bookbinding machines***
1 la brocheuse automatique sans couture *f* (l'encolleuse *f*) pour faibles tirages *m*
– ***adhesive binder*** *(perfect binder) for short runs*
2 le poste d'alimentation *f* manuelle
– *manual feed station*
3 le poste de rognage *m*
– *cutoff knife and roughing station*
4 le dispositif d'encollage *m*
– *gluing mechanism*
5 la sortie de livres *m*
– *delivery (book delivery)*
6 la machine à faire les couvertures *f*
– ***case maker*** *(case-making machine)*
7 les magasins *m* de couvertures *f* en carton *m*
– *board feed hopper*
8 les pinces *f* tire-carton
– *pickup sucker*
9 le bac à colle *f*
– *glue tank*
10 le cylindre porte-recouvrement
– *cover cylinder*
11 le bras suceur
– *picker head*
12 la table d'alimentation *f* en matières *f* de recouvrement *m* [toile *f*, carton *m*, cuir *m*]
– *feed table for covering materials [linen, paper, leather]*
13 le mécanisme de pression *f*
– *pressing mechanism*
14 la table de réception *f*
– *delivery table*
15 l'encarteuse-piqueuse *f*
– ***gang stitcher*** *(gathering and wire-stitching machine, gatherer and wire stitcher)*
16 le margeur de feuilles *f*
– *sheet feeder (sheet-feeding station)*
17 le margeur de pliage *m*
– *folder-feeding station*
18 le dévidoir de fil *m* métallique
– *stitching wire feed mechanism*
19 la table de réception *f*
– *delivery table*
20 la cisaille circulaire à carton *m*
– ***rotary board cutter*** *(rotary board-cutting machine)*
21 la table de marge *f* échancrée
– *feed table with cut-out section*
22 la molette de coupe *f*
– *rotary cutter*
23 le guide d'entrée *f*
– *feed guide*

1-35 machines *f* de reliure *f*
– ***bookbinding machines***
1 le massicot automatique (massiquot *m*)
– *guillotine (guillotine cutter, automatic guillotine cutter)*
2 le pupitre de commande *f*
– *control panel*
3 le sommier de pression *f*
– *clamp*
4 l'équerre *f* de massicot *m*
– *back gauge* (Am. *gage)*
5 le cadran d'ajustement *m* de la pression
– *calibrated pressure adjustment [to clamp]*
6 l'indicateur de format *m* de coupe *f*
– *illuminated cutting scale*
7 la commande à une main de l'équerre *f*
– *single-hand control for the back gauge* (Am. *gage)*
8 la plieuse mixte à poches *f* et à couteaux *m*
– *combined buckle and knife folding machine (combined buckle and knife folder)*
9 la table de marge *f*
– *feed table (feed board)*
10 les poches de pliage *m*
– *fold plates*
11 la butée de poche *f*
– *stop for making the buckle fold*
12 les couteaux *m* de plis *m* croisés
– *cross fold knives*
13 la sortie à cordons *m* pour plis *m* parallèles
– *belt delivery for parallel-folded signatures*
14 le dispositif de troisième pli *m*
– *third cross fold unit*
15 la sortie après le troisième pli *m*
– *delivery tray for cross-folded signatures*
16 la couseuse à fil *m*
– *sewing machine (book-sewing machine)*
17 le dévidoir à fil *m*
– *spool holder*
18 la cannette
– *thread cop (thread spool)*
19 le dévidoir à mousseline *f*
– *gauze roll holder (mull roll holder, scrim roll holder)*
20 la mousseline
– *gauze (mull, scrim)*
21 les cylindres *m* porte-aiguilles
– *needle cylinder with sewing needles*
22 le volume cousu
– *sewn book*
23 la sortie
– *delivery*
24 le chariot porte-aiguilles
– *reciprocating saddle*
25 le margeur (de feuilles *f*)
– *sheet feeder (feeder)*
26 le magasin de margeur *m*
– *feed hopper*
27 la machine à emboîter les livres *m*
– *casing-in machine*
28 l'encolleuse *f* de mors *m*
– *joint and side pasting attachment*
29 le couteau
– *blade*
30 le préchauffage
– *preheater unit*
31 l'encolleuse *f* pour encollage *m* en plein *m*, en réserve *f*, en bandes *f* ou des bords *m*
– *gluing machine for whole-surface, stencil, edge, and strip gluing*
32 le bac à colle *f*
– *glue tank*
33 le rouleau encolleur
– *glue roller*
34 la table d'alimentation *f*
– *feed table*
35 le dispositif d'évacuation *f*
– *delivery*
36 le livre
– ***book***
37 la jaquette (la couverture de protection*f*, la chemise), une jaquette publicitaire
– *dust jacket (dust cover, bookjacket, wrapper), a publisher's wrapper*
38 le rabat de jaquette *f*
– *jacket flap*
39 le texte sur le rabat
– *blurb*
40-42 la reliure
– *binding*
40 la couverture
– *cover (book cover, case)*
41 le dos
– *spine (backbone, back)*
42 la tranchefile
– *tailband (footband)*
43-47 les feuilles *f* de titre *m* (préliminaires *f*)
– *preliminary matter (prelims, front matter)*
43 la page de faux titre *m*
– *half-title*
44 le faux titre
– *half-title (bastard title, fly title)*
45 la page de titre *m*
– *title page*
46 le titre (grand titre *m*)
– *full title (main title)*
47 le sous-titre
– *subtitle*
48 la marque d'éditeur *m*
– *publisher's imprint (imprint)*
49 la feuille de garde *f* (la garde, la page de garde *f*)
– *fly leaf (endpaper, endleaf)*
50 la dédicace manuscrite
– *handwritten dedication*
51 l'ex-libris *m*
– *bookplate (ex libris)*
52 le livre ouvert
– *open book*
53 la page
– *page*
54 le pli
– *fold*
55-58 les marges *f*
– *margin*
55 la marge intérieure (la marge de petit fond *m*)
– *back margin (inside margin, gutter)*
56 la marge supérieure (la marge de tête *f*)
– *head margin (upper margin)*
57 la marge extérieure (la marge de grand fond *m*)
– *fore edge margin (outside margin, fore edge)*
58 la marge inférieure (la marge de pied *m*)
– *tail margin (foot margin, tail, foot)*
59 la surface imprimée
– *type area*
60 le titre de chapitre *m*
– *chapter heading*
61 l'astérisque *m*
– *asterisk*
62 la note en bas *m* de page *f*, une note
– *footnote, a note*
63 le numéro de page *f* (le folio)
– *page number*
64 la page sur deux colonnes *f*
– *double-column page*
65 la colonne
– *column*
66 le titre courant
– *running title (running head)*
67 le sous-titre courant
– *caption*
68 la note marginale
– *marginal note (side note)*
69 la signature
– *signature (signature code)*
70 le signet fixe
– *attached bookmark (attached bookmarker)*
71 le signet mobile
– *loose bookmark (loose bookmarker)*

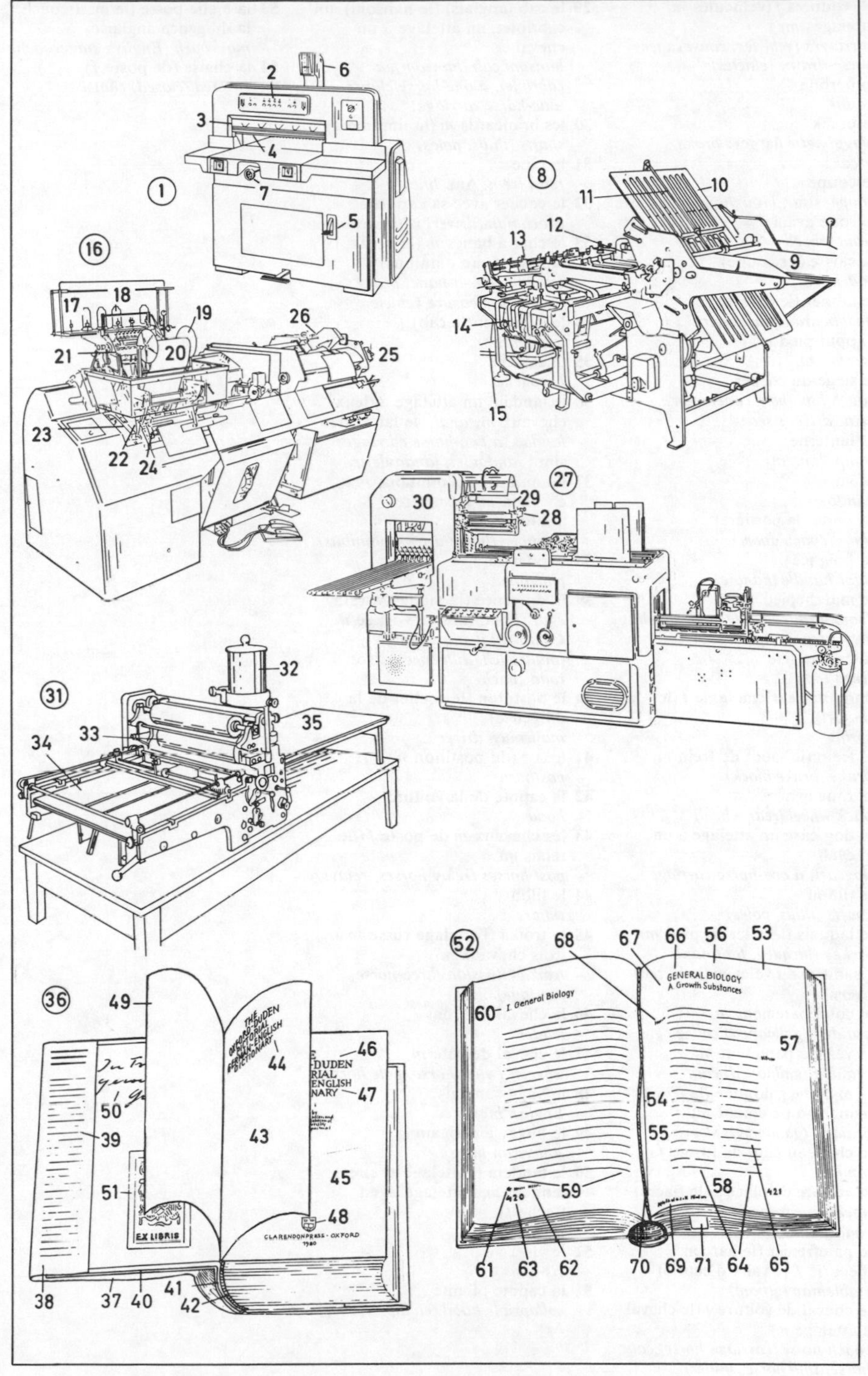
1 2 3 4 5 6 7 8 9 10 11 12 13 14 15 16 17 18 19 20 21 22 23 24 25 26 27 28 29 30 31 32 33 34 35 36 37 38 39 40 41 42 43 44 45 46 47 48 49 50 51 52 53 54 55 56 57 58 59 60 61 62 63 64 65 66 67 68 69 70 71
THE OXFORD-DUDEN PICTORIAL FRENCH-ENGLISH DICTIONARY
CLARENDON PRESS · OXFORD
1980
EX LIBRIS
GENERAL BIOLOGY
A Growth Substances
I. General Biology
420
421

1-54 voitures *f* (véhicules *m*, attelages *m*)
– *carriages (vehicles, conveyances, horse-drawn vehicles)*
1 la berline
– *berlin*
2 le break
– *waggonette (*larger: *brake, break)*
3 le coupé
– *coupé;* sim.: *brougham*
4 la roue avant
– *front wheel*
5 la caisse (de coupé)
– *coach body*
6 le tablier (le pare-boue)
– *dashboard (splashboard)*
7 l'appui-pied *m*
– *footboard*
8 le siège du cocher
– *coach box (box, coachman's seat, driver's seat)*
9 la lanterne
– *lamp (lantern)*
10 la vitre
– *window*
11 la porte (la portière)
– *door (coach door)*
12 la poignée
– *door handle (handle)*
13 le marchepied
– *footboard (carriage step, coach step, step, footpiece)*
14 la capote fixe
– *fixed top*
15 l'amortisseur *m* à lame *f* (le ressort)
– *spring*
16 le frein (le sabot de frein *m*)
– *brake (brake block)*
17 la roue arrière
– *back wheel (rear wheel)*
18 le dog-cart, un attelage à un cheval
– *dogcart, a one-horse carriage*
19 le timon
– *shafts (thills, poles)*
20 le laquais (le valet de pied *m*)
– *lackey (lacquey, footman)*
21 l'habit *m* du valet *m* (la livrée)
– *livery*
22 le col à parement *m*
– *braided (gallooned) collar*
23 la veste à parement *m*
– *braided (gallooned) coat*
24 la manche galonnée (la manche à parement *m*)
– *braided (gallooned) sleeve*
25 le chapeau haut de forme *f*
– *top hat*
26 la voiture de place *f* (le fiacre)
– *hackney carriage (hackney coach, cab, growler,* Am. *hack)*
27 le palefrenier (le garçon d'écurie *f*, le valet d'écurie)
– *stableman (groom)*
28 le cheval de voiture *f* (le cheval d'attelage *m*)
– *coach horse (carriage horse, cab horse, thill horse, thiller)*
29 le cab (anglais) (le hansom), un cabriolet, un attelage à un cheval
– *hansom cab (hansom), a cabriolet, a one-horse chaise (one-horse carriage)*
30 les brancards *m* (la limonière)
– *shafts (thills, poles)*
31 la rêne
– *reins (rein,* Am. *line)*
32 le cocher avec sa capuche
– *coachman (driver) with inverness*
33 le char à bancs *m* (le break, la tapissière, un omnibus)
– *covered char-a-banc (brake, break), a pleasure vehicle*
34 le cabriolet (le cab)
– *gig (chaise)*
35 la calèche
– *barouche*
36 le landau, un attelage à deux chevaux *m*; *anal.:* le landaulet
– *landau, a two-horse carriage;* sim.: *landaulet, landaulette*
37 l'omnibus *m* (l'omnibus *m* à chevaux *m*, la voiture publique)
– *omnibus (horse-drawn omnibus)*
38 le phaéton
– *phaeton*
39 la diligence (la malle-poste); *égal.:* la voiture de voyage *m*
– *Continental stagecoach (mailcoach, diligence);* also: *road coach*
40 le postillon (le cocher de la diligence)
– *mailcoach driver*
41 le cor (du postillon *m*)
– *posthorn*
42 la capote de la voiture
– *hood*
43 les chevaux *m* de poste *f* (de relais *m*)
– *post horses (relay horses, relays)*
44 le tilbury
– *tilbury*
45 la troïka (l'attelage russe *m* à trois chevaux *m*)
– *troika (Russian three-horse carriage)*
46 le cheval de front
– *leader*
47 le cheval de côté *m*
– *wheeler (wheelhorse, pole horse)*
48 le buggy anglais
– *English buggy*
49 le buggy américain
– *American buggy*
50 le tandem (l'attelage *m* en tandem *m*, l'attelage *m* en flèche *f*)
– *tandem*
51 le vis-à-vis
– *vis-à-vis*
52 la capote pliante
– *collapsible hood (collapsible top)*
53 la malle-poste (le mail-coach, la diligence anglaise)
– *mailcoach (English stagecoach)*
54 la chaise (de poste *f*)
– *covered (closed) chaise*

1
2
3
4
5
6
7
8
9
10
11
12
13
14
15
16
17
18
19
20
21
22
23
24
25
26
27
28
29
30
31
32
33
34
35
36
37
38
39
40
41
42
43
44
45
46
47
48
49
50
51
52
53
54

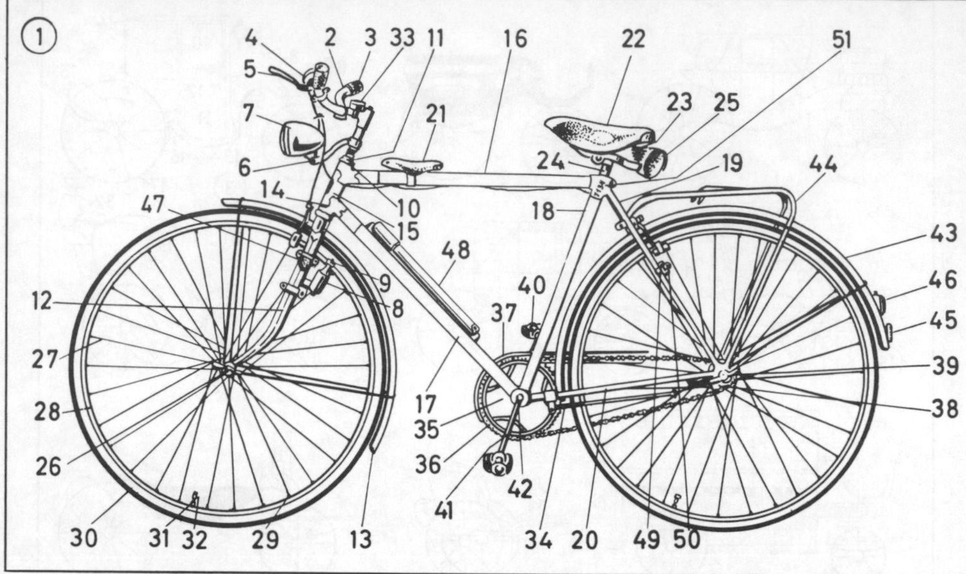

1 la bicyclette (le vélo), une bicyclette (pour) homme, une bicyclette de tourisme *m*
– *bicycle (cycle,* coll. *bike,* Am. *wheel), a gent's bicycle, a touring bicycle (touring cycle, roadster)*

2 le guidon, un guidon de randonnée *f*
– *handlebar (handlebars), a touring cycle handlebar*

3 la poignée
– *handlebar grip (handgrip, grip)*

4 le timbre avertisseur (la sonnette de vélo *m*)
– *bicycle bell*

5 le frein avant (un frein sur jante *f*)
– *hand brake (front brake), a rim brake*

6 le support de phare *m*
– *lamp bracket*

7 le projecteur de vélo *m*
– *headlamp (bicycle lamp)*

8 la dynamo de vélo *m*
– *dynamo*

9 la molette de dynamo *f*
– *pulley*

10-12 la fourche de roue *f* avant
– *front forks*

10 le tube de fourche *f*
– *handlebar stem*

11 la tête de fourche *f*
– *steering head*

12 les lames *f* de fourche *f*
– *fork blades (fork ends)*

13 le garde-boue avant
– *front mudguard* (Am. *front fender)*

14-20 le cadre de vélo *m*
– *bicycle frame*

14 le tube de direction *f*
– *steering tube (fork column)*

15 l'écusson *m* du constructeur
– *head badge*

16 le tube supérieur du cadre
– *crossbar (top tube)*

17 le tube inférieur du cadre (le tube du pédalier)
– *down tube*

18 le tube de selle *f*
– *seat tube*

19 les bases *f* du cadre
– *seat stays*

20 les haubans *m* du cadre
– *chain stays*

21 la selle d'enfant *m*
– *child's seat (child carrier seat)*

22 la selle de vélo *m* (selle *f* souple)
– *bicycle saddle*

23 les ressorts *m* de selle *f*
– *saddle springs*

24 le tube porte-selle
– *seat pillar*

25 la sacoche à outils *m*
– *saddle bag (tool bag)*

26-32 la roue (roue *f* avant)
– *wheel (front wheel)*

26 le moyeu
– *hub*

27 le rayon
– *spoke*

28 la jante
– *rim (wheel rim)*

29 l'écrou *m* de rayon *m*
– *spoke nipple (spoke flange, spoke end)*

30 le pneumatique (le pneu, le pneu haute pression *f*); *à l'intérieur:* la chambre à air *m*, *à l'extérieur:* l'enveloppe *f*
– *tyres* (Am. *tires) (tyre, pneumatic tyre, high-pressure tyre);* inside: *tube (inner tube),* outside: *tyre (outer case, cover)*

31 la valve, une valve de chambre *f* à air *m* avec raccord *m* souple ou valve *f* brevetée à bille *f*
– *valve, a tube valve with valve tube or a patent valve with ball*

32 le capuchon de valve *f*
– *valve sealing cap*

33 le compteur de vitesse *f* avec compteur *m* kilométrique
– *bicycle speedometer with milometer*

34 la béquille latérale
– *kick stand (prop stand)*

35-42 la transmission à chaîne *f*
– *bicycle drive (chain drive)*

35-39 le pédalier
– *chain transmission*

35 le plateau de pédalier *m* (la roue dentée avant)
– *chain wheel*

36 la chaîne, une chaîne à rouleaux *m*
– *chain, a roller chain*

37 le couvre-chaîne (le carter en tôle *f*)
– *chain guard*

38 le pignon (la roue dentée arrière)
– *sprocket wheel (sprocket)*

39 l'écrou *m* papillon
– *wing nut (fly nut, butterfly nut)*

40 la pédale
– *pedal*

41 la manivelle de pédalier *m*
– *crank*

42 le palier de pédalier *m*
– *bottom bracket bearing*

43 le garde-boue arrière
– *rear mudguard* (Am. *rear fender)*

44 le porte-bagages
– *luggage carrier (carrier)*

45 le cataphote
– *reflector*

46 le feu arrière
– *rear light (rear lamp)*

47 le repose-pied
– *footrest*

48 la pompe à vélo *m* (pompe *f* à air *m*)
– *bicycle pump*

49 l'antivol *m* de bicyclette *f*, un cadenas s'engageant dans les rayons *m*
– *bicycle lock, a wheel lock*

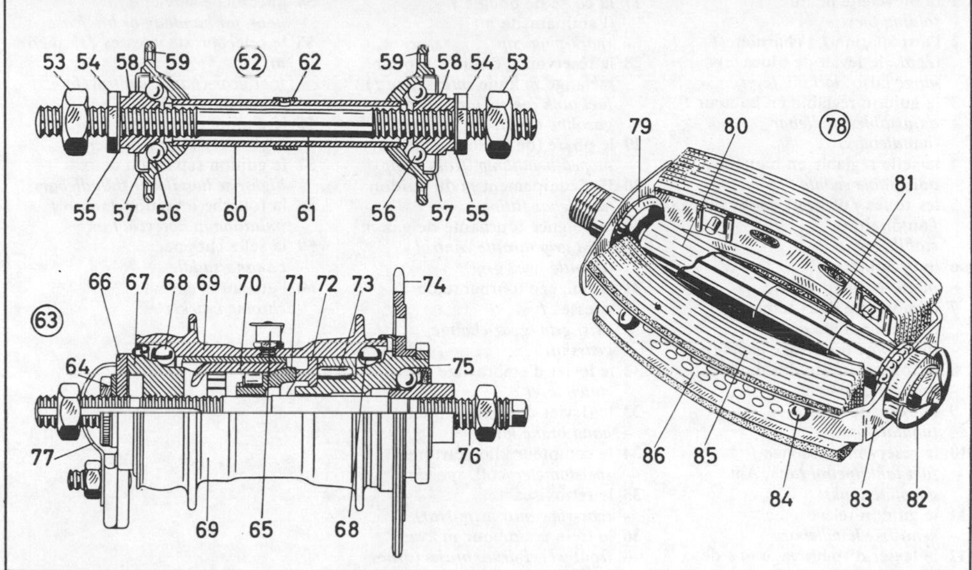

50 la clé d'antivol *m*
– *patent key*
51 le numéro de fabrication *f* de la bicyclette
– *cycle serial number (factory number, frame number)*
52 le moyeu de la roue avant
– *front hub (front hub assembly)*
53 l'ecrou *m*
– *wheel nut*
54 le contre-écrou freiné
– *locknut (locking nut)*
55 le couvre-cuvette
– *washer (slotted cone adjusting washer)*
56 la bille
– *ball bearing*
57 la couronne antipoussière
– *dust cap*
58 le cône
– *cone (adjusting cone)*
59 le flasque
– *centre* (Am. *center*) *hub*
60 le tube
– *spindle*
61 l'axe *m*
– *axle*
62 le clips obturant le trou de graissage *m*
– *clip covering lubrication hole (lubricator)*
63 le moyeu à roue *f* libre avec frein *m* à contre-pédalage *m*
– *free-wheel hub with back-pedal brake (with coaster brake)*
64 le contre-écrou de bielle *f* (l'écrou *m* de blocage *m*)
– *safety nut*
65 le graisseur à chapeau (graisseur *m*)
– *lubricator*
66 la bielle de frein *m*
– *brake arm*
67 la cuvette de frein *m* (le cône de frein *m*)
– *brake arm cone*
68 la bague à billes *f* de roulement *m*
– *bearing cup with ball bearings in ball race*
69 le corps de moyeu *m*
– *hub shell (hub body, hub barrel)*
70 la bague de frein *m*
– *brake casing*
71 le cône-frein
– *brake cone*
72 l'anneau *m* de transmission *f*
– *driver*
73 le rouleau d'entraînement *m*
– *driving barrel*
74 la couronne dentée
– *sprocket*
75 la tête de filetage *m*
– *thread head*
76 l'axe *m*
– *axle*
77 l'étrier *m* d'arrêt *m*
– *bracket*
78 la pédale de vélo *m* (la pédale, la pédale réflectorisée)
– *bicycle pedal (pedal, reflector pedal)*
79 le flasque
– *cup*
80 le tube de pédale *f*
– *spindle*
81 l'axe *m* de pédale *f*
– *axle*
82 la couronne antipoussière
– *dust cap*
83 le bâti de pédale *f*
– *pedal frame*
84 le piton de fixation *f* en caoutchouc *m*
– *rubber stud*
85 la garniture de pédale *f* en caoutchouc *m*
– *rubber block (rubber tread)*
86 le verre rétroréflecteur
– *glass reflector*

1 la bicyclette pliante
– *folding bicycle*
2 l'articulation *f* à charnière *f* (*égal.:* le levier de blocage)
– *hinge (*also: *locking lever)*
3 le guidon réglable en hauteur *f*
– *adjustable handlebar (handlebars)*
4 la selle réglable en hauteur *f*
– *adjustable saddle*
5 les roues *f* d'appui *m* (les roues *f* auxiliaires)
– *stabilizers*
6 le cyclomoteur
– *motor-assisted bicycle*
7 le moteur à deux temps *m* refroidi par air *m*
– *air-cooled two-stroke engine*
8 la fourche téléhydraulique
– *telescopic forks*
9 le cadre tubulaire
– *tubular frame*
10 le réservoir d'essence *f*
– *fuel tank (petrol tank,* Am. *gasoline tank)*
11 le guidon relevé
– *semi-rise handlebars*
12 le levier d'embrayage *m* à deux vitesses *f*
– *two-speed gear-change (gearshift)*
13 la selle relevée
– *high-back polo saddle*
14 le bras oscillant de fourche *f* arrière
– *swinging-arm rear fork*
15 le pot d'échappement *m* relevé
– *upswept exhaust*
16 la grille de protection *f* (contre le pot d'échappement *m*)
– *heat shield*
17 la chaîne (la transmission secondaire)
– *drive chain*
18 l'arceau *m* de protection
– *crash bar (roll bar)*
19 le compteur kilométrique
– *speedometer (*coll. *speedo)*
20 la bicyclette à accumulateurs *m* (la bicyclette électrique, le city-bike)
– *battery-powered moped, an electrically-powered vehicle*
21 la selle à suspension *f* centrale
– *swivel saddle*
22 le compartiment des accumulateurs *m*
– *battery compartment*
23 le porte-bagages (le panier en fil *m* métallique)
– *wire basket*
24 le cyclomoteur (de randonnée *f*)
– *touring moped (moped)*
25 la pédale
– *pedal crank (pedal drive, starter pedal)*
26 le moteur monocylindrique à deux temps *m*
– *single-cylinder two-stroke engine*
27 la cosse de bougie *f* (l'antiparasite *m*)
– *spark-plug cap*
28 le réservoir d'essence *f* (pour mélange *m* huile *m*/essence *f*)
– *fuel tank (petrol tank,* Am. *gasoline tank)*
29 le phare (de cyclomoteur *m*)
– *moped headlamp (front lamp)*
30-35 l'équipement *m* du guidon
– *handlebar fittings*
30 la poignée tournante de gaz *m*
– *twist grip throttle control (throttle twist grip)*
31 la poignée tournante de vitesses *f*
– *twist grip (gear-change, gearshift)*
32 le levier d'embrayage *m*
– *clutch lever*
33 le (levier de) frein à main *f*
– *hand brake lever*
34 le compteur kilométrique
– *speedometer (*coll. *speedo)*
35 le rétroviseur
– *rear-view mirror (mirror)*
36 le frein à tambour *m* avant
– *front wheel drum brake (drum brake)*
37 les câbles *m* Bowden
– *Bowden cables (brake cables)*
38 le feu arrière complet (le feu stop)
– *stop and tail light unit*
39 le vélomoteur [50 à 125 cm^3]
– *light motorcycle with kickstarter*
40 le tableau de bord *m* avec compteur *m* kilométrique et compte-tours *m* électronique
– *housing for instruments with speedometer and electronic rev counter (revolution counter)*
41 la fourche téléhydraulique avec caoutchouc *m* de protection *f*
– *telescopic shock absorber*
42 la selle biplace
– *twin seat*
43 le kick
– *kickstarter*
44 le repose-pied [du passager *m*]
– *pillion footrest, a footrest*
45 le guidon sport
– *handlebar (handlebars)*
46 le carter de chaîne *f* étanche
– *chain guard*
47 le scooter
– *motor scooter (scooter)*
48 le carter latéral amovible
– *removable side panel*
49 le cadre tubulaire
– *tubular frame*
50 le coffrage de fourche *f*
– *metal fairings*
51 la béquille
– *prop stand (stand)*
52 la pédale de frein *m*
– *foot brake*
53 l'avertisseur *m* (le klaxon)
– *horn (hooter)*
54 l'accroche-serviette *m*
– *hook for handbag or briefcase*
55 le sélecteur de vitesses *f* (à pied *m*)
– *foot gear-change control (foot gearshift control)*
56 le chopper
– *high-riser;* sim.: *Chopper*
57 le guidon séparé en deux
– *high-rise handlebar (handlebars)*
58 la fourche imitation *f* moto *f*
– *imitation motorcycle fork*
59 la selle chopper
– *banana saddle*
60 l'arceau *m* chromé
– *chrome bracket*

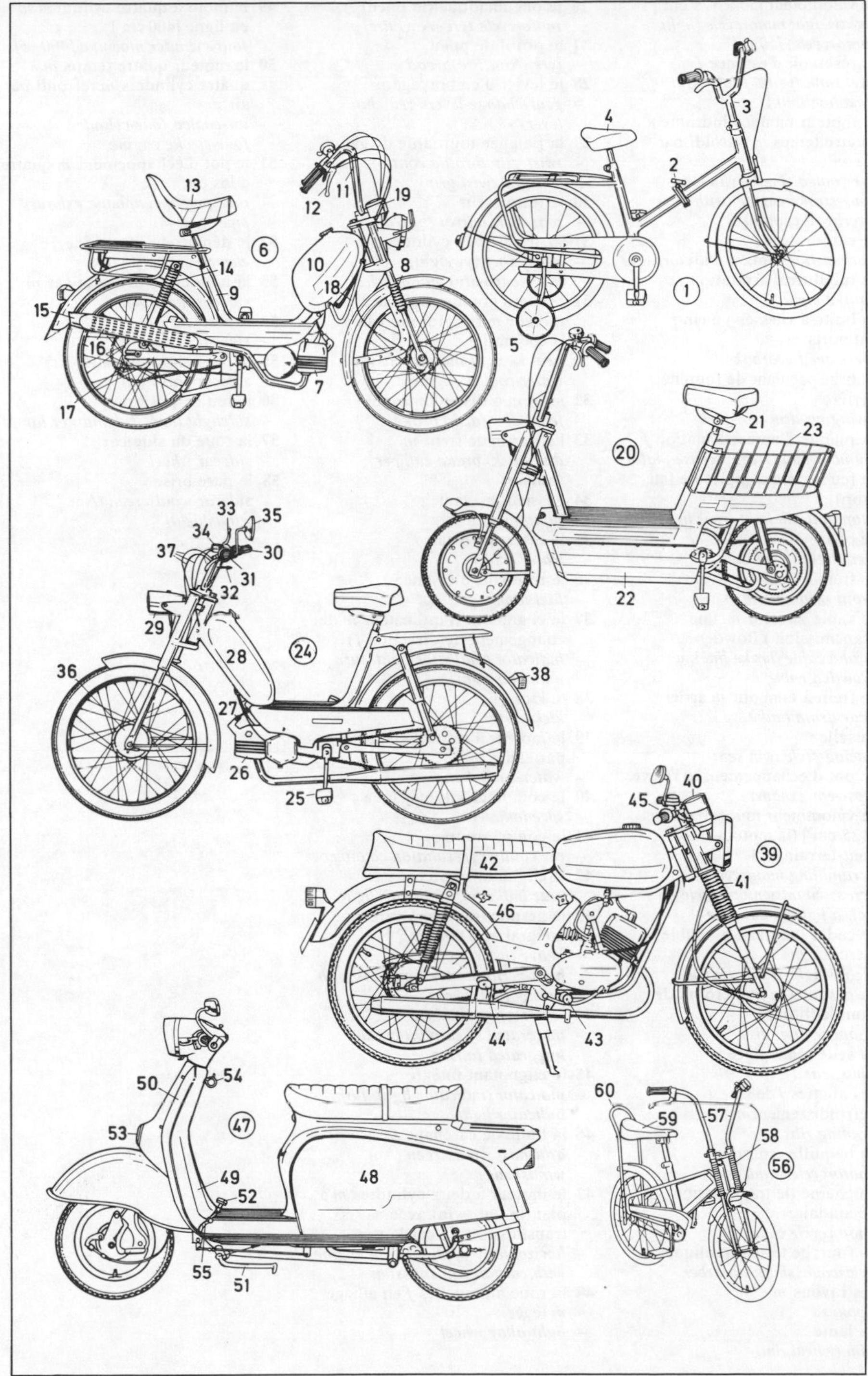
1
2
3
4
5
6
7
8
9
10
11
12
13
14
15
16
17
18
19
20
21
22
23
24
25
26
27
28
29
30
31
32
33
34
35
36
37
38
39
40
41
42
43
44
45
46
47
48
49
50
51
52
53
54
55
56
57
58
59
60

1 le vélomoteur [50 à 125 cm^3]
– *lightweight motorcycle (light motorcycle) [50 cc]*
2 le réservoir d'essence *f*
– *fuel tank (petrol tank,* Am. *gasoline tank)*
3 le moteur monocylindrique à quatre temps *m* refroidi par air *m*
– *air-cooled single-cylinder four-stroke engine (with overhead camshaft)*
4 le carburateur
– *carburettor* (Am. *carburetor)*
5 la tubulure d'aspiration *f*
– *intake pipe*
6 la boîte à vitesses *f* à cinq rapports *m*
– *five-speed gearbox*
7 le bras oscillant de fourche *f* arrière
– *swinging-arm rear fork*
8 la plaque d'immatriculation *f*
– *number plate* (Am. *license plate)*
9 le feu arrière complet (le feu stop)
– *stop and tail light (rear light)*
10 le phare
– *headlight (headlamp)*
11 le frein à tambour avant
– *front drum brake*
12 le câble de frein *m*, une transmission *f* Bowden
– *brake cable (brake line), a Bowden cable*
13 le frein à tambour *m* arrière
– *rear drum brake*
14 la selle
– *racing-style twin seat*
15 le pot d'échappement *m* relevé
– *upswept exhaust*
16 le vélomoteur tout-terrain *m* [125 cm^3] (la motocylette tout-terrain)
– *scrambling motorcycle (cross-country motorcycle) [125 cc], a light motorcycle*
17 le cadre tubulaire à double berceau *m*
– *lightweight cradle frame*
18 la plaque (de numéro *m*) de compétition *f*
– *number disc (disk)*
19 la selle monoplace
– *solo seat*
20 les ailettes *f* de refroidissement *m*
– *cooling ribs*
21 la béquille centrale
– *motorcycle stand*
22 la chaîne (la transmission secondaire)
– *motorcycle chain*
23 la fourche téléhydraulique
– *telescopic shock absorber*
24 les rayons *m*
– *spokes*
25 la jante
– *rim (wheel rim)*
26 le pneumatique (le pneu)
– *motorcycle tyre* (Am. *tire)*
27 le profil de pneu
– *tyre* (Am. *tire) tread*
28 le levier d'embrayage *m*
– *gear-change lever (gearshift lever)*
29 la poignée tournante de gaz *m*
– *twist grip throttle control (throttle twist grip)*
30 le rétroviseur
– *rear-view mirror (mirror)*
31-58 les grosses cylindrées *f*
– *heavy (heavyweight, large-capacity) motorcycles*
31 la moto grande routière à moteur *m* refroidi par eau *f* [1 000 cm^3]
– *heavyweight motorcycle with water-cooled engine*
32 le frein à disque *m* avant
– *front disc (disk) brake*
33 l'étrier *m* de frein *m*
– *disc (disk) brake calliper (caliper)*
34 l'essieu *m* avant
– *floating axle*
35 le réservoir d'eau *f*
– *water cooler*
36 le réservoir d'essence *f*
– *fuel tank*
37 le clignotant (l'indicateur *m* de changement de direction *f*)
– *indicator (indicator light, turn indicator light)*
38 le kick
– *kickstarter*
39 le moteur à refroidissement *m* par eau *f*
– *water-cooled engine*
40 le compteur kilométrique
– *speedometer*
41 le compte-tours
– *rev counter (revolution counter)*
42 le clignotant arrière
– *rear indicator (indicator light)*
43 la grande routière à carénage intégral *m* [1 000 cm^3]
– *heavy (heavyweight, high-performance) machine with fairing [1000 cc]*
44 le carénage intégral
– *integrated streamlining, an integrated fairing*
45 le clignotant intégré
– *indicator (indicator light, turn indicator light)*
46 la bulle de carénage *m*
– *anti-mist windscreen* (Am. *windshield)*
47 le moteur à deux cylindres *m* à plat (le flat twin) avec transmission *f* à cardan *m*
– *horizontally-opposed twin engine with cardan transmission*
48 la roue à branches *f* en alliage *m* léger
– *light alloy wheel*
49 la moto à quatre cylindres *m* en ligne [400 cm^3]
– *four-cylinder machine [400 cc]*
50 le moteur quatre temps *m* à quatre cylindres *m* refroidi par air *m*
– *air-cooled four-cylinder four-stroke engine*
51 le pot d'échappement *m* quatre dans un
– *four-pipe megaphone exhaust pipe*
52 le démarreur électrique
– *electric starter button*
53 la motocyclette à side-car *m*
– *sidecar machine*
54 le side-car
– *sidecar body*
55 le pare-chocs du side-car
– *sidecar crash bar*
56 le feu de position *f*
– *sidelight* (Am. *sidemarker lamp)*
57 la roue du side-car
– *sidecar wheel*
58 le pare-brise
– *sidecar windscreen* (Am. *windshield)*

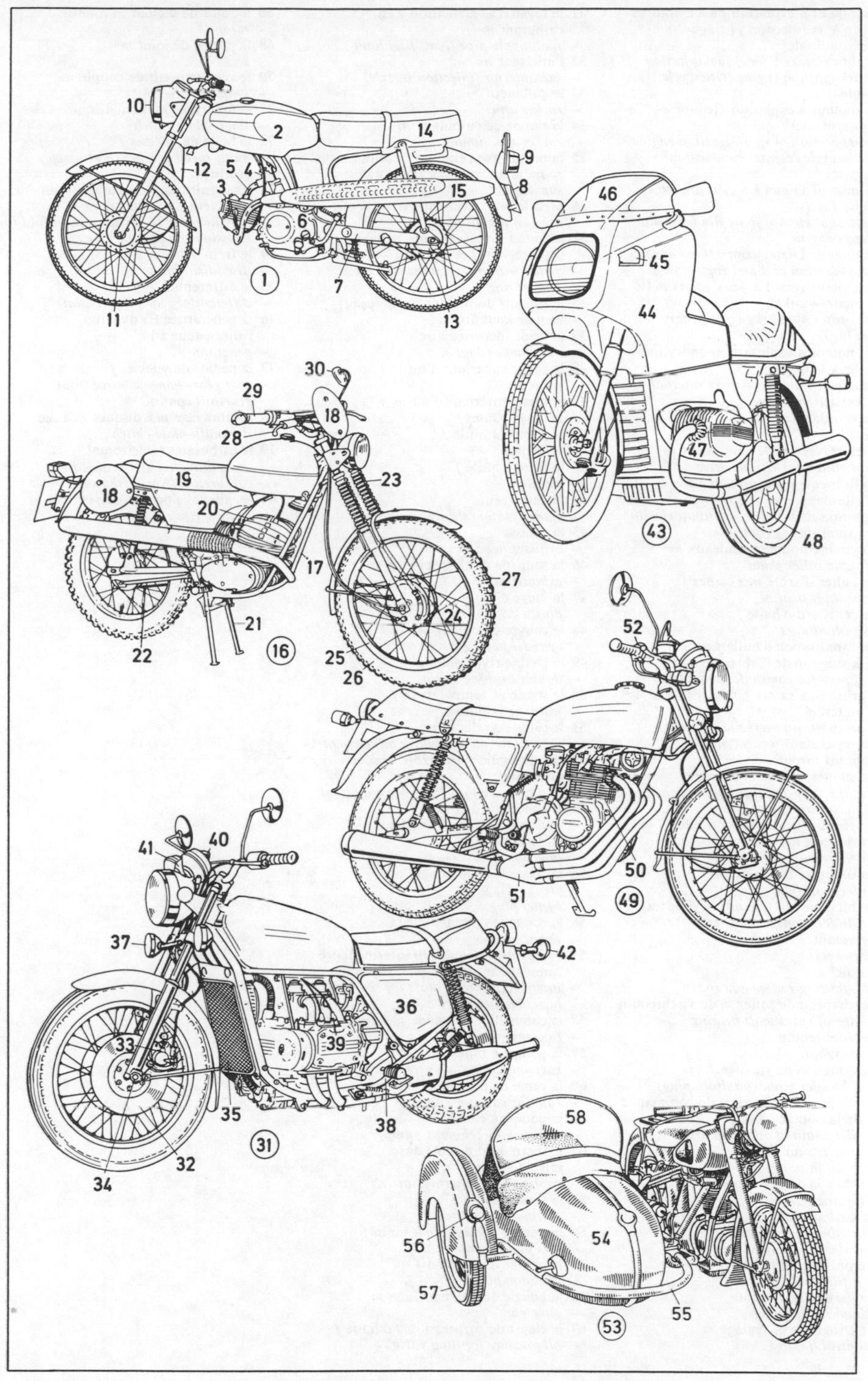
1
2
3
4
5
6
7
8
9
10
11
12
13
14
15
16
17
18
19
20
21
22
23
24
25
26
27
28
29
30
31
32
33
34
35
36
37
38
39
40
41
42
43
44
45
46
47
48
49
50
51
52
53
54
55
56
57
58

1 le moteur à explosion *f* à 8 cylindres *m* en V et injection *f* [coupe longitudinale]
– *eight-cylinder V (vee) fuel-injection spark-ignition engine (Otto-cycle engine)*
2 le moteur à explosion *f* [coupe transversale]
– *cross-section of spark-ignition engine (Otto-cycle internal combustion engine)*
3 le moteur Diesel à 5 cylindres *m* en ligne *f*
– *sectional view of five-cylinder in-line diesel engine*
4 le moteur Diesel [coupe transversale]
– *cross-section of diesel engine*
5 le moteur rotatif à deux rotors *m* (le moteur Wankel)
– *two-rotor Wankel engine (rotary engine)*
6 le moteur à explosion *f* monocylindre à deux temps *m*
– *single-cylinder two-stroke internal combustion engine*
7 le ventilateur
– *fan*
8 l'embrayage *m* de ventilateur *m*
– *fan clutch for viscous drive*
9 l'allumeur *m* à commande *f* d'allumage *m* par dépression *f*
– *ignition distributor (distributor) with vacuum timing control*
10 la chaîne double à rouleaux *m*
– *double roller chain*
11 le palier d'arbre *m* à cames *f*
– *camshaft bearing*
12 le reniflard d'huile *f*
– *air-bleed duct*
13 la canalisation d'huile *f* pour graissage *m* de l'arbre à cames *f*
– *oil pipe for camshaft lubrication*
14 l'arbre *m* à cames *f*, un arbre à cames *f* en tête *f*
– *camshaft, an overhead camshaft*
15 le répartiteur à papillon *m*
– *venturi throat*
16 le silencieux d'admission *f*
– *intake silencer (absorption silencer,* Am. *absorption muffler)*
17 le régulateur de pression *f* de carburant *m*
– *fuel pressure regulator*
18 la tubulure d'admission *f*
– *inlet manifold*
19 le bloc-moteur (le carter-cylindres)
– *cylinder crankcase*
20 le volant
– *flywheel*
21 la bielle
– *connecting rod (piston rod)*
22 le chapeau de palier *m* du vilebrequin
– *cover of crankshaft bearing*
23 le vilebrequin
– *crankshaft*
24 le bouchon de vidange *f*
– *oil bleeder screw (oil drain plug)*
25 la chaîne à rouleaux *m* de commande *f* de la pompe à huile *f*
– *roller chain of oil pump drive*
26 l'amortisseur *m*
– *vibration damper*
27 l'arbre *m* de commande *f* de l'allumeur *m*
– *distributor shaft for the ignition distributor (distributor)*
28 l'orifice *m* (la tubulure) de remplissage d'huile *f*
– *oil filler neck*
29 la cartouche filtrante
– *diaphragm spring*
30 la tringlerie de réglage *m*
– *control linkage*
31 le tuyau d'alimentation *f* en carburant *m*
– *fuel supply pipe (*Am. *fuel line)*
32 l'injecteur *m*
– *fuel injector (injection nozzle)*
33 le culbuteur
– *rocker arm*
34 la rampe de culbuteur *m*
– *rocker arm mounting*
35 la bougie avec embout *m* antiparasite
– *spark plug (sparking plug) with suppressor*
36 le collecteur d'échappement *m*
– *exhaust manifold*
37 le piston avec segments *m* de compression *f* et segment *m* racleur
– *piston with piston rings and oil scraper ring*
38 le support du moteur (le berceau)
– *engine mounting*
39 la bride intermédiaire
– *dog flange (dog)*
40 le carter supérieur d'huile *f*
– *crankcase*
41 le carter inférieur d'huile *f*
– *oil sump (sump)*
42 la pompe à huile *f*
– *oil pump*
43 le filtre à huile *f*
– *oil filter*
44 le démarreur
– *starter motor (starting motor)*
45 la culasse
– *cylinder head*
46 la soupape d'échappement *m*
– *exhaust valve*
47 la jauge d'huile *f*
– *dipstick*
48 le couvre-culbuteur *m*
– *cylinder head gasket*
49 la chaîne rivée double
– *double bushing chain*
50 la sonde de température *f*
– *warm-up regulator*
51 le câble de ralenti *m*
– *tapered needle for idling adjustment*
52 la canalisation de gazole *m* sous pression *f*
– *fuel pressure pipe (fuel pressure line)*
53 le collecteur de fuites *f*
– *fuel leak line (drip fuel line)*
54 l'injecteur *m*
– *injection nozzle (spray nozzle)*
55 la fixation de la bougie de préchauffage *m*
– *heater plug*
56 la rondelle de butée *f*
– *thrust washer*
57 l'arbre *m* de pignon *m* intermédiaire commandant la pompe d'injection *f*
– *intermediate gear shaft for the injection pump drive*
58 la commande d'avance *f* à l'injection *f*
– *injection timer unit*
59 la pompe à vide *m*
– *vacuum pump (low-pressure regulator)*
60 la came de pompe *f* à vide *m*
– *cam for vacuum pump*
61 la pompe à eau *f*
– *water pump (coolant pump)*
62 le thermostat d'eau *f* de refroidissement *m*
– *cooling water thermostat*
63 le thermocontact
– *thermo time switch*
64 la pompe à gazole *m* à main *f*
– *fuel hand pump*
65 la pompe d'injection *f*
– *injection pump*
66 la bougie de préchauffage *m*
– *glow plug*
67 le clapet de surpression *f* d'huile *f*
– *oil pressure limiting valve*
68 le rotor de moteur *m* rotatif
– *rotor*
69 la portée de joint *m*
– *seal*
70 le convertisseur de couple *m*
– *torque converter*
71 l'embrayage *m* monodisque
– *single-plate clutch*
72 la boîte de vitesses *f*
– *multi-speed gearing (multi-step gearing)*
73 les garnitures *f* antipollution du collecteur d'échappement *m*
– *port liners in the exhaust manifold for emission control*
74 le frein à disque *m*
– *disc (disk) brake*
75 le différentiel
– *differential gear (differential)*
76 la génératrice (la dynamo, l'alternateur *m*)
– *generator*
77 la pédale de vitesses *f*
– *foot gear-change control (foot gearshift control)*
78 l'embrayage *m* à disques *m* à sec
– *dry multi-plate clutch*
79 le carburateur horizontal
– *cross-draught (*Am. *cross-draft) carburettor (*Am. *carburetor)*
80 les ailettes *f* de refroidissement *m*
– *cooling ribs*

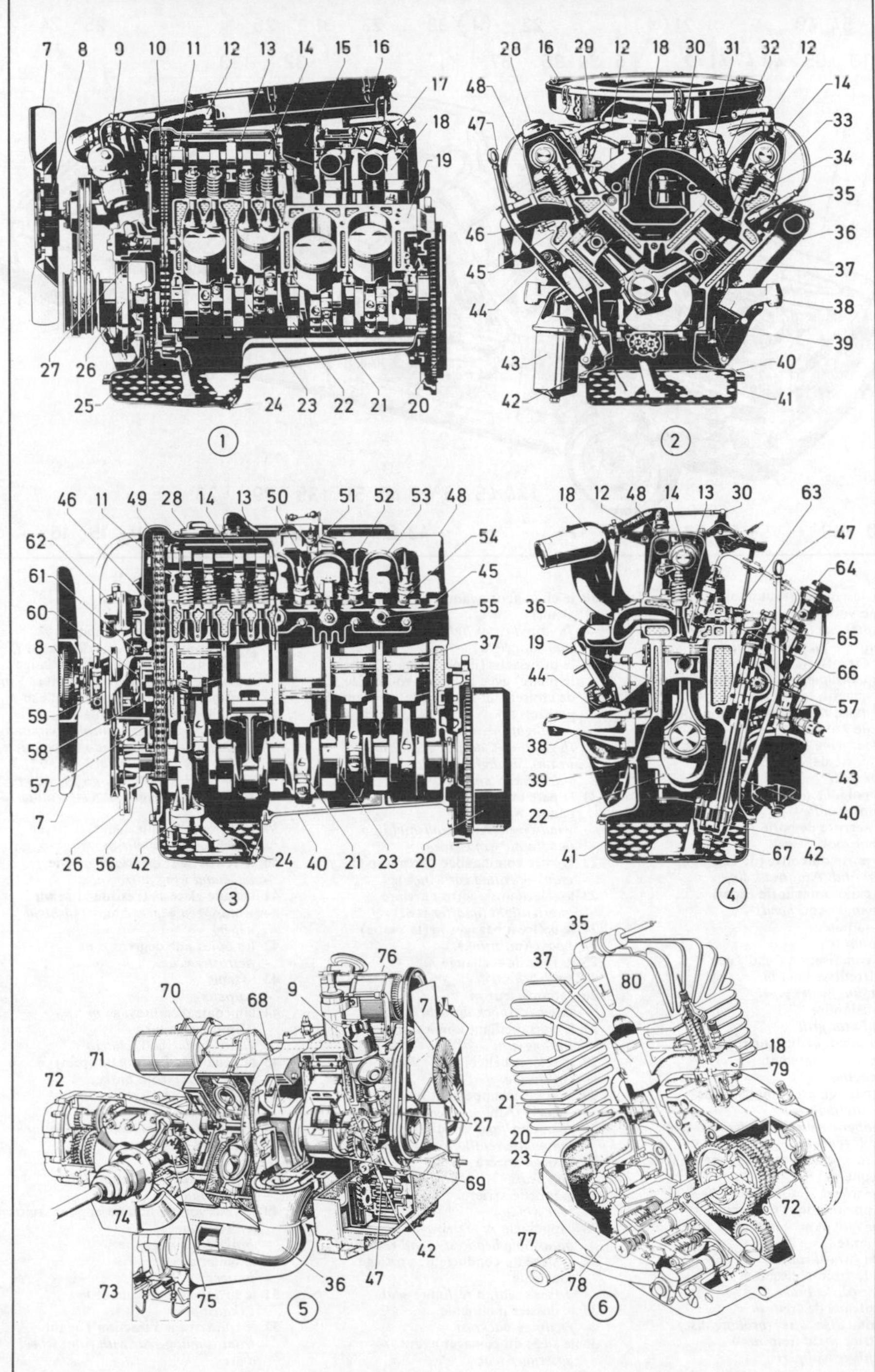
7 8 9 10 11 12 13 14 15 16
17 18 19
27 26
25 24 23 22 21 20
1
28 16 29 12 18 30 31 32 12
48 47 46 45 44 43 42
14 33 34 35 36 37 38 39 40 41
2
46 11 49 28 14 13 50 51 52 53 48
62 61 60 8 59 58 57 7
54 45 55 37
26 56 42 24 40 21 23 20
3
18 12 48 14 13 30 63
36 19 44 38 39 22 41
47 64 65 66 57 43 40 67 42
4
76 9 7 70 68 71 72
27 69 42 47 36
74 73 75
5
35 37 80
18 79 21 20 23 72
77 78
6

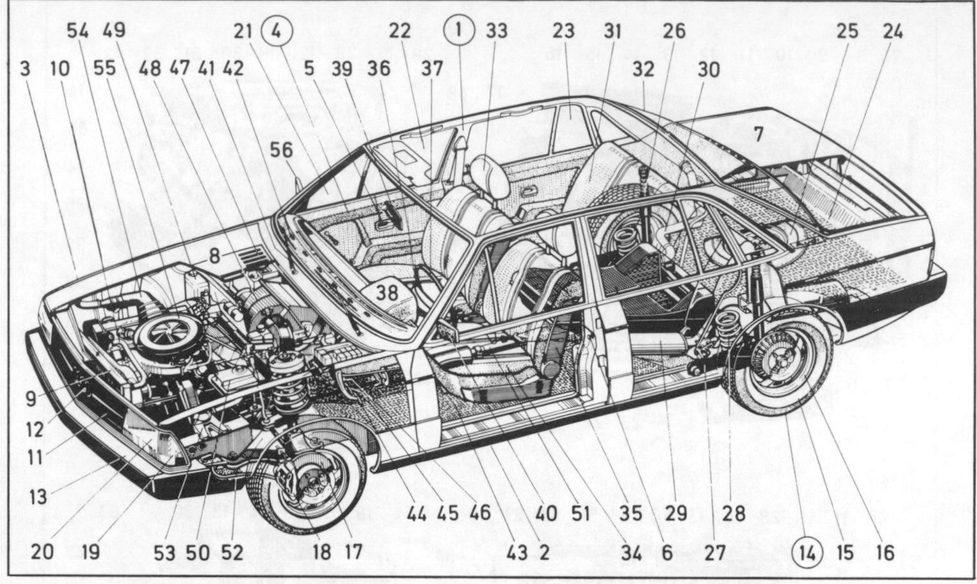

1-56 la voiture (l'automobile *f*, l'auto *f*), une voiture de tourisme *m*
– *motor car (car,* Am. *automobile, auto), a passenger vehicle*
1 la carrosserie autoporteuse
– *monocoque body (unitary body)*
2 le châssis, la caisse
– *chassis, the understructure of the body*
3 l'aile *f* avant
– *front wing (*Am. *front fender)*
4 la porte de voiture *f*
– *car door*
5 la poignée de porte *f*
– *door handle*
6 la serrure de porte *f*
– *door lock*
7 la porte du coffre (de la malle)
– *boot lid (*Am. *trunk lid)*
8 le capot-moteur (le capot)
– *bonnet (*Am. *hood)*
9 le radiateur
– *radiator*
10 la canalisation d'eau *f* de refroidissement *m*
– *cooling water pipe*
11 la calandre
– *radiator grill*
12 l'écusson *m* du constructeur (le monogramme)
– *badging*
13 le pare-chocs avant garni de caoutchouc *m*
– *rubber-covered front bumper (*Am. *front fender)*
14 la roue d'automobile *f*, une roue à disque *m*
– *car wheel, a disc (disk) wheel*
15 le pneumatique (le pneu)
– *car tyre (*Am. *automobile tire)*
16 la jante
– *rim (wheel rim)*
17-18 le frein à disque *m*
– *disc (disk) brake*
17 le disque de frein *m*
– *brake disc (disk) (braking disc)*
18 l'étrier *m* de frein *m*
– *calliper (caliper)*
19 le clignoteur avant (le feu clignotant avant)
– *front indicator light (front turn indicator light)*
20 le projecteur (improprement appelé le phare) avec le feu de route *f*, le feu de croisement *m* (le code) et le feu de position *f*
– *headlight (headlamp) with main beam (high beam), dipped beam (low beam), sidelight (side lamp,* Am. *sidemarker lamp)*
21 le pare-brise, un pare-brise panoramique
– *windscreen (*Am. *windshield), a panoramic windscreen*
22 la vitre commandée par manivelle *f*
– *crank-operated car window*
23 le sélecteur de vitre *f* arrière
– *quarter light (quarter vent)*
24 le coffre à bagages *m* (la malle)
– *boot (*Am. *trunk)*
25 la roue de rechange *m*
– *spare wheel*
26 l'amortisseur *m*
– *damper (shock absorber)*
27 le bras oscillant longitudinal
– *trailing arm*
28 le ressort hélicoïdal
– *coil spring*
29 le pot d'échappement *m*
– *silencer (*Am. *muffler)*
30 l'aération *f* par circulation *f* forcée
– *automatic ventilation system*
31 le siège arrière
– *rear seats*
32 la lunette arrière
– *rear window*
33 l'appui-tête *m* réglable
– *adjustable headrest (head restraint)*
34 le siège du conducteur, un siège couchette
– *driver's seat, a reclining seat*
35 le dossier inclinable
– *reclining backrest*
36 le siège du passager avant
– *passenger seat*
37 le volant
– *steering wheel*
38 le combiné d'instrumentation *f* regroupant le compteur de vitesse *f*, le compte-tours, la montre, la jauge d'essence (l'indicateur *m* de niveau *m* d'essence *f*), le thermomètre d'eau *f* et le thermomètre d'huile *f*
– *centre (*Am. *center) console containing speedometer (*coll. *speedo), revolution counter (rev counter, tachometer), clock, fuel gauge (*Am. *gage), water temperature gauge, oil temperature gauge*
39 le rétroviseur intérieur
– *inside rear-view mirror*
40 le rétroviseur extérieur gauche
– *left-hand wing mirror*
41 l'essuie-glace *m* (l'essuie-vitre *m*)
– *windscreen wiper (*Am. *windshield wiper)*
42 les ouïes *f* de dégivrage *m*
– *defroster vents*
43 le tapis
– *carpeting*
44 la pédale d'embrayage *m* (l'embrayage *m*)
– *clutch pedal (*coll. *clutch)*
45 la pédale de frein *m* (le frein)
– *brake pedal (*coll. *brake)*
46 la pédale d'accélérateur *m* (l'accélérateur *m*)
– *accelerator pedal (*coll. *accelerator)*
47 la prise d'air *m*
– *inlet vent*
48 le ventilateur d'aération *f*
– *blower fan*
49 le réservoir de liquide *m* pour frein *m* hydraulique
– *brake fluid reservoir*
50 la batterie
– *battery*
51 le tuyau d'échappement *m*
– *exhaust pipe*
52 le train avant à traction *f* avant
– *front running gear with front wheel drive*

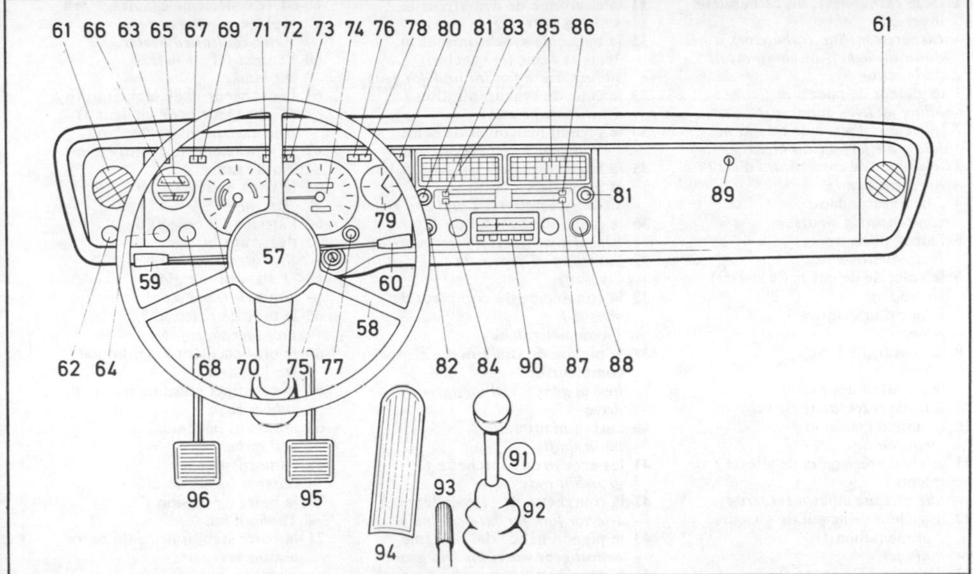

53 le support du moteur (le berceau)
– *engine mounting*
54 le silencieux d'admission *f*
– *intake silencer* (Am. *intake muffler)*
55 le filtre à air *m*
– *air filter (air cleaner)*
56 le rétroviseur extérieur droit
– *right-hand wing mirror*
57-90 le tableau de bord *m*
– *dashboard (fascia panel)*
57 le moyeu anticollision du volant
– *controlled-collapse steering column*
58 la branche du volant
– *steering wheel spoke*
59 le commutateur indicateur *m* de direction *f* - feux *m* de croisement *m*
– *indicator and dimming switch*
60 le commutateur essuie-glace *m* - lave-glace - avertisseur *m* sonore
– *wiper/washer switch and horn*
61 l'aérateur *m* latéral
– *side window blower*
62 l'interrupteur *m* feux *m* de position - projecteurs *m* - feux de stationnement *m*
– *sidelight, headlight, and parking light switch*
63 le témoin de feux *m* antibrouillard
– *fog lamp warning light*
64 l'interrupteur *m* des feux *m* antibrouillard avant et arrière
– *fog headlamp and rear lamp switch*
65 l'indicateur *m* d'essence *f* (la jauge d'essence *f*)
– *fuel gauge* (Am. *gage)*
66 le thermomètre d'eau *f*
– *water temperature gauge* (Am. *gage)*
67 le témoin de feu *m* antibrouillard arrière
– *warning light for rear fog lamp*
68 l'interrupteur *m* des feux *m* de détresse *f*
– *hazard flasher switch*
69 le témoin des feux *m* de route
– *main beam warning light*
70 le compte-tours *m* éléctrique
– *electric rev counter (revolution counter)*
71 le témoin du niveau d'essence *f*
– *fuel warning light*
72 le témoin du frein à main *f* et du système de freinage *m* à deux circuits *m* indépendants
– *warning light for the hand brake and dual-circuit brake system*
73 le témoin de pression *f* d'huile *f*
– *oil pressure warning light*
74 le compteur de vitesse *f* avec le compteur journalier (le totalisateur partiel)
– *speedometer* (coll. *speedo) with trip mileage recorder*
75 l'antivol *m*
– *starter and steering lock*
76 le témoin des feux *m* indicateurs de direction *f* et de détresse *f*
– *warning lights for turn indicators and hazard flashers*
77 le potentiomètre de réglage *m* de l'éclairage *m* intérieur avec remise *f* à zéro du compteur journalier (du totalisateur partiel)
– *switch for the courtesy light and reset button for the trip mileage recorder*
78 le témoin de charge *f*
– *ammeter*
79 la montre électrique
– *electric clock*
80 le témoin de désembuage *m* de la lunette arrière
– *warning light for heated rear window*
81 l'interrupteur *m* de ventilation *f* vers le bas
– *switch for the leg space ventilation*
82 l'interrupteur *m* de désembuage *m* de la lunette arrière
– *rear window heating switch*
83 la manette de ventilation *f*
– *ventilation switch*
84 la manette de chauffage *m*
– *temperature regulator*
85 l'aérateur *m* orientable (air *m* frais)
– *fresh-air inlet and control*
86 le répartiteur d'air *m* frais
– *fresh-air regulator*
87 le répartiteur de chauffage *m*
– *warm-air regulator*
88 l'allume-cigares *m*
– *cigar lighter*
89 la serrure de la boîte à gants *m* (du vide-poches)
– *glove compartment (glove box) lock*
90 l'autoradio *m*
– *car radio*
91 le levier de changement *m* de vitesse *f* au plancher (le levier de vitesses *f*)
– *gear lever (gearshift lever, floor-type gear-change)*
92 la manchette en cuir *m*
– *leather gaiter*
93 le levier de frein *m* à main *f*
– *hand brake lever*
94 la pédale d'accélérateur *m* (l'accélérateur *m*)
– *accelerator pedal*
95 la pédale de frein *m* (le frein)
– *brake pedal*
96 la pédale d'embrayage *m* (l'embrayage *m*)
– *clutch pedal*

1-15 le carburateur, un carburateur inversé
- ***carburettor*** (Am. *carburetor), a down-draught* (Am. *down-draft) carburettor*

1 le gicleur de ralenti *m*
- *idling jet (slow-running jet)*

2 le gicleur d'air *m* de ralenti *m*
- *idling air jet (idle air bleed)*

3 le gicleur de correction *f* d'air *m*
- *air correction jet*

4 l'air *m* secondaire
- *compensating airstream*

5 l'air *m* primaire
- *main airstream*

6 le volet de départ *m* (le starter)
- *choke flap*

7 le bec de giclage *m*
- *plunger*

8 le venturi (la buse)
- *venturi*

9 le papillon des gaz *m*
- *throttle valve (butterfly valve)*

10 le tube d'émulsion *f*
- *emulsion tube*

11 la vis de réglage *m* de vitesse *f* au ralenti
- *idle mixture adjustment screw*

12 le gicleur principal (le gicleur d'alimentation *f*)
- *main jet*

13 l'arrivée *f* d'essence *f*
- *fuel inlet* (Am. *gasoline inlet) (inlet manifold)*

14 la cuve à niveau *m* constant
- *float chamber*

15 le flotteur
- *float*

16-27 le graissage sous pression *f*
- ***pressure-feed lubricating system***

16 la pompe à huile *f*
- *oil pump*

17 le carter d'huile *f*
- *oil sump*

18 la crépine
- *sump filter*

19 le réfrigérant d'huile *f*
- *oil cooler*

20 le filtre à huile *f*
- *oil filter*

21 le canal principal du carter-cylindres
- *main oil gallery (drilled gallery)*

22 le canal de graissage *m*
- *crankshaft drilling (crankshaft tributary, crankshaft bleed)*

23 le palier de vilebrequin *m*
- *crankshaft bearing (main bearing)*

24 le palier d'arbre *m* à cames *f*
- *camshaft bearing*

25 le palier de tête *f* de bielle *f*
- *connecting-rod bearing*

26 l'alésage *m* pour l'axe *m* de piston *m*
- *gudgeon pin (piston pin)*

27 le canal secondaire du carter-cylindres
- *bleed*

28-47 la boîte de vitesses *f* **synchronisée à quatre rapports** *m*
- ***four-speed synchromesh gearbox***

28 la pédale d'embrayage *m*
- *clutch pedal*

29 le vilebrequin
- *crankshaft*

30 l'arbre *m* secondaire
- *drive shaft (propeller shaft)*

31 la couronne de démarreur *m*
- *starting gear ring*

32 la bague de synchroniseur *m* 3ème et 4ème (le synchro)
- *sliding sleeve for 3rd and 4th gear*

33 le cône de synchronisation *f*
- *synchronizing cone*

34 le pignon hélicoïdal de 3ème
- *helical gear wheel for 3rd gear*

35 la bague de synchroniseur *m* 1ère et 2ème (le synchro)
- *sliding sleeve for 1st and 2nd gear*

36 le pignon hélicoïdal de 1ère
- *helical gear wheel for 1st gear*

37 l'arbre *m* de renvoi *m*
- *lay shaft*

38 la commande du compteur de vitesse *f*
- *speedometer drive*

39 le pignon de câble *m* du compteur *m*
- *helical gear wheel for speedometer drive*

40 l'arbre *m* primaire
- *main shaft*

41 les axes *m* de fourchette *f*
- *gearshift rods*

42 la fourchette de 1ère et 2ème
- *selector fork for 1st and 2nd gear*

43 le pignon hélicoïdal de 2ème
- *helical gear wheel for 2nd gear*

44 la fourchette de marche *f* arrière
- *selector head with reverse gear*

45 la fourchette de 3ème et 4ème
- *selector fork for 3rd and 4th gear*

46 le levier de vitesses *f*
- *gear lever (gearshift lever)*

47 la grille de vitesses *f*
- *gear-change pattern (gearshift pattern, shift pattern)*

48-55 le frein à disque
- ***disc (disk) brake*** *[assembly]*

48 le disque de frein *m*
- *brake disc (disk) (braking disc)*

49 l'étrier *m* de frein *m*, un étrier fixe avec les plaquettes *f*
- *calliper (caliper), a fixed calliper with friction pads*

50 le tambour de servofrein *m* (le tambour de frein *m* à main *f*)
- *servo cylinder (servo unit)*

51 la mâchoire de frein *m*
- *brake shoes*

52 la garniture de frein *m*
- *brake lining*

53 le raccord de canalisation *f* de freinage *m*
- *outlet to brake line*

54 le cylindre de roue *f*
- *wheel cylinder*

55 le ressort de rappel
- *return spring*

56-59 la direction (la direction à vis *f* sans fin *f* ou à vis *f* globique)
- ***steering gear*** *(worm-and-nut steering gear)*

56 la colonne de direction *f*
- *steering column*

57 le galet de vis *f* globique
- *worm gear sector*

58 le levier de commande *f* de direction *f*
- *steering drop arm*

59 la vis sans fin *f*
- *worm*

60-64 le système de chauffage *m* **à réglage** *m* **par eau** *f*
- ***water-controlled heater***

60 l'entrée *f* d'air *m* frais
- *air intake*

61 l'échangeur *m* de température *f* (l'échangeur *m* de chaleur *f*)
- *heat exchanger (heater box)*

62 le ventilateur de chauffage *m*
- *blower fan*

63 le volet de réglage *m*
- *flap valve*

64 l'arrivée *f* (l'ouïe *f*) de dégivrage *m*
- *defroster vent*

65-71 l'essieu *m* **rigide**
- ***live axle*** *(rigid axle)*

65 le tube de réaction *f*
- *propeller shaft*

66 le bras oscillant longitudinal
- *trailing arm*

67 le coussinet en caoutchouc *m*
- *rubber bush*

68 le ressort hélicoïdal
- *coil spring*

69 l'amortisseur *m*
- *damper (shock absorber)*

70 la barre de torsion *f*
- *Panhard rod*

71 la barre stabilisatrice (la barre antidévers)
- *stabilizer bar*

72-84 la suspension MacPherson
- ***MacPherson strut unit***

72 la plaque de fixation *f* sur la caisse
- *body-fixing plate*

73 le support de fixation *f* supérieure
- *upper bearing*

74 le ressort hélicoïdal
- *suspension spring*

75 la tige de piston *m*
- *piston rod*

76 l'amortisseur de suspension *f*
- *suspension damper*

77 la jante
- *rim (wheel rim)*

78 la fusée de roue *f*
- *stub axle*

79 le pivot de fusée *f*
- *steering arm*

80 la rotule de pivot *m* de fusée *f*
- *track-rod ball-joint*

81 le bras arrière de triangle *m*
- *trailing link arm*

82 le coussinet élastique (le coussinet en caoutchouc *m*)
- *bump rubber (rubber bonding)*

83 le support de fusée *f*
- *lower bearing*

84 la traverse principale
- *lower suspension arm*

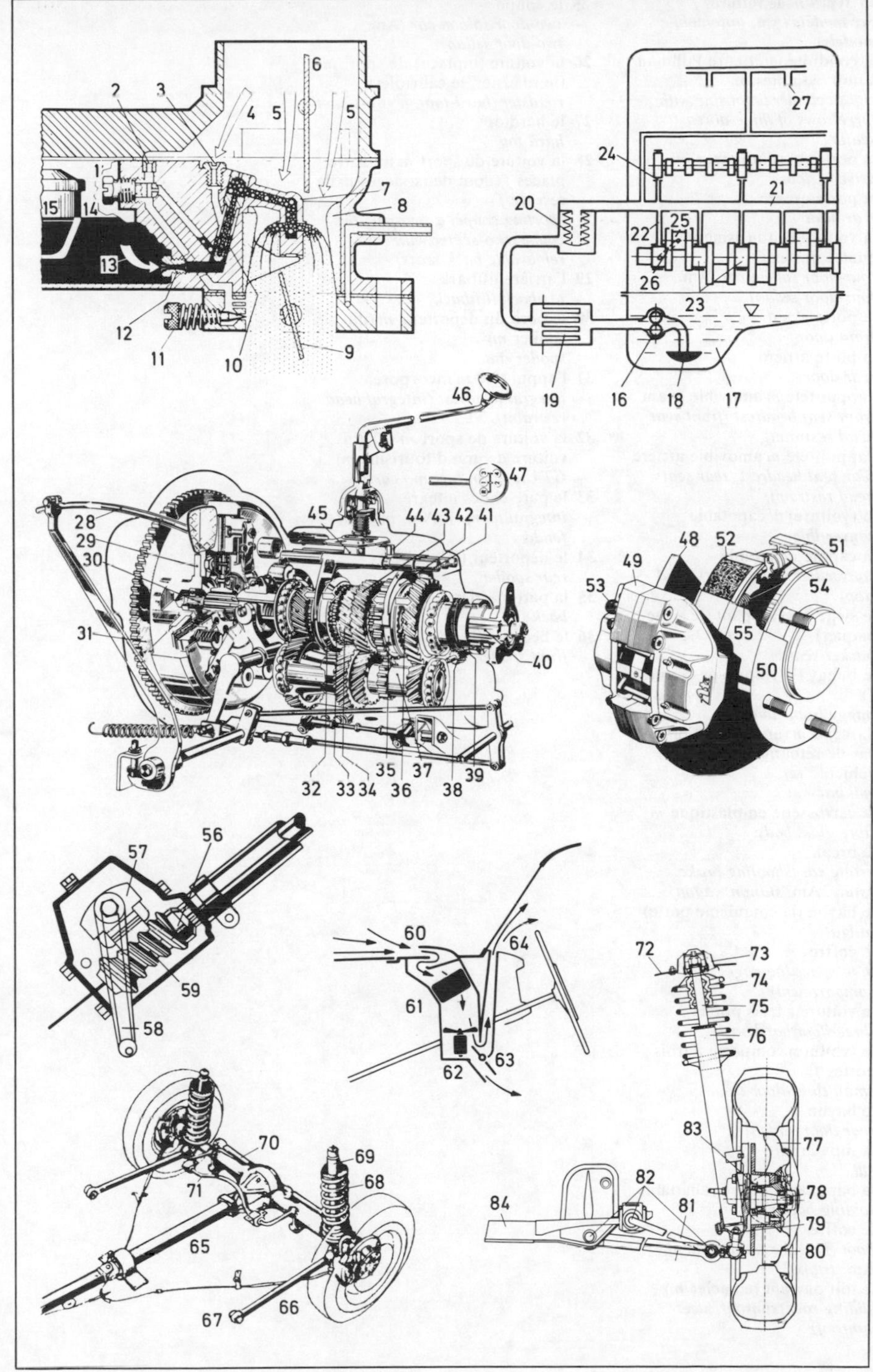
1
2
3
4
5
5
6
7
8
9
10
11
12
13
14
15
16
17
18
19
20
21
22
23
24
25
26
27
28
29
30
31
32
33
34
35
36
37
38
39
40
41
42
43
44
45
46
47
48
49
50
51
52
53
54
55
56
57
58
59
60
61
62
63
64
65
66
67
68
69
70
71
72
73
74
75
76
77
78
79
80
81
82
83
84

1-36 types *m* **de voitures** *f*
– ***car models*** (Am. *automobile models)*
1 la conduite intérieure Pullman à huit cylindres *m*
– *eight-cylinder limousine with three rows of three-abreast seating*
2 la porte du conducteur *m*
– *driver's door*
3 la porte arrière
– *rear door*
4 la voiture de tourisme *m* à quatre portes *f*
– *four-door saloon car (*Am. *four-door sedan)*
5 la porte avant
– *front door*
6 la porte arrière
– *rear door*
7 l'appui-tête *m* amovible avant
– *front seat headrest (front seat head restraint)*
8 l'appui-tête *m* amovible arrière
– *rear seat headrest (rear seat head restraint)*
9 la (voiture) décapotable
– *convertible*
10 la capote rabattable
– *convertible (collapsible) hood (top)*
11 le siège enveloppant (le siège baquet)
– *bucket seat*
12 le buggy (la voiture des dunes *f*)
– *buggy (dune buggy)*
13 l'arceau *m* (une protection en cas de retournement *m* du véhicule *m*)
– *roll bar*
14 la carrosserie en plastique *m*
– *fibre glass body*
15 le break
– *estate car (shooting brake, estate,* Am. *station wagon)*
16 le hayon (la cinquième porte)
– *tailgate*
17 le coffre
– *boot space (luggage compartment)*
18 la voiture à trois portes *f*
– *three-door hatchback*
19 la (voiture) compacte à trois portes *f*
– *small three-door car*
20 le hayon
– *rear door (tailgate)*
21 la jupe arrière
– *sill*
22 la banquette arrière rabattable
– *folding back seat*
23 le coffre
– *boot (luggage compartment,* Am. *trunk)*
24 le toit ouvrant (en acier *m*)
– *sliding roof (sunroof, steel sunroof)*
25 le coupé
– *two-door saloon car (*Am. *two-door sedan)*
26 la voiture (biplace) de sport *m* (le roadster, le cabriolet)
– *roadster (hard-top), a two-seater*
27 le hardtop
– *hard top*
28 la voiture de sport *m* à quatre places *f* (dont deux sièges *m* de réserve *f*)
– *sporting coupé, a two-plus-two coupé (two-seater with removable back seats)*
29 l'arrière liftback
– *fastback (liftback)*
30 le bord du déporteur *m* (du spoiler *m*)
– *spoiler rim*
31 l'appui-tête *m* incorporé
– *integral headrest (integral head restraint)*
32 la voiture de sport *m* GT (la voiture de grand tourisme *m*)
– *GT car (gran turismo car)*
33 le pare-chocs intégré
– *integral bumper (*Am. *integral fender)*
34 le déporteur (le spoiler)
– *rear spoiler*
35 la partie arrière
– *back*
36 le becquet (le spoiler avant)
– *front spoiler*

1
2
3
4
5
6
7
8
9
10
11
12
13
14
15
16
17
18
19
20
21
22
23
24
25
26
27
28
29
30
31
32
33
34
35
36

1 le (petit) camion tout-terrain *m* à quatre roues *f* motrices
– *light cross-country lorry (light truck, pickup truck) with all-wheel drive (four-wheel drive)*
2 la cabine
– *cab (driver's cab)*
3 la plate-forme de chargement *m*
– *loading platform (body)*
4 la roue de secours *m*, un pneu tout-terrain *m*
– *spare tyre* (Am. *spare tire), a cross-country tyre*
5 la camionnette
– *light lorry (light truck, pickup truck)*
6 la camionnette-plateau (la camionnette-plate-forme)
– *platform truck*
7 le fourgon (la camionnette fermée)
– *medium van*
8 la porte latérale coulissante (la porte de chargement *m*)
– *sliding side door [for loading and unloading]*
9 le minibus
– *minibus*
10 le toit pliant (toit *m* ouvrant)
– *folding top (sliding roof)*
11 la porte arrière
– *rear door*
12 la porte latérale pivotante
– *hinged side door*
13 le coffre à bagages *m*
– *luggage compartment*
14 le siège de passager *m*
– *passenger seat*
15 la cabine
– *cab (driver's cab)*
16 la grille d'aération *f*
– *air inlet*
17 l'autocar *m* (le car de voyage *m*, le car long-courrier)
– *motor coach (coach, bus)*
18 le compartiment à bagages *m*
– *luggage locker*
19 les bagages *m* (une valise)
– *hand luggage (suitcase, case)*
20 le train routier (le convoi routier), un poids
– *heavy lorry (heavy truck, heavy motor truck)*
21 le camion-tracteur
– *tractive unit (tractor, towing vehicle)*
22 la remorque
– *trailer (drawbar trailer)*
23 le plateau (la plate-forme) amovible
– *swop platform (body)*
24 le camion à triple mouvement *m* de bascule *f* de la benne
– *three-way tipper (three-way dump truck)*
25 la benne basculante (le plateau basculant)
– *tipping body (dump body)*
26 le mécanisme de bascule *f* (le vérin hydraulique)
– *hydraulic cylinder*
27 le container (*ELF:* le conteneur) déposé
– *supported container platform*
28 la semi-remorque, un camion-citerne *f*
– *articulated vehicle, a vehicle tanker*
29 le tracteur routier, le tracteur de semi-remorque *f*
– *tractive unit (tractor, towing vehicle)*
30-33 la citerne remorquée
– *semi-trailer (skeletal)*
30 le réservoir (la citerne)
– *tank*
31 la plaque tournante
– *turntable*
32 les béquilles *f* à roues *f*
– *undercarriage*
33 la roue de secours *m*
– *spare wheel*
34 le petit autocar en version *f* urbaine
– *midi bus [for short-route town operations]*
35 la porte va-et-vient
– *outward-opening doors*
36 l'autobus *m* à impériale *f*
– *double-deck bus (double-decker bus)*
37 l'étage *m* inférieur
– *lower deck (lower saloon)*
38 l'impériale *f* (l'étage *m* supérieur)
– *upper deck (upper saloon)*
39 la montée
– *boarding platform*
40 le trolleybus
– *trolley bus*
41 la perche pivotante du trolley *m*
– *current collector*
42 le trolley (à galet *m*)
– *trolley (trolley shoe)*
43 la ligne aérienne double (bifilaire)
– *overhead wires*
44 la remorque de trolleybus *m*
– *trolley bus trailer*
45 le soufflet d'accouplement *m*
– *pneumatically sprung rubber connection*

1
2
3
4
5
6
7
8
9
10
11
12
13
14
15
16
17
18
18
18
18
19
20
21
22
23
24
25
26
27
28
29
30
31
32
33
34
35
36
37
38
39
40
41
42
43
44
45

1-55 l'atelier *m* **spécialisé** (un atelier agréé)
– ***agent's garage*** *(distributor's garage,* Am. *specialty shop)*
1-23 le poste de diagnostic *m* auto
– *diagnostic test bay*
1 l'appareil *m* à diagnostic *m*
– *computer*
2 le connecteur mâle de diagnostic *m*
– *main computer socket*
3 le câble de diagnostic *m*
– *computer harness (computer cable)*
4 l'inverseur *m* automatique manuel
– *switch from automatic to manual*
5 la fente d'introduction *f* de cartes *f* programme
– *slot for program cards*
6 l'imprimante *f*
– *print-out machine (printer)*
7 le compte-rendu de diagnostic *m* (le diagnostic)
– *condition report (data print-out)*
8 la commande manuelle
– *master selector (hand control)*
9 les lampes *f* de résultat *m* [vert: bon; rouge: mauvais]
– *light read-out [green: OK; red: not OK]*
10 le fichier de cartes *f* programme
– *rack for program cards*
11 l'interrupteur *m* secteur
– *mains button*
12 la touche de programme *m* rapide
– *switch for fast readout*
13 le tiroir de séquence *f* d'allumage *m*
– *firing sequence insert*
14 la case de réception *f* de cartes *f*
– *shelf for used cards*
15 la potence porte-câbles
– *cable boom*
16 le câble de mesure *f* de température *f* d'huile *f*
– *oil temperature sensor*
17 le contrôleur de pincement *m* et de carrossage *m* à droite *f*
– *test equipment for wheel and steering alignment*
18 la plaque optique droite
– *right-hand optic plate*
19 les transistors *m* de déclenchement *m*
– *actuating transistors*
20 le commutateur de projecteur *m*
– *projector switch*
21 la ligne photoréceptrice pour la mesure du carrossage
– *check light for wheel alignment, a row of photocells*
22 la ligne photoréceptrice pour la mesure du pincement
– *check light for steering alignment, a row of photocells*
23 le tournevis électrique
– *power screwdriver*
24 le contrôleur de réglage *m* de projecteurs *m*
– *beam setter*
25 le pont-élévateur hydraulique
– *hydraulic lift*
26 le bras ajustable de pont-élévateur *m*
– *adjustable arm of hydraulic lift*
27 le tampon de pont-élévateur *m*
– *hydraulic lift pad*
28 la cavité pour roue *f*
– *excavation*
29 le contrôleur de pression *f* des pneus *m* (le manomètre, le contrôleur de gonflage *m*)
– *pressure gauge* (Am. *gage)*
30 le pistolet graisseur
– *grease gun*
31 la boîte à petites pièces *f*
– *odds-and-ends box*
32 la nomenclature des pièces *f* de rechange *m*
– *wall chart [of spare parts]*
33 le diagnostic automatique
– *automatic computer test*
34 l'automobile *f* (l'auto *f*, la voiture), une voiture de tourisme *m*
– *motor car (car,* Am. *automobile, auto), a passenger vehicle*
35 le compartiment moteur
– *engine compartment*
36 le capot moteur
– *bonnet* (Am. *hood)*
37 la béquille du capot moteur
– *bonnet support* (Am. *hood support)*
38 le câble de diagnostic *m*
– *computer harness (computer cable)*

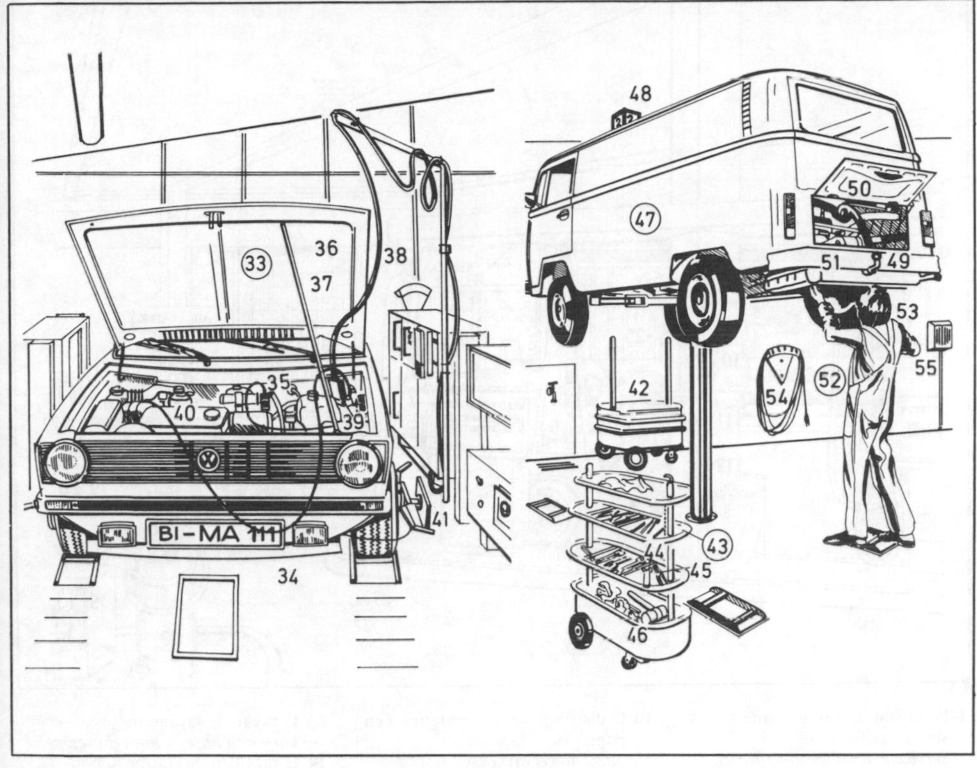

39 le connecteur femelle de diagnostic *m*
– *main computer socket;* also: *multi-outlet socket*
40 le câble de sonde *f* de température *f* d'huile *f*
– *oil temperature sensor*
41 le miroir de roue *f* pour mesure *f* optique du pincement *m* et du carrossage *m*
– *wheel mirror for visual wheel and steering alignment*
42 le chariot d'outillage *m* (la servante d'atelier *m*)
– *tool trolley*
43 l'outil *m*
– *tools*
44 la clé
– *impact wrench*
45 la clé dynamométrique
– *torque wrench*
46 le marteau à planer
– *body hammer (roughing-out hammer)*
47 le véhicule en réparation *f*, un minibus
– *vehicle under repair, a minibus*
48 le numéro de réparation *f*
– *car location number*
49 le moteur arrière
– *rear engine*
50 le volet du moteur arrière
– *tailgate*
51 l'échappement *m*
– *exhaust system*
52 la réparation de l'échappement *m*
– *exhaust repair*
53 le mécanicien automobile
– *motor car mechanic (motor vehicle mechanic,* Am. *automotive mechanic)*
54 le tuyau à air *m* comprimé
– *air hose*
55 l'interphone *m*
– *intercom*

1-29 la station-service, une station self-service
– *service station (petrol station, filling station,* Am. *gasoline station, gas station), a self-service station*
1 le distributeur d'essence *f* super ou normale (*anal.:* de gazole *m*); la pompe à essence *f*
– *petrol (*Am. *gasoline) pump (blending pump) for regular and premium grade petrol (*Am. *gasoline) (*sim.: *for derv)*
2 le tuyau du distributeur
– *hose (petrol pump,* Am. *gasoline pump, hose)*
3 le pistolet distributeur
– *nozzle*
4 la somme à payer
– *cash readout*
5 le volume débité
– *volume readout*
6 le prix du litre
– *price display*
7 le voyant lumineux
– *indicator light*
8 l'automobiliste *m* utilisant la pompe à essence *f* self-service
– *driver using self-service petrol pump (*Am. *gasoline pump)*
9 l'extincteur *m*
– *fire extinguisher*
10 le distributeur de serviettes *f* en papier *m*
– *paper-towel dispenser*
11 la serviette en papier *m*
– *paper towel*
12 la corbeille à papiers *m*
– *litter receptacle*
13 le réservoir de mélange *m* deux-temps
– *two-stroke blending pump*
14 le verre gradué
– *meter*
15 l'huile *f* pour moteur *m* (l'huile *f* moteur)
– *engine oil*
16 le broc à huile *f* moteur
– *oil can*
17 le contrôleur de pression *f* des pneus *m*
– *tyre pressure gauge (*Am. *tire pressure gage)*
18 le tuyau à air *m* comprimé
– *air hose*
19 le réservoir d'air *m*
– *static air tank*
20 le manomètre (le contrôleur de gonflage *m*)
– *pressure gauge (*Am. *gage) (manometer)*
21 l'embout *m* de gonflage *m*
– *air filler neck*
22 le box de réparation *f*
– *repair bay (repair shop)*
23 le tuyau de lavage *m*
– *car-wash hose, a hose (hosepipe)*
24 le magasin de station-service *f*
– *accessory shop*
25 le bidon d'essence *f* (le jerrycan)
– *petrol can (*Am. *gasoline can)*
26 la pèlerine
– *rain cape*
27 les pneumatiques (les pneus *m*)
– *car tyres (*Am. *automobile tires)*
28 les accessoires *m* auto
– *car accessories*
29 la caisse
– *cash desk (console)*

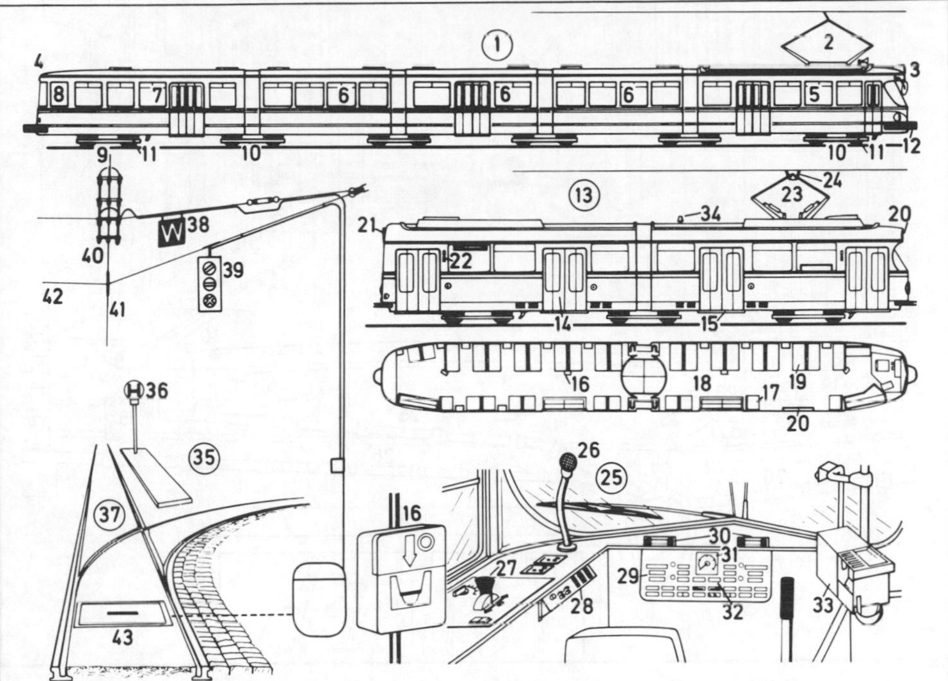

1 l'autorail *m* articulé à 12 essieux *m* du réseau interurbain
– *twelve-axle articulated railcar for interurban rail service*
2 le pantographe
– *current collector*
3 la tête de train *m* (l'avant *m* de l'autorail *m*)
– *head of the railcar*
4 la queue de train *m* (l'arrière *m* de l'autorail *m*)
– *rear of the railcar*
5 la voiture de tête *f* A (la motrice)
– *carriage A containing the motor*
6 la voiture B (*égal.:* voiture C ou D)
– *carriage B (*also: *carriages C and D)*
7 la voiture de queue *f* E (la motrice)
– *carriage E containing the motor*
8 le combinateur arrière
– *rear controller*
9 le bogie moteur
– *bogie*
10 le bogie porteur
– *carrying bogie*
11 le couvre-roue (chasse-pierres *m*)
– *wheel guard*
12 le tampon
– *bumper (*Am. *fender)*
13 l'autorail *m* (l'automotrice *f*) urbain et interurbain à six essieux *m type «Mannheim»*
– *six-axle articulated railcar ('Mannheim' type) for tram (*Am. *streetcar, trolley) and urban rail services*
14 la porte pliante (la porte accordéon, la portière)
– *entrance and exit door, a double folding door*
15 le marchepied
– *step*
16 le composteur de billets *m*
– *ticket-cancelling machine*
17 la place assise individuelle
– *single seat*
18 les places *f* debout (le couloir)
– *standing room portion*
19 la banquette double
– *double seat*
20 le panneau indicateur du numéro de ligne *f* et de direction *f*
– *route (number) and destination sign*
21 le panneau indicateur du numéro de ligne *f*
– *route sign (number sign)*
22 l'indicateur *m* de direction *f* (le clignotant)
– *indicator (indicator light)*
23 le pantographe
– *pantograph (current collector)*
24 les semelles *f* d'archet *m* du pantographe en carbone *m* ou en alliage *m* d'aluminium *m*
– *carbon or aluminium (*Am. *aluminum) alloy trolley shoes*
25 la cabine (le poste) de conduite *f*
– *driver's position*
26 le microphone
– *microphone*
27 le combinateur
– *controller*
28 l'appareil *m* de radio *f*
– *radio equipment (radio communication set)*
29 le tableau de bord *m*
– *dashboard*
30 l'éclairage *m* du tableau de bord *m*
– *dashboard lighting*
31 l'indicateur *m* de vitesse *f* (le tachymètre, le compteur de vitesse *f*
– *speedometer*
32 les touches *f* de commande *f* d'ouverture *f* des portes *f*, d'essuie-glaces *m* et d'éclairage *m* intérieur et extérieur
– *buttons controlling doors, windscreen wipers, internal and external lighting*
33 le distributeur de billets *m* avec changeur *m* de monnaie *f*
– *ticket counter with change machine*
34 l'antenne *f* radio
– *radio antenna*
35 l'arrêt *m* (la station, la halte)
– *tram stop (*Am. *streetcar stop, trolley stop)*
36 le panneau du point d'arrêt *m*
– *tram stop sign (*Am. *streetcar stop sign, trolley stop sign)*
37 l'aiguillage *m* électrique
– *electric change points*
38 le signal d'aiguillage *m*
– *points signal (switch signal)*
39 le signal lumineux d'aiguillage *m* à 3 feux *m* (les signaux *m* lumineux de position *f* d'aiguille *f*)
– *points change indicator*
40 le contact de la caténaire
– *trolley wire contact point*
41 le caténaire
– *trolley wire (overhead contact wire)*
42 l'antibalançant *m*
– *overhead cross wire*
43 le mécanisme de commande *f* électromagnétique (*égal.:* électro-hydraulique, électrique) de l'aiguille *f*
– *electric (*also: *electrohydraulic, electromechanical) points mechanism*

1-5 les différentes couches *f* de la chaussée
– road layers

1 la couche de protection *f* contre le gel (la couche antigel)
– *anti-frost layer*

2 la couche de base *f* bitumineuse
– *bituminous sub-base course*

3 la couche de profilage *m* (la sous-couche) inférieure
– *base course*

4 la couche de profilage *m* (la sous-couche) supérieure
– *binder course*

5 la couche de circulation *f* (le revêtement de la chaussée)
– *bituminous surface*

6 la bordure de trottoir *m*
– *kerb (curb)*

7 la pierre de bordure *f* sur chant *m*
– *kerbstone (curbstone)*

8 le pavage (du trottoir *m*)
– *paving (pavement)*

9 le trottoir
– *pavement* (Am. *sidewalk, walkway)*

10 le caniveau
– *gutter*

11 le passage pour piétons *m* (le passage zébré) [*anc.:* le passage clouté]
– *pedestrian crossing (zebra crossing,* Am. *crosswalk)*

12 le coin de la rue
– *street corner*

13 la chaussée
– *street*

14 les câbles *m* électriques
– *electricity cables*

15 les câbles téléphoniques
– *telephone cables*

16 la ligne téléphonique de transit *m*
– *telephone cable pipeline*

17 le puits (de visite *f*) à câbles *m* avec dalle *f* de recouvrement *m*
– *cable manhole with cover (with manhole cover)*

18 le lampadaire, une lampe d'éclairage *m* public
– *lamp post with lamp*

19 les câbles *m* électriques pour installations *f* techniques
– *electricity cables for technical installations*

20 la ligne de raccordement *m* téléphonique d'immeuble *m*
– *subscribers'* (Am. *customers') telephone lines*

21 la conduite de gaz *m*
– *gas main*

22 la conduite d'eau *f* (potable)
– *water main*

23 la fosse d'écoulement *m* avec séparateur *m* (le siphon de sédimentation *f*)
– *drain*

24 la bouche d'égout *m* avec grille *f*
– *drain cover*

25 le branchement de la fosse d'écoulement *m* à l'égout *m* mixte
– *drain pipe*

26 le branchement d'immeuble *m* pour les eaux *f* usées
– *waste pipe*

27 l'égout *m* mixte (pour eaux usées et eaux de surface *f*)
– *combined sewer*

28 la conduite de chauffage *m* urbain
– *district heating main*

29 le tunnel de métro(politain) *m*
– *underground tunnel*

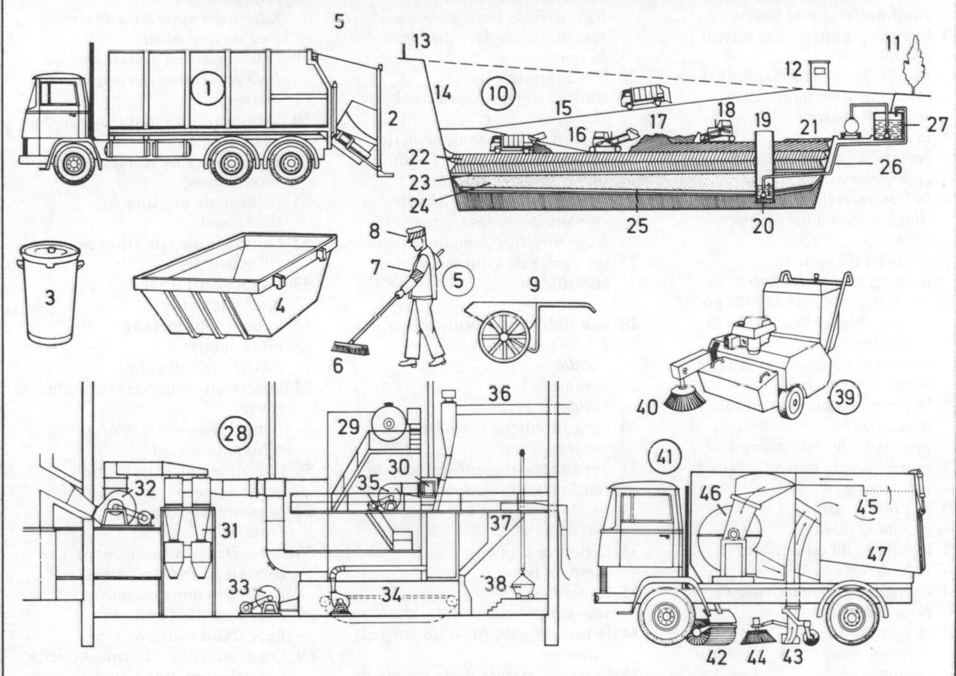

1 le camion d'enlèvement *m* des ordures *f* ménagères (le camion de collecte *f*)
– *refuse collection vehicle (*Am. *garbage truck)*

2 le dispositif de basculement *m* des poubelles *f*, un dispositif de vidage *f* étanche
– *dustbin-tipping device (*Am. *garbage can dumping device), a dust-free emptying system*

3 la poubelle
– *dustbin (*Am. *garbage can, trash can)*

4 le container (*ELF:* le conteneur)
– *refuse container (*Am. *garbage container)*

5 le balayeur
– *road sweeper* (Am. *street sweeper)*

6 le balai
– *broom*

7 le brassard (à bandes *f* réfléchissantes)
– *fluorescent armband*

8 la casquette (à bandes *f* réfléchissantes)
– *cap with fluorescent band*

9 la brouette (de balayeur *m*)
– *road sweeper's (*Am. *street sweeper's) barrow*

10 la décharge contrôlée (*ELF:* un dépôt de déchets *m*)
– *controlled tip (*Am. *sanitary landfill, sanitary fill)*

11 la rangée d'arbres *m* (formant écran *m*)
– *screen*

12 le contrôle d'entrée *f*
– *weigh office*

13 la clôture de protection *f* pour le gibier
– *fence*

14 la paroi (de la décharge)
– *embankment*

15 la rampe d'accès *m*
– *access ramp*

16 le bulldozer (*ELF:* le bouteur)
– *bulldozer*

17 les ordures *f* ménagères
– *refuse (*Am. *garbage)*

18 le bulldozer-compresseur (d'ordures *f*)
– *bulldozer for dumping and compacting*

19 le puits d'épuisement *m*
– *pump shaft*

20 la pompe pour eaux *f* usées
– *waste water pump*

21 le recouvrement poreux
– *porous cover*

22 les ordures *f* compactées en décomposition *f*
– *compacted and decomposed refuse*

23 la couche filtrante de gravier *m*
– *gravel filter layer*

24 la couche filtrante morainique
– *morainic filter layer*

25 la couche de drainage *m*
– *drainage layer*

26 la canalisation d'évacuation *f* (des eaux *f* usées)
– *drain pipe*

27 le réservoir d'eaux *f* usées
– *water tank*

28 l'usine d'incinération *f* d'ordures *f* ménagères
– *refuse (*Am. *garbage) incineration unit*

29 la chaudière
– *furnace*

30 le foyer à mazout *m* (le foyer à fuel-oil *m*)
– *oil-firing system*

31 le séparateur de poussières *f*
– *separation plant*

32 le ventilateur à tirage *m* forcé par aspiration *f*
– *extraction fan*

33 la soufflante sous grille *f*
– *low-pressure fan for the grate*

34 la grille mobile
– *continuous feed grate*

35 la soufflante (du foyer *m* à mazout *m*)
– *fan for the oil-firing system*

36 le transporteur de déchets *m* incinérés séparément
– *conveyor for separately incinerated material*

37 l'installation *f* d'enfournement *m* du charbon *m* (d'alimentation *f* en charbon *m*)
– *coal feed conveyor*

38 le chariot transporteur de terre *f* à foulon *m*
– *truck for carrying fuller's earth*

39 la balayeuse
– *mechanical sweeper*

40 le balai circulaire
– *circular broom*

41 la balayeuse-ramasseuse automobile, une éboueuse
– *road-sweeping lorry (street-cleaning lorry, street cleaner)*

42 le balai cylindrique (le rouleau à brosse *f* métallique)
– *cylinder broom*

43 le tuyau d'aspiration *f*
– *suction port*

44 le balai d'alimentation *f*
– *feeder broom*

45 la circulation d'air *m* (la chambre de déflection *f* d'air *m*)
– *air flow*

46 le ventilateur
– *fan*

47 le collecteur de boues *f*
– *dust collector*

1-54 engins *m* **de construction** *f* **routière** (engins *m* routiers)
- ***road-building machinery***

1 la pelle équipée pour travail *m* en butte *f*
- *shovel (power shovel, excavator)*

2 la cabine de commande *f*
- *machine housing*

3 la chenille
- *caterpillar mounting (*Am. *caterpillar tractor)*

4 la flèche de la pelle
- *digging bucket arm (dipper stick)*

5 le godet de la pelle
- *digging bucket (bucket)*

6 les dents *f* de fouille *f* du godet
- *digging bucket (bucket) teeth*

7 le tombereau
- *tipper (dump truck), a heavy lorry (*Am. *truck)*

8 la benne basculante en tôle *f* d'acier *m*
- *tipping body (*Am. *dump body)*

9 la nervure de renforcement *f*
- *reinforcing rib*

10 le protège-cabine
- *extended front*

11 la cabine du conducteur
- *cab (driver's cab)*

12 les matériaux *m* en vrac *m*
- *bulk material*

13 la benne racleuse
- *concrete scraper, an aggregate scraper*

14 la benne d'approvisionnement *m*
- *skip hoist*

15 la bétonnière
- *mixing drum (mixer drum), a mixing machine*

16 le scraper sur chenilles *f* (le scrapdozer) (*ELF:* la décapeuse)
- *caterpillar hauling scraper*

17 la benne racleuse (le scraper)
- *scraper blade*

18 la lame
- *levelling (*Am. *leveling) blade (smoothing blade)*

19 la niveleuse (la niveleuse à lame *f*)
- *grader (motor grader)*

20 le carificateur
- *scarifier (ripper, road ripper, rooter)*

21 la lame niveleuse
- *grader levelling (*Am. *leveling) blade (grader ploughshare,* Am. *plowshare)*

22 la couronne de rotation *f* de la lame
- *blade-slewing gear (slew turntable)*

23 le chemin de fer *m* de chantier *m* (chemin *m* de fer *m* à voie *f* étroite)
- *light railway (narrow-gauge,* Am. *narrow-gage, railway)*

24 le locotracteur (la locomotive Diesel à voie *f* étroite)
- *light railway (narrow-gauge,* Am. *narrow-gage) diesel locomotive*

25 le wagonnet
- *trailer wagon (wagon truck, skip)*

26 la grenouille à moteur *m* (le dameur à explosion *f*) [*plus lourd:* la dame à moteur]
- *tamper (rammer) [with internal combustion engine];* heavier: *frog (frog-type jumping rammer)*

27 les tiges *f* de guidage *m* et de contrôle *m*
- *guide rods*

28 le bulldozer (le bouldozeur, *ELF:* le bouteur)
- *bulldozer*

29 la lame
- *bulldozer blade*

30 l'encadrement *m* du boutoir
- *pushing frame*

31 l'épandeur-régleur-dameur *m*
- *road-metal spreading machine (macadam spreader, stone spreader)*

32 la poutre dameuse
- *tamping beam*

33 les dames *f*
- *sole-plate*

34 la tôle de gabarit *m* (le gabarit)
- *side stop*

35 la paroi latérale de la trémie de stockage *m*
- *side of storage bin*

36 le rouleau compresseur trijante
- *three-wheeled roller, a road roller*

37 le cylindre (le rouleau)
- *roller*

38 le toit tout temps *m*
- *all-weather roof*

39 le tracteur-compresseur Diesel
- *mobile diesel-powered air compressor*

40 la bouteille à oxygène *m*
- *oxygen cylinder*

41 la gravillonneuse automotrice
- *self-propelled gritter*

42 le clapet d'épandage *m*
- *spreading flap*

43 le finisseur de revêtements *m* noirs
- *surface finisher*

44 la tôle de gabarit *m*
- *side stop*

45 la trémie de stockage *m*
- *bin*

46 la goudronneuse avec fondoir *m* de goudron *m* et de bitume *m*
- *tar-spraying machine (bituminous distributor) with tar and bitumen heater*

47 la chaudière à goudron *m*
- *tar storage tank*

48 la centrale d'enrobage *m* bitumineux
- *fully automatic asphalt drying and mixing plant*

49 l'élévateur *m* à godets *m*
- *bucket elevator (elevating conveyor)*

50 le tambour de malaxage *m* de l'asphalte *m*
- *asphalt-mixing drum (asphalt mixer drum)*

51 l'élévateur de filler *m*
- *filler hoist*

52 l'adjonction *f* de filler *m*
- *filler opening*

53 l'injection *f* du liant
- *binder injector*

54 la sortie du mélange bitumineux
- *mixed asphalt outlet*

55 la section transversale d'une route
- *typical cross-section of a bituminous road*

56 l'accotement *m* gazonné
- *grass verge*

57 la pente transversale
- *crossfall*

58 le revêtement bitumineux
- *asphalt surface (bituminous layer, bituminous coating)*

59 la couche de fondation *f*
- *base (base course)*

60 la sous-couche (la sous-couche à gravier *m*), une couche antigel
- *gravel sub-base course (hardcore sub-base course, Telford base), an anti-frost layer*

61 le fossé souterrain de drainage *m*
- *sub-drainage*

62 le drain de ciment *m*
- *perforated cement pipe*

63 le caniveau d'écoulement *m*
- *drainage ditch*

64 le revêtement de terre végétale contre le gel
- *soil covering*

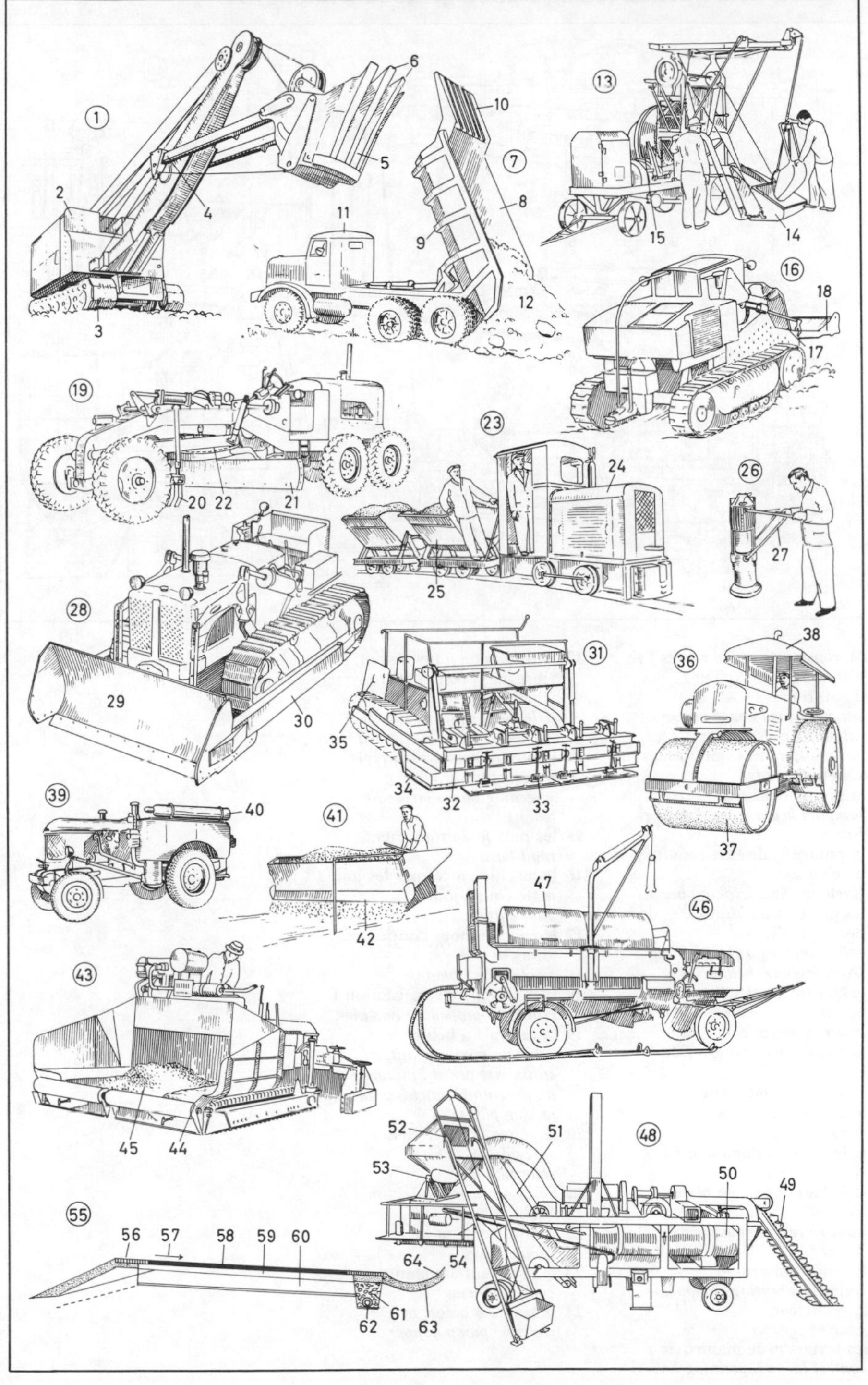
1
2
3
4
5
6
7
8
9
10
11
12
13
14
15
16
17
18
19
20
21
22
23
24
25
26
27
28
29
30
31
32
33
34
35
36
37
38
39
40
41
42
43
44
45
46
47
48
49
50
51
52
53
54
55
56
57
58
59
60
61
62
63
64

201 Construction routière II
Road Construction (Road Building, Road Making) II

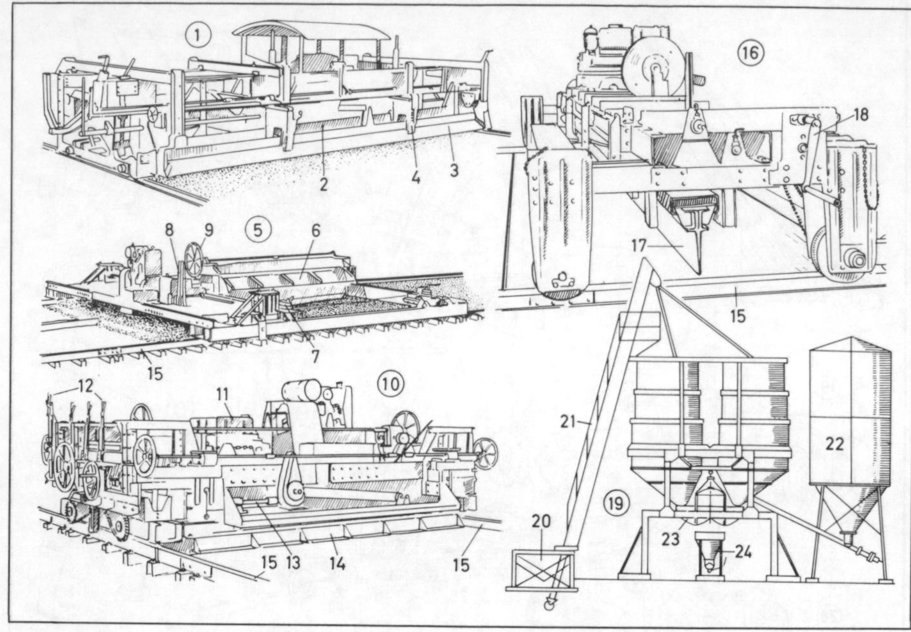

1-24 construction *f* **de routes** *f* **en béton** *m* (construction *f* d'autoroutes *f*)
– ***concrete road construction*** *(highway construction)*

1 le finisseur, un engin routier
– *subgrade grader*

2 la poutre dameuse
– *tamping beam (consolidating beam)*

3 la poutre égaliseuse (poutre *f* niveleuse)
– *levelling (*Am. *leveling) beam*

4 les galets *m* de guidage *m* de la poutre égaliseuse
– *roller guides for the levelling (*Am. *leveling) beam*

5 le chariot répartiteur de béton *m*
– *concrete spreader*

6 le bac de distribution *f* de béton *m*
– *concrete spreader box*

7 le guidage du câble
– *cable guides*

8 le levier de commande *f*
– *control levers*

9 le volant de vidage *m* des bacs *m*
– *handwheel for emptying the boxes*

10 le vibro-finisseur
– *concrete-vibrating compactor*

11 le réducteur
– *gearing (gears)*

12 les leviers *m* de manœuvre *f*
– *control levers (operating levers)*

13 l'arbre *m* de transmission *f* aux vibreurs *m* de la poutre vibrante
– *axle drive shaft to vibrators (tampers) of vibrating beam*

14 la poutre lisseuse (la règle lisseuse)
– *screeding board (screeding beam)*

15 les rails *m* de roulement *m*
– *road form*

16 la machine à couper les joints *m* (le coupe-joint)
– *joint cutter*

17 le couteau pour couper les joints *m*
– *joint-cutting blade*

18 la manivelle de translation *f*
– *crank for propelling machine*

19 la centrale à béton *m*
– *concrete-mixing plant, a stationary central mixing plant, an automatic batching and mixing plant*

20 la benne collectrice des agrégats *m*
– *collecting bin*

21 l'élévateur *m* à godets *m*
– *bucket elevator*

22 le silo à ciment *m*
– *cement store*

23 le malaxeur à mélange *m* forcé
– *concrete mixer*

24 la benne à béton *m*
– *concrete pump hopper*

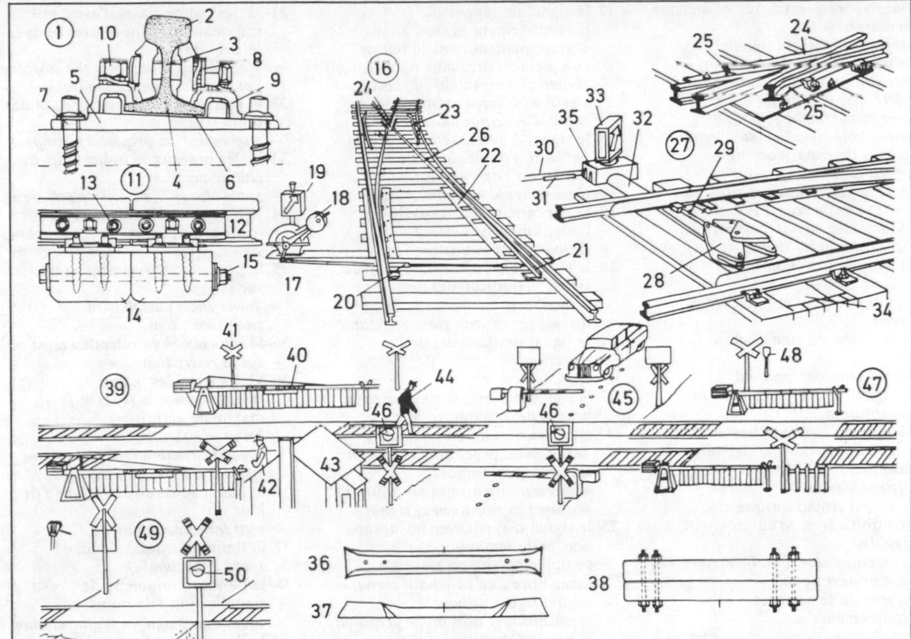

1-38 la voie
– *line (track)*
1 le rail
– *rail*
2 le champignon du rail
– *rail head*
3 l'âme *f* du rail
– *web (rail web)*
4 le patin du rail
– *rail foot (rail bottom)*
5 la selle de rail *m*
– *sole-plate (base plate)*
6 la semelle de rail *m*
– *cushion*
7 le tirefond
– *coach screw (coach bolt)*
8 la rondelle élastique
– *lock washers (spring washers)*
9 le crapaud (la plaque de serrage *m*)
– *rail clip (clip)*
10 le boulon à crochet *m*
– *T-head bolt*
11 le joint de rail *m*
– *rail joint (joint)*
12 l'éclisse *f*
– *fishplate*
13 le boulon d'éclisse *f*
– *fishbolt*
14 la traverse jumelée
– *coupled sleeper* (Am. *coupled tie, coupled crosstie)*
15 le boulon de jumelage *m*
– *coupling bolt*
16 l'aiguille *f* manœuvrée à pied d'œuvre
– *manually-operated points (switch)*
17 le levier de commande *f* à main *f*
– *switch stand*
18 le contrepoids
– *weight*
19 le signal d'aiguille *f* (le signal de position *f* d'aiguille *f*, la lanterne d'aiguille *f*)
– *points signal (switch signal, points signal lamp, switch signal lamp)*
20 la tringle de commande *f*
– *pull rod*
21 la lame d'aiguille *f*
– *switch blade (switch tongue)*
22 le coussinet de glissement *m* (la plaque de glissement *m*)
– *slide chair*
23 le contre-rail
– *check rail (guard rail)*
24 le cœur d'aiguille *f*
– *frog*
25 la patte de lièvre *m*
– *wing rail*
26 le rail compensateur
– *closure rail*
27 l'aiguille manœuvrée à distance *f*
– *remote-controlled points (switch)*
28 le verrou d'aiguille *f*
– *point lock (switch lock)*
29 la tringle de connexion *f*
– *stretcher bar*
30 la transmission funiculaire
– *point wire*
31 le tendeur
– *turnbuckle*
32 le caniveau de transmission *f* funiculaire
– *channel*
33 le signal lumineux d'aiguille *f*
– *electrically illuminated points signal (switch signal)*
34 le châssis d'aiguillage *m*
– *trough*
35 le mécanisme de commande *f* d'aiguille *f* sous carter *m* de protection *f*
– *points motor with protective casing*
36 la traverse en acier *m* (la traverse métallique)
– *steel sleeper* (Am. *steel tie, steel crosstie)*
37 la traverse en béton
– *concrete sleeper* (Am. *concrete tie, concrete crosstie)*
38 la traverse jumelée
– *coupled sleeper* (Am. *coupled tie, coupled crosstie)*
39-50 les passages *m* à niveau *m*
– ***level crossings*** (Am. *grade crossings)*
39 le passage à niveau *m* gardé
– *protected level crossing* (Am. *protected grade crossing)*
40 la barrière
– *barrier (gate)*
41 le croix d'avertissement *m* (la croix de Saint-André)
– *warning cross* (Am. *crossbuck)*
42 le garde-barrière
– *crossing keeper* (Am. *gateman)*
43 la maison du garde-barrière
– *crossing keeper's box* (Am. *gateman's box)*
44 le surveillant de la voie
– *linesman* (Am. *trackwalker)*
45 le passage à demi-barrière *f*
– *half-barrier crossing*
46 le feu clignotant
– *warning light*
47 la barrière à poste *m* d'appel *m*
– *intercom-controlled crossing;* sim.: *telephone-controlled crossing*
48 l'interphone *m*
– *intercom system*
49 le passage non gardé
– *unprotected level crossing* (Am. *unprotected grade crossing)*
50 le feu clignotant
– *warning light*

203 Le voie ferrée II (la signalisation)

1-6 sémaphores *m* (carrés *m*, signaux *m* d'arrêt)
– ***stop signals*** *(main signals)*
1 le sémaphore, un signal sémaphorique en position *f* «arrêt» *m* (un signal d'arrêt *m*)
– *stop signal (main signal), a semaphore signal in 'stop' position*
2 le bras de sémaphore *m*
– *signal arm (semaphore arm)*
3 le signal électrique en position «arrêt» *m* (le signal lumineux)
– *electric stop signal (colour light,* Am. *color light, signal) at 'stop'*
4 la position du signal «ralentissement» *m*
– *signal position: 'proceed at low speed'*
5 la position du signal «voie *f* libre»
– *signal position: 'proceed'*
6 le signal de remplacement *m*
– *substitute signal*
7-24 signaux *m* **d'avertissement** *m* (signaux *m* avancés, signaux *m* à distance *f*)
– ***distant signals***
7 le signal sémaphorique en position «arrêt *m* au prochain signal»
– *semaphore signal at 'be prepared to stop at next signal'*
8 le bras de sémaphore complémentaire
– *supplementary semaphore arm*
9 le signal lumineux d'avertissement *m* «arrêt *m* au prochain signal»
– *colour light (*Am. *color light) distant signal at 'be prepared to stop at next signal'*
10 la position du signal «ralentissement *m* au prochain signal»
– *signal position: 'be prepared to proceed at low speed'*
11 la position du signal «voie *f* libre au prochain signal»
– *signal position: 'proceed main signal ahead'*
12 le signal sémaphorique d'avertissement *m* avec panneau *m* complémentaire annonçant un raccourcissement de la distance de freinage *m* de plus de 5 %
– *semaphore signal with indicator plate showing a reduction in braking distance of more than 5%*
13 le panneau triangulaire
– *triangle (triangle sign)*
14 le signal d'avertissement *m* lumineux avec feu *m* complémentaire de réduction *f* de la distance de freinage *m*
– *colour light (*Am. *color light) distant signal with indicator light for showing reduced braking distance*
15 la lampe blanche complémentaire
– *supplementary white light*
16 le signal lumineux d'avertissement *m* d'arrêt *m* au prochain signal (le feu d'avertissement *m* jaune)
– *distant signal indicating 'be prepared to stop at next signal' (yellow light)*
17 le signal de rappel *m* d'avertissement *m* (le signal d'avertissement *m* avec feu *m* complémentaire, sans panneau *m*)
– *second distant signal (distant signal with supplementary light, without indicator plate)*
18 le signal d'avertissement *m* avec pancarte *f* (tableau *m*) de limitation *f* de vitesse *f*
– *distant signal with speed indicator*
19 la pancarte (le tableau) de limitation *f* de vitesse *f*
– *distant speed indicator*
20 le signal d'avertissement *m* avec signal *m* (indicateur) de direction *f*
– *distant signal with route indicator*
21 le signal (indicateur) de direction *f*
– *route indicator*
22 le signal d'avertissement *m* sans bras *m* de sémaphore *m* complémentaire en position *f* «arrêt *m* au prochain signal» *m*
– *distant signal without supplementary arm in position: 'be prepared to stop at next signal'*
23 le signal d'avertissement *m* sans bras *m* de sémaphore *m* complémentaire en position *f* «voie libre *f* au prochain signal»
– *distant signal without supplementary arm in 'be prepared to proceed' position*
24 le panneau d'avertissement *m*
– *distant signal identification plate*
25-44 signaux *m* **complémentaires**
– ***supplementary signals***
25 le panneau trapézoïdal annonçant l'arrêt *m* devant un poste d'exploitation *f*
– *stop board for indicating the stopping point at a control point*
26-29 les mirlitons *m* (avertisseurs *m* optiques, poteaux *m* avertisseurs de signal *m*)
– ***approach signs***
26 le mirliton placé à 100 m avant le signal d'avertissement *m*
– *approach sign 100 m from distant signal*
27 le mirliton placé à 175 m avant le signal d'avertissement *m*
– *approach sign 175 m from distant signal*
28 le mirliton placé à 250 m avant le signal d'avertissement *m*
– *approach sign 250 m from distant signal*
29 le mirliton placé à une distance réduite de 5% par rapport à la distance de freinage *m* sur le canton
– *approach sign at a distance of 5% less than the braking distance on the section*
30 le panneau à damier *m* annonçant des sémaphores *m* placés ni immédiatement à droite ni directement au-dessus de la voie
– *chequered sign indicating stop signals (main signals) not positioned immediately to the right of or over the line (track)*
31-32 les panneaux *m* d'arrêt *m* indiquant le point d'arrêt *m* de la tête du train
– *stop boards to indicate the stopping point of the front of the train*
33 le panneau d'avertissement *m* du point d'arrêt *m*
– *stop board (be prepared to stop)*
34-35 les poteaux *m* indicateurs de chasse-neige *m*
– *snow plough (*Am. *snowplow) signs*
34 le poteau «relèvement *m* du soc»
– *'raise snow plough (*Am. *snowplow)' sign*
35 le poteau «abaissement *m* du soc»
– *'lower snow plough (*Am. *snowplow)' sign*
36-44 signaux *m* **de ralentissement** *m*
– ***speed restriction signs***
36-38 les triangles *m* **de ralentissement** *m* [vitesse *f* maximale autorisée: 3 x 10 = 30 km/h]
– ***speed restriction sign*** *[maximum speed 3 x 10 = 30 kph]*
36 le panneau de signalisation *f* de jour *m*
– *sign for day running*
37 la limite de vitesse *f* codée
– *speed code number*
38 le panneau lumineux de signalisation *f* de nuit *f*
– *illuminated sign for night running*
39 le début du tronçon (de la section) de ralentissement *m* provisoire
– *commencement of temporary speed restriction*
40 la fin du tronçon (de la section) de ralentissement *m* provisoire
– *termination of temporary speed restriction*
41 le panneau de limitation *f* de vitesse *f* sur un tronçon (une section) de ralentissement *m* permanent [vitesse *f* maximale autorisée: 5 x 10 = 50 km/h]
– *speed restriction sign for a section with a permanent speed restriction [maximum speed 5 x 10 = 50 kph]*
42 le début du tronçon (de la section) de ralentissement *m* permanent
– *commencement of permanent speed restriction*
43 le signal d'annonce *f* de vitesse *f* limite [uniquement sur les grandes lignes *f*]
– *speed restriction warning sign [only on main lines]*
44 le signal de limitation *f* de vitesse *f* [uniquement sur les grandes lignes *f*]
– *speed restriction sign [only on main lines]*
45-52 signaux *m* d'aiguillage *m* (de position *f* d'aiguille *f*)
– ***point signals*** *(switch signals)*
45-48 aiguillages *m* **simples**
– ***single points*** *(single switches)*
45 l'embranchement *m* droit
– *route straight ahead (main line)*
46 l'embranchement *m* cintré [à droite]
– *[right] branch*

47 l'embranchement *m* cintré [à gauche]
– *[left] branch*
48 l'embranchement *m* courbe [vu du cœur du croisement]
– *branch [seen from the frog]*
49-52 traversées-jonctions *f* doubles
– ***double crossover***
49 la traversée-jonction rectiligne de gauche à droite
– *route straight ahead from left to right*
50 la traversée-jonction rectiligne de droite à gauche
– *route straight ahead from right to left*
51 la traversée-jonction cintrée à gauche
– *turnout to the left from the left*
52 la traversée-jonction cintrée à droite
– *turnout to the right from the right*
53 le poste d'aiguillage *m* mécanique
– ***manually-operated signal box*** *(*Am. *signal tower, switch tower)*
54 le châssis d'enclenchement *m*
– *lever mechanism*
55 le levier d'aiguille *f* [bleu], un levier de verrouillage *m* d'aiguille *f*
– *points lever (switch lever) [blue], a lock lever*
56 le levier de signal *m* [rouge]
– *signal lever [red]*
57 la manette
– *catch*
58 le levier d'itinéraire *m* (levier *m* de parcours *m*)
– *route lever*
59 le block-système (le block, le cantonnement)
– *block instruments*
60 le panneau de section *f* (canton *m*) de block *m*
– *block section panel*
61 le poste (d'aiguillage *m*) **électrique**
– ***electrically-operated signal box*** *(*Am. *signal tower, switch tower)*
62 les leviers *m* d'aiguille *f* et de signal *m*
– *points (switch) and signal knobs*
63 la table d'enclenchements *m*
– *lock indicator panel*
64 le panneau de contrôle *m* (les voyants *m* lumineux)
– *track and signal indicator*
65 le poste de commande *f* à tableau *m* de contrôle *m* optique
– ***track diagram control layout***
66 le pupitre de commande *f* avec diagramme *m* figuratif des voies *f* (avec tableau *m* ou schéma *m* des voies *f*)
– *track diagram control panel (domino panel)*
67 les boutons-poussoirs *m* (les touches *f*)
– *push buttons*
68 les itinéraires *m* (les parcours *m* topographiques)
– *routes*
69 l'interphone *m*
– *intercom system*

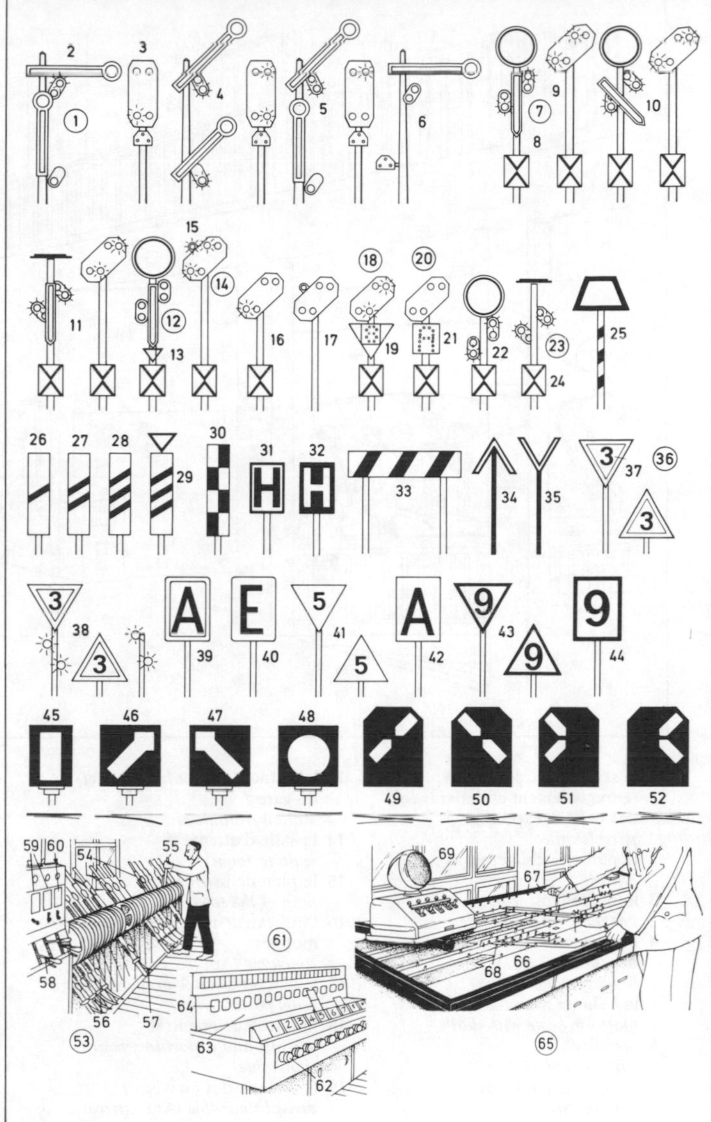

1 le service des colis *m* express (enregistrement et délivrance des colis *m* express)
– *parcels office*
2 le panier à couvercle *m*
– *parcels*
3 la malle d'osier *m*
– *basket*
4 l'enregistrement *m* des bagages *m*
– *luggage counter*
5 la balance automatique
– *platform scale with dial*
6 la valise
– *suitcase (case)*
7 l'étiquette *f* autocollante
– *luggage sticker*
8 le bulletin de bagages *m*
– *luggage receipt*
9 le préposé aux bagages *m*
– *luggage clerk*
10 l'affiche *f* (le placard) publicitaire
– *poster (advertisement)*
11 la boîte à lettres *f*
– *station post box (*Am. *station mailbox)*
12 le tableau indicateur du retard des trains *m*
– *notice board indicating train delays*
13 le restaurant (*anal.:* le buffet) de gare *f*
– *station restaurant*
14 la salle d'attente *f*
– *waiting room*
15 le plan de la ville
– *map of the town (street map)*
16 l'indicateur *m* à panneaux *m* mobiles
– *timetable (*Am. *schedule)*
17 le garçon d'hotel *m* (le groom)
– *hotel porter*
18 l'indicateur *m* mural
– *arrivals and departures board (timetable)*
19 le tableau des arrivées *f*
– *arrival timetable (*Am. *arrival schedule)*
20 le tableau des départs *m*
– *departure timetable (*Am. *departure schedule)*

21 la consigne automatique
– *left luggage lockers*
22 le changeur de monnaie *f*
– *change machine*
23 le passage souterrain d'accès *m* aux voies *f*
– *tunnel to the platforms*
24 les voyageurs *m* (les voyageuses *f*)
– *passengers*
25 l'escalier *m* d'accès *m* aux quais *m*
– *steps to the platforms*
26 la librairie de la gare
– *station bookstall (*Am. *station bookstand)*
27 la consigne des bagages *m* à main *f*
– *left luggage office (left luggage)*
28 l'agence *f* de voyages *m* (le bureau de tourisme; *égal.:* le bureau de réservation *f* des chambres *f* d'hôtel *m*)
– *travel centre (*Am. *center);* also: *accommodation bureau*
29 le bureau de renseignements *m*
– *information office (*Am. *information bureau)*
30 l'horloge *f* de gare *f*
– *station clock*
31 l'agence *f* bancaire avec le bureau de change *m*
– *bank branch with foreign exchange counter*
32 le tableau des taux *m* de change *m*
– *indicator board showing exchange rates*
33 le plan du réseau ferroviaire
– *railway map (*Am. *railroad map)*
34 la délivrance des billets *m*
– *ticket office*
35 le guichet des billets *m*
– *ticket counter*
36 le billet (le titre de transport *m*)
– *ticket (railway ticket,* Am. *railroad ticket)*
37 le plateau tournant [guichet *m*]
– *revolving tray*
38 l'hygiaphone *m*
– *grill*
39 l'employé *m* affecté à la vente des billets *m*
– *ticket clerk (*Am. *ticket agent)*
40 la machine *f* à billets *m* (la machine à imprimer les billets *m*)
– *ticket-printing machine (ticket-stamping machine)*
41 l'imprimante *f* manuelle de billets *m*
– *hand-operated ticket printer*
42 l'indicateur *m* de poche *f*
– *pocket timetable (*Am. *pocket train schedule)*
43 la banquette à bagages *m*
– *luggage rest*
44 l'antenne *f* médicale (l'infirmerie *f*)
– *first aid station*
45 le centre d'accueil *m*
– *Travellers' (*Am. *Travelers') Aid*
46 la cabine téléphonique publique
– *telephone box (telephone booth, telephone kiosk, call box)*
47 le bureau de tabac *m*
– *cigarettes and tobacco kiosk*
48 la boutique de fleuriste *m*
– *flower stand*
49 l'agent *m* chargé de l'information *f* du public
– *railway information clerk*
50 l'indicateur *m* (officiel) des (horaires *m* de) chemins *m* de fer *m*
– *official timetable (official railway guide,* Am. *train schedule)*

1 le quai de gare *f*
– *platform*
2 l'escalier *m* d'accès *m* aux quais
– *steps to the platform*
3 le passage supérieur d'accès *m* aux quais
– *bridge to the platforms*
4 le numéro de quai *m*
– *platform number*
5 la marquise (l'abri *m*) de gare *f*
– *platform roofing*
6 les voyageurs *m* (les voyageuses *f*)
– *passengers*
7-12 les bagages *m*
– ***luggage***
7 la valise
– *suitcase (case)*
8 le porte-adresse
– *luggage label*
9 l'autocollant *m* d'hôtel *m*
– *hotel sticker*
10 le sac de voyage *m*
– *travelling* (Am. *traveling) bag*
11 le carton à chapeaux *m*
– *hat box*
12 le parapluie, un parapluie-canne
– *umbrella, a walking-stick umbrella*

13 le bâtiment des voyageurs *m* (des recettes *f*)
– *main building;* also: *offices*
14 le quai numéro 1
– *platform*
15 le passage à niveau *m* de quai *m*
– *crossing*
16 le kiosque roulant
– *news trolley*
17 le vendeur de journaux *m*
– *news vendor* (Am. *news dealer)*
18 la lecture de voyage *m*
– *reading matter for the journey*
19 la bordure de quai *m*
– *edge of the platform*
20 l'agent *m* de police *f* de la gare
– *railway policeman* (Am. *railroad policeman)*
21 le panneau indicateur de direction *f*
– *destination board*
22 la case d'affichage *m* de la destination
– *destination indicator*
23 la case d'affichage *m* de l'heure *f* de départ *m*
– *departure time indicator*
24 la case d'affichage *m* du retard du train
– *delay indicator*

25 le train du réseau régional, un train automoteur (rame *f* automotrice)
– *suburban train, a railcar*
26 le compartiment réservé
– *special compartment*
27 le haut-parleur de quai *m*
– *platform loudspeaker*
28 le panneau de gare *f*
– *station sign*
29 le chariot électrique
– *electric trolley (electric truck)*
30 le cariste
– *loading foreman*
31 le porteur (de bagages *m*)
– *porter* (Am. *redcap)*
32 le chariot à bagages *m*
– *barrow*
33 la fontaine à eau *f* potable
– *drinking fountain*
34 le Trans-Europ-Express électrique (le T.E.E.); *égal.:* le train rapide interurbain
– *electric Trans-Europe Express;* also: *Intercity train*
35 la locomotive électrique, une locomotive de (grande) vitesse *f*
– *electric locomotive, an express locomotive*
36 l'archet *m* de pantographe *m*
– *collector bow (sliding bow)*

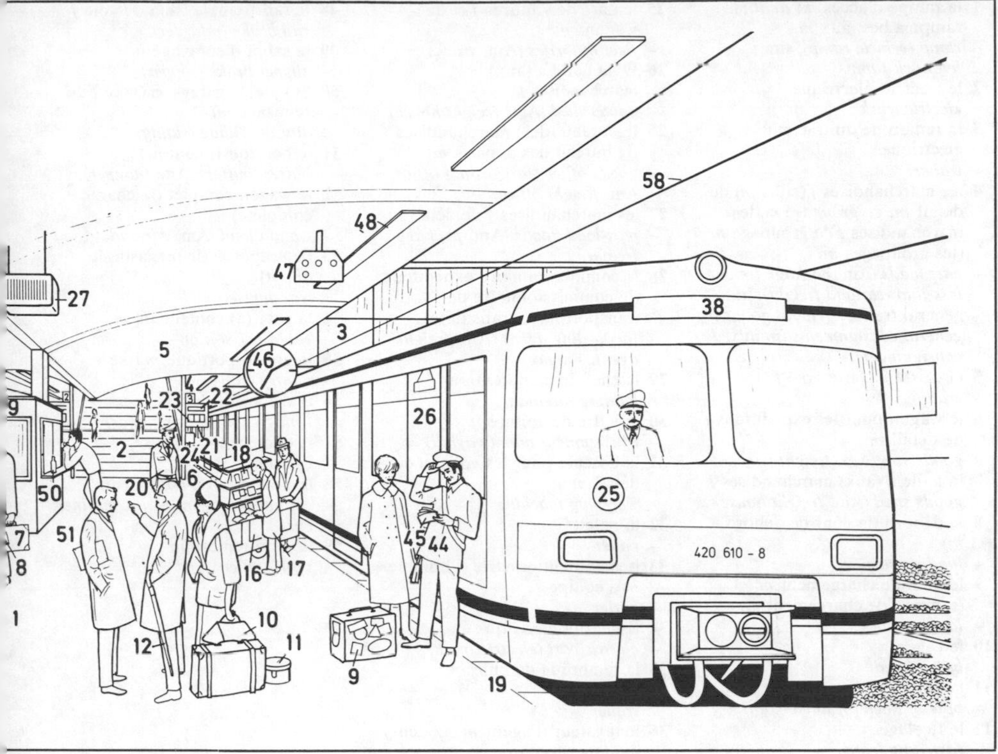

37 le compartiment de secrétariat *m*
– *secretarial compartment*
38 la plaque d'itinéraire *m*
– *destination board*
39 le visiteur (matériel *m* roulant)
– *wheel tapper*
40 le marteau de sondage *m* des bandages *m*
– *wheel-tapping hammer*
41 le chef de sécurité *f*
– *station foreman*
42 le guidon de départ *m*
– *signal*
43 la casquette rouge [inconnue en France]
– *red cap*
44 l'agent *m* chargé de l'information *f* du public
– *inspector*
45 l'indicateur *m* de poche *f*
– *pocket timetable* (Am. *pocket train schedule)*
46 la pendule de quai *m*
– *platform clock*
47 le signal de départ *m*
– *starting signal*
48 la rampe d'éclairage *m* de quai *m*
– *platform lighting*
49 la buvette de quai *m*
– *refreshment kiosk*
50 la bouteille de bière *f*
beer bottle
51 le journal
– *newspaper*
52 le baiser d'adieu *m*
– *parting kiss*
53 l'étreinte *f*
– *embrace*
54 le banc de quai *m*
– *platform seat*
55 la corbeille à détritus *m*
– *litter bin* (Am. *litter basket)*
56 la boîte à lettres *f* de quai *m*
– *platform post box* (Am. *platform mailbox)*
57 la cabine téléphonique de quai *m*
– *platform telephone*
58 le fil de contact *m*
– *trolley wire (overhead contact wire)*
59-61 la voie
– *track*
59 le rail
– *rail*
60 la traverse
– *sleeper* (Am. *tie, crosstie)*
61 le ballast (le lit de ballast *m*)
– *ballast (bed)*

1 la rampe d'accès *m*; *anal.:* la rampe à bestiaux *m*
– *ramp (vehicle ramp);* sim.: *livestock ramp*
2 le tracteur électrique
– *electric truck*
3 la remorque du tracteur électrique
– *trailer*
4 les marchandises *f* (colis *m*) de détail *m*; *en groupage m:* les marchandises *f* de groupage *m* (les groupages *m*)
– *part loads (*Am. *package freight, less-than-carload freight);* in general traffic: *general goods in general consignments (in mixed consignments)*
5 la caisse à claire-voie *f*
– *crate*
6 le wagon pour les expéditions *f* de détail *m*
– *goods van (*Am. *freight car)*
7 la halle à (aux) marchandises *f*
– *goods shed (*Am. *freight house)*
8 le débord (la cour de débord *m*)
– *loading strip*
9 le quai de chargement *m* (rampe *f* de chargement *m*)
– *loading dock*
10 le cageot
– *bale of peat*
11 la balle
– *bale of linen (of linen cloth)*
12 le ficelage
– *fastening (cord)*
13 la bonbonne (la tourie)
– *wicker bottle (wickered bottle, demijohn)*
14 le diable
– *trolley*
15 le camion de fret *m*
– *goods lorry (*Am. *freight truck)*
16 le chariot élévateur à fourche *f*
– *forklift truck (fork truck, forklift)*
17 la voie de chargement *m*
– *loading siding*
18 les marchandises *f* encombrantes
– *bulky goods*
19 le petit conteneur [propriété *f* des chemins *m* de fer *m*]
– *small railway-owned (*Am. *railroad-owned) container*
20 la roulotte de forain *m*; *anal.:* la roulotte de cirque *m*
– *showman's caravan (*sim.: *circus caravan)*
21 le wagon plat
– *flat wagon (*Am. *flat freight car)*
22 le gabarit de chargement *m* (profil *m* d'encombrement *m*)
– *loading gauge (*Am. *gage)*
23 la balle de paille *f*
– *bale of straw*
24 le wagon à ranchers *m*
– *flat wagon (*Am. *flatcar) with side stakes*
25 le parc de voitures *f* et de wagons *m*
– *fleet of lorries (*Am. *trucks)*
26-39 la halle à (aux) **marchandises** *f*
– ***goods shed*** (Am. *freight house)*
26 le bureau (des) marchandises *f* (le bureau des départs *m*)
– *goods office (forwarding office,* Am. *freight office)*
27 les marchandises *f* de détail *m*
– *part-load goods (*Am. *package freight)*
28 le commissionnaire-expéditeur (le commissionnaire de transport *m*, le transitaire)
– *forwarding agent (*Am. *freight agent, shipper)*
29 le chef de manutention *f*
– *loading foreman*
30 la lettre de voiture *f*
– *consignment note (waybill)*
31 la bascule pour les colis *m* de détail *m*
– *weighing machine*
32 la palette
– *pallet*
33 le manutentionnaire (l'homme *m* d'équipe *f*)
– *porter*
34 le chariot électrique
– *electric cart (electric truck)*
35 la remorque du chariot électrique
– *trailer*
36 le taxateur (l'agent *m* taxateur)
– *loading supervisor*
37 la porte de la halle
– *goods shed door (*Am. *freight house door)*
38 la glissière
– *rail (slide rail)*
39 le galet de roulement *m*
– *roller*
40 l'abri *m* de bascule *f*
– *weighbridge office*
41 la bascule à wagon *m* (le pont-bascule)
– *weighbridge*
42 le chantier de triage *m*
– *marshalling yard (*Am. *classification yard, switch yard)*
43 la locomotive de manœuvre *f*
– *shunting engine (shunting locomotive, shunter,* Am. *switch engine, switcher)*
44 le poste de butte *f* (poste *m* de bosse *f*)
– *marshalling yard signal box (*Am. *classification yard switch tower)*
45 le brigadier (le chef d'équipe *f*) de manœuvre *f*
– *yardmaster*
46 la rampe (la bosse) de triage *m* (la butte, le dos d'âne *m*)
– *hump*
47 la voie de triage *m*
– *sorting siding (classification siding, classification track)*
48 le rail-frein, le frein de voie *f*
– *rail brake (retarder)*
49 le sabot d'enrayage *m*
– *slipper brake (slipper)*
50 la voie de garage *m* (voie *f* de remisage *m*)
– *storage siding (siding)*
51 le heurtoir (le butoir)
– *buffer (buffers,* Am. *bumper)*
52 le wagon complet (la charge complète)
– *wagon load (*Am. *carload)*
53 l'entrepôt *m* (le magasin, le dépôt)
– *warehouse*
54 la gare (à) conteneurs *m*
– *container station*
55 la grue à portique *m* fixe
– *gantry crane*
56 le dispositif de levage *m*
– *lifting gear (hoisting gear)*
57 le conteneur
– *container*
58 le wagon porte-conteneurs
– *container wagon (*Am. *container car)*
59 la semi-remorque
– *semi-trailer*

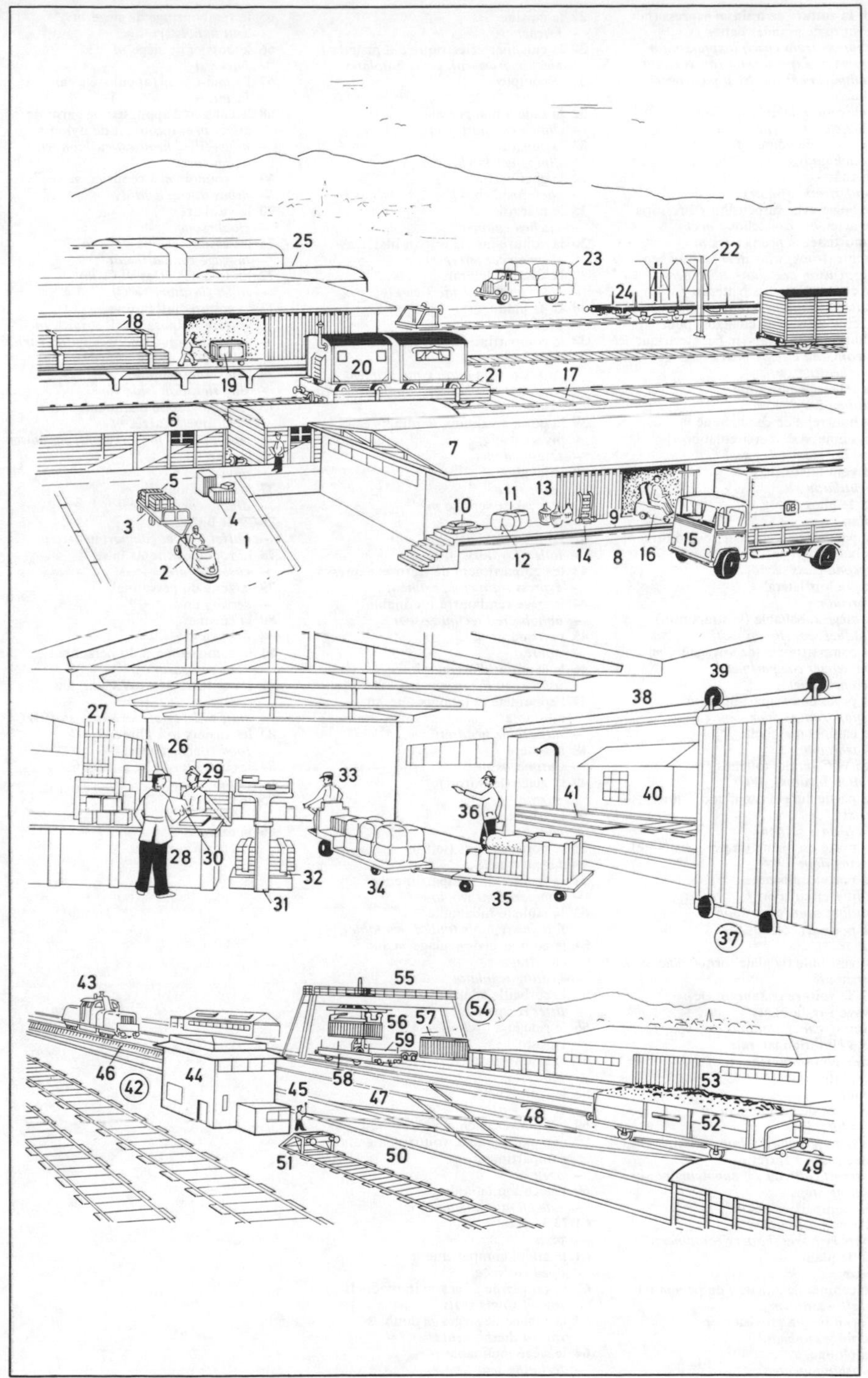
25
23
22
24
18
20
19
21
17
6
7
5
4
3
1
2
11
13
10
9
12
14
8
16
15
DB
39
38
27
26
29
33
36
40
41
28
30
32
31
34
35
37
43
55
54
56
57
59
58
46
44
42
45
47
53
48
52
51
50
49

1-21 la voiture de train *m* **express** (la voiture de grandes lignes *f*)
– ***express train coach*** *(express train carriage, express train car, corridor compartment coach), a passenger coach*
1 l'élévation latérale
– *side elevation (side view)*
2 la caisse de voiture *f*
– *coach body*
3 le châssis
– *underframe (frame)*
4 le bogie avec suspension *f* à ressorts *m* acier *m* - caoutchouc *m* et amortisseurs *m* de chocs *m*
– *bogie (truck) with steel and rubber suspension and shock absorbers*
5 le compartiment à batteries *f*
– *battery containers (battery boxes)*
6 l'échangeur *m* de chaleur *f* pour chauffage *m* à vapeur *f* et électrique
– *steam and electric heat exchanger for the heating system*
7 la fenêtre coulissante
– *sliding window*
8 le bourrelet en caoutchouc *m* [système *m* d'intercirculation *f*]
– *rubber connecting seal*
9 le ventilateur statique
– *ventilator*
10-21 le plan
– ***plan***
10 la partie 2ème classe d'une voiture mixte
– *second-class section*
11 le couloir latéral
– *corridor*
12 le siège rabattable (le strapontin)
– *folding seat (tip-up seat)*
13 le compartiment [de voyageurs *m*]
– *passenger compartment (compartment)*
14 la porte de compartiment *m*
– *compartment door*
15 le cabinet de toilette *f*
– *washroom*
16 les W.C. *m* (les toilettes *f*)
– *toilet (lavatory, WC)*
17 la partie 1ère classe d'une voiture mixte
– *first-class section*
18 la porte oscillante (la porte battante)
– *swing door*
19 la porte coulissante d'intercirculation *f*
– *sliding connecting door*
20 la porte d'accès *m*
– *door*
21 le vestibule (la plate-forme) d'accès *m*
– *vestibule*
22-32 la voiture restaurant (le wagon-restaurant)
– ***dining car*** *(restaurant car, diner)*
22-25 l'élévation latérale
– ***side elevation*** *(side view)*
22 la porte
– *door*
23 la porte de chargement *m*
– *loading door*
24 le pantographe d'alimentation *f* électrique à l'arrêt *m*
– *current collector for supplying power during stops*
25 les compartiments *m* d'accumulateur *m*
– *battery boxes (battery containers)*
26-32 le plan
– ***plan***
26 le cabinet de toilette *f* du personnel
¬ *staff washroom*
27 l'armoire *f* à provisions *f*
– *storage cupboard*
28 la plonge
– *washing-up area*
29 la cuisine
– *kitchen*
30 la cuisinière électrique à 8 plaques *f*
– *electric oven with eight hotplates*
31 le comptoir
– *counter*
32 la salle à manger *m*
– *dining compartment*
33 la cuisine
– *dining car kitchen*
34 le chef cuisinier
– *chef (head cook)*
35 le placard
– *kitchen cabinet*
36 la voiture-lits (le wagon-lits)
– *sleeping car (sleeper)*
37 l'élévation latérale
– *side elevation (side view)*
38-42 le plan
– ***plan***
38 le compartiment de voiture-lit *f* pour deux voyageurs *m*
– *two-seat twin-berth compartment (two-seat two-berth compartment,* Am. *bedroom)*
39 la porte à vantaux *m* pliants et pivotants
– *folding doors*
40 le lavabo
– *washstand*
41 le local de service *m*
– *office*
42 les toilettes *f* (les W.C. *m*)
– *toilet (lavatory, WC)*
43 le compartiment de train *m* express
– *express train compartment*
44 le siège rembourré inclinable
– *upholstered reclining seat*
45 l'accoudoir *m*
– *armrest*
46 le cendrier d'accoudoir *m*
– *ashtray in the armrest*
47 l'appui-tête *m* (appuie-tête *m*) ajustable
– *adjustable headrest*
48 la têtière
– *antimacassar*
49 la glace (le miroir)
– *mirror*
50 la patère
– *coat hook*
51 le porte-bagages (le filet àbagages *m*)
– *luggage rack*
52 la fenêtre de compartiment
– *compartment window*
53 la tablette rabattable
– *fold-away table (pull-down table)*
54 le bouton *m* de réglage *m* du chauffage
– *heating regulator*
55 la corbeille àdétritus *m*
– *litter receptacle*
56 le rideau à tirette *f*
– *curtain*
57 le repose-pieds
– *footrest*
58 le coin fenêtre
– *corner seat*
59 la voiture-coach, voiture *f* non compartimentée, voiture *f* à grand compartiment *m*
– *open car*
60 l'élévation latérale
– *side elevation (side view)*
61-72 le plan
– ***plan***
61 le grand compartiment
– *open carriage*
62 la rangée de sièges *m* individuels
– *row of single seats*
63 la rangée de sièges *m* doubles
– *row of double seats*
64 le siège inclinable
– *reclining seat*
65 le rembourrage de siège *m*
– *seat upholstery*
66 le dossier de siège *m*
– *backrest*
67 l'appui-tête *m* (appuie-tête *m*)
– *headrest*
68 le coussin d'appui-tête *m* garni de duvet *m* et recouvert de nylon *m*
– *down-filled headrest cushion with nylon cover*
69 l'accoudoir *m* à cendrier *m*
– *armrest with ashtray*
70 le vestiaire
– *cloakroom*
71 les casiers *m* à bagages *m*
– *luggage compartment*
72 les toilettes *f* (les W.C. *m*)
– *toilet (lavatory, WC)*
73 la voiture-buffet, une voiture-restaurant self-service *m*
– *buffet car (quick-service buffet car), a self-service restaurant car*
74 l'élévation latérale
– *side elevation (side view)*
75 le pantographe d'alimentation *f* électrique à l'arrêt *m*
– *current collector for supplying power*
76 le plan
– *plan*
77 la salle à manger *m*
– *dining compartment*
78-79 le buffet
– ***buffet*** *(buffet compartment)*
78 la zone des clients *m*
– *customer area*
79 la zone du personnel
– *serving area*
80 la cuisine
– *kitchen*
81 le compartiment du personnel
– *staff compartment*
82 les toilettes *f* (les W.C. *m*) du personnel
– *staff toilet (staff lavatory, staff WC)*
83 les casiers *m* à aliments *m*
– *food compartments*
84 les serviettes *f*
– *plates*
85 le couvert
– *cutlery*
86 la caisse
– *till (cash register)*

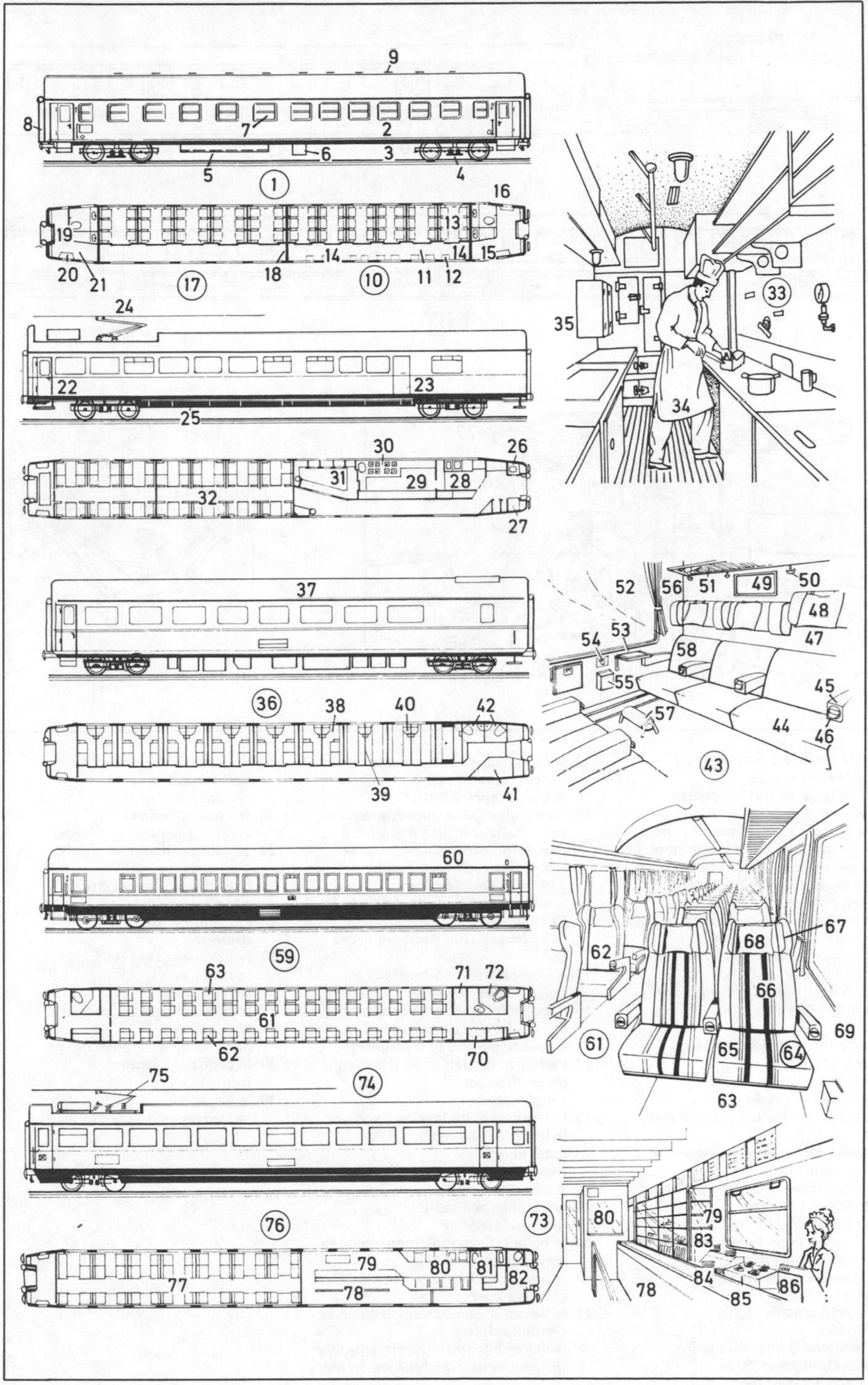
9
8
7
2
3
4
5
6
1
16
19
13
14
15
20
21
18
11
12
10
17
24
22
23
25
30
26
31
29
28
32
27
33
35
34
37
36
38
40
42
39
41
52
56
51
49
50
48
47
54
53
58
55
45
57
44
46
43
60
59
67
68
62
66
63
71
72
61
69
65
64
62
70
74
63
75
76
73
80
79
83
79
80
81
82
77
78
84
86
78
85

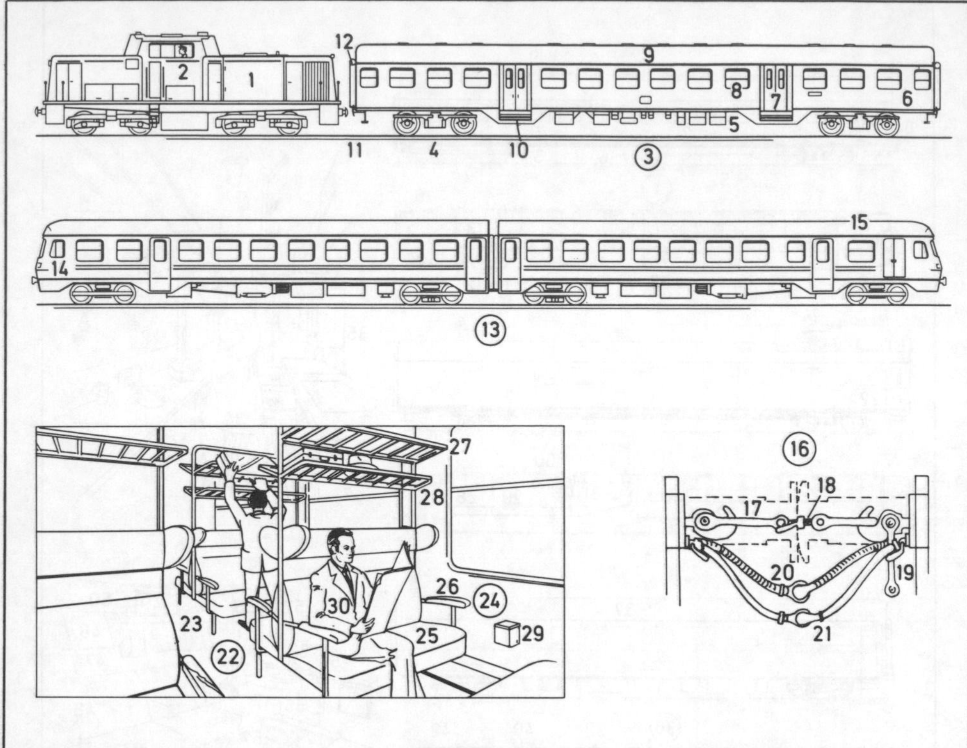

1-30 le trafic à courte distance *f*
– ***local train service***

1-12 le train de trafic à courte distance *f*
– ***local train*** *(short-distance train)*

1 la locomotive Diesel monomoteur
– *single-engine diesel locomotive*

2 le mécanicien de locomotive *f*
– *engine driver* (Am. *engineer)*

3 la voiture à quatre essieux *m*, une voiture à voyageurs *m*
– *four-axled coach (four-axled car) for short-distance routes, a passenger coach (passenger car)*

4 le bogie [avec frein *m* à disques *m*]
– *bogie (truck) [with disc (disk) brakes]*

5 le châssis
– *underframe (frame)*

6 la caisse de voiture *f* à panneaux *m* en tôle *f*
– *coach body with metal panelling* (Am. *paneling)*

7 la double porte à vantaux *m* pliants et pivotants
– *double folding doors*

8 la fenêtre du compartiment
– *compartment window*

9 le grand compartiment
– *open carriage*

10 la porte d'accès *m*
– *entrance*

11 le système d'intercirculation *f* (intercirculation *f*)
– *connecting corridor*

12 le bourrelet en caoutchouc *m* (intercirculation *f*)
– *rubber connecting seal*

13 l'autorail *m*, une automotrice pour trafic à courte distance *f*, une automotrice Diesel
– *light railcar, a short-distance railcar, a diesel railcar*

14 la cabine de conduite *f* de l'automotrice *f*
– *cab (driver's cab,* Am. *engineer's cab)*

15 le compartiment à bagages *m*
– *luggage compartment*

16 l'accouplement *m* de conduites *f* et l'attelage *m* de voitures *f*
– *connecting hoses and coupling*

17 l'étrier *m* d'attelage *m* (la manille de tendeur *m*)
– *coupling link*

18 le tendeur d'attelage *m* (la vis et le levier de manœuvre *f* du tendeur *m*)
– *tensioning device (coupling screw with tensioning lever)*

19 la manille pendante
– *unlinked coupling*

20 le boyau d'accouplement *m* de la conduite de chauffage *m*
– *heating coupling hose (steam coupling hose)*

21 le boyau d'accouplement *m* de la conduite du frein
– *coupling hose (connecting hose) for the compressed-air braking system*

22 la partie 2ème classe d'une voiture mixte
– *second-class section*

23 le couloir central
– *central gangway*

24 le compartiment
– *compartment*

25 la banquette rembourrée
– *upholstered seat*

26 l'accoudoir *m*
– *armrest*

27 le porte-bagages (le filet à bagages *m*)
– *luggage rack*

28 le filet à chapeaux et petits bagages *m*
– *hat and light luggage rack*

29 le cendrier pivotant
– *ashtray*

30 le voyageur
– *passenger*

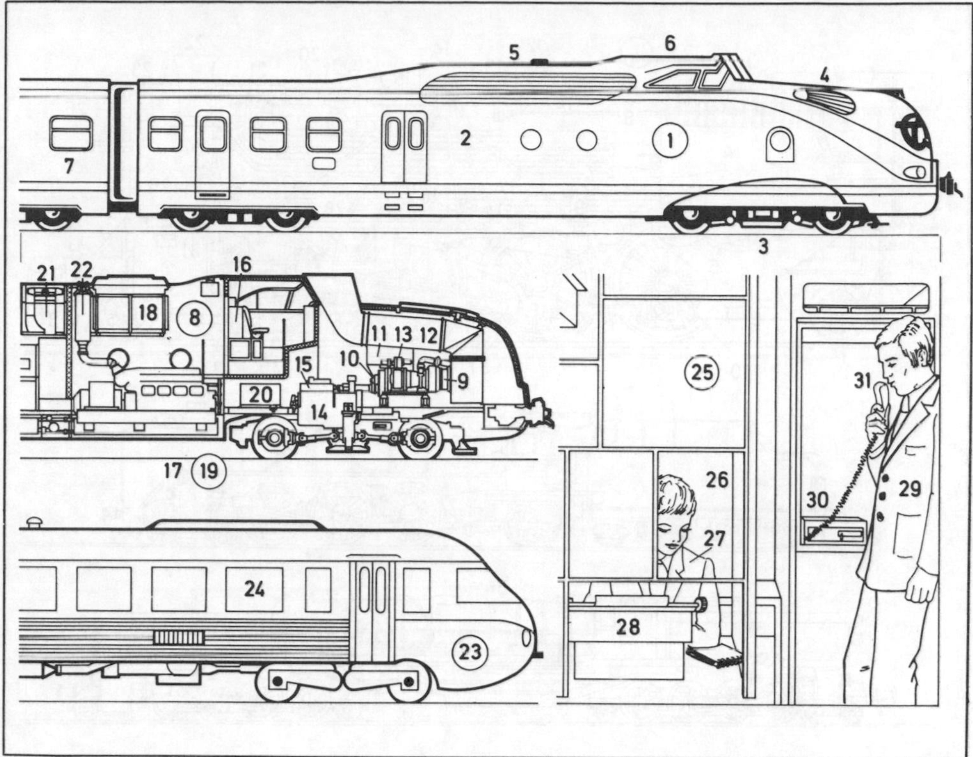

1-22 le train T.E.E. (I.C.) (le train Trans-Europe-Express interurbain)
– ***Trans-Europe Express***

1 la rame automotrice (le train automoteur) des Chemins de fer fédéraux allemands (D.B.), une rame automotrice Diesel ou une rame automotrice à turbine *f*à gaz *m*
– *German Federal Railway trainset, a diesel trainset or gas turbine trainset*

2 la voiture motrice (la motrice)
– *driving unit*

3 l'essieu *m* monté moteur
– *drive wheel unit*

4 le moteur Diesel de traction *f*
– *main engine*

5 le générateur thermoélectrique
– *diesel generator unit*

6 la cabine de conduite *f* (poste *m* de conduite *f*)
– *cab (driver's cab,* Am. *engineer's cab)*

7 la remorque intermédiaire
– *second coach*

8 la motrice à turbine *f* à gaz *m* [coupe]
– *gas turbine driving unit [diagram]*

9 la turbine à gaz *m*
– *gas turbine*

10 la transmission de turbine *f*
– *turbine transmission*

11 le conduit d'admission *f* d'air *m*
– *air intake*

12 la conduite d'échappement *m* avec silencieux *m*
– *exhaust with silencers (*Am. *mufflers)*

13 le démarreur électrique
– *dynastarter*

14 la transmission Voith
– *Voith transmission*

15 l'échangeur *m* de chaleur *f* pour refroidissement *m* de l'huile *f* de transmission *f*
– *heat exchanger for the transmission oil*

16 l'armoire *f* de commande *f* et de la turbine à gaz *m*
– *gas turbine controller*

17 le réservoir de carburant *m* de la turbine à gaz *m*
– *gas turbine fuel tank*

18 le refroidisseur par air *m* de l'huile *f* de la transmission et de la turbine
– *oil-to-air cooling unit for transmission and turbine*

19 le moteur Diesel auxiliaire
– *auxiliary diesel engine*

20 le réservoir de carburant *m*
– *fuel tank*

21 l'installation *f* de refroidissement *m*
– *cooling unit*

22 le tuyau d'échappement *m* à silencieux *m*
– *exhaust with silencers (*Am. *mufflers)*

23 la rame automotrice expérimentale de la Société Nationale des Chemins de fer Français (S.N.C.F.) avec un moteur Diesel 6 cylindres *m* sous plancher *m* (sous caisse *f*) et une turbine à gaz *m* à deux arbres *m*
– ***experimental trainset*** *of the Société Nationale des Chemins de Fer Français (SNCF) with six-cylinder underfloor diesel engine and twin-shaft gas turbine*

24 le turbogroupe à silencieux *m*
– *turbine unit with silencers (*Am. *mufflers)*

25 le compartiment secrétariat
– *secretarial compartment*

26 le compartiment dactylo
– *typing compartment*

27 la secrétaire
– *secretary*

28 la machine à écrire
– *typewriter*

29 l'homme d'affaires *f* en voyage *m*
– *travelling (*Am. *traveling) salesman*

30 la machine à dicter
– *dictating machine*

31 le microphone (*fam.:* le micro)
– *microphone*

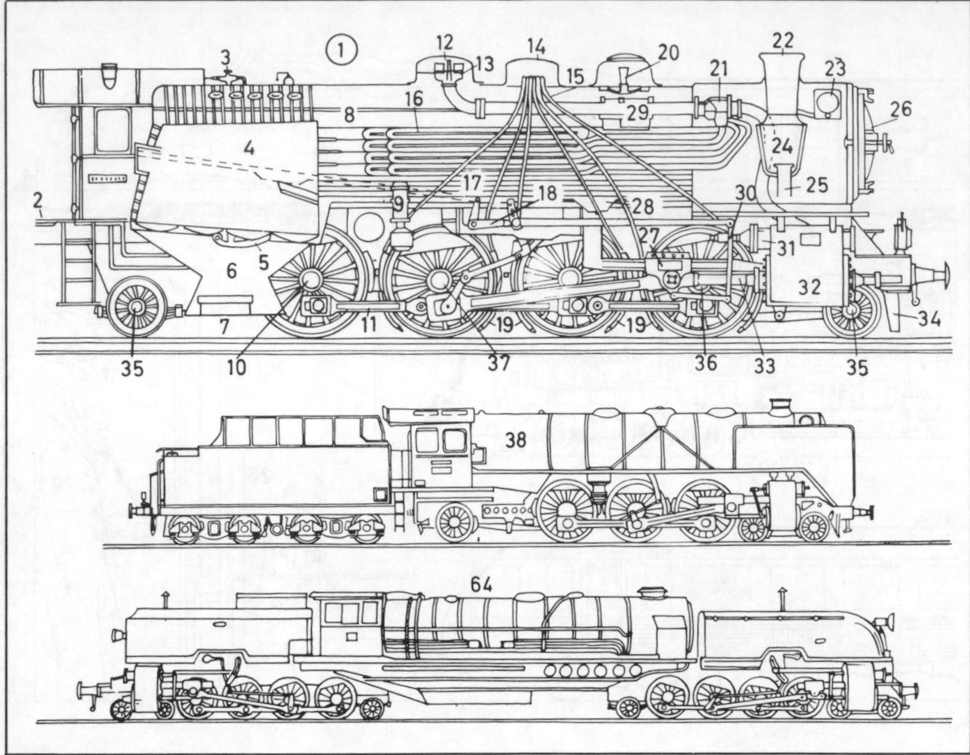

1-69 locomotives *f* **à vapeur** *f*
– ***steam locomotives***
2-37 la chaudière et le mécanisme moteur de la locomotive
– ***locomotive boiler and driving gear***
2 le tablier de tender *m* avec attelage *m*
– *tender platform with coupling*
3 la soupape de sûreté pour surpression *f* de vapeur *f*
– *safety valve for excess boiler pressure*
4 le foyer
– *firebox*
5 la grille basculante (le jette-feu)
– *drop grate*
6 le cendrier ventilé
– *ashpan with damper doors*
7 la trappe du cendrier
– *bottom door of the ashpan*
8 les tubes *m* à fumée *f*
– *smoke tubes (flue tubes)*
9 la pompe d'alimentation *f* en eau *f*
– *feed pump*
10 la boîte d'essieu *m*
– *axle bearing*
11 la bielle d'accouplement *m*
– *connecting rod*
12 le dôme de vapeur *f*
– *steam dome*
13 le régulateur de vapeur *f*
– *regulator valve (regulator main valve)*
14 la sablière
– *sand dome*
15 les tubes de descente *f* du sable
– *sand pipes (sand tubes)*
16 la chaudière tubulaire
– *boiler (boiler barrel)*
17 les tubes *m* de fumée *f* ou bouilleurs
– *fire tubes or steam tubes*
18 le changement de marche *f*
– *reversing gear (steam reversing gear)*
19 les tuyères *f* d'écoulement *m* du sable
– *sand pipes*
20 la soupape d'alimentation *f*
– *feed valve*
21 le collecteur de vapeur *f*
– *steam collector*
22 la cheminée (l'évacuation *f* des fumées *f* et de la vapeur d'échappement *m*)
– *chimney (smokestack, smoke outlet and waste steam exhaust)*
23 le réchauffeur à vapeur *f* d'échappement *m* (réchauffeur *m* à surface *f*)
– *feedwater preheater (feedwater heater, economizer)*
24 la grille à flammèches *f* (le pare-étincelles)
– *spark arrester*
25 la tuyère d'échappement *m*
– *blast pipe*
26 la porte de boîte *f* à fumée *f*
– *smokebox door*
27 la tête de piston *m*
– *cross head*
28 le collecteur de boues *f*
– *mud drum*
29 le plateau de ruissellement *m* de l'eau *f* d'alimentation *f*
– *top feedwater tray*
30 la tige de tiroir *m*
– *combination lever*
31 la boîte de tiroir *m*
– *steam chest*
32 le cylindre à vapeur *f*
– *cylinder*
33 la tige de piston *m* avec boîte *f* à garniture *f*
– *piston rod with stuffing box (packing box)*
34 le chasse-pierre
– *guard iron (rail guard,* Am. *pilot, cowcatcher)*
35 l'essieu *m* porteur
– *carrying axle (running axle, dead axle)*
36 l'essieu *m* couplé
– *coupled axle*
37 l'essieu moteur
– *driving axle*
38 la locomotive à tender *m* séparé pour train *m* rapide
– *express locomotive with tender*

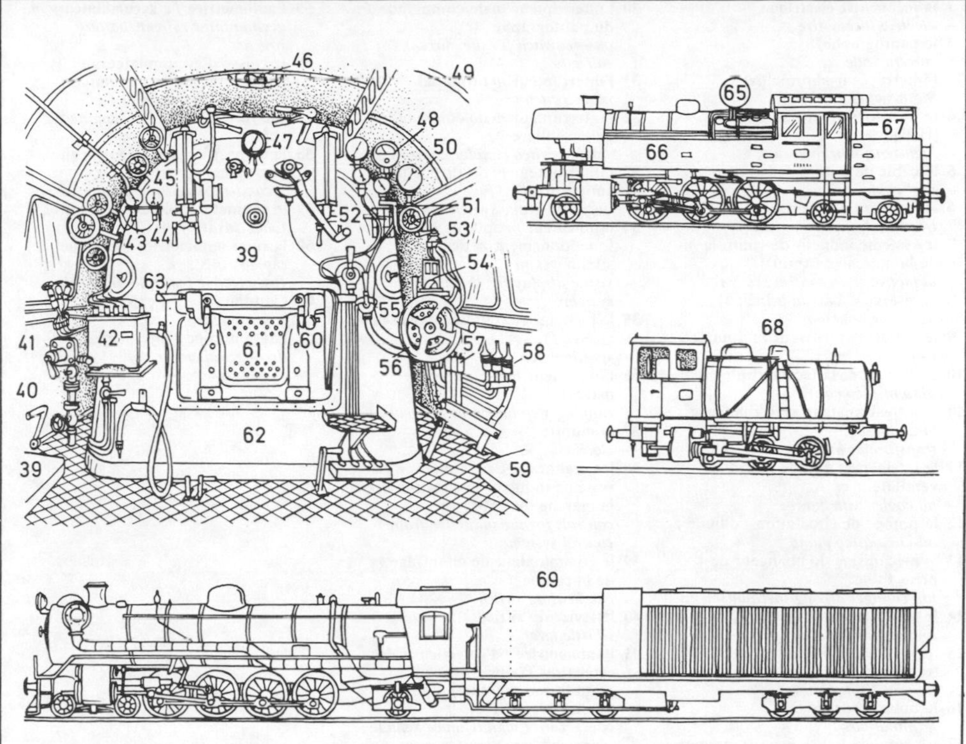

39-63 le poste de conduite *f* (la cabine de conduite *f*) **d'une locomotive à vapeur** *f*
– ***cab** (driver's cab,* Am. *engineer's cab)*

39 le siège du chauffeur
– *fireman's seat*

40 la manivelle de la grille basculante (du jette-feu)
– *drop grate lever*

41 l'injecteur *m*
– *line steam injector*

42 la pompe de graissage *m* automatique
– *automatic lubricant pump (automatic lubricator)*

43 le manomètre du réchauffeur
– *preheater pressure gauge (*Am. *gage)*

44 le manomètre du chauffage
– *carriage heating pressure gauge (*Am. *gage)*

45 l'indicateur de niveau *m* d'eau *f*
– *water gauge (*Am. *gage)*

46 l'éclairage *m*
– *light*

47 le manomètre de chaudière *f*
– *boiler pressure gauge (*Am. *gage)*

48 le téléthermomètre
– *distant-reading temperature gauge (*Am. *gage)*

49 l'abri *m* du mécanicien
– *cab (driver's cab,* Am. *engineer's cab)*

50 le manomètre de frein *m*
– *brake pressure gauge (*Am. *gage)*

51 le robinet du sifflet à vapeur *f*
– *whistle valve handle*

52 le livret-horaire
– *driver's timetable (*Am. *engineer's schedule)*

53 le robinet (de frein *m*) du mécanicien
– *driver's brake valve (*Am. *engineer's brake valve)*

54 le tachygraphe
– *speed recorder (tachograph)*

55 le robinet de sablière *f*
– *sanding valve*

56 le volant de changement *m* de marche *f*
– *reversing wheel*

57 le robinet du frein de secours *m*
– *emergency brake valve*

58 la valve de purge *f*
– *release valve*

59 le siège du mécanicien
– *driver's seat (*Am. *engineer's seat)*

60 l'écran *m* anti-éblouissant
– *firehole shield*

61 la porte du foyer
– *firehole door*

62 la boîte à feu *m*
– *vertical boiler*

63 la poignée de l'ouvre-porte *m* du foyer
– *firedoor handle handgrip*

64 la locomotive articulée (locomotive *f* Garratt)
– *articulated locomotive (Garratt locomotive)*

65 la locomotive-tender
– *tank locomotive*

66 la soute à eau *f*
– *water tank*

67 le tender à combustible *m*
– *fuel tender*

68 la locomotive à accumulateur *m* de vapeur *f* (locomotive *f* sans foyer *m*)
– *steam storage locomotive (fireless locomotive)*

69 la locomotive à condensation *f*
– *condensing locomotive (locomotive with condensing tender)*

1 **la locomotive électrique**
- ***electric locomotive***
2 le pantographe
- *current collector*
3 l'interrupteur *m* principal
- *main switch*
4 le transformateur haute tension *f* [H.T.]
- *high-tension transformer*
5 le câble de toiture *f* (de toit *m*)
- *roof cable*
6 le moteur de traction *f*
- *traction motor*
7 le système inductif de contrôle *m* de la marche du train
- *inductive train control system*
8 le réservoir d'air *m* principal
- *main air reservoir*
9 le sifflet (l'avertisseur *m* sonore)
- *whistle*
10-18 **le plan de la locomotive**
- ***plan of locomotive***
10 le transformateur avec changeur *m* de prise *f*
- *transformer with tap changer*
11 le réfrigérant d'huile *f* avec ventilateur *m*
- *oil cooler with blower*
12 la pompe de circulation *f* d'huile *f*
- *oil-circulating pump*
13 le mécanisme du changeur de prise *f*
- *tap changer driving mechanism*
14 le compresseur d'air *m*
- *air compressor*
15 le ventilateur du moteur de traction *f*
- *traction motor blower*
16 la boîte à bornes *f*
- *terminal box*
17 les condensateurs *m* pour moteurs *m* auxiliaires
- *capacitors for auxiliary motors*
18 le cache-collecteur
- *commutator cover*
19 la cabine de conduite *f*
- *cab (driver's cab,* Am. *engineer's cab)*
20 le volant du manipulateur
- *controller handwheel*
21 le dispositif d'homme *m* mort
- *dead man's handle*
22 le robinet (de frein *m*) du mécanicien
- *driver's brake valve (*Am. *engineer's brake valve)*
23 le robinet de commande *f* du frein direct
- *ancillary brake valve (auxiliary brake valve)*
24 le manomètre à air *m* comprimé
- *pressure gauge (*Am. *gage)*
25 l'inverseur *m* de pontage *m* du dispositif d'homme *m* mort
- *bypass switch for the dead man's handle*
26 l'indicateur *m* d'effort *m* de traction *f*
- *tractive effort indicator*
27 le voltmètre de chauffage *m*
- *train heating voltage indicator*
28 le voltmètre du fil de contact *m*
- *contact wire voltage indicator (overhead wire voltage indicator)*
29 le voltmètre haute tension [H.T.]
- *high-tension voltage indicator*
30 l'interrupteur *m* de commande *f* du pantographe
- *on/off switch for the current collector*
31 l'interrupteur *m* principal
- *main switch*
32 l'interrupteur *m* de commande *f* de la sablière
- *sander switch (sander control)*
33 l'interrupteur *m* du dispositif antipatinage
- *anti-skid brake switch*
34 l'indicateur *m* optique de fonctionnement *m* des auxiliaires *m*
- *visual display for the ancillary systems*
35 le tachymètre (l'indicateur *m* de vitesse *f*)
- *speedometer*
36 l'indicateur *m* du cran de marche *f*
- *running step indicator*
37 la montre
- *clock*
38 les organes *m* de commande *f* du système inductif de contrôle *m* de la marche du train
- *controls for the inductive train control system*
39 le commutateur de chauffage *m* de la cabine
- *cab heating switch*
40 le levier du sifflet
- *whistle lever*
41 **l'automotrice *f* d'entretien *m* des caténaires *f*** (automotrice *f* à plate-forme *f* mobile), une automotrice Diesel
- ***contact wire maintenance vehicle*** *(overhead wire maintenance vehicle), a diesel railcar*
42 la plate-forme de travail *m*
- *work platform (working platform)*
43 l'échelle *f*
- *ladder*
44-54 **l'équipement *m* mécanique de l'automotrice *f* d'entretien *m* des caténaires *f***
- ***mechanical equipment of the contact wire maintenance vehicle***
44 le compresseur d'air *m*
- *air compressor*
45 la pompe à huile *f* du ventilateur
- *blower oil pump*
46 la génératrice d'éclairage *m*
- *generator*
47 le moteur Diesel
- *diesel engine*
48 la pompe d'injection *f*
- *injection pump*
49 le silencieux
- *silencer (*Am. *muffler)*
50 le changement de vitesse *f*
- *change-speed gear*
51 l'arbre *m* articulé (l'arbre *m* à cardan *m*)
- *cardan shaft*
52 le dispositif de graissage *m* des boudins *m*
- *wheel flange lubricator*
53 le mécanisme de renversement *m* de marche *f*
- *reversing gear*
54 le bras de réaction *f*
- *torque converter bearing*
55 **l'automotrice *f* à accumulateurs *m***
- ***accumulator railcar*** *(battery railcar)*
56 la caisse d'accumulateurs *m*
- *battery box (battery container)*
57 la cabine de conduite *f*
- *cab (driver's cab,* Am. *engineer's cab)*
58 la disposition des sièges *m* en 2ème classe *f*
- *second-class seating arrangement*
59 le cabinet de toilette *f*
- *toilet (lavatory, WC)*
60 **la rame automotrice électrique rapide**
- ***fast electric multiple-unit train***
61 l'automotrice *f* d'extrémité *f*
- *front railcar*
62 l'automotrice *f* intermédiaire
- *driving trailer car*

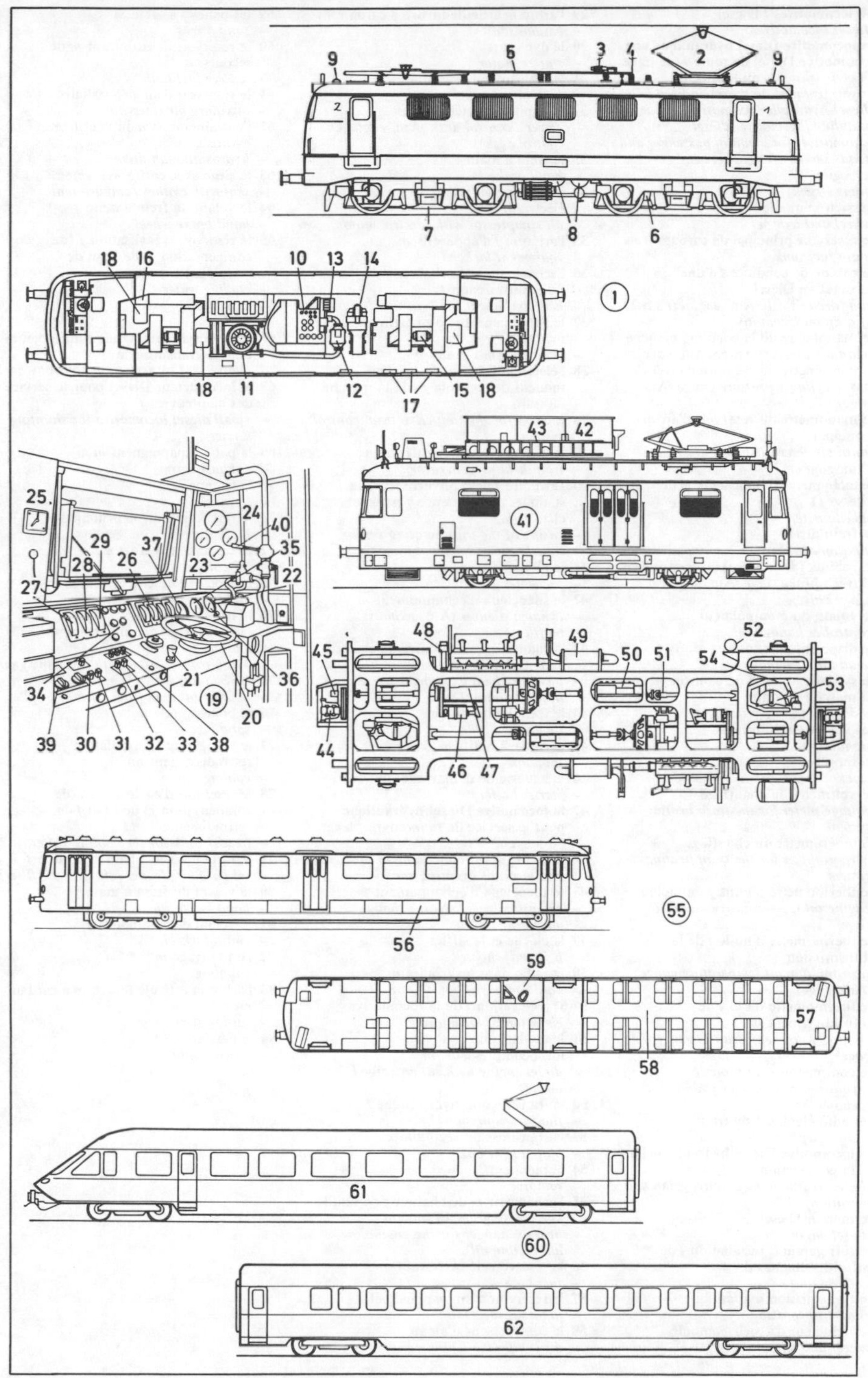
1
2
3
4
5
6
7
8
9
10
11
12
13
14
15
16
17
18
19
20
21
22
23
24
25
26
27
28
29
30
31
32
33
34
35
36
37
38
39
40
41
42
43
44
45
46
47
48
49
50
51
52
53
54
55
56
57
58
59
60
61
62

1-84 locomotives *f* Diesel
- ***diesel locomotives***

1 la locomotive Diesel hydraulique une locomotive Diesel de route *f* (de ligne *f*) pour trains *m* mi-lourds de voyageurs *m* et de marchandises *f*
- ***diesel-hydraulic locomotive**, a mainline locomotive (diesel locomotive) for medium passenger and goods service (freight service)*

2 le bogie
- *bogie (truck)*

3 l'essieu *m* monté
- *wheel and axle set*

4 le réservoir principal de carburant *m*
- *main fuel tank*

5 la cabine de conduite *f* d'une locomotive Diesel
- *cab (driver's cab,* Am. *engineer's cab) of a diesel locomotive*

6 le manomètre de la conduite blanche
- *main air pressure gauge (*Am. *gage)*

7 le manomètre du cylindre de frein *m*
- *brake cylinder pressure gauge (*Am. *gage)*

8 le manomètre du réservoir d'air *m* principal
- *main air reservoir pressure gauge (*Am. *gage)*

9 le tachymètre (l'indicateur *m* de vitesse *f*)
- *speedometer*

10 le frein direct
- *auxiliary brake*

11 le robinet (de frein *m*) du mécanicien
- *driver's brake valve (*Am. *engineer's brake valve)*

12 le volant du manipulateur
- *controller handwheel*

13 le dispositif d'homme *m* mort
- *dead man's handle*

14 le système inductif de contrôle *m* de la marche du train
- *inductive train control system*

15 les voyants *m* lumineux
- *signal lights*

16 la montre
- *clock*

17 le voltmètre du chauffage
- *voltage meter for the train heating system*

18 l'ampèremètre du chauffage
- *current meter for the train heating system*

19 le thermomètre d'huile *f* du moteur
- *engine oil temperature gauge (*Am. *gage)*

20 le thermomètre d'huile *f* de la transmission
- *transmission oil temperature gauge (*Am. *gage)*

21 le thermomètre d'eau *f* de refroidissement *m*
- *cooling water temperature gauge (*Am. *gage)*

22 le compte-tours du moteur
- *revolution counter (rev counter, tachometer)*

23 le radiotéléphone du train
- *radio telephone*

24 la locomotive Diesel hydraulique [en plan et élévation]
- *diesel-hydraulic locomotive [plan and elevation]*

25 le moteur Diesel
- *diesel engine*

26 le réfrigérant (l'installation *f* de refroidissement *m*)
- *cooling unit*

27 la transmission hydraulique
- *fluid transmission*

28 le réducteur d'essieu *m* monté
- *wheel and axle drive*

29 l'arbre *m* articulé (arbre à cardan *m*)
- *cardan shaft*

30 le dynastart
- *starter motor*

31 le tableau de bord
- *instrument panel*

32 le pupitre du mécanicien
- *driver's control desk (*Am. *engineer's control desk)*

33 le frein à main *f*
- *hand brake*

34 le compresseur d'air *m* à moteur *m* électrique
- *air compressor with electric motor*

35 l'armoire *f* d'appareils *m*
- *equipment locker*

36 l'échangeur *m* de chaleur *f* de l'huile *f* de transmission *f*
- *heat exchanger for transmission oil*

37 le ventilateur du compartiment moteur
- *engine room ventilator*

38 l'électro-aimant *m* du système inductif de contrôle *m* de la marche du train
- *magnet for the inductive train control system*

39 la génératrice de chauffage *m*
- *train heating generator*

40 l'armoire *f* des convertisseurs *m* statiques de fréquence *f* pour le chauffage
- *casing of the train heating system transformer*

41 le réchauffeur
- *preheater*

42 le silencieux d'échappement *m*
- *exhaust silencer (*Am. *exhaust muffler)*

43 l'échangeur *m* auxiliaire de chaleur *f* de l'huile *f* de transmission *f*
- *auxiliary heat exchanger for the transmission oil*

44 le frein hydraulique
- *hydraulic brake*

45 la caisse à outils *m*
- *tool box*

46 la batterie de démarrage *m*
- *starter battery*

47 la locomotive Diesel hydraulique pour le service de manœuvre *f* léger ou moyen
- ***diesel-hydraulic locomotive** for light and medium shunting service*

48 le silencieux d'échappement *m*
- *exhaust silencer (*Am. *exhaust muffler)*

49 la cloche et le sifflet
- *bell and whistle*

50 la radio dans les triages *m*
- *yard radio*

51-67 l'élévation *f* de la locomotive
- *elevation of locomotive*

51 le moteur Diesel à turbocompresseur *m*
- *diesel engine with supercharged turbine*

52 la transmission hydraulique
- *fluid transmission*

53 la transmission secondaire
- *output gear box*

54 le radiateur
- *radiator*

55 l'échangeur *m* de chaleur *f* de l'huile *f* de graissage *m* du moteur
- *heat exchanger for the engine lubricating oil*

56 le réservoir de carburant *m*
- *fuel tank*

57 le réservoir d'air *m* principal
- *main air reservoir*

58 le compresseur d'air *m*
- *air compressor*

59 les boîtes *f* à sable *m*
- *sand boxes*

60 le réservoir de carburant *m* de secours *m*
- *reserve fuel tank*

61 le réservoir d'air *m* auxiliaire
- *auxiliary air reservoir*

62 l'entraînement *m* du ventilateur hydrostatique
- *hydrostatic fan drive*

63 le siège avec coffre *m* à vêtements *m*
- *seat with clothes compartment*

64 le volant du frein à main *f*
- *hand brake wheel*

65 le réservoir d'égalisation *f* (de compensation *f*) de l'eau de refroidissement *m*
- *cooling water*

66 le ballast
- *ballast*

67 le volant de commande *f* du moteur et de la transmission
- *engine and transmission control wheel*

68 le locotracteur Diesel pour le service des manœuvres *f*
- ***small diesel locomotive** for shunting service*

69 le pot d'échappement *m*
- *exhaust casing*

70 la trompe
- *horn*

71 le réservoir d'air *m* principal
- *main air reservoir*

72 le compresseur d'air *m*
- *air compressor*

73 le moteur Diesel 8 cylindres *m*
- *eight-cylinder diesel engine*

74 la transmission Voith avec mécanisme *m* de renversement *m* de marche *f*
- *Voith transmission with reversing gear*

75 le réservoir à gasole *m*
- *heating oil tank (fuel oil tank)*

76 la boîte à sable *m*
- *sand box*

77 le réfrigérant (l'installation *f* de refroidissement *m*)
- *cooling unit*

78 le réservoir d'égalisation *f* (de compensation *f*) de l'eau *f* de refroidissement *m*
- *header tank for the cooling water*

79 le filtre à air *m* à bain *m* d'huile *f*
- *oil bath air cleaner (oil bath air filter)*

80 le volant du frein à main *f*
- *hand brake wheel*

81 le volant de commande *f*
- *control wheel*

82 l'embrayage *m*
- *coupling*

83 l'arbre *m* articulé (arbre *m* à cardan *m*)
- *cardan shaft*

84 la persienne
- *louvred shutter*

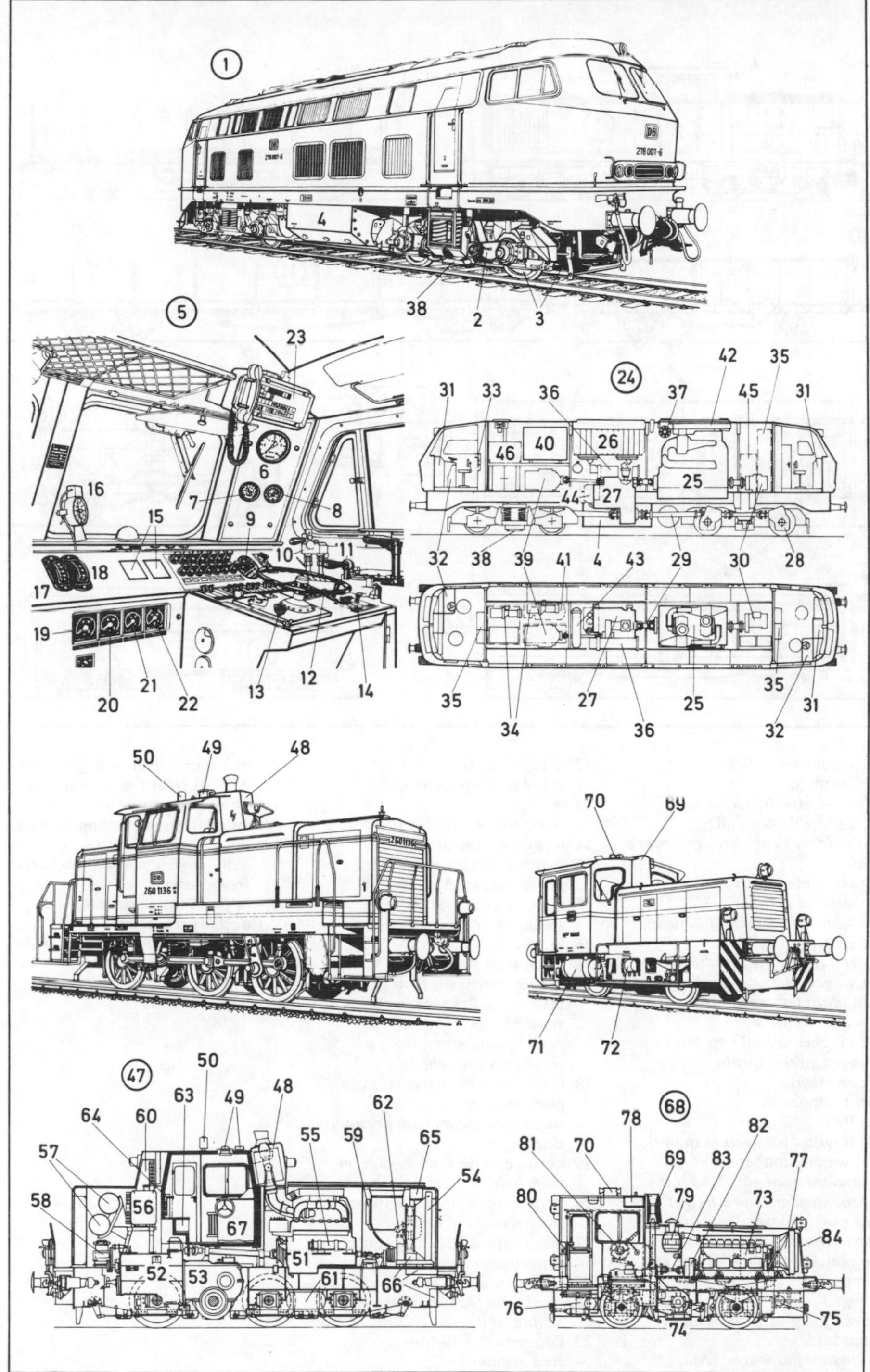
1
218 001-6
4
38
2
3
5
23
16
6
7
8
15
9
10
11
18
17
19
21
20
22
13
12
14
24
31
33
36
37
42
35
45
31
46
40
26
27
25
44
32
38
39
41
4
43
29
30
28
35
34
27
36
25
35
32
31
50
49
48
260 1136
70
69
71
72
47
50
63
49
48
64
60
57
58
56
67
52
53
51
55
59
62
65
54
61
66
68
78
81
70
69
82
83
77
80
79
73
84
76
74
75

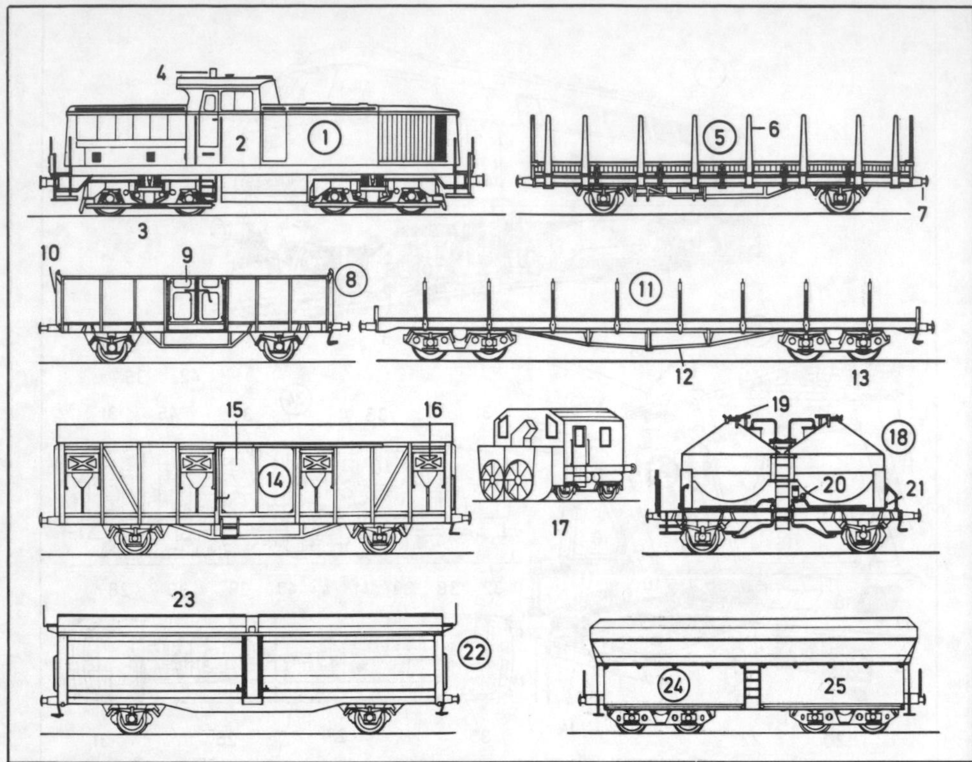

1 la locomotive Diesel hydraulique
– *diesel-hydraulic locomotive*
2 la cabine de conduite *f*
– *cab (driver's cab,* Am. *engineer's cab)*
3 l'essieu *m* monté
– *wheel and axle set*
4 l'antenne *f* de radio *f* dans les triages *m*
– *aerial for the yard radio*
5 le wagon plat standard
– *standard flat wagon (*Am. *standard flatcar)*
6 le rancher articulé en acier *m*
– *hinged steel stanchion (stanchion)*
7 les tampons *m*
– *buffers*
8 le wagon découvert standard (le wagon tombereau)
– *standard open goods wagon (*Am. *standard open freight car)*
9 les portes *f* latérales pivotantes
– *revolving side doors*
10 le bout amovible (l'about *m* amovible)
– *hinged front*
11 le wagon plat à bogies *m* standard
– *standard flat wagon (*Am. *standard flatcar) with bogies*
12 le tirant de brancard *m*
– *sole bar reinforcement*
13 le bogie
– *bogie (truck)*
14 le wagon couvert
– *covered goods van (covered goods wagon,* Am. *boxcar)*
15 la porte coulissante
– *sliding door*
16 le volet d'aération *f*
ventilation flap
17 le chasse-neige à turbine *f*, une machine à dégager les voies *f*
– *snow blower (rotary snow plough,* Am. *snowplow), a track-clearing vehicle*
18 le wagon à déchargement *m* pneumatique
– *wagon (*Am. *car) with pneumatic discharge*
19 l'orifice *m* de remplissage *m*
– *filler hole*
20 le raccord d'air *m* comprimé
– *compressed-air supply*
21 le raccord de déchargement *m*
– *discharge connection valve*
22 le wagon à toit *m* coulissant
– *goods van (*Am. *boxcar) with sliding roof*
23 l'ouverture *f* du toit
– *roof opening*
24 le wagon ouvert à bogies *m* à déchargement *m* automatique (le wagon ouvert autodéchargeur à bogies *m*)
– *bogie open self-discharge wagon (*Am. *bogie open self-discharge freight car)*
25 la paroi basculante de déchargement *m*
– *discharge flap (discharge door)*

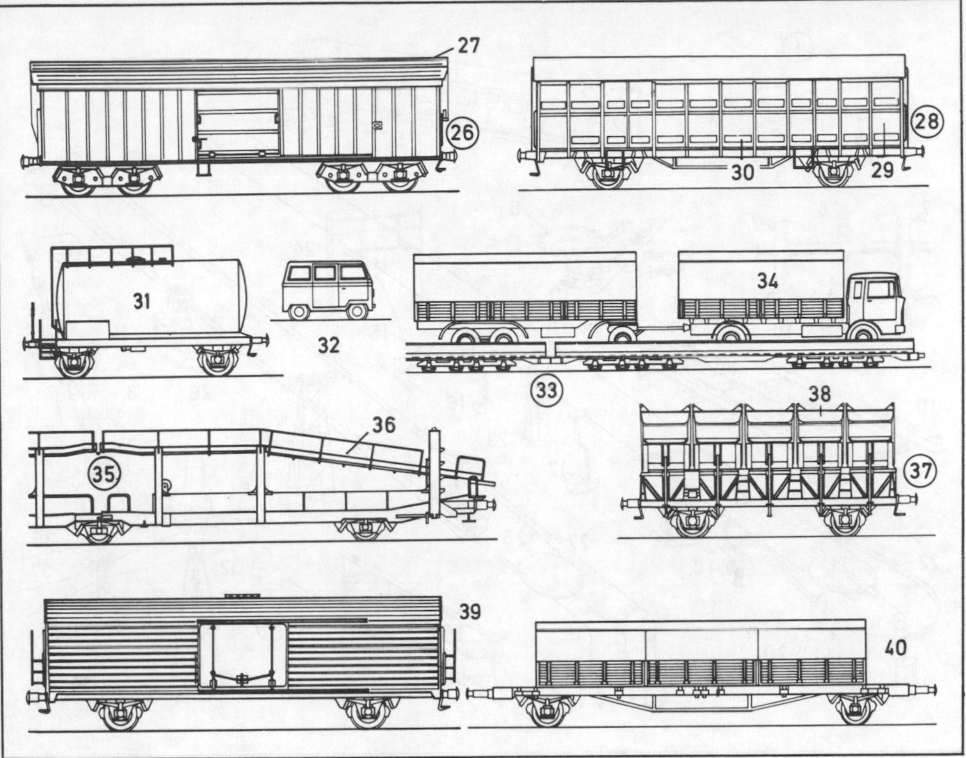

26 le wagon à bogies *m* à toit *m*pivotant
– *bogie wagon with swivelling (Am. swiveling) roof*
27 le toit pivotant
– *swivelling (Am. swiveling) roof*
28 le wagon à cloisons *f* à étages *m* de grande capacité *f* pour le transport de petits bestiaux *m*
– *large-capacity wagon (Am. large-capacity car) for small livestock*
29 la paroi latérale à claire-voie *f*
– *sidewall with ventilation flaps (slatted wall)*
30 le volet d'aération *f*
– *ventilation flap*
31 le wagon-citerne
– *tank wagon (Am. tank car)*
32 la draisine
– *track inspection railcar*
33 les wagons *m* à plate-forme *f* surbaissée
– *open special wagons (Am. open special freight cars)*
34 le poids lourd avec remorque *f*
– *lorry (Am. truck) with trailer*
35 le wagon à deux étages *m* pour le transport d'automobiles *f*
– *two-tier car carrier (double-deck car carrier)*
36 la rampe d'accès *m*
– *hinged upper deck*
37 le wagon à bennes *f* basculantes
– *tipper wagon (Am. dump car) with skips*
38 la benne basculante
– *skip*
39 le wagon frigorifique universel
– *general-purpose refrigerator wagon (refrigerator van, Am. refrigerator car)*
40 les équipements *m* interchangeables pour wagons *m* plats
– *interchangeable bodies for flat wagons (Am. flatcars)*

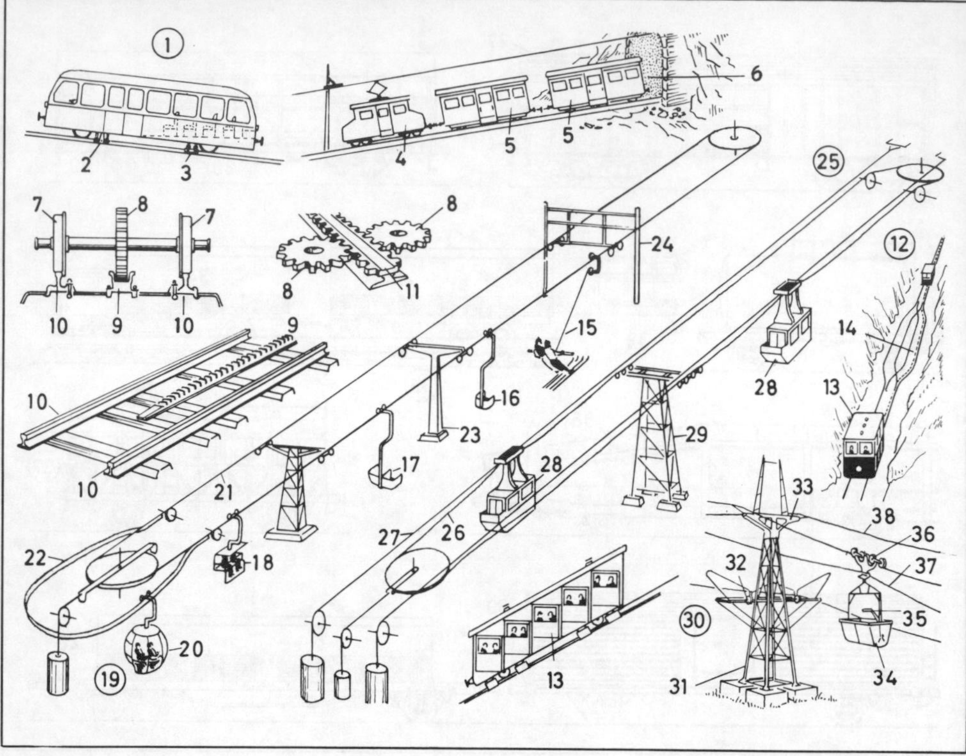

1-14 chemins *m* **de fer** *m* **de montagne** *f*
– ***mountain railways*** (Am. *mountain railroads)*

1 l'automotrice *f* à adhérence *f*
– *adhesion railcar*

2 l'entraînement *m*
– *drive*

3 le frein de secours *m*
– *emergency brake*

4-5 le chemin de fer *m* de montagne *f* à crémaillère *f*
– *rack mountain railway (rack-and-pinion railway, cog railway,* Am. *cog railroad, rack railroad)*

4 la locomotive électrique à crémaillère *f*
– *electric rack railway locomotive (*Am. *electric rack railroad locomotive)*

5 la voiture de chemin *m* de fer *m* à crémaillère *f*
– *rack railway coach (rack railway trailer,* Am. *rack railroad car)*

6 le tunnel
– *tunnel*

7-11 chemins *m* de fer *m* à crémaillère *f* [système *m*]
– *rack railways (rack-and-pinion railways,* Am. *rack railroads) [systems]*

7 la roue porteuse
– *running wheel (carrying wheel)*

8 le pignon moteur
– *driving pinion*

9 la crémaillère
– *rack [with teeth machined on top edge]*

10 le rail
– *rail*

11 la crémaillère horizontale double
– *rack [with teeth on both outer edges]*

12 le funiculaire fixe à câble *m* (le funiculaire)
– *funicular railway (funicular, cable railway)*

13 la voiture de funiculaire *m*
– *funicular railway car*

14 le câble tracteur
– *haulage cable*

15-38 téléphériques *m*
– ***cableways*** *(ropeways, cable suspension lines)*

15-24 téléphériques *m* monocâbles (téléphériques *m* à câble *m* unique sans fin *f*)
– *single-cable ropeways (single-cable suspension lines), endless ropeways*

15 le téléski (le remonte-pente)
– *drag lift*

16-18 le télésiège
– *chair lift*

16 le siège, une chaise monoplace
– *lift chair, a single chair*

17 le siège double, une chaise biplace
– *double lift chair, a two-seater chair*

18 le siège double à attelage *m*
– *double chair (two-seater chair) with coupling*

19 la télécabine (la télébenne), un téléphérique à câble *m* sans fin *f*
– *gondola cableway, an endless cableway*

20 la cabine circulante
– *gondola (cabin)*

21 le câble sans fin *f*, un câble porteur et moteur
– *endless cable, a suspension (supporting) and haulage cable*

22 le rail de retour *m*
– *U-rail*

23 le pylône support
– *single-pylon support*

24 le portique support
– *gantry support*

25 le téléphérique bicâble, un téléphérique va-et-vient
– *double-cable ropeway (double-cable suspension line), a suspension line with balancing cabins*

26 le câble tracteur
– *haulage cable*

27 le câble porteur
– *suspension cable (supporting cable)*

28 la cabine de passagers *m*
– *cabin*

29 le pylône intermédiaire
– *intermediate support*

30 le téléphérique, un téléphérique bicâble
– *cableway (ropeway, suspension line), a double-cable ropeway (double-cable suspension line)*

31 le pylône en treillis *m*
– *pylon*

32 le galet de câble *m* tracteur
– *haulage cable roller*
33 le sabot de câble *m* (le coussinet de câble *m* porteur)
– *cable guide rail (suspension cable bearing)*
34 la benne, une benne basculante
– *skip, a tipping bucket* (Am. *dumping bucket*)
35 la butée de basculement *m*
– *stop*
36 le train de galets *m*
– *pulley cradle*
37 le câble tracteur
– *haulage cable*
38 le câble porteur
– *suspension cable (supporting cable)*
39 la station inférieure
– ***valley station*** *(lower station)*
40 la fosse de déplacement *m* des contrepoids *m*
– *tension weight shaft*
41 le contrepoids du câble porteur
– *tension weight for the suspension cable (supporting cable)*
42 le contrepoids du câble tracteur
– *tension weight for the haulage cable*
43 la poulie du câble tendeur (la poulie de tension *f*)
– *tension cable pulley*
44 le câble porteur
– *suspension cable (supporting cable)*
45 le câble tracteur
– *haulage cable*
46 le câble lest (le câble d'équilibre *m*)
– *balance cable (lower cable)*
47 le câble de secours *m*
– *auxiliary cable (emergency cable)*
48 l'appareil *m* tendeur du câble de secours *m*
– *auxiliary-cable tensioning mechanism (emergency-cable tensioning mechanism)*
49 les galets *m* porteurs du câble tracteur
– *haulage cable rollers*
50 l'amortisseur *m* de démarrage *m* (l'amortisseur *m* à ressort *m*)
– *spring buffer* (Am. *spring bumper*)
51 le quai de la station inférieure
– *valley station platform (lower station platform)*
52 la cabine de passagers *m* (la benne de téléphérique *m*), une benne de grande capacité *f*
– *cabin (cableway gondola, ropeway gondola, suspension line gondola), a large-capacity cabin*
53 le train de galets *m*
– *pulley cradle*
54 la suspente
– *suspension gear*
55 l'amortisseur *m* d'oscillations *f*
– *stabilizer*
56 le butoir
– *guide rail*
57 la station supérieure
– ***top station*** *(upper station)*
58 le sabot du câble porteur
– *suspension cable guide (supporting cable guide)*
59 l'ancrage du câble porteur
– *suspension cable anchorage (supporting cable anchorage)*
60 la batterie de galets *m* du câble tracteur
– *haulage cable rollers*
61 la poulie de renvoi *m* du câble tracteur
– *haulage cable guide wheel*
62 la poulie motrice du câble tracteur
– *haulage cable driving pulley*
63 le treuil de commande *f*
– *main drive*
64 le treuil de réserve *f*
– *standby drive*
65 le poste du conducteur (le poste de commande *f*)
– *control room*
66 le train de galets *m* (les organes *m* de roulement *m*) de la cabine
– ***cabin pulley cradle***
67 le longeron du train de galets *m*
– *main pulley cradle*
68 le berceau double
– *double cradle*
69 le berceau à deux galets *m*
– *two-wheel cradle*
70 les galets *m* de roulement *m*
– *running wheels*
71 le frein de câble *m* porteur, un frein de secours *m* en cas *m* de rupture *f* du câble tracteur
– *suspension cable brake (supporting cable brake), an emergency brake in case of haulage cable failure*
72 l'axe *m* de suspension *f*
– *suspension gear bolt*
73 le manchon du câble tracteur
– *haulage cable sleeve*
74 le manchon du câble lest
– *balance cable sleeve (lower cable sleeve)*
75 le dispositif antidérailleur (l'antidérailleur *m*)
– *derailment guard*
76 pylônes *m* de téléphérique *m* (pylônes *m* intermédiaires)
– ***cable supports*** *(ropeway supports, suspension line supports, intermediate supports)*
77 le pylône en treillis *m* métallique, un pylône en charpente *f* métallique
– *pylon, a framework support*
78 le pylône en tubes *m* d'acier *m*, un pylône tubulaire en acier *m*
– *tubular steel pylon, a tubular steel support*
79 le sabot du câble porteur (le sabot d'appui *m*)
– *suspension cable guide rail (supporting cable guide rail, support guide rail)*
80 les potences *f* du pylône, un dispositif pour les travaux *m* sur câbles *m*
– *support truss, a frame for work on the cable*
81 la fondation des pylônes *m*
– *base of the support*

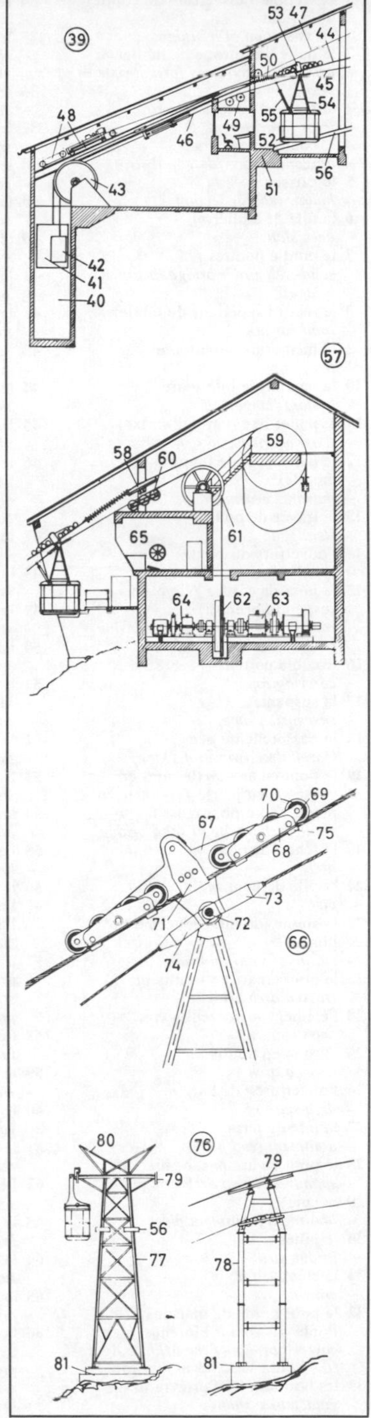

1 la section transversale (la coupe) d'un pont
– *cross-section of a bridge*
2 la dalle orthotrope de tablier *m*
– *orthotropic roadway (orthotropic deck)*
3 la ferme à jambes *f* de force *f*
– *truss (bracing)*
4 le contreventement
– *diagonal brace (diagonal strut)*
5 le caisson
– *hollow tubular section*
6 la tôle de tablier *m*
– *deck slab*
7 le pont à poutres *f*
– *solid-web girder bridge (beam bridge)*
8 le rebord supérieur du tablier
– *road surface*
9 la membrure supérieure
– *top flange*
10 la membrure inférieure
– *bottom flange*
11 le palier fixe (l'appui *m* fixe)
– *fixed bearing*
12 le palier mobile (l'appui *m* mobile)
– *movable bearing*
13 la travée de pont *m*
– *clear span*
14 l'ouverture du pont
– *span*
15 le pont de cordes *f* (le pont suspendu primitif)
– *rope bridge (primitive suspension bridge)*
16 le câble porteur
– *carrying rope*
17 la suspente
– *suspension rope*
18 la passerelle tressée
– *woven deck (woven decking)*
19 le pont en arcs *m* (le pont en voûtes *f*) en pierre *f* (pont *m* en pierre *f*), un pont massif
– *stone arch bridge, a solid bridge*
20 l'arche *f* de pont *m*
– *arch*
21 la pile de pont *m*
– *pier*
22 la statue (de saint *m*) ornant le pont
– *statue of saint on bridge*
23 le pont en arc en treillis *m*
– *trussed arch bridge*
24 l'élément *m* de treillis *m*
– *truss element*
25 l'arc *m* en treillis *m*
– *trussed arch*
26 l'ouverture *f* de l'arc *m*
– *arch span*
27 la pile de terre *f*
– *abutment (end pier)*
28 le pont en arc *m* sur piliers *m*
– *spandrel-braced arch bridge*
29 la culée
– *abutment (abutment pier)*
30 le pilier
– *bridge strut*
31 la clé d'arc *m*
– *crown*
32 le pont bordé de maisons *f* (le Ponte Vecchio à Florence)
– *covered bridge of the Middle Ages (the* Ponte Vecchio *in* Florence*)*
33 les boutiques *f* d'orfèvre *m*
– *goldsmiths' shops*
34 le pont en treillis *m* métallique
– *steel lattice bridge*
35 le contreventement
– *counterbrace (crossbrace, diagonal member)*
36 le montant (la barre verticale)
– *vertical member*
37 le nœud du treillis
– *truss joint*
38 le portique d'extrémité *f*
– *portal frame*
39 le pont suspendu
– *suspension bridge*
40 le câble porteur
– *suspension cable*
41 la suspente
– *suspender (hanger)*
42 le pylône
– *tower*
43 l'ancrage *m* du câble porteur
– *suspension cable anchorage*
44 les longerons *m* [portant le tablier]
– *tied beam [with roadway]*
45 la culée
– *abutment*
46 le pont à haubans *m* (le pont haubané, le pont à suspentes *f* obliques)
– *cable-stayed bridge*
47 le câble d'ancrage *m* (le hauban)
– *inclined tension cable*
48 l'ancrage *m* de hauban *m*
– *inclined cable anchorage*
49 le pont en béton *m* armé
– *reinforced concrete bridge*
50 l'arc *m* en béton *m* armé
– *reinforced concrete arch*
51 le système de suspentes *f* obliques
– *inclined cable system (multiple cable system)*
52 le pont plat
– *flat bridge, a plate girder bridge*
53 le raidisseur transversal
– *stiffener*
54 la pile
– *pier*
55 l'appui *m* de pont *m*
– *bridge bearing*
56 le bec *m* de pont *m* [*en amont:* l'avant-bec *m*; *en aval:* l'arrière-bec *m*]
– *cutwater*
57 le pont en éléments *m* préfabriqués
– *straits bridge, a bridge built of precast elements*
58 l'élément *m* préfabriqué
– *precast construction unit*
59 le viaduc
– *viaduct*
60 le fond *m* de la vallée
– *valley bottom*
61 le pilier en béton *m* armé
– *reinforced concrete pier*
62 l'échafaudage *m*
– *scaffolding*
63 le pont tournant en treillis *m*
– *lattice swing bridge*
64 la couronne de pivotement *m*
– *turntable*
65 la pile de pivotement *m*
– *pivot pier*
66 la moitié mobile du pont (le demi-pont)
– *pivoting half (pivoting section, pivoting span, movable half) of bridge*
67 le pont tournant plat
– *flat swing bridge*
68 la volée du pont
– *middle section*
69 le pivot
– *pivot*
70 le parapet
– *parapet (handrailing)*

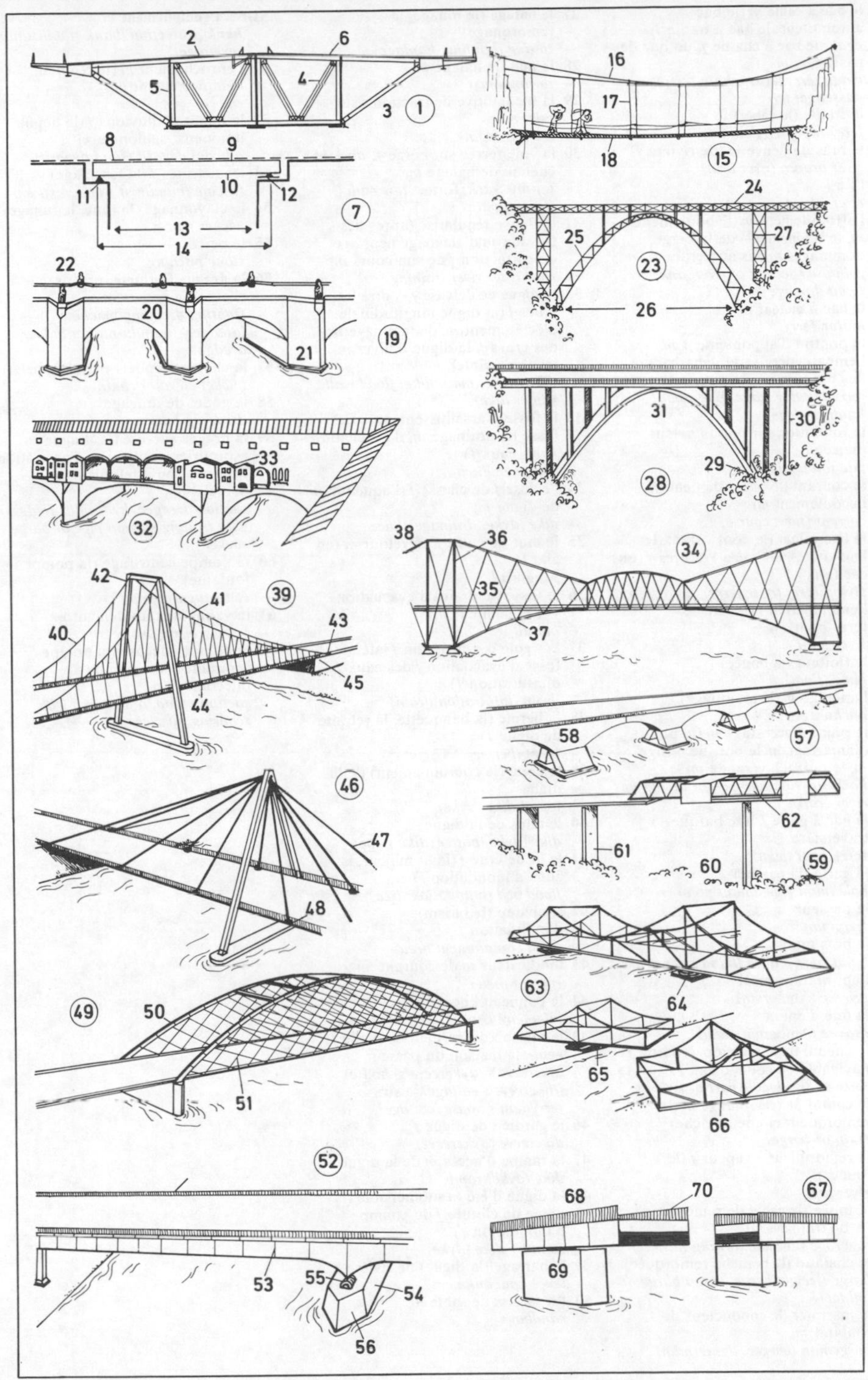
1
2
3
4
5
6
7
8
9
10
11
12
13
14
15
16
17
18
19
20
21
22
23
24
25
26
27
28
29
30
31
32
33
34
35
36
37
38
39
40
41
42
43
44
45
46
47
48
49
50
51
52
53
54
55
56
57
58
59
60
61
62
63
64
65
66
67
68
69
70

1 le bac à câble *m* (le bac automoteur: le bac à traille *f*; *égal.:* le bac à chaîne *f*, un bac de passagers *m*
– ***cable ferry*** (also: *chain ferry), a passenger ferry*
2 la traille (le câble)
– *ferry rope (ferry cable)*
3 le bras de fleuve *m* (de rivière *f*)
– *river branch (river arm)*
4 l'île *f*
– *river island (river islet)*
5 l'affouillement *m* (l'éboulement *m*, le ravinement) de la berge, dommages *m* dus aux crues *f*
– *collapsed section of riverbank, flood damage*
6 le bac à moteur *m*
– ***motor ferry***
7 le ponton (l'appontement *m*, l'embarcadère *m*, le débarcadère des bateaux *m* à moteur *m*)
– *ferry landing stage (motorboat landing stage)*
8 la fondation sur pilotis *m* (sur pieux *m*)
– *pile foundations*
9 le courant (le cours de l'eau *f*, l'écoulement *m*)
– *current (flow, course)*
10 le bac volant (le pont volant, le bac ancré), un bac à voitures *f* (un car-ferry)
– ***flying ferry*** *(river ferry), a car ferry*
11 l'embarcation *f* (le bac, le ferry-boat)
– *ferry boat*
12 le flotteur (la bouée)
– *buoy (float)*
13 l'ancrage *m* (le mouillage)
– *anchorage*
14 le point d'accostage *m* (le point d'amarrage *m*, le port de refuge *m*, le port d'hivernage *m*)
– *harbour* (Am. *harbor) for laying up river craft*
15 le bac à gaffe *f*, une barque traversière
– ***ferry boat*** *(punt)*
16 la gaffe (la perche)
– *pole (punt pole, quant pole)*
17 le passeur
– *ferryman*
18 le bras mort
– *blind river branch (blind river arm)*
19 l'épi *m* transversal
– *groyne* (Am. *groin)*
20 la tête d'épi *m*
– *groyne* (Am. *groin) head*
21 le chenal de navigation *f* (partie *f* navigable du cours d'eau *f*)
– *fairway (navigable part of river)*
22 le convoi de remorquage *m* (le remorqueur et une péniche)
– ***train of barges***
23 le remorqueur à vapeur *f* (le toueur)
– *river tug*
24 la touée (le câble de remorquage *m*, de traînage *m*)
– *tow rope (tow line, towing hawser)*
25 le chaland (la péniche remorquée)
– *barge (freight barge, cargo barge, lighter)*
26 le marinier (le conducteur de chaland *m*)
– *bargeman (bargee, lighterman)*
27 le halage (le touage, le remorquage)
– ***towing*** *(hauling, haulage)*
28 le mât de halage *m*
– *towing mast*
29 la locomotive de traction *f* sur rails *m*
– *towing engine*
30 la voie ferrée sur berge *f*; *anc.:* le chemin de halage *m*
– *towing track;* form.: *tow path (towing path)*
31 le fleuve régularisé (après des travaux *m* d'aménagement *m* et de correction *f* de son cours *m*)
– *river after river training*
32 la digue de défense *f* contre les crues *f* (la digue longitudinale d'écrêtement *m*, de laminage *m* des crues *f*, la digue d'hiver *m* insubmersible)
– ***dike*** *(dyke, main dike, flood wall, winter dike)*
33 le fossé d'assainissement *m* (le fossé de drainage *m*, d'évacuation *f* des eaux *f*)
– *drainage ditch*
34 l'écluse *f* de chasse *f* (l'aqueduc *m* de digue *f*)
– *dike (dyke) drainage sluice*
35 le mur de culée *f* en retour *m* (en aile *f*)
– *wing wall*
36 le fossé (le drain) d'évacuation *f* (l'évacuateur *m*)
– *outfall*
37 la rigole d'évacuation *f* latérale (le fossé d'évacuation *f* des eaux *f* d'infiltration *f*)
– *drain (infiltration drain)*
38 la berme (la banquette, la retraite de digue *f*)
– *berm (berme)*
39 la crête (le couronnement) de la digue
– *top of dike (dyke)*
40 le talus de la digue
– *dike (dyke) batter (dike slope)*
41 le lit de crue *f* (le lit majeur, la zone d'inondation *f*)
– *flood bed (inundation area)*
42 le champ (le bassin) d'inondation *f*
– *flood containment area*
43 l'indicateur *m* de courant *m*
– *current meter*
44 le panneau kilométrique
– *kilometre* (Am. *kilometer) sign*
45 la maison du gardien de digue *f*; *égal.:* la maison du passeur
– *dikereeve's (dykereeve's) house (dikereeve's cottage);* also: *ferryman's house (cottage)*
46 le gardien de digue *f*
– *dikereeve (dykereeve)*
47 la rampe d'accès *m* de la digue
– *dike (dyke) ramp*
48 la digue d'été *m* submersible (la digue de clôture *f* du champ d'inondation *f*)
– *summer dike (dyke)*
49 le barrage (la digue) de rivière *f*
– *levee (embankment)*
50 les sacs *m* de sable *m*
– *sandbags*
51-55 l'endiguement *m*
– ***bank protection*** *(bank stabilization, revetment)*
51 l'enrochement *m* (le remblai, l'empierrement *m*)
– *riprap*
52 le dépôt d'alluvions *f* (le dépôt limoneux, sablonneux)
– *alluvial deposit (sand deposit)*
53 les fascines *f* (le fascinage)
– *fascine (bundle of wooden sticks)*
54 le clayonnage (la tune, le tunage)
– *wicker fences*
55 le perré
– *stone pitching*
56 la drague flottante, une drague à chaîne *f* à godets *m*
– ***floating dredging machine*** *(dredger), a multi-bucket ladder dredge*
57 la chaîne à godets *m* (le chapelet)
– *bucket elevator chain*
58 le godet de dragage
– *dredging bucket*
59 la drague suceuse (la drague aspiratrice) à tuyau *m* d'aspiration *f* traînant ou à refouleur *m* à déblais *m*
– ***suction dredger*** *(hydraulic dredger) with trailing suction pipe or barge sucker*
60 la pompe centrifuge (la pompe foulante)
– *centrifugal pump*
61 la vanne de refoulement *m*
– *back scouring valve*
62 la pompe suceuse (la pompe aspirante), une pompe à injection *f*
– *suction pump, a jet pump with scouring nozzles*

1
3
49
2
5
4
9
42
48
6
7
8
14
10
11
15
17
47
44
44
12
46
16
18
19
20
45
13
43
21
22
23
26
24
27
25
32
28
29
41
31
30
33
39
38
35
40
55
34
37
54
36
53
59
60
61
50
52
51
56
62
57
58

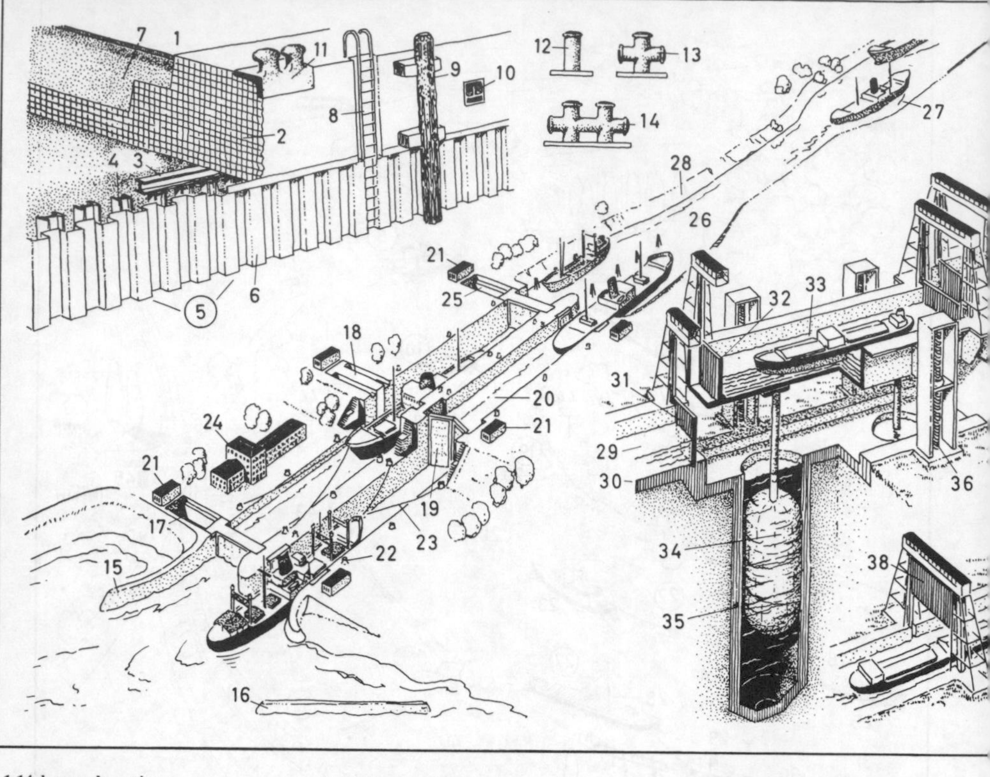

1-14 le mur de quai *m*
– ***quay wall***
1 le revêtement de la chaussée
– *road surface*
2 le massif de maçonnerie *f* (le perré)
– *body of wall*
3 la poutre (la traverse) métallique (en acier *m*)
– *steel sleeper*
4 le pilier métallique (en acier *m*)
– *steel pile*
5 la paroi de palplanches *f*
– *sheet pile wall (sheet pile bulkhead, sheet piling)*
6 la palplanche en acier *m*
– *box pile*
7 le remblai (le terre-plein)
– *backfilling (filling)*
8 l'échelle *f*
– *ladder*
9 la défense (le pieu d'accostage *m*)
– *fender (fender pile)*
10 le renfoncement (la niche) d'amarrage *m*
– *recessed bollard*
11 le double bollard d'amarrage *m*
– *double bollard*
12 le bollard (la bitte d'amarrage *m* à terre *f*)
– *bollard*
13 la bitte d'enroulement *m* en croix *f*
– *cross-shaped bollard (cross-shaped mooring bitt)*
14 la bitte en double croix *f*
– *double cross-shaped bollard (double cross-shaped mooring bitt)*
15-28 le canal
– ***canal***
15-16 l'entrée *f* du canal (le musoir)
– *canal entrance*
15 le môle (la jetée)
– *mole*
16 le brise-lames
– *breakwater*
17-25 les écluses *f* en échelle *f* (l'échelle *f* d'écluses *f*)
– *staircase of locks*
17 la tête aval
– *lower level*
18 la porte d'écluse *f*, une porte coulissante
– *lock gate, a sliding gate*
19 la porte d'écluse *f*, une porte busquée
– *mitre (Am. miter) gate*
20 le sas d'écluse *f* (le bassin)
– *lock (lock chamber)*
21 la salle des machines *f*
– *power house*
22 le cabestan enrouleur pour halage *m*
– *warping capstan (hauling capstan), a capstan*
23 l'(h)aussière (la touée), un grelin
– *warp*
24 le bâtiment administratif (*exemple m:* administration *f* du canal, service *m* de protection *f* des eaux *f*, douanes *f*)
– *offices (e.g. canal administration, river police, customs)*
25 la tête amont
– *upper level (head)*
26 le port-écluse, un avant-port
– *lock approach*
27 la voie d'évitement *m* du canal (le point d'élargissement *m*)
– *lay-by*
28 le talus de rive *f*
– *bank slope*
29-38 l'ascenseur *m* **à bateaux** *m*
– ***boat lift*** *(Am. boat elevator)*
29 le bief d'aval *m*
– *lower pound (lower reach)*
30 le radier du canal
– *canal bed*
31 la porte de bief *m*, une porte levante
– *pound lock gate, a vertical gate*
32 la porte du sas d'écluse *f*
– *lock gate*
33 le sas (le bassin)
– *boat tank (caisson)*
34 le flotteur, un dispositif de levage *m*
– *float*
35 le puits du flotteur
– *float shaft*
36 le vérin hydraulique (la tige de montée *f* et descente *f*)
– *lifting spindle*
37 le bief d'amont *m* (le bief supérieur)
– *upper pound (upper reach)*
38 la porte levante
– *vertical gate*
39-46 la centrale hydraulique de pied *m* **de barrage** *m* (l'usine *f* de pompage *m*)
– ***pumping plant and reservoir***
39 le barrage-réservoir (le réservoir d'accumulation *f*, le bassin de retenue *f*)
– *forebay*
40 la prise d'eau *f* (la chambre de mise *f* en charge *f*)
– *surge tank*
41 la conduite forcée
– *pressure pipeline*

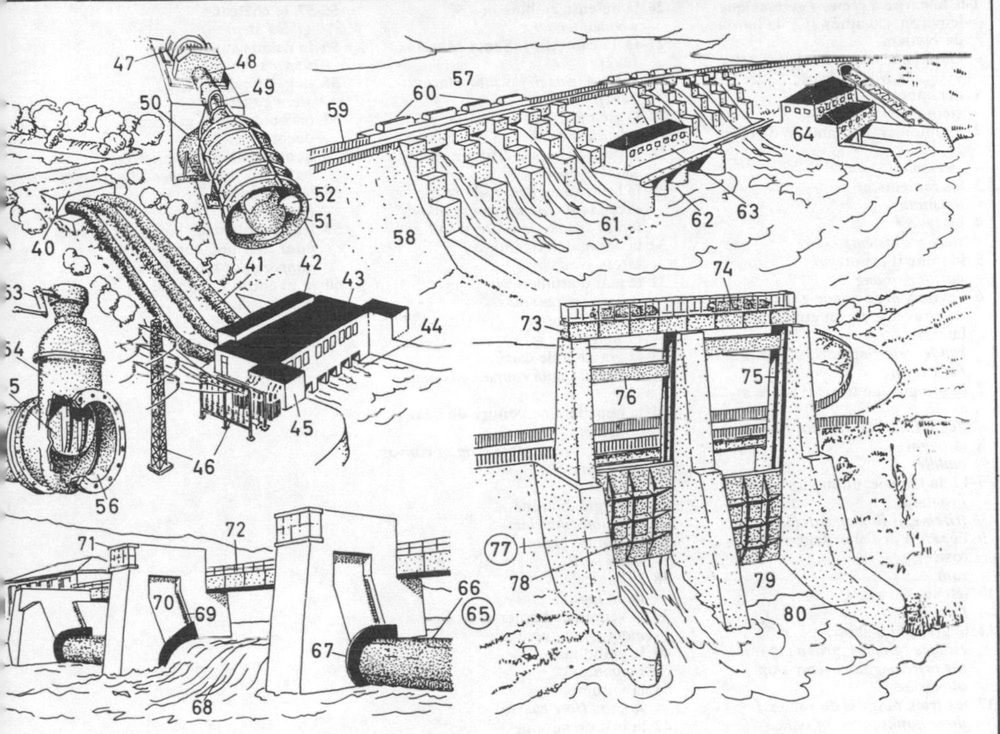

42 le bâtiment des vannes *f*
– *valve house (valve control house)*
43 la salle des turbines *f* (la station de pompage *m*)
– *turbine house (pumping station)*
44 l'installation *f* de restitution *f* (de décharge *f*)
– *discharge structure (outlet structure)*
45 la salle de commande *f*
– *control station*
46 le poste de transformation *f*
– *transformer station*
47-52 la pompe hélice (la pompe à rotor *m*, à roue *f* à ailettes *f*)
– ***axial-flow pump*** *(propeller pump)*
47 le moteur d'entraînement *m*
– *drive motor*
48 le réducteur
– *gear*
49 l'arbre *m* de transmission *f*
– *drive shaft*
50 la conduite forcée
– *pressure pipe*
51 le conduit d'aspiration *f*
– *suction head*
52 l'hélice *f* (le rotor, la couronne mobile, la roue à ailettes *f*, les pales *f*)
– *impeller wheel*
53-56 la vanne (la vanne d'arrêt *m*)
– ***sluice valve*** *(sluice gate)*
53 la commande à manivelle *f*
– *crank drive*
54 le corps de vanne *f*
– *valve housing*
55 la vanne
– *sliding valve (sliding gate)*
56 l'orifice *m* d'écoulement *m* (la bouche)
– *discharge opening*
57-64 le barrage de vallée *f*
– ***dam*** *(barrage)*
57 le bassin de retenue *f* (le barrage-réservoir, le lac d'accumulation *f*)
– *reservoir (storage reservoir, impounding reservoir, impounded reservoir)*
58 le barrage en béton *m*
– *masonry dam*
59 la crête (le couronnement) du barrage
– *crest of dam*
60 l'évacuateur *m* de crues *f* (le déversoir)
– *spillway (overflow spillway)*
61 le bassin d'amortissement *m* (le bassin de restitution *f*, de repos *m*)
– *stilling basin (stilling box, stilling pool)*
62 l'évacuateur *m* de fond *m* (la décharge *f* de fond *m*)
– *scouring tunnel (outlet tunnel, waste water outlet)*
63 le bâtiment des vannes *f*
– *valve house (valve control house)*
64 le bâtiment des turbines *f*
– *power station*
65-72 le barrage mobile à cylindres *m* (le barrage-écluse), un barrage réservoir; *autre système m:* le barrage à clapets *m*
– ***rolling dam*** *(weir), a barrage;* other system: *shutter weir*
65 le cylindre, une vanne cylindrique
– *roller, a barrier*
66 le haut du cylindre
– *roller top*
67 le collet (le bouclier latéral)
– *flange*
68 le cylindre (la vanne) submersible (immergé(e))
– *submersible roller*
69 la crémaillère
– *rack track*
70 la niche
– *recess*
71 le bâtiment des treuils *m*
– *hoisting gear cabin*
72 la passerelle de service *m* (de manœuvre *f*)
– *service bridge (walkway)*
73-80 le barrage à vannes *f* (le barrage-vannes)
– ***sluice dam***
73 la passerelle des treuils *m*
– *hoisting gear bridge*
74 le treuil de halage *m*
– *hoisting gear (winding gear)*
75 la rainure de guidage *m* (la rainure-guide, le rail de guidage *m* de la vanne)
– *guide groove*
76 le contrepoids
– *counterweight (counterpoise)*
77 la vanne (la hausse)
– *sluice gate (floodgate)*
78 les nervures *f* de renforcement *m*
– *reinforcing rib*
79 le radier du barrage
– *dam sill (weir sill)*
80 le bajoyer
– *wing wall*

1-6 le navire à rames *f* **germanique** [environ 400 après JC]; la barque de Nydam
– ***Germanic rowing boat*** *[ca. AD 400], the Nydam boat*
1 l'étambot *m*
– *stern post*
2 le timonier (l'homme *m* de barre *f*)
– *steersman*
3 les rameurs *m*
– *oarsman*
4 l'étrave *f*
– *stem post (stem)*
5 la rame (l'aviron *m*)
– *oar, for rowing*
6 l'aviron *m* de queue *f* (l'aviron *m* de gouverne *f*), un gouvernail latéral
– *rudder (steering oar), a side rudder, for steering*
7 la pirogue, un tronc d'arbre *m* évidé
– ***dugout****, a hollowed-out tree trunk*
8 la pagaie
– *paddle*
9-12 la trirème, un navire de guerre *f* romain
– ***trireme****, a Roman warship*
9 l'éperon *m* d'abordage *m* (le rostre)
– *ram*
10 le château avant
– *forecastle (fo'c'sle)*
11 le grappin d'abordage *m*
– *grapple (grapnel, grappling iron), for fastening the enemy ship alongside*
12 les trois rangs *m* de rames *f*
– *three banks (tiers) of oars*
13-17 le drakkar viking (le navire à tête *f* de dragon *m*)
– ***Viking ship*** *(longship, dragon ship) [Norse]*
13 la barre du gouvernail
– *helm (tiller)*
14 le support de tente *f* à têtes *f* de cheval *m* sculptées
– *awning crutch with carved horses' heads*
15 la tente
– *awning*
16 la figure de proue *f* à tête *f* de dragon *m*
– *dragon figurehead*
17 le bouclier
– *shield*
18-26 le kog de la Hanse à deux châteaux *m*
– ***cog*** *(Hansa cog, Hansa ship)*
18 le câble d'ancre *f*
– *anchor cable (anchor rope, anchor hawser)*
19 le château avant (le gaillard)
– *forecastle (fo'c'sle)*
20 le beaupré
– *bowsprit*
21 la voile carrée carguée sur la vergue
– *furled (brailed-up) square sail*
22 l'oriflamme *m*
– *town banner (city banner)*
23 le château arrière
– *aftercastle (sterncastle)*
24 le gouvernail d'étambot *m*
– *rudder, a stem rudder*
25 l'arrière *m* arrondi
– *elliptical stern (round stern)*
26 la défense en bois *m*
– *wooden fender*
27-43 la caravelle [«Santa Maria» 1492]
– ***caravel*** *(carvel) ['Santa Maria' 1492]*
27 la chambre de l'amiral *m*
– *admiral's cabin*
28 le bout-dehors d'artimon *m*
– *spanker boom*
29 la brigantine, une voile latine
– *mizzen (mizen, mutton spanker, lateen spanker), a lateen sail*
30 la corne de brigantine *f*
– *lateen yard*
31 le mât d'artimon *m*
– *mizzen (mizen) mast*
32 l'assemblage *m*
– *lashing*
33 la grand-voile carrée
– *mainsail (main course), a square sail*
34 la bonette, une voilure de beau temps *m*
– *bonnet, a removable strip of canvas*
35 la bouline
– *bowline*
36 la cargue-bouline
– *bunt line (martinet)*
37 la grand-vergue
– *main yard*
38 le hunier
– *main topsail*
39 la vergue de hunier *m*
– *main topsail yard*
40 le grand mât
– *mainmast*
41 la misaine
– *foresail (fore course)*
42 le mât de misaine *f*
– *foremast*
43 la civadière
– *spritsail*
44-50 la galère [XVe - XVIIIe siècles], une galère d'esclaves *m*
– ***galley*** *[15th to 18th century], a slave galley*
44 le fanal
– *lantern*
45 le gavon, la chambre du capitaine
– *cabin*
46 la coursie
– *central gangway*
47 le garde-chiourme avec son fouet *m*
– *slave driver with whip*
48 la chiourme (les galériens *m*, les forçats *m*)
– *galley slaves*
49 la rambate, une plate-forme de combat *m* à l'avant *m*
– *covered platform in the forepart of the ship*
50 l'artillerie *f*
– *gun*
51-60 le vaisseau de ligne *f* [XVIIIe - XIXe siècles] à trois ponts
– ***ship of the line*** *(line-of-battle ship) [18th to 19th century], a three-decker*
51 le bout-dehors (le bâton de foc *m*)
– *jib boom*
52 le petit perroquet
– *fore topgallant sail*
53 le grand perroquet
– *main topgallant sail*
54 la perruche
– *mizzen (mizen) topgallant sail*
55-57 le château
– *gilded stern*
55 la galerie supérieure
– *upper stern*
56 la galerie de poupe *f*
– *stern gallery*
57 les bouteilles *f*, galeries *f* décoratives
– *quarter gallery, a projecting balcony with ornamental portholes*
58 le tableau arrière
– *lower stern*
59 les sabords *m* de batterie *f* ouverts pour tirer une bordée
– *gunports for broadside fire*
60 le panneau de sabord *m*
– *gunport shutter*

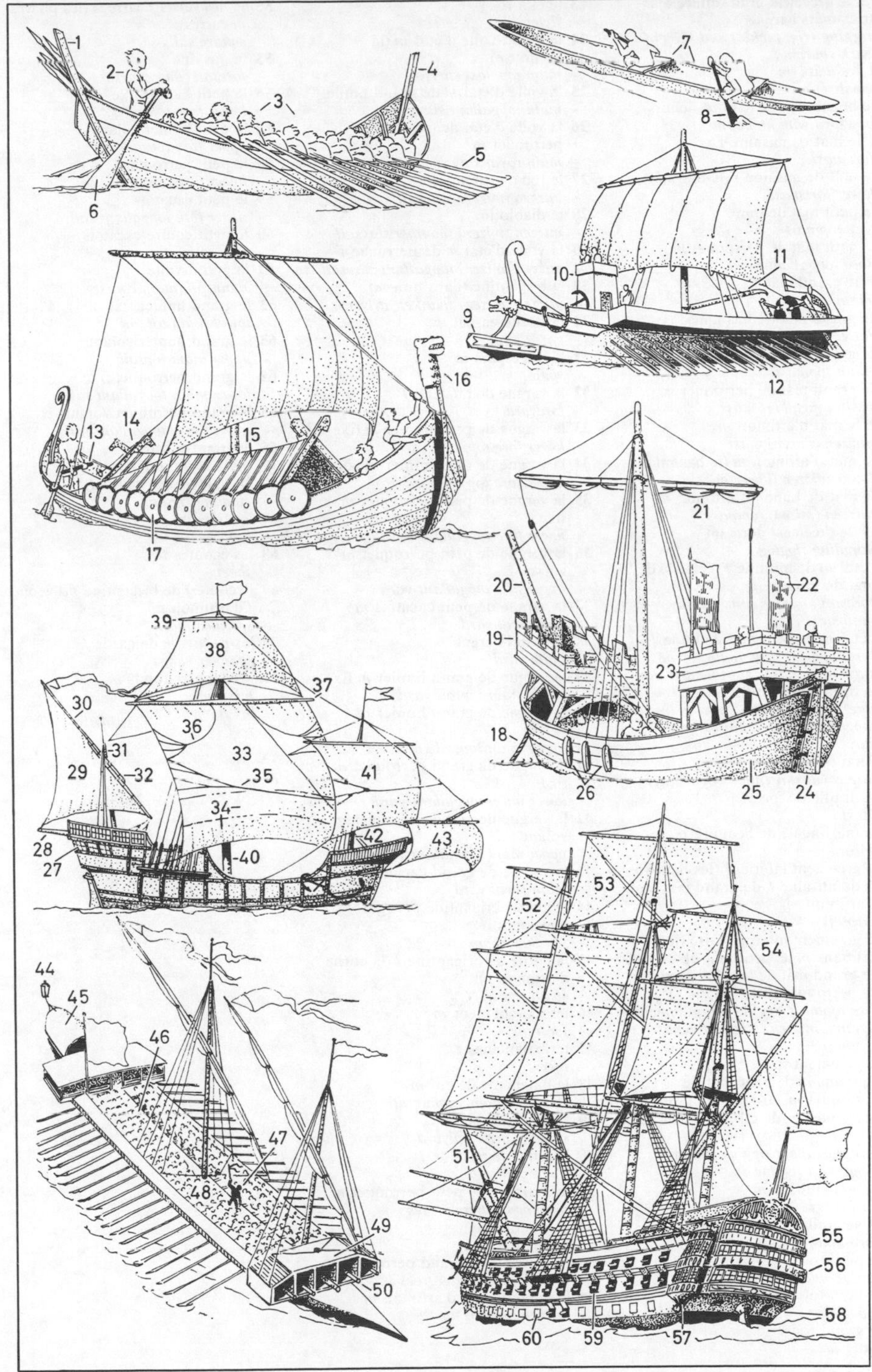
1
2
3
4
5
6
7
8
9
10
11
12
13
14
15
16
17
18
19
20
21
22
23
24
25
26
27
28
29
30
31
32
33
34
35
36
37
38
39
40
41
42
43
44
45
46
47
48
49
50
51
52
53
54
55
56
57
58
59
60

1-72 le gréement et la voilure d'un trois-mâts barque
- ***rigging (rig, tackle) and sails of a bark (barque)***

1-9 les mâts *m*
- ***masts***

1 le beaupré avec le bout-dehors
- *bowsprit with jib boom*

2-4 le mât de misaine *f*
- *foremast*

2 le mât de misaine *f* (le bas-mât)
- *lower foremast*

3 le petit mât de hune *f*
- *fore topmast*

4 le petit mât de perroquet *m*
- *fore topgallant mast*

5-7 le grand mât
- *mainmast*

5 le grand mât (le bas-mât)
- *lower mainmast*

6 le grand mât de hune *f*
- *main topmast*

7 le grand mât de perroquet *m*
- *main topgallant mast*

8-9 le mât d'artimon *m*
- *mizzen (mizen) mast*

8 le mât d'artimon *m* (le bas-mât)
- *lower mizzen (lower mizen)*

9 le mât de hune *f* d'artimon *m*
- *mizzen (mizen) topmast*

10-19 le gréement dormant
- ***standing rigging***

10 l'étai *m* de misaine *f* (l'étai *m* de mât de misaine *f*)
- *forestay, mizzen (mizen) stay, mainstay*

11 l'étai *m* de petit mât de hune *f*
- *fore topmast stay, main topmast stay, mizzen (mizen) topmast stay*

12 la draille de clin-foc *m*
- *fore topgallant stay, mizzen (mizen) topgallant stay, main topgallant stay*

13 l'étai de petit cacatois *m*
- *fore royal stay (main royal stay)*

14 la draille de foc *m*
- *jib stay*

15 la martingale de beaupré *m*
- *bobstay*

16 le gréement inférieur (les haubans *m* de misaine *f*, de grand mât *m*, d'artimon *m*)
- *shrouds*

17 le gréement intermédiaire (les haubans *m* de petit mât de hune *f*, de grand mât de hune *f*, de mât de perroquet *m* de fougue *f*)
- *fore topmast rigging (main topmast rigging, mizzen (mizen) topmast rigging)*

18 le gréement supérieur (les haubans *m* de petit mât de perroquet *m*, de grand mât de perroquet *m*, de mât de perruche *f*)
- *fore topgallant rigging (main topgallant rigging)*

19 les galhaubans *m*
- *backstays*

20-31 les voiles *f* **longitudinales**
- ***fore-and-aft sails***

20 le petit foc
- *fore topmast staysail*

21 le faux-foc (le second foc)
- *inner jib*

22 le grand foc
- *outer jib*

23 le clin-foc
- *flying jib*

24 la grand-voile d'étai *m* (la poillouse)
- *main topmast staysail*

25 la voile d'étai *m* de grand hunier
- *main topgallant staysail*

26 la voile d'étai de grand perroquet *m*
- *main royal staysail*

27 le foc d'artimon *m*
- *mizzen (mizen) staysail*

28 le diablotin
- *mizzen (mizen) topmast staysail*

29 la voile d'étai *m* de perruche *f*
- *mizzen (mizen) topgallant staysail*

30 la brigantine (l'artimon *m*)
- *mizzen (mizen, spanker, driver)*

31 le flèche-en-cul *m*
- *gaff topsail*

32-45 les espars *m*
- ***spars***

32 la vergue de misaine *f*
- *foreyard*

33 la vergue de petit hunier *m* fixe
- *lower fore topsail yard*

34 la vergue de petit hunier *m* volant
- *upper fore topsail yard*

35 la vergue de petit perroquet *m* fixe
- *lower fore topgallant yard*

36 la vergue de petit perroquet *m* volant
- *upper fore topgallant yard*

37 la vergue de petit cacatois *m*
- *fore royal yard*

38 la grand-vergue
- *main yard*

39 la vergue de grand hunier *m* fixe
- *lower main topsail yard*

40 la vergue de grand hunier *m* volant
- *upper main topsail yard*

41 la vergue de grand perroquet *m* fixe
- *lower main topgallant yard*

42 la vergue de grand perroquet *m* volant
- *upper main topgallant yard*

43 la vergue de grand cacatois *m*
- *main royal yard*

44 le gui de brigantine *f* (le gui d'artimon *m*)
- *spanker boom*

45 la corne de brigantine *f* (la corne d'artimon *m*)
- *spanker gaff*

46 les marchepieds *m*
- *footrope*

47 les balancines *f*
- *lifts*

48 la balancine de gui *m*
- *spanker boom topping lift*

49 la drisse de pic *m*
- *spanker peak halyard*

50 la hune de misaine *f*
- *foretop*

51 les barres *f* de petit perroquet *m*
- *fore topmast crosstrees*

52 la grand-hune
- *maintop*

53 les barres *f* de grand perroquet *m*
- *main topmast crosstrees*

54 la hune de mât d'artimon *m*
- *mizzen (mizen) top*

55-66 les voiles *f* carrées (les phares *m* carrés)
- ***square sails***

55 la misaine
- *foresail (fore course)*

56 le petit hunier fixe
- *lower fore topsail*

57 le petit hunier volant
- *upper fore topsail*

58 le petit perroquet
- *lower fore topgallant sail*

59 le petit cacatois
- *upper fore topgallant sail*

60 le petit contre-cacatois
- *fore royal*

61 la grand-voile
- *mainsail (main course)*

62 le grand hunier fixe
- *lower main topsail*

63 le grand hunier volant
- *upper main topsail*

64 le grand perroquet fixe
- *lower main topgallant sail*

65 le grand perroquet volant
- *upper main topgallant sail*

66 le grand cacatois
- *main royal sail*

67-71 le gréement courant
- ***running rigging***

67 les bras *m*
- *braces*

68 les écoutes *f*
- *sheets*

69 l'écoute *f* de brigantine *f* (l'écoute *f* d'artimon *m*)
- *spanker sheet*

70 les palans *m* de garde *f*
- *spanker vangs*

71 les cargues-fonds *m*
- *bunt line*

72 les ris *m*
- *reef*

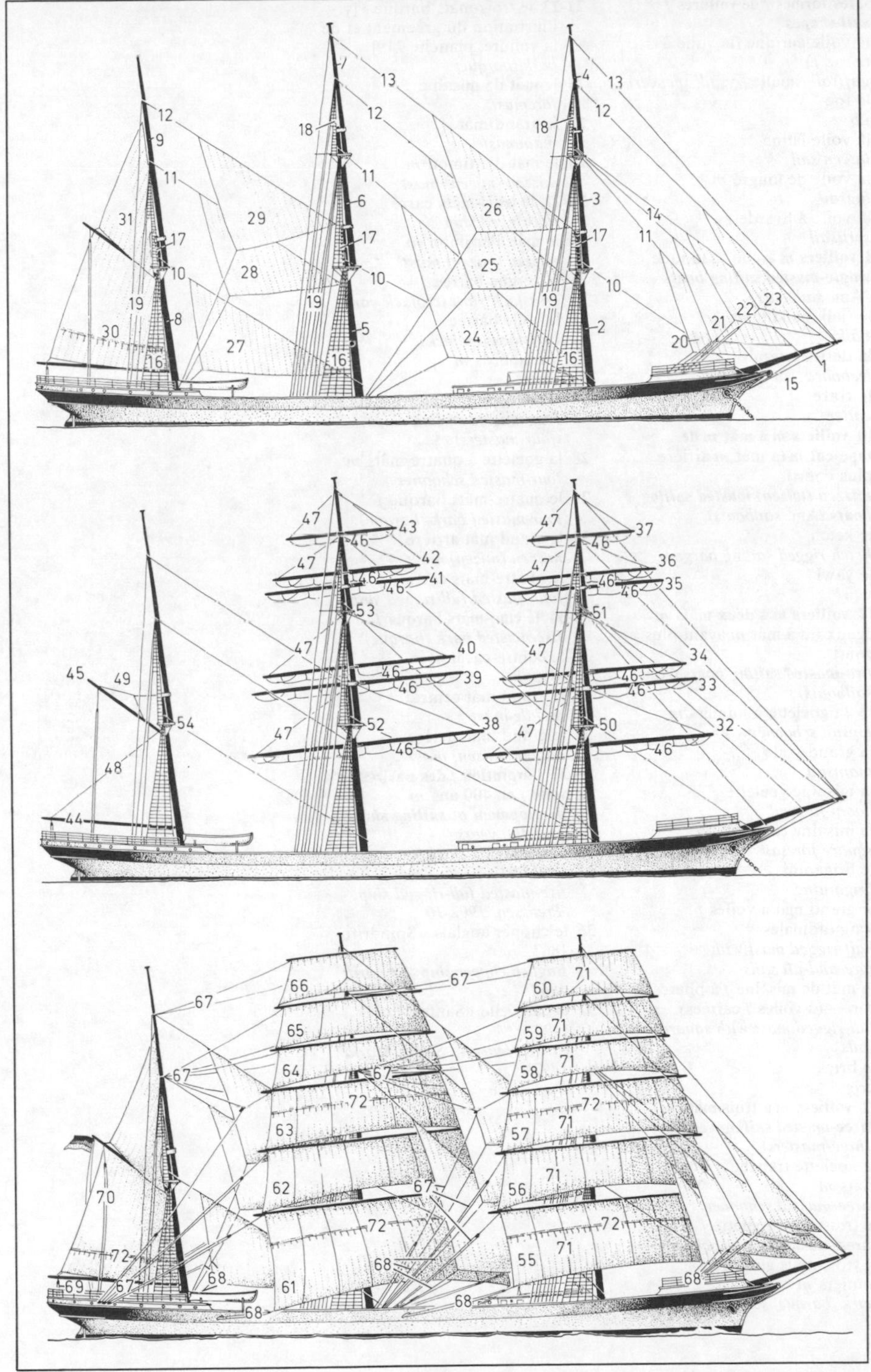

1-5 les formes *f* **de voilures** *f*
– ***sail shapes***
1 la voile aurique (la voile à corne *f*)
– *gaffsail* (small: *trysail, spencer)*
2 le foc
– *jib*
3 la voile latine
– *lateen sail*
4 la voile de lougre *m*
– *lugsail*
5 la voile à livarde *f*
– *spritsail*
6-8 voiliers *m* à mât *m* unique
– ***single-masted sailing boats*** *(*Am. *sailboats)*
6 le tjalk hollandais
– *tjalk*
7 la dérive latérale
– *leeboard*
8 le cotre
– *cutter*
9-10 voiliers *m* **à mât** *m* **de tape-cul** *m* (à mât *m* arrière plus court)
– ***mizzen (mizen) masted sailing boats (***Am. *sailboats)*
9 le ketch
– *ketch-rigged sailing barge*
10 le yawl
– *yawl*
11-17 voiliers *m* **à deux mâts** *m* égaux ou à mât *m* avant plus court
– ***two-masted sailing boats (***Am. *sailboats)*
11-13 la goélette à huniers *m*
– *topsail schooner*
11 la grand-voile
– *mainsail*
12 la misaine-goélette
– *boom foresail*
13 la misaine carrée
– *square foresail*
14 le brigantin
– *brigantine*
15 le grand mât à voiles *f* longitudinales
– *half-rigged mast with fore-and-aft sails*
16 le mât de misaine *f* à phares *m* carrés (à voiles *f* carrées)
– *full-rigged mast with square sails*
17 le brick
– *brig*
18-27 voiliers *m* **à trois mâts** *m*
– ***three-masted sailing vessels*** *(three-masters)*
18 la goélette franche à trois mâts *m*
– *three-masted schooner*
19 le trois-mâts goélette *f*
– *three-masted topsail schooner*
20 le trois-mâts goélette *f* à huniers *m*
– *bark (barque) schooner*
21-23 le trois-mâts barque *f* [v. illustration du gréement et de la voilure, planche 219]
– *bark (barque)*
21 le mât de misaine *f*
– *foremast*
22 le grand-mât
– *mainmast*
23 le mât d'artimon *m*
– *mizzen (mizen) mast*
24-27 le trois-mâts carré
– *full-rigged ship*
24 le mât d'artimon *m*
– *mizzen (mizen) mast*
25 la vergue barrée
– *crossjack yard (crojack yard)*
26 la voile barrée
– *crossjack (crojack)*
27 les sabords *m*
– *ports*
28-31 voiliers *m* **à quatre mâts** *m*
– ***four-masted sailing ships*** *(four-masters)*
28 la goélette à quatre mâts *m*
– *four-masted schooner*
29 le quatre-mâts barque *f*
– *four-masted bark (barque)*
30 le grand mât arrière
– *mizzen (mizen) mast*
31 le quatre-mâts carré
– *four-masted full-rigged ship*
32-34 le cinq-mâts barque *f*
– ***five-masted bark*** *(barque)*
32 le contre-cacatois
– *skysail*
33 le grand-mât central
– *middle mast*
34 le grand-mât arrière
– *mizzen (mizen) mast*
35-37 l'évolution *f* **des navires** *m* **à voile** *f* en 400 ans *m*
– ***development of sailing ships*** *over 400 years*
35 le cinq-mâts carré «Preussen», 1902-1910
– *five-masted full-rigged ship 'Preussen' 1902-10*
36 le clipper anglais «Spindrift», 1867
– *English clipper ship 'Spindrift' 1867*
37 la caravelle «Santa Maria», 1492
– *caravel (carvel) 'Santa Maria' 1492*

1
2
3
4
5
6
7
8
9
10
11
12
13
14
15
16
17
18
19
20
21
22
23
24
25
26
27
28
29
30
31
32
33
34
35
36
37

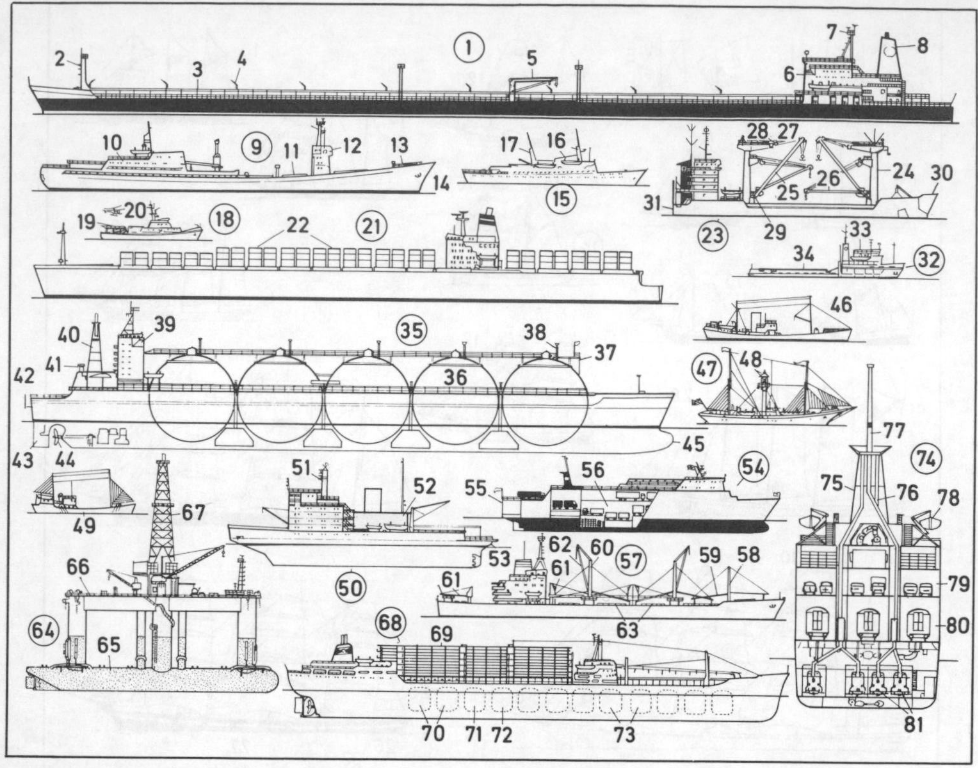

1 **le super-tanker** (ULCC, Ultra Large Crude Carrier) du type à passerelle *f* arrière
– ***ULCC*** *(ultra large crude carrier) of the 'all-aft' type*
2 le mât avant
– *foremast*
3 le passavant avec les conduites *f*
– *catwalk with the pipes*
4 la bouche d'incendie *m*
– *fire gun (fire nozzle)*
5 la grue de pont *m*
– *deck crane*
6 le château et la passerelle
– *deckhouse with the bridge*
7 le mât de signaux *m* et l'antenne *f* radar
– *aft signal (signalling) and radar mast*
8 la cheminée
– *funnel*
9 **un navire expérimental à propulsion** *f* **nucléaire,** le transporteur de vrac *m* «Otto Hahn»
– ***nuclear research ship*** *'Otto Hahn', a bulk carrier*
10 les superstructures *f* arrière (la chambre des machines *f*)
– *aft superstructure (engine room)*
11 le panneau de charge *f*
– *cargo hatchway for bulk goods (bulk cargoes)*
12 la passerelle
– *bridge*
13 le gaillard
– *forecastle (fo'c'sle)*
14 l'étrave *f*
– *stem*
15 **le navire d'excursion** *f*
– ***seaside pleasure boat***
16 la fausse cheminée
– *dummy funnel*
17 la conduite d'échappement *m*
– *exhaust mast*
18 **le navire de sauvetage** *m*
– ***rescue cruiser***
19 la plate-forme d'atterrissage *m* pour hélicoptères *m*
– *helicopter platform (working deck)*
20 l'hélicoptère *m*
– *rescue helicopter*
21 **le navire porte-conteneurs** *m*
– ***all-container ship***
22 les conteneurs *m* chargés en pontée *f*
– *containers stowed on deck*
23 **le cargo**
– ***cargo ship***
24-29 l'installation *f* de manutention *f*
– *cargo gear (cargo-handling gear)*
24 le mât bipode
– *bipod mast*
25 le mât de charge *f* à grande capacité *f*
– *jumbo derrick boom (heavy-lift derrick boom)*
26 la flèche
– *derrick boom (cargo boom)*
27 le palan
– *tackle*
28 la poulie
– *block*
29 la butée
– *thrust bearing*
30 la porte d'étrave *f*
– *bow doors*
31 la porte arrière de chargement *m*
– *stern loading door*
32 **le ravitailleur de forage** *m* offshore (forage *m* en mer *f*)
– ***offshore drilling rig supply vessel***
33 les superstructures *f*
– *compact superstructure*
34 la plate-forme de travail *m*
– *loading deck (working deck)*
35 **le méthanier**
– ***liquefied-gas tanker***
36 le réservoir sphérique
– *spherical tank*
37 le système de télévision *f* pour la navigation
– *navigational television receiver mast*
38 l'évent *m*
– *vent mast*
39 la passerelle
– *deckhouse*
40 la cheminée
– *funnel*
41 le ventilateur
– *ventilator*
42 l'arrière *m* à tableau *m*
– *transom stern (transom)*
43 le gouvernail
– *rudder blade (rudder)*
44 l'hélice *f*
– *ship's propeller (ship's screw)*
45 le bulbe d'étrave *f*
– *bulbous bow*
46 le chalutier
– *steam trawler*
47 **le bateau-feu**
– ***lightship*** *(light vessel)*
48 le phare (le feu)
– *lantern (characteristic light)*
49 le bateau de pêche *f*
– *smack*
50 **le brise-glace**
– ***ice breaker***
51 le feu de route *f*
– *steaming light mast*
52 l'abri *m* de l'hélicoptère *m*
– *helicopter hangar*
53 le point de fixation *f* à l'arrière *f* pour remorquer un navire par l'avant *m*
– *stern towing point, for gripping the bow of ships in tow*
54 **le cargo roll-on - roll-off** (le navire transroulier, le cargo à manutention *f* horizontale)
– ***roll-on-roll-off (ro-ro) trailer ferry***
55 la porte arrière avec rampe *f* d'accès *m*
– *stern port (stern opening) with ramp*
56 le monte-charge pour véhicules *m* lourds
– *heavy vehicle lifts* (Am. *heavy vehicle elevators)*
57 **le cargo**
– ***multi-purpose freighter***
58 le mât auxiliaire servant d'aérateur *m*
– *ventilator-type samson (sampson) post (ventilator-type king post)*
59 la flèche
– *derrick boom (cargo boom, cargo gear, cargo-handling gear)*
60 le mât de charge *f*
– *derrick mast*
61 la grue de pont *m*
– *deck crane*
62 le mât de charge *f* à grande capacité *f*
– *jumbo derrick boom (heavy-lift derrick boom)*
63 le panneau de chargement *m*
– *cargo hatchway*
64 **la plate-forme de forage** *m* semi-submersible
– ***semisubmersible drilling vessel***
65 le navire-support avec les machines *f*
– *floating vessel with machinery*
66 la plate-forme de forage *m*
– *drilling platform*
67 le derrick
– *derrick*
68 **le transport de bétail** *m*
– ***cattleship*** *(cattle vessel)*
69 les superstructures *f* pour le transport du bétail
– *superstructure for transporting livestock*
70 les réservoirs *m* d'eau *f* douce
– *fresh water tanks*
71 le réservoir de carburant *m*
– *fuel tank*
72 la cuve à fumier *m*
– *dung tank*
73 les réservoirs *m* de fourrage *m*
– *fodder tanks*
74 **le ferry** (un navire de transport *m* automobile ou ferroviaire) [coupe *f*]
– ***train ferry*** *[cross section]*
75 la cheminée
– *funnel*
76 les tuyaux *m* d'échappement *m*
– *exhaust pipes*
77 le mât
– *mast*
78 le canot de sauvetage *m* dans ses bossoirs *m* (porte-manteau *m*)
– *ship's lifeboat hanging at the davit*
79 le pont des voitures *f*
– *car deck*
80 le pont ferroviaire
– *main deck (train deck)*

81 la machine principale
– *main engines*
82 le paquebot (le transatlantique)
– ***passenger liner*** *(liner, ocean liner)*
83 l'étrave *f*
– *stem*
84 la cheminée à structure *f* en treillis *m*
– *funnel with lattice casing*
85 le grand pavois (série *f* de pavillons *m* hissés de l'avant à l'arrière pour les fêtes *f* ou le premier voyage)
– *flag dressing (rainbow dressing, string of flags extending over mastheads, e.g., on the maiden voyage)*
86 un chalutier, un navire-usine
– ***trawler****, a factory ship*
87 le portique
– *gallows*
88 la rampe arrière
– *stern ramp*
89 le cargo porte-conteneurs
– ***container ship***
90 le chargement en pontée *f*
– *loading bridge (loading platform)*
91 l'échelle *f* de coupée *f*
– *sea ladder (jacob's ladder, rope ladder)*
92 un pousseur et une barge
– *barge and push tug assembly*
93 le pousseur
– *push tug*
94 la barge sans moteur *m*
– *tug-pushed dumb barge (tug-pushed lighter)*
95 le bateau-pilote
– *pilot boat*
96 le cargo mixte, un navire de transport *m* de marchandises *f* et de passagers *m*
– ***combined cargo and passenger liner***
97 le débarquement des passagers *m*
– *passengers disembarking by boat*
98 l'échelle *f* de coupée *f*
– *accommodation ladder*
99 le caboteur
– *coaster (coasting vessel)*
100 la vedette de la douane
– *customs* or *police launch*

101-128 le paquebot de croisière *f* (le navire d'excursion *f*)
– ***excursion steamer*** *(pleasure steamer)*
101-106 l'installation *f* de mise à l'eau *f* des canots *m*
– *lifeboat launching gear*
101 le bossoir
– *davit*
102 l'entremise *f* de bossoir *m*
– *wire rope span*
103 la sauvegarde
– *lifeline*
104 le palan
– *tackle*
105 la poulie
– *block*
106 le garrant
– *fall*
107 le canot de sauvetage *m* avec son taud
– *ship's lifeboat (ship's boat) covered with tarpaulin*
108 l'étrave *f*
– *stem*
109 le passager
– *passenger*
110 le steward
– *steward*
111 le fauteuil de pont *m* (le transatlantique)
– *deck-chair*
112 le mousse
– *deck hand*
113 le seau
– *deck bucket*
114 le maître d'équipage *m*
– *boatswain (bo's'n, bo'sun, bosun)*
115 la vareuse
– *tunic*
116 la tente
– *awning*
117 le montant de tente *f*
– *stanchion*
118 l'arbalétrier *m*
– *ridge rope (jackstay)*
119 la ligne d'amarrage *m*
– *lashing*
120 le pavois
– *bulwark*

121 le garde-corps
– *guard rail*
122 la rambarde
– *handrail (top rail)*
123 l'échelle *f* de descente *f*
– *companion ladder (companionway)*
124 la bouée de sauvetage *m*
– *lifebelt (lifebuoy)*
125 le feu de la bouée
– *lifebuoy light (lifebelt light, signal light)*
126 l'officier *m* de quart *m*
– *officer of the watch (watchkeeper)*
127 le caban
– *reefer (Am. pea jacket)*
128 les jumelles *f*
– *binoculars*

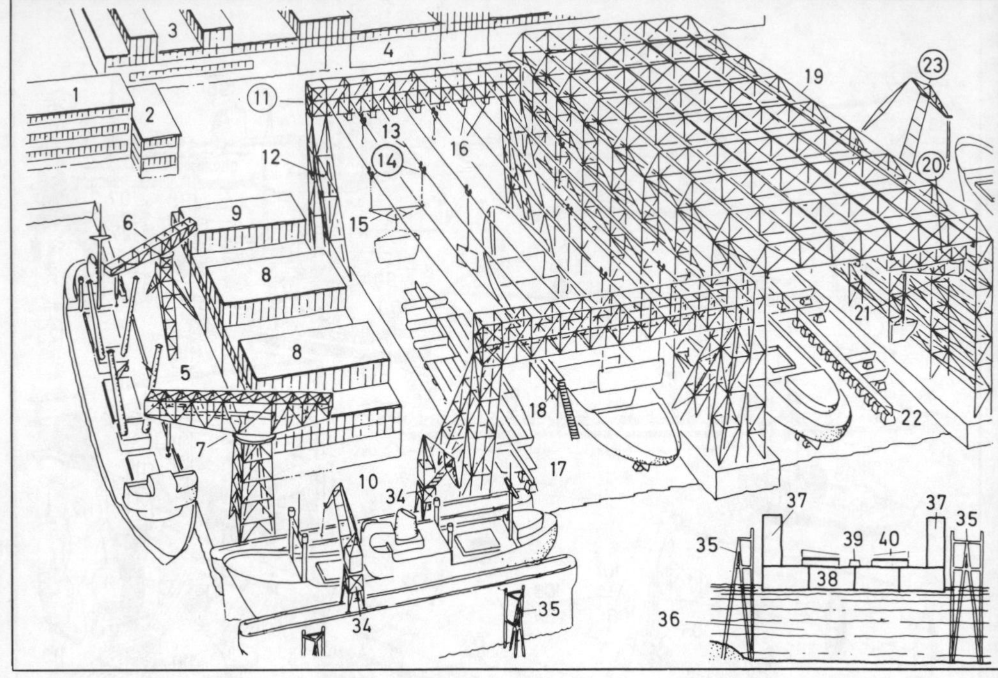

1-43 le chantier de construction *f* navale (le chantier naval)
– ***shipyard*** *(shipbuilding yard, dockyard,* Am. *navy yard)*
1 le bâtiment administratif
– *administrative offices*
2 le bureau d'études *f*
– *ship-drawing office*
3-4 les halles *f* de construction *f*
– *shipbuilding sheds*
3 la salle de tracé *m*
– *mould (*Am. *mold) loft*
4 la halle de montage *m*
– *erection shop*
5-9 le quai d'armement *m*
– *fitting-out quay*
5 le quai
– *quay*
6 la grue tripode
– *tripod crane*
7 la grue marteau *m*
– *hammer-headed crane*
8 l'atelier *m* des machines *f*
– *engineering workshop*
9 l'atelier *m* des chaudières *f*
– *boiler shop*
10 le quai de réparation *f*
– *repair quay*
11-26 les installations *f* de la cale de construction *f*
– *slipways (slips, building berths, building slips, stocks)*
11-18 la cale à portique *m*, une cale de construction *f*
– *cable crane berth, a slipway (building berth)*
11 le portique de cale *f*
– *slipway portal*
12 la palée
– *bridge support*
13 le câble
– *crane cable*
14 le chariot-treuil *m* (le chariot roulant, le treuil roulant)
– *crab (jenny)*
15 le palonnier
– *cross piece*
16 la cabine du grutier
– *crane driver's cabin (crane driver's cage)*
17 le radier de la cale de construction *f*
– *slipway floor*
18 l'échafaudage *m*
– *staging, a scaffold*
19-21 la cale à échafaudage *m*
– *frame slipway*
19 l'échafaudage *m* de cale *f*
– *slipway frame*
20 la grue àchevalet *m*
– *overhead travelling (*Am. *traveling) crane (gantry crane)*
21 le chariot à bec *m* pivotant (le pont roulant orientable)
– *slewing crab*
22 la quille sur forme *f*
– *keel in position*
23 la grue pivotante à volée *f* variable, une grue de cale *f*
– *luffing jib crane, a slipway crane*
24 le chemin de roulement *m*
– *crane rails (crane track)*
25 la grue à portique *m* (la grue-portique, le portique roulant)
– *gantry crane*
26 le portique
– *gantry (bridge)*
27 les portants *m* de portique *m*
– *trestles (supports)*
28 le chariot roulant (le treuil roulant, le pont roulant)
– *crab (jenny)*
29 les couples *m* de construction *f*
– *hull frames in position*
30 le navire en construction *f*
– *ship under construction*
31-33 la cale sèche (le bassin de radoub *m*, de carénage *m*)
– *dry dock*
31 le radier de la cale (du bassin)
– *dock floor (dock bottom)*
32 les portes *f* du bassin
– *dock gates (caisson)*
33 la station de pompage *m*
– *pumping station (power house)*
34-43 le dock flottant (la forme flottante)
– *floating dock (pontoon dock)*
34 la grue de dock *m*, une grue à portique *m*
– *dock crane (dockside crane), a jib crane*
35 la défense en pilotis *m* (le duc d'albe)
– *fender pile*
36-43 l'installation *f* du dock flottant
– *working of docks*
36 la souille (la fosse) du dock flottant
– *dock basin*
37-38 la structure du dock flottant
– *dock structure*
37 le ballast latéral (la paroi, le caisson vertical)
– *side tank (side wall)*
38 le ballast de fond *m* (le caisson horizontal)
– *bottom tank (bottom pontoon)*

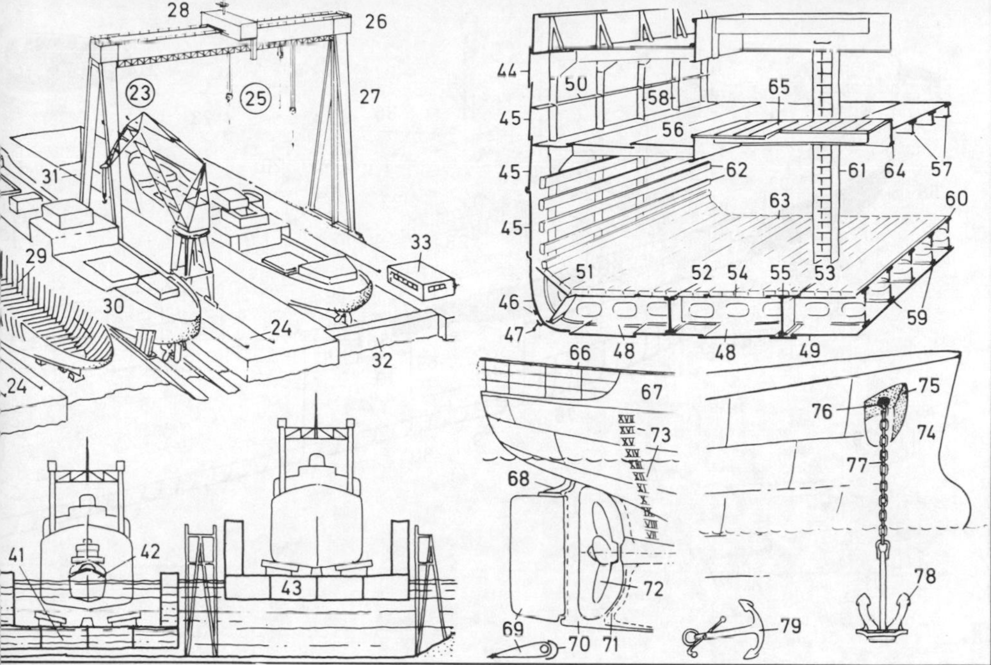

39 le tin de construction *f*
– *keel block*
40 le tin latéral (le tin de bouchain *m*)
– *bilge block (bilge shore, side support)*
41-43 l'entrée *f* d'un navire au bassin
– *docking a ship*
41 le dock flottant immergé
– *flooded floating dock*
42 le remorqueur du navire
– *tug towing the ship*
43 le dock flottant remonté, après pompage *m* de l'eau *f*
– *emptied (pumped-out) dock*
44-61 la charpente du navire
– ***structural parts of the ship***
44-56 la charpente longitudinale
– *longitudinal structure*
44-49 le bordé extérieur
– *shell (shell plating, skin)*
44 la virure de carreau *m*
– *sheer strake*
45 le bordé de côté *m*
– *side strake*
46 la virure de bouchain *m*
– *bilge strake*
47 la quille de roulis *m* (la quille de bouchain *m*)
– *bilge keel*
48 le bordé de fond *m*
– *bottom plating*
49 la quille plate
– *flat plate keel (keel plate)*
50 la serre
– *stringer (side stringer)*
51 le support de côté *m* (la virure latérale)
– *tank margin plate*
52 la carlingue latérale
– *longitudinal side girder*
53 la quille-carlingue (la carlingue centrale)
– *centre* (Am. *center) plate girder (centre girder, kelson, keelson, vertical keel)*
54 le plafond (la plate-forme) du ballast
– *tank top plating (tank top, inner bottom plating)*
55 la virure centrale
– *centre* (Am. *center) strake*
56 la tôle de pont *m*
– *deck plating*
57 le barrot de pont *m*
– *deck beam*
58 la membrure (le couple)
– *frame (rib)*
59 la varangue
– *floor plate*
60 le double fond cellulaire
– *cellular double bottom*
61 l'épontille *f* de cale *f*
– *hold pillar (pillar)*
62-63 le vaigrage
– *dunnage*
62 le vaigrage latéral
– *side battens (side ceiling, spar ceiling)*
63 le vaigrage de fond *m*
– *ceiling (floor ceiling)*
64-65 l'écoutille *f*
– *hatchway*
64 l'hiloire *f* (le surbau)
– *hatch coaming*
65 le panneau d'écoutille *f*
– *hatch cover (hatchboard)*
66-72 l'arrière *m* (la poupe)
– *stern*
66 la rambarde (le garde-corps)
– *guard rail*
67 le pavois
– *bulwark*
68 la mèche du gouvernail
– *rudder stock*
69-70 le gouvernail
– *Oertz rudder*
69 le safran
– *rudder blade (rudder)*
70-71 l'étambot *m*
– *stern frame*
70 l'étambot *m* arrière
– *rudder post*
71 l'étambot *m* avant
– *propeller post (screw post)*
72 l'hélice *f*
– *ship's propeller (ship's screw)*
73 l'échelle *f* de tirants *m* d'eau *f*
– *draught (draft) marks*
74-79 l'avant *m* (la proue, l'étrave *f*)
– *bow*
74 l'étrave *f*, une étrave à bulbe *m*
– *stem, a bulbous stem (bulbous bow)*
75 l'écubier *m*
– *hawse*
76 le manchon d'écubier *m*
– *hawse pipe*
77 la chaîne d'ancre *f* (la chaîne de mouillage *m*)
– *anchor cable (chain cable)*
78 l'ancre *f* sans jas
– *stockless anchor (patent anchor)*
79 l'ancre *f* à jas
– *stocked anchor*

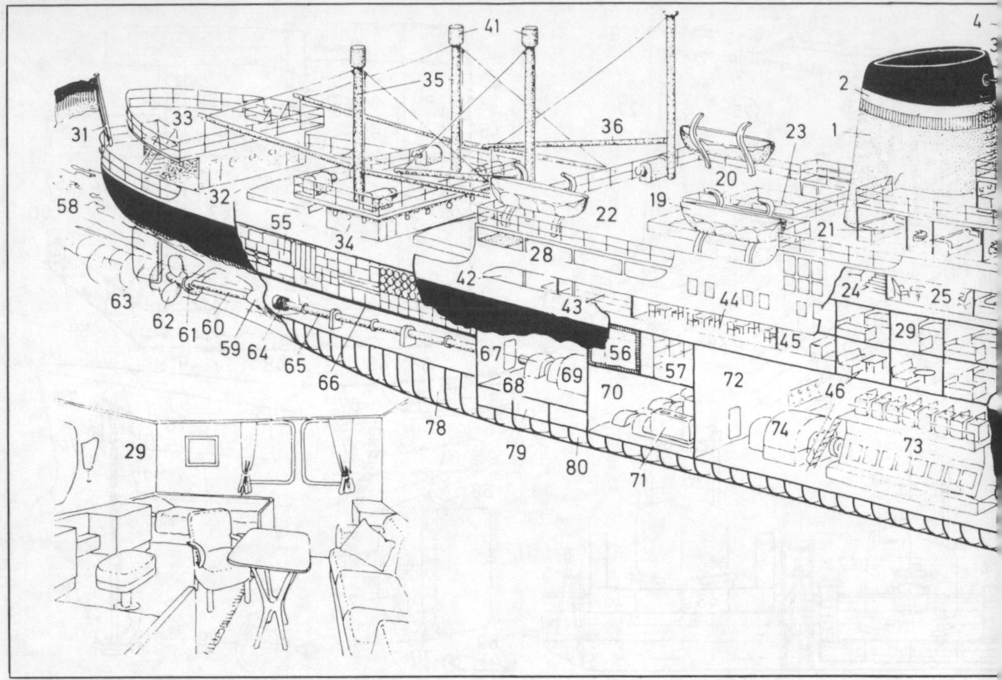

1-71 le cargo mixte passagers *m* **- marchandises** *f* [d'un type ancien]
– ***combined cargo and passenger ship*** *[of the older type]*
1 la cheminée
– *funnel*
2 la marque de cheminée *f*
– *funnel marking*
3 la sirène (le signal de brume *f*)
– *siren (fog horn)*
4-11 la passerelle de navigation *f*
– ***compass platform*** *(compass bridge, compass flat, monkey bridge)*
4 les antennes *f*
– *antenna lead-in (antenna down-lead)*
5 l'antenne *f* radiogoniométrique (le cadre gonio)
– *radio direction finder (RDF) antenna (direction finder antenna, rotatable loop antenna, aural null loop antenna)*
6 le compas magnétique
– *magnetic compass (mariner's compass)*
7 la lampe morse
– *morse lamp (signalling,* Am. *signaling, lamp)*
8 l'antenne *f* radar *m*
– *radar antenna (radar scanner)*
9 le pavillon signalétique
– *code flag signal*
10 la drisse de pavillons *m*
– *code flag halyards*
11 l'étai *m* de pavillons *m*
– *triatic stay (signal stay)*
12-18 la passerelle
– ***bridge deck*** *(bridge)*
12 le poste radiotélégraphique
– *radio room*
13 la chambre du capitaine
– *captain's cabin*
14 la chambre de navigation *f*
– *navigating bridge*
15 le feu de route *f* tribord *m* [vert; le feu de route bâbord *m* est rouge]
– *starboard sidelight [green; port sidelight red]*
16 l'aileron *m* de passerelle *f*
– *wing of bridge*
17 le cagnard
– *shelter (weather cloth, dodger)*
18 la timonerie
– *wheelhouse*
19-21 le pont des embarcations *f*
– ***boat deck***
19 le canot de sauvetage *m*
– *ship's lifeboat*
20 le bossoir (le porte-manteau)
– *davit*
21 la chambre d'un officier
– *officer's cabin*
22-27 le pont-promenade
– ***promenade deck***
22 le sun-deck
– *sun deck (lido deck)*
23 la piscine
– *swimming pool*
24 la descente (l'escalier *m*)
– *companion ladder (companionway)*
25 la bibliothèque
– *library (ship's library)*
26 le salon
– *lounge*
27 la galerie
– *promenade*
28-30 le pont A
– ***A-deck***
28 le pont couvert
– *semi-enclosed deck space*
29 une cabine double
– *double-berth cabin, a cabin*
30 une cabine de luxe *m*
– *de luxe cabin*
31 le mât de pavillon *m*
– *ensign staff*
32-42 le pont B (le pont principal)
– ***B-deck*** *(main deck)*
32 la plage arrière
– *after deck*
33 la dunette
– *poop*
34 le rouf
– *deckhouse*
35 le mât de charge *f*
– *samson (sampson) post (king post)*
36 la flèche
– *derrick boom (cargo boom)*
37 les barres de flèche *f*
– *crosstrees (spreader)*
38 le nid de pie *f*
– *crow's nest*
39 le mât de hune *f*
– *topmast*
40 le feu de route *f* avant
– *forward steaming light*
41 le capuchon de ventilateur *m*
– *ventilator lead*
42 la cuisine
– *galley (caboose, cookroom, ship's kitchen)*
43 la cambuse
– *ship's pantry*
44 la salle à manger
– *dining room*
45 le bureau du commissaire
– *purser's office*

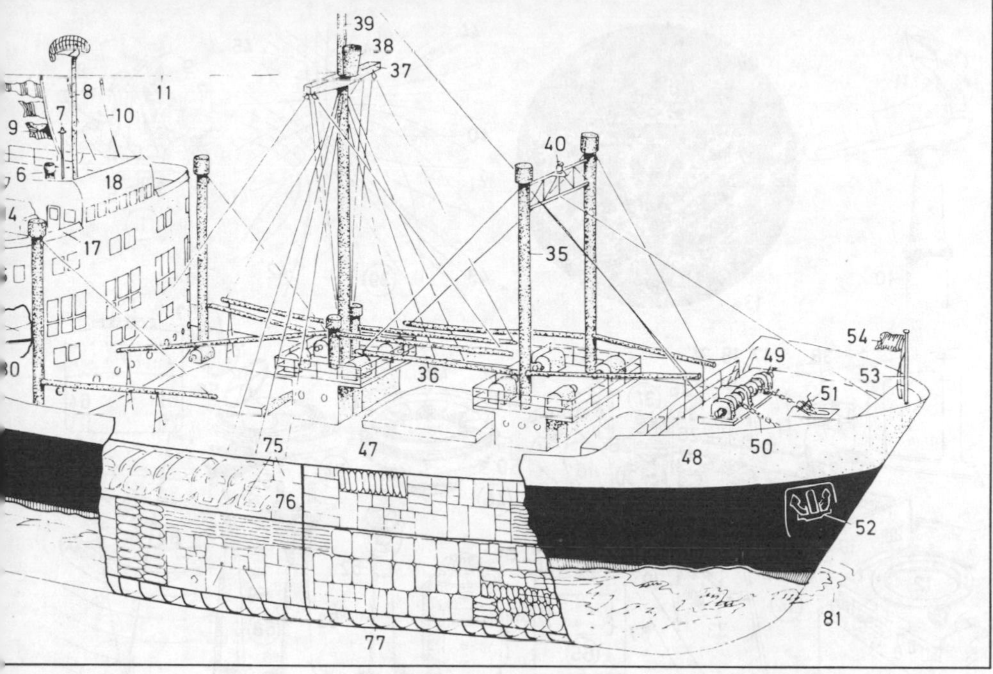

46 une cabine simple
– *single-berth cabin*
47 le pont avant
– *foredeck*
48 le gaillard
– *forecastle (fo'c'sle)*
49-51 les apparaux *m* **de mouillage** *m* **(le mouillage)**
– ***ground tackle***
49 le guindeau (le treuil)
– *windlass*
50 la chaîne d'ancre *f*
– *anchor cable (chain cable)*
51 l'étrangloir *m* (le stoppeur)
– *compressor (chain compressor)*
52 l'ancre *f*
anchor
53 le mât de pavillon *m* d'étrave *f*
– *jackstaff*
54 le pavillon d'étrave *f*
– *jack*
55 les soutes *f* arrière
– *after holds*
56 la chambre froide
– *cold storage room (insulated hold)*
57 la soute aux vivres *f*
– *store room*
58 le sillage
– *wake*
59 l'aileron *m*
– *shell bossing (shaft bossing)*
60 la ligne d'arbres *m*
– *tail shaft (tail end shaft)*
61 le support d'arbre *m*
– *shaft strut (strut, spectacle frame, propeller strut, propeller bracket)*
62 l'hélice *f* à trois pales *f*
– *three-blade ship's propeller (ship's screw)*
63 le gouvernail
– *rudder blade (rudder)*
64 le presse-étoupe
– *stuffing box*
65 l'arbre *m* porte-hélice
– *propeller shaft*
66 le tunnel d'arbre *m*
– *shaft alley (shaft tunnel)*
67 la butée
– *thrust block*
68-74 le propulseur diesel-électrique
– ***diesel-electric drive***
68 la chambre des moteurs *m* électriques
electric engine room
69 le moteur électrique
– *electric motor*
70 la chambre des machines *f* auxiliaires
– *auxiliary engine room*
71 les machines *f* auxiliaires
– *auxiliary engines*
72 la chambre du moteur principal
– *main engine room*
73 le moteur principal, un moteur Diesel
– *main engine, a diesel engine*
74 la génératrice
– *generator*
75 les soutes *f* avant
– *forward holds*
76 l'entrepont *m*
– *tween deck*
77 la cargaison
cargo
78 les réservoirs *m* de ballast *m* pour lest *m* d'eau *f*
ballast tank (deep tank) for water ballast
79 le réservoir d'eau *f* douce
– *fresh water tank*
80 le réservoir de carburant *m*
– *fuel tank*
81 la vague d'étrave *f*
– *bow wave*

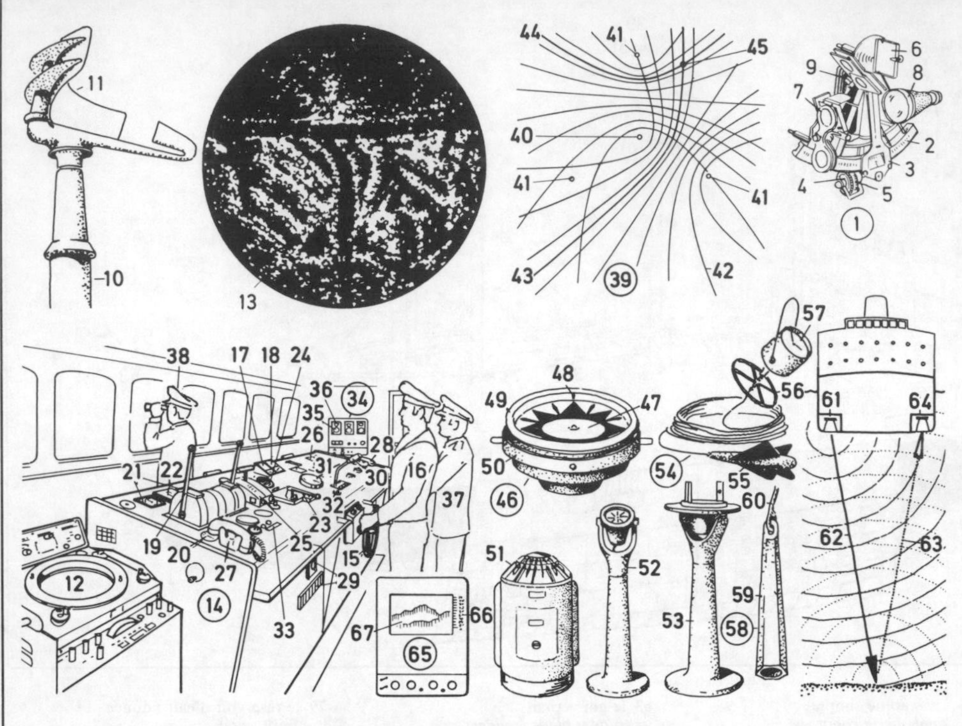

1 le sextant
– ***sextant***
2 le limbe
– *graduated arc*
3 l'alidade *f*
– *index bar (index arm)*
4 la vis micrométrique
– *decimal micrometer*
5 le vernier
– *vernier*
6 le grand miroir
– *index mirror*
7 le petit miroir
– *horizon glass (horizon mirror)*
8 la lunette
– *telescope*
9 la poignée
– *grip (handgrip)*
10-13 **l'installation *f* du radar** (la passerelle de navigation *f*)
– ***radar equipment*** *(radar apparatus)*
10 le mât radar
– *radar pedestal*
11 l'antenne *f* pivotante
– *revolving radar reflector*
12 l'écran *m* radar (l'indicateur *m* radar)
– *radar display unit (radar screen)*
13 l'image *f* radar
– *radar image (radar picture)*
14-38 **la timonerie** (la passerelle de navigation *f*)
– ***wheelhouse***
14 le poste de commandement *m*
– *steering and control position*
15 la roue du gouvernail (la barre)
– *ship's wheel for controlling the rudder mechanism*
16 le barreur (l'homme *m* de barre *f*)
– *helmsman* (Am. *wheelsman)*
17 l'indicateur *m* d'angle *m* de barre *f*
– *rudder angle indicator*
18 le pilote automatique
– *automatic pilot (autopilot)*
19 le levier de commande *f* de l'hélice *f* à pas *m* variable
– *control lever for the variable-pitch propeller (reversible propeller, feathering propeller, feathering screw)*
20 l'indicateur *m* de pas *m*
– *propeller pitch indicator*
21 le compte-tours du moteur principal
– *main engine revolution indicator*
22 le speedomètre (l'indicateur *m* de vitesse *f*)
– *ship's speedometer (log)*
23 le commutateur de commande *f* du gouvernail d'étrave *f*
– *control switch for bow thruster (bow-manoeuvring,* Am. *maneuvering, propeller)*
24 l'écho-sondeur *m*
– *echo recorder (depth recorder, echograph)*
25 le transmetteur d'ordres *m* aux machines *f* (le chadburn)
– *engine telegraph (engine order telegraph)*
26 la commande des stabilisateurs *m* antiroulis *m*
– *controls for the anti-rolling system (for the stabilizers)*
27 le téléphone de liaison *f* intérieure
– *local-battery telephone*
28 l'appareil *m* de radiotéléphonie *f*
– *shipping traffic radio telephone*
29 le tableau indicateur des feux *m* de route *f*
– *navigation light indicator panel (running light indicator panel)*
30 le micro du système *m* de diffusion *f* générale
– *microphone for ship's address system*
31 le gyrocompas, un compas répétiteur
– *gyro compass (gyroscopic compass), a compass repeater*
32 le bouton de commande *f* de la sirène (le signal de brume *f*)
– *control button for the ship's siren (ship's fog horn)*
33 l'indicateur *m* de surcharge *f* du moteur principal
– *main engine overload indicator*
34 le récepteur de l'appareil *m* de localisation *f* hyperbolique Decca
– *detector indicator unit for fixing the ship's position*
35 le cadran de dégrossissage *m*
– *rough focusing indicator*
36 le cadran d'identification *f* fine
– *fine focusing indicator*
37 l'officier *m* de quart *m*
– *navigating officer*
38 le commandant
– *captain*
39 **le système de navigation** *f* Decca
– ***Decca navigation system***
40 la station maître
– *master station*
41 la station esclave
– *slave station*
42 l'hyperbole *f* de base *f*
– *null hyperbola*
43 l'hyperbole *f* de position *f* (1)
– *hyperbolic position line 1*
44 l'hyperbole *f* de position *f* (2)
– *hyperbolic position line 2*
45 le point (la position)
– *position (fix, ship fix)*
46-53 **les compas** *m*
– ***compasses***
46 le compas magnétique, un con à liquide *m*
– *liquid compass (fluid compass, spirit compass, wet compass), a magnetic compass*
47 la rose des vents *f*
– *compass card*
48 la ligne de foi *f*
– *lubber's line (lubber's mark, lubber's point)*
49 la cuvette du compas *m*
– *compass bowl*
50 la suspension à la Cardan
– *gimbal ring*
51-53 le compas gyroscopique (le gyrocompas)
– *gyro compass (gyroscopic comp gyro compass unit)*
51 le compas principal
– *master compass (master gyro compass)*
52 le compas répétiteur
– *compass repeater (gyro repeate*
53 le compas répétiteur avec l'alidade *f* de relèvement *m*
– *compass repeater with pelorus*
54 **le loch à hélice** *f*, un loch remorqué
– ***patent log*** *(screw log, mechani log, towing log, taffrail log, speedometer), a log*
55 l'hélice *f* du loch (le poisson c loch *m*)
– *rotator*
56 le régulateur
– *governor*
57 le compteur (le cadran)
– *log clock*
58-67 **les sondes** *f*
– ***leads***

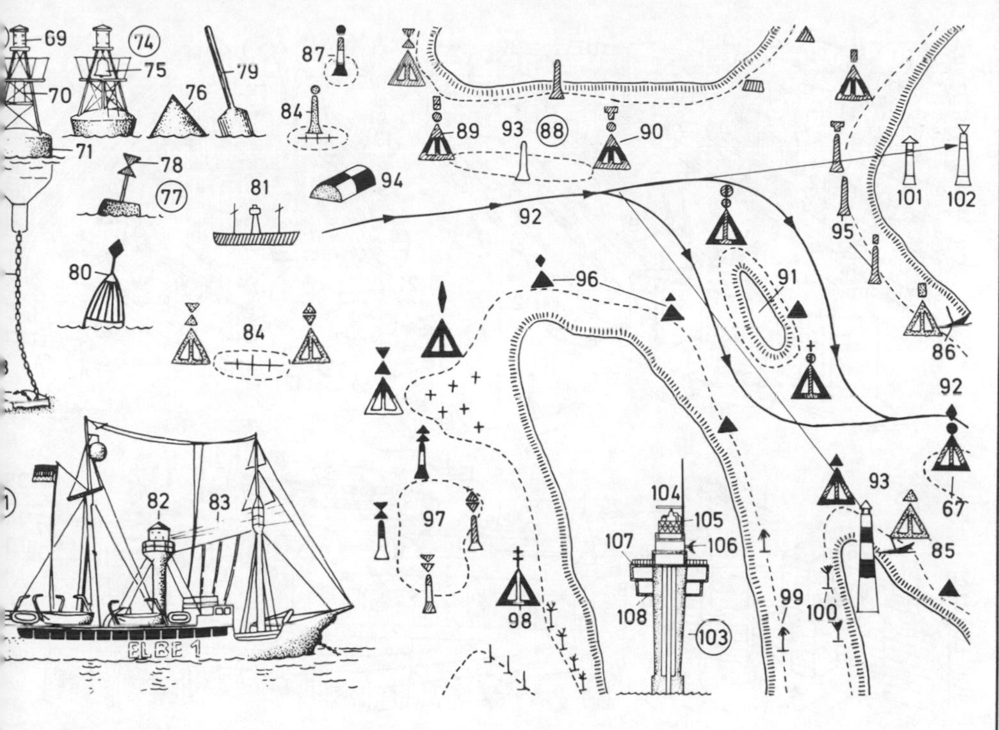

58 la sonde à main *f*
– *hand lead*
59 le plomb de sonde *f*
– *lead (lead sinker)*
60 la ligne de sonde*f*
– *leadline*
61-67 l'écho-sondeur *m* (le sondeur acoustique, le sondeur par ultra-sons *m*)
– *echo sounder (echo sounding machine)*
61 le transducteur-émetteur
– *sound transmitter*
62 l'onde *f* acoustique
– *sound wave (sound impulse)*
63 l'onde *f* réfléchie(l'écho *m*)
– *echo (sound echo, echo signal)*
64 le transducteur-récepteur
– *echo receiver (hydrophone)*
65 l'enregistreur *m*
– *echograph (echo sounding machine recorder)*
66 l'échelle *f* d'enregistrement *m*
– *depth scale*
67 la ligne du fond *m*
– *echogram (depth recording, depth reading)*
68-108 la signalisation maritime par balises *f* et feux *m*
– ***sea marks** (floating navigational marks)* ***for buoyage and lighting systems***
68-83 les marques *f* de balisage *m*
– *fairway marks (channel marks)*
68 la bouée lumineuse à sifflet *m*
– *light and whistle buoy*
69 le feu
– *light (warning light)*
70 le sifflet
– *whistle*
71 le flotteur
– *buoy*
72 la chaîne de mouillage *m*
– *mooring chain*
73 le mouillage (le corps mort)
– *sinker (mooring sinker)*
74 la bouée lumineuse à cloche *f*
– *light and bell buoy*
75 la cloche
– *bell*
76 la bouée conique
– *conical buoy*
77 la bouée cylindrique
– *can buoy*
78 le voyant
– *topmark*
79 la bouée à espar *m*
– *spar buoy*
80 la balise
– *topmark buoy*
81 le bateau-feu
– *lightship (light vessel)*
82 le phare (le feu)
– *lantern mast (lantern tower)*
83 le faisceau lumineux
– *beam of light*
84-102 le balisage d'un chenal (système *m* latéral, système *m* cardinal)
– *fairway markings (channel markings) [German type]*
84 épave *f* (bouée *f* verte)
– *wreck [green buoys]*
85 épave *f* à droite *f* du chenal
– *wreck to starboard*
86 épave *f* à gauche *f* du chenal
– *wreck to port*
87 haut-fond *m* isolé
– *shoals (shallows, shallow water,* Am. *flats)*
88 banc *m* médian à gauche *f* du chenal
– *middle ground to port*
89 marque *f* de bifurcation *f* (voyant *m* rouge, cylindre *m* sur sphère *f*)
– *division (bifurcation) [beginning of the middle ground; topmark: red cylinder above red ball]*
90 marque *f* de jonction *f* (voyant *m* rouge, croix *f* sur sphère *f*)
– *convergence (confluence) [end of the middle ground; topmark: red St. Antony's cross above red ball]*
91 banc *m* médian
– *middle ground*
92 le chenal principal
– *main fairway (main navigable channel)*
93 le chenal secondaire
– *secondary fairway (secondary navigable channel)*
94 la tonne
– *can buoy*
95 la marque de bâbord *m* (rouge)
– *port hand buoys (port hand marks) [red]*
96 la marque de tribord *m* (noire)
– *starboard hand buoys (starboard hand marks) [black]*
97 un danger isolé (balisage *m* cardinal)
– *shoals (shallows, shallow water,* Am. *flats) outside the fairway*
98 marque *f* de transition *f* (voyant *m*: croix *f* à deux barres *f*)
– *middle of the fairway (mid-channel)*
99 perches *f* de tribord *m* (signalisation *f* fédérale)
– *starboard markers [inverted broom]*
100 perches *f* de bâbord *m* (signalisation *f* fédérale)
– *port markers [upward-pointing broom]*
101-102 un alignement lumineux
– *range lights (leading lights)*
101 le feu de direction *f* inférieur
– *lower range light (lower leading light)*
102 le feu de direction *f* supérieur
– *higher range light (higher leading light)*
103 le phare
– *lighthouse*
104 l'antenne *f* radar
– *radar antenna (radar scanner)*
105 le feu (la lanterne du phare)
– *lantern (characteristic light)*
106 l'antenne *f* radiogoniométrique
– *radio direction finder (RDF) antenna*
107 la plate-forme d'observation *f* et des machines *f*
– *machinery and observation platform (machinery and observation deck)*
108 l'habitation *f* du gardien
– *living quarters*

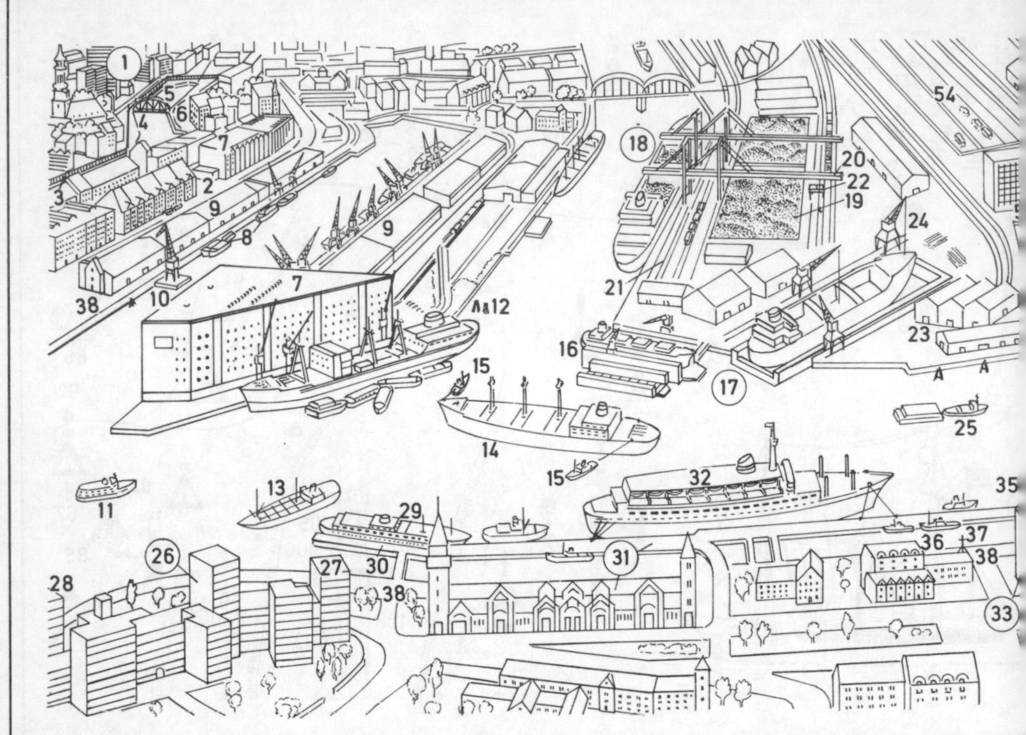

1 le quartier du port
– *dock area*
2 le port franc
– *free port (foreign trade zone)*
3 la frontière de la zone franche
– *free zone frontier (free zone enclosure)*
4 le poste de douane *f*
– *customs barrier*
5 l'entrée *f* en douane *f*
– *customs entrance*
6 le bureau des douanes *f*
– *port custom house*
7 l'entrepôt *m*
– *entrepôt*
8 la barge (la gabare, l'allège *f*, la péniche)
– *barge (dumb barge, lighter)*
9 l'entrepôt *m* de transit *m* de marchandises *f* diverses
– *break-bulk cargo transit shed (general cargo transit shed, package cargo transit shed)*
10 le ponton-grue
– *floating crane*
11 le bac
– *harbour* (Am. *harbor*) *ferry (ferryboat)*
12 les ducs *m* d'albe
– *fender (dolphin)*
13 le bateau-citerne
– *bunkering boat*
14 le transport de marchandises *f* diverses
– *break-bulk carrier (general cargo ship)*
15 le remorqueur
– *tug*
16 le dock flottant
– *floating dock (pontoon dock)*
17 la cale sèche
– *dry dock*
18 le quai de charbonnage *m*
– *coal wharf*
19 le parc à charbon *m*
– *coal bunker*
20 le portique de chargement *m*
– *transporter loading bridge*
21 le chemin de fer *m* desservant le port
– *quayside railway*
22 la trémie de pesage *m*
– *weighing bunker*
23 l'entrepôt
– *warehouse*
24 la grue à flèche *f*
– *quayside crane*
25 l'allège *f* et son remorqueur
– *launch and lighter*
26 l'hôpital *m* du port
– *port hospital*
27 le pavillon de quarantaine *f*
– *quarantine wing*
28 l'institut *m* de médecine *f* tropicale
– *Institute of Tropical Medicine*
29 le navire d'excursion *f*
– *excursion steamer (pleasure steamer)*
30 la jetée
– *jetty*
31 la gare maritime
– *passenger terminal*
32 le paquebot (le transatlantique, le navire de ligne *f*)
– *liner (passenger liner, ocean liner)*
33 la station météorologique
– *meteorological office, a weather station*
34 le mât de signalisation *f*
– *signal mast (signalling mast)*
35 le signal de tempête *f*
– *storm signal*
36 les bureaux du port
– *port administration offices*
37 l'échelle *f* de marée *f*
– *tide level indicator*
38 la rue bordant le quai
– *quayside road (quayside roadway)*
39 le poste de chargement *m* roll-on roll-off
– *roll-on roll-off (ro-ro) system (roll-on roll-off operation)*
40 le portique
– *gantry*
41 le poste de chargement *m* par chariots *m* (truck-to-truck)
– *truck-to-truck system (truck-to-truck operation)*
42 la charge unitaire emballée
– *foil-wrapped unit loads*

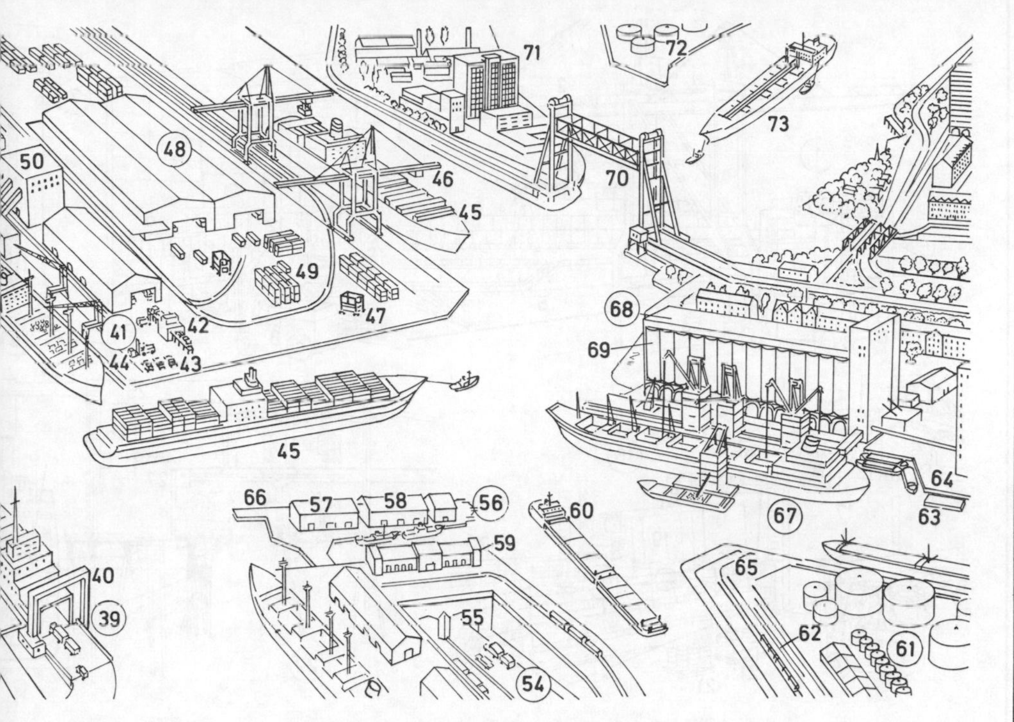

43 les palettes *f*
– *pallets*
44 le chariot élévateur à fourche *f*
– *forklift truck (fork truck, forklift)*
45 le cargo porte-conteneurs *m*
– *container ship*
46 le pont-roulant de chargement *m* de conteneurs *m*
– *transporter container-loading bridge*
47 le camion porte-conteneurs *m*
– *container carrier truck*
48 l'entrepôt *m* pour conteneurs *m* (terminal *m* pour conteneurs *m*)
– *container terminal (container berth)*
49 l'unité *f* de charge *f*
– *unit load*
50 la chambre froide de stockage *f*
– *cold store*
51 le transporteur à bande *f* (la bande transporteuse)
– *conveyor belt (conveyor)*
52 l'entrepôt *m* à fruits *m*
– *fruit storage shed (fruit warehouse)*
53 le bâtiment administratif
– *office building*
54 l'autoroute *f* urbaine
– *urban motorway (Am. freeway)*
55 le tunnel passant sous le port
– *harbour (Am. harbor) tunnels*
56 le port de pêche *f*
– *fish dock*
57 le marché au poisson *m*
– *fish market*
58 la criée au poisson *m*
– *auction room*
59 la conserverie de poisson *m*
– *fish-canning factory*
60 le pousseur
– *push tow*
61 les réservoirs *m* de pétrole *m*
– *tank farm*
62 l'embranchement *m* ferroviaire
– *railway siding*
63 le ponton d'accostage *m*
– *landing pontoon (landing stage)*
64 le quai
– *quay*
65 le brise-lames
– *breakwater (mole)*
66 la jetée, un prolongement du quai
– *pier (jetty), a quay extension*
67 le transporteur de vrac *m*
– *bulk carrier*
68 le silo
– *silo*
69 la cuve du silo
– *silo cylinder*
70 le pont élévateur
– *lift bridge*
71 la zone industrielle du port
– *industrial plant*
72 les réservoirs *m* de stockage *m*
– *storage tanks*
73 le pétrolier
– *tanker*

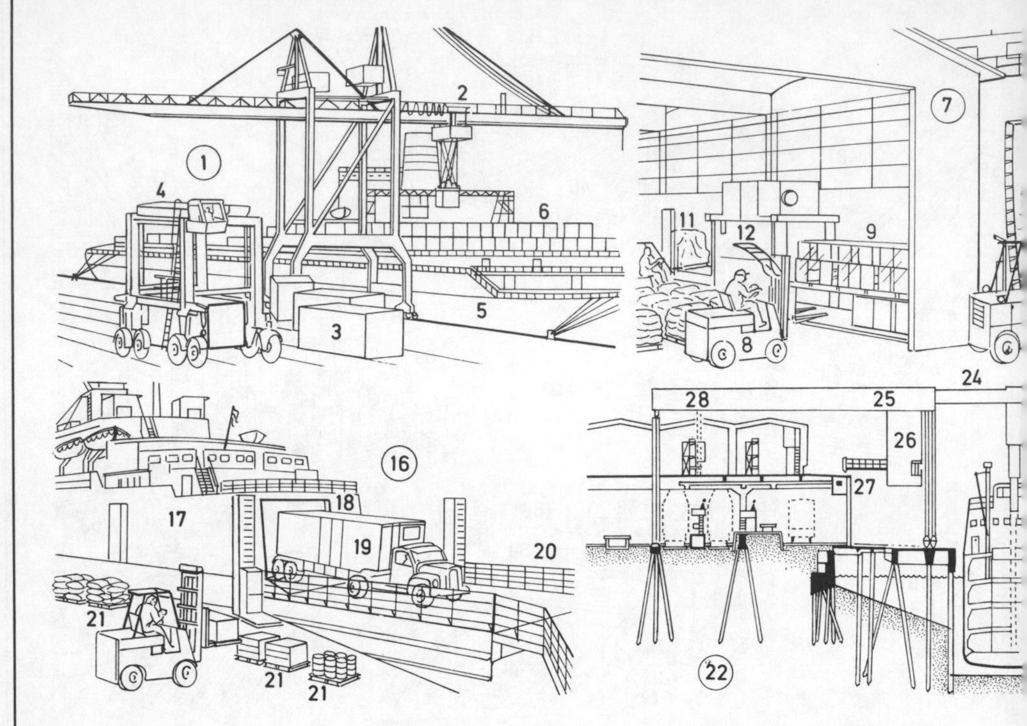

1 le terminal pour conteneurs *m* (entrepôt *m* pour conteneurs *m*), une installation moderne de manutention *f* de marchandises *f*
– *container terminal (container berth), a modern cargo-handling berth*
2 le pont roulant de chargement *m*
– *transporter container-loading bridge (loading bridge);* sim.: *transtainer crane (transtainer)*
3 le conteneur
– *container*
4 le chariot transporteur
– *truck (carrier)*
5 le cargo porte-conteneurs
– *all-container ship*
6 les conteneurs *m* chargés en pontée *f*
– *containers stowed on deck*
7 la manutention horizontale des conteneurs *m* par chariots *m* à fourche *f*
– *truck-to-truck handling (horizontal cargo handling with pallets)*
8 le chariot à fourche *f*
– *forklift truck (fork truck, forklift)*
9 la charge unitaire emballée
– *unitized foil-wrapped load (unit load)*
10 la palette normalisée
– *flat pallet, a standard pallet*
11 la charge unitaire emballée de marchandises *f* diverses
– *unitized break-bulk cargo*
12 la machine d'emballage *m* sous film *m* rétractable
– *heat sealing machine*
13 le transporteur de marchandises *f* diverses
– *break-bulk carrier (general cargo ship)*
14 le sabord de charge *f*
– *cargo hatchway*
15 le chariot récepteur à bord *m*
– *receiving truck on board ship*
16 le terminal à usages *m* multiples
– *multi-purpose terminal*
17 le cargo de transport *m* roll-on roll-off (le navire transroulier, le cargo à manutention *f* horizontale)
– *roll-on roll-off ship (ro-ro-ship)*
18 la porte arrière
– *stern port (stern opening)*
19 un camion chargé
– *driven load, a lorry* (Am. *truck*)
20 le dépôt de marchandises *f* roll-on roll-off (l'installation *f* de manutention *f* horizontale)
– *ro-ro depot*
21 la charge unitaire
– *unitized load (unitized package)*
22 le terminal à bananes *f* [coupe *f*]
– *banana-handling terminal [section]*
23 l'élévateur *m* de cale *f*
– *seaward tumbler*
24 la flèche
– *jib*
25 le pont élévateur
– *elevator bridge*
26 l'élingue *f* en chaîne *f*
– *chain sling*
27 le poste d'éclairage *m*
– *lighting station*
28 le système de chargement *m* des camions *m* et wagons *m*
– *shore-side tumbler for loading trains and lorries* (Am. *trucks*)
29 le poste de chargement *m* de vrac *m*
– *bulk cargo handling*
30 le transporteur de vrac *m* (*ELF:* le vraquier)
– *bulk carrier*

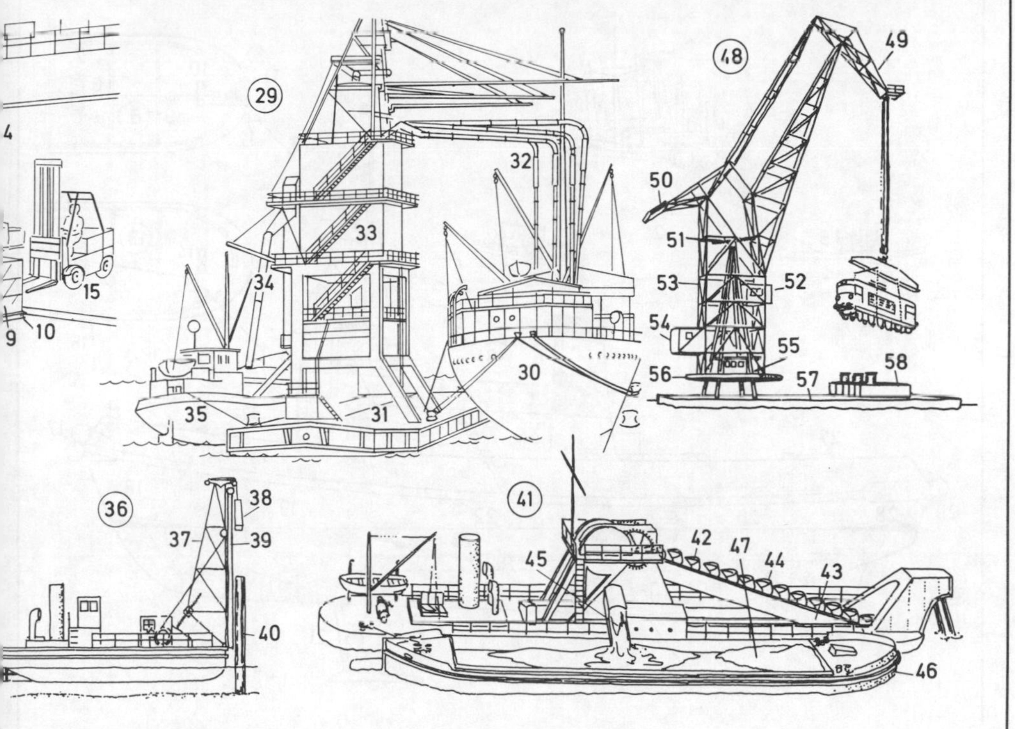

31 le ponton-grue de chargement *m*
– *floating bulk-cargo elevator*
32 les conduites d'aspiration *f*
– *suction pipes*
33 le récepteur
– *receiver*
34 la conduite de sortie *f*
– *delivery pipe*
35 la barge de transport *m* de vrac *m*
– *bulk transporter barge*
36 le batteur de pieux *m*
– *floating pile driver*
37 l'installation de battage *m*
– *pile driver frame*
38 le marteau de battage *m*
pile hammer
39 le rail de guidage *m*
– *driving guide rail*
40 le pieu
– *pile*
41 la drague à godets *m*
– *bucket dredger, a dredger*
42 la chaîne à godets *m* (le chapelet)
– *bucket chain*
43 l'élévateur à godets *m*
– *bucket ladder*
44 le godet de dragage *m*
– *dredger bucket*
45 le déversoir
– *chute*
46 le chaland de transport *m* (la marie-salope)
– *hopper barge*
47 les déchets *m*
– *spoil*
48 la grue flottante
– *floating crane*
49 la flèche de la grue
– *jib (boom)*
50 le contrepoids
– *counterweight (counterpoise)*
51 l'axe *m* de réglage *m*
– *adjusting spindle*
52 la cabine du grutier
– *crane driver's cabin (crane driver's cage)*
53 la charpente de la grue
– *crane framework*
54 la cabine du treuil
– *winch house*
55 la plate-forme de commande *m*
– *control platform*
56 la plaque tournante
– *turntable*
57 le ponton
– *pontoon, a pram*
58 l'abri *m* du moteur
– *engine superstructure (engine mounting)*

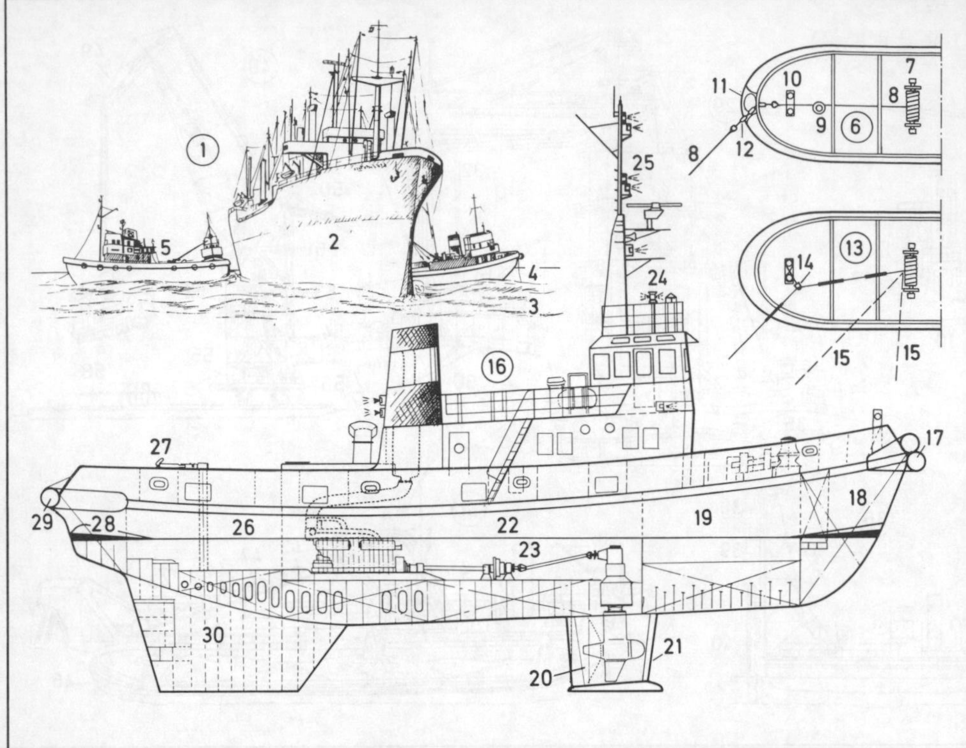

1 le sauvetage d'un navire échoué
– *salvaging (salving) of a ship run aground*

2 le navire échoué
– *ship run aground (damaged vessel)*

3 le banc de sable *m*
– *sandbank;* also: *quicksand*

4 la haute mer (le large, la pleine mer)
– *open sea*

5 le remorqueur de sauvetage *m*
– *tug (salvage tug)*

6-15 l'installation *f* de remorquage *m*
– *towing gear*

6 le matériel de remorquage *m* en mer *f*
– *towing gear for towing at sea*

7 le treuil de remorque *f*
– *towing winch (towing machine, towing engine)*

8 la remorque (le câble de remorque *f*)
– *tow rope (tow line, towing hawser)*

9 le guidage de la remorque
– *tow rope guide*

10 le chaumard
– *cross-shaped bollard*

11 l'écubier *m*
– *hawse hole*

12 le câble-chaîne
– *anchor cable (chain cable)*

13 le matériel de remorquage *m* au port *m*
– *towing gear for work in harbours* (Am. *harbors)*

14 la retenue
– *guest rope*

15 la position de la remorque en l'absence *f* de retenue *f*
– *position of the tow rope (tow line, towing hawser)*

16 le remorqueur (le remorqueur de sauvetage *m*) [coupe *f*]
– *tug (salvage tug) [vertical elevation]*

17 la défense d'étrave *f*
– *bow fender (pudding fender)*

18 le poste avant
– *forepeak*

19 les emménagements *m*
– *living quarters*

20 l'hélice *f* carénée
– *Schottel propeller*

21 la carène d'hélice *f*
– *Kort vent*

22 la salle des machines *f*
– *engine and propeller room*

23 le système d'accouplement *m*
– *clutch coupling*

24 la passerelle de navigation *f*
– *compass platform (compass bridge, compass flat, monkey bridge)*

25 le matériel de lutte *f* contre l'incendie *m*
– *fire-fighting equipment*

26 la soute
– *stowage*

27 le croc de remorquage *m*
– *tow hook*

28 le coqueron arrière
– *afterpeak*

29 la défense arrière
– *stern fender*

30 l'aileron *m* de manœuvre *f*
– *main manoeuvring* (Am. *maneuvering) keel*

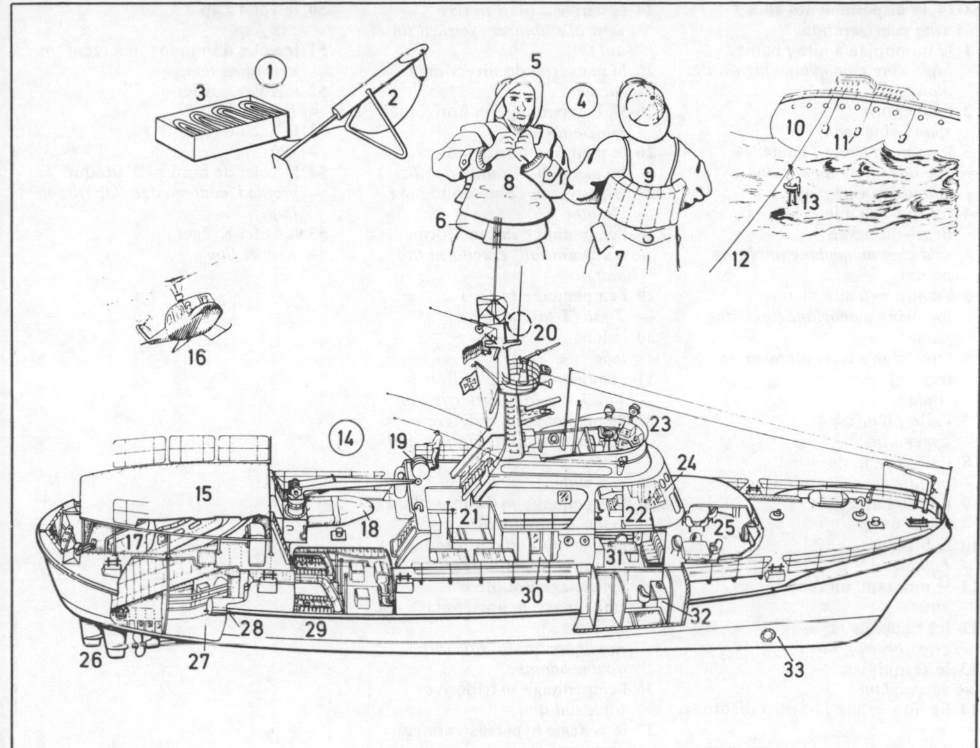

1 le lance-amarre (le porte-amarre, le canon porte-amarre)
– *rocket apparatus (rocket gun, line-throwing gun)*
2 la fusée porte-amarre
– *life rocket (rocket)*
3 la ligne de sauvetage *m*
– *rocket line (whip line)*
4 le ciré (le vêtement ciré)
– *oilskins*
5 le suroît
– *sou'wester (southwester)*
6 la veste de ciré *m*
– *oilskin jacket*
7 le manteau de ciré *m*
– *oilskin coat*
8 le gilet de sauvetage *m* gonflable
– *inflatable life jacket*
9 le gilet de sauvetage *m* en liège *m*
– *cork life jacket (cork life preserver)*
10 le navire échoué (le navire naufragé)
– *stranded ship (damaged vessel)*
11 le sac à huile *f* pour filer de l'huile *f* à la surface de l'eau *f*
– *oil bag, for trickling oil on the water surface*
12 le câble de sauvetage *m*
– *lifeline*
13 la bouée-culotte
– *breeches buoy*
14 la vedette de sauvetage *m* (le canot de sauvetage *m*)
– *rescue cruiser*
15 la plate-forme d'atterrissage *m* pour hélicoptère *m*
– *helicopter landing deck*
16 l'hélicoptère *m* de sauvetage *m*
– *rescue helicopter*
17 l'annexe *f*
– *daughter boat*
18 le canot pneumatique
– *inflatable boat (inflatable dinghy)*
19 le radeau de sauvetage *m*
– *life raft*
20 le matériel de lutte *f* contre l'incendie *m*
– *fire-fighting equipment for fires at sea*
21 l'infirmerie *f* avec la salle d'opération *f* et l'unité *f* de réanimation *f*
– *hospital unit with operating cabin and exposure bath*
22 la chambre de navigation *f*
– *navigating bridge*
23 la passerelle supérieure
– *upper tier of navigating bridge*
24 la passerelle inférieure
– *lower tier of navigating bridge*
25 le carré
– *messroom*
26 l'hélice *f* et le gouvernail
– *rudders and propeller (screw)*
27 la soute
– *stowage*
28 le réservoir de mousse *f* anti-incendie
– *foam can*
29 les moteurs *m* latéraux
– *side engines*
30 les douches *f*
– *shower*
31 la cabine du patron
– *coxswain's cabin*
32 la cabine d'un membre de l'équipage *m*
– *crew member's single-berth cabin*
33 l'hélice *f* d'étrave *f*
– *bow propeller*

1-14 la disposition des ailes *f*
– ***wing configurations***
1 le monoplan à aile *f* haute
– *high-wing monoplane (high-wing plane)*
2 l'envergure *f*
– *span (wing span)*
3 l'avion *m* à aile *f* haute
– *shoulder-wing monoplane (shoulder-wing plane)*
4 l'avion *m* à aile *f* demi-surélevée
– *midwing monoplane (midwing plane)*
5 l'avion *m* à aile *f* basse
– *low-wing monoplane (low-wing plane)*
6 l'avion *m* à trois plans *m* (le triplan)
– *triplane*
7 l'aile *f* haute
– *upper wing*
8 l'aile *f* centrale
– *middle wing (central wing)*
9 l'aile *f* basse
– *lower wing*
10 le biplan
– *biplane*
11 le montant, un renfort
– *strut*
12 les haubans *m*
– *cross bracing wires*
13 le sesquiplan
– *sesquiplane*
14 l'avion *m* aile *f* basse à dièdre *m*
– *low-wing monoplane (low-wing plane) with cranked wings (inverted gull wings)*
15-22 les formes *f* **d'ailes** *f*
– ***wing shapes***
15 l'aile *f* elliptique
– *elliptical wing*
16 l'aile *f* rectangulaire
– *rectangular wing*
17 l'aile *f* trapézoïdale
– *tapered wing*
18 l'aile *f* à double flèche *f*
– *crescent wing*
19 l'aile *f* delta
– *delta wing*
20 l'aile *f* à faible flèche *f*
– *swept-back wing with semi-positive sweepback*
21 l'aile *f* à forte flèche *f*
– *swept-back wing with positive sweepback*
22 l'aile *f* ogivale
– *ogival wing (ogee wing)*
23-36 les différentes formes *f* **d'empennage** *m*
– ***tail shapes*** *(tail unit shapes, empennage shapes)*
23 l'empennage *m* courant
– *normal tail (normal tail unit)*
24-25 l'empennage *m* de direction *f*
– *vertical tail (vertical stabilizer and rudder)*
24 la dérive à plan *m* fixe
– *vertical stabilizer (vertical fin, tail fin)*
25 la gouverne de direction *f*
– *rudder*
26-27 l'empennage *m* horizontal
– *horizontal tail*
26 le plan fixe horizontal
– *tailplane (horizontal stabilizer)*
27 la gouverne de profondeur *f*
– *elevator*
28 l'empennage *m* cruciforme
– *cruciform tail (cruciform tail unit)*
29 l'empennage *m* en T
– *T-tail (T-tail unit)*
30 le lobe
– *lobe*
31 l'empennage *m* papillon *m*
– *V-tail (vee-tail, butterfly tail)*
32 l'empennage *m* bidérive
– *double tail unit (twin tail unit)*
33 la dérive gauche
– *end plate*
34 l'empennage *m* double (d'un avion *m* bipoutre)
– *double tail unit (twin tail unit) of a twin-boom aircraft*
35 le fuselage double à empennage *m* horizontal surélevé
– *raised horizontal tail with double booms*
36 l'empennage *m* tridérive
– *triple tail unit*
37 le système hypersustentateur
– ***system of flaps***
38 le bec de sécurité *f* mobile
– *extensible slat*
39 le spoiler (*ELF:* le déporteur)
– *spoiler*
40 le volet à double courbure *f*
– *double-slotted Fowler flap*
41 l'aileron *m* extérieur
– *outer aileron (low-speed aileron)*
42 les aérofreins *m* internes
– *inner spoiler (landing flap, lift dump)*
43 l'aileron *m* intérieur
– *inner aileron (all-speed aileron)*
44 les aérofreins *m* externes
– *brake flap (air brake)*
45 le profil lisse (le profil de base *f*)
– *basic profile*
46-48 les volets *m* de courbure *f*
– *plain flaps (simple flaps)*
46 le volet de courbure *f*
– *normal flap*
47 le volet de courbure *f* à fente *f*
– *slotted flap*
48 le volet de courbure *f* à double fente *f*
– *double-slotted flap*
49-50 les volets *m* d'intrados *m*
– *split flaps*
49 le volet d'intrados *m*
– *plain split flap (simple split flap)*
50 le volet Zap
– *zap flap*
51 le volet d'intrados *m* à recul *m*
– *extending flap*
52 le volet Fowler
– *Fowler flap*
53 le bec de sécurité *f*
– *slat*
54 le volet de bord *m* d'attaque *f*
– *profiled leading-edge flap (droop flap)*
55 le volet Krüger
– *Krüger flap*

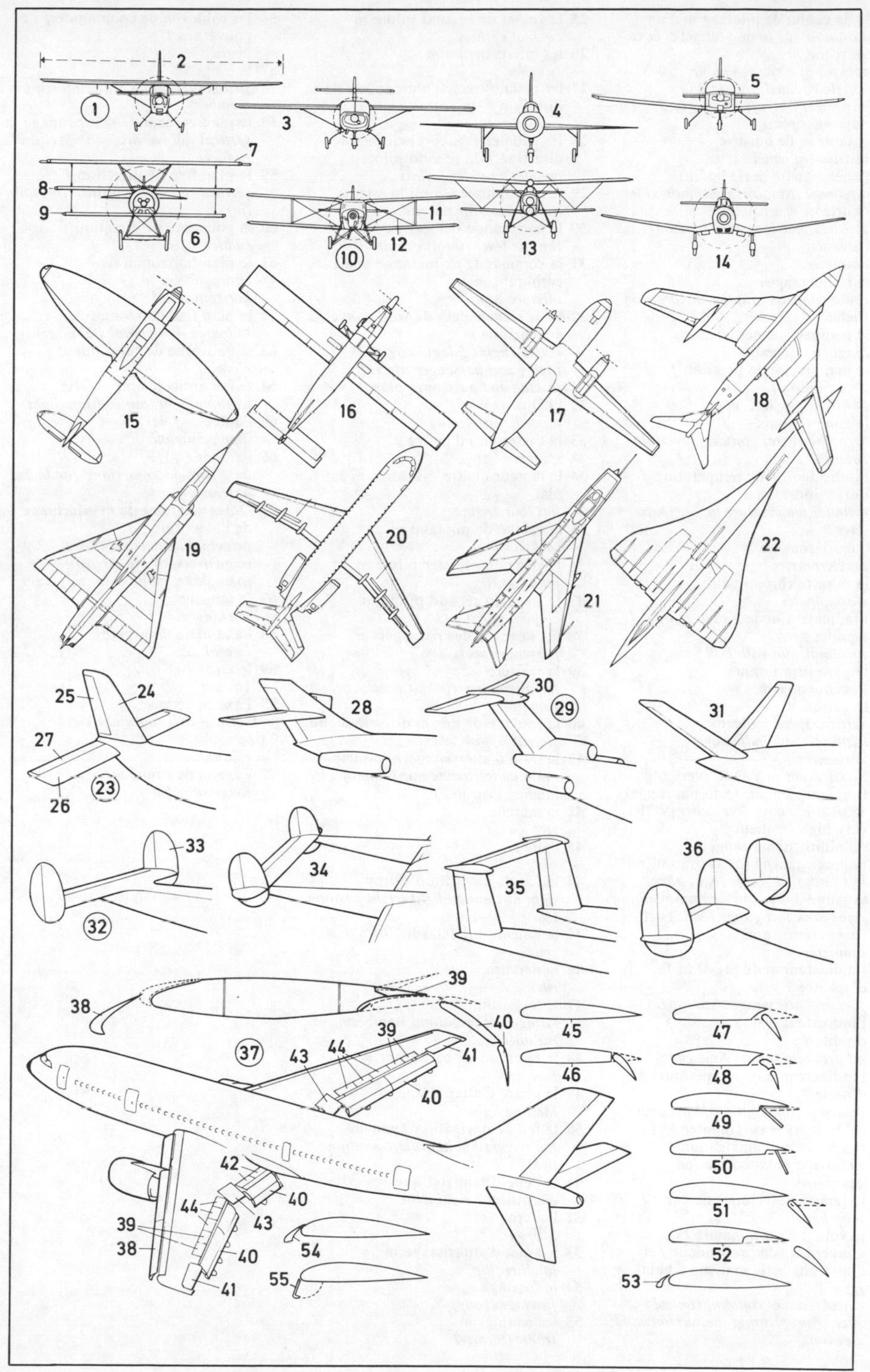

1
2
3
4
5
6
7
8
9
10
11
12
13
14
15
16
17
18
19
20
21
22
23
24
25
26
27
28
29
30
31
32
33
34
35
36
37
38
39
40
41
42
43
44
45
46
47
48
49
50
51
52
53
54
55

1-31 la cabine de pilotage *m* d'un monomoteur *m* de voltige *m* et de tourisme *m*
– ***cockpit*** *of a single-engine (single-engined) racing and passenger aircraft (racing and passenger plane)*
1 le tableau de bord *m*
– *instrument panel*
2 l'anémomètre *m* (le badin)
– *air-speed* (Am. *airspeed) indicator*
3 l'horizon *m* artificiel
– *artificial horizon (gyro horizon)*
4 l'altimètre *m*
– *altimeter*
5 le radiocompas
– *radio compass (automatic direction finder)*
6 le compas magnétique
– *magnetic compass*
7 le manomètre de pression *f* d'admission *f*
– *boost gauge* (Am. *gage)*
8 le compte-tours
– *tachometer (rev counter, revolution counter)*
9 l'indicateur *m* de température *f* des cylindres *m*
– *cylinder temperature gauge* (Am. *gage)*
10 l'accéléromètre *m*
– *accelerometer*
11 la montre chronomètre
– *chronometer*
12 l'indicateur *m* de virage *m* bille *f* aiguille *f*
– *turn indicator with ball*
13 le gyro directionnel
– *directional gyro*
14 le variomètre
– *vertical speed indicator (rate-of-climb indicator, variometer)*
15 l'indicateur *m* V.O.R. (very high frequency omnidirectional range)
– *VOR radio direction finder* [VOR: very high frequency omnidirectional range]
16 la jauge gauche (de carburant *m*)
– *left tank fuel gauge* (Am. *gage)*
17 la jauge droite (de carburant *m*)
– *right tank fuel gauge* (Am. *gage)*
18 l'ampèremètre *m*
– *ammeter*
19 l'indicateur *m* de pression *f* d'essence *f*
– *fuel pressure gauge* (Am. *gage)*
20 l'indicateur *m* de pression *f* d'huile *f*
– *oil pressure gauge* (Am. *gage)*
21 l'indicateur *m* de température *f* d'huile *f*
– *oil temperature gauge* (Am. *gage)*
22 les boîtiers *m* de commande *f* radio *f* et radionavigation *f*
– *radio and radio navigation equipment*
23 la lampe de lecture *f* de carte *f*
– *map light*
24 le volant de commande *f* des gouvernes *f* de profondeur *f* et d'ailerons *m* (le manche à balai *m*)
– *wheel (control column, control stick) for operating the ailerons and elevators*
25 le volant du second pilote *m*
– *co-pilot's wheel*
26 les interrupteurs *m*
– *switches*
27 les pédales *m* de commande *f* de direction *f*
– *rudder pedals*
28 les pédales *f* de commande *f* de direction *f* du second pilote
– *co-pilot's rudder pedals*
29 le microphone (*fam.:* le micro)
– *microphone for the radio*
30 la commande des gaz *m*
– *throttle lever (throttle control)*
31 la commande de mélange *m* air - carburant *m*
– *mixture control*

32-66 le monomoteur de voltige *m* **et de tourisme** *m*
– ***single-engine (single-engined) racing and passenger aircraft (racing and passenger plane)***
32 l'hélice *f*
– *propeller (airscrew)*
33 la casserole *f* d'hélice *f*
– *spinner*
34 le moteur quatre cylindres *m* à plat
– *flat four engine*
35 la cabine de pilotage *m*
– *cockpit*
36 le siège du premier pilote *m*
– *pilot's seat*
37 le siège du second pilote *m*
– *co-pilot's seat*
38 les sièges *m* des passagers *m*
– *passenger seats*
39 la verrière
– *hood (canopy, cockpit hood, cockpit canopy)*
40 la roulette de nez *m* directionnelle
– *steerable nose wheel*
41 le train d'atterrissage *m* principal
– *main undercarriage unit (main landing gear unit)*
42 la marche
– *step*
43 l'aile *f*
– *wing*
44 le feu de navigation *f* droit
– *right navigation light (right position light)*
45 le longeron (l'extrados *m*)
– *spar*
46 la nervure
– *rib*
47 le longeron
– *stringer (longitudinal reinforcing member)*
48 le réservoir de carburant *m*
– *fuel tank*
49 le phare d'atterrissage *m*
– *landing light*
50 le feu de navigation *f* gauche
– *left navigation light (left position light)*
51 le déperditeur statique
– *electrostatic conductor*
52 l'aileron *m*
– *aileron*
53 le volet d'atterrissage *m*
– *landing flap*
54 le fuselage
– *fuselage (body)*
55 les couples *m*
– *frame (former)*
56 les câbles *m* de commande *f* des gouvernes *f*
– *chord*
57 le longeron
– *stringer (longitudinal reinforcing member)*
58 le plan vertical de l'empennage *m*
– *vertical tail (vertical stabilizer and rudder)*
59 le plan fixe de direction *f*
– *vertical stabilizer (vertical fin, tail fin)*
60 la gouverne de direction *f*
– *rudder*
61 le plan horizontal de l'empennage *m*
– *horizontal tail*
62 le plan fixe horizontal
– *tailplane (horizontal stabilizer)*
63 la gouverne de profondeur *f*
– *elevator*
64 le feu anticollision
– *warning light (anticollision light)*
65 l'antenne *f* VHF
– *dipole antenna*
66 l'antenne *f* HF
– *long-wire antenna (long-conductor antenna)*

67-72 les mouvements *m* **principaux** de l'avion *m*
– ***principal manoeuvres*** (Am. *maneuvers) of the aircraft (aeroplane, plane,* Am. *airplane)*
67 le tangage
– *pitching*
68 l'axe *m* de tangage *m*
– *lateral axis*
69 le lacet
– *yawing*
70 l'axe *m* de lacet *m*
– *vertical axis (normal axis)*
71 le roulis
– *rolling*
72 l'axe *m* de roulis *m*
– *longitudinal axis*

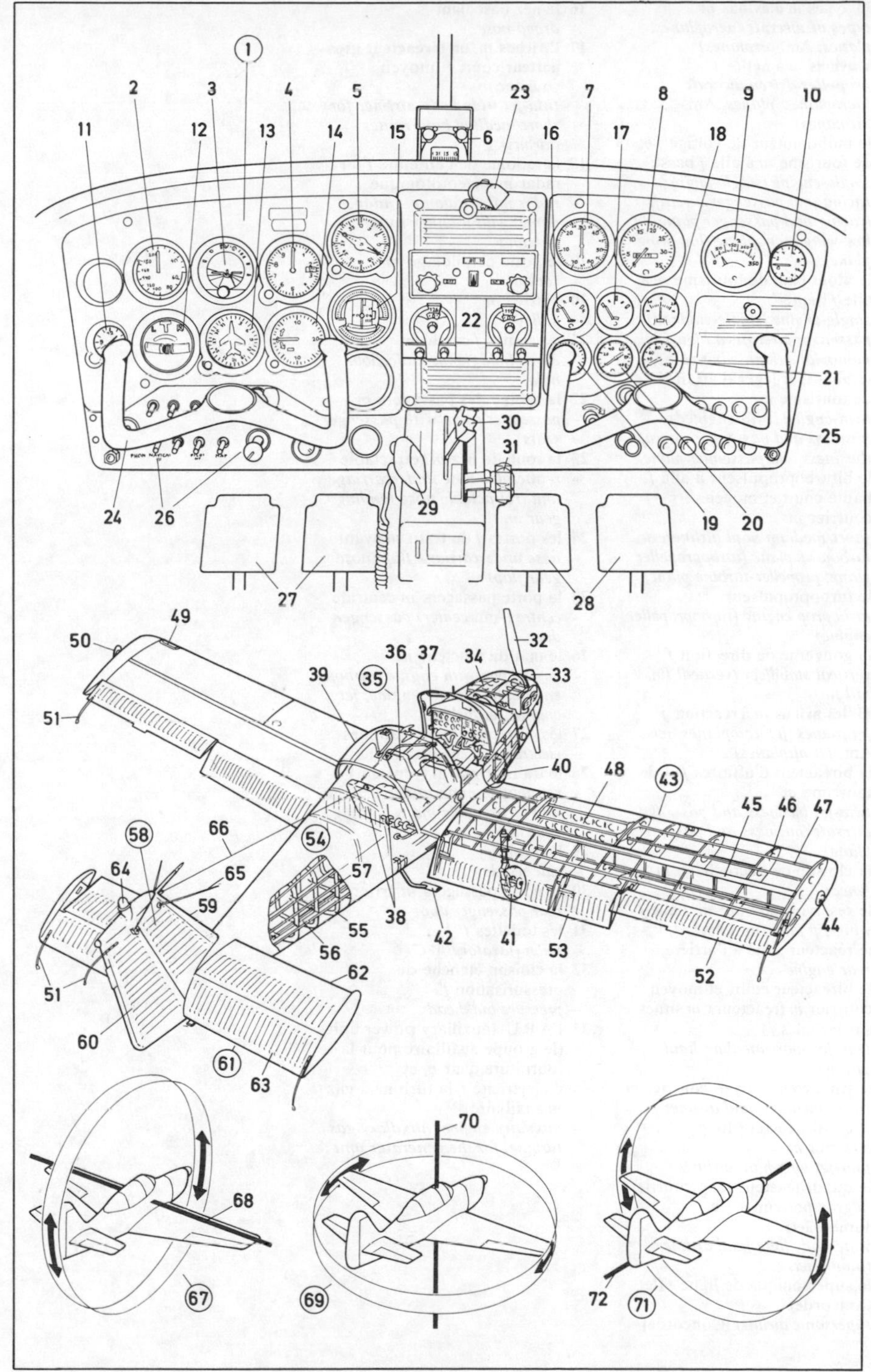
1
2
3
4
5
6
7
8
9
10
11
12
13
14
15
16
17
18
19
20
21
22
23
24
25
26
27
28
29
30
31
32
33
34
35
36
37
38
39
40
41
42
43
44
45
46
47
48
49
50
51
52
53
54
55
56
57
58
59
60
61
62
63
64
65
66
67
68
69
70
71
72

1-33 types *m* **d'avions** *m*
- ***types of aircraft*** *(aeroplanes, planes,* Am. *airplanes)*

1-6 avions *m* **à hélice** *f*
- ***propeller-driven aircraft*** *(aeroplanes, planes,* Am. *airplanes)*

1 le monomoteur de voltige *f* et de tourisme *m* à aile *f* basse
- *single-engine (single-engined) racing and passenger aircraft (racing and passenger plane), a low-wing monoplane (low-wing plane)*

2 le monoplan de tourisme *m* à aile *f* haute
- *single-engine (single-engined) passenger aircraft, a high-wing monoplane (high-wing plane)*

3 le bimoteur léger d'affaires *f* et de tourisme *m*
- *twin-engine (twin-engined) business and passenger aircraft (business and passenger plane)*

4 le biturbopropulseur à aile *f* haute court et moyen courrier *m*
- *short/medium haul airliner, a turboprop plane (turbopropeller plane, propeller-turbine plane)*

5 le turbopropulseur
- *turboprop engine (turbopropeller engine)*

6 la gouverne de direction *f*
- *vertical stabilizer (vertical fin, tail fin)*

7-33 les avions *m* **à réaction** *f*
- ***jet planes*** *(jet aeroplanes, jets,* Am. *jet airplanes)*

7 le biréacteur d'affaires *f* et de tourisme *m*
- *twin-jet business and passenger aircraft (business and passenger plane)*

8 la cloison de décrochage *m*
- *fence*

9 le réservoir de bout *m* d'aile *f*
- *wing-tip tank (tip tank)*

10 le réacteur situé à l'arrière
- *rear engine*

11 le biréacteur court et moyen courrier *m* (réacteurs *m* situés sur les ailes *f*)
- *twin-jet short/medium haul airliner*

12 le triréacteur moyen courrier *m*
- *tri-jet medium haul airliner*

13 le quadriréacteur long courrier *m*
- *four-jet long haul airliner*

14 le quadriréacteur long courrier *m* gros porteur *m* (le Jumbo-Jet)
- *wide-body long haul airliner (jumbo jet)*

15 le supersonique de ligne *f* (le Concorde)
- *supersonic airliner* [Concorde]

16 le nez basculant
- *droop nose*

17 l'Airbus *m*, **un biréacteur gros porteur** court et moyen courrier *m*
- ***twin-jet wide-body airliner*** *for short/medium haul routes (airbus)*

18 le radome de l'antenne *f* du radar *m* météorologique
- *radar nose (radome, radar dome) with weather radar antenna*

19 le poste de pilotage *m*
- *cockpit*

20 l'office *m*
- *galley*

21 les soutes *f* cargo *m*
- *cargo hold (hold, underfloor hold)*

22 la cabine des passagers *m*
- *passenger cabin with passenger seats*

23 la roue de nez *m* rétractable
- *retractable nose undercarriage unit (retractable nose landing gear unit)*

24 les portes *f* du train *m* avant
- *nose undercarriage flap (nose gear flap)*

25 la porte passagers *m* centrale
- *centre (*Am. *center) passenger door*

26 le mât du réacteur *m*
- *engine pod with engine (turbojet engine, jet turbine engine, jet engine, jet turbine)*

27 les déperditeurs *m* statiques
- *electrostatic conductors*

28 le train principal (rentrant)
- *retractable main undercarriage unit (retractable main landing gear unit)*

29 le hublot
- *side window*

30 la porte passagers *m* arrière
- *rear passenger door*

31 les toilettes *f*
- *toilet (lavatory, WC)*

32 la cloison étanche de pressurisation *f*
- *pressure bulkhead*

33 l'A.P.U. (auxiliary power unit) (le groupe auxiliaire pour la fourniture d'air *m* et d'électricité *f*, la turbine à gaz *m* auxiliaire)
- *auxiliary engine (auxiliary gas turbine) for the generator unit*

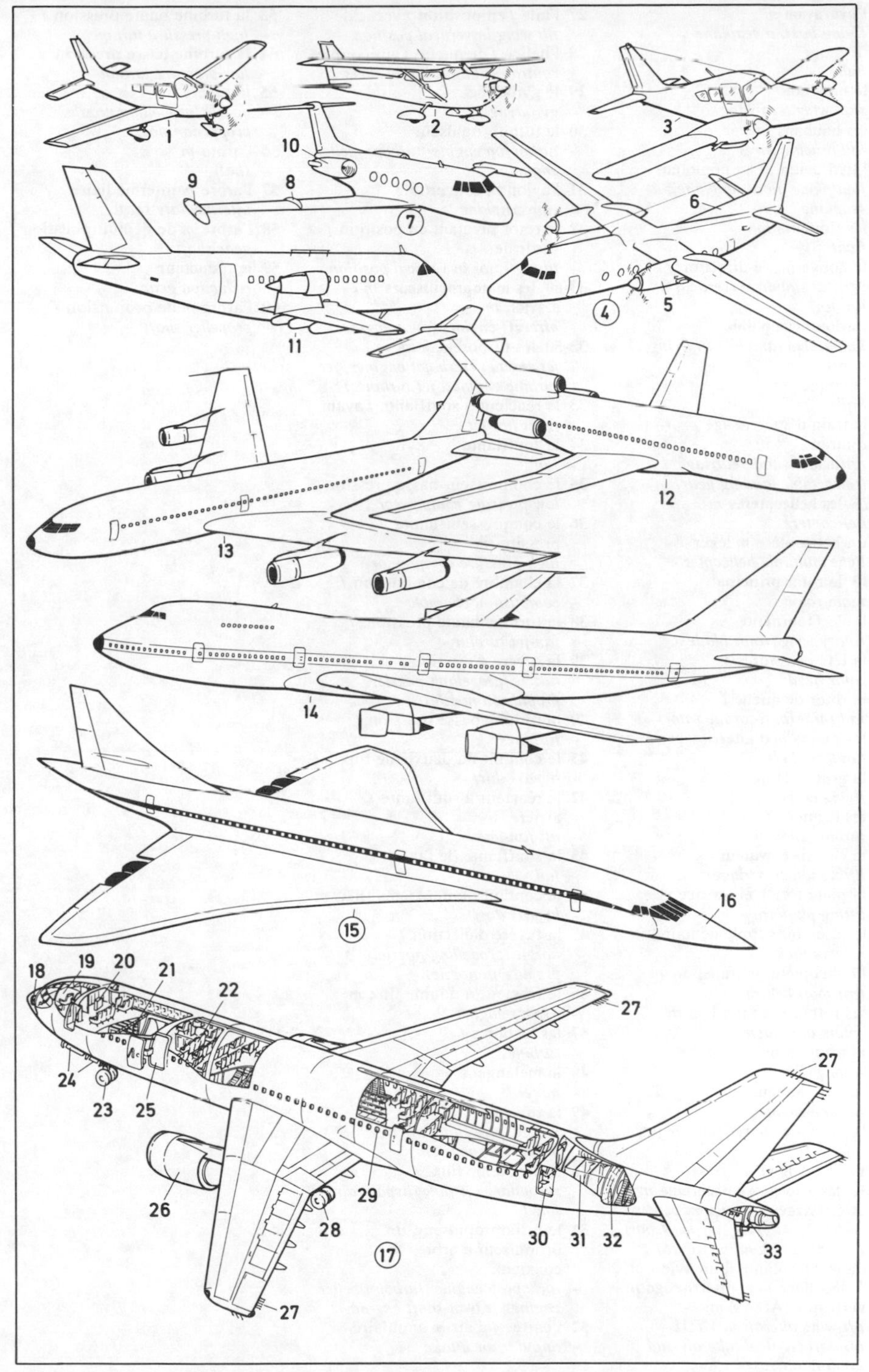
1
2
3
4
5
6
7
8
9
10
11
12
13
14
15
16
17
18
19
20
21
22
23
24
25
26
27
28
29
30
31
32
33

1 l'hydravion *m*
– ***flying boat****, a seaplane*
2 la coque
– *hull*
3 le moignon
– *stub wing (sea wing)*
4 les haubans *m*
– *tail bracing wires*
5 l'hydravion *m* monomoteur
– *floatplane (float seaplane), a seaplane*
6 les flotteurs *m*
– *float*
7 la gouverne de direction *f*
– *vertical stabilizer (vertical fin, tail fin)*
8 l'avion *m* **amphibie**
– ***amphibian*** *(amphibian flying boat)*
9 la coque
– *hull*
10 le train d'atterrissage *m* rentrant
– *retractable undercarriage (retractable landing gear)*
11-25 les hélicoptères *m*
– ***helicopters***
11 un hélicoptère *m* léger
– *light multirole helicopter*
12-13 le rotor principal
– *main rotor*
12 l'aile *f* tournante
– *rotary wing (rotor blade)*
13 la tête de rotor *m*
– *rotor head*
14 le rotor de queue *f*
– *tail rotor (anti-torque rotor)*
15 les patins *m* d'atterrissage *m*
– *landing skids*
16 la grue volante
– *flying crane*
17 les turbines *f*
– *turbine engines*
18 le châssis élévateur
– *lifting undercarriage*
19 la plate-forme élévatrice
– *lifting platform*
20 le réservoir supplémentaire
– *reserve tank*
21 l'hélicoptère de transport *m*
– *transport helicopter*
22 les rotors *m* en tandem *m*
– *rotors in tandem*
23 le rotor en pylone *m*
– *rotor pylon*
24 le turbomoteur
– *turbine engine*
25 la porte de chargement *m* (en queue *f*)
– *tail loading gate*
26-32 les avions *m* **à décollage** *m* **et atterrissage** *m* **verticaux courts**
– ***V/STOL aircraft*** *(vertical/short take-off and landing aircraft)*
26 l'aile *f* pivotante d'un avion *m* à décollage *m* et atterrissage *m* verticaux (ADAV *m*)
– *tilt-wing aircraft, a VTOL aircraft (vertical take-off and landing aircraft)*
27 l'aile *f* en position *f* verticale
– *tilt wing in vertical position*
28 l'hélice *f* de queue *f* anticouple
– *contrarotating tail propellers*
29 le gyrodyne
– *gyrodyne*
30 le turbopropulseur
– *turboprop engine (turbopropeller engine)*
31 l'avion *m* convertible
– *convertiplane*
32 le rotor pivotant en position *f* verticale
– *tilting rotor in vertical position*
33-60 les motopropulseurs *m* **d'avion** *m*
– ***aircraft engines*** *(aero engines)*
33-50 les turboréacteurs *m*
– *jet engines (turbojet engines, jet turbine engines, jet turbines)*
33 le réacteur à soufflante *f* avant
– *front fan-jet*
34 la soufflante
– *fan*
35 le compresseur basse pression *f*
– *low-pressure compressor*
36 le compresseur haute pression *f*
– *high-pressure compressor*
37 la chambre de combustion *f*
– *combustion chamber*
38 la turbine haute pression *f*
– *fan-jet turbine*
39 la tuyère d'éjection *f*
– *nozzle (propelling nozzle, propulsion nozzle)*
40 la turbine basse pression *f*
– *turbines*
41 le conduit du deuxième flux *m*
– *bypass duct*
42 le réacteur à soufflante *f* arrière
– *aft fan-jet*
43 la soufflante (le fan)
– *fan*
44 le conduit du deuxième flux *m*
– *bypass duct*
45 la tuyère d'éjection *f*
– *nozzle (propelling nozzle, propulsion nozzle)*
46 le réacteur à double flux *m*
– *bypass engine*
47 les turbines *f*
– *turbines*
48 le mélangeur
– *mixer*
49 la tuyère
– *nozzle (propelling nozzle, propulsion nozzle)*
50 le deuxième flux
– *secondary air flow (bypass air flow)*
51 le turbopropulseur, un propulseur à arbres *m* coaxiaux
– *turboprop engine (turbopropeller engine), a twin-shaft engine*
52 l'entrée *f* d'air *m* annulaire
– *annular air intake*
53 la turbine haute pression *f*
– *high-pressure turbine*
54 la turbine basse pression *f*
– *low-pressure turbine*
55 la tuyère
– *nozzle (propelling nozzle, propulsion nozzle)*
56 l'arbre *m*
– *shaft*
57 l'arbre *m* intermédiaire
– *intermediate shaft*
58 l'arbre *m* de démultiplication *f*
– *gear shaft*
59 le réducteur
– *reduction gear*
60 l'arbre *m* de propulsion *f*
– *propeller shaft*

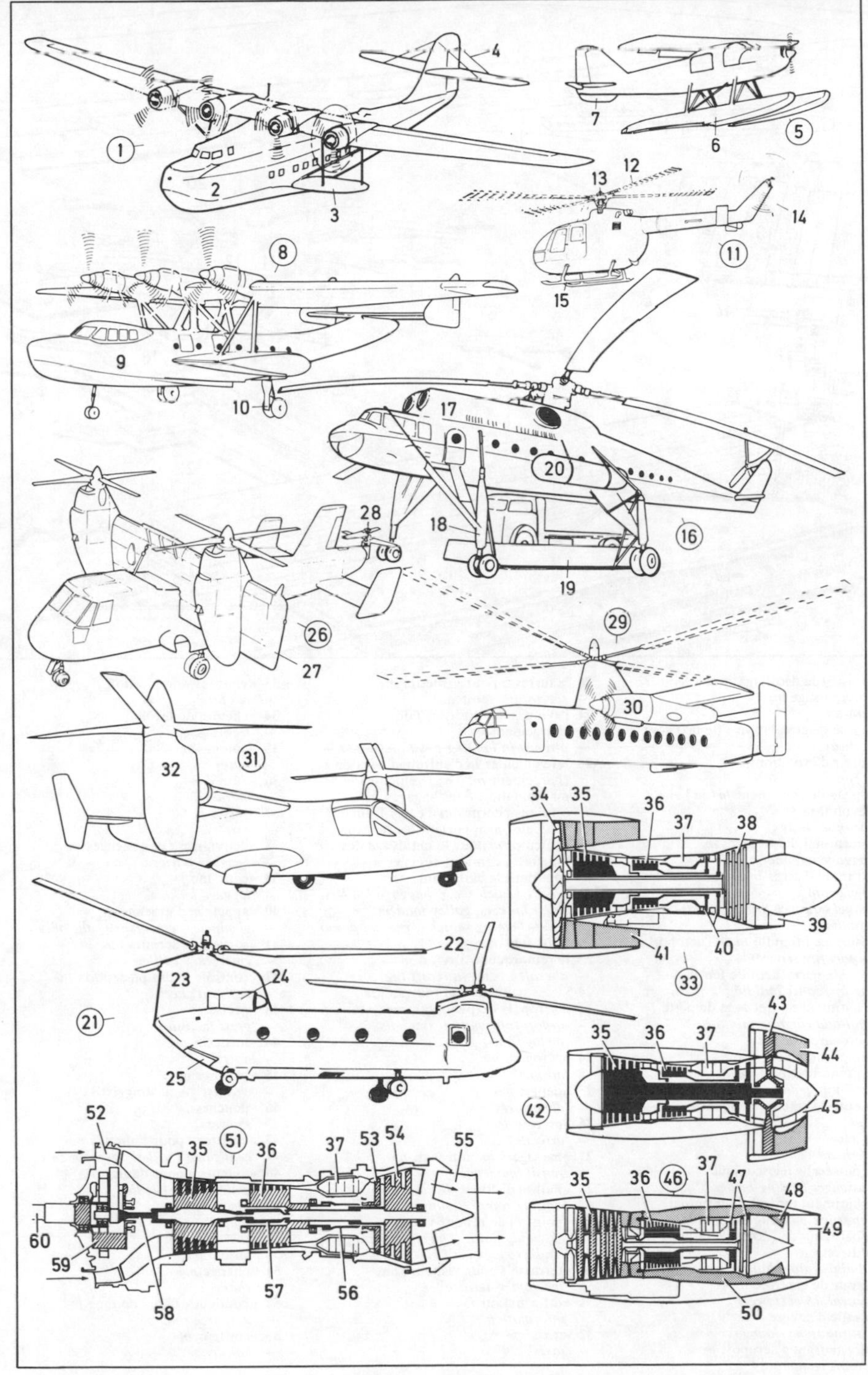
4
7
5
6
1
2
3
13 12
14
11
15
8
9
10
17
20
16
18
19
28
26
27
29
30
31
32
34 35 36 37 38
39
40
41
33
22
23 24
21
25
43
35 36 37
44
42
45
52
51
35 36 37 53 54 55
60
59
57 56
58
37 46
35 36 47
48
49
50

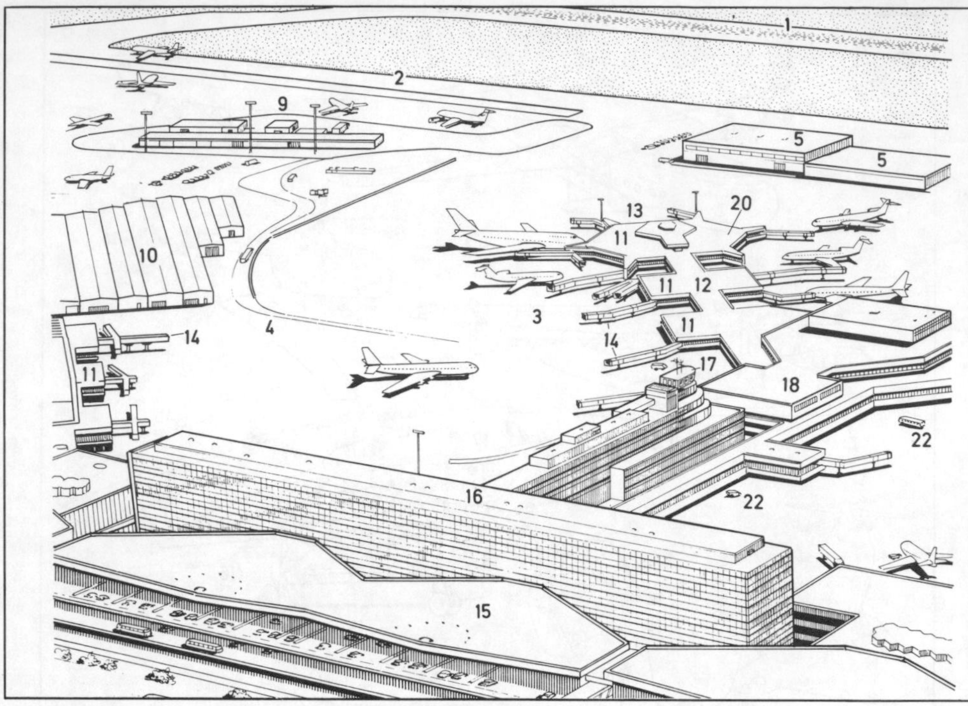

1 la piste (de décollage *m* et d'atterrissage *m*)
– *runway*
2 la voie de circulation *f* (le taxiway)
– *taxiway*
3 l'aire *f* d'évolution *f*
– *apron*
4 la piste de roulement *m* (de l'aire *f* d'évolution *f*)
– *apron taxiway*
5 le terminal des bagages *m*
– *baggage terminal*
6 le tunnel d'accès *m* au terminal des bagages *m*
– *tunnel entrance to the baggage terminal*
7 le service incendie *m* de l'aéroport *m*
– *airport fire service*
8 le poste permanent de feu *m*
– *fire appliance building*
9 le bâtiment de fret *m* et de poste *f*
– *mail and cargo terminal*
10 l'aérogare *f* du fret
– *cargo warehouse*
11 le point de départ *m*
– *assembly point*
12 la porte d'embarquement *m*
– *pier*
13 la jetée
– *pierhead*
14 la passerelle téléscopique
– *passenger loading bridge*
15 le bâtiment central (le terminal)
– *departure building (terminal)*
16 le bâtiment de l'administration *f* et de la direction
– *administration building*
17 la tour de contrôle *m*
– *control tower (tower)*
18 la salle d'attente *f*
– *waiting room (lounge)*
19 le restaurant d'aéroport *m*
– *airport restaurant*
20 la terrasse pour visiteurs *m*
– *spectators' terrace*
21 l'avion *m* en position *f* de chargement *m*
– *aircraft in loading position (nosed in)*
22 les véhicules *m* d'entretien *m* et de chargement *m*; p.ex.: véhicules *m* de manipulation *f* des bagages *m*, camions-citernes *m* d'eau *f* fraîche, véhicules *m* apportant les repas *m*, véhicules *m* pour le nettoyage des toilettes *f*, camions-citernes *m* apportant le carburant
– *service vehicles, e.g. baggage loaders, water tankers, galley loaders, toilet-cleaning vehicles, ground power units, tankers*
23 le remorqueur d'avion *m*
– *aircraft tractor (aircraft tug)*
24-53 les panneaux *m* indicateurs d'aéroport *m* (pictogrammes *m*)
– *airport information symbols (pictographs)*
24 «aéroport *m*»
– *'airport'*
25 «départ *m*»
– *'departures'*
26 «arrivée *f*»
– *'arrivals'*
27 «passagers *m* en transit *m*»
– *transit 'passengers'*
28 «hall *m* d'attente *f*»
– *'waiting room' ('lounge')*
29 «point *m* de rendez-vous *m*»
– *'assembly point' ('meeting point', 'rendezvous point')*
30 «terrasse *f* pour visiteurs *m*»
– *'spectators' terrace'*
31 «information *f*»
– *'information'*
32 «taxis *m*»
– *'taxis'*
33 «voitures *f* de location *f*»
– *'car hire'*
34 «chemin de fer *m*»
– *'trains'*
35 «autobus *m*»
– *'buses'*
36 «entrée *f*»
– *'entrance'*
37 «sortie *f*»
– *'exit'*
38 «délivrance *f* des bagages *m*»
– *'baggage retrieval'*
39 «consigne *f*»
– *'luggage lockers'*
40 «appels *m* d'urgence *f*»
– *telephone - 'emergency calls only'*
41 «sortie *f* de secours *m*»
– *'emergency exit'*
42 «contrôle *m* des passeports *m*»
– *'passport check'*
43 «presse *f*»
– *'press facilities'*
44 «médecin *m*»
– *'doctor'*
45 «pharmacie *f*»
– *'chemist'* (Am. *druggist'*)
46 «douches *f*»
– *'showers'*
47 «toilettes *f* pour hommes *m*»
– *'gentlemen's toilet' ('gentlemen')*
48 «toilettes *f* pour dames *f*»
– *'ladies toilet' ('ladies')*
49 «chapelle *f*»
– *'chapel'*
50 «restaurant *m*»
– *'restaurant'*
51 «change *m*»
– *'change'*
52 «boutiques *f* hors douane *f*»
– *'duty free shop'*
53 «coiffeur *m*»
– *'hairdresser'*

2
4
6
7
2
8
3
19
20
14
11
13
14
4
21
23
22
3
22
12
11
11

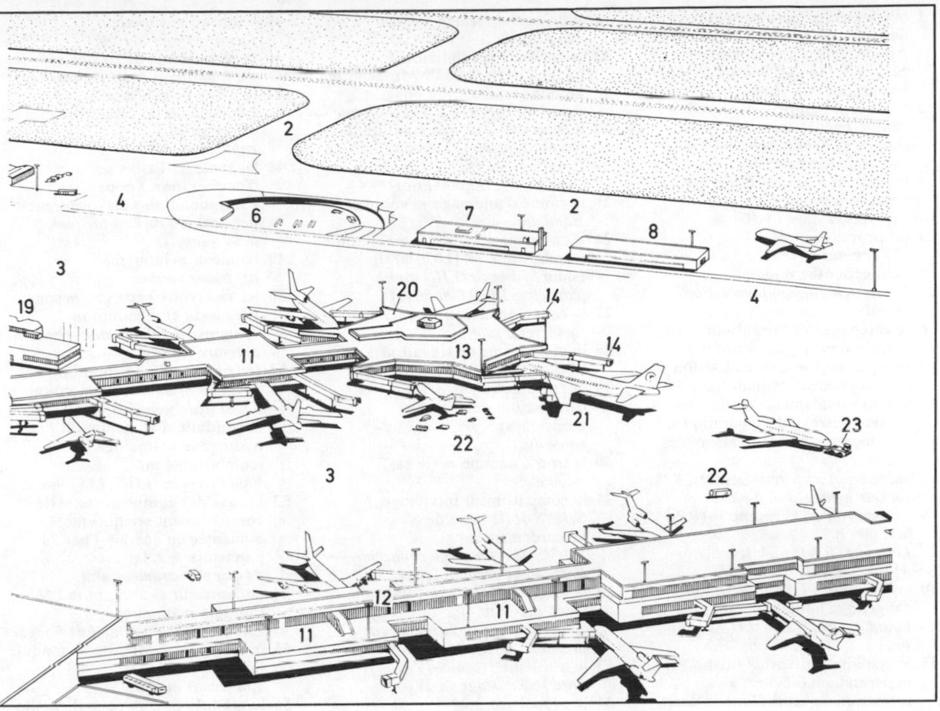

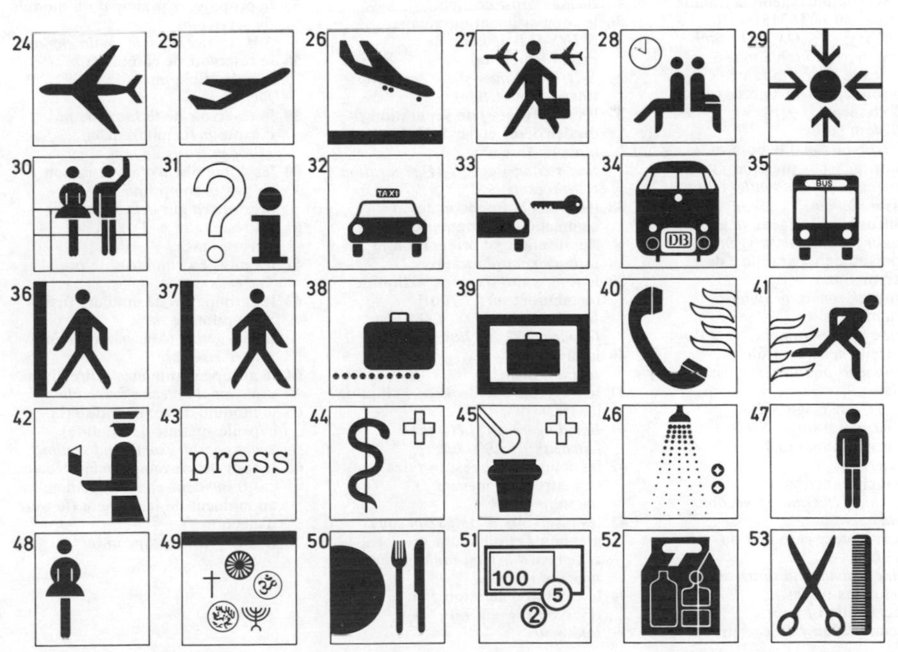

24
25
26
27
28
29
30
31
32
TAXI
33
34
DB
35
BUS
36
37
38
39
40
41
42
43
press
44
45
46
47
48
49
50
51
100
5
2
52
53

1 **le lanceur (la fusée porteuse) Saturn V d'«Apollo»** (du satellite Apollo) [vue *f* d'ensemble *m*]
– ***Saturn V 'Apollo' booster*** *(booster rocket) [overall view]*
2 le lanceur Saturn V d'«Apollo» [coupe *f* générale]
– *Saturn V 'Apollo' booster (booster rocket) [overall sectional view]*
3 le premier étage *S-1C* (l'étage *m* de décollage *m*)
– *first rocket stage (S-IC)*
4 les propulseurs *m* F-1
– *F-1 engines*
5 le bouclier thermique
– *heat shield (thermal protection shield)*
6 le carénage des propulseurs *m*
– *aerodynamic engine fairings*
7 l'empennage *m* de stabilisation *f* (le stabilisateur, le plan fixe)
– *aerodynamic stabilizing fins*
8 les rétrofusées *f* de séparation *f*, huit moteurs-fusées *m* assemblés par paires *f*
– *stage separation retro-rockets, 8 rockets arranged in 4 pairs*
9 le réservoir de kérosène *m* (RP-1) [811 000 l]
– *kerosene (RP-1) tank [capacity: 811,000 litres]*
10 les conduites *f* d'alimentation *f* en oxygène *m* liquide (comburant *m*)
– *liquid oxygen (LOX, LO_2) supply lines*
11 le système anti-vortex (dispositif *m* permettant d'éviter la formation de tourbillons *m* dans le carburant)
– *anti-vortex system (device for preventing the formation of vortices in the fuel)*
12 le réservoir d'oxygène *m* liquide (comburant *m*) [1 315 000 l]
– *liquid oxygen (LOX, LO_2) tank [capacity: 1,315,000 litres]*
13 la chicane antiballottante (cloisonnement *m* amortissant le ballottement)
– *anti-slosh baffles*
14 les réservoirs *m* d'hélium *m* comprimé (sous pression *f*)
– *compressed-helium bottles (helium pressure bottles)*
15 le diffuseur d'oxygène *m* gazeux
– *diffuser for gaseous oxygen*
16 la cloison de séparation *f* des réservoirs *m*
– *inter-tank connector (inter-tank section)*
17 le bloc des instruments *m* et des appareils *m* de contrôle *m*
– *instruments and system-monitoring devices*
18 le deuxième étage *S-II*
– *second rocket stage (S-II)*
19 les propulseurs *m* J-2
– *J-2 engines*
20 le bouclier thermique
– *heat shield (thermal protection shield)*
21 le bâti moteur et le bâti de poussée *f*
– *engine mounts and thrust structure*
22 les moteurs-fusées *m* d'accélération *f* pour l'accumulation *f* du carburant
– *acceleration rockets for fuel acquisition*
23 la conduite d'admission *f* (d'aspiration *f*) de l'hydrogène *m* liquide (combustible *m*)
– *liquid hydrogen (LH_2) suction line*
24 le réservoir d'oxygène *m* liquide (comburant *m*) [1 315 000 l]
– *liquid oxygen (LOX, LO_2) tank [capacity: 1,315,000 litres]*
25 la canne d'allumage *m* verticale
– *standpipe*
26 le réservoir d'hydrogène *m* liquide (combustible *m*) [1 020 000 l]
– *liquid hydrogen (LH_2) tank [capacity: 1,020,000 litres]*
27 la canne de niveau *m*
– *fuel level sensor*
28 la plate-forme de travail *m*
– *work platform (working platform)*
29 la gaine de câbles *m* (la canalisation de câbles *m* électriques)
– *cable duct*
30 le trou d'homme *m* (le sas)
– *manhole*
31 le compartiment interétage *S-IC/S-II* (le cône de raccordement *m*)
– *S-IC/S-II inter-stage connector (inter-stage section)*
32 le réservoir de gaz *m* comprimé (sous pression *f*)
– *compressed-gas container (gas pressure vessel)*
33 le troisième étage *S-IV B*
– *third rocket stage (S-IVB)*
34 le propulseur J-2
– *J-2 engine*
35 le cône de poussée *f* (d'échappement *m*) de la tuyère d'éjection *f*
– *nozzle (thrust nozzle)*
36 le compartiment interétage *S-II/S-IVB* (le cône de raccordement *m*)
– *S-II/S-IVB inter-stage connector (inter-stage section)*
37 les rétrofusées *f* de séparation *f* du deuxième étage *S-II*, 4 moteurs-fusées *m*
– *four second-stage (S-II) separation retro-rockets*
38 les moteurs-fusées *m* de commande *f* d'orientation *f* (de stabilisation *f* d'orientation *f*)
– *attitude control rockets*
39 le réservoir d'oxygène *m* liquide (comburant *m*) [77 200 l]
– *liquid oxygen (LOX, LO_2) tank [capacity: 77,200 litres]*
40 la tuyauterie
– *fuel line duct*
41 le réservoir d'hydrogène *m* liquide [253 000 l]
– *liquid hydrogen (LH_2) tank [capacity: 253,000 litres]*
42 les sondes *f* de mesure *f* (les capteurs *m* de mesure *f*)
– *measuring probes*
43 les réservoirs *m* de gaz *m* sous pression *f* et d'hélium *m*
– *compressed-helium tanks (helium pressure vessels)*
44 le conduit d'aération *f* du réservoir (l'évent *m*)
– *tank vent*
45 l'anneau *m* supérieur
– *forward frame section*
46 la plate-forme de travail *m*
– *work platform (working platform)*
47 la gaine de câbles *m* (la canalisation de câbles *m* électriques)
– *cable duct*
48 les moteurs-fusées *m* d'accélération *f* pour l'accumulation *f* du carburant
– *acceleration rockets for fuel acquisition*
49 l'anneau *m* inférieur
– *aft frame section*
50 les réservoirs *m* de gaz *m* sous pression *f* et d'hélium *m*
– *compressed-helium tanks (helium pressure vessels)*
51 la conduite d'alimentation *f* en oxygène *m* liquide (comburant *m*)
– *liquid hydrogen (LH_2) line*
52 la conduite d'alimentation *f* en hydrogène *m* liquide (combustible *m*)
– *liquid oxygen (LOX, LO_2) line*
53 la case des équipements *m* (le compartiment scientifique) alimentée en énergie *f* par 24 panneaux *m* solaires
– *24-panel instrument unit*
54 l'adaptateur *m* abritant le LM (module *m* lunaire)
– *LM hangar (lunar module hangar)*
55 le LM (Lunar Module, le module lunaire)
– *LM (lunar module)*
56 le module de service *m* d'Apollo (Service Module, le compartiment moteur)
– *Apollo SM (service module), containing supplies and equipment*
57 le propulseur principal du module de service *m*
– *SM (service module) main engine*
58 le réservoir de carburant *m* (combustible *m*)
– *fuel tank*
59 le réservoir de tétraoxyde *m* d'azote *m* (comburant *m*)
– *nitrogen tetroxide tank*
60 les appareils *m* d'alimentation *f* en gaz *m* comprimé
– *pressurized gas delivery system*
61 les réservoirs *m* d'oxygène *m*
– *oxygen tanks*
62 les piles *f* à combustible *m*
– *fuel cells*
63 les groupes *m* de moteurs-fusées *m* de pilotage *m*
– *manoeuvring* (Am. *maneuvering) rocket assembly*
64 le groupe d'antennes *f* directives
– *directional antenna assembly*
65 le module de commande *f* (la capsule spatiale, le satellite)
– *space capsule (command section)*
66 la tour de sauvetage *m* éjectée en cas d'incident *m* ou d'accident *m* au moment du lancement (la tour d'éjection *f*)
– *launch phase escape tower*

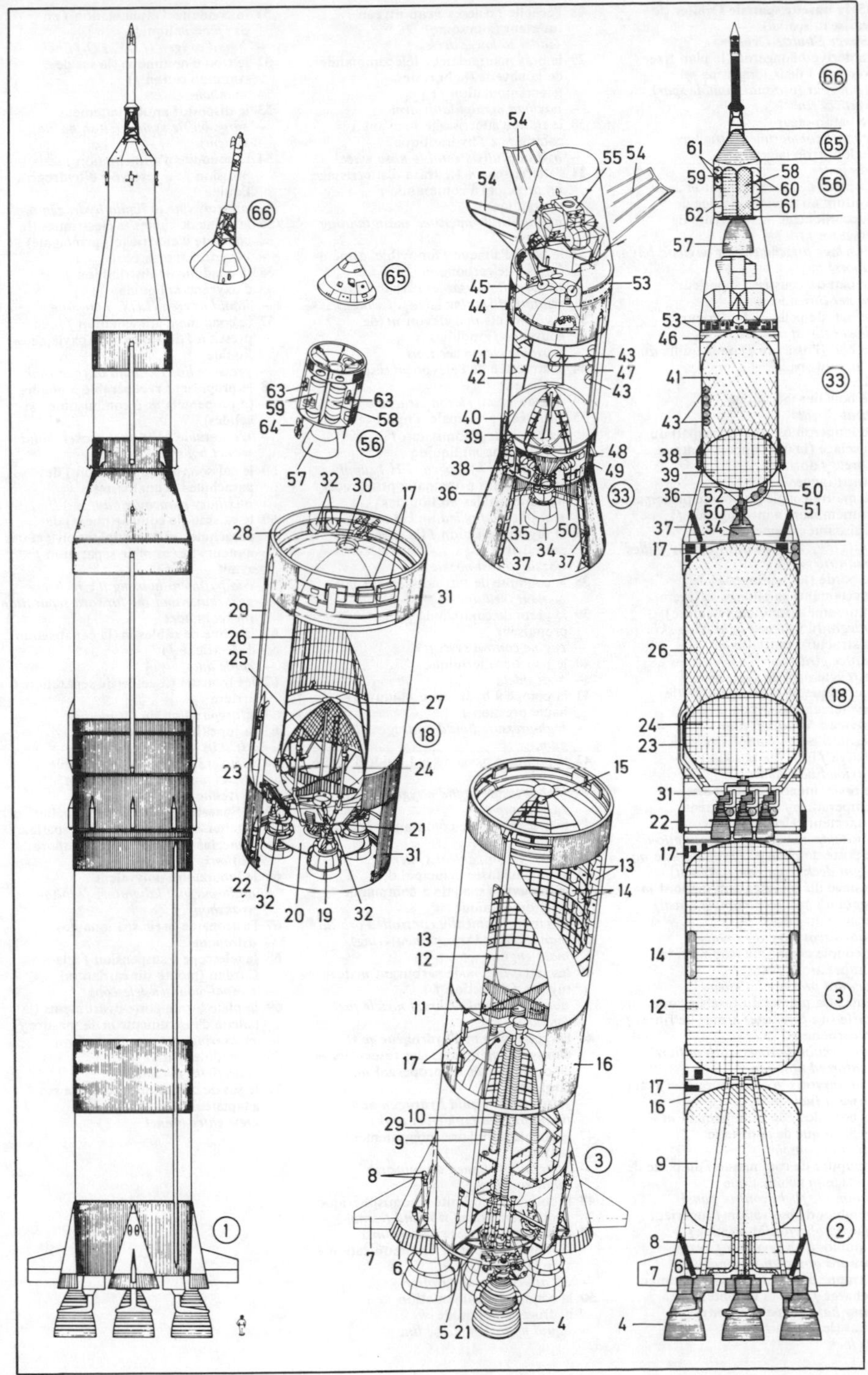
66
65
63
59
64
58
56
57
32
30
17
36
28
31
29
26
25
27
18
24
23
21
22
32
20
19
54
55
45
44
53
41
42
43
47
40
39
38
48
49
33
35
34
50
37
15
13
14
12
11
16
10
9
8
7
6
5
21
4
3
1
61
60
62
46
52
51
2

1-45 la navette spatiale Orbiter (le vaisseau spatial)
– ***Space Shuttle-Orbiter***
1 la dérive bilongeron (le plan fixe vertical à deux longerons *m*)
– *twin-spar (two-spar, double-spar) vertical fin*
2 le bâti-moteur
– *engine compartment structure*
3 le longeron latéral
– *fin post*
4 la pièce de raccordement *m* de la voilure au fuselage (la tige de raccordement *m*, la ferrure de fixation *f*)
– *fuselage attachment [of payload bay doors]*
5 le bâti de poussée *f* supérieur
– *upper thrust mount*
6 le bâti de poussée *f* inférieur
– *lower thrust mount*
7 le bâti (l'ossature *f*) de la quille du vaisseau spatial
– *keel*
8 le bouclier thermique
– *heat shield*
9 le longeron central (principal) du fuselage (la tige support centrale, l'arête *f* dorsale)
– *waist longeron*
10 le maître-couple (le couple principal, la membrure à mi-longueur *f*) fraisé intégralement
– *integrally machined (integrally milled) main rib*
11 le bordé (les bordages *m*, le revêtement) en alliages *m* légers entièrement renforcé (stabilisé)
– *integrally stiffened light alloy skin*
12 la structure en treillis *m*
– *lattice girder*
13 le revêtement de protection *f* thermique de la charge utile (le revêtement isolant de la soute)
– *payload bay insulation*
14 l'écoutille *f* du compartiment à charge *f* utile (de la soute)
– *payload bay door*
15 le revêtement isolant à basse température *f* (le revêtement protecteur réfrigérant)
– *low-temperature surface insulation*
16 le poste de pilotage *m* (l'habitacle *m*)
– *flight deck (crew compartment)*
17 le siège du commandant de bord *m*
– *captain's seat (commander's seat)*
18 le siège du pilote
– *pilot's seat (co-pilot's seat)*
19 le couple comprimé (soumis à la compression) avant
– *forward pressure bulkhead*
20 le nez (la pointe) du fuselage, une coiffe (un carénage) armée de fibres *f* de carbone *m*
– *nose-section fairings, carbon fibre reinforced nose cone*
21 les réservoirs *m* de carburant *m* avant
– *forward fuel tanks*
22 les consoles *f* de l'équipement *m* électronique de la navette
– *avionics consoles*
23 le pupitre de commande *f* du poste de pilotage *m* automatique
– *automatic flight control panel*
24 le hublot d'observation *f* supérieur
– *upward observation windows*
25 le hublot d'observation *f* avant
– *forward observation windows*
26 la trappe d'accès *m* au compartiment à charge *f* utile (à la soute)
– *entry hatch to payload bay*
27 le sas (le sas à air *m*)
– *air lock*
28 l'échelle *f* d'accès *m* au niveau inférieur (à la soute)
– *ladder to lower deck*
29 le bras manipulateur télécommandé de la navette (le bras de télémanipulation *f*)
– *payload manipulator arm*
30 le train d'atterrissage *m* avant à commande *f* hydraulique
– *hydraulically steerable nose wheel*
31 l'atterrisseur *m* (le train d'atterrissage *m*) principal à commande *f* hydraulique
– *hydraulically operated main landing gear*
32 le bord d'attaque *f* amovible, armé de fibres *f* de carbone *m*
– *removable (reusable) carbon fibre reinforced leading edge [of wing]*
33 les éléments *m* d'élevon *m* (de gouverne *f*) mobiles
– *movable elevon sections*
34 la structure de l'élevon *m* résistant à la chaleur
– *heat-resistant elevon structure*
35 l'arrivée *f* principale d'hydrogène *m* (la conduite d'admission *f* d'hydrogène *m*) liquide
– *main liquid hydrogen (LH_2) supply*
36 le propulseur principal à propergols *m*(combustibles *m*) liquides
– *main liquid-fuelled rocket engine*
37 la tuyère d'éjection *f* (la tuyère propulsive)
– *nozzle (thrust nozzle)*
38 la conduite de refroidissement *m*
– *coolant feed line*
39 le vérin de commande *f* du propulseur
– *engine control system*
40 le bouclier thermique
– *heat shield*
41 la pompe à hydrogène *m*liquide à haute pression *f*
– *high-pressure liquid hydrogen (LH_2) pump*
42 la pompe à oxygène *m* liquide à haute pression *f*
– *high-pressure liquid oxygen (LOX, LO_2) pump*
43 le mécanisme de commande *f* de la poussée
– *thrust vector control system*
44 le moteur-fusée principal de manœuvre *f* spatiale à commande *f* électromécanique
– *electromechanically controlled orbital manoeuvring (*Am.* maneuvering) main engine*
45 les réservoirs *m* de carburant *m* des tuyères *f* d'éjection *f*
– *nozzle fuel tanks (thrust nozzle fuel tanks)*
46 **les réservoirs *m* d'hydrogène *m* et d'oxygène *m*** liquides (les réservoirs *m* de carburant *m*, de propergol *m*) **largables**
– ***jettisonable liquid hydrogen and liquid oxygen tank*** *(fuel tank)*
47 le couple annulaire intégralement renforcé
– *integrally stiffened annular rib (annular frame)*
48 le couple d'extrémité *f* hémisphérique
– *hemispherical end rib (end frame)*
49 la passerelle arrière d'accès *m* à l'Orbiter (le pont de communication *f* avec l'Orbiter)
– *aft attachment to Orbiter*
50 la conduite d'alimentation *f* en hydrogène *m* liquide
– *liquid hydrogen (LH_2) line*
51 la conduite d'alimentation *f* en oxygène *m* liquide
– *liquid oxygen (LOX, LO_2) line*
52 le trou d'homme *m* (le sas de communication *f*)
– *manhole*
53 le dispositif antiballottement
– *surge baffle system (slosh baffle system)*
54 la conduite d'alimentation *f* sous pression *f* du réservoir d'hydrogène *m* liquide
– *pressure line to liquid hydrogen tank*
55 la gaine de câbles *m* électriques (la conduite d'électricité *f* principale)
– *electrical system bus*
56 la conduite de distribution *f* d'oxygène *m* liquide
– *liquid oxygen (LOX, LO_2) line*
57 la conduite d'alimentation *f* sous pression *f* du réservoir d'oxygène *m* liquide
– *pressure line to liquid oxygen tank*
58 **le propulseur récupérable à poudre** *f* (à propergols *m*, à combustibles *m* solides)
– ***recoverable solid-fuel rocket*** *(solid rocket booster)*
59 le caisson (le compartiment) des parachutes *m* auxiliaires
– *auxiliary parachute bay*
60 le caisson (le compartiment) des parachutes *m* de récupération *f* et des moteurs-fusées *m* de séparation *f* avant
– *compartment housing the recovery parachutes and the forward separation rocket motors*
61 la gaine de câbles *m* (la canalisation d'électricité *f*)
– *cable duct*
62 les moteurs-fusées *m* de séparation *f* arrière
– *aft separation rocket motors*
63 la jupe (le carénage) arrière
– *aft skirt*
64 la tuyère d'éjection *f* orientable
– *swivel nozzle (swivelling,* Am. *swiveling, nozzle)*
65 **le Spacelab** (le laboratoire spatial, l'atelier *m* orbital, la station spatiale)
– ***Spacelab*** *(space laboratory, space station)*
66 le laboratoire polyvalent
– *multi-purpose laboratory (orbital workshop)*
67 l'astronaute *m* (le spationaute)
– *astronaut*
68 le télescope à suspension *f* à la Cardan (monté sur cardan *m*)
– *gimbal-mounted telescope*
69 la plate-forme porte-instruments (la palette d'instruments *m* de mesure *f*)
– *measuring instrument platform*
70 le module spatial
– *spaceflight module*
71 le sas de communication *f* (le sas adaptateur, d'amarrage *m*)
– *crew entry tunnel*

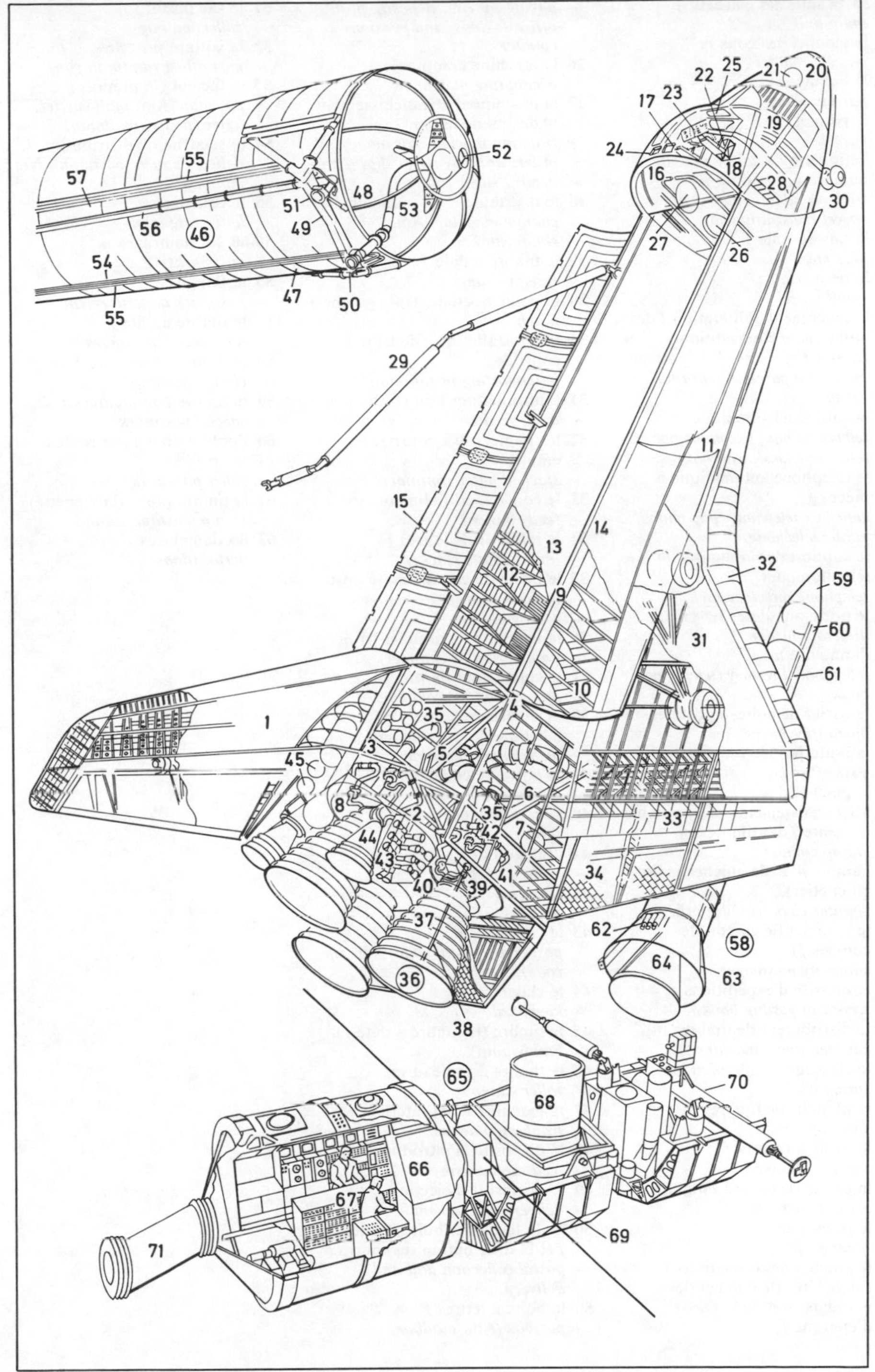
1
2
3
4
5
6
7
8
9
10
11
12
13
14
15
16
17
18
19
20
21
22
23
24
25
26
27
28
29
30
31
32
33
34
35
36
37
38
39
40
41
42
43
44
45
46
47
48
49
50
51
52
53
54
55
56
57
58
59
60
61
62
63
64
65
66
67
68
69
70
71

1-30 la salle des guichets *m*
– ***main hall***
1 le guichet des colis *m*
– *parcels counter*
2 la balance
– *parcels scales*
3 le paquet
– *parcel*
4 l'étiquette *f* à coller avec le numéro d'expédition *f*
– *stick-on address label with parcel registration slip*
5 le pot de colle *f*
– *glue pot*
6 le petit paquet
– *small parcel*
7 la machine d'oblitération *f* des bulletins *m* d'expédition *f*
– *franking machine (*Am. *postage meter) for parcel registration cards*
8 la cabine téléphonique
– *telephone box (telephone booth, telephone kiosk, call box)*
9 le téléphone automatique à pièces *f*
– *coin-box telephone (pay phone, public telephone)*
10 le support des annuaires *m* téléphoniques
– *telephone directory rack*
11 le porte-annuaires basculant
– *directory holder*
12 l'annuaire *m*
– *telephone directory (telephone book)*
13 le casier de boîtes *f* postales
– *post office boxes*
14 la boîte postale
– *post office box*
15 le guichet des affranchissements *m* (le guichet de vente *f* des timbres *m*)
– *stamp counter*
16 l'employé *m* de guichet *m* (le guichetier)
– *counter clerk (counter officer)*
17 le coursier (le garçon de courses *f*)
– *company messenger*
18 le registre d'expéditions *f*
– *record of posting book*
19 le distributeur de timbres *m*
– *counter stamp machine*
20 le classeur à timbres *m*
– *stamp book*
21 la planche de timbres *m*
– *sheet of stamps*
22 le tiroir à valeurs *f*
– *security drawer*
23 la caisse (le tiroir à monnaie *f*)
– *change rack*
24 le pèse-lettres
– *letter scales*
25 le guichet des opérations *f* financières (le guichet des mandats *m* et de la caisse d'épargne *f*)
– *paying-in (*Am. *deposit), post office savings, and pensions counter*
26 la machine comptable
– *accounting machine*
27 la machine d'affranchissement *m* des mandats *m*
– *franking machine for money orders and paying-in slips (*Am. *deposit slips)*
28 le distributeur de monnaie *f*
– *change machine (*Am. *changemaker)*
29 le timbre à date *f*
– *receipt stamp*
30 le passe-documents (le guichet)
– *hatch*
31-44 l'installation *f* de tri *m* du courrier
– *letter-sorting installation*
31 l'introduction *f* du courrier *m*
– *letter feed*
32 les paniers *m* à courrier *m* empilés
– *stacked letter containers*
33 le convoyeur d'alimentation *f*
– *feed conveyor*
34 le releveur de lettres *f*
– *intermediate stacker*
35 le poste de codage *m* (le poste d'indexation *f*)
– *coding station*
36 la machine de premier tri *m*
– *pre-distributor channel*
37 le calculateur de processus *m*
– *process control computer*
38 la trieuse de lettres *f* (la machine de tri *m* de lettres *f*)
– *distributing machine*
39 le poste de codage *m* vidéo
– *video coding station*
40 l'écran *m* vidéo
– *screen*
41 l'image *f* de l'adresse *f*
– *address display*
42 l'adresse *f*
– *address*
43 le code postal
– *post code (postal code,* Am. *zip code)*
44 le clavier
– *keyboard*
45 le timbre (le timbre à date *f*)
– *handstamp*
46 le timbre à rouleau *m*
– *roller stamp*
47 la machine à oblitérer
– *franking machine*
48 le dispositif d'introduction *f*
– *feed mechanism*
49 le dispositif d'éjection *f*
– *delivery mechanism*
50-55 la levée des boîtes *f* à lettres *f* et la distribution du courrier
– *postal collection and and delivery*
50 la boîte à lettres *f*
– *postbox (*Am. *mailbox)*
51 le sac postal
– *collection bag*
52 la voiture postale
– *post office van (mail van)*
53 le facteur (le préposé)
– *postman (*Am. *mail carrier, letter carrier, mailman)*
54 la sacoche de distribution *f*
– *delivery pouch (postman's bag, mailbag)*
55 le courrier
– *letter-rate item*
56-60 les timbrages *m*
– *postmarks*
56 la flamme
– *postmark advertisement*
57 le timbre à date *f*
– *date stamp postmark*
58 le timbre de surtaxe *f*
– *charge postmark*
59 le timbre commémoratif
– *special postmark*
60 l'oblitération *f* par rouleau *m* à main *f*
– *roller postmark*
61 le timbre-poste (la vignette)
– *stamp (postage stamp)*
62 les dentelures *f*
– *perforations*

OXFORD OX2 6DP
BERLIN ist eine Reise wert
Come and see BERLIN
OXFORD
22.5.79
GREAT BRITAIN
POSTAGE PAID
07
LP.B.R 208F
ROTARY
INTERNATIONAL
LUXEMBOURG
BITTE AUCH IN DER
ABSENDERANGABE
VERGISS
MEIN
NICHT:
DIE POSTLEITZAHL
GUMMERSBACH 31
me
25.2.76-16
5270

237 Poste II (téléphone et télégraphe)

1 **la cabine téléphonique**, un téléphone public
– ***telephone box*** *(telephone booth, telephone kiosk, call box), a public telephone*
2 l'usager *m* du téléphone (*avec raccordement m individuel:* l'abonné *m* au téléphone *m*)
– *telephone user (*with own telephone: *telephone subscriber, telephone customer)*
3 le téléphone automatique à pièces *f* pour communications *f* locales et interurbaines
– *coin-box telephone (pay phone, public telephone) for local and long-distance calls (trunk calls)*
4 le dispositif d'appel *m* d'alarme *f*
– *emergency telephone*
5 l'annuaire *m* du téléphone *m*
– *telephone directory (telephone book)*
6-26 **les postes** *m* téléphoniques (appareils *m* téléphoniques)
– ***telephone instruments*** *(telephones)*
6 le téléphone (l'appareil *m* téléphonique) de bureau *m* en version *f* standard
– *standard table telephone*
7 le combiné
– *telephone receiver (handset)*
8 l'écouteur *m*
– *earpiece*
9 le microphone [*fam.:* le micro]
– *mouthpiece (microphone)*
10 le cadran d'appel *m*
– *dial (push-button keyboard)*
11 le disque de cadran *m*
– *finger plate (dial finger plate, dial wind-up plate)*
12 la butée
– *finger stop (dial finger stop)*
13 le support commutateur
– *cradle (handset cradle, cradle switch)*
14 le cordon du combiné *m*
– *receiver cord (handset cord)*
15 le boîtier de l'appareil *m* téléphonique
– *telephone casing (telephone cover)*
16 le compteur de taxes *f* à domicile *m*
– *subscriber's (customer's) private meter*
17 le poste principal d'un central privé relié au réseau *m* public
– *switchboard (exchange) for a system of extensions*
18 la touche de ligne *f* réseau *m*
– *push button for connecting main exchange lines*
19 les touches *f* de sélection *f* des postes *m* supplémentaires
– *push buttons for calling extensions*
20 le téléphone à clavier *m*
– *push-button telephone*
21 la touche de mise *f* à la terre des postes *m* supplémentaires
– *earthing button for the extensions*
22-26 le standard privé
– *switchboard with extensions*
22 le poste principal
– *exchange*
23 le poste dirigeur (le poste central)
– *switchboard operator's set*
24 la ligne réseau *m*
– *main exchange line*
25 l'armoire *f* de commutation *f*
– *switching box (automatic switching system, automatic connecting system, switching centre,* Am. *center)*
26 le poste supplémentaire
– *extension*
27-41 **le central téléphonique**
– ***telephone exchange***
27 le service des perturbations *f* radioélectriques
– *fault repair service*
28 le technicien d'antiparasitage *m*
– *maintenance technician*
29 la position d'essais *m* et de mesures *f*
– *testing board (testing desk)*
30 la télégraphie
– *telegraphy*
31 l'appareil *m* télégraphique (le télégraphe, le téléimprimeur)
– *teleprinter (teletypewriter)*
32 la bande perforée
– *paper tape*
33 les renseignements *m* téléphoniques
– *directory enquiries*
34 le poste de renseignements *m*
– *information position (operator's position)*
35 la «demoiselle du téléphone», l'opératrice *f*
– *operator*
36 le lecteur de microfilms *m* (de microfiches *f*)
– *microfilm reader*
37 le classeur de microfilms *m* (de microfiches *f*)
– *microfilm file*
38 la projection sur l'écran *m* du microfilm des numéros *m* d'appel *m*
– *microfilm card with telephone numbers*
39 l'indication *f* de la date
– *date indicator display*
40 la table de mesures *f* et d'essais *m*
– *testing and control station*
41 les équipements *m* d'autocommutation *f* pour le téléphone, le télex et la transmission de données *f*
– *switching centre (*Am. *center) for telephone, telex, and data transmission services*
42 **le sélecteur** (le commutateur rotatif motorisé à contacts *m* en métaux *m* précieux; *dans l'avenir m:* le dispositif de commutation *f* électronique)
– ***selector*** *(motor uniselector made of noble metals;* in the future: *electronic selector)*
43 le banc
– *contact arc (bank)*
44 le balai
– *contact arm (wiper)*
45 l'empilage *m* de contacts *m*
– *contact field*
46 l'élément *m* de contact *m*
– *contact arm tag*
47 l'électroaimant *m*
– *electromagnet*
48 le moteur de sélecteur *m*
– *selector motor*
49 l'élément *m* de réglage *m*
– *restoring spring (resetting spring)*
50 **les radiocommunications** *f*
– ***communication links***
51-52 la transmission par satellite *m*
– *satellite radio link*
51 la station terrienne avec antenne *f* directive
– *earth station with directional antenna*
52 le satellite de télécommunication *f* avec antenne *f* directive
– *communications satellite with directional antenna*
53 la station côtière
– *coastal station*
54-55 les radiocommunications *f* intercontinentales
– *intercontinental radio link*
54 la station à ondes *f* courtes
– *short-wave station*
55 l'ionosphère *f*
– *ionosphere*
56 le câble sous-marin
– *submarine cable (deep-sea cable)*
57 l'amplificateur *m* (le répéteur) de câble *m*
– *underwater amplifier*
58 **la transmission de données** *f* (le traitement de données *f* à distance *f*)
– ***data transmission*** *(data services)*
59 l'équipement *m* d'entrée *f* - sortie *f* de données *f* sur bande *f*
– *input/output device for data carriers*
60 l'équipement *m* de traitement *m* de données *f*
– *data processor*
61 la téléimprimante
– *teleprinter*
62-64 les supports *m* de données *f*
– *data carriers*
62 la bande perforée
– *punched tape (punch tape)*
63 la bande magnétique
– *magnetic tape*
64 la carte perforée
– *punched card (punch card)*
65 le poste télex
– *telex link*
66 le téléimprimeur
– *teleprinter (page printer)*
67 le coffret de raccordement *m*
– *dialling (*Am. *dialing) unit*
68 la bande perforée télex pour transmission *f* du texte *m* à la vitesse maximale
– *telex tape (punched tape, punch tape) for transmitting the text at maximum speed*
69 le télex
– *telex message*
70 le clavier
– *keyboard*

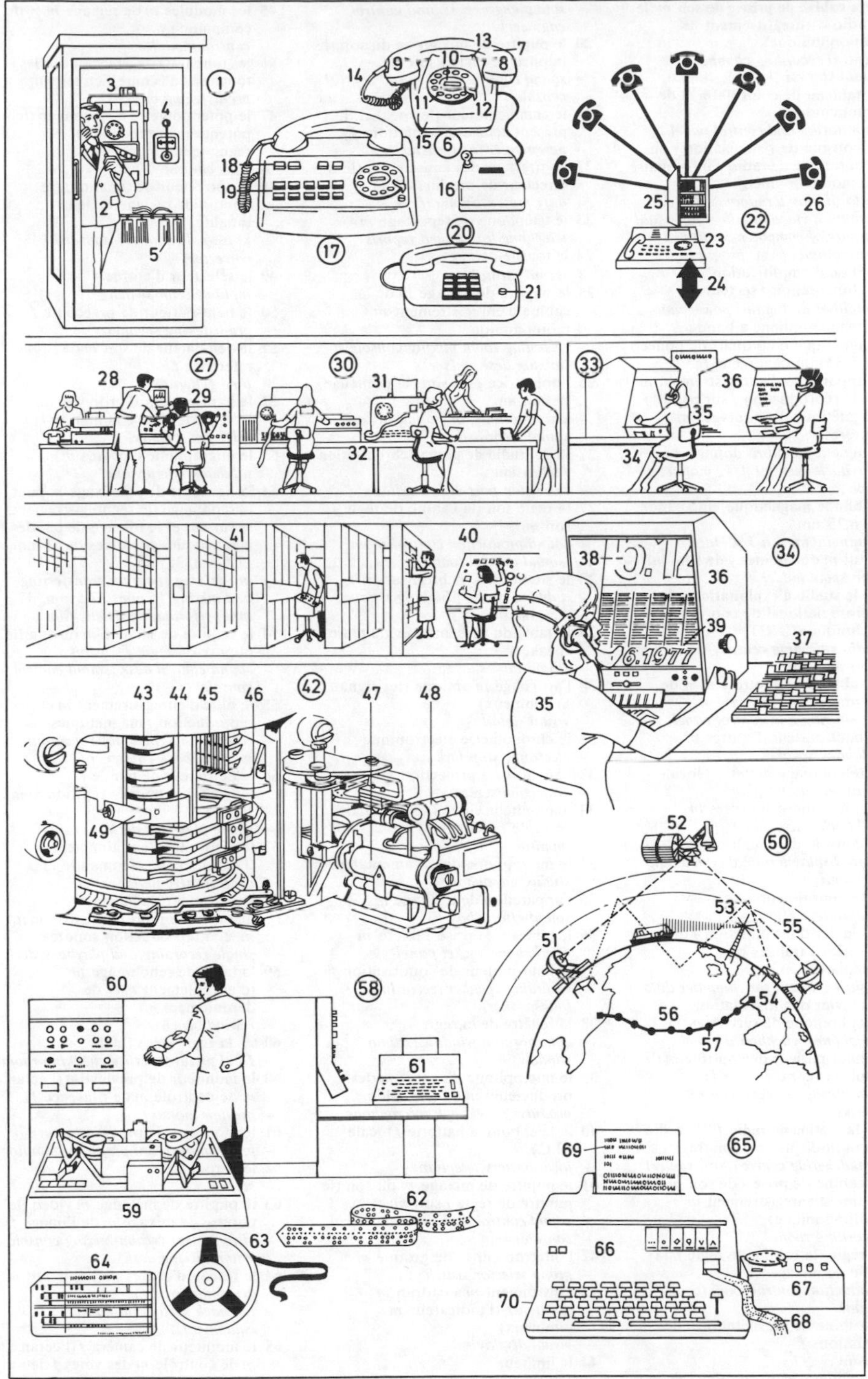

1
2
3
4
5
6
7
8
9
10
11
12
13
14
15
16
17
18
19
20
21
22
23
24
25
26
27
28
29
30
31
32
33
34
35
36
37
38
39
40
41
42
43
44
45
46
47
48
49
50
51
52
53
54
55
56
57
58
59
60
61
62
63
64
65
66
67
68
69
70

1-6 la cabine de prise *f* **de son** *m* (le studio d'enregistrement *m* radiophonique)
– ***central recording channel of a radio station***
1 le tableau de contrôle *m* et de commande *f*
– *monitoring and control panel*
2 la console de visualisation *f* du programme de radio *f* informatisé (le moniteur vidéo)
– *data display terminal (video data terminal, video monitor) for visual display of computer-controlled programmes (*Am.* programs)*
3 le bloc d'amplification *f* et d'alimentation *f* secteur *m*
– *amplifier and mains power unit*
4 le magnétophone à bande *f* magnétique d'un quart de pouce ou 6,35 mm de largeur *f* (l'appareil *m* d'enregistrement *m* et de reproduction *f* sur bande *f* magnétique de montages *m* sonores)
– *magnetic sound recording and playback deck for 1/4" magnetic tape*
5 la bande magnétique, une bande de 6,35 mm
– *magnetic tape, a 1/4" tape*
6 l'étui *m* de bobines *f* de film *m*
– *film spool holder*
7-15 le studio d'exploitation *f* du Centre national de coordination *f* technique (CNCT)
– ***radio switching centre (****Am.* *center) control room*
7 le tableau de contrôle *m* et de commande *f*
– *monitoring and control panel*
8 le haut-parleur d'ordres *m*
– *talkback speaker*
9 le téléphone à batterie *f* locale
– *local-battery telephone*
10 le microphone d'ordres *m*
– *talkback microphone*
11 la console de visualisation *f*
– *data display terminal (video data terminal)*
12 le téléimprimeur
– *teleprinter*
13 le clavier d'introduction *f* de données f traitées par calculateur *m*
– *input keyboard for computer data*
14 le clavier de l'installation téléphonique de service *m*
– *telephone switchboard panel*
15 le haut-parleur de contrôle *m* (le haut-parleur d'écoute *f*)
– *monitoring speaker (control speaker)*
16-26 la station de radio *f* (le studio de radiodiffusion *f* sonore)
– ***broadcasting centre*** *(*Am. *center)*
16 la cabine de prise *f* de son *m* (la cabine d'enregistrement *m* radiophonique)
– *recording room*
17 la régie (la cabine de régie *f*, la salle de mixage *m*)
– *production control room (control room)*
18 la cabine de présentation *f* des émissions *f*
– *studio*
19 l'ingénieur *m* du son (le régisseur du son)
– *sound engineer (sound control engineer)*
20 le pupitre de mixage *m* du son (le pupitre de régie *f* son *m*)
– *sound control desk (sound control console)*
21 le commentateur (le speaker, le présentateur d'informations *f*)
– *newsreader (newscaster)*
22 le directeur des émissions *f* (le directeur de production *f*)
– *duty presentation officer*
23 le téléphone de reportage *m*
– *telephone for phoned reports*
24 le tourne-disque
– *record turntable*
25 le pupitre de mixage *m* de la cabine d'enregistrement *m* radiophonique
– *recording room mixing console (mixing desk, mixer)*
26 l'opératrice *f* du son (la preneuse de son *m*)
– *sound technician (sound mixer, sound recordist)*
27-53 le studio de postsynchronisation *f* **télévision**
– ***television post-sync studio***
27 la régie son (la cabine de régie *f* son *m*)
– *sound production control room (sound control room)*
28 le studio de synchronisation *f*
– *dubbing studio (dubbing theatre,* Am. *theater)*
29 la table du présentateur (la table speaker)
– *studio table*
30 l'affichage *m* optique (les signaux *m* lumineux)
– *visual signal*
31 le chronomètre électronique
– *electronic stopclock*
32 l'écran *m* de projection *f*
– *projection screen*
33 le moniteur vidéo (l'écran *m* de contrôle *m* d'image *f*)
– *monitor*
34 le microphone du commentateur
– *studio microphone*
35 l'appareil *m* de bruitage *m*
– *sound effects box*
36 le tableau de prise *f* micro *m*
– *microphone socket panel*
37 le haut-parleur de sonorisation *f*
– *recording speaker (recording loudspeaker)*
38 la fenêtre de la régie
– *control room window (studio window)*
39 le microphone d'ordres *m* des producteurs *m* de télévision *f*
– *producer's talkback microphone*
40 le téléphone à batterie *f* locale (B.L.)
– *local-battery telephone*
41 le pupitre de mixage *m* du son (le pupitre de régie *f* son *m*)
– *sound control desk (sound control console)*
42 l'interrupteur *m* de groupe *m*
– *group selector switch*
43 l'instrument *m* à cadran *m* lumineux (l'indicateur *m* lumineux)
– *visual display*
44 le limiteur
– *limiter display (clipper display)*
45 les modules *m* de réglage *m* et de commande *f*
– *control modules*
46 les touches *f* de préécoute *f* (les touches *f* d'écoute *f* en test *m*)
– *pre-listening buttons*
47 le potentiomètre à curseur *m* (le potentiomètre rectiligne, le régulateur à curseur *m*)
– *slide control*
48 le correcteur de tonalité *f* (le bouton de réglage *m* de la tonalité)
– *universal equalizer (universal corrector)*
49 le sélecteur d'entrée *f*
– *input selector switch*
50 le haut-parleur de préécoute *f*
– *pre-listening speaker*
51 le générateur de son *m* de référence *f*
– *tone generator*
52 le haut-parleur d'ordres *m* (le haut-parleur de commande *f*)
– *talkback speaker*
53 le microphone d'ordres *m*
– *talkback microphone*
54-59 le studio de prémixage *m* pour le repiquage (le réenregistrement, le surjeu) et le mixage de bandes *f* magnétiques perforées de 16 mm, 17,5 mm, 35 mm
– ***pre-mixing room*** *for transferring and mixing 16 mm, 17.5 mm, 35 mm perforated magnetic film*
54 le pupitre de mixage *m* du son (le pupitre de régie *f* son *m*)
– *sound control desk (sound control console)*
55 le bloc d'enregistrement *m* et de reproduction *f* magnétiques
– *compact magnetic tape recording and playback equipment*
56 le dérouleur de bande *f* magnétique pour la reproduction sonore
– *single playback deck*
57 le dispositif d'entraînement *m* (l'organe *m* de commande *f*)
– *central drive unit*
58 le dérouleur de bande *f* magnétique pour l'enregistrement *m* et la reproduction sonores
– *single recording and playback deck*
59 la table de rebobinage *m* (d'enroulement *m* et de déroulement *m*)
– *rewind bench*
60-65 la régie vidéo finale
– ***final picture quality checking room***
60 le moniteur de preview *m* (l'écran *m* de contrôle *m* de présence *f*)
– *preview monitor*
61 le moniteur de programme *m*
– *programme (*Am. *program) monitor*
62 le chronomètre
– *stopclock*
63 le pupitre de mélange *m* vidéo (le pupitre de mixage *m* de l'image *f*)
– *vision mixer (vision-mixing console, vision-mixing desk)*
64 le réseau d'ordres *m* (l'appareil *m* de commande *f*)
– *talkback system (talkback equipment)*
65 le moniteur de caméra *f* (l'écran *m* de contrôle *m* des voies *f* de caméra *f*)
– *camera monitor (picture monitor)*

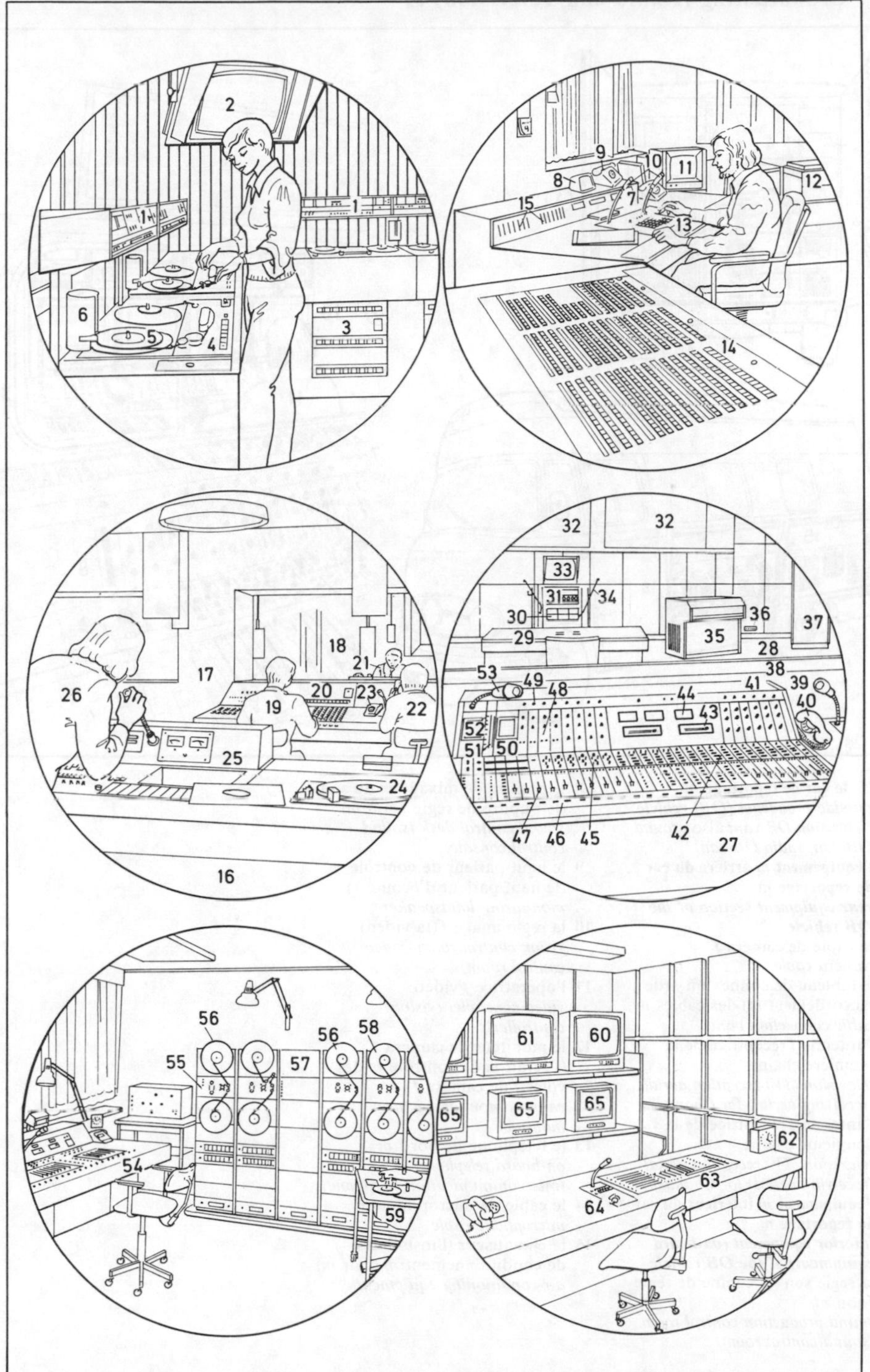
1
2
3
4
5
6
7
8
9
10
11
12
13
14
15
16
17
18
19
20
21
22
23
24
25
26
27
28
29
30
31
32
33
34
35
36
37
38
39
40
41
42
43
44
45
46
47
48
49
50
51
52
53
54
55
56
57
58
59
60
61
62
63
64
65

239 La radiodiffusion (radio et télévision) II
Broadcasting (Radio and Television) II

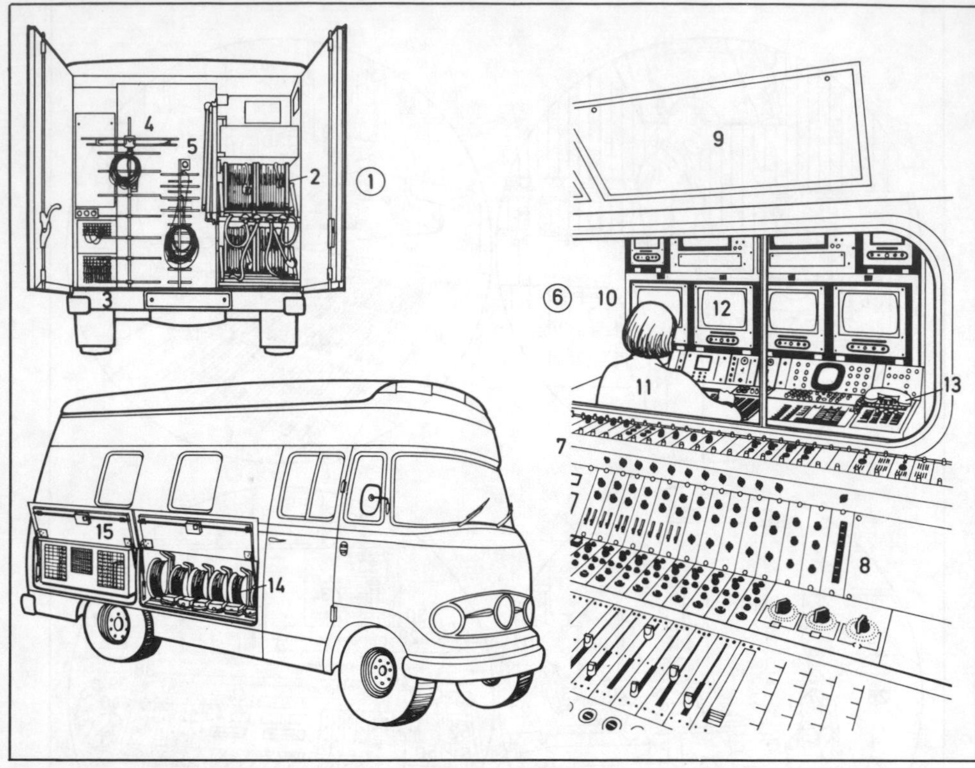

1-15 le car de reportage *m*
– ***outside broadcast (OB) vehicle*** *(television OB van;* also: *sound OB van, radio OB van)*

1 l'équipement *m* **arrière du car de reportage** *m*
– ***rear equipment section of the OB vehicle***

2 le câble de caméra *f*
– *camera cable*

3 le tableau de connexion *f* (de raccordement *m*) des câbles *m*
– *cable connection panel*

4 l'antenne *f* réceptrice de la première chaîne
– *television (TV) reception aerial (receiving aerial) for Channel I*

5 l'antenne *f* réceptrice de la deuxième chaîne
– *television (TV) reception aerial (receiving aerial) for Channel II*

6 l'équipement *m* **intérieur du car de reportage** *m*
– ***interior equipment (on-board equipment) of the OB vehicle***

7 la régie son (la cabine de régie *f* son *m*)
– *sound production control room (sound control room)*

8 le pupitre de mixage *m* du son (le pupitre de régie *f* son *m*)
– *sound control desk (sound control console)*

9 le haut-parleur de contrôle *m* (le haut-parleur d'écoute *f*)
– *monitoring loudspeaker*

10 la régie image *f* (la vidéo)
– *vision control room (video control room)*

11 l'opératrice *f* vidéo
– *video controller (vision controller)*

12 le moniteur de caméra *f* (l'écran *m* de contrôle *m* des voies *f* de caméra *f*)
– *camera monitor (picture monitor)*

13 le téléphone de bord *m*
– *on-board telephone (intercommunication telephone)*

14 le câble de microphone *m*
– *microphone cable*

15 le climatiseur (l'installation *f* de conditionnement *m* d'air *m*)
– *air-conditioning equipment*

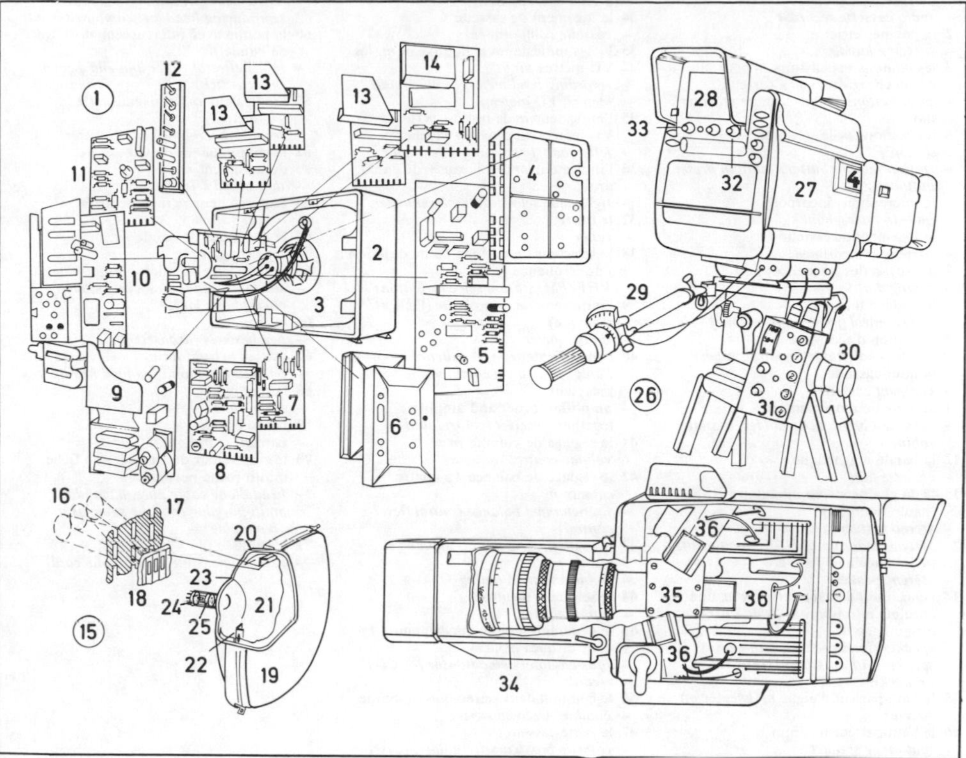

1 **le téléviseur couleur** (le récepteur de télévision *f* en couleur *f*)
– ***colour (Am. color) television (TV) receiver*** *(colour television set) of modular design*

2 le coffret de télévision *f* (le châssis du téléviseur)
– *television cabinet*

3 le tube cathodique (le tube-image)
– *television tube (picture tube)*

4 le module amplificateur de fréquence *f* intermédiaire (F.I.)
– *IF (intermediate frequency) amplifier module*

5 le module de décodage *m* couleur *f* (le décodeur couleur *f*)
– *colour* (Am. *color*) *decoder module*

6 le sélecteur VHF et UHF (le sélecteur ondes *f* métriques et décimétriques)
– *VHF and UHF tuner*

7 le module de synchronisation *f* horizontale (le module de synchronisation *f* lignes *f*)
– *horizontal synchronizing module*

8 le module de balayage *m* vertical (balayage *m* trames *f*)
– *vertical deflection module*

9 le module de cadrage *m*
– *horizontal linearity control module*

10 le module de balayage *m* horizontal (balayage *m* lignes *f*)
– *horizontal deflection module*

11 le module de réglage *m*
– *control module*

12 le module de convergence *f*
– *convergence module*

13 le module d'étage *m* final de couleur *f* (le module d'étage *m* de sortie *f* vidéo)
– *colour* (Am. *color*) *output stage module*

14 le module son *m*
– *sound module*

15 l'écran *m* couleur *f*
– *colour* (Am. *color*) *picture tube*

16 le faisceau d'électrons *m* (électronique)
– *electron beams*

17 le masque perforé (à trous *m*, à rainures *f*)
– *shadow mask with elongated holes*

18 les bandes *f* fluorescentes
– *strip of fluorescent (luminescent, phosphorescent) material*

19 l'écran *m* fluorescent (l'écran *m* à pastilles *f* de luminophores *m*)
– *coating (film) of fluorescent material*

20 le blindage magnétique
– *inner magnetic screen (screening)*

21 le vide
– *vacuum*

22 le support du masque compensé thermiquement
– *temperature-compensated shadow mask mount*

23 la bague de centrage *m* du module de balayage *m*
– *centring (centering) ring for the deflection system*

24 les canons *m* électroniques
– *electron gun assembly*

25 la cathode à chauffage *m* direct
– *rapid heat-up cathode*

26 **la caméra de télévision** *f*
– ***television (TV) camera***

27 la tête de caméra *f*
– *camera head*

28 le moniteur de caméra *f* (l'écran *m* de contrôle *m* des voies *f* de caméra *f*)
– *camera monitor*

29 la manette de guidage *m*
– *control arm (control lever)*

30 la mise au point
– *focusing adjustment*

31 le boîtier de commande *f*
– *control panel*

32 le réglage du contraste
– *contrast control*

33 le réglage de la luminosité
– *brightness control*

34 le zoom
– *zoom lens*

35 le prisme de division *f* optique (le diviseur optique)
– *beam-splitting prism (beam splitter)*

36 le module de prise *f* de vue *f* (le tube couleur *f*)
– *pickup unit (colour,* Am. *color, pickup tube)*

1 l'appareil *m* **radio à mini-cassette** *f* (le radio-cassette)
– ***radio cassette recorder***
2 la poignée étrier *m*
– *carrying handle*
3 les boutons *m* poussoirs *m* pour la partie enregistreur *m* à cassette *f*
– *push buttons for the cassette recorder unit*
4 les boutons *m* de sélection *f* de station *f*
– *station selector buttons (station preset buttons)*
5 le microphone incorporé
– *built-in microphone*
6 le logement de cassette *f*
– *cassette compartment*
7 le cadran des fréquences *f*
– *tuning dial*
8 le réglage linéaire
– *slide control [for volume or tone]*
9 le bouton d'accord *m*
– *tuning knob (tuning control, tuner)*
10 la mini-cassette
– ***compact cassette***
11 la boîte de rangement *m*
– *cassette box (cassette holder, cassette cabinet)*
12 la bande magnétique
– *cassette tape*
13-48 la chaîne stéréo modulaire Hi-Fi (haute fidélité *f*)
– ***stereo system*** *(*also: *quadraphonic system) made up of Hi-Fi components*
13-14 les enceintes *f* **stéréo**
– ***stereo speakers***
14 l'enceinte *f* de haut-parleurs *m*, une enceinte à trois voies *f* avec filtres *m* d'aiguillage *m*
– *speaker (loudspeaker), a three-way speaker with crossover (crossover network)*
15 le haut-parleur d'aigus *m* (tweeter *m*)
– *tweeter*
16 le haut-parleur médium
– *mid-range speaker*
17 le haut-parleur de graves *m*
– *woofer*
18 la platine tourne-disques *m*
– ***record player***
19 le chassis de la platine
– *record player housing (record player base)*
20 le plateau
– *turntable*
21 le bras de lecture *f*
– *tone arm*
22 le contrepoids d'équilibrage *m*
– *counterbalance (counterweight)*
23 la suspension à la Cardan
– *gimbal suspension*
24 le réglage de pression *f* de tête *f*
– *stylus pressure control (stylus force control)*
25 le dispositif anti-skating
– *anti-skate control*
26 la cellule de lecture *f* magnétique à diamant *m* conique ou elliptique
– *magnetic cartridge with (conical or elliptical) stylus, a diamond*
27 le repose-bras
– *tone arm lock*
28 le dispositif de soulèvement *m* du bras *m*
– *tone arm lift*
29 le sélecteur de vitesse *f* de rotation *f*
– *speed selector (speed changer)*
30 le bouton de start *m*
– *starter switch*
31 le réglage de tonalité *f*
– *treble control*
32 le capot
– *dust cover*
33 la platine de cassette *f* **stéréo**
– ***stereo cassette deck***
34 le logement de cassette *f*
– *cassette compartment*
35-36 les indicateurs *m* de niveau *m* (les VU-mètres *m*)
– *recording level meters (volume unit meters, VU meters)*
35 l'indicateur *m* de niveau *m* (le VU-mètre) du canal *m* gauche
– *left-channel recording level meter*
36 l'indicateur *m* de niveau *m* du canal droit
– *right-channel recording level meter*
37 le tuner
– ***tuner***
38 le sélecteur de stations *f* à modulation *f* de fréquence *f*
– *VHF (FM) station selector buttons*
39 l'indicateur *m* d'accord *m* (l'œil *m* magique)
– *tuning meter*
40 l'amplificateur *m*; *le tuner et l'amplificateur m combinés:* le récepteur
– ***amplifier;*** tuner and amplifier together: *receiver (control unit)*
41 le réglage de volume *m*
– *volume control*
42 le réglage de balance *f* à quatre canaux *m*
– *four-channel balance control (level control)*
43 le réglage de tonalité *f* aigus *m* et graves *m*
– *treble and bass tuning*
44 le sélecteur d'entrées *f*
– *input selector*
45 le démodulateur de quadriphonie *f* pour disques *m* CD4
– ***four-channel demodulator*** *for CD4 records*
46 le commutateur stéréo-quadriphonie
– *quadra/stereo converter*
47 le porte-cassettes
– *cassette box (cassette holder, cassette cabinet)*
48 le rangement des disques *m*
– *record storage slots (record storage compartments)*
49 le microphone (*fam.:* le micro)
– ***microphone***
50 la grille de microphone *m*
– *microphone screen*
51 le pied de microphone *m*
– *microphone base (microphone stand)*
52 la chaîne compacte (radio *f*, cassette *f*, tourne-disques *m*)
– ***three-in-one stereo component system*** *(automatic record changer, cassette deck, and stereo receiver)*
53 le système d'équilibrage *m* du bras *m*
– *tone arm balance*
54 le réglage d'accord *m*
– *tuning meters*
55 les indicateurs *m* de commutation *f* automatique oxyde *m* de fer *m* / oxyde *m* de chrome *m*
– *indicator light for automatic FeO/CrO$_2$ tape switch-over*
56 le magnétophone, un appareil à bobines *f* à deux ou quatre pistes *f*
– ***open-reel-type recorder****, a two or four-track unit*
57 la bobine de bande *f* magnétique
– *tape reel (open tape reel)*
58 la bande magnétique (une bande 1/4 de pouce *m*)
– *open-reel tape (recording tape, 1/4" tape)*
59 l'ensemble *m* de têtes *f* avec tête *f* d'effacement *m* tête *f* d'enregistrement *m*, tête *f* de lecture *f* (*ou:* tête *f* combinée)
– *sound head housing with erasing head (erase head), recording head, and reproducing head (*or: *combined head)*
60 la poulie avec interrupteur *m* de fin *f* de bande *f*
– *tape deflector roller and end switch (limit switch)*
61 l'indicateur *m* de niveau *m* (le VU-mètre)
– *recording level meter (VU meter)*
62 le commutateur de vitesse *f* de déroulement *m*
– *tape speed selector*
63 l'interrupteur *m* marche-arrêt
– *on/off switch*
64 le compteur de bande *f*
– *tape counter*
65 les entrées *f* du microphone *m* stéréo
– *stereo microphone sockets (stereo microphone jacks)*
66 le casque
– ***headphones*** *(headset)*
67 l'étrier *m* capitonné
– *padded headband (padded headpiece)*
68 la membrane
– *membrane*
69 l'écouteur *m*
– *earcups (earphones)*
70 le connecteur du casque, une fiche multibroche normalisée
– *headphone cable plug, a standard multi-pin plug (not the same as a phono plug)*
71 le câble
– *headphone cable (headphone cord)*

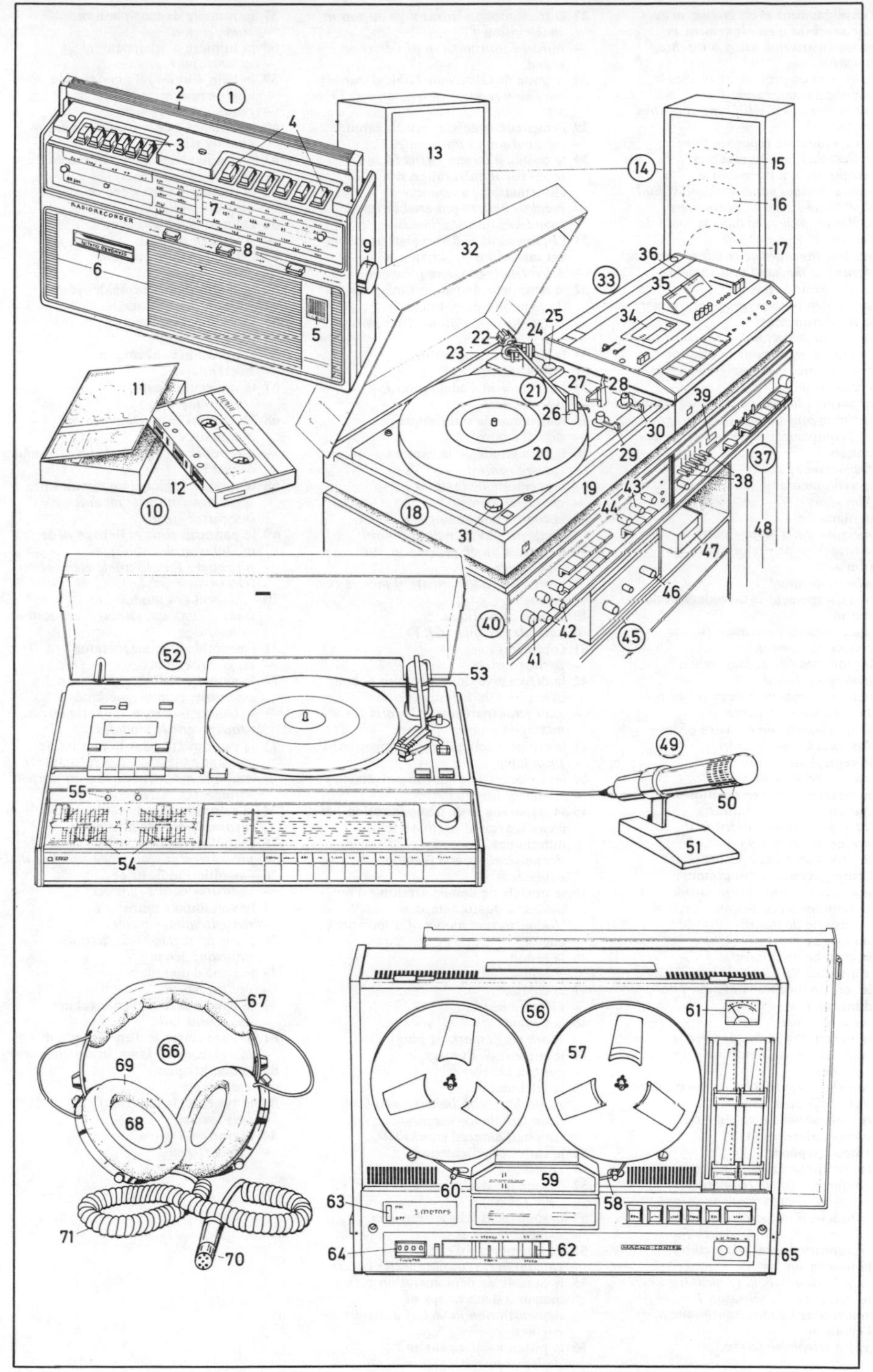
1
2
3
4
5
6
7
8
9
10
11
12
13
14
15
16
17
18
19
20
21
22
23
24
25
26
27
28
29
30
31
32
33
34
35
36
37
38
39
40
41
42
43
44
45
46
47
48
49
50
51
52
53
54
55
56
57
58
59
60
61
62
63
64
65
66
67
68
69
70
71
RADIORECORDER
3 motors

1 l'enseignement *m* en groupe *m* avec une **machine d'enseignement** *m*
– *group instruction using a* ***teaching machine***
2 le bureau du professeur *m* avec le pupitre de commande *f*
– *instructor's desk with central control unit*
3 le répétiteur de réponses *f* avec indicateurs *m* individuels et compteurs *m* à tri *m* croisé
– *master control panel with individual diplays and cross total counters*
4 le clavier d'élève *m* dans la main de l'élève *m*
– *student input device (student response device) in the hand of a student*
5 le compteur de pas *m*
– *study step counter (progress counter)*
6 le rétroprojecteur
– *overhead projector*
7 l'équipement *m* pour la création de programmes *m* d'enseignement *m* audio-visuel
– *apparatus for producing audio-visual learning programmes (*Am. *programs)*
8-10 l'équipement *m* de codage *m* des images *f*
– *frame coding device*
8 la visionneuse
– *film viewer*
9 la mémoire
– *memory unit (storage unit)*
10 le dispositif de perforation *f* du film *m*
– *film perforator*
11-14 l'équipement *m* de codage *m* du son *m*
– *audio coding equipment (sound coding equipment)*
11 les touches *f* de codage *m*
– *coding keyboard*
12 le magnétophone à deux pistes *f*
– *two-track tape recorder*
13 le magnétophone à quatre pistes *f*
– *four-track tape recorder*
14 le réglage de niveau *m*
– *recording level meter*
15 le système PIP (présentation *f* individuelle programmée)
– *PIP (programmed individual presentation) system*
16 le projecteur audio-visuel pour l'enseignement *m* programmé
– *AV (audio-visual) projector for programmed instruction*
17 la cassette de son *m*
– *audio cassette*
18 la cassette de film *m*
– *video cassette*
19 le terminal de transmission *f* de données *f*
– *data terminal*
20 la liaison téléphonique avec la centrale de concentration *f* de données *f*
– *telephone connection with the central data collection station*
21 **le vidéophone** (le système de vidéoconférence *f*)
– ***video telephone***
22 le commutateur de conférence *f*
– *conference circuit (conference hook-up, conference connection)*
23 la touche d'image *f* locale
– *camera tube switch (switch for transmitting speaker's picture)*
24 la touche son *m*
– *talk button (talk key, speaking key)*
25 les touches *f* de sélection *f*
– *touch-tone buttons (touch-tone pad)*
26 l'écran *m*
– *video telephone screen*
27 la transmission infrarouge du son *m* de télévision *f*
– *infrared transmission of television sound*
28 le poste de télévision *f* (téléviseur *m*)
– *television receiver (television set, TV set)*
29 l'émetteur *m* de son *m* à infrarouge
– *infrared sound transmitter*
30 le casque d'écoute *f* sans fil *m* à récepteur *m* infrarouge et alimentation *f* autonome
– *cordless battery-powered infrared sound headphones (headset)*
31 **l'équipement** *m* **d'enregistrement** *m* **sur microfilm** *m* [schéma *m*]
– ***microfilming system*** *[diagram]*
32 le dérouleur de bande *f* magnétique (la mémoire de données *f*)
– *magnetic tape station (data storage unit)*
33 la mémoire tampon *m*
– *buffer storage*
34 l'interface *m* d'adaptation *f*
– *adapter unit*
35 la commande numérique
– *digital control*
36 la commande de la caméra
– *camera control*
37 la mémoire de texte *m*
– *character storage*
38 la commande analogique
– *analogue (*Am. *analog) control*
39 la correction de géométrie *f* du tube-image
– *correction (adjustment) of picture tube geometry*
40 le tube cathodique
– *cathode ray tube (CRT)*
41 l'optique *f*
– *optical system*
42 la diapositive de formulaire *m* pour insertion *f* de formulaires *m*
– *slide (transparency) of a form for mixing-in images of forms*
43 la lampe à éclairs *m* (la lampe flash)
– *flash lamp*
44 les cassettes *f* de film *m* universelles
– *universal film cassettes*
45-84 **appareils** *m* **de démonstration** *f* **et d'enseignement** *m* (matériel *m* didactique)
– ***demonstration and teaching equipment***
45 le modèle de démonstration *f* d'un moteur à quatre temps *m*
– *demonstration model of a four-stroke engine*
46 le piston
– *piston*
47 la culasse
– *cylinder head*
48 la bougie
– *spark plug (sparking plug)*
49 le rupteur d'allumage *m*
– *contact breaker*
50 le vilebrequin
– *crankshaft with balance weights (counterbalance weights) (counterbalanced crankshaft)*
51 le carter du vilebrequin
– *crankcase*
52 la soupape d'admission *f*
– *inlet valve*
53 la soupape d'échappement *m*
– *exhaust valve*
54 les chambres *f* d'eau *f*
– *coolant bores (cooling water bores)*
55 le modèle de démonstration *f* d'un moteur à deux temps *m*
– *demonstration model of a two-stroke engine*
56 le piston à déflecteur *m*
– *deflector piston*
57 la lumière de trop-plein *m*
– *transfer port*
58 la lumière d'échappement *m*
– *exhaust port*
59 le bain d'huile *f* du carter *m* de vilebrequin *m*
– *crankcase scavenging*
60 les ailettes *f* de refroidissement *m*
– *cooling ribs*
61-67 les modèles *m* de molécules *f*
– *models of molecules*
61 la molécule d'éthylène *m*
– *ethylene molecule*
62 l'atome *m* d'hydrogène *m*
– *hydrogen atom*
63 l'atome *m* de carbone *m*
– *carbon atom*
64 la molécule de formaldéhyde *m*
– *formaldehyde atom*
65 l'atome d'oxygène *m*
– *oxygen molecule*
66 l'anneau *m* benzénique
– *benzene ring*
67 la molécule d'eau *f*
– *water molecule*
68-72 circuits *m* en éléments *m* modulaires
– *electronic circuits made up of modular elements*
68 le module logique, un circuit intégré
– *logic element (logic module), an integrated circuit*
69 le panneau pour enfichage *m* de modules *m* électroniques
– *plugboard for electronic elements (electronic modules)*
70 la liaison des modules *m*
– *linking (link-up, joining, connection) of modules*
71 l'assemblage *m* magnétique
– *magnetic contact*
72 le montage de circuits *m* avec des assemblages *m* magnétiques
– *assembly (construction) of a circuit, using magnetic modules*
73 le multimètre pour la mesure de courant *m*, tension *f* et résistance *f*
– *multiple meter for measuring current, voltage and resistance*
74 le commutateur de calibre *m*
– *measurement range selector*
75 l'échelle *f* de mesure *f*
– *measurement scale (measurement dial)*
76 l'aiguille *f* indicatrice
– *indicator needle (pointer)*
77 le voltampèremètre
– *current/voltage meter*
78 la vis de réglage *m* de zéro *m*
– *adjusting screw*
79 le banc d'optique *f*
– *optical bench*
80 le banc à section *f* triangulaire
– *triangular rail*
81 le laser (laser *m* d'enseignement *m*)
– *laser (teaching laser, instruction laser)*
82 le diaphragme
– *diaphragm*
83 le système de lentilles *f*
– *lens system*
84 l'écran *m*
– *target (screen)*

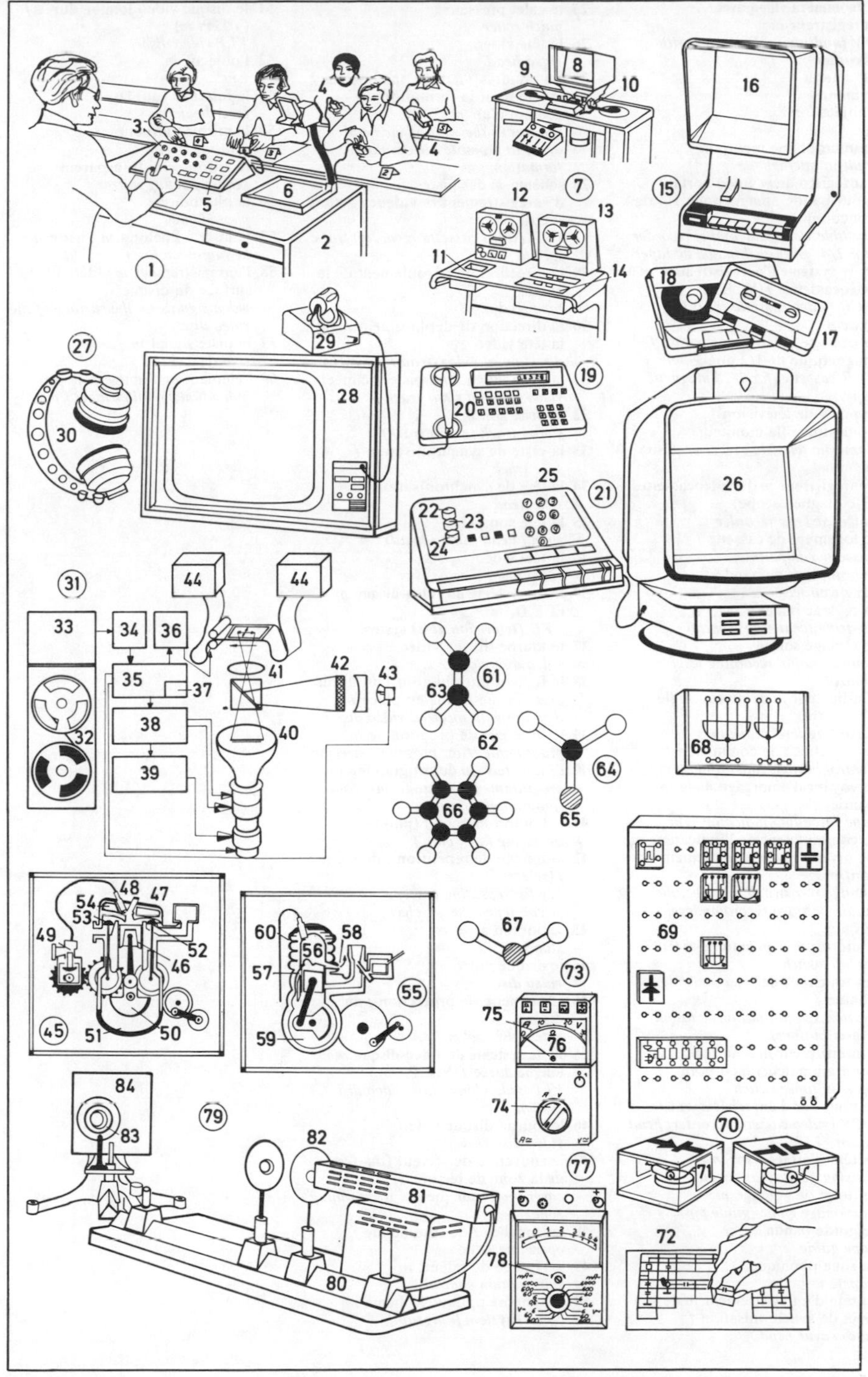
1
2
3
4
5
6
7
8
9
10
11
12
13
14
15
16
17
18
19
20
21
22
23
24
25
26
27
28
29
30
31
32
33
34
35
36
37
38
39
40
41
42
43
44
45
46
47
48
49
50
51
52
53
54
55
56
57
58
59
60
61
62
63
64
65
66
67
68
69
70
71
72
73
74
75
76
77
78
79
80
81
82
83
84

1-4 la caméra vidéo avec enregistreur *m*
– ***AV (audio-visual) camera with recorder***
1 la caméra
– *camera*
2 l'objectif *m*
– *lens*
3 le microphone incorporé
– *built-in microphone*
4 l'enregistreur *m* vidéo portatif (pour bande *f* magnétique 1/4 de pouce *m*)
– *portable video (videotape) recorder (for 1/4" open-reel magnetic tape)*
5-36 le système d'enregistrement *m* **à vidéocassettes** *f* (VCR *m*)
– ***VCR (video cassette recorder) system***
5 la cassette vidéo (pour bande *f* magnétique de 1/2 pouce *m*)
– *VCR cassette (for 1/2" magnetic tape)*
6 le poste de télévision *f* domestique (le moniteur)
– *domestic television receiver (*also: *monitor)*
7 l'enregistreur *m* de vidéocassettes *f* (le magnétoscope)
– *video cassette recorder*
8 le logement de cassette *f*
– *cassette compartment*
9 le compteur de bande *f*
– *tape counter*
10 le réglage image *f*
– *centring (centering) control*
11 le réglage son *m*
– *sound (audio) recording level control*
12 l'indicateur *m* de niveau *m* (le VU-mètre)
– *recording level indicator*
13 les touches *f* de commande *f*
– *control buttons (operating keys)*
14 le voyant d'amorçage *m* de la bande
– *tape threading indicator light*
15 le commutateur de l'indicateur *m* de niveau *m* d'enregistrement *m* son/image
– *changeover switch for selecting audio or video recording level display*
16 l'interrupteur *m* marche-arrêt
– *on/off switch*
17 les touches *f* de sélection *f* de chaîne *f*
– *station selector buttons (station preset buttons)*
18 l'interrupteur *m* à horloge *f* (le programmateur) incorporé
– *built-in timer switch*
19 le tambour d'enregistrement *m*
– *VCR (video cassette recorder) head drum*
20 la tête d'effacement *m*
– *erasing head (erase head)*
21 le doigt de guidage *m*
– *stationary guide (guide pin)*
22 le guide-bande
– *tape guide*
23 la roue phonique
– *capstan*
24 la tête d'enregistrement *m* de son *m* et de synchronisation *f*
– *audio sync head*
25 le galet presseur
– *pinch roller*
26 la tête vidéo
– *video head*
27 les rainures *f* dans le tambour de la tête pour la formation du coussin d'air *m*
– *grooves in the wall of the head drum to promote air cushion formation*
28 schéma *m* des pistes *f* d'enregistrement *m* vidéocassette *f* [VCR]
– *VCR (video cassette recorder) track format*
29 la direction du déroulement de la bande
– *tape feed*
30 la direction de déplacement *m* de la tête vidéo
– *direction of video head movement*
31 la piste vidéo, une piste inclinée
– *video track, a slant track*
32 la piste son *m*
– *sound track (audio track)*
33 la piste de synchronisation *f*
– *sync track*
34 la tête de synchronisation *f*
– *sync head*
35 la tête son *m*
– *sound head (audio head)*
36 la tête vidéo
– *video head*
37-45 le système de vidéo-disque *m* **(T.E.D.** *m***)**
– ***TED (television disc) system***
37 le tourne-disque vidéo
– *video disc player*
38 la fente d'introduction *f* du disque avec disque *m* mis en place *f*
– *disc slot with inserted video disc*
39 le sélecteur de programme *m*
– *programme (*Am. *program) selector*
40 l'indicateur *m* de programme *m*
– *programme (*Am. *program) scale (programme dial)*
41 le bouton marche *f* (play)
– *operating key ('play')*
42 la touche de répétition *f* de scène *f* (select)
– *key for repeating a scene (scene-repeat key, 'select')*
43 le bouton arrêt *m*
– *stop key*
44 le disque vidéo
– *video disc*
45 la pochette de protection *f* du disque
– *video disc jacket*
46-60 le système de vidéo-disque *m* **longue durée** *f* **(V.L.P.** *m***)**
– *VLP (video long play) video disc system*
46 le tourne-disque vidéo
– *video disc player*
47 le couvercle du lecteur (*au-dessus de* la zone de lecture *f*)
– *cover projection (*below it: *scanning zone)*
48 les touches *f* de commande *f*
– *operating keys*
49 le réglage de ralenti *m*
– *slow motion control*
50 le système optique [schéma *m*]
– *optical system [diagram]*
51 le disque vidéo longue durée *f* (V.L.P. *m*)
– *VLP video disc*
52 l'objectif *m*
– *lens*
53 le faisceau (du) laser
– *laser beam*
54 le miroir tournant
– *rotating mirror*
55 le miroir semi-transparent
– *semi-reflecting mirror*
56 la photodiode
– *photodiode*
57 le laser à l'hélium *m* - néon *m*
– *helium-neon laser*
58 l'enregistrement *m* vidéo à la surface du disque
– *video signals on the surface of the video disc*
59 la piste signal *m*
– *signal track*
60 l'élément *m* d'image *f* (le pit)
– *individual signal element ('pit')*

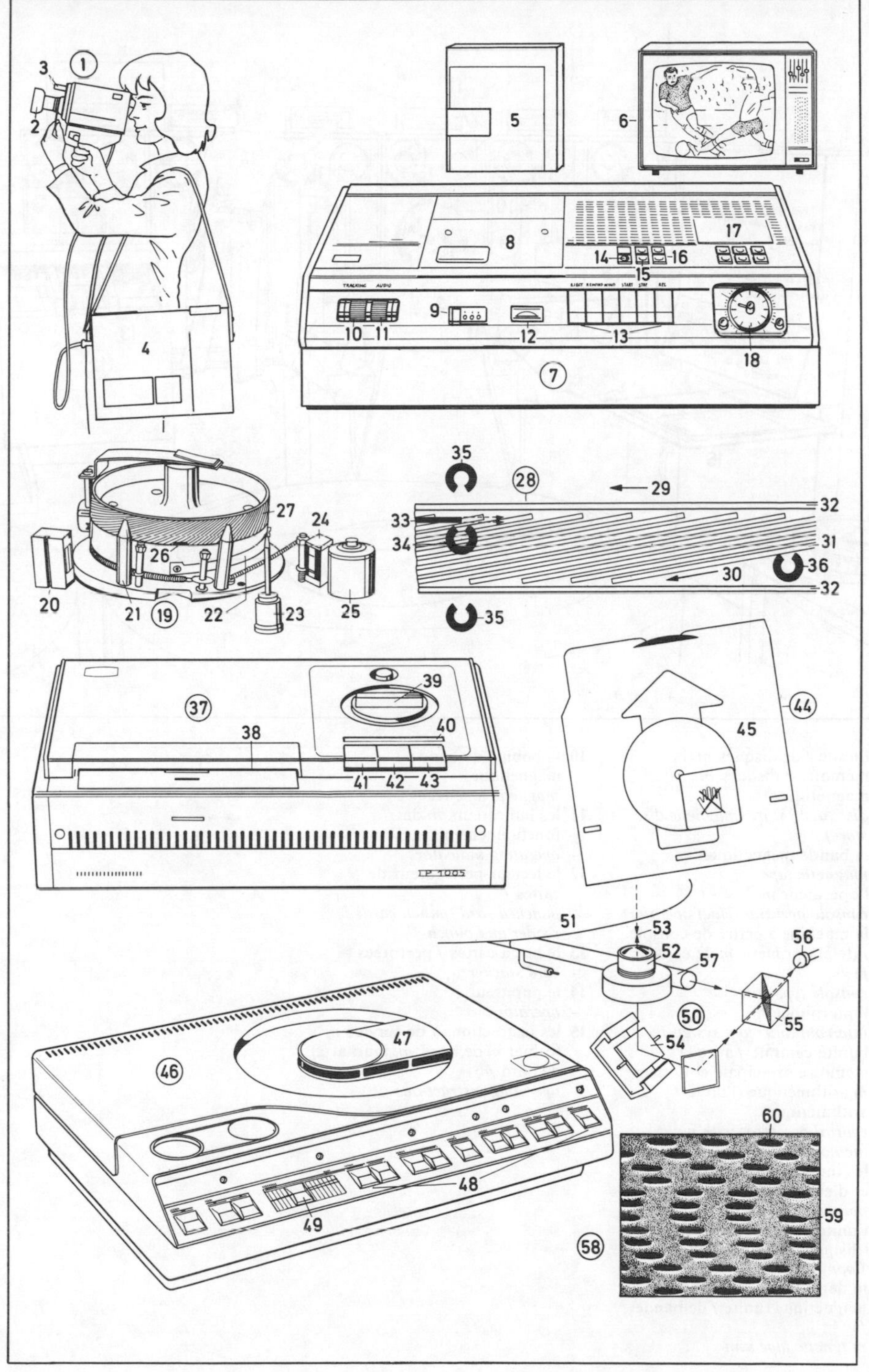
1
2
3
4
5
6
7
8
9
10
11
12
13
14
15
16
17
18
TRACKING AUDIO
EJECT REWIND WIND START STOP REC
19
20
21
22
23
24
25
26
27
28
29
30
31
32
33
34
35
36
37
38
39
40
41
42
43
44
45
46
47
48
49
50
51
52
53
54
55
56
57
58
59
60

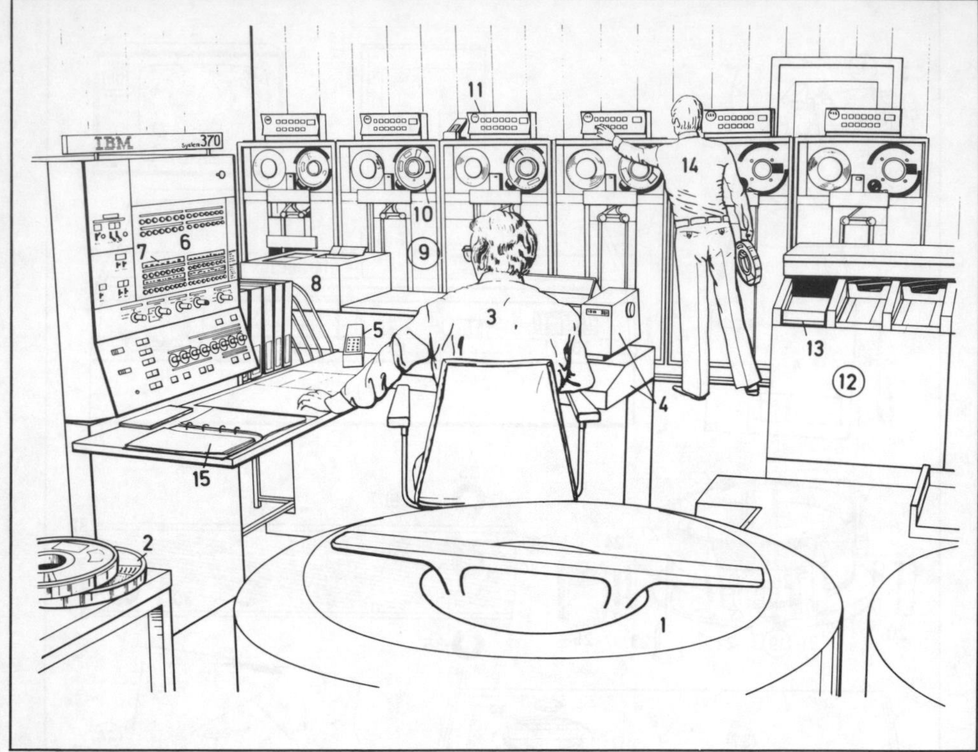

1 l'unité *f* de disques *m* (la mémoire à disques *m* magnétiques)
– *disc (disk) store (magnetic disc store)*
2 la bande magnétique
– *magnetic tape*
3 l'opérateur *m*
– *console operator (chief operator)*
4 la machine à écrire de console *f* (téléimprimeur *m* de console *f*)
– *console typewriter*
5 l'interphone *m*
– *intercom (intercom system)*
6 l'unité centrale *f* avec la mémoire principale et l'organe *m* arithmétique (l'unité *f* arithmétique)
– *central processor with main memory and arithmetic unit*
7 les indicateurs *m* d'opérations *f* et d'erreurs *f*
– *operation and error indicators*
8 l'unité *f* de disquettes *f* (disques *m* souples)
– *floppy disc (disk) reader*
9 le dérouleur de bande *f* magnétique (unité *f* de bande *f*)
– *magnetic tape unit*
10 la bobine de bande *f* magnétique
– *magnetic tape reel*
11 les indicateurs *m* de fonctionnement *m*
– *operating indicators*
12 le lecteur-perforateur de cartes *f*
– *punched card (punch card) reader and punch*
13 le bac à cartes *f* perforées
– *card stacker*
14 le pupitreur
– *operator*
15 les instructions *f* de service *m* (cahier *m* de bord *m*, journal *m* de bord *m*)
– *operating instructions*

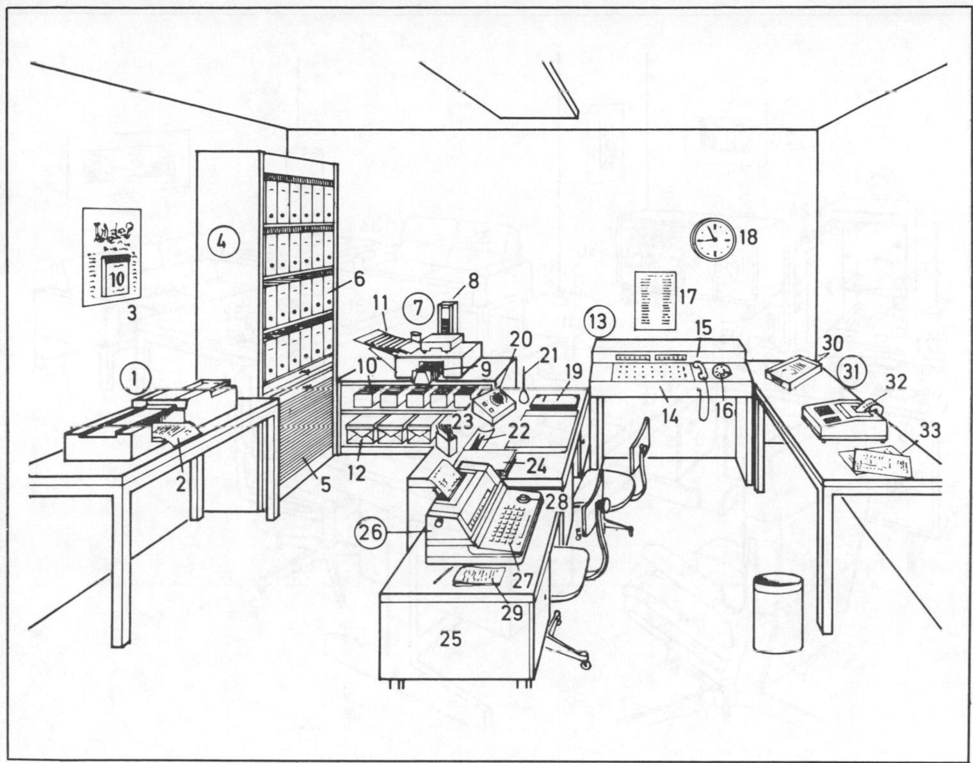

1-33 le bureau d'accueil *m* (le secrétariat)
– ***receptionist's office*** *(secretary's office)*

1 le télécopieur (l'émetteur-récepteur *m* de fac-similé *m*)
– *facsimile telegraph*

2 la télécopie (le fac-similé)
– *transmitted copy (received copy)*

3 le calendrier mural
– *wall calendar*

4 le (meuble-)classeur (le casier)
– *filing cabinet*

5 le rideau articulé à glissière *f*
– *tambour door (roll-up door)*

6 le (dossier-)classeur
– *file (document file)*

7 l'adressographe-duplicateur *m* à alcool *m* (la machine à adresser)
– *transfer-type addressing machine*

8 le magasin vertical à clichés *m*
– *vertical stencil magazine*

9 le dispositif de réception *f* des clichés *m*
– *stencil ejection*

10 la boîte de rangement *m* des clichés *m* (le panier, le casier à clichés)
– *stencil storage drawer*

11 le dispositif d'alimentation *f* en papier *m* (le plateau de chargement *m* du papier)
paper feed

12 la réserve de papier *m* à lettres *f*
– *stock of notepaper*

13 le central téléphonique privé
– *switchboard (internal telephone exchange)*

14 le clavier à boutons *m* poussoirs (à touches *f*) pour la transmission des communications *f* internes
– *push-button keyboard for internal connections*

15 le combiné (l'écouteur *m*)
– *handset*

16 le cadran d'appel *m*
– *dial*

17 le répertoire téléphonique des postes *m* d'abonnés *m* privés
– *internal telephone list*

18 l'horloge *f* mére (l'horloge *f* synchrone)
– *master clock (main clock)*

19 le parapheur
– *folder containing documents, correspondence, etc. for signing (to be signed)*

20 l'interphone *m*
– *intercom (office intercom)*

21 le stylo
– *pen*

22 le plumier plateau
– *pen and pencil tray*

23 le fichier
– *card index*

24 la pile de formulaires *m*
– *stack (set) of forms*

25 le bureau de dactylo *f* (la table de machine *f* à écrire)
– *typing desk*

26 la machine à écrire à mémoire *f*
– *memory typewriter*

27 le clavier de machine *f* à écrire
– *keyboard*

28 l'interrupteur *m* rotatif de la mémoire de travail *m* et de la boucle de bande *f* magnétique
– *rotary switch for the main memory and the magnetic tape loop*

29 le bloc sténo
– *shorthand pad* (Am. *steno pad)*

30 la corbeille à courrier *m* (le casier à correspondance *f*)
– *letter tray*

31 la calculatrice de bureau *m*
– *office calculator*

32 l'imprimante *f*
– *printer*

33 la lettre commerciale
– *business letter*

1-36 le bureau de direction *f*
– ***executive's office***
1 le siège de bureau, un fauteuil tournant capitonné
– *swivel chair*
2 le bureau
– *desk*
3 le plan de travail *m* bureau *m*
– *writing surface (desk top)*
4 le tiroir de bureau *m*
– *desk drawer*
5 le coffre (à tiroirs *m*) avec trappe *f* abattante
– *cupboard (storage area) with door*
6 le sous-main
– *desk mat (blotter)*
7 la lettre commerciale
– *business letter*
8 l'agenda *m* de bureau *m*
– *appointments diary*
9 le plumier avec porte-stylo *m*
– *desk set*
10 l'interphone *m*
– *intercom (office intercom)*
11 la lampe de bureau *m*
– *desk lamp*
12 la calculatrice de poche *f* (la calculatrice électronique)
– *pocket calculator (electronic calculator)*
13 le téléphone, un poste d'intercommunication *f*
– *telephone, an executive-secretary system*
14 le cadran d'appel *m*; *égal.*: le clavier à touches *f*
– *dial;* also: *push-button keyboard*
15 les touches *f* d'appel *m*
– *call buttons*
16 le combiné (l'écouteur *m*)
– *receiver (telephone receiver)*
17 la machine à dicter
– *dictating machine*
18 l'indicateur *m* de longueur *f* de dictée *f*
– *position indicator*
19 les touches *f* de commande *f*
– *control buttons (operating keys)*
20 l'armoire *f* basse (le meuble-classeur)
– *cabinet*
21 le fauteuil du visiteur
– *visitor's chair*
22 le coffre-fort (le coffre-bloc)
– *safe*
23 la gâchette (serrure *f*)
– *bolts (locking mechanism)*
24 le blindage (la paroi blindée en acier *m*)
– *armour (*Am. *armor) plating*
25 les documents *m* (les dossiers *m*) confidentiels
– *confidential documents*
26 le brevet (le titre de propriété *f* industrielle)
– *patent*
27 l'argent *m* liquide
– *petty cash*
28 le tableau
– *picture*
29 le meuble-bar
– *bar (drinks cabinet)*
30 le service de verres *m*
– *bar set*
31-36 l'ensemble *m* de conférence *f*
– *conference grouping*
31 la table de conférence *f*
– *conference table*
32 l'enregistreur *m* de poche *f*
– *pocket-sized dictating machine (micro cassette recorder)*
33 le cendrier
– *ashtray*
34 la table d'angle *m*
– *corner table*
35 la lampe de table *f*
– *table lamp*
36 le fauteuil de conférence *f* capitonné
– *two-seater sofa [part of the conference grouping]*

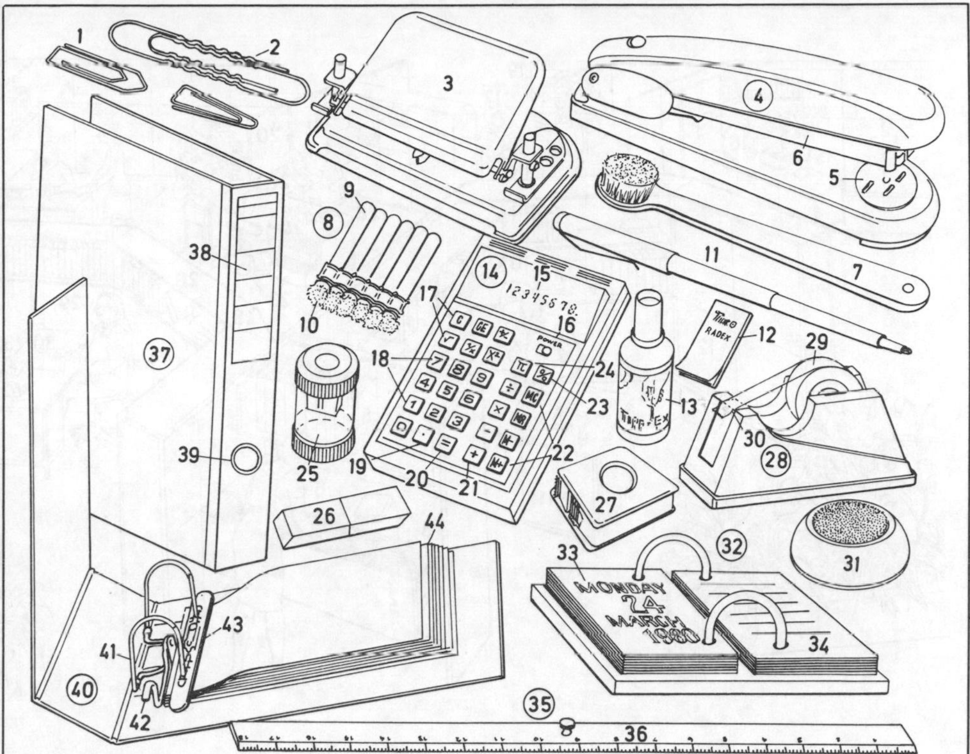

1-44 le matériel (les fournitures *f*) de bureau
– ***office equipment*** *(office supplies, office materials)*
1 l'attache *f* de bureau *m* (le trombone)
– *[small] paper clip*
2 le trombone géant
– *[large] paper clip*
3 le perforateur
– *punch*
4 *l'agrafeuse* f *de bureau* m
– *stapler*
5 l'enclume *f*
– *anvil*
6 le poussoir de chargement *m*
– *spring-loaded magazine*
7 la brosse de nettoyage des caractères *m* de machine *f* à écrire
– *type-cleaning brush for typewriters*
8 les bâtons *m* pour nettoyer les caractères *m*
– *type cleaner (type-cleaning kit)*
9 le tube de dissolvant *m*
– *fluid container (fluid reservoir)*
10 le pinceau de nettoyage *m*
– *cleaning brush*
11 le stylo-feutre
– *felt tip pen*
12 le correcteur de frappe *f*
– *correcting paper [for typing errors]*
13 le liquide correcteur
– *correcting fluid [for typing errors]*
14 la calculatrice électronique de poche *f* (la calculette)
– *electronic pocket calculator*
15 l'affichage *m* électroluminescent à 8 chiffres *m*
– *eight-digit fluorescent display*
16 l'interrupteur *m* marche *f*/arrêt *m*
– *on/off switch*
17 les touches *f* de fonction *f*
– *function keys*
18 les touches *f* de chiffre *m* (les touches *f* numériques)
– *number keys*
19 la touche de virgule *f* (la touche de virgulage *m*, de décimalisation *f*)
– *decimal key*
20 la touche de résultat *m* (la touche de totalisation *f*)
– *equals' key*
21 les touches *f* d'instruction *f* (les touches *f* d'opération *f*)
– *instruction keys (command keys)*
22 les touches *f* de mémoire *f* (les touches *f* de mise *f* en mémoire *f*, d'enregistrement *m* en mémoire *f*)
– *memory keys*
23 la touche de pourcentage *m* (la touche de calcul *m* d'intérêts *m*)
– *percent key (percentage key)*
24 la touche π (pour le calcul de la circonférence d'un cercle)
– *π-key (pi-key) for mensuration of circles*
25 le taille-crayon (taille-crayons *m*)
– *pencil sharpener*
26 la gomme (pour) machine *f* à écrire
– *typewriter rubber*
27 le distributeur de ruban *m* adhésif
– *adhesive tape dispenser*
28 le dévidoir de table *f* de ruban *m* adhésif
– *adhesive tape holder (roller-type adhesive tape dispenser)*
29 le rouleau de ruban *m* adhésif
– *roll of adhesive tape*
30 l'arête *f* coupante (le bord denté)
– *tear-off edge*
31 le mouilleur de bureau *m* avec éponge *f*
– *moistener*
32 le bloc éphéméride
– *desk diary*
33 la feuille (la page) de calendrier *m*
– *date sheet (calendar sheet)*
34 la feuille (la page) de notes *f* (d'annotation *f*)
– *memo sheet*
35 la règle graduée
– *ruler*
36 le biseau gradué (la graduation) en centimètres *m* et millimètres *m*
– *centimetre and millimetre (*Am. *centimeter and millimeter) graduations*
37 le classeur à levier *m*
– *file (document file)*
38 l'étiquette *f* d'indexage *m*
– *spine label (spine tag)*
39 la perforation (le trou) de manipulation *f*
– *finger hole*
40 le classeur de relevés *m*
– *arch board file*
41 la mécanique du classeur
– *arch unit*
42 le levier classeur *m*
– *release lever (locking lever, release/lock lever)*
43 le curseur de blocage *m*
– *compressor*
44 le relevé (l'extrait *m*) de compte *m*
– *bank statement (statement of account)*

1-48 le bureau en espace *m* ouvert ou bureau *m* collectif (le bureau-paysage)
– ***open plan office***

1 la cloison séparatrice (la cloisonnette, le panneau-écran)
– *partition wall (partition screen)*

2 le fichier d'archivage *m* (l'armoire *f* de classement *m* d'archives *f*) avec coffre *m* pour dossiers *m* suspendus (avec classeur-tiroir *m* à visibilité *f* horizontale)
– *filing drawer with suspension file system*

3 le dossier suspendu
– *suspension file*

4 *file tab*

5 le classeur
– *file (document file)*

6 l'archiviste *m*
– *filing clerk*

7 l'employé *m* de bureau *m* (le rédacteur)
– *clerical assistant*

8 la fiche de dossier *m*
– *note for the files*

9 le téléphone
– *telephone*

10 l'étagère *f* à dossiers *m* (l'étagère *f* de rangement *m* des classeurs *m*)
– *filing shelves*

11 le bureau
– *clerical assistant's desk*

12 l'armoire *f* de rangement *m* (de classement *m*)
– *office cupboard*

13 le bac à plantes *f* (la jardinière, le jardin d'appartement *m*)
– *plant stand (planter)*

14 les plantes *f* d'intérieur *m* (d'appartement *m*)
– *indoor plants (houseplants)*

15 la programmeuse
– *programmer*

16 l'écran *m* de visualisation *f*
– *data display terminal (visual display unit)*

17 l'employé *m* du service après-vente
– *customer service representative*

18 le client
– *customer*

19 le dessin réalisé par ordinateur *m*
– *computer-generated design (computer-generated art)*

20 la cloison d'insonorisation *f* (la cloison acoustique, d'absorption *f* du son)
– *sound-absorbing partition*

21 la dactylo(graphe)
– *typist*

22 la machine à écrire
– *typewriter*

23 le tiroir-fichier
– *filing drawer*

24 le fichier (de la) clientèle
– *customer card index*

25 le siège de bureau *m*, une chaise tournante réglable en hauteur *f*
– *office chair, a swivel chair*

26 le bureau de dactylo *f* (la table de machine *f* à écrire)
– *typing desk*

27 la boîte à fiches *f*
– *card index box*

28 l'étagère *f* modulaire (l'étagère *f* démontable, le rayonnage à usages *m* multiples, polyvalent)
– *multi-purpose shelving*

29 le directeur (le chef de service *m*)
– *proprietor*

30 la lettre commerciale
– *business letter*

31 la secrétaire de direction *f*
– *proprietor's secretary*
32 le bloc sténo
– *shorthand pad* (Am. *steno pad)*
33 l'audiotypiste *f*
– *audio typist*
34 la machine à dicter
– *dictating machine*
35 l'écouteur *m* auriculaire (d'oreille *f*) placé dans le pavillon de l'oreille *f*
– *earphone*
36 le graphique (le diagramme) de statistiques *f*
– *statistics chart*
37 le coffre (le caisson) à tiroirs *m* du bureau-ministre
– *pedestal containing a cupboard or drawers*
38 le placard à portes glissantes (à glissière *f*, à coulisse *f*)
– *sliding-door cupboard*
39 les éléments *m* de bureau *m* (les cloisonnettes *f*, les panneaux-écrans *m*) disposés en angle *m*
– *office furniture arranged in an angular configuration*
40 l'étagère *f* suspendue (le rayonnage suspendu)
– *wall-mounted shelf*
41 la corbeille à courrier *m* (le bac à correspondance *f*)
– *letter tray*
42 le calendrier mural
– *wall calendar*
43 le centre de transmission *f* de données *f* (la banque de données *f*, le fichier central, le serveur en informations *f* factuelles)
– *data centre (*Am. *center)*
44 la demande d'informations *f* inscrite sur l'écran de visualisation *f*
– *calling up information on the data display terminal (visual display unit)*
45 la corbeille à papier *m*
– *waste paper basket*
46 le graphique statistique des ventes *f*
– *sales statistics*
47 la liste informatique (de traitement *m* électronique de l'information *f*), un imprimé à pliage *m* accordéon (paravent *m*)
– *EDP print-out, a continuous fan-fold sheet*
48 l'élément *m* modulaire d'assemblage *m*
– *connecting element*

1 **la machine à écrire électrique,** une machine à écrire à sphère *f* (à tête *f* d'impression *f*, d'écriture *f* cylindrique, à boule *f*)
– ***electric typewriter**, a golf ball typewriter*
2-6 le clavier
– *keyboard*
2 la barre d'espacement *m*
– *space bar*
3 la touche majuscule
– *shift key*
4 la touche d'interligne *m* et de retour *m* à la ligne
– *line space and carrier return key*
5 la touche fixe-majuscule
– *shift lock*
6 la touche passe-marge
– *margin release key*
7 la touche de tabulation *f* (la commande de pose *f* des taquets *m* de tabulateur *m*)
– *tabulator key*
8 la touche d'annulation *f* de tabulation *f* (la commande de dépose *f* des taquets *m* du tabulateur)
– *tabulator clear key*
9 l'interrupteur *m* marche *f*/arrêt *m*
– *on/off switch*
10 le levier de réglage *m* de la force d'impression *f*
– *striking force control (impression control)*
11 le sélecteur de position *f* du ruban encreur (encré, bicolore)
– *ribbon selector*
12 l'échelle *f* graduée
– *margin scale*
13 le margeur gauche
– *left margin stop*
14 le margeur droit
– *right margin stop*
15 la sphère (la boule) mobile portant les caractères *m* (la tête d'impression *f*, d'écriture *f* cylindrique, l'imprimante-caractères)
– *golf ball (spherical typing element) bearing the types*
16 la cartouche de ruban *m* encreur (encré, bicolore)
– *ribbon cassette*
17 la barre presse-papier avec guide-papier *m* mobiles
– *paper bail with rollers*
18 le cylindre
– *platen*
19 le guide-ligne transparent
– *typing opening (typing window)*
20 le levier de dégagement *m* du papier
– *paper release lever*
21 le levier de recul *m* (le levier de frappe *f*, de marche *f* arrière, le levier de rappel *m*, de retour *m* du chariot)
– *carrier return lever*
22 le bouton d'entraînement *m* du cylindre *m*
– *platen knob*
23 le sélecteur d'interligne *m* à positions *f* multiples
– *line space adjuster*
24 le levier de libération *f* du cylindre
– *variable platen action lever*
25 le bouton de débrayage *m* du cylindre
– *push-in platen variable*
26 la tablette d'appui *m* pour annotations *f* et gommage *m*
– *erasing table*
27 le capot de protection *f* transparent
– *transparent cover*
28 la sphère (la boule, la tête d'impression *f*) interchangeable
– *exchange golf ball (exchange typing element)*
29 le caractère
– *type*
30 le couvercle de la sphère (de la boule, de la tête d'impression *f*)
– *golf ball cap (cap of typing element)*
31 les segments *m* dentés
– *teeth*
32 **le copieur (le polycopieur, le photocopieur) automatique à bobine** *f*
– ***web-fed automatic copier***
33 le magasin (le compartiment) à bobine *f*
– *magazine for paper roll*
34 le curseur de réglage *m* (de sélection *f*) du format
– *paper size selection (format selection)*
35 le présélecteur de copies *f* (le totalisateur de copies *f*)
– *print quantity selection*
36 le bouton de réglage *m* du contraste (le bouton de commande *f* de la qualité des copies *f*)
– *contrast control*
37 l'interrupteur *m* principal
– *main switch (on/off switch)*
38 le bouton de commande *f* de copie *f*
– *start print button*
39 la glace porte-original
– *document glass*
40 la bande entraîneuse en caoutchouc *m*
– *transfer blanket*
41 le porte-toner (le rouleau encreur)
– *toner roll*
42 le système d'exposition *f* (d'éclairement *m*)
– *exposure system*
43 le distributeur de copies *f* (le plateau récepteur)
– *print delivery (copy delivery)*
44 **la machine à plier les lettres** *f* (la plieuse)
– ***letter-folding machine***
45 le plateau de chargement *m* du papier (le bloc d'alimentation *f* en papier *m*)
– *paper feed*
46 le dispositif de pliage *m*
– *folding mechanism*
47 le plateau récepteur
– *receiving tray*
48 **la petite presse offset**
– ***small offset press***
49 le margeur
– *paper feed*
50 le levier d'encrage *m* des plaques *f* offset
– *lever for inking the plate cylinder*
51-52 l'encrage *m*
– *inking unit (inker unit)*
51 le rouleau distributeur (le distributeur)
– *distributing roller (distributor)*
52 le rouleau encreur (l'encreur *m*)
– *ink roller (inking roller, fountain roller)*
53 le bouton de réglage *m* de la pression
– *pressure adjustment*
54 la sortie
– *sheet delivery (receiving table)*
55 le bouton de réglage *m* de la vitesse d'impression *f*
– *printing speed adjustment*
56 la taqueuse vibrante de pile *f* (de liasse *f*) de feuilles *f*
– *jogger for aligning the piles of sheets*
57 la pile (la liasse) de feuilles *f*
– *pile of paper (pile of sheets)*
58 la machine à plier (la plieuse)
– *folding machine*
59 l'assembleuse f pour faibles tirages *m*
– *gathering machine (collating machine, assembling machine) for short runs*
60 le bloc d'assemblage *m*
– *gathering station (collating station, assembling station)*
61 la brocheuse automatique pour reliure *f* thermique sans couture *f*
– *adhesive binder (perfect binder) for hot adhesives*
62 **la machine à dicter à bande** *f* **magnétique**
– ***magnetic tape dictating machine***
63 le casque d'écoute *f* (l'écouteur *m* auriculaire)
– *headphones (headset, earphones)*
64 l'interrupteur *m* marche *f*/arrêt *m*
– *on/off switch*
65 le berceau du microphone
– *microphone cradle*
66 la prise pédale *f* dactylo (la prise extérieure, la prise de raccordement *m* à la pédale dactylo)
– *foot control socket*
67 la prise (de) téléphone *m* (la prise auxiliaire pour téléphone *m*)
– *telephone adapter socket*
68 la prise (d')écouteur *m* (la prise (de) casque *m* d'écoute *f*)
– *headphone socket (earphone socket, headset socket)*
69 la prise (de) micro *m*
– *microphone socket*
70 le haut-parleur incorporé
– *built-in loudspeaker*
71 le voyant lumineux (la lampe témoin)
– *indicator lamp (indicator light)*
72 le chargeur de cassette *f*
– *cassette compartment*
73 les touches *f* d'avance *f* rapide (d'enroulement *m* rapide, de rebobinage *m* rapide avant), de retour *m* arrière (de déroulement *m* rapide, de rebobinage *m* rapide arrière) et de pause *f* (d'arrêt *m*)
– *forward wind, rewind, and stop buttons*
74 le compteur horaire (le compteur de durée *f* de fonctionnement *m*) avec graduation *f*
– *time scale with indexing marks*
75 le curseur d'arrêt *m* du compteur horaire
– *time scale stop*

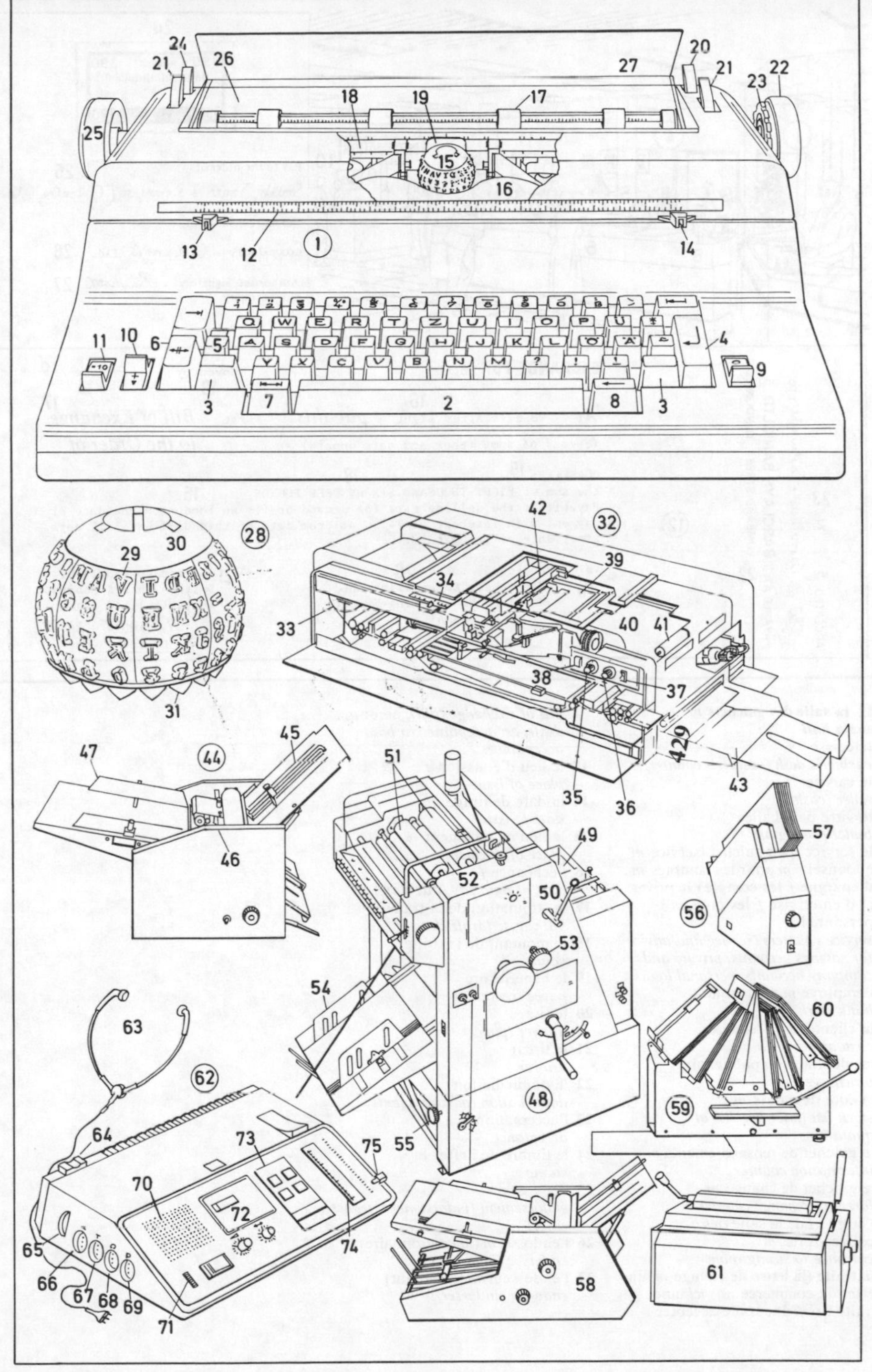
24
21
26
27
20
21
22
23
25
18
19
17
15
16
13
12
1
14
11
10
6
5
4
9
3
7
2
8
3
30
28
29
31
42
32
39
34
33
40
41
38
37
429
35
36
43
45
44
47
46
51
49
52
50
56
57
53
54
60
63
62
48
59
64
73
75
55
70
72
74
65
66
67
68
69
58
61
71

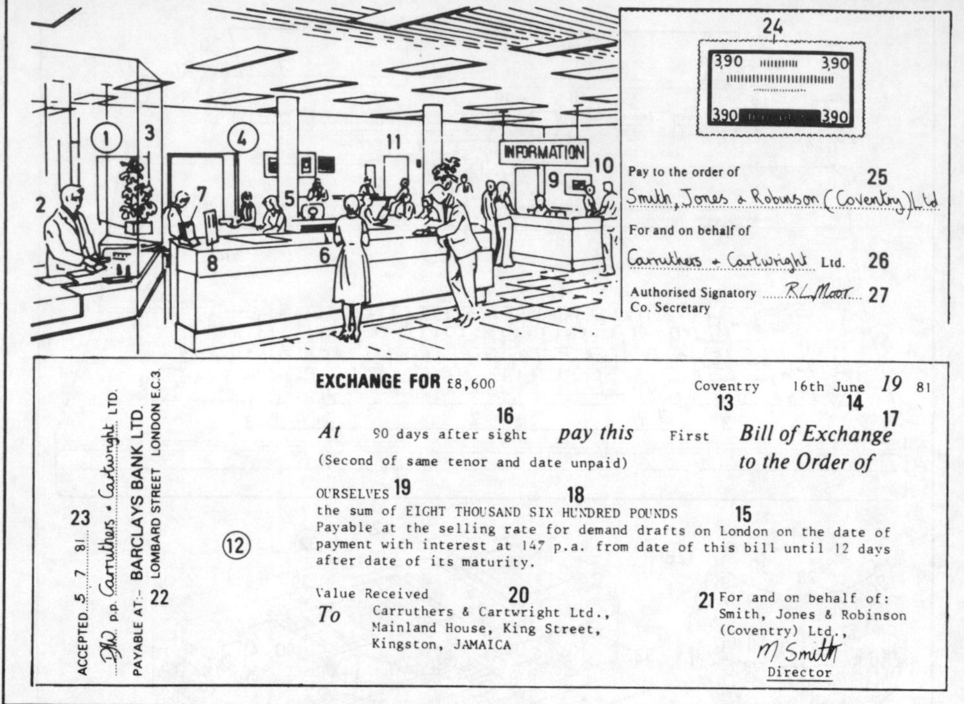

1
2
3
4
5
6
7
8
9
10
11
INFORMATION
24
3,90
3,90
3,90
3,90
Pay to the order of
25
Smith, Jones & Robinson (Coventry) Ltd
For and on behalf of
Carruthers & Cartwright Ltd.
26
Authorised Signatory R.L.Moor 27
Co. Secretary
EXCHANGE FOR £8,600
Coventry
13
16th June
14
19 81
17
16
At 90 days after sight pay this First Bill of Exchange
(Second of same tenor and date unpaid) to the Order of
OURSELVES 19
18
the sum of EIGHT THOUSAND SIX HUNDRED POUNDS
15
Payable at the selling rate for demand drafts on London on the date of payment with interest at 14% p.a. from date of this bill until 12 days after date of its maturity.
Value Received
20
To Carruthers & Cartwright Ltd., Mainland House, King Street, Kingston, JAMAICA
21 For and on behalf of: Smith, Jones & Robinson (Coventry) Ltd.,
M Smith
Director
12
23
ACCEPTED 5 7 81
DW p.p. Carruthers & Cartwright LTD.
PAYABLE AT:- BARCLAYS BANK LTD. LOMBARD STREET LONDON E.C.3.
22

1-11 la salle des guichets *m*
– ***main hall***

1 la caisse
– *cashier's desk (cashier's counter)*

2 le caissier
– *teller (cashier)*

3 la vitre pare-balles
– *bullet-proof glass*

4 le service d'un guichet (service *m* et conseils *m* pour les comptes *m* d'épargne *f*, les comptes *m* privés et d'entreprise *f*, les prêts *m* personnels)
– *service counters (service and advice for savings accounts, private and company accounts, personal loans)*

5 l'employé *m* de banque *f*
– *bank clerk*

6 la cliente de la banque
– *customer*

7 les dépliants *m* publicitaires
– *brochures*

8 la cote des cours *m*
– *stock list (price list, list of quotations)*

9 le guichet de renseignements *m*
– *information counter*

10 le guichet de change *m*
– *foreign exchange counter*

11 l'entrée *f* de la salle des coffres-forts *m*
– *entrance to strong room*

12 la traite (la lettre de change *m*, un effet de commerce *m*); *ici:* une traite tirée, une traite acceptée
– ***bill of exchange*** *(bill);* here: *a draft, an acceptance (a bank acceptance)*

13 le lieu d'émission *f*
– *place of issue*

14 la date de tirage *m*
– *date of issue*

15 le lieu de paiement *m*
– *place of payment*

16 l'échéance *f*
– *date of maturity (due date)*

17 la stipulation de la traite
– *bill clause (draft clause)*

18 le montant de la traite
– *value*

19 le bénéficiaire
– *payee (remittee)*

20 le tiré
– *drawee (payer)*

21 le tireur
– *drawer*

22 la domiciliation
– *domicilation (paying agent)*

23 l'acceptation *f*
– *acceptance*

24 le timbre de l'effet *m*
– *stamp*

25 l'endos *m*
– *endorsement (indorsement, transfer entry)*

26 l'endossé *m* (le cessionnaire)
– *endorsee (indorsee)*

27 l'endosseur *m* (le cédant)
– *endorser (indorser)*

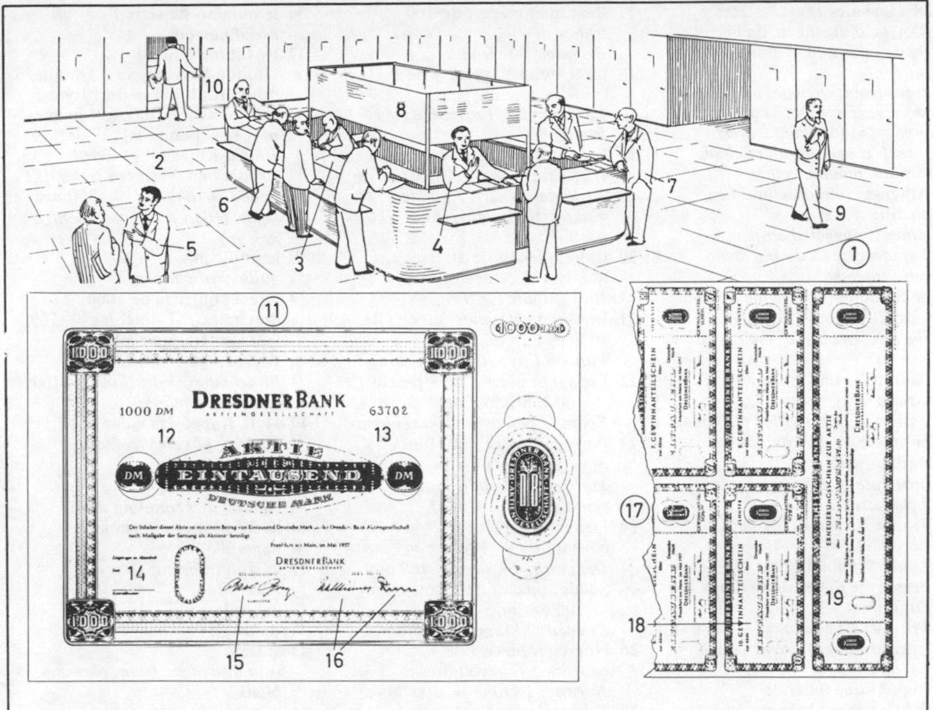

1-10 la Bourse (la Bourse des effets *m,* la Bourse des valeurs *f*)
- ***stock exchange*** *(exchange for the sale of securities, stocks, and bonds)*

1 la salle de la Bourse
- *exchange hall (exchange floor)*

2 le marché des valeurs *f*
- *market for securities*

3 la corbeille
- *broker's post*

4 l'agent *m* de change *m* (le courtier assermenté), un courtier
- *sworn stockbroker (exchange broker, stockbroker,* Am. *specialist), an inside broker*

5 le courtier libre pour les transactions *f* sur le marché libre
- *kerbstone broker (kerbstoner, curbstone broker, curbstoner, outside broker), a commercial broker dealing in unlisted securities*

6 le membre de la Bourse, un particulier admis aux transactions *f*
- *member of the stock exchange (stockjobber,* Am. *floor trader, room trader)*

7 l'agent *m* en Bourse *f,* un employé de banque *f*
- *stock exchange agent (boardman), a bank employee*

8 la cote de la Bourse
- *quotation board*

9 le garçon à la Bourse
- *stock exchange attendant (waiter)*

10 la cabine téléphonique
- *telephone box (telephone booth, telephone kiosk, call box)*

11-19 les valeurs *f*; *catégories f:* action *f,* valeur *f* à revenu *m* fixe, emprunt *m,* obligation *f* hypothécaire, obligation *f* communale, obligation *f* industrielle, obligation *f* convertible
- ***securities;*** kinds: *share (*Am. *stock), fixed-income security, annuity, bond, debenture bond, municipal bond (corporation stock), industrial bond, convertible bond*

11 l'action *f* (le titre); *ici:* l'action *f* au porteur
- *share certificate (*Am. *stock certificate);* here: *bearer share (share warrant)*

12 la valeur nominale de l'action *f*
- *par (par value, nominal par, face par) of the share*

13 le numéro d'ordre *m*
- *serial number*

14 le numéro de page *f* de l'inscription *f* au registre *m* des actions *f* de la banque
- *page number of entry in bank's share register (bank's stock ledger)*

15 la signature du président du conseil de surveillance *f*
- *signature of the chairman of the board of governors*

16 la signature du président du conseil de direction *f* (le directeur général)
- *signature of the chairman of the board of directors*

17 la feuille de coupons *m*
- *sheet of coupons (coupon sheet, dividend coupon sheet)*

18 le coupon du dividende
- *dividend warrant (dividend coupon)*

19 le talon de renouvellement *m*
- *talon*

252 Argent (pièces de monnaie et billets de banque)

1-28 monnaies *f* (*var.*: pièces *f* d'or *m*, d'argent *m*, de nickel *m*, de cuivre *m*, d'aluminium *m*)
– ***coins*** *(coin, coinage, metal money, specie,* Am. *hard money;* kinds: *gold, silver, nickel, copper, or aluminium,* Am. *aluminum, coins)*

1 Athènes: tétradrachme *f* en pastille *f*
– *Athens: nugget-shaped tetradrachm (tetradrachmon, tetradrachma)*

2 la chouette (l'emblème *m* de la ville d'Athènes)
– *the owl (emblem of the city of Athens)*

3 l'aureus *m* de Constantin le Grand
– *aureus of Constantine the Great*

4 la bractéate de Frédéric Ier Barberousse
– *bracteate of Emperor Frederick I Barbarossa*

5 France: le louis d'or *m* de Louis XIV
– *Louis XIV louis-d'or*

6 Prusse: le thaler de Frédéric le Grand
– *Prussia: 1 reichstaler (speciestaler) of Frederick the Great*

7 République fédérale d'Allemagne: la pièce de 5 deutschemark *m* (DM); 1 DM = 100 pfennig *m*
– *Federal Republic of Germany: 5 Deutschmarks (DM); 1 DM = 100 pfennigs*

8 l'avers *m* (le droit, la face)
– *obverse*

9 le revers (la pile)
– *reverse (subordinate side)*

10 l'indicatif *m* du lieu *m* de frappe *f*
– *mint mark (mintage, exergue)*

11 l'inscription *f* sur la tranche
– *legend (inscription on the edge of a coin)*

12 l'effigie *f*, une allégorie nationale
– *device (type), a provincial coat of arms*

13 Autriche: pièce *f* de 25 schilling *m*; 1 schilling = 100 groschen *m*
– *Austria: 25 schillings; 1 sch = 100 groschen*

14 les écussons *m* des provinces *f*
– *provincial coats of arms*

15 Suisse: pièce *f* de 5 francs *m*; 1 franc suisse = 100 centimes *m*
– *Switzerland: 5 francs; 1 franc = 100 centimes*

16 France: pièce *f* de 1 franc *m*; 1 franc = 100 centimes *m*
– *France: 1 franc = 100 centimes*

17 Belgique: pièce *f* de 100 francs *m*
– *Belgium: 100 francs*

18 Luxembourg: pièce *f* de 1 franc *m*
– *Luxembourg (Luxemburg): 1 franc*

19 Pays-Bas: pièce *f* de 2 florins 1/2; 1 florin *m* = 100 cents *m*
– *Netherlands: 2 1/2 guilders; 1 guilder (florin, gulden) = 100 cents*

20 Italie: pièce *f* de 10 lires *f*; 1 lire = 100 centesimi *m*
– *Italy: 10 lire* (sg. *lira)*

21 Etat *m* du Vatican: pièce *f* de 10 lires *f*
– *Vatican City: 10 lire* (sg. *lira)*

22 Espagne: pièce *f* de 1 peseta *f* = 100 céntimos *m*
– *Spain: 1 peseta = 100 céntimos*

23 Portugal: pièce *f* de 1 escudo *m* = 100 centavos *m*
– *Portugal: 1 escudo = 100 centavos*

24 Danemark: pièce de 1 couronne *f* = 100 re *m*
– *Denmark: 1 krone = 100 öre*

25 Suède: pièce *f* de 1 couronne *f* = 100 öre *m*
– *Sweden: 1 krona = 100 öre*

26 Norvège: pièce *f* de 1 couronne *f* = 100 öre *m*
– *Norway: 1 krone = 100 öre*

27 Tchécoslovaquie: pièce de 1 couronne *f* = 100 haléři *m* [1 heller *m*]
– *Czechoslovakia: 1 koruna = 100 heller*

28 Yougoslavie: pièce de 1 dinar *m* = 100 para *m*
– *Yugoslavia: 1 dinar = 100 paras*

29-39 billets *m* **de banque**
– ***banknotes*** (Am. *bills) (paper money, notes, treasury notes)*

29 République fédérale d'Allemagne: billet *m* de 20 DM *m*
– *Federal Republic of Germany: 20 DM*

30 indication *f* de la banque d'émission *f*
– *bank of issue (bank of circulation)*

31 le filigrane (le médaillon en camaïeu *m*)
– *watermark [a portrait]*

32 la valeur nominale
– *denomination*

33 États-Unis *m* d'Amérique (USA): billet *m* de 1 dollar *m* ($) = 100 cents *m*
– *USA: 1 dollar ($) = 100 cents*

34 les signatures *f* en fac-similé *m*
– *facsimile signatures*

35 le timbre de contrôle *m*
– *impressed stamp*

36 le numéro de série *f*
– *serial number*

37 Royaume-Uni de Grande-Bretagne et d'Irlande du Nord: billet *m* de 1 livre *f* sterling (£) = 100 new pence *m* [1 new penny *m*]
– *United Kingdom of Great Britain and Northern Ireland: 1 pound sterling (£1) = 100 new pence (100p.); (sg. new penny, new p.)*

38 le guillochis
– *guilloched pattern*

39 Grèce: billet *m* de 1000 drachmes *f*; 1 drachme = 100 lepta *m* [1 lepton *m*]
– *Greece: 1,000 drachmas (drachmae); 1 drachma = 100 lepta* (sg. *lepton)*

40-44 la frappe des monnaies *f*
– ***striking of coins*** *(coinage, mintage)*

40-41 les coins *m*
– *coining dies (minting dies)*

40 le coin supérieur (mobile)
– *upper die*

41 le coin inférieur (fixe)
– *lower die*

42 la virole
– *collar*

43 le flan
– *coin disc (disk) (flan, planchet, blank)*

44 la presse monétaire
– *coining press (minting press)*

1
2
3
4
5
EIN REICHSTHALER
17A85
6
7
BUNDESREPUBLIK DEUTSCHLAND
5
DEUTSCHE MARK
8
12
1975
9
10
11
13
14
REPUBLIK ÖSTERREICH
25
SCHILLING
5FR
1968
15
LIBERTE · EGALITE · FRATERNITE
1
FRANC
1960
16
BELGIË
FRK
17
1
F
18
19
70
$2\frac{1}{2}$
G
NEDERLAND
19
10
20
CITTA DEL VATICANO
L.100
21
UNA PESETA
22
1
ESCUDO
23
19
75
1 KRONE
24
19
73
1
KR
PLIKTEN FRAMFÖR ALLT
25
NORGE
19
54
1 KRONE
26
J 7743002 Y
31
Banknote
32
ZWANZIG
DEUTSCHE MARK
20
30
DEUTSCHE
BUNDESBANK
ZWANZIG
DEUTSCHE
MARK
J 7743002 Y
29
CERTIFICATE
STATES OF AMERICA
A 37400134 B
ONE DOLLAR
35
36
WASHINGTON DC
34
A 37400134 B
ONE DOLLAR
33
1
DINAR
1965
28
100
REPUBLIKA ČESKOSLOVENSKA
27
37
sum of
One Pound
LONDON
For the Gov. and Comp. of
the BANK of ENGLAND
Chief Cashier
ES47 994350
38
ΔΡΑΧΜΑΙ
ΧΙΛΙΑΙ
09 Α 788763
39
09 Α 788763
1000
1000
40
43
42
44
41

1-3 le drapeau de l'ONU (l'Organisation *f* des Nations *f* unies)
– *flag of the United Nations*
1 le mât de drapeau *m* surmonté de la pomme
– *flagpole (flagstaff) with truck*
2 la drisse (la corde)
– *halyard (halliard, haulyard)*
3 l'étoffe *f* (le tablier du drapeau)
– *bunting*
4 le drapeau du Conseil de l'Europe *f* (le drapeau européen)
– *flag of the Council of Europe*
5 le drapeau des Jeux *m* olympiques (le drapeau olympique)
– *Olympic flag*
6 le drapeau en berne *f* (le drapeau hissé à mi-mât) [en signe *m* de deuil *m* ou de détresse *f*]
– *flag at half-mast* (Am. *at half-staff) [as a token of mourning]*
7-11 le drapeau
– *flag*
7 la hampe
– *flagpole (flagstaff)*
8 le clou décoratif (le cloutage)
– *ornamental stud*
9 la cravate (l'écharpe *f* nouée en cravate *f*)
– *streamer*
10 la pointe de hampe *f* (le fer de lance *f*)
– *pointed tip of the flagpole*
11 l'étoffe *f* (le tablier du drapeau)
– *bunting*
12 la bannière (l'oriflamme *m*)
– *banner (gonfalon)*
13 l'étendard *m* de cavalerie *f* [l'emblème *m* d'un régiment de cavalerie *f*]
– *cavalry standard (flag of the cavalry)*
14 l'étendard *m* du président de la République fédérale d'Allemagne *f* [les armes *f* du chef de l'Etat *m* en RFA *f*]
– *standard of the German Federal President [ensign of head of state]*
15-21 drapeaux *m* (pavillons *m* à bord *m* d'un navire) nationaux
– *national flags*
15 l'Union Jack *m* (Grande-Bretagne *f*)
– *the Union Jack (Great Britain)*
16 le drapeau tricolore (France *f*)
– *the Tricolour* (Am. *Tricolor*) *(France)*
17 le Danebrog (Danemark *m*)
– *the Danebrog (Dannebrog) (Denmark)*
18 la bannière étoilée (Etats-Unis *m* d'Amérique *f*)
– *the Stars and Stripes (Star-Spangled Banner) (USA)*
19 le croissant (Turquie *f*)
– *the Crescent (Turkey)*
20 la bannière du soleil levant (Japon *m*)
– *the Rising Sun (Japan)*
21 la faucille et le marteau (URSS ou Union *f* des Républiques *f* Socialistes Soviétiques)
– *the Hammer and Sickle (USSR)*
22-34 pavillons *m* à signaux *m*, un jeu de pavillons *m*
– *signal flags, a hoist*
22-28 les pavillons *m* à lettre *f*
– *letter flags*
22 lettre *f* «A», un pavillon à deux pointes *f* (un fanion dentelé, échancré, un guidon)
– *letter A, a burgee (swallow-tailed flag)*
23 «G», le pavillon pilote (le signal d'appel *m* du pilote)
– *G, pilot flag*
24 «H» (le pilote est à bord *m*)
– *H ('pilot on board')*
25 «L», le signal d'arrêt *m* pour communication *f* importante
– *L ('you should stop, I have something important to communicate')*
26 «P», le Pierrot bleu, un signal de départ *m*
– *P, the Blue Peter ('about to set sail')*
27 «W», le signal de demande *f* d'assistance *f* médicale
– *W ('I require medical assistance')*
28 «Z», un pavillon (fanion) rectangulaire
– *Z, an oblong pennant (oblong pendant)*
29 la flamme (la banderole) «Aperçu» du code des pavillons *m*, une flamme du Code international des signaux *m*
– *code pennant (code pendant), used in the International Signals Code*
30-32 fanions *m* auxiliaires, fanions *m* triangulaires
– *substitute flags (repeaters), triangular flags (pennants, pendants)*
33-34 flammes *f* numériques (chiffrées)
– *numeral pennants (numeral pendants)*
33 le chiffre 1
– *number 1*
34 le chiffre 0
– *number 0*
35-38 pavillons *m* de douane *f*
– *customs flags*
35 le pavillon «douane» des navires *m* du service des douanes *f*
– *customs boat pennant (customs boat pendant)*
36 le pavillon signalant que le navire a été inspecté par le service des douanes *f*
– *'ship cleared through customs'*
37 le signal d'appel *m* de la douane
– *customs signal flag*
38 le pavillon de transport *m* de poudre *f* [«cargaison *f* inflammable»]
– *powder flag ['inflammable (flammable) cargo']*

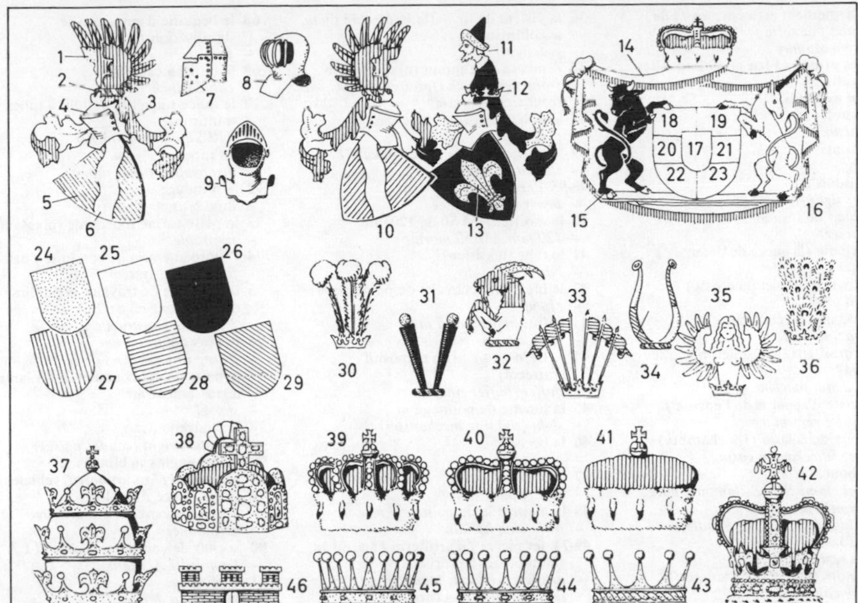

1-36 héraldique *f* (science *f* du blason *m*)
– *heraldry (blazonry)*
1-6 le blason
– *coat-of-arms (achievement of arms, hatchment, achievement)*
1 le cimier
– *crest*
2 le bourrelet (le tortil)
– *wreath of the colours* (Am. *colors)*
3 le lambrequin
– *mantle (mantling)*
4 le timbre
– *tilting helmet (jousting helmet)*
5 l'écu *m*
– *shield*
6 la fasce ondée
– *bend sinister wavy*
7 le grand heaume
– *pot-helmet (pot-helm, heaume)*
8 le timbre à grilles *f*
– *barred helmet (grilled helmet)*
9 le timbre à visière *f* relevée
– *helmet affronty with visor open*
10-13 le blason d'alliance *f*
– *marital achievement (marshalled,* Am. *marshaled, coat-of-arms)*
10 le blason d'homme *m*
– *arms of the baron (of the husband)*
11-13 le blason de femme *f*
– *arms of the family of the femme (of the wife)*
11 le pantin
– *demi-man;* also: *demi-woman*
12 la couronne de feuilles *f*
– *crest coronet*
13 la fleur de lis *m*
– *fleur-de-lis*
14 le manteau
– *heraldic tent (mantling)*
15-16 les tenants *m*, les animaux *m* héraldiques
– *supporters (heraldic beasts)*
15 le taureau
– *bull*
16 la licorne
– *unicorn*
17-23 la figuration des blasons *m*, les partitions *f*
– *blazon*
17 le centre (le cœur, l'abîme *m*)
– *inescutcheon (heart-shield)*
18-23 les six cantons *m* de l'écu *m*
– *quarterings one to six*
18-19 le chef
– *chief*
22-23 la pointe
– *base*
24-29 les émaux *m* héraldiques
– *tinctures*
24-25 les métaux *m*
– *metals*
24 or *m* [jaune]
– *or (gold) [yellow]*
25 argent *m* [blanc]
– *argent (silver) [white]*
26 sable *m* [noir]
– *sable*
27 gueules *m* [rouge]
– *gules*
28 azur *m* [bleu]
– *azure*
29 sinople *m* [vert]
– *vert*
30 le plumet (les plumes *f* d'autruche *f*)
– *ostrich feathers (treble plume)*
31 les bâtons *m*
– *truncheon*
32 l'animal *m* naissant
– *demi-goat*
33 le vol banneret
– *tournament pennons*
34 la lyre (les cornes *f* de buffle *m*)
– *buffalo horns*
35 la harpie
– *harpy*
36 les plumes *f* de paon *m*
– *plume of peacock's feathers*
37 la tiare pontificale
– *tiara (papal tiara)*
38 la couronne impériale [allemande, jusqu'en 1806]
– *Imperial Crown [German, until 1806]*
39 la couronne ducale [en Allemagne]
– *ducal coronet (duke's coronet)*
40 le bonnet de prince [en Allemagne]
– *prince's coronet*
41 le bonnet de prince-électeur *m* [Allemagne]
– *elector's coronet*
42 la couronne royale anglaise
– *English Royal Crown*
43-45 couronnes *f* héraldiques
– *coronets of rank*
43 la couronne de noble *m* non titré [en Allemagne]
– *baronet's coronet*
44 la couronne de baron [en Allemagne]
– *baron's coronet (baronial coronet)*
45 la couronne de comte [en Allemagne et en France]
– *count's coronet*
46 la couronne murale d'un blason de ville *f*
– *mauerkrone (mural crown) of a city crest*

1-98 l'armement *m* (les armes *f*) de l'armée *f* de terre *f*
– *army weaponry*
1-39 les armes *f* à feu *m* individuelles (portatives)
– ***hand weapons***
1 le pistolet P1, le P1
– *P1 pistol*
2 le canon
– *barrel*
3 le guidon
– *front sight (foresight)*
4 le chien de fusil *m*
– *hammer*
5 la détente (la queue de détente *f*)
– *trigger*
6 la poignée pistolet (la crosse)
– *pistol grip*
7 le magasin du chargeur
– *magazine holder*
8 la mitraillette (le pistolet-mitrailleur, le PM)
– *MP 2 sub-machine gun*
9 la crosse d'appui *m* de l'épaule *f*
– *shoulder rest (butt)*
10 la boîte de culasse *f* (la chambre)
– *casing (mechanism casing)*
11 l'embouchoir *m*
– *barrel clamp (barrel-clamping nut)*
12 le levier d'armement *m*
– *cocking lever (cocking handle)*
13 le garde-main (le fût)
– *palm rest*
14 l'arrêtoir *m* (le cran de sureté *f*)
– *safety catch*
15 le chargeur
– *magazine*
16 le fusil-mitrailleur (FM) G3-A3
– *G3-A3 self-loading rifle*
17 le canon
– *barrel*
18 le cache-flammes (le cache-lueur, l'antilueur *m*)
– *flash hider (flash eliminator)*
19 le garde-main (le fût)
– *palm rest*
20 le dispositif de détente *f* (la queue de détente *f* et le pontet ou sous-garde *f*)
– *trigger mechanism*
21 le chargeur
– *magazine*
22 la hausse de tir *m* (l'œilleton *m*, le cran de mire *f*)
– *notch (sighting notch, rearsight)*
23 l'embase *f* (la monture) du guidon
– *front sight block (foresight block) with front sight (foresight)*
24 la crosse de fusil *m*
– *rifle butt (butt)*
25 le lance-roquettes antichar de 44 mm (le bazooka de 44 mm)
– *44 mm anti-tank rocket launcher*
26 la roquette
– *rocket (projectile)*
27 le frein de tir *m* (le tube amortisseur de recul *m*)
– *buffer*
28 la lunette de visée *f* (la visière de tir *m*, la hausse de tir *m*)
– *telescopic sight (telescope sight)*
29 le mécanisme de tir *m*
– *firing mechanism*
30 l'appui-joue *m*
– *cheek rest*
31 la pièce d'appui *m* pour épauler
– *shoulder rest (butt)*
32 la mitrailleuse MG3
– *MG3 machine gun (Spandau)*
33 la boîte de culasse *f* (le fût du canon)
– *barrel casing*
34 l'obturateur *m* de gaz brûlés
– *gas regulator*
35 le volet de changement *m* de canon *m*
– *belt-changing flap*
36 la visière de tir *m* (la hausse de tir *m*, le collimateur)
– *rearsight*
37 l'embase *f* (la monture) du guidon
– *front sight block (foresight block) with front sight (foresight)*
38 la poignée pistolet (la crosse)
– *pistol grip*
39 la crosse d'appui *m* de l'épaule *f*
– *shoulder rest (butt)*
40-95 l'armement *m* lourd
– ***heavy weapons***
40 le mortier AM 50 de 120 mm
– *120 mm AM 50 mortar*
41 le tube (le canon)
– *barrel*
42 le bipied (le chevalet de pointage *m*)
– *bipod*
43 l'affût *m* de canon *m*
– *gun carriage*
44 le frein de tir *m* (le dispositif antirecul)
– *buffer (buffer ring)*
45 la lunette de pointage *m*
– *sight (sighting mechanism)*
46 la bêche
– *base plate*
47 le coussinet
– *striker pad*
48 la manivelle de pointage *m*
– *traversing handle*
49-74 les pièces *f* d'artillerie *f* à affût *m* automoteur (motorisées)
– *artillery weapons mounted on self-propelled gun carriages*
49 le canon SF M 107 de 175 mm
– *175 mm SFM 107 cannon*
50 le barbotin (la roue d'entraînement *m*)
– *drive wheel*
51 le vérin de levage *m* hydraulique
– *elevating piston*
52 le frein de tir *m* (le frein récupérateur)
– *buffer (buffer recuperator)*
53 le système hydraulique (le tourillon)
– *hydraulic system*
54 la culasse
– *breech ring*
55 la bêche du dispositif de levage *m*
– *spade*
56 le vérin
– *spade piston*
57 l'obusier *m* M 109 G de 155 mm
– *155 mm M 109 G self-propelled gun*
58 le frein de bouche *f*
– *muzzle*
59 l'extracteur *m* de gaz *m* brûlés (de fumée *f*)
– *fume extractor*
60 le berceau du canon
– *barrel cradle*
61 le récupérateur
– *barrel recuperator*
62 la flèche support de canon *m* (l'étrier *m* d'appui *m*)
– *barrel clamp*
63 la mitrailleuse de défense *f* antiaérienne (de DCA ou défense contre avions *m*)
– *light anti-aircraft (AA) machine gun*
64 le lance-missiles (le lance-fusées) *Honest John* M 386
– *Honest John M 386 rocket launcher*
65 le missile (la fusée) à ogive *f* (tête *f*) explosive (nucléaire)
– *rocket with warhead*
66 la rampe de lancement *m*
– *launching ramp*
67 le vérin de levage *m* (d'érection *f*) de la rampe
– *elevating gear*
68 le béquille d'appui *m* (de stabilisation *f*)
– *jack*
69 le treuil à câble *m*
– *cable winch*
70 le lance-roquettes 110 SF à tubes *m* multiples
– *110 SF rocket launcher*
71 les tubes *m*
– *disposable rocket tubes*
72 le blindage
– *tube bins*
73 la plate-forme tournante (pivotante)
– *turntable*
74 l'équipement *m* de conduite *f* de tir *m*
– *fire control system*
75 le véhicule de travaux *m* publics (de déblaiement *m*) de 2,5 t
– *2.5 tonne construction vehicle*
76 le bras de levage *m*
– *lifting arms (lifting device)*
77 la pelle de déblaiement *m* (la lame de terrassement *m*)
– *shovel*
78 le contrepoids
– *counterweight (counterpoise)*
79-95 les engins *m* blindés
– ***armoured*** (Am. *armored*) **vehicles**
79 l'ambulance *f* M 113
– *M113 armoured* (Am. *armored*) *ambulance*
80 le char de combat *m Leopard* 1 A 3
– *Leopard 1 A 3 tank*
81 le blindage
– *protection device*
82 le télémètre laser et infrarouge
– *infrared laser rangefinder*
83 les pots *m* lance-fumigènes
– *smoke canisters (smoke dispensers)*
84 la tourelle blindée
– *armoured* (Am. *armored*) *turret*
85 le blindage de protection *f* de la chenille
– *skirt*
86 le galet porteur (le galet de roulement *m*)
– *road wheel*
87 la chenille
– *track*
88 le char (le tank) de lutte *f* antichar
– *anti-tank tank*
89 l'extracteur *m* de gaz *m* brûlés
– *fume extractor*
90 le blindage
– *protection device*
91 le véhicule blindé de transport *m* du personnel *Marder*
– *armoured* (Am. *armored*) *personnel carrier*
92 le canon automatique
– *cannon*
93 le véhicule blindé de remblai *m Standard*
– *armoured* (Am. *armored*) *recovery vehicle*
94 la lame de terrassement *m* et de soutènement *m*
– *levelling* (Am. *leveling*) *and support shovel*
95 la flèche de la grue
– *jib*
96 la jeep de 0,25 t (le véhicule à usages *m* multiples)
– *.25 tonne all-purpose vehicle*
97 le pare-brise rabattable
– *drop windscreen* (Am. *drop windshield*)
98 la capote de toile *f* (la bâche)
– *canvas cover*

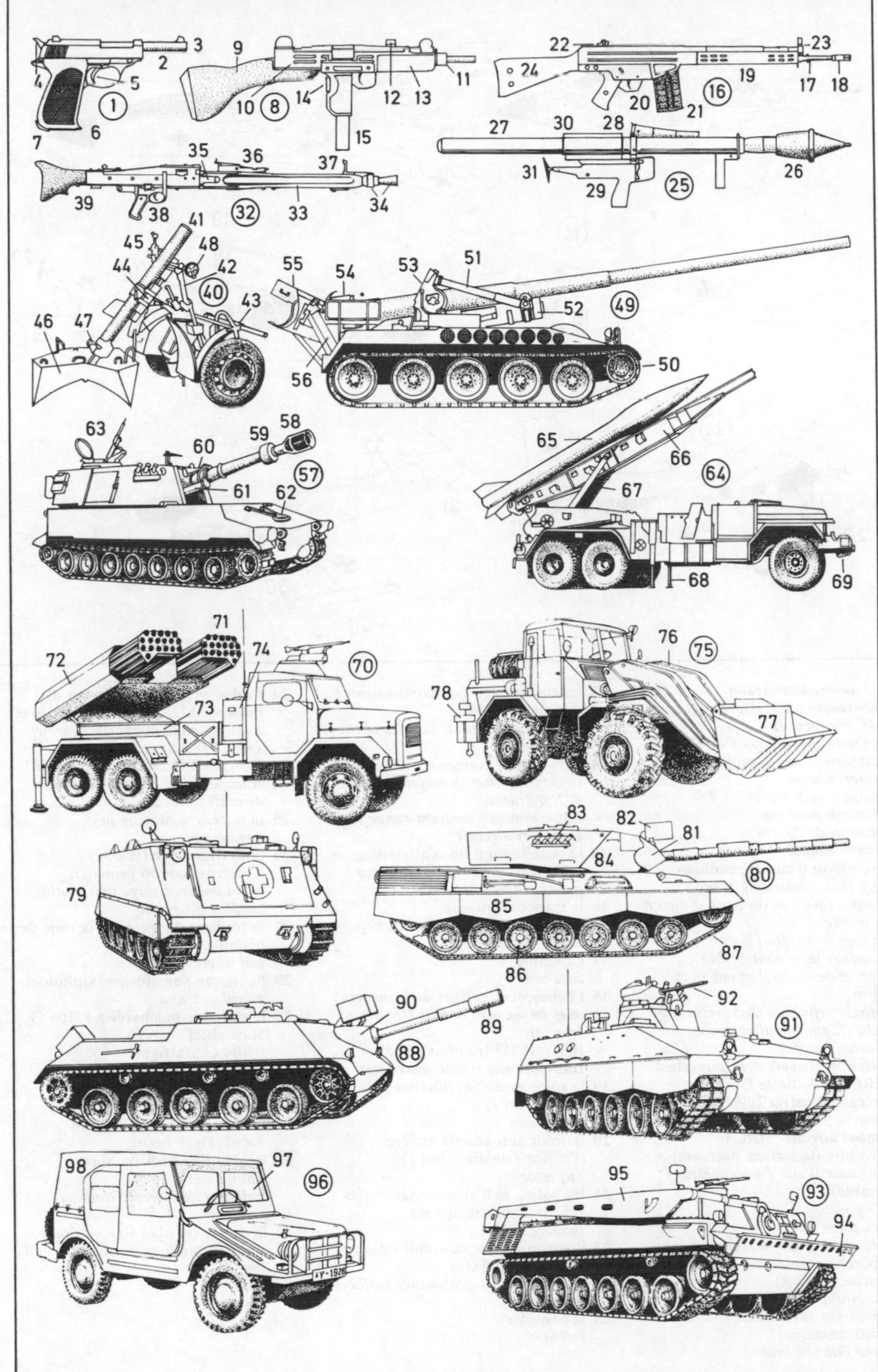
1
2
3
4
5
6
7
8
9
10
11
12
13
14
15
16
17
18
19
20
21
22
23
24
25
26
27
28
29
30
31
32
33
34
35
36
37
38
39
40
41
42
43
44
45
46
47
48
49
50
51
52
53
54
55
56
57
58
59
60
61
62
63
64
65
66
67
68
69
70
71
72
73
74
75
76
77
78
79
80
81
82
83
84
85
86
87
88
89
90
91
92
93
94
95
96
97
98

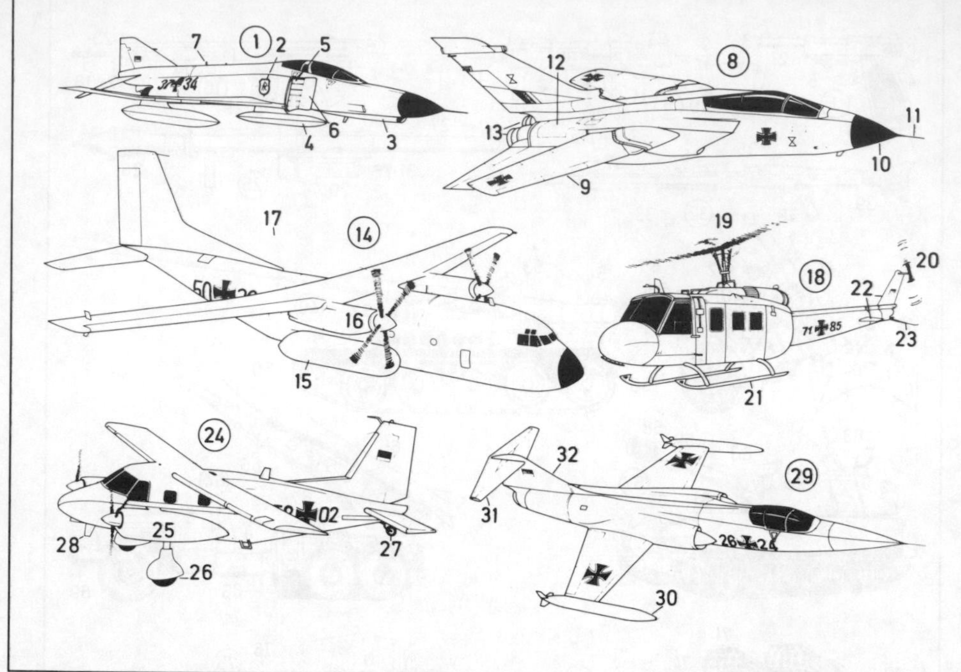

1 le chasseur-bombardier d'interception *f McDonell-Douglas F-4F Phantom II*
- McDonnell-Douglas F-4F Phantom II ***interceptor and fighter-bomber***

2 l'insigne *m* de l'escadre *f*
- *squadron marking*

3 le canon de 20 mm
- *aircraft cannon*

4 le réservoir d'aile *f* (pendulaire)
- *wing tank (underwing tank)*

5 l'entrée *f* d'air *m* (la prise d'air *m*)
- *air intake*

6 le piège à couche *f* limite
- *boundary layer control flap*

7 la prise de ravitaillement *m* en vol *m*
- *in-flight refuelling (*Am. *refueling) probe (flight refuelling probe, air refuelling probe)*

8 l'avion *m* **de combat** *m* **polyvalent** (MRCA, Multirole Combat Aircraft) *Panavia 200 Tornado*
- Panavia 200 Tornado ***multirole combat aircraft*** *(MRCA)*

9 la voilure (la surface portante) tournante (l'aile *f* à géométrie *f* variable)
- *swing wing*

10 le radome
- *radar nose (radome, radar dome)*

11 la perche anémométrique (le tube, la prise de Pitot)
- *pitot-static tube (pitot tube)*

12 l'aérofrein *m* (le frein aérodynamique)
- *brake flap (air brake)*

13 les tuyères *f* de postcombustion *f* des réacteurs *m*
- *afterburner exhaust nozzles of the engines*

14 l'avion *m* **de transport** *m* (l'avion *m* cargo, porteur) **moyen courrier** *C 160 Transall*
- C160 Transall ***medium-range transport aircraft***

15 la nacelle du train d'atterissage *m*
- *undercarriage housing (landing gear housing)*

16 le turbopropulseur
- *propeller-turbine engine (turboprop engine)*

17 l'antenne *f*
- *antenna*

18 l'hélicoptère *m* **léger de transport** *m* **et de secours** *m Bell UH-1D Iroquois*
- Bell UH-ID Iroquois ***light transport and rescue helicopter***

19 le rotor principal (l'hélice *f* de propulsion *f*)
- *main rotor*

20 le rotor anti-couple arrière (l'hélice *f* de direction *f*)
- *tail rotor*

21 les patins *m* d'atterrissage *m* (les skis *m* d'atterrissage *m*)
- *landing skids*

22 l'empennage *m* de stabilisation *f* (les plans *m* fixes)
- *stabilizing fins (stabilizing surfaces, stabilizers)*

23 la béquille
- *tail skid*

24 l'avion *m* **de transport** *m* **et de liaison** *f* ADAC (à décollage *m* et à atterrissage *m* courts) *Dornier DO 28 D-2 Skyservant*
- Dornier DO 28 D-2 Skyservant ***transport and communications aircraft***

25 la nacelle à moteur *m*
- *engine pod*

26 l'atterrisseur *m* (le train d'atterrissage *m*) principal
- *main undercarriage unit (main landing gear unit)*

27 la roulette de queue *f* (la roue de béquille *f*)
- *tail wheel*

28 l'antenne *f* ensiforme (xiphoïde)
- *sword antenna*

29 le chasseur-bombardier F-104 G Starfighter
- F-104 G Starfighter ***fighter-bomber***

30 le réservoir en bout *m* d'aile *f*
- *wing-tip tank (tip tank)*

31-32 l'empennage *m* en T *m*
- *T-tail (T-tail unit)*

31 le plan fixe horizontal (le stabilisateur)
- *tailplane (horizontal stabilizer, stabilizer)*

32 la dérive (le plan fixe vertical)
- *vertical stabilizer (vertical fin, tail fin)*

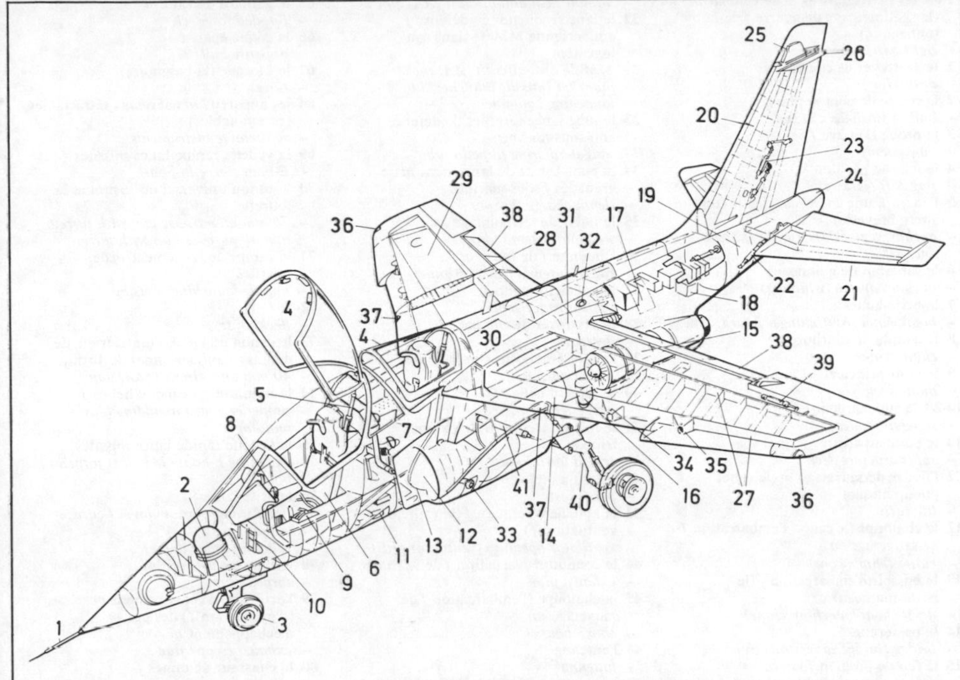

1-41 l'avion *m* à réaction *f* d'entraînement *m* franco-allemand *Dornier-Dassault-Breguet Alpha Jet*
– Dornier-Dassault-Breguet Alpha Jet *Franco-German jet trainer*

1 la perche anémométrique (la prise, le tube de Pitot)
– *pitot-static tube (pitot tube)*

2 le réservoir d'oxygène *m*
– *oxygen tank*

3 le train d'atterrissage *m* repliable (escamotable) vers l'avant *m*
– *forward-retracting nose wheel*

4 la verrière (le capot de l'habitacle *m*, de la carlingue)
– *cockpit canopy (cockpit hood)*

5 le vérin de relevage *m* de la verrière
– *canopy jack*

6 le siège du pilote (le siège de l'élève pilote *m*), un siège éjectable
– *pilot's seat (student pilot's seat), an ejector seat (ejection seat)*

7 le siège de l'observateur *m* (le siège de l'instructeur *m*), un siège éjectable
– *observer's seat (instructor's seat), an ejector seat (ejection seat)*

8 le levier de commande *f* (le manche à balai *m*)
– *control column (control stick)*

9 la manette des gaz *m*
– *thrust lever*

16 le réservoir d'alimentation *f* du système hydraulique
– *reservoir for the hydraulic system*

17 le compartiment des batteries *f* d'accumulateurs *m*
– *battery housing*

18 le bloc électronique arrière
– *rear avionics bay*

19 la soute à bagages *m*
– *baggage compartment*

20 la dérive (l'empennage *m*) trilongeron
– *triple-spar tail construction*

21 le gouvernail de profondeur *f*
– *horizontal tail*

22 la servocommande *f* (la tringlerie de commande *f*) du gouvernail de profondeur *f*
– *servo-actuating mechanism for the elevator*

23 la servocommande *f* du gouvernail de direction *f*
– *servo-actuating mechanism for the rudder*

24 le caisson du parachute de freinage *m*
– *brake chute housing (drag chute housing)*

25 l'antenne *f* VHF profilée [*VHF: Very high frequency*]
VHF (very high frequency) antenna (UHF antenna)

26 l'antenne *f* de direction *f* (l'antenne *f* VOR) [*VOR: Very high frequency omnidirectional range*]
– *VOR (very high frequency omnidirectional range) antenna*

27 la voilure (la surface portante) bilongeron
– *twin-spar wing construction*

28 le revêtement intégré aux longerons *m*
– *former with integral spars*

29 le réservoir structural (le réservoir intégré dans le caisson d'aile *f*)
– *integral wing tanks*

30 le réservoir central
– *centre-section (Am. center-section) fuel tank*

31 les réservoirs *m* du fuselage
– *fuselage tanks*

32 la tubulure de remplissage *m* par gravité *f*
– *gravity fuelling (Am. fueling) point*

33 la prise de ravitaillement *m* sous pression *f*
– *pressure fuelling (Am. fueling) point*

34 la suspension intérieure de l'aile *f*
– *inner wing suspension*

35 la suspension extérieure de l'aile *f*
– *outer wing suspension*

36 les feux *m* de position *f*
– *navigation lights (position lights)*

37 le phare d'atterrissage *m*
– *landing lights*

38 le volet de profondeur *f*
– *landing flap*

39 la servocommande (la tringlerie, le guignol) de l'aileron *m* de profondeur *f*
– *aileron actuator*

40 le train d'atterrissage *m* principal repliable (escamotable) vers l'avant
– *forward-retracting main undercarriage unit (main landing gear unit)*

41 le vérin de relevage *m* du train principal
– *undercarriage hydraulic cylinder (landing gear hydraulic cylinder)*

1-63 les petits navires *m* **de combat** *m* (les bâtiments *m* de guerre *f* de faible tonnage *m*)
– ***light battleships***
1 le destroyer de combat *m*
– ***destroyer***
2 la coque de pont *m* plat
– *hull of flush-deck vessel*
3 la proue (l'étrave *f*)
– *bow (stem)*
4 le mât de pavillon *m*
– *flagstaff (jackstaff)*
5 l'ancre *f*, une ancre sans jas *m* (une ancre brevetée)
– *anchor, a stockless anchor (patent anchor)*
6 le cabestan (le guindeau)
– *anchor capstan (windlass)*
7 le brise-lames
– *breakwater* (Am. *manger board)*
8 le couple de courbure *f*
– *chine strake*
9 le pont principal
– *main deck*
10-28 la superstructure
– *superstructures*
10 le pont supérieur
– *superstructure deck*
11 l'îlot *m* de sauvetage *m* (le canot pneumatique)
– *life rafts*
12 la chaloupe (le canot, l'embarcation *f* de sauvetage *m*)
– *cutter (ship's boat)*
13 le bossoir d'embarcation *f* (le porte-manteau)
– *davit (boat-launching crane)*
14 la passerelle
– *bridge (bridge superstructure)*
15 le feu de position *f* latéral
– *side navigation light (side running light)*
16 l'antenne *f*
– *antenna*
17 le cadre radiogoniométrique (le radiogoniomètre, le poste de radiodétection *f*)
– *radio direction finder (RDF) frame*
18 le mât en treillis *m* (le pylône)
– *lattice mast*
19 la cheminée avant
– *forward funnel*
20 la cheminée arrière
– *aft funnel*
21 la mitre de cheminée *f* (le capuchon)
– *cowl*
22 la dunette (le château d'arrière *f*, de poupe *f*)
– *aft superstructure (poop)*
23 le cabestan (le guindeau)
– *capstan*
24 la descente (l'escalier *m* d'accès *m* au pont inférieur)
– *companion ladder (companionway, companion hatch)*
25 le mât du pavillon national
– *ensign staff*
26 la poupe, une poupe à arcasse *f*
– *stern, a transom stern*
27 la ligne de flottaison *f*
– *waterline*
28 le projecteur
– *searchlight*
29-37 l'armement *m*
– *armament*
29 la tourelle contenant un canon *m* de 100 mm
– *100 mm gun turret*
30 le lance-roquettes de défense *f* anti-sous-marine, un lance-roquettes quadruple
– *four-barrel anti-submarine rocket launcher (missile launcher)*
31 l'affût *m* de deux canons *m* de 40 mm de défense *f* antiaérienne (canons *m* antiaériens, de DCA: défense *f* contre avions *m*)
– *40 mm twin anti-aircraft (AA) gun*
32 le lance-roquettes de défense *f* antiaérienne MM 38 dans son logement
– *MM 38 anti-aircraft (AA) rocket launcher (missile launcher) in launching container*
33 le tube lance-torpilles de défense *f* anti-sous-marine
– *anti-submarine torpedo tube*
34 la plate-forme de lancement *m* de grenades *f* sous-marines
– *depth-charge thrower*
35 le radar de télépointage *m*
– *weapon system radar*
36 l'antenne *f* de radar *m*
– *radar antenna (radar scanner)*
37 le télémètre optique
– *optical rangefinder*
38 le destroyer de combat *m*
– ***destroyer***
39 l'ancre *f* de bossoir *m* (de touée *f*)
– *bower anchor*
40 le capot d'hélice *f*
– *propeller guard*
41 le mât en treillis *m* (le pylône) tripode
– *tripod lattice mast*
42 le mât à pible
– *pole mast*
43 la bouche d'aération *f* (la grille de ventilation *f*)
– *ventilator openings (ventilator grill)*
44 le conduit d'évacuation *f* de la fumée
– *exhaust pipe*
45 la chaloupe (l'embarcation *f* de sauvetage *m*)
– *ship's boat*
46 l'antenne *f*
– *antenna*
47 le canon universel de 127 mm à télépointage *m* dans sa tourelle
– *radar-controlled 127 mm all-purpose gun in turret*
48 le canon universel de 127 mm
– *127 mm all-purpose gun*
49 la rampe de lancement *m* de missiles *m* Tartar mer-air
– *launcher for Tartar missiles*
50 le lance-roquettes de défense *f* anti-sous-marine
– *anti-submarine rocket (ASROC) launcher (missile launcher)*
51 les antennes *f* du radar de conduite *f* de tir *m*
– *fire control radar antennas*
52 le radome
– *radome (radar dome)*
53 la frégate
– ***frigate***
54 l'écubier *m* d'ancre *f* (de mouillage *m*)
– *hawse pipe*
55 le feu (le fanal) de tête *f* de mât *m*
– *steaming light*
56 le feu de position *f*
– *navigation light (running light)*
57 la bouche d'aspiration *f* d'air *m*
– *air extractor duct*
58 la cheminée
– *funnel*
59 la mitre de cheminée *f*
– *cowl*
60 l'antenne fouet
– *whip antenna (fishpole antenna)*
61 la chaloupe (le canot, l'embarcation *f* de sauvetage *m*)
– *cutter*
62 le feu de poupe *f*
– *stern light*
63 le bourrelet du capot d'hélice *f*
– *propeller guard boss*
64-91 les navires *m* **(les bâtiments** *m*) **de combat** *m*
– ***fighting ships***
64 le sous-marin
– ***submarine***
65 le gaillard d'avant *m*
– *flooded foredeck*
66 la coque épaisse
– *pressure hull*
67 le kiosque (la baignoire)
– *turret*
68 les appareils *m* «aériens» rétractables (escamotables)
– *retractable instruments*
69 la vedette rapide lance-missiles
– *E-boat (torpedo boat)*
70 le canon universel de 76 mm et la tourelle
– *76 mm all-purpose gun with turret6 mm all-purpose gun with turret*
71 la rampe de lancement *m* des missiles *m*
– *missile-launching housing*
72 le rouf
– *deckhouse*
73 le canon de DCA *f* (antiaérien, de défense *f* antiaérienne) de 40 mm
– *40 mm anti-aircraft (AA) gun*
74 la moulure du capot d'hélice *f*
– *propeller guard moulding* (Am. *molding)*
75 la vedette rapide lance-missiles
– *143 class E-boat (143 class torpedo boat)*
76 le brise-lames
– *breakwater* (Am. *manger board)*
77 le radome
– *radome (radar dome)*
78 le tube lance-torpilles
– *torpedo tube*
79 l'orifice *m* d'échappement *m* (d'évacuation *f*) des gaz *m* d'échappement *m*
– *exhaust escape flue*
80 le chasseur de mines *f*
– ***mine hunter***
81 la nervure de renforcement *m*
– *reinforced rubbing strake*
82 le canot pneumatique
– *inflatable boat (inflatable dinghy)*
83 le bossoir d'embarcation *f* (le porte-manteau)
– *davit*
84 le dragueur de mines *f* **rapide**
– ***minesweeper***
85 le treuil à tambour *m* à câble *m*
– *cable winch*
86 le treuil (le guindeau) de remorque *f*
– *towing winch (towing machine, towing engine)*
87 la drague (le poisson autopropulsé, le flotteur)
– *mine-sweeping gear (paravanes)*
88 la grue
– *crane (davit)*
89 la péniche (le chaland, le navire) de débarquement *m*
– ***landing craft***
90 la porte d'étrave *f* (de proue *f*)
– *bow ramp*
91 la porte de poupe *f*
– *stern ramp*
92-97 les bâtiments *m* auxiliaires (de soutien *m* logistique)
– ***auxiliaries***
92 le ravitailleur
– *tender*
93 le bâtiment de soutien *m*, version *f* atelier *m* de réparation *f*
– *servicing craft*
94 le mouilleur de mines *f*
– *minelayer*
95 le navire-école
– *training ship*
96 le remorqueur de sauvetage *m* en haute mer *f*
– *deep-sea salvage tug*
97 le pétrolier ravitailleur
– *fuel tanker (replenishing ship)*

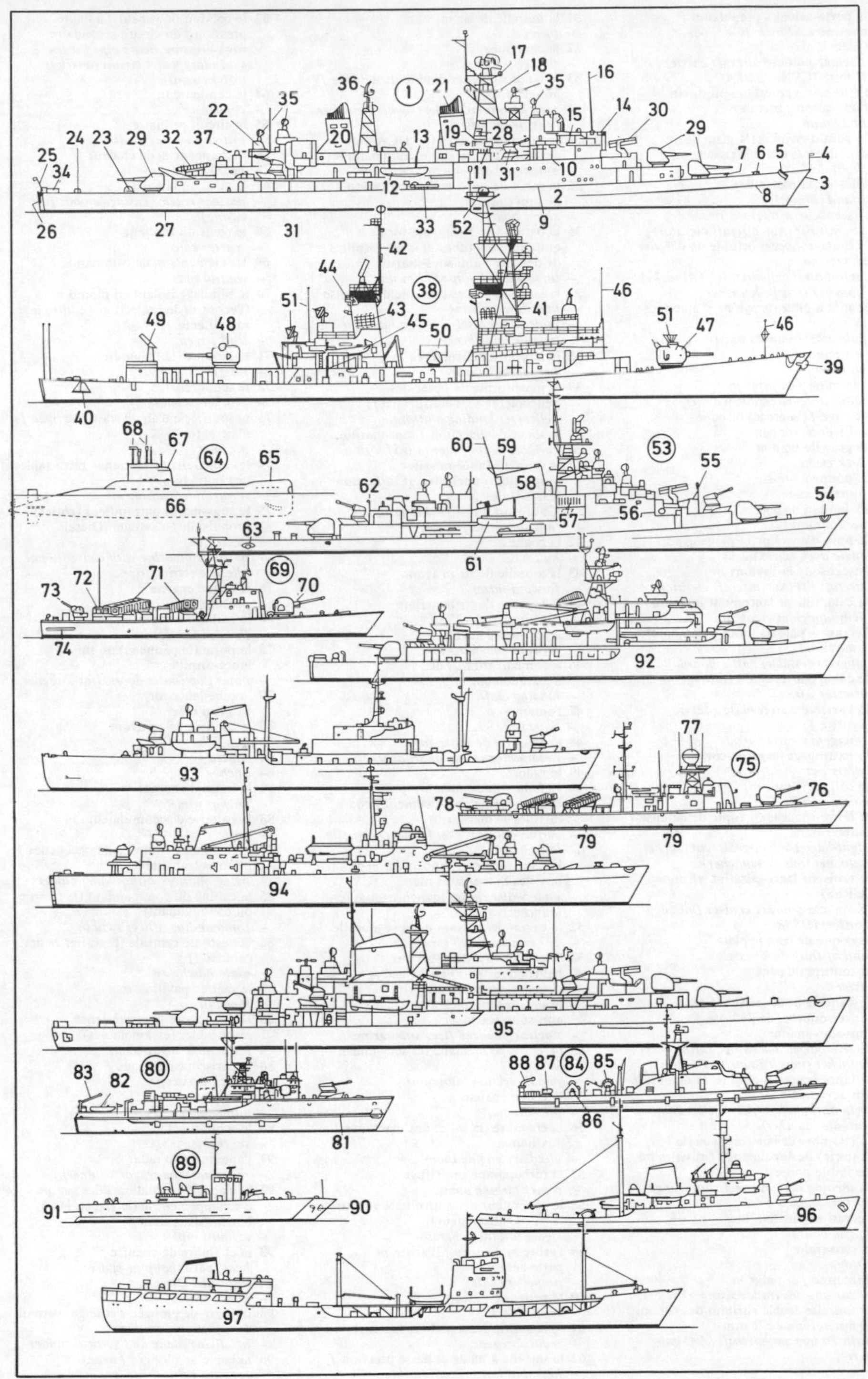
1
2
3
4
5
6
7
8
9
10
11
12
13
14
15
16
17
18
19
20
21
22
23
24
25
26
27
28
29
30
31
32
33
34
35
36
37
38
39
40
41
42
43
44
45
46
47
48
49
50
51
52
53
54
55
56
57
58
59
60
61
62
63
64
65
66
67
68
69
70
71
72
73
74
75
76
77
78
79
80
81
82
83
84
85
86
87
88
89
90
91
92
93
94
95
96
97

1 **le porte-avions à propulsion** *f* **nucléaire** *«Nimitz ICVN 68»* (États-Unis)
– ***nuclear-powered aircraft carrier*** Nimitz ICVN68' *(USA)*
2-11 le plan vertical longitudinal (l'élevation *f* latérale)
– *body plan*
2 le pont d'envol *m* (la piste de décollage *m* et d'atterrissage *m*)
– *flight deck*
3 l'îlot *m* (la passerelle)
– *island (bridge)*
4 l'ascenseur *m* d'avions *m*
– *aircraft lift* (Am. *aircraft elevator)*
5 le lance-roquettes octuple de défense *f* antiaérienne
– *eight-barrel anti-aircraft (AA) rocket launcher (missile launcher)*
6 le mât à pible (le pylône d'antennes *f*)
– *pole mast (antenna mast)*
7 l'antenne *f*
– *antenna*
8 l'antenne *f* de radar *m*
– *radar antenna (radar scanner)*
9 l'étrave *f* (la proue) blindée
– *fully enclosed bow*
10 la grue de bord *m*
– *deck crane*
11 la poupe à arcasse *f*
– *transom stern*
12-20 le plan du pont
– *deck plan*
12 le pont d'envol *m* (la plage avant)
– *angle deck (flight deck)*
13 l'ascenseur *m* d'avions *m*
– *aircraft lift* (Am. *aircraft elevator)*
14 la catapulte de lancement *m* double
– *twin launching catapult*
15 l'écran *m* pare-flammes escamotable (amovible)
– *hinged (movable) baffle board*
16 le câble d'arrêt *m* (de freinage *m*)
– *arrester wire*
17 la barrière d'arrêt *m* (le filet de sécurité *f*)
– *emergency crash barrier*
18 le bastingage (le garde-corps)
– *safety net*
19 le coffre (le caisson)
– *caisson (cofferdam)*
20 le lance-roquettes octuple de défense *f* antiaérienne
– *eight-barrel anti-aircraft (AA) rocket launcher (missile launcher)*
21 **le croiseur lance-missiles** *«Kara»* (URSS)
– 'Kara' class ***rocket cruiser*** *(missile cruiser) (USSR)*
22 la coque de pont *m* plat
– *hull of flush-deck vessel*
23 la tonture du pont
– *sheer*
24 la batterie de douze tubes *m* lance-roquettes de défense *f* anti-sous-marine
– *twelve-barrel underwater salvo rocket launcher (missile launcher)*
25 le lance-roquettes double de défense *f* antiaérienne
– *twin anti-aircraft (AA) rocket launcher (missile launcher)*
26 la chambre de lancement *m* (la batterie) de 4 roquettes *f* (missiles *m*) de faible portée *f*
– *launching housing for 4 short-range rockets (missiles)*
27 l'écran *m* pare-flammes
– *baffle board*
28 la passerelle
– *bridge*
29 l'antenne *f* de radar *m*
– *radar antenna (radar scanner)*
30 la tourelle double abritant des canons *m* antiaériens de 76 mm
– *twin 76 mm anti-aircraft (AA) gun turret*
31 la tourelle de tir *m*
– *turret*
32 la cheminée
– *funnel*
33 le lance-roquettes double de défense *f* antiaérienne
– *twin anti-aircraft (AA) rocket launcher (missile launcher)*
34 le canon antiaérien (de DCA *f*, de défense *f* antiaérienne) automatique
– *automatic anti-aircraft (AA) gun*
35 le canot de bord *m* (l'embarcation *f* de sauvetage *m*)
– *ship's boat*
36 la batterie de 5 (la plate-forme quintuple de) tubes *m* lance-torpilles de défense *f* anti-sous-marine
– *underwater 5-torpedo housing*
37 le lance-roquettes sextuple de défense *f* anti-sous-marine
– *underwater 6-salvo rocket launcher (missile launcher)*
38 le hangar d'hélicoptères *m*
– *helicopter hangar*
39 la plate-forme de poser des hélicoptères *m* (l'hélisurface *f*)
– *helicopter landing platform*
40 le sonar de détection *f* sous-marine
– *variable depth sonar (VDS)*
41 **le croiseur lance-missiles à propulsion** *f* **nucléaire** *«California»* (États-Unis)
– 'California' class ***rocket cruiser*** *(missile cruiser) (USA)*
42 la coque
– *hull*
43 la tourelle de tir *m* avant
– *forward turret*
44 la tourelle de tir *m* arrière
– *aft turret*
45 le gaillard d'avant *m*
– *forward superstructure*
46 les embarcations *f* de débarquement *m*
– *landing craft*
47 l'antenne *f*
– *antenna*
48 l'antenne *f* de radar *m*
– *radar antenna (radar scanner)*
49 le radome
– *radome (radar dome)*
50 la plate-forme de lancement *m* de missiles *m* mer-air
– *surface-to-air rocket launcher (missile launcher)*
51 la plate-forme de lancement *m* de missiles *m* mer-sous-mer
– *underwater rocket launcher (missile launcher)*
52 le canon de 127 mm dans sa tourelle
– *127 mm gun with turret*
53 la plate-forme de poser des hélicoptères *m* (l'hélisurface *f*)
– *helicopter landing platform*
54 **le sous-marin nucléaire anti-sous-marin**
– ***nuclear-powered fleet submarine***
55-74 la coupe médiane du sous-marin [schéma]
– *middle section [diagram]*
55 la coque épaisse
– *pressure hull*
56 la chambre (la salle) des machines *f* auxiliaires
– *auxiliary engine room*
57 la turbopompe centrifuge
– *rotary turbine pump*
58 le générateur de la turbine à vapeur *f* (le turbo-alternateur)
– *steam turbine generator*
59 l'arbre *m* d'hélice *f* (l'arbre *m* porte-hélice)
– *propeller shaft*
60 le palier de butée *f*
– *thrust block*
61 le démultiplicateur (le réducteur)
– *reduction gear*
62 la turbine à haute et basse pression *f*
– *high and low pressure turbine*
63 le conduit de vapeur *f* à haute pression *f* du circuit secondaire
– *high-pressure steam pipe for the secondary water circuit (auxiliary water circuit)*
64 le condenseur
– *condenser*
65 le circuit primaire
– *primary water circuit*
66 l'échangeur *m* de chaleur *f*
– *heat exchanger*
67 la cuve du réacteur
– *nuclear reactor casing (atomic pile casing)*
68 le cœur du réacteur
– *reactor core*
69 les éléments *m* de commande *f*
– *control rods*
70 le blindage isolant en plomb *m* (l'écran *m* de protection *f* contre le rayonnement)
– *lead screen*
71 le kiosque (la baignoire)
– *turret*
72 le schnorchel
– *snorkel (schnorkel)*
73 la soufflerie d'air *m* frais (l'arrivée *f* d'air *m* frais)
– *air inlet*
74 les appareils *m* «aériens» rétractables (escamotables)
– *retractable instruments*
75 **le sous-marin patrouilleur (côtier)** à propulsion *f* classique (Diesel électrique)
– ***patrol submarine*** *with conventional (diesel-electric) drive*
76 la coque épaisse
– *pressure hull*
77 le gaillard d'avant *m*
– *flooded foredeck*
78 la porte (le panneau) du tube lance-torpilles
– *outer flap (outer doors) [for torpedoes]*
79 le tube lance-torpilles
– *torpedo tube*
80 le fond de cale *f* avant
– *bow bilge*
81 l'ancre *f*
– *anchor*
82 le treuil d'ancrage *m*
– *anchor winch*
83 la batterie d'accumulateurs *m*
– *battery*
84 les cabines *f* équipées de couchettes *f* pliantes (rabattables)
– *living quarters with folding bunks*
85 la cabine du commandant (le quartier du commandant)
– *commanding officer's cabin*
86 la descente centrale (l'escalier *m* des cabines *f*)
– *main hatchway*
87 le mât de pavillon *m*
– *flagstaff*
88-91 les appareils *m* «aériens» rétractables (escamotables)
– *retractable instruments*
88 le périscope d'attaque *f*
– *attack periscope*
89 l'antenne *f*
– *antenna*
90 le schnorchel
– *snorkel (schnorkel)*
91 l'antenne *f* de radar *m*
– *radar antenna (radar scanner)*
92 le clapet d'évacuation *f* des gaz *m* d'échappement *m* (le clapet, la bouche d'aération *f*)
– *exhaust outlet*
93 la chambre de chauffe *f*
– *heat space (hot-pipe space)*
94 le groupe Diesel
– *diesel generators*
95 la barre de plongée *f* et le gouvernail de direction *f* arrière
– *aft diving plane and vertical rudder*
96 la barre de plongée *f* avant
– *forward vertical rudder*

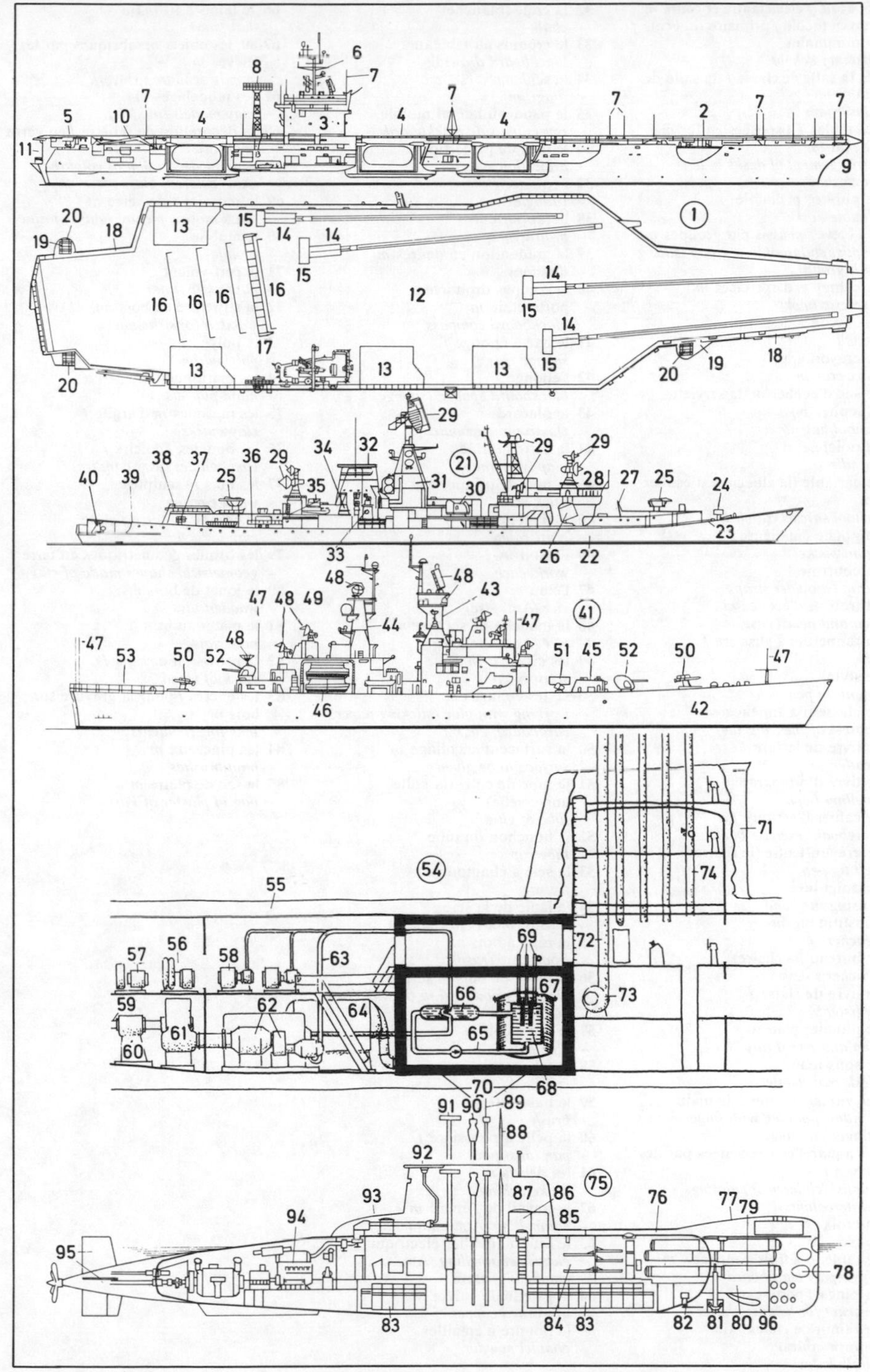
6 7
8
7 10 4 3 4 7 4 7 2 7 7
5
11 9
1
20 13 15
19 18 14 14
15
16 16 16 16 12 14
15
14
17
13 13 13 15 19 18
20 20
29
32 29 29
38 37 36 29 34 21
25 31 30 28 27 25
40 39 35 24
23
33 26 22
48 48 43
47 48 49 44 41 47
-47 48 51 45 52 50 47
53 50 52
46 42
71
54 74
55
69 72
57 56 58 63
67 73
59 62 66
64
61 65
60 68
70
91 90 89
88
92
75
93 87 86
94 85 76 77 79
95 78
83 84 83 82 81 80 96

1-85 école *f* **élémentaire et cours** *m* **moyen** (école *f* primaire ou école *f* communale)
– ***primary school***
1-45 la salle de classe *f* (la salle de cours *m*)
– ***classroom***
1 les tables *f* disposées en fer *m* à cheval *m*
– *arrangement of desks in a horseshoe*
2 le pupitre *m* double
– *double desk*
3 les élèves *m* assis par groupes *m*
– *pupils (children) in a group (sitting in a group)*
4 le cahier *m* d'exercices *m*
– *exercise book*
5 le crayon à dessin *m*
– *pencil*
6 le crayon gras
– *wax crayon*
7 le sac d'écolier *m* (la serviette d'écolier *m*)
– *school bag*
8 la poignée
– *handle*
9 le cartable (la gibecière d'écolier *m*)
– *school satchel (satchel)*
10 la poche antérieure
– *front pocket*
11 la courroie
– *strap (shoulder strap)*
12 la trousse d'écolier *m*
– *pen and pencil case*
13 la fermeture à glissière *f*
– *zip*
14 le stylo
– *fountain pen (pen)*
15 le classeur à anneaux *m*
– *loose-leaf file (ring file)*
16 le livre de lecture *f*
– *reader*
17 le livre d'orthographe *f*
– *spelling book*
18 le cahier d'écriture *f*
– *notebook (exercise book)*
19 le crayon-feutre (le feutre)
– *felt tip pen*
20 le doigt levé
– *raising the hand*
21 l'instituteur *m*
– *teacher*
22 le bureau (la chaire)
– *teacher's desk*
23 le livre de classe *f*
– *register*
24 le plumier plateau
– *pen and pencil tray*
25 le sous-main
– *desk mat (blotter)*
26 les vitres *f* peintes à la main
– *window painting with finger paints (finger painting)*
27 les aquarelles *f* exécutées par des élèves *m*
– *pupils' (children's) paintings (watercolours)*
28 la croix
– *cross*
29 le tableau à trois panneaux *m*
– *three-part blackboard*
30 la pince *f* porte-carte
– *bracket for holding charts*
31 la rainure à craies *f* (le repose-craies)
– *chalk ledge*
32 la craie (blanche)
– *chalk*
33 le croquis au tableau
– *blackboard drawing*
34 le schéma
– *diagram*
35 le panneau latéral mobile
– *reversible side blackboard*
36 le mur de projection *f*
– *projection screen*
37 l'equerre *f*
– *triangle*
38 le rapporteur
– *protractor*
39 la graduation en degrés *m*
– *divisions*
40 le compas droit avec porte-craie *m*
– *blackboard compass*
41 le bac à éponge *f*
– *sponge tray*
42 l'éponge *f*
– *blackboard sponge (sponge)*
43 le placard
– *classroom cupboard*
44 la carte murale
– *map (wall map)*
45 le mur de briques *f*
– *brick wall*
46-85 l'atelier *m*
– ***craft room***
46 l'établi *m*
– *workbench*
47 l'étau *m*
– *vice* (Am. *vise)*
48 la manette de serrage *m*
– *vice* (Am. *vise) bar*
49 les ciseaux *m*
– *scissors*
50-52 les collages *m*
– *working with glue (sticking paper, cardboard, etc.)*
50 la surface d'encollage *m*
– *surface to be glued*
51 le tube de colle (la colle universelle)
– *tube of glue*
52 le bouchon du tube
– *tube cap*
53 la scie à chantourner
– *fretsaw*
54 la lame de la scie
– *fretsaw blade (saw blade)*
55 la râpe à bois *m*
– *wood rasp (rasp)*
56 la pièce de bois *m* serrée
– *piece of wood held in the vice* (Am. *vise)*
57 le pot à colle *f*
– *glue pot*
58 le tabouret
– *stool*
59 la balayette
– *brush*
60 la pelle à poussière *f*
– *pan (dust pan)*
61 les débris *m*
– *broken china*
62 le travail de l'émail *m*
– *enamelling* (Am. *enameling)*
63 le four à émailler électrique
– *electric enamelling* (Am. *enameling) stove*
64 la galette de cuivre *m*
– *unworked copper*
65 la poudre à émailler
– *enamel powder*
66 le tamis à fil *m* fin
– *hair sieve*
67-80 les objets *m* fabriqués par les élèves *m*
– *pupils' (children's) work*
67 les modelages *m*
– *clay models (models)*
68 la décoration de fenêtre *f* en verre *m* coloré
– *window decoration of coloured* (Am. *colored) glass*
69 la mosaïque de verre *m*
– *glass mosaic picture (glass mosaic)*
70 le mobile
– *mobile*
71 le cerf-volant
– *paper kite (kite)*
72 la structure en bois *m*
– *wooden construction*
73 le polyèdre
– *polyhedron*
74 les marionnettes *f*
– *hand puppets*
75 les masques *m* d'argile *f*
– *clay masks*
76 les bougies *f* de cire *f*
– *cast candles (wax candles)*
77 les bois *m* sculptés
– *wood carving*
78 la cruche en terre *f* cuite
– *clay jug*
79 les formes géométriques en terre *f*
– *geometrical shapes made of clay*
80 le jouet de bois *m*
– *wooden toys*
81 le matériau brut
– *materials*
82 la provision de bois *f*
– *stock of wood*
83 les encres *f* pour la gravure sur bois *m*
– *inks for wood cuts*
84 les pinceaux *m*
– *paintbrushes*
85 le sac de plâtre *m*
– *bag of plaster of Paris*

water cycle
condensation
beaker
icecubes
drops of water
steam
water
READER
DUDEN
GYPSUM POWDER
GLUE

261 Ecole II (enseignement secondaire)

1-45 le lycée; *anal.:* le collège d'enseignement *m* secondaire (le C.E.S.)
– ***grammar school;*** also: *comprehensive school*
1-13 le cours de chimie *f*
– ***chemistry***
1 la salle de chimie *f* avec les bancs *m* étagés en gradins *m*
– *chemistry lab (chemistry laboratory) with tiered rows of seats*
2 le professeur de chimie *f*
– *chemistry teacher*
3 la table d'expérimentation *f*
– *demonstration bench (teacher's bench)*
4 la prise d'eau *f*
– *water pipe*
5 le plan de travail *m* carrelé
– *tiled working surface*
6 le bassin d'évier *m*
– *sink*
7 le moniteur vidéo *f*, un récepteur pour la diffusion de programmes *m* pédagogiques
– *television monitor, a screen for educational programmes* (Am. *programs)*
8 le rétroprojecteur
– *overhead projector*
9 le plan de projection *f* pour les transparents *m* (les rhodoïdes *m*)
– *projector top for skins*
10 l'optique *f* de projection *f* avec le miroir incliné
– *projection lens with right-angle mirror*
11 la table d'élèves *m* équipée pour les expériences *f*
– *pupils'* (Am. *students') bench with experimental apparatus*
12 la prise de courant *m* (la prise femelle)
– *electrical point (socket)*
13 la table de projection *f*
– *projection table*
14-34 la salle de préparation *f* **pour le cours de biologie** *f*
– ***biology preparation room*** *(biology prep room)*
14 le squelette
– *skeleton*
15 la collection de crânes *m*, les moulages *m* de crânes *m*
– *casts of skulls*
16 la calotte crânienne du Pithecanthropus erectus *m*
– *calvarium of Pithecanthropus Erectus*
17 le crâne de l'Homo steinheimensis *m*
– *skull of Steinheim man*
18 la calotte crânienne du sinanthrope
– *calvarium of Peking man (of Sinanthropus)*
19 le crâne de l'Homme *m* de Néanderthal, un crâne d'hominidé *m*
– *skull of Neanderthal man*
20 le crâne de l'australopithèque *m*
– *Australopithecine skull (skull of Australopithecus)*
21 le crâne de l'Homo sapiens *m*
– *skull of present-day man*
22 la table de préparation *f*
– *dissecting bench*
23 les flacons *m* à produits *m* chimiques
– *chemical bottles*
24 la prise de gaz *m*
– *gas tap*
25 la boîte de Petri
– *petri dish*
26 l'éprouvette *f* graduée
– *measuring cylinder*
27 les fiches *f* de travail *m* (le matériel pédagogique)
– *work folder (teaching material)*
28 le livre du maître (le manuel)
– *textbook*
29 les cultures *f* bactériologiques
– *bacteriological cultures*
30 l'étuve *f* d'incubation *f*
– *incubator*
31 le séchoir à éprouvettes *f*
– *test tube rack*
32 le flacon-laveur (le barboteur)
– *washing bottle*
33 la cuve à eau *f*
– *water tank*
34 l'évier *m*
– *sink*
35 le laboratoire de langues *f*
– ***language laboratory***
36 le tableau mural
– *blackboard*
37 l'unité *f* d'enseignement *m* (la console centrale)
– *console*
38 le casque d'écoute *f*
– *headphones (headset)*
39 le microphone
– *microphone*
40 l'écouteur *m* (l'oreillette *f*)
– *earcups*
41 le ressort de casque *m* matelassé
– *padded headband (padded headpiece)*
42 l'enregistreur *m* de programmes *m* pédagogiques, un appareil d'enregistrement *m* à cassettes *f*
– *programme* (Am. *program) recorder, a cassette recorder*
43 le bouton de réglage *m* du volume pour la piste «élève»
– *pupil's* (Am. *student's) volume control*
44 le bouton de réglage *m* du volume pour la piste «maître»
– *master volume control*
45 le clavier de service *m*
– *control buttons (operating keys)*

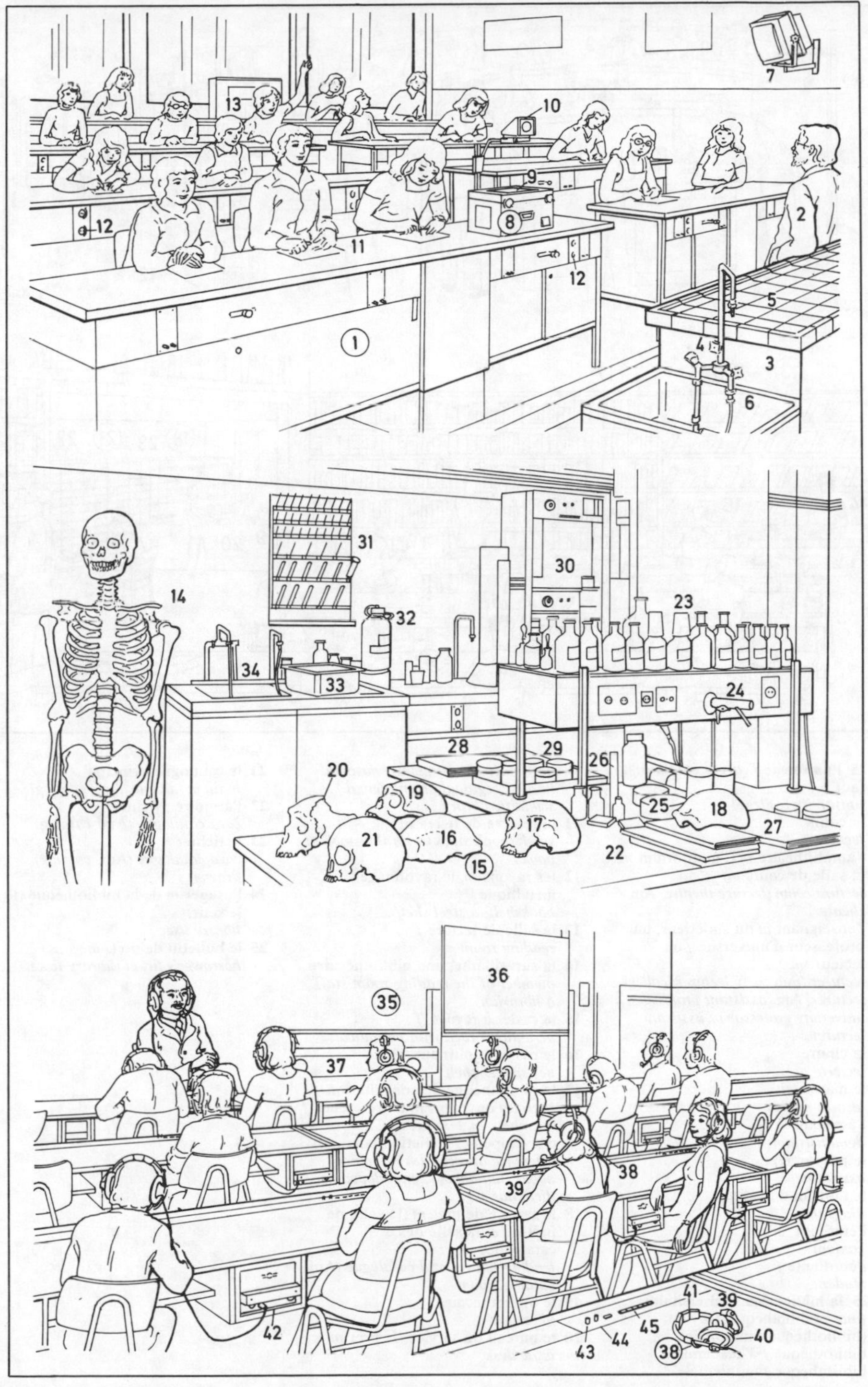
1
2
3
4
5
6
7
8
9
10
11
12
13
14
15
16
17
18
19
20
21
22
23
24
25
26
27
28
29
30
31
32
33
34
35
36
37
38
39
40
41
42
43
44
45

1-25 l'université *f* (*argot étudiant:* la fac)
– ***university*** *(college)*
1 le cours
– *lecture*
2 l'amphithéâtre *m* (l'auditorium *m*, la salle de cours *m*)
– *lecture room (lecture theatre,* Am. *theater)*
3 l'enseignant *m* du supérieur, un professeur d'université *f* ou lecteur *m*
– *lecturer (university lecturer, college lecturer,* Am. *assistant professor), a university professor or assistant lecturer*
4 la chaire
– *lectern*
5 le manuscrit
– *lecture notes*
6 l'assistant
– *demonstrator*
7 le préparateur
– *assistant*
8 le tableau didactique
– *diagram*
9 l'étudiant *m*
– *student*
10 l'étudiante *f*
– *student*
11-25 la bibliothèque universitaire; *anal.:* bibliothèque *f* d'Etat (bibliothèque *f* nationale), bibliothèque *f* d'académie *f*, bibliothèque *f* municipale
– ***university library;*** sim.: *national library, regional or municipal scientific library*
11 la réserve de livres *m*
– *stack (book stack) with the stock of books*
12 les rayons *m*, le rayonnage métallique
– *bookshelf, a steel shelf*
13 la salle de lecture *f*
– *reading room*
14 la surveillante, une bibliothécaire
– *member of the reading room staff, a librarian*
15 le casier à revues *f*
– *periodicals rack with periodicals*
16 le casier à journaux *m*
– *newspaper shelf*
17 la bibliothèque de consultation *f* avec les ouvrages *m* de référence *f* (manuels *m*, lexiques *m*, encyclopédies *f*, dictionnaires *m*)
– *reference library with reference books (handbooks, encyclopedias, dictionaries)*
18 le service de prêt *m* (la salle de prêt *m*) et la salle des catalogues *m*
– *lending library and catalogue (*Am. *catalog) room*
19 le bibliothécaire
– *librarian*
20 le bureau du service de prêt *m*
– *issue desk*
21 le catalogue principal
– *main catalogue (*Am. *catalog)*
22 l'armoire *f* fichier
– *card catalogue (*Am. *catalog)*
23 le fichier
– *card catalogue (*Am. *catalog) drawer*
24 l'usager *m* de la bibliothèque (le lecteur)
– *library user*
25 le bulletin de prêt *m*
– *borrower's ticket (library ticket)*

1-15 la réunion électorale, un meeting électoral
– *election meeting, a public meeting*
1-2 le comité
– *committee*
1 le président
– *chairman*
2 l'assesseur *m*
– *committee member*
3 la table du comité
– *committee table*
4 la sonnette
– *bell*
5 l'orateur *m*
– *election speaker (speaker)*
6 la tribune
– *rostrum*
7 le microphone
– *microphone*
8 l'assemblée *f* (l'assistance *f*)
– *meeting (audience)*
9 le distributeur de tracts *m*
– *man distributing leaflets*
10 le service d'ordre *m*
– *stewards*
11 le brassard
– *armband (armlet)*
12 la banderole électorale
– *banner*
13 la pancarte électorale
– *placard*
14 la proclamation
– *proclamation*
15 le contradicteur
– *heckler*
16-30 le scrutin
– *election*
16 le bureau de vote *m*
– *polling station (polling place)*
17 l'assesseur *m*
– *election officer*
18 le fichier électoral
– *electoral register*
19 la carte d'électeur *m* avec le numéro d'électeur *m*
– *polling card with registration number (polling number)*
20 le bulletin de vote *m* avec les noms *m* des partis *m* et des candidats *m*
– *ballot paper with the names of the parties and candidates*
21 l'enveloppe *f* électorale
– *ballot envelope*
22 l'électrice *f*
– *voter*
23 l'isoloir *m*
– *polling booth*
24 l'électeur *m* exerçant son droit *m* de vote *m*
– *elector (qualified voter)*
25 le règlement électoral
– *election regulations*
26 le secrétaire
– *clerk*
27 la tête de liste *f* de l'opposition *f*
– *clerk with the duplicate list*
28 le président du bureau de vote *m*
– *election supervisor*
29 l'urne *f* électorale
– *ballot box*
30 la fente de l'urne *f*
– *slot*

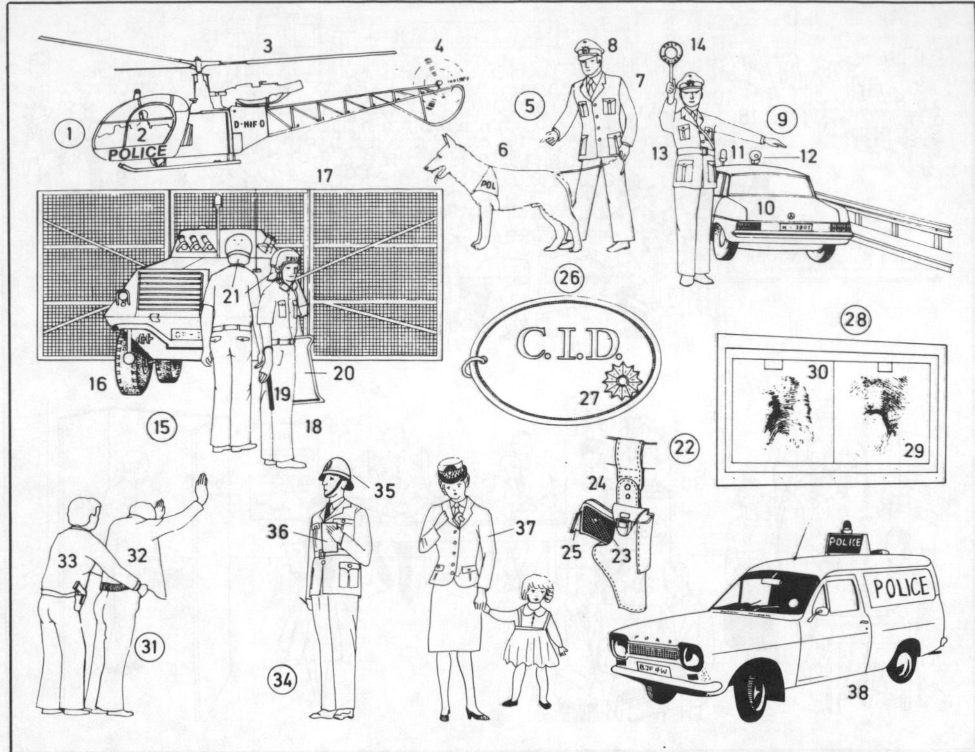

1-33 le service d'intervention *f* **de la police**
– ***police duties***

1 l'hélicoptère *m* **de surveillance** *f* de la circulation
– ***police helicopter*** *(traffic helicopter) for controlling (*Am. *controling) traffic from the air*

2 la cabine du pilote
– *cockpit*

3 le rotor (le rotor principal)
– *rotor (main rotor)*

4 l'hélice *f* de queue *f* (le rotor anticouple)
– *tail rotor*

5 le service des chiens *m* **policiers**
– ***use of police dogs***

6 le chien policier (chien de police *f*)
– *police dog*

7 l'uniforme *m*
– *uniform*

8 la casquette de service *m*, une casquette à visière avec cocarde *f*
– *uniform cap, a peaked cap with cockade*

9 le contrôle de la circulation par une patrouille
– ***traffic control*** *by a mobile traffic patrol*

10 la voiture de patrouille *f*
– *patrol car*

11 le gyrophare
– *blue light*

12 le haut-parleur
– *loud hailer (loudspeaker)*

13 l'agent *m* de patrouille *f*
– *patrolman (police patrolman)*

14 le panneau de police *f*
– *police signalling* (Am. *signaling) disc (disk)*

15 la surveillance des manifestations *f*
– ***riot duty***

16 le véhicule d'intervention *f*
– *special armoured* (Am. *armored) car*

17 la grille de déblaiement *m*
– *barricade*

18 l'agent *m* de police en tenue *f* de combat *m*
– *policeman (police officer) in riot gear*

19 l'arme *f* d'intervention *f* (la matraque)
– *truncheon (baton)*

20 le bouclier de protection *f*
– *riot shield*

21 le casque de protection *f*
– *protective helmet (helmet)*

22 le pistolet de service *m*
– ***service pistol***

23 la poignée du pistolet
– *pistol grip*

24 l'étui *m* du pistolet
– *quick-draw holster*

25 le magasin du pistolet
– *magazine*

26 l'insigne *m* **de la police** judiciaire
– ***police identification disc (disk)***

27 l'étoile de la police
– *police badge*

28 la dactyloscopie (la comparaison des empreintes *f* digitales)
– ***fingerprint identification*** *(dactyloscopy)*

29 l'empreinte *f* digitale
– *fingerprint*

30 le tableau lumineux
– *illuminated screen*

31 la fouille à corps *m*
– ***search***

32 le suspect
– *suspect*

33 l'officier *m* de police *f* en civil
– *detective (plainclothes policeman)*

34 le policier anglais (le bobby)
– *English policeman*

35 le casque
– *helmet*

36 le calepin
– *pocket book*

37 l'auxiliaire féminine de police *f*
– *policewoman*

38 le fourgon cellulaire
– *police van*

1-26 le café; *anal.:* le bar-express, le salon de thé *m*
– ***café,*** sim.: *espresso bar, tea room*
1 le comptoir
– *counter (cake counter)*
2 le percolateur
– *coffee urn*
3 le passe-monnaie
– *tray for the money*
4 la tarte
– *gateau*
5 la meringue, un gâteau fait de blancs *m* d'œufs *m* battus et de sucre *m* en poudre *f,* additionné de crème *f* fouettée
– *meringue with whipped cream*
6 l'apprenti *m* pâtissier
– *trainee pastry cook*
7 la demoiselle (la dame) du comptoir
– *girl (lady) at the counter*
8 le casier à journaux *m* (le porte-revues)
– *newspaper shelves (newspaper rack)*
9 l'applique *f* murale
– *wall lamp*
10 la banquette d'angle *m*
– *corner seat, an upholstered seat*
11 la table de café *m*
– *café table*
12 la plaque de marbre *m*
– *marble top*
13 la serveuse
– *waitress*
14 le plateau à servir
– *tray*
15 la bouteille de limonade *f*
– *bottle of lemonade*
16 le verre à limonade *f*
– *lemonade glass*
17 les joueurs *m* d'échecs *m* disputant une partie d'échecs
– *chess players playing a game of chess*
18 le couvert à café *m*
– *coffee set*
19 la tasse à café *m*
– *cup of coffee*
20 le petit sucrier
– *small sugar bowl*
21 le crémier
– *cream jug (Am. creamer)*
22-24 les clients *m* du café (les consommateurs *m*)
– *café customers*
22 le monsieur
– *gentleman*
23 la dame
– *lady*
24 le lecteur de journaux *m*
– *man reading a newspaper*
25 le journal
– *newspaper*
26 la tringle à journaux *m*
– *newspaper holder*

1-29 le restaurant (l'auberge *f*); *plus ancien:* le cabaret
– ***restaurant***
1-11 le comptoir (le buffet)
– *bar (counter)*
1 la pompe à bière *f*
– *beer pump (beerpull)*
2 l'égouttoir *m*
– *drip tray*
3 le bock (la chope)
– *beer glass, a tumbler*
4 la mousse de la bière (le faux col)
– *froth (head)*
5 le cendrier sphérique
– *spherical ashtray for cigarette and cigar ash*
6 le verre à bière *f*
– *beer glass (beer mug)*
7 le chauffe-bière
– *beer warmer*
8 le barman
– *bartender (barman,* Am. *barkeeper, barkeep)*
9 l'étagère *f* à verres *m*
– *shelf for glasses*
10 l'étagère *f* à bouteilles *f*
– *shelf for bottles*
11 la pile d'assiettes *f* (de vaisselle *f*)
– *stack of plates*
12 le portemanteau
– *coat stand*
13 la patère à chapeaux *m*
– *hat peg*
14 la patère à vêtements *m*
– *coat hook*
15 le ventilateur mural
– *wall ventilator*
16 la bouteille
– *bottle*
17 le plat
– *complete meal*
18 la serveuse (le personnel de salle *f*)
– *waitress*
19 le plateau
– *tray*
20 le vendeur de billets *m* de loterie *f*
– *lottery ticket seller*
21 le menu (la carte du jour)
– *menu (menu card)*
22 l'huilier *m*
– *cruet stand*
23 la boîte de cure-dents *m*
– *toothpick holder*
24 le porte-allumettes
– *matchbox holder*
25 le client (le consommateur), la cliente
– *customer*
26 le rond de feutre *m*
– *beer mat*
27 le couvert
– *meal of the day*
28 la vendeuse de fleurs *f*
– *flower seller (flower girl)*
29 la corbeille à fleurs *f*
– *flower basket*
30-44 la taverne (le débit de boissons *f*)
– ***wine restaurant*** *(wine bar)*
30 le sommelier (un chef de rang *m*)
– *wine waiter, a head waiter*
31 la carte des vins *m*
– *wine list*
32 le carafon (le pichet) de vin *m*
– *wine carafe*
33 le verre à vin *m*
– *wineglass*
34 le poêle en faïence *f*
– *tiled stove*
35 le carreau de poêle *m* en faïence *f*
– *stove tile*
36 la banquette du poêle
– *stove bench*
37 le panneau de bois *m*
– *wooden panelling* (Am. *paneling*)
38 la banquette de coin *m*
– *corner seat*
39 la table d'hôte *m* (la table des habitués *m*)
– *table reserved for regular customers*
40 l'habitué *m*
– *regular customer*
41 le dressoir (le vaisselier)
– *cutlery chest*
42 le seau à glace *f*
– *wine cooler*
43 la bouteille de vin *m*
– *bottle of wine*
44 les cubes *m* de glace *f*
– *ice cubes (ice, lumps of ice)*
45-78 le restaurant self-service (*f*am.: le self)
– ***self-service restaurant***

45 la pile de plateaux *m*
– *stack of trays*
46 les pailles *f* pour boire (chalumeaux *m*)
– *drinking straws (straws)*
47 les serviettes *f*
– *serviettes (napkins)*
48 les casiers à couverts *m*
– *cutlery holders*
49 la vitrine réfrigérante pour plats *m* froids
– *cool shelf*
50 la tranche de melon *m*
– *slice of honeydew melon*
51 l'assiette *f* de salades *f*
– *plate of salad*
52 le plateau de fromages *m*
– *plate of cheeses*
53 le plat de poisson *m*
– *fish dish*
54 le sandwich
– *filled roll*
55 le plat de viande *f* garni
– *meat dish with trimmings*
56 le demi-poulet
– *half chicken*
57 la corbeille de fruits *m*
– *basket of fruit*
58 le jus de fruit *m*
– *fruit juice*
59 le rayon des boissons *f*
– *drinks shelf*
60 la bouteille de lait *m*
– *bottle of milk*
61 la bouteille d'eau *f* minérale
– *bottle of mineral water*
62 le menu diététique
– *vegetarian meal (diet meal)*
63 le plateau
– *tray*
64 la glissière à plateaux *m*
– *tray counter*
65 l'affichage *m* des plats *m*
– *food price list*
66 le passe-plats
– *serving hatch*
67 le plat chaud
– *hot meal*
68 l'appareil *m* distributeur de bière *f*
– *beer pump (beerpull)*
69 la caisse
– *cash desk*
70 la caissière
– *cashier*
71 le propriétaire
– *proprietor*
72 la barrière
– *rail*
73 la salle de restaurant *m*
– *dining area*
74 la table de restaurant *m*
– *table*
75 le sandwich au fromage
– *open sandwich*
76 la coupe glacée
– *ice-cream sundae*
77 la salière et la poivrière
– *salt cellar and pepper pot*
78 la décoration de table *f* (la parure florale)
– *table decoration (flower arrangement)*

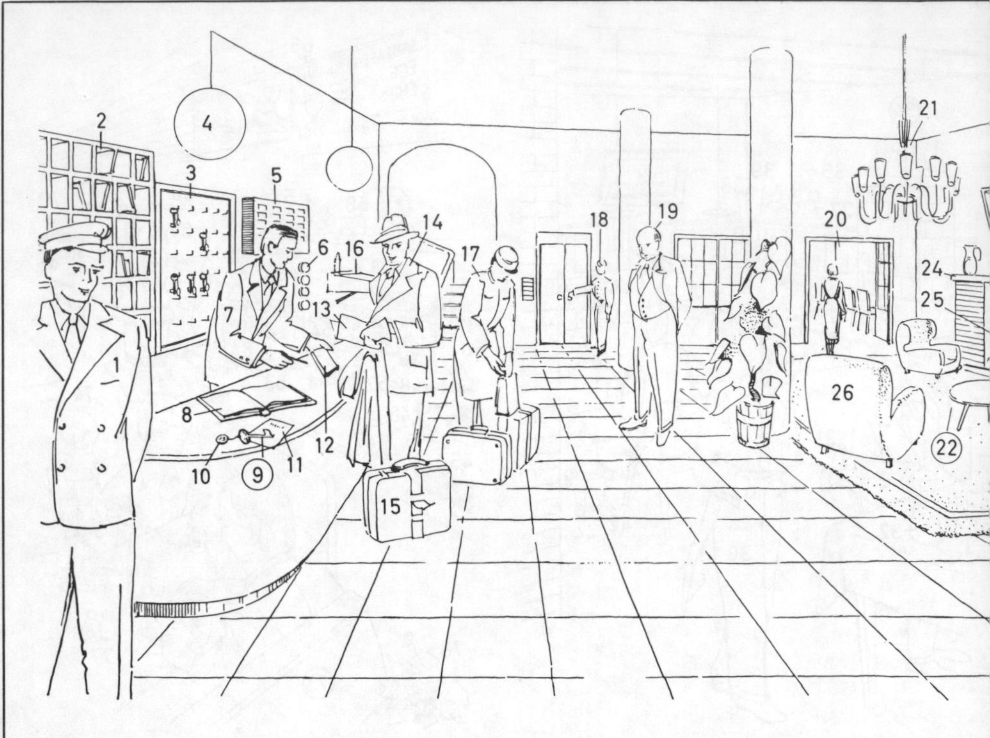

1-26 la réception (le hall d'accueil *m*)
– ***vestibule** (foyer, reception hall)*
1 le portier
– *doorman (commissionaire)*
2 le casier du courrier avec les cases *f*
– *letter rack with pigeon holes*
3 le tableau des clefs *f*
– *key rack*
4 le globe électrique, un globe de verre *m* dépoli (la suspension en verre *m* dépoli)
– *globe lamp, a frosted glass globe*
5 le tableau avertisseur
– *indicator board (drop board)*
6 le voyant lumineux d'appel *m*
– *indicator light*
7 le chef de réception *f*
– *chief receptionist*
8 le registre des voyageurs *m*
– *register (hotel register)*
9 la clef de la chambre
– *room key*
10 la plaque numérotée avec le numéro de la chambre
– *number tag (number tab) showing room number*
11 la facture de l'hôtel *m*
– *hotel bill*
12 le bloc des fiches *f* d'arrivée *f*
– *block of registration forms*
13 le passeport
– *passport*
14 le client de l'hôtel *m*
– *hotel guest*
15 la valise avion *m*, une valise légère
– *lightweight suitcase, a light suitcase for air travel*
16 le pupitre mural
– *wall desk*
17 le bagagiste
– *porter (*Am. *baggage man)*
18-26 le hall de l'hôtel *m*
– *lobby (hotel lobby)*
18 le groom (le chasseur)
– *page (pageboy,* Am. *bell boy)*
19 le directeur (le gérant) de l'hôtel *m*
– *hotel manager*
20 la salle à manger (le restaurant de l'hôtel *m*)
– *dining room (hotel restaurant)*
21 le lustre, un luminaire à sources *f* multiples
– *chandelier*
22 le coin du feu
– *fireside*
23 la cheminée (l'âtre *m*)
– *fireplace*
24 le linteau
– *mantelpiece (mantelshelf)*
25 le feu de bois *m* (la flambée)
– *fire (open fire)*
26 le fauteuil club
– *armchair*
27-38 la chambre d'hôtel *m*, une chambre à deux lits *m* avec salle *f* de bains *m*
– ***hotel room**, a double room with bath*
27 la double porte
– *double door*
28 la plaque des sonneries *f*
– *service bell panel*
29 l'armoire *f* de rangement *m*
– *wardrobe trunk*
30 la penderie
– *clothes compartment*
31 la lingère
– *linen compartment*
32 le lavabo double
– *double washbasin*
33 le garçon d'étage *m*
– *room waiter*
34 le téléphone intérieur
– *room telephone*
35 la moquette veloutée
– *velour (velours) carpet*
36 le guéridon à fleurs *f*
– *flower stand*
37 le bouquet de fleurs *f* (la présentation florale)
– *flower arrangement*
38 les lits *m* jumeaux
– *double bed*
39 la salle commune (la salle des fêtes *f*, la salle de banquet *m*)
– ***banquet room***

40-43 les convives *m* (la réunion privée) d'un repas de fête *f* (d'un banquet)
– *party (private party) at table (at a banquet)*
40 l'orateur *m* portant un toast
– *speaker proposing a toast*
41 le voisin de table *f* du 42
– *42's neighbour (Am. neighbor)*
42 le commensal de la convive du 43
– *43's partner*
43 la convive du 42
– *42's partner*
44-46 le thé (le five o'clock) dans le bar de l'hôtel *m*
– ***thé dansant** (tea dance) in the foyer*
44 le trio (l'orchestre *m*) du bar
– *bar trio*
45 le violoniste ambulant
– *violinist*
46 le couple de danseurs *m*
– *couple dancing (dancing couple)*
47 le garçon
– *waiter*
48 la serviette du garçon
– *napkin*
49 le vendeur de cigares *m* et cigarettes *f*
– *cigar and cigarette boy*
50 l'éventaire *m*
– *cigarette tray*
51 le bar de l'hôtel *m*
– ***hotel bar***
52 la barre d'appui *m* pour les pieds *m*
– *foot rail*
53 le tabouret de bar *m*
– *bar stool*
54 le bar (le comptoir)
– *bar*
55 le client du bar
– *bar customer*
56 le verre à cocktail *m*
– *cocktail glass (Am. highball glass)*
57 le verre à whisky *m*
– *whisky (whiskey) glass*
58 le bouchon de champagne *m*
– *champagne cork*
59 le seau à champagne *m* (le seau à frapper)
– *champagne bucket (champagne cooler)*
60 le verre à graduations *f*
– *measuring beaker (meusure)*
61 le shaker à cocktails *m*
– *cocktail shaker*
62 le barman
– *bartender (barman,* Am. *barkeeper, barkeep)*
63 la barmaid
– *barmaid*
64 l'étagère *f* à bouteilles *f*
– *shelf for bottles*
65 l'étagère *f* à verres *m*
– *shelf for glasses*
66 le revêtement en panneaux *m* de verre *m*
– *mirrored panel*
67 le seau à glace *f*
– *ice bucket*

1 le parcmètre
– *parking meter*
2 le plan directeur (plan *m* de la ville)
– *map of the town (street map)*
3 le panneau lumineux
– *illuminated board*
4 la légende
– *key*
5 la corbeille à papiers *m*
– *litter bin* (Am. *litter basket)*
6 le lampadaire
– *street lamp (street light)*
7 la plaque de nom *m* de rue *f*
– *street sign showing the name of the street*
8 la grille d'égout *m*
– *drain*
9 le magasin de mode *f*
– *clothes shop (fashion house)*
10 la vitrine
– *shop window*
11 l'étalage *m*
– *window display (shop window display)*
12 les accessoires *m* de vitrine *f* (la décoration de vitrine *f*)
– *window decoration (shop window decoration)*
13 l'entrée *f*
– *entrance*
14 la fenêtre
– *window*
15 le bac à fleurs *f*
– *window box*
16 l'enseigne *f* lumineuse
– *neon sign*
17 l'atelier *m* de tailleur *m*
– *tailor's workroom*
18 le passant
– *pedestrian*
19 le sac à provisions *f*
– *shopping bag*
20 le balayeur de rues *f*
– *road sweeper* (Am. *street sweeper)*
21 le balai
– *broom*
22 les ordures *f* (les détritus *m*)
– *rubbish (litter)*
23 les rails *m* de tramway *m*
– *tramlines* (Am. *streetcar tracks)*
24 le passage piétons *m* (le passage zébré); *anc.:* le passage clouté, les clous
– *pedestrian crossing (zebra crossing,* Am. *crosswalk)*
25 l'arrêt *m* de tramway *m*
– *tram stop* (Am. *streetcar stop, trolley stop)*
26 le panneau d'arrêt *m*
– *tram stop sign* (Am. *streetcar stop sign, trolley stop sign)*
27 le panneau horaire *m*
– *tram timetable* (Am. *streetcar schedule)*
28 le distributeur automatique de billets *m*
– *ticket machine*
29 le panneau de signalisation *f* «passage *m* piétons» *m*
– *'pedestrian crossing' sign*
30 l'agent *m* de la circulation en train de régler la circulation
– *traffic policeman on traffic duty (point duty)*
31 la manchette blanche
– *traffic control cuff*
32 la casquette blanche
– *white cap*
33 le geste de la main
– *hand signal*
34 le motocycliste
– *motorcyclist*
35 la motocylette
– *motorcycle*
36 la passagère
– *pillion passenger (pillion rider)*
37 la librairie
– *bookshop*
38 la chapellerie
– *hat shop (hatter's shop);* for ladies' hats: *milliner's shop*
39 l'enseigne *f* du magasin
– *shop sign*
40 l'agence *f* d'assurances *f*
– *insurance company office*
41 le grand magasin
– *department store*
42 la devanture
– *shop front*
43 le panneau-réclame
– *advertisement*

44 les oriflammes *f*
– *flags*
45 l'enseigne *f* de toit *m* (l'enseigne *f* principale) en lettres *f* lumineuses
– *illuminated letters*
46 la rame de tramway *m*
– *tram* (Am. *streetcar, trolley)*
47 le camion de déménagement *m*
– *furniture lorry* (Am. *furniture truck)*
48 le passage supérieur pour piétons *m*
– *flyover*
49 l'éclairage *m* de la rue, un lampadaire central
– *suspended street lamp*
50 la bande stop
– *stop line*
51 la matérialisation du passage piétons *m*
– *pedestrian crossing* (Am. *crosswalk)*
52 les feux *m* de signalisation *f*
– *traffic lights*
53 le poteau des feux *m* de signalisation *f*
– *traffic light post*
54 le dispositif de signalisation *f*
– *set of lights*
55 les feux *m* piétons *m*
– *pedestrian lights*
56 la cabine téléphonique
– *telephone box (telephone booth, telephone kiosk, call box)*
57 le panneau publicitaire de cinéma *m* (la réclame de cinéma *m)*
– *cinema advertisement (film poster)*
58 la zone piétonnière (piétonne)
– *pedestrian precinct (paved zone)*
59 le café
– *street café*
60 la terrasse
– *group seated (sitting) at a table*
61 le parasol
– *sunshade*
62 l'escalier *m* de descente *f* aux toilettes *f*
– *steps to the public lavatories (public conveniences)*
63 la station de taxis *m*
– *taxi rank (taxi stand)*
64 le taxi
– *taxi (taxicab, cab)*
65 l'enseigne *f* du taxi
– *taxi sign*
66 le panneau de signalisation *f* «station *f* de taxis» *m*
– *traffic sign showing 'taxi rank' ('taxi stand')*
67 la borne d'appel *m* taxis *m*
– *taxi telephone*
68 le bureau de poste *f*
– *post office*
69 le distributeur automatique de cigarettes *f*
– *cigarette machine*
70 la colonne Morris
– *advertising pillar*
71 l'affiche *f*
– *poster (advertisement)*
72 la bande matérialisée
– *white line*
73 la présélection de gauche *f*
– *lane arrow for turning left*
74 la présélection de continuité *f*
– *lane arrow for going straight ahead*
75 le marchand de journaux *m*
– *news vendor* (Am. *news dealer)*

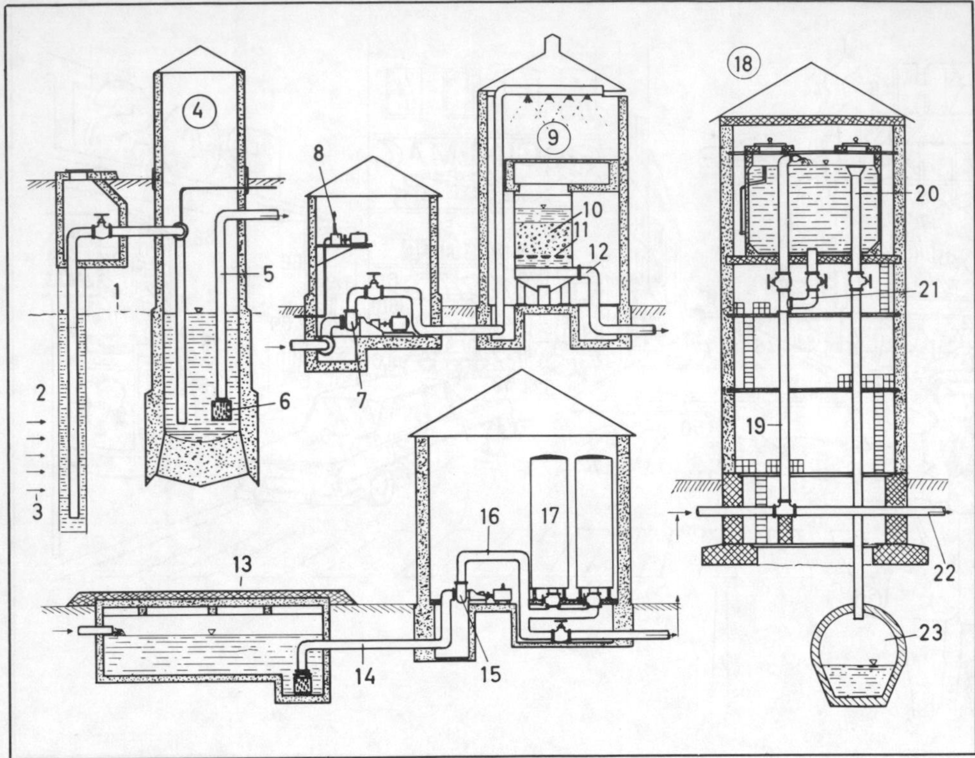

1-66 l'approvisionnement *m* **en eau** *f* **potable** (la distribution d'eau *f* potable)
– ***drinking water supply***
1 le niveau de la nappe d'eau *f* souterraine (le niveau de la nappe phréatique)
– *water table (groundwater level)*
2 la couche perméable
– *water-bearing stratum (aquifer, aquafer)*
3 le courant d'eau *f* souterraine
– *groundwater stream (underground stream)*
4 le puits de captage *m* d'eau *f* brute
– *collector well for raw water*
5 la conduite d'aspiration *f*
– *suction pipe*
6 la crépine à clapet *m* de pied *m*
– *pump strainer (with foot valve)*
7 la pompe d'épuisement *m* à moteur *m*
– *bucket pump with motor*
8 la pompe à vide *m* à moteur *m*
– *vacuum pump with motor*
9 la station de filtration *f* rapide
– *rapid-filter plant*
10 le gravier filtrant
– *filter gravel (filter bed)*
11 le plancher de filtre *m*, une grille
– *filter bottom, a grid*
12 la conduite de sortie *f* de l'eau *f* filtrée
– *filtered water outlet*
13 le réservoir d'eau *f* filtrée
– *purified water tank*
14 la conduite d'aspiration *f* avec crépine *f* et clapet *m* de pied *m*
– *suction pipe with pump strainer and foot valve*
15 la pompe principale à moteur *m*
– *main pump with motor*
16 la conduite de refoulement *m*
– *delivery pipe*
17 le réservoir d'air *m*
– *compressed-air vessel (air vessel, air receiver)*
18 le château d'eau *f*
– *water tower*
19 la conduite ascensionnelle
– *riser pipe (riser)*
20 le tuyau de trop-plein *m*
– *overflow pipe*
21 le tuyau de sortie *f*
– *outlet*
22 la conduite de distribution *f*
– *distribution main*
23 le canal des eaux *f* de trop-plein *m*
– *excess water conduit*
24-39 le captage d'une source *f*
– *tapping a spring*
24 la chambre de captage *m* d'une source *f*
– *chamber*
25 le mur de la chambre (l'arrêt *m* de sable *m*)
– *chamber wall*
26 le puits de visite *f* (le puits d'accès *m*)
– *manhole*
27 la cheminée d'aération *f*
– *ventilator*
28 les échelons *m* en fer *m*
– *step irons*
29 le remblai
– *filling (backing)*
30 le robinet-vanne (la vanne d'arrêt *m*)
– *outlet control valve*
31 le robinet de vidange *f*
– *outlet valve*
32 la crépine
– *strainer*
33 le trop-plein
– *overflow pipe (overflow)*
34 l'écoulement *m* de fond *m* (la décharge de fond *m*)
– *bottom outlet*
35 les tuyaux *m* en terre *f* cuite (tuyaux *m* en grès *m*)
– *earthenware pipes*
36 la couche imperméable
– *impervious stratum (impermeable stratum)*
37 le mur de moellons *m*
– *rough rubble*
38 la couche perméable
– *water-bearing stratum (aquifer, aquafer)*
39 la couche d'argile *f* damée
– *loam seal (clay seal)*

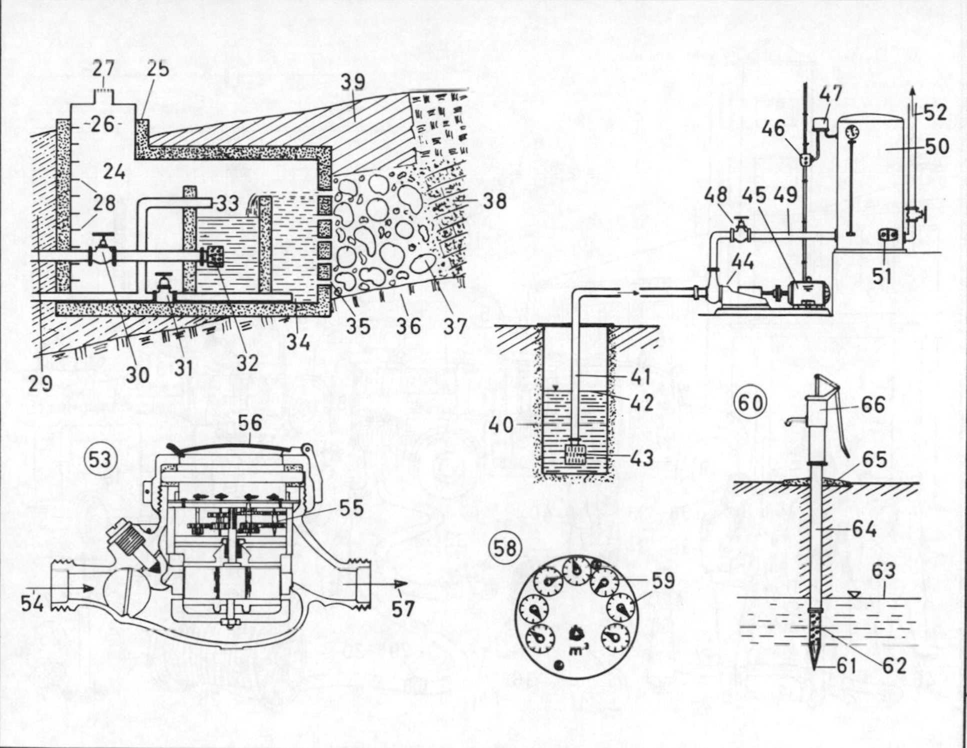

40-52 l'approvisionnement *m* privé en eau *f*
– *individual water supply*
40 le puits
– *well*
41 la conduite d'aspiration *f*
– *suction pipe*
42 la surface de la nappe d'eau *f* souterraine
– *water table (groundwater level)*
43 la crépine à clapet *m* de pied *m*
– *pump strainer with foot valve*
44 la pompe centrifuge
– *centrifugal pump*
45 le moteur
– *motor*
46 le disjoncteur (de protection *f*) du moteur
– *motor safety switch*
47 le contrôleur de pression *f*, un appareil de couplage *m*
– *manostat, a switching device*
48 le robinet-vanne (la vanne d'arrêt *m*)
– *stopcock*
49 la conduite de refoulement *m*
– *delivery pipe*
50 le réservoir d'air *m*
– *compressed-air vessel (air vessel, air receiver)*
51 le trou d'homme *m* (l'orifice *m* de nettoiement *m*)
– *manhole*
52 le branchement vers l'usager *m*
– *delivery pipe*
53 le compteur d'eau *f*, un compteur d'eau *f* à turbine *f*
– *water meter, a rotary meter*
54 l'arrivée *f* d'eau *f*
– *water inlet*
55 le mécanisme compteur
– *counter gear assembly*
56 le couvercle vitré
– *cover with glass lid*
57 la sortie de l'eau *f*
– *water outlet*
58 le cadran du compteur *m* d'eau *f*
– *water-meter dial*
59 l'indicateur *m*
– *counters*
60 la pompe pour puits instantané
– *driven well (tube well, drive well)*
61 la pointe de pénétration *f*
– *pile shoe*
62 le tube à trous *m* (formant crépine *f*)
– *filter*
63 le niveau de la nappe d'eau *f* souterraine
– *water table (groundwater level)*
64 le tuyau de la pompe (la gaine)
– *well casing*
65 la bordure de pompe *f*
– *well head*
66 la pompe à main *f* (la pompe à bras *m*, la pompe à piston *m*)
– *hand pump*

1-46 **l'exercice** *m* **de lutte** *f* **contre le feu** (l'exercice *m* des sapeurs-pompiers *m*, l'exercice *m* d'extinction *f*, d'escalade *f*, d'échelle *f* et de sauvetage *m*)
– ***fire service drill*** *(extinguishing, climbing, ladder, and rescue work)*

1-3 le poste d'incendie *m* (le poste permanent de feu *m*)
– *fire station*

1 le garage pour les véhicules *m* et la remise pour le matériel *m*
– *engine and appliance room*

2 la caserne des sapeurs-pompiers *m*
– *firemen's quarters*

3 la tour d'entraînement *m*
– *drill tower*

4 la sirène d'alerte *f* (au feu *m*)
– *fire alarm (fire alarm siren, fire siren)*

5 la voiture de premier secours *m* (le fourgon-pompe)
– *fire engine*

6 le feu avertisseur, un feu tournant à éclats *m* (un feu intermittent)
– *blue light (warning light), a flashing light* (Am. *flashlight)*

7 l'avertisseur *m* sonore
– *horn (hooter)*

8 la motopompe, une pompe centrifuge
– *motor pump, a centrifugal pump*

9 l'échelle *f* orientable automobile
– *motor turntable ladder (*Am. *aerial ladder)*

10 la grande échelle, une échelle en acier *m* (une échelle mécanique)
– *ladder, a steel ladder (automatic extending ladder)*

11 le mécanisme de l'échelle *f*
– *ladder mechanism*

12 la béquille (d'appui *m*)
– *jack*

13 le conducteur
– *ladder operator*

14 l'échelle *f* coulissante
– *extension ladder*

15 le croc à incendie *m* (la gaffe)
– *ceiling hook* (Am. *preventer)*

16 l'échelle *f* à crochets *m*
– *hook ladder* (Am. *pompier ladder)*

17 les sapeurs *m* tenant la toile de sauvetage *m*
– *holding squad*

18 la toile de sauvetage *m*
– *jumping sheet (sheet)*

19 l'ambulance *f* (la voiture de secours *m*)
– *ambulance car (ambulance)*

20 l'appareil *m* de réanimation *f*, un inhalateur d'oxygène *m*
– *resuscitator (resuscitation equipment), oxygen apparatus*

21 l'infirmier *m*
– *ambulance attendant (ambulance man)*

22 le brassard
– *armband (armlet, brassard)*

23 le brancard (la civière)
– *stretcher*

24 le blessé, un homme ayant perdu connaissance *f*
– *unconscious man*

25 la bouche d'incendie *m*
– *pit hydrant*

26 le tuyau vertical à embranchement *m* double
– *standpipe (riser, vertical pipe)*

27 la clé tricoise
– *hydrant key*

28 le dévidoir mobile pour tuyaux *m* souples
– *hose reel* (Am. *hose cart, hose wagon, hose truck, hose carriage)*

29 le raccord à griffes *f* pour boyaux *m* (le raccord pompiers)
– *hose coupling*

30 le tuyau d'aspiration *f*, un boyau (un tuyau souple)
– *soft suction hose*

31 le tuyau de refoulement *m*
– *delivery hose*

32 la pièce d'embranchement *m* (le raccord en T *m*)
– *dividing breeching*

33 la lance
– *branch*

34 l'équipe *f* de pompiers *m* [le porte-lance et son aide *m*]
– *branchmen*

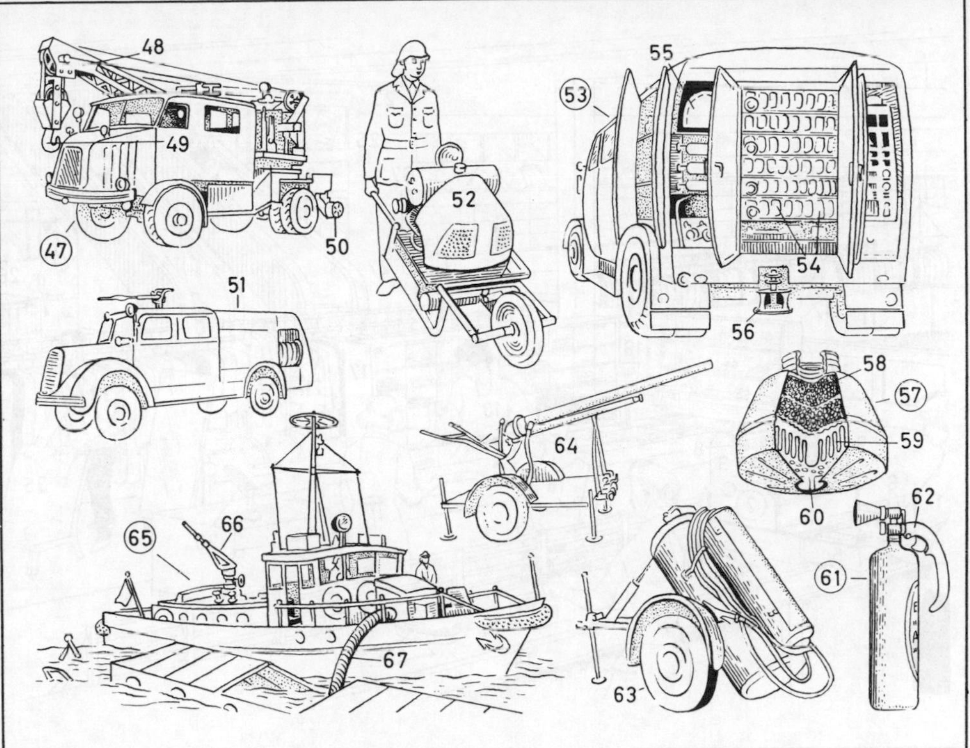

35 la borne d'incendie *m*
– *surface hydrant (fire plug)*
36 le chef de poste *m*
– *officer in charge*
37 le sapeur-pompier
– *fireman* (Am. *firefighter)*
38 le casque antifeu avec couvre-nuque *m*
– *helmet (fireman's helmet,* Am. *fire hat) with neck guard (neck flap)*
39 l'appareil *m* respiratoire protecteur (le respirateur)
– *breathing apparatus*
40 le masque à gaz *m*
– *face mask*
41 le talkie-walkie (*ELF:* l'émetteur *m* - récepteur *m* radio)
– *walkie-talkie set*
42 le projecteur portatif
– *hand lamp*
43 la hache de sapeur-pompier *m*
– *small axe* (Am. *ax, pompier hatchet)*
44 le ceinturon à mousquetons *m*
– *hook belt*
45 la corde de sauvetage *m*
– *beltline*
46 le vêtement antifeu en amiante *m* ou en toile *f* métallisée
– *protective clothing of asbestos (asbestos suit) or of metallic fabric*
47 la grue automobile
– *breakdown lorry* (Am. *crane truck, wrecking crane)*
48 la grue de dépannage *m*
– *lifting crane*
49 le crochet de traction *f*
– *load hook (draw hook,* Am. *drag hook)*
50 le galet support
– *support roll*
51 le fourgon-réservoir
– *water tender*
52 la motopompe portative
– *portable pump*
53 le fourgon à tuyaux *m* et d'outillage *m*
– *hose layer*
54 les tuyaux *m* enroulés
– *flaked lengths of hose*
55 le tambour (l'enrouleur *m,* le touret) de câble *m*
– *cable drum*
56 le cabestan
– *winch*
57 le filtre du masque *m* à gaz *m*
– *face mask filter*
58 le charbon actif
– *active carbon (activated carbon, activated charcoal)*
59 le filtre à poussière *f*
– *dust filter*
60 l'entrée *f* d'air *m*
– *air inlet*
61 l'extincteur *m* à main *f*
– *portable fire extinguisher*
62 la soupape pistolet
– *trigger valve*
63 l'extincteur *m* mobile
– *large mobile extinguisher (wheeled fire extinguisher)*
64 le projecteur de mousse *f* d'air *m* et d'eau *f*
– *foam-making branch* (Am. *foam gun)*
65 le bateau-pompe
– *fireboat*
66 la lance d'incendie *m* à grande puissance *f* (la lance «Monitor»)
– *monitor (water cannon)*
67 le tuyau flexible d'aspiration *f*
– *suction hose*

1 la caissière
– *cashier*
2 la caisse enregistreuse
– *electric cash register (till)*
3 les touches *f* numériques
– *number keys*
4 la touche d'annulation *f*
– *cancellation button*
5 le tiroir-caisse
– *cash drawer (till)*
6 les compartiments *m* pour la monnaie et les billets *m* de banque *f*
– *compartments (money compartments) for coins and notes* (Am. *bills)*
7 la fiche de caisse *f* acquittée (la quittance)
– *receipt (sales check)*
8 le montant (le total enregistré)
– *amount [to be paid]*
9 le compteur
– *adding mechanism*
10 la marchandise
– *goods*
11 le hall central
– *glass-roofed well*
12 le rayon hommes *m*
– *men's wear department*
13 la vitrine, l'étalage *m* intérieur
– *showcase (display case, indoor display window)*
14 le comptoir de délivrance *f* des marchandises *f*
– *wrapping counter*
15 la corbeille à marchandises *f*
– *tray for purchases*
16 la cliente
– *customer*
17 le rayon bonneterie *f*
– *hosiery department*
18 la vendeuse
– *shop assistant* (Am. *salesgirl, saleslady)*
19 le panneau des prix *m*
– *price card*
20 l'appuie-bras *m* de gantier *m*
– *glove stand*
21 le duffle-coat, un manteau trois-quarts
– *duffle coat, a three-quarter length coat*
22 l'escalier *m* roulant
– *escalator*
23 le tube fluorescent (le tube au néon *m*)
– *fluorescent light (fluorescent lamp)*
24 le bureau (p.ex.: bureau *m* de crédit *m*, bureau *m* de voyages *m*, bureau *m* de la direction)
– *office (e.g. customer accounts office, travel agency, manager's office)*
25 le panneau publicitaire
– *poster (advertisement)*
26 le guichet de l'agence *f* des spectacles *m*
– *theatre* (Am. *theater) and concert booking office (advance booking office)*
27 le rayonnage
– *shelves*
28 le rayon de confection *f* pour dames *f*
– *ladies' wear department*
29 la robe prêt-à-porter *m*
– *ready-made dress (ready-to-wear dress,* coll. *off-the-peg dress)*
30 le protège-vêtements
– *dust cover*
31 la tringle à vêtements *m*
– *clothes rack*
32 la cabine d'essayage *m*
– *changing booth (fitting booth)*
33 le chef de réception *f*
– *shop walker* (Am. *floorwalker, floor manager)*
34 le mannequin
– *dummy*
35 le fauteuil
– *seat (chair)*
36 le journal de modes *f*
– *fashion journal (fashion magazine)*
37 le retoucheur [*en France généralement:* une retoucheuse]
– *tailor marking a hemline*
38 le mètre-ruban
– *measuring tape (tape measure)*
39 la craie-tailleur
– *tailor's chalk (French chalk)*
40 l'arrondisseur *m* de bas *m* de jupe *f*
– *hemline marker*
41 le manteau vague
– *loose-fitting coat*

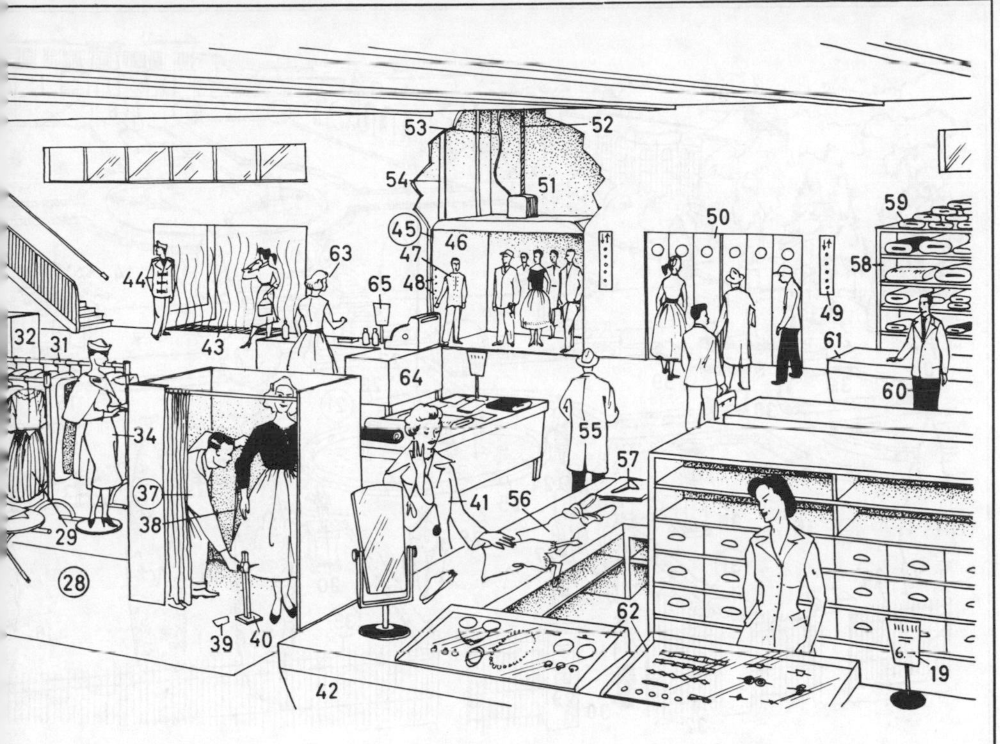

42 le comptoir de vente *f*
– *sales counter*
43 le rideau d'air *m* chaud
– *warm-air curtain*
44 le portier
– *doorman (commissionaire)*
45 l'ascenseur *m*
– *lift* (Am. *elevator)*
46 la cabine d'ascenseur *m*
– *lift cage (lift car,* Am. *elevator car)*
47 le garçon d'ascenseur *m*
– *lift operator (*Am. *elevator operator)*
48 le levier de commande *f*
– *controls (lift controls,* Am. *elevator controls)*
49 l'indicateur *m* d'étage *m*
– *floor indicator*
50 la porte coulissante
– *sliding door*
51 la cage d'ascenseur *m*
– *lift shaft* (Am. *elevator shaft)*
52 le câble porteur
– *bearer cable*
53 le câble de commande *f*
– *control cable*
54 le rail de guidage *m*
– *guide rail*
55 le client
– *customer*
56 le rayon lingerie *f*
– *hosiery*
57 le rayon de blanc *m* de maison *f*
– *linen goods (table linen and bed linen)*
58 le rayon tissus *m*
– *fabric department*
59 la pièce de tissu *m*
– *roll of fabric (roll of material, roll of cloth)*
60 le chef de rayon *m*
– *head of department (department manager)*
61 le comptoir
– *sales counter*
62 le rayon de bijouterie *f* (bijouterie *f* de fantaisie *f*, articles *m* de Paris)
– *jewellery* (Am. *jewelry) department*
63 la vendeuse du rayon de nouveautés *f*
– *assistant* (Am. *salesgirl, saleslady), selling new lines (new products)*
64 la table des offres *f* spéciales
– *special counter (extra counter)*
65 le panneau d'offres *f* spéciales
– *placard advertising special offers*
66 le rayon rideaux *m* et voilages *m*
– *curtain department*
67 l'étalage *m* de rayon *m*
– *display on top of the shelves*

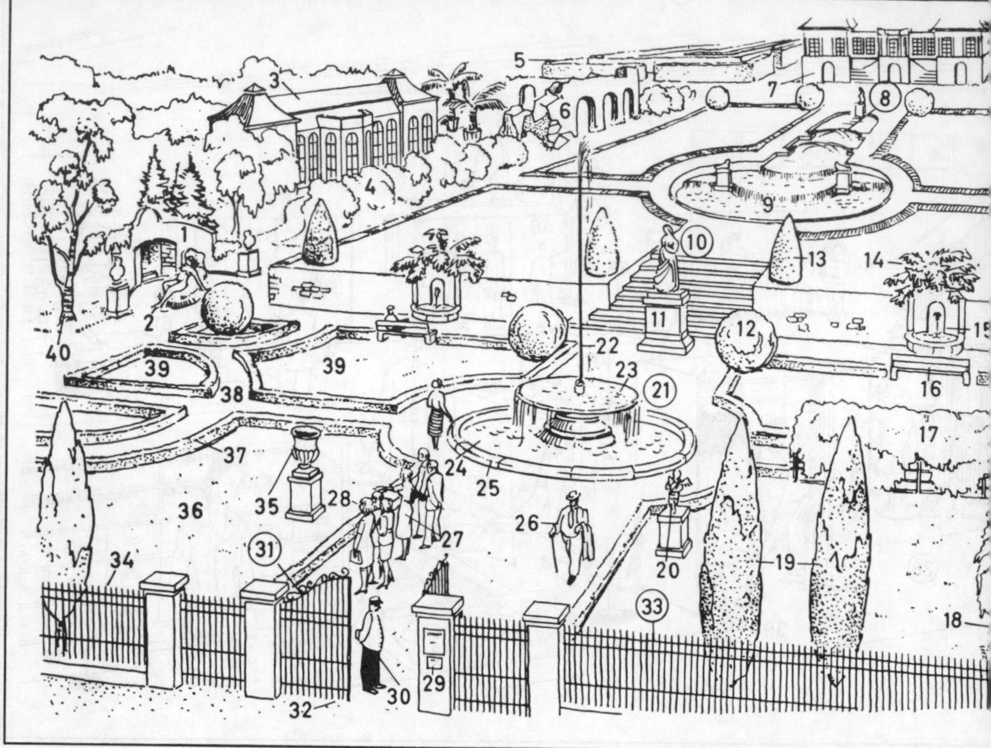

1-40 le jardin à la française, un parc de château *m*
– ***formal garden*** *(French Baroque garden), palace gardens*
1 la grotte
– *grotto (cavern)*
2 la statue, une nymphe
– *stone statue, a river nymph*
3 l'orangerie *f*
– *orangery (orangerie)*
4 le bosquet
– *boscage (boskage)*
5 le labyrinthe
– *maze (labyrinth of paths and hedges)*
6 le théâtre de verdure *f*
– *open-air theatre* (Am. *theater)*
7 le château du XVIIe siècle (un château de style *m* Louis XIV)
– *Baroque palace*
8 les jeux *m* d'eau *f*
– *fountains*
9 la cascade (la cascade artificielle à gradins *m*)
– *cascade (broken artificial waterfall, artificial falls)*
10 la statue, un monument
– *statue, a monument*
11 le socle
– *pedestal (base of statue)*
12 l'arbre *m* taillé en boule *f*
– *globe-shaped tree*
13 l'arbre *m* taillé en cône *m*
– *conical tree*
14 le buisson d'ornement *m*
– *ornamental shrub*
15 la fontaine murale
– *wall fountain*
16 le banc de jardin *m*
– *park bench*
17 la pergola
– *pergola (bower, arbour,* Am. *arbor)*
18 le sentier recouvert de gravier *m*
– *gravel path (gravel walk)*
19 l'arbre *m* taillé en pyramide *f*
– *pyramid tree (pyramidal tree)*
20 l'amour *m*
– *cupid (cherub, amoretto, amorino)*
21 la fontaine
– *fountain*
22 le jet d'eau *f*
– *fountain (jet of water)*
23 la coupe
– *overflow basin*
24 le bassin
– *basin*
25 la margelle
– *kerb (curb)*
26 le promeneur
– *man out for a walk*
27 la conférencière (l'hôtesse *f*)
– *tourist guide*
28 le groupe de touristes *m*
– *group of tourists*
29 le règlement du parc
– *park by-laws (bye-laws)*
30 le gardien
– *park keeper*
31 le portail (la grille), une grille en fer *m* forgé
– *garden gates, wrought iron gates*
32 le passage d'entrée *f*
– *park entrance*
33 le grillage
– *park railings*
34 le barreau
– *railing (bar)*
35 le vase de pierre *f*
– *stone vase*
36 la pelouse (le gazon)
– *lawn*
37 la bordure d'allée *f*, une haie taillée
– *border, a trimmed (clipped) hedge*
38 l'allée *f*
– *park path*
39 le parterre
– *parterre*
40 le bouleau
– *birch (birch tree)*
41-72 le parc à l'anglaise (le jardin anglais)
– ***landscaped park*** *(jardin anglais)*
41 la plate-bande fleurie
– *flower bed*
42 le banc de jardin *m*
– *park bench (garden seat)*
43 la corbeille à papiers *m*
– *litter bin (Am. litter basket)*
44 la pelouse de jeux *m*
– *play area*
45 le cours d'eau *f*
– *stream*

46 la passerelle
– *jetty*
47 le pont
– *bridge*
48 le fauteuil de jardin *m*
– *park chair*
49 l'enclos *m* des animaux *m*
– *animal enclosure*
50 la pièce d'eau *f*
– *pond*
51-54 les oiseaux *m* aquatiques
– *waterfowl*
51 le canard sauvage avec ses canetons *m*
– *wild duck with young*
52 l'oie *f* sauvage
– *goose*
53 le flamant
– *flamingo*
54 le cygne
– *swan*
55 l'île *f*
– *island*
56 le nénuphar
– *water lily*
57 le café avec terrasse *f*
– *open-air café*
58 le parasol
– *sunshade*
59 l'arbre *m*
– *park tree (tree)*
60 le faîte
– *treetop (crown)*
61 le bosquet
– *group of trees*
62 le jet d'eau *f*
– *fountain*
63 le saule pleureur
– *weeping willow*
64 la sculpture moderne
– *modern sculpture*
65 la serre
– *hothouse*
66 le jardinier
– *park gardener*
67 le balai de branchages *m*
– *broom*
68 le mini-golf
– *minigolf course*
69 le joueur de mini-golf *m*
– *minigolf player*
70 le parcours du mini-golf
– *minigolf hole*
71 la mère avec la voiture d'enfant *m*
– *mother with pram (baby carriage)*
72 le couple d'amoureux *m*
– *courting couple (young couple)*

1 le ping-pong (le tennis de table *f*)
– *table tennis game*
2 la table de ping-pong *m*
– *table*
3 le filet de ping-pong *m*
– *table tennis net*
4 la raquette de ping-pong *m*
– *table tennis racket (raquet) (table tennis bat)*
5 la balle de ping-pong *m*
– *table tennis ball*
6 le badminton
– *badminton game (shuttlecock game)*
7 le volant
– *shuttlecock*
8 le pas-de-géant (le vindas)
– *maypole swing*
9 la bicyclette (le vélo) d'enfant *m*
– *child's bicycle*
10 le football
– *football game (soccer game)*
11 le but de football *m* (la cage)
– *goal (goalposts)*
12 le ballon de football *m*
– *football*
13 le buteur (le marqueur de buts *m*)
– *goal scorer*
14 le gardien de but *m* (le goal)
– *goalkeeper*
15 le saut à la corde
– *skipping* (Am. *jumping rope)*
16 la corde à sauter
– *skipping rope* (Am. *skip rope, jump rope, jumping rope)*
17 le pylône d'escalade *f* en bois *m*
– *climbing tower*
18 la balançoire (l'escarpolette *f*) à pneu *m*
– *rubber tyre* (Am. *tire) swing*
19 le pneu de camion *m*
– *lorry tyre* (Am. *truck tire)*
20 le ballon à rebonds *m*
– *bouncing ball*
21 l'ouvrage *m* de jeux *m* en plein air *m*
– *adventure playground*
22 l'échelle *f* de rondins *m*
– *log ladder*
23 la plate-forme d'observation *f* (le mirador)
– *lookout platform*
24 le toboggan
– *slide*
25 la boîte à ordures *f* (la poubelle)
– *litter bin* (Am. *litter basket)*
26 l'ours *m* en peluche *f*
– *teddy bear*
27 le train miniature en bois *m*
– *wooden train set*
28 la grenouillère (la pataugeoire) pour enfants *m*
– *paddling pool*
29 le voilier miniature
– *sailing boat (yacht,* Am. *sailboat)*
30 le canard, un jouet d'enfant *m*
– *toy duck*
31 la voiture d'enfant *m* (le landau)
– *pram (baby carriage)*
32 la barre fixe
– *high bar (bar)*
33 le kart
– *go-cart (soap box)*
34 le drapeau à damier *m* (le drapeau de départ *m*)
– *starter's flag*
35 la bascule (la balançoire, le tape(-)cul)
– *seesaw*
36 l'automate *m* (le robot)
– *robot*
37 l'aéromodélisme *m*
– *flying model aeroplanes* (Am. *airplanes)*

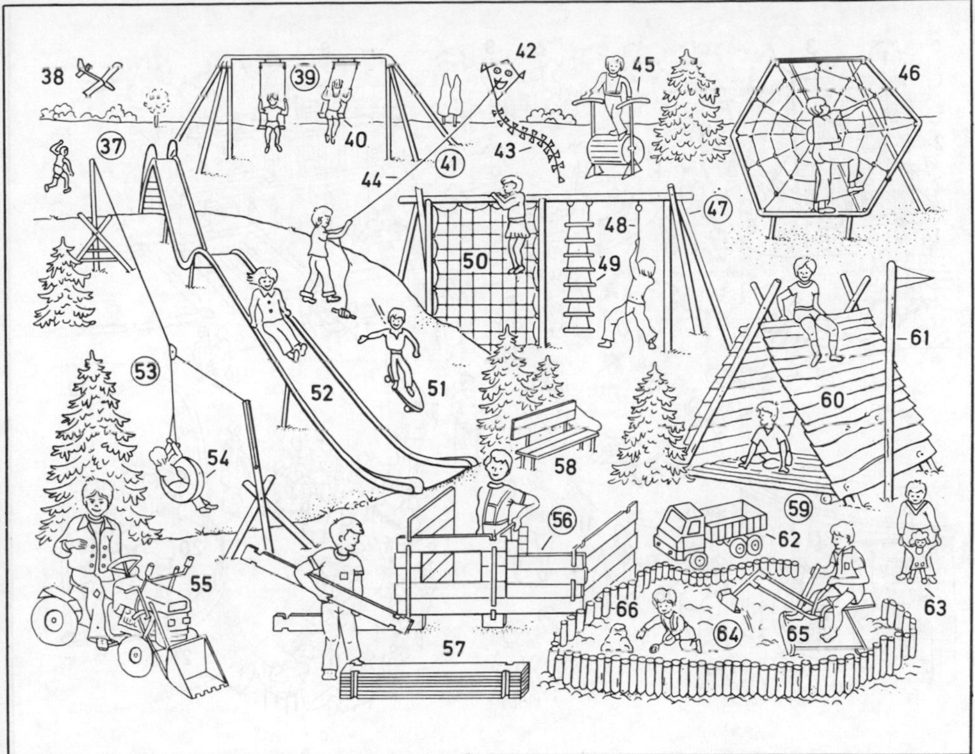

38 l'avion *m* miniature (le modèle réduit d'avion *m*, l'avion *m* de modèle *m* réduit)
– *model aeroplane* (Am. *airplane*)
39 le portique à 2 balançoires *f*
– *double swing*
40 le siège (la planche) de balançoire *f*
– *swing seat*
41 le lancer du cerf-volant *m*
– *flying kites*
42 le cerf-volant
– *kite*
43 la queue du cerf-volant
– *tail of the kite*
44 la ficelle (le fil, la cordelette) du cerf-volant
– *kite string*
45 le cylindre rotatif (le tambour d'entraînement *m* à la course à pied *m*)
– *revolving drum*
46 la toile d'araignée *f*
– *spider's web*
47 le portique
– *climbing frame*
48 la corde lisse
– *climbing rope*
49 l'échelle *f* de corde *f*
– *rope ladder*
50 le filet de grimper *m*
– *climbing net*
51 la planche à roulettes *f* (le skateboard, le roll-surf)
– *skateboard*
52 le toboggan en montagnes *f* russes
– *up-and-down slide*
53 le transporteur aérien à pneu *m*
– *rubber tyre* (Am. *tire*) *cable car*
54 le pneu servant de siège *m*
– *rubber tyre* (Am. *tire*)
55 le tracteur, un véhicule à pédales *f*
– *tractor, a pedal car*
56 la maison miniature à éléments *m* de construction *f* interchangeables
– *den*
57 la planche d'assemblage *m*
– *presawn boards*
58 le banc
– *seat (bench)*
59 la tente (la cabane, la hutte) d'Indien *m*
– *Indian hut*
60 le toit d'escalade *f*
– *climbing roof*
61 le mât de drapeau *m*
– *flagpole (flagstaff)*
62 le camion, un jouet d'enfant *m*
– *toy lorry* (Am. *toy truck*)
63 la poupée
– *walking doll*
64 le bac à sable *m*
– *sandpit* (Am. *sandbox*)
65 l'excavateur *m* (l'excavatrice *f*, la pelle mécanique), un jouet d'enfant *m*
– *toy excavator (toy digger)*
66 le monticule de sable *m* (le pâté, le tas de sable *m*)
– *sandhill*

1-21 le parc de la station thermale
– *spa gardens*
1-7 les bains *m*
– *salina (salt works)*
1 le bâtiment de graduation *f*
– *thorn house (graduation house)*
2 les fascines *f* de prunelliers *m*
– *thorns (brushwood)*
3 la rigole de répartition *f* des eaux *f*
– *brine channels*
4 la conduite d'eau *f* salée à partir de la pompe
– *brine pipe from the pumping station*
5 le gardien du bâtiment de graduation *f*
– *salt works attendant*
6-7 la cure d'inhalation *f*
– *inhalational therapy*
6 l'inhalatorium *m* de plein air *m*
– *open-air inhalatorium (outdoor inhalatorium)*
7 le malade à la cure d'inhalation *f*
– *patient inhaling (taking an inhalation)*
8 l'établissement *m* de cure *f* avec le casino
– *hydropathic (pump room) with kursaal (casino)*
9 le promenoir (les colonnades *f*)
– *colonnade*
10 la promenade de la station balnéaire
– *spa promenade*
11 l'allée *f* de la source
– *avenue leading to the mineral spring*
12-14 la cure de repos *m*
– *rest cure*
12 la pelouse de repos *m*
– *sunbathing area (lawn)*
13 la chaise longue
– *deck-chair*
14 la marquise
– *sun canopy*
15 le pavillon de la source
– *pump room*
16 l'étagère *f* à verres *m*
– *rack for glasses*
17 le distributeur d'eau *f*
– *tap*
18 le curiste en train de boire l'eau *f*
– *patient taking the waters*
19 le kiosque à musique *f*
– *bandstand*
20 l'orchestre *m* de la station donnant un concert
– *spa orchestra giving a concert*
21 le chef d'orchestre *m*
– *conductor*

Roulette 275

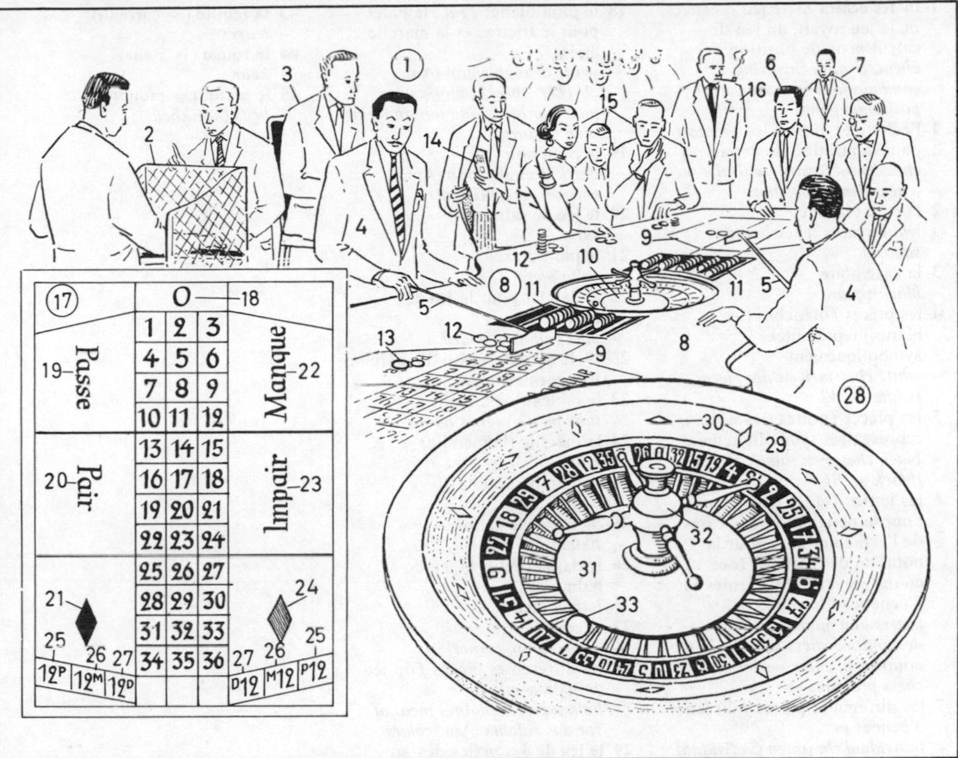

1-33 la roulette, un jeu de hasard *m*
– ***roulette**, a game of chance (gambling game)*

1 la salle de roulette *f* (la salle de jeu *m*) au casino *m*
– *gaming room in the casino (in the gambling casino)*

2 la caisse
– *cash desk*

3 le chef de partie *f*
– *tourneur (dealer)*

4 le croupier
– *croupier*

5 le râteau
– *rake*

6 le croupier de tête *f*
– *head croupier*

7 le chef de salle *f*
– *hall manager*

8 la table de roulette *f*
– *roulette table (gaming table, gambling table)*

9 le tableau du jeu
– *roulette layout*

10 la roulette
– *roulette wheel*

11 la banque
– *bank*

12 le jeton (la plaque)
– *chip (check, plaque)*

13 la mise
– *stake*

14 la carte *f* d'entrée au casino
– *membership card*

15 le joueur de roulette *f*
– *roulette player*

16 le détective privé
– *private detective (house detective)*

17 le tableau
– *roulette layout*

18 le zéro
– *zero (nought, O)*

19 Passe *f* [nombres *m* de 19 à 36]
– *passe (high) [numbers 19 to 36]*

20 Pair *m* [nombres *m* pairs]
– *pair (even numbers)*

21 Noir *m*
– *noir (black)*

22 Manque *m* [nombres *m* de 1 à 18]
– *manque (low) [numbers 1 to 18]*

23 Impair *m* [nombres *m* impairs]
– *impair [odd numbers]*

24 Rouge *m*
– *rouge (red)*

25 les douze premiers *m* (la première douzaine) [nombres *m* de 1 à 12]
– *douze premier (first dozen) [numbers 1 to 12]*

26 les douze du milieu *m* (la douzaine intermédiaire) [nombres *m* de 13 à 24]
– *douze milieu (second dozen) [numbers 13 to 24]*

27 les douze derniers *m* (la dernière douzaine) [nombres *m* de 25 à 36]
– *douze dernier (third dozen) [numbers 25 to 36]*

28 la roulette (un cylindre tournant)
– *roulette wheel (roulette)*

29 le bassin de la roulette
– *roulette bowl*

30 le séparateur
– *fret (separator)*

31 le cylindre tournant avec les numéros de 0 à 36
– *revolving disc (disk) showing numbers 0 to 36*

32 le moulinet
– *spin*

33 la bille
– *roulette ball*

1-16 les échecs *m* (le jeu d'échecs *m*, le jeu royal), un jeu de calcul *m* ou de position *f*
– ***chess,*** *a game involving combinations of moves, a positional game*
1 l'échiquier *m* avec les pièces *f* dans la position de départ *m*
– *chessboard (board) with the men (chessmen) in position*
2 la case blanche
– *white square (chessboard square)*
3 la case noire
– *black square*
4 les pièces *f* blanches (les blancs) représentées symboliquement
– *white chessmen (white pieces) [white = W]*
5 les pièces *f* noires (les noirs *m*) représentées symboliquement
– *black chessmen (black pieces) [black = B]*
6 les lettres *f* et les chiffres *m* pour la désignation des cases de l'échiquier *m* et pour la notation des parties *f* (des coups *m*) et des problèmes *m* d'échecs *m*
– *letters and numbers for designating chess squares in the notation of chess moves and chess problems*
7 les différentes pièces *f* du jeu d'échecs *m*
– *individual chessmen (individual pieces)*
8 le roi
– *king*
9 la dame
– *queen*
10 le fou
– *bishop*
11 le cavalier
– *knight*
12 la tour
– *rook (castle)*
13 le pion
– *pawn*
14 la marche (le déplacement) de chaque pièce *f*
– *moves of the individual pieces*
15 le mat (l'échec *m* et mat), un mat du cavalier
– *mate (checkmate), a mate by knight*
16 la pendule d'échecs *m*, une pendule à double cadran *m* pour tournois *m* d'échecs *m* (championnats *m* d'échecs *m*)
– *chess clock, a double clock for chess matches (chess championships)*
17-19 le jeu de dames *f*
– ***draughts*** (Am. *checkers)*
17 le damier
– *draughtboard* (Am. *checkerboard)*
18 le pion blanc; *égal.:* le palet pour le trictrac et la marelle assise
– *white draughtsman* (Am. *checker, checkerman);* also: *piece for backgammon and nine men's morris*
19 le pion noir
– *black draughtsman* (Am. *checker, checkerman)*
20 le jeu de salta *m*
– ***salta***
21 le pion du salta
– *salta piece*
22 le damier pour le **jeu de trictrac** *m*
– *backgammon board*
23-25 la marelle assise (la mérelle)
– ***nine men's morris***
23 le tableau de marelle *f*
– *nine men's morris board*
24 la marelle (la mérelle)
– *mill*
25 la marelle double
– *double mill*
26-28 le jeu de halma
– ***halma***
26 le damier pour le jeu de halma *m*
– *halma board*
27 le coin
– *yard (camp, corner)*
28 les différentes pièces *f* du jeu de halma *m*
– *halma pieces (halma men) of various colours* (Am. *colors)*
29 le jeu de dés *m* (les dés *m*)
– ***dice*** *(dicing)*
30 le cornet à dés *m*
– *dice cup*
31 les dés *m*
– *dice*
32 les points *m*
– *spots (pips)*
33 le jeu de domino *m* (les dominos *m*)
– ***dominoes***
34 le domino
– *domino (tile)*
35 le double
– *double*
36 les cartes *f* **à jouer**
– ***playing cards***
37 le jeu de cartes *f* françaises
– *French playing card (card)*
38-45 les couleurs *f*
– *suits*
38 le trèfle
– *clubs*
39 le pique
– *spades*
40 le cœur
– *hearts*
41 le carreau
– *diamonds*
42-45 cartes *f* allemandes
– *German suits*
42 le gland (= trèfle)
– *acorns*
43 la feuille (= carreau)
– *leaves*
44 le rouge (= cœur)
– *hearts*
45 le grelot (= pique)
– *bells (hawkbells)*

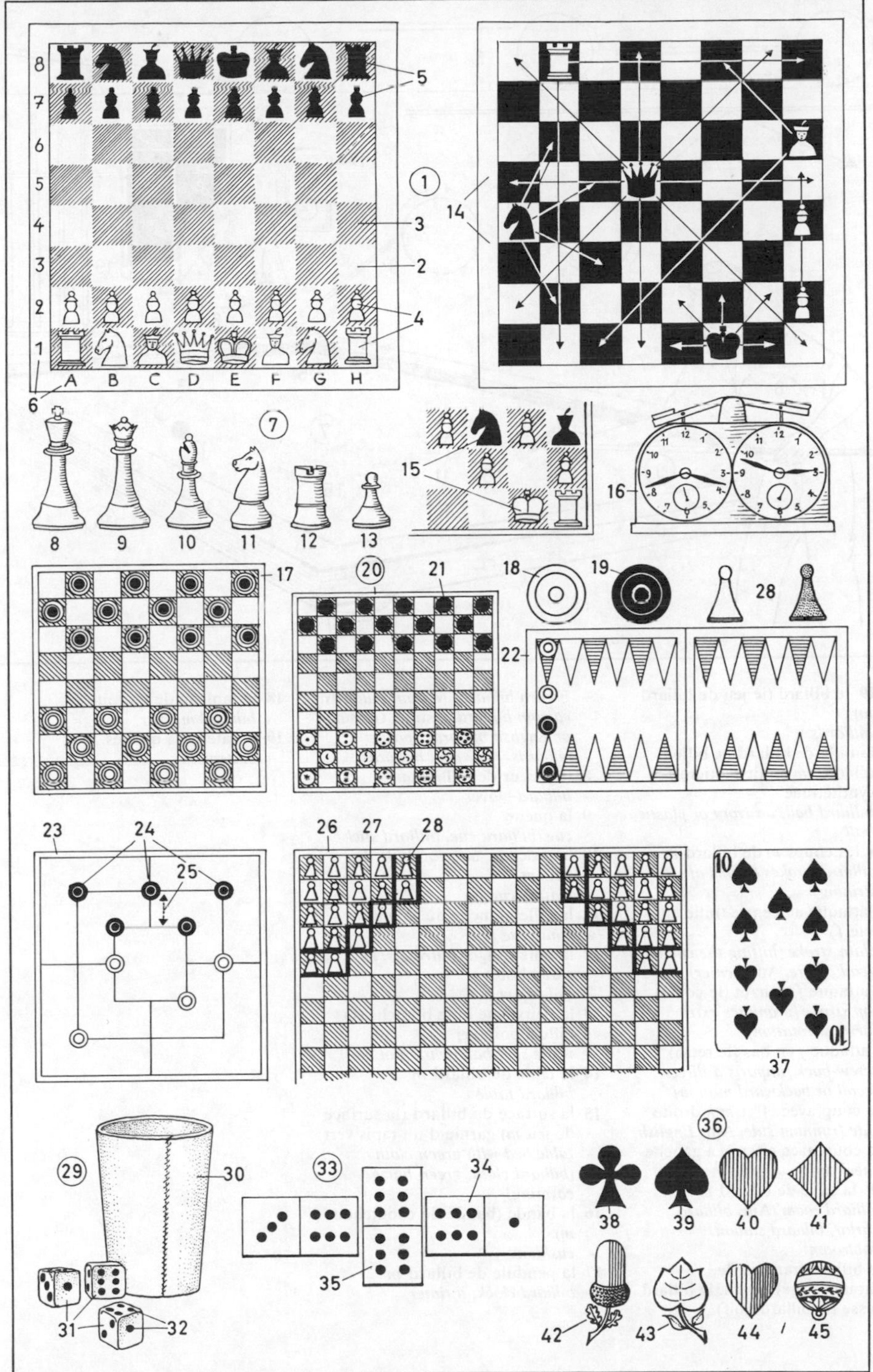
8
7
6
5
4
3
2
1
A B C D E F G H
1
2
3
4
5
6
7
8
9
10
11
12
13
14
15
16
17
18
19
20
21
22
23
24
25
26
27
28
29
30
31
32
33
34
35
36
37
38
39
40
41
42
43
44
45

1-19 le billard (le jeu de billard *m*)
– *billiards*

1 la bille de billard *m*, bille d'ivoire *m* ou de matière *f* synthétique
– *billiard ball, an ivory or plastic ball*

2-6 les coups *m* de billard *m*
– *billiard strokes (forms of striking)*

2 l'attaque au centre (bille en tête *f*)
– *plain stroke (hitting the cue ball dead centre,* Am. *center)*

3 l'attaque *f* en haut (le coulé)
– *top stroke [promotes extra forward rotation]*

4 l'attaque *f* en bas (le rétro)
– *screw-back [imparts a direct recoil or backward motion]*

5 le coup avec effet *m* à droite
– *side (running side,* Am. *English)*

6 le coup avec effet *m* à gauche
– *check side*

7-19 la salle de billard *m*
– *billiard room (*Am. *billiard parlor, billiard saloon, poolroom)*

7 le billard français (le carambolage); *anal.:* le billard russe (le billard-golf)
– *French billiards (carom billiards, carrom billiards);* sim.: *German or English billiards (pocket billiards,* Am. *pool billiards)*

8 le joueur de billard *m*
– *billiard player*

9 la queue
– *cue (billiard cue, billiard stick)*

10 le procédé, une rondelle de cuir *m*
– *leather cue tip*

11 la bille blanche du joueur
– *white cue ball*

12 la bille rouge (*autrefois:* la carambole)
– *red object ball*

13 la deuxième bille blanche (la bille à pointer)
– *white spot ball (white dot ball)*

14 la table de billard *m*
– *billiard table*

15 la surface du billard (la surface de jeu *m*) garnie d'un tapis vert
– *table bed with green cloth (billiard cloth, green baize covering)*

16 la bande (bande de caoutchouc *m*)
– *cushions*

17 la pendule de billard *m*
– *billiard clock, a timer*

18 le tableau de marque *f*
– *billiard marker*

19 le râtelier à queues *f*
– *cue rack*

1-59 le terrain de camping *m*
– ***camp site*** *(camping site,* Am. *campground)*
1 la réception
– *reception (office)*
2 le gardien du camping *m*
– *camp site attendant*
3 la caravane pliante
– *folding trailer (collapsible caravan, collapsible trailer)*
4 le hamac
– *hammock*
5-6 les sanitaires *m*
– *washing and toilet facilities*
5 les cabinets *m* de toilette *f* et les WC *m*
– *toilets and washrooms (*Am. *lavatories)*
6 les lavabos *m*
– *washbasins and sinks*
7 le bungalow [*en Suisse:* le chalet]
– *bungalow (chalet)*
8-11 le camp de scouts *m* (le camp d'éclaireurs *m*, le jamboree)
– ***scout camp***
8 la tente ronde (le marabout)
– *bell tent*
9 le fanion de troupe *f*
– *pennon*
10 le feu de camp *m*
– *camp fire*
11 le scout (l'éclaireur *m*)
– *boy scout (scout)*
12 le bateau à voile *f* (le canot à voile *f*)
– *sailing boat (yacht,* Am. *sailboat)*
13 l'embarcadère *m* (l'appontement *m*)
– *landing stage (jetty)*
14 le bateau gonflable
– *inflatable boat (inflatable dinghy)*
15 le moteur hors-bord *m*
– *outboard motor (outboard)*
16 le trimaran
– *trimaran*
17 le banc de nage *f* (la banquette)
– *thwart (oarsman's bench)*
18 le tolet
– *rowlock (oarlock)*
19 la rame
– *oar*
20 la remorque à bateau *m*
– *boat trailer (boat carriage)*
21 la tente canadienne
– ***ridge tent***
22 le double toit
– *flysheet*
23 le tendeur
– *guy line (guy)*
24 le piquet de tente *f*
– *tent peg (peg)*
25 le maillet
– *mallet*
26 l'attache *f* de sol *m*
– *groundsheet ring*
27 l'abside *f*
– *bell end*
28 l'auvent *m* ouvert
– *erected awning*
29 la lampe tempête *f*, une lampe à pétrole *m*
– *storm lantern, a paraffin lamp*
30 le sac de couchage *m*, le duvet
– *sleeping bag*
31 le matelas pneumatique (le matelas gonflable)
– *air mattress (inflatable air-bed)*
32 la vache à eau *f* (le sac à eau *f*)
– *water carrier (drinking water carrier)*
33 le réchaud à deux brûleurs *m* à propane *m* ou à butane *m*
– *double-burner gas cooker for propane gas or butane gas*
34 la bouteille de gaz *m* propane *m* (butane *m*)
– *propane or butane gas bottle*
35 la marmite à pression *f* (la cocotte minute *f*)
– *pressure cooker*
36 la tente de caravaning *m*
– ***frame tent***
37 l'avancée *f*
– *awning*
38 le mât de tente *f*
– *tent pole*
39 l'ouverture *f* d'entrée *f*
– *wheelarch doorway*
40 la fenêtre d'aération *f*
– *mesh ventilator*
41 la fenêtre transparente
– *transparent window*
42 le numéro d'emplacement *m*
– *pitch number*
43 la chaise de camping *m*, une chaise pliante
– *folding camp chair*
44 la table de camping *m*, une table pliante
– *folding camp table*
45 la vaisselle de camping *m*
– *camping eating utensils*
46 le campeur
– *camper*
47 le barbecue
– *charcoal grill (barbecue)*
48 le charbon de bois *m*
– *charcoal*
49 le soufflet
– *bellows*
50 le porte-bagages de toit *m*
– *roof rack*
51 la pieuvre (une fixation à sandows *m*)
– *roof lashing*
52 la remorque de camping *m* (la caravane)
– ***caravan*** (Am. *trailer)*
53 le compartiment à bouteilles *f* de gaz *m*
– *box for gas bottle*
54 la roulette de timon *m*
– *jockey wheel*
55 le coupleur de remorque *f*
– *drawbar coupling*
56 l'aération *f* de toit *m*
– *roof ventilator*
57 l'auvent *m* de caravane *f*
– *caravan awning*
58 la tente igloo *m* gonflable
– *inflatable igloo tent*
59 la chaise bain *m* de soleil *m*
– *camp bed (Am. camp cot)*

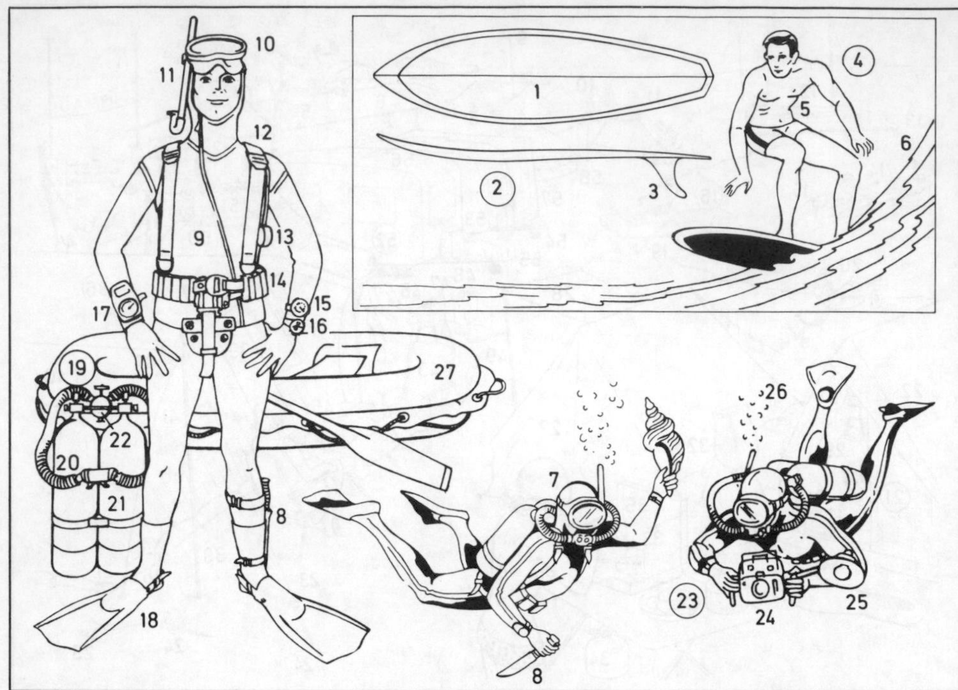

1-6 le surf
– *surf riding (surfing)*
1 la planche de surf *m* vue de dessus *m*
– *plan view of surfboard*
2 la planche de surf *m* vue en coupe *f*
– *section of surfboard*
3 la dérive
– *skeg (stabilizing fin)*
4 l'évolution *f* au point de déferlement *m* de la vague
– *big wave riding*
5 le surfer
– *surfboarder (surfer)*
6 la vague déferlante (le rouleau)
– *breaker*
7-27 la plongée subaquatique (sous-marine)
– *skin diving (underwater swimming)*
7 le plongeur
– *skin diver (underwater swimmer)*
8-22 l'équipement *m* de plongée *f*
– *underwater swimming set*
8 le couteau de plongeur *m*
– *knife*
9 la combinaison (la tenue) de plongée *f* en néoprène *m*, une combinaison chauffante
– *neoprene wetsuit*
10 le masque de plongée *f* (le masque facial, le masque respiratoire), un masque à compensateur *m*
– *diving mask (face mask, mask), a pressure-equalizing mask*
11 le tube respiratoire (le tuba)
– *snorkel (schnorkel)*
12 la bretelle de l'appareil *m* de plongée *f* à air *m* comprimé
– *harness of diving apparatus*
13 le manomètre de contrôle *m* de pression *f* [il indique le volume d'air *m* restant dans les deux bouteilles *f*]
– *compressed-air pressure gauge (Am. gage)*
14 la ceinture de plomp *m* (la ceinture de plongée *f* alourdie par des tares *f* en plomb *m*)
– *weight belt*
15 le bathymètre (le profondimètre)
– *depth gauge (Am. gage)*
16 la montre de plongée *f* étanche pour le contrôle de la durée de séjour *m* sous l'eau *f*
– *waterproof watch for checking duration of dive*
17 le décompressimètre de contrôle *m* de la vitesse de remontée *f* (la table de décompression *f* indiquant les paliers *m* de décompression *f*)
– *decometer for measuring stages of ascent*
18 la palme
– *fin (flipper)*
19 l'appareil *m* respiratoire, une batterie de deux bouteilles *f*
– *diving apparatus (also: aqualung, scuba), with two cylinders (bottles)*
20 le régulateur de débit *m* prolongé de deux flexibles *m* annelés
– *two-tube demand regulator*
21 la bouteille d'air *m* comprimé
– *compressed-air cylinder (compressed-air bottle)*
22 le détendeur (le bloc de détente *f*) des bouteilles *f* d'air *m* comprimé
– *on/off valve*
23 la photographie subaquatique (sous-marine)
– *underwater photography*
24 le boîtier photo sous-marin (*égal.*: l'appareil *m* photo sous-marin, étanche)
– *underwater camera*
25 le flash sous-marin (étanche)
– *underwater flashlight*
26 les bulles *f* d'air *m* expiré
– *exhaust bubbles*
27 le canot pneumatique
– *inflatable boat (inflatable dinghy)*

1 le sauveteur (le surveillant de baignade *f*)
– *lifesaver (lifeguard)*
2 la corde de sauvetage *m*
– *lifeline*
3 la bouée de sauvetage *m*
– *lifebelt (lifebuoy)*
4 la boule de tempête *f* (le signal de tempête *f*), une bombe à signaux *m* (une boule de signaux m)
– *storm signal*
5 la boule horaire (le signal horaire)
– *time ball*
6 le panneau avertisseur
– *warning sign*
7 le tableau des marées *f*, un panneau indicateur des heures *f* de marées *f* (de flux *m* et de reflux *m*, de marée *f* montante et de marée *f* descendante)
– *tide table, a notice board showing times of low tide and high tide*
8 le panneau indicateur des températures *f* de l'eau *f* et de l'air *m*
– *board showing water and air temperature*
9 le ponton de bord *m* de mer *f*
– *bathing platform*
10 le mât portant les fanions *m* (flammes *f*) triangulaires
– *pennon staff*
11 le fanion (la flamme)
– *pennon*
12 le pédalo
– *paddle boat (peddle boat)*
13 l'aquaplane *m* tiré par un canot à moteur *m* (automobile)
– *surf riding (surfing) behind motorboat*
14 l'amateur *m* d'aquaplane *m*
– *surfboarder (surfer)*
15 la planche d'aquaplane *m*
– *surfboard*
16 le ski nautique
– *water ski*
17 le matelas pneumatique
– *inflatable beach mattress*
18 le ballon de plage *f* en matière *f* plastique, en caoutchouc *m*
– *beach ball*
19-23 la tenue de plage *f*
– *beachwear*
19 l'ensemble *m* (le costume, le vêtement) de plage *f*
– *beach suit*
20 le chapeau de plage *f* (le chapeau de soleil *m*)
– *beach hat*
21 la veste de plage *f* (en toile *f* légère)
– *beach jacket*
22 le pantalon de plage *f* (en toile *f* légère)
beach trousers
23 les chaussures *f* de plage *f* (les sandales *f*, les nu-pieds *m*)
– *beach shoe (bathing shoe)*
24 le sac de plage *f*
– *beach bag*
25 le peignoir
– *bathing gown (bathing wrap)*
26 le bikini (le maillot de bain *m* pour femmes *f*, le deux-pièces)
– *bikini (ladies' two-piece bathing suit)*
27 le slip de bain *m*
– *bikini bottom*
28 le soutien-gorge
– *bikini top*
29 le bonnet de bain *m*
– *bathing cap (swimming cap)*
30 le baigneur
– *bather*
31 le jeu de l'anneau *m* volant (l'anno-tennis, le deck-tennis)
– *deck tennis (quoits)*
32 l'anneau *m* de caoutchouc *m*
– *rubber ring (quoit)*
33 l'animal *m* gonflable
– *inflatable rubber animal*
34 le surveillant de plage *f*
– *beach attendant*
35 le château de sable *m*
– *sand den [built as a wind-break]*
36 l'abri *m* de plage *f* en osier *m*
– *roofed wicker beach chair*
37 le chasseur (le plongeur) sous-marin
– *underwater swimmer*
38 le masque (les lunettes *f*) de plongée *f*
– *diving goggles*
39 le tube respiratoire (le tuba)
– *snorkel (schnorkel)*
40 le harpon manuel (le trident)
– *hand harpoon (fish spear, fish lance)*
41 les palmes *f* de plongée *f*
– *fin (flipper) for diving (for underwater swimming)*
42 le maillot de bain *m*
– *bathing suit (swimsuit)*
43 le slip de bain *m*
– *bathing trunks (swimming trunks)*
44 le bonnet de bain *m*
– *bathing cap (swimming cap)*
45 la tente de plage *f*
– *beach tent, a ridge tent*
46 la station de sauvetage *m* (le poste de secours *m*)
– *lifeguard station*

281 Baignade II (centre de loisirs)

1-9 la piscine à vagues *f* artificielles (à houle *f* artificielle), une piscine couverte
– *swimming pool with artificial waves, an indoor pool*

1 les vagues *f* artificielles (la houle artificielle)
– *artificial waves*

2 la plage (le rivage)
– *beach area*

3 le bord du bassin (de la piscine)
– *edge of the pool*

4 le maître-nageur (le surveillant de piscine *f*)
– *swimming pool attendant (pool attendant, swimming bath attendant)*

5 le fauteuil de relaxation *f*
– *sun bed*

6 la bouée de natation *f*
– *lifebelt*

7 les flotteurs *m* de natation *f* en liège *m*, ceints en haut des bras *m*
– *water wings*

8 le bonnet de bain *m*
– *bathing cap*

9 le canal d'accès *m* au bassin des bains *m* bouillonnants en plein air *m*
– *channel to outdoor mineral bath*

10 le solarium (le bain de soleil *m* artificiel)
– *solarium*

11 la zone (la terrasse) d'insolation *f* (la salle de bronzage *m*)
– *sunbathing area*

12 la femme prenant un bain *m* de soleil *m* artificiel (la femme allongée en séance *f* de bronzage *m*)
– *sun bather*

13 le soleil artificiel (les lampes *f* à arcs *m*, à rayons *m* ultraviolets)
– *sun ray lamp*

14 la serviette de bain *m*
– *bathing towel*

15 le camp de naturisme *m* (le camp de nudisme *m*)
– *nudist sunbathing area*

16 le nudiste (l'adepte *m* du nudisme, de la vie au grand air en état *m* de nudité *f* totale)
– *nudist (naturist)*

17 l'enceinte *f* (le mur de clôture *f*)
– *screen (fence)*

18 le sauna (le bain de vapeur *f* finnois, finlandais, un sauna mixte)
– *sauna (mixed sauna)*

19 le revêtement mural en bois *m*
– *wood panelling (*Am. *paneling)*

20 les gradins *m* de repos *m*
– *tiered benches*

21 le four de l'étuve *f* humide
– *sauna stove*

22 les galets (les pierres *f* poreuses)
– *stones*

23 l'hygromètre *m*
– *hygrometer*

24 le thermomètre
– *thermometer*

25 la serviette
– *towel*

26 le baquet d'eau *f* pour l'humidification *f* des galets *m* du four
– *water tub for moistening the stones in the stove*

27 les verges *f* de bouleau *m* pour se flageller
– *birch rods (birches) for beating the skin*

28 la salle de refroidissement *m* pour se rafraîchir après la séance de sauna *m*
– *cooling room for cooling off (cooling down) after the sauna*

29 la douche tiède
– *lukewarm shower*

30 le bassin d'eau *f* froide
– *cold bath*

31 le bassin à remous *m* d'eau *f* chaude (le bain bouillonnant, le bain de massage *m*)
– *hot whirlpool (underwater massage bath)*

32 la marche d'accès *m*
– *step into the bath*

33 le bain bouillonnant (le bain de massage *m*)
– *massage bath*

34 le ventilateur d'injection *f*
– *jet blower*

35 le bassin à remous *m* d'eau *f* chaude [schéma *m*]
– *hot whirlpool [diagram]*

36 la coupe transversale du bassin
– *section of the bath*

37 l'entrée *f* (la marche d'accès *m*)
– *step*

38 la banquette circulaire
– *circular seat*

39 le dispositif d'aspiration *f* d'eau *f*
– *water extractor*

40 la canalisation d'eau *f* (le tuyau d'alimentation *f* en eau *f*)
– *water jet pipe*

41 la canalisation d'air *m* (le tuyau d'aspiration *f*)
– *air jet pipe*

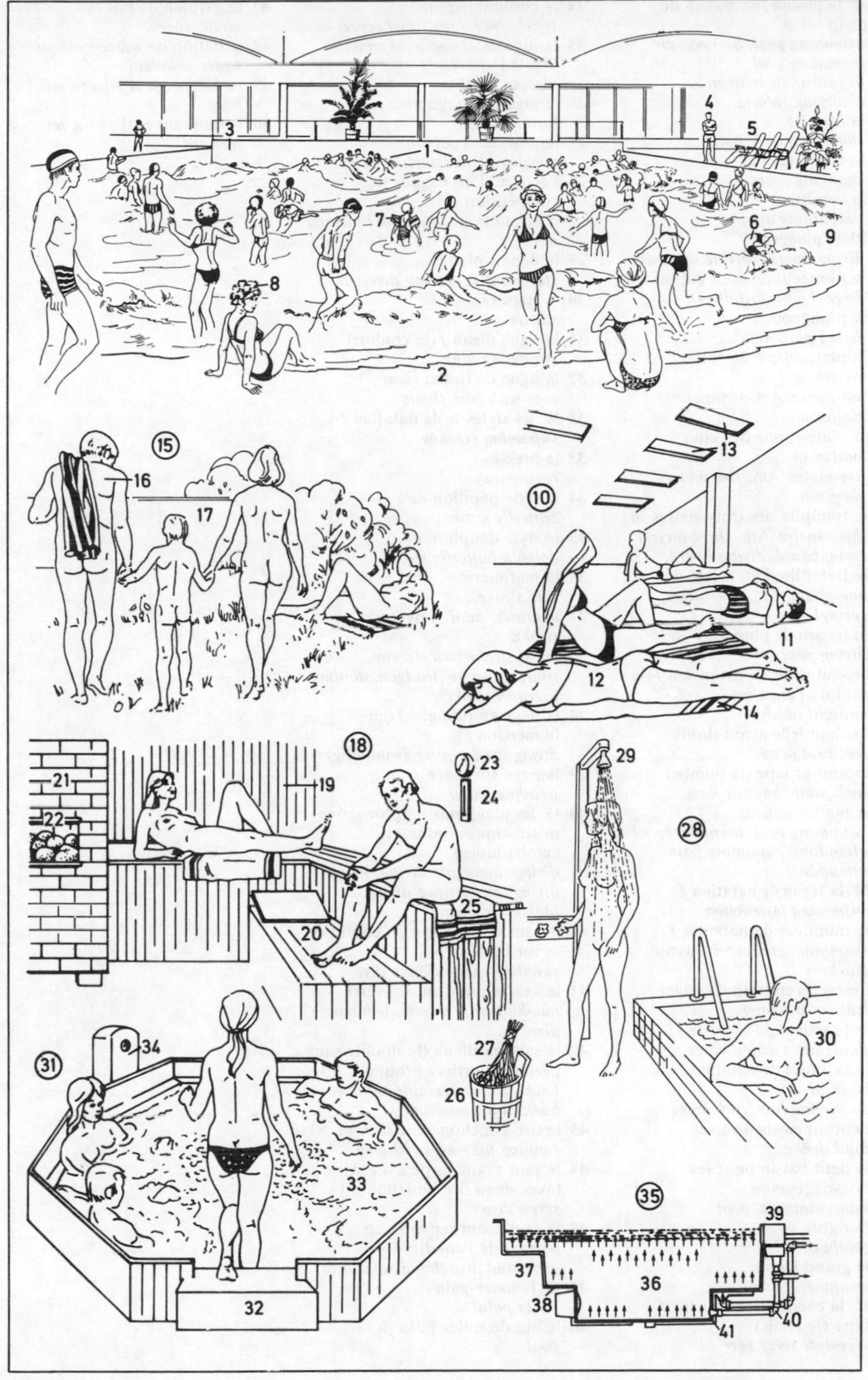
1
2
3
4
5
6
7
8
9
10
11
12
13
14
15
16
17
18
19
20
21
22
23
24
25
26
27
28
29
30
31
32
33
34
35
36
37
38
39
40
41

1-32 la piscine, un bassin de plein air *m*
– ***swimming pool****, an open-air swimming pool*
1 la cabine de bain *m*
– *changing cubicle*
2 la douche
– *shower (shower bath)*
3 le vestiaire
– *changing room*
4 le solarium
– *sunbathing area*
5-10 le plongeoir
– ***diving boards*** *(diving apparatus)*
5 le plongeur de haut vol *m*
– *diver (highboard diver)*
6 le plongeoir
– *diving platform*
7 la plate-forme des dix mètres *m*
– *ten-metre (*Am. *ten-meter) platform*
8 la plate-forme des cinq mètres *m*
– *five-metre (*Am. *five-meter) platform*
9 le tremplin des trois mètres *m*
– *three-metre (*Am. *three-meter) springboard (diving board)*
10 le tremplin d'un mètre *m*
– *one-metre (*Am. *one-meter) springboard*
11 le bassin de plongée *f*
– *diving pool*
12 le saut droit en extension *f* (le saut de l'ange *m*)
– *straight header*
13 la chandelle avant droite
– *feet-first jump*
14 le saut groupé (la bombe)
– *tuck jump (haunch jump)*
15 le maître-nageur
– *swimming pool attendant (pool attendant, swimming bath attendant)*
16-20 la leçon de natation *f*
– ***swimming instruction***
16 le moniteur de natation *f*
– *swimming instructor (swimming teacher)*
17 l'élève *m* en train de nager
– *learner-swimmer*
18 la brassière de sécurité *f*
– *float;* sim.: *water wings*
19 la ceinture de natation *f* en liège *m*
– *swimming belt (cork jacket)*
20 l'entraînement *m* à sec
– *land drill*
21 le petit bassin pour les non-nageurs *m*
– *non-swimmers' pool*
22 la rigole
– *footbath*
23 le grand bassin
– *swimmers' pool*
24-32 la compétition de nage *f* libre (le relais)
– ***freestyle relay race***
24 le chronométreur
– *timekeeper (lane timekeeper)*
25 le juge de classement *m* (le juge à l'arrivée *f*)
– *placing judge*
26 le juge de virage *m*
– *turning judge*
27 le plot de départ *m*
– *starting block (starting place)*
28 l'arrivée d'un nageur de compétition *f*
– *competitor touching the finishing line*
29 le départ plongé
– *starting dive (racing dive)*
30 le starter
– *starter*
31 la ligne d'eau *f* (le couloir)
– *swimming lane*
32 la ligne de flotteurs *m*
– *rope with cork floats*
33-39 les styles *m* **de natation** *f*
– ***swimming strokes***
33 la brasse
– *breaststroke*
34 le style papillon *m*
– *butterfly stroke*
35 le style dauphin *m*
– *dolphin butterfly stroke*
36 la marinière
– *side stroke*
37 le crawl; *anal.:* l'overarm stroke
– *crawl stroke (crawl);* sim.: *trudgen stroke (trudgen, double overarm stroke)*
38 la nage en plongée *f* (en immersion *f*)
– *diving (underwater swimming)*
39 la nage sur place *f*
– *treading water*
40-45 les plongeons *m* (plongeons *m* artistiques, sauts *m* acrobatiques)
– ***diving*** *(acrobatic diving, fancy diving, competitive diving, highboard diving)*
40 le saut avant carpé en équilibre *m* sur les bras *m*
– *standing take-off pike dive*
41 le saut avant droit renversé
– *one-half twist isander (reverse dive)*
42 le saut périlleux (le double saut périlleux) arrière groupé
– *backward somersault (double backward somersault)*
43 le tire-bouchon avec élan *m*
– *running take-off twist dive*
44 le saut avant carpé avec vrille *f* (avec demi tire-bouchon *m*)
– *screw dive*
45 le saut avant renversé en partant de l'équilibre *m*
– *armstand dive (handstand dive)*
46-50 le water-polo
– ***water polo***
46 le but de water-polo *m*
– *goal*
47 le gardien de but *m*
– *goalkeeper*
48 le ballon de water-polo *m*
– *water polo ball*
49 le défenseur (l'arrière *m*)
– *back*
50 l'attaquant *m* (l'avant *m*)
– *forward*

1
2
3
4
5
6
7
8
9
10
11
12
13
14
15
16
17
18
19
20
21
22
23
24
25
26
27
28
29
30
31
32
33
34
35
36
37
38
39
40
41
42
43
44
45
46
47
48
49
50

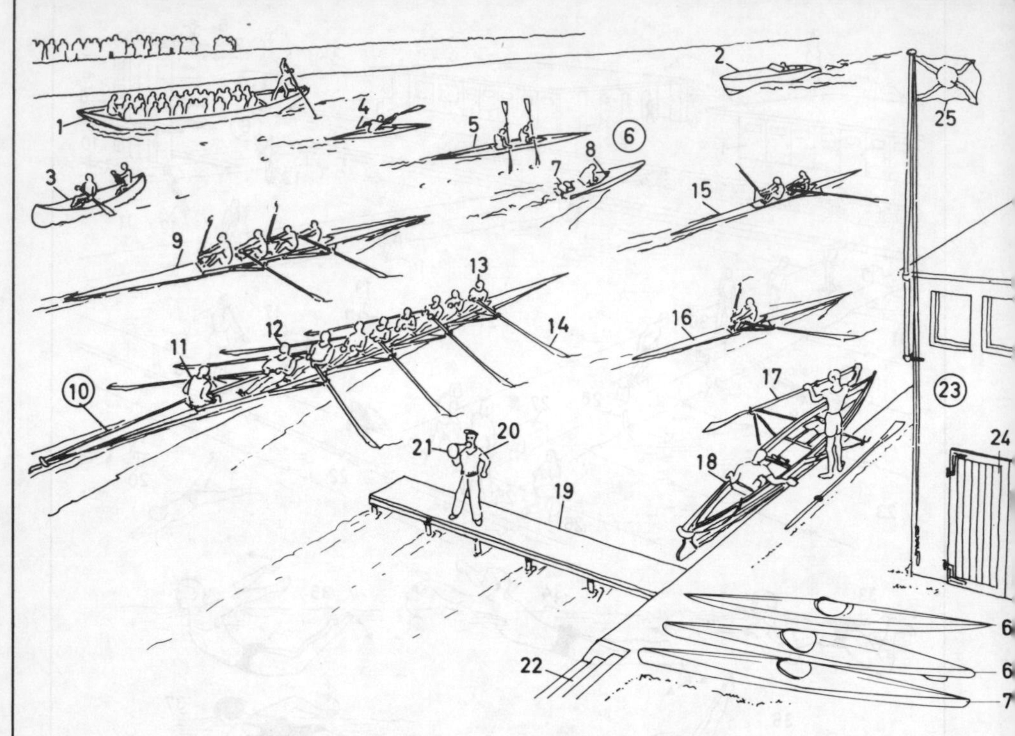

1-18 les préparatifs *m* de la régate (la course à l'aviron *m*)
– *taking up positions for the regatta*
1 la barque de promenade *f*, maniée à la perche
– *punt, a pleasure boat*
2 le canot à moteur *m*
– *motorboat*
3 le canoë canadien
– *Canadian canoe*
4 le kayak monoplace
– *kayak (Alaskan canoe, slalom canoe), a canoe*
5 le kayak biplace
– *tandem kayak*
6 le canot hors-bord (à moteur *m* hors-bord)
– *outboard motorboat (outboard speedboat, outboard)*
7 le hors-bord (le moteur hors-bord)
– *outboard motor (outboard)*
8 le cockpit
– *cockpit*
9-16 les outriggers *m* de course *f* (embarcations *f* de course *f* à l'aviron *m*)
– *racing boats (sportsboats, outriggers)*
9-15 les outriggers *m* de course *f* à plusieurs équipiers *m*
– *shells (rowing boats,* Am. *rowboats)*
9 le quatre sans barreur *m* (l'outrigger *m* à quatre rameurs *m* sans barreur *m*), une embarcation construite à franc-bord *m*
– *coxless four, a carvel-built boat*
10 le huit barré (l'outrigger *m* à huit rameurs *m* avec barreur *m*)
– *eight (eight-oared racing shell)*
11 le barreur
– *cox*
12 le chef de nage *f*, un rameur (un nageur), le numéro 1
– *stroke, an oarsman*
13 le nageur de pointe *f* (le rameur de pointe *f*)
– *bow ('number one')*
14 l'aviron *m*
– *oar*
15 le deux sans barreur *m* (le pair-oar)
– *coxless pair*
16 le skiff (le simple)
– *single sculler (single skuller, racing sculler, racing skuller, skiff)*
17 l'aviron *m*
– *scull (skull)*
18 l'outrigger *m* à un rameur avec barreur *m*, une embarcation construite à clins *m*
– *coxed single, a clinker-built single*
19 le ponton (l'appontement *m*)
– *jetty (landing stage, mooring)*
20 l'entraîneur *m*
– *rowing coach*
21 le porte-voix (le mégaphone)
– *megaphone*
22 l'escalier *m* du quai
– *quayside steps*
23 le club (le club-house)
– *clubhouse (club)*
24 le hangar à bateaux *m*
– *boathouse*
25 le pavillon du club
– *club's flag*
26-33 la yole à quatre rameurs *m*, un canot de promenade *f*
– *four-oared gig, a touring boat*
26 le gouvernail
– *oar*
27 le siège du barreur
– *cox's seat*
28 le banc de nage *f*
– *thwart (seat)*
29 la dame de nage *f* (le tolet)
– *rowlock (oarlock)*
30 le plat-bord
– *gunwale (gunnel)*
31 la glissière de banquette *f*
– *rising*
32 la quille
– *keel*
33 le bordé à clins *m*
– *skin (shell, outer skin) [clinker-built]*
34 la pagaie
– *single-bladed paddle (paddle)*
35-38 la rame (l'aviron *m*)
– *oar (scull, skull)*
35 la poignée
– *grip*
36 la garniture de cuir *m*
– *leather sheath*
37 le manche
– *shaft (neck)*
38 la pelle
– *blade*

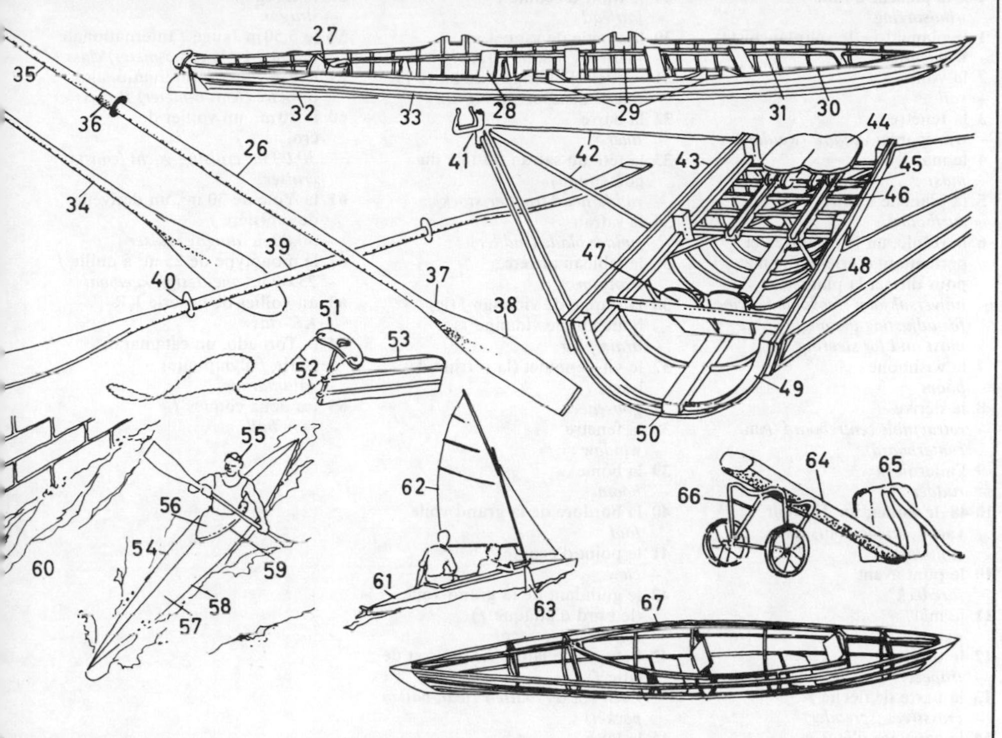

39 la pagaie double
– *double-bladed paddle (double-ended paddle)*

40 le paragouttes
– *drip ring*

41-50 le siège coulissant
– *sliding seat*

41 la dame de nage *f* (le tolet)
– *rowlock (oarlock)*

42 le porte-nage
– *outrigger*

43 la lisse (l'hiloire *f*)
– *saxboard*

44 le siège (la sellette)
– *sliding seat*

45 la glissière
– *runner*

46 l'entretoise *f*
– *strut*

47 le repose-pieds
– *stretcher*

48 le bordé
– *skin (shell, outer skin)*

49 la membrure
– *frame (rib)*

50 la carlingue
– *kelson (keelson)*

51-53 le gouvernail
– *rudder (steering rudder)*

51 la traverse
– *yoke*

52 les tire-veilles *f*
– *lines (steering lines)*

53 le safran
– *blade (rudder blade, rudder)*

54-66 le kayak pliant
– *folding boats (foldboats, canoes)*

54 le kayak monoplace
– *one-man kayak*

55 le canoéiste
– *canoeist*

56 la jupe (le pontage)
– *spraydeck*

57 le pont en toile *f*
– *deck*

58 la coque couverte de toile *f* caoutchoutée
– *rubber-covered canvas hull*

59 l'hiloire *f*
– *cockpit coaming (coaming)*

60 le canal ménagé le long d'un barrage
– *channel for rafts alongside weir*

61 le kayak pliant biplace, un kayak de promenade *f*
– *two-seater folding kayak, a touring kayak*

62 la voile d'un kayak pliant
– *sail of folding kayak*

63 la dérive latérale
– *leeboard*

64 la housse de protection pour la carcasse du kayak
– *bag for the rods*

65 l'enveloppe *f* de toile *f* dans son sac *m*
– *rucksack*

66 le chariot de transport *m*
– *boat trailer (boat carriage)*

67 la carcasse du kayak pliant
– *frame of folding kayak*

68-70 types *m* de kayaks *m*
– *kayaks*

68 le kayak lapon
– *Eskimo kayak*

69 le kayak de sport *m* et de course *f*
– *wild-water racing kayak*

70 le kayak de promenade *f*
– *touring kayak*

1-9 la planche à voile *f*
– ***windsurfing***
1 le planchiste (le véliplanchiste)
– *windsurfer*
2 la voile
– *sail*
3 la fenêtre
– *transparent window (window)*
4 le mât
– *mast*
5 la planche à voile *f*
– *surfboard*
6 la rotule, un joint universel permettant d'orienter le mât pour diriger la planche
– *universal joint (movable bearing) for adjusting the angle of the mast and for steering*
7 le wishbone
– *boom*
8 la dérive
– *retractable centreboard (*Am. *centerboard)*
9 l'aileron *m*
– *rudder*
10-48 le voilier, un dériveur
– ***yacht*** *(sailing boat,* Am. *sailboat)*
10 le pont avant
– *foredeck*
11 le mât
– *mast*
12 le trapèze
– *trapeze*
13 la barre de flèche *f*
– *crosstrees (spreader)*
14 le capelage d'étai *m*
– *hound*
15 l'étai *m* avant (la draille de foc *m*)
– *forestay*
16 le génois, un foc
– *jib (Genoa jib)*
17 le palan d'étarquage *m*
– *jib downhaul*
18 le hauban
– *side stay (shroud)*
19 le ridoir
– *lanyard (bottlescrew)*
20 le pied de mât *m* (l'emplanture *f*)
– *foot of the mast*
21 le hale-bas de bôme *f*
– *kicking strap (vang)*
22 le taquet coinceur
– *jam cleat*
23 l'écoute *f* de foc *m*
– *foresheet (jib sheet)*
24 le puits de dérive *f*
– *centreboard (*Am. *centerboard) case*
25 la tête de la dérive
– *bitt*
26 la dérive
– *centreboard (*Am. *centerboard)*
27 la barre d'écoute *f*
– *traveller (*Am. *traveler)*
28 la grande écoute
– *mainsheet*
29 le filoir d'écoute *f*
– *fairlead*
30 la sangle de rappel *m*
– *toestraps (hiking straps)*
31 le stick (l'allonge *f* de barre *f*)
– *tiller extension (hiking stick)*
32 la barre
– *tiller*
33 la tête du safran (la tête du gouvernail)
– *rudderhead (rudder stock)*
34 le safran
– *rudder blade (rudder)*
35 le tableau arrière
– *transom*
36 la trappe de vidange *f* (le bouchon de vidange *f*)
– *drain plug*
37 le vit-de-mulet (la ferrure de bôme *f*)
– *gooseneck*
38 la fenêtre
– *window*
39 la bôme
– *boom*
40 la bordure de la grand-voile
– *foot*
41 le point d'écoute *f*
– *clew*
42 le guindant de la grand-voile (le bord d'attaque *f*)
– *luff (leading edge)*
43 l'étui *m* de latte *f* (le gousset de latte *f*)
– *leech pocket (batten cleat, batten pocket)*
44 la latte
– *batten*
45 la chute de la grand-voile (le bord de fuite *f*)
– *leech (trailing edge)*
46 la grand-voile
– *mainsail*
47 la têtière (la planchette de tête *f*)
– *headboard*
48 la girouette
– *racing flag (burgee)*
49-65 les séries *f* de voiliers ***m*** (les classes *f* de voiliers *m*)
– ***yacht classes***
49 le Flying Dutchman (série *f* olympique)
– *Flying Dutchman*
50 la Yole OK
– *O-Joller*
51 le Finn (série *f* olympique)
– *Finn dinghy (Finn)*
52 le Pirat
– *pirate*
53 le sharpie de 12 m²
– *12.00 m² sharpie*
54 le Tempest
– *tempest*
55 le Star (série *f* olympique)
– *star*
56 le Soling (série *f* olympique)
– *soling*
57 le Dragon
– *dragon*
58 le 5,50 m Jauge *f* Internationale
– *5.5-metre (*Am. *5.5-meter) class*
59 le 6 m Jauge *f* Internationale
– *6-metre (*Am. *6-meter) R-class*
60 le 30 m², un voilier de croisière *f*
– *30.00 m² cruising yacht (coastal cruiser)*
61 la Yole de 30 m², un dériveur de croisière *f*
– *30.00 m² dinghy cruiser*
62 le monotype de 25 m² à quille *f*
– *25.00 m² one-design keelboat*
63 un voilier de la série KR
– *KR-class*
64 le Tornado, un catamaran (série *f* olympique)
– *catamaran*
65 les deux coques *f*
– *twin hull*

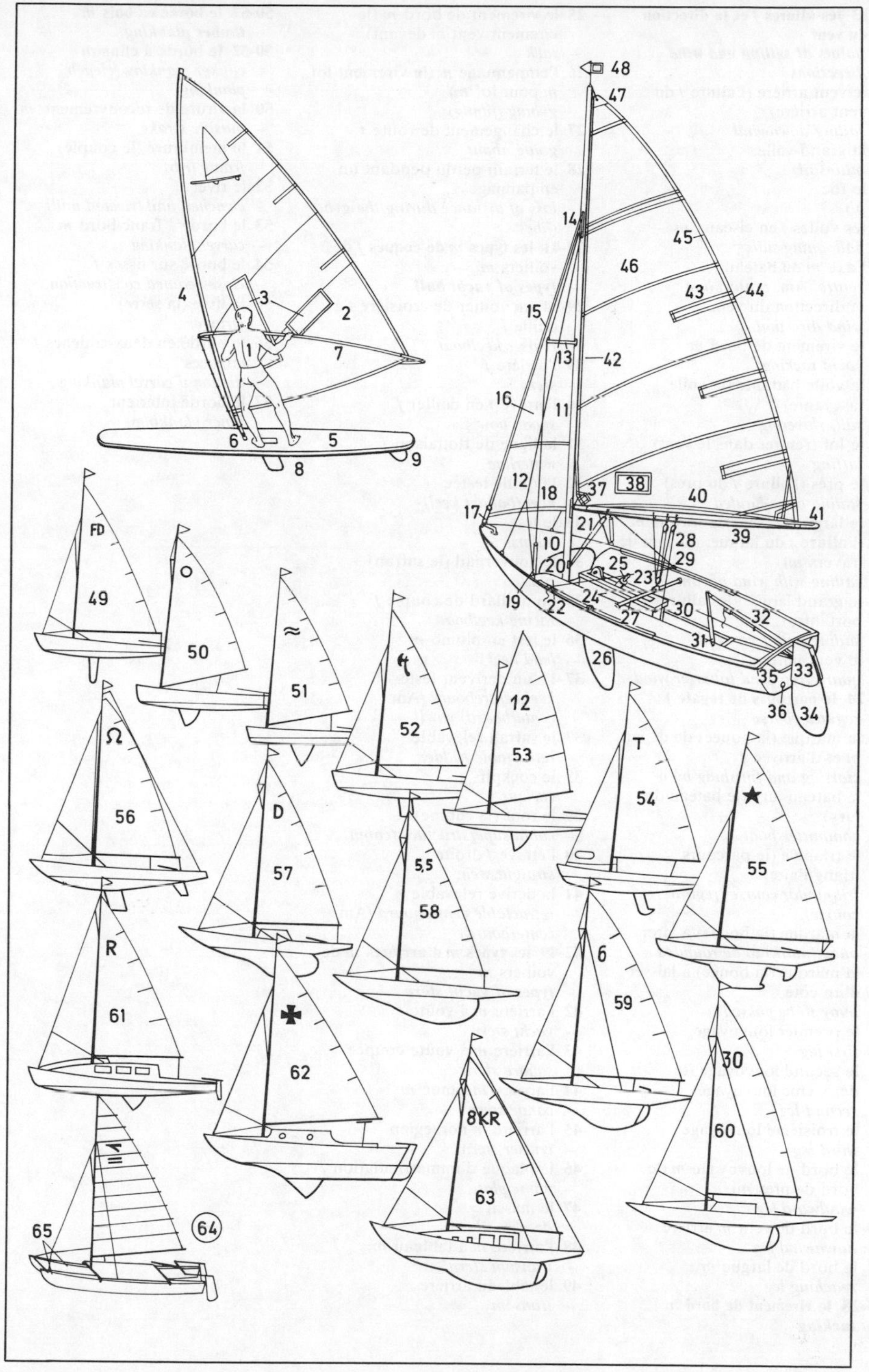
1
2
3
4
5
6
7
8
9
10
11
12
13
14
15
16
17
18
19
20
21
22
23
24
25
26
27
28
29
30
31
32
33
34
35
36
37
38
39
40
41
42
43
44
45
46
47
48
FD
49
O
50
51
52
12
53
T
54
55
56
D
57
5,5
58
6
59
30
60
R
61
62
8KR
63
64
65

1-13 les allures *f* **et la direction du vent**
– ***points of sailing and wind directions***
1 le vent arrière (l'allure *f* du vent arrière)
– *sailing downwind*
2 la grand-voile
– *mainsail*
3 le foc
– *jib*
4 les voiles *f* en ciseaux *m*
– *ballooning sails*
5 l'axe *m* du bateau
– *centre (*Am. *center) line*
6 la direction du vent
– *wind direction*
7 le virement de bord *m*
– *yacht tacking*
8 la voile battante (la voile faseyante)
– *sail, shivering*
9 le lof (rentrer dans le vent)
– *luffing*
10 le près (l'allure *f* du près)
– *sailing close-hauled*
11 le largue, le vent de travers *m* (l'allure *f* du largue, du vent de travers *m*)
– *sailing with wind abeam*
12 le grand largue (les allures *f* portantes)
– *sailing with free wind*
13 le vent portant
– *quartering wind (quarter wind)*
14-24 le parcours de régate *f*
– ***regatta course***
14 la marque (la bouée) de départ *m* et d'arrivée *f*
– *starting and finishing buoy*
15 le bateau-jury (le bateau du jury)
– *committee boat*
16 le triangle (le parcours triangulaire)
– *triangular course (regatta course)*
17 la marque (la bouée) à virer
– *buoy (mark) to be rounded*
18 la marque (la bouée) à laisser d'un côté
– *buoy to be passed*
19 le premier louvoyage
– *first leg*
20 le second louvoyage (le deuxième louvoyage)
– *second leg*
21 le troisième louvoyage
– *third leg*
22 le bord de louvoyage *m* (le bord de près *m*)
– *windward leg*
23 le bord de vent *m* arrière
– *downwind leg*
24 le bord de largue *m*
– *reaching leg*
25-28 le virement de bord *m*
– ***tacking***
25 le virement de bord *m* (le virement vent *m* devant)
– *tack*
26 l'empannage *m* (le virement lof *m* pour lof *m*)
– *gybing (jibing)*
27 le changement de route *f*
– *going about*
28 le terrain perdu pendant un empannage
– *loss of distance during the gybe (jibe)*
29-41 les types *m* **de coques** *f* de voiliers *m*
– ***types of yacht hull***
29-34 un voilier de croisière *f* à quille *f*
– *cruiser keelboat*
29 l'arrière *f*
– *stern*
30 l'étrave *f* en cuiller *f*
– *spoon bow*
31 la ligne de flottaison *f*
– *waterline*
32 la quille lestée
– *keel (ballast keel)*
33 le lest
– *ballast*
34 le gouvernail (le safran)
– *rudder*
35 un quillard de course *f*
– *racing keelboat*
36 le lest en plomb *m*
– *lead keel*
37-41 un dériveur lesté
– *keel-centreboard (*Am. *centerboard) yawl*
37 le safran relevable
– *retractable rudder*
38 le cockpit
– *cockpit*
39 le rouf (la cabine)
– *cabin superstructure (cabin)*
40 l'étrave *f* droite
– *straight stem*
41 la dérive relevable
– *retractable centreboard (*Am. *centerboard)*
42-49 les types *m* **d'arrières** *m* de voiliers *m*
– ***types of yacht stern***
42 l'arrière *m* à voûte *f*
– *yacht stern*
43 l'arrière *m* à voûte coupée
– *square stern*
44 l'arrière *m* canoé *m*
– *canoe stern*
45 l'arrière *m* norvégien
– *cruiser stern*
46 la plaque d'immatriculation *f*
– *name plate*
47 le massif
– *deadwood*
48 l'arrière *m* à tableau *m*
– *transom stern*
49 le tableau arrière
– *transom*
50-57 le bordé en bois *m*
– ***timber planking***
50-52 le bordé à clins *m*
– *clinker planking (clench planking)*
50 la virure de recouvrement *m*
– *outside strake*
51 la membrure (le couple)
– *frame (rib)*
52 le rivet
– *clenched nail (riveted nail)*
53 le bordé à franc-bord *m*
– *carvel planking*
54 le bordé sur lisses *f*
– *close-seamed construction*
55 la lisse (la serre)
– *stringer*
56 le bordé en deux couches *f* croisées
– *diagonal carvel planking*
57 le bordé intérieur
– *inner planking*

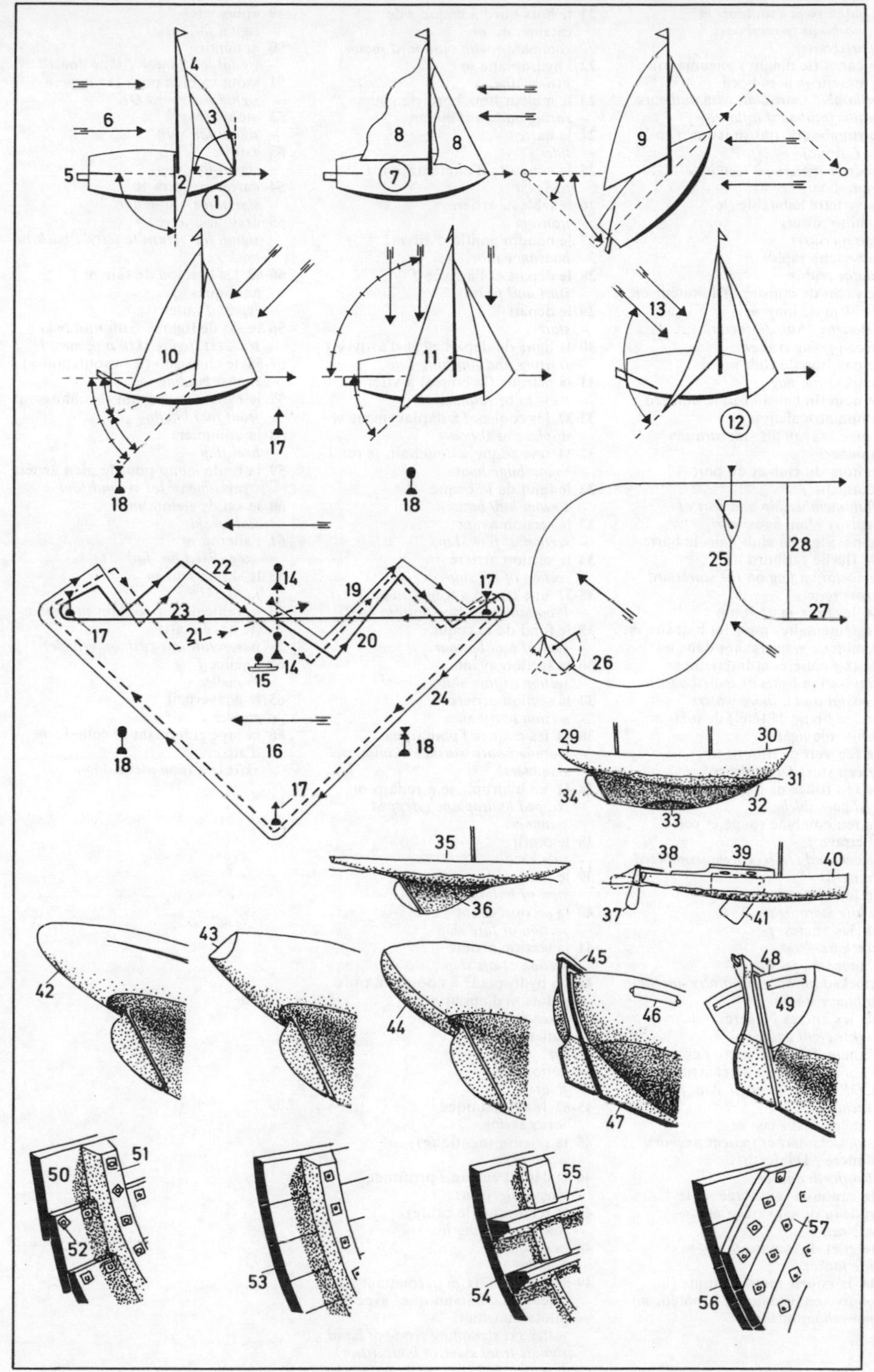
1
2
3
4
5
6
7
8
8
9
10
11
12
13
14
14
15
16
17
17
17
17
18
18
18
18
19
20
21
22
23
24
25
26
27
28
29
30
31
32
33
34
35
36
37
38
39
40
41
42
43
44
45
46
47
48
49
50
51
52
53
54
55
56
57

1-5 bateaux *m* à moteur *m*
– *motorboats (powerboats, sportsboats)*
1 le canot (le dinghy) pneumatique à moteur *m* hors-bord
– *inflatable sportsboat with outboard motor (outboard inflatable)*
2 le runabout à transmission *f* en Z (à Z-drive)
– *Z-drive motorboat (outdrive motorboat)*
3 la vedette habitable (le cabin-cruiser)
– *cabin cruiser*
4 la vedette rapide
– *motor cruiser*
5 le yacht de croisière *f* à moteur *m* de 30 m de long *m*
– *30-metre (*Am. *30-meter) ocean-going cruiser*
6 le pavillon de club *m*
– *association flag*
7 le nom du bateau (ou le numéro d'immatriculation *f*)
– *name of craft (*or: *registration number)*
8 le nom du club et du port d'attache *f*
– *club membership and port of registry (*Am. *home port)*
9 le pavillon du club dans la barre de flèche *f* tribord
– *association flag on the starboard crosstrees*
10-14 les feux *m* de route *f* réglementaires pour les bateaux *m* à moteur *m* naviguant dans les eaux *f* côtières et intérieures
– *navigation lights of sportsboats in coastal and inshore waters*
10 le feu blanc de tête *f* de mât *m*
– *white top light*
11 le feu vert de tribord *m*
– *green starboard sidelight*
12 le feu rouge de bâbord *m*
– *red port sidelight*
13 le feu combiné rouge et vert d'étrave *f*
– *green and red bow light (combined lantern)*
14 le feu blanc de poupe *f*
– *white stern light*
15-18 les ancres *f*
– *anchors*
15 l'ancre *f* à jas *m*
– *stocked anchor (Admiralty anchor), a bower anchor*
16-18 les ancres *f* légères
– *lightweight anchor*
16 l'ancre *f* CQR (l'ancre *f* charrue *f*, l'ancre *f* à soc *m* de charrue *f*)
– *CQR anchor (plough,* Am. *plow, anchor)*
17 l'ancre *f* sans jas *m*
– *stockless anchor (patent anchor)*
18 l'ancre *f* Danforth
– *Danforth anchor*
19 le canot de sauvetage *m* (le radeau de sauvetage *m*)
– *life raft*
20 le gilet de sauvetage *m*
– *life jacket*
21-44 la course motonautique (la course en bateaux *m* à moteur *m*)
– *powerboat racing*
21 le hors-bord à coque *f* de catamaran *m*
– *catamaran with outboard motor*
22 l'hydroplane *m*
– *hydroplane*
23 le moteur hors-bord de course *f*
– *racing outboard motor*
24 la barre
– *tiller*
25 la conduite d'alimentation *f*
– *fuel pipe*
26 le tableau arrière
– *transom*
27 le boudin gonflé d'air *m*
– *buoyancy tube*
28 le départ et l'arrivée *f*
– *start and finish*
29 le départ
– *start*
30 la ligne de départ *m* et d'arrivée *f*
– *starting and finishing line*
31 la marque (la bouée) à virer
– *buoy to be rounded*
32-37 les coques *f* à déplacement *m*
– *displacement boats*
32-34 une coque à bouchain *m* rond
– *round-bilge boat*
32 le fond de la coque
– *view of hull bottom*
33 la section avant
– *section of fore ship*
34 la section arrière
– *section of aft ship*
35-37 une coque à fonds *m* en V
– *V-bottom boat (vee-bottom boat)*
35 le fond de la coque
– *view of hull bottom*
36 la section avant
– *section of fore ship*
37 la section arrière
– *section of aft ship*
38-44 les coques *f* planantes
– *planing boats (surface skimmers, skimmers)*
38-41 un hydroplane à redans *m*
– *stepped hydroplane (stepped skimmer)*
38 le profil
– *side view*
39 le fond de la coque
– *view of hull bottom*
40 la section avant
– *section of fore ship*
41 la section arrière
– *section of aft ship*
42 un hydroplane à coque *f* à trois points *m* d'appui *m*
– *three-point hydroplane*
43 l'aileron *m*
– *fin*
44 le flotteur
– *float*
45-62 le ski nautique
– *water skiing*
45 la skieuse (nautique)
– *water skier*
46 le départ en eau *f* profonde
– *deep-water start*
47 la remorque (le câble)
– *tow line (towing line)*
48 la poignée
– *handle*
49-55 les signaux *m* permettant au skieur de communiquer avec le pilote du canot
– *water-ski signalling (code of hand signals from skier to boat driver)*
49 «plus vite»
– *signal for 'faster'*
50 «ralentir»
– *signal for 'slower' ('slow down')*
51 «tout va bien pour la vitesse»
– *signal for 'speed OK'*
52 «tourner»
– *signal for 'turn'*
53 «stop»
– *signal for 'stop'*
54 «arrêt moteur» *m*
– *signal for 'cut motor'*
55 «retour à terre» *f*
– *signal for 'return to jetty' ('back to dock')*
56-62 les types *m* de skis *m* nautiques
– *types of water ski*
56 le ski de figures *f*, un monoski
– *trick ski (figure ski), a monoski*
57-58 le chausson (les caoutchoucs)
– *rubber binding*
57 le caoutchouc avant (le chausson)
– *front foot binding*
58 la talonnière
– *heel flap*
59 la bride mono pour le pied arrière
– *strap support for second foot*
60 le ski de slalom *m*
– *slalom ski*
61 l'aileron *m*
– *skeg (fixed fin, fin)*
62 le ski de saut *m*
– *jump ski*
63 le véhicule sur coussin *m* d'air *m* (le hovercraft)
– *hovercraft (air-cushion vehicle)*
64 l'hélice *f*
– *propeller*
65 le gouvernail
– *rudder*
66 la jupe enfermant le coussin *m* d'air *m*
– *skirt enclosing air cushion*

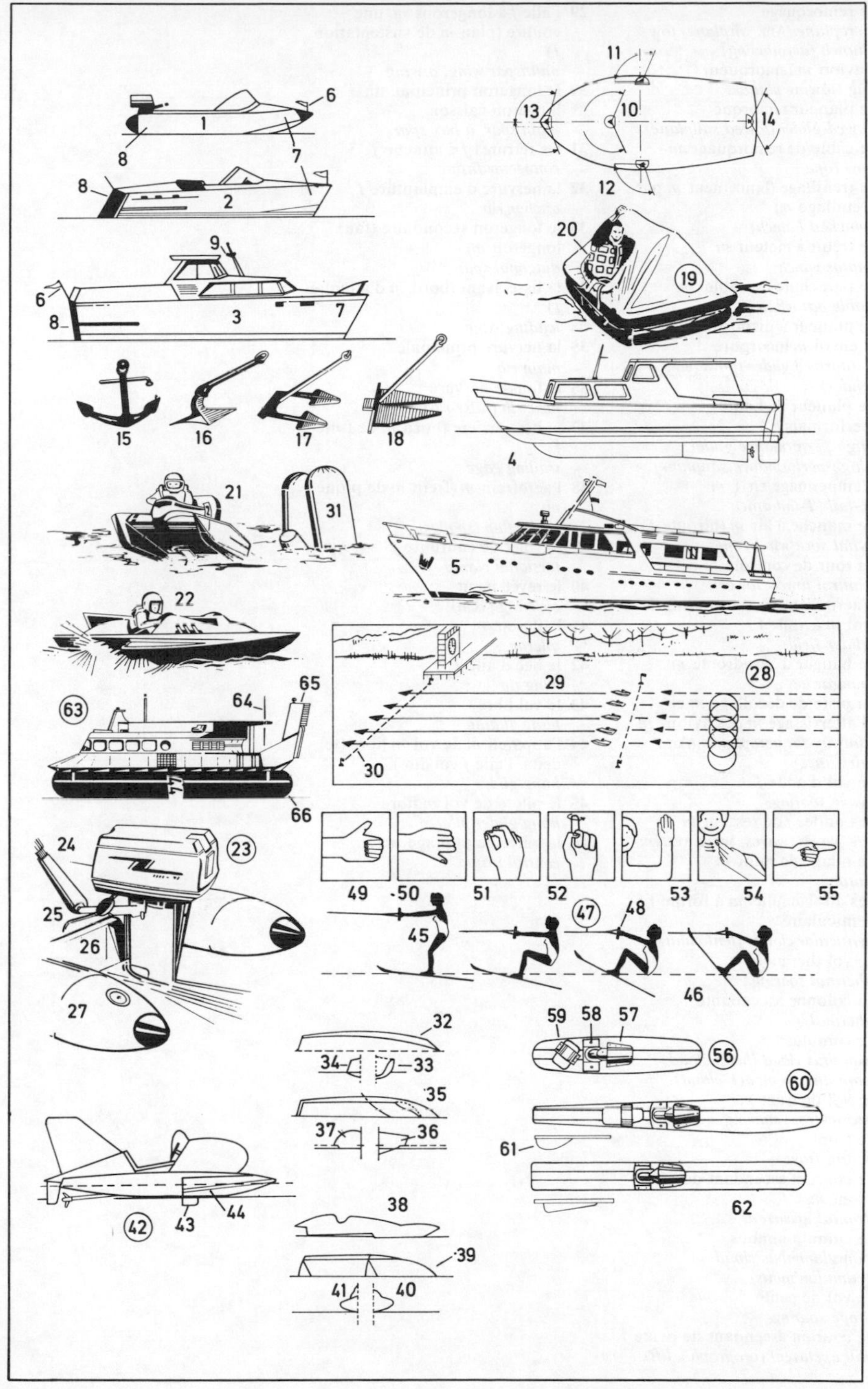
1
2
3
4
5
6
7
8
9
10
11
12
13
14
15
16
17
18
19
20
21
22
23
24
25
26
27
28
29
30
31
32
33
34
35
36
37
38
39
40
41
42
43
44
45
46
47
48
49
50
51
52
53
54
55
56
57
58
59
60
61
62
63
64
65
66

1 le remorquage
- *aeroplane* (Am. *airplane*) *tow launch (aerotowing)*
2 l'avion *m* remorqueur
- *tug (towing plane)*
3 le planeur remorqué
- *towed glider (towed sailplane)*
4 le câble de remorquage *m*
- *tow rope*
5 le treuillage (lancement *m* par treuillage *m*)
- *winched launch*
6 le treuil à moteur *m*
- *motor winch*
7 le parachute de câble *m*
- *cable parachute*
8 le planeur à dispositif *m* d'envol *m* incorporé
- *motorized glider (powered glider)*
9 le planeur de haute performance *f*
- *high-performance glider (high-performance sailplane)*
10 l'empennage en T *m*
- *T-tail (T-tail unit)*
11 le manche à air *m* (biroute *f*)
- *wind sock(wind cone)*
12 la tour de contrôle *m*
- *control tower (tower)*
13 l'aérodrome *m* (terrain *m*) de vol *m* à voile *f*
- *glider field*
14 le hangar d'aérodrome *m*
- *hangar*
15 la piste de décollage *m* et d'atterrissage *m* des avions *m*
- *runway for aeroplanes* (Am. *airplanes)*
16 le vol d'onde *f*
- *wave soaring*
17 les ondes *f* de ressaut *m*
- *lee waves (waves, wave system)*
18 le nuage de rotor *m*
- *rotor*
19 les altocumulus *m* à forme *f* lenticulaire
- *lenticular clouds (lenticulars)*
20 le vol thermique
- *thermal soaring*
21 la colonne ascendante
- *thermal*
22 le cumulus
- *cumulus cloud (heap cloud, cumulus, woolpack cloud)*
23 le vol de front *m*
- *storm-front soaring*
24 le front
- *storm front*
25 le courant ascendant de front *m*
- *frontal upcurrent*
26 le cumulo-nimbus
- *cumulonimbus cloud (cumulonimbus)*
27 le vol de pente *f*
- *slope soaring*
28 le courant ascendant de pente *f*
- *hill upcurrent (orographic lift)*
29 l'aile *f* à longerons *m*, une voilure (plan *m* de sustentation *f*)
- *multispar wing, a wing*
30 le longeron principal, un longeron-caisson
- *main spar, a box spar*
31 les ferrures *f* d'attache *f*
- *connector fitting*
32 la nervure d'emplanture *f*
- *anchor rib*
33 le longeron secondaire (faux longeron *m*)
- *diagonal spar*
34 la lisse avant (bord *m* d'attaque *f*)
- *leading edge*
35 la nervure principale
- *main rib*
36 la fausse nervure
- *nose rib (false rib)*
37 la lisse arrière (bord *m* de fuite *f*)
- *trailing edge*
38 l'aérofrein *m* (frein *m* de piqué *m*)
- *brake flap (spoiler)*
39 le volet de courbure *f*
- *torsional clamp*
40 le revêtement
- *covering (skin)*
41 l'aileron *m*
- *aileron*
42 le bec d'aile *f*
- *wing tip*
43 le vol libre
- *hang gliding*
44 l'appareil *m* de vol *m* libre (le delta, l'aile *f* volante)
- *hang glider*
45 le pilote de vol *m* libre
- *hang glider pilot*
46 la barre de pilotage *m*
- *control frame*

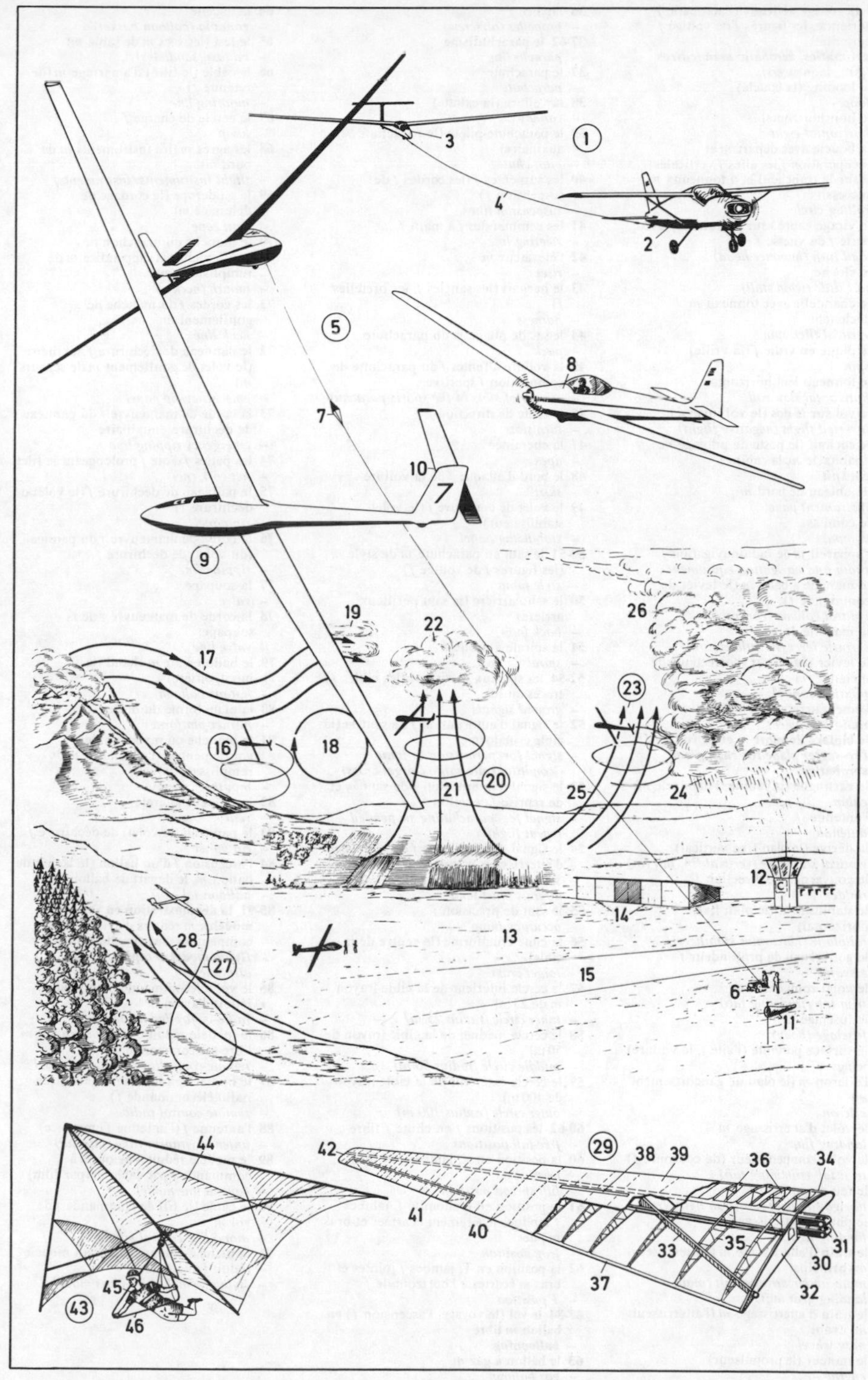
1
3
4
2
5
8
7
10
9
19
22
26
17
23
16
18
20
21
25
24
12
14
13
28
27
15
6
11
29
44
42
38
39
36
34
41
40
33
35
31
30
37
32
45
43
46

1-9 la voltige aérienne (l'acrobatie *f* aérienne, les figures *f* de voltige *f* aérienne)
– ***aerobatics, aerobatic manoeuvres*** *(*Am. *maneuvers)*
1 le looping (la boucle)
– *loop*
2 le huit horizontal
– *horizontal eight*
3 la boucle avec départ *m* et récupération *f* les ailes *f* verticales («sur la tranche») et 4 tonneaux *m* successifs
– *rolling circle*
4 le virage cabré «sur la tranche» avec perte *f* de vitesse *f*
– *stall turn (hammer head)*
5 la cloche
– *tail slide (whip stall)*
6 la chandelle avec tonneau *m* déclenché
– *vertical flick spin*
7 le piqué en vrille *f* (la vrille)
– *spin*
8 le tonneau lent horizontal
– *horizontal slow roll*
9 le vol sur le dos (le vol inversé)
– *inverted flight (negative flight)*
10 le cockpit (le poste de pilotage *m*, l'habitacle *m*, la cabine)
– ***cockpit***
11 le tableau de bord *m*
– *instrument panel*
12 le compas
– *compass*
13 l'appareil *m* de radionavigation *f*
– *radio and navigation equipment*
14 le manche à balai *m* (le levier de commande *f*)
– *control column (control stick)*
15 la manette des gaz *m*
– *throttle lever (throttle control)*
16 le levier régulateur (correcteur) de mélange *m*
– *mixture control*
17 l'émetteurrécepteur *m*
– *radio equipment*
18 le biplace de sport *m* **et de voltige** *f*
– ***two-seater plane for racing and aerobatics***
19 la carlingue (la cabine, l'habitacle *m*)
– *cabin*
20 l'antenne *f*
– *antenna*
21 la dérive (le plan fixe vertical)
– *vertical stabilizer (vertical fin, tail fin)*
22 le gouvernail de direction *f*
– *rudder*
23 le stabilisateur (le plan fixe horizontal)
– *tailplane (horizontal stabilizer)*
24 le gouvernail de profondeur *f*
– *elevator*
25 le volet compensateur
– *trim tab (trimming tab)*
26 le fuselage
– *fuselage (body)*
27 la surface portante (l'aile *f*, la voilure)
– *wing*
28 l'aileron *m* (le plan de gauchissement *m*)
– *aileron*
29 le volet d'atterrissage *m*
– *landing flap*
30 le volet compensateur (de courbure *f*)
– *trim tab (trimming tab)*
31 le feu de position *f*
– *navigation light (position light) [red]*
32 le phare d'atterrissage *m*
– *landing light*
33 le train d'atterrissage *m* (l'atterrisseur *m*) principal
– *main undercarriage unit (main landing gear unit)*
34 le train d'atterrissage *m* (l'atterrisseur *m*) avant
– *nose wheel*
35 le moteur (le propulseur)
– *engine*
36 l'hélice *f*
– *propeller (airscrew)*
37-62 le parachutisme
– ***parachuting***
37 le parachute
– *parachute*
38 la voilure (la calotte)
– *canopy*
39 le parachute-pilote (le parachute auxiliaire)
– *pilot chute*
40 les suspentes *f* (les cordes *f* de suspension *f*)
– *suspension lines*
41 les commandes *f* à main *f*
– *steering line*
42 l'élévateur *m*
– *riser*
43 le harnais (les sangles *f*, les bretelles *f*)
– *harness*
44 le sac de pliage *m* du parachute
– *pack*
45 la voilure à fentes *f* du parachute de compétition *f* sportive
– *system of slots of the sports parachute*
46 la fente de direction *f*
– *turn slots*
47 la cheminée
– *apex*
48 le bord d'attaque *f* de la voilure
– *skirt*
49 le volet de courbure *f* (le volet stabilisateur)
– *stabilizing panel*
50-51 le saut en parachute *m* de style *m* (les figures *f* de voltige *f*)
– *style jump*
50 le salto arrière (le saut périlleux arrière)
– *back loop*
51 la spirale à droite *f*
– *spiral*
52-54 les signaux *m* visuels (les cibles *f*) tracés au sol
– *ground signals*
52 le signal d'autorisation *f* de saut *m* (la cible cruciforme)
– *signal for 'permission to jump' ('conditions are safe') (target cross)*
53 le signal d'interdiction *f* de saut *m* et de reprise *f* de vol *m*
– *signal for 'parachuting suspended - repeat flight'*
54 le signal d'interdiction *f* de saut *m* et d'atterrissage *m* immédiat
– *signal for 'parachuting suspended - aircraft must land'*
55 le saut de précision *f*
– *accuracy jump*
56 la cible cruciforme (le centre de la cible)
– *target cross*
57 le cercle intérieur de la cible [rayon *m* de 25 m]
– *inner circle [radius 25 m]*
58 le cercle médian de la cible [rayon de 50 m]
– *middle circle [radius 50 m]*
59 le cercle extérieur de la cible [rayon de 100 m]
– *outer circle [radius 100 m]*
60-62 les positions *f* en chute *f* libre
– *free-fall positions*
60 la position en X, jambes *f* et bras *m* écartés
– *full spread position*
61 la position en grenouille *f*, jambes *f* tendues légèrement écartées et bras *m* pliés
– *frog position*
62 la position en T, jambes *f* jointes et bras *m* écartés à l'horizontale *f*
– *T position*
63-84 le vol (le voyage, l'ascension *f*) **en ballon** *m* **libre**
– ***ballooning***
63 le ballon à gaz *m*
– *gas balloon*
64 la nacelle
– *gondola (balloon basket)*
65 le lest (les sacs *m* de sable *m*)
– *ballast (sandbags)*
66 le câble (le filin) d'amarrage *m* (de retenue *f*)
– *mooring line*
67 le cercle de charge *f*
– *hoop*
68 les agrès *m* (les instruments *m* de bord *m*)
– *flight instruments (instruments)*
69 le guiderope (le cordage de délestage *m*)
– *trail rope*
70 le manche ou manchon de gonflement *m* (l'appendice *m* de remplissage *m*)
– *mouth (neck)*
71 les cordes *f* du manche de gonflement *m*
– *neck line*
72 le panneau de déchirure *f* auxiliaire (le volet de gonflement *m* de secours *m*)
– *emergency rip panel*
73 la corde de manœuvre *f* du panneau de déchirure *f* auxiliaire
– *emergency ripping line*
74 les pattes *f* d'oie *f* prolongeant le filet
– *network (net)*
75 le panneau de déchirure *f* (le volet de déchirure *f*)
– *rip panel*
76 la corde de manœuvre *f* du panneau (du volet) de déchirure *f*
– *ripping line*
77 la soupape
– *valve*
78 la corde de manœuvre *f* de la soupape
– *valve line*
79 le ballon à air *m* chaud (la montgolfière)
– *hot-air balloon*
80 la plate-forme du brûleur
– *burner platform*
81 le manche ou manchon de gonflement *m* (l'appendice *m* de remplissage *m*)
– *mouth*
82 la soupape latérale
– *vent*
83 le panneau (le volet) de déchirure *f*
– *rip panel*
84 l'ascension *f* d'un ballon (le lâcher de ballon *m*, le départ de ballon *m*)
– *balloon take-off*
85-91 la démonstration en vol *m* **de modèles** *m* réduits d'avions *m* (la compétition d'aéromodélisme *m*)
– ***flying model aeroplanes*** *(*Am. *airplanes)*
85 le vol télécommandé d'un modèle réduit d'avion *m*
– *radio-controlled model flight*
86 le modèle réduit d'avion *m* en vol *m* libre télécommandé
– *remote-controlled free flight model*
87 le boîtier de radiocommande *f* (de radiotélécommande *f*)
– *remote control radio*
88 l'antenne *f* (l'antenne *f* émettrice)
– *antenna (transmitting antenna)*
89 le modèle réduit d'avion *m* à commande *f* par câble *m* (par film)
– *control line model*
90 le câble (le fil) de commande *f* de vol *m*
– *mono-line control system*
91 la niche à chien volante, un modèle réduit fantaisiste
– *flying kennel, a K9-class model*

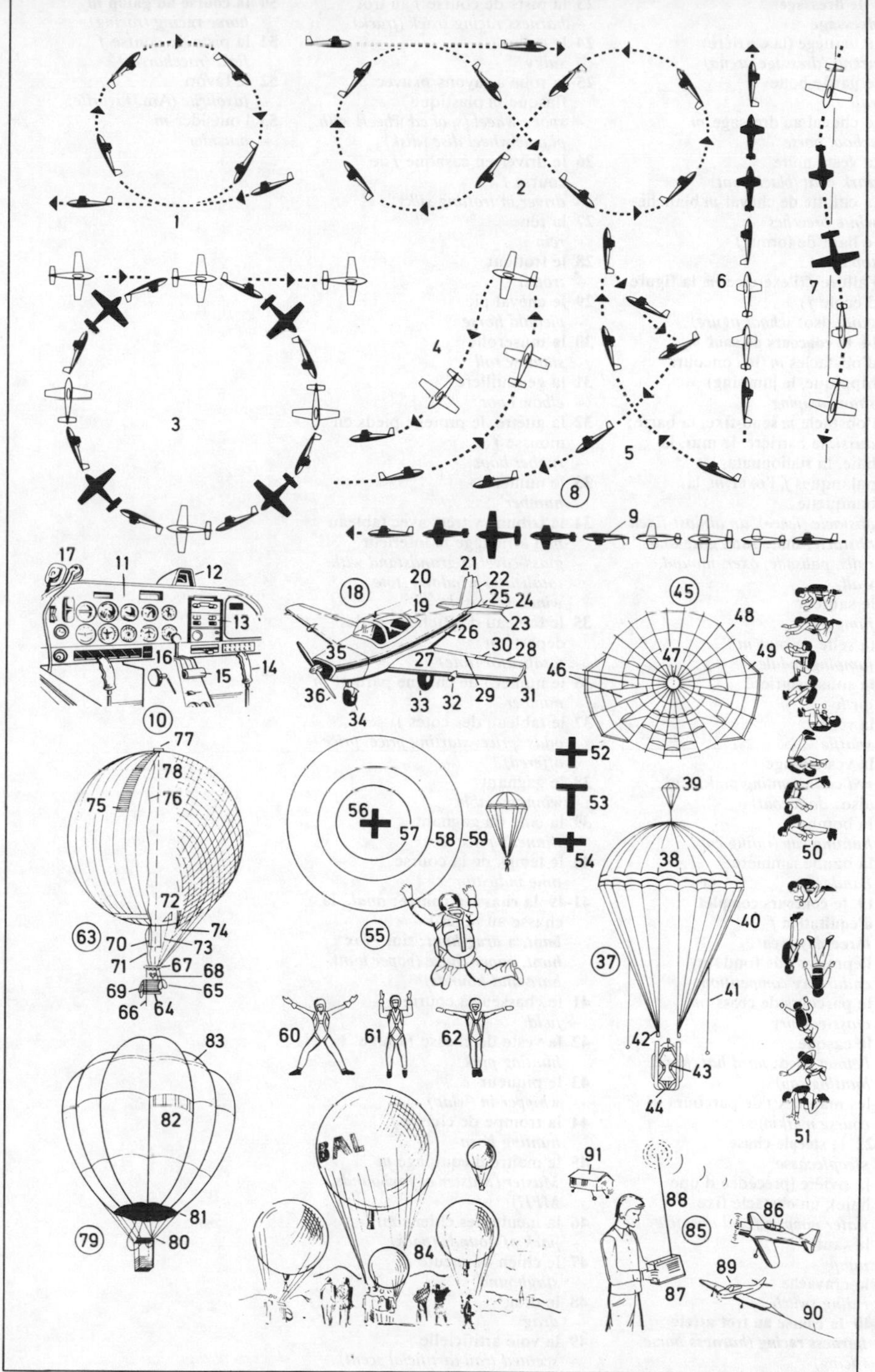

1-7 le dressage
– ***dressage***
1 le manège (la carrière)
– *arena (dressage arena)*
2 le garde-botte
– *rail*
3 le cheval au dressage *m*
– *school horse*
4 la veste noire
– *dark coat (black coat)*
5 la culotte de cheval *m* blanche
– *white breeches*
6 le haut de forme *f*
– *top hat*
7 l'allure *f* (l'exercice *m*, la figure d'école *f*)
– *gait* (also: *school figure)*
8-14 le concours de saut *m* d'obstacles *m* (le concours hippique, le jumping)
– ***show jumping***
8 l'obstacle *m* semi-fixe, la barre; *aussi:* la barrière, le mur, la haie, la stationnata, les palanques *f*, l'oxer *m*, la banquette
– *obstacle (fence), an almost-fixed obstacle;* sim.: *gate, gate and rails, palisade, oxer, mound, wall*
9 le sauteur
– *jumper*
10 la selle de saut *m*
– *jumping saddle*
11 la sous-ventrière
– *girth*
12 la rêne
– *snaffle*
13 la veste rouge
– *red coat (hunting pink, pink;* also: *dark coat)*
14 la bombe
– *hunting cap (riding cap)*
15 la bande jambière
– *bandage*
16-19 le concours complet d'équitation *f*
– ***three-day event***
16 l'épreuve *f* de fond *m*
– *endurance competition*
17 le parcours de cross *m*
– *cross-country*
18 le casque
– *helmet* (also: *hard hat, hard hunting cap)*
19 les marques *f* de parcours *m*
– *course markings*
20-22 le steeple-chase
– ***steeplechase***
20 la rivière (précédée d'une haie), un obstacle fixe
– *water jump, a fixed obstacle*
21 le saut
– *jump*
22 la cravache
– *riding switch*
23-40 la course au trot attelé
– ***harness racing*** *(harness horse racing)*
23 la piste de course *f* au trot
– *harness racing track (track)*
24 le sulky
– *sulky*
25 la roue à rayons *m* avec flasque *m* plastique
– *spoke wheel (spoked wheel) with plastic wheel disc (disk)*
26 le driver en casaque *f* de course *f*
– *driver in trotting silks*
27 la rêne
– *rein*
28 le trotteur
– *trotter*
29 le cheval pie
– *piebald horse*
30 la muserolle
– *shadow roll*
31 la genouillère
– *elbow boot*
32 la guêtre, le protège-pieds en mousse *f*
– *rubber boot*
33 le numéro
– *number*
34 la tribune vitrée, avec tableau *m* d'affichage *m* intérieur
– *glass-covered grandstand with totalizator windows (tote windows) inside*
35 le tableau d'affichage *m* des départs *m*
– *totalizator (tote)*
36 le numéro de chaque partant *m*
– *number*
37 le tableau des cotes *f*
– *odds (price, starting price, price offered)*
38 le gagnant
– *winners' table*
39 la cote du gagnant
– *winner's price*
40 le temps de la course
– *time indicator*
41-49 la chasse à courre; *anal.:* la chasse au renard
– ***hunt, a drag hunt;*** sim.: *fox hunt, paper chase (paper hunt, hare-and-hounds)*
41 le chasseur à courre
– *field*
42 la veste de chasse *f* rouge
– *hunting pink*
43 le piqueur
– *whipper-in (whip)*
44 la trompe de chasse *f*
– *hunting horn*
45 le maître d'équipage *m*
– *Master (Master of foxhounds, MFH)*
46 la meute (les chiens *m*)
– *pack of hounds (pack)*
47 le chien de meute *m*
– *staghound*
48 le drag
– *drag*
49 la voie artificielle
– *scented trail (artificial scent)*
50 la course au galop *m*
– ***horse racing*** *(racing)*
51 la piste de course *f*
– *field (racehorses)*
52 le favori
– *favourite* (Am. *favorite)*
53 l'outsider *m*
– *outsider*

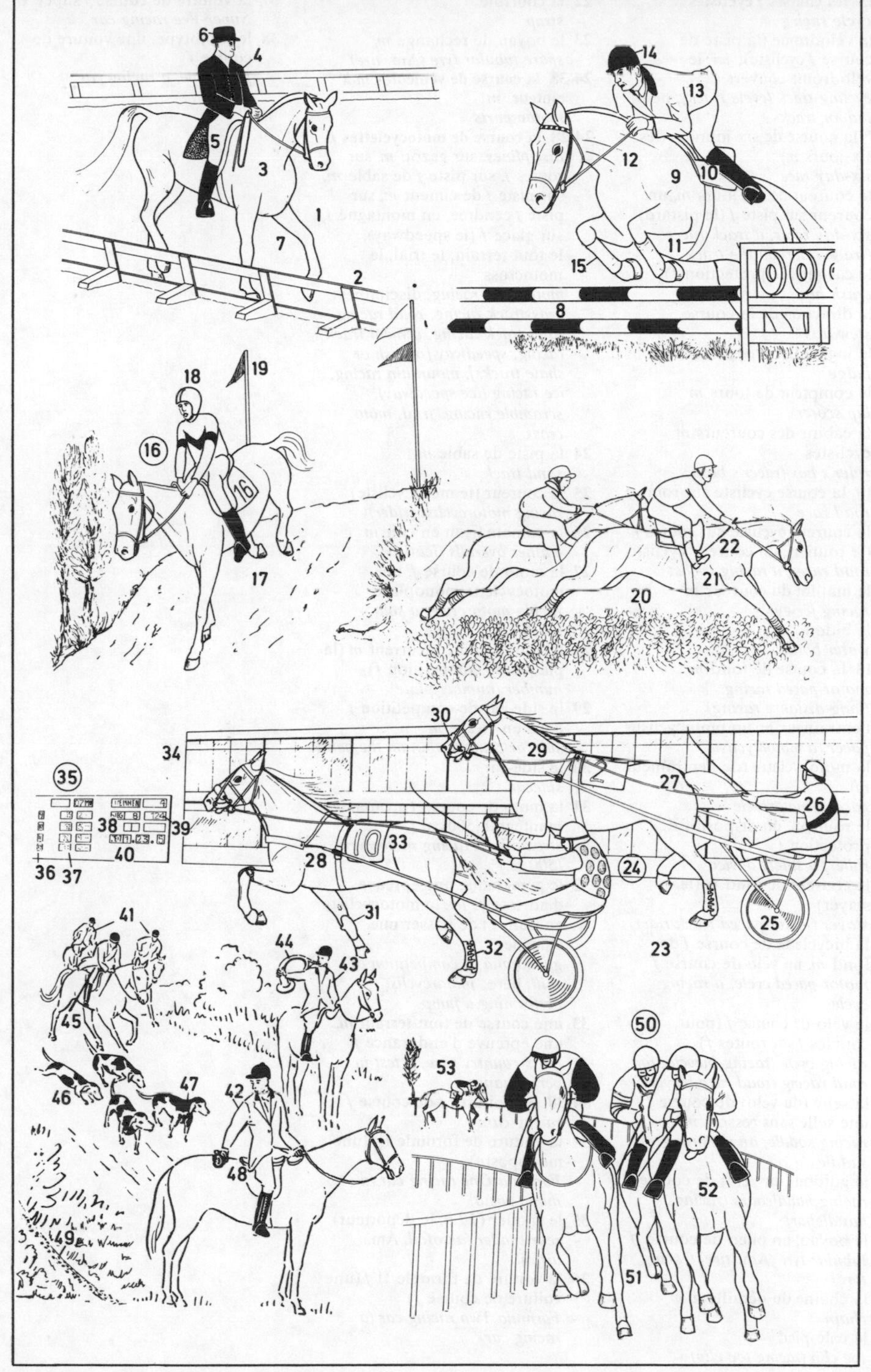
1
2
3
4
5
6
7
8
9
10
11
12
13
14
15
16
17
18
19
20
21
22
23
24
25
26
27
28
29
30
31
32
33
34
35
36
37
38
39
40
41
42
43
44
45
46
47
48
49
50
51
52
53

290 Course cycliste, course de véhicules à moteur

1-23 les courses *f* cyclistes
– ***cycle racing***
1 le vélodrome (la piste de course *f* cycliste); *ici:* le vélodrome couvert
– *cycling track (cycle track);* here: *indoor track*
2-7 la course de six jours *m* (les six-jours *m*)
– *six-day race*
2 le coureur de six jours *m*, un coureur sur piste *f* (le pistard)
– *six-day racer, a track racer (track rider) on the track*
3 le casque (de protection *f*)
– *crash hat*
4 la direction de la course
– *stewards*
5 le juge à l'arrivée *f*
– *judge*
6 le compteur de tours *m*
– *lap scorer*
7 la cabine des coureurs *m* cyclistes
– *rider's box (racer's box)*
8-10 la course cycliste sur route *f*
– *road race*
8 le coureur cycliste sur routes *f* (le routier), un coureur cycliste
– *road racer, a racing cyclist*
9 le maillot du coureur *m*
– *racing jersey*
10 le bidon
– *water bottle*
11-15 la course de fond *m*
– *motor-paced racing (long-distance racing)*
11 l'entraîneur *m*, un motocycliste
– *pacer, a motorcyclist*
12 la motocyclette (de l'entraîneur *m*)
– *pacer's motorcycle*
13 le rouleau, un dispositif de protection *f*
– *roller, a safety device*
14 le coureur de fond *m* (le stayer)
– *stayer (motor-paced track rider)*
15 la bicyclette de course *f* de fond *m*, un vélo de course *f*
– *motor-paced cycle, a racing cycle*
16 le vélo de course *f* (pour courses *f* sur routes *f*)
– *racing cycle (racing bicycle) for road racing (road race bicycle)*
17 la selle (du vélo) de course *f*, une selle sans ressort *m*
– *racing saddle, an unsprung saddle*
18 le guidon (du vélo) de course *f*
– *racing handlebars (racing handlebar)*
19 le boyau, un pneu de course *f*
– *tubular tyre* (Am. *tire) (racing tyre)*
20 la chaîne du dérailleur *m*
– *chain*
21 le cale-pied
– *toe clip (racing toe clip)*
22 la courroie
– *strap*
23 le boyau de rechange *m*
– *spare tubular tyre* (Am. *tire)*
24-38 la course de véhicules *m* à moteur *m*
– ***motorsports***
24-28 la course de motocyclettes *f*, *disciplines:* sur gazon *m*, sur routes *f*, sur piste *f* de sable *m*, sur piste *f* de ciment *m*, sur piste *f* cendrée, en montagne *f*, sur glace *f* (le speedway), le tout-terrain, le trial, le motocross
– *motorcycle racing;* disciplines: *grasstrack racing, road racing, sand track racing, cement track racing, speedway [on ash or shale tracks], mountain racing, ice racing (ice speedway), scramble racing, trial, moto cross*
24 la piste de sable *m*
– *sand track*
25 le coureur (le motocycliste)
– *racing motorcyclist (rider)*
26 la combinaison en cuir *m*
– *leather overalls (leathers)*
27 la moto de course *f*, une motocyclette monoplace
– *racing motorcycle, a solo machine*
28 le numéro du concurrent *m* (la plaque de compétition *f*)
– *number (number plate)*
29 le side-car de compétition *f* dans un virage *m*
– *sidecar combination on the bend*
30 le side-car
– *sidecar*
31 la moto de course *f* à carénage *m* intégral [500 cm^3]
– *streamlined racing motorcycle [500 cc.]*
32 le gymkhana, une épreuve d'adresse *f*; *ici:* le motocycliste en train *m* de passer une chicane
– *gymkhana, a competition of skill;* here: *motorcyclist performing a jump*
33 une course de tout-terrain *m*, une épreuve d'endurance *f*
– *cross-country race, a test in performance*
34-38 les voitures *f* de course *f*
– *racing cars*
34 la voiture de formule I *f* (une monoposto)
– *Formula One racing car (a mono posto)*
35 le spoiler (*ELF:* le déporteur)
– *rear spoiler (aerofoil,* Am. *airfoil)*
36 la voiture de formule II *f* (une voiture de course *f*)
– *Formula Two racing car (a racing car)*
37 la voiture de course *f* super V
– *Super-Vee racing car*
38 le prototype, une voiture de course *f*
– *prototype, a racing car*

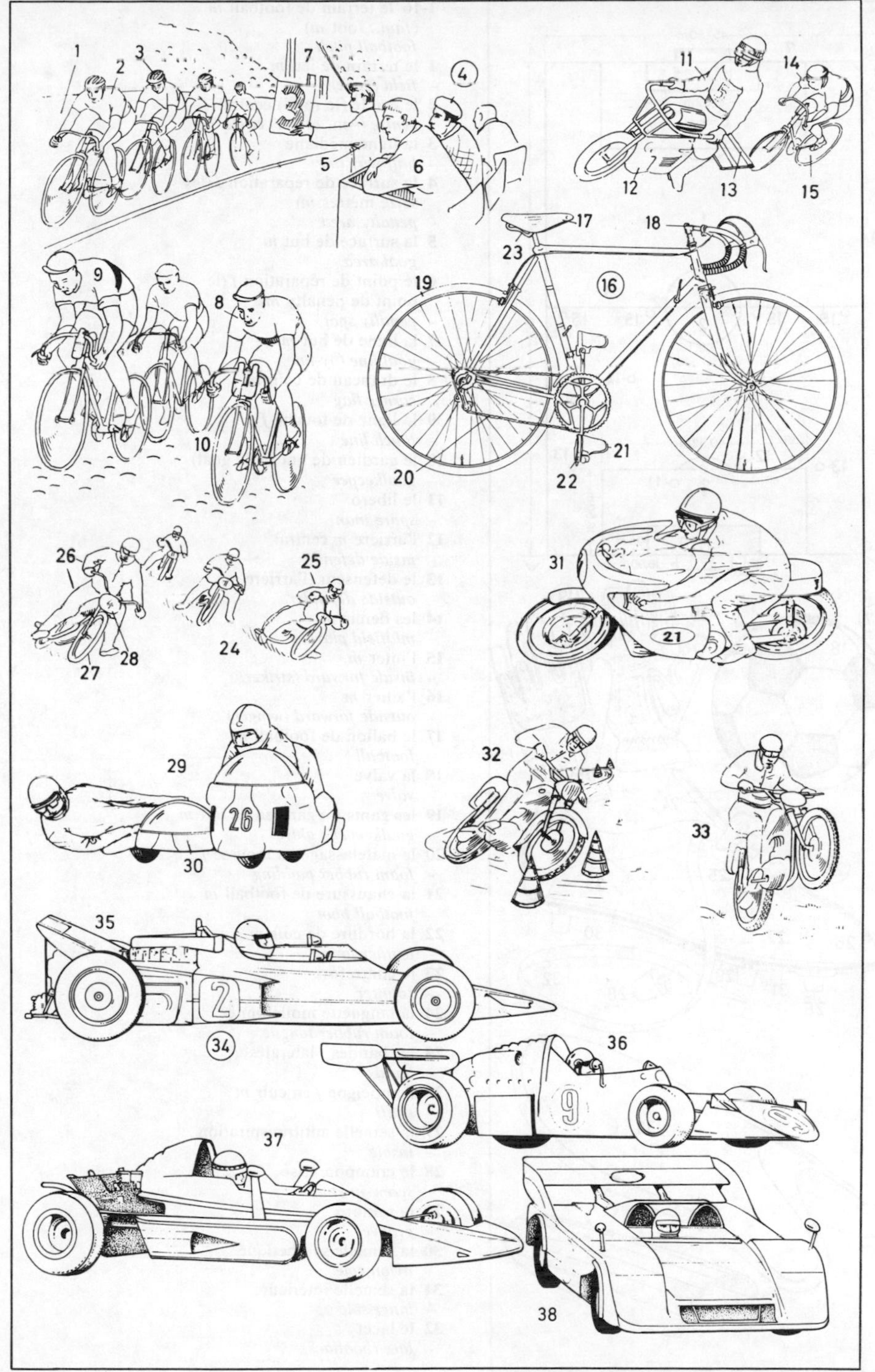
1
2
3
4
5
6
7
8
9
10
11
12
13
14
15
16
17
18
19
20
21
22
23
24
25
26
27
28
29
30
31
32
33
34
35
36
37
38

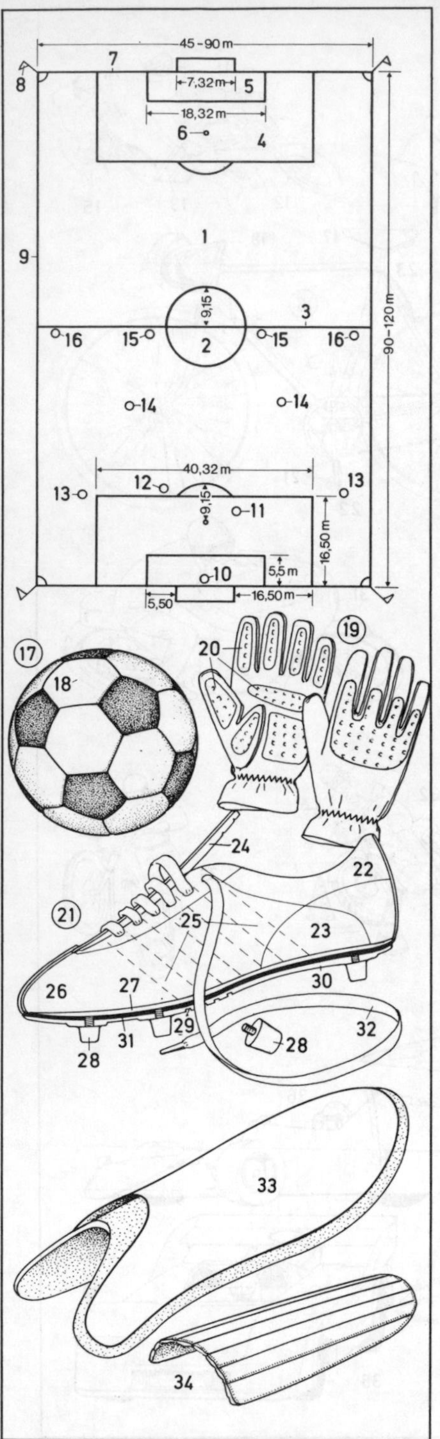

1-16 le terrain de football *m* (*fam.:* foot *m*)
– *football pitch*
1 le terrain de jeu *m*
– *field (park)*
2 le cercle (le rond) central
– *centre (*Am. *center) circle*
3 la ligne médiane
– *half-way line*
4 la surface de réparation *f* (les seize mètres *m*)
– *penalty area*
5 la surface de but *m*
– *goal area*
6 le point de réparation *f* (le point de penalty *m*)
– *penalty spot*
7 la ligne de but *m*
– *goal line (by-line)*
8 le drapeau de coin *m*
– *corner flag*
9 la ligne de touche *f*
– *touch line*
10 le gardien de but *m* (le goal)
– *goalkeeper*
11 le libero
– *spare man*
12 l'arrière *m* central
– *inside defender*
13 le défenseur (l'arrière *m*)
– *outside defender*
14 les demis *m*
– *midfield players*
15 l'inter *m*
– *inside forward (striker)*
16 l'ailier *m*
– *outside forward (winger)*
17 le ballon de football *m*
– *football*
18 la valve
– *valve*
19 les gants du gardien de but *m*
– *goalkeeper's gloves*
20 le matelassage en mousse *f*
– *foam rubber padding*
21 la chaussure de football *m*
– *football boot*
22 la bordure de cuir *m*
– *leather lining*
23 le contrefort
– *counter*
24 la languette molletonnée
– *foam rubber tongue*
25 les bandes *f* latérales
– *bands*
26 l'empeigne *f* en cuir *m*
– *shaft*
27 la semelle antitranspiration
– *insole*
28 le crampon vissé
– *screw-in stud*
29 la rainure
– *groove*
30 la semelle synthétique
– *nylon sole*
31 la semelle intérieure
– *inner sole*
32 le lacet
– *lace (bootlace)*

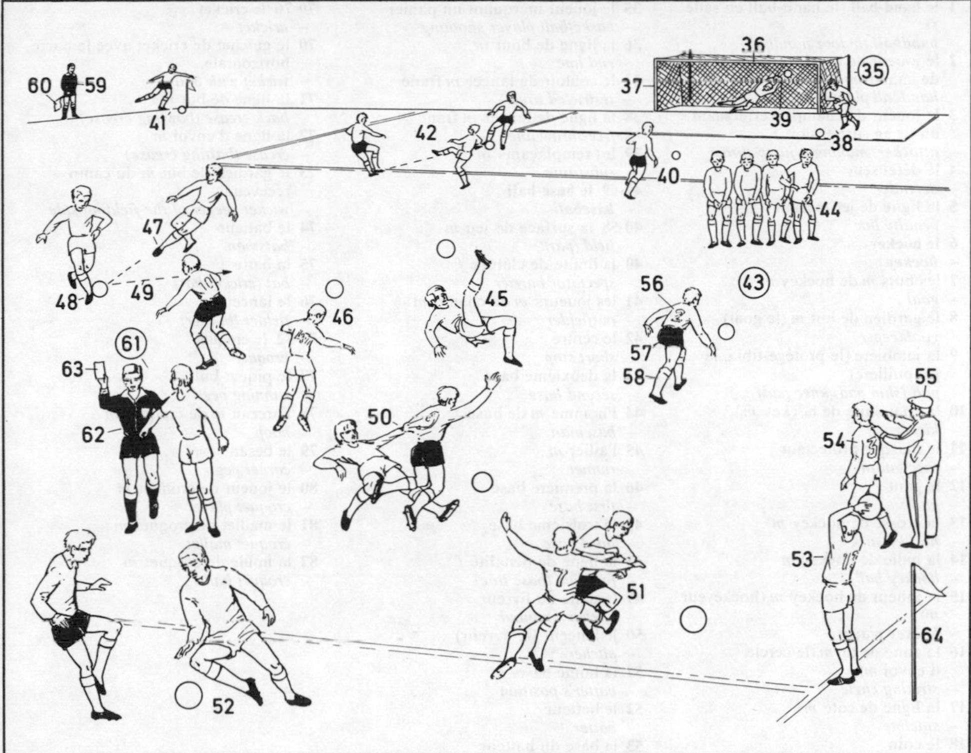

33 la jambière avec sa chevillère
– *football pad with ankle guard*
34 le protège-tibia
– *shin guard*
35 le but
– *goal*
36 la barre transversale (la transversale)
– *crossbar*
37 le poteau (le poteau de but *m*)
– *post (goalpost)*
38 le dégagement (la remise en jeu *m*)
– *goal kick*
39 le dégagement du poing *m*
– *save with the fists*
40 le coup de pied *m* de réparation *f* (*fam.:* le penalty)
– *penalty (penalty kick)*
41 le coup de pied *m* de coin *m* (*fam.:* le corner)
– *corner (corner kick)*
42 le hors-jeu
– *offside*
43 le coup franc
– *free kick*
44 le mur
– *wall*
45 le coup de pied *m* retourné
– *bicycle kick (overhead bicycle kick)*
46 le tir de la tête (la tête)
– *header*
47 la passe
– *pass (passing the ball)*
48 la réception du ballon
– *receiving the ball (taking a pass)*
49 la passe courte (la passe redoublée, le une-deux)
– *short pass (one-two)*
50 la faute
– *foul (infringement)*
51 le tacle
– *obstruction*
52 le dribble
– *dribble*
53 la rentrée en touche *f*
– *throw-in*
54 le remplaçant
– *substitute*
55 l'entraîneur *m*
– *coach*
56 le maillot
– *shirt (jersey)*
57 la culotte (le short)
– *shorts*
58 la chaussette
– *sock (football sock)*
59 le juge de ligne *f*
– *linesman*
60 le drapeau du juge de touche *f*
– *linesman's flag*
61 l'expulsion *f* hors du terrain
– *sending-off*
62 l'arbitre *m*
– *referee*
63 le carton d'expulsion *f* (le carton rouge; *égal.:* le carton d'avertissement, le carton jaune)
– *red card; as a caution* also: *yellow card*
64 le drapeau de ligne *f* médiane
– *centre (Am. center) flag*

1 le hand-ball (le hand-ball en salle *f*)
– ***handball*** *(indoor handball)*
2 le joueur de hand-ball, une joueur de champ *m*
– *handball player, a field player*
3 le joueur de champ *m* effectuant un tir en suspension *f*
– *attacker, making a jump throw*
4 le défenseur
– *defender*
5 la ligne de jet *m* franc
– *penalty line*
6 le hockey
– ***hockey***
7 les buts *m* de hockey *m*
– *goal*
8 le gardien de but *m* (le goal)
– *goalkeeper*
9 la jambière (le protège-tibia, la genouillère)
– *pad (shin pad, knee pad)*
10 la chaussure de hockey *m*
– *kicker*
11 le masque protecteur
– *face guard*
12 le gant
– *glove*
13 la crosse de hockey *m*
– *hockey stick*
14 la balle de hockey *m*
– *hockey ball*
15 le joueur de hockey *m* (hockeyeur *m*)
– *hockey player*
16 la zone de tir *m* (le cercle d'envoi *m*)
– *striking circle*
17 la ligne de côté *m*
– *sideline*
18 le coin
– *corner*
19 le rugby
– ***rugby*** *(rugby football)*
20 la mêlée
– *scrum (scrummage)*
21 le ballon de rugby *m* (le ballon ovale)
– *rugby ball*
22 le football américain
– ***American football*** (Am. *football*)
23 le porteur du ballon, un joueur de football *m*
– *player carrying the ball, a football player*
24 le casque
– *helmet*
25 le masque protecteur
– *face guard*
26 le maillot rembourré
– *padded jersey*
27 le ballon
– *ball (pigskin)*
28 le basket-ball (*fam.:* le basket)
– ***basketball***
29 le ballon de basket *m*
– *basketball*
30 le panneau
– *backboard*
31 le montant des panneaux *m*
– *basket posts*
32 le panier
– *basket*
33 l'anneau du panier
– *basket ring*
34 le rectangle d'encadrement *m*
– *target rectangle*
35 le joueur marquant un panier
– *basketball player shooting*
36 la ligne de bout *m*
– *end line*
37 le couloir de lancer *m* franc
– *restricted area*
38 la ligne de lancer *m* franc
– *free-throw line*
39 les remplaçants *m*
– *substitute*
40-69 le base-ball
– ***baseball***
40-58 la surface de jeu *m*
– *field (park)*
40 la limite de clôture *f*
– *spectator barrier*
41 les joueurs *m* de champ *m*
– *outfielder*
42 le centre
– *short stop*
43 la deuxième base
– *second base*
44 l'homme *m* de base *f*
– *baseman*
45 l'ailier *m*
– *runner*
46 la première base
– *first base*
47 la troisième base
– *third base*
48 la ligne de pénalité *f*
– *foul line (base line)*
49 la dalle du livreur
– *pitcher's mound*
50 le lanceur (le livreur)
– *pitcher*
51 la home base
– *batter's position*
52 le batteur
– *batter*
53 la base du batteur
– *home base (home plate)*
54 le receveur
– *catcher*
55 le juge-arbitre en chef *m*
– *umpire*
56 la loge du manager
– *coach's box*
57 l'entraîneur *m* (le manager)
– *coach*
58 les batteurs *m* suivants
– *batting order*
59-60 les gants *m* de base-ball *m*
– *baseball gloves (baseball mitts)*
59 le gant du joueur de champ *m*
– *fielder's glove (fielder's mitt)*
60 le gant du receveur
– *catcher's glove (catcher's mitt)*
61 la balle de base-ball *m*
– *baseball*
62 la batte
– *bat*
63 le batteur en position *f* de frappe *f*
– *batter at bat*
64 le receveur
– *catcher*
65 l'arbitre *m*
– *umpire*
66 l'ailier *m*
– *runner*
67 le tamis du lanceur
– *base plate*
68 le lanceur
– *pitcher*
69 le mont du lanceur
– *pitcher's mound*
70-76 le cricket
– ***cricket***
70 le guichet de cricket avec la barre horizontale
– *wicket with bails*
71 la ligne de but *m*
– *back crease (bowling crease)*
72 la ligne d'envoi *m*
– *crease (batting crease)*
73 le gardien de but *m* du camp receveur
– *wicket keeper of the fielding side*
74 le batteur
– *batsman*
75 la batte
– *bat (cricket bat)*
76 le lanceur
– *fielder (bowler)*
77-82 le croquet
– ***croquet***
77 le piquet-but
– *winning peg*
78 l'arceau *m* de croquet *m*
– *hoop*
79 le besan
– *corner peg*
80 le joueur de croquet *m*
– *croquet player*
81 le maillet de croquet *m*
– *croquet mallet*
82 la boule de croquet *m*
– *croquet ball*

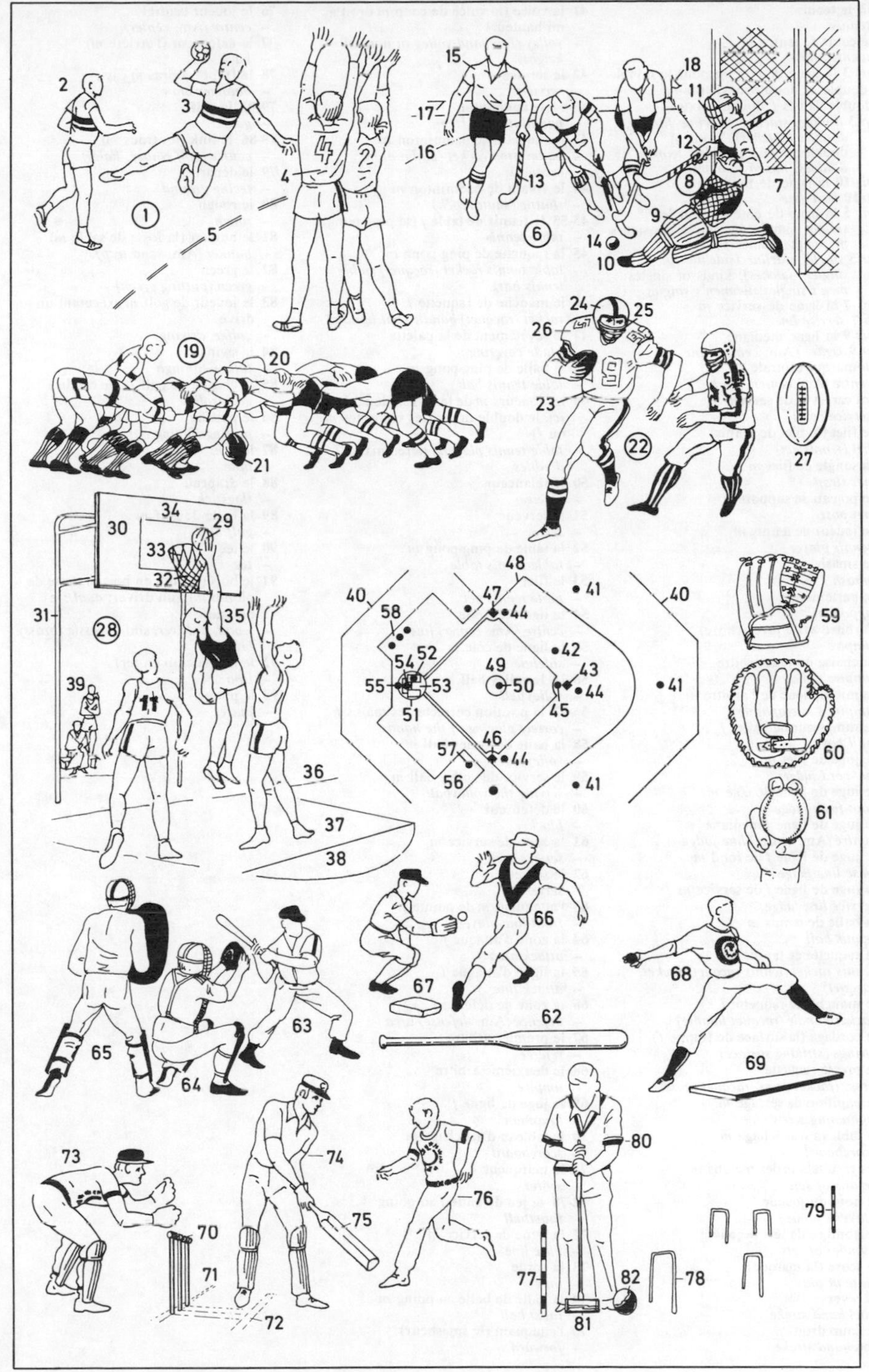

1-42 le tennis
– ***tennis***
1 le court de tennis *m*
– *tennis court*
2 *bis* 3 la ligne de côté *m* pour le double (double *m*; double messieurs *m*; double dames *f*; double mixte)
2 *to* 3 *doubles sideline (sideline for doubles matches)*; kinds of doubles: *men's doubles, women's doubles, mixed doubles*
3 *bis* 10 la ligne de fond *m*
3 *to* 10 *base line*
4 *bis* 5 la ligne de côté *m* pour le *simple* (simple *m*; simple messieurs *m*; simple dames *f*)
4 *to* 5 *singles sideline (sideline for singles matches);* kinds of singles: *men's singles, women's singles*
6 *bis* 7 la ligne de service *m*
6 *to* 7 *service line*
8 *bis* 9 la ligne médiane
8 *to* 9 *centre* (Am. *center) line*
11 la marque centrale
– *centre* (Am. *center) mark*
12 les carrés *m* de service *m*
– *service court*
13 le filet (le filet de tennis)
– *net (tennis net)*
14 la sangle de filet *m*
– *net strap*
15 le poteau de support *m*
– *net post*
16 le joueur de tennis *m*
– *tennis player*
17 le smash
– *smash*
18 le partenaire
– *opponent*
19 l'arbitre *m* (le juge-arbitre)
– *umpire*
20 la chaise du juge-arbitre
– *umpire's chair*
21 le microphone de l'arbitre *m*
– *umpire's microphone*
22 le ramasseur de balles *f*
– *ball boy*
23 le juge de filet *m*
– *net-cord judge*
24 le juge de ligne de côté *m*
– *foot-fault judge*
25 le juge de ligne *f* médiane
– *centre* (Am. *center) line judge*
26 le juge de ligne *f* de fond *m*
– *base line judge*
27 le juge de ligne *f* de service *m*
– *service line judge*
28 la balle de tennis *m*
– *tennis ball*
29 la raquette de tennis *m*
– *tennis racket (tennis racquet, racket, racquet)*
30 le manche de raquette *f*
– *racket handle (racquet handle)*
31 le cordage (la surface de frappe *f*)
– *strings (striking surface)*
32 le presse-raquette
– *press (racket press, racquet press)*
33 le papillon de serrage *m*
– *tightening screw*
34 le tableau d'affichage *m*
– *scoreboard*
35 les résultats *m* des matchs *m*
– *results of sets*
36 le nom du joueur
– *player's name*
37 le nombre de sets *m* joués
– *number of sets*
38 le score (la marque)
– *state of play*
39 le revers
– *backhand stroke*
40 le coup droit
– *forehand stroke*
41 la volée (la volée de coup *m* droit à mi-hauteur)
– *volley (forehand volley at normal height)*
42 le service
– *service*
43-44 le badminton
– ***badminton***
43 la raquette de badminton *m*
– *badminton racket (badminton racquet)*
44 le volant de badminton *m*
– *shuttle (shuttlecock)*
45-55 le tennis de table *f* (le ping-pong)
– ***table tennis***
45 la raquette de ping-pong *m*
– *table tennis racket (racquet) (table tennis bat)*
46 le manche de raquette *f*
– *racket (racquet) handle (bat handle)*
47 le revêtement de la palette
– *blade covering*
48 la balle de ping-pong *m*
– *table tennis ball*
49 les joueurs *m* de tennis *m* de table *f*; *ici:* le double mixte (les pongistes *m* ou *f*)
– *table tennis players;* here: *mixed doubles*
50 le relanceur
– *receiver*
51 le serveur
– *server*
52 la table de ping-pong *m*
– *table tennis table*
53 le filet
– *table tennis net*
54 la ligne centrale
– *centre* (Am. *center) line*
55 la ligne de côté *m*
– *sideline*
56-71 le volley-ball
– ***volleyball***
56-57 la position correcte des mains *f*
– *correct placing of the hands*
58 la balle de volley-ball *m*
– *volleyball*
59 le service de volley-ball *m*
– *serving the volleyball*
60 le défenseur
– *blocker*
61 la zone de service *m*
– *service area*
62 le serveur
– *server*
63 l'attaquant *m* de pointe *f*
– *front-line player*
64 la zone d'attaque *f*
– *attack area*
65 la ligne d'attaque *f*
– *attack line*
66 la zone de défense *f*
– *defence* (Am. *defense) area*
67 le premier arbitre
– *referee*
68 le deuxième arbitre
– *umpire*
69 le juge de ligne *f*
– *linesman*
70 le tableau d'affichage *m*
– *scoreboard*
71 le marqueur
– *scorer*
72-78 le jeu de balle *f* au poing
– ***faustball***
72 la ligne de service *m*
– *base line*
73 la corde
– *tape*
74 la balle de balle au poing *m*
– *faust ball*
75 l'attaquant (le smasheur)
– *forward*
76 le joueur central
– *centre* (Am. *center)*
77 le défenseur (l'arrière *m*)
– *back*
78 la frappe à bras *m* cassé
– *hammer blow*
79-93 le golf
– ***golf***
79-86 le link (les trous *m*)
– *course (golf course, holes)*
79 le départ
– *teeing ground*
80 le rough
– *rough*
81 le bunker (la fosse de sable *m*)
– *bunker* (Am. *sand trap)*
82 le green
– *green (putting green)*
83 le joueur de golf *m* exécutant un drive
– *golfer, driving*
84 le swing
– *follow-through*
85 le chariot de golf *m* (le caddie)
– *golf trolley*
86 le putting
– *putting (holing out)*
87 le trou
– *hole*
88 le drapeau
– *flagstick*
89 la balle de golf *m*
– *golf ball*
90 le tee
– *tee*
91 le bois (le club en bois *m* (lesté de plomb *m*)), un driver; *anal.:* le brassie
– *wood, a driver;* sim.: *brassie (brassy, brassey)*
92 le fer (le club en fer)
– *iron*
93 le putter
– *putter*

SCORES
SETS GAMES
BORG
ASHE

1-33 l'escrime *f*
– ***fencing*** *(modern fencing)*
1-18 l'assaut *m* au fleuret
– *foil*
1 le maître d'armes *f*
– *fencing master (fencing instructor)*
2 la piste (d'escrime *f*)
– *piste*
3 la ligne de mise *f* en garde *f*
– *on guard line*
4 la ligne médiane
– *centre* (Am. *center) line*
5-6 les escrimeurs *m* (les fleuretistes *m*) tirant en assaut *m*
– *fencers (foil fencers, foilsmen, foilists) in a bout*
5 l'attaquant *m* fendu
– *attacker (attacking fencer) in lunging position (lunging)*
6 le tireur parant
– *defender (defending fencer), parrying*
7 le coup droit, une attaque d'escrime *f*
– *straight thrust, a fencing movement*
8 la parade de tierce *f* ou de sixte *f*
– *parry of the tierce*
9 l'axe *m* de l'assaut *m*
– *line of fencing*
10 les trois distances *f* entre tireurs *m* (grande, moyenne ou faible distance *f*)
– *the three fencing measures (short, medium, and long measure)*
11 le fleuret, une arme d'estoc *m*
– *foil, a thrust weapon*
12 le gant (d'escrime *f*)
– *fencing glove*
13 le masque (d'escrime *f*)
– *fencing mask (foil mask)*
14 la bavette du masque d'escrime *f*
– *neck flap (neck guard) on the fencing mask*
15 la veste métallique
– *metallic jacket*
16 la veste d'escrime *f*
– *fencing jacket*
17 les chaussures d'escrime *f* sans talon *m*
– *heelless fencing shoes*
18 la position de salut *m* avant l'assaut *m*
– *first position for fencer's salute (initial position, on guard position)*
19-24 l'assaut *m* au sabre
– *sabre* (Am. *saber) fencing*
19 le sabreur
– *sabreurs (sabre fencers,* Am. *saber fencers)*
20 le sabre d'escrime *f*
– *(light) sabre* (Am. *saber)*
21 le gant (de sabre *m*)
– *sabre* (Am. *saber) glove (sabre gauntlet)*
22 le masque (de sabre *m*)
– *sabre* (Am. *saber) mask*
23 l'attaque *f* à la tête, un coup de figure *f* à droite *f*
– *cut at head*
24 la parade de quinte *f*
– *parry of the fifth (quinte)*
25-33 l'assaut *m* à l'épée *f* électrique
– *épée, with electrical scoring equipment*
25 l'épéiste *m*
– *épéeist*
26 l'épée *f* électrique; *égal.:* le fleuret électrique
– *electric épée;* also: *electric foil*
27 le coup de pointe *f*
– *épée point*
28 le compteur optique de touches *f*
– *scoring lights*
29 l'enrouleur *m*
– *spring-loaded wire spool*
30 les lampes *f* de touche *f*
– *indicator light*
31 le fil sur enrouleur *m*
– *wire*
32 le dispositif électronique d'arbitrage *m*
– *electronic scoring equipment*
33 la position en garde *f*
– *on guard position*
34-45 les armes *f* **d'escrime** *f*
– ***fencing weapons***
34 le sabre, une arme de taille *f* et d'estoc *m*
– *light sabre* (Am. *saber), a cut and thrust weapon*
35 la garde (la corbeille)
– *guard*
36 l'épée *f*, une arme d'estoc *m*
– *épée, a thrust weapon*
37 le fleuret français, une arme d'estoc *m*
– *French foil, a thrust weapon*
38 la garde
– *guard (coquille)*
39 le fleuret italien
– *Italian foil*
40 le pommeau du fleuret
– *foil pommel*
41 la poignée
– *handle*
42 le quillon
– *cross piece (quillons)*
43 la coquille
– *guard (coquille)*
44 la lame
– *blade*
45 la mouche
– *button*
46 les engagements *m*
– *engagements*
47 l'engagement *m* en quarte *f*
– *quarte (carte) engagement*
48 l'engagement *m* en tierce *f* ou en sixte *f*
– *tierce engagement (*also: *sixte engagement)*
49 l'enveloppement *m*
– *circling engagement*
50 l'engagement *m* en seconde *f* ou en octave *f*
– *seconde engagement (*also: *octave engagement)*
51-53 les surfaces *f* valables
– *target areas*
51 toute la surface du corps à l'épée *f* (hommes *m*)
– *the whole body in épée fencing (men)*
52 toute la partie du corps située au-dessus de la ligne des hanches *f* au sabre (hommes *m*)
– *head and upper body down to the groin in sabre* (Am. *saber) fencing (men)*
53 le tronc entre le cou et la ligne des hanches *f* au fleuret *m* (dames *f* et hommes *m*)
– *trunk from the neck to the groin in foil fencing (ladies and men)*

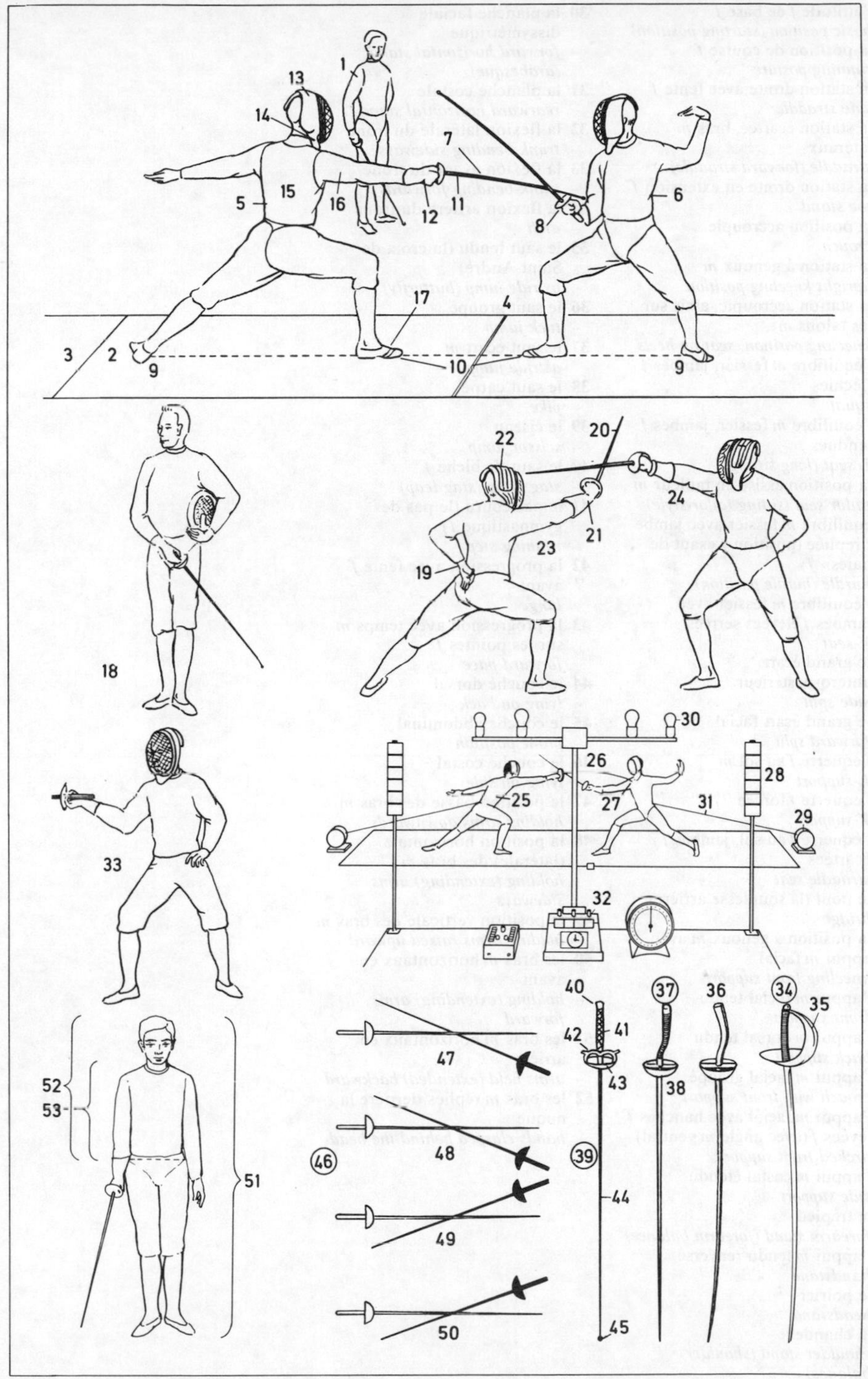
1
2
3
4
5
6
7
8
9
10
11
12
13
14
15
16
17
18
19
20
21
22
23
24
25
26
27
28
29
30
31
32
33
34
35
36
37
38
39
40
41
42
43
44
45
46
47
48
49
50
51
52
53

1 l'attitude *f* de base *f*
– *basic position (starting position)*
2 la position de course *f*
– *running posture*
3 la station droite avec fente *f*
– *side straddle*
4 la station écartée, bras *m* latéraux
– *straddle (forward straddle)*
5 la station droite en extension *f*
– *toe stand*
6 la position accroupie
– *crouch*
7 la station à genoux *m*
– *upright kneeling position*
8 la station accroupie, assis sur les talons *m*
– *kneeling position, seat on heels*
9 l'équilibre *m* fessier, jambes *f* fléchies
– *squat*
10 l'équilibre *m* fessier, jambes *f* tendues
– *L seat (long sitting)*
11 la position assise en tailleur *m*
– *tailor seat (sitting tailor-style)*
12 équilibre *m* fessier avec jambe *f* repliée (position *f* «saut de haies» *f*)
– *hurdle (hurdle position)*
13 l'équilibre *m* fessier avec jambes *f* élevées serrées
– *V-seat*
14 le grand écart antéro-postérieur
– *side split*
15 le grand écart facial
– *forward split*
16 l'équerre *f* au sol *m*
– *L-support*
17 l'équerre *f* forcée
– *V-support*
18 l'équerre *f* au sol, jambes *f* écartées
– *straddle seat*
19 le pont (la souplesse arrière)
– *bridge*
20 la position à genoux *m* avec appui *m* facial
– *kneeling front support*
21 l'appui *m* facial tendu
– *front support*
22 l'appui *m* dorsal tendu
– *back support*
23 l'appui *m* facial groupé
– *crouch with front support*
24 l'appui *m* facial avec hanches *f* levées *f* (avec angle *m* ventral)
– *arched front support*
25 l'appui *m* costal étendu
– *side support*
26 le trépied
– *forearm stand (forearm balance)*
27 l'appui *m* tendu renversé
– *handstand*
28 le poirier
– *headstand*
29 la chandelle
– *shoulder stand (shoulder balance)*
30 la planche faciale dissymétrique
– *forward horizontal stand (arabesque)*
31 la planche costale
– *rearward horizontal stand*
32 la flexion latérale du tronc
– *trunk-bending sideways*
33 la flexion avant du tronc
– *trunk-bending forwards*
34 la flexion arrière du tronc
– *arch*
35 le saut tendu (la croix de Saint-André)
– *astride jump (butterfly)*
36 le saut groupé
– *tuck jump*
37 le saut écart *m*
– *astride jump*
38 le saut carpé
– *pike*
39 le ciseau
– *scissor jump*
40 le saut de biche *f*
– *stag jump (stag leap)*
41 le pas couru (le pas de gymnastique *f*)
– *running step*
42 la progression avec fente *f* avant
– *lunge*
43 la progression avec temps *m* sur les pointes *f*
– *forward pace*
44 le couché dorsal
– *lying on back*
45 le couché abdominal
– *prone position*
46 le couché costal
– *lying on side*
47 la position basse des bras *m*
– *holding arms downwards*
48 la position horizontale (latérale) des bras *m*
– *holding (extending) arms sideways*
49 la position verticale des bras *m*
– *holding arms raised upward*
50 les bras *m* horizontaux en avant
– *holding (extending) arms forward*
51 les bras *m* horizontaux en arrière
– *arms held (extended) backward*
52 les bras *m* repliés derrière la nuque
– *hands clasped behind the head*

47
48
49
50
51
1
2
3
4
5
6
7
8
9
52
10
11
12
13
20
21
22
14
15
23
24
16
17
18
19
25
26
27
28
29
30
31
32
33
34
35
36
37
38
41
42
39
40
43
44
45
46

1-11 les agrès *m* du concours olympique de gymnastique *f* masculine
– *gymnastics apparatus in men's Olympic gymnastics*
1 le cheval (le cheval-sautoir)
– *long horse (horse, vaulting horse)*
2 les barres parallèles *f*
– *parallel bars*
3 la barre
– *bar*
4 les anneaux *m*
– *rings (stationary rings)*
5 le cheval d'arçon *m* (cheval-arçons)
– *pommel horse (side horse)*
6 l'arçon *m*
– *pommel*
7 la barre fixe
– *horizontal bar (high bar)*
8 la barre
– *bar*
9 le montant de barre *f*
– *upright*
10 le haubanage
– *stay wires*
11 le praticable (surface *f* de 12 x 12 mètres)
– *floor (12 m x 12 m floor area)*
12-21 le matériel d'apport *m* et les agrès *m* pour la gymnastique scolaire ou la gymnastique de club *m*
– *auxiliary apparatus and apparatus for school and club gymnastics*
12 le tremplin
– *springboard (Reuther board)*
13 le tapis de sol *m*
– *landing mat*
14 le banc suédois
– *bench*
15 le plinth (le plint)
– *box*
16 l'élément *m* de plinth *m*
– *small box*
17 le mouton (le boc)
– *buck*
18 le tapis mousse *f* (le tapis Pleyel)
– *mattress*
19 la corde (lisse)
– *climbing rope (rope)*
20 l'espalier *m*
– *wall bars*
21 l'échelle *f* verticale
– *window ladder*
22-39 les positions *f* face à l'engin *m*
– *positions in relation to the apparatus*
22 la station faciale latérale
– *side, facing*
23 la station dorsale latérale
– *side, facing away*
24 la station faciale transversale
– *end, facing*
25 la station dorsale transversale
– *end, facing away*
26 la station faciale latérale
– *outside, facing*
27 la station faciale transversale en bout *m* de barres *f*
– *inside, facing*
28 l'appui *m* facial tendu
– *front support*
29 l'appui *m* dorsal tendu
– *back support*
30 le siège écarté
– *straddle position*
31 le siège latéral extérieur
– *seated position outside*
32 le siège transversal en amazone *f*
– *riding seat outside*
33 la suspension faciale tendue
– *hang*
34 la suspension tendue en supination *f*
– *reverse hang*
35 la suspension inclinée
– *hang with elbows bent*
36 la suspension renversée
– *piked reverse hang*
37 la suspension renversée tendue
– *straight inverted hang*
38 l'appui *m* transversal tendu
– *straight hang*
39 l'appui *m* transversal fléchi
– *bent hang*
40-46 les prises *f*
– *grasps* *(kinds of grasp)*
40 la prise simple (la pronation) à la barre fixe
– *overgrasp on the horizontal bar*
41 la prise inversée (la supination) à la barre fixe
– *undergrasp on the horizontal bar*
42 la prise mixte à la barre fixe
– *combined grasp on the horizontal bar*
43 la prise croisée à la barre fixe
– *cross grasp on the horizontal bar*
44 la prise cubitale à la barre fixe
– *rotated grasp on the horizontal bar*
45 la prise radiale aux barres *f* parallèles
– *outside grip on the parallel bars*
46 la prise cubitale aux barres *f* parallèles
– *rotated grasp on the parallel bars*
47 la manique
– *leather handstrap*
48-60 les exercices *m* aux agrès *m*
– *exercises*
48 le saut de brochet *m* au cheval
– *long-fly on the horse*
49 le rétablissement en siège *m* écarté aux barres *f* parallèles
– *rise to straddle on the parallel bars*
50 la croix de fer *m* aux anneaux *m*
– *crucifix on the rings*
51 le passé de jambe *f* au cheval d'arçon *m*
– *scissors (scissors movement) on the pommel horse*
52 le placement du dos jambes *f* tendues au sol
– *legs raising into a handstand on the floor*
53 le saut fléchi au cheval
– *squat vault on the horse*
54 le cercle transversal au cheval d'arçon *m*
– *double leg circle on the pommel horse*
55 la dislocation avant aux anneaux *m*
– *hip circle backwards on the rings*
56 la bascule dorsale aux anneaux *m*
– *lever hang on the rings*
57 le fouetter-balancer aux barres *f* parallèles
– *rearward swing on the parallel bars*
58 la bascule mi-renversée aux barres *f* parallèles
– *forward kip into upper arm hang on the parallel bars*
59 la sortie filée à la barre
– *backward underswing on the horizontal bar*
60 la lune à la barre
– *backward grand circle on the horizontal bar*
61-63 l'équipement *m* du gymnaste
– *gymnastics kit*
61 le maillot de gymnastique *f*
– *singlet (vest,* Am. *undershirt)*
62 le pantalon de gymnastique *f*
– *gym trousers*
63 les chaussures *f* (les chaussons *m*) de gymnastique *f*
– *gym shoes*
64 le bandeau de poignet *m*
– *wristband*

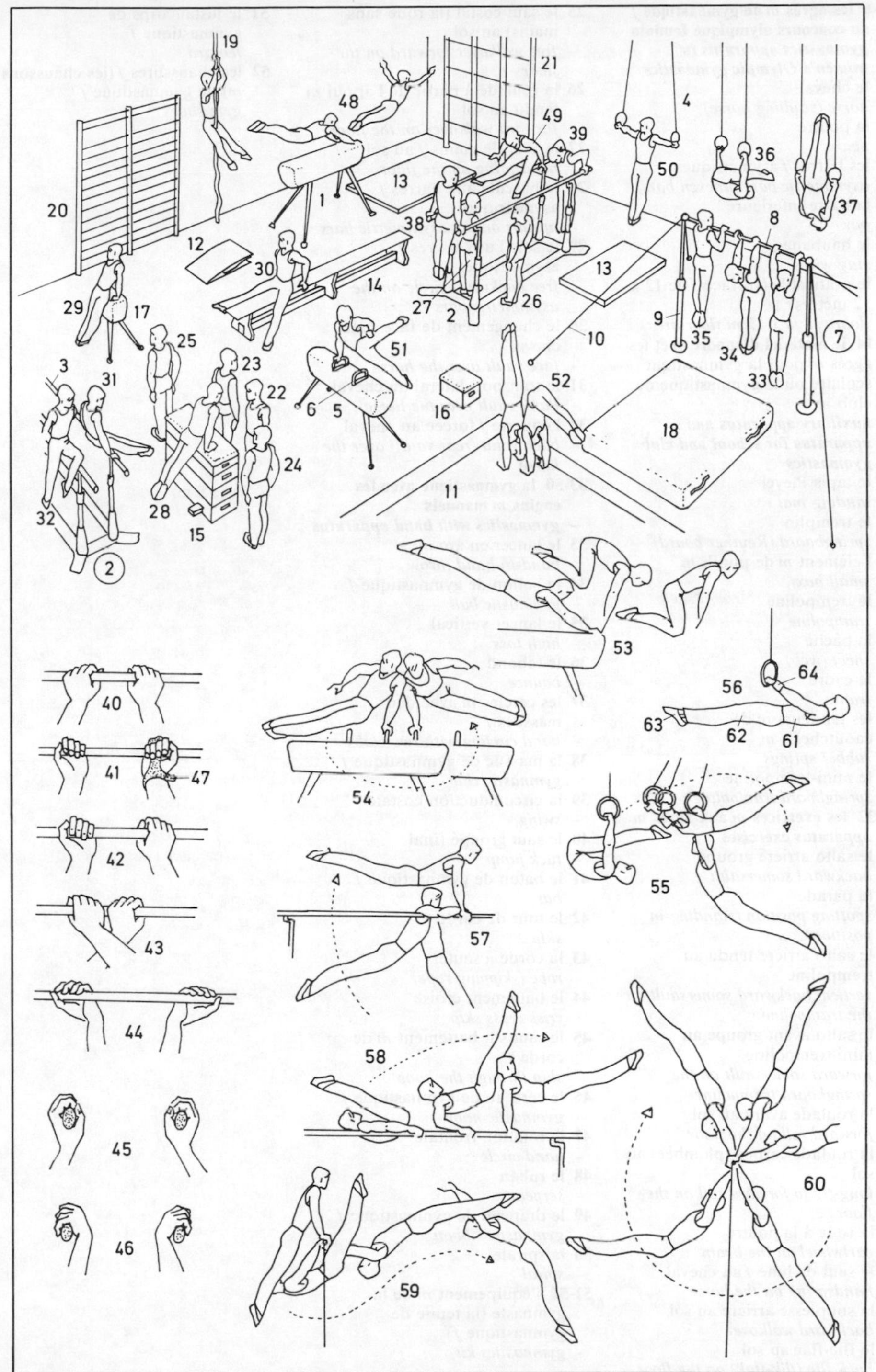
19
21
48
4
49
39
36
50
37
20
1
13
38
8
12
30
13
14
27
2
26
29
17
10
9
35
7
34
33
25
51
3
31
23
52
22
6
5
16
18
28
24
11
32
15
2
53
40
64
56
63
62
61
41
47
54
42
55
43
57
44
58
45
60
46
59

297 Gymnastique aux agrès II (gymnastique féminin)

1-6 les agrès *m* de gymnastique *f* au concours olympique féminin
– ***gymnastics apparatus in women's Olympic gymnastics***
1 le cheval
– *horse (vaulting horse)*
2 la poutre
– *beam*
3 les barres *f* asymétriques
– *asymmetric bars (uneven bars)*
4 la barre inférieure
– *bar*
5 le haubanage
– *stay wires*
6 le praticable (surface *f* de 12 x 12 mètres)
– *floor (12 m x 12 m floor area)*
7-14 le matériel d'apport *m* et les agrès *m* pour la gymnastique scolaire ou la gymnastique de club *m*
– ***auxiliary apparatus and apparatus for school and club gymnastics***
7 le tapis Pleyel
– *landing mat*
8 le tremplin
– *springboard (Reuther board)*
9 l'élément *m* de plinth *m*
– *small box*
10 le trempoline
– *trampoline*
11 la bâche
– *sheet (web)*
12 le cadre
– *frame*
13 les tendeurs *m* de caoutchouc *m*
– *rubber springs*
14 le mini-trempoline
– *springboard trampoline*
15-32 les exercices *m* **aux agrès** *m*
– ***apparatus exercises***
15 le salto arrière groupé
– *backward somersault*
16 la parade
– *spotting position (standing-in position)*
17 le salto arrière tendu au trempoline
– *vertical backward somersault on the trampoline*
18 le salto avant groupé au mini-trempoline
– *forward somersault on the springboard trampoline*
19 la roulade avant au sol
– *forward roll on the floor*
20 la roulade carpée (plombée) au sol
– *long-fly to forward roll on the floor*
21 la roue à la poutre
– *cartwheel on the beam*
22 le saut de lune *f* au cheval
– *handspring on the horse*
23 la souplesse arrière au sol
– *backward walkover*
24 le flic-flac au sol
– *back flip (flik-flak) on the floor*
25 le saut costal (la roue sans mains) au sol
– *free walkover forward on the floor*
26 la roulade à partir de l'appui *m* tendu au sol
– *forward walkover on the floor*
27 le saut de mains *f* au sol
– *headspring on the floor*
28 la bascule aux barres *f* asymétriques
– *upstart on the asymmetric bars*
29 le soleil aux barres *f* asymétriques
– *free backward circle on the asymmetric bars*
30 le changement de face *f* au cheval
– *face vault over the horse*
31 le transport latéral au cheval
– *flank vault over the horse*
32 l'équerre *f* forcée au cheval
– *back vault (rear vault) over the horse*
33-50 la gymnastique avec les engins *m* **manuels**
– ***gymnastics with hand apparatus***
33 le lancer en arc *m*
– *hand-to-hand throw*
34 le ballon de gymnastique *f*
– *gymnastic ball*
35 le lancer vertical
– *high toss*
36 le rebond
– *bounce*
37 les cercles *m* avec deux massues *f*
– *hand circling with two clubs*
38 la massue de gymnastique *f*
– *gymnastic club*
39 la circumduction costale
– *swing*
40 le saut groupé final
– *tuck jump*
41 le bâton de gymnastique *f*
– *bar*
42 le tour de corde *f*
– *skip*
43 la corde à sauter
– *rope (skipping rope)*
44 le battement croisé
– *criss-cross skip*
45 le saut sur battement *m* de corde *f*
– *skip through the hoop*
46 le cerceau de gymnastique *f*
– *gymnastic hoop*
47 la rotation frontale
– *hand circle*
48 le ruban
– *serpent*
49 le drapeau de gymnastique *f*
– *gymnastic ribbon*
50 la spirale
– *spiral*
51-52 l'équipement *m* de la gymnaste (la tenue de gymnastique *f*)
– *gymnastics kit*
51 le justaucorps de gymnastique *f*
– *leotard*
52 les chaussures *f* (les chaussons *m*) de gymnastique *f*
– *gym shoes*

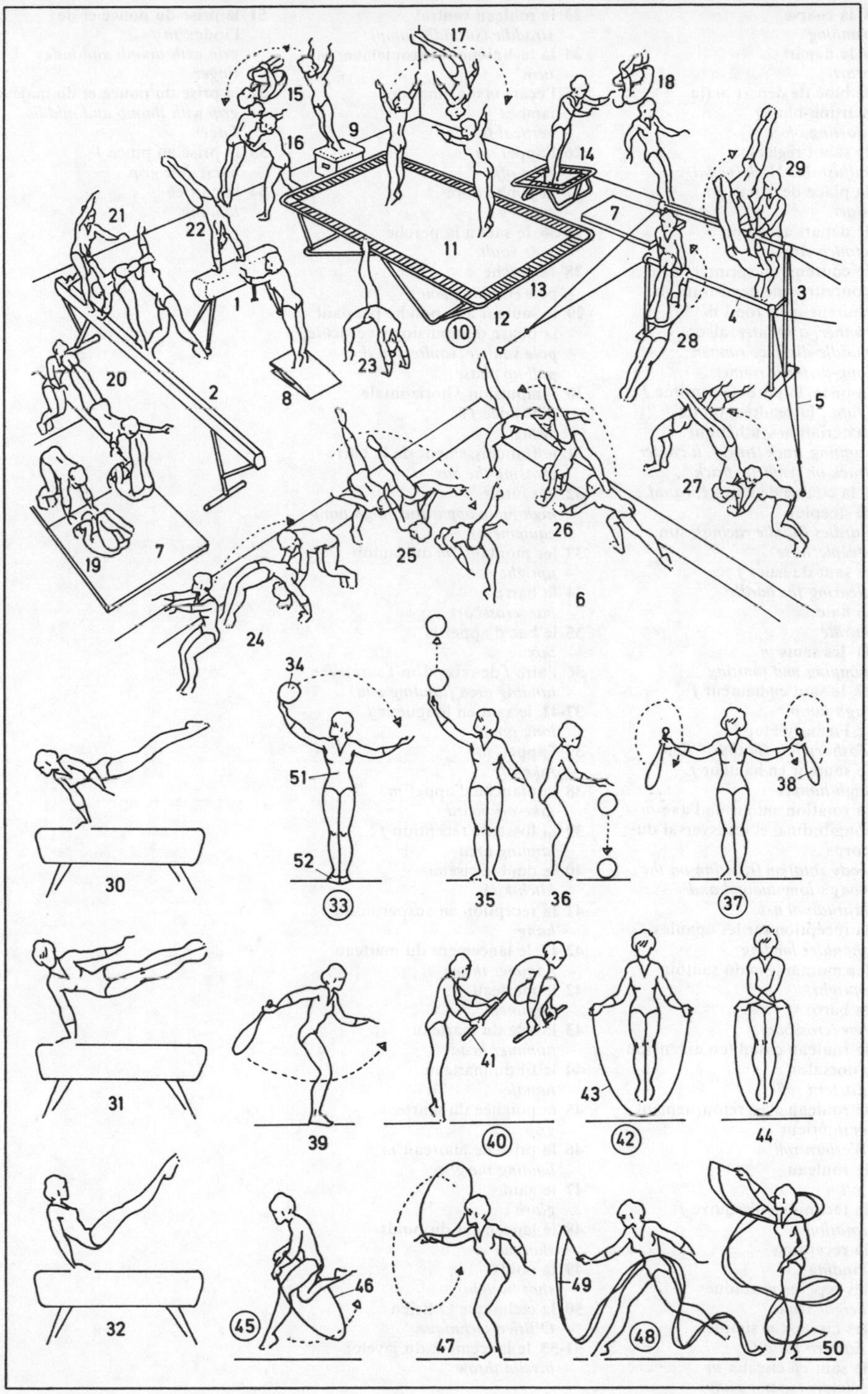
1
2
3
4
5
6
7
7
8
9
10
11
12
13
14
15
16
17
18
19
20
21
22
23
24
25
26
27
28
29
30
31
32
33
34
35
36
37
38
39
40
41
42
43
44
45
46
47
48
49
50
51
52

1-8 la course
– ***running***
1-6 le départ
– *start*
1 le bloc de départ *m* (le starting-block)
– *starting block*
2 le sabot réglable
– *adjustable block (pedal)*
3 la place de départ *m*
– *start*
4 le départ accroupi
– *crouch start*
5 le coureur, un sprinter; *égal.:* coureur *m* de demi-fond *m*, coureur *m* de fond *m*
– *runner, a sprinter;* also: *middle-distance runner, long-distance runner*
6 la piste, la piste de cendrée *f* (*fam.:* la cendrée) ou de matériau *m* synthétique
– *running track (track), a cinder track or synthetic track*
7-8 la course de haies *f*; (*anal.:* le steeple)
– *hurdles (hurdle racing);* sim.: *steeplechase*
7 le saut de haies *f*
– *clearing the hurdle*
8 la haie
– *hurdle*
9-41 les sauts *m*
– ***jumping and vaulting***
9-27 le saut en hauteur *f*
– *high jump*
9 le Fosbury Flop
– *Fosbury flop (Fosbury, flop)*
10 le sauteur en hauteur *f*
– *high jumper*
11 la rotation autour de l'axe *m* longitudinal et transversal du corps
– *body rotation (rotation on the body's longitudinal and latitudinal axes)*
12 la réception sur les épaules *f*
– *shoulder landing*
13 les montants *m* du sautoir
– *upright*
14 la barre
– *bar (crossbar)*
15 le rouleau costal (en extension *f* dorsale)
– *Eastern roll*
16 le rouleau avec retournement *m* intérieur
– *Western roll*
17 le rouleau
– *roll*
18 la technique d'esquive *f*
– *rotation*
19 la réception
– *landing*
20 les repères *m* gradués
– *height scale*
21 les ciseaux *m* simples
– *Eastern cut-off*
22 le saut en ciseaux *m*
– *scissors (scissor jump)*
23 le rouleau ventral
– *straddle (straddle jump)*
24 la technique d'enroulement *m*
– *turn*
25 l'écart *m* maximal des jambes *f*
– *vertical free leg*
26 l'appel *m*
– *take-off*
27 la jambe libre
– *free leg*
28-36 le saut à la perche
– *pole vault*
28 la perche
– *pole (vaulting pole)*
29 le sauteur à la perche pendant la phase d'impulsion *f* verticale
– *pole vaulter (vaulter) in the pull-up phase*
30 l'impulsion *f* horizontale (l'esquive *f*)
– *swing*
31 le franchissement de la barre
– *crossing the bar*
32 le sautoir
– *high jump apparatus (high jump equipment)*
33 les montants *m* du sautoir
– *upright*
34 la barre
– *bar (crossbar)*
35 le bac d'appel *m*
– *box*
36 l'aire *f* de réception *f* surélevée
– *landing area (landing pad)*
37-41 le saut en longueur *f*
– *long jump*
37 l'appel *m*
– *take-off*
38 la planche d'appel *m*
– *take-off board*
39 la fosse de réception *f*
– *landing area*
40 le double ciseau
– *hitch-kick*
41 la réception en suspension *f*
– *hang*
42-47 le lancement du marteau
– *hammer throw*
42 le marteau
– *hammer*
43 la tête du marteau
– *hammer head*
44 le fil du marteau
– *handle*
45 la poignée du marteau
– *grip*
46 la prise de marteau *m*
– *holding the grip*
47 le gant
– *glove*
48 le lancement du poids
– *shot put*
49 le poids
– *shot (weight)*
50 la technique O'Brien
– *O'Brien technique*
51-53 le lancement du javelot
– *javelin throw*
51 la prise du pouce et de l'index *m*
– *grip with thumb and index finger*
52 la prise du pouce et du majeur
– *grip with thumb and middle finger*
53 la prise en pince *f*
– *horseshoe grip*
54 la cordée
– *binding*

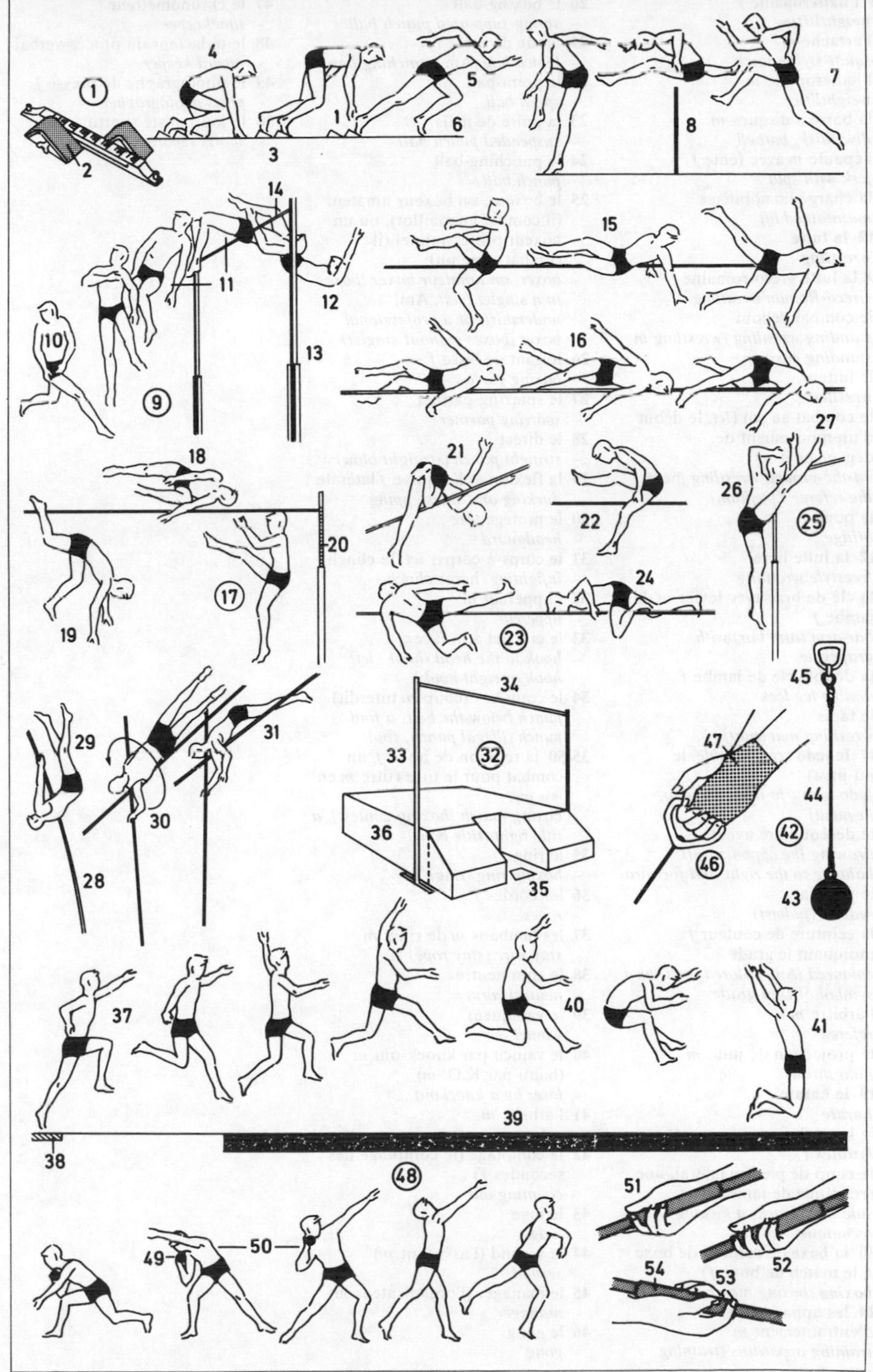
1
2
3
4
5
6
7
8
9
10
11
12
13
14
15
16
17
18
19
20
21
22
23
24
25
26
27
28
29
30
31
32
33
34
35
36
37
38
39
40
41
42
43
44
45
46
47
48
49
50
51
52
53
54

1-5 l'haltérophilie *f*
– ***weightlifting***
1 l'arraché *m*
– *squat-style snatch*
2 l'haltérophile *m*
– *weightlifter*
3 la barre à disques *m*
– *disc (disk) barbell*
4 l'épaulé *m* avec fente *f*
– *jerk with split*
5 la charge immobilisée
– *maintained lift*
6-12 la lutte
– ***wrestling***
6-9 la lutte gréco-romaine
– *Greco-Roman wrestling*
6 le combat debout
– *standing wrestling (wrestling in standing position)*
7 le lutteur
– *wrestler*
8 le combat au sol (*ici:* le début d'un mouvement de dégagement *m*)
– *on-the-ground wrestling (*here: *the referee's position)*
9 le pont
– *bridge*
10-12 la lutte libre
– *freestyle wrestling*
10 la clé de bras avec levier *m* de jambe *f*
– *bar arm (arm bar) with grapevine*
11 la double clé de jambe *f*
– *double leg lock*
12 le tapis
– *wrestling mat (mat)*
13-17 le judo (*comparable:* le jiu-jitsu)
– ***judo*** (sim.: *ju-jitsu, jiu jitsu, ju-jutsu)*
13 le déséquilibre avant
– *drawing the opponent off balance to the right and forward*
14 le judoka
– *judoka (judoist)*
15 la ceinture de couleur *f* indiquant le grade
– *coloured (*Am. *colored) belt, as a symbol of Dan grade*
16 l'arbitre *m*
– *referee*
17 la projection de judo *m*
– *judo throw*
18-19 le karaté
– ***karate***
18 le karateka
– *karateka*
19 le coup de pied *m* latéral, une technique de jambe *f*
– *side thrust kick, a kicking technique*
20-50 la boxe (le combat de boxe *f*, le match de boxe *f*)
– ***boxing*** *(boxing match)*
20-24 les appareils *m* d'entraînement *m*
– *training apparatus (training equipment)*
20 le boxing-ball
– *spring-supported punch ball*
21 le sac de sable *m*
– *punch bag (*Am. *punching bag)*
22 le point-ball
– *speed ball*
23 la poire de maïs
– *suspended punch ball*
24 le punching-ball
– *punch ball*
25 le boxeur, un boxeur amateur (il combat en maillot), ou un boxeur professionnel (il combat torse nu)
– *boxer, an amateur boxer (boxes in a singlet, vest,* Am. *undershirt) or a professional boxer (boxes without singlet)*
26 le gant de boxe *f*
– *boxing glove*
27 le sparring-partner
– *sparring partner*
28 le direct
– *straight punch (straight blow)*
29 la flexion et l'esquive *f* latérale
– *ducking and sidestepping*
30 le protège-tête
– *headguard*
31 le corps-à-corps; *ici:* le clinch
– *infighting;* here: *clinch*
32 l'uppercut *m*
– *uppercut*
33 le crochet à la face
– *hook to the head (hook, left hook or right hook)*
34 le coup bas (coup *m* interdit)
– *punch below the belt, a foul punch (illegal punch, foul)*
35-50 la réunion de boxe *f*, un combat pour le titre (titre *m* en jeu *m*)
– *boxing match (boxing contest), a title fight (title bout)*
35 le ring
– *boxing ring (ring)*
36 les cordes *f*
– *ropes*
37 les haubans *m* de ring *m*
– *stay wire (stay rope)*
38 le coin neutre
– *neutral corner*
39 le vainqueur
– *winner*
40 le vaincu par knock-out *m* (battu par K.O. *m*)
– *loser by a knockout*
41 l'arbitre *m*
– *referee*
42 le comptage (le comptage des secondes *f*)
– *counting out*
43 le juge
– *judge*
44 le second (l'assistant *m*)
– *second*
45 le manager (l'organisateur *m*)
– *manager*
46 le gong
– *gong*
47 le chronométreur
– *timekeeper*
48 le rédacteur du procès-verbal
– *record keeper*
49 le photographe de presse *f*
– *press photographer*
50 le journaliste sportif
– *sports reporter (reporter)*

1
2
3
4
5
6
7
8
9
10
11
12
13
14
15
16
17
18
19
20
21
22
23
24
25
26
27
28
29
30
31
32
33
34
35
36
37
38
39
40
41
42
43
44
45
46
47
48
49
50

1-57 l'alpinisme *m* (la randonnée de haute montagne *f*)
– ***mountaineering*** *(mountain climbing, Alpinism)*
1 le refuge (l'abri *m*)
– *hut (Alpine Club hut, mountain hut, base)*
2-13 l'escalade *f* (l'escalade *f* de rocher *m*) [la technique de rocher *m*, la varappe]
– ***climbing*** *(rock climbing) [rock climbing technique]*
2 la paroi rocheuse (le mur, la dalle rocheuse)
– *rock face (rock wall)*
3 la fissure (horizontale, verticale ou oblique)
– *fissure (vertical, horizontal, or diagonal fissure)*
4 la vire (rocheuse, herbeuse, caillouteuse, neigeuse ou de glace *f*)
– *ledge (rock ledge, grass ledge, scree ledge, snow ledge, ice ledge)*
5 l'alpiniste *m*
– *mountaineer (climber, mountain climber, Alpinist)*
6 l'anorak *m* (le blouson matelassé)
– *anorak (high-altitude anorak, snowshirt, padded jacket)*
7 la culotte d'escalade *f*
– *breeches (climbing breeches)*
8 la cheminée
– *chimney*
9 le becquet (la pointe rocheuse)
– *belay (spike, rock spike)*
10 l'auto-assurance *f*
– *belay*
11 la boucle d'assurance *f*
– *rope sling (sling)*
12 la corde d'alpinisme *m*
– *rope*
13 la plate-forme
– *spur*
14-21 la progression sur glace *f*
– ***snow and ice climbing*** *[snow and ice climbing technique]*
14 la paroi glaciaire (la paroi de glace *f*)
– *ice slope (firn slope)*
15 l'alpiniste *m* sur une paroi de glace *f*
– *snow and ice climber*
16 le piolet
– *ice axe* (Am. *ax)*
17 la marche (la marche taillée dans la glace)
– *step (ice step)*
18 les lunettes *f* de glacier *m*
– *snow goggles*
19 la capuche (le capuchon de l'anorak *m*)
– *hood (anorak hood)*
20 la corniche
– *cornice (snow cornice)*
21 l'arête *f* (l'arête *f* glaciaire)
– *ridge (ice ridge)*
22-27 la cordée [la traversée en cordée *f*]
– ***rope*** *(roped party)*
22 le glacier
– *glacier*
23 la crevasse
– *crevasse*
24 le pont de neige *f*
– *snow bridge*
25 le premier de cordée *f*
– *leader*
26 l'alpiniste *m* en second
– *second man (belayer)*
27 le dernier de cordée *f*
– *third man*
28-30 la descente en rappel *m* (le rappel)
– ***roping down*** *(abseiling, rapelling)*
28 la boucle de rappel *m*
– *abseil sling*
29 la descente avec freinage *m* du pied
– *sling seat*
30 la méthode Dulfer (le rappel en Dulfer)
– *Dülfer seat*
31-57 l'équipement *m* **de l'alpiniste** *m* (équipement *m* de haute montagne *f*, équipement *m* pour la course de rocher *m* ou de glace *f*)
– ***mountaineering equipment*** *(climbing equipment, snow and ice climbing equipment)*
31 le piolet
– *ice axe* (Am. *ax)*
32 la dragonne
– *wrist sling*
33 la pique
– *pick*
34 la panne
– *adze* (Am. *adz)*
35 l'œilleton *m*
– *karabiner hole*
36 le piolet pour course *f* de glace *f* (piolet *m* à ancrage *m*)
– *short-shafted ice axe* (Am. *ax)*
37 le marteau-piolet (marteau *m* pour courses *f* mixtes, neige *f* et glace *f*)
– *hammer axe* (Am. *ax)*
38 le piton universel
– *general-purpose piton*
39 le piton de rappel *m* (piton à anneau *m*)
– *abseil piton (ringed piton)*
40 la broche à glace *f* (broche *f* tire-bouchon)
– *ice piton (semi-tubular screw ice piton, corkscrew piton)*
41 la broche crantée (broche *f* à glace *f*)
– *drive-in ice piton*
42 la chaussure de montagne *f*
– *mountaineering boot*
43 la semelle profilée
– *corrugated sole*
44 la chaussure d'escalade *f*
– *climbing boot*
45 la pointe en caoutchouc *m* renforcé
– *roughened stiff rubber upper*
46 le mousqueton
– *karabiner*
47 la fermeture à vis *f*
– *screwgate*
48 les crampons *m* à dix ou à douze pointes *f*
– *crampons (lightweight crampons, twelve-point crampons, ten-point crampons)*
49 les pointes *f* d'attaque *f*
– *front points*
50 le protège-pointes
– *point guards*
51 les lanières *f* de fixation *f*
– *crampon strap*
52 la fixation à câble *m*
– *crampon cable fastener*
53 le casque
– *safety helmet (protective helmet)*
54 la lampe frontale
– *helmet lamp*
55 les guêtres *f* de montagne *f* (les manchons-guêtres *m*)
– *snow gaiters*
56 le baudrier
– *climbing harness*
57 le harnais pelvien
– *sit harness*

1
2
3
4
5
6
7
8
9
10
11
12
13
14
15
16
17
18
19
20
21
22
23
24
25
26
27
28
29
30
31
32
33
34
35
36
37
38
39
40
41
42
43
44
45
46
47
48
49
50
51
52
53
54
55
56
57

1-72 le ski
– *skiing*
1 le ski compact
– *compact ski*
2 la fixation de sécurité *f*
– *safety binding (release binding)*
3 la lanière (la courroie de sécurité *f*)
– *strap*
4 la carre d'acier *m*
– *steel edge*
5 le bâton de ski *m*
– *ski stick (ski pole)*
6 la poignée du bâton
– *grip*
7 la dragonne
– *loop*
8 la rondelle (le disque)
– *basket*
9 la combinaison de ski *m* pour dames *f*
– *ladies' one-piece ski suit*
10 le bonnet de ski *m*
– *skiing cap (ski cap)*
11 les lunettes *f* de ski *m*
– *skiing goggles*
12 la chaussure monocoque
– *cemented sole skiing boot*
13 le casque de ski *m*
– *crash helmet*
14-20 l'équipement *m* de ski *m* de fond *m*
– *cross-country equipment*
14 le ski de fond *m*
– *cross-country ski*
15 la fixation rottefella
– *cross-country rat trap binding*
16 la chaussure de ski *m* de fond *m*
– *cross-country boot*
17 la combinaison de fond *m*
– *cross-country gear*
18 la casquette de ski *m*
– *peaked cap*
19 les lunettes *f* de soleil *m*
– *sunglasses*
20 les bâtons *m* Tonkin Bambou de ski *m* de fond *m*
– *cross-country poles made of bamboo*
21-24 le matériel de fartage *m*
– *ski-waxing equipment*
21 le fart
– *ski wax*
22 la lampe de fartage *m* (le skiwaxer)
– *waxing iron (blowlamp, blowtorch)*
23 l'applicateur *m* en liège *m*
– *waxing cork*
24 le grattoir en métal *m*
– *wax scraper*
25 le bâton de compétition *f*
– *downhill racing pole*
26 le pas de montée *f* (pas *m* alternatif)
– *herringbone, for climbing a slope*
27 la montée en escalier *m*
– *sidestep, for climbing a slope*
28 la sacoche «banane» *f*
– *ski bag*
29 le slalom
– *slalom*
30 le piquet de porte *f*
– *gate pole*
31 la combinaison de compétition *f*
– *racing suit*
32 la descente
– *downhill racing*
33 «l'œuf» *m*, la position de recherche *f* de vitesse *f*
– *'egg' position, the ideal downhill racing position*
34 le ski de descente *f*
– *downhill ski*
35 le saut
– *ski jumping*
36 le sauteur en vol *m*
– *lean forward*
37 le dossard
– *number*
38 le ski de saut *m*
– *ski jumping ski*
39 les rainures *f* de guidage *m* (3 à 5 rainures *f*)
– *grooves (3 to 5 grooves)*
40 la fixation à câble *m*
– *cable binding*
41 la chaussure de saut *m*
– *ski jumping boots*
42 le ski de fond *m*
– *cross-country*
43 la combinaison de ski *m* de fond *m*
– *cross-country stretch-suit*
44 la trace
– *course*
45 les fanions *m* de balisage *m*
– *course-marking flag*
46 les différentes strates *f* d'un ski moderne
– *layers of a modern ski*
47 le noyau
– *special core*
48 les lames *f*
– *laminates*
49 la lame d'amortissement *m*
– *stabilizing layer (stabilizer)*
50 la carre d'acier *m*
– *steel edge*
51 la carre supérieure en aluminium *m*
– *aluminium (*Am.* aluminum) upper edge*
52 la semelle de polyester *m*
– *synthetic bottom (artificial bottom)*
53 l'anticroiseur *m*
– *safety jet*
54-56 les éléments *m* de la fixation
– *parts of the binding*
54 la talonnière
– *automatic heel unit*
55 la butée
– *toe unit*
56 le frein
– *ski stop*
57-63 les remontées *f* mécaniques
– *ski lift*
57 le télésiège biplace
– *double chair lift*
58 la barre de protection *f* avec repose-pieds *m*
– *safety bar with footrest*
59 le téléski (le monte-pente; *fam.*: le tire-fesses)
– *ski lift*
60 la trace
– *track*
61 la suspente
– *hook*
62 le boîtier d'enroulement *m* du cordon
– *automatic cable pulley*
63 le câble tracteur
– *haulage cable*
64 la course de slalom *m*
– *slalom*
65 la porte ouverte
– *open gate*
66 la porte verticale aveugle (fermée)
– *closed vertical gate*
67 la porte verticale ouverte
– *open vertical gate*
68 la salvis
– *transversal chicane*
69 l'épingle *f* à cheveux *m*
– *hairpin*
70 la double porte verticale décalée
– *elbow*
71 le couloir
– *corridor*
72 la chicane Allais
– *Allais chicane*

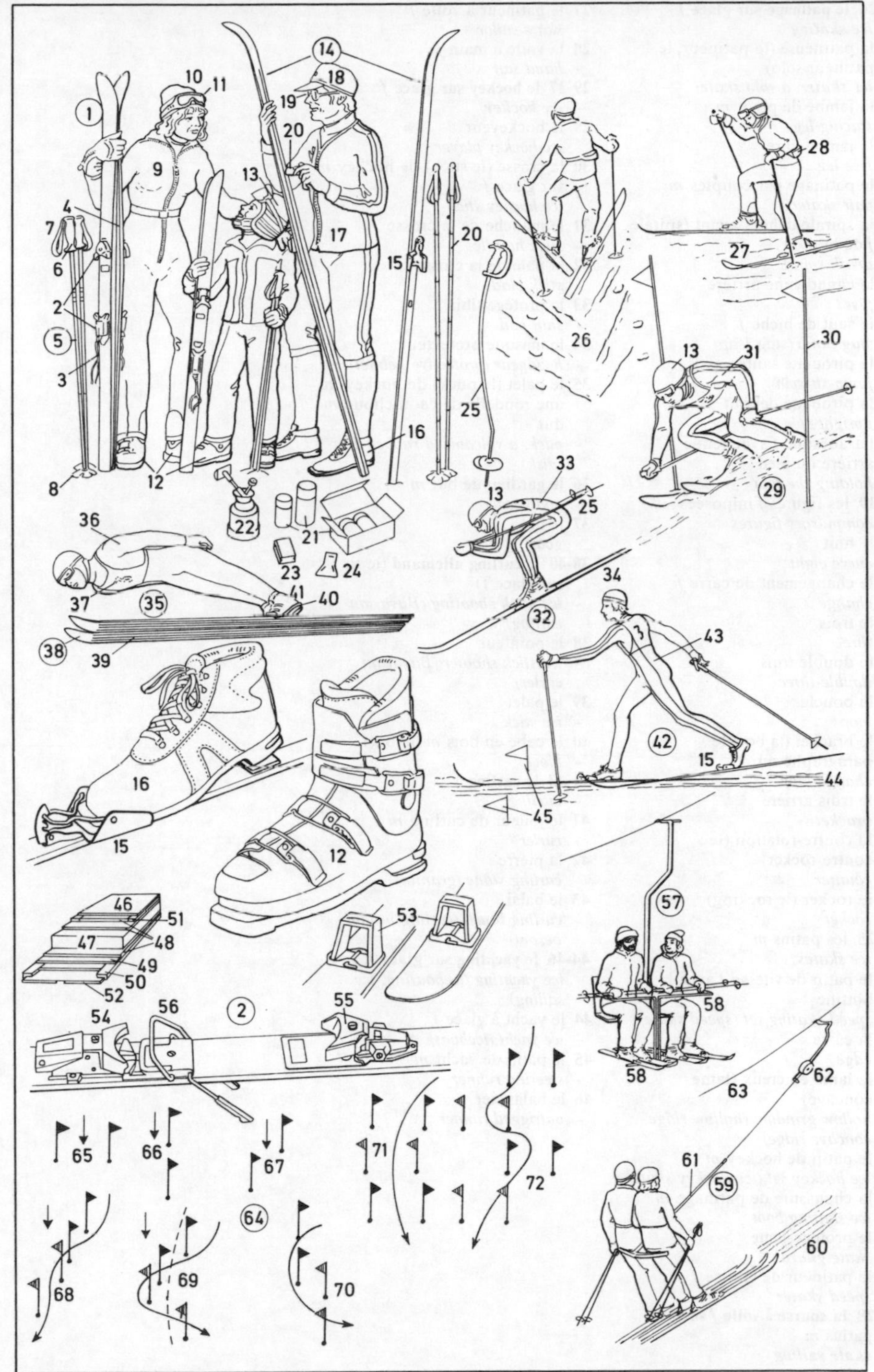
1
2
3
4
5
6
7
8
9
10
11
12
13
14
15
16
17
18
19
20
21
22
23
24
25
26
27
28
29
30
31
32
33
34
35
36
37
38
39
40
41
42
43
44
45
46
47
48
49
50
51
52
53
54
55
56
57
58
59
60
61
62
63
64
65
66
67
68
69
70
71
72

1-26 le patinage sur glace *f*
– ***ice skating***
1 la patineuse (le patineur, le patineur solo)
– *ice skater, a solo skater*
2 la jambe de pivot *m*
– *tracing leg*
3 la jambe libre
– *free leg*
4 le patinage par couples *m*
– *pair skaters*
5 la spirale dehors avant (spirale *f* de la mort)
– *death spiral*
6 la canadienne arrière
– *pivot*
7 le saut de biche *f*
– *stag jump (stag leap)*
8 la pirouette sautée assise
– *jump-sit-spin*
9 la pirouette debout
– *upright spin*
10 l'arabesque *f* avec tenue *f* arrière du pied
– *holding the foot*
11-19 les figures *f* imposées
– *compulsory figures*
11 le huit
– *curve eight*
12 le changement de carre *f*
– *change*
13 le trois
– *three*
14 le double trois
– *double-three*
15 la boucle
– *loop*
16 le bracket (la boucle paragraphe *m*)
– *change-loop*
17 le trois arrière
– *bracket*
18 la contre-rotation (le contre-rocker)
– *counter*
19 le rocker (le rocking)
– *rocker*
20-25 les patins *m*
– *ice skates*
20 le patin de vitesse *f* avec la bottine
– *speed skating set (speed skate)*
21 la carre
– *edge*
22 la lame en creux (lame concave)
– *hollow grinding (hollow ridge, concave ridge)*
23 le patin de hockey *m*
– *ice hockey set (ice hockey skate)*
24 la chaussure de patinage *m*
– *ice skating boot*
25 le protège-lame
– *skate guard*
26 le patineur de vitesse *f*
– *speed skater*
27-28 la course à voile *f* sur patins *m*
– ***skate sailing***
27 le patineur à voile *f*
– *skate sailor*
28 la voile à main *f*
– *hand sail*
29-37 le hockey sur glace *f*
– ***ice hockey***
29 le hockeyeur
– *ice hockey player*
30 la crosse (le stick) de hockey *m* sur glace *f*
– *ice hockey stick*
31 le manche de la crosse
– *stick handle*
32 la pale de la crosse
– *stick blade*
33 le protège-tibia
– *shin pad*
34 le masque protecteur
– *headgear (protective helmet)*
35 le palet (le puck) de hockey *m*, une rondelle de caoutchouc *m* dur
– *puck, a vulcanized rubber disc (disk)*
36 le gardien de but *m*
– *goalkeeper*
37 le but
– *goal*
38-40 le curling allemand (le tir sur glace *f*)
– ***ice-stick shooting*** *(Bavarian curling)*
38 le pointeur
– *ice-stick shooter (Bavarian curler)*
39 le palet
– *ice stick*
40 le cube en bois *m* (le but)
– *block*
41-43 le curling
– ***curling***
41 le joueur de curling *m*
– *curler*
42 la pierre
– *curling stone (granite)*
43 le balai
– *curling brush (curling broom, besom)*
44-46 le yachting sur glace *f*
– ***ice yachting*** *(iceboating, ice sailing)*
44 le yacht à glace *f*
– *ice yacht (iceboat)*
45 le patin de yacht *m*
– *steering runner*
46 le balancier
– *outrigged runner*

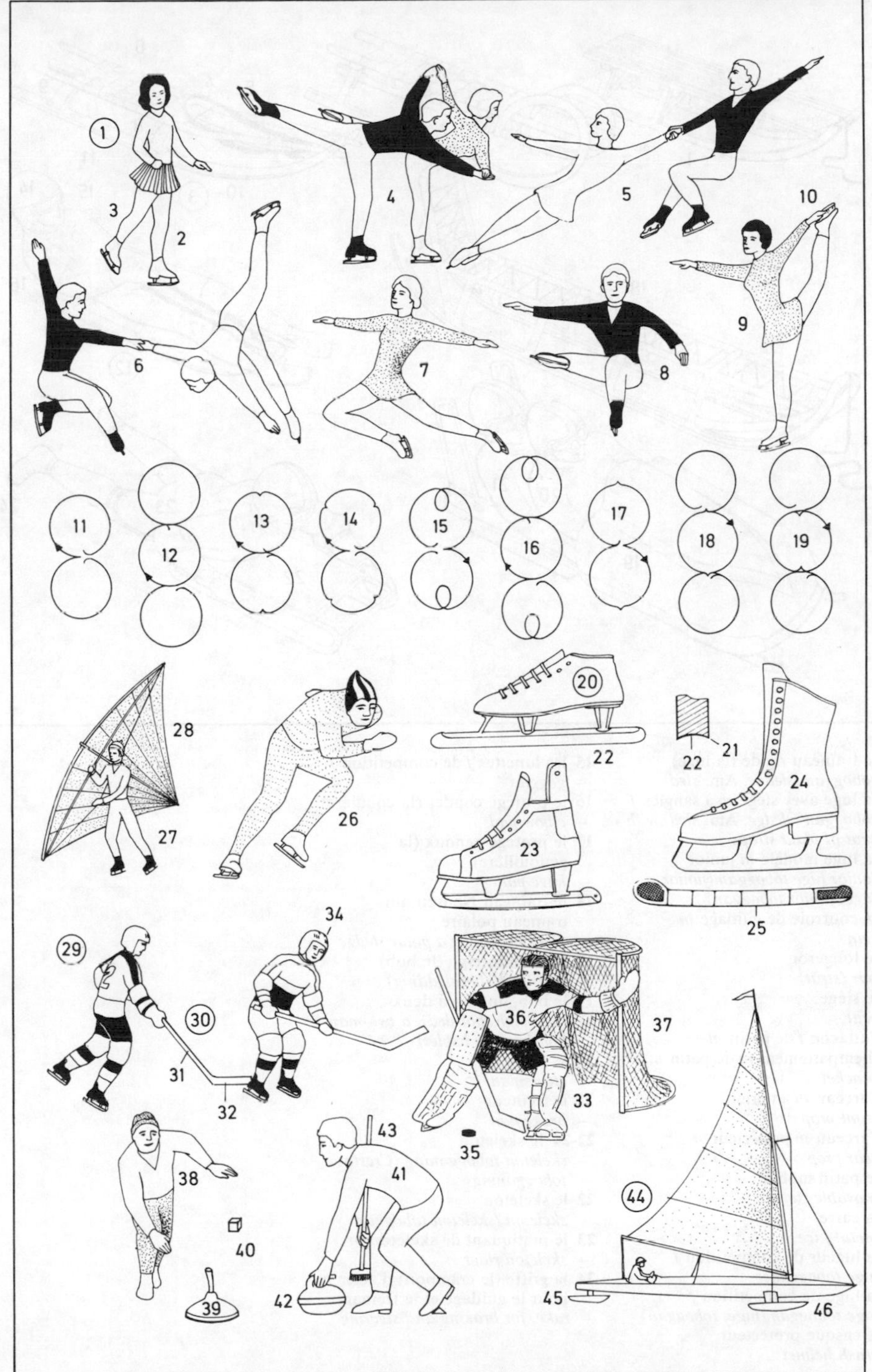
1
3
2
4
5
10
6
7
8
9
11
12
13
14
15
16
17
18
19
20
28
21
22
22
27
26
24
23
25
29
34
30
36
37
31
32
33
35
38
43
41
44
40
39
42
45
46

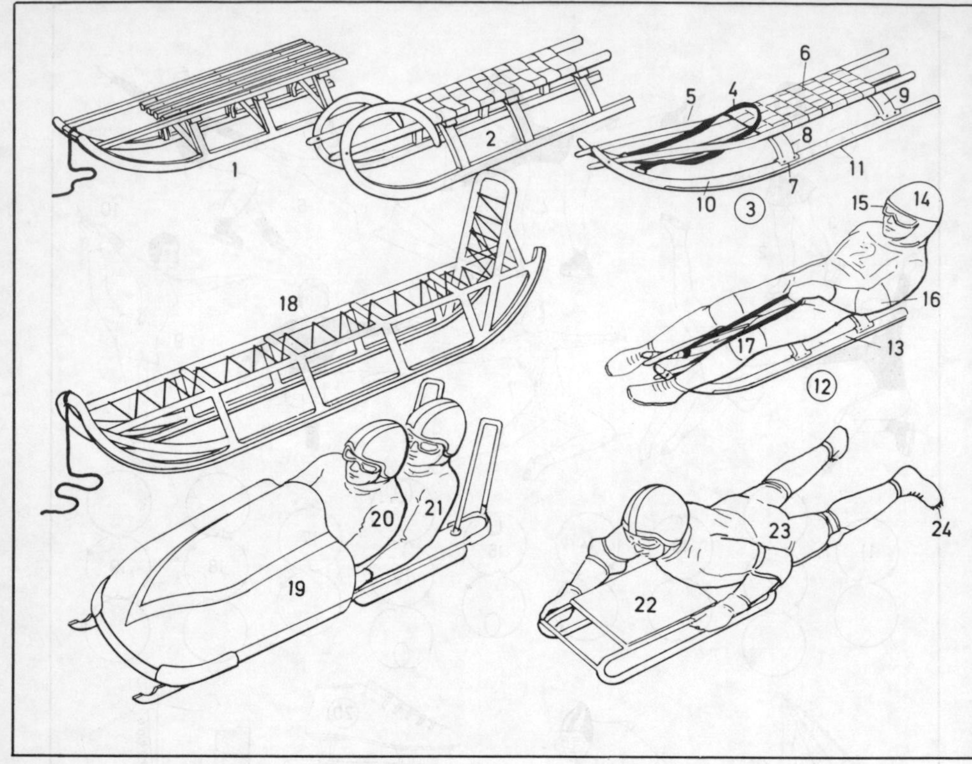

1 le traîneau rigide (la luge)
– *toboggan (sledge,* Am. *sled)*
2 la luge avec siège *m* à sangles *f*
– *toboggan (sledge,* Am. *sled) with seat of plaid straps*
3 la luge modèle *m* junior
– *junior luge toboggan (junior luge, junior toboggan)*
4 la courroie de guidage *m*
– *rein*
5 le longeron
– *bar (strut)*
6 le siège
– *seat*
7 l'attache *f* de patin *m* (l'empattement *m* de patin *m*)
– *bracket*
8 l'arceau *m* antérieur
– *front prop*
9 l'arceau *m* postérieur
– *rear prop*
10 le patin mobile
– *movable runner*
11 la carre
– *metal face*
12 le lugeur de compétition *f*
– *luge tobogganer*
13 la luge de compétition *f*
– *luge toboggan (luge, toboggan)*
14 le casque protecteur
– *crash helmet*
15 les lunettes *f* de compétition *f*
– *goggles*
16 le protège-coudes (la coudière)
– *elbow pad*
17 le protège-genoux (la genouillère)
– *knee pad*
18 le traîneau Nansen, un traîneau polaire
– *Nansen sledge, a polar sledge*
19-21 le bobsleigh (le bob)
– *bobsleigh (bobsledding)*
19 le bob, un bob à deux
– *bobsleigh (bobsled), a two-man bobsleigh (a boblet)*
20 le capitaine
– *steersman*
21 le freineur
– *brakeman*
22-24 le skeleton
– *skeleton tobogganing (Cresta tobogganing)*
22 le skeleton
– *skeleton (skeleton toboggan)*
23 le pratiquant de skeleton *m*
– *skeleton rider*
24 la griffe (le crampon) d'acier *m* pour le guidage et le freinage
– *rake, for braking and steering*

1 l'avalanche *f* de neige *f*; *var.*: l'avalanche *f* de poudreuse *f*, l'avalanche *f* de fond *m*
– *avalanche (snow avalanche,* Am. *snowslide);* kinds: *wind avalanche, ground avalanche*

2 le pare-avalanche, un mur de déviation *f* (un mur d'arrêt *m*); *anal.*: le déflecteur, le coin freineur
– *avalanche wall, a deflecting wall (diverting wall);* sim.: *avalanche wedge*

3 la galerie pare-avalanche (le toit à neige *f*)
– *avalanche gallery*

4 la tempête de neige *f*
– *snowfall*

5 la congère
– *snowdrift*

6 le chevalet freineur (le râtelier)
– *snow fence*

7 la forêt de protection *f*
– *avalanche forest [planted as protection against avalanches]*

8 le camion de voirie *f*
– *street-cleaning lorry (street cleaner)*

9 l'élément *m* chasse-neige
– *snow plough (*Am. *snowplow) attachment*

10 les chaînes *f* antidérapantes
– *snow chain (skid chain, tyre chain,* Am. *tire chain)*

11 le couvre-radiateur
– *radiator bonnet (*Am. *radiator hood)*

12 le volet aérateur et le rideau de radiateur *m*
– *radiator shutter and shutter opening (louvre shutter)*

13 le bonhomme de neige *f*
– *snowman*

14 la bataille de boules *f* de neige *f*
– *snowball fight*

15 la boule de neige *f*
– *snowball*

16 le vélo des neiges *f*
– *ski bob*

17 la glissoire
– *slide*

18 le garçonnet effectuant une glissade
– *boy, sliding*

19 le verglas
– *icy surface (icy ground)*

20 la couche de neige *f* sur le toit
– *covering of snow, on the roof*

21 le glaçon (la stalactite)
– *icicle*

22 le balayeur de neige *f*
– *man clearing snow*

23 la pelle à neige *f*
– *snow push (snow shovel)*

24 le tas de neige *f*
– *heap of snow*

25 le traîneau à chevaux *m*
– *horse-drawn sleigh (horse sleigh)*

26 les grelots *m* (les sonnailles *f*)
– *sleigh bells (bells, set of bells)*

27 la chancelière
– *foot muff (*Am. *foot bag)*

28 le couvre-oreilles (le protège-oreilles)
– *earmuff*

29 le fauteuil-traîneau
– *handsledge (tread sledge);* sim.: *push sledge*

30 la neige fondante
– *slush*

1-13 le jeu de quilles *f* (la quille Saint-Gall, la quille à neuf)
– ***skittles***
1-11 la disposition des quilles *f*
– *skittle frame*
1 la quille de tête *f*
– *front pin (front)*
2 la quille de passage *m* avant gauche, une servante
– *left front second pin (left front second)*
3 le passage avant gauche
– *running three [left]*
4 la quille de passage *m* avant droit, une servante
– *right front second pin (right front second)*
5 le passage avant droit
– *running three [right]*
6 la quille coin *m* arrière gauche, un valet
– *left corner pin (left corner), a corner (copper)*
7 le roi
– *landlord*
8 la quille coin *m* arrière droit, un valet
– *right corner pin (right corner), a corner (copper)*
9 la quille de passage *m* arrière gauche, une servante
– *back left second pin (back left second)*
10 la quille de passage *m* arrière droit, une servante
– *back right second pin (back right second)*
11 la quille de coin *m* arrière
– *back pin (back)*
12 la quille
– *pin*
13 la quille du milieu
– *landlord*
14-20 le bowling
– ***tenpin bowling***
14 la disposition des quilles *f*
– *frame*
15 la boule à trous *m*
– *bowling ball (ball with finger holes)*
16 le trou pour la prise
– *finger hole*
17-20 les lancers *m*
– *deliveries*
17 le lancer droit
– *straight ball*
18 le crochet
– *hook ball (hook)*
19 la courbe
– *curve*
20 la courbe inverse
– *back-up ball (back-up)*
21 le jeu de boules *f*; *anal.:* la boccia italienne, les bowls anglais
– ***boules;*** sim.: *Italian game of boccie, green bowls (bowls)*
22 le joueur de boules *f*
– *boules player*
23 le cochonnet
– *jack (target jack)*
24 la boule métallique striée
– *grooved boule*
25 le groupe de joueurs *m*
– *group of players*
26 le tir à la carabine
– ***rifle shooting***
27-29 les positions *f* de tir *m*
– *shooting positions*
27 la position de tir «debout»
– *standing position*
28 la position de tir «à genoux»
– *kneeling position*
29 la position de tir «couché»
– *prone position*
30-33 les cibles *f* de tir *m* (les cartons-cibles)
– *targets*
30 la cible pour le tir à 50 mètres *m*
– *target for 50 m events (50 m target)*
31 le cordon
– *circle*
32 la cible pour le tir à 100 mètres *m*
– *target for 100 m events (100 m target)*
33 la cible mobile (le sanglier courant)
– *bobbing target (turning target, running-boar target)*
34-39 les munitions *f*
– *ammunition*
34 la balle à air *m* (le diabolo) pour carabine *f* à air *m*
– *air rifle cartridge*
35 la cartouche à percussion *f* annulaire pour carabine courte
– *rimfire cartridge for zimmerstutzen (indoor target rifle), a smallbore German single-shot rifle*
36 la douille
– *case head*
37 la balle ronde
– *caseless round*
38 la cartouche calibre *m* 22 *long rifle*
– *.22 long rifle cartridge*
39 la cartouche calibre *m* 222 *Remington*
– *.222 Remington cartridge*
40-49 les carabines *f* de compétition *f*
– *sporting rifles*
40 la carabine à air *m*
– *air rifle*
41 le dioptre (l'œilleton)
– *optical sight*
42 le guidon
– *front sight (foresight)*
43 l'arme *f* standard de petit calibre *m*
– *smallbore standard rifle*
44 l'arme *f* libre de petit calibre *m*
– *international smallbore free rifle*
45 le cale-main pour la visée debout
– *palm rest for standing position*
46 l'arceau *m* de la plaque de couche *f*
– *butt plate with hook*
47 la crosse à trou *m*
– *butt with thumb hole*
48 la carabine de petit calibre *m* pour le tir au sanglier *m* courant
– *smallbore rifle for bobbing target (turning target)*
49 la lunette de visée *f*
– *telescopic sight (riflescope, telescope sight)*
50 le dioptre de visée avec guidon *m* à trou *m*
– *optical ring sight*
51 le dioptre de visée *f* avec guidon *m* à lame *f*
– *optical ring and bead sight*
52-66 le tir à l'arc *m*
– ***archery*** *(target archery)*
52 l'armé *m*
– *shot*
53 le tireur à l'arc *m* (l'archer *m*)
– *archer*
54 l'arc *m* de compétition *f*
– *competition bow*
55 la branche
– *riser*
56 le viseur (la hausse)
– *point-of-aim mark*
57 la poignée
– *grip (handle)*
58 le stabilisateur
– *stabilizer*
59 la corde de l'arc *m*
– *bow string (string)*
60 la flèche
– *arrow*
61 la pointe de la flèche
– *pile (point) of the arrow*
62 l'empennage *m*
– *fletching*
63 l'encoche *f*
– *nock*
64 le fût (le tube)
– *shaft*
65 les marques *f* du tireur
– *cresting*
66 la cible
– *target*
67 la **pelote** basque
– *Basque game of* ***pelota*** *(jai alai)*
68 le joueur de pelote *f* basque
– *pelota player*
69 la chistera
– *wicker basket (cesta)*
70-78 la fosse olympique (le skeet, le tir au pigeon *m*, le ball-trap)
– ***skeet*** *(skeet shooting), a kind of clay pigeon shooting*
70 le superposé de skeet *m*
– *skeet over-and-under shotgun*
71 la bouche du canon avec l'alésage *m* spécial pour tir *m* au pigeon *m*
– *muzzle with skeet choke*
72 la position de préparation *f* (la position de chasse *f*)
– *ready position on call*
73 l'arme *f* en joue *f*
– *firing position*
74 le terrain de skeet *m*
– *shooting range*
75 la cabine haute
– *high house*
76 la cabine basse
– *low house*
77 la trajectoire du plateau
– *target's path*
78 le poste de tir *m*
– *shooting station (shooting box)*
79 la roue américaine
– ***aero wheel***
80 la poignée
– *handle*
81 le repose-pied
– *footrest*
82 le karting
– ***go-karting*** *(karting)*
83 le kart
– *go-kart (kart)*
84 la plaque avec le numéro de départ *m*
– *number plate (number)*
85 les pédales *f*
– *pedals*
86 le pneu lisse
– *pneumatic tyre* (Am. *tire)*
87 le réservoir d'essence *f*
– *petrol tank* (Am. *gasoline tank)*
88 le cadre (le châssis)
– *frame*
89 le volant
– *steering wheel*
90 le siège-baquet
– *bucket seat*
91 la cloison pare-feu
– *protective bulkhead*
92 le moteur à deux temps *m*
– *two-stroke engine*
93 le silencieux d'échappement *m*
– *silencer* (Am. *muffler)*

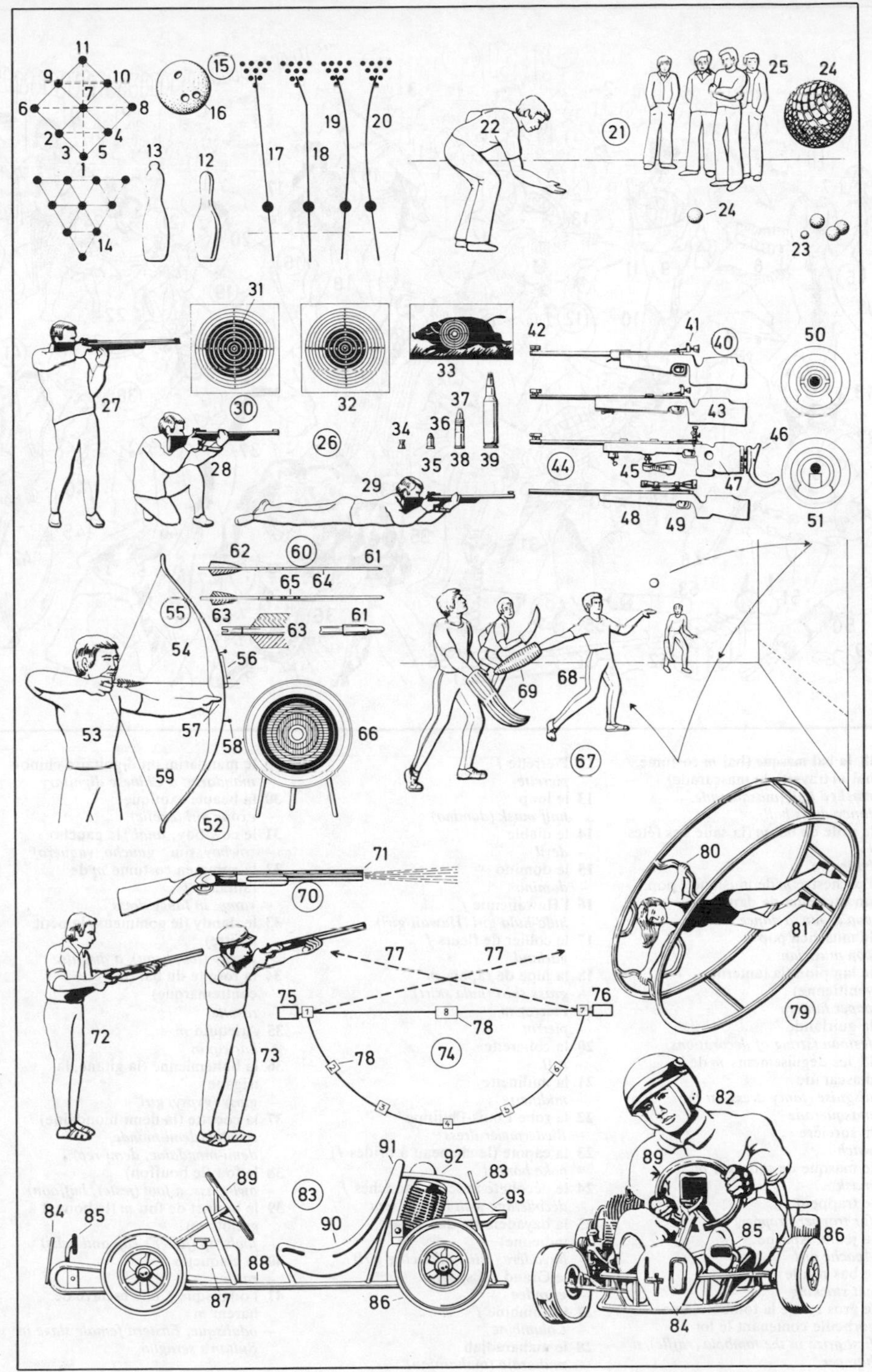

1-48 le bal masqué (bal *m* costumé, bal *m* travesti, la mascarade)
– ***masked ball*** *(masquerade, fancy-dress ball)*
1 la salle de bal *m* (la salle des fêtes *f*)
– *ballroom*
2 l'orchestre *m* de musique *f* pop, un orchestre de danse *f*
– *pop-group, a dance band*
3 le musicien pop
– *pop musician*
4 le lampion (la lanterne vénitienne)
– *paper lantern*
5 la guirlande
– *festoon (string of decorations)*
6-48 les déguisements *m* de la mascarade
– *disguise (fancy dress) at the masquerade*
6 la sorcière
– *witch*
7 le masque de carnaval *m*
– *mask*
8 le trappeur
– *fur trapper (trapper)*
9 la jeune Apache
– *Apache girl*
10 le bas résille
– *net stocking*
11 le gros lot de la tombola, une corbeille contenant le lot
– *first prize in the tombola (raffle), a hamper*
12 Pierrette *f*
– *pierette*
13 le loup
– *half mask (domino)*
14 le diable
– *devil*
15 le domino
– *domino*
16 l'Hawaiienne *f*
– *hula-hula girl (Hawaii girl)*
17 le collier de fleurs *f*
– *garland*
18 la jupe de raphia *m*
– *grass skirt (hula skirt)*
19 Pierrot *m*
– *pierrot*
20 la collerette
– *ruff*
21 la midinette
– *midinette*
22 la robe Louis-Philippe
– *Biedermeier dress*
23 la capote (le chapeau à brides *f*)
– *poke bonnet*
24 le décolleté avec les mouches *f*
– *décolletage with beauty spot*
25 la bayadère (la danseuse indienne)
– *bayadère (Hindu dancing girl)*
26 le Grand d'Espagne
– *grandee*
27 Colombine *f*
– *Columbine*
28 le maharadjah
– *maharaja (maharajah)*
29 le mandarin, un dignitaire chinois
– *mandarin, a Chinese dignitary*
30 la beauté exotique
– *exotic girl (exotic)*
31 le cow-boy; *anal.:* le gaucho
– *cowboy;* sim.: *gaucho (vaquero)*
32 la vamp en costume *m* de fantaisie *f*
– *vamp, in fancy dress*
33 le dandy (le gommeux, le petit maître)
– *dandy (fop, beau), a disguise*
34 la rosette du bal (la contremarque)
– *rosette*
35 Arlequin *m*
– *harlequin*
36 la bohémienne (la gitane, la tsigane)
– *gipsy (gypsy) girl*
37 la cocotte (la demi-mondaine)
– *cocotte (demi-monde, demi-mondaine, demi-rep)*
38 le fou (le bouffon)
– *owl-glass, a fool (jester, buffoon)*
39 le bonnet de fou *m* (le bonnet à grelots *m*)
– *foolscap (jester's cap and bells)*
40 la claquette
– *rattle*
41 l'odalisque *f*, une esclave de harem *m*
– *odalisque, Eastern female slave in Sultan's seraglio*

42 le pantalon turc (le chalvar)
– *chalwar (pantaloons)*
43 le pirate (le corsaire)
– *pirate (buccaneer)*
44 le tatouage
– *tattoo*
45 le bonnet en papier *m*
– *paper hat*
46 le faux nez (le nez en carton *m*)
– *false nose*
47 la crécelle
– *clapper (rattle)*
48 la batte (batte *f* de fou *m*)
– *slapstick*
49-54 pièces *f* d'artifice *m*
– ***fireworks***
49 l'amorce *f* fulminante
– *percussion cap*
50 le pétard (la papillotte)
– *cracker*
51 le pois fulminant
– *banger*
52 le pétard à répétition *f*
– *jumping jack*
53 la fusée
– *cannon cracker (maroon, marroon)*
54 la fusée volante
– *rocket*
55 la boule de papier *m*
– *paper ball*
56 la boîte à surprise *f* (l'attrape *f*)
– *jack-in-the-box, a joke*
57-70 le cortège de carnaval
– ***carnival procession***
57 le char de carnaval *m*
– *carnival float (carnival truck)*
58 le prince carnaval
– *King Carnival*
59 la marotte (le sceptre de fou *m*)
– *bauble (fool's sceptre,* Am. *scepter)*
60 l'ordre *m* de fou *m* (la décoration de carnaval *m*)
– *fool's badge*
61 la princesse carnaval
– *Queen Carnival*
62 les confetti *m*
– *confetti*
63 le géant, une tête de Turc *m*
– *giant figure, a satirical figure*
64 la reine de beauté *f*
– *beauty queen*
65 le personnage de conte *m* de fée *f*
– *fairy-tale figure*
66 le serpentin
– *paper streamer*
67 la marquise
– *majorette*
68 le garde du prince
– *king's guard*
69 le paillasse
– *buffoon, a clown*
70 le tambour de lansquenet *m*
– *lansquenet's drum*

1-63 le cirque ambulant
– *travelling (Am. traveling) circus*
1 le chapiteau du cirque, un chapiteau à quatre mâts de corniche *f*
– *circus tent (big top), a four-pole tent*
2 le mât du chapiteau
– *tent pole*
3 le projecteur
– *spotlight*
4 l'éclairagiste *m*
– *lighting technician*
5 la plate-forme de départ *m*
– *trapeze platform*
6 le trapèze (le trapèze volant)
– *trapeze*
7 l'acrobate *m* aérien; *fam.:* l'aérien (le voltigeur)
– *trapeze artist*
8 l'échelle de corde *f*
– *rope ladder*
9 la tribune de l'orchestre *m*
– *bandstand*
10 l'orchestre *m* du cirque
– *circus band*
11 l'entrée *f* de la piste
– *ring entrance (arena entrance)*
12 le montoir
– *wings*
13 le hauban
– *tent prop (prop)*
14 le filet de protection *f*
– *safety net*
15 les gradins *m*
– *seats for the spectators*
16 la loge de cirque *m*
– *circus box*
17 le directeur de cirque *m*
– *circus manager*
18 l'imprésario *m*
– *artiste agent (agent)*
19 les accès *m* (entrée *f* et sortie *f*)
– *entrance and exit*
20 l'accès *m* des gradins *m*
– *steps*
21 la piste, l'arène *f*, le manège
– *ring (arena)*
22 la banquette
– *ring fence*
23 le clown musical
– *musical clown (clown)*
24 le clown (le bouffon, le paillasse)
– *clown*
25 l'entrée *f* comique (l'entrée *f* des clowns *m*), un numéro de cirque *m*
– *comic turn (clown act), a circus act*
26 les écuyers *m* (les voltigeurs *m*)
– *circus riders (bareback riders)*
27 le garçon de piste *f*, un garçon de cirque *m*
– *ring attendant, a circus attendant*
28 la pyramide
– *pyramid*
29 l'homme *m* de base *f* (le porteur)
– *support*
30-31 le dressage en liberté *f*
– *performance by liberty horses*
30 le cheval de cirque *m* cabré (la levade)
– *circus horse, performing the levade (pesade)*
31 le dresseur, un maître de manège *m*
– *ringmaster, a trainer*
32 le voltigeur (l'écuyer *m* dans un numéro de voltige *f* équestre)
– *vaulter*
33 l'issue *f* de secours *m*
– *emergency exit*
34 la caravane (*vieux:* la roulotte)
– *caravan (circus caravan,* Am. *trailer)*

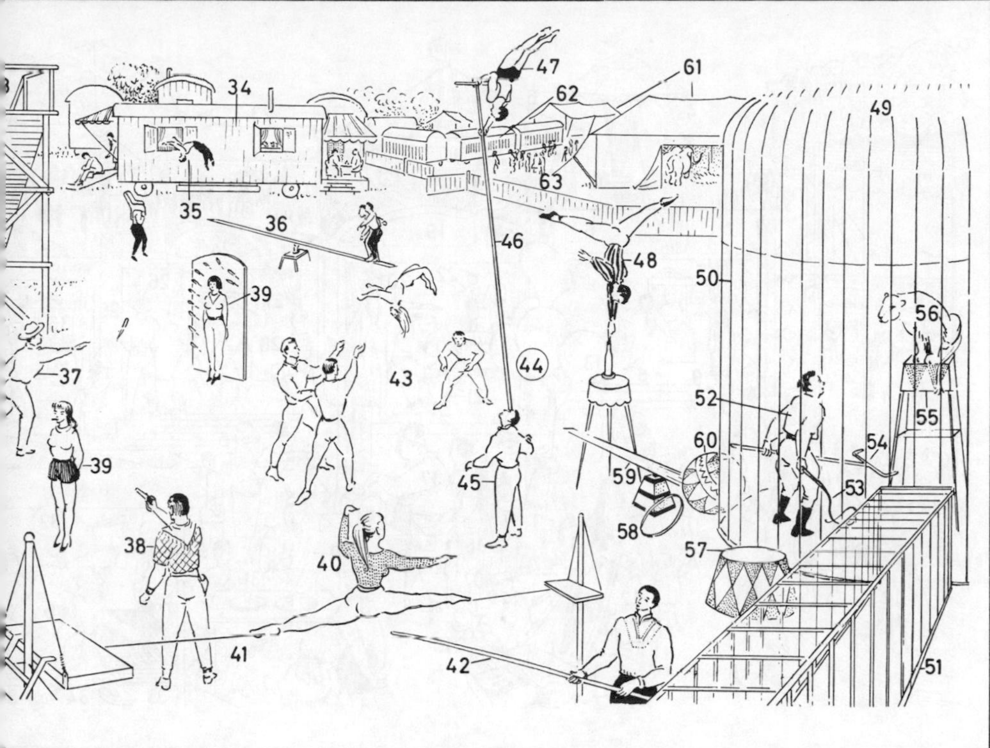

35 l'acrobate *m* à la basculc
– *springboard acrobat (springboard artist)*
36 la bascule
– *springboard*
37 le lanceur de couteaux *m*
– *knife thrower*
38 le virtuose du tir
– *circus marksman*
39 la comparse (la cible vivante)
– *assistant*
40 la funambule (la fil-de-fériste)
– *tightrope dancer*
41 le fil (la corde)
– *tightrope*
42 le balancier
– *balancing pole*
43 le numéro de mains-à-mains
– *throwing act*
44 l'équilibre *m*
– *balancing act*
45 le porteur
– *support*
46 la perche aérienne (la perche de bambou *m*)
– *pole (bamboo pole)*
47 l'acrobate *m*
– *acrobat*
48 l'équilibriste *m*
– *equilibrist (balancer)*
49 la cage aux fauves *m*, une cage circulaire
– *wild animal cage, a round cage*
50 la grille de la cage aux fauves *m*
– *bars of the cage*
51 le tunnel de la cage aux fauves *m*
– *passage (barred passage, passage for the wild animals)*
52 le dompteur (le dresseur)
– *tamer (wild animal tamer)*
53 la chambrière
– *whip*
54 la fourche de garde *f*
– *fork*
55 le piédestal
– *pedcstal*
56 le fauve (le tigre, le lion)
– *wild animal (tiger, lion)*
57 le socle
– *stand*
58 le cerceau
– *hoop (jumping hoop)*
59 la batoude
– *seesaw*
60 la boule
– *ball*
61 le village de toile *f*
– *camp*
62 la voiture-cage
– *cage caravan*
63 la ménagerie
– *menagerie*

1-69 la foire (la fête foraine, la kermesse, la fête de village *m*, la frairie, la fête patronale)
– *fair (annual fair)*
1 le champ de foire *f*
– *fairground*
2 le manège de chevaux *m* de bois *m*
– *children's merry-go-round, (whirligig), a roundabout (*Am. *carousel)*
3 la buvette
– *refreshment stall (drinks stall)*
4 le manège d'avions *m*
– *chairoplane*
5 les montagnes *f* russes (le train fantôme)
– *up-and-down roundabout, a ghost train*
6 la baraque foraine
– *show booth (booth)*
7 la caisse
– *box (box office)*
8 l'aboyeur *m* (l'annonceur *m*)
– *barker*
9 le médium
– *medium*
10 le camelot (le marchand forain)
– *showman*
11 la tête de Turc *m* (le dynamomètre)
– *try-your-strength machine*
12 le marchand ambulant (le marchand forain, le camelot, le charlatan)
– *hawker*
13 le ballon, un jouet d'enfant *m*
– *balloon*
14 le serpentin
– *paper serpent*
15 le moulinet, une éolienne miniature
– *windmill*
16 le pickpocket (le voleur à la tire)
– *pickpocket (thief)*
17 le vendeur (le camelot)
– *vendor*
18 le rahat loukoum
– *Turkish delight*
19 la scène d'exhibition *f* des monstres *m*
– *freak show*
20 le géant
– *giant*
21 la femme colosse
– *fat lady*
22 les nains *m* (les nabots *m*)
– *dwarfs (midgets)*
23 la brasserie foraine
– *beer marquee*
24 la baraque de forain *m*
– *sideshow*
25-28 les (artistes *m*) forains *m* (le baladin, le saltimbanque, l'histrion *m*, le bateleur)
– *travelling (*Am. *traveling) artistes (travelling show people)*
25 le cracheur de feu *m*
– *fire eater*
26 l'avaleur de sabres *m*
– *sword swallower*
27 l'hercule *m* forain
– *strong man*
28 le briseur de chaînes *f*
– *escapologist*
29 les spectateurs *m*
– *spectators*
30 le glacier (le marchand de glaces *f*, de crèmes *f* glacées)
– *ice-cream vendor (ice-cream man)*
31 le cornet de glace *f*
– *ice-cream cornet, with ice cream*
32 le stand de saucisses *f* grillées
– *sausage stand*
33 le gril pour saucisses *f* grillées
– *grill (Am. broiler)*
34 la saucisse grillée
– *bratwurst (grilled sausage,* Am. *broiled sausage)*
35 la pince à saucisses *f*
– *sausage tongs*
36 la cartomancienne (la tireuse de cartes *f*, la voyante), une diseuse de bonne aventure *f*
– *fortune teller*
37 la grande roue
– *big wheel (Ferris wheel)*
38 l'orgue *m* limonaire (l'orgue *m* de Barbarie), un instrument de musique automatique
– *orchestrion (automatic organ), an automatic musical instrument*
39 le grand huit (les montagnes *f* russes)
– *scenic railway (switchback)*
40 le toboggan
– *toboggan slide (chute)*
41 les bateaux-balançoires *m*
– *swing boats*
42 le bateau-balançoire renversable
– *swing boat, turning full circle*
43 le renversement (la culbute)
– *full circle*
44 la baraque de loterie *f*
– *lottery booth (tombola booth)*
45 la roue de fortune *f* (la roue de loterie *f*)
– *wheel of fortune*

46 le globe infernal
– *devil's wheel (typhoon wheel)*
47 l'anneau *m*
– *throwing ring (quoit)*
48 les lots *m*
– *prizes*
49 l'homme-sandwich *m* monté sur des échasses *f*
– *sandwich man on stilts*
50 le panneau-réclame (la pancarte publicitaire)
– *sandwich board (placard)*
51 le marchand de cigarettes *f*, un marchand ambulant
– *cigarette seller, an itinerant trader (a hawker)*
52 l'éventaire *m*
– *tray*
53 l'étalage *m* de fruits *m*
– *fruit stall*
54 le motocycliste exécutant le numéro du mur de la mort
– *wall-of-death rider*
55 la galerie de miroirs *m* déformants
– *hall of mirrors*
56 le miroir concave
– *concave mirror*
57 le miroir convexe
– *convex mirror*
58 le stand de tir *m*
– *shooting gallery*
59 l'hippodrome *m*
– *hippodrome*
60 le bric-à-brac (le marché aux puces *f*, les décrochez-moi-ça *m*, les baraques *f* de brocanteurs *m*, de fripiers *m*)
– *junk stalls (second-hand stalls)*
61 la tente de secours *m* médical (le poste de secours *m*)
– *first aid tent (first aid post)*
62 la piste d'autos *f* tamponneuses
– *dodgems (bumper cars)*
63 l'auto *f* tamponneuse
– *dodgem car (bumper car)*
64-66 la vente de poteries *f*
– *pottery stand*
64 le camelot (le crieur, le bonimenteur)
– *barker*
65 la femme de la halle (la marchande)
– *market woman*
66 les poteries *f* (les objets *m* de céramique *f*)
– *pottery*
67 les visiteurs *m* de la foire
– *visitors to the fair*
68 l'exposition *f* de figurines *f* de cire *f*
– *waxworks*
69 la figurine de cire *f* (la statuette de cire *f*, la poupée de cire *f*)
– *wax figure*

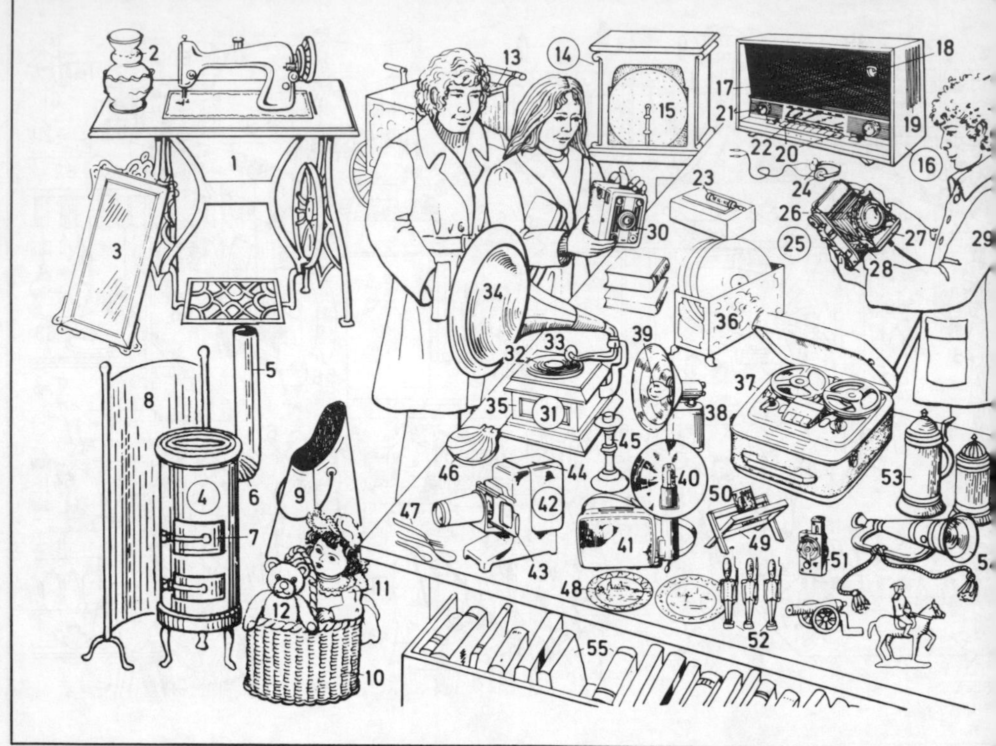

1 la machine à coudre à pédalier *m*
– *treadle sewing machine*
2 le vase à fleurs *m*
– *flower vase*
3 le trumeau
– *wall mirror*
4 le poêle
– *cylindrical stove*
5 le tuyau de poêle *m*
– *stovepipe*
6 le coude de tuyau *m* de poêle *m*
– *stovepipe elbow*
7 la porte de poêle *m*
– *stove door*
8 le garde-feu
– *stove screen*
9 le seau à charbon *m*
– *coal scuttle*
10 le panier à bois *m*
– *firewood basket*
11 la poupée
– *doll*
12 l'ours en peluche *f*
– *teddy bear*
13 l'orgue *m* de Barbarie
– *barrel organ*
14 l'orchestrion *m*
– *orchestrion*
15 le disque métallique (le disque perforé)
– *metal disc (disk)*
16 le poste de radio *f* (le récepteur de radio *f*, la radio; *anc.:* le poste de T.S.F. *f*), un récepteur superhétérodyne
– *radio (radio set,* joc.: *'steam radio'), a superheterodyne (superhet)*
17 l'écran *m* acoustique (le baffle)
– *baffle board*
18 l'œil *m* magique, un tube indicateur d'accord *m*
– *'magic eye', a tuning indicator valve*
19 la grille acoustique (les ouïes *f*)
– *loudspeaker aperture*
20 les touches *f* de sélection *f* des stations *f*
– *station selector buttons (station preset buttons)*
21 le bouton d'accord *m*
– *tuning knob*
22 les cadrans *m* de réglage *m* de fréquence *f* (de longueur *f* d'onde *f*)
– *frequency bands*
23 le détecteur (le récepteur à galène *f*)
– *crystal detector (crystal set)*
24 le casque (à écouteurs *m*)
– *headphones (headset)*
25 l'appareil *m* de photo *f* à soufflet *m* (appareil *m* pliant, type folding)
– *folding camera*
26 le soufflet
– *bellows*
27 l'abattant *m*
– *hinged cover*
28 les tendeurs *m*
– *spring extension*
29 le vendeur
– *salesman*
30 l'appareil *m* de photo *f* box (le box)
– *box camera*
31 le phonographe (le gramophone, le phono)
– *gramophone*
32 le disque
– *record (gramophone record)*
33 le pick-up (la tête de lecture *f*) équipé d'une aiguille
– *needle head with gramophone needle*
34 le pavillon
– *horn*
35 le coffret de phonographe *m*
– *gramophone box*
36 le porte-disques
– *record rack*
37 le magnétophone à bande *f*
– *tape recorder, a portable tape recorder*
38 le flash
– *flashgun*
39 la lampe de flash *m*
– *flash bulb*
40-41 le flash électronique
– *electronic flash (electronic flashgun)*
40 la torche
– *flash head*
41 le compartiment accu du flash
– *accumulator*

42 le projecteur de diapositives *f*
– *slide projector*
43 le passe-vues
– *slide holder*
44 le boîtier de lampe *f*
– *lamphouse*
45 le bougeoir
– *candlestick*
46 la coquille Saint-Jacques (la coquille de pèlerin *m*)
– *scallop shell*
47 le couvert
– *cutlery*
48 l'assiette *f* souvenir
– *souvenir plate*
49 le séchoir pour plaques *f* photographiques
– *drying rack for photographic plates*
50 la plaque photographique
– *photographic plate*
51 le déclencheur automatique
– *delayed-action release*
52 les soldats *m* d'étain *m* (*anal.:* les soldats *m* de plomb *m*)
– *tin soldiers* (*sim.: lead soldiers*)
53 la chope
– *beer mug (stein)*
54 la trompette
– *bugle*
55 les livres *m* anciens
– *second-hand books*
56 l'horloge *f* (la pendule de parquet *m*)
– *grandfather clock*
57 le coffre d'horloge *f*
– *clock case*
58 la pendule d'horloge *f*
– *pendulum*
59 le poids de marche *f*
– *time weight*
60 le poids de sonnerie *f*
– *striking weight*
61 le fauteuil à bascule *f* (le rocking-chair)
– *rocking chair*
62 le costume de marin *m*
– *sailor suit*
63 le béret de marin *m*
– *sailor's hat*
64 la toilette
– *washing set*
65 la cuvette
– *washing basin*
66 le broc à eau *f*
– *water jug*
67 le support de toilette *f*
– *washstand*
68 le fouloir à lessive *f*
– *dolly*
69 le baquet à lessive *f* (le cuvier)
– *washtub*
70 la planche à laver
– *washboard*
71 la toupie d'Allemagne
– *humming top*
72 l'ardoise *f*
– *slate*
73 le plumier
– *pencil box*
74 la machine à additionner
– *adding and subtracting machine*
75 le rouleau de papier *m*
– *paper roll*
76 les touches *f* de chiffre *m*
– *number keys*
77 le boulier
– *abacus*
78 l'encrier *m*, un encrier à couvercle *m*
– *inkwell, with lid*
79 la machine à écrire
– *typewriter*
80 la machine à calculer
– *[hand-operated] calculating machine (calculator)*
81 la manivelle de commande *f*
– *operating handle*
82 le totalisateur de résultat *m*
– *result register (product register)*
83 le totalisateur
– *rotary counting mechanism (rotary counter)*
84 la balance de ménage *m*
– *kitchen scales*
85 le cotillon (le jupon)
– *waist slip (underskirt)*
86 le chariot à ridelles *f*
– *wooden handcart*
87 la pendule
– *wall clock*
88 la bouillotte en métal *m*
– *bed warmer*
89 le bidon à lait *m*
– *milk churn*

1-13 le complexe cinématographique (les studios *m*)
- ***film studios*** *(studio complex,* Am. *movie studios)*

1 le terrain de prise *f* de vues *f* (tournage *m*) en extérieur *m*
- *lot (studio lot)*

2 les laboratoires *m* de tirage *m*
- *processing laboratories (film laboratories, motion picture laboratories)*

3 les salles *f* de montage *m*
- *cutting rooms*

4 le bâtiment administratif (les bureaux *m*)
- *administration building (office building, offices)*

5 le blockhaus pour films *m* (la filmothèque)
- *film (motion picture) storage vault (film library, motion picture library)*

6 les ateliers *m*
- *workshop*

7 les décors *m* construits
- *film set (*Am. *movie set)*

8 la station électrique
- *power house*

9 les laboratoires *m* techniques et de recherche *f*
- *technical and research laboratories*

10 les plateaux *m*
- *groups of stages*

11 le bassin en béton *m* pour scènes *f* nautiques
- *concrete tank for marine sequences*

12 le cyclorama
- *cyclorama*

13 la colline du cyclorama
- *hill*

14-60 les prises *f* de vues *f* (tournages *m*)
- ***shooting*** *(filming)*

14 l'auditorium *m* (le studio d'enregistrement *m*)
- *music recording studio (music recording theatre,* Am. *theater)*

15 les parois *f* acoustiques (panneaux *m* acoustiques)
- *'acoustic' wall lining*

16 l'écran *m* de projection *f* (l'écran *m*)
- *screen (projection screen)*

17 l'orchestre *m* du film
- *film orchestra*

18 la prise de vues *f* (le tournage) en extérieur *f* (les extérieurs *m*)
- *exterior shooting (outdoor shooting, exterior filming, outdoor filming)*

19 la caméra synchrone pilotée par quartz *m*
- *camera with crystal-controlled drive*

20 le chef opérateur (le cameraman, le cadreur)
- *cameraman*

21 l'assistante *f* du réalisateur
- *assistant director*

22 le perchman
- *boom operator (boom swinger)*

23 le chef opérateur du son
- *recording engineer (sound recordist)*

24 le magnétophone portatif piloté par quartz *m*
- *portable sound recorder with crystal-controlled drive*

25 la girafe
- *microphone boom*

26-60 la prise de vues *f* (le tournage) en studio *m*
- *shooting (filming) in the studio (on the sound stage, on the stage, in the filming hall)*

26 le directeur de production *f*
- *production manager*

27 la vedette féminine (l'actrice *f* de cinéma *m*, la vedette de cinéma *m*, la star)
- *leading lady (film actress, film star, star)*

28 la vedette masculine (l'acteur *m* de cinéma *m*, le héros de cinéma *m*, le héros)
- *leading man (film actor, film star, star)*

29 le figurant (la silhouette)
- *film extra (extra)*

30 la disposition des microphones *m* (micros *m*) pour l'enregistrement *m* stéréophonique et des effets *m* sonores
- *arrangement of microphones for stereo and sound effects*

31 le microphone (micro *m*) de studio *m*
- *studio microphone*

32 le câble de microphone *m* (micro *m*)
– *microphone cable*
33 la coulisse et l'arrière-plan *m*
– *side flats and background*
34 le clapman
– *clapper boy*
35 la claquette (le clap) avec l'ardoise *f* portant le titre du film, le numéro de plan *m* et le numéro de la prise
– *clapper board (clapper) with slates (boards) for the film title, shot number (scene number), and take number*
36 le maquilleur (le coiffeur)
– *make-up artist (hairstylist)*
37 l'électricien *m* de plateau *m*
– *lighting electrician (studio electrician, lighting man,* Am. *gaffer)*
38 le diffuseur
– *diffusing screen*
39 la script-girl (*ELF:* la scripte)
– *continuity girl (script girl)*
40 le réalisateur (le metteur en scène *f*)
– *film director (director)*
41 le chef opérateur (le cameraman)
– *cameraman (first cameraman)*
42 le cadreur (l'opérateur *m*)
– *camera operator, an assistant cameraman (camera assistant)*
43 l'architecte-chef-décorateur *m*
– *set designer (art director)*
44 le régisseur général
– *director of photography*
45 le script
– *filmscript (script, shooting script,* Am. *movie script)*
46 l'assistant-réalisateur *m*
– *assistant director*
47 la caméra insonorisée (caméra *f* de prise *f* de vues *f*), une caméra à film *m* large (caméra *f* Cinémascope)
– *soundproof film camera (soundproof motion picture camera), a wide screen camera (cinemascope camera)*
48 le caisson insonore
– *soundproof housing (soundproof cover, blimp)*
49 la grue américaine (le dolly)
– *camera crane (dolly)*
50 le socle (l'embase *f*) hydraulique
– *hydraulic stand*
51 l'écran *m* opaque (anti-halo), arrêtant la lumière parasite
– *mask (screen) for protection from spill light (gobo, nigger)*
52 le projecteur sur trépied *m* (la lumière d'appoint *m*)
– *tripod spotlight (fill-in light, filler light, fill light, filler)*
53 la passerelle de projecteurs *m*
– *spotlight catwalk*
54 la cabine de prise *f* de son *m*
– *recording room*
55 l'ingénieur *m* du son
– *recording engineer (sound recordist)*
56 le pupitre de mixage *m*
– *mixing console (mixing desk)*
57 le recorder (l'adjoint *m* de l'ingénieur *m* du son)
– *sound assistant (assistant sound engineer)*
58 l'équipement *m* d'enregistrement *m* magnétique du son
– *magnetic sound recording equipment (magnetic sound recorder)*
59 l'équipement *m* d'amplification *f* et de trucage *m*, pour la réverbération *f* et les effets *m* sonores par exemple
– *amplifier and special effects equipment, e.g. for echo and sound effects*
60 la caméra sonore (la caméra à son *m* optique)
– *sound recording camera (optical sound recorder)*

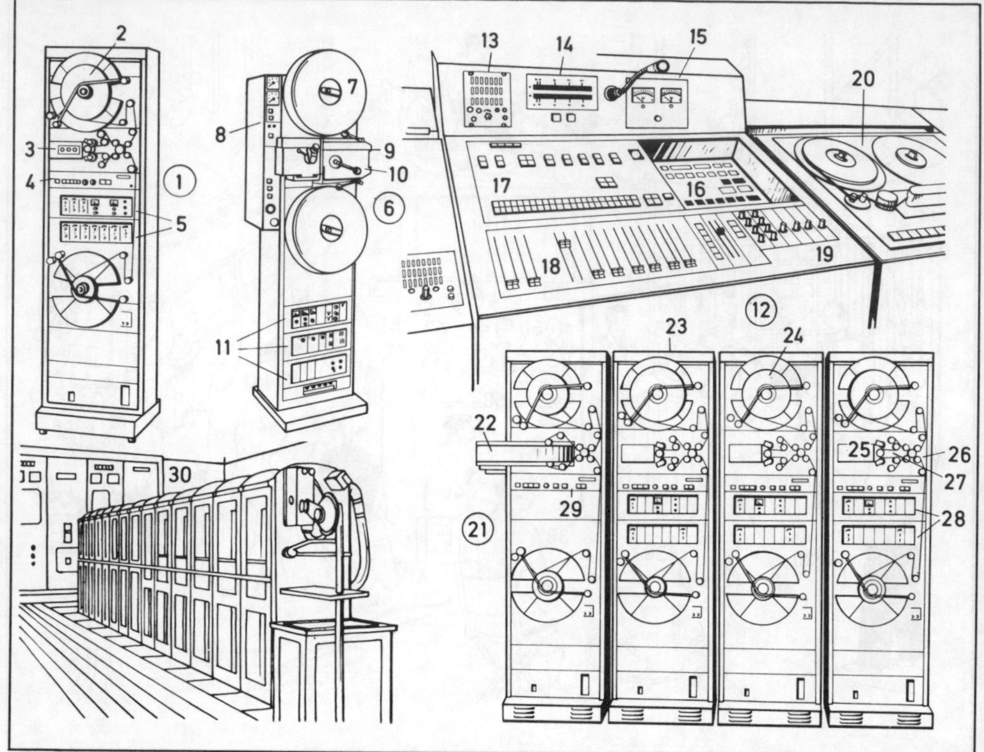

1-46 enregistrement *m* et copie *f* du son
– ***sound recording and re-recording** (dubbing)*

1 l'équipement *m* d'enregistrement *m* magnétique du son
– *magnetic sound recording equipment (magnetic sound recorder)*

2 la bobine de film *m* magnétique
– *magnetic film spool*

3 le porte-têtes magnétiques
– *magnetic head support assembly*

4 le panneau de commande *f*
– *control panel*

5 l'amplificateur *m* d'enregistrement *m* et de lecture *f* du son magnétique
– *magnetic sound recording and playback amplifier*

6 l'enregistreur *m* de son *m* optique (la caméra sonore)
– *optical sound recorder (sound recording camera, optical sound recording equipment)*

7 le magasin (le chargeur) de film *m* en lumière *f* du jour
– *daylight film magazine*

8 le panneau de commande *f* et de contrôle *m*
– *control and monitoring panel*

9 l'oculaire *m* pour contrôle *m* visuel de l'enregistrement *m* optique du son
– *eyepiece for visual control of optical sound recording*

10 le dérouleur
– *deck*

11 l'amplificateur *m* d'enregistrement *m* et l'alimentation *f* secteur
– *recording amplifier and mains power unit*

12 le pupitre de commande *f*
– *control desk (control console)*

13 le haut-parleur de contrôle *m*
– *monitoring loudspeaker (control loudspeaker)*

14 les indicateurs *m* de niveau *m* d'enregistrement *m* (vumètres *m*)
– *recording level indicators*

15 les appareils *m* de contrôle *m*
– *monitoring instruments*

16 le panneau de commutation *f*
– *jack panel*

17 le panneau de commande *f*
– *control panel*

18 les potentiomètres *m* à curseur *m*
– *sliding control*

19 les correcteurs *m* d'affaiblissement *m* (atténuateurs *m*, filtres *m* correcteurs, égalisateurs *m*)
– *equalizer*

20 la platine de son *m* magnétique
– *magnetic sound deck*

21 l'équipement *m* de mixage *m* pour film *m* magnétique
– *mixer for magnetic film*

22 le projecteur de film *m*
– *film projector*

23 l'équipement *m* d'enregistrement *m* et de lecture *f*
– *recording and playback equipment*

24 la bobine de film *m*
– *film reel (film spool)*

25 le porte-têtes avec la tête d'enregistrement *m*, la tête de lecture *f* et la tête d'effacement *m*
– *head support assembly for the recording head, playback head, and erasing head (erase head)*

26 le mécanisme d'entraînement *m* du film
– *film transport mechanism*
27 le filtre de synchronisation *f*
– *synchronizing filter*
28 l'amplificateur *m* de son *m* magnétique
– *magnetic sound amplifier*
29 le panneau de commande *f*
– *control panel*
30 les machines *f* de développement *m* du film dans le laboratoire de tirage *m*
– *film-processing machines (film-developing machines) in the processing laboratory (film laboratory, motion picture laboratory)*
31 la chambre de réverbération *f*
– *echo chamber*
32 le haut-parleur de la chambre de réverbération *f*
– *echo chamber loudspeaker*
33 le microphone (le micro) de la chambre de réverbération *f*
– *echo chamber microphone*
34-36 le mixage de sons *m* (le mixage *m* de plusieurs bandes *f* son *m*)
– *sound mixing (sound dubbing, mixing of several sound tracks)*
34 le studio de mixage *m*
– *mixing room (dubbing room)*
35 le pupitre de mixage *m* pour son *m* mono ou stéréo
– *mixing console (mixing desk) for mono or stereo sound*
36 les ingénieurs *m* du son effectuant le mixage
– *dubbing mixers (recording engineers, sound recordists) dubbing (mixing)*
37-41 la post-synchronisation (le doublage)
– *synchronization (syncing, dubbing, post-synchronization, post-syncing)*
37 le studio de post-synchronisation *f* (doublage *m*)
– *dubbing studio (dubbing theatre,* Am. *theater)*
38 le directeur de post-synchronisation *f* (doublage *m*)
– *dubbing director*
39 l'actrice *f* de post-synchronisation *f* (doublage *m*)
– *dubbing speaker (dubbing actress)*
40 le microphone (micro *m*) sur girafe *f*
– *boom microphone*
41 le câble de microphone *m* (micro *m*)
– *microphone cable*
42-46 le montage
– *cutting (editing)*
42 la table de montage *m*
– *cutting table (editing table, cutting bench)*
43 le monteur
– *film editor (cutter)*
44 le plateau pour les bandes *f* son *m* et image *f*
– *film turntable, for picture and sound tracks*
45 la projection de l'image *f*
– *projection of the picture*
46 le haut-parleur
– *loudspeaker*

1-23 la projection cinématographique
– ***film projection*** *(motion picture projection)*

1 le cinéma (la salle de cinéma *m*)
– *cinema (picture house,* Am. *movie theater, movie house)*

2 la caisse du cinéma
– *cinema box office (*Am. *movie theater box office)*

3 le billet de cinéma *m*
– *cinema ticket (*Am. *movie theater ticket)*

4 l'ouvreuse *f*
– *usherette*

5 les spectateurs *m* (le public du cinéma)
– *cinemagoers (filmgoers, cinema audience,* Am. *moviegoers, movie audience)*

6 l'éclairage *m* de sécurité *f* (l'éclairage *m* de secours *m*)
– *safety lighting (emergency lighting)*

7 la sortie de secours *m*
– *emergency exit*

8 la scène
– *stage*

9 les rangées *f* de fauteuils *m*
– *rows of seats (rows)*

10 les rideaux *m* de scène *f*
– *stage curtain (screen curtain)*

11 l'écran *m* de projection *f* (l'écran *m*)
– *screen (projection screen)*

12 la cabine de projection *f*
– *projection room (projection booth)*

13 le projecteur gauche
– *lefthand projector*

14 le projecteur droit
– *righthand projector*

15 la fenêtre de projection *f* et de surveillance *f*
– *projection room window with projection window and observation port*

16 le tambour à pellicule *f* (la bobine)
– *reel drum (spool box)*

17 le gradateur d'éclairage *m* de la salle
– *house light dimmers (auditorium lighting control)*

18 le redresseur, un redresseur au sélénium ou à vapeur *f* de mercure *m* alimentant les lampes *f* de projection *f*
– *rectifier, a selenium or mercury vapour rectifier for the projection lamps*

19 l'amplificateur *m*
– *amplifier*

20 l'opérateur *m* de projection *f* (le projectionniste)
– *projectionist*

21 la table de rebobinage *m* du film
– *rewind bench for rewinding the film*

22 la colle pour film *m*
– *film cement (splicing cement)*

23 le projecteur de diapositives *f* (publicitaires)
– *slide projector for advertisements*

24-52 les projecteurs ***m*** **de cinéma** ***m*** (appareils *m* de projection *f*)
– ***film projectors***

24 le projecteur sonore (le projecteur de films *m* sonores, l'appareil *m* de projection *f* de films *m* sonores)
– *sound projector (film projector, cinema projector, theatre projector,* Am. *movie projector)*

25-38 le mécanisme du projecteur
– *projector mechanism*

25 les tambours *m* ignifuges à refroidissement *m* par circulation *f* d'huile *f*
– *fireproof reel drums (spool boxes) with circulating oil cooling system*

26 le cylindre à picots *m* (tambour *m*) débiteur
– *feed sprocket (supply sprocket)*

27 le cylindre à picots *m* (tambour *m*) récepteur
– *take-up sprocket*

28 le lecteur de son *m* magnétique
– *magnetic head cluster*

29 le galet-guide (le tambour-guide) avec commande *f* de cadrage *m*
– *guide roller (guiding roller) with framing control*

30 le galet forme-boucle pour stabilisation *f* du film entraîné par saccades *f*; *égal.:* le contact de rupture *f* du film

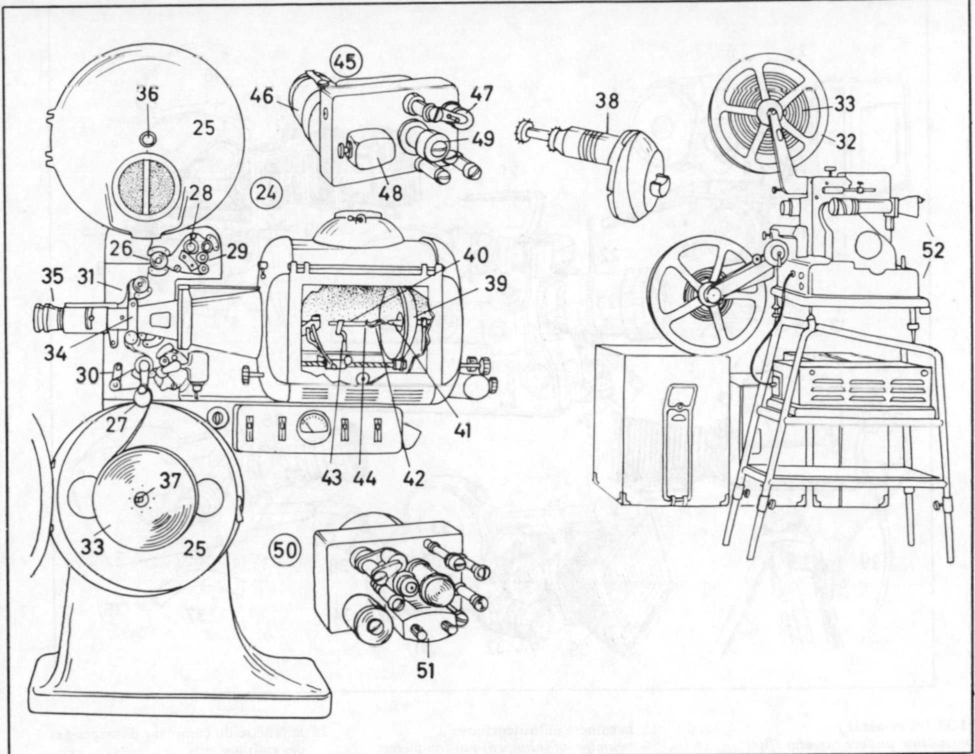

- *loop former for smoothing out the intermittent movement;* also: *film break detector*

31 le couloir du film
- *film path*

32 la bobine du film
- *film reel (film spool)*

33 le rouleau de film *m*
- *reel of film*

34 la fenêtre de projection *f* avec soufflante *f* de ventilation *f*
- *film gate (picture gate, projector gate) with cooling fan*

35 l'objectif *m* de projection *f*
- *projection lens (projector lens)*

36 l'axe *m* débiteur
- *feed spindle*

37 l'axe *m* récepteur à friction *f*
- *take-up spindle with friction drive*

38 le mécanisme à croix *f* de Malte
- *maltese cross mechanism (maltese cross movement, Geneva movement)*

39-44 la lanterne
- *lamphouse*

39 la lampe à arc *m* à réflecteur *m* concave non-sphérique et aimant *m* de soufflage *m* pour stabilisation *f* de l'arc *m*; *égal.:* la lampe au xénon très haute pression *f*
- *mirror arc lamp, with aspherical (non-spherical) concave mirror and blowout magnet for stabilizing the arc* (also: *high-pressure xenon arc lamp)*

40 le charbon positif
- *positive carbon (positive carbon rod)*

41 le charbon négatif
- *negative carbon (negative carbon rod)*

42 l'arc *m* électrique
- *arc*

43 le porte-charbon
- *carbon rod holder*

44 le cratère du charbon
- *crater (carbon crater)*

45 le lecteur de son *m* optique [également conçu pour le son stéréo multivoie et pour trace *f* acoustique symétrique]
- *optical sound unit [also designed for multi-channel optical stereophonic sound and for push-pull sound tracks]*

46 l'optique *f* de lecture *f* du son
- *sound optics*

47 la tête de lecture *f* du son
- *sound head*

48 la lampe excitatrice dans le boîtier
- *exciter lamp in housing*

49 la cellule photoélectrique dans l'axe *m* creux
- *photocell in hollow drum*

50 le lecteur de son *m* magnétique à quatre pistes *f*
- *attachable four-track magnetic sound unit (penthouse head, magnetic sound head)*

51 la tête magnétique à quatre pistes *f*
- *four-track magnetic head*

52 le projecteur de films *m* de format *m* réduit pour cinéma *m* ambulant
- *narrow-gauge (Am. narrow-gage) cinema projector for mobile cinema*

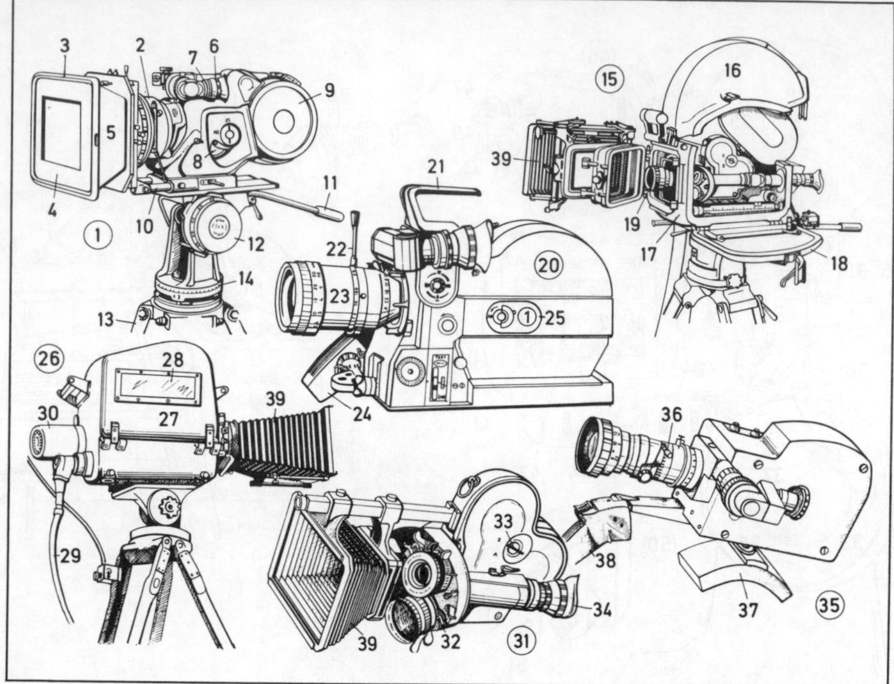

1-39 les caméras *f*
– ***motion picture cameras** (film cameras)*
1 la caméra pour film *m* (de format *m*) standard (la caméra pour film *m* de 35 mm)
– *standard-gauge* (Am. *standard-gage) motion picture camera (standard-gauge,* Am. *standard-gage, 35 mm camera)*
2 l'objectif *m* (l'optique *f* de prise *f* de vues *f*)
– *lens (object lens, taking lens)*
3 le parasoleil avec porte-filtres *m* et porte-caches *m*
– *lens hood (sunshade) with matte box*
4 le cache
– *matte (mask)*
5 le soufflet réglable de contre-jour *m*
– *lens hood barrel*
6 l'oculaire *m* du viseur
– *viewfinder eyepiece*
7 la mise au point *m* de l'oculaire *m*
– *eyepiece control ring*
8 le réglage d'ouverture *f* du diaphragme à secteurs *m*
– *opening control for the segment disc (disk) shutter*
9 le boîtier de cassette *f* de film *m* (de chargeur *m*)
– *magazine housing*
10 la glissière de parasoleil *m*
– *slide bar for the lens hood*
11 le levier de commande *f*
– *control arm (control lever)*
12 la plate-forme à panoramique *m* horizontal et vertical
– *pan and tilt head*
13 le trépied en bois
– *wooden tripod*
14 la graduation angulaire
– *degree scale*
15 la caméra autosilencieuse
– *soundproof (blimped) motion picture camera (film camera)*
16-18 le caisson insonore
– *soundproof housing (blimp)*
16 la partie supérieure du caisson insonore
– *upper section of the soundproof housing*
17 la partie inférieure du caisson insonore
– *lower section of the soundproof housing*
18 la paroi rabattue du caisson insonore
– *open sidewall of the soundproof housing*
19 l'objectif *m* de caméra *f*
– *camera lens*
20 la caméra légère professionnelle
– *lightweight professional motion picture camera*
21 la poignée
– *grip (handgrip)*
22 le levier de variation *f* de la focale (levier *m* de zoom *m*)
– *zooming lever*
23 l'objectif *m* à focale *f* continûment variable (le zoom *m*)
– *zoom lens (variable focus lens, varifocal lens) with infinitely variable focus*
24 la poignée à déclencheur *m*
– *handgrip with shutter release*
25 la porte de caméra *f*
– *camera door*
26 la caméra sonore (la caméra de reportage *m*) pour enregistrement *m* simultané de l'image *f* et du son
– *sound camera (newsreel camera) for recording sound and picture*
27 le caisson insonore
– *soundproof housing (blimp)*
28 la fenêtre du compteur d'images *f* et des cadrans *m*
– *window for the frame counters and indicator scales*
29 le câble de synchronisation *f* (le câble de fréquence *f* pilote)
– *pilot tone cable (sync pulse cable)*
30 le générateur de fréquence *f* pilote
– *pilot tone generator (signal generator, pulse generator)*
31 la caméra pour films *m* de format *m* réduit, une caméra 16 mm
– *professional narrow-gauge* (Am. *narrow-gage) motion picture camera, a 16 mm camera*
32 la tourelle porte-objectifs (tourelle *f* à objectifs *m*)
– *lens turret (turret head)*
33 le verrouillage du carter
– *housing lock*
34 l'œilleton *m* d'oculaire *m*
– *eyecup*
35 la caméra à grande vitesse *f*, une caméra spéciale pour films *m* de format *m* réduit
– *high-speed camera, a special narrow-gauge* (Am. *narrow-gage) camera*
36 le levier de variation *f* de la focale (levier *m* de zoom *m*)
– *zooming lever*
37 la crosse
– *rifle grip*
38 le poignée à déclencheur *m*
– *handgrip with shutter release*
39 le soufflet du parasoleil
– *lens hood bellows*

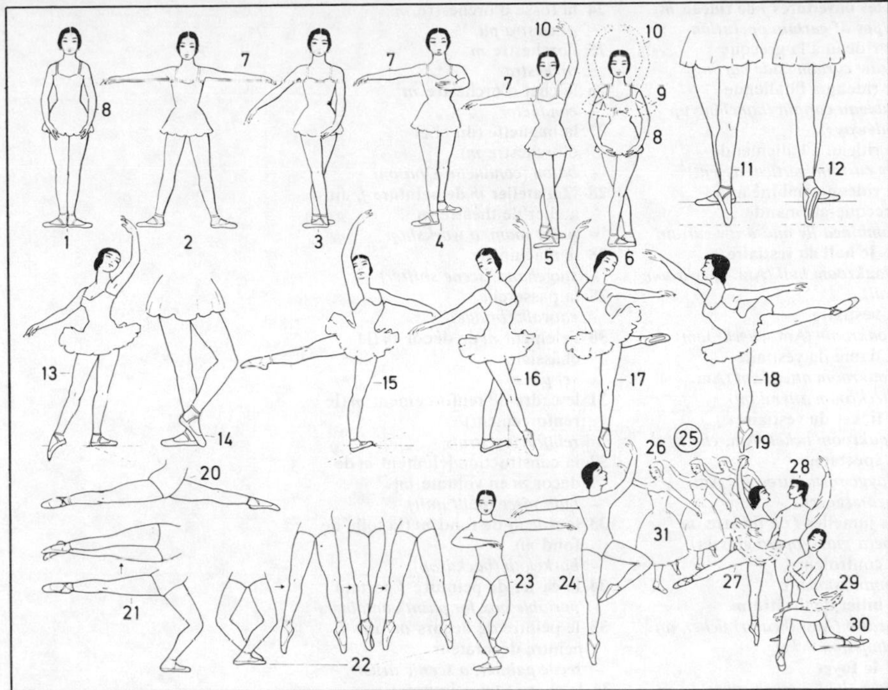

1-6 les cinq positions *f*
– *the five positions (ballet positions)*
1 la première position
– *first position*
2 la deuxième position
– *second position*
3 la troisième position
– *third position*
4 la quatrième position [avancée]
– *fourth position [open]*
5 la quatrième position [croisée; cinquième position ouverte]
– *fourth position [crossed; extended fifth position]*
6 la cinquième position
– *fifth position*
7-10 les ports *m* de bras *m*
– *ports de bras (arm positions)*
7 le port de bras *m* à côté
– *port de bras à coté*
8 le port de bras *m* en bas
– *port de bras en bas*
9 le port de bras *m* en avant
– *port de bras en avant*
10 le port de bras *m* en haut
– *port de bras en haut*
11 le dégagé à la quatrième devant
– *dégagé à la quatrième devant*
12 le dégagé à la quatrième derrière
– *dégagé à la quatrième derrière*
13 l'effacé *m*
– *effacé*
14 le sur le cou-de-pied
– *sur le cou-de-pied*
15 l'écarté *m*
– *écarté*
16 le croisé
– *croisé*
17 l'attitude *f*
– *attitude*
18 l'arabesque *f*
– *arabesque*
19 la pointe
– *à pointe (on full point)*
20 le grand écart
– *splits*
21 la cabriole
– *cabriole (capriole)*
22 l'entrechat *m* (entrechat *m* quatre, soubresaut *m* battu)
– *entrechat (entrechat quatre)*
23 la préparation [pour la pirouette par exemple]
– *préparation [e.g. for a pirouette]*
24 la pirouette
– *pirouette*
25 le corps de ballet *m*
– *corps de ballet*
26 la danseuse de ballet *m* (la ballerine)
– *ballet dancer (ballerina)*
27-28 le pas de trois
– *pas de trois*
27 la danseuse étoile
– *prima ballerina*
28 le danseur étoile
– *principal male dancer (leading soloist)*
29 le tutu
– *tutu*
30 le chausson de danse *f*
– *point shoe, a ballet shoe (ballet slipper)*
31 le jupon de danse *f*
– *ballet skirt*

1-4 les ouvertures *f* **de rideau** *m*
– ***types of curtain operation***
1 le rideau à la grecque
– *draw curtain (side parting)*
2 le rideau à l'italienne
– *tableau curtain (bunching up sideways)*
3 le rideau à l'allemande
– *fly curtain (vertical ascent)*
4 le rideau combiné à la grecque-allemande
– *combined fly and draw curtain*
5-11 le hall du vestiaire
– ***cloakroom hall*** (Am. *checkroom hall)*
5 le vestiaire
– *cloakroom* (Am. *checkroom)*
6 la dame du vestiaire
– *cloakroom attendant* (Am. *checkroom attendant)*
7 le ticket du vestiaire
– *cloakroom ticket* (Am. *check)*
8 le spectateur
– *playgoer (theatregoer,* Am. *theatergoer)*
9 les jumelles *f* de théâtre *m*
– *opera glass (opera glasses)*
10 le contrôleur
– *commissionaire*
11 le billet de théâtre *m*
– *theatre* (Am. *theater) ticket, an admission ticket*
12-13 le foyer
– ***foyer*** *(lobby, crush room)*
12 l'ouvreur *m*; *anc.:* l'ouvreur *m* de loge *f* [*en France:* l'ouvreuse *f*]
– *usher;* form.: *box attendant*
13 le programme
– *programme* (Am. *program)*
14-27 le lieu théâtral
– ***auditorium and stage***
14 la scène
– *stage*
15 le proscenium
– *proscenium*
16-20 la salle de théâtre *m*
– ***auditorium***
16 la galerie (le poulailler)
– *gallery (balcony)*
17 le deuxième balcon
– *upper circle*
18 le premier balcon
– *dress circle* (Am. *balcony, mezzanine)*
19 l'orchestre *m*
– *front stalls*
20 le fauteuil (la place de théâtre *m*)
– *seat (theatre seat,* Am. *theater seat)*
21-27 la répétition
– ***rehearsal*** *(stage rehearsal)*
21 le chœur
– *chorus*
22 le chanteur
– *singer*
23 la cantatrice
– *singer*
24 la fosse d'orchestre *m*
– *orchestra pit*
25 l'orchestre *m*
– *orchestra*
26 le chef d'orchestre *m*
– *conductor*
27 la baguette (du chef d'orchestre *m*)
– *baton (conductor's baton)*
28-42 l'atelier *m* **de peinture** *f*, un atelier de théâtre *m*
– ***paint room,*** *a workshop*
28 le machiniste
– *stagehand (scene shifter)*
29 la passerelle
– *catwalk (bridge)*
30 l'élément *m* de décor *m* (le châssis)
– *set piece*
31 le cadre de renforcement *m* (le renforcement)
– *reinforcing struts*
32 la construction [élément *m* de décor *m* en volume *m*]
– *built piece (built unit)*
33 le rideau de fond *m* (la toile de fond *m*)
– *backcloth (backdrop)*
34 le casier de peinture *f* portatif
– *portable box for paint containers*
35 le peintre de décors *m*, un peintre décorateur
– *scene painter, a scenic artist*
36 le chariot de peinture *f*
– *paint trolley*
37 le décorateur
– *stage designer (set designer)*
38 le dessinateur de costumes *m*
– *costume designer*
39 l'esquisse *f* de costumes *m*
– *design for a costume*
40 le croquis
– *sketch for a costume*
41 la maquette de scène *f*
– *model stage*
42 la maquette de décors *m*
– *model of the set*
43-52 la loge d'artiste *m*
– ***dressing room***
43 le miroir à maquillage *m*
– *dressing room mirror*
44 la serviette de maquillage *m*
– *make-up gown*
45 la table de maquillage *m*
– *make-up table*
46 le bâton de fard *m*
– *greasepaint stick*
47 le chef maquilleur
– *chief make-up artist (chief make-up man)*
48 le maquilleur (le perruquier)
– *make-up artist (hairstylist)*
49 la perruque
– *wig*
50 les accessoires *m* de théâtre *m*
– *props (properties)*
51 le costume de théâtre *m*
– *theatrical costume*
52 la lampe d'appel *m* en scène *f*
– *call light*

1-60 la cage de scène *f* avec la machinerie des cintres *m* et des dessous *m*
– ***stagehouse with machinery*** *(machinery in the flies and below stage)*
1 le poste de commande *f*
– *control room*
2 le pupitre de commande *f* (le jeu d'orgue *m*) à mémorisation *f* des effets *m* lumineux
– *control console (lighting console, lighting control console) with preset control for presetting lighting effects*
3 la conduite d'éclairage *m*
– *lighting plot (light plot)*
4 le gril
– *grid (gridiron)*
5 la passerelle de service *m*
– *fly floor (fly gallery)*
6 le dispositif d'arrosage *m* (de protection *f* contre l'incendie *m*)
– *sprinkler system for fire prevention (for fire protection)*
7 le brigadier des cintres *m*
– *fly man*
8 les fils *m*
– *fly lines (lines)*
9 le cyclorama
– *cyclorama*
10 la toile de fond (le rideau de fond *m*)
– *backcloth (backdrop, background)*
11 la principale
– *arch, a drop cloth*
12 la frise
– *border*
13 la herse cloisonnée
– *compartment (compartment-type, compartmentalized) batten* (Am. *border light)*
14 les appareils *m* d'éclairage *m* de scène *f*
– *stage lighting units (stage lights)*
15 l'éclairage *m* d'horizon *m*
– *horizon lights (backdrop lights)*
16 les projecteurs *m* de scène *f* pivotants
– *adjustable acting area lights (acting area spotlights)*
17 les appareils *m* de projection *f* de décor *m*
– *scenery projectors (projectors)*
18 la lance d'incendie *m* «Monitor»
– *monitor (water cannon) (a piece of safety equipment)*
19 le pont d'éclairage *m* mobile
– *travelling* (Am. *traveling) lighting bridge (travelling lighting gallery)*
20 l'électricien *m*
– *lighting operator (lighting man)*
21 le projecteur d'avant-scène *f*
– *portal spotlight (tower spotlight)*
22 le cadre (de scène *f*) mobile
– *adjustable proscenium*
23 le rideau de scène *f*
– *curtain (theatrical curtain)*
24 le rideau de fer *m*
– *iron curtain (safety curtain, fire curtain)*
25 l'avant-scène *f*
– *forestage (apron)*
26 la rampe
– *footlight (footlights, floats)*
27 le trou (la boîte) du souffleur
– *prompt box*
28 le souffleur (la souffleuse)
– *prompter*
29 le pupitre du régisseur de scène *f*
– *stage manager's desk*
30 le régisseur de scène *f*
– *stage director (stage manager)*
31 la scène tournante
– *revolving stage*
32 la trappe
– *trap opening*
33 la table de trappe *f*
– *lift* (Am. *elevator)*
34 l'estrade *f* abaissable
– *bridge* (Am. *elevator), a rostrum*
35 les éléments *m* de décor *m*
– *pieces of scenery*
36 la scène (le plateau)
– *scene*
37 l'acteur *m* (le comédien)
– *actor*
38 l'actrice *f* (la comédienne)
– *actress*
39 les figurants *m*
– *extras (supers, supernumeraries)*
40 le metteur en scène *f*
– *director (producer)*
41 le manuscrit (le texte)
– *prompt book (prompt script)*
42 la table du metteur en scène *f*
– *director's table (producer's table)*
43 l'assistant-metteur en scène
– *assistant director (assistant producer)*
44 la conduite générale
– *director's script (producer's script)*
45 le brigadier de plateau *m*
– *stage carpenter*
46 le machiniste
– *stagehand (scene shifter)*
47 l'élément *m* de décor *m* (le châssis)
– *set piece*
48 la lanterne de scène *f*
– *mirror spot (mirror spotlight)*
49 le panneau rotatif de filtres *m* colorés
– *automatic filter change (with colour filters, colour mediums, gelatines)*
50 la salle de presse *f* hydraulique
– *hydraulic plant room*
51 le réservoir d'eau *f*
– *water tank*
52 la canalisation d'aspiration *f*
– *suction pipe*
53 la pompe hydraulique
– *hydraulic pump*
54 la canalisation de refoulement *m*
– *pressure pipe*
55 le réservoir (l'accumulateur *m*) de pression *f*
– *pressure tank (accumulator)*
56 le manomètre à contact *m*
– *pressure gauge* (Am. *gage)*
57 l'indicateur *m* de niveau *m* d'eau *f*
– *level indicator (liquid level indicator)*
58 le levier de commande *f*
– *control lever*
59 le brigadier des machines *f*
– *operator*
60 les pistons *m* hydrauliques
– *rams*

4
8
6
5
3
2
1
7
9
10
11
12
13
16
17
18
15
13
20
19
14
24
8
17
21
22
23
36
37
39
35
30
17
29
25
27
31
38
33
34
28
26
32
44
43
47
40
41
47
42
50
55
33
45
51
56
58
60
46
52
57
17
53
59
48
54
49

1 le bar
– *bar*
2 la dame du bar (la barmaid)
– *barmaid*
3 le tabouret de bar *m*
– *bar stool*
4 l'étagère *f* à bouteilles *f*
– *shelf for bottles*
5 l'étagère *f* à verres *m*
– *shelf for glasses*
6 le verre à bière *f*
– *beer glass*
7 les verres *m* à vin *m* et à liqueur *f*
– *wine and liqueur glasses*
8 le robinet distributeur de bière *f*
– *beer tap (tap)*
9 le comptoir du bar (comptoir *m*)
– *bar*
10 le réfrigérateur
– *refrigerator (fridge,* Am. *icebox)*
11 les lampes *f* du bar
– *bar lamps*
12 l'éclairage *m* indirect
– *indirect lighting*
13 la batterie de projecteurs *m*
– *colour* (Am. *color) organ (clavilux)*
14 l'éclairage *m* de piste *f*
– *dance floor lighting*
15 l'enceinte *f* (acoustique)
– *speaker (loudspeaker)*
16 la piste de danse *f*
– *dance floor*
17-18 le couple de danseurs *m*
– *dancing couple*
17 la danseuse
– *dancer*
18 le danseur
– *dancer*
19 l'électrophone *m*
– *record player*
20 le microphone (*fam:* le micro)
– *microphone*
21 le magnétophone
– *tape recorder*
22-23 la chaîne haute-fidélité
– *stereo system (stereo equipment)*
22 le tuner
– *tuner*
23 l'amplificateur *m* (*fam:* l'ampli *m*)
– *amplifier*
24 les disques *m*
– *records (discs)*
25 le discjockey (*ELF:* le présentateur)
– *disc jockey*
26 le pupitre de mixage
– *mixing console (mixing desk, mixer)*
27 le tambourin
– *tambourine*
28 la cloison vitrée
– *mirrored wall*
29 le revêtement de plafond *m*
– *ceiling tiles*
30 le système d'aération *f*
– *ventilators*
31 les toilettes *f*
– *toilets (lavatories, WC)*
32 le long drink
– *long drink*
33 le cocktail
– *cocktail* (Am. *highball)*

1-33 la boîte de nuit *f* (le nightclub)
– ***nightclub*** *(night spot)*
1 le vestiaire
– *cloakroom (*Am. *checkroom)*
2 la demoiselle du vestiaire
– *cloakroom attendant (*Am. *checkroom attendant)*
3 l'orchestre *m*
– *band*
4 la clarinette
– *clarinet*
5 le clarinettiste
– *clarinettist (*Am. *clarinetist)*
6 la trompette
– *trumpet*
7 le trompettiste
– *trumpeter*
8 la guitare
– *guitar*
9 le guitariste
– *guitarist (guitar player)*
10 la batterie
– *drums*
11 le batteur
– *drummer*
12 l'enceinte *f* (acoustique)
– *speaker (loudspeaker)*
13 le bar
– *bar*
14 la dame du bar (la barmaid)
– *barmaid*
15 le comptoir du bar
– *bar*
16 le tabouret de bar *m*
– *bar stool*
17 le magnétophone
– *tape recorder*
18 l'appareil *m* (récepteur *m*) de radio *f*
– *receiver*
19 les alcools *m*
– *spirits*
20 le projecteur pour films *m* pornographiques en huit millimètres *m*
– *cine projector for porno films (sex films, blue movies)*
21 l'écran *m* dans son logement *m*
– *box containing screen*
22 la scène
– *stage*
23 l'éclairage *m* de scène *f*
– *stage lighting*
24 le projecteur de scène *f*
– *spotlight*
25 la rampe
– *festoon lighting*
26 la lampe de la rampe
– *festoon lamp (lamp, light bulb)*
27-32 le strip-tease (le numéro de strip-tease *m*)
– *striptease act (striptease number)*
27 la strip-teaseuse
– *striptease artist (stripper)*
28 la jarretelle
– *suspender (*Am. *garter)*
29 le soutien-gorge
– *brassière (bra)*
30 l'étole *f* de fourrure
– *fur stole*
31 les gants *m*
– *gloves*
32 le bas
– *stocking*
33 l'entraîneuse *f*
– *hostess*

1-33 la corrida (le combat de taureaux *m*, la course de taureaux *m*)
– ***bullfight** (corrida, corrida de toros)*
1 la passe de corrida *f* (le «quiebro», la passe de banderilles *f*)
– *mock bullfight*
2 le novillero (le torero débutant, l'apprenti *m* torero)
– *novillero*
3 le taureau factice [le chariot orné de cornes *f* et monté sur une roue de bicyclette *f*]
– *mock bull (dummy bull)*
4 l'apprenti *m* banderillero
– *novice banderillero (apprentice banderillero)*
5 l'arène *f* (la «Plaza de toros», l'amphithéâtre *m*) [schéma]
– *bullring (plaza de toros) [diagram]*
6 l'entrée *f* principale
– *main entrance*
7 les loges *f*
– *boxes*
8 les places *f* assises (les gradins *m*)
– *stands*
9 l'arène *f* proprement dite (le «ruedo», le redondel)
– *arena (ring)*
10 la porte d'entrée *f* des toreros *m* (des toréadors *m*)
– *bullfighters' entrance*
11 la sortie du toril (la sortie des «corrales»)
– *torril door*
12 la porte de service *m* d'arrastre *m* [pour évacuer les cadavres *m* de taureaux *m*]
– *exit gate for killed bulls*
13 la cour d'équarrissage *m* (le «desolladero», l'abattoir *m*)
– *slaughterhouse*
14 le toril (les étables *f* de taureaux *m*)
– *bull pens (corrals)*
15 la cour des chevaux *m* (le «patio de los caballeros», les écuries *f*)
– *paddock*
16 le picador
– *lancer on horseback (picador)*
17 la pique
– *lance (pike pole, javelin)*
18 le cheval caparaçonné
– *armoured* (Am. *armored*) *horse*
19 la jambière en fer *m* (la «mona»)
– *leg armour* (Am. *armor*)
20 le chapeau rond de picador *m* (le «castoreño»)
– *picador's round hat*
21 le banderillero (le péon), un torero (un toréador)
– *banderillero, a torero*
22 les banderilles *f*
– *banderillas (barbed darts)*
23 la ceinture en soie *f* (la «faja»)
– *shirtwaist*
24 le combat (la passe)
– *bullfight*
25 le matador (l'espada *m*), un torero (un toréador)
– *matador (swordsman), a torero*
26 la petite queue de cheval *m* (tresse *f* de cheveux *m*) maintenue par une résille ornée d'un ruban noir (la «coleta», un insigne de la classe des toreros *m*)
– *queue, a distinguishing mark of the matador*
27 la cape (l'étoffe *f* rouge)
– *red cloak (capa)*
28 le taureau de combat *m* (le «toro»)
– *fighting bull*
29 le chapeau rond et noir du torero (la «montera»)
– *montera [hat made of tiny black silk chenille balls]*
30 l'estocade *f* (la mise à mort du taureau «a volaque»)
– *killing the bull (kill)*
31 le matador des corridas *f* de bienfaisance *f* [sans costume *m* de combat *m*]
– *matador in charity performances [without professional uniform]*
32 l'épée *f* (l'«estoque»)
– *estoque (sword)*
33 la muleta
– *muleta*
34 le rodéo
– ***rodeo***
35 le jeune taureau (le novillo)
– *young bull*
36 le cow-boy
– *cowboy*
37 le chapeau mou de cow-boy *m* (le stetson)
– *stetson (stetson hat)*
38 le foulard
– *scarf (necktie)*
39 le cavalier de rodéo *m*
– *rodeo rider*
40 le lasso
– *lasso*

1
2
3
4
5
6
7
8
8
9
10
11
12
13
14
15
16
17
18
19
20
21
22
22
23
24
25
26
26
27
28
29
30
31
32
33
34
35
36
37
38
39
40

1-2 la notation médiévale
– ***medieval (mediaeval) notes***
1 la notation du plain-chant
– *plainsong notation (neumes, neums, pneumes, square notation)*
2 la notation mesurée
– *mensural notation*
3-7 la note de musique *f*
– ***musical note*** *(note)*
3 la tête
– *note head*
4 la queue
– *note stem (note tail)*
5 le crochet
– *hook*
6 la barre
– *stroke*
7 le point
– *dot indicating augmentation of note's value*
8-11 les clés *f*
– ***clefs***
8 la clé de sol
– *treble clef (G-clef, violin clef)*
9 la clé de fa
– *bass clef (F-clef)*
10 la clé d'ut troisième
– *alto clef (C-clef)*
11 la clé d'ut quatrième
– *tenor clef*
12-19 les valeurs *f* des notes *f*
– ***note values***
12 la double ronde
– *breve (brevis,* Am. *double-whole note)*
13 la ronde
– *semibreve (*Am. *whole note)*
14 la blanche
– *minim (*Am. *half note)*
15 la noire
– *crotchet (*Am. *quarter note)*
16 la croche
– *quaver (*Am. *eighth note)*
17 la double croche
– *semiquaver (*Am. *sixteenth note)*
18 la triple croche
– *demisemiquaver (*Am. *thirty-second note)*
19 la quadruple croche
– *hemidemisemiquaver (*Am. *sixty-fourth note)*
20-27 les silences *m*
– ***rests***
20 la double pause
– *breve rest*
21 la pause
– *semibreve rest (*Am. *whole rest)*
22 la demi-pause
– *minim rest (*Am. *half rest)*
23 le soupir
– *crotchet rest (*Am. *quarter rest)*
24 le demi-soupir
– *quaver rest (*Am. *eighth rest)*
25 le quart de soupir *m*
– *semiquaver rest (*Am. *sixteenth rest)*
26 le huitième de soupir *m*
– *demisemiquaver rest (*Am. *thirty-second rest)*
27 le seizième de soupir *m*
– *hemidemisemiquaver rest (*Am. *sixty-fourth rest)*
28-42 la mesure
– ***time*** *(time signatures, measure,* Am. *meter)*
28 la mesure à deux-huit
– *two-eight time*
29 la mesure à deux-quatre
– *two-four time*
30 la mesure à deux-deux
– *two-two time*
31 la mesure à quatre-huit
– *four-eight time*
32 la mesure à quatre-quatre
– *four-four time (common time)*
33 la mesure à quatre-deux
– *four-two time*
34 la mesure à six-huit
– *six-eight time*
35 la mesure à six-quatre
– *six-four time*
36 la mesure à trois-huit
– *three-eight time*
37 la mesure à trois-quatre
– *three-four time*
38 la mesure à trois-deux
– *three-two time*
39 la mesure à neuf-huit
– *nine-eight time*
40 la mesure à neuf-quatre
– *nine-four time*
41 la mesure à cinq-quatre
– *five-four time*
42 la barre de mesure
– *bar (bar line, measure line)*
43-44 la portée
– ***staff*** *(stave)*
43 la ligne
– *line of the staff*
44 l'interligne *m*
– *space*
45-49 les gammes *f*
– ***scales***
45 la gamme d'ut *m* majeur; *notes f fondamentales:* ut (do), ré, mi, fa, sol, la, si, do (ut)
– *C major scale naturals: c, d, e, f, g, a, b, c*
46 la gamme de la mineur (naturelle); *notes f fondamentales:* la, si, do, ré, mi, fa, sol, la
– *A minor scale [natural] naturals: a, b, c, d, e, f, g, a*
47 la gamme de la *m* mineur (harmonique)
– *A minor scale [harmonic]*
48 la gamme de la *m* mineur (mélodique)
– *A minor scale [melodic]*
49 la gamme chromatique
– *chromatic scale*
50-54 les altérations *f*
– ***accidentals*** *(inflections, key signatures)*
50-51 les signes *m* d'élévation *f*
– *signs indicating the raising of a note*
50 le dièse (l'élévation *f* d'un demi-ton)
– *sharp (raising the note a semitone or half-step)*
51 le double dièse (l'élévation *f* d'un ton)
– *double sharp (raising the note a tone or full-step)*
52-53 les signes *m* d'abaissement *m*
– *signs indicating the lowering of a note*
52 le bémol (l'abaissement *m* d'un demi-ton)
– *flat (lowering the note a semitone or half-step)*
53 le double bémol (l'abaissement *m* d'un ton)
– *double flat (lowering the note a tone or full-step)*
54 le bécarre
– *natural*
55-68 les tonalités *f* (tonalités *f* en mode *m* majeur et leurs relatifs *m* en mode *m* mineur avec les mêmes altérations *f*)
– ***keys*** *(major keys and the related minor keys having the same signature)*
55 ut *m* majeur (la *m* mineur)
– *C major (A minor)*
56 sol *m* majeur (mi *m* mineur)
– *G major (E minor)*
57 ré *m* majeur (si *m* mineur)
– *D major (B minor)*
58 la *m* majeur (fa *m* dièse mineur)
– *A major (F sharp minor)*
59 mi *m* majeur (ut *m* dièse mineur)
– *E major (C sharp minor)*
60 si *m* majeur (sol *m* dièse majeur)
– *B major (G sharp minor)*
61 fa *m* dièse majeur (ré *m* dièse mineur)
– *F sharp major (D sharp minor)*
62 ut *m* majeur (la *m* mineur)
– *C major (A minor)*
63 fa *m* majeur (ré *m* mineur)
– *F major (D minor)*
64 si *m* bémol majeur (sol *m* mineur)
– *B flat major (G minor)*
65 mi *m* bémol majeur (ut *m* mineur)
– *E flat major (C minor)*
66 la *m* bémol majeur (fa *m* mineur)
– *A flat major (F minor)*
67 ré *m* bémol majeur (si *m* bémol mineur)
– *D flat major (B flat minor)*
68 sol *m* bémol majeur (mi *m* bémol mineur)
– *G flat major (E flat minor)*

1
Magni - fí-cat
2
Nu kom der heidē Heiland,
3
4
5
6
7
8
9
10
11
12
13
14
15
16
17
18
19
20
21
22
23
24
25
26
27
28
29
30
31
32
33
34
35
36
37
38
39
40
41
42
43
44
45
46
47
48
49
50
51
52
53
54
55
56
57
58
59
60
61
62
63
64
65
66
67
68

1-5 l'accord *m*
– ***chord***
1-4 les accords *m* parfaits
– *triad*
1 l'accord *m* parfait majeur
– *major triad*
2 l'accord *m* parfait mineur
– *minor triad*
3 l'accord *m* de quinte *f* diminuée
– *diminished triad*
4 l'accord *m* de quinte *f* augmentée
– *augmented triad*
5 l'accord *m* de septième
– *chord of four notes, a chord of the seventh (seventh chord, dominant seventh chord)*
6-13 les intervalles *m*
– ***intervals***
6 l'unisson *m*
– *unison (unison interval)*
7 la seconde majeure
– *major second*
8 la tierce majeure
– *major third*
9 la quarte
– *perfect fourth*
10 la quinte
– *perfect fifth*
11 la sixte majeure
– *major sixth*
12 la septième majeure
– *major seventh*
13 l'octave *f*
– *perfect octave*
14-22 les ornements *m*
– ***ornaments*** *(graces, grace notes)*
14 l'appogiature *f* longue
– *long appoggiatura*
15 l'appogiature *f* brève
– *acciaccatura (short appoggiatura)*
16 l'appogiature *f* double
– *slide*
17 le mordant
– *trill (shake) without turn*
18 la trille
– *trill (shake) with turn*
19 le trémolo
– *upper mordent (inverted mordent, pralltriller)*
20 le mordant inférieur
– *lower mordent (mordent)*
21 le gruppetto
– *turn*
22 l'arpège *m*
– *arpeggio*
23-26 les autres signes *m*
– *other signs in musical notation*
23 le triolet (*par analogie:* le duolet, le quartolet, le sextolet et, *peu usités:* le quintolet, le heptolet)
– *triplet;* corresponding groupings: *duplet (couplet), quadruplet, quintuplet, sextolet (sextuplet), septolet (septuplet, septimole)*
24 la liaison
– *tie (bind)*
25 le point d'orgue *m*, un signe d'arrêt *m* et de repos *m*
– *pause (pause sign)*
26 le signe de reprise *f*
– *repeat mark*
27-41 les indications *f* d'expression *f*
– ***expression marks*** *(signs of relative intensity)*
27 l'accent *m*
– *marcato (marcando, markiert, attack, strong accent)*
28 presto (rapide)
– *presto (quick, fast)*
29 portato (note *f* filée)
– *portato (lourer, mezzo staccato, carried)*
30 tenuto (note tenue)
– *tenuto (held)*
31 crescendo (en augmentant)
– *crescendo (increasing gradually in power)*
32 decrescendo (en diminuant)
– *decrescendo (diminuendo, decreasing or diminishing gradually in power)*
33 legato (lié)
– *legato (bound)*
34 staccato (pointé)
– *staccato (detached)*
35 piano (doucement)
– *piano (soft)*
36 pianissimo (très doucement)
– *pianissimo (very soft)*
37 pianissimo piano (le plus doucement possible)
– *pianissimo piano (as soft as possible)*
38 forte (fort)
– *forte (loud)*
39 fortissimo (très fort)
– *fortissimo (very loud)*
40 forte fortissimo (le plus fort possible)
– *forte fortissimo (double fortissimo, as loud as possible)*
41 fortepiano (attaque *f* forte, résonance *f* douce)
– *forte piano (loud and immediately soft again)*
42-50 l'échelle *f* **musicale**
– ***divisions of the compass***
42 la double contre-octave
– *subcontra octave (double contra octave)*
43 la contre-octave
– *contra octave*
44 la première octave
– *great octave*
45 la deuxième octave
– *small octave*
46 la troisième octave
– *one-line octave*
47 la quatrième octave
– *two-line octave*
48 la cinquième octave
– *three-line octave*
49 la sixième octave
– *four-line octave*
50 la septième octave
– *five-line octave*

1
2
3
4
5
6
7
8
9
10
11
12
13
14
15
16
17
18
19
20
21
22
23
3
27
24
25
26
28
Presto
29
30
ten.
33
cresc.
decresc.
cresc.
31
decresc.
32
34
p
35
pp
36
ppp
37
f
38
ff
39
fff
40
fp
41
8va sopra
42
43
44
45
46
47
48
49
50
8va bassa
in Britain:
A2 B♭2 B2 C1 etc.
B1 C B c β c' b' c'' b'' c''' b''' c'''' b'''' c'''''
en France:
la02 si b02 si02 do01 etc.
si01 do1 si1 do2 si2 do3 si3 do4 si4 do5 si5 do6 si6 do7

1 le lur (lour *m*), une trompe de bronze *m*
– *lur, a bronze trumpet*
2 la flûte de Pan (la syrinx)
– *panpipes (Pandean pipes, syrinx)*
3 la diaule (l'aulos *m*), une flûte double
– *aulos, a double shawm*
4 la flûte
– *aulos pipe*
5 la phorbéïa
– *phorbeia (peristomion, capistrum, mouth band)*
6 le cromorne (le tournebout)
– *crumhorn (crummhorn, cromorne, krumbhorn, krummhorn)*
7 la flûte à bec *m*
– *recorder (fipple flute)*
8 la cornemuse; *anal.:* la musette, le biniou
– *bagpipe;* sim.: *musette*
9 le réservoir d'air *m* (l'outre *f*)
– *bag*
10 le tuyau de mélodie *f* (le chalumeau)
– *chanter (melody pipe)*
11 le tuyau de bourdon *m* (le bourdon)
– *drone (drone pipe)*
12 le cornet à bouquin *m*
– *curved cornett (zink)*
13 le serpent
– *serpent*
14 le chalumeau; *plus grands:* la bombarde, le pommer
– *shawm (schalmeyes);* larger: *bombard (bombarde, pommer)*
15 la cithare; *anal. et plus petite:* la lyre
– *cythara (cithara);* sim. and smaller: *lyre*
16 le montant de cithare *f*
– *arm*
17 le chevalet
– *bridge*
18 la caisse de résonance
– *sound box (resonating chamber, resonator)*
19 le plectre
– *plectrum, a plucking device*
20 la pochette (le violon de petit format *m*)
– *kit (pochette), a miniature violin*
21 le cistre, un instrument à cordes *f* pincées; *anal.:* la pandore
– *cittern (cithern, cither, cister, citole), a plucked instrument;* sim.: *pandora (bandora, bandore)*
22 la rose (la rosace)
– *sound hole*
23 la viole, une viole de gambe *f*; *plus grandes:* la basse de viole *f*, la violone (contrebasse de viole *f*)
– *viol (descant viol, treble viol), a viola da gamba;* larger: *tenor viol, bass viol (viola da gamba, gamba), violone (double bass viol)*
24 l'archet *m* de viole *f*
– *viol bow*
25 la vielle (vielle *f* à roue *f*, vielle *f* de ménétrier *m*, vielle *f* de mendiant *m*, la chifonie, l'organistrum *m*)
– *hurdy-gurdy (vielle à roue, symphonia, armonie, organistrum)*
26 la roue de vielle *f*
– *friction wheel*
27 le couvercle
– *wheel cover (wheel guard)*
28 le clavier
– *keyboard (keys)*
29 la caisse de résonance *f*
– *resonating body (resonator, sound box)*
30 les cordes *f* mélodiques
– *melody strings*
31 les cordes *f* bourdons
– *drone strings (drones, bourdons)*
32 le tympanon (le czimbalum, le cymbalum)
– *dulcimer*
33 le cadre
– *rib (resonator wall)*
34 la batte de tympanon *m* valaisan
– *beater for the Valasian dulcimer*
35 le marteau de tympanon *m* appenzellois
– *hammer (stick) for the Appenzell dulcimer*
36 le clavicorde; *types:* clavicorde *m* lié, clavicorde *m* libre
– *clavichord;* kinds: *fretted or unfretted clavichord*
37 la mécanique du clavicorde
– *clavichord mechanism*
38 la touche (levier *m* de touche *f*)
– *key (key lever)*
39 la sellette de bascule *f*
– *balance rail*
40 le tenon de guidage *m*
– *guiding blade*
41 la fente de guidage *m*
– *guiding slot*
42 l'appui *m*
– *resting rail*
43 la tangente
– *tangent*
44 la corde
– *string*
45 le clavecin, un instrument à clavier *m* à cordes *f* griffées; *anal.:* l'épinette *f*, le virginal (la virginale)
– *harpsichord (clavicembalo, cembalo), a wing-shaped stringed keyboard instrument;* sim.: *spinet (virginal)*
46 le clavier (manuel) supérieur
– *upper keyboard (upper manual)*
47 le clavier (manuel) inférieur
– *lower keyboard (lower manual)*
48 la mécanique du clavecin
– *harpsichord mechanism*
49 la touche (levier *m* de touche *f*)
– *key (key lever)*
50 le sautereau
– *jack*
51 le registre à mortaises *f*
– *slide (register)*
52 la languette de sautereau *m*
– *tongue*
53 le bec de plume *f*
– *quill plectrum*
54 l'étouffoir *m*
– *damper*
55 la corde
– *string*
56 l'orgue *m* portatif (le régal); *plus grand:* un (orgue) positif [l'orgue est masculin au singulier et féminin au pluriel]
– *portative organ, a portable organ;* larger: *positive organ (positive)*
57 le tuyau (d'orgue *m*)
– *pipe (flue pipe)*
58 le soufflet
– *bellows*

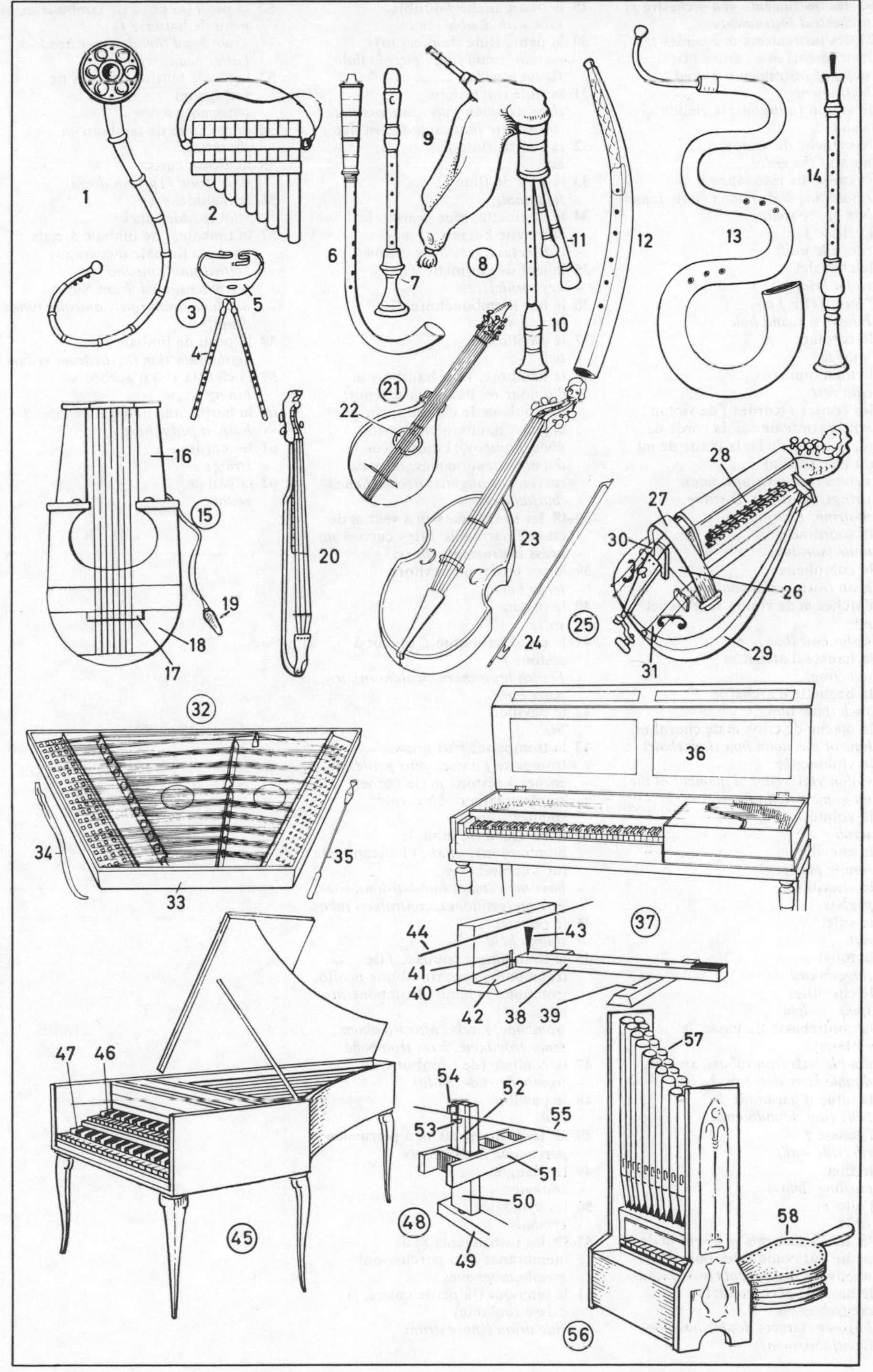
1
2
3
4
5
6
7
8
9
10
11
12
13
14
15
16
17
18
19
20
21
22
23
24
25
26
27
28
29
30
31
32
33
34
35
36
37
38
39
40
41
42
43
44
45
46
47
48
49
50
51
52
53
54
55
56
57
58

1-62 les instruments *m* **d'orchestre** *m*
– ***orchestral instruments***
1-27 les instruments *m* **à cordes** *f*, instruments *m* à cordes *f* frottées
– ***stringed instruments**, bowed instruments*
1 le violon (*autrefois:* la vielle)
– *violin*
2 le manche du violon
– *neck of the violin*
3 la caisse de résonance *f*
– *resonating body (violin body, sound box of the violin)*
4 l'éclisse *f*
– *rib (side wall)*
5 le chevalet
– *violin bridge*
6 l'ouïe *f* (FF *f pl*)
– *F-hole, a sound hole*
7 le cordier
– *tailpiece*
8 la mentonnière
– *chin rest*
9 les cordes *f* (cordes *f* de violon *m*); la corde de sol, la corde de ré, la corde de la, la corde de mi (la chanterelle)
– *strings (violin strings, fiddle strings): G-string, D-string, A-string, E-string*
10 la sourdine
– *mute (sordino)*
11 la colophane
– *resin (rosin, colophony)*
12 l'archet *m* de violon *m* (l'archet *m*)
– *violin bow (bow)*
13 la hausse d'archet *m*
– *nut (frog)*
14 la baguette d'archet *m*
– *stick (bow stick)*
15 la mèche de crins *m* de cheval *m*
– *hair of the violin bow (horsehair)*
16 le violoncelle
– *violoncello (cello), a member of the da gamba violin family*
17 la volute
– *scroll*
18 la cheville
– *tuning peg (peg)*
19 le chevillier
– *pegbox*
20 le sillet
– *nut*
21 la touche
– *fingerboard*
22 le chevillier
– *spike (tailpin)*
23 la contrebasse (la basse, la violone)
– *double bass (contrabass, violone, double bass viol,* Am. *bass)*
24 la table d'harmonie *f*
– *belly (top, soundboard)*
25 l'éclisse *f*
– *rib (side wall)*
26 le filet
– *purfling (inlay)*
27 l'alto *m*
– *viola*
28-38 les instruments *m* **à vent** *m* de petite harmonie *f* (les bois *m*)
– ***woodwind instruments** (woodwinds)*
28 le basson; *plus grand:* le contrebasson
– *bassoon;* larger: *double bassoon (contrabassoon)*
29 le bec à anche *f* double
– *tube with double reed*
30 la petite flûte (le piccolo)
– *piccolo (small flute, piccolo flute, flauto piccolo)*
31 la flûte traversière
– *flute (German flute), a cross flute (transverse flute, side-blown flute)*
32 la clef de flûte *f*
– *key*
33 le trou de flûte *f*
– *fingerhole*
34 la clarinette; *plus grande:* la clarinette basse
– *clarinet;* larger: *bass clarinet*
35 la clef de clarinette *f*
– *key (brille)*
36 le bec (l'embouchure *f*)
– *mouthpiece*
37 le pavillon
– *bell*
38 le hautbois; *var.:* hautbois *m* d'amour *m*; hautbois *m* ténor: hautbois *m* de chasse *f*, cor *m* anglais; hautbois *m* baryton
– *oboe (hautboy);* kinds: *oboe d'amore; tenor oboes: oboe da caccia, cor anglais; heckelphone (baritone oboe)*
39-48 les instruments *m* **à vent** *m* de grande harmonie *f* (les cuivres *m*)
– ***brass instruments** (brass)*
39 le cor ténor, un saxhorn
– *tenor horn*
40 le piston
– *valve*
41 le cor d'harmonie *f*, un cor à pistons *f*
– *French horn (horn, waldhorn), a valve horn*
42 le pavillon
– *bell*
43 la trompette; *plus grande:* trompette *f* basse; *plus petite:* le cornet à pistons *m* (le cornet)
– *trumpet;* larger: *Bb cornet;* smaller: *cornet*
44 le basstuba (le tuba, le bombardon); *anal.:* l'hélicon *m*, le tuba contrebasse
– *bass tuba (tuba, bombardon);* sim.: *helicon (pellitone), contrabass tuba*
45 le poucier
– *thumb hold*
46 le trombone à coulisse *f* (le trombone); *var.:* trombone *m* alto, trombone *m* ténor; trombone *m* basse
– *trombone;* kinds: *alto trombone, tenor trombone, bass trombone*
47 la coulisse (de trombone *m*)
– *trombone slide (slide)*
48 le pavillon
– *bell*
49-59 les instruments *m* **à percussion** *f*
– ***percussion instruments***
49 le triangle
– *triangle*
50 les cymbales *f*
– *cymbals*
51-59 les instruments *m* à membranes *f* (la percussion)
– *membranophones*
51 le tambour (la petite caisse, la caisse roulante)
– *side drum (snare drum)*
52 la peau (la peau de tambour *m*, la peau de batterie *f*)
– *drum head (head, upper head, batter head, vellum)*
53 la vis de tension *f* (la vis de serrage *m*)
– *tensioning screw*
54 la baguette de tambour *m*
– *drumstick*
55 la grosse caisse
– *bass drum (Turkish drum)*
56 la mailloche
– *stick (padded stick)*
57 la timbale, une timbale à clefs *f*; *anal.:* la timbale mécanique
– *kettledrum (timpano), a screw-tensioned drum;* sim.: *machine drum (mechanically tuned drum)*
58 la peau de timbale *f*
– *kettledrum skin (kettledrum vellum)*
59 la clef (la vis) d'accord *m*
– *tuning screw*
60 la harpe, une harpe à pédales *f*
– *harp, a pedal harp*
61 les cordes
– *strings*
62 la pédale
– *pedal*

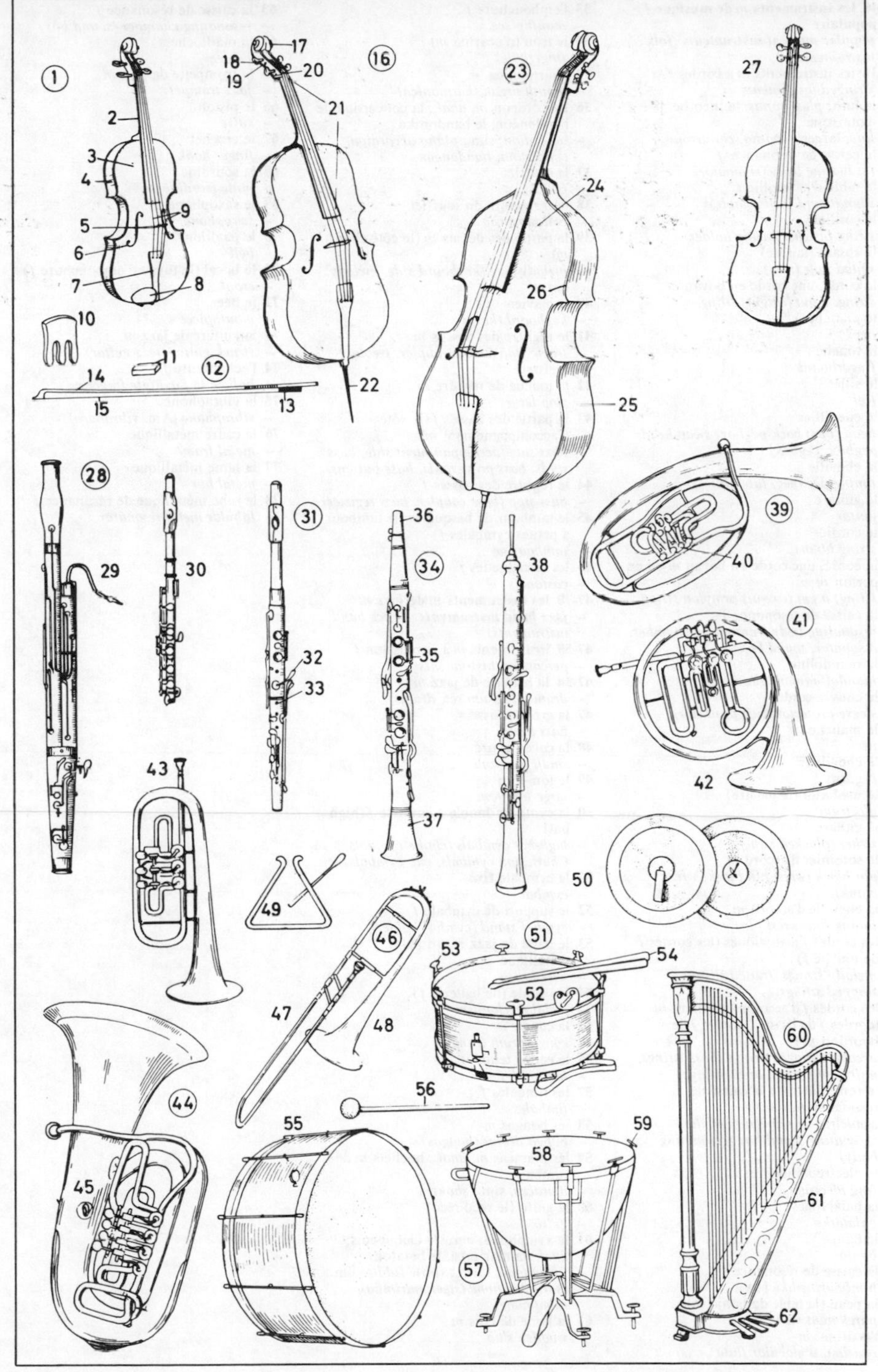
1
2
3
4
5
6
7
8
9
10
11
12
13
14
15
16
17
18
19
20
21
22
23
24
25
26
27
28
29
30
31
32
33
34
35
36
37
38
39
40
41
42
43
44
45
46
47
48
49
50
51
52
53
54
55
56
57
58
59
60
61
62

1-46 les instruments *m* **de musique** *f* **populaire**
- ***popular musical instruments*** *(folk instruments)*

1-31 les instruments *m* à cordes *f*
- *stringed instruments*

1 le luth; *plus grands:* la théorbe, le chitarrone
- *lute;* larger: *theorbo, chitarrone*

2 la caisse de résonance *f*
- *resonating body (resonator)*

3 la table d'harmonie *f*
- *soundboard (belly, table)*

4 le cordier
- *string fastener (string holder)*

5 la rosace (la rose)
- *sound hole (rose)*

6 la corde, une corde en boyau *m*
- *string, a gut (catgut) string*

7 le manche
- *neck*

8 la touche
- *fingerboard*

9 le sillet
- *fret*

10 le chevillier
- *head (bent-back pegbox, swan-head pegbox, pegbox)*

11 la cheville
- *tuning peg (peg, lute pin)*

12 la guitare
- *guitar*

13 le cordier
- *string holder*

14 la corde, une corde en boyau *m* ou en perlon *m*
- *string, a gut (catgut) or nylon string*

15 la caisse de résonance *f*
- *resonating body (resonating chamber, resonator, sound box)*

16 la mandoline
- *mandolin (mandoline)*

17 le couvre-cordes
- *sleeve protector (cuff protector)*

18 le manche
- *neck*

19 le chevillier
- *pegdisc*

20 le médiator (le plectre)
- *plectrum*

21 la cithare
- *zither (plucked zither)*

22 le sommier d'accord *m*
- *pin block (wrest pin block, wrest plank)*

23 la cheville d'accord *m*
- *tuning pin (wrest pin)*

24 les cordes *f* mélodiques (les cordes *f* de touche *f*)
- *melody strings (fretted strings, stopped strings)*

25 les cordes *f* d'accompagnement *m* (cordes *f* de basse *f*, cordes *f* de bourdon *m*)
- *accompaniment strings (bass strings, unfretted strings, open strings)*

26 le renflement de la caisse de résonance *f*
- *semicircular projection of the resonating sound box (resonating body)*

27 le plectre annulaire
- *ring plectrum*

28 la balalaïka
- *balalaika*

29 le banjo
- *banjo*

30 la caisse de résonance *f*
- *tambourine-like body*

31 la peau (la table de banjo *m*)
- *parchment membrane*

32 l'ocarina *m*
- *ocarina, a globular flute*

33 l'embouchure *f*
- *mouthpiece*

34 le trou (d'ocarina *m*)
- *fingerhole*

35 l'harmonica *m*
- *mouth organ (harmonica)*

36 l'accordéon *m*; *anal.:* la concertina, le bandonéon, le bandonika
- *accordion;* sim.: *piano accordion, concertina, bandoneon*

37 le soufflet
- *bellows*

38 la fermeture du soufflet
- *bellows strap*

39 la partie des dessus *m* (le côté chant *m*)
- *melody side (keyboard side, melody keys)*

40 le clavier
- *keyboard (keys)*

41 le registre des dessus *m*
- *treble stop (treble coupler, treble register)*

42 la touche de registre *m*
- *stop lever*

43 la partie des basses *f* (le côté d'accompagnement *m*)
- *bass side (accompaniment side, bass studs, bass press-studs, bass buttons)*

44 le registre des basses *f*
- *bass stop (bass coupler, bass register)*

45 le tambour de basque *m* (le tambour à petites cymbales *f*)
- *tambourine*

46 les castagnettes *f*
- *castanets*

47-78 les instruments *m* **de jazz** *m*
- ***jazz band instruments*** *(dance band instruments)*

47-58 instruments *m* à percussion *f*
- *percussion instruments*

47-54 la batterie de jazz *m*
- *drum kit (drum set, drums)*

47 la grosse caisse
- *bass drum*

48 la caisse claire
- *small tom-tom*

49 le tom-tom
- *large tom-tom*

50 la cymbale double à coulisse *f* (high hat)
- *high-hat cymbals (choke cymbals, Charleston cymbals, cup cymbals)*

51 la cymbale fixe
- *cymbal*

52 le support de cymbale *f*
- *cymbal stand (cymbal holder)*

53 le balai de jazz *m*, un balai métallique
- *wire brush*

54 la pédale (de batterie *f*)
- *pedal mechanism*

55 la conga
- *conga drum (conga)*

56 le cercle tendeur
- *tension hoop*

57 les timbales *f*
- *timbales*

58 les bongos *m*
- *bongo drums (bongos)*

59 les maracas *m*; *anal.:* hochets *m* de rumba *f*
- *maracas;* sim.: *shakers*

60 le guiro (le reco-reco)
- *guiro*

61 le xylophone; *anc.:* le claquebois; *anal.:* la marimba, le balafon
- *xylophone;* form.: *straw fiddle;* sim.: *marimbaphone (steel marimba), tubaphone*

62 la lame de bois *m*
- *wooden slab*

63 la caisse de résonance *f*
- *resonating chamber (sound box)*

64 la mailloche
- *beater*

65 la trompette de jazz *m*
- *jazz trumpet*

66 le piston
- *valve*

67 le crochet
- *finger hook*

68 la sourdine
- *mute (sordino)*

69 le saxophone
- *saxophone*

70 le pavillon
- *bell*

71 le bocal (le tuyau d'embouchure *f*)
- *crook*

72 le bec
- *mouthpiece*

73 la guitare de jazz *m*
- *struck guitar (jazz guitar)*

74 l'échancrure *f*
- *hollow to facilitate fingering*

75 le vibraphone
- *vibraphone* (Am. *vibraharp)*

76 le cadre métallique
- *metal frame*

77 la lame métallique
- *metal bar*

78 le tube métallique de résonance *f*
- *tubular metal resonator*

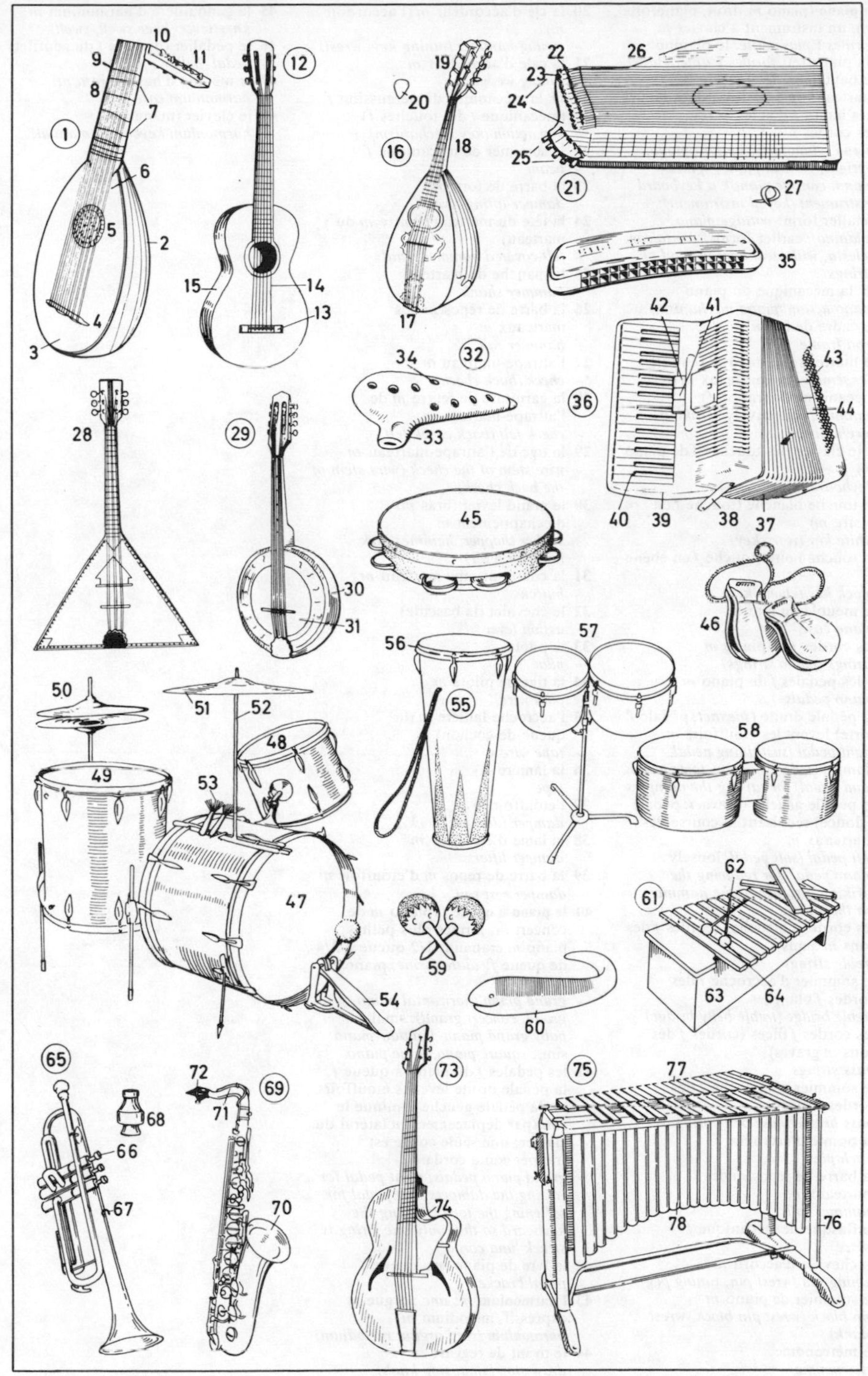
1
2
3
4
5
6
7
8
9
10
11
12
13
14
15
16
17
18
19
20
21
22
23
24
25
26
27
28
29
30
31
32
33
34
35
36
37
38
39
40
41
42
43
44
45
46
47
48
49
50
51
52
53
54
55
56
57
58
59
60
61
62
63
64
65
66
67
68
69
70
71
72
73
74
75
76
77
78

1 **le piano** (piano *m* droit, pianoforte *m*), un instrument à clavier *m*; *formes* f *plus petite:* le pianino (la pianette); *formes* f *antérieures:* le pantaléon, le clavecin à marteaux *m*, le célesta dans lequel des lames *f* d'acier *m* remplacent les cordes *f*
– ***piano*** *(pianoforte, upright piano, upright, vertical piano, spinet piano, console piano), a keyboard instrument (keyed instrument);* smaller form: *cottage piano (pianino);* earlier forms: *pantaleon, celesta, with steel bars instead of strings*
2-18 la mécanique du piano
– *piano action (piano mechanism)*
2 le cadre de fer *m*
– *iron frame*
3 le marteau (marteau *m* feutré); *l'ensemble:* les marteaux *m* (le mécanisme de frappe *f*)
– *hammer;* collectively: *striking mechanism*
4-5 le clavier (les touches *f* de piano *m*)
– *keyboard (piano keys)*
4 la touche blanche (touche *f* en ivoire *m*)
– *white key (ivory key)*
5 la touche noire (touche *f* en ébène *f*)
– *black key (ebony key)*
6 le meuble du piano
– *piano case*
7 les cordes *f* de piano *m*
– *strings (piano strings)*
8-9 les pédales *f* de piano *m*
– *piano pedals*
8 la pédale droite (*inexact:* pédale *f* forte) levant les étouffoirs *m*
– *right pedal (sustaining pedal, damper pedal;* loosely: *forte pedal, loud pedal) for raising the dampers*
9 la pédale gauche (*inexact:* pédale *f* douce) réduisant la course des marteaux *m*
– *left pedal (soft pedal;* loosely: *piano pedal) for reducing the striking distance of the hammers on the strings*
10 les cordes *f* blanches (cordes *f* des sons *m* aigus)
– *treble strings*
11 le sommier d'accroche *f* des cordes *f* blanches
– *treble bridge (treble belly bridge)*
12 les cordes *f* filées (cordes *f* des sons *m* graves)
– *bass strings*
13 le sommier d'accroche *f* des cordes *f* filées
– *bass bridge (bass belly bridge)*
14 la pointe d'accroche *f*
– *hitch pin*
15 la barre de repos *m* des marteaux *m*
– *hammer rail*
16 le flasque de mécanique *f*
– *brace*
17 la cheville d'accord *m*
– *tuning pin (wrest pin, tuning peg)*
18 le sommier de piano *m*
– *pin block (wrest pin block, wrest plank)*
19 le métronome
– *metronome*
20 la clé d'accordeur *m* (l'accordoir *m*)
– *tuning hammer (tuning key, wrest)*
21 la cale d'accordeur *m*
– *tuning wedge*
22-39 la mécanique de percussion *f* (mécanique *f* des touches *f*)
– *key action (key mechanism)*
22 le sommier de mécanique *f*
– *beam*
23 la barre de forte *m*
– *damper-lifting lever*
24 la tête du marteau (feutre *m* du marteau)
– *felt-covered hammer head*
25 le manche du marteau
– *hammer shank*
26 la barre de repos *m* des marteaux *m*
– *hammer rail*
27 l'attrape-marteau *m*
– *check (back check)*
28 la garniture de feutre *m* de l'attrape-marteau *m*
– *check felt (back check felt)*
29 la tige de l'attrape-marteau *m*
– *wire stem of the check (wire stem of the back check)*
30 le grand levier (bras *m*) d'échappement *m*
– *sticker (hopper, hammer jack, hammer lever)*
31 la contre-attrape marteau *m*
– *button*
32 le chevalet (la bascule)
– *action lever*
33 le pilote
– *pilot*
34 la tige de pilote *m*
– *pilot wire*
35 l'accroche-lanière *m* (la queue-de-cochon)
– *tape wire*
36 la lanière
– *tape*
37 l'étouffoir *m*
– *damper (damper block)*
38 la lame d'étouffoir *m*
– *damper lifter*
39 la barre de repos *m* d'étouffoir *m*
– *damper rest rail*
40 **le piano à queue** *f* (piano *m* de concert *m*; *formes* plus petites: piano *m* crapaud; 1/2 queue *f*, 3/4 de queue *f*; *autre forme:* piano *m* carré)
– ***grand piano*** *(horizontal piano, grand, concert grand);* smaller: *baby grand piano, boudoir piano;* sim.: *square piano, table piano*
41 les pédales *f* du piano à queue *f*; la pédale droite lève les étouffoirs *m*; la pédale gauche diminue le son (par déplacement *m* latéral du clavier; une seule corde est frappée «una corda»)
– *grand piano pedals; right pedal for raising the dampers; left pedal for softening the tone (shifting the keyboard so that only one string is struck 'una corda')*
42 la lyre de piano *m* à queue *f*
– *pedal bracket*
43 **l'harmonium** *m*; *anc.:* orgue *m* expressif, mélodium *m*
– ***harmonium*** *(reed organ, melodium)*
44 le tirant de registre *m*
– *draw stop (stop, stop knob)*
45 la genouillère d'harmonium *m*
– *knee lever (knee swell, swell)*
46 le pédalier (pédales *f* du soufflet)
– *pedal (bellows pedal)*
47 le meuble d'harmonium *m*
– *harmonium case*
48 le clavier (manuel *m*)
– *harmonium keyboard (manual)*

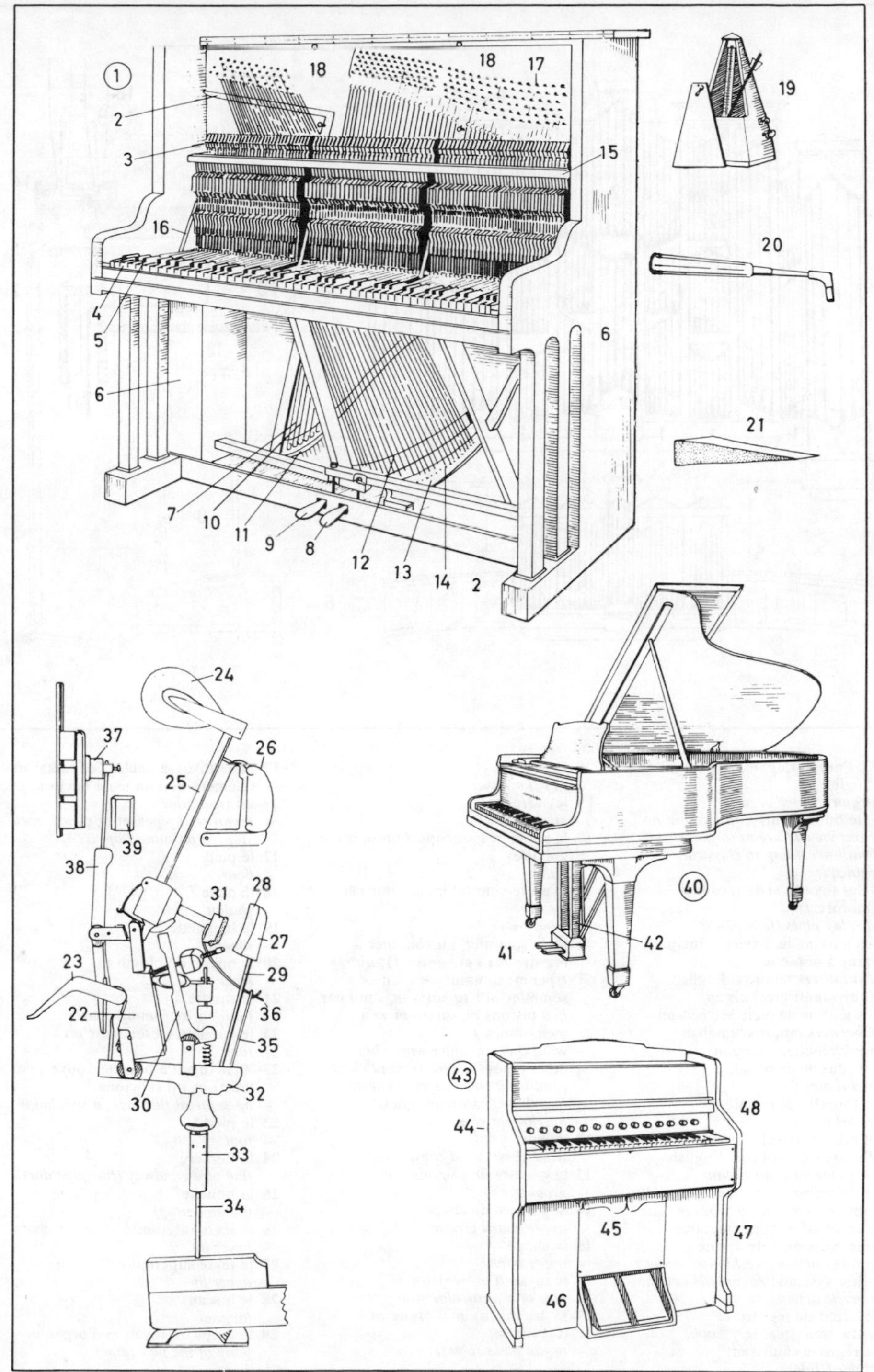
1
2
3
4
5
6
7
8
9
10
11
12
13
14
15
16
17
18
19
20
21
22
23
24
25
26
27
28
29
30
31
32
33
34
35
36
37
38
39
40
41
42
43
44
45
46
47
48

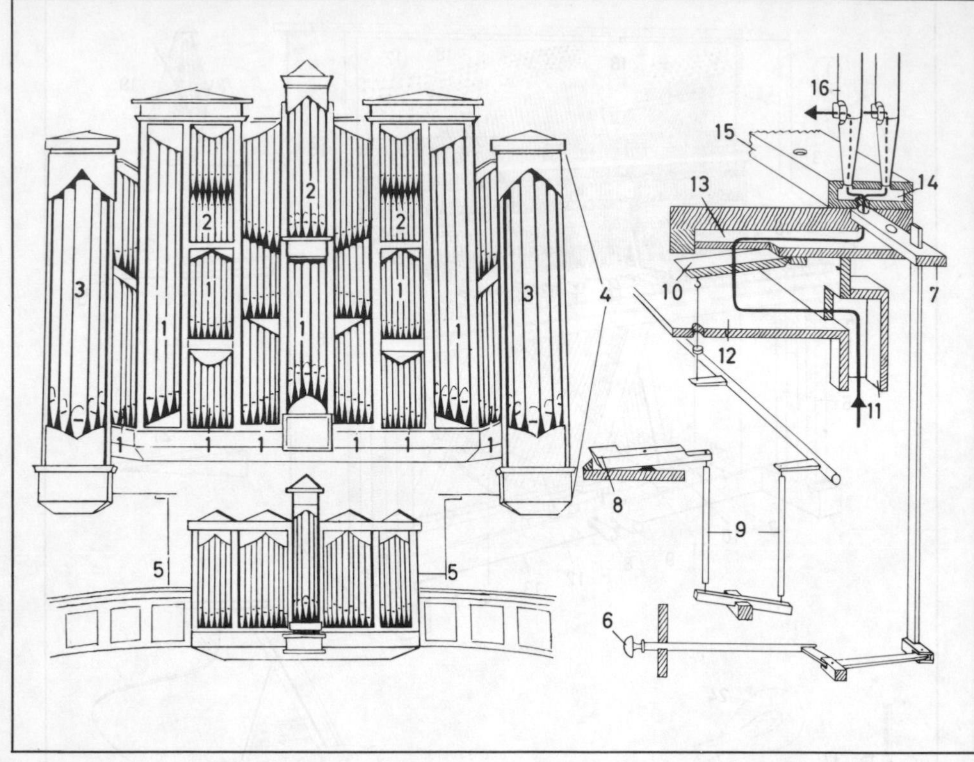

1-52 l'orgue *sing. m, pl. f* (orgue *m* d'église *f*)
– ***organ*** *(church organ)*
1-5 le buffet (buffet *m* d'orgue *m*)
– *front view of organ (organ case) [built according to classical principles]*
1-3 les tuyaux *m* de façade *f* (montre *f*)
– *display pipes (face pipes)*
1 les jeux *m* du clavier principal (grand orgue *m*)
– *Hauptwerk* (approx. English equivalent: *great organ)*
2 les jeux *m* de récit *m* (récit *m*)
– *Oberwerk* (approx. English equivalent: *swell organ)*
3 les jeux *m* de pédale *f*
– *pedal pipes*
4 la tourelle de pédale *f*
– *pedal tower*
5 le positif dorsal
– *Rückpositiv* (approx. English equivalent: *choir organ)*
6-16 la transmission mécanique du mouvement; *autres types m:* transmission *f* pneumatique, transmission *f* électrique
– *tracker action (mechanical action);* other systems: *pneumatic action, electric action*
6 le tirant de registre *m*
– *draw stop (stop, stop knob)*
7 le registre coulissant
– *slider (slide)*
8 la touche
– *key (key lever)*
9 les vergettes *f*
– *sticker*
10 la soupape (soupape *f* obturant la gravure)
– *pallet*
11 le porte-vent (alimentation *f* en air *m*)
– *wind trunk*
12-14 le sommier, un sommier à registre *m* (à glissières *f*); *autres types* m: sommier *m* à caisse *f*, sommier *m* à ressorts *m*, sommier *m* à pistons *m*, sommier *m* à membranes *f*
– *wind chest, a slider wind chest;* other types: *sliderless wind chest (unit wind chest), spring chest, kegellade chest (cone chest), diaphragm chest*
12 la laye
– *wind chest (wind chest box)*
13 la gravure de sommier *m*
– *groove*
14 la gravure de chape *f*
– *upper board groove*
15 la chape
– *upper board*
16 le tuyau d'un registre
– *pipe of a particular stop*
17-35 les tuyaux *m* d'orgue *m* (tuyaux *m*)
– *organ pipes (pipes)*
17-22 le tuyau à anche *f* en métal *m* (élément *m* d'un jeu à anches *f*), un trombone
– *metal reed pipe (*set of pipes: *reed stop), a posaune stop*
17 le pied
– *boot*
18 l'anche *f*
– *shallot*
19 la languette
– *tongue*
20 le noyau de plomb *m*
– *block*
21 la rasette
– *tuning wire (tuning crook)*
22 le pavillon (résonateur *m*)
– *tube*
23-30 le tuyau à bouche *f* ouvert en métal *m*, un salicional
– *open metal flue pipe, a salicional*
23 le pied
– *foot*
24 la lumière
– *flue pipe windway (flue pipe duct)*
25 la bouche
– *mouth (cutup)*
26 la lèvre inférieure
– *lower lip*
27 la lèvre supérieure
– *upper lip*
28 le biseau
– *languid*
29 le corps du tuyau *m* d'orgue *m*
– *body of the pipe (pipe)*

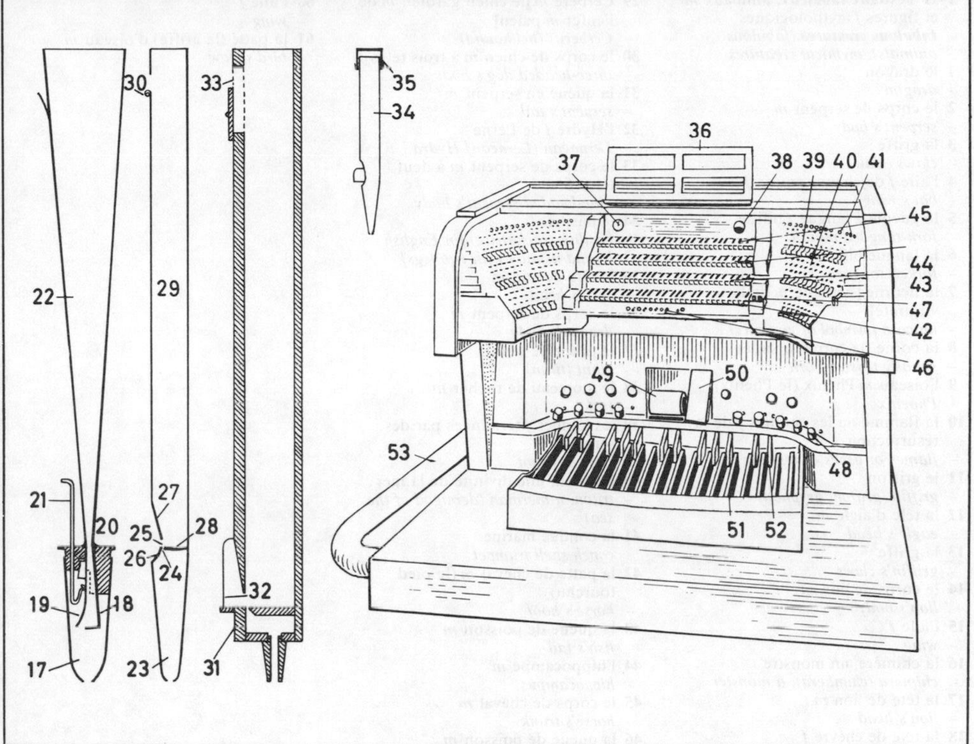

30 le rouleau d'accordage *m* (rouleau *m* d'entaille *f*), un dispositif d'accord *m*
- *tuning flap (tuning tongue), a tuning device*

31-33 le tuyau à bouche *f* ouvert en bois *m*, un principal (prestant *m*)
- *open wooden flue pipe (open wood), principal (diapason)*

31 la lèvre inférieure
- *cap*

32 le frein harmonique
- *ear*

33 la fenêtre d'accordage *m* à coulisse *f*
- *tuning hole (tuning slot), with slide*

34 le tuyau à bouche *f* bouché (bourdon *m*)
- *stopped flue pipe*

35 la calotte
- *stopper*

36-52 la console d'un orgue à transmission *f* électrique
- *organ console (console) of an electric action organ*

36 le pupitre
- *music rest (music stand)*

37 l'indicateur *m* de position *f* des rouleaux *m*
- *crescendo roller indicator*

38 le voltmètre
- *voltmeter*

39 la touche de registre *m* (domino *m* basculant)
- *stop tab (rocker)*

40 la touche de combinaison *f* libre
- *free combination stud (free combination knob)*

41 les interrupteurs *m* des jeux *m* à anche *f*, accouplements *m*, etc.
- *cancel buttons for reeds, couplers etc.*

42 le manuel I (clavier *m* manuel I) du positif dorsal
- *manual I, for the Rückpositiv (choir organ)*

43 le manuel II (clavier *m* manuel II) du grand orgue
- *manual II, for the Hauptwerk (great organ)*

44 le manuel III (clavier *m* manuel III) de récit *m*
- *manual III, for the Oberwerk (swell organ)*

45 le manuel IV (clavier *m* manuel IV) de bombarde *f*
- *manual IV, for the Schwellwerk (solo organ)*

46 les boutons-poussoirs *m* et les boutons *m* de combinaison *f* pour la registration manuelle, les combinaisons *f* libres ou fixes et les appels *m* de jeux *m* composés
- *thumb pistons controlling the manual stops (free or fixed combinations) and buttons for setting the combinations*

47 les interrupteurs *m* de ventilateur *m* et de transmission *f* électrique
- *switches for current to blower and action*

48 la pédale de tirasse *f*
toe piston, for the coupler

49 le rouleau de crescendo *m* (pédale *f* d'introduction *f* des tutti *m*)
- *crescendo roller (general crescendo roller)*

50 la pédale d'expression *f*
- *balanced swell pedal*

51 la touche inférieure de pédalier *m* [notes *f* naturelles]
- *pedal key [natural]*

52 la touche supérieure de pédalier [notes *f* altérées]
- *pedal key [sharp or flat]*

53 le câble (de transmission *f* électrique)
- *cable (transmission cable)*

1-61 bestiaire fabuleux, animaux *m* et figures *f* mythologiques
- ***fabulous creatures*** *(fabulous animals), mythical creatures*

1 le dragon
- *dragon*

2 le corps de serpent *m*
- *serpent's body*

3 la griffe
- *claws (claw)*

4 l'aile *f* de chauve-souris *f*
- *bat's wing*

5 la gueule à langue *f* bifide
- *fork-tongued mouth*

6 la langue bifide
- *forked tongue*

7 la licorne [symbole *m* de la virginité]
- *unicorn [symbol of virginity]*

8 la corne (la corne torsadée)
- *spirally twisted horn*

9 l'oiseau *m* Phénix (le Phénix)
- *Phoenix*

10 la flamme ou les cendres *f* de la résurrection
- *flames or ashes of resurrection*

11 le griffon
- *griffin (griffon, gryphon)*

12 la tête d'aigle *m*
- *eagle's head*

13 la griffe
- *griffin's claws*

14 le corps de lion *m*
- *lion's body*

15 l'aile *f*
- *wing*

16 la chimère, un monstre
- *chimera (chimaera), a monster*

17 la tête de lion *m*
- *lion's head*

18 la tête de chèvre *f*
- *goat's head*

19 le corps de dragon *m* (le corps de serpent *m*)
- *dragon's body*

20 le sphinx, une figure symbolique
- *sphinx, a symbolic figure*

21 la tête humaine
- *human head*

22 le corps de lion *m*
- *lion's body*

23 la sirène, la sirène-poisson (l'ondine *f*, la naïade, la nymphe); *anal.:* la néréide, l'océanide *f* (nymphes de la mer, divinités de la mer); *masc.:* l'ondin
- *mermaid (nix, nixie, water nixie, sea maid, sea maiden, naiad, water nymph, water elf, ocean nymph, sea nymph, river nymph);* sim.: *Nereids, Oceanids (sea divinities, sea deities, sea goddesses);* male: *nix (merman, seaman)*

24 le corps de femme *f*
- *woman's trunk*

25 la queue de poisson *m*
- *fish's tail (dolphin's tail)*

26 Pégase *m* (le cheval du poète, le cheval ailé)
- *Pegasus (favourite,* Am. *favorite, steed of the Muses, winged horse);* sim.: *hippogryph*

27 le corps de cheval *m*
- *horse's body*

28 les ailes *f*
- *wings*

29 Cerbère *m* [le chien gardien *m* de l'enfer *m* païen]
- *Cerberus (hellhound)*

30 le corps de chien *m* à trois têtes *f*
- *three-headed dog's body*

31 la queue en serpent *m*
- *serpent's tail*

32 l'Hydre *f* de Lerne
- *Lernaean (Lernean) Hydra*

33 le corps de serpent *m* à neuf têtes *f*
- *nine-headed serpent's body*

34 le basilic
- *basilisk (cockatrice) [in English legend usually with two legs]*

35 la tête de coq *m*
- *cock's head*

36 le corps de serpent *m*
- *dragon's body*

37 le géant (le titan)
- *giant (titan)*

38 le morceau de rocher *m*
- *rock*

39 les jambes *f* terminées par des serpents *m*
- *serpent's foot*

40 le triton, une divinité de la mer
- *triton, a merman (demigod of the sea)*

41 la conque marine
- *conch shell trumpet*

42 la patte de cheval *m* (le pied fourchu)
- *horse's hoof*

43 la queue de poisson *m*
- *fish's tail*

44 l'hippocampe *m*
- *hippocampus*

45 le corps de cheval *m*
- *horse's trunk*

46 la queue de poisson *m*
- *fish's tail*

47 le taureau marin, un monstre marin
- *sea ox, a sea monster*

48 le corps de taureau *m*
- *monster's body*

49 la queue de poisson *m*
- *fish's tail*

50 la Bête de l'Apocalypse *f* (la Bête à sept têtes *f* de l'Apocalypse *f*)
- *seven-headed dragon of St. John's Revelation (Revelations, Apocalypse)*

51 l'aile *f*
- *wing*

52 le centaure, un être mi-homme *m* mi-cheval *m*
- *centaur (hippocentaur), half man and half beast*

53 le torse d'homme *m* tenant un arc et une flèche
- *man's body with bow and arrow*

54 le corps de cheval *m*
- *horse's body*

55 la harpie, un esprit des vents *m* (esprit *m* de la tempête)
- *harpy, a winged monster*

56 la tête de femme *f*
- *woman's head*

57 le corps d'oiseau *m*
- *bird's body*

58 la sirène, la sirène-oiseau, un être démoniaque
- *siren, a daemon*

59 le corps de femme *f*
- *woman's body*

60 l'aile *f*
- *wing*

61 la patte (la griffe) d'oiseau *m*
- *bird's claw*

1
2
3
4
5
6
7
8
9
10
11
12
13
14
15
16
17
18
19
20
21
22
23
24
25
26
27
28
29
30
31
32
33
34
35
36
37
38
39
40
41
42
43
44
45
46
47
48
49
50
51
52
53
54
55
56
57
58
59
60
61

1-40 les objets *m* de fouilles *f* préhistoriques
- *prehistoric finds*

1-9 le paléolithique et **le mésolithique**
- ***Old Stone Age** (Palaeolithic, Paleolithic, period) and **Mesolithic period***

1 le biface de silex *m*
- *hand axe* (Am. *ax) (fist hatchet), a stone tool*

2 la pointe de sagaie *f*, en os *m*
- *head of throwing spear, made of bone*

3 le harpon, en os *m*
- *bone harpoon*

4 la pointe triangulaire
- *head*

5 le propulseur en bois *m* de renne *m*
- *harpoon thrower, made of reindeer antler*

6 le galet teint
- *painted pebble*

7 la tête de cheval *m*, une sculpture
- *head of a wild horse, a carving*

8 l'idole *f* paléolithique, une statuette en ivoire *m*
- *Stone Age idol, an ivory statuette*

9 le bison, une peinture rupestre (peinture *f* pariétale)
- *bison, a cave painting (rock painting) [cave art, cave painting]*

10-20 le néolithique
- ***New Stone Age** (Neolithic period)*

10 l'amphore *f* (céramique *f* cordée)
- *amphora [corded ware]*

11 le vase en bombe *f* (civilisation *f* mégalithique)
- *bowl [menhir group]*

12 la bouteille à collerette *f* (civilisation *f* des gobelets *m* en entonnoir *m*)
- *collared flask [Funnel-Beaker culture]*

13 le récipient orné de spirales *f* (céramique *f* rubanée)
- *vessel with spiral pattern [spiral design pottery]*

14 le gobelet campaniforme (civilisation *f* des gobelets *m* campaniformes)
- *bell beaker [beaker pottery]*

15 la maison sur pilotis *m*, une construction sur pilotis *m*
- *pile dwelling (lake dwelling, lacustrine dwelling)*

16 le dolmen, une tombe mégalithique; *autres types:* le dolmen à couloir *m*, l'allée *f* couverte; *recouvert de terre f, graviers m, pierres f:* le tumulus
- *dolmen (cromlech), a megalithic tomb* (coll.: *giant's tomb);* other kinds: *passage grave, gallery grave (long cist);* when covered with earth: *tumulus (barrow, mound)*

17 le coffre de pierre *f* avec inhumation *f* en position *f* fléchie
- *stone cist, a contracted burial*

18 le menhir (un mégalithe)
- *menhir (standing stone), a monolith*

19 la hache-marteau, une hache de combat *m* en pierre *f*
- *boat axe* (Am. *ax), a stone battle axe*

20 la figurine de terre *f* cuite (une idole)
- *clay figurine (an idol)*

21-40 l'âge *m* **de bronze** *m* et **l'âge** *m* **de fer** *m*
- ***Bronze Age and Iron Age;*** epochs: *Hallstatt period, La Tène period*

21 la pointe de lance *f* en bronze *m*
- *bronze spear head*

22 le poignard de bronze *m* à manche *m* riveté
- *hafted bronze dagger*

23 la hache à douille *f*, une hache de bronze *m* emmanchée
- *socketed axe* (Am. *ax) with haft fastened to rings, a bronze axe*

24 la plaque de ceinture *f*
- *girdle clasp*

25 le gorgerin
- *necklace (lunula)*

26 le torque d'or *m*
- *gold neck ring*

27 la fibule en archet *m*, une fibule (épingle *f* à étrier *m*)
- *violin-bow fibula (safety pin)*

28 la fibule serpentiforme; *autres types:* fibule *f* en barque *f*, fibule *f* en arbalète *f*
- *serpentine fibula;* other kinds: *boat fibula, arc fibula*

29 l'épingle *f* à tête *f* globulaire, une épingle de bronze *m*
- *bulb-head pin, a bronze pin*

30 la fibule à deux pièces *f* à spirales *f*; *type voisin:* la fibule à plaques *f* rondes
- *two-piece spiral fibula;* sim.: *disc (disk) fibula*

31 le couteau de bronze *m* à manche *m* de bronze *m*
- *hafted bronze knife*

32 la clé en fer *m*
- *iron key*

33 le soc de charrue *f*
- *ploughshare* (Am. *plowshare)*

34 la situle en tôle *f* de bronze *m*, une offrande funéraire
- *sheet-bronze situla, a funerary vessel*

35 la cruche à anse *f* (céramique *f* incisée)
- *pitcher [chip-carved pottery]*

36 le chariot cultuel miniature (le chariot cultuel)
- *miniature ritual cart (miniature ritual chariot)*

37 la pièce d'argent *m* celte
- *Celtic silver coin*

38 l'urne *f* anthropomorphe, une urne contenant des cendres *f*; *autres types:* urne *f* en forme *f* de maison *f*, urne *f* mamelonnée
- *face urn, a cinerary urn;* other kinds: *domestic urn, embossed urn*

39 la tombe à urne *f* protégée par des pierres *f*
- *urn grave in stone chamber*

40 l'urne *f* à col *m* cylindrique
- *urn with cylindrical neck*

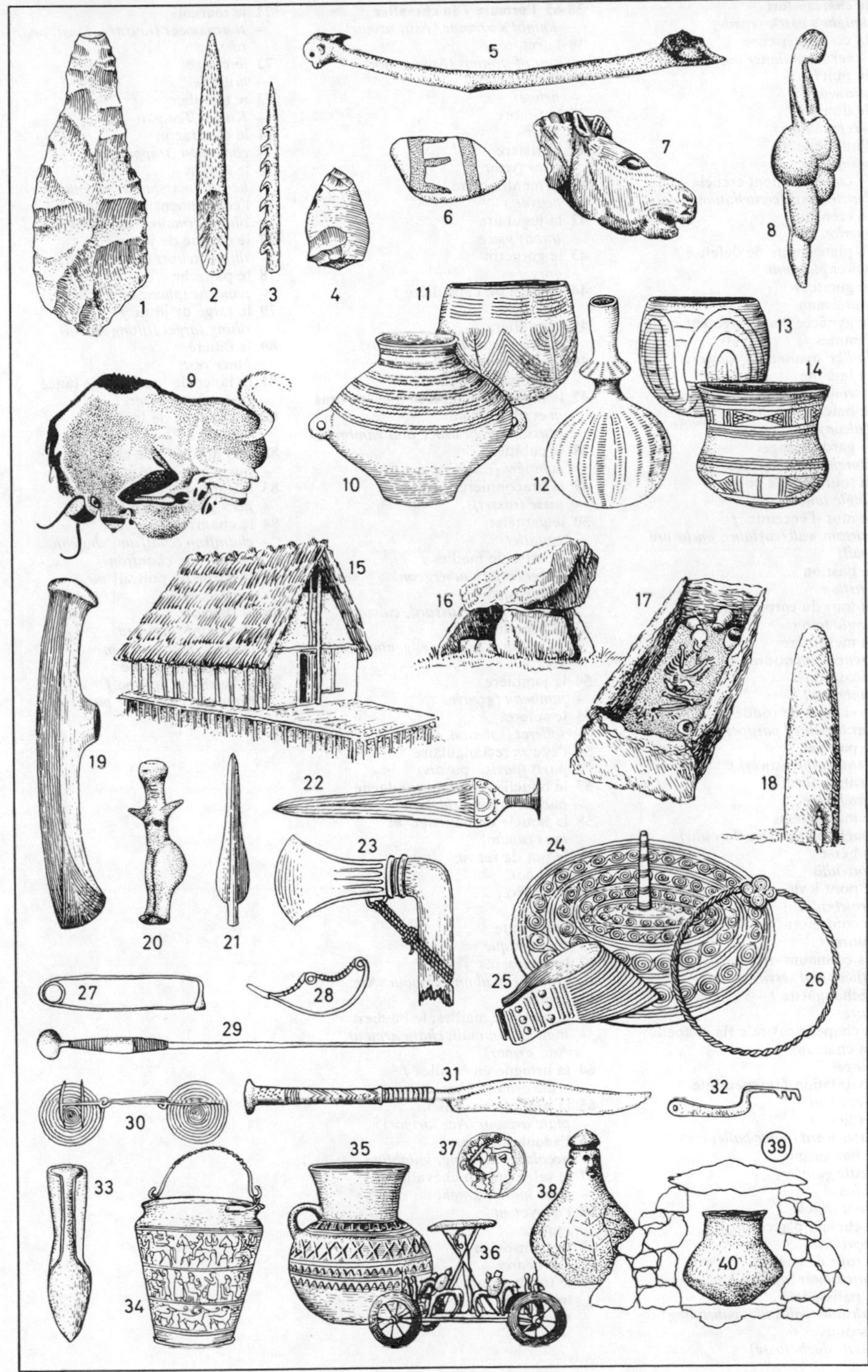
1
2
3
4
5
6
7
8
9
10
11
12
13
14
15
16
17
18
19
20
21
22
23
24
25
26
27
28
29
30
31
32
33
34
35
36
37
38
39
40

1 le château-fort
– ***knight's castle*** *(castle)*
2 la cour intérieure
– *inner ward (inner bailey)*
3 le puits
– *draw well*
4 le donjon
– *keep (donjon)*
5 l'oubliette *f*
– *dungeon*
6 le couronnement crénelé
– *battlements (crenellation)*
7 le créneau
– *merlon*
8 la plate-forme de défense *f*
– *tower platform*
9 le guetteur
– *watchman*
10 le gynécée (l'appartement *m* des femmes *f*)
– *ladies' apartments (bowers)*
11 la lucarne
– *dormer window (dormer)*
12 le balcon
– *balcony*
13 le garde-manger
– *storehouse (magazine)*
14 la tour d'angle *m*
– *angle tower*
15 le mur d'enceinte *f*
– *curtain wall (curtains, enclosure wall)*
16 le bastion
– *bastion*
17 la tour du corps de garde *f*
– *angle tower*
18 la meurtrière
– *crenel (embrasure)*
19 la courtine
– *inner wall*
20 le chemin de ronde *f*
– *battlemented parapet*
21 le parapet
– *parapet (breastwork)*
22 l'entrée fortifiée
– *gatehouse*
23 le mâchicoulis
– *machicolation (machicoulis)*
24 la herse
– *portcullis*
25 le pont-levis
– *drawbridge*
26 le contrefort
– *buttress*
27 les communs *m*
– *offices and service rooms*
28 l'échauguette *f*
– *turret*
29 la chapelle castrale (la chapelle du château)
– *chapel*
30 l'habitation *f* seigneuriale
– *great hall*
31 les lices *f*
– *outer ward (outer bailey)*
32 la barbacane
– *castle gate*
33 le fossé
– *moat (ditch)*
34 le chemin d'accès *m*
– *approach*
35 la tour de guet *m*
– *watchtower (turret)*
36 la palissade
– *palisade (pallisade, palisading)*
37 les douves *f*
– *moat (ditch, fosse)*

38-65 l'armure *f* du chevalier
– ***knight's armour*** *(*Am. *armor)*
38 l'armure *f*
– *suit of armour* (Am. *armor)*
39-42 le casque
– *helmet*
39 le timbre
– *skull*
40 la visière
– *visor (vizor)*
41 la mentonnière
– *beaver*
42 la jugulaire
– *throat piece*
43 le gorgerin
– *gorget*
44 la crête de l'épaulière *f*
– *epaulière*
45 l'épaulière *f*
– *pallette (pauldron, besageur)*
46 le plastron
– *breastplate (cuirass)*
47 le brassard (canon *m* d'avant-bras *m* et du bras *m*)
– *brassard (rear brace and vambrace)*
48 la cubitière
– *cubitière (coudière, couter)*
49 la braconnière
– *tasse (tasset)*
50 le gantelet
– *gauntlet*
51 la cotte de mailles *f*
– *habergeon (haubergeon)*
52 le cuissard
– *cuisse (cuish, cuissard, cuissart)*
53 la genouillère
– *knee cap (knee piece, genouillère, poleyn)*
54 la jambière
– *jambeau (greave)*
55 le soleret
– *solleret (sabaton, sabbaton)*
56 l'écu *m* rectangulaire
– *pavis (pavise, pavais)*
57 le bouclier rond, la rondache
– *buckler (round shield)*
58 la boucle de bouclier *m*
– *boss (umbo)*
59 le pot de fer *m*
– *iron hat*
60 le morion
– *morion*
61 la barbute
– *light casque*
62 les cuirasses *f*
– *types of mail and armour (*Am. *armor)*
63 la cotte de mailles, le haubert
– *mail (chain mail, chain armour,* Am. *armor)*
64 la broigne en écailles *f*
– *scale armour* (Am. *armor)*
65 la broigne en écus *m*
– *plate armour* (Am. *armor)*

66 l'adoubement *m*
– ***accolade*** *(dubbing, knighting)*
67 le seigneur, un chevalier
– *liege lord, a knight*
68 l'écuyer *m*
– *esquire*
69 l'échanson *m*
– *cup bearer*
70 le troubadour (*m*éridional: le trouvère)
– *minstrel (minnesinger, troubadour)*

71 le tournoi
– ***tournament*** *(tourney, joust, just, tilt)*
72 le croisé
– *crusader*
73 le templier
– *Knight Templar*
74 le caparaçon
– *caparison (trappings)*
75 le héraut
– *herald (marshal at tournament)*
76 l'équipement *m* de joute *f*
– *tilting armour* (Am. *armor)*
77 le casque de joute *f*
– *tilting helmet (jousting helmet)*
78 le panache
– *panache (plume of feathers)*
79 la targe de joute *f*
– *tilting target (tilting shield)*
80 le faucre
– *lance rest*
81 la lance de joute *f*, une lance
– *tilting lance (lance)*
82 la rondelle de lance *f*
– *vamplate*
83-88 l'armure *f* de cheval *m*
– *horse armour* (Am. *armor)*
83 le garde-encolure
– *neck guard (neck piece)*
84 le chanfrein
– *chamfron (chaffron, chafron, chamfrain, chanfron)*
85 la barde de poitrail *m*
– *poitrel*
86 le flancois
– *flanchard (flancard)*
87 la selle de tournoi *m*
– *tournament saddle*
88 la barde de croupe *f*
– *rump piece (quarter piece)*

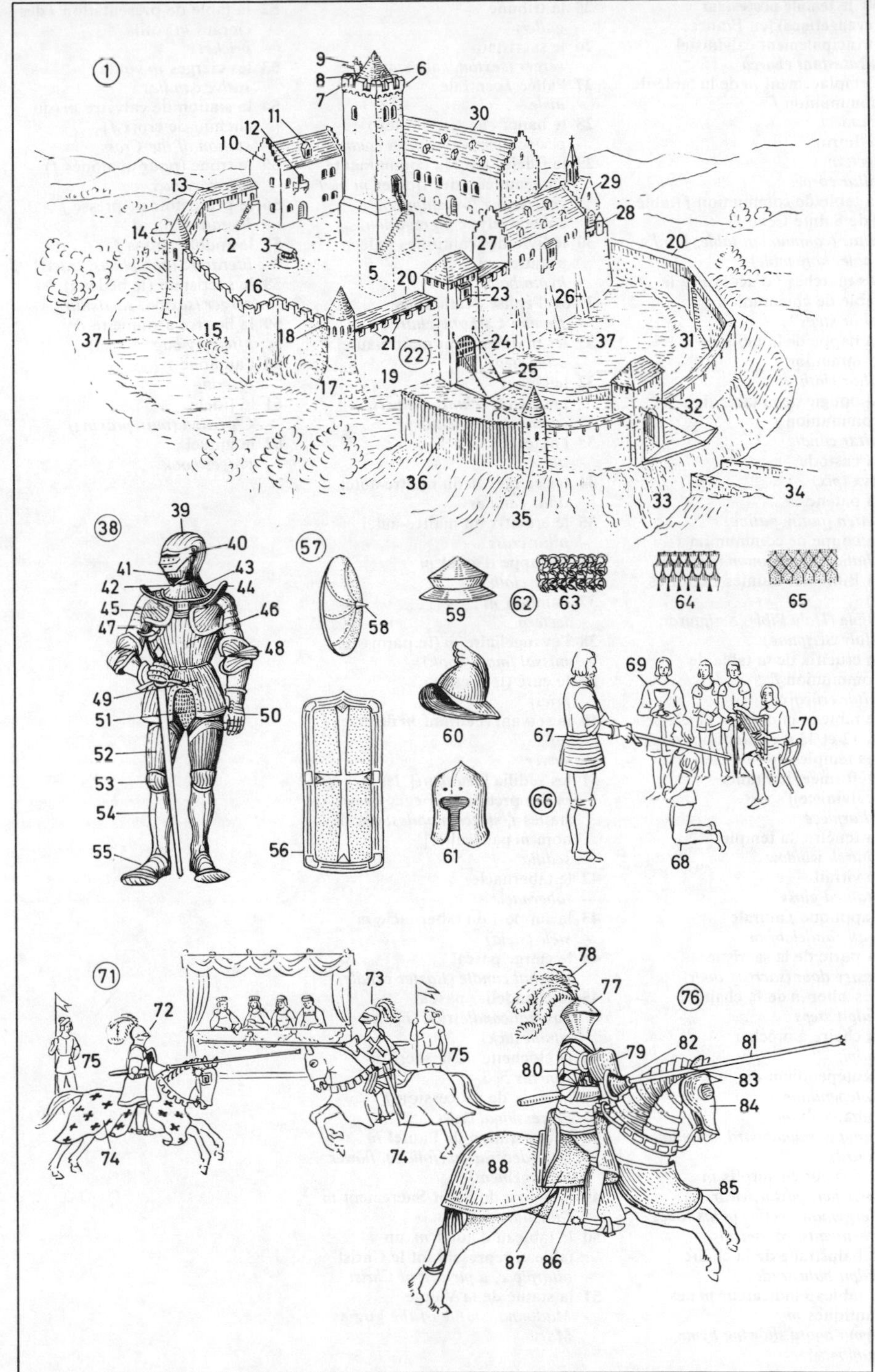
1
2
3
5
6
7
8
9
10
11
12
13
14
15
16
17
18
19
20
21
22
23
24
25
26
27
28
29
30
31
32
33
34
35
36
37
38
39
40
41
42
43
44
45
46
47
48
49
50
51
52
53
54
55
56
57
58
59
60
61
62
63
64
65
66
67
68
69
70
71
72
73
74
75
76
77
78
79
80
81
82
83
84
85
86
87
88

1-30 le temple protestant (évangélique) [en France: principalement calviniste]
– ***Protestant church***
1 l'emplacement *m* de la table de communion *f*
– *chancel*
2 le lutrin
– *lectern*
3 *altar carpet*
4 la table de communion *f* (table *f* de Sainte-Cène *f*)
– *altar (communion table, Lord's table, holy table)*
5 les marches *f* d'accès *m* à la table de communion *f*
– *altar steps*
6 la nappe de la table de communion *f*
– *altar cloth*
7 la bougie de la table de communion *f*
– *altar candle*
8 la custode
– *pyx (pix)*
9 la patène
– *paten (patin, patine)*
10 la coupe de communion *f*
– *chalice (communion cup)*
11 la Bible (les Saintes Ecritures *f*)
– *Bible (Holy Bible, Scriptures, Holy Scripture)*
12 le crucifix de la table de communion *f*
– *altar crucifix*
13 le tableau mural [les objets 8, 9, 12 et 13 n'existent pas dans les temples de l'Eglise Réformée de France (calviniste)]
– *altarpiece*
14 la fenêtre du temple
– *church window*
15 le vitrail
– *stained glass*
16 l'applique *f* murale
– *wall candelabrum*
17 la porte de la sacristie
– *vestry door (sacristy door)*
18 l'escalier *m* de la chaire
– *pulpit steps*
19 la chaire à prêcher
– *pulpit*
20 l'antépendium *m*
– *antependium*
21 l'abat-voix *m*
– *canopy (soundboard, sounding board)*
22 le pasteur en surplis *m*
– *preacher (pastor, vicar, clergyman, rector) in his robes (vestments, canonicals)*
23 la balustrade de la chaire
– *pulpit balustrade*
24 le tableau indicateur *m* des cantiques *m*
– *hymn board showing hymn numbers*
25 la tribune
– *gallery*
26 le sacristain
– *verger (sexton, sacristan)*
27 l'allée *f* centrale
– *aisle*
28 le banc; *ens.:* les stalles *f*
– *pew;* collectively: *pews (seating)*
29 le fidèle; *ens.:* la communauté, l'assemblée *f* des fidèles *m ou f*
– *churchgoer (worshipper);* collectively: *congregation*
30 le livre des cantiques *m*(le psautier *m*)
– *hymn book*
31-62 l'église *f* catholique
– ***Roman Catholic church***
31 les marches *f* du maître-autel
– *altar steps*
32 le chœur
– *presbytery (choir, chancel, sacrarium, sanctuary)*
33 l'autel *m*
– *altar*
34 les cierges *m* du maître-autel
– *altar candles*
35 le crucifix du maître-autel
– *altar cross*
36 la nappe d'autel *m*
– *altar cloth*
37 l'ambon *m*
– *lectern*
38 l'évangéliaire *m* (le paroissien)
– *missal (mass book)*
39 le curé (le prêtre)
– *priest*
40 le servant (l'enfant *m* de chœur *m*)
– *server*
41 les sedilia [*peu usité*], les sièges *m* des prêtres *m* [*sièges fixes:* stalles *f*, *sièges mobiles:* pas de nom *m* particulier]
– *sedilia*
42 le tabernacle
– *tabernacle*
43 le support du tabernacle *m*
– *stele (stela)*
44 le cierge pascal
– *paschal candle (Easter candle)*
45 le chandelier pascal
– *paschal candlestick (Easter candlestick)*
46 la clochette de la sacristie
– *sanctus bell*
47 la croix de procession *f*
– *processional cross*
48 la décoration de l'autel *m*
– *altar decoration (foliage, flower arrangement)*
49 la lampe du Saint-Sacrement *m*
– *sanctuary lamp*
50 le tableau d'autel *m*, un tableau représentant le Christ
– *altarpiece, a picture of Christ*
51 la statue de la Vierge
– *Madonna, statue of the Virgin Mary*
52 la table de présentation *f* des cierges *m* votifs
– *pricket*
53 les cierges *m* votifs
– *votive candles*
54 la station de calvaire *m* (du chemin de croix *f*)
– *station of the Cross*
55 le tronc (pour aumônes *f*)
– *offertory box*
56 le présentoir de presse *f*
– *literature stand*
57 les publications *f*
– *literature (pamphlets, tracts)*
58 le sacristain (le bedeau)
– *verger (sexton, sacristan)*
59 la bourse à sonnette *f*
– *offertory bag*
60 l'aumône *f*
– *offering*
61 le fidèle
– *Christian (man praying)*
62 le missel
– *prayer book*

1 2 3 4 5 6 7 8 9 10 11 12 13 14 15 16 17 18 19 20
21 22 23 24 25 26 27 28 29 30 31 32 33 34 35 36 37 38 39 40
41 42 43 44 45 46 47 48 49 50 51 52 53 54 55 56 57 58 59 60
61 62
123
1-4
26

1 **l'église** *f*
– ***church***
2 le clocher
– *steeple*
3 le coq du clocher
– *weathercock*
4 la girouette
– *weather vane (wind vane)*
5 la boule de la flèche
– *apex*
6 la flèche du clocher *m*
– *church spire (spire)*
7 l'horloge *f* de l'église *f*
– *church clock (tower clock)*
8 l'ouïe *f*
– *belfry window*
9 la cloche à fonctionnement *m* électrique
– *electrically operated bell*
10 la croix de faîte *m*
– *ridge cross*
11 la toiture de l'église *f*
– *church roof*
12 la chapelle commémorative (votive)
– *memorial chapel*
13 la sacristie, une annexe
– *vestry (sacristy), an annexe (annex)*
14 la plaque (la dalle) commémorative, l'épitaphe *f*
– *memorial tablet (memorial plate, wall memorial, wall stone)*
15 l'entrée *f* latérale
– *side entrance*
16 le portail (la porte) de l'église *f*
– *church door (main door, portal)*
17 le fidèle
– *churchgoer*
18 le mur du cimetière (le mur d'enclos *m* de l'église *f*)
– *graveyard wall (churchyard wall)*
19 la porte du cimetière (de l'enclos *m* de l'église *f*)
– *graveyard gate (churchyard gate, lichgate, lychgate)*
20 le presbytère
– *vicarage (parsonage, rectory)*
21-41 le cimetière
– ***graveyard*** *(churchyard, God's acre,* Am. *burying ground)*
21 la chapelle mortuaire
– *mortuary*
22 le fossoyeur
– *grave digger*
23 la tombe (le tombeau)
– *grave (tomb)*
24 le tertre funéraire
– *grave mound*
25 la croix tombale
– *cross*
26 la pierre tombale (le monument funéraire)
– *gravestone (headstone, tombstone)*
27 le caveau de famille *f*
– *family grave (family tomb)*
28 la chapelle du cimetière
– *graveyard chapel*
29 la tombe d'enfant *m*
– *child's grave*
30 le tombeau à urne *f*
– *urn grave*
31 l'urne *f*
– *urn*
32 la tombe militaire
– *soldier's grave*
33-41 l'enterrement *m* (l'inhumation *f*, les funérailles *f*, les obsèques *f*)
– *funeral (burial)*
33 les personnes *f* venues assister à l'enterrement *m*
– *mourners*
34 la fosse
– *grave*
35 le cercueil
– *coffin* (Am. *casket)*
36 la pelle
– *spade*
37 le prêtre
– *clergyman*
38 la famille (les parents *m*) du défunt *m*
– *the bereaved*
39 le voile de veuve *f*, un voile de deuil *m*
– *widow's veil, a mourning veil*
40 les employés *m* des pompes *f* funèbres (croque-morts *m*)
– *pallbearers*
41 la civière
– *bier*
42-50 la procession
– ***procession*** *(religious procession)*
42 la croix de procession *f*
– *processional crucifix*
43 le porteur de croix *f*
– *cross bearer (crucifer)*
44 la bannière, une bannière d'église *f*
– *processional banner, a church banner*
45 l'enfant *m* de chœur *m*
– *acolyte*
46 le porteur du dais *m*
– *canopy bearer*
47 le prêtre
– *priest*
48 l'ostensoir *m* avec le Saint-Sacrement
– *monstrance with the Blessed Sacrament (consecrated Host)*
49 le dais
– *canopy (baldachin, baldaquin)*
50 les religieuses *f*
– *nuns*
51 le cortège
– *participants in the procession*
52-58 le couvent (le monastère)
– ***monastery***
52 le cloître
– *cloister*
53 le jardin du cloître
– *monastery garden*
54 le moine, un (moine) bénédictin
– *monk, a Benedictine monk*
55 l'habit *m* monacal
– *habit (monk's habit)*
56 le capuchon
– *cowl (hood)*
57 la tonsure
– *tonsure*
58 le bréviaire
– *breviary*
59 **la catacombe,** une sépulture souterraine paléochrétienne
– ***catacomb****, an early Christian underground burial place*
60 l'arcosolium *m*
– *niche (tomb recess, arcosolium)*
61 la dalle (la plaque) de pierre *f*
– *stone slab*

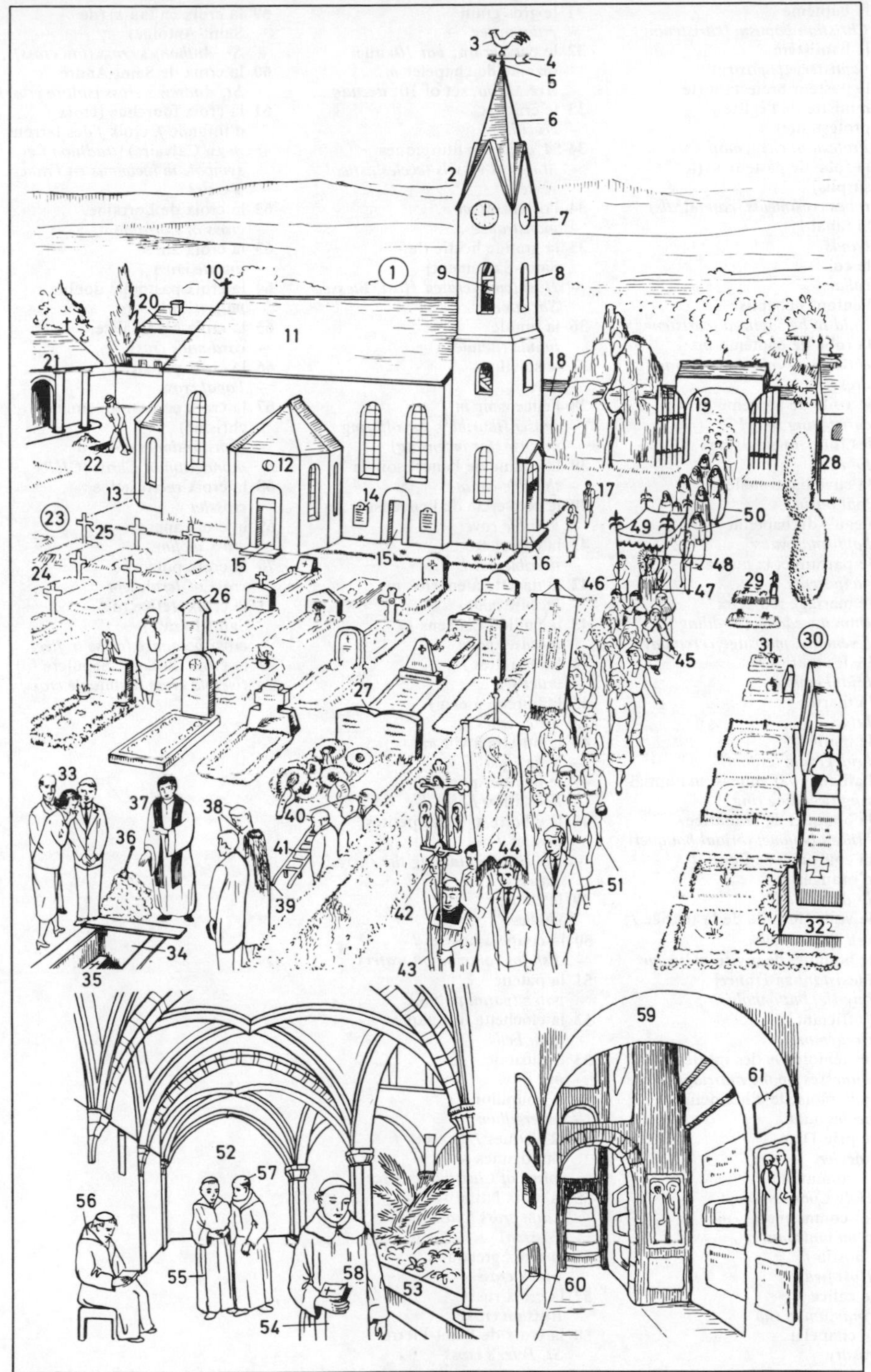
1
2
3
4
5
6
7
8
9
10
11
12
13
14
15
16
17
18
19
20
21
22
23
24
25
26
27
28
29
30
31
32
33
34
35
36
37
38
39
40
41
42
43
44
45
46
47
48
49
50
51
52
53
54
55
56
57
58
59
60
61

1 le baptême
– *Christian baptism (christening)*
2 le baptistère
– *baptistery (baptistry)*
3 le pasteur protestant (le ministre de l'église *f* protestante)
– *Protestant clergyman*
4 la robe de pasteur *m* (le surplis)
– *robes (vestments, canonicals)*
5 le rabat
– *bands*
6 le col
– *collar*
7 l'enfant *m* baptisé
– *child to be baptized (christened)*
8 la robe de baptême *m*
– *christening robe (christening dress)*
9 le voile de baptême *m*
– *christening shawl*
10 les fonts *m* baptismaux
– *font*
11 la cuve baptismale
– *font basin*
12 l'eau *f* du baptême
– *baptismal water*
13 le parrain et la marraine
– *godparents*
14 le mariage religieux
– *church wedding (wedding ceremony, marriage ceremony)*
15-16 les mariés *m*
– *bridal couple*
15 la mariée
– *bride*
16 le marié
– *bridegroom (groom)*
17 l'alliance *f* (l'anneau *m* nuptial)
– *ring (wedding ring)*
18 le bouquet de la mariée
– *bride's bouquet (bridal bouquet)*
19 la couronne de fleurs *f* d'oranger *m*
– *bridal wreath*
20 le voile (le voile de la mariée *f*)
– *veil (bridal veil)*
21 le bouquet de myrte *m* [*usage inexistant en France*]
– *[myrtle] buttonhole*
22 l'officiant *m*
– *clergyman*
23 les témoins *m* des mariés *m*
– *witnesses [to the marriage]*
24 la demoiselle d'honneur *m*
– *bridesmaid*
25 le prie-Dieu
– *kneeler*
26 la communion
– *Holy Communion*
27 les communiants *m*
– *communicants*
28 l'hostie *f*
– *Host (wafer)*
29 le calice
– *communion cup*
30 le chapelet
– *rosary*
31 le gros grain
– *paternoster*
32 le petit grain; *par 10:* une dizaine de chapelet *m*
– *Ave Maria;* set of 10: *decade*
33 le crucifix
– *crucifix*
34-54 objets *m* liturgiques
– *liturgical vessels (ecclesiastical vessels)*
34 l'ostensoir *m*
– *monstrance*
35 la grande hostie (le Saint-Sacrement)
– *Host (consecrated Host, Blessed Sacrament)*
36 la lunule
– *lunula (lunule)*
37 le soleil
– *rays*
38 l'encensoir *m*
– *censer (thurible), for offering incense (for incensing)*
39 la chaîne de l'encensoir *m*
– *thurible chain*
40 le couvercle de l'encensoir *m*
– *thurible cover*
41 la cassolette
– *thurible bowl*
42 la navette à encens *m*
– *incense boat*
43 la cuiller à encens *m*
– *incense spoon*
44 les burettes *f*
– *cruet set*
45 la burette à eau *f*
– *water cruet*
46 la burette à vin *m*
– *wine cruet*
47 le bénitier portatif
– *holy water basin*
48 le ciboire avec les petites hosties *f*
– *ciborium containing the sacred wafers*
49 le calice
– *chalice*
50 la coupe à hosties *f*
– *dish for communion wafers*
51 la patène
– *paten (patin, patine)*
52 la clochette liturgique
– *altar bells*
53 la custode
– *pyx (pix)*
54 le goupillon
– *aspergillum*
55-72 formes *f* de croix *f* chrétiennes
– *forms of Christian crosses*
55 la croix latine
– *Latin cross (cross of the Passion)*
56 la croix grecque
– *Greek cross*
57 la croix russe
– *Russian cross*
58 la croix de Saint-Pierre
– *St. Peter's cross*
59 la croix en tau *m* (de Saint-Antoine)
– *St. Anthony's cross (tau cross)*
60 la croix de Saint-André
– *St. Andrew's cross (saltire cross)*
61 la croix fourchue (croix *f* d'infamie *f*, croix *f* des larrons *m* au Calvaire) [*tradition f et symbole m inconnus en France*]
– *Y-cross*
62 la croix de Lorraine
– *cross of Lorraine*
63 la croix ansée
– *ansate cross*
64 la croix pastorale double
– *patriarchal cross*
65 la croix cardinalice
– *cardinal's cross*
66 la croix papale
– *Papal cross*
67 la croix constantinienne (le chrisme)
– *Constantinian cross, a monogram of Christ (CHR)*
68 la croix recroisettée
– *crosslet*
69 la croix ancrée
– *cross moline*
70 la croix potencée
– *cross of Jerusalem*
71 la croix tréflée (de Saint-Lazare)
– *cross botonnée (cross treflée)*
72 la croix du Saint-Sépulcre
– *fivefold cross (quintuple cross)*

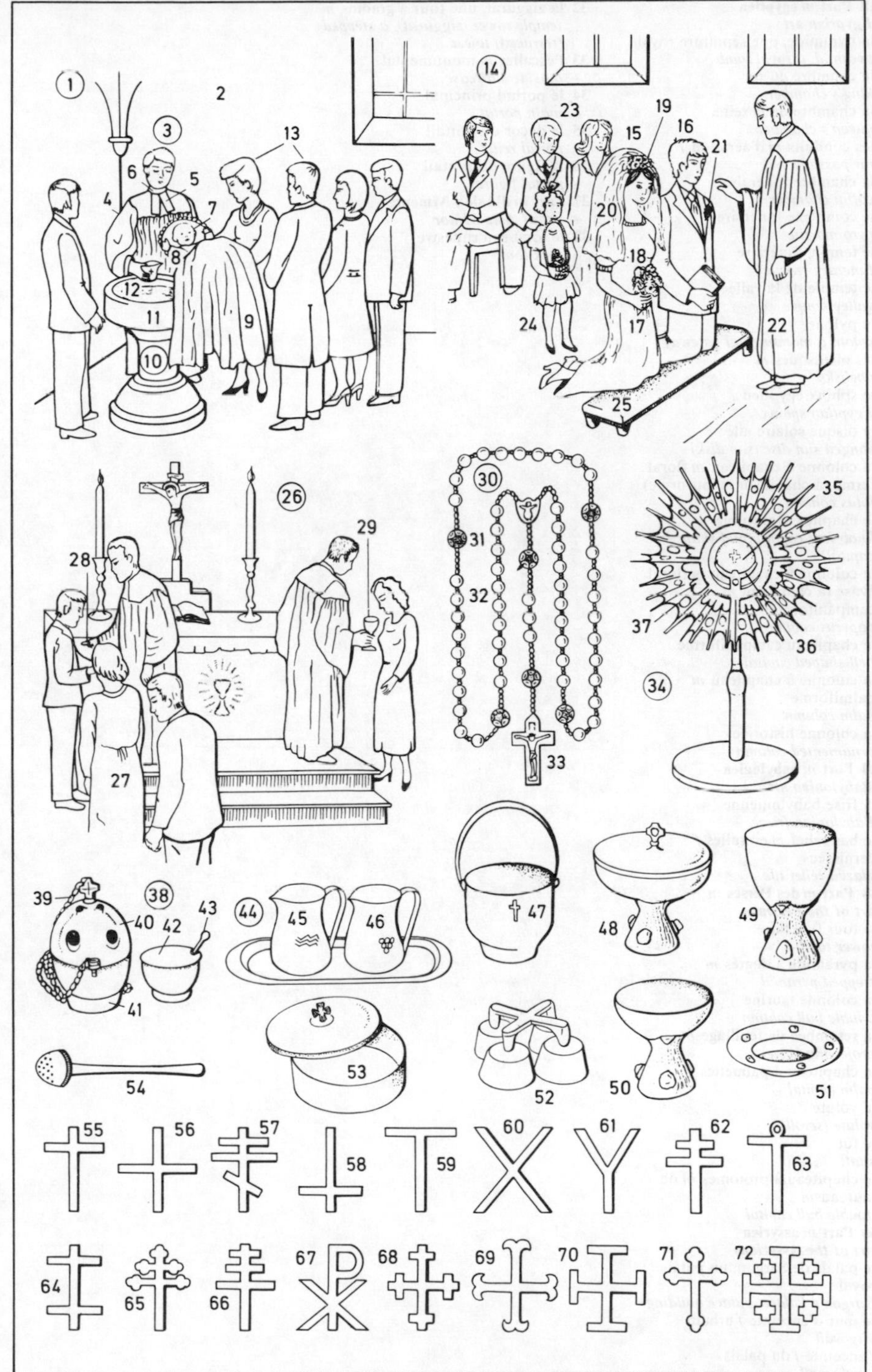

1-18 l'art *m* égyptien
– *Egyptian art*
1 la pyramide, une sépulture royale
– *pyramid, a royal tomb*
2 la chambre du roi
– *king's chamber*
3 la chambre de la reine
– *queen's chamber*
4 les conduits *m* d'aération *f*
– *air passage*
5 la chambre funéraire
– *coffin chamber*
6 le complexe funéraire
– *pyramid site*
7 le temple funéraire
– *funerary temple*
8 le temple de la vallée
– *valley temple*
9 le pylône
– *pylon, a monumental gateway*
10 les obélisques *m*
– *obelisks*
11 le sphinx égyptien
– *Egyptian sphinx*
12 le disque solaire ailé
– *winged sun disc (sun disk)*
13 la colonne à chapiteau *m* floral fermé (à chapiteau *m* lotiforme)
– *lotus column*
14 le chapiteau lotiforme
– *knob-leaf capital (bud-shaped capital)*
15 la colonne à chapiteau *m* floral évasé (à chapiteau *m* campaniforme)
– *papyrus column*
16 le chapiteau campaniforme
– *bell-shaped capital*
17 la colonne à chapiteau *m* palmiforme
– *palm column*
18 la colonne historiée
– *ornamented column*
19-20 l'art *m* babylonien
– *Babylonian art*
19 la frise babylonienne
– *Babylonian frieze*
20 le bas-relief *m* en tuiles *f* vernissées
– *glazed relief tile*
21-28 l'art *m* des Perses *m*
– *art of the Persians*
21 la tour funéraire
– *tower tomb*
22 la pyramide à degrés *m*
– *stepped pyramid*
23 la colonne taurine
– *double bull column*
24 la retombée de feuillage *m*
– *projecting leaves*
25 le chapiteau à palmettes *f*
– *palm capital*
26 la volute
– *volute (scroll)*
27 le fût
– *shaft*
28 le chapiteau à protomes *m* de taureau *m*
– *double bull capital*
29-36 l'art *m* assyrien
– *art of the Assyrians*
29 le palais de Sargon, un palais royal
– *Sargon's Palace, palace buildings*
30 le mur d'enceinte *f* urbain
– *city wall*
31 l'enceinte *f* du palais
– *castle wall*
32 la ziggurat, une tour à gradins *m*
– *temple tower (ziggurat), a stepped (terraced) tower*
33 l'escalier *m* monumental
– *outside staircase*
34 le portail principal
– *main portal*
35 le décor du portail
– *portal relief*
36 la figure du portail
– *portal figure*
37 l'art *m* d'Asie *f* Mineure
– *art of Asia Minor*
38 le tombeau rupestre
– *rock tomb*

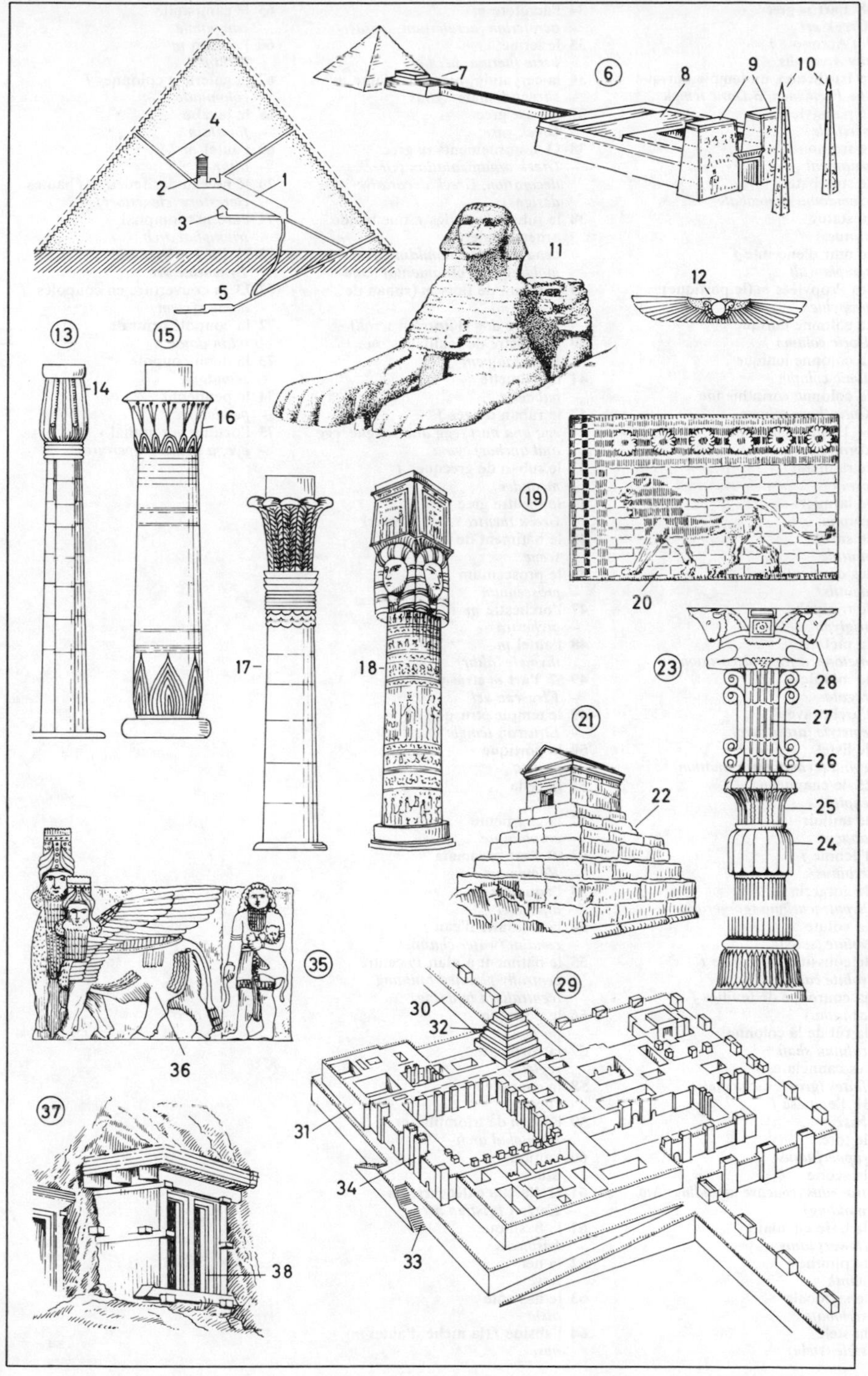
1
2
3
4
5
6
7
8
9
10
11
12
13
14
15
16
17
18
19
20
21
22
23
24
25
26
27
28
29
30
31
32
33
34
35
36
37
38

1-48 l'art *m* grec
– Greek art
1-7 l'Acropole *f*
– *the Acropolis*
1 le Parthénon, un temple dorique
– *the Parthenon, a Doric temple*
2 le péristyle
– *peristyle*
3 le fronton
– *pediment*
4 le stylobate
– *crepidoma (stereobate)*
5 la statue
– *statue*
6 le mur d'enceinte *f*
– *temple wall*
7 les Propylées *m* (le portique)
– *propylaea*
8 la colonne dorique
– *Doric column*
9 la colonne ionique
– *Ionic column*
10 la colonne corinthienne
– *Corinthian column*
11-14 l'entablement *m*
– *cornice*
11 le rampant
– *cyma*
12 le larmier
– *corona*
13 le soffite
– *mutule*
14 les denticules *m*
– *dentils*
15 le triglyphe
– *triglyph*
16 la métope
– *metope, a frieze decoration*
17 la mutule
– *regula*
18 l'architrave *f*
– *epistyle (architrave)*
19 le listel
– *cyma (cymatium, kymation)*
20-25 le chapiteau
– *capital*
20 le tailloir
– *abacus*
21 l'échine *f*
– *echinus*
22 le gorgerin
– *hypotrachelium (gorgerin)*
23 la volute
– *volute (scroll)*
24 le coussinet de volute *f*
– *volute cushion*
25 la couronne de feuilles *f*
– *acanthus*
26 le fût de la colonne
– *column shaft*
27 les cannelures *f*
– *flutes (grooves, channels)*
28-31 l'embase *f*
– *base*
28 le tore
– *[upper] torus*
29 la scotie
– *trochilus (concave moulding,* Am. *molding)*
30 la base circulaire
– *[lower] torus*
31 la plinthe
– *plinth*
32 le stylobate
– *stylobate*
33 la stèle
– *stele (stela)*
34 l'acrotère *m*
– *acroterion (acroterium, acroter)*
35 le terme
– *herm (herma, hermes)*
36 la caryatide; *masc.:* l'atlante *m*
– *caryatid;* male: *Atlas*
37 le vase grec
– *Greek vase*
38-43 les ornements *m* grecs
– *Greek ornamentation (Greek decoration, Greek decorative designs)*
38 le ruban de perles *f*, une bande ornementale
– *bead-and-dart moulding (*Am. *molding), an ornamental band*
39 le ruban de flots *m* (ruban de postes *m*)
– *running dog (Vitruvian scroll)*
40 le registre de feuillages *m*
– *leaf ornament*
41 la palmette
– *palmette*
42 le ruban d'oves *f*
– *egg and dart (egg and tongue, egg and anchor) cyma*
43 le ruban de grecques *f*
– *meander*
44 le théâtre grec
– *Greek theatre* (Am. *theater)*
45 le bâtiment de scène *f*
– *scene*
46 le proscenium
– *proscenium*
47 l'orchestre *m*
– *orchestra*
48 l'autel *m*
– *thymele (altar)*
49-52 l'art *m* étrusque
– Etruscan art
49 le temple étrusque
– *Etruscan temple*
50 le portique
– *portico*
51 la cella
– *cella*
52 la charpente
– *entablature*
53-60 l'art *m* romain
– Roman art
53 l'aqueduc *m*
– *aqueduct*
54 la conduite d'eau *f*
– *conduit (water channel)*
55 le bâtiment à plan *m* centré
– *centrally-planned building (centralized building)*
56 le portique
– *portico*
57 la corniche
– *reglet*
58 la coupole
– *cupola*
59 l'arc *m* de triomphe *m*
– *triumphal arch*
60 l'attique *m*
– *attic*
61-71 l'art *m* paléochrétien
– Early Christian art
61 la basilique
– *basilica*
62 la nef
– *nave*
63 le bas-côté
– *aisle*
64 l'abside *f* (la niche d'autel *m*)
– *apse*
65 le campanile
– *campanile*
66 l'atrium *m*
– *atrium*
67 la galerie à colonnes *f*
– *colonnade*
68 le lavabo
– *fountain*
69 l'autel *m*
– *altar*
70 le niveau des fenêtres *f* hautes
– *clerestory (clearstory)*
71 l'arc *m* triomphal
– *triumphal arch*
72-75 l'art *m* byzantin
– Byzantine art
72-73 la couverture en coupoles *f*
– *dome system*
72 la coupole centrale
– *main dome*
73 la demi-coupole
– *semidome*
74 le pendentif
– *pendentive*
75 l'oculus *m* zénithal
– *eye, a lighting aperture*

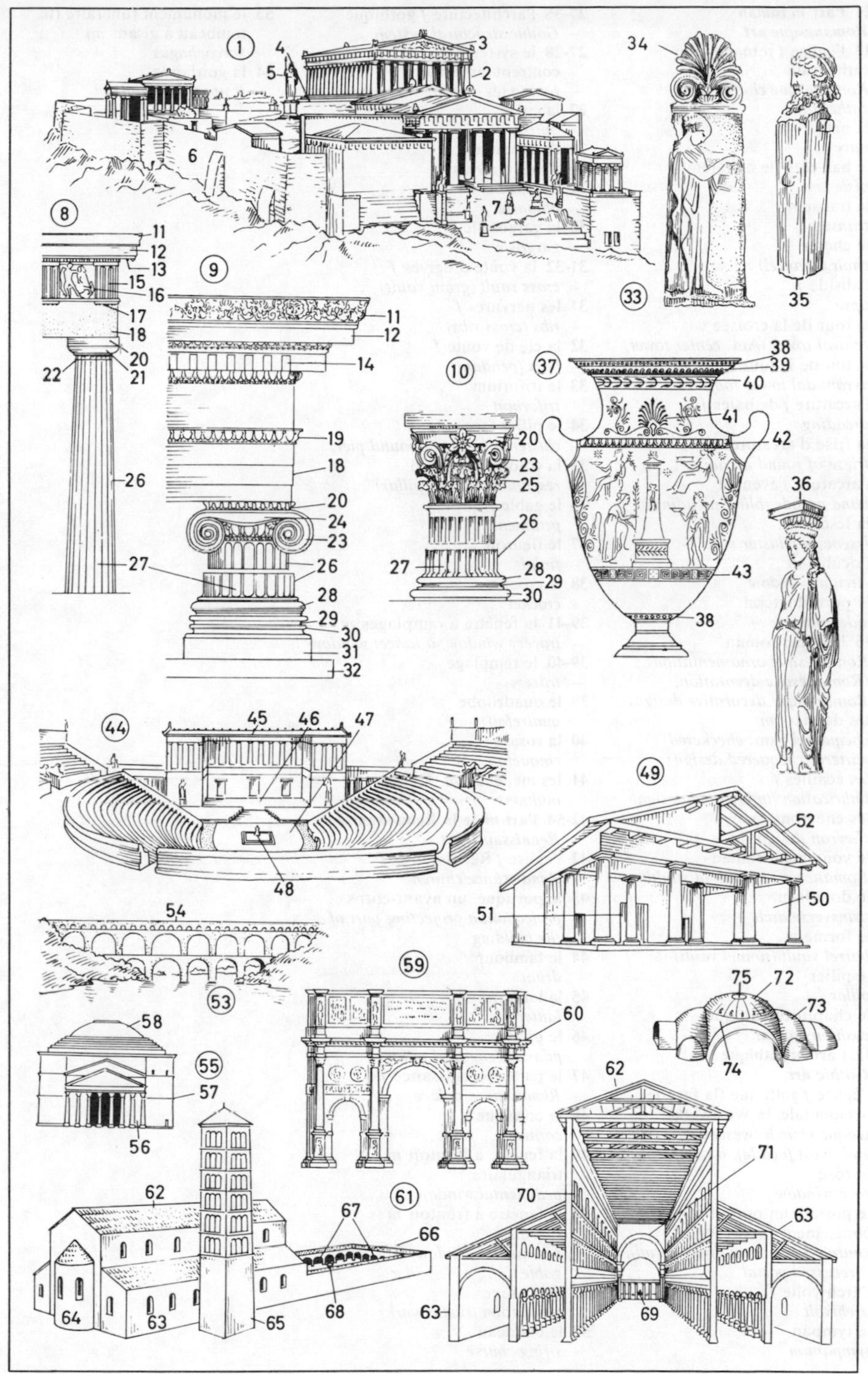
1
2
3
4
5
6
7
8
9
10
11
12
13
14
15
16
17
18
19
20
21
22
23
24
25
26
27
28
29
30
31
32
33
34
35
36
37
38
39
40
41
42
43
44
45
46
47
48
49
50
51
52
53
54
55
56
57
58
59
60
61
62
63
64
65
66
67
68
69
70
71
72
73
74
75

1-21 l'art *m* roman
– ***Romanesque art***
1-13 l'église *f* romane, une cathédrale
– *Romanesque church, a cathedral*
1 la nef
– *nave*
2 le bas-côté (le collatéral)
– *aisle*
3 le transept
– *transept*
4 le chœur
– *choir (chancel)*
5 l'abside *f*
– *apse*
6 la tour de la croisée
– *central tower (*Am. *center tower)*
7 le toit de la tour
– *pyramidal tower roof*
8 l'arcature *f* de baies *f*
– *arcading*
9 la frise d'arcatures *f*
– *frieze of round arcading*
10 l'arcature *f* aveugle
– *blind arcade (blind arcading)*
11 la lésène
– *lesene, a pilaster strip*
12 l'oculus *m*
– *circular window*
13 le portail latéral
– *side entrance*
14-16 le décor roman
– *Romanesque ornamentation (Romanesque decoration, Romanesque decorative designs)*
14 les damiers *m*
– *chequered (*Am. *checkered) pattern (chequered design)*
15 les écailles *f*
– *imbrication (imbricated design)*
16 les chevrons *m*
– *chevron design*
17 le voûtement roman
– *Romanesque system of vaulting*
18 le doubleau
– *transverse arch*
19 le formeret
– *barrel vault (tunnel vault)*
20 le pilier
– *pillar*
21 le chapiteau cubique
– *cushion capital*
22-41 l'art *m* gothique
– ***Gothic art***
22 l'église *f* gothique (la façade occidentale, le Westwerk).
– *Gothic church [westwork, west end, west façade], a cathedral*
23 la rose
– *rose window*
24 le portail, un portail à ébrasements *m* profonds
– *church door (main door, portal), a recessed portal*
25 l'archivolte *f*
– *archivolt*
26 le tympan
– *tympanum*
27-35 l'architecture *f* gothique
– *Gothic structural system*
27-28 le système de contrebutement *m*
– *buttresses*
27 la culée
– *buttress*
28 l'arc-boutant *m*
– *flying buttress*
29 le pinacle
– *pinnacle*
30 la gargouille
– *gargoyle*
31-32 la voûte d'ogives *f*
– *cross vault (groin vault)*
31 les nervures *f*
– *ribs (cross ribs)*
32 la clé de voûte *f*
– *boss (pendant)*
33 le triforium
– *triforium*
34 le pilier fasciculé
– *clustered pier (compound pier)*
35 la colonne engagée
– *respond (engaged pillar)*
36 le gâble
– *pediment*
37 le fleuron
– *finial*
38 le crochet
– *crocket*
39-41 la fenêtre à remplages *m*
– *tracery window, a lancet window*
39-40 le remplage
– *tracery*
39 le quadrilobe
– *quatrefoil*
40 la rosace
– *cinquefoil*
41 les meneaux *m*
– *mullions*
42-54 l'art *m* de la Renaissance
– ***Renaissance art***
42 l'église *f* Renaissance *f*
– *Renaissance church*
43 le portique, un avant-corps
– *projection, a projecting part of the building*
44 le tambour
– *drum*
45 la lanterne
– *lantern*
46 le pilastre
– *pilaster (engaged pillar)*
47 le palais Renaissance *f*
– *Renaissance palace*
48 la corniche
– *cornice*
49 la fenêtre à fronton *m* triangulaire
– *pedimental window*
50 la fenêtre à fronton *m* surbaissé
– *pedimental window with round gable*
51 le bossage
– *rustication (rustic work)*
52 le bandeau
– *string course*
53 le monument funéraire (le tombeau à gisant *m*)
– *sarcophagus*
54 la guirlande
– *festoon (garland)*

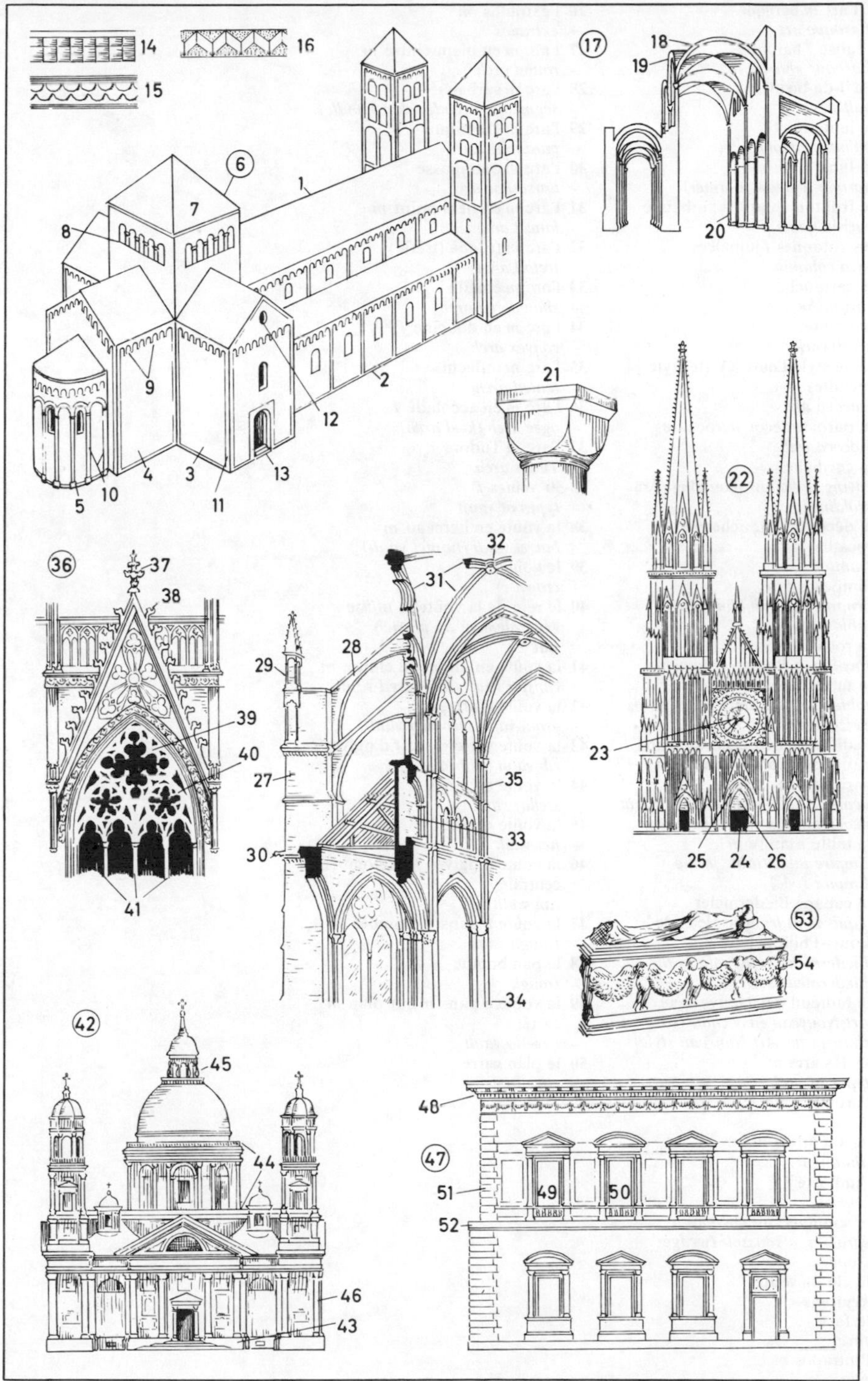
14
16
15
17
18
19
20
6
7
1
8
9
2
12
21
5
10
4
3
11
13
22
36
37
38
32
31
28
29
39
40
23
27
35
33
30
25
24
26
41
34
53
54
42
45
48
44
47
51
49
50
52
46
43

1-8 l'art *m* baroque
– ***Baroque art***
1 l'église *f* baroque
– *Baroque church*
2 l'œil-de-bœuf *m*
– *bull's eye*
3 le lanternon
– *bulbous cupola*
4 la lucarne
– *dormer window (dormer)*
5 le fronton en arc *m* surbaissé
– *curved gable*
6 les colonnes *f* jumelées
– *twin columns*
7 le cartouche
– *cartouche*
8 la volute
– *scrollwork*
9-13 le style Louis XV (le style rocaille)
– ***Rococo art***
9 la paroi à décor *m* rocaille
– *Rococo wall*
10 la corniche
– *coving, a hollow moulding (*Am. *molding)*
11 le décor à cartouches *m* rocaille
– *framing*
12 l'imposte *f*
– *ornamental moulding (*Am. *molding)*
13 la rocaille
– *rocaille, a Rococo ornament*
14 la table Louis XVI
– *table in Louis Seize style (Louis Seize table)*
15 l'édifice *m* néo-classique, un bâtiment *m* à portique *m* (à péristyle *m*)
– *neoclassical building (building in neoclassical style), a gateway*
16 la table Empire *m*
– *Empire table (table in the Empire style)*
17 le canapé Biedermeier [*équivalent français:* le style Louis-Philippe]
– *Biedermeier sofa (sofa in the Biedermeier style)*
18 le fauteuil Art Nouveau *m*
– *Art Nouveau easy chair (easy chair in the Art Nouveau style)*
19-37 les arcs *m*
– ***types of arch***
19 l'arc *m*
– *arch*
20 les piédroits *m*
– *abutment*
21 l'imposte *f*
– *impost*
22 le sommier, un claveau
– *springer, a voussoir (wedge stone)*
23 la clé de voûte *f*
– *keystone*
24 la face
– *face*
25 l'intrados *m*
– *pier*
26 l'extrados *m*
– *extrados*
27 l'arc *m* en plein cintre *m*
– *round arch*
28 l'arc *m* surbaissé
– *segmental arch (basket handle)*
29 l'arc *m* elliptique
– *parabolic arch*
30 l'arc *m* outrepassé
– *horseshoe arch*
31 l'arc *m* en tiers-point *m*
– *lancet arch*
32 l'arc *m* trilobé (tréflé)
– *trefoil arch*
33 l'arc *m* épaulé
– *shouldered arch*
34 l'arc *m* en doucine *f*
– *convex arch*
35 l'arc *m* infléchi
– *tented arch*
36 l'arc *m* en accolade *f*
– *ogee arch (keel arch)*
37 l'arc *m* Tudor
– *Tudor arch*
38-50 voûtes *f*
– ***types of vault***
38 la voûte en berceau *m*
– *barrel vault (tunnel vault)*
39 le voûtain
– *crown*
40 le rein de la voûte (*s'utilise généralement au pluriel*)
– *side*
41 la voûte en arc *m* de cloître *m*
– *cloister vault (cloistered vault)*
42 la voûte d'arêtes *f*
– *groin vault (groined vault)*
43 la voûte sur croisée *f* d'ogives *f*
– *rib vault (ribbed vault)*
44 la voûte en étoile *f*
– *stellar vault*
45 la voûte nervée
– *net vault*
46 la voûte d'ogives *f* à retombée *f* centrale
– *fan vault*
47 la voûte à pans *m* bombés
– *trough vault*
48 le pan bombé
– *trough*
49 la voûte à pans *m* sur plan *m* carré
– *cavetto vault*
50 le plan carré
– *cavetto*

1
3
2
4
5
6
10
11
9
12
13
14
16
7
8
17
18
15
19
26
23
22
21
20
24
25
27
28
29
30
31
32
33
34
35
36
37
39
40
38
40
40
41
42
43
44
45
46
47
48
40
49
50

Art V 337

1-6 l'art *m* chinois
– ***Chinese art***
1 la pagode
– *pagoda, a temple tower*
2 le toit à gradins *m*
– *storey (story) roof (roof of storey)*
3 le portique
– *pailou (pailoo), a memorial archway*
4 le passage
– *archway*
5 le vase de porcelaine *f*
– *porcelain vase*
6 l'objet *m* en laque *f* sculptée
– *incised lacquered work*
7-11 l'art *m* japonais
– ***Japanese art***
7 le temple
– *temple*
8 le campanile
– *bell tower*
9 la charpente
– *supporting structure*
10 le bodisattva, un saint bouddhique
– *bodhisattva (boddhisattva), a Buddhist saint*
11 le toril, un portique
– *torii, a gateway*
12-18 l'art *m* de l'Islam
– ***Islamic art***
12 la mosquée
– *mosque*
13 le minaret
– *minaret, a prayer tower*
14 le mirhab (la niche à prières *f*)
– *mihrab*
15 le minbar (la chaire à prêcher)
– *minbar (mimbar, pulpit)*
16 le mausolée, un monument funéraire
– *mausoleum, a tomb*
17 la voûte à stalactites *f*
– *stalactite vault (stalactitic vault)*
18 le chapiteau arabe
– *Arabian capital*
19-28 l'art *m* de l'Inde
– ***Indian art***
19 Shiva dansant, une divinité hindoue
– *dancing Siva (Shiva), an Indian god*
20 la statue de Bouddha (un Bouddha)
– *statue of Buddha*
21 le stupa (le stoupa), un tumulus en forme de coupole *f*, un monument religieux bouddhique
– *stupa (Indian pagoda), a mound (dome), a Buddhist shrine*
22 le parasol
– *umbrella*
23 la balustrade de pierre *f*
– *stone wall* (Am. *stone fence)*
24 le portique
– *gate*
25 le temple
– *temple buildings*
26 la çikkara (la tour du temple)
– *shikara (sikar, sikhara, temple tower)*
27 l'intérieur *m* d'un sanctuaire rupestre (un çaïtya)
– *chaitya hall*
28 le dagoba (un petit stupa)
– *chaitya, a small stupa*

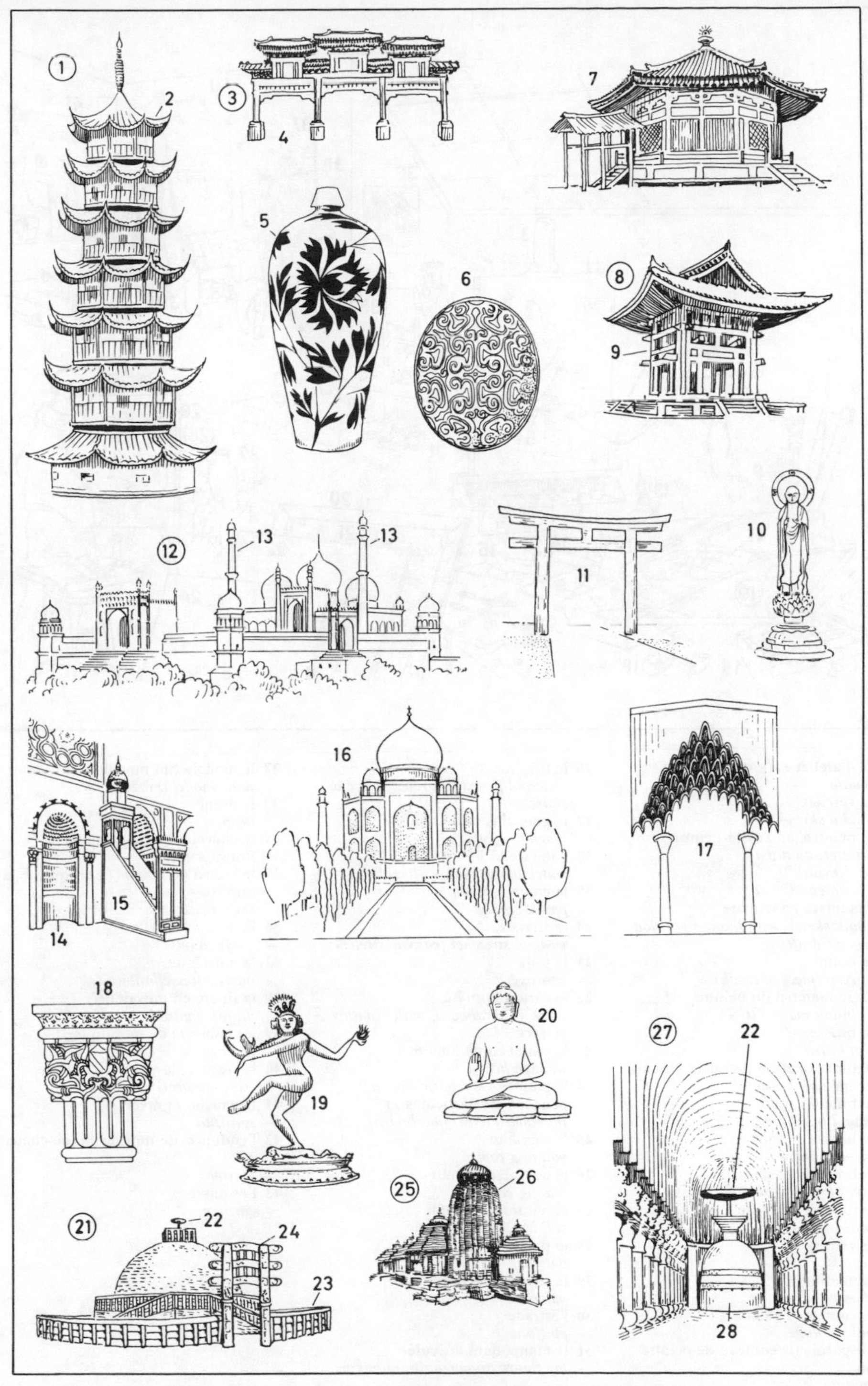
1
2
3
4
5
6
7
8
9
10
11
12
13
13
14
15
16
17
18
19
20
21
22
23
24
25
26
27
22
28

1-43 l'atelier *m* (le studio)
- ***studio***

1 la verrière
- *studio skylight*

2 le peintre, un artiste-peintre
- *painter, an artist*

3 le chevalet
- *studio easel*

4 l'esquisse *f* à la craie
- *chalk sketch, with the composition (rough draft)*

5 la craie
- *crayon (piece of chalk)*

6-19 le matériel du peintre
- *painting materials*

6 la brosse
- *flat brush*

7 le pinceau effilé (la queue-de-rat)
- *camel hair brush*

8 le pinceau rond
- *round brush*

9 la brosse à fonds *m*
- *priming brush*

10 la boîte de couleurs *f*
- *box of paints (paintbox)*

11 le tube de peinture *f* à l'huile *f*
- *tube of oil paint*

12 le vernis
- *varnish*

13 le médium
- *thinner*

14 le couteau à palette *f*
- *palette knife*

15 la spatule (le couteau de peintre *m*)
- *spatula*

16 le fusain
- *charcoal pencil (charcoal, piece of charcoal)*

17 la gouache, la détrempe
- *tempera (gouache)*

18 l'aquarelle *f*
- *watercolour* (Am. *watercolor)*

19 le crayon pastel
- *pastel crayon*

20 le châssis
- *wedged stretcher (canvas stretcher)*

21 la toile
- *canvas*

22 le carton apprêté
- *piece of hardboard, with painting surface*

23 le panneau de bois *m*
- *wooden board*

24 le panneau d'aggloméré *m* (le panneau de particules *f*)
- *fibreboard* (Am. *fiberboard)*

25 la servante
- *painting table*

26 le chevalet portatif
- *folding easel*

27 la nature-morte, un sujet
- *still life group, a motif*

28 la palette
- *palette*

29 le support de pinceau *m*
- *palette dipper*

30 l'estrade *f*
- *platform*

31 le mannequin articulé
- *lay figure (mannequin, manikin)*

32 le modèle (un modèle pour le nu)
- *nude model (model, nude)*

33 le drapé
- *drapery*

34 le chevalet de dessinateur *m*
- *drawing easel*

35 le bloc à dessins *m* (à croquis *m*, à esquisses *f*)
- *sketch pad*

36 l'étude *f* à l'huile *f*
- *study in oils*

37 la mosaïque
- *mosaic (tessellation)*

38 la figure en mosaïque *f*
- *mosaic figure*

39 les cubes *m* de mosaïque *f*
- *tesserae*

40 la fresque, la peinture murale
- *fresco (mural)*

41 l'ébauche *f* gravée
- *sgraffito*

42 l'enduit *m* de mortier *m* (de chaux *f*)
- *plaster*

43 l'esquisse *f*
- *cartoon*

1-38 l'atelier *m*
– ***studio***
1 le sculpteur
– *sculptor*
2 le compas de réduction *f*
– *proportional dividers*
3 le compas d'épaisseur *f*
– *calliper (caliper)*
4 le modèle en plâtre *m*
– *plaster model, a plaster cast*
5 le bloc de pierre (un bloc non épannelé)
– *block of stone (stone block)*
6 le sculpteur en terre *f* glaise *f*
– *modeller* (Am. *modeler)*
7 la figure de terre *f* glaise *f* (d'argile *f* à modeler)
– *clay figure, a torso*
8 le rouleau de terre *f* glaise *f* (d'argile *f*, de pâte *f* à modeler)
– *roll of clay, a modelling (*Am. *modeling) substance*
9 la selle
– *modelling* (Am. *modeling) stand*
10 l'ébauchoir *m*
– *wooden modelling* (Am. *modeling) tool*
11 la mirette
– *wire modelling* (Am. *modeling) tool*
12 la spatule
– *beating wood*
13 la gradine grain *m* d'orge *m*
– *claw chisel (toothed chisel, tooth chisel)*
14 le ciseau plat
– *flat chisel*
15 la pointe (le poinçon)
– *point (punch)*
16 la masse (la massette)
– *iron-headed hammer*
17 la gouge
– *gouge (hollow chisel)*
18 la gouge coudée
– *spoon chisel*
19 le ciseau plat
– *wood chisel, a bevelled-edge chisel*
20 le burin
– *V-shaped gouge*
21 le maillet
– *mallet*
22 l'armature *f*
– *framework*
23 le socle
– *baseboard*
24 la potence
– *armature support (metal rod)*
25 les papillons *m*
– *armature*
26 la cire (la figurine en cire *f*)
– *wax model*
27 le bloc de bois *m*
– *block of wood*
28 le sculpteur sur bois *m*
– *wood carver (wood sculptor)*
29 le sac de plâtre *m*
– *sack of gypsum powder (gypsum)*
30 la caisse à terre *f* glaise *f*
– *clay box*
31 la terre glaise *f* (la terre à modeler, l'argile *f* à modeler)
– *modelling (Am. modeling) clay (clay)*
32 la statue (une sculpture en ronde-bosse *f*)
– *statue, a sculpture*
33 le bas-relief
– *low relief (bas-relief)*
34 le châssis grillagé de modelage *m*
– *modelling (*Am. *modeling) board*
35 le grillage
– *wire frame, wire netting*
36 le médaillon
– *circular medallion (tondo)*
37 le masque
– *mask*
38 la plaquette
– *plaque*

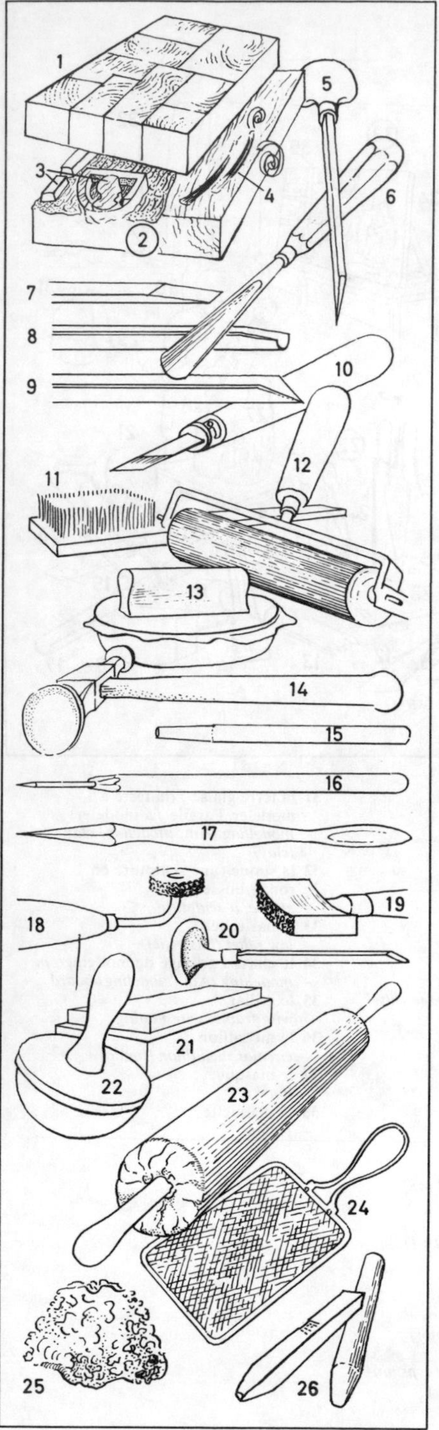

1-13 la gravure sur bois *m* (la xylographie), un procédé de gravure *f* (d'impression *f*) en relief *m*
– ***wood engraving*** *(xylography), a relief printing method (a letterpress printing method)*

1 la planche de bois *m* de bout *m* pour la gravure à teintes *f* (sur bois *m* de bout *m*), un bloc de bois *m*
– *end-grain block for wood engravings, a wooden block*

2 la planche de bois *m* de fil *m* pour la gravure en taille *f* d'épargne *f* (sur bois *m* de fil *m*), un modèle en bois *m*
– *wooden plank for woodcutting, a relief image carrier*

3 la gravure en relief *m* (parties *f* épargnées, reproduites après encrage *m*, la réserve)
– *positive cut*

4 la taille (l'évidement *m*) dans le fil du bois
– *plank cut*

5 le burin à contours *m*
– *burin (graver)*

6 la gouge creuse
– *U-shaped gouge*

7 le ciseau (le burin plat)
– *scorper (scauper, scalper)*

8 la gouge
– *scoop*

9 la gouge en V *m* (triangulaire)
– *V-shaped gouge*

10 le couteau à contours *m*
– *contour knife*

11 la brosse
– *brush*

12 le rouleau à gélatine *f*
– *roller (brayer)*

13 le frottoir
– *pad (wiper)*

14-24 la gravure sur cuivre *m* (la chalcographie, la gravure en taille-douce, la gravure au burin), un procédé de gravure *f* (d'impression *f*) en creux *m*; *var.:* l'eau-forte *f*, la gravure au lavis, à la manière noire (le mezzo-tinto), l'aquatinte *f* (la gravure au grain de résine *f*), la gravure en manière *f* de crayon *m* (la gravure à la roulette, au pointillé)
– ***copperplate engraving*** *(chalcography), an intaglio process;* kinds: *etching, mezzotint, aquatint, crayon engraving*

14 le marteau à emboutir (l'emboutissoir *m*)
– *hammer*

15 le poinçon (le repoussoir)
– *burin*

16 la pointe sèche pour la gravure en taille-douce *f*
– *etching needle (engraver)*

17 le racloir-brunissoir (l'ébarboir *m*, le grattoir avec brunissoir *m*, avec polissoir)
– *scraper and burnisher*

18 la roulette de pointillage *m* (la molette à pointiller)
– *roulette*

19 le berceau à poncer (le grenoir)
– *rocking tool (rocker)*

20 le burin à bout *m* rond, un traçoir (une échoppe)
– *round-headed graver, a graver (burin)*

21 la pierre à huile *f* (la pierre à aiguiser, l'aiguisoir *m*)
– *oilstone*

22 le tampon encreur
– *dabber (inking ball, ink ball)*

23 le rouleau encreur en cuir *m*
– *leather roller*

24 le crible à grenure *f*
– *sieve*

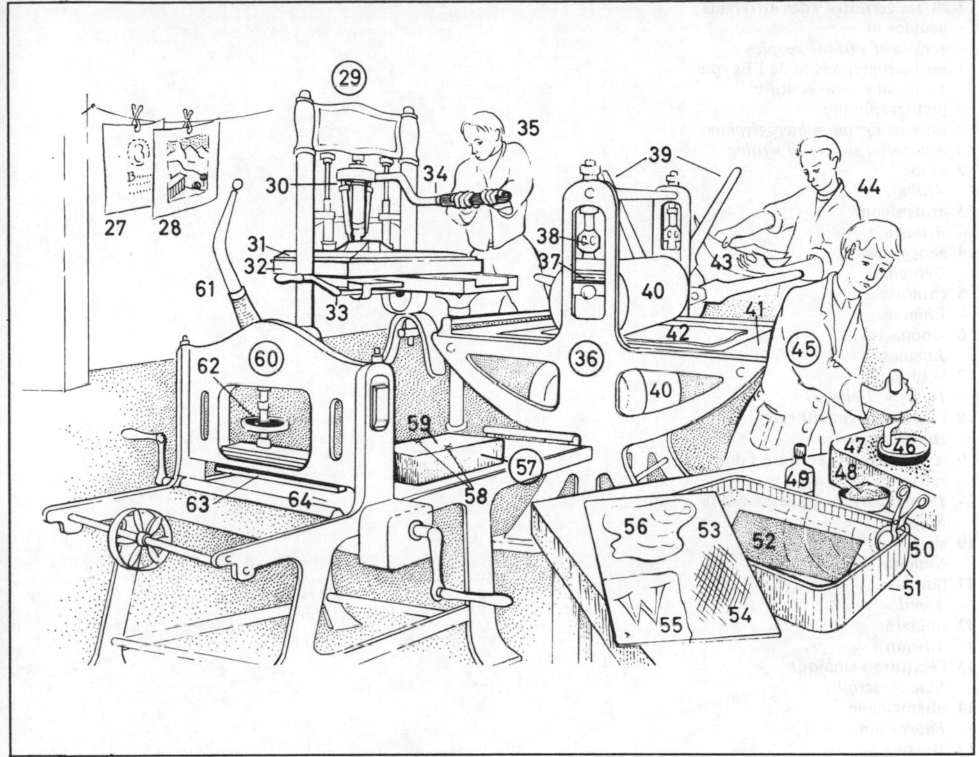

25-26 la lithographie (la gravure sur pierre *f*), un procédé de gravure *f* (d'impression *f*) à plat *m* ou planographique
– ***lithography** (stone lithography), a planographic printing method*

25 l'éponge *f* pour humidifier la pierre lithographique
– *sponge for moistening the lithographic stone*

26 le crayon (la craie) lithographique (le crayon gras), une craie
– *lithographic crayons (greasy chalk)*

27-64 l'atelier *m* **d'impression** *f* (de reproduction *f* graphique), une imprimerie
– ***graphic art studio**, a printing office* (Am. *printery)*

27 la feuille imprimée (l'impression *f* en blanc *m*, à recto *m* simple)
– *broadside (broadsheet, single sheet)*

28 l'impression *f* (en) couleur *f* (la chromolithographie, la lithochromie)
– *full-colour* (Am. *full-color) print (colour print, chromolithograph)*

29 la presse à platine *f*, une presse à bras *m*
– *platen press, a hand press*

30 la genouillère (la rotule)
– *toggle*

31 la platine, une plaque de foulage *m* (d'impression *f*)
– *platen*

32 la forme (la matrice, le bloc d'impression *f*)
– *type forme* (Am. *form)*

33 la manivelle de tirage *m*
– *feed mechanism*

34 le bras de la manivelle de relevage *m*
– *bar (devil's tail)*

35 l'imprimeur *m*
– *pressman*

36 la presse à taille-douce *f*
– *copperplate press*

37 la garniture en carton *m*
– *tympan*

38 le régulateur de pression *f*
– *pressure regulator*

39 le levier à plusieurs bras *m* en étoile *f*
– *star wheel*

40 le cylindre de pression *f*
– *cylinder*

41 le tympan (la table d'impression *f*, le marbre)
– *bed*

42 le feutre (le blanchet, le lange)
– *felt cloth*

43 l'épreuve *f*
– *proof (pull)*

44 l'imprimeur *m* chalcographe (le graveur sur cuivre *m*, au burin, en taille-douce *f*)
– *copperplate engraver*

45 l'imprimeur *m* lithographe ponçant la pierre (le greneur)
– *lithographer (litho artist), grinding the stone*

46 le polissoir (la meule)
– *grinding disc (disk)*

47 la grenure (la granulation, les grains *m*)
– *grain (granular texture)*

48 le sable à faire le verre
– *pulverized glass*

49 la dissolution
– *rubber solution*

50 la pince
– *tongs*

51 le bain d'eau-forte *f* (de mordant *m*, d'acide *m*) attaquant les parties *f* dévernies de la plaque de zinc *m*
– *etching bath for etching*

52 la plaque de zinc *m* (le cliché de zinc *m*)
– *zinc plate*

53 la plaque de cuivre *m* (le cliché de cuivre *m*)
– *polished copperplate*

54 l'empreinte *f* quadrillée (le guillochis)
– *cross hatch*

55 le creux d'attaque *f* (partie *f* de la plaque de cuivre *m* mise à nu par une pointe sèche et attaquée et creusée par l'acide *m*)
– *etching ground*

56 la couche protectrice de vernis *m* (la réserve)
– *non-printing area*

57 la pierre lithographique
– *lithographic stone*

58 les repères *m* (les piqûres *f*)
– *register marks*

59 le cliché (la plaque d'impression *f*)
– *printing surface (printing image carrier)*

60 la presse lithographique (d'impression *f* à plat *m*)
– *lithographic press*

61 le levier de pression *f*
– *lever*

62 la vis de serrage *m*
– *scraper adjustment*

63 le plateau presseur
– *scraper*

64 le marbre
– *bed*

1-20 les écritures *f* des différents peuples *m*
– ***scripts of various peoples***
1 les hiéroglyphes *m* de l'Egypte *f* ancienne, une écriture pictographique
– *ancient Egyptian hieroglyphics, a pictorial system of writing*
2 arabe
– *Arabic*
3 arménienne
– *Armenian*
4 géorgienne
– *Georgian*
5 chinoise
– *Chinese*
6 japonaise
– *Japanese*
7 hébraïque
– *Hebrew (Hebraic)*
8 l'écriture *f* cunéïforme
– *cuneiform script*
9 le dévanâgari (écriture *f* du sanscrit)
– *Devanagari, script employed in Sanskrit*
10 siamoise
– *Siamese*
11 tamoule
– *Tamil*
12 tibétaine
– *Tibetan*
13 l'écriture *f* sinaïque
– *Sinaitic script*
14 phénicienne
– *Phoenician*
15 grecque
– *Greek*
16 capitale romaine
– *Roman capitals*
17 onciale (l'écriture *f* onciale)
– *uncial (uncials, uncial script)*
18 minuscule *f* caroline
– *Carolingian (Carlovingian, Caroline) minuscule*
19 runes *f* (écriture *f* runique)
– *runes*
20 russe
– *Russian*
21-26 instruments *m* d'écriture *f* anciens
– ***ancient* writing implements**
21 le stylet d'acier *m* hindou, poinçon *m* pour l'écriture *f* sur papyrus *m*
– *Indian steel stylus for writing on palm leaves*
22 le poinçon égyptien, une tige de roseau *m*
– *ancient Egyptian reed pen*
23 la plume creuse de roseau *m*
– *writing cane*
24 le pinceau
– *brush*
25 le style (stylet *m*) romain en métal *m*
– *Roman metal pen (stylus)*
26 la plume d'oie *f*
– *quill (quill pen)*

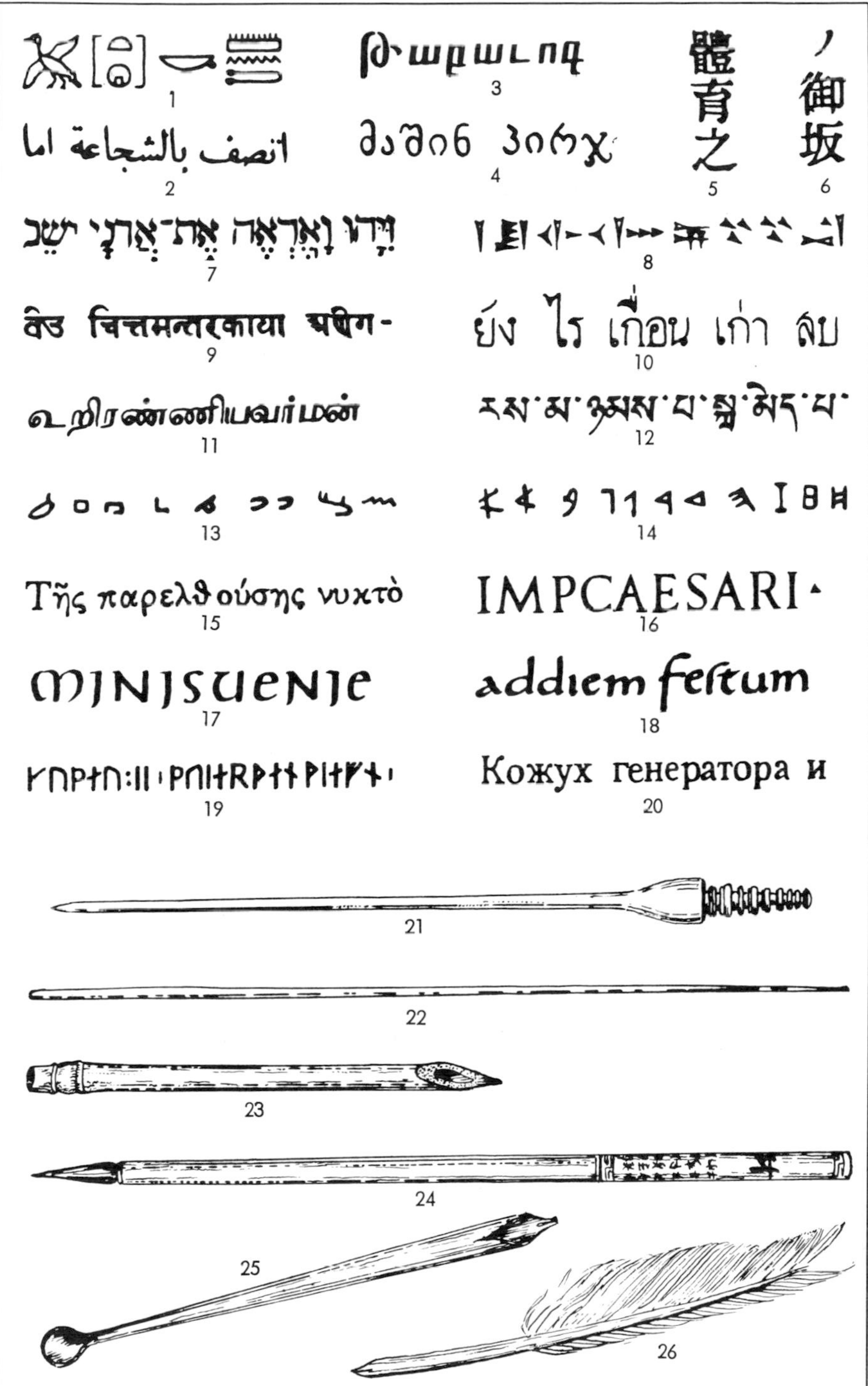
1
3
體
育
之
5
御
坂
6
2
4
7
8
9
10
11
12
13
14
Τῆς παρελθούσης νυκτὸ
15
IMPCAESARI
16
17
addiem feſtum
18
19
Кожух генератора и
20
21
22
23
24
25
26

1-15 les caractères *m*
– ***types*** *(type faces)*
1 la gothique
– *Gothic type (German black-letter type)*
2 le Schwabach
– *Schwabacher type (German black-letter type)*
3 l'antique *f* (la fracture) allemande
– *Fraktur (German black-letter type)*
4 l'antique *f* médiévale
– *Humanist (Mediaeval)*
5 le garamond
– *Transitional*
6 le Didot
– *Didone*
7 le bâton
– *Sanserif (Sanserif type, Grotesque)*
8 l'égyptienne *f*
– *Egyptian*
9 le caractère machine *f*
– *typescript (typewriting)*
10 l'anglaise *f*
– *English hand (English handwriting, English writing)*
11 l'allemande *f*
– *German hand (German handwriting, German writing)*
12 la latine
– *Latin script*
13 la notation sténographique (la sténographie)
– *shorthand (shorthand writing, stenography)*
14 la transcription phonétique
– *phonetics (phonetic transcription)*
15 le braille
– *Braille*
16-29 les signes *m* **de ponctuation** *f*
– ***punctuation marks*** *(stops)*
16 le point
– *full stop (period, full point)*
17 le deux-points *m*
– *colon*
18 la virgule
– *comma*
19 le point-virgule
– *semicolon*
20 le point d'interrogation *f*
– *question mark (interrogation point, interrogation mark)*
21 le point d'exclamation *f*
– *exclamation mark (*Am. *exclamation point)*
22 l'apostrophe *f*
– *apostrophe*
23 le tiret
– *dash (em rule)*
24 les parenthèses *f*
– *parentheses (round brackets)*
25 les crochets *m*
– *square brackets*
26 les guillemets *m*
– *quotation mark (double quotation marks, paired quotation marks, inverted commas)*
27 les guillemets *m* à la française
– *guillemet (French quotation mark)*
28 le trait d'union *f*
– *hyphen*
29 les points *m* de suspension *f*
– *marks of omission (ellipsis)*
30-35 les signes *m* **d'accentuation** *f* **et les signes** *m* **diacritiques**
– ***accents and diacritical marks*** *(diacritics)*
30 l'accent *m* aigu
– *acute accent (acute)*
31 l'accent *m* grave
– *grave accent (grave)*
32 l'accent *m* circonflexe
– *circumflex accent (circumflex)*
33 la cédille
– *cedilla [under c]*
34 le tréma
– *diaeresis (*Am. *dieresis) [over e]*
35 le tilde
– *tilde [over n]*
36 le paragraphe
– *section mark*
37-70 le journal, un quotidien national
– ***newspaper****, a national daily newspaper*
37 la page de journal *m*
– *newspaper page*
38 la première page (la une)
– *front page*
39 le titre du journal
– *newspaper heading*
40 la table des matières *f*
– *contents*
41 le prix
– *price*
42 la date de publication *f*
– *date of publication*
43 le lieu de parution *f*
– *place of publication*
44 la manchette
– *headline*
45 la colonne
– *column*
46 le surtitre (le titre d'appel *m*)
– *column heading*
47 la colombelle
– *column rule*
48 l'éditorial *m*
– *leading article (leader, editorial)*
49 le sommaire
– *reference to related article*
50 la nouvelle brève
– *brief news item*
51 la rubrique politique
– *political section*
52 le titre de page *f* intérieure
– *page heading*
53 le dessin humoristique
– *cartoon*
54 le reportage du correspondant
– *report by newspaper's own correspondent*
55 le sigle de l'agence *f* de presse *f*
– *news agency's sign*
56 l'annonce publicitaire (*fam.:* la publicité)
– *advertisement (*coll. *ad)*
57 la rubrique sportive
– *sports section*
58 la photo de presse *f*
– *press photo*
59 la légende
– *caption*
60 le reportage sportif
– *sports report*
61 les nouvelles *f* sportives
– *sports news item*
62 la rubrique des informations *f* générales
– *home and overseas news section*
63 les faits *m* divers
– *news in brief (miscellaneous news)*
64 les programmes *m* de télévision *f* (un aperçu des programmes *m* de la semaine)
– *television programmes (*Am. *programs)*
65 le bulletin météorologique
– *weather report*
66 la carte météorologique
– *weather chart (weather map)*
67 la rubrique de la vie culturelle
– *arts section (feuilleton)*
68 la rubrique nécrologique
– *death notice*
69 la rubrique des annonces *f*
– *advertisements (classified advertising)*
70 les offres *f* et les demandes *f* d'emploi *m*, une offre d'emploi *m*
– *job advertisement, a vacancy (a situation offered)*

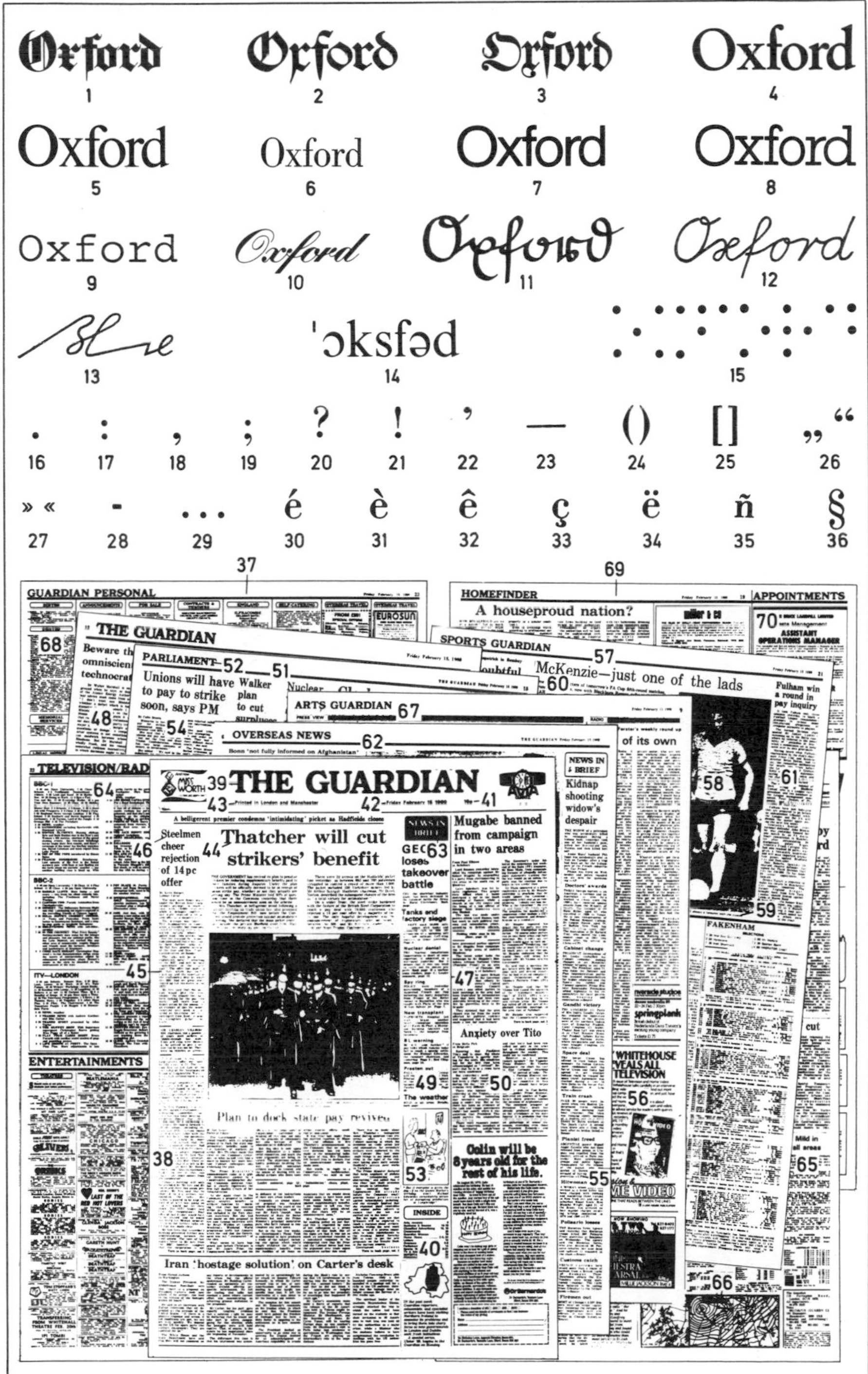
Oxford
1
Oxford
2
Oxford
3
Oxford
4
Oxford
5
Oxford
6
Oxford
7
Oxford
8
Oxford
9
Oxford
10
Oxford
11
Oxford
12
13
ˈɔksfəd
14
15
. 16
: 17
, 18
; 19
? 20
! 21
’ 22
— 23
() 24
[] 25
„ “ 26
» « 27
- 28
... 29
é 30
è 31
ê 32
ç 33
ë 34
ñ 35
§ 36
37
GUARDIAN PERSONAL
EUROSUN
68
THE GUARDIAN
Beware the omniscient technocrat
48
PARLIAMENT 52
51
Unions will have to pay to strike soon, says PM
Walker plan to cut surpluses
54
Nuclear
ARTS GUARDIAN 67
OVERSEAS NEWS 62
Bonn 'not fully informed on Afghanistan'
TELEVISION/RADIO
BBC-1
64
46
BBC-2
ITV—LONDON
45
ENTERTAINMENTS
38
39
THE GUARDIAN
43 Printed in London and Manchester
42 Friday February 15 1980
41
A belligerent premier condemns 'intimidating' picket as Hadfields closes
Steelmen cheer rejection of 14pc offer
44
Thatcher will cut strikers' benefit
NEWS IN BRIEF
GEC loses takeover battle
63
Tanks and factory siege
Mugabe banned from campaign in two areas
47
Anxiety over Tito
49
50
Plan to dock state pay revived
53
INSIDE
40
Colin will be 8 years old for the rest of his life.
Iran 'hostage solution' on Carter's desk
NEWS IN BRIEF
Kidnap shooting widow's despair
Doctors' awards
55
56
69
HOMEFINDER
A houseproud nation?
APPOINTMENTS
70
ASSISTANT OPERATIONS MANAGER
SPORTS GUARDIAN
57
McKenzie—just one of the lads
60
of its own
58
Fulham win a round in pay inquiry
61
59
FAKENHAM
springplank
WHITEHOUSE REVEALS ALL TELEVISION
65
66

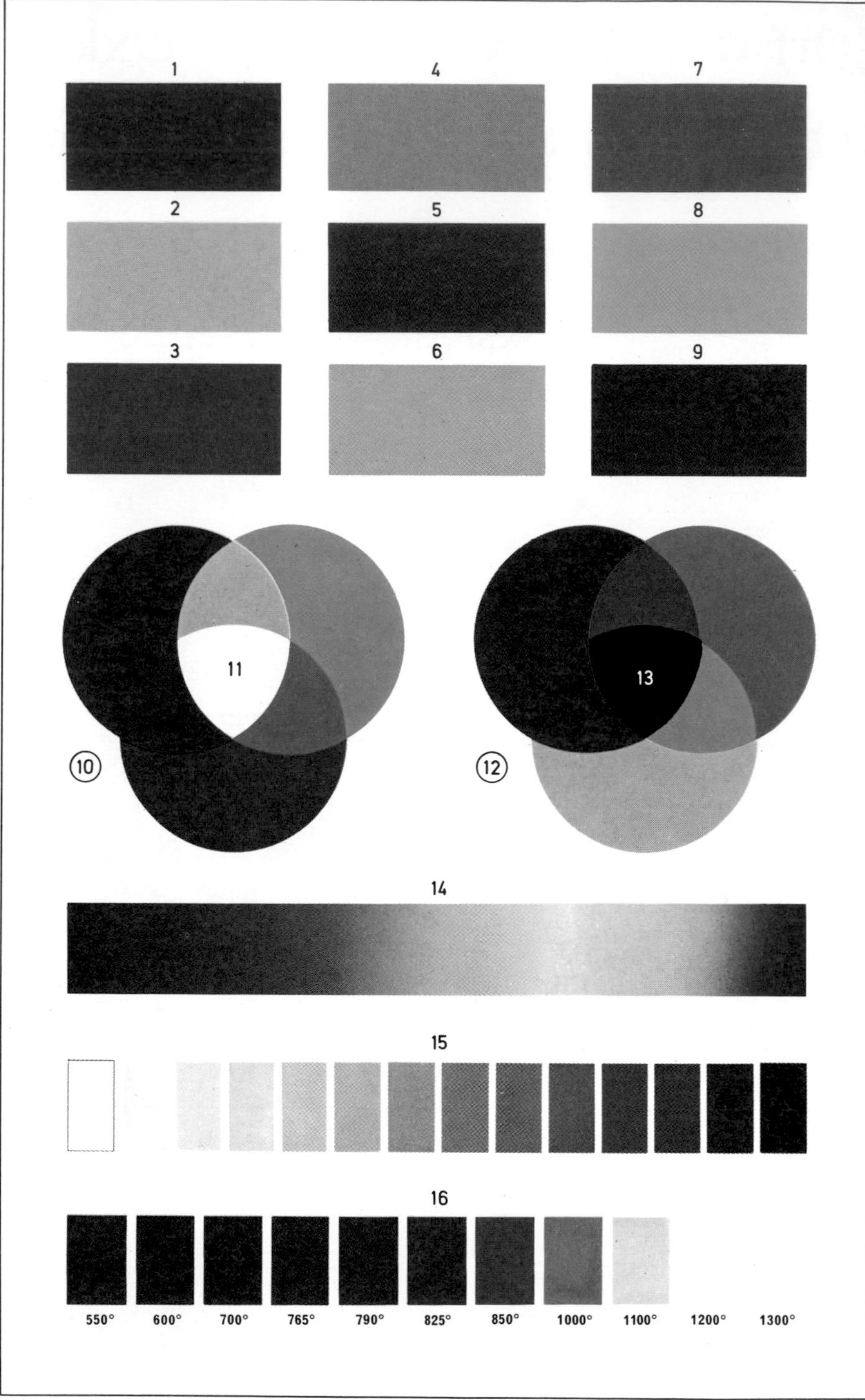
1
4
7
2
5
8
3
6
9
11
10
13
12
14
15
16
550°
600°
700°
765°
790°
825°
850°
1000°
1100°
1200°
1300°

1 rouge
– *red*
2 jaune
– *yellow*
3 bleu
– *blue*
4 rose
– *pink*
5 brun
– *brown*
6 bleu ciel
– *azure (sky blue)*
7 orange
– *orange*
8 vert
– *green*
9 violet
– *violet*
10 le mélange additif de couleurs *f*
– *additive mixture of colours* (Am. *colors)*
11 blanc
– *white*
12 le mélange soustractif de couleurs *f*
– *subtractive mixture of colours* (Am. *colors)*
13 noir
– *black*
14 le spectre solaire (les couleurs *f* de l'arc-en-ciel *m*)
– *solar spectrum (colours,* Am. *colors, of the rainbow)*
15 l'échelle *f* des gris *m*
– *grey* (Am. *gray) scale*
16 les couleurs *f* d'incandescence *f*
– *heat colours* (Am. *colors)*

① I II III IV V VI VII VIII IX X

② 1 2 3 4 5 6 7 8 9 10

① XX XXX XL XLIX IL L LX LXX LXXX XC

② 20 30 40 49 50 60 70 80 90

① XCIX IC C CC CCC CD D DC DCC DCCC

② 99 100 200 300 400 500 600 700 800

① CM CMXC M

② 900 990 1000

③ 9658 ④ 5 kg. ⑤ 2 ⑥ 2nd ⑦ +5 ⑧ -5

1-26 l'arithmétique *f*
– ***arithmetic***
1-22 le nombre
– ***numbers***
1 les chiffres *m* romains
– *Roman numerals*
2 les chiffres *m* arabes
– *Arabic numerals*
3 le nombre abstrait, un nombre à quatre chiffres *m* [8: le chiffre des unités *f*, 5: le chiffre des dizaines *f*, 6: le chiffre des centaines *f*, 9: le chiffre des milliers *m*]
– *abstract number, a four-figure number [8: units; 5: tens; 6: hundreds; 9: thousands]*
4 le nombre concret
– *concrete number*
5 le nombre cardinal
– *cardinal number (cardinal)*
6 le nombre ordinal
– *ordinal number (ordinal)*
7 le nombre positif [affecté du signe plus]
– *positive number [with plus sign]*
8 le nombre négatif [affecté du signe moins]
– *negative number [with minus sign]*
9 les symboles *m* algébriques
– *algebraic symbols*
10 le nombre fractionnaire [3: le nombre entier, $\frac{1}{3}$: la fraction]
– *mixed number [3: whole number (integer); $\frac{1}{3}$: fraction]*
11 les nombres *m* pairs
– *even numbers*
12 les nombres *m* impairs
– *odd numbers*
13 les nombres *m* premiers
– *prime numbers*
14 le nombre complexe [3: la partie réelle, $2\sqrt{-1}$: la partie imaginaire]
– *complex number [3: real part; $2\sqrt{-1}$: imaginary part]*
15-16 les fractions *f* ordinaires
– *vulgar fractions*
15 la fraction irréductible [2: le numérateur, le trait de fraction, 3: le dénominateur]
– *proper fraction [2: numerator, horizontal line; 3: denominator]*
16 le nombre fractionnaire égal à l'inverse *m* de la fraction 15
– *improper fraction, also the reciprocal of item 15*
17 la fraction de fraction *f*
– *compound fraction (complex fraction)*
18 l'expression *f* fractionnaire
– *improper fraction [when cancelled down produces a whole number]*
19 les fractions *f* à dénominateur *m* différent [35: le dénominateur commun]
– *fractions of different denominations [35: common denominator]*
20 la fraction décimale finie, avec virgule *f* et décimales *f* [3: le chiffre des dixièmes *m*; 5: le chiffre des centièmes *m*; 7: le chiffre des millièmes *m*]
– *proper decimal fraction with decimal point and decimal places [3: tenths; 5: hundredths; 7: thousandths]*
21 la fraction décimale périodique infinie
– *recurring decimal*
22 la période
– *recurring decimal*
23-26 le calcul (les 4 opérations *f* de base *f*, les 4 opérations *f* fondamentales)
– ***fundamental arithmetical operations***

⑨ a,b,c... ⑩ $3\frac{1}{3}$ ⑪ 2,4,6,8 ⑫ 1,3,5,7

⑬ 3,5,7,11 ⑭ $3+2\sqrt{-1}$ ⑮ $\frac{2}{3}$ ⑯ $\frac{3}{2}$

⑰ $\frac{\frac{5}{6}}{\frac{3}{4}}$ ⑱ $\frac{12}{4}$ ⑲ $\frac{4}{5}+\frac{2}{7}=\frac{38}{35}$ ⑳ 0·357

㉑ $0{\cdot}6666.... = 0{\cdot}\overline{6}$ ㉒ ㉓ 3 + 2 = 5

㉔ 3 - 2 = 1 ㉕ 3 · 2 = 6, 3 x 2 = 6 ㉖ 6 ÷ 2 = 3

en France: ⑥ 2ème ⑳ 0,357

㉑ $0{,}6666.... = 0{,}\overline{6}$ ㉒ ㉖ 6/2 = 3

23 l'addition *f* [3 et 2: les termes *m* de la somme; + : le signe plus (le signe d'addition *f*; = : le signe d'égalité *f*, 5: la somme (le résultat)]
– *addition (adding) [3 and 2: the terms of the sum; + : plus sign; = : equals sign; 5: the sum]*

24 la soustraction [3: le diminuende; - : le signe moins (le signe de soustraction *f*); 2: le diminuteur; 1: le reste (la différence)]
– *subtraction (subtracting); [3: the minuend; - : minus sign; 2: the subtrahend; 1: the remainder (difference)]*

25 la multiplication [3: le multiplicande; x (ou .): le signe de multiplication; 2: le multiplicateur; 2 et 3: les facteurs *m*; 6: le produit]
– *multiplication (multiplying); [3: the multiplicand; × : multiplication sign; 2: the multiplier; 2 and 3: factors; 6: the product]*

26 la division [6: le dividende; : (ou /) = le signe de division *f*; 2: le diviseur; 3: le quotient]
– *division (dividing); [6: the dividend; ÷ division sign; 2: the divisor; 3: the quotient]*

① $3^2 = 9$

② $\sqrt[3]{8} = 2$

③ $\sqrt{4} = 2$

④ $3x + 2 = 12$

⑤ $4a + 6ab - 2ac = 2a(2 + 3b - c)$

⑥ $\log_{10} 3 = 0{\cdot}4771$

⑦ $\dfrac{P[£1000] \times R[5\%] \times T[2\text{years}]}{100} = I[£100]$

1-24 arithmétique *f*
– ***arithmetic***
1-10 les opérations *f* **d'arithmétique supérieure**
– ***advanced arithmetical operations***
1 l'élévation *f* à une puissance (l'exponentiation *f*) [3: la base, 2: l'exposant *m*, 9: la valeur de la puissance]
– *raising to a power [three squared (3^2) the power; 3: the base; 2: the exponent (index); 9: value of the power]*
2 l'extraction *f* de la racine [la racine cubique de 8; 8: la quantité radicale, 3: l'indice *m* de la racine, √‾: le signe radical, 2: la racine]
– *evolution (extracting a root); [cube-root of 8: cube root; 8: the radical; 3: the index (degree) of the root; √‾: radical sign; 2: value of the root]*
3 la racine carrée
– *square root*
4-5 le calcul algébrique (l'algèbre *f*)
– *algebra*
4 l'équation *f* [3, 2: les coefficients *m*, x: l'inconnue *f*]
– *simple equation [3, 2: the coefficients; x: the unknown quantity]*
5 l'équation *f* d'identité *f* [a, b, c: les symboles *m* algébriques]
– *identical equation; [a, b, c: algebraic symbols]*
6 le calcul logarithmique [log: le symbole du logarithme, 3: l'antilogarithme *m*, 10: la base, 0: la caractéristique, 4771: la mantisse, 0,4771: le logarithme]
– *logarithmic calculation (taking the logarithm, log); [log: logarithm sign; 3: number whose logarithm is required; 10: the base; 0: the characteristic; 4771: the mantissa; 0.4771: the logarithm]*
7 le calcul des intérêts *m* [k: le capital, p: le taux, t: le temps de placement *m*, z: l'intérêt *m* (le rapport, le gain), %: le signe de pourcentage *m*]
– *simple interest formula; [P: the principal; R: rate of interest; T: time; I: interest (profit); %: percentage sign]*
8-10 la règle de trois [≙ équivaut à]
– *rule of three (rule-of-three sum, simple proportion)*
8 la mise en équation *f* avec l'inconnue *f* x *m*
– *statement with the unknown quantity x*
9 l'équation *f*
– *equation (conditional equation)*
10 la solution
– *solution*
11-14 les mathématiques *f* **supérieures**
– ***higher mathematics***
11 la série arithmétique avec les termes *m* 2, 4, 6, 8
– *arithmetical series with the elements 2, 4, 6, 8*
12 la série géométrique
– *geometrical series*
13-14 le calcul infinitésimal
– ***infinitesimal calculus***
13 la dérivée (le quotient différentiel) [dx, dy: les différentielles *f*, d: le signe de différentiation *f*]
– *derivative [dx, dy: the differentials; d: differential sign]*

(8) 2 years @ £50 / 4 years @ £x

(9) $2 : 50 = 4 : x$

(10) $x = £100$

(11) $2+4+6+8 \ldots$

(12) $2+4+8+16+32 \ldots$

(13) $\frac{dy}{dx}$

(14) $\int ax\,dx = a\int x\,dx = \frac{ax^2}{2} + C$

(15) ∞ (16) $\equiv$ (17) $\approx$ (18) $\neq$ (19) $>$

(20) $<$ (21) $\parallel$ (22) $\sim$ (23) $\sphericalangle$ (24) $\triangle$

en France: (6) $\log_{10} 3 = 0{,}4771$ ou $\log 3 = 0{,}4771$

(8) 2 ans ≙ 50F / 4 ans ≙ xF

(9) $2/50 = 4/x$

(10) $x = 100F$

(7) $\frac{k\,1000F \cdot p\,5\% \cdot t\,2\text{ ans}}{100} = z\,100F$

14 l'intégrale *f* (l'intégration *f*) [x: la variable d'intégration *f*, C: la constante d'intégration *f*, dx: la différentielle]
– *integral (integration); [x: the variable; C: constant of integration; ∫: the integral sign; dx: the differential]*

15-24 les symboles *m* mathématiques
– ***mathematical symbols***

15 infini
– *infinity*

16 identique à (le signe d'identité *f*)
– *identically equal to (the sign of identity)*

17 sensiblement égal à
– *approximately equal to*

18 différent de (le signe d'inégalité *f*)
– *unequal to*

19 supérieur à (plus grand que)
– *greater than*

20 inférieur à (plus petit que)
– *less than*

21-24 les symboles *m* géométriques
– ***geometrical symbols***

21 parallèle à
– *parallel (sign of parallelism)*

22 semblable à
– *similar to (sign of similarity)*

23 le symbole d'angle *m*
– *angle symbol*

24 le symbole de triangle *m*
– *triangle symbol*

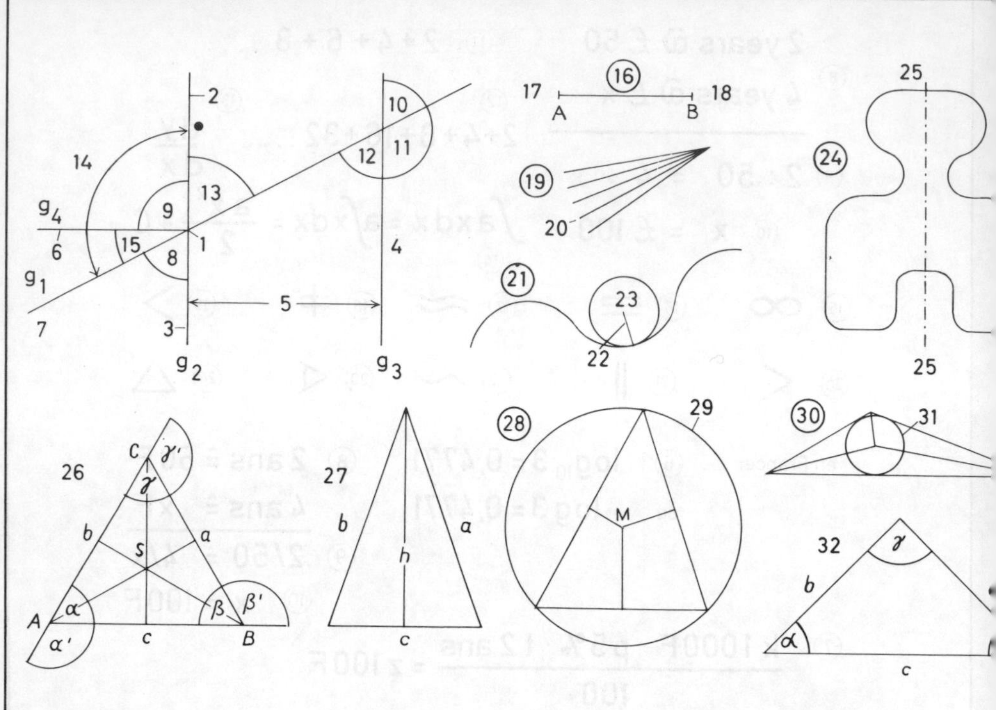

1-58 la géométrie plane (la géométrie euclidienne)
– ***plane geometry*** *(elementary geometry, Euclidian geometry)*
1-23 le point, la ligne, l'angle *m*
– ***point, line, angle***
1 le point [le point d'intersection *f* de g_1 et g_2], le sommet de l'angle *m* 8
– *point [point of intersection of g_1 and g_2], the angular point of 8*
4 la parallèle à g_2
– *the parallel to g_2*
5 la distance des droites *f* g_1 et g_2
– *distance between the straight lines g_2 and g_3*
6 la perpendiculaire (g_4) à g_2
– *perpendicular (g_4) on g_2*
8 l'angle *m*
– *angle*
9 l'angle *m* droit [90°]
– *right angle [90°]*
10 l'angle *m* aigu, alterne externe de l'angle *m* 8
– *acute angle, also the alternate angle to 8*
11 l'angle *m* obtus
– *obtuse angle*
12 l'angle *m* correspondant de l'angle *m* 8
– *corresponding angle to 8*
14 l'angle *m* adjacent; *ici:* l'angle *m* supplémentaire de l'angle *m* 13
– *adjacent angle;* here: *supplementary angle to 13*
15 l'angle *m* complémentaire de l'angle *m* 8
– *complementary angle to 8*
16 le segment de droite *f*
– *straight line AB*
17 l'extrémité *f* A
– *end A*
18 l'extrémité *f* B
– *end B*
19 le faisceau de droites *f*
– *pencil of rays*
20 la droite du faisceau
– *ray*
21 la courbe
– *curved line*
22 un rayon de courbure *f*
– *radius of curvature*
23 un centre de courbure *f*
– *centre* (Am. *center) of curvature*
24-58 les surfaces *f* **planes**
– ***plane surfaces***
24 la figure symétrique
– *symmetrical figure*
25 l'axe *m* de symétrie *f*
– *axis of symmetry*
26-32 les triangles *m*
– ***plane triangles***
26 le triangle équilatéral [A, B, C: les sommets *m*; a, b, c: les côtés *m*; α (alpha), β (bêta), γ (gamma): les angles *m* intérieurs; α', β', γ': les angles *m* extérieurs; S: le centre de gravité *f*]
– *equilateral triangle; [A, B, C: the vertices; a, b, c: the sides; α (alpha), β (beta), γ (gamma): the interior angles; α', β', γ': the exterior angles; S: the centre* (Am. *center)]*
27 le triangle isocèle [a, b: les côtés *m* égaux; c: la base; h: une hauteur]
– *isoceles triangle [a, b: the sides (legs); c: the base; h: the perpendicular, an altitude]*
28 le triangle acutangle avec les médiatrices *f*
– *acute-angled triangle with perpendicular bisectors of the sides*
29 le cercle circonscrit
– *circumcircle (circumscribed circle)*
30 le triangle obtusangle avec les bissectrices *f*
– *obtuse-angled triangle with bisectors of the angles*
31 le cercle inscrit
– *inscribed circle*
32 le triangle rectangle et les fonctions *f* trigonométriques [a, b: les côtés *m* de l'angle *m* droit; c: l'hypoténuse *f*; γ: l'angle *m* droit; a/c = sin α (sinus); b/c = cos α (cosinus); a/b = tg α (tangente); b/a = cotg α (cotangente)]

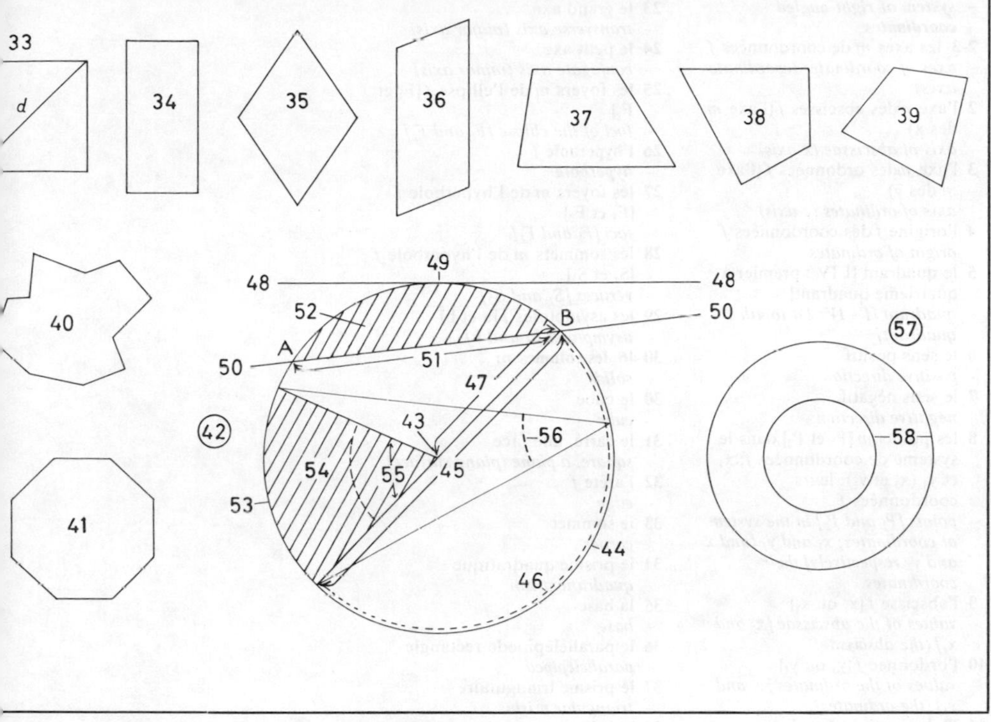

– *right-angled triangle and the trigonometrical functions of angles; [a, b: the catheti; c: the hypotenuse; γ:* the right angle; a:c = sin α *(sine); b:c =* cos α *(cosine); a:b =* tan α *(tangent); a:b =* cot α *(cotangent)*

33-39 les quadrilatères ***m***
– ***quadrilaterals***

33-36 les parallélogrammes ***m***
– ***parallelograms***

33 le carré [d: une diagonale]
– *square [d: a diagonal]*

34 le rectangle
– *rectangle*

35 le losangle (le rhombe)
– *rhombus (rhomb, lozenge)*

36 le rhomboïde
– *rhomboid*

37 le trapèze
– *trapezium*

38 le deltoïde (le cerf-volant)
– *deltoid (kite)*

39 le quadrilatère irrégulier
– *irregular quadrilateral*

40 le polygone
– *polygon*

41 le polygone régulier
– *regular polygon*

42 le cercle
– ***circle***

43 le centre
– *centre* (Am. *center)*

44 la circonférence
– *circumference (periphery)*

45 le diamètre
– *diameter*

46 le demi-cercle
– *semicircle*

47 le rayon [r]
– *radius (r)*

48 la tangente
– *tangent*

49 le point de tangente *f* [P]
– *point of contact (P)*

50 la sécante
– *secant*

51 la corde AB
– *the chord AB*

52 le segment circulaire
– *segment*

53 l'arc *m* de cercle *m*
– *arc*

54 le secteur circulaire
– *sector*

55 l'angle *m* au centre
– *angle subtended by the arc at the centre (Am. center) (centre,* Am. *center, angle)*

56 l'angle *m* inscrit
– *circumferential angle*

57 la couronne circulaire
– *ring (annulus)*

58 les cercles *m* concentriques
– *concentric circles*

1 le système de coordonnées cartésiennes (orthogonales)
– *system of right-angled coordinates*
2-3 les axes *m* de coordonnées *f*
– *axes of coordinates (coordinate axes)*
2 l'axe *m* des abscisses *f* (l'axe *m* des x)
– *axis of abscissae (x-axis)*
3 l'axe *m* des ordonnées *f* (l'axe *m* des y)
– *axis of ordinates (y-axis)*
4 l'origine *f* des coordonnées *f*
– *origin of ordinates*
5 le quadrant [I IV : premier à quatrième quadrant]
– *quadrant [I - IV: 1st to 4th quadrant]*
6 le sens positif
– *positive direction*
7 le sens négatif
– *negative direction*
8 les points *m* [P_1 et P_2] dans le système de coordonnées *f*; x_1 et y_1 (x_2 et y_2): leurs coordonnées *f*
– *points [P_1 and P_2] in the system of coordinates; x_1 and y_1 [and x_2 and y_2 respectively] their coordinates*
9 l'abscisse *f* [x_1 ou x_2]
– *values of the abscissae [x_1 and x_2] (the abscissae)*
10 l'ordonnée *f* [y_1 ou y_1]
– *values of the ordinates [y_1 and y_2] (the ordinates)*
11-29 les sections *f* coniques
– *conic sections*
11 les courbes planes
– *curves in the system of coordinates*
12 les droites *f* [a: la pente de la droite; b: l'ordonnée *f* à l'origine *f*; c: la racine de l'équation *f* de la droite]
– *plane curves [a: the gradient (slope) of the curve; b: the ordinates' intersection of the curve; c: the root of the curve]*
13 les courbes *f*
– *inflected curves*
14 **la parabole,** une courbe du second degré *m*
– ***parabola**, a curve of the second degree*
15 les branches *f* de la parabole
– *branches of the parabola*
16 le sommet de la parabole
– *vertex of the parabola*
17 l'axe *m* de la parabole
– *axis of the parabola*
18 une courbe du troisième degré
– *a curve of the third degree*
19 le maximum de la courbe
– *maximum of the curve*
20 le minimum de la courbe
– *minimum of the curve*
21 le point d'inflexion *f*
– *point of inflexion (of inflection)*
22 l'ellipse *f*
– *ellipse*
23 le grand axe
– *transverse axis (major axis)*
24 le petit axe
– *conjugate axis (minor axis)*
25 les foyers *m* de l'ellipse *f* [F_1 et F_2]
– *foci of the ellipse [F_1 and F_2]*
26 l'hyperbole *f*
– *hyperbola*
27 les foyers *m* de l'hyperbole *f* [F_1 et F_2]
– *foci [F_1 and F_2]*
28 les sommets *m* de l'hyperbole *f* [S_1 et S_2]
– *vertices [S_1 and S_2]*
29 les asymptotes *f* [a et b]
– *asymptotes [a and b]*
30-46 les volumes *m*
– *solids*
30 le cube
– *cube*
31 le carré, une face
– *square, a plane (plane surface)*
32 l'arête *f*
– *edge*
33 le sommet
– *corner*
34 le prisme quadratique
– *quadratic prism*
35 la base
– *base*
36 le parallélépipède rectangle
– *parallelepiped*
37 le prisme triangulaire
– *triangular prism*
38 le cylindre, un cylindre droit
– *cylinder, a right cylinder*
39 la base, un cercle
– *base, a circular plane*
40 l'enveloppe *f*
– *curved surface*
41 la sphère
– *sphere*
42 l'ellipsoïde *m* de révolution *f*
– *ellipsoid of revolution*
43 le cône
– *cone*
44 la hauteur
– *height of the cone (cone height)*
45 le tronc de cône *m*
– *truncated cone (frustum of a cone)*
46 la pyramide quadrangulaire
– *quadrilateral pyramid*

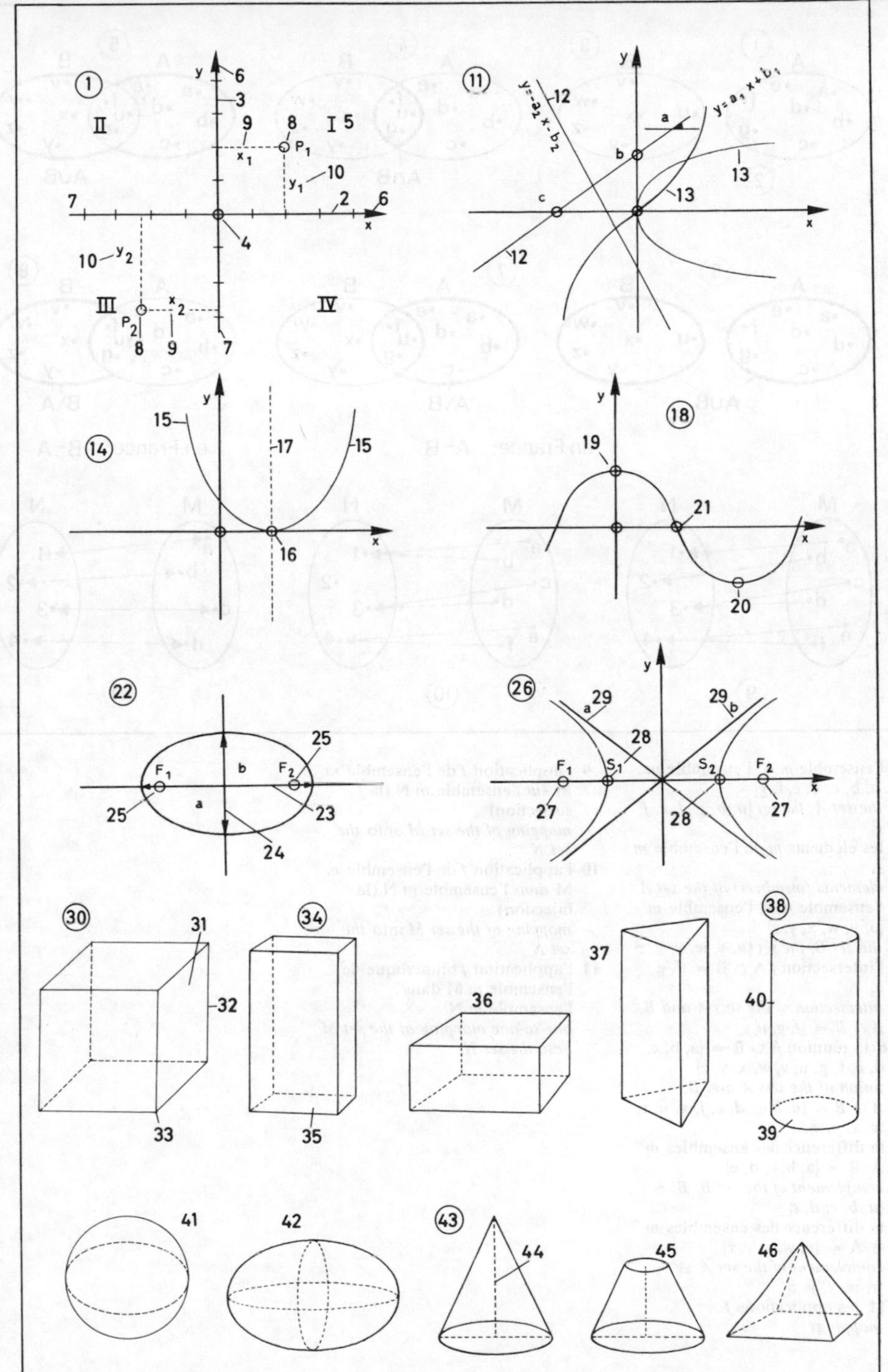

1
y
6
3
II
9
8
I 5
x_1
P_1
y_1
10
7
2
6
x
4
10 y_2
III
P_2
x
2
IV
8
9
7
11
y
$y=a_2x+b_2$
12
$y=a_1x+b_1$
a
b
13
13
c
x
12
14
y
15
17
15
16
x
18
y
19
21
x
20
22
b
a
F_1
F_2
25
25
23
24
26
y
29
a
29
b
28
F_1
S_1
S_2
F_2
x
27
28
27
30
31
32
33
34
35
36
37
38
40
39
41
42
43
44
45
46

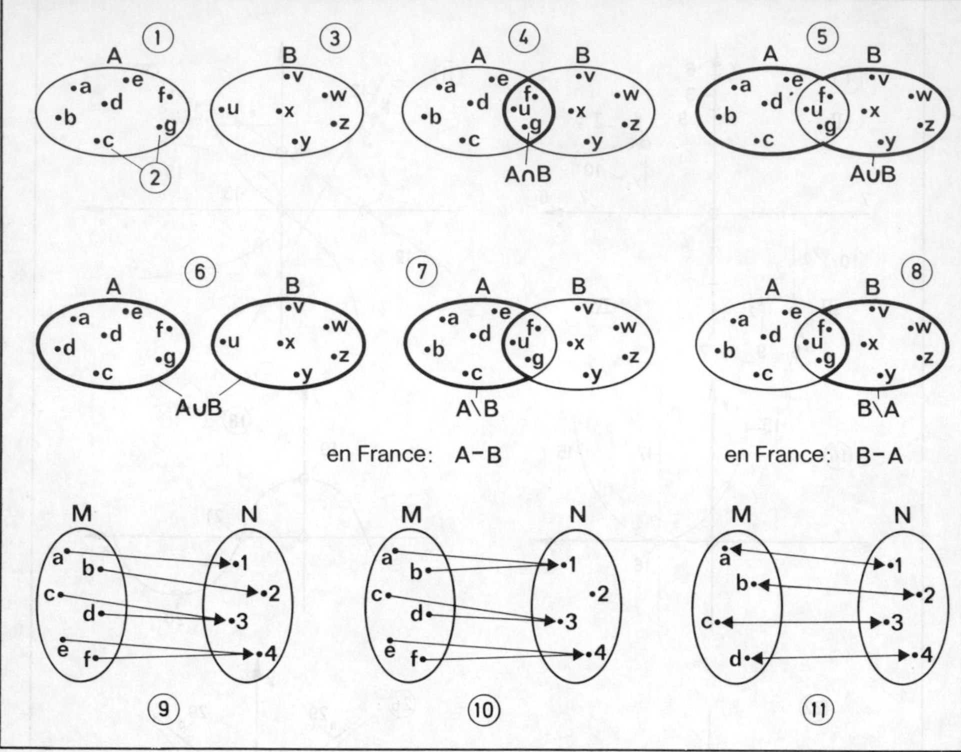

1 l'ensemble *m* A, l'ensemble *m* {a, b, c, d, e, f, g}
– *the set A, the set {a, b, c, d, e, f, g}*

2 les éléments *m* de l'ensemble *m* A
– *elements (members) of the set A*

3 l'ensemble *m* B, l'ensemble *m* {u, v, w, x, y, z}
– *the set B, the set {u, v, w, x, y, z}*

4 l'intersection *f* A ∩ B = {f, g, u}
– *intersection of the sets A and B, A ∩ B = {f, g, u}*

5-6 la réunion A ∪ B = {a, b, c, d, e, f, g, u, v, w, x, y, z}
– *union of the sets A and B, A ∪ B = {a, b, c, d, e, f, g, u, v, w, x, y, z}*

7 la différence des ensembles *m* A B = {a, b, c, d, e}
– *complement of the set B, B′ = {a, b, c, d, e}*

8 la différence des ensembles *m* B A = {v, w, x, y, z}
– *complement of the set A, A′ = {v, w, x, y, z}*

9-11 les applications *f*
– *mappings*

9 l'application *f* de l'ensemble *m* M *sur* l'ensemble *m* N (la surjection)
– *mapping of the set M* onto *the set N*

10 l'application *f* de l'ensemble *m* M *dans* l'ensemble *m* N (la bijection)
– *mapping of the set M* into *the set N*

11 l'application *f* biunivoque de l'ensemble *m* M dans l'ensemble *m* N
– *one-to-one mapping of the set M onto the set N*

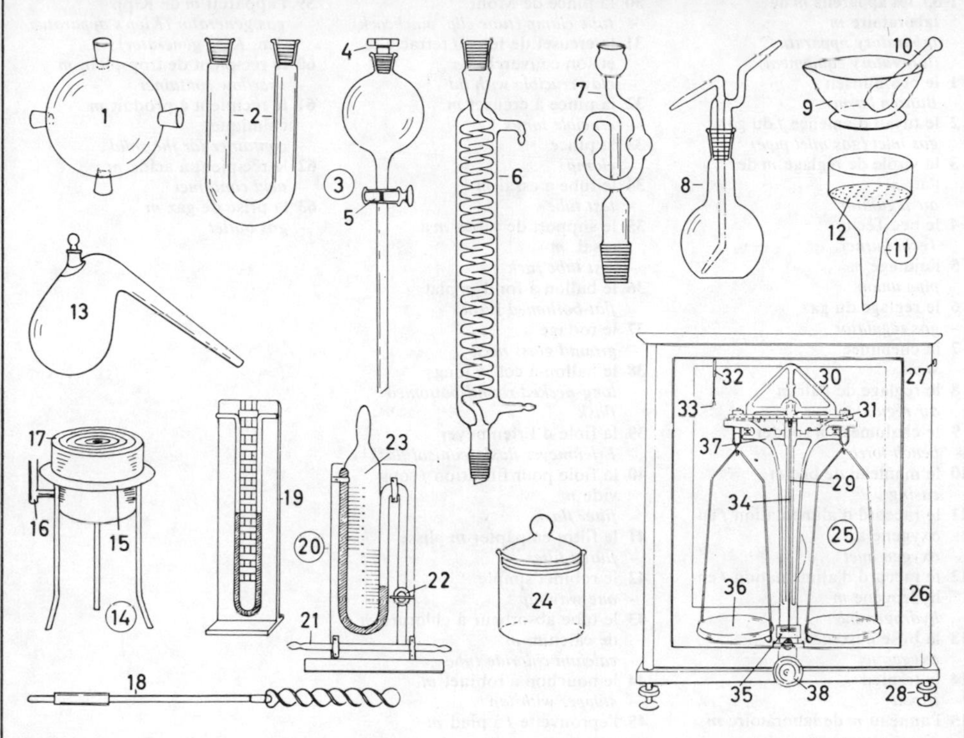

1-38 les appareils *m* de laboratoire *m*
– ***laboratory apparatus** (laboratory equipment)*
1 le ballon de Scheidt
– *Scheidt globe*
2 le tube en U *m*
– *U-tube*
3 l'ampoule *f* à décanter (l'ampoule *f* à brome *m*)
– *separating funnel*
4 le bouchon à tête *f* octogonale [en France : hexagonale]
– *octagonal ground-glass stopper*
5 le robinet
– *tap* (Am. *faucet*)
6 le réfrigérant à serpentin *m*
– *coiled condenser*
7 le tube de sûreté *f*
– *air lock*
8 la pissette
– *wash-bottle*
9 le mortier
– *mortar*
10 le pilon
– *pestle*
11 l'entonnoir *m* de Büchner
– *filter funnel (Büchner funnel)*
12 le filtre
– *filter (filter plate)*
13 la cornue
– *retort*
14 le bain-marie
– *water bath*
15 le trépied
– *tripod*
16 l'indicateur *m* de niveau *m* d'eau *f*
– *water gauge (Am. gage)*
17 les rondelles *f*
– *insertion rings*
18 l'agitateur *m*
– *stirrer*
19 le manomètre à minimum *m* et à maximum *m* de pression *f*
– *manometer for measuring positive and negative pressures*
20 le manomètre à vide *m*
– *mirror manometer for measuring small pressures*
21 la tubulure de prise *f* de pression *f*
– *inlet*
22 le robinet
– *tap (Am. faucet)*
23 la graduation mobile
– *sliding scale*
24 le flacon à tare *f*
– *weighing bottle*
25 la balance d'analyse *f*
– *analytical balance*
26 la cage de balance *f*
– *case*
27 la paroi antérieure amovible
– *sliding front panel*
28 la vis calante
– *three-point support*
29 le fléau
– *column (balance column)*
30 le bras du balancier
– *balance beam (beam)*
31 le rail du curseur
– *rider bar*
32 la manette du curseur
– *rider holder*
33 le curseur
– *rider*
34 l'aiguille *f*
– *pointer*
35 la règle de lecture *f*
– *scale*
36 la graduation
– *scale pan*
37 le dispositif d'arrêt *m*
– *stop*
38 le bouton d'arrêt *m*
– *stop knob*

1-63 les appareils *m* **de laboratoire** *m*
– ***laboratory apparatus** (laboratory equipment)*
1 le bec Bunsen
– *Bunsen burner*
2 le tuyau d'amenée *f* du gaz
– *gas inlet (gas inlet pipe)*
3 la virole de réglage *m* de l'air *m*
– *air regulator*
4 le bec Téclu
– *Teclu burner*
5 l'ajutage *m*
– *pipe union*
6 le réglage du gaz
– *gas regulator*
7 la cheminée
– *stem*
8 le réglage de l'air *m*
– *air regulator*
9 le chalumeau à souder
– *bench torch*
10 le manteau de bec *m*
– *casing*
11 le raccord d'alimentation *f* en oxygène *m*
– *oxygen inlet*
12 le raccord d'alimentation *f* en hydrogène *m*
– *hydrogen inlet*
13 la buse à oxygène *m*
– *oxygen jet*
14 le trépied
– *tripod*
15 l'anneau *m* de laboratoire *m*
– *ring (retort ring)*
16 l'entonnoir *m*
– *funnel*
17 le triangle de terre *f* cuite
– *pipe clay triangle*
18 la toile métallique
– *wire gauze*
19 la plaque d'amiante *m*
– *wire gauze with asbestos centre* (Am. *center)*
20 le bécher
– *beaker*
21 la burette
– *burette (for measuring the volume of liquids)*
22 le statif
– *burette stand*
23 la pince à burette *f*
– *burette clamp*
24 la pipette graduée
– *graduated pipette*
25 la pipette jaugée
– *pipette*
26 l'éprouvette *f* graduée
– *measuring cylinder (measuring glass)*
27 l'éprouvette *f* graduée avec bouchon *m*
– *measuring flask*
28 la fiole jaugée
– *volumetric flask*
29 la capsule en porcelaine *f*
– *evaporating dish (evaporating basin), made of porcelain*
30 la pince de Mohr
– *tube clamp (tube clip, pinchcock)*
31 le creuset de terre *f* réfractaire et son couvercle *m*
– *clay crucible with lid*
32 la pince à creuset *m*
– *crucible tongs*
33 la pince
– *clamp*
34 le tube à essai *m*
– *test tube*
35 le support de tubes *m* à essai *m*
– *test tube rack*
36 le ballon à fond *m* plat
– *flat-bottomed flask*
37 le rodage
– *ground glass neck*
38 le ballon à col *m* long
– *long-necked round-bottomed flask*
39 la fiole d'Erlenmeyer
– *Erlenmeyer flask (conical flask)*
40 la fiole pour filtration *f* sous vide *m*
– *filter flask*
41 le filtre en papier *m* plissé
– *fluted filter*
42 le robinet simple
– *one-way tap*
43 le tube absorbeur à chlorure *m* de calcium *m*
– *calcium chloride tube*
44 le bouchon à robinet *m*
– *stopper with tap*
45 l'éprouvette *f* à pied *m*
– *cylinder*
46 l'appareil *m* à distiller
– *distillation apparatus (distilling apparatus)*
47 le ballon
– *distillation flask (distilling flask)*
48 le réfrigérant
– *condenser*
49 le robinet à deux voies *f* et trois branches *f*
– *return tap, a two-way tap*
50 le ballon à distiller
– *distillation flask (distilling flask, Claisen flask)*
51 le dessicateur
– *desiccator*
52 le couvercle à robinet *m*
– *lid with fitted tube*
53 le robinet
– *tap*
54 le disque en porcelaine *f*
– *desiccator insert made of porcelain*
55 le ballon tricol
– *three-necked flask*
56 le tube de jonction *f* (le tube en Y *m*)
– *connecting piece (Y-tube)*
57 le flacon à trois tubulures *f*
– *three-necked bottle*
58 le flacon laveur
– *gas-washing bottle*
59 l'appareil *m* de Kipp
– *gas generator (Kipp's apparatus,* Am. *Kipp generator)*
60 le récipient de trop-plein *m*
– *overflow container*
61 le récipient à produit *m* chimique
– *container for the solid*
62 le récipient à acide *m*
– *acid container*
63 la prise de gaz *m*
– *gas outlet*

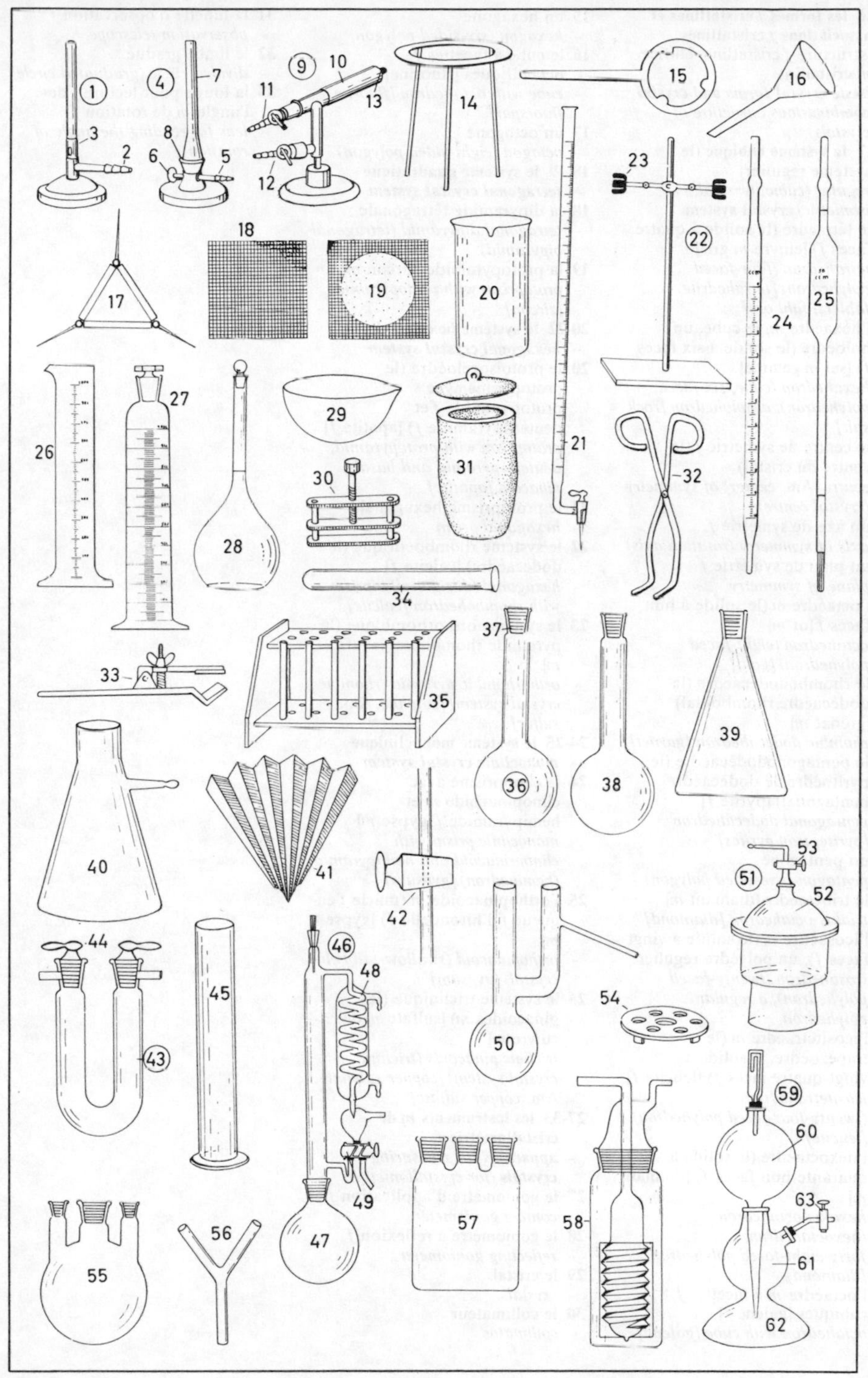
1
2
3
4
5
6
7
8
9
10
11
12
13
14
15
16
17
18
19
20
21
22
23
24
25
26
27
28
29
30
31
32
33
34
35
36
37
38
39
40
41
42
43
44
45
46
47
48
49
50
51
52
53
54
55
56
57
58
59
60
61
62
63

1-26 les formes *f* cristallines et associations *f* cristallines (structure *f* cristalline, édifice *m* cristallin)
- ***basic crystal forms and crystal combinations*** *(structure of crystals)*

1-17 le système cubique (le système régulier)
- ***regular*** *(cubic, tesseral, isometric)* **crystal system**

1 le tétraèdre (le solide à quatre faces *f*) [cuivre *m* gris]
- *tetrahedron (four-faced polyhedron) [tetrahedrite, fahlerz, fahl ore]*

2 l'héxaèdre *m*, le cube, un holoèdre (le solide à six faces *f*) [sel *m* gemme]
- *hexahedron (cube, six-faced polyhedron), a holohedron [rock salt]*

3 le centre de symétrie *f* (le centre du cristal)
- *centre (*Am. *center) of symmetry (crystal centre)*

4 un axe de symétrie *f*
- *axis of symmetry (rotation axis)*

5 un plan de symétrie *f*
- *plane of symmetry*

6 l'octaèdre *m* (le solide à huit faces *f* [or *m*]
- *octahedron (eight-faced polyhedron) [gold]*

7 le rhombododécaèdre (le dodécaèdre rhomboïdal) [grenat *m*]
- *rhombic dodecahedron [garnet]*

8 le pentagonododécaèdre (le pyritoèdre, le dodécaèdre pentagonal) [pyrite *f*]
- *pentagonal dodecahedron [pyrite, iron pyrites]*

9 un pentagone
- *pentagon (five-sided polygon)*

10 le trioctaèdre [diamant *m*]
- *triakis-octahedron [diamond]*

11 l'icosaèdre *m* (le solide à vingt faces *f*), un polyèdre régulier
- *icosahedron (twenty-faced polyhedron), a regular polyhedron*

12 l'icositétraèdre *m* (le trapézoèdre, le solide à vingt-quatre faces *f*) [leucite *f*]
- *icositetrahedron (twenty-four-faced polyhedron) [leucite]*

13 l'hexoctaèdre (le solide à quarante-huit faces *f*) [diamant *m*]
- *hexakis-octahedron (hexoctahedron, forty-eight-faced polyhedron) [diamond]*

14 l'octaèdre *m* à facettes *f* cubiques [galène *f*]
- *octahedron with cube [galena]*

15 un hexagone
- *hexagon (six-sided polygon)*

16 le cube à facettes *f* octaèdriques [fluorine]
- *cube with octahedron [fluorite, fluorspar]*

17 un octogone
- *octagon (eight-sided polygon)*

18-19 le système quadratique
- ***tetragonal crystal system***

18 la dipyramide tétragonale
- *tetragonal dipyramid (tetragonal bipyramid)*

19 la protopyramide [zircon *m*]
- *protoprism with protopyramid [zircon]*

20-22 le système hexagonal
- ***hexagonal crystal system***

20 le protoisocéloèdre (le protoprisme avec protopyramide *f* et deutéropyramide *f*) [apatite *f*]
- *protoprism with protopyramid, deutero-pyramid and basal pinacoid [apatite]*

21 le protoprisme hexagonal
- *hexagonal prism*

22 le système rhomboédrique (le dodécaèdre) [calcite *f*]
- *hexagonal (ditrigonal) biprism with rhombohedron [calcite]*

23 le système orthorhombique (la pyramide rhombique) [soufre *m*]
- *orthorhombic pyramid (rhombic crystal system) [sulphur,* Am. *sulfur]*

24-25 le système monoclinique
- ***monoclinic crystal system***

24 le clinoprisme avec clinopinacoïde *m* et hémipyramide *f* [gypse *m*]
- *monoclinic prism with clinoprinacoid and hemipyramid (hemihedron) [gypsum]*

25 l'orthopinacoïde *m* (mâcle *f* en queue *f* d'hirondelle *f*) [gypse *m*]
- *orthopinacoid (swallow-tail twin crystal) [gypsum]*

26 le système triclinique (les pinacoïdes *m*) [sulfate *m* de cuivre *m*]
- *triclinic pinacoids (triclinic crystal system) [copper sulphate,* Am. *copper sulfate]*

27-33 les instruments *m* de cristallométrie *f*
- ***apparatus for measuring crystals*** *(for crystallometry)*

27 le goniomètre d'application *f*
- *contact goniometer*

28 le goniomètre à réflexion *f*
- *reflecting goniometer*

29 le cristal
- *crystal*

30 le collimateur
- *collimator*

31 la lunette d'observation *f*
- *observation telescope*

32 le limbe gradué
- *divided circle (graduated circle)*

33 la loupe pour lecture *f* de l'angle *m* de rotation *f*
- *lens for reading the angle of rotation*

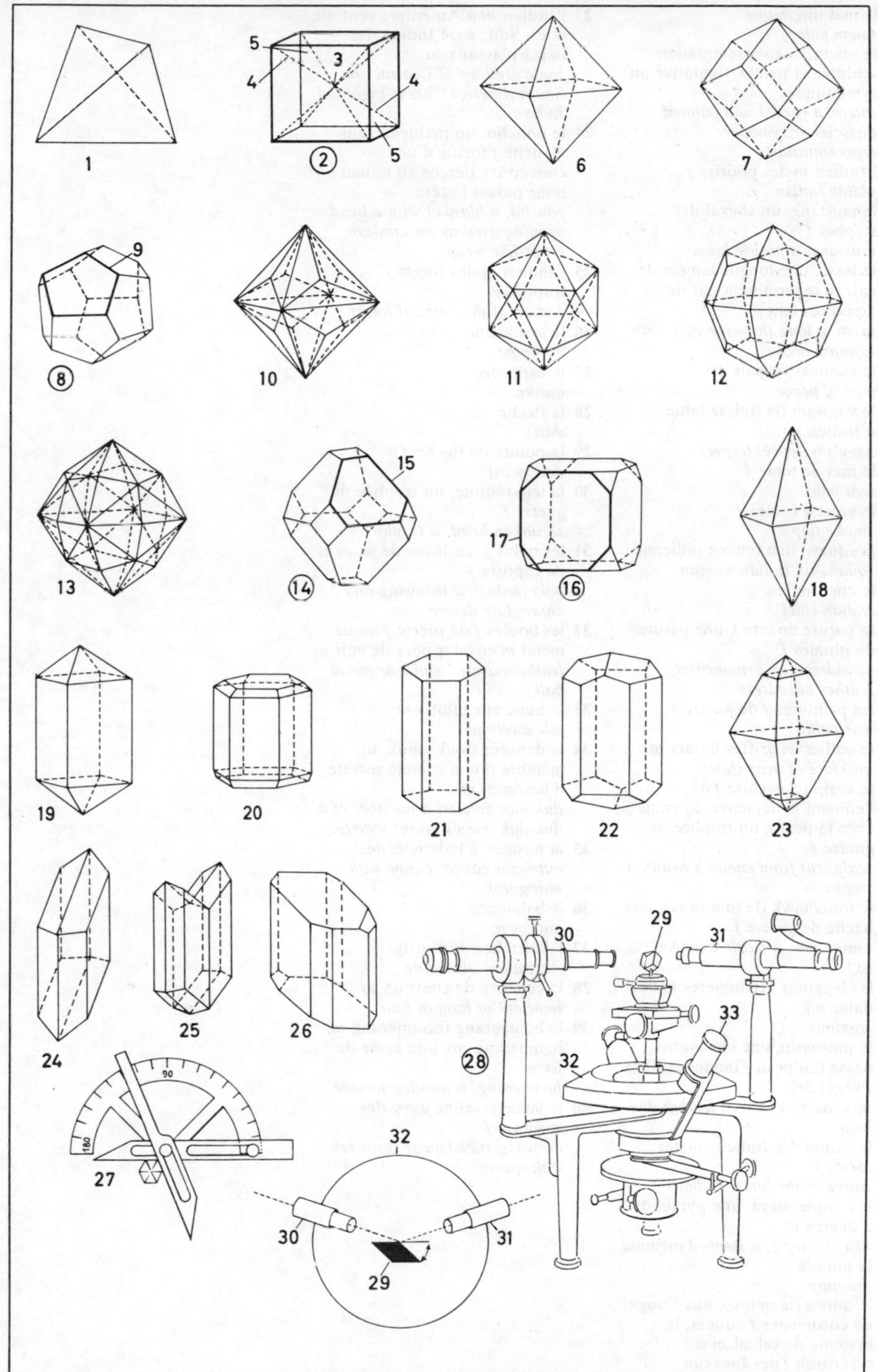
1
2
3
4
5
6
7
8
9
10
11
12
13
14
15
16
17
18
19
20
21
22
23
24
25
26
27
90
180
28
29
30
31
32
33

1 le mât totémique
- *totem pole*
2 le totem, une représentation sculptée et peinte, figurative ou symbolique
- *totem, a carved and painted pictorial or symbolic representation*
3 l'Indien *m* des prairies *f*
- *plains Indian*
4 le mustang, un cheval des steppes *f*
- *mustang, a prairie horse*
5 le lasso, une longue lanière de cuir *m* se terminant par un nœud coulant
- *lasso, a long throwing-rope with running noose*
6 le calumet de paix *f*
- *pipe of peace*
7 le wigwam (le tipi, la tente d'Indien *m*)
- *wigwam (tepee, teepee)*
8 le mât de tente *f*
- *tent pole*
9 le volet à fumée *f*
- *smoke flap*
10 la squaw, une femme indienne
- *squaw, an Indian woman*
11 le chef indien
- *Indian chief*
12 la parure de tête *f*, une parure de plumes *f*
- *headdress, an ornamental feather headdress*
13 les peintures *f* de guerre *f*
- *war paint*
14 le collier de griffes d'ours *m*
- *necklace of bear claws*
15 le scalp (chevelure *f* de l'ennemi *m* détachée du crâne avec la peau), un trophée de guerre *f*
- *scalp (cut from enemy's head), a trophy*
16 le tomahawk (le tomawak), une hache de guerre *f*
- *tomahawk, a battle axe (*Am. *ax)*
17 les leggings *f* (jambières *m* de daim *m*)
- *leggings*
18 le mocassin, une chaussure basse (en peau *f* tannée et fibre *f* végétale)
- *moccasin, a shoe of leather and bast*
19 le canoë des Indiens *m* des forets *f*
- *canoe of the forest Indians*
20 le temple maya, une pyramide à degrés *m*
- *Maya temple, a stepped pyramid*
21 la momie
- *mummy*
22 le quipu (le quipo), une frange de cordelettes *f* nouées, le système de calcul *m* et d'écriture *f* des Incas *m*
- *quipa (knotted threads, knotted code of the Incas)*
23 l'Indien *m* d'Amérique centrale et du Sud; *ici:* l'Indien des hauts plateaux *m*
- *Indio (Indian of Central and South America);* here: *highland Indian*
24 le poncho, un manteau sans manche *f* formé d'une couverture percée au milieu pour passer la tête
- *poncho, a blanket with a head opening used as an armless cloak-like wrap*
25 l'Indien *m* des forêts *f* tropicales
- *Indian of the tropical forest*
26 la sarbacane
- *blowpipe*
27 le carquois
- *quiver*
28 la flèche
- *dart*
29 la pointe de flèche *f*
- *dart point*
30 la tête réduite, un trophée de guerre *f*
- *shrunken head, a trophy*
31 les bolas *f*, un lasso de jet *m* et de capture *f*
- *bola (bolas), a throwing and entangling device*
32 les boules *f* de pierre *f* ou de métal *m* enveloppées de cuir *m*
- *leather-covered stone or metal ball*
33 la hutte sur pilotis *m*
- *pile dwelling*
34 le danseur douk-douk, un membre d'une société secrète d'hommes *m*
- *duk-duk dancer, a member of a duk-duk (men's secret society)*
35 la pirogue à balancier *m*
- *outrigger canoe (canoe with outrigger)*
36 le balancier
- *outrigger*
37 l'Australien *m* aborigène
- *Australian aborigine*
38 la ceinture de cheveux *m*
- *loincloth of human hair*
39 le boomerang (boumerang *m*, boumarang *m*), une arme de jet *m*
- *boomerang, a wooden missile*
40 le lance-javeline avec des javelines *f*
- *throwing stick (spear thrower) with spears*

1 2 3 4 5 6 7 8 9 10 11 12 13 14 15 16 17 18 19 20 21 22 23 24 25 26 27 28 29 30 31 32 33 34 35 36 37 38 39 40

1 l'Esquimau *m*
– *Eskimo*
2 le chien de traîneau *m* (le chien d'Esquimau *m*)
– *sledge dog (sled dog), a husky*
3 le traîneau à chiens *m*
– *dog sledge (dog sled)*
4 l'igloo *m*, une habitation de neige *f* en forme *f* de coupole *f*
– *igloo, a dome-shaped snow hut*
5 le bloc de neige *f*
– *block of snow*
6 le tunnel d'entrée *f*
– *entrance tunnel*
7 la lampe à huile *f* de phoque *m*
– *blubber-oil lamp*
8 le lance-javelot
– *wooden missile*
9 le javelot
– *lance*
10 le harpon
– *harpoon*
11 le flotteur de harpon *m*
– *skin float*
12 le kayak (le kayac), une embarcation individuelle légère
– *kayak, a light one-man canoe*
13 la carcasse de bois *m* ou d'os *m* recouverte de peaux *f*
– *skin-covered wooden or bone frame*
14 la pagaie
– *paddle*
15 l'attelage *m* de rennes *m*
– *reindeer harness*
16 le renne
– *reindeer*
17 l'Ostyak *m* (l'Ostiack *m*)
– *Ostyak (Ostiak)*
18 le traîneau à dossier *m*
– *passenger sledge*
19 la yourte *f* (la iourte), une tente d'habitation *f* des nomades *m* de l'Asie *f* occidentale et centrale
– *yurt (yurta), a dwelling tent of the western and central Asiatic nomads*
20 la couverture de feutre *m*
– *felt covering*
21 la cheminée
– *smoke outlet*
22 le Kirghiz
– *Kirghiz*
23 le bonnet en peau *f* de mouton *m*
– *sheepskin cap*
24 le chaman (le chamane)
– *shaman*
25 la parure à frange *f*
– *decorative fringe*
26 le tambour à cadre *m*
– *frame drum*
27 le Tibétain
– *Tibetan*
28 le fusil à baguette *f*
– *flintlock with bayonets*
29 le moulin à prières *f*
– *prayer wheel*
30 la botte de feutre *m*
– *felt boot*
31 le sampan (l'habitation *f* flottante)
– *houseboat (sampan)*
32 la jonque
– *junk*
33 la voile en nattes *f*
– *mat sail*
34 le pousse-pousse
– *rickshaw (ricksha)*
35 le traîneur de pousse-pousse *m*
– *rickshaw coolie (cooly)*
36 le lampion
– *Chinese lantern*
37 le samurai (le samouraï)
– *samurai*
38 l'armure *f* ouatinée
– *padded armour (*Am. *armor)*
39 la geisha
– *geisha*
40 le kimono
– *kimono*
41 l'obi *f*
– *obi*
42 l'éventail *m*
– *fan*
43 le coolie
– *coolie (cooly)*
44 le criss (le kriss), un poignard malais
– *kris (creese, crease), a Malayan dagger*
45 le charmeur de serpents *m*
– *snake charmer*
46 le turban
– *turban*
47 la flûte
– *flute*
48 le serpent dansant
– *dancing snake*

1
2
3
4
5
6
7
8
9
10
11
12
13
14
15
16
17
18
19
20
21
22
23
24
25
26
27
28
29
30
31
32
33
34
35
36
37
38
39
40
41
42
43
44
45
46
47
48

1 la caravane de chameaux *m*
– *camel caravan*
2 la bête de selle *f*
– *riding animal*
3 la bête de somme *f*
– *pack animal*
4 l'oasis *f*
– *oasis*
5 la palmeraie
– *grove of palm trees*
6 le Bédouin
– *bedouin (beduin)*
7 le burnous
– *burnous*
8 le guerrier Masaï (Massai)
– *Masai warrior*
9 la coiffure
– *headdress (hairdress)*
10 le bouclier
– *shield*
11 la peau de bœuf *m* peinte
– *painted ox hide*
12 la lance à long fer *m*
– *long-bladed spear*
13 le Nègre (le Noir)
– *negro*
14 le tambour de danse *f*
– *dance drum*
15 le poignard de jet *m*
– *throwing knife*
16 le masque de bois *m*
– *wooden mask*
17 l'idole *f* d'un ancêtre
– *figure of an ancestor*
18 le tam-tam
– *slit gong*
19 la baguette de tam-tam *m*
– *drumstick*
20 la pirogue, une embarcation faite d'un seul tronc d'arbre *m* évidé
– *dugout, a boat hollowed out of a tree trunk*
21 la hutte de Nègre *m*
– *negro hut*
22 la Négresse
– *negress*
23 le plateau de lèvre *f*
– *lip plug (labret)*
24 le mortier
– *grinding stone*
25 la femme Herero
– *Herero woman*
26 la coiffe de cuir *m*
– *leather cap*
27 la calebasse
– *calabash (gourd)*
28 la hutte en ruche *f*
– *beehive-shaped hut*
29 le Bochiman (le Boschiman)
– *bushman*
30 la pièce insérée dans le lobe de l'oreille *f*
– *earplug*
31 le pagne
– *loincloth*
32 l'arc *m*
– *bow*
33 le kirri, une massue à grosse tête *f* ronde
– *knobkerry (knobkerrie), a club with round, knobbed end*
34 la femme Bochiman en train de faire du feu par frottement *m*
– *bushman woman making a fire by twirling a stick*
35 le paravent
– *windbreak*
36 le Zoulou en costume *m* de danse *f*
– *Zulu in dance costume*
37 le bâton de danse *f*
– *dancing stick*
38 l'anneau *m* jambier
– *bangle*
39 le cor de guerre *f* en ivoire *m*
– *ivory war horn*
40 le collier d'amulettes *f* et d'os *m*
– *string of amulets and bones*
41 le Pygmée
– *pigmy*
42 le sifflet magique pour conjurer les mauvais esprits *m*
– *magic pipe for exorcising evil spirits*
43 le fétiche
– *fetish*

1
2
3
4
5
6
7
8
9
10
11
12
13
14
15
16
17
18
19
20
21
22
23
24
25
26
27
28
29
30
31
32
33
34
35
36
37
38
39
40
41
42
43

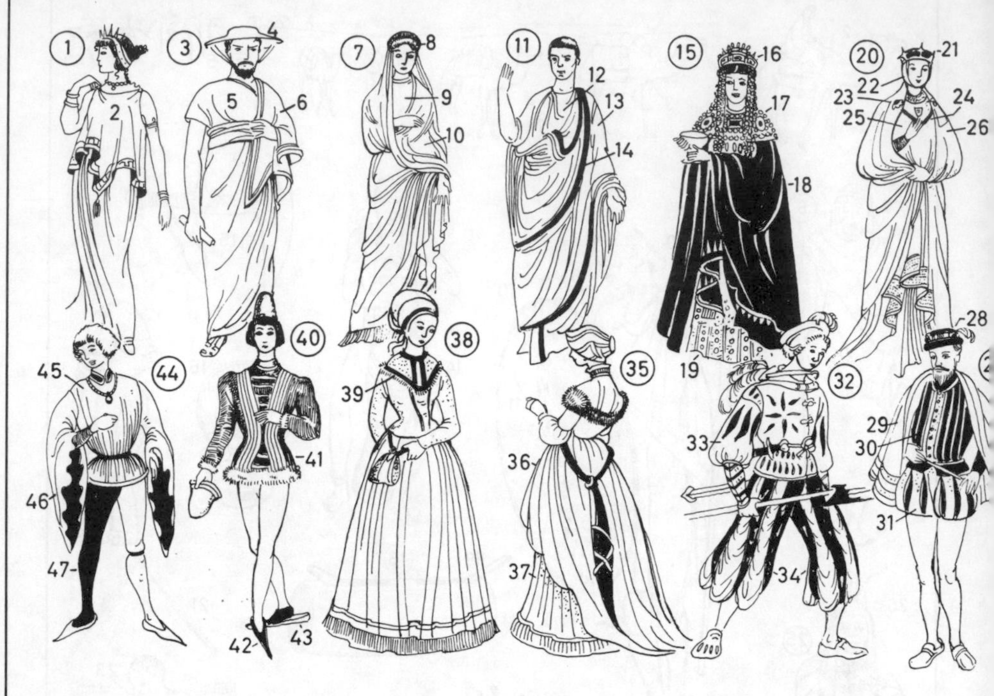

1 la femme grecque
– *Greek woman*
2 le péplum (le péplos)
– *peplos*
3 un Grec
– *Greek*
4 le pétase (le chapeau thessalien)
– *petasus (Thessalonian hat)*
5 le chiton, un vêtement de dessous *m* en lin *m*
– *chiton, a linen gown worn as a basic garment*
6 l'himation *m*, un vêtement de dessus *m* en laine *f*
– *himation, woollen (*Am. *woolen) cloak*
7 la femme romaine
– *Roman woman*
8 le toupet frontal
– *toupee wig (partial wig)*
9 la stola
– *stola*
10 la palla, un châle de couleur *f*
– *palla, a coloured (*Am. *colored) wrap*
11 le Romain
– *Roman*
12 la tunique
– *tunica (tunic)*
13 la toge
– *toga*
14 la bande prétexte
– *purple border (purple band)*
15 une impératrice byzantine
– *Byzantine empress*
16 le diadème de perles *f*
– *pearl diadem*
17 le pendentif
– *jewels*
18 le manteau de pourpre *f*
– *purple cloak*
19 la robe
– *long tunic*
20 une princesse germanique [XIIIe siècle *m*]
– *German princess [13th cent.]*
21 le diadème
– *crown (diadem)*
22 la mentonnière
– *chinband*
23 la boucle
– *tassel*
24 la bride de la chape
– *cloak cord*
25 le surcot
– *girt-up gown (girt-up surcoat, girt-up tunic)*
26 la chape
– *cloak*
27 un Allemand en costume *m* espagnol [vers 1575]
– *German dressed in the Spanish style [ca. 1575]*
28 la toque
– *wide-brimmed cap*
29 la cape à l'espagnole
– *short cloak (Spanish cloak, short cape)*
30 le pourpoint rembourré
– *padded doublet (stuffed doublet, peasecod)*
31 le haut-de-chausses rembourré
– *stuffed trunk-hose*
32 un lansquenet [vers 1530]
– *lansquenet (German mercenary soldier) [ca. 1530]*
33 le pourpoint tailladé
– *slashed doublet (paned doublet)*
34 le haut-de-chausses bouffant
– *Pluderhose (loose breeches, paned trunk-hose, slops)*
35 une Bâloise [vers 1525]
– *woman of Basle [ca. 1525]*
36 la robe retroussée
– *overgown (gown)*
37 la cotte
– *undergown (petticoat)*
38 une Nurembergeoise [vers 1500]
– *woman of Nuremberg [ca. 1500]*
39 le collet (le fichu)
– *shoulder cape*
40 un Bourguignon [XVe siècle *m*]
– *Burgundian [15th cent.]*
41 le pourpoint court
– *short doublet*
42 les poulaines *f*
– *piked shoes (peaked shoes, copped shoes, crackowes, poulaines)*
43 les patins de bois *m*
– *pattens (clogs)*
44 un damoiseau [vers 1400]
– *young nobleman [ca. 1400]*

45 la jaquette courte
– *short, padded doublet (short, quilted doublet, jerkin)*
46 les manches en entonnoir *m*
– *dagged sleeves (petal-scalloped sleeves)*
47 les chausses *f*
– *hose*
48 une dame patricienne d'Augsbourg [vers 1575]
– *Augsburg patrician lady [ca. 1575]*
49 la manche à gigot *m*
– *puffed sleeve*
50 la marlotte
– *overgown (gown, open gown, sleeveless gown)*
51 une dame française [vers 1600]
– *French lady [ca. 1600]*
52 la fraise
– *millstone ruff (cartwheel ruff, ruff)*
53 la taille lacée (la taille de guêpe *f*)
– *corseted waist (wasp waist)*
54 un seigneur [vers 1650]
– *gentleman [ca. 1650]*
55 le feutre à larges bords *m*
– *wide-brimmed felt hat (cavalier hat)*
56 le collet (le rabat)
– *falling collar (wide-falling collar) of linen*
57 la doublure de toile *f*
– *white lining*
58 la botte à revers *m*
– *jack boots (bucket-top boots)*
59 une dame [vers 1650]
– *lady [ca. 1650]*
60 les manches *f* bouillonnées
– *full puffed sleeves (puffed sleeves)*
61 un seigneur [vers 1700]
– *gentleman [ca. 1700]*
62 le tricorne
– *three-cornered hat*
63 l'épée *f* de cour *f*
– *dress sword*
64 une dame [vers 1700]
– *lady [ca. 1700]*
65 la fontange
– *lace fontange (high headdress of lace)*
66 la mante de dentelle *f*
– *lace-trimmed loose-hanging gown (loose-fitting housecoat, robe de chambre, negligée, contouche)*
67 la bordure brodée
– *band of embroidery*
68 une dame [vers 1880]
– *lady [ca. 1880]*
69 la tournure (le pouf)
– *bustle*
70 une dame [vers 1858]
– *lady [ca. 1858]*
71 le cabriolet (la capote)
– *poke bonnet*
72 la crinoline
– *crinoline*
73 un bourgeois sous Louis-Philippe
– *gentleman of the Biedermeier period*
74 le faux col
– *high collar (choker collar)*
75 le gilet à ramages *m*
– *embroidered waistcoat (vest)*
76 l'habit *m* à basques *f*
– *frock coat*
77 la perruque à la Cadogan
– *pigtail wig*
78 le nœud du catogan
– *ribbon (bow)*
79 une dame en costume *m* de cour *f*
– *ladies in court dress [ca. 1780]*
80 la traîne
– *train*
81 la coiffure de style *m* Louis XVI
– *upswept Rococo coiffure*
82 la parure de plumes *f* (le panache)
– *hair decoration*
83 la robe à paniers *m*
– *panniered overskirt*

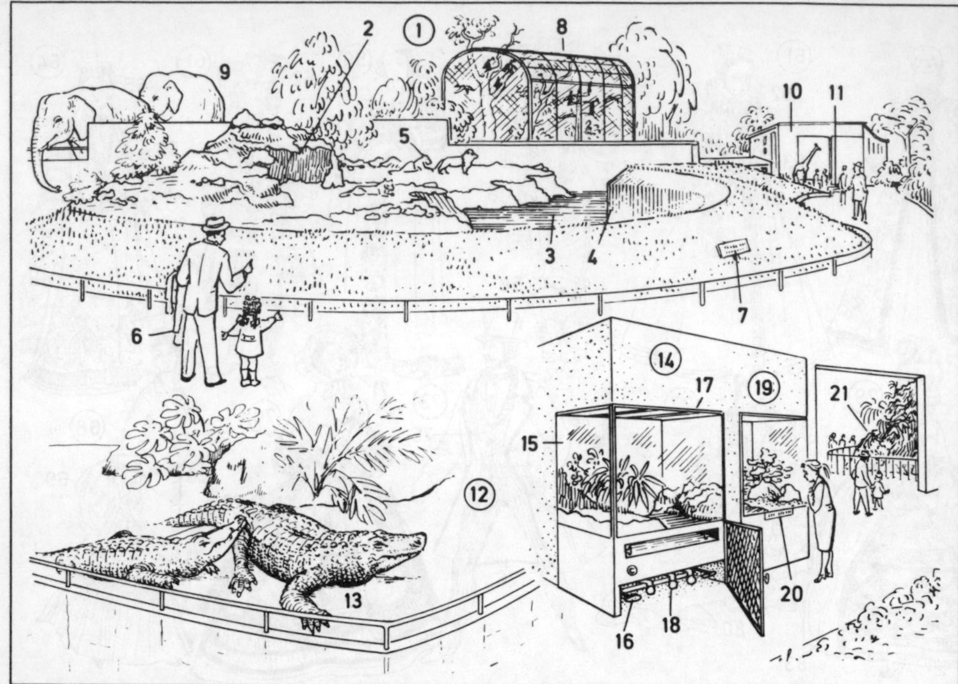

1 l'installation *f* à ciel *m* ouvert
– *outdoor enclosure (enclosure)*

2 le rocher naturel
– *rocks*

3 le fossé de séparation *f*, une douve
– *moat*

4 le mur de protection *f*
– *enclosing wall*

5 les animaux *m* présentés; *ici:* une troupe de lions *m*
– *animals on show;* here: *a pride of lions*

6 le visiteur du zoo
– *visitor to the zoo*

7 le panneau d'interdiction *f*
– *notice*

8 la volière
– *aviary*

9 l'enclos *m* des éléphants *m*
– *elephant enclosure*

10 le logement (la loge) des animaux (p.ex.: des fauves *m*, des girafes *f*, des éléphants *m*, des singes *m*)
– *animal house (e.g. carnivore house, giraffe house, elephant house, monkey house)*

11 la cage extérieure
– *outside cage (summer quarters)*

12 l'enclos *m* des reptiles *m*
– *reptile enclosure*

13 le crocodile du Nil
– *Nile crocodile*

14 le vivarium
– *terrarium and aquarium*

15 la vitrine
– *glass case*

16 l'arrivée *f* d'air *m* frais
– *fresh-air inlet*

17 l'évacuation *f* d'air *m* (le système d'aération *f*)
– *ventilator*

18 le chauffage au sol
– *underfloor heating*

19 l'aquarium *m*
– *aquarium*

20 le panneau explicatif
– *information plate*

21 le paysage tropical
– *flora in artificially maintained climate*

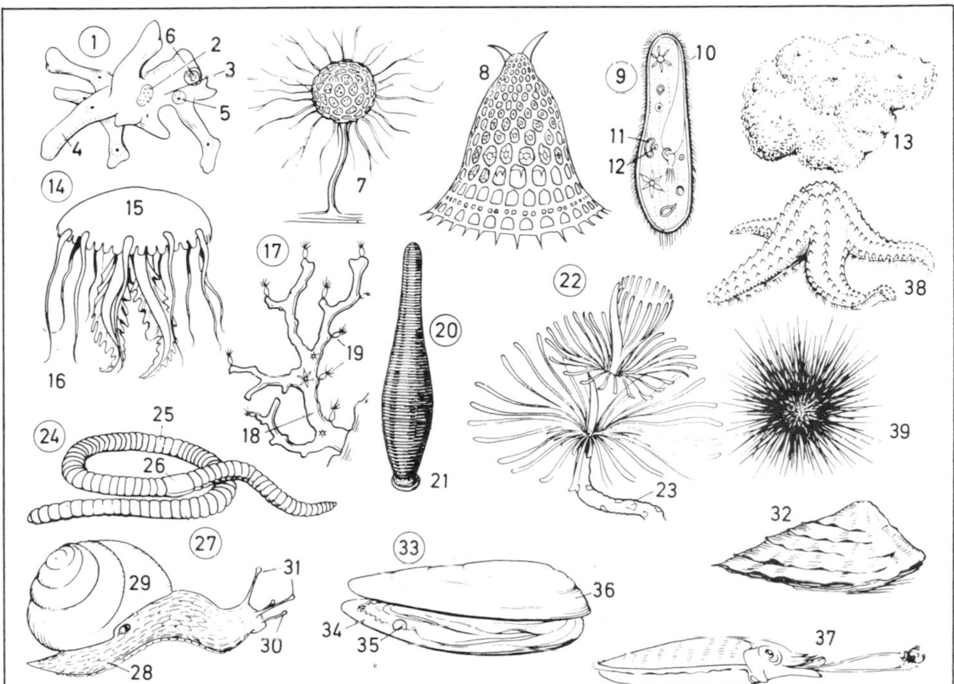

1-12 les protozoaires *m* (les unicellulaires *m*, les infusoires *m*)
– ***unicellular (one-celled, single-celled) animals*** *(protozoans)*
1 l'amibe *f*, un rhizopode, un rhizopode
– *amoeba, a rhizopod*
2 le nucléus
– *cell nucleus*
3 le protoplasme
– *protoplasm*
4 le pseudopode
– *pseudopod*
5 la vacuole contractile
– *excretory vacuole (contractile vacuole, an organelle)*
6 la vacuole nutritive
– *food vacuole*
7 l'héliozoaire *m*
– *Actinophrys, a heliozoan*
8 le radiolaire (*ici:* le squelette silicieux)
– *radiolarian;* here: *siliceous skeleton*
9 la paramécie, un infusoire à cils *m*, un infusoire à cils *m*
– *slipper animalcule, a Paramecium (ciliate infusorian)*
10 les cils *m* vibratiles
– *cilium*
11 le macronucléus
– *macronucleus (meganucleus)*
12 le micronucléus
– *micronucleus*
13-39 les métazoaires *m* (animaux *m* multicellulaires)
– ***multicellular animals*** *(metazoans)*
13 l'éponge *f*, un spongiaire
– *bath sponge, a porifer (sponge)*
14 la méduse (méduse *f* à ombrelle *f*, la gelée de mer *f*) un cœlentéré
– *medusa, a discomedusa (jellyfish), a coelenterate*
15 l'ombrelle *f*
– *umbrella*
16 le tentacule
– *tentacle*
17 l'anthozoaire *m*, un madrépore
– *red coral (precious coral), a coral animal (anthozoan, reef-building animal)*
18 la branche de corail *m*
– *coral colony*
19 le polype corallier
– *coral polyp*
20-26 les vers *m*
– *worms (Vermes)*
20 la sangsue, un annélide (ver *m* à segments *m*)
– *leech, an annelid*
21 la ventouse
– *sucker*
22 le spirographe (le spirorbe), un polychète
– *Spirographis, a bristle worm*
23 le tube d'habitation *f*
– *tube*
24 le lombric (le ver de terre *f*)
– *earthworm*
25 le segment
– *segment*
26 le clitellum (la zone d'accouplement *m*)
– *clitellum [accessory reproductive organ]*
27-36 les mollusques *m*
– *molluscs (*Am. *mollusks)*
27 l'escargot *m* (l'escargot *m* des vignes *f*), un limaçon
– *edible snail, a snail*
28 la sole pédieuse (le pied abdominal)
– *creeping foot*
29 la coquille
– *shell (snail shell)*
30 la tentacule oculaire
– *stalked eye*
31 les tentacules *m*
– *tentacle (horn, feeler)*
32 l'huître *f*
– *oyster*
33 la mulette perlière
– *freshwater pearl mussel*
34 la nacre
– *mother-of-pearl (nacre)*
35 la perle
– *pearl*
36 la valve d'un bivalve
– *mussel shell*
37 la seiche, un céphalopode
– *cuttlefish, a cephalopod*
38-39 les échinodermes *m*
– *echinoderms*
38 l'étoile *f* de mer *f*
– *starfish (sea star)*
39 l'oursin *m*
– *sea urchin (sea hedgehog)*

1-2 les crustacés *m*
– ***crustaceans***
1 la dromie, un crabe, un crustacé
– *mitten crab, a crab*
2 l'asellus *m*
– *water slater*
3-23 les insectes *m*
– ***insects***
3 la libellule (la demoiselle), un insecte
– *water nymph (dragonfly), a homopteran (homopterous insect), a dragonfly*
4 la nèpe cendrée (le scorpion d'eau *f*, la punaise aquatique), un insecte hémiptère
– *water scorpion (water bug), a rhynchophore*
5 la patte préhensile
– *raptorial leg*
6 l'éphémère *m*
– *mayfly (dayfly, ephemerid)*
7 l'œil *m* à facettes *f*
– *compound eye*
8 la sauterelle (le criquet, la locuste), un orthoptère sauteur
– *green grasshopper (green locust, meadow grasshopper), an orthopteron (orthopterous insect)*
9 la larve
– *larva (grub)*
10 l'insecte *m* parfait, une imago
– *adult insect, an imago*
11 la patte sauteuse
– *leaping hind leg*
12 la phrygane, un insecte névroptère
– *caddis fly (spring fly, water moth), a neuropteran*
13 le puceron, un insecte hémiptère aphidien
– *aphid (greenfly), a plant louse*
14 le puceron aptère
– *wingless aphid*
15 le puceron ailé
– *winged aphid*
16-20 les diptères *m*
– ***dipterous insects*** *(dipterans)*
16 le moustique (le cousin, la tipule), un moucheron, un longicorne
– *gnat (mosquito, midge), a culicid*
17 le dard (la trompe)
– *proboscis (sucking organ)*
18 la mouche à viande *f* (mouche *f* bleue), un muscidé
– *bluebottle (blowfly), a fly*
19 la larve
– *maggot (larva)*
20 la nymphe
– *chrysalis (pupa)*
21-23 les hyménoptères *m*
– ***Hymenoptera***
21-22 la fourmi
– *ant*
21 la reine (la femelle ailée)
– *winged female*
22 l'ouvrière *f*
– *worker*
23 le bourdon
– *bumblebee (humblebee)*
24-39 les coléoptères *m*
– ***beetles*** *(Coleoptera)*
24 le lucane (le cerf-volant), un scarabéidé
– *stag beetle, a lamellicorn beetle*
25 les mandibules *f*
– *mandibles*
26 les mâchoires *f*
– *trophi*
27 l'antenne *f* (le *ou* la palpe)
– *antenna (feeler)*
28 la tête
– *head*
29-30 le thorax
– *thorax*
29 le pronotum
– *thoracic shield (prothorax)*
30 l'écusson *m*
– *scutellum*
31 les tergites *m* (les arceaux *m* dorsaux des segments *m*)
– *tergites*
32 l'orifice *m* respiratoire (le stigmate)
– *stigma*
33 l'aile *f*
– *wing (hind wing)*
34 la veine de l'aile *f*
– *nervure*
35 le pli de l'aile *f*
– *point at which the wing folds*
36 l'élytre *m*
– *elytron (forewing)*
37 la coccinelle (la bête à bon Dieu), un coccinellidé
– *ladybird (ladybug), a coccinellid*
38 l'ergate *m* (le forgeron), un longicorne
– *Ergates faber, a longicorn beetle (longicorn)*
39 le bousier (le coléoptère stercoraire), un carabidé, un coléoptère ravisseur
– *dung beetle, a lamellicorn beetle*
40-47 les arachnides *m*
– ***arachnids***
40 le scorpion domestique, un scorpion
– *Euscorpius flavicandus, a scorpion*
41 la mandibule (la patte-mâchoire)
– *cheliped with chelicer*
42 l'antenne *f* maxillaire
– *maxillary antenna (maxillary feeler)*
43 l'aiguillon *m* caudal
– *tail sting*
44-46 les araignées *f*
– ***spiders***
44 l'ixode *m* (la tique), un acarien
– *wood tick (dog tick), a tick*
45 l'épeire *f* diadème *f* (l'araignée *f* porte-croix), une araignée
– *cross spider (garden spider), an orb spinner*
46 la glande à liquide *m* gommeux
– *spinneret*
47 la toile d'araignée *f*
– *spider's web (web)*
48-56 les papillons *m*
– ***Lepidoptera*** *(butterflies and moths)*
48 le bombyx du mûrier, un bombyx
– *mulberry-feeding moth (silk moth), a bombycid moth*
49 les œufs *m*
– *eggs*
50 le ver à soie *f* (la chenille)
– *silkworm*
51 le cocon
– *cocoon*
52 le macaon (le grand porte-queue), un papillon diurne
– *swallowtail, a butterfly*
53 l'antenne *f*
– *antenna (feeler)*
54 la tache oculée
– *eyespot*
55 le sphinx du troène (sphinx à tête *f* de mort *f*, l'achérontia *m*), un papillon nocturne
– *privet hawkmoth, a hawkmoth (sphinx)*
56 la trompe
– *proboscis*

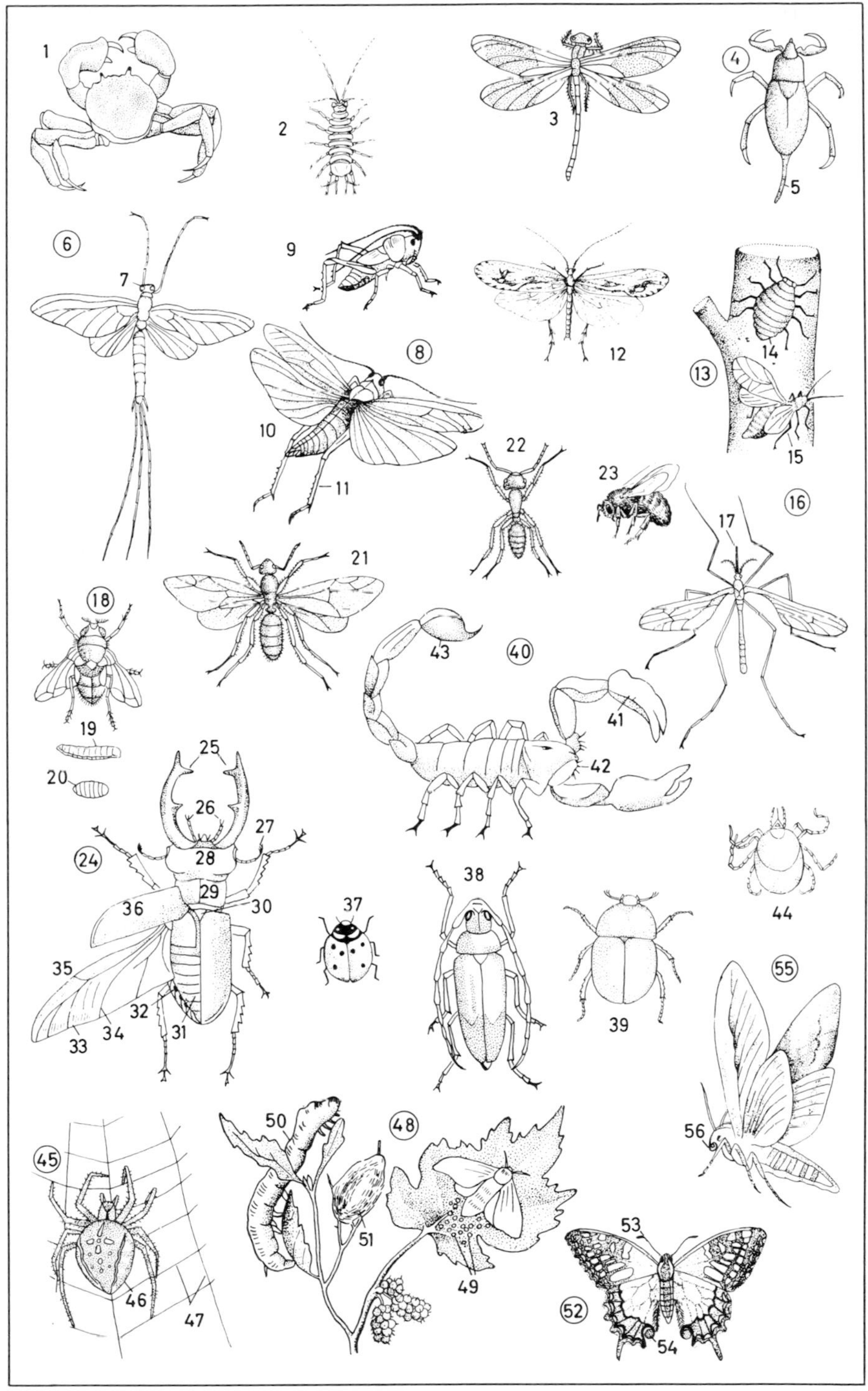
1
2
3
4
5
6
7
9
12
8
10
11
13
14
15
22
23
16
17
18
21
43
40
41
42
19
20
25
26
27
24
28
29
30
36
37
38
39
44
35
32
34
33
31
55
56
50
48
45
51
49
53
46
47
52
54

1-3 les oiseaux *m* **coureurs,** oiseaux *m* terrestres
- ***flightless birds***

1 le casoar; *anal.:* l'émeu *m*
- *cassowary;* sim.: *emu*

2 l'autruche *f*
- *ostrich*

3 la couvée d'œufs *m* d'autruche *f* [12-14 œufs *m*]
- *clutch of ostrich eggs [12 - 14 eggs]*

4 le manchot, un oiseau aquatique
- *king penguin, a penguin, a flightless bird*

5-10 les oiseaux *m* **palmipèdes**
- ***web-footed birds***

5 le pélican blanc, un pélican
- *white pelican (wood stork, ibis, wood ibis, spoonbill, brent-goose,* Am. *brant-goose, brant), a pelican*

6 le pied palmé
- *webfoot (webbed foot)*

7 la palmure
- *web (palmations) of webbed foot (palmate foot)*

8 la mandibule inférieure, avec la poche de la gorge
- *lower mandible with gular pouch*

9 le fou de bassan, un fou
- *northern gannet (gannet, solan goose), a gannet*

10 le grand cormoran, avec les ailes *f* déployées
- *green cormorant (shag), a cormorant displaying with spread wings*

11-14 les oiseaux *m* **de mer** *f*
- ***long-winged birds*** *(seabirds)*

11 la sterne naine, l'hirondelle *f* de mer *f*, plongeant à la recherche de nourriture *f*
- *common sea swallow, a sea swallow (tern), diving for food*

12 le fulmar
- *fulmar*

13 le guillemot de troïl, un pingouin
- *guillemot, an auk*

14 la mouette rieuse, une mouette (un goéland)
- *black-headed gull (mire crow), a gull*

15-17 les ansérinés *m*
- ***Anseres***

15 le harle bièvre, un canard plongeur, un anatidé
- *goosander (common merganser), a sawbill*

16 le cygne tuberculé, un cygne
- *mute swan, a swan*

17 le tubercule du bec
- *knob on the bill*

18 le héron cendré, un héron, un échassier
- *common heron, a heron*

19-21 limicoles *m*, oiseaux *m* de rivage *m*
- ***plovers***

19 l'échasse *f* blanche
- *stilt (stilt bird, stilt plover)*

20 la foulque macroule (la poule d'eau *f*)
- *coot, a rail*

21 le vanneau huppé
- *lapwing (green plover, peewit, pewit)*

22 la caille des blés, un gallinacé
- *quail, a gallinaceous bird*

23 la tourterelle des bois *m*, un columbidé
- *turtle dove, a pigeon*

24 le martinet noir, un grand voilier
- *swift*

25 la huppe fasciée
- *hoopoe, a roller*

26 la huppe érectile
- *erectile crest*

27 le pic épeiche, un pic (*genres voisins:* le pic vert, le torcol)
- *spotted woodpecker, a woodpecker;* related: *wryneck*

28 l'entrée *f* du nid
- *entrance to the nest*

29 la cavité de nidification *f*
- *nesting cavity*

30 le coucou gris
- *cuckoo*

1
2
3
4
5
6
7
8
9
10
11
12
13
14
15
16
17
18
19
20
21
22
23
24
25
26
27
28
29
30

360 Oiseaux II (oiseaux indigènes)

1 le chardonneret, un passereau
- *goldfinch, a finch*

2 le guêpier d'Europe *f*
- *bee eater*

3 le rouge-queue à front *m* blanc, le rossignol des murailles *f*, un turdiné
- *redstart (star finch), a thrush*

4 la mésange bleue, une mésange, un oiseau sédentaire
- *bluetit, a tit (titmouse), a resident bird (non-migratory bird)*

5 le bouvreuil pivoine
- *bullfinch*

6 le rollier d'Europe *f*
- *common roller (roller)*

7 le loriot, un oiseau migrateur
- *golden oriole, a migratory bird*

8 le martin-pêcheur
- *kingfisher*

9 la bergeronnette grise, la bergeronnette hochequeue
- *white wagtail, a wagtail*

10 le pinson des arbres *m*, un fringille
- *chaffinch*

1
2
3
4
5
6
7
8
9
10
S. Vogel

1-20 les oiseaux *m* **chanteurs**
- ***songbirds***

1-3 les corvidés *m*
- ***Corvidae*** *(corvine birds, crows)*

1 le geai des chênes *m* (le geai)
- *jay (nutcracker)*

2 le corbeau freux; *anal.:* la corneille, le choucas
- *rook, a crow*

3 la pie bavarde
- *magpie*

4 l'étourneau *m* sansonnet (le sansonnet)
- *starling (pastor, shepherd bird)*

5 le moineau domestique (le pierrot, le piaf)
- *house sparrow*

6-8 les fringillidés *m*, fringilles *m*
- ***finches***

6-7 les bruants *m*
- *buntings*

6 le bruant jaune
- *yellowhammer (yellow bunting)*

7 le bruant ortolan (l'ortolan *m*)
- *ortolan (ortolan bunting)*

8 le tarin des aulmes *m*; *anal.:* le verdier, le serin cini
- *siskin (aberdevine)*

9 la mésange charbonnière
- *great titmouse (great tit, ox eye), a titmouse (tit)*

10 le roitelet huppé; *anal.:* le roitelet triple bandeau *m*
- *golden-crested wren (goldcrest);* sim.: *firecrest*

11 le grimpereau; *anal.:* la sittelle
- *nuthatch*

12 le troglodyte mignon
- *wren*

13-17 les turdidés *m*
- ***thrushes***

13 le merle noir
- *blackbird*

14 le rossignol philomèle (le rossignol)
- *nightingale* (poet.: *philomel, philomela)*

15 le rouge-gorge
- *robin (redbreast, robin redbreast)*

16 la grive musicienne
- *song thrush (throstle, mavis)*

17 le rossignol progné
- *thrush nightingale*

18-19 les alaudidés *m*, alouettes *f*
- *larks*

18 l'alouette *f* lulu; *anal.:* l'alouette *f* des champs *m*
- *woodlark*

19 le cochevis huppé
- *crested lark (tufted lark)*

20 l'hirondelle *f* (l'hirondelle *f* de fenêtre *f*, l'hirondelle *f* de cheminée *f*)
- *common swallow (barn swallow, chimney swallow), a swallow*

1-13 les rapaces *m* **diurnes**
– ***diurnal birds of prey***
1-4 les faucons *m*
– *falcons*
1 le faucon émerillon
– *merlin*
2 le faucon pèlerin
– *peregrine falcon*
3 les culottes *f*, les cuisses *f* emplumées
– *leg feathers*
4 le tarse
– *tarsus*
5-9 les aigles *m*
– *eagles*
5 le pygargue à queue *f* blanche
– *white-tailed sea eagle (white-tailed eagle, grey sea eagle, erne)*
6 le bec crochu
– *hooked beak*
7 la serre (la griffe)
– *claw (talon)*
8 la queue
– *tail*
9 la buse variable (la buse)
– *common buzzard*
10-13 les accipitridés *m*
– *accipiters*
10 l'autour *m* des palombes *f*
– *goshawk*
11 le milan royal
– *common European kite (glede, kite)*
12 l'épervier *m* d'Europe *f*
– *sparrow hawk (spar-hawk)*
13 le busard des roseaux *m* (l'harpaye *m*)
– *marsh harrier (moor buzzard, moor harrier, moor hawk)*
14-19 les rapaces *m* **nocturnes**
– ***owls*** *(nocturnal birds of prey)*
14 le hibou moyen-duc (le moyen-duc)
– *long-eared owl (horned owl)*
15 le hibou grand-duc (le grand-duc)
– *eagle-owl (great horned owl)*
16 l'oreille *f*, l'aigrette *f*
– *plumicorn (feathered ear, ear tuft, ear, horn)*
17 la chouette effraie (l'effraie *f*)
– *barn owl (white owl, silver owl, yellow owl, church owl, screech owl)*
18 le disque facial (le visage)
– *facial disc (disk)*
19 la chouette chevêche (la chevêche)
– *little owl (sparrow owl)*

1 le cacatoès à huppe *f* jaune, un perroquet (un psittacidé)
– *sulphur-crested cockatoo, a parrot*
2 l'ara *m* bleu et jaune
– *blue-and-yellow macaw*
3 le paradisier bleu (l'oiseau *m* de paradis *m*)
– *blue bird of paradise*
4 l'oiseau-mouche *m* sapho, un colibri
– *sappho*
5 le cardinal
– *cardinal (cardinal bird)*
6 le toucan, un piciforme
– *red-billed toucan, a toucan*

1
2
3
4
5
6

1-18 les poissons *m*
- ***fishes***

1 le requin bleu, un squale
- *man-eater (blue shark, requin), a shark*

2 le museau
- *nose (snout)*

3 les fentes *f* branchiales
- *gill slit (gill cleft)*

4 la carpe miroir, un cyprinidé (la carpe)
- *mirror carp, a carp*

5 l'opercule *m* branchial
- *gill cover (operculum)*

6 la nageoire dorsale
- *dorsal fin*

7 la nageoire pectorale
- *pectoral fin*

8 la nageoire abdominale
- *pelvic fin (abdominal fin, ventral fin)*

9 la nageoire anale
- *anal fin*

10 la nageoire caudale
- *caudal fin (tail fin)*

11 l'écaille *f* (la plaque)
- *scale*

12 le silure (le poisson chat)
- *catfish (sheatfish, sheathfish, wels)*

13 le barbillon
- *barbel*

14 le hareng
- *herring*

15 la truite de rivière *f* (la truite fario); *anal.:* la truite de lac *m*, la truite arc-en-ciel *m*, la truite saumonée
- *brown trout, a trout*

16 le brochet
- *pike (northern pike)*

17 l'anguille *f*
- *freshwater eel (eel)*

18 l'hippocampe *m* (le cheval marin)
- *sea horse (Hippocampus, horsefish)*

19 les branchies *f* en houppe *f* (les lophobranchies *f*)
- *tufted gills*

20-26 les amphibiens *m* (batraciens *m*)
- ***Amphibia*** *(amphibians)*

20-22 les urodèles *m*
- *salamanders*

20 le triton à crête *f*, un urodèle aquatique
- *greater water newt (crested newt), a water newt*

21 la crête dorsale
- *dorsal crest*

22 la salamandre, un urodèle terrestre
- *fire salamander, a salamander*

23-26 les anoures *m*
- *salientians (anurans, batrachians)*

23 le crapaud
- *European toad, a toad*

24 la rainette, la grenouille verte
- *tree frog (tree toad)*

25 le sac vocal
- *vocal sac (vocal pouch, croaking sac)*

26 la ventouse
- *adhesive disc (disk)*

27-41 les reptiles *m*
- ***reptiles***

27 le lézard
- *sand lizard*

28 la tortue
- *hawksbill turtle (hawksbill)*

29 la carapace
- *carapace (shell)*

30 le basilic, un iguanidé
- *basilisk*

31 le varan du désert
- *desert monitor, a monitor lizard (monitor)*

32 l'iguane *m* vert
- *common iguana, an iguana*

33 le caméléon, un reptile lacertilien
- *chameleon*

34 le pied préhensile
- *prehensile foot*

35 la queue préhensile
- *prehensile tail*

36 le gecko (la tarente)
- *wall gecko, a gecko*

37 l'orvet *m* (le serpent de verre *m*), un lézard sans pattes *f*
- *slowworm (blindworm)*

38-41 les serpents *m*
- ***snakes***

38 la couleuvre à collier *m*, un serpent sans venin *m*
- *ringed snake (ring snake, water snake, grass snake), a colubrid*

39 les taches du collier
- *collar*

40-41 les vipères *f*, des serpents *m* venimeux
- *vipers (adders)*

40 la vipère péliade (la péliade)
- *common viper, a poisonous (venomous) snake*

41 la vipère aspic (l'aspic *m*)
- *asp (asp viper)*

1
2
3
4
5
6
7
8
9
10
11
12
13
14
15
16
17
18
19
20
21
22
23
24
25
26
27
28
29
30
31
32
33
34
35
36
37
38
39
40
41

365 Lépidoptères (papillons de jour et de nuit)

1-6 les papillons *m* **de jour** *m*
- ***butterflies***

1 le vulcain, (l'amiral *m*), une vanesse
- *red admiral*

2 le paon du jour, une vanesse
- *peacock butterfly*

3 l'aurore *f*, une piéride
- *orange tip (orange tip butterfly)*

4 le citron, une piéride
- *brimstone (brimstone butterfly)*

5 le morio, une vanesse
- *Camberwell beauty (mourning cloak, mourning cloak butterfly)*

6 le lycène
- *blue (lycaenid butterfly, lycaenid)*

7-11 les papillons *m* **de nuit** *f*
- ***moths*** *(Heterocera)*

7 l'écaille *f* martée (la martre, la hérisonne)
- *garden tiger*

8 l'écaille *f* chinée
- *red underwing*

9 le sphinx tête *f* de mort *f*
- *death's-head moth (death's-head hawkmoth), a hawkmoth (sphinx)*

10 la chenille
- *caterpillar*

11 la chrysalide (la nymphe)
- *chrysalis (pupa)*

1
2
3
4
5
6
7
8
9
10
11
S. Vogel

1 l'ornithorynque *m*, un monotrème, un mammifère ovipare
- *platypus (duck-bill, duck-mole), a monotreme (oviparous mammal)*

2-3 les marsupiaux *m*
- ***marsupial mammals** (marsupials)*

2 l'opossum *m* d'Amérique *f* du Nord, un didelphidé
- *New World opossum, a didelphid*

3 le kangourou roux, un diprotodonte d'Australasie *f*
- *red kangaroo (red flyer), a kangaroo*

4-7 les insectivores *m*
- ***insectivores** (insect-eating mammals)*

4 la taupe
- *mole*

5 le hérisson
- *hedgehog*

6 les piquants *m*
- *spine*

7 la musaraigne, un soricidé
- *shrew (shrew mouse)*

8 le tatou
- *nine-banded armadillo (peba)*

9 l'oreillard *m*, une chauve-souris, un chiroptère, un mammifère volant
- *long-eared bat (flitter-mouse), a flying mammal (chiropter, chiropteran)*

10 le pangolin, un mammifère écailleux
- *pangolin (scaly ant-eater)*

11 le paresseux
- *two-toed sloth (unau)*

12-19 les rongeurs *m*
- ***rodents***

12 le cobaye (le cochon d'Inde)
- *guinea pig (cavy)*

13 le porc-épic
- *porcupine*

14 le castor
- *beaver*

15 la souris sauteuse, la gerboise
- *jerboa*

16 le hamster
- *hamster*

17 le rat d'eau *f*
- *water vole*

18 la marmotte
- *marmot*

19 l'écureuil *m*
- *squirrel*

20 l'éléphant *m* d'Afrique *f*, un proboscidien
- *African elephant, a proboscidean (proboscidian)*

21 la trompe
- *trunk (proboscis)*

22 la défense
- *tusk*

23 le lamantin, un sirénien
- *manatee (manati, lamantin), a sirenian*

24 le daman d'Afrique *f* du Sud, un procaviidé
- *South African dassie (das, coney, hyrax), a procaviid*

25-31 les ongulés *m*
- ***ungulates***

25-27 les périssodactyles *m*
- ***odd-toed ungulates***

25 le rhinocéros noir d'Afrique *f*, à deux cornes *f*
- *African black rhino, a rhinoceros (nasicorn)*

26 le tapir
- *Brazilian tapir, a tapir*

27 le zèbre
- *zebra*

28-31 les artiodactyles *m*
- ***even-toed ungulates***

28-30 les ruminants *m*
- ***ruminants***

28 le lama
- *llama*

29 le chameau (à deux bosses *f*)
- *Bactrian camel (two-humped camel)*

30 le guanaco
- *guanaco*

31 l'hippopotame *m*
- *hippopotamus*

1
2
3
4
5
6
7
8
9
10
11
12
13
14
15
16
17
18
19
20
21
22
23
24
25
26
27
28
29
30
31

1-10 les ongulés *m*, ruminants *m*
– ***ungulates, ruminants***
1 l'élan *m*
– *elk (moose)*
2 le cerf wapiti
– *wapiti* (Am. *elk)*
3 le chamois
– *chamois*
4 la girafe
– *giraffe*
5 l'antilope *f*
– *black buck, an antelope*
6 le mouflon
– *mouflon (moufflon)*
7 le bouquetin
– *ibex (rock goat, bouquetin, steinbock)*
8 le buffle
– *water buffalo (Indian buffalo, water ox)*
9 le bison
– *bison*
10 le bœuf musqué
– *musk ox*
11-22 les carnassiers *m*, les carnivores *m*
– ***carnivores*** *(beasts of prey)*
11-13 les canidés *m*
– ***Canidae***
11 le chacal
– *black-backed jackal (jackal)*
12 le renard roux
– *red fox*
13 le loup
– *wolf*
14-17 les martes *f* (martres *f*), mustélidés *m*
– ***martens***
14 la fouine
– *stone marten (beach marten)*
15 la zibeline
– *sable*
16 la belette
– *weasel*
17 la loutre de mer *f*
– *sea otter, an otter*
18-22 les pinnipèdes *m*
– ***seals*** *(pinnipeds)*
18 le phoque à fourrure *f*
– *fur seal (sea bear, ursine seal)*
19 l'otarie *f*
– *common seal (sea calf, sea dog)*
20 le morse
– *walrus (morse)*
21 la moustache
– *whiskers*
22 la défense
– *tusk*
23-29 les cétacés *m*
– ***whales***
23 le dauphin
– *bottle-nosed dolphin (bottle-nose dolphin)*
24 le marsouin
– *common dolphin*
25 le cachalot
– *sperm whale (cachalot)*
26 l'évent *m*
– *blowhole (spout hole)*
27 la nageoire dorsale, l'aileron *m* dorsal
– *dorsal fin*
28 la nageoire pectorale, l'aileron *m* pectoral
– *flipper*
29 la queue, la nageoire caudale, l'aileron *m* caudal
– *tail flukes (tail)*

1
2
3
4
5
6
7
8
9
10
11
12
13
14
15
16
17
18
19
20
21
22
23
24
25
26
27
28
29

1-11 les carnassiers *m* (carnivores *m*, bêtes *f* de proie *f*)
– ***carnivores*** *(beasts of prey)*
1 l'hyène *f* rayée
– *striped hyena, a hyena*
2-8 les félins *m*
– ***felines*** *(cats)*
2 le lion
– *lion*
3 la crinière
– *mane (lion's mane)*
4 la patte
– *paw*
5 le tigre
– *tiger*
6 le léopard
– *leopard*
7 le guépard
– *cheetah (hunting leopard)*
8 le lynx
– *lynx*
9-11 les ursidés *m*
– ***bears***
9 le raton laveur
– *raccoon (racoon,* Am. *coon)*
10 l'ours *m* brun
– *brown bear*
11 l'ours *m* blanc, l'ours *m* polaire
– *polar bear (white bear)*
12-16 les primates *m*
– ***primates***
12-13 les singes *m*
– *monkeys*
12 le singe rhésus
– *rhesus monkey (rhesus, rhesus macaque)*
13 le babouin
– *baboon*
14-16 les anthropoïdes *m*
– ***anthropoids*** *(anthropoid apes, great apes)*
14 le chimpanzé
– *chimpanzee*
15 l'orang-outang *m*
– *orang-utan (orang-outan)*
16 le gorille
– *gorilla*

1
2
3
4
5
6
7
8
9
10
11
12
13
14
15
16

1 Gigantocypris agassizi, un crustacé
- *Gigantocypris agassizi*
2 Macropharynx longicaudatus, un poisson abyssal
- *Macropharynx longicaudatus (pelican eel)*
3 le pentacrinus, un échinoderme
- *Pentacrinus (feather star), a sea lily, an echinoderm*
4 Thaumatolampas diadema, un céphalopode (luminescent)
- *Thaumatolampas diadema, a cuttlefish [luminescent]*
5 l'atolla *m*, une méduse abyssale, un cœlenthéré
- *Atolla, a deep-sea medusa, a coelenterate*
6 le mélanocète, un brachioptère (luminescent)
- *Melanocetes, a pediculate [luminescent]*
7 Lophocalyx philippensis, une éponge siliceuse
- *Lophocalyx philippensis, a glass sponge*
8 le mopsea, un polype (luminescent) (colonie *f*)
- *Mopsea, a sea fan [colony]*
9 l'hydrallmania *m*, un polype hydroïde, un polype, un cœlenthéré (colonie *f*)
- *Hydrallmania, a hydroid polyp, a coelenterate [colony]*
10 Malacosteus indicus, un stomiatidé (luminescent)
- *Malacosteus indicus, a stomiatid [luminescent]*
11 Brisinga endecacnemos, un ophiuridé, un échinoderme (luminescent après stimulation *f*)
- *Brisinga endecacnemos, a sand star (brittle star), an echinoderm [luminescent only when stimulated]*
12 la pasiphæa, une crevette abyssale, un crustacé
- *Pasiphaea, a shrimp, a crustacean*
13 l'échiostoma *m*, un stomiatidé, un poisson abyssal (luminescent)
- *Echiostoma, a stomiatid, a fish [luminescent]*
14 Umbellula encrinus, une pennatule, une plume de mer *f*, un cœlenthéré
- *Umbellula encrinus, a sea pen (sea feather), a coelenterate [colony, luminescent]*
15 le polycheles, un crustacé
- *Polycheles, a crustacean*
16 le lithodes, un crabe, un crustacé
- *Lithodes, a crustacean, a crab*
17 l'archaster *m*, une étoile de mer *f*, un échinoderme
- *Archaster, a starfish (sea star), an echinoderm*
18 l'oneirophanta *m*, une holothurie, un échinoderme
- *Oneirophanta, a sea cucumber, an echinoderm*
19 Palaeopneustes niasicus, un oursin, un échinoderme
- *Palaeopneustes niasicus, a sea urchin (sea hedgehog), an echinoderm*
20 le chitonactis, une anémone de mer *f*, une actinie, un cœlenthéré
- *Chitonactis, a sea anemone (actinia), a coelenterate*

1
2
3
4
5
6
7
8
9
10
11
12
13
14
15
16
17
18
19
20
S. Vogel

1 l'arbre *m*
– *tree*
2 le tronc
– *bole (tree trunk, trunk, stem)*
3 la couronne de l'arbre *m*
– *crown of tree (crown)*
4 la cime
– *top of tree (treetop)*
5 la branche
– *bough (limb, branch)*
6 le rameau
– *twig (branch)*
7 le tronc [coupe *f* transversale]
– *bole (tree trunk) [cross section]*
8 l'écorce *f*
– *bark (rind)*
9 le liber
– *phloem (bast sieve tissue, inner fibrous bark)*
10 le cambium
– *cambium (cambium ring)*
11 les rayons *m* médullaires
– *medullary rays (vascular rays, pith rays)*
12 l'aubier *m*
– *sapwood (sap, alburnum)*
13 le cœur du bois
– *heartwood (duramen)*
14 le vaisseau médullaire
– *pith*
15 la plante
– ***plant***
16-18 la racine
– *root*
16 la racine principale
– *primary root*
17 la racine secondaire
– *secondary root*
18 la radicelle
– *root hair*
19-25 la pousse
– *shoot (sprout)*
19 la feuille
– *leaf*
20 la tige
– *stalk*
21 la pousse latérale
– *side shoot (offshoot)*
22 le bourgeon terminal
– *terminal bud*
23 la fleur
– *flower*
24 le bouton floral
– *flower bud*
25 l'aisselle *f* foliaire avec le bourgeon axillaire
– *leaf axil with axillary bud*
26 la feuille
– ***leaf***
27 le pétiole
– *leaf stalk (petiole)*
28 le limbe
– *leaf blade (blade, lamina)*
29 la nervure secondaire
– *venation (veins, nervures, ribs)*
30 la nervure principale
– *midrib (nerve)*
31-38 les formes *f* de feuilles *f*
– *leaf shapes*
31 linéaire
– *linear*
32 lancéolée
– *lanceolate*
33 ronde
– *orbicular (orbiculate)*
34 aciculaire, en aiguille *f*
– *acerose (acerous, acerate, acicular, needle-shaped)*
35 cordée
– *cordate*
36 ovoïde
– *ovate*
37 sagittée
– *sagittate*
38 réniforme
– *reniform*
39-42 feuilles *f* composées
– *compound leaves*
39 composée palmée (digitée)
– *digitate (digitated, palmate, quinquefoliolate)*
40 composée pennée
– *pinnatifid*
41 composée paripennée
– *abruptly pinnate*
42 composée imparipennée
– *odd-pinnate*
43-50 divers bords *m* du limbe
– *leaf margin shapes*
43 feuille *f* à bord *m* entier
– *entire*
44 dentelée
– *serrate (serrulate, saw-toothed)*
45 denticulée
– *doubly toothed*
46 crénelée
– *crenate*
47 dentée
– *dentate*
48 lobée
– *sinuate*
49 poilue
– *ciliate (ciliated)*
50 le poil
– *cilium*
51 la fleur
– ***flower***
52 le pédoncule, le pédicelle
– *flower stalk (flower stem, scape)*
53 le réceptacle
– *receptacle (floral axis, thalamus, torus)*
54 l'ovaire *m*
– *ovary*
55 le style
– *style*
56 le stigmate
– *stigma*
57 l'étamine *f*
– *stamen*
58 le sépale
– *sepal*
59 le pétale
– *petal*
60 l'ovaire *m* et l'étamine *f* [coupe *f*]
– *ovary and stamen [section]*
61 la paroi de l'ovaire *m*
– *ovary wall*
62 la cavité de l'ovaire *m*
– *ovary cavity*
63 l'ovule *m*
– *ovule*
64 le sac embryonnaire
– *embryo sac*
65 le grain de pollen (le pollen)
– *pollen*
66 le tube pollinique
– *pollen tube*
67-77 inflorescences *f*
– *inflorescences*
67 l'épi *m*
– *spike (racemose spike)*
68 la grappe
– *raceme (simple raceme)*
69 le panicule
– *panicle*
70 la cyme bipare
– *cyme*
71 le spadice
– *spadix (fleshy spike)*
72 l'ombelle *f*
– *umbel (simple umbel)*
73 le capitule
– *capitulum*
74 le capitule convexe
– *composite head (discoid flower head)*
75 le capitule concave
– *hollow flower head*
76 la cyme unipare scorpioïde
– *bostryx (helicoid cyme)*
77 la cyme unipare hélicoïde
– *cincinnus (scorpioid cyme, curled cyme)*
78-82 les racines *f*
– *roots*
78 les racines *f* adventives
– *adventitious roots*
79 la racine pivotante
– *tuber (tuberous root, swollen taproot)*
80 les crampons *m*
– *adventitious roots (aerial roots)*
81 les racines *f* munies d'épines *f*
– *root thorns*
82 les racines *f* aériennes
– *pneumatophores*
83-85 le brin d'herbe *f*
– *blade of grass*
83 la graine
– *leaf sheath*
84 la ligule
– *ligule (ligula)*
85 le limbe
– *leaf blade (lamina)*
86 le germe
– *embryo (seed, germ)*
87 le cotylédon
– *cotyledon (seed leaf, seed lobe)*
88 la radicule
– *radicle*
89 la tigelle
– *hypocotyl*
90 la gemmule
– *plumule (leaf bud)*
91-102 les fruits *m*
– *fruits*
91-96 les fruits *m* déhiscents
– *dehiscent fruits*
91 le follicule
– *follicle*
92 la gousse
– *legume (pod)*
93 la silique
– *siliqua (pod)*
94 la capsule loculicide
– *schizocarp*
95 la pyxide
– *pyxidium (circumscissile seed vessel)*
96 la capsule poricide
– *poricidal capsule (porose capsule)*
97-102 les fruits *m* charnus
– *indehiscent fruits*
97 la baie
– *berry*
98 la noix
– *nut*
99 la drupe (la cerise)
– *drupe (stone fruit) (cherry)*
100 le faux fruit (l'églantier *m*)
– *aggregate fruit (compound fruit) (rose hip)*
101 le fruit composé (la framboise)
– *aggregate fruit (compound fruit) (raspberry)*
102 le fruit à pépins *m* (la pomme)
– *pome (apple)*

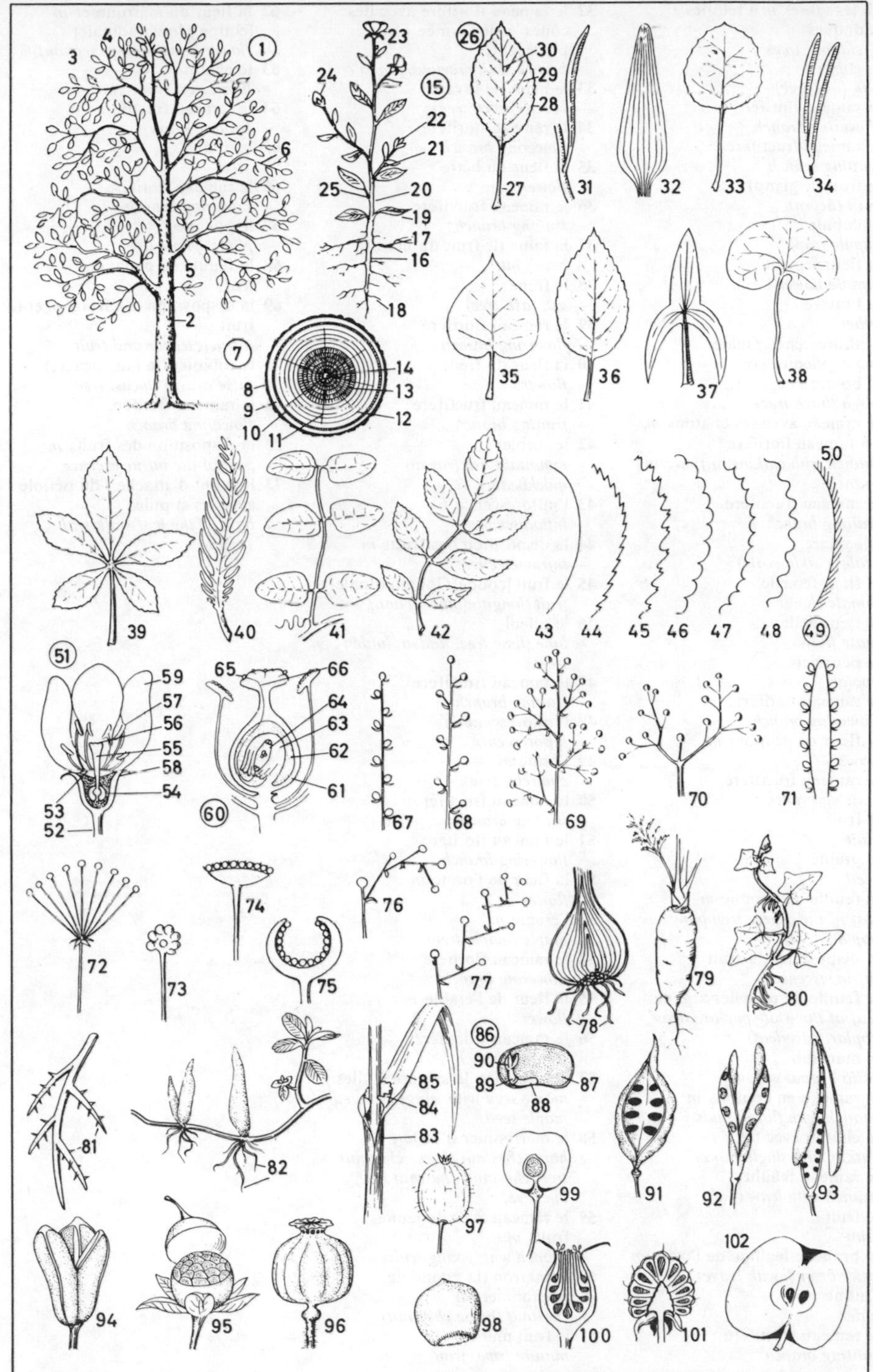
1 2 3 4 5 6 7 8 9 10 11 12 13 14 15 16 17 18 19 20 21 22 23 24 25 26 27 28 29 30 31 32 33 34 35 36 37 38 39 40 41 42 43 44 45 46 47 48 49 50 51 52 53 54 55 56 57 58 59 60 61 62 63 64 65 66 67 68 69 70 71 72 73 74 75 76 77 78 79 80 81 82 83 84 85 86 87 88 89 90 91 92 93 94 95 96 97 98 99 100 101 102

1-73 les arbres *m* à feuilles *f* caduques
– *deciduous trees*
1 le chêne
– *oak (oak tree)*
2 le rameau florifère
– *flowering branch*
3 le rameau fructifère
– *fruiting branch*
4 le fruit (le gland)
– *fruit (acorn)*
5 la cupule
– *cupule (cup)*
6 la fleur femelle
– *female flower*
7 la bractée
– *bract*
8 l'inflorescence *f* mâle
– *male inflorescence*
9 le bouleau
– *birch (birch tree)*
10 le rameau avec ses chatons *m*, un rameau florifère
– *branch with catkins, a flowering branch*
11 le rameau fructifère
– *fruiting branch*
12 la samare
– *scale (catkin scale)*
13 la fleur femelle
– *female flower*
14 la fleur mâle
– *male flower*
15 le peuplier
– *poplar*
16 le rameau florifère
– *flowering branch*
17 la fleur de peuplier *m*
– *flower*
18 le rameau fructifère
– *fruiting branch*
19 le fruit
– *fruit*
20 la graine
– *seed*
21 la feuille de tremble *m*
– *leaf of the aspen (trembling poplar)*
22 la disposition du fruit
– *infructescence*
23 la feuille du peuplier argenté
– *leaf of the white poplar (silver poplar, silverleaf)*
24 le marsault
– *sallow (goat willow)*
25 le rameau en boutons *m*
– *branch with flower buds*
26 le chaton avec fleur *f*
– *catkin with single flower*
27 le rameau feuillu
– *branch with leaves*
28 le fruit
– *fruit*
29 la branche feuillue de l'osier *m*
– *osier branch with leaves*
30 l'aulne *m*
– *alder*
31 le rameau fructifère
– *fruiting branch*
32 le rameau florifère avec des cônes *m* de l'année *f* précédente
– *branch with previous year's cone*
33 le hêtre (le fayard)
– *beech (beech tree)*
34 le rameau florifère
– *flowering branch*
35 la fleur du hêtre
– *flower*
36 le rameau fructifère
– *fruiting branch*
37 la faine (le fruit du hêtre)
– *beech nut*
38 le frêne
– *ash (ash tree)*
39 le rameau florifère
– *flowering branch*
40 la fleur du frêne
– *flower*
41 le rameau fructifère
– *fruiting branch*
42 le sorbier
– *mountain ash (rowan, quickbeam)*
43 l'inflorescence *f*
– *inflorescence*
44 la disposition des fruits *m*
– *infructescence*
45 le fruit [coupe *f* longitudinale]
– *fruit [longitudinal section]*
46 le tilleul
– *lime (lime tree, linden, linden tree)*
47 le rameau fructifère
– *fruiting branch*
48 l'inflorescence *f*
– *inflorescence*
49 l'orme *m*
– *elm (elm tree)*
50 le rameau fructifère
– *fruiting branch*
51 le rameau florifère
– *flowering branch*
52 la fleur de l'orme *m*
– *flower*
53 l'érable *m*
– *maple (maple tree)*
54 le rameau florifère
– *flowering branch*
55 la fleur de l'érable *m*
– *flower*
56 le rameau fructifère
– *fruiting branch*
57 la disamare, la samare à ailes *f*
– *maple seed with wings (winged maple seed)*
58 le marronnier d'Inde *f*
– *horse chestnut (horse chestnut tree, chestnut, chestnut tree, buckeye)*
59 le rameau avec de jeunes fruits *m*
– *branch with young fruits*
60 le marron (la graine de marronnier *m*)
– *chestnut (horse chestnut)*
61 le fruit mûr
– *mature (ripe) fruit*
62 la fleur du marronnier *m* [coupe *f* longitudinale]
– *flower [longitudinal section]*
63 le charme
– *hornbeam (yoke elm)*
64 le rameau fructifère
– *fruiting branch*
65 la graine
– *seed*
66 le rameau florifère
– *flowering branch*
67 le platane
– *plane (plane tree)*
68 la feuille de platane *m*
– *leaf*
69 la disposition des fruits *m* et le fruit
– *infructescence and fruit*
70 le robinier (le faux acacia)
– *false acacia (locust tree)*
71 le rameau florifère
– *flowering branch*
72 la disposition des fruits *m*
– *part of the infructescence*
73 le point d'attache *f* du pétiole avec les stipules *f*
– *base of the leaf stalk with stipules*

1
2
3
4
5
6
7
8
9
10
11
12
13
14
15
16
17
18
19
20
21
22
23
24
25
26
27
28
29
30
31
32
33
34
35
36
37
38
39
40
41
42
43
44
45
46
47
48
49
50
51
52
53
54
55
56
57
58
59
60
61
62
63
64
65
66
67
68
69
70
71
72
73
♀
♂

1-71 les conifères *m*
– *coniferous trees (conifers)*
1 le sapin blanc
– *silver fir (European silver fir, common silver fir)*
2 le cône, un fruit
– *fir cone, a fruit cone*
3 l'axe *m* du cône
– *cone axis*
4 le cône femelle
– *female flower cone*
5 l'écaille *f*
– *bract scale (bract)*
6 le cône mâle
– *male flower shoot*
7 l'étamine *f*
– *stamen*
8 l'écaille *f* du cône
– *cone scale*
9 la graine ailée
– *seed with wing (winged seed)*
10 la graine [coupe *f* longitudinale]
– *seed [longitudinal section]*
11 l'aiguille *f* de sapin *m*
– *fir needle (needle)*
12 l'épicéa *m*
– *spruce (spruce fir)*
13 le cône
– *spruce cone*
14 l'écaille *f* du cône
– *cone scale*
15 la graine
– *seed*
16 le cône femelle
– *female flower cone*
17 le cône mâle
– *male inflorescence*
18 l'étamine *f*
– *stamen*
19 l'aiguille *f* d'épicéa *m*
– *spruce needle*
20 le pin sylvestre
– *pine (Scots pine)*
21 le pin nain
– *dwarf pine*
22 le cône femelle
– *female flower cone*
23 les feuilles *f* aciculaires géminées
– *short shoot with bundle of two leaves*
24 le cône mâle
– *male inflorescences*
25 la pousse de l'année
– *annual growth*
26 le cône de pin *m* (la pomme de pin *m*)
– *pine cone*
27 l'écaille *f* du cône
– *cone scale*
28 la graine
– *seed*
29 le cône du pin cembro (pin *m* cembrot, arole *m*)
– *fruit cone of the arolla pine (Swiss stone pine)*
30 le cône du pin Weymouth
– *fruit cone of the Weymouth pine (white pine)*
31 la pousse [coupe *f* transversale]
– *short shoot [cross section]*
32 le mélèze
– *larch*
33 le rameau florifère
– *flowering branch*
34 l'écaille *f* du cône femelle
– *scale of the female flower cone*
35 l'anthère *f*
– *anther*
36 le rameau avec un cône
– *branch with larch cones (fruit cones)*
37 la graine
– *seed*
38 l'écaille *f*
– *cone scale*
39 le thuya
– *arbor vitae (tree of life, thuja)*
40 le rameau fructifère
– *fruiting branch*
41 le cône
– *fruit cone*
42 l'écaille *f*
– *scale*
43 le rameau avec des fleurs *f* mâles et des fleurs *f* femelles
– *branch with male and female flowers*
44 la pousse mâle
– *male shoot*
45 l'écaille *f* avec sacs *m* polliniques
– *scale with pollen sacs*
46 la pousse femelle
– *female shoot*
47 le genévrier
– *juniper (juniper tree)*
48 la pousse femelle [coupe *f* longitudinale]
– *female shoot [longitudinal section]*
49 la pousse mâle
– *male shoot*
50 l'écaille *f* avec sacs *m* polliniques
– *scale with pollen sacs*
51 le rameau fructifère
– *fruiting branch*
52 la baie de genièvre *m*
– *juniper berry*
53 le fruit [coupe *f* transversale]
– *fruit [cross section]*
54 la graine
– *seed*
55 le pin pignon
– *stone pine*
56 la pousse mâle
– *male shoot*
57 le cône avec les graines *f* (pignes *f*) [coupe *f* longitudinale]
– *fruit cone with seeds [longitudinal section]*
58 le cyprès
– *cypress*
59 le rameau fructifère
– *fruiting branch*
60 la graine
– *seed*
61 l'if *m*
– *yew (yew tree)*
62 le cône mâle et le cône femelle
– *male flower shoot and female flower cone*
63 le rameau fructifère
– *fruiting branch*
64 le fruit
– *fruit*
65 le cèdre
– *cedar (cedar tree)*
66 le rameau fructifère
– *fruiting branch*
67 l'écaille *f* du fruit
– *fruit scale*
68 le cône mâle et le cône femelle
– *male flower shoot and female flower cone*
69 le séquoia
– *mammoth tree (Wellingtonia, sequoia)*
70 le rameau fructifère
– *fruiting branch*
71 la graine
– *seed*

1 le forsythia
– *forsythia*
2 l'ovaire *m* et l'étamine *f*
– *ovary and stamen*
3 la feuille du forsythia
– *leaf*
4 le jasmin jaune
– *yellow-flowered jasmine (jasmin, jessamine)*
5 la fleur [coupe *f* longitudinale] avec le style, l'ovaire *m* et les étamines *f*
– *flower [longitudinal section] with styles, ovaries, and stamens*
6 le troène
– *privet (common privet)*
7 la fleur de troène *m*
– *flower*
8 la disposition des fruits *m* (baies *f*)
– *infructescence*
9 le seringat
– *mock orange (sweet syringa)*
10 la boule de neige *f* (la viorne)
– *snowball (snowball bush, guelder rose)*
11 la fleur
– *flower*
12 les fruits *m*
– *fruits*
13 le laurier-rose
– *oleander (rosebay, rose laurel)*
14 la fleur de laurier-rose *m* [coupe *f* longitudinale]
– *flower [longitudinal section]*
15 le magnolia
– *red magnolia*
16 la feuille de magnolia *m*
– *leaf*
17 le cognassier du Japon
– *japonica (japanese quince)*
18 le fruit
– *fruit*
19 le buis
– *common box (box, box tree)*
20 la fleur femelle
– *female flower*
21 la fleur mâle
– *male flower*
22 le fruit du buis [coupe *f* longitudinale]
– *fruit [longitudinal section]*
23 le weigelia
– *weigela (weigelia)*
24 le yucca [partie *f* de l'inflorescence *f*]
– *yucca [part of the inflorescence]*
25 la feuille
– *leaf*
26 l'églantier *m*
– *dog rose (briar rose, wild briar)*
27 le fruit de l'églantier *m* (le cynorrhodon)
– *fruit*
28 la kerrie (la spirée du Japon)
– *kerria*
29 le fruit
– *fruit*
30 le cornouiller sanguin
– *cornelian cherry*
31 la fleur du cornouiller sanguin
– *flower*
32 le fruit
– *fruit (cornelian cherry)*
33 le galé (le piment royal)
– *sweet gale (gale)*

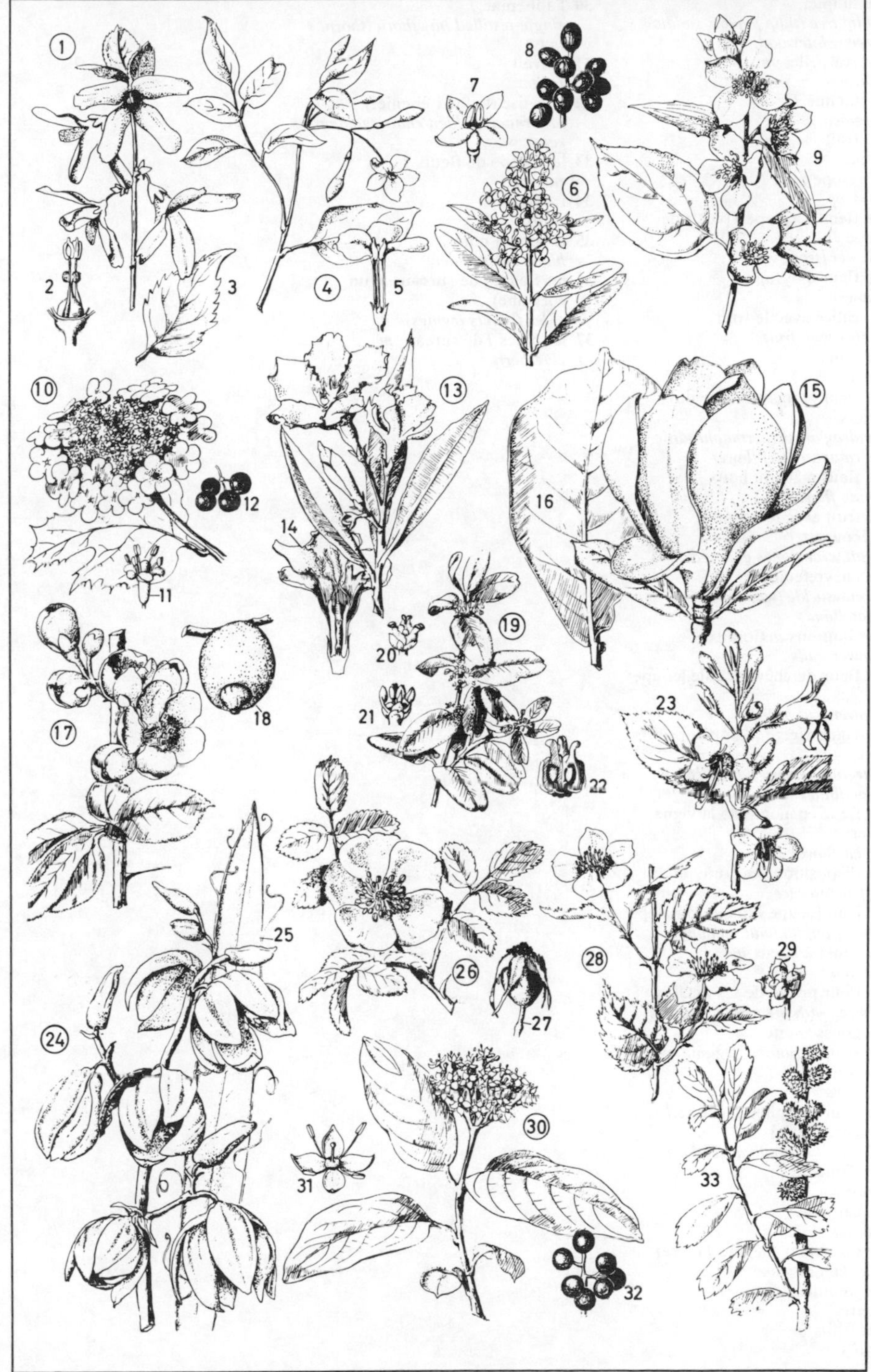
1
2
3
4
5
6
7
8
9
10
11
12
13
14
15
16
17
18
19
20
21
22
23
24
25
26
27
28
29
30
31
32
33

1 le tulipier
- *tulip tree (tulip poplar, saddle tree, whitewood)*

2 les carpelles *m*
- *carpels*

3 l'étamine *f*
- *stamen*

4 le fruit
- *fruit*

5 l'hysope *f*
- *hyssop*

6 la fleur d'hysope *f* [vue *f* de face *f*]
- *flower [front view]*

7 la fleur d'hysope *f*
- *flower*

8 le calice avec le fruit
- *calyx with fruit*

9 le houx
- *holly*

10 la fleur hermaphrodite du houx
- *androgynous (hermaphroditic, hermaphrodite) flower*

11 la fleur mâle du houx
- *male flower*

12 le fruit avec le noyau découvert
- *fruit with stones exposed*

13 le chèvrefeuille
- *honeysuckle (woodbine, woodbind)*

14 les boutons *m* floraux
- *flower buds*

15 la fleur du chèvrefeuille [coupe *f*]
- *flower [cut open]*

16 la vigne vierge (l'ampélopsis *m*)
- *Virginia creeper (American ivy, woodbine)*

17 la fleur épanouie de la vigne vierge
- *open flower*

18 la disposition des fruits *m*
- *infructescence*

19 le fruit [coupe *f* longitudinale]
- *fruit [longitudinal section]*

20 le genêt à balais *m*
- *broom*

21 la fleur privée de ses pétales *m*
- *flower with the petals removed*

22 la gousse verte
- *immature (unripe) legume (pod)*

23 la spirée
- *spiraea*

24 la fleur de spirée *f* [coupe *f* longitudinale]
- *flower [longitudinal section]*

25 les fruits *m*
- *fruit*

26 le carpelle
- *carpel*

27 le prunellier (l'épine *f* noire)
- *blackthorn (sloe)*

28 les feuilles *f*
- *leaves*

29 les fruits *m*
- *fruits*

30 l'aubépine *f*
- *single-pistilled hawthorn (thorn, may)*

31 le fruit
- *fruit*

32 le cytise (le faux ébénier)
- *laburnum (golden chain, golden rain)*

33 la grappe de fleurs *f*
- *raceme*

34 les fruits *m*
- *fruits*

35 le sureau noir
- *black elder (elder)*

36 les fleurs *f* de sureau *m* (un corymbe)
- *elder flowers (cymes)*

37 les baies *f* de sureau *m*
- *elderberries*

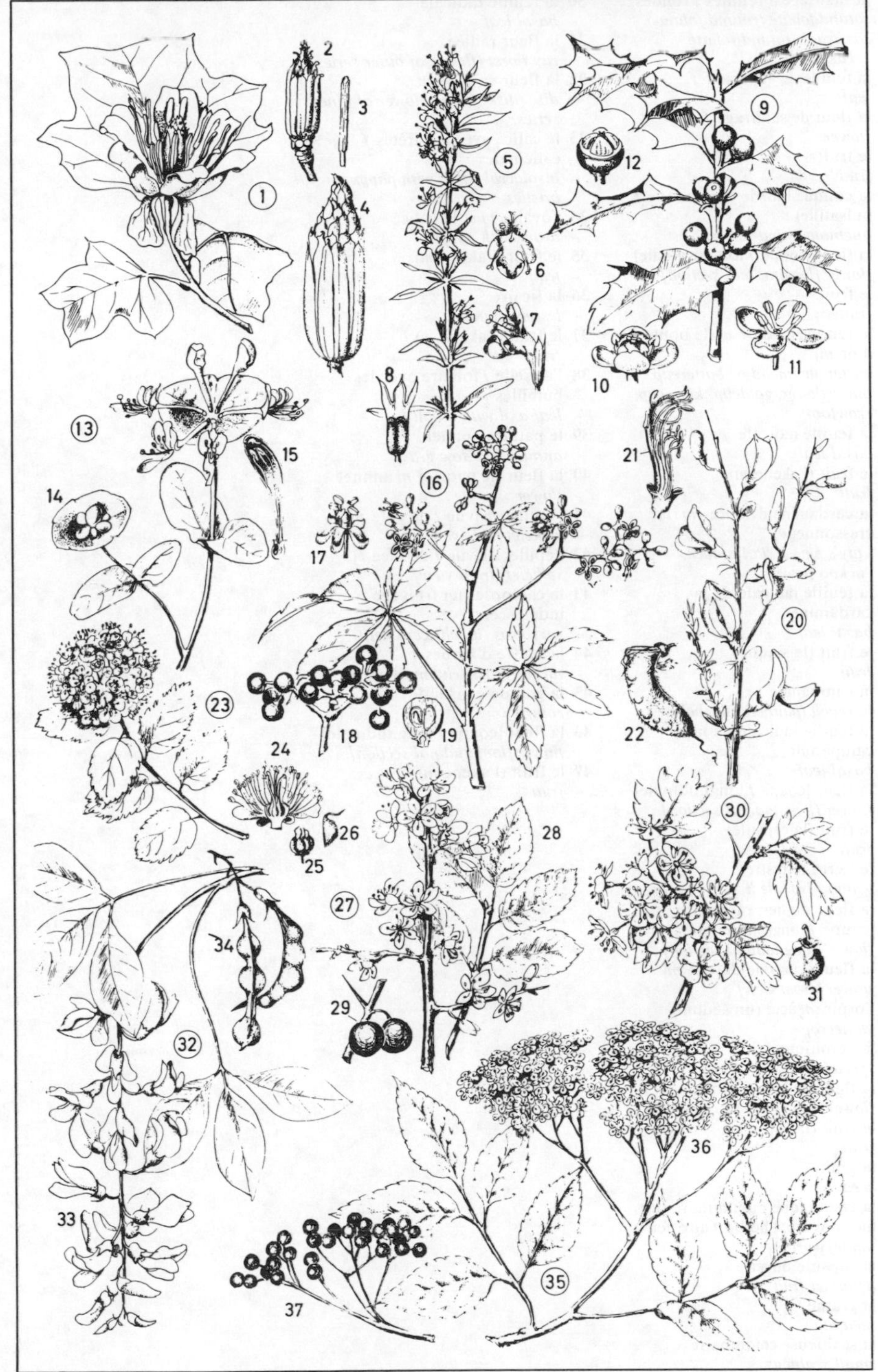
1
2
3
4
5
6
7
8
9
10
11
12
13
14
15
16
17
18
19
20
21
22
23
24
25
26
27
28
29
30
31
32
33
34
35
36
37

375 Fleurs des prés et des champs I

1 la saxifrage à feuilles *f* rondes
– *rotundifoliate (rotundifolious) saxifrage (rotundifoliate breakstone)*
2 la feuille de saxifrage *f*
– *leaf*
3 la fleur de saxifrage *f*
– *flower*
4 le fruit
– *fruit*
5 la couque lourde (l'anémone *f* pulsatille)
– *anemone (windflower)*
6 la fleur [coupe *f* longitudinale]
– *flower [longitudinal section]*
7 le fruit
– *fruit*
8 la renoncule d'or *m* (le bouton d'or *m*)
– *buttercup (meadow buttercup, butterflower, goldcup, king cup, crowfoot)*
9 la feuille radicale
– *basal leaf*
10 le fruit (l'akène *m*)
– *fruit*
11 la cardamine des prés *m* (la cressonnette)
– *lady's smock (ladysmock, cuckoo flower)*
12 la feuille radicale de la cardamine
– *basal leaf*
13 le fruit (la silique)
– *fruit*
14 la campanule
– *harebell (hairbell, bluebell)*
15 la feuille radicale de la campanule
– *basal leaf*
16 la fleur [coupe *f* longitudinale]
– *flower [longitudinal section]*
17 le fruit (la capsule)
– *fruit*
18 le lierre terrestre
– *ground ivy (ale hoof)*
19 la fleur du lierre terrestre [coupe *f* longitudinale]
– *flower [longitudinal section]*
20 la fleur [vue *f* de devant *m*]
– *flower [front view]*
21 l'orpin *m* âcre (un sédum)
– *stonecrop*
22 la véronique
– *speedwell*
23 la fleur de la véronique
– *flower*
24 le fruit (la capsule)
– *fruit*
25 la graine
– *seed*
26 la lysimiaque nummulaire (la monnoyère, l'herbe *f* aux écus)
– *moneywort*
27 la capsule ouverte
– *dehisced fruit*
28 la graine
– *seed*
29 la scabieuse colombaire
– *small scabious*
30 la feuille radicale
– *basal leaf*
31 la fleur radiée
– *ray floret (flower of outer series)*
32 la fleur en tube *m*
– *disc (disk) floret (flower of inner series)*
33 le calice avec les arêtes *f* calicinales
– *involucral calyx with pappus bristles*
34 l'ovaire *m* et le calice
– *ovary with pappus*
35 le fruit (l'akène *m*)
– *fruit*
36 la ficaire
– *lesser celandine*
37 le fruit (l'akène *m*)
– *fruit*
38 l'aisselle *f* foliaire avec les bulbilles *f*
– *leaf axil with bulbil*
39 le paturin annuel
– *annual meadow grass*
40 la fleur de paturin *m* annuel
– *flower*
41 l'épillet *m* [vue *f* de côté *m*]
– *spikelet [side view]*
42 l'épillet *m* [vue *f* de face *f*]
– *spikelet [front view]*
43 le caryopse (un fruit sec indéhiscent)
– *caryopsis (indehiscent fruit)*
44 la touffe d'herbes *f*
– *tuft of grass (clump of grass)*
45 la grande consoude
– *comfrey*
46 la fleur [coupe *f* longitudinale]
– *flower [longitudinal section]*
47 le fruit (l'akène *m*)
– *fruit*

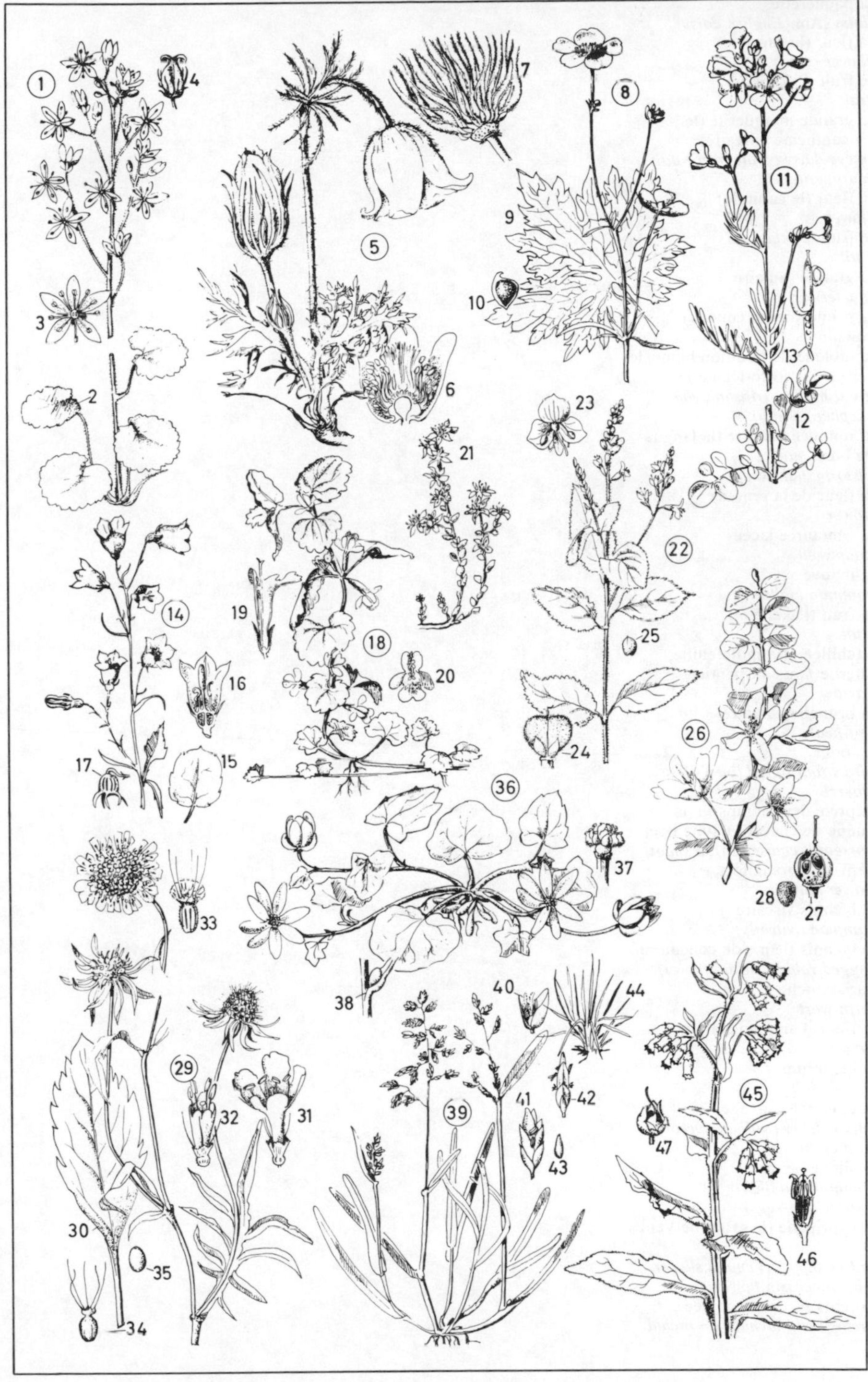
1
2
3
4
5
6
7
8
9
10
11
12
13
14
15
16
17
18
19
20
21
22
23
24
25
26
27
28
29
30
31
32
33
34
35
36
37
38
39
40
41
42
43
44
45
46
47

1 la pâquerette
- *daisy (*Am. *English daisy)*

2 la fleur (le capitule)
- *flower*

3 le fruit (l'akène *m*)
- *fruit*

4 la grande marguerite (le leucanthème vulgaire)
- *oxeye daisy (white oxeye daisy, marguerite)*

5 la fleur (le capitule)
- *flower*

6 le fruit (l'akène *m*)
- *fruit*

7 la grande radiaire
- *masterwort*

8 la primevère (le coucou)
- *cowslip*

9 la molène (le bouillon blanc, le cierge de Notre-Dame *f*)
- *great mullein (Aaron's rod, shepherd's club)*

10 la renouée bistorte (la langue de bœuf *m*)
- *bistort (snakeweed)*

11 la fleur de la renouée
- *flower*

12 la centaurée jacée
- *knapweed*

13 la mauve
- *common mallow*

14 le fruit (l'akène *m*)
- *fruit*

15 l'achillée *f* (la millefeuille, l'herbe *f* au charpentier)
- *yarrow*

16 la brunelle vulgaire
- *self-heal*

17 le lotier
- *bird's foot trefoil (bird's foot clover)*

18 la prêle des champs *m* (la queue de cheval *m*) [une tige]
- *horsetail (equisetum) [a shoot]*

19 l'épi *m* sporangifère
- *flower (strobile)*

20 le lychnis viscaire
- *campion (catchfly)*

21 le lychnis fleur *f* de coucou *m*
- *ragged robin (cuckoo flower)*

22 l'aristoloche *f*
- *birth-wort*

23 la fleur d'aristoloche
- *flower*

24 le géranium
- *crane's bill*

25 la chicorée sauvage
- *wild chicory (witloof, succory, wild endive)*

26 le silène penché
- *common toadflax (butter-and-eggs)*

27 le cypripède (le sabot de Vénus *f*)
- *lady's slipper (Venus's slipper,* Am. *moccasin flower)*

28 l'orchis *m*, une orchidée
- *orchis (wild orchid), an orchid*

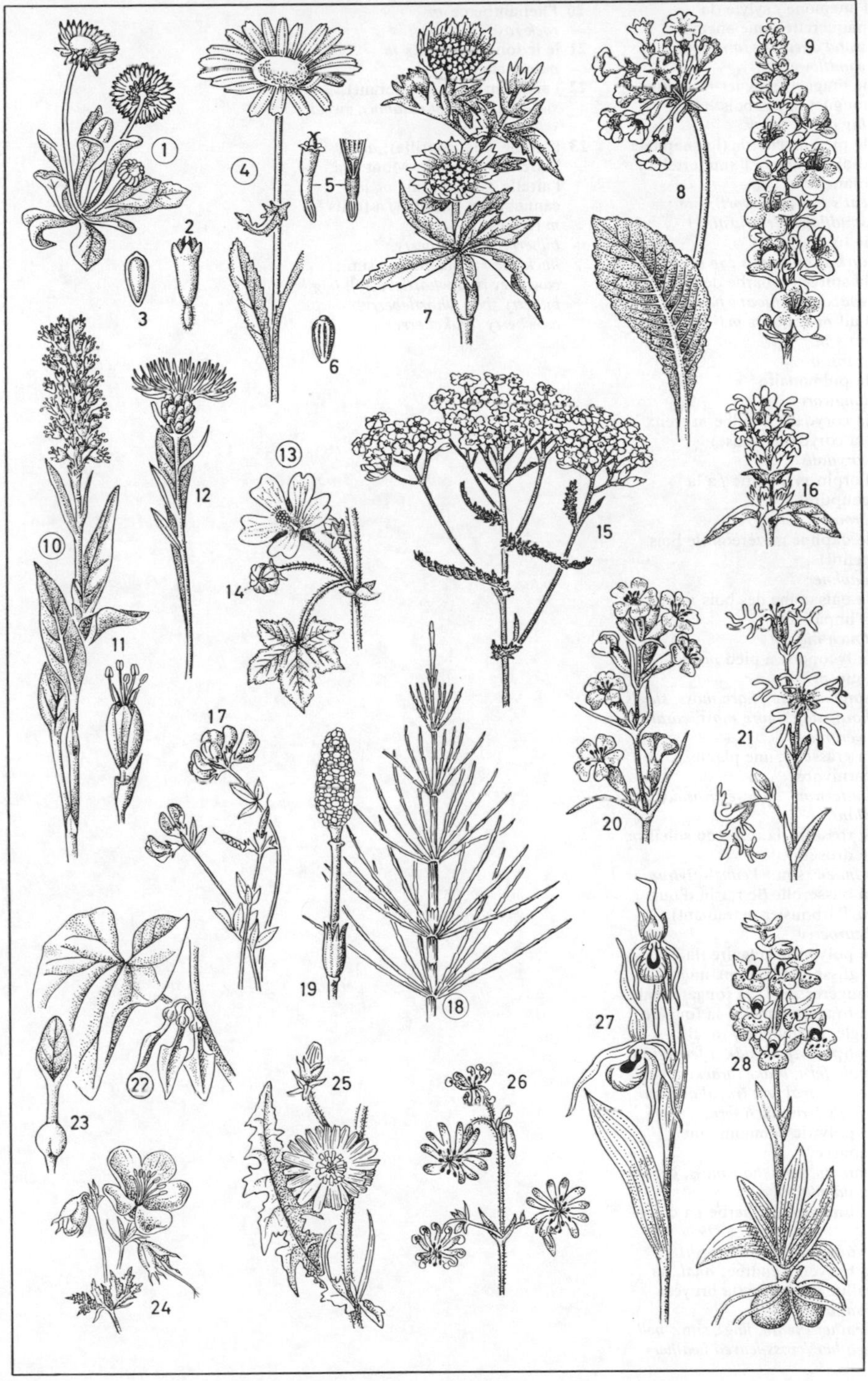
1
2
3
4
5
6
7
8
9
10
11
12
13
14
15
16
17
18
19
20
21
22
23
24
25
26
27
28

377 Plantes des bois, des tourbières et des laudes

1 l'anémone *f* sylvie (la pâquerette), une anémone
– *wood anemone (anemone, windflower)*
2 le muguet (muguet *m* de mai, muguet *m* des bois *m*)
– *lily of the valley*
3 le pied de chat *m* (le gnaphale dioïque, *anal.:* l' immortelle *f* blanche)
– *cat's foot (milkwort);* sim.: *sandflower (everlasting)*
4 le lis martagon
– *turk's cap (turk's cap lily)*
5 la spirée (la barbe de bouc *m*)
– *goatsbeard (goat's beard)*
6 l'ail *m* des ours *m* (l'ail *m* des bois *m*)
– *ramson*
7 la pulmonaire
– *lungwort*
8 la corydalle à bulbe *m* creux (la corydalle creuse)
– *corydalis*
9 l'orpin *m* (l'herbe *f* à la coupure)
– *orpine (livelong)*
10 le daphné mézéréon (le bois gentil)
– *daphne*
11 la balsamine des bois *m* (l'impatiente *f*)
– *touch-me-not*
12 le lycopode à pied *m* de loup *m*
– *staghorn (stag horn moss, stag's horn, stag's horn moss, coral evergreen)*
13 la grassette, une plante carnivore
– *butterwort, an insectivorous plant*
14 le rossolis (la rosée du soleil *m*, le droséra)
– *sundew;* sim.: *Venus's flytrap*
15 la busserolle (le raisin d'ours *m*, l'arbousier *m* traînant)
– *bearberry*
16 le polypode vulgaire (la réglisse des bois *m*), une fougère; *anal.:* la fougère mâle, la fougère femelle, la fougère aigle, l'osmonde *f* royale
– *polypody (polypod), a fern;* sim.: *male fern, brake (bracken, eagle fern), royal fern (royal osmund, king's fern, ditch fern)*
17 le polytric commun, une mousse
– *haircap moss (hair moss, golden maidenhair), a moss*
18 la linaigrette (l'herbe *f* à coton *m*)
– *cotton grass (cotton rush)*
19 la bruyère cendrée; *anal.:* la callune vulgaire (la bruyère commune)
– *heather (heath, ling);* sim.: *bell heather (cross-leaved heather)*
20 l'hélianthème *m*
– *rock rose (sun rose)*
21 le lédon des marais *m*
– *marsh tea*
22 l'acore *m* (le jonc odorant)
– *sweet flag (sweet calamus, sweet sedge)*
23 l'airelle *f* (la myrtille); *anal.:* l'airelle *f* vigne du Mont Ida, l'airelle *f* des marais *m*, la canneberge, l'airelle *f* à fruits *m* rouges
– *bilberry (whortleberry, huckleberry, blueberry);* sim.: *cowberry (red whortleberry), bog bilberry (bog whortleberry), crowberry (crakeberry)*

1
2
3
4
5
6
7
8
9
10
11
12
13
14
15
16
17
18
19
20
21
22
23

1-13 la flore alpine
– ***alpine plants***
1 le rhododendron
– *alpine rose (alpine rhododendron)*
2 le rameau florifère
– *flowering shoot*
3 la soldanelle
– *alpine soldanella (soldanella)*
4 la corolle étalée
– *corolla opened out*
5 la capsule et le style
– *seed vessel with the style*
6 l'armoise *f* mutelline (le génépi)
– *alpine wormwood*
7 l'inflorescence *f* (le capitule)
– *inflorescence*
8 l'oreille *f* d'ours *m*
– *auricula*
9 l'edelweiss *m* (le pied de lion *m*, l'étoile *f* d'argent *m*)
– *edelweiss*
10 les types *m* de fleurs *f*
– *flower shapes*
11 le fruit (l'akène *f*) avec son aigrette *f*
– *fruit with pappus tuft*
12 une partie de l'involucre *m*
– *part of flower head (of capitulum)*
13 la gentiane acaule
– *stemless alpine gentian*
14-57 la flore aquatique et la flore des marais *m*
– ***aquatic plants*** *(water plants)* **and marsh plants**
14 le nénuphar
– *white water lily*
15 la feuille
– *leaf*
16 la fleur
– *flower*
17 le victoria regia (la reine des eaux *f*, le maïs d'eau *f*)
– *Queen Victoria water lily (Victoria regia water lily, royal water lily, Amazon water lily)*
18 la feuille
– *leaf*
19 la face inférieure de la feuille
– *underside of the leaf*
20 la fleur
– *flower*
21 le typha (la massette, les quenouilles *f*)
– *reed mace bulrush (cattail, cat's tail, cattail flag, club rush)*
22 la partie mâle de l'épi *m* (l'épi *m* staminé)
– *male part of the spadix*
23 la fleur mâle
– *male flower*
24 la partie femelle de l'épi *m*
– *female part*
25 la fleur femelle
– *female flower*
26 le myosotis
– *forget-me-not*
27 le rameau en fleur *f*
– *flowering shoot*
28 la fleur [coupe *f*]
– *flower [section]*
29 la morène
– *frog's bit*
30 le cresson de fontaine *f*
– *watercress*
31 la tige avec fleurs *f* et fruits *m* (siliques *f*) jeunes
– *stalk with flowers and immature (unripe) fruits*
32 la fleur
– *flower*
33 la silique avec les graines *f*
– *siliqua (pod) with seeds*
34 deux graines *f*
– *two seeds*
35 la lentille d'eau *f*
– *duckweed (duck's meat)*
36 la plante en fleurs *f*
– *plant in flower*
37 la fleur
– *flower*
38 le fruit
– *fruit*
39 le butome en ombelle *f* (le jonc fleuri)
– *flowering rush*
40 l'ombelle *f*
– *flower umbel*
41 les feuilles *f*
– *leaves*
42 le fruit (la follicule)
– *fruit*
43 l'algue *f* verte
– *green alga*
44 le plantain d'eau *f* (le flûteau)
– *water plantain*
45 la feuille
– *leaf*
46 l'inflorescence *f*
– *panicle*
47 la fleur
– *flower*
48 la laminaire, une algue brune
– *honey wrack, a brown alga*
49 le thalle
– *thallus (plant body, frond)*
50 les sores *m*
– *holdfast*
51 la sagittaire (la flèche d'eau *f*)
– *arrow head*
52 les formes de feuilles *f*
– *leaf shapes*
53 les fleurs *f* [mâles au sommet, femelles à la base *f*]
– *inflorescence with male flowers [above] and female flowers [below]*
54 la zostère
– *sea grass*
55 l'inflorescence *f*
– *inflorescence*
56 l'élodée *f* du Canada (la peste d'eau *f*)
– *Canadian waterweed (Canadian pondweed)*
57 la fleur
– *flower*

1
2
3
4
5
6
7
8
9
10
11
12
13
14
15
16
17
18
19
20
21
22
23
24
25
26
27
28
29
30
31
32
33
34
35
36
37
38
39
40
41
42
43
44
45
46
47
48
49
50
51
52
53
54
55
56
57

1 l'aconit *m*
– *aconite (monkshood, wolfsbane, helmet flower)*
2 la digitale pourprée
– *foxglove (Digitalis)*
3 la colchique
– *meadow saffron (naked lady, naked boys)*
4 la grande ciguë
– *hemlock (Conium)*
5 la morelle noire
– *black nightshade (common nightshade, petty morel)*
6 la jusquiame noire (l'herbe *f* aux chevaux *m*)
– *henbane*
7 la belladone, une solanacée
– *deadly nightshade (belladonna, banewort, dwale), a solanaceous herb*
8 la stramoine (la datura stramoine, la pomme épineuse)
– *thorn apple (stramonium, stramony,* Am. *jimson weed, jimpson weed, Jamestown weed, stinkweed)*
9 l'arum *m* tacheté (le gouet, le pied de veau *m*)
– *cuckoo pint (lords-and-ladies, wild arum, wake-robin)*
10-13 les champignons vénéneux
– *poisonous fungi (poisonous mushrooms, toadstools)*
10 l'amanite *f* tue-mouches *m* (la fausse oronge, un champignon à lamelles *f*)
– *fly agaric (fly amanita, fly fungus), an agaric*
11 l'amanite phalloïde
– *amanita*
12 le bolet de Satan *m*
– *Satan's mushroom*
13 le lactaire toisonné
– *woolly milk cap*

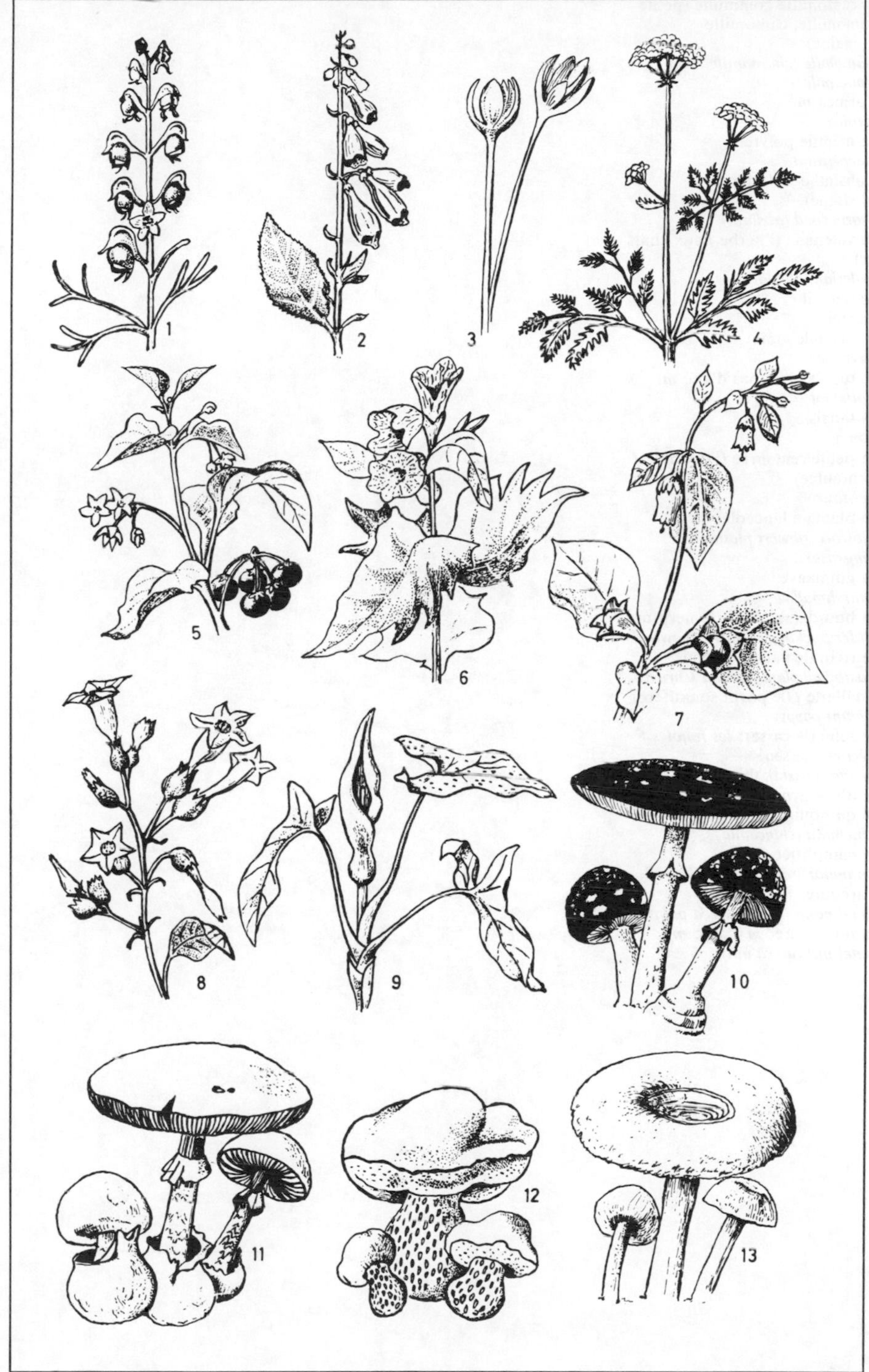
1
2
3
4
5
6
7
8
9
10
11
12
13

1 la camomille commune (petite camomille, camomille romaine)
- *camomile (chamomile, wild camomile)*

2 l'arnica *m*
- *arnica*

3 la menthe poivrée
- *peppermint*

4 l'absinthe *f* (l'armoise *f* absinthe)
- *wormwood (absinth)*

5 la valériane (l'herbe *f* aux chats *m*)
- *valerian (allheal)*

6 le fenouil
- *fennel*

7 la lavande vraie
- *lavender*

8 le tussilage (le pas d'âne *m*)
- *coltsfoot*

9 la tanaisie
- *tansy*

10 la petite centaurée (l'érythrée *f* centaurée)
- *centaury*

11 le plantain lancéolé
- *ribwort (ribwort plantain, ribgrass)*

12 la guimauve
- *marshmallow*

13 la bourdaine; *anal.:* le nerprun
- *alder buckthorn (alder dogwood)*

14 le ricin (le palma-Christi)
- *castor-oil plant (Palma Christi)*

15 l'œillette *f* (le pavot somnifère)
- *opium poppy*

16 le séné (la casse); *les folioles f séchées:* le séné
- *senna (cassia);* the dried leaflets: *senna leaves*

17 le quinquina
- *cinchona (chinchona)*

18 le camphrier
- *camphor tree (camphor laurel)*

19 l'aréquier *m*
- *betel palm (areca, areca palm)*

20 la noix d'arec *m* (l'arec *m*)
- *betel nut (areca nut)*

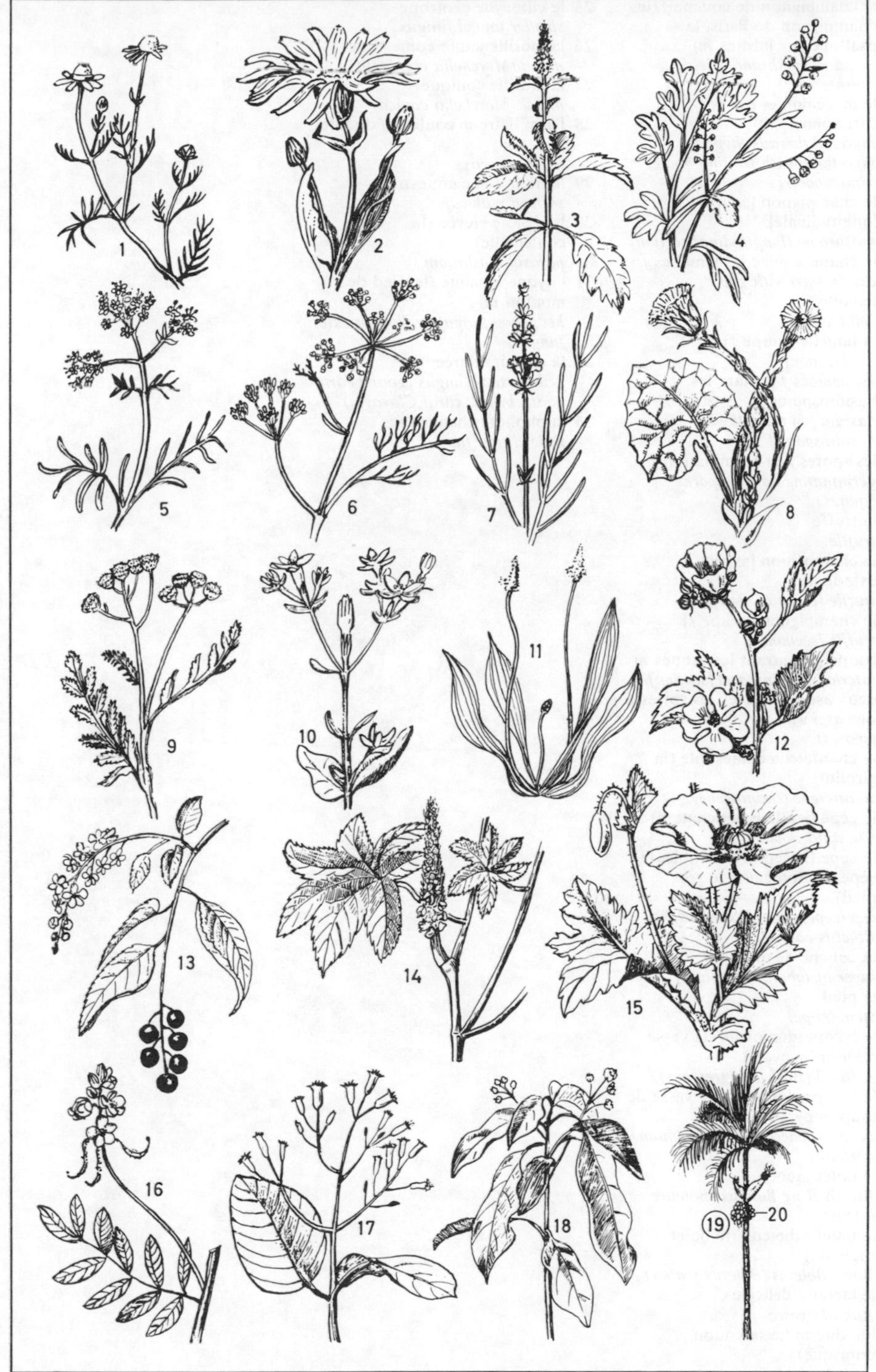
1
2
3
4
5
6
7
8
9
10
11
12
13
14
15
16
17
18
19
20

1 le champignon de couche *f* (le champignon de Paris, la psalliote des jardins *m*)
– *meadow mushroom (field mushroom)*
2 le mycélium et les carpophores *m*
– *mycelial threads (hyphae, mycelium) with fruiting bodies (mushrooms)*
3 le champignon [coupe *f* longitudinale]
– *mushroom [longitudinal section]*
4 le chapeau avec les lamelles *f*
– *cap (pileus) with gills*
5 le voile
– *veil (velum)*
6 la lamelle [coupe *f*]
– *gill [section]*
7 les basides *f* portant les basidiospores *f*
– *basidia [on the gill with basidiospores]*
8 les spores *f* en germination *f*
– *germinating basidiospores (spores)*
9 la truffe
– *truffle*
10 le champignon [aspect *m* extérieur]
– *truffle [external view]*
11 le champignon [coupe *f*]
– *truffle [section]*
12 coupe *f* montrant les asques *m*
– *interior showing asci [section]*
13 deux asques *m* avec les spires *f*
– *two asci with the ascospores (spores)*
14 la chanterelle comestible (la girolle)
– *chanterelle (chantarelle)*
15 le cèpe bai (le bolet châtain)
– *Chestnut Boletus*
16 le cèpe (le cèpe comestible, le cèpe de Bordeaux, le gros pied)
– *cep (cepe, squirrel's bread, Boletus edulis)*
17 la couche de tubes *m*
– *layer of tubes (hymenium)*
18 le pied
– *stem (stipe)*
19 le lycoperdon ovale (la vesse de loup *m* ovale)
– *puffball (Bovista nigrescens)*
20 le lycoperdon rond (la vesse de loup *m* perlée)
– *devil's tobacco pouch (common puffball)*
21 le bolet jaune
– *Brown Ring Boletus (Boletus luteus)*
22 le bolet raboteux (le bolet rugueux)
– *Birch Boletus (Boletus scaber)*
23 le lactaire délicieux
– *Russula vesca*
24 l'hydne *m* (le sarcodon imbriqué)
– *scaled prickle fungus*
25 le clitocybe géotrope
– *slender funnel fungus*
26 la morille jaune comestible
– *morel (Morchella esculenta)*
27 la morille conique
– *morel (Morchella conica)*
28 l'armillaire *m* couleur *f* de miel *m*
– *honey fungus*
29 le tricholome équestre
– *saffron milk cap*
30 la lépiote élevée (la coulemelle)
– *parasol mushroom*
31 l'hydne *m* sinué (le pied de mouton *m*)
– *hedgehog fungus (yellow prickle fungus)*
32 la clavaire dorée
– *yellow coral fungus (goatsbeard, goat's beard, coral Clavaria)*
33 la pholiote changeante
– *little cluster fungus*

1
2
3
4
5
6
7
8
9
10
11
12
13
14
15
16
17
18
19
20
21
22
23
24
25
26
27
28
29
30
31
32
33

382 Stimulants et épices tropicaux

1 le caféier
– *coffee tree (coffee plant)*
2 le rameau fructifère
– *fruiting branch*
3 le rameau florifère
– *flowering branch*
4 la fleur
– *flower*
5 le fruit avec les deux graines *f* [coupe *f* longitudinale]
– *fruit with two beans [longitudinal section]*
6 le grain de café *m*; *après traitement m:* le café
– *coffee bean;* when processed: *coffee*
7 le théier
– *tea plant (tea tree)*
8 le rameau florifère
– *flowering branch*
9 la feuille de thé *m*; *après traitement m:* le thé
– *tea leaf;* when processed: *tea*
10 le fruit (capsule *f*)
– *fruit*
11 le maté (*feuilles séchées:* le maté, le thé du Paraguay, le thé des jésuites)
– *maté shrub (maté, yerba maté, Paraguay tea)*
12 le rameau florifère avec les fleurs *f* hermaphrodites
– *flowering branch with androgynous (hermaphroditic, hermaphrodite) flowers*
13 la fleur mâle
– *male flower*
14 la fleur hermaphrodite
– *androgynous (hermaphroditic, hermaphrodite) flower*
15 le fruit (baie *f*)
– *fruit*
16 le cacaoyer (le cacaotier)
– *cacao tree (cacao)*
17 le rameau avec fleurs *f* et fruits *m* (cabosses *f*)
– *branch with flowers and fruits*
18 la fleur [coupe *f* longitudinale]
– *flower [longitudinal section]*
19 les graines *f* (fèves *f*) de cacao; *après traitement m:* le cacao, la poudre de cacao *m*
– *cacao beans (cocoa beans);* when processed: *cocoa, cocoa powder*
20 la graine [coupe *f* longitudinale]
– *seed [longitudinal section]*
21 la plantule
– *embryo*
22 le cannelier
– *cinnamon tree (cinnamon)*
23 le rameau florifère
– *flowering branch*
24 le fruit (baie *f*)
– *fruit*
25 l'écorce *f* du cannelier; *broyée:* la canelle
– *cinnamon bark;* when crushed: *cinnamon*
26 le giroflier
– *clove tree*
27 le rameau florifère
– *flowering branch*
28 le bouton floral; *séché:* le clou de girofle *m*
– *flower bud;* when dried: *clove*
29 la fleur
– *flower*
30 le muscadier
– *nutmeg tree*
31 le rameau florifère
– *flowering branch*
32 la fleur femelle [coupe *f* longitudinale]
– *female flower [longitudinal section]*
33 le fruit mûr
– *mature (ripe) fruit*
34 la fleur, une graine entourée d'un arille (macis *m*)
– *nutmeg with mace, a seed with laciniate aril*
35 la graine [coupe *f* transversale]; *séchée:* la noix de muscade *f*
– *seed [cross section];* when dried: *nutmeg*
36 le poivrier
– *pepper plant*
37 le rameau fructifère
– *fruiting branch*
38 l'inflorescence *f*
– *inflorescence*
39 le fruit (baie *f*) [coupe *f* longitudinale] avec la graine (grain *m* de poivre *m*); *moulu:* le poivre
– *fruit [longitudinal section] with seed (peppercorn);* when ground: *pepper*
40 le tabac de Virginie *f*
– *Virginia tobacco plant*
41 le rameau florifère
– *flowering shoot*
42 la fleur
– *flower*
43 la feuille de tabac *m*; *après traitement m:* le tabac
– *tobacco leaf;* when cured: *tobacco*
44 le fruit (la capsule) mûr
– *mature (ripe) fruit capsule*
45 la graine
– *seed*
46 le vanillier
– *vanilla plant*
47 le rameau florifère
– *flowering shoot*
48 le fruit (la capsule); *après traitement m:* la gousse de vanille
– *vanilla pod;* when cured: *stick of vanilla*
49 le pistachier
– *pistachio tree*
50 le rameau florifère avec fleurs *f* femelles
– *flowering branch with female flowers*
51 *le fruit:* une drupe; *la graine:* la pistache
– *drupe (pistachio, pistachio nut)*
52 la canne à sucre *m*
– *sugar cane*
53 la plante à la floraison
– *plant in bloom*
54 l'inflorescence *f*
– *panicle*
55 la fleur
– *flower*

1 2 3 4 5 6 7 8 9 10 11 12 13 14 15 16 17 18 19 20 21 22 23 24 25 26 27 28 29 30 31 32 33 34 35 36 37 38 39 40 41 42 43 44 45 46 47 48 49 50 51 52 53 54 55

1 le colza
– *rape (cole, coleseed)*
2 la feuille radicale de colza *m*
– *basal leaf*
3 la fleur de colza *m* [coupe *f* longitudinale]
– *flower [longitudinal section]*
4 la silique mûre
– *mature (ripe) siliqua (pod)*
5 la graine oléagineuse
– *oleiferous seed*
6 le lin
– *flax*
7 la tige fleurie
– *peduncle (pedicel, flower stalk)*
8 la capsule (le fruit)
– *seed vessel (boll)*
9 le chanvre
– *hemp*
10 la plante femelle en fruits *m*
– *fruiting female (pistillate) plant*
11 l'inflorescence *f* femelle
– *female inflorescence*
12 la fleur du chanvre
– *flower*
13 l'inflorescence *f* mâle
– *male inflorescence*
14 le fruit
– *fruit*
15 la graine (le chènevis)
– *seed*
16 le cotonnier
– *cotton*
17 la fleur du cotonnier
– *flower*
18 le fruit
– *fruit*
19 les poils *m* des graines *f* (le coton)
– *lint [cotton wool]*
20 le kapokier
– *silk-cotton tree (kapok tree, capoc tree, ceiba tree)*
21 le fruit
– *fruit*
22 le rameau florifère
– *flowering branch*
23 la graine
– *seed*
24 la graine [coupe *f* longitudinale]
– *seed [longitudinal section]*
25 le jute
– *jute*
26 le rameau florifère
– *flowering branch*
27 la fleur du jute
– *flower*
28 le fruit
– *fruit*
29 l'olivier *m*
– *olive tree (olive)*
30 le rameau florifère
– *flowering branch*
31 la fleur d'olivier *m*
– *flower*
32 le fruit
– *fruit*
33 l'hévéa *m* (l'arbre *m* à caoutchouc *m*)
– *rubber tree (rubber plant)*
34 le rameau florifère
– *fruiting branch*
35 la figue d'hévéa *m*
– *fig*
36 la fleur d'hévéa *m*
– *flower*
37 le palaquium [fournit la gutta-percha]
– *gutta-percha tree*
38 le rameau florifère
– *flowering branch*
39 la fleur du palaquium *m*
– *flower*
40 le fruit
– *fruit*
41 l'arachide *f*
– *peanut (ground nut, monkey nut)*
42 le rameau florifère
– *flowering shoot*
43 la racine fructifère
– *root with fruits*
44 le fruit d'arachide *f* [coupe *f* longitudinale]
– *nut (kernel) [longitudinal section]*
45 le sésame
– *sesame plant (simsim, benniseed)*
46 le rameau avec fleurs *f* et fruits *m*
– *flowers and fruiting branch*
47 la fleur de sésame *m* [coupe *f* longitudinale]
– *flower [longitudinal section]*
48 le cocotier
– *coconut palm (coconut tree, coco palm, cocoa palm)*
49 l'inflorescence *f*
– *inflorescence*
50 la fleur femelle
– *female flower*
51 la fleur mâle [coupe *f* longitudinale]
– *male flower [longitudinal section]*
52 le fruit du cocotier [coupe *f* longitudinale]
– *fruit [longitudinal section]*
53 la noix de coco *m*
– *coconut (cokernut)*
54 le palmier à huile *f*
– *oil palm*
55 le spadice mâle avec la fleur mâle
– *male spadix*
56 le régime de fruits *m*
– *infructescence with fruit*
57 la graine avec les pores *m* germinatifs
– *seed with micropyles (foramina) (foraminate seed)*
58 le sagoutier
– *sago palm*
59 le fruit de sagoutier *m*
– *fruit*
60 le bambou
– *bamboo stem (bamboo culm)*
61 le rameau feuillu
– *branch with leaves*
62 l'épi *m* de fleurs *f*
– *spike*
63 le chaume avec ses nœuds *m*
– *part of bamboo stem with joints*
64 le papyrus (le souchet à papier *m*)
– *papyrus plant (paper reed, paper rush)*
65 l'inflorescence *f*
– *umbel*
66 l'épillet *m*
– *spike*

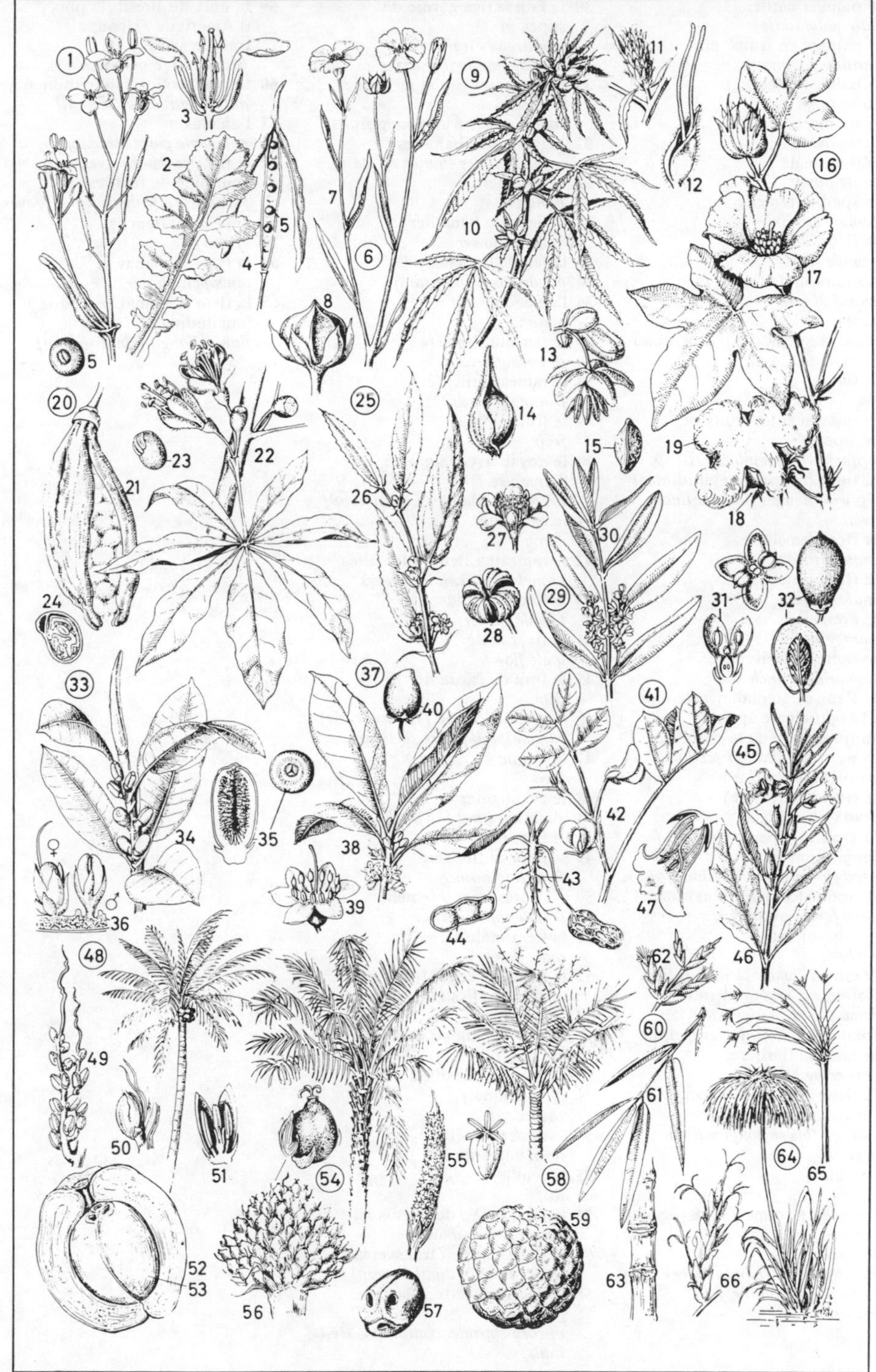
1
2
3
4
5
5
6
7
8
9
10
11
12
13
14
15
16
17
18
19
20
21
22
23
24
25
26
27
28
29
30
31
32
33
34
35
36
37
38
39
40
41
42
43
44
45
46
47
48
49
50
51
52
53
54
55
56
57
58
59
60
61
62
63
64
65
66
♀
♂

1 le palmier dattier
– *date palm (date)*
2 le palmier en fruits *m*
– *fruiting palm*
3 la palme (la feuille)
– *palm frond*
4 le spadice mâle
– *male spadix*
5 la fleur mâle
– *male flower*
6 le spadice femelle
– *female spadix*
7 la fleur femelle
– *female flower*
8 un rameau de dattes *f*
– *stand of fruit*
9 *date*
10 le noyau de la datte (la graine)
– *date kernel (seed)*
11 le figuier
– *fig*
12 le rameau et les fruits *m* composés
– *branch with pseudocarps*
13 la figue [coupe *f* longitudinale]
– *fig with flowers [longitudinal section]*
14 la fleur femelle
– *female flower*
15 la fleur mâle
– *male flower*
16 le grenadier
– *pomegranate*
17 le rameau florifère
– *flowering branch*
18 la fleur de grenadier *m* [coupe *f* longitudinale après suppression *f* de la corolle]
– *flower [longitudinal section, corolla removed]*
19 le fruit (la grenade)
– *fruit*
20 la graine (le pépin) [coupe *f* longitudinale]
– *seed [longitudinal section]*
21 la graine [coupe *f* transversale]
– *seed [cross section]*
22 l'embryon *m*
– *embryo*
23 le citron; *anal.:* la mandarine, l'orange *f*, le pamplemousse
– *lemon;* sim.: *tangerine (mandarin), orange, grapefruit*
24 le rameau florifère
– *flowering branch*
25 la fleur d'oranger *m* [coupe *f* longitudinale]
– *orange flower [longitudinal section]*
26 le fruit
– *fruit*
27 l'orange *f* [coupe *f* transversale]
– *orange [cross section]*
28 le bananier
– *banana plant (banana tree)*
29 la touffe de feuille *f*
– *crown*
30 la fausse tige garnie de stipes *m*
– *herbaceous stalk with overlapping leaf sheaths*
31 l'inflorescence *f* et les jeunes fruits *m*
– *inflorescence with young fruits*
32 le régime de bananes *f*
– *infructescence (bunch of fruit)*
33 la banane
– *banana*
34 la fleur du bananier
– *banana flower*
35 la feuille [schéma *m*]
– *banana leaf [diagram]*
36 l'amandier *m*
– *almond*
37 le rameau florifère
– *flowering branch*
38 le rameau fructifère
– *fruiting branch*
39 le fruit
– *fruit*
40 le noyau avec la graine [l'amande *f*]
– *drupe containing seed [almond]*
41 le caroubier
– *carob*
42 le rameau à fleurs *f* femelles
– *branch with female flowers*
43 la fleur femelle
– *female flower*
44 la fleur mâle
– *male flower*
45 le fruit de caroubier *m*
– *fruit*
46 la gousse [coupe *f* transversale]
– *siliqua (pod) [cross section]*
47 la graine
– *seed*
48 le châtaignier
– *sweet chestnut (Spanish chestnut)*
49 le rameau florifère
– *flowering branch*
50 l'inflorescence *f* femelle
– *female inflorescence*
51 la fleur mâle
– *male flower*
52 la bogue avec les fruits *m* (akènes *m*) [les marrons *m*, les châtaignes *f*]
– *cupule containing seeds (nuts, chestnuts)*
53 la noix du Brésil (la noix d'Amérique *f*)
– *Brazil nut*
54 le rameau florifère
– *flowering branch*
55 la feuille
– *leaf*
56 la fleur [vue *f* de dessus *m*]
– *flower [from above]*
57 la fleur [coupe *f* transversale]
– *flower [longitudinal section]*
58 la coque ouverte avec les graines *f*
– *opened capsule, containing seeds (nuts)*
59 la noix du Brésil (la noix d'Amérique *f*) [coupe *f* transversale]
– *Brazil nut [cross section]*
60 la noix [coupe *f* longitudinale]
– *nut [longitudinal section]*
61 l'ananas *m*
– *pineapple plant (pineapple)*
62 le fruit composé avec une couronne de feuilles *f*
– *pseudocarp with crown of leaves*
63 l'épi *m* de fleurs *f*
– *syncarp*
64 la fleur d'ananas *m*
– *pineapple flower*
65 la fleur d'ananas *m* [coupe *f* longitudinale]
– *flower [longitudinal section]*

Acknowledgements

ADB GmbH, Bestwig; AEG-Telefunken, Abteilung Werbung, Wolfenbüttel; Agfa-Gevaert AG, Presse-Abteilung, Leverkusen; Eduard Ahlborn GmbH, Hildesheim; AID, Land- und Hauswirtschaftlicher Auswertungs- und Informationsdienst e. V., Bonn-Bad Godesberg; Arbeitsausschuß der Waldarbeitsschulen beim Kuratorium für Waldarbeit und Forsttechnik, Bad Segeberg; Arnold & Richter KG, München; Atema AB, Härnösand (Schweden); Audi NSU Auto-Union AG, Presseabteilung, Ingolstadt; Bêché & Grohs GmbH, Hückeswagen/Rhld.; Big Dutchman (Deutschland) GmbH, Bad Mergentheim und Calveslage über Vechta; Biologische Bundesanstalt für Land- und Forstwirtschaft, Braunschweig; Black & Decker, Idstein/Ts.; Braun AG, Frankfurt am Main; Bolex GmbH, Ismaning; Maschinenfabrik zum Bruderhaus GmbH, Reutlingen; Bund Deutscher Radfahrer e. V., Gießen; Bundesanstalt für Arbeit, Nürnberg; Bundesanstalt für Wasserbau, Karlsruhe; Bundesbahndirektion Karlsruhe, Presse- u. Informationsdienst, Karlsruhe; Bundesinnungsverband des Deutschen Schuhmacher-Handwerks, Düsseldorf; Bundeslotsenkammer, Hamburg; Bundesverband Bekleidungsindustrie e. V., Köln; Bundesverband der Deutschen Gas- und Wasserwirtschaft e. V., Frankfurt am Main; Bundesverband der Deutschen Zementindustrie e. V., Köln; Bundesverband Glasindustrie e. V., Düsseldorf; Bundesverband Metall, Essen-Kray und Berlin; Burkhardt + Weber KG, Reutlingen; Busatis-Werke KG, Remscheid; Claas GmbH, Harsewinkel; Copygraph GmbH, Hannover; Dr. Irmgard Correll, Mannheim; Daimler-Benz AG, Presse-Abteilung, Stuttgart; Dalex-Werke Niepenberg & Co. GmbH, Wissen; Elisabeth Daub, Mannheim; John Deere Vertrieb Deutschland, Mannheim; Deutsche Bank AG, Filiale Mannheim, Mannheim; Deutsche Gesellschaft für das Badewesen e. V., Essen; Deutsche Gesellschaft für Schädlingsbekämpfung mbH, Frankfurt am Main; Deutsche Gesellschaft zur Rettung Schiffbrüchiger, Bremen; Deutsche Milchwirtschaft, Molkerei- und Käserei-Zeitung (Verlag Th. Mann), Gelsenkirchen-Buer; Deutsche Eislauf-Union e. V., München; Deutscher Amateur-Box-Verband e. V., Essen; Deutscher Bob- und Schlittensportverband e. V., Berchtesgaden; Deutscher Eissport-Verband e. V., München; Deutsche Reiterliche Vereinigung e. V., Abteilung Sport, Warendorf; Deutscher Fechter-Bund e. V., Bonn; Deutscher Fußball-Bund, Frankfurt am Main; Deutscher Handball-Bund, Dortmund; Deutscher Hockey-Bund e. V., Köln; Deutscher Leichtathletik Verband, Darmstadt; Deutscher Motorsport Verband e. V., Frankfurt am Main; Deutscher Schwimm-Verband e. V., München; Deutscher Turner-Bund, Würzburg; Deutscher Verein von Gas- und Wasserfachmännern e. V., Eschborn; Deutscher Wetterdienst, Zentralamt, Offenbach; DIN Deutsches Institut für Normung e. V., Köln; Deutsches Institut für Normung e. V., Fachnormenausschuß Theatertechnik, Frankfurt am Main; Deutsche Versuchs- und Prüf-Anstalt für Jagd- und Sportwaffen e. V., Altenbeken-Buke; Friedrich Dick GmbH, Esslingen; Dr. Maria Dose, Mannheim; Dual Gebrüder Steidinger, St. Georgen/Schwarzwald; Durst AG, Bozen (Italien); Gebrüder Eberhard, Pflug- und Landmaschinenfabrik, Ulm; Gabriele Echtermann, Hemsbach; Dipl.-Ing. W. Ehret GmbH, Emmendingen-Kollmarsreute; Eichbaum-Brauereien AG, Worms/Mannheim; ER-WE-PA, Maschinenfabrik und Eisengießerei GmbH, Erkrath bei Düsseldorf; Escher Wyss GmbH, Ravensburg; Eumuco Aktiengesellschaft für Maschinenbau, Leverkusen; Euro-Photo GmbH, Willich; European Honda Motor Trading GmbH, Offenbach; Fachgemeinschaft Feuerwehrfahrzeuge und -geräte, Verein Deutscher Maschinenbau-Anstalten e. V., Frankfurt am Main; Fachnormenausschuß Maschinenbau im Deutschen Normenausschuß DNA, Frankfurt am Main; Fachnormenausschuß Schmiedetechnik in DIN Deutsches Institut für Normung e. V., Hagen; Fachverband des Deutschen Tapetenhandels e. V., Köln; Fachverband der Polstermöbelindustrie e. V., Herford; Fachverband Rundfunk und Fernsehen im Zentralverband der Elektrotechnischen Industrie e. V., Frankfurt am Main; Fahr AG Maschinenfabrik, Gottmadingen; Fendt & Co., Agrartechnik, Marktoberndorf; Fichtel & Sachs AG, Schweinfurt; Karl Fischer, Pforzheim; Heinrich Gerd Fladt, Ludwigshafen am Rhein; Forschungsanstalt für Weinbau, Gartenbau, Getränketechnologie und Landespflege, Geisenheim am Rhein; Förderungsgemeinschaft des Deutschen Bäckerhandwerks e. V., Bad Honnef; Forschungsinstitut der Zementindustrie, Düsseldorf; Johanna Förster, Mannheim; Stadtverwaltung Frankfurt am Main, Straßen- und Brückenbauamt, Frankfurt am Main; Freier Verband Deutscher Zahnärzte e. V., Bonn-Bad Godesberg; Fuji Photo Film (Europa) GmbH, Düsseldorf; Gesamtverband der Deutschen Maschen-Industrie e. V., Gesamtmasche, Stuttgart; Gesamtverband des Deutschen Steinkohlenbergbaus, Essen; Gesamtverband der Textilindustrie in der BRD, Gesamttextil, e. V., Frankfurt am Main; Geschwister-Scholl-Gesamtschule, Mannheim-Vogelstang; Eduardo Gomez, Mannheim; Gossen GmbH, Erlangen; Rainer Götz, Hemsbach; Grapha GmbH, Ostfildern; Ines Groh, Mannheim; Heinrich Groos, Geflügelzuchtbedarf, Bad Mergentheim; A. Gruse, Fabrik für Landmaschinen, Großberkel; Hafen Hamburg, Informationsbüro, Hamburg; Hagedorn Landmaschinen GmbH, Warendorf/Westf.; kino-hähnel GmbH, Erftstadt Liblar; Dr. Adolf Hanle, Mannheim; Hauptverband Deutscher Filmtheater e. V., Hamburg; Dr.-Ing. Rudolf Hell GmbH, Kiel; W. Helwig Söhne KG, Ziegenhain; Geflügelfarm Hipp, Mannheim; Gebrüder Holder, Maschinenfabrik, Metzingen; Horten Aktiengesellschaft, Düsseldorf; IBM Deutschland GmbH, Zentrale Bildstelle, Stuttgart; Innenministerium Baden-Württemberg, Pressestelle, Stuttgart; Industrieverband Gewebe, Frankfurt am Main; Industrievereinigung Chemiefaser e. V., Frankfurt am Main; Instrumentation Marketing Corporation, Burbank (Calif.); ITT Schaub-Lorenz Vertriebsgesellschaft mbH, Pforzheim; M. Jakoby KG, Maschinenfabrik, Hetzerath/Mosel; Jenoptik Jena GmbH, Jena (DDR); Brigitte Karnath, Wiesbaden; Wilhelm Kaßbaum, Hockenheim; Van Katwijk's Industrieën N. V., Staalkat Div., Aalten (Holland); Kernforschungszentrum Karlsruhe; Leo Keskari, Offenbach; Dr. Rolf Kiesewetter, Mannheim; Ev. Kindergarten, Hohensachsen; Klambt-Druck GmbH, Offset-Abteilung, Speyer; Maschinenfabrik Franz Klein, Salzkotten; Dr. Klaus-Friedrich Klein, Mannheim; Klimsch + Co., Frankfurt am Main; Kodak AG, Stuttgart; Alfons Kordecki, Eckernförde; Heinrich Kordecki, Mannheim; Krefelder Milchhof GmbH, Krefeld; Dr. Dieter Krickeberg, Musikinstrumenten-Museum, Berlin; Bernard Krone GmbH, Spelle; Pelz-Kunze, Mannheim; Kuratorium für Technik und Bauwesen in der Landwirtschaft, Darmstein-Kranichstein; Landesanstalt für Pflanzenschutz, Stuttgart; Landesinnungsverband des Schuhmacherhandwerks Baden-Württemberg, Stuttgart; Landespolizeidirektion Karlsruhe, Karlsruhe; Landwirtschaftskammer, Hannover; Metzgerei Lebold, Mannheim; Ernst Leitz Wetzlar GmbH, Wetzlar; Louis Leitz, Stuttgart; Christa Leverkinck, Mannheim; Franziska Liebisch, Mannheim; Linhof GmbH, München; Franz-Karl Frhr. von Linden, Mannheim; Loewe Opta GmbH, Kronach; Beate Lüdicke, Mannheim; MAN AG, Werk Augsburg, Augsburg; Mannheimer Verkehrs-Aktiengesellschaft (MVG), Mannheim; Milchzentrale Mannheim-Heidelberg AG, Mannheim; Ing. W. Möhlenkamp, Melle; Adolf Mohr Maschinenfabrik, Hofheim; Mörtl Schleppergerätebau KG, Gemünden/Main; Hans-Heinrich Müller, Mannheim; Müller Martini AG, Zofingen; Gebr. Nubert KG, Spezialeinrichtungen, Schwäbisch Gmünd; Nürnberger Hercules-Werke GmbH, Nürnberg; Olympia Werke AG, Wilhelmshaven; Ludwig Pani Lichttechnik und Projektion, Wien (Österreich); Ulrich Papin, Mannheim; Pfalzmilch Nord GmbH, Ludwigshafen/Albisheim; Adolf Pfeiffer GmbH, Ludwigshafen am Rhein; Philips Pressestelle, Hamburg; Carl Platz GmbH Maschinenfabrik, Frankenthal/Pfalz; Posttechnisches Zentralamt, Darmstadt; Rabe-Werk Heinrich Clausing, Bad Essen; Rahdener Maschinenfabrik August Kolbus, Rahden; Rank Strand Electric, Wolfenbüttel; Stephan Reinhardt, Worms; Nic. Reisinger, Graphische Maschinen, Frankfurt-Rödelheim; Rena Büromaschinenfabrik GmbH & Co., Deisenhofen bei München; Werner Ring, Speyer; Ritter Filmgeräte GmbH, Mannheim; Röber Saatreiniger KG, Minden; Rollei Werke, Braunschweig; Margarete Rossner, Mannheim; Roto-Werke GmbH, Königslutter; Ruhrkohle Aktiengesellschaft, Essen; Papierfabrik Salach GmbH, Salach/Württ.; Dr. Karl Schaifers, Heidelberg; Oberarzt Dr. med. Hans-Jost Schaumann, Städt. Krankenanstalten, Mannheim; Schlachthof, Mannheim; Dr. Schmitz + Apelt, Industrieofenbau GmbH, Wuppertal; Maschinenfabrik Schmotzer GmbH, Bad Windsheim; Mälzerei Schragmalz, Berghausen b. Speyer; Schutzgemeinschaft Deutscher Wald, Bonn; Siemens AG, Bereich Meß- und Prozeßtechnik, Bild- und Tontechnik, Karlsruhe; Siemens AG, Dental-Depot, Mannheim; Siemens-Reiniger-Werke, Erlangen; Sinar AG Schaffhausen, Feuerthalen (Schweiz); Spitzenorganisation der Filmwirtschaft e. V., Wiesbaden; Stadtwerke–Verkehrsbetriebe, Mannheim; W. Steenbeck & Co., Hamburg; Streitkräfteamt, Dezernat Werbemittel, Bonn-Duisdorf; Bau- und Möbelschreinerei Fritz Ströbel, Mannheim; Gebrüder Sucker GmbH & Co. KG, Mönchengladbach; Gebrüder Sulzer AG, Winterthur (Schweiz); Dr. med. Alexander Tafel, Weinheim; Klaus Thome, Mannheim; Prof. Dr. med. Michael Trede, Städt. Krankenanstalten, Mannheim; Trepel AG, Wiesbaden; Verband der Deutschen Hochseefischereien e. V., Bremerhaven; Verband der Deutschen Schiffbauindustrie e. V., Hamburg; Verband der Korbwaren-, Korbmöbel- und Kinderwagenindustrie e. V., Coburg; Verband des Deutschen Drechslerhandwerks e. V., Nürnberg; Verband des Deutschen Faß- und Weinküfer-Handwerks, München; Verband Deutscher Papierfabriken e. V., Bonn; Verband Kommunaler Städtereinigungsbetriebe, Köln-Marienburg; Verband technischer Betriebe für Film und Fernsehen e. V., Berlin; Verein Deutscher Eisenhüttenleute, Düsseldorf; Verein Deutscher Zementwerke, Düsseldorf; Vereinigung Deutscher Elektrizitätswerke, VDEW, e. V., Frankfurt am Main; Verkehrsverein, Weinheim/Bergstr.; J. M. Voith GmbH, Heidenheim; Helmut Volland, Erlangen; Dr. med. Dieter Walter, Weinheim; W. E. G. Wirtschaftsverband Erdöl- und Erdgasgewinnung e. V., Hannover; Einrichtungshaus für die Gastronomie Jürgen Weiss & Co., Düsseldorf; Wella Aktiengesellschaft, Darmstadt; Optik-Welzer, Mannheim; Werbe & Graphik Team, Schriesheim; Wiegand Karlsruhe GmbH, Ettlingen; Dr. Klaus Wiemann, Gevelsburg; Wirtschaftsvereinigung Bergbau, Bonn; Wirtschaftsvereinigung Eisen- und Stahlindustrie, Düsseldorf; Wolf-Dietrich Wyrwas, Mannheim; Yashica Europe GmbH, Hamburg; Zechnersche Buchdruckerei, Speyer; Carl Zeiss, Oberkochen; Zentralverband der Deutschen Elektrohandwerke, ZVEH, Frankfurt am Main; Zentralverband der deutschen Seehafenbetriebe e. V., Hamburg; Zentralverband der elektrotechnischen Industrie e. V., Fachverband Phonotechnik, Hamburg; Zentralverband des Deutschen Bäckerhandwerks e. V., Bad Honnef; Zentralverband des Deutschen Friseurhandwerks, Köln; Zentralverband des Deutschen Handwerks ZDH, Pressestelle, Bonn; Zentralverband des Kürschnerhandwerks, Bad Homburg; Zentralverband für das Juwelier-, Gold- und Silberschmiedehandwerk der BRD, Ahlen; Zentralverband für Uhren, Schmuck und Zeitmeßtechnik, Bundesinnungsverband des Uhrmacherhandwerks, Königstein; Zentralverband Sanitär-, Heizungs- und Klimatechnik, Bonn; Erika Zöller, Edingen; Zündapp-Werke GmbH, München.

Index

Les nombres en caractères semi-gras situés derrière les entrées correspondent aux numéros des planches d'illustrations, ceux en caractères maigres, aux numéros des illustrations figurant sur les planches. Les homonymes de signification différente ou les mots dont l'illustration apparaît sur plusieurs planches sont distingués par des indications concernant les divers domaines lexicaux, imprimées en cursives.

La liste suivante contient les abréviations utilisées pour indiquer les différents domaines lexicaux dans la mesure où leur signification n'est pas évidente et sans équivoque.

Abatt.	Abattoir
Aéron:	Aéronautique
App. mén.:	Appareils ménagers
Astr.:	Astronomie
Astron.:	Astronautique
Athl.:	Athlétisme
Atm.:	L'atmosphère
Best. fabul.:	Bestiaire fabuleux
Bouch.:	Boucherie-charcuterie
Brass.:	Brasserie
Briq.:	Briqueterie
Carr.:	Carrière
Ch. de f.:	Chemin de fer
Centr.:	Centrale électrique
Comm.:	Commerce
Compos.:	Composition
Constr.:	Construction
Cord.:	Cordonnerie
Cost.:	Costume
Cout.:	Couture
Elect.:	Elections
Electr.:	Electricien
Electr. gd. public:	Electronique grand public
Ferbl.:	Ferblantier
Inst. fluv.:	Installations fluviaux
Mach. agric.:	Machines agricoles
Mar.:	Marine
Méc.:	Mécanique
Mil.:	Militaire
Min.:	Mine de charbon
Nett.:	Nettoiement
Opt.:	Opticien
Parc attr.:	Parc d'attractions
Pétr.:	Pétrole
Piscic.:	Pisciculture
Rest.:	Restaurant
Serr.:	Serrurier
Serv. eaux:	Services des eaux
Soud.:	Soudage
Sylvic.:	Sylviculture
Ust. cuis.:	Ustensiles de cuisine
Vitic.:	Viticulture
Vitr.:	Vitrerie
Voit. chev.:	Voiture à chevaux

A

~ automatique pour la batterie **74** 23
~ autonome **242** 30
~ électrique **155** 21
~ en acide sulfurique **156** 33
~ en air **147** 17
~ en eau *Méd.* **27** 46
~ en eau *Agric.* **74** 26
~ en gaz **139** 54
~ en gaz inerte **142** 34
~ en hydrogène **170** 15
~ en hydroxylamine **170** 21
~ en riblons **147** 65
~ en tissu **168** 9
~ externe **115** 79
~ par le cuvier de tête **173** 13
~ secteur **311** 11
~ sous pression **235** 54
alimenteur automatique **174** 40
alinéa **175** 15
alizé du nord-est **9** 48
~ du sud-est **9** 49
allée **272** 38
~ centrale *Jard.* **55** 42
~ centrale *Eglise* **330** 27
~ couverte **328** 16
~ de jardin **51** 14; **52** 23
~ de la source **274** 11
allège *Constr.* **118** 12; **120** 33
~ *Ports* **225** 8
~ de fenêtre **37** 24
~ et son remorqueur **225** 25
allégorie nationale **252** 12
Allemand en costume espagnol **355** 27
allemande **342** 11
aller **155** 10
alliage léger **235** 11
alliance *Joaill.* **36** 5
~ *Eglise* **332** 17
allonge *Abatt.* **94** 21
~ *Bouch.* **96** 55
~ de barre **284** 31
alluchon **91** 9
allumage, rupteur d' **242** 49
allume-cigares **191** 88
allumette **107** 22
allumeur **190** 9
~ de chalumeau **141** 27
allure *Cheval* **72** 39-44
~ *Sports* **285** 1-13
~ *Equitation* **289** 7
~ du largue **285** 11
~ du près **285** 10
~ du vent arrière **285** 1
~ du vent de travers **285** 11
~ portante **285** 12
alluvions, cône d' **13** 9
aloès **53** 13
alouette **361** 18-19
~ des champs **361** 18
~ lulu **361** 18
aloyau **95** 17
alpinisme **300** 1-57
alpiniste **300** 5
~ en second **300** 26
~ sur une paroi de glace **300** 15
Altaïr **3** 9
altération **320** 50-54
alternateur *Nucl.* **154** 15, 47, 53
~ *Energ.* **155** 46
~ *Moteur* **190** 76
~ triphasé *Centr.* **153** 1, 26
~ triphasé *Nucl.* **154** 34
altimètre **230** 4
altise des crucifères **80** 39
alto **323** 27
altocumulus **8** 15
~ à forme lenticulaire **287** 19
~ castellanus **8** 16
~ floccus **8** 16
altostratus **8** 8
~ precipitans **8** 9
alucite des céréales **81** 29
alvéole **77** 26-30
~ à couvain **77** 31
~ à miel operculé **77** 33
~ contenant l'œuf **77** 27
~ de bouchon fusible **127** 35
~ de mâle **77** 36
~ de stockage de pollen **77** 35
~ d'ouvrière **77** 34
~ operculé contenant la nymphe **77** 32
alysson **61** 17
amande *Ust. table* **45** 41
~ *Bot.* **59** 8; **384** 40
amandier **384** 36
amanite phalloïde **379** 11
~ tue-mouches **379** 10
amarante **60** 21
amaryllidac'ee **53** 8
amas d'étoiles ouvert **3** 26
amateur d'aquaplane **280** 14
amble **72** 40
ambon **330** 37
ambulance **270** 19
~ M 113 **255** 79
âme **121** 75
~ du rail **202** 3
aménagement des cours d'eau **216**
amenée de courant **142** 25
~ du gaz **350** 2
Amérique **14** 12-13
~ du Nord **14** 12
~ du Sud **14** 13
amiante *Pompiers* **270** 46
~ *Chim.* **350** 19
amibe **357** 1
amiral **365** 1
ammoniac *Cokerie* **156** 23
~ *Text.* **170** 24
amorçage de la bande **243** 14
amorce **86** 21; **87** 59
~ fulminante **306** 49
amortisseur *Moteur* **190** 26
~ *Autom.* **191** 26; **192** 69
~ à lame **186** 15
~ à ressort **214** 50
~ de chocs **207** 4
~ de d'emarrage **214** 50
~ de suspension **192** 76
~ d'oscillations **214** 55
~ électromagnétique **11** 40
~ principal d'atterrissage **6** 32
amour **272** 20
ampélopsis **374** 16
ampèremètre **230** 18
~ du chauffage **212** 18
amphibien **364** 20-26
amphithéâtre **262** 2
amphore **328** 10
ampli **317** 23
amplificateur *Electr. gd public* **241** 40
~ *Ciné* **312** 19
~ *Discoth.* **317** 23
~ de brillance **27** 16
~ de câble **237** 57
~ de son magnétique **311** 28
~ d'enregistrement **311** 11
~ d'enregistrement et de lecture du son magnétique **311** 5
ampoule a brome **349** 3
~ à décanter **349** 3
~ de verre **127** 57
amulette **354** 40
amygdale **19** 23
analyse, balance d' **349** 25
~ automatique du rythme de l'E.C.G. sur papier **25** 48
analyseur couleur **116** 36
~ d'E.C.G. de longue durée **25** 45
ananas *Comm.* **99** 85
~ *Bot.* **384** 61
anatidé **359** 15
anatomie humaine **16; 17; 18; 19; 20**
ancêtre **354** 17
anche **326** 18
~ double **323** 29
ancolie **60** 10
ancrage *Constr.* **120** 34
~ *Cours d'eau* **216** 13
~ de hauban **215** 48
~ du câble porteur *Ch. de f.* **214** 59
~ du câble porteur *Ponts* **215** 43
~ par câbles métalliques **155** 44
ancre *Mar.* **223** 52
~ *Mil.* **258** 5; **259** 81
~ *Sports* **286** 15-18
~, chaîne d' **223** 50
~ à jas *Mar.* **222** 79
~ à jas *Sports* **286** 15
~ à soc de charrue **286** 16
~ brevetée **258** 5
~ charrue **286** 16
~ CQR **286** 16
~ Danforth **286** 18
~ de bossoir **258** 39
~ de touée **258** 39
~ légère **286** 16-18
~ sans jas *Mar.* **222** 78
~ sans jas *Mil.* **258** 5
~ sans jas *Sports* **286** 17
andain **63** 23
andaineur rotatif **64** 40-45
Andromeda **3** 24
andouiller de fer **88** 7
~ d'œil **88** 6
~ moyen **88** 8
Andromède **3** 24
âne **73** 3
anémomètre *Météor.* **10** 28
~ *Aéron.* **230** 2
anémone **377** 1
~ de mer **369** 20
~ pulsatille **375** 5
~ sylvie **377** 1
anéroïde, baromètre **10** 4
~, capsule **10** 6
ânesse **73** 3
anesthésie du nerf **24** 53
ange, nid d' **28** 17
~, saut de l' **282** 12
angiographie, salle d' **27** 12
anglaise **342** 10
angle **346** 1-23, 8
~, côtés de l' **346** 7, 3
~, sommet de l' **346** 1
~, symbole d' **345** 23
~ adjacent **346** 14
~ aigu **346** 10
~ alterne externe **346** 10
~ au centre **346** 55
~ au niveau **87** 75
~ complémentaire **346** 15
~ correspondant **346** 12
~ de barre **224** 17
~ de chute **87** 78
~ de rotation **351** 33
~ d'élévation **87** 76
~ droit **346** 9, 32
~ extérieur **346** 26
~ inscrit **346** 56
~ intérieur **346** 26
~ obtus **346** 11
~ plat **346** 13, 9, 15
~ rentrant **346** 10, 11, 12
~ supplémentaire **346** 14
angles opposés par le sommet **346** 8, 13
angrois **137** 31
anguille **364** 17
anguillule de la betterave **80** 51
anhydrite limite **154** 67
animal d'embouche **94** 2
~ domestique **73**
~ en tissu **46** 13
~ gonflable **280** 33
~ héraldique **254** 15-16
~ multicellulaire **357** 13-39
~ mythologique **327** 1-61
~ naissant **254** 32
~ présenté **356** 5
anneau *Sylvic.* **84** 24
~ *Serr.* **140** 34
~ *Gymnast.* **296** 4
~ *Parc attr.* **308** 47
~ benzénique **242** 66
~ bridge **89** 58
~ d'attelage **64** 60
~ de caoutchouc **280** 32
~ de corps amovible **89** 56
~ de dentition **28** 12
~ de départ **89** 51
~ de laboratoire **350** 15
~ de levage du moteur **164** 37
~ de microprismes **115** 62, 63
~ de transmission **187** 72
~ dépoli **115** 53
~ du panier **292** 33
~ encastré dans la plate-bande porte-anneaux **164** 54
~ inférieur **234** 49
~ jambier **354** 38
~ nuptial **332** 17
~ porteur **147** 46
~ supérieur *Opt.* **113** 7
~ supérieur *Astron.* **234** 45
~ volant **280** 31
annélide **357** 20
annelier **108** 27
annexe *Mar.* **228** 17
~ *Eglise* **331** 13
annonce **342** 69
~ publicitaire **342** 56
annonceur **308** 8
anno-tennis **280** 31
annuaire **236** 12
~ du téléphone **237** 5
~ téléphonique **236** 10
annulaire **19** 67
annulation, touche d' **271** 4
anode de cuivre **178** 5
anophèle **81** 44
anorak *Cost.* **29** 62
~ *Alpin.* **300** 6
anoure **364** 23-26
anse **55** 27

~ facial groupé **295** 23
~ facial tendu **295** 21; **296** 28
~ fixe **215** 11
~ mobile **215** 12
~ tendu renversé **295** 27
~ transversal fléchi **296** 39
~ transversal tendu **296** 38
appuie-bras de gantier **271** 20
appui-joue **255** 30
appui-pied **186** 7
appui-tête **207** 67
~ ajustable **207** 47
~ amovible arrière **193** 8
~ amovible avant **193** 7
~ incorporé **193** 31
~ réglable **191** 33
A.P.U. **231** 33
aquaplane tiré par un canot à moteur **280** 13
aquarelle *Maison* **48** 5, 7
~ *Ecole* **260** 27
~ *Peintre* **338** 18
aquarium **356** 19
Aquarius **4** 63
aquatinte **340** 14-24
aqueduc **334** 53
~ de digue **216** 34
Aquila **3** 9
ara bleu et jaune **363** 2
arabe **341** 2
~, chiffre **344** 2
arabesque **314** 18
~ avec tenue arrière du pied **302** 10
arachide **383** 41
arachnide **358** 40-47
araignée **358** 44-46, 45
~, toile d' *Jeux enf.* **273** 46
~, toile d' *Zool.* **358** 47
~ domestique **81** 9
~ porte-croix **358** 45
arasement **122** 39
~ sanitaire **123** 4
araucaria **53** 16
arbalétrier *Constr.* **121** 55
~ *Mar.* **221** 118
arbitre **291** 62; **292** 65; **293** 19; **299** 16, 41
arbousier traînant **377** 15
arbre *Moulins* **91** 5
~ *Méc.* **143** 61
~ *Aéron.* **232** 56
~ *Parc* **272** 59
~ *Bot.* **370** 1
~ à cames *Moteur* **190** 11, 13, 14
~ à cames *Autom.* **192** 24
~ à cames en tête **190** 14
~ à caoutchouc **383** 33
~ à cardan *Agric.* **67** 16
~ à cardan *Ch. de f.* **211** 51; **212** 29, 83
~ à excentrique **166** 56
~ à feuilles caduques **371** 1-73
~ à palettes **178** 25
~ articulé *Agric.* **67** 16
~ articulé *Ch. de f.* **211** 51; **212** 29, 83
~ d'accouplement **148** 58
~ de commande de l'allumeur **190** 27
~ de démultiplication **232** 58
~ de frein **143** 99
~ de pignon intermédiaire **190** 57
~ de propulsion **232** 60
~ de renvoi **192** 37
~ de transmission *Mach. agric.* **64** 30
~ de transmission *Inst. fluv.* **217** 49
~ de transmission à cardan **64** 40, 48
~ de transmission aux vibreurs **201** 13
~ d'entraînement du volant batteur **163** 24
~ d'hélice **259** 59
~ en espalier **52** 1
~ en espalier détaché **52** 16
~ en espalier mural **52** 17
~ et montant d'entraînement de la plate-bande porte-anneaux **164** 42
~ fruitier à haute tige **52** 30
~ fruitier en espalier **52** 1, 2, 16, 17, 29
~ fruitier nain **52** 1, 2, 16, 17, 29
~ incliné par le vent **13** 43
~ intermédiaire **232** 57
~ porte-hélice *Mar.* **223** 65
~ porte-hélice *Mil.* **259** 59
~ primaire **192** 40
~ secondaire **192** 30
~ taillé **52** 1, 2, 16, 17, 29
~ taillé en boule **272** 12
~ taillé en cône **272** 13
~ taillé en cordon **52** 2
~ taillé en pyramide *Jard.* **52** 16
~ taillé en pyramide *Parc* **272** 19
arbrisseau **52** 9
~ de pose **86** 47
arbuste à baies **52** 19
~ à baies à haute tige **52** 11
arc *Best. fabul.* **327** 53
~ *Arts* **336** 19
~ *Ethnol.* **354** 32
~, lampe à **312** 39
~, tir à l' **305** 52-66
~ de cercle **346** 53
~ de cloître **336** 41
~ de compétition **305** 54
~ de réglage micrométrique à ressort **151** 66
~ de triomphe **334** 59
~ électrique **312** 42
~ elliptique **336** 29
~ en accolade **336** 36
~ en béton armé **215** 50
~ en doucine **336** 34
~ en plein cintre **336** 27
~ en tiers-point **336** 31
~ en treillis **215** 23, 25
~ épaulé **336** 33
~ infléchi **336** 35
~ outrepassé **336** 30
~ surbaissé **336** 5, 28
~ tréflé **336** 32
~ trilobé **336** 32
~ triomphal **334** 71
~ Tudor **336** 37
arcature aveugle **335** 10
~ de baies **335** 8
arcatures, frise d' **335** 9
arc-boutant **335** 28
arceau **193** 13
~ antérieur **303** 8
~ chromé **188** 60
~ de croquet **292** 78
~ de la plaque de couche **305** 46
~ de protection **188** 18
~ de réglage **106** 17
~ de sécurité *Mach.agric.* **65** 21
~ de sécurité *Sylvic.* **85** 36
~ dorsal des segments **358** 31
~ en espalier **52** 12
~ postérieur **303** 9
arc-en-ciel **7** 4
~, couleurs de l' **343** 14
archaster **369** 17
arche de glacier **12** 51
~ de pont **215** 20
archer **305** 53
archet **323** 12
~ de pantographe **205** 36
~ de scie **150** 17
~ de viole **322** 24
~ de violon **323** 12
architecte-chef-décorateur **310** 43
architecture gothique **335** 27-35
architrave **334** 18
archiviste **248** 6
archivolte **335** 25
arçon **296** 6
~ arrière **71** 39
~ avant **71** 38
arcosolium **331** 60
arcs **336** 19-37
Arctique **14** 21
Arcturus **3** 30
ardillon **89** 80
ardoise *Constr.* **122** 85
~ *Marché puces* **309** 72
~ cornière **122** 77
~ d'angle **122** 77
~ de batellement **122** 76
~ de chéneau **122** 76
~ de pignon **122** 80
~ débordeuse **122** 76
~ faîtière **122** 79
arec **380** 20
arène *Cirque* **307** 21
~ *Taurom.* **319** 5, 9
aréole **16** 29
arécquier **380** 19
arête *Agric.* **68** 12
~ *Alpin.* **300** 21
~ *Math.* **347** 32
~ calicinale **375** 33
~ coupante **247** 30
~ dorsale **235** 9
~ glaciaire **300** 21
arêtes, voûte d' **336** 42
arêtier **121** 12, 62
argent *Argent* **252**
~ *Hérald.* **254** 25
~ liquide **246** 27
argile **160** 1
~ à modeler **339** 7, 31
~ brute **159** 2
Argo **3** 45
Aries **4** 53
arille **382** 34
aristoloche **376** 22
arithmétique **344** 1-26; **345** 1-24
~ supérieure **345** 1-10
Arlequin **306** 35
armature *Constr.* **119** 68; **123** 37
~ *Sculpteur* **339** 22
arme à feu individuelle **255** 1-39
~ à feu portative **87** 2
~ à plusieurs coups **87** 2
~ de chasse **87**
~ de jet **352** 39
~ de taille et d'estoc **294** 34
~ d'escrime **294** 34-45
~ d'estoc **294** 11, 36, 37
~ d'intervention **264** 19
~ du chef de l'Etat en RFA **253** 14
~ en joue **305** 73
~ libre de petit calibre **305** 44
~ sportive **87** 1-40
~ standard de petit calibre **305** 43
armé **305** 52
armée de l'air **256; 257**
~ de terre **255** 1-98
armement **258** 29-37
~ de l'armée de terre **255** 1-98
~ lourd **255** 40-95
arménienne **341** 3
armes, maître d' **294** 1
~ de l'armée de terre **255** 1-98
armillaire couleur de miel **381** 28
armoire à chaussures fourre-tout **41** 8
~ à pharmacie **22** 35
~ à provisions **207** 27
~ à vaisselle **39** 8; **44** 26
~ accolée **177** 69
~ basse **246** 20
~ d'appareils **212** 35
~ de chambre à coucher **43** 1
~ de chambre d'enfant **47** 21
~ de classement **248** 12
~ de classement d'archives **248** 2
~ de commande **93** 20
~ de commande et de la turbine à gaz **209** 16
~ de commutation **237** 25
~ de rangement *Bureau* **248** 12
~ de rangement *Hôtel* **267** 29
~ de toilette à miroirs **49** 31
~ des convertisseurs statiques de fréquence **212** 40
~ d'incubation et d'éclosion **74** 28
~ d'outils pour le bricolage **134** 1-34
~ fichier **262** 22
~ haute **43** 1
~ murale **22** 40
armoise absinthe **380** 4
~ mutelline **378** 6
armure *Text.* **171** 1-29
~ *Chevalerie* **329** 38
~, rapport d' **171** 12
~ cheviotte **171** 11
~ de cheval **329** 83-88
~ drap anglais **171** 11
~ du chevalier **329** 38-65
~ du tricot longitudinal **171** 26
~ en feuillard **153** 50
~ en fils d'acier **153** 50
~ «natté» **171** 11
~ «nid d'abeille» **171** 29
~ ouatinée **353** 38
~ textile **171**
~ «toile» **171** 1, 4, 24
arnica **380** 2
arole **372** 29
arôme pour potages **98** 30
arpège **321** 22
arrachage **163** 71
arraché **299** 1
arrache-clous **120** 75

attaque à la tête **294** 23
~ au centre **277** 2
~ de coulée **148** 21
~ d'escrime **294** 7
~ en bas **277** 4
~ en haut **277** 3
~ forte **321** 41
attelage *Voit. chev.* **186** 1-54
~ *Ch. de f.* **210** 2
~, étrier d' **208** 17
~, tendeur d' **208** 18
~ à deux chevaux **186** 36
~ à trois points **65** 72
~ à un cheval **186** 18, 29
~ de bœufs **63** 16
~ de rennes **353** 15
~ de voitures **208** 16
~ en flèche **186** 50
~ en tandem **186** 50
~ herse-émotteuse **65** 87
~ russe à trois chevaux **186** 45
attelle **21** 10, 12
attente, hall d' **233** 28
~, salle d' **233** 18
atténuateur **311** 19
atterrissage, patin d' *Aéron.* **232** 15
~, patin d' *Mil.* **256** 21
~, phare d' *Aéron.* **230** 49
~, phare d' *Mil.* **257** 37
~, ski d' **256** 21
~, train d' *Aéron.* **230** 41; **232** 10
~, train d' *Astron.* **235** 30, 31
~, train d' *Mil.* **256** 15
~, volet d' *Aéron.* **230** 53
~, volet d' *Sports* **288** 29
~ avant, train d' **288** 34
~ principal, train d' *Mil.* **256** 26
~ principal, train d' *Sports* **288** 33
~ principal repliable, train d' **257** 40
~ repliable, train d' **257** 3
~ sur la Lune **6**
atterrisseur avant **288** 34
~ principal *Mil.* **256** 26
~ principal *Sports* **288** 33
~ principal à commande hydraulique **235** 31
attique *Maison* **37** 83
~ *Arts* **334** 60
attisoir **137** 4
attitude **314** 17
~ de base **295** 1
attrape **306** 56
attrape-marteau **325** 27
aube courbée **91** 38
~ droite **91** 40
~ rectiligne **91** 40
aubépine **374** 30
auberge **266** 1-29
aubier *Constr.* **120** 85
~ *Bot.* **370** 12
aubrietia **51** 7
audiotypiste **248** 33
audio-visuel **243**
auditorium *Univ.* **262** 2
~ *Ciné* **310** 14
auge à mortier **118** 20, 84
~ des rouleaux de nappe **163** 15
~ d'incubation **89** 18
~ extérieure **62** 9
auget *Moulins* **91** 36
~ *Constr.* **122** 22
~ à plâtre **134** 18
aulne **371** 30
aulos **322** 3
aumône **330** 60
aureus **252** 3
auriculaire **19** 68
Auriga **3** 27
aurore **365** 3
~ boréale **7** 30
aussière *Pêche* **90** 4
~ *Inst. fluv.* **217** 23
Australie **14** 17
Australien aborigène **352** 37
australopithèque **261** 20
autel *Eglise* **330** 33
~ *Arts* **334** 48, 69
~, niche d' **334** 64
auto **191** 1-56; **195** 34
~ tamponneuse **308** 63
auto-assurance **300** 10
autobus *Autom.* **194**
~ *Aéroport* **233** 35
~ à impériale **194** 36
autocar **194** 17
autoclave **170** 12
autocollant d'hôtel **205** 9
automate **273** 36
automatisme du diaphragme **117** 20
automobile **191** 1-56; **192; 193; 195** 34
automobiliste utilisant la pompe à essence self-service **196** 8
automotrice à accumulateurs **211** 55
~ à adhérence **214** 1
~ à plate-forme mobile **211** 41
~ d'entretien **211** 44-54
~ d'entretien des caténaires **211** 41
~ d'extrémité **211** 61
~ Diesel **208** 13; **211** 41
~ intermédiaire **211** 62
~ pour trafic à courte distance **208** 13
~ urbaine et interurbaine à six essieux **197** 13
autoradio **191** 90
autorail **208** 13
~ articulé à 12 essieux du réseau interurbain **197** 1
~ urbain et interurbain à six essieux **197** 13
autoroute **201** 1-24
~ avec rampe d'accès **15** 16
~ urbaine **225** 54
auto-sauvetage **21** 33
autour des palombes **362** 10
Autriche **252** 13
autruche **359** 2
~, plumes d' **254** 30
auvent **37** 67
~ de caravane **278** 57
~ ouvert **278** 28
auxiliaire féminine de police **264** 37
avalanche de fond **304** 1
~ de neige **304** 1
~ de poudreuse **304** 1
avaleur de sabres **308** 26
avance, pas d' **149** 9
avancée **278** 37
avancement, cylindre d' **85** 19
avant *Mar.* **222** 74-79
~ *Sports* **282** 50
~ de l'autorail **197** 3
avant-bassin **162** 5
avant-bec **215** 56
avant-bras *Anat.* **16** 46
~ *Cheval* **72** 21
avant-corps **335** 43
avant-creuset basculant **148** 5
avant-port **217** 26
avant-scène **316** 25
avant-toit *Maison* **37** 9
~ *Constr.* **121** 3
~ à chevrons **37** 9
avant-train **65** 14-19
avers **252** 8
averse **8** 19; **9** 37
avertissement **291** 63
avertisseur **188** 53
~ optique **203** 26-29
~ sonore *Autom.* **191** 60
~ sonore *Ch. de f.* **211** 9
~ sonore *Pompiers* **270** 7
aviculture **74**
avion **229; 230; 231; 232**
~ à aile basse **229** 5
~ à aile demi-surélevée **229** 4
~ à aile haute **229** 3
~ à décollage et atterrissage verticaux courts **232** 26-32
~ à hélice **231** 1-6
~ à réaction **231** 7-33
~ à réaction d'entraînement franco-allemand **257** 1-41
~ à trois plans **229** 6
~ aile basse à dièdre **229** 14
~ amphibie **232** 8
~ bipoutre **229** 34
~ cargo **256** 14
~ convertible **232** 31
~ de combat polyvalent **256** 8
~ de modèle réduit **273** 38
~ de transport **256** 14
~ de transport et de liaison ADAC **256** 24
~ en position de chargement **233** 21
~ miniature **273** 38
~ porteur **256** 14
~ remorqueur **287** 2
~ stratosphérique **7** 15
aviron *Mar.* **218** 5
~ *Sports* **283** 14, 17, 35-38
~ de gouverne **218** 6
~ de queue **218** 6
avoine **68** 27
~ élevée **69** 22
axe *Dess.* **151** 30
~ *Bicycl.* **187** 61, 76
~, grand **347** 23
~, petit **347** 24
~ de coordonnées **347** 2-3
~ de fourchette **192** 41
~ de la parabole **347** 17
~ de lacet **230** 70
~ de l'âme **87** 38
~ de l'anticlinal **12** 17
~ de l'assaut **294** 9
~ de l'écliptique **4** 22
~ de pédale **187** 81
~ de piston **192** 26
~ de prise de force **63** 21
~ de réglage **226** 51
~ de roulis **230** 72
~ de suspension **214** 72
~ de symétrie *Math.* **346** 25
~ de symétrie *Cristallogr.* **351** 4
~ de tangage **230** 68
~ débiteur **312** 36
~ des abscisses **347** 2
~ des déclinaisons **113** 5, 17
~ des ordonnées **347** 3
~ des x **347** 2
~ des y **347** 3
~ du bateau **285** 5
~ du cône **372** 3
~ du monde *Astr.* **4** 10
~ du monde *Opt.* **113** 18
~ horaire *Astr.* **5** 7, 8
~ horaire *Opt.* **113** 18
~ instantané de rotation **4** 25
~ moyen de rotation **4** 27
~ récepteur à friction **312** 37
~ repère de piquetage **118** 70
~ synclinal **12** 19
axonge **96** 5
azalée **53** 12
azur **254** 28

B

babine **70** 26
bâbord **286** 12
~, marque de **224** 95
~, perche de **224** 100
babouin **368** 13
bac *Cartogr.* **15** 12
~ *Cours d'eau* **216** 11
~ *Ports* **225** 11
~ à câble **216**
~ à cartes perforées **244** 13
~ à chaîne **216** 1
~ à chutes **141** 15
~ à ciment **146** 15
~ à colle **184** 9; **185** 32
~ à copeaux et à huile **149** 44
~ à cops **165** 16
~ à correspondance **248** 41
~ à eau *Jard.* **55** 29
~ à eau *Soud.* **141** 17
~ à éponge **260** 41
~ à fleurs **268** 15
~ à gaffe **216** 15
~ à herbe **56** 29
~ à légumes **39** 4
~ à mortier **118** 39
~ à moteur **216** 6
~ à plantes **248** 13
~ à produits lessiviels **50** 27
~ à sable **273** 64
~ à tissu **167** 10
~ à traille **216** 1
~ à voitures *Cartogr.* **15** 47
~ à voitures *Cours d'eau* **216** 10
~ ancré **216** 10
~ automoteur **216** 1
~ d'alevinage **89** 18
~ d'appel **298** 35
~ d'aspiration de vapeur **103** 25
~ de distribution de béton **201** 6
~ de passagers **216** 1
~ de teinture en matière thermoplastique **130** 15
~ de trempage **136** 13
~ de trempe **137** 8
~ d'éclosion **89** 15
~ pour piétons **15** 60
~ récupérateur **56** 29
~ refroidisseur **93** 5
~ volant **216** 10
bâche *Mil.* **255** 98
~ *Gymnast.* **297** 11
~ de mouillage **165** 44

~ élastique **32** 33
~ entraîneuse en caoutchouc **249** 40
~ fluorescente **240** 18
~ jambière **289** 15
~ latérale **291** 25
~ magnétique *Poste* **237** 63
~ magnétique *Radiodiff.* **238** 5
~ magnétique *Electr. gd public* **241** 12, 58
~ magnétique *Informat.* **244** 2
~ magnétique de 1/2 pouce **243** 5
~ magnétique d'enregistrement des impulsions de l'E.C.G. analysé **25** 46
~ magnétique 1/4 de pouce **243** 4
~ matérialisée **268** 72
~ mobile **180** 26
~ ornementale **334** 38
~ perforée *Photocomp.* **176** 6, 8, 12
~ perforée *Poste* **237** 32, 62
~ perforée télex **237** 68
~ prétexte **355** 14
~ stop **268** 50
~ transporteuse *Agric.* **74** 35
~ transporteuse *Constr.* **118** 77
~ transporteuse *Text.* **169** 32
~ transporteuse *Imprim.* **182** 30
~ transporteuse *Ports* **225** 51
~ transporteuse d'alimentation **74** 25
~ transporteuse d'alimentation en pâte chimique ou mécanique **172** 79
~ transporteuse des déjections **74** 27
~ transporteuse des œufs **74** 22
~ 1/4 de pouce **241** 58
bandeau **335** 52
~ de poignet **296** 64
banderille **319** 22
banderillero **319** 21
banderole «Aperçu» **253** 29
~ électorale **263** 12
bandonéon **324** 36
bandonika **324** 36
banjo **324** 29
bannière *Drapeaux* **253** 12
~ *Eglise* **331** 44
~ d'église **331** 44
~ du soleil levant **253** 20
~ étoilée **253** 18
banque *Banque* **250**
~ *Roulette* **275** 11
~, billet de **252** 29-39
~, employé de *Banque* **250** 5
~, employé de *Bourse* **251** 7
~ de données **248** 43
~ d'émission **252** 30
banquette *Géogr.* **13** 64
~ *Cours d'eau* **216** 38
~ *Camping* **278** 17
~ *Equitation* **289** 8
~ *Cirque* **307** 22
~ à bagages **204** 43
~ arrière rabattable **193** 22
~ circulaire **281** 38
~ d'angle **265** 10
~ de coin **266** 38
~ double **197** 19
~ du poêle **266** 36
~ rembourrée **208** 25
baptême **332** 1
~, eau du **332** 12
~, robe de **332** 8
~, voile de **332** 9
baptistère **332** 2
baquet à lessive **309** 69
~ à plante **55** 48
~ à vendange **78** 10
~ d'eau pour l'humidification des galets du four **281** 26
~ en bois **91** 27
bar *Maison* **42** 20
~ *Hôtel* **267** 54
~ *Discoth.* **317** 1
~ *Boîte nuit* **318** 13
~, tabouret de **267** 53
~ de l'hôtel **267** 44-46, 51
baraque de brocanteurs **308** 60
~ de chantier **118** 48; **119** 44
~ de forain **308** 24
~ de loterie **308** 44
~ foraine **308** 6
baratte industrielle en continu **76** 33
barbacane **329** 32
barbe *Barbes, coiffures* **34**
~ *Chasse* **88** 73
~ carrée **34** 16
~ de bouc **377** 5
~ de trois jours **34** 23
~ du dard **77** 10
~ en pointe **34** 10
~ longue **34** 15
barbecue **278** 47
barbiche **73** 15
barbillon *Zool.* **73** 24
~ *Piscic.* **89** 80
~ *Zool.* **364** 13
barboteur **261** 32
~ à eau basse pression **141** 8
barboteuse **29** 21
barbotin **255** 50
barbotine **161** 15
barbute **329** 61
barde de croupe **329** 88
~ de poitrail **329** 85
bardière **95** 40
bar-express **265** 1-26
barge **225** 8
~ de transport de vrac **226** 35
~ sans moteur **221** 94
barillet *Horlog.* **110** 38
~ *Mach.-out.* **149** 64
~ d'objectif **115** 3
barmaid *Hôtel* **267** 63
~ *Discoth.* **317** 2
~ *Boîte nuit* **318** 14
barman *Rest.* **266** 8
~ *Hôtel* **267** 62
barographe **10** 4
baromètre à liquide **10** 1
~ à mercure **10** 1
~ à siphon **10** 1
~ anéroïde **10** 4
baroque, art **336** 1-8
~, église **336** 1
barque de Nydam **218** 1-6
~ de pêche **89** 27
~ de promenade **283** 1
~ traversière **216** 15
barrage *Cartogr.* **15** 66
~ *Sports* **283** 60
~ à clapets **217** 65-72
~ à vannes **217** 73-80
~ de rivière **216** 49
~ de séparation **155** 38
~ de vallée **217** 57-64
~ en béton **217** 58
~ mobile à cylindres **217** 65-72
~ réservoir **217** 65-72
barrage-écluse **217** 65-72
barrage-réservoir **217** 39, 57
barrage-vannes **217** 73-80
barre *Agric.* **75** 5
~ *Navig.* **224** 15
~ *Sports* **284** 32; **286** 24
~ *Equitation* **289** 8
~ *Gymnast.* **296** 3, 8
~ *Athl.* **298** 14, 34
~ *Mus.* **320** 6
~, angle de **224** 17
~, homme de **218** 2
~ à aiguille **100** 23
~ à battre les tapis **37** 51
~ à disques **299** 3
~ à pinces **180** 56
~ à trous **64** 47
~ absorbante **154** 24
~ antidévers **192** 71
~ conductrice *Atome* **2** 42
~ conductrice *Centr.* **152** 29
~ conductrice inférieure **65** 28
~ conductrice supérieure **65** 27
~ d'accouplement **65** 47
~ d'aiguilles **167** 28
~ d'anode **178** 5
~ d'appui pour les pieds **267** 52
~ d'attelage *Agric.* **63** 20
~ d'attelage *Mach. agric.* **64** 61
~ de chariotage **149** 33
~ de commande **154** 24
~ de coulée **148** 9
~ de coupe **64** 3
~ de fixation **75** 16
~ de fixation de la plaque **179** 8
~ de flèche *Mar.* **223** 37
~ de flèche *Sports* **284** 13
~ de flèche tribord **286** 9
~ de forte **325** 23
~ de mesure **320** 42
~ de mise bas **75** 43
~ de pilotage **287** 46
~ de plongée **259** 95
~ de plongée avant **259** 96
~ de protection **84** 8
~ de protection avec repose-pieds **301** 58
~ de réglage **106** 17
~ de repos des marteaux **325** 15, 26
~ de repos d'étouffoir **325** 39
~ de torsion **192** 70
~ de traction *Agric.* **62** 20
~ de traction *Mach. agric.* **65** 18
~ d'écoute **284** 27
~ d'espacement **249** 2
~ d'évacuation du fumier **75** 21
~ d'inversion **149** 34
~ du gouvernail **218** 13
~ fixe *Jeux enf.* **273** 32
~ fixe *Gymnast.* **296** 7
~ horizontale **292** 70
~ inférieure **297** 4
~ porte-moules **178** 6
~ presse-papier avec guide-papier mobiles **249** 17
~ stabilisatrice **192** 71
~ transversale **291** 36
~ verticale **215** 36
barreau *Maison* **38** 17
~ *Constr.* **123** 51
~ *Parc* **272** 34
barres asymétriques **297** 3
~ de grand perroquet **219** 53
~ de petit perroquet **219** 51
~ parallèles **296** 2
barrette **105** 11
~ avec brillant **36** 18
~ de dominos **127** 29
~ de plots de raccordement thermoplastiques **127** 29
~ flash **114** 75
barreur *Navig.* **224** 16
~ *Sports* **283** 9, 10, 11, 18
barrière *Comm.* **99** 5
~ *Ch. de f.* **202** 40
~ *Rest.* **266** 72
~ *Equitation* **289** 8
~ à poste d'appel **202** 47
~ d'arrêt **259** 17
barrique **130** 5
barrot de pont **222** 57
barysphère **11** 5
bas **318** 32
~ de jambe **33** 41
~ de ligne **89** 78
~ fourneau électrique Siemens **147** 51-54
~ résille **306** 10
bas-côté **334** 63; **335** 2
bascule *Text.* **170** 29
~ *Jeux enf.* **273** 35
~ *Cirque* **307** 36
~ *Mus.* **325** 32
~ à wagon **206** 41
~ aux barres asymétriques **297** 28
~ dorsale aux anneaux **296** 56
~ mi-renversée aux barres parallèles **296** 58
~ pour les colis de détail **206** 31
basculeur **147** 44, 59
base *Reliure* **183** 25
~ *Math.* **345** 1, 6; **346** 27; **347** 35, 39
~, attitude de **295** 1
~ circulaire **334** 30
~ cylindrique **178** 10
~ du batteur **292** 53
~ du cadre **187** 19
~ en forme d'étoile **136** 19
base-ball **292** 40-69
bas-flanc **75** 38
baside **381** 7
basidiospore **381** 7
basilic *Best. fabul.* **327** 34
~ *Zool.* **364** 30
basilique **334** 61
basket **292** 28
basket-ball **292** 28
bas-mât **219** 2, 5, 8
basque **33** 14
bas-relief *Arts* **333** 20
~ *Sculpteur* **339** 33
~ en tuiles vernissées **333** 20
basse **323** 23
~ de viole **322** 23
basse-cour **73** 18-36
basses côtes **95** 19
basset allemand **70** 39
bassin *Anat.* **17** 18-21

~ *Jard.* **51** 16
~ *Inst. fluv.* **217** 20, 33
~ *Parc* **272** 24
~ à remous d'eau chaude **281** 31, 35
~ d'affinage **162** 4
~ d'amortissement **217** 61
~ de carénage **222** 31-33
~ de coulée **147** 34
~ de fusion **162** 3, 14
~ de la roulette **275** 29
~ de plein air **282** 1-32
~ de plongée **282** 11
~ de radoub **222** 31-33
~ de repos **217** 61
~ de restitution **217** 61
~ de retenue **217** 39, 57
~ d'eau froide **281** 30
~ d'élevage **89** 6
~ d'élevage de truites **89** 6
~ d'évier **261** 6
~ d'inondation **216** 42
~ en béton pour scènes nautiques **310** 11
~ versant **12** 24
bassine à friture **97** 66
bassinet **20** 31
basson **323** 28
basstuba **323** 44
bastingage **259** 18
bastion **329** 16
bas-ventre **16** 37
bât **73** 4
bataille de boules de neige **304** 14
batardeau de moulin **91** 42
bateau à moteur *Cours d'eau* **216** 7
~ à moteur *Sports* **286** 1-5
~ à voile **278** 12
~ de pêche *Pêche* **90** 24
~ de pêche *Mar.* **221** 49
~ de sauvetage **146** 19
~ du jury **285** 15
~ gonflable **278** 14
bateau-balançoire **308** 41
~ renversable **308** 42
bateau-citerne **225** 13
bateau-feu *Mar.* **221** 47
~ *Navig.* **224** 81
bateau-jury **285** 15
bateau-phare **15** 13
bateau-pilote **221** 95
bateau-pompe **270** 65
bateleur **308** 25-28
batellement **122** 49
batholite **11** 29
bathymètre **279** 15
bâti *Menuis.* **133** 50
~ *Vann.* **136** 22
~ *Text.* **167** 33; **168** 15, 54
~ *Photogr.* **177** 40
~ d'arrosage **62** 28
~ de dérouleur **165** 41
~ de la quille du vaisseau spatial **235** 7
~ de pédale **187** 83
~ de pilon **139** 16
~ de poussée **234** 21
~ de poussée inférieur **235** 6
~ de poussée supérieur **235** 5
~ de scie **138** 25
~ d'ensouple de l'ourdissoir **165** 27
~ du métier à tisser **166** 24
~ en C **26** 19; **27** 17
~ en col de cygne *Méd.* **27** 17
~ en col de cygne *Compos.* **175** 50
~ fixe **65** 90
~ moteur **234** 21
bâtiment à péristyle **336** 15
~ à plan centré **334** 55
~ à portique **336** 15
~ administratif *Min.* **144** 18
~ administratif *Inst. fluv.* **217** 24
~ administratif *Mar.* **222** 1
~ administratif *Ports* **225** 53
~ administratif *Ciné* **310** 4
~ annexe *Agric.* **62** 14
~ annexe *Nucl.* **154** 36
~ auxiliaire **258** 92-97
~ central **233** 15
~ de combat **258** 64-91
~ de fosse **144** 4
~ de fret et de poste **233** 9
~ de guerre de faible tonnage **258** 1-63
~ de l'administration et de la direction **233** 16
~ de puits **144** 4
~ de scène **334** 45
~ de soutien **258** 93
~ de soutien logistique **258** 92-97
~ des machines **144** 2
~ des recettes **205** 13
~ des treuils **217** 71
~ des turbines **217** 64
~ des vannes **217** 42, 63
~ des voyageurs **205** 13
~ d'exploitation **62** 14
~ du réacteur **154** 20
~ public **15** 54
bâti-moteur **235** 2
bâton *Hérald.* **254** 31
~ *Ecriture* **342** 7
~ de compétition **301** 25
~ de craie **48** 15
~ de danse **354** 37
~ de fard **315** 46
~ de foc **218** 51
~ de gymnastique **297** 41
~ de peinture **129** 47
~ de ski **301** 5
~ pour nettoyer les caractères **247** 8
~ Tonkin Bambou **301** 20
bâtonnet au cumin **97** 31
~ salé **97** 31
bâtons de croisée ligaturés **136** 21
batoude **307** 59
batracien **364** 20-26
battant *Maison* **37** 21
~ *Tiss.* **166** 6, 41
batte *Vann.* **136** 36
~ *Carr.* **158** 36
~ *Sports* **292** 62, 75
~ *Carnaval* **306** 48
~ de fou **306** 48
~ de tympanon valaisan **322** 34
battement croisé **297** 44
batterie *Mach. agric.* **65** 53
~ *Photo* **114** 66
~ *Autom.* **191** 50
~ *Boîte nuit* **318** 10
~ à mercure **25** 32
~ d'accumulateurs **257** 17; **259** 83
~ de bouteilles **141** 1
~ de 5 tubes lance-torpilles de défense anti-sous-marine **259** 36
~ de démarrage **212** 46
~ de deux bouteilles **279** 19
~ de douze tubes lance-roquettes de défense anti-sous-marine **259** 24
~ de fours à coke *Min.* **144** 7
~ de fours à coke *Cokerie* **156** 8
~ de galets du câble tracteur **214** 60
~ de jazz **324** 47-54
~ de ponte **74** 18
~ de projecteurs **317** 13
~ de 4 roquettes de faible portée **259** 26
~ de rectification **92** 51
~ locale **238** 40
batteur *Maison* **39** 22
~ *Mach. agric.* **64** 12
~ *Boul.-pâtiss.* **97** 59
~ *Filat. coton* **163** 47
~ *Sports* **292** 52, 74
~ *Boîte nuit* **318** 11
~ de pieux **226** 36
~ double **163** 14
~ en position de frappe **292** 63
~ suivant **292** 58
batteur-mélangeur **97** 70
batteuse **131** 4
battu par K.O. **299** 40
battue **86** 34-39
baudrier **300** 56
bavette **30** 24
~ du masque d'escrime **294** 14
bavoir **28** 43
bayadère **306** 25
bazooka de 44 mm **255** 25
beaupré **218** 20
~, martingale de **219** 15
~ avec le bout-dehors **219** 1
beauté exotique **306** 30
bébé **28** 5
bec *Chasse* **88** 84
~ *Mus.* **323** 36; **324** 72
~ à anche double **323** 29
~ à maïs **64** 35
~ brûleur sous revêtement **38** 60
~ Bunsen *Papet.* **173** 5
~ Bunsen *Chim.* **350** 1
~ crochu **362** 6
~ d'aile **287** 42
~ d'âne **132** 8
~ d'aspersion **83** 28
~ de convertisseur **147** 45
~ de coulée **147** 43
~ de gaz **37** 62
~ de giclage **192** 7
~ de mesure extérieure **149** 70
~ de mesure intérieure **149** 71
~ de plume **322** 53
~ de pont **215** 56
~ de sécurité **229** 53
~ de sécurité mobile **229** 38
~ Téclu **350** 4
bécarre **320** 54
bécasse **88** 83
bec-de-cane **41** 28
bêche *Jard.* **56** 2
~ *Mil.* **255** 46
~ du dispositif de levage **255** 55
~ semi-automatique **56** 12
bécher **350** 20
becquet *Autom.* **193** 36
~ *Alpin.* **300** 9
bédane **140** 25
~ à bois **132** 8
bedeau **330** 58
bedlington **70** 18
bedlington-terrier **70** 18
Bédouin **354** 6
bégonia **53** 10
~ tubéreux **51** 19
bégoniacée **53** 10
beignet soufflé **97** 29
~ viennois **97** 29
belette **367** 16
Belgique **252** 17
Bélier *Astr.* **4** 53
bélier *Zool.* **73** 13
~ hydraulique **65** 24
belladone **379** 7
Bellatrix **3** 13
belle-mère, coussin de **53** 14
bémol **320** 52
bénédictin **331** 54
bénéficiaire **250** 19
bénitier portatif **332** 47
benne **214** 34
~ à béton *Constr.* **119** 38
~ à béton *Constr. rout.* **201** 24
~ basculante *Autom.* **194** 25
~ basculante *Ch. de f.* **213** 37, 38; **214** 34
~ basculante à trois panneaux latéraux amovibles **62** 18
~ basculante en tôle d'acier **200** 8
~ collectrice des agrégats **201** 20
~ d'approvisionnement **200** 14
~ de grande capacité **214** 52
~ de téléphérique **214** 52
~ racleuse **200** 13, 17
benne-trémie **147** 5
benzène *Cokerie* **156** 24
~ *Text.* **170** 6, 8
~ brut **156** 41, 42
béquille *Mach. agric.* **64** 62
~ *Motocycl.* **188** 51
~ *Mil.* **256** 23
~ à roues **194** 32
~ ajustable **67** 22
~ centrale **189** 21
~ d'appui *App. mén.* **50** 37
~ d'appui *Mil.* **255** 68
~ (d'appui) *Pompiers* **270** 12
~ du capot moteur **195** 37
~ hydraulique **85** 45
~ latérale **187** 34
berceau *Puéricult.* **28** 30
~ *Moteur* **190** 38
~ *Autom.* **191** 53
~, voûte en **336** 38
~ à deux galets **214** 69
~ à poncer **340** 19
~ de poupée **48** 24
~ d'osier **48** 24
~ double **214** 68
~ du canon **255** 60
~ du microphone **249** 65
~ en osier **28** 30
béret basque **35** 27
~ de marin **309** 63
berger allemand **70** 25
bergerie **75** 9
bergeronnette grise **360** 9
~ hochequeue **360** 9
berline *Min.* **144** 45
~ *Voit. chev.* **186** 1
berme **216** 38
bermuda **31** 44
berne, drapeau en **253** 6

bertholée **128** 46
bertholet **128** 46
besaïgue **120** 72
besan **292** 79
bestiaire fabuleux **327** 1-61
bétail, gros **73** 1-2
~ de boucherie **94** 2
~ de pâturage **62** 45
bête à bon Dieu **358** 37
~ à cornes **73** 1
Bête à sept têtes de l'Apocalypse **327** 50
~ de l'Apocalypse **327** 50
bête de proie **368** 1-11
~ de selle **354** 2
~ de somme **354** 3
~ noire **88** 51
Bételgeuse **3** 13
béton **119** 72
~, centrale à **201** 19
~ armé **118** 13; **119** 1-89, 1, 2, 8
~ compact **119** 72
~ coulé **119** 7
~ damé **118** 1
~ de fondation **123** 13
~ de ponce **119** 24
~ de semelle **123** 13
~ lourd **119** 72
bétonneur au lissage **119** 9
bétonnière *Maison* **47** 40
~ *Constr.* **118** 33; **119** 29
~ *Constr. rout.* **200** 15
bette **57** 28
betterave fourragère **69** 21
~ sucrière **68** 44
beurre *Epic.* **98** 22
~ *Comm.* **99** 47
~ de marque en pains de 250 g **76** 37
beurrier **45** 36
biberon **28** 19
Bible **330** 11
bibliothécaire **262** 14, 19
bibliothèque **223** 25
~ d'académie **262** 11-25
~ de consultation **262** 17
~ d'Etat **262** 11-25
~ municipale **262** 11-25
~ nationale **262** 11-25
~ universitaire **262** 11-25
biceps **18** 37
~ crural **18** 61
biche **88** 1
~, jeune **88** 1
~ adulte **88** 1
~ en train de viander **86** 13
bicyclette **187** 1
~ (pour) homme **187** 1
~ à accumulateurs **188** 20
~ de course de fond **290** 15
~ de tourisme **187** 1
~ d'enfant **273** 9
~ électrique **188** 20
~ pliante **188** 1
bidet **49** 7
bidon *Sylvic.* **84** 35
~ *Tonell.* **130** 13
~ *Sports* **290** 10
~ à lait **309** 89
~ de diluant **129** 16
~ de transport des poissons **89** 4
~ d'essence *Sylvic.* **84** 36
~ d'essence *Autom.* **196** 25
Biedermeier, canapé **336** 17
bief d'amont *Moulins* **91** 41
~ d'amont *Inst. fluv.* **217** 37
~ d'aval *Moulins* **91** 44
~ d'aval *Inst. fluv.* **217** 29
~ du moulin **91** 44
~ supérieur **217** 37
bielle **190** 21
~ d'accouplement **210** 11
~ de frein **187** 66
~ de semelle **166** 52
bière **205** 50
~, distributeur de **266** 68
~, filtre à **93** 15
~, pompe à **266** 1
~, verre à *Ust. table* **45** 91
~, verre à *Brass.* **93** 30
~, verre à *Rest.* **266** 6
~, verre à *Discoth.* **317** 6
~ Ale **93** 26
~ blonde **93** 26
~ brune **93** 26
~ de froment **93** 26
~ en boîtes **99** 73
~ faiblement alcoolisée **93** 26
~ forte **93** 26
~ Gose **93** 26
~ munichoise **93** 26
~ Pils **93** 26
~ Porter **93** 26
~ Salvator **93** 26
~ sans alcool **93** 26
~ Stout **93** 26
biface de silex **328** 1
bifide, langue **327** 6
bigarreau **59** 5
bigorne **125** 19
~ conique **137** 12
~ pyramidale **137** 13
bigorneau pour façonnage de bourrelets **125** 8
bigoudi **105** 12
bijou **36**
bijouterie de fantaisie **271** 62
bijoutier **108** 17
bikini **280** 26
billard **277** 1-19
~, salle de **277** 7-19
~, table de **277** 14
~ français **277** 7
~ russe **277** 7
billard-golf **277** 7
bille *Sylvic.* **84** 19
~ *Bicycl.* **187** 56
~ *Roulette* **275** 33
~, crayon à **47** 26
~, stylo à **47** 26
~ à pointer **277** 13
~ blanche du joueur **277** 11
~ d'acier **143** 70
~ de billard **277** 1
~ d'ivoire **277** 1
~ en tête **277** 2
~ rouge **277** 12
billet **204** 36
~ de banque *Argent* **252** 29-39
~ de banque *Magasin* **271** 6
~ de cinéma **312** 3
~ de loterie **266** 20
~ de théâtre **315** 11
billot **125** 21
bimoteur léger d'affaires et de tourisme **231** 3
biniou **322** 8
binoculaire **23** 6
biopsie, pince à **23** 17
bipied **255** 42
biplace de sport et de voltige **288** 18
biplan **229** 10
biréacteur court et moyen courrier **231** 11
~ d'affaires et de tourisme **231** 7
~ gros porteur court et moyen courrier **231** 17
biroute **287** 11
bisaïgue **120** 72
biscotte **97** 54
biscuit de chien **99** 37
~ roulé **97** 19
~ saupoudré de rognures de pâte **97** 35
biseau **326** 28
~ du cliché **178** 44
~ gradué **247** 36
bison *Préhist.* **328** 9
~ *Zool.* **367** 9
bissectrice **346** 30
bistouri **26** 43
bitte d'amarrage à terre **217** 12
~ d'enroulement en croix **217** 13
~ en double croix **217** 14
bitume **145** 64
biturbopropulseur à aile haute court et moyen courrier **231** 4
bivalve **357** 36
blague à tabac **107** 43
blaireau *Chasse* **88** 48
~ *Coiff.* **105** 10; **106** 27
blanc *Hérald.* **254** 25
~ *Couleurs* **343** 11
~ de l'œuf **74** 62
~ de maison **271** 57
blanc-étoc **84** 4-14
blanche **320** 14
blanchet *Text.* **168** 56
~ *Imprim.* **180** 24, 37, 63, 79
~ *Arts graph.* **340** 42
~ de caoutchouc **180** 54
blanchiment **169** 21
blancs *Compos.* **174** 8
~ *Jeux* **276** 4
blason **254** 1-6
~ d'alliance **254** 10-13
~ de femme **254** 11-13
~ de ville **254** 46
~ d'homme **254** 10
blastocœle **74** 67
blastoderme **74** 65
blatte domestique **81** 17
blazer **33** 54
blé **68** 23
~ de l'Inde **68** 31
~ de Turquie **68** 31
~ d'Espagne **68** 31
blessé **270** 24
~ de la route **21** 18
~ sans connaissance **21** 20
blessure **21** 8
blette **57** 28
bleu *Hérald.* **254** 28
~ *Couleurs* **343** 3
~ ciel **343** 6
bleuet **61** 1
blindage *Bureau* **246** 24
~ *Mil.* **255** 72, 81, 90
~ de protection de la chenille **255** 85
~ isolant en plomb **259** 70
~ magnétique **240** 20
bloc à croquis **338** 35
~ à dessins **338** 35
~ à esquisses **338** 35
~ à poncer *Tapiss.* **128** 13
~ à poncer *Peint.* **129** 26
~ d'alimentation en papier **249** 45
~ d'amplification et d'alimentation secteur **238** 3
~ d'assemblage **249** 60
~ de bois *Sculpteur* **339** 27
~ de bois *Arts graph.* **340** 1
~ de chauffage **183** 27
~ de cire d'abeilles **77** 67
~ de commande **177** 51
~ de coupe **56** 41
~ de départ **298** 1
~ de distribution **157** 67
~ de l'assistante **24** 9
~ de montage **178** 41
~ de neige **353** 5
~ de pierre **339** 5
~ de rangement de la tablette porte-instrumentation **24** 8
~ de roche **158** 8
~ de serrage **132** 31
~ d'éjection **157** 56
~ d'enregistrement et de reproduction magnétiques **238** 55
~ des fiches d'arrivée **267** 12
~ des instruments et des appareils de contrôle **234** 17
~ d'habitations à étages **37** 77-81
~ électronique **112** 53
~ électronique arrière **257** 18
~ électronique avant **257** 11
~ éphéméride **247** 32
~ faillé **12** 4-11, 10
~ moteur *App. mén.* **50** 82
~ moteur *Scierie* **157** 15
~ non épannelé **339** 5
~ sténo **245** 29; **248** 32
blocage de l'accélérateur **85** 17
~ de rotation **14** 57
~ d'inclinaison **14** 55
bloc-couronne **145** 4
block **203** 59
blockhaus pour films **310** 5
block-système **203** 59
bloc-moteur **190** 19
bloomer **32** 21
blouse blanche **33** 56
~ de cocktail **30** 55
~ de coiffeur **106** 2
~ de travail **33** 56
~ paysanne **31** 29
blouson **30** 38; **31** 42
~ de survêtement **33** 28
~ imitation fourrure **29** 44
~ matelassé **300** 6
blue-jeans **31** 60; **33** 22
bob **303** 19-21, 19
~ à deux **303** 19
bobby **264** 34
bobinage de canette **104** 16
bobine *Coord.* **100** 29
~ *Photo* **114** 20
~ *Verr.* **162** 55
~ *Filat. coton* **164** 23
~ *Ciné* **312** 16
~ à enroulement automatique **117** 80
~ croisée *Filat. coton* **164** 58
~ croisée *Tiss.* **165** 7, 13, 24
~ croisée à fils croisés **165** 8
~ de bande magnétique *Electr. gd public* **241** 57
~ de bande magnétique *Informat.* **244** 10

~ de fil **103** 12
~ de fil à coudre **104** 9
~ de film *Ciné* **117** 79
~ de film *Radiodiff.* **238** 6
~ de film *Ciné* **311** 24
~ de film magnétique **311** 2
~ de papier **181** 46
~ de papier couché **173** 35
~ de papier non imprimé **180** 2
~ de papier vierge **180** 2
~ de pellicule **114** 8
~ débitrice **117** 31
~ d'induction **11** 44
~ du film **312** 32
~ réceptrice **117** 32, 80
bobine-bouteille **167** 4
bobineuse **148** 72
bobinoir **169** 26
~ à renvidage croisé **165** 1
bobsleigh **303** 19-21
boc **296** 17
bocal *Ust. cuis.* **40** 25
~ *Apicult.* **77** 63
~ *Mus.* **324** 71
~ de légumes **96** 51
~ de sauce remoulade **96** 29
boccia italienne **305** 21
Bochiman **354** 29
bock **266** 3
bodisattva **337** 10
bœuf *Zool.* **73** 1
~ *Abatt.* **94** 2
~ *Viande* **95** 14-37
~, cimier de **95** 35
~, filet de **95** 24
~, poitrine de **95** 23
~, quartier de **94** 22
~ musqué **367** 10
boggie **152** 41
bogie *Centr.* **152** 41
~ *Ch. de f.* **208** 4; **212** 2; **213** 13
~ avec suspension à ressorts acier - caoutchouc **207** 4
~ moteur **197** 9
~ porteur **197** 10
bogue avec les fruits **384** 52
bohémienne **306** 36
Bohr-Sommerfeld **1** 26
bois *Sylvic.* **84** 1-34
~ *Chasse* **88** 5-11, 29-31
~ *Sports* **293** 91
~ *Mus.* **323** 28-38
~, charbon de **278** 48
~, cheval de **308** 2
~, cœur du **120** 84
~, demi- **120** 88
~, faux **120** 85
~, gravure sur **340** 1-13
~, long **84** 19
~, menu **84** 37
~ avivé **120** 10
~ coupé en croix **120** 90
~ de bout *Constr.* **120** 92
~ de bout *Arts graph.* **340** 1
~ de brin **120** 87
~ de charpente **120** 83-96
~ de chauffage **157** 54
~ de coffrage **119** 18
~ de conifères **15** 1
~ de construction **120** 2, 10, 83-96
~ de feuillus **15** 4
~ de fil **340** 2
~ de grume *Constr.* **120** 35
~ de grume *Scierie* **157** 30
~ de lit **43** 5
~ de long **120** 2
~ de renne **328** 5
~ défibré **172** 68
~ d'équarrissage **120** 88
~ d'œuvre **120** 10, 83-96
~ en défen(d)s **84** 10
~ en état **120** 87
~ équarri *Constr.* **119** 64; **120** 10
~ équarri *Scierie* **157** 36
~ équarri boulonné **119** 74
~ fendu **120** 85
~ gentil **377** 10
~ imparfait **120** 85
~ mi-plat **120** 88
~ non usiné **135** 21
~ parfait **120** 84
~ refendu **120** 88
~ rond *Constr.* **120** 35
~ rond *Scierie* **157** 30
~ sculpté **260** 77
boisseau **159** 28
boissons rafraîchissantes **96** 30
boîte à bornes *Centr.* **153** 60
~ à bornes *Ch. de f.* **211** 16
~ à compartiments **134** 39
~ à coupes **132** 43
~ à déchets **96** 46
~ à engrenage *Filat. coton* **163** 57; **164** 39
~ à engrenage *Text.* **168** 10, 32
~ à engrenage avec moteur incorporé **164** 2
~ à engrenage portant le moteur **164** 33
~ à feu **210** 62
~ à fiches **248** 27
boîte à fumée **210** 26
~ à garniture **210** 33
boîte à lettres *Ch. de f.* **204** 11
~ à lettre-s *Poste* **236** 50-55, 50
~ à lettres de quai **205** 56
~ à lumière *Opt.* **112** 28, 59
~ à lumière *Photo* **116** 29
~ à navettes **166** 9
boîte à onglets **132** 43
boîte à ordures *Bouch.* **96** 46
~ à ordures *Jeux enf.* **273** 25
~ à outils **134** 35
~ à petites pièces **195** 31
~ à poinçons **108** 30
~ à recaler **124** 31
~ à rideaux **44** 15
~ à sable **212** 59, 76
~ à semence **65** 75
~ à surprise **306** 56
~ à vitesses à cinq rapports **189** 6
~ d'allumettes **107** 21
~ d'aspiration **108** 45
~ d'aspiration des mèches cassées **164** 44
~ de boutons **103** 15
~ de chocolats **98** 79
~ de cigares **107** 1
~ de cirage **50** 39
~ de compresses non stériles **26** 23
~ de conserve **96** 26
~ de conserve de légumes **96** 27
~ de conserve de poisson **96** 28
~ de conserves **99** 91
~ de couleurs **338** 10
~ de crème **28** 13
~ de culasse *Chasse* **87** 16
~ de culasse *Mil.* **255** 10, 33
~ de cure-dents **266** 23
~ de nuit **318** 1-33
~ de parquet **127** 22
boîte de parquet à clapet **127** 24
boîte de parquet à couvercle pivotant **127** 24
~ de parquet pivotante **127** 23
~ de peinture **129** 6
~ de peintures **48** 6
~ de Petri **261** 25
~ de poudre **99** 29
~ de rangement **241** 11
~ de rangement de petites pièces **134** 34
~ de rangement des clichés **245** 10
~ de talc **28** 14
~ de tiroir **210** 31
~ de vitesses *Tourn.* **135** 4
~ de vitesses *Mach.-out.* **150** 36
~ de vitesses *Moteur* **190** 72
boîte de vitesses réglables **149** 2
boîte de vitesses synchronisée à quatre rapports **192** 28-47
~ d'engrenages **65** 79
~ des avances **149** 8
~ d'esches **89** 24
~ d'essai de verres **111** 45
~ d'essieu **210** 10
~ d'extrémité **153** 33
~ du souffleur **316** 27
~ métallique **93** 25
~ portoir de semis **55** 51
~ postale **236** 13, 14
boîte-piège **86** 20
boîtier *Météor.* **10** 18, 39
~ *Photo* **115** 2
~ *Centr.* **153** 37
~ contenant les instruments **10** 59
~ de cassette de film **313** 9
~ de chargeur **313** 9
~ de commande **240** 31
~ de commande radio et radionavigation **230** 22
~ de commande suspendu et pivotant **177** 6
~ de lampe **309** 44
~ de lampe au xénon **177** 42
~ de l'appareil **2** 5
~ de l'appareil téléphonique **237** 15
~ de l'instrument **2** 22
~ de mixage **117** 26
~ de radiocommande **288** 87
~ de télécommande **157** 14
~ d'enroulement du cordon **301** 62
~ des tubes de canette **166** 21
~ isolant en bois **10** 26
~ photo sous-marin **279** 24
~ pour prises de vues sous-marines **117** 57
bolas **352** 31
bolet châtain **381** 15
~ de Satan **379** 12
~ jaune **381** 21
~ raboteux **381** 22
~ rugueux **381** 22
bollard **217** 12
bombarde **322** 14; **326** 45
bombardement neutronique **1** 36
~ par un neutron **1** 50
bombardon **323** 44
bombe *Sports* **282** 14
~ *Equitation* **289** 14
~ à hydrogène **7** 12
~ à signaux **280** 4
~ atomique **7** 11
~ au cobalt **2** 28
~ de fixatif pour cheveux **106** 23
~ pour l'entretien des chaussures **50** 40
bombyx **358** 48
~ à livrée **80** 13
~ disparate **80** 1
~ du mûrier **358** 48
~ moine **82** 17
bôme **284** 39
bonbon **98** 75
~ acidulé **98** 76
bonbonne **206** 13
bonbonnière **46** 12
bonbons assortis **47** 31
bonde **130** 7
bonette **218** 34
bongo **324** 58
bonhomme de neige **304** 13
bonimenteur **308** 64
bonne aventure **308** 36
bonnet *Puéricult.* **28** 26
~ *Cost.* **29** 2
~ à grelots **306** 39
~ à pointe **35** 39
~ de bain *Plage* **280** 29, 44
~ de bain *Natation* **281** 8
~ de dame **35** 1-21
~ de fou **306** 39
~ de grosse laine **35** 9
~ de laine *Cost.* **29** 57
~ de laine *Coiffures* **35** 26
~ de musc **35** 33
~ de prince **254** 40
~ de prince-électeur **254** 41
~ de renard **35** 19
~ de ski *Coiffures* **35** 39
~ de ski *Sports hiver* **301** 10
~ de vison **35** 20
~ d'homme **35** 22-40
~ en papier **306** 45
~ en peau de mouton **353** 23
~ en tissu mohair **35** 11
~ tricoté **35** 10
bonneterie **167**
~, rayon **271** 17
bonnette **117** 55
boomerang **352** 39
Boötes **3** 30
borax **108** 39
bord **62** 25
~ apparent **122** 86
~ cubital de la main **19** 70
~ d'attaque **284** 42; **287** 34
~ d'attaque amovible **235** 32
~ d'attaque de la voilure **288** 48
~ de fuite **284** 45; **287** 37
~ de largue **285** 24
~ de louvoyage **285** 22
~ de près **285** 22
~ de vent arrière **285** 23
~ denté **247** 30
~ du bassin **281** 3
~ du déporteur **193** 30
~ du disque lunaire **4** 41
~ du limbe **370** 43-50
~ du spoiler **193** 30
~ entier **370** 43
~ non visible **151** 24
~ radial de la main **19** 69
~ recouvert **122** 88
~ visible **151** 23

bordage **235** 11
bord-côtes **31** 70
~ élastique **31** 43
~ tricot **29** 65
bordé *Astron.* **235** 11
~ *Sports* **283** 48
~ à clins **283** 33; **285** 50-52
~ à franc-bord **285** 53
~ de côté **222** 45
~ de fond **222** 48
~ en bois **285** 50-57
~ en deux couches croisées **285** 56
~ extérieur **222** 44-49
~ intérieur **285** 57
~ sur lisses **285** 54
bordure **136** 17
~ brodée **355** 67
~ d'allée **272** 37
~ d'arceaux **55** 38
~ de ciment **52** 20
~ de cuir **291** 22
~ de la grand-voile **284** 40
~ de l'allée **51** 15
~ de papier peint **128** 29
~ de pompe **269** 65
~ de quai **205** 19
~ de rive **122** 26
~ de trottoir **198** 6
borne cadastrale **63** 2
~ d'appel taxis **268** 67
~ d'incendie **270** 35
~ kilométrique **15** 109
borraginacée **69** 13
Boschiman **354** 29
bosquet **272** 4, 61
bossage **335** 51
bosse *Ch. de f.* **206** 44
~ *Zool.* **366** 29
~ de triage **206** 46
~ frontale latérale **16** 4
bossoir **221** 78, 101; **223** 20
~ d'embarcation **258** 13, 83
bostryche de l'épicéa **82** 22
botanique générale **370**
botillon **101** 18
botte **136** 14
~ à fourrure de poulain **101** 10
~ à revers **355** 58
~ à toute épreuve **101** 14
~ de cow-boy **101** 9
~ de femme **101** 12
~ de feutre **353** 30
~ de ville pour hommes **101** 13
~ d'hiver **101** 1
~ en PVC injecté sans couture **101** 14
~ haute pour hommes **101** 7
bottillon isotherme **101** 1
bottine d'homme **101** 5
bouc *Barbes, coiffures* **34** 10
~ *Zool.* **73** 14
bouche *Anat.* **16** 13
~ *Cheval* **72** 9
~ *Inst. fluv.* **217** 56
~ *Mus.* **326** 25
~ d'aération *Maison* **49** 20
~ d'aération *Mil.* **258** 43; **259** 92
~ d'aspiration d'air **258** 57
~ de coulée **178** 17
~ de soufflage **165** 5
~ d'égout avec grille **198** 24
~ d'incendie *Mar.* **221** 4
~ d'incendie *Pompiers* **270** 25
~ du canon **305** 71
~ et pharynx **19** 14-37
bouche-à-bouche **21** 26
bouche-à-nez **21** 26
bouchée **97** 18
~ à la liqueur **98** 83
bouche-pores **128** 3
boucher *Abatt.* **94** 1
~ *Bouch.* **96** 38
~, couteaux de **96** 31-37
boucherie, bétail de **94** 2
~, cochon de **94** 11
boucherie-charcuterie **96** 1-30
bouchon *Agric.* **67** 36
~ *Piscic.* **89** 43-48
~ à robinet **350** 44
~ à tête octogonale **349** 4
~ à vis **115** 11
~ de champagne **267** 58
~ de vidange *Moteur* **190** 24
~ de vidange *Sports* **284** 36
~ du tube **260** 52
~ fileté **83** 40
~ fusiforme **89** 43
boucle *Barbes, coiffures* **34** 3
~ *Chauss.* **101** 52
~ *Sports* **288** 1
~ *Sports hiver* **302** 15
~ *Hist. cost.* **355** 23
~ à liage de tête **171** 39
~ avec départ et récupération **288** 3
~ d'assurance **300** 11
~ de bande magnétique **245** 28
~ de bouclier **329** 58
~ de ceinture **31** 12
~ de charge **171** 37
~ de platine **23** 15
~ de rappel **300** 28
~ d'oreille **36** 13
~ paragraphe **302** 16
boucleteau d'attelle **71** 14
bouclier *Constr.* **118** 57
~ *Mar.* **218** 17
~ *Ethnol.* **354** 10
~ de protection **264** 20
~ rond **329** 57
~ thermique **234** 5, 20; **235** 8, 40
Bouddha **337** 20
boudin *Comm.* **99** 56
~ *Ch. de f.* **211** 52
~ d'argile **159** 14
~ de pâte **161** 8
~ gonflé d'air **286** 27
bouée *Pêche* **90** 2
~ *Cours d'eau* **216** 12
~, feu de **221** 125
~ à espar **224** 79
~ à laisser d'un côté **285** 18
~ à virer **285** 17; **286** 31
~ conique **224** 76
~ cylindrique **224** 77
~ de départ et d'arrivée **285** 14
~ de natation **281** 6
~ de sauvetage *Mar.* **221** 124
~ de sauvetage *Plage* **280** 3
~ lumineuse à cloche **224** 74
~ lumineuse à sifflet **224** 68
~ verte **224** 84
bouée-culotte **228** 13
bouffon *Carnaval* **306** 38
~ *Cirque* **307** 24
bouge **130** 6
bougeoir **309** 45
bougie *Apicult.* **77** 66
~ *Enseign.* **242** 48
~ avec embout antiparasite **190** 35
~ de cire **260** 76
~ de la table de communion **330** 7
~ de préchauffage **190** 55, 66
bougnou **144** 47
bouilloire **39** 16
~ à sifflet *Maison* **39** 16
~ à sifflet *Ust. cuis.* **40** 10
~ en laiton **42** 14
bouillon blanc **376** 9
bouillotte en métal **309** 88
boulangerie **97** 1-54
boulangerie-pâtisserie **97** 1-54
bouldozeur **200** 28
boule *Joaill.* **36** 82-86
~ *Boul.-pâtiss.* **97** 6
~ *Bureau* **249** 1
~ *Cirque* **307** 60
~, petite **97** 7
~ à trous **305** 15
~ de Berlin **97** 29
~ de croquet **292** 82
~ de graveur **108** 34
~ de la flèche **331** 5
~ de métal **352** 32
~ de neige *Hiver* **304** 15
~ de neige *Bot.* **373** 10
~ de papier **306** 55
~ de pierre **352** 32
~ de signaux **280** 4
~ de tempête **280** 4
~ horaire **280** 5
~ interchangeable **249** 28
~ lisse **36** 82
~ métallique striée **305** 24
~ mobile **249** 15
bouleau *Jard.* **51** 13
~ *Parc* **272** 40
~ *Bot.* **371** 9
~, verge de **281** 27
bouledogue **70** 1
boules, jeu de **305** 21
boulet **72** 24
boulier *Maison* **47** 14
~ *Marché puces* **309** 77
boulin **118** 27; **119** 49
bouline **218** 35
boulon *Constr.* **119** 75
~ *Méc.* **143** 13-50
~ à crochet **202** 10
~ à embase **143** 32
~ à tête carrée **143** 39
~ à tête cylindrique **143** 36
~ à tête en T **143** 41
~ à tête fraisée **143** 28
~ à tête hexagonale **143** 13
~ à tête six-pans **143** 13
~ de jumelage **202** 15
~ d'éclisse **202** 13
~ fileté **121** 98
boumarang **352** 39
boumerang **352** 39
bouquet **35** 7
~ de faîtage **120** 8
~ de fleurs **267** 37
~ de la mariée **332** 18
~ de myrte **332** 21
bouquetin **367** 7
bouquin **73** 18
bourdaine **380** 13
bourdon *Mus.* **322** 11; **326** 34
~ *Zool.* **358** 23
bourgeois sous Louis-Philippe **355** 73
bourgeon *Plantes* **54** 26
~ *Bot.* **59** 22
~ apical **59** 47
~ axillaire **370** 25
~ terminal **370** 22
Bourguignon **355** 40
bourrage **153** 45
bourre **87** 52
bourrelet **254** 2
~ du capot d'hélice **258** 63
~ en caoutchouc **207** 8; **208** 12
bourre-pipe **107** 46
bourriche **89** 28
Bourse **251** 1-10
bourse à pasteur **61** 9
~ à sonnette **330** 59
~ au-dessus du trou de sortie **86** 27
~ de capucin **61** 9
Bourse des effets **251** 1-10
~ des valeurs **251** 1-10
bousier **358** 39
bout **107** 13
~ amovible **213** 10
~ bombé **100** 58
~ coupé **107** 4
~ de botte **101** 16
~ d'entrait **121** 33
~ doré **107** 13
~ du doigt **19** 79
~ du goujon **143** 23
~ dur **100** 58
~ en attente **118** 61
~ en escalier **118** 61
~ renforcé *Coord.* **100** 58
~ renforcé *Chauss.* **101** 40
~ rond **143** 20
~ soufré **107** 23
~ sphérique **143** 50
bout-dehors **218** 51; **219** 1
~ d'artimon **218** 28
bouteille *Mar.* **218** 57
~ *Rest.* **266** 16
~ à collerette **328** 12
~ à oxygène **200** 40
~ à vin **79** 14
~ d'acétylène **141** 2, 22
~ d'air comprimé **279** 21
~ de bière *Brass.* **93** 26
~ de bière *Ch. de f.* **205** 50
~ de chianti **99** 77
~ de CO_2 **138** 32
~ de gaz **278** 53
~ de gaz propane **278** 34
~ de jus de fruits **99** 74
~ de lait **266** 60
~ de limonade **265** 15
~ de shampooing **105** 32
~ de vin *Comm.* **99** 76
~ de vin *Rest.* **266** 43
~ de vin mousseux **99** 78
~ de whisky **42** 31
~ de Zug **89** 17
~ d'eau minérale **266** 61
~ d'oxygène *Méd.* **27** 45
~ d'oxygène *Soud.* **141** 3, 21
~ non consignée **93** 29
~ propre **93** 21
bouterolle **108** 19
bouteur *Nett.* **199** 16
~ *Constr. rout.* **200** 28
boutique de fleuriste **204** 48
~ d'orfèvre **215** 33
~ hors douane **233** 52
bout-liège **107** 13
boutoir **88** 53
bouton *Cost.* **33** 64
~ *Plantes* **54** 23
~ *Bot.* **61** 3
~ arrêt **243** 43
~ d'accord *Electr. gd public* **241** 9
~ d'accord *Marché puces* **309** 21

brin *Piscic.* **89** 54
~ *Vann.* **136** 14
~ de clôture **136** 5
~ dépassant du pied de la monture **136** 23
~ d'herbe **370** 83-85
~ moteur **145** 7
brique à perforation verticale **159** 21
~ creuse **159** 21-22
~ creuse tubulaire **159** 22
~ crue **159** 16
~ cuite **159** 20
~ de cheminée **159** 25
~ de lait **76** 22
~ de maçonnerie **159** 20
~ de mur **159** 20
~ de pavement **159** 27
~ perforée en losanges **159** 23
~ pleine **159** 20
~ pleine calibrée **118** 58
~ pontée de plancher **159** 24
~ radiale **159** 25
~ verte **159** 16
briquet à essence **107** 27
~ à gaz **107** 30
~ à jeter **107** 30
briqueterie *Cartogr.* **15** 89
~ *Briq.* **159**
brise-balles de cotons mélangés **163** 7
brise-glace **221** 50
brise-lames *Géogr.* **13** 37
~ *Inst. fluv.* **217** 16
~ *Ports* **225** 65
~ *Mil.* **258** 7, 76
briseur **163** 53
~ de chaînes **308** 28
Brisinga endecacnemos **369** 11
broc à eau **309** 66
~ à huile moteur **196** 16
brocard **86** 17; **88** 28
brochage **183** 8, 32
broche *Joaill.* **36** 7
~ *Ust. cuis.* **40** 33
~ *Mach.-out.* **149** 20; **150** 27
~ à glace **300** 40, 41
~ avec antimariages **164** 43
~ crantée **300** 41
~ de fraisage horizontale **150** 39
~ de fraisage verticale **150** 37
~ de perçage **150** 23
~ en ivoire **36** 30
~ horizontale **150** 40
~ moderne **36** 19
~ nue **164** 52
~ porte-fraise **175** 60
~ principale **149** 11
~ standard **164** 45
~ tire-bouchon **300** 40
brochet **364** 16
brocheuse automatique **249** 61
~ automatique sans couture **184** 1
broderie **29** 29; **30** 42
~ anglaise **102** 11
~ sur filet **102** 27
~ sur tulle **102** 15
broigne en écailles **329** 64
~ en écus **329** 65
brome, ampoule à **349** 3
bronche **20** 5
bronze, âge de **328** 21-40
brosse *Chasse* **87** 62
~ *Peintre* **338** 6
~ *Arts graph.* **340** 11
~, cheveux en **34** 11
~, coupe en **34** 11
~, moustache en **34** 19
~ à badigeonner **129** 3
~ à boucler les cheveux **105** 13
~ à chaussures **50** 41
~ à cheveux **28** 7
~ à cheveux en soies dures **105** 16
~ à cheveux radiale **105** 13
~ à chien **70** 28
~ à cirage **50** 42
~ à démêler les cheveux **105** 2
~ à dents électrique **49** 29
~ à encoller *Tapiss.* **128** 27
~ à encoller *Peint.* **129** 18
~ à étaler **128** 49
~ à fonds **338** 9
~ à habits *App. mén.* **50** 44
~ à habits *Cout.* **104** 31
~ à jet d'air chaud **106** 30
~ à polir *Coord.* **100** 11
~ à polir *Orfèvre* **108** 44
~ à pollen **77** 7
~ à récurer **50** 56
~ à tapis **50** 45
~ à tapisser **128** 40
~ à vaisselle **50** 51
~ aspirante **50** 79
~ chauffante **106** 30
~ circulaire **134** 24
~ de crin **100** 12
~ de nettoyage **247** 7
~ de pansage **71** 55
~ de rechange **49** 30
~ d'orfèvre **108** 33
~ métallique **141** 26; **142** 18
~ rotative **168** 46
~ universelle **50** 67
brosse-émoussoir **56** 23
brou **59** 42
brouette *Jard.* **56** 47
~ *Constr.* **118** 37; **119** 42
~ *Nett.* **199** 9
brouillard **9** 31
broussaille **15** 15
broyage et séchage simultanés des matières premières **160** 4
broyeur **159** 8
~ à boulets **161** 1
~ à charbon **152** 4
~ à cylindres **159** 9
~ à gypse **160** 14
~ à meules verticales **159** 8
~ centrifuge **172** 5
~ de ciment **160** 12
~ de matière **160** 4, 7
~ tubulaire **161** 1
bruant **361** 6-7
~ jaune **361** 6
~ ortolan **361** 7
brucelles **109** 14
bruche du haricot **81** 19
~ du pois **81** 19
bruine **9** 33
brûleur **162** 6
~ à gaz **139** 3, 48
~ à mazout **38** 58-60
brume **9** 31
brun **343** 5
brunelle vulgaire **376** 16
brunissoir **108** 48
Bruxelles, chou de **57** 30
~, dentelle de **102** 18
bruyère, pipe de **107** 39
~ cendrée **377** 19
~ commune **377** 19
buanderie **118** 5, 6
Büchner, entonnoir de **349** 11
buffet *Ch. de f.* **207** 78-79
~ *Rest.* **266** 1-11
~ *Mus.* **326** 1-5
~ bas **44** 20
~ de gare **204** 13
~ d'orgue **326** 1-5
buffle **367** 8
buggy **193** 12
~ américain **186** 49
~ anglais **186** 48
buis *Coord.* **100** 48
~ *Bot.* **373** 19
buisson d'ornement **272** 14
bulbe *Anat.* **17** 47
~ *Plantes* **54** 28
~ à double sens **155** 39
~ d'étrave **221** 45
~ rachidien **18** 24
bulbille **375** 38
buldo oval **89** 47
bulldozer *Nett.* **199** 16
~ *Constr. rout.* **200** 28
bulldozer-compresseur **199** 18
bulle d'air expiré **279** 26
~ de carénage **189** 46
bulles, chambre à **1** 58
bulletin de bagages **204** 8
~ de prêt **262** 25
~ de vote **263** 20
~ d'expédition **236** 7
~ météorologique **342** 65
bull-terrier **70** 16
bungalow **278** 7
bunker **293** 81
Bunsen, bec **350** 1
bure **144** 27
bureau *Pétr.* **146** 14
~ *Bureau* **245**; **246** 2; **247**; **248** 11; **249**
~ *Ecole* **260** 22
~ *Magasin* **271** 24
~ *Ciné* **310** 4
~, employé de **248** 7
~ collectif **248** 1-48
~ d'accueil **245** 1-33
~ de change **204** 31
~ de crédit **271** 24
~ de dactylo **245** 25; **248** 26
~ de dessin **151**
~ de direction **246** 1-36
~ de la direction **271** 24
~ de poste **268** 68
~ de renseignements **204** 29
~ de réservation des chambres d'hôtel **204** 28
~ de tabac **204** 47
~ de tourisme **204** 28
~ de vote **263** 16, 28
~ de voyages **271** 24
~ des départs **206** 26
~ des douanes **225** 6
~ (des) marchandises **206** 26
~ d'études *Dess.* **151**
~ d'études *Mar.* **222** 2
~ du commissaire **223** 45
~ du port **225** 36
~ du professeur **242** 2
~ du service de prêt **262** 20
~ en espace ouvert **248** 1-48
bureau-paysage **248** 1-48
burette **350** 21
~, pince à **350** 23
~ à eau **332** 45
~ à vin **332** 46
burettes **332** 44
burin *Serr.* **140** 26
~ *Compos.* **175** 33
~ *Sculpteur* **339** 20
~ à bout rond **340** 20
~ à contours **340** 5
~ de tourneur **135** 24
~ plat **340** 7
~ pneumatique **148** 45
burnous **354** 7
busard des roseaux **362** 13
buse *Agric.* **67** 33
~ *Autom.* **192** 8
~ *Oiseaux* **362** 9
~ à oxygène **350** 13
~ d'arrosage **67** 27
~ d'aspiration des copeaux **140** 17
~ de chalumeau coupeur **141** 38
~ de chalumeau soudeur **141** 33
~ de coupe **141** 19
~ de tuyère d'aspiration **64** 15
~ d'éjection à jet plan **83** 4
~ variable **362** 9
busserolle **377** 15
buste **42** 17
bustier **32** 4
but *Sports* **291** 35
~ *Sports hiver* **302** 37, 40
~, gardien de *Jeux enf.* **273** 14
~, gardien de *Sports* **282** 47; **291** 10; **292** 8
~ de football **273** 11
~ de hockey **292** 7
~ de water-polo **282** 46
butane *Pétr.* **145** 53
~ *Camping* **278** 33
butée *Chasse* **87** 70
~ *Menuis.* **133** 11
~ *Mar.* **221** 29; **223** 67
~ *Poste* **237** 12
~ *Sports hiver* **301** 55
~ de basculement **214** 35
~ de poche **185** 11
~ de profondeur **134** 47
~ longitudinale **157** 68
buteur **273** 13
butoir *Scierie* **157** 18
~ *Tiss.* **166** 44
~ *Ch. de f.* **206** 51; **214** 56
~ du sabre de chasse **166** 65
butome en ombelle **378** 39
butte **206** 44, 46
buttoir **56** 5
buvette **308** 3
~ de quai **205** 49

C

cab **186** 29, 34
caban *Cost.* **33** 63
~ *Mar.* **221** 127
cabane à outils **52** 3
~ d'Indien **273** 59
cabaret **266** 1-29
cabestan *Ciné* **117** 34
~ *Mach.-out.* **149** 43

canapé **42** 24
~ Biedermeier **336** 17
canard *Zool.* **73** 35
~ *Jeux enf.* **273** 30
~ de caoutchouc **49** 4
~ plongeur **359** 15
~ sauvage avec ses canetons **272** 51
Cancer **4** 56
~, tropique du **3** 4
cancrelat **81** 17
candidat **263** 20
cane **73** 35
canelle **382** 25
caneton **73** 35
canette *Coord.* **100** 29
~ *Tiss.* **166** 7, 30
caniche **70** 36
~ nain **70** 36
canidé **367** 11-13
canine **19** 17
Canis major **3** 14
~ minor **3** 15
caniveau **198** 10
~ de transmission funiculaire **202** 32
~ d'écoulement **200** 63
canne *Maison* **41** 5
~ *Vann.* **136** 24
~ à lancer **89** 20
~ à pêche **89** 49-58
~ à sucre **382** 52
~ d'allumage verticale **234** 25
~ de niveau **234** 27
~ du souffleur **162** 39
~ en fibre de carbone **89** 57
~ en fibre de verre **89** 49
~ en fibre de verre creux **89** 57
~ télescopique **89** 53
~ utilisée pour serrer le garrot **21** 16
canneberge **377** 23
cannelier **382** 22
cannelure *Géogr.* **13** 30
~ *Métall.* **148** 59
~ *Scierie* **157** 6
~ *Arts* **334** 27
canne-siège de chasse **86** 10
cannette *Tiss.* **166** 5
~ *Reliure* **185** 18
~ de fil de nylon **133** 4
~ pour filés **163** 2
canoë **283**
~ canadien **283** 3
~ des Indiens des forêts **352** 19
canoéiste **283** 55
canon *Cheval* **72** 23
~ *Mil.* **255** 2, 17, 41
~, affût de **255** 43
~ à âme rayée **87** 26
~ à électrons **113** 31
~ à plombs **87** 27
~ antiaérien **258** 31, 73; **259** 34
~ antiaérien de 76 mm **259** 30
~ automatique **255** 92
~ d'avant-bras et du bras **329** 47
~ de 127 mm dans sa tourelle **259** 52
~ de DCA **258** 73
~ de défense antiaérienne **258** 73
~ de 20 mm **256** 3
~ électronique **240** 24
~ lisse **87** 27
~ porte-amarre **228** 1
~ rayé **87** 34
~ SF M 107 de 175 mm **255** 49
~ universel de 127 mm **258** 47, 48
~ universel de 76 mm et la tourelle **258** 70
cañon **13** 45
canot **258** 61
~ à moteur *Plage* **280** 13
~ à moteur *Sports* **283** 2
~ à rames **89** 27
~ à voile **278** 12
~ de bord **259** 35
~ de promenade **283** 26-33
~ de sauvetage *Mar.* **223** 19; **228** 14
~ de sauvetage *Mil.* **258** 12
~ de sauvetage *Sports* **286** 19
~ de sauvetage avec son taud **221** 107
~ de sauvetage dans ses bossoirs **221** 78
~ hors-bord **283** 6
~ pneumatique *Mar.* **228** 18
~ pneumatique *Mil.* **258** 11, 82
~ pneumatique *Sports* **279** 27
~ pneumatique à moteur hors-bord **286** 1
canotier **35** 35
cantatrice **315** 23
cantine **119** 45
cantique **330** 24
canton de block **203** 60
~ d'écu **254** 18-23
cantonnement **203** 59
cantre *Filat. coton* **164** 28
~ *Tiss.* **165** 25
~ à cônes **165** 9
~ chargé **164** 41
~ garni de bobines croisées **164** 58
canyon **13** 45
caoutchouc **286** 57-58
~ avant **286** 57
caparaçon **329** 74
cape *Ust. fumeurs* **107** 5
~ *Taurom.* **319** 27
~ à l'espagnole **355** 29
~ imperméable **41** 4
capelage d'étai **284** 14
Capella **3** 27
capitaine **303** 20
capital **345** 7
capitale romaine **341** 16
capitule **61** 14; **370** 73; **376** 2, 5; **378** 7
~ concave **370** 75
~ convexe **370** 74
caporal **107** 25
capot *Autom.* **191** 8
~ *Electr. gd public* **241** 32
~ de l'habitacle **257** 4
~ de protection transparent **249** 27
~ d'évacuation des copeaux **132** 48
~ d'hélice **258** 40, 74
~ moteur **195** 36
capotage de la bande abrasive **133** 31
capote *Carnaval* **306** 23
~ *Hist. cost.* **355** 71
~ de la voiture **186** 42
~ de toile **255** 98
~ fixe **186** 14
~ pliante **186** 52
~ rabattable **193** 10
~ repliable **28** 35
capot-moteur **191** 8
câpres **98** 42
Capricorne **3** 36; **4** 62
Capricornus **3** 36; **4** 62
caprolactame **170** 28
capselle **61** 9
capsule *Agric.* **57** 6
~ *Brass.* **93** 27
~ *Papet.* **173** 7
~ *Bot.* **375** 17, 24; **378** 5; **382** 10, 48; **383** 8
~ anéroïde **10** 6
~ avec les graines **61** 5
~ en porcelaine **350** 29
~ loculicide **370** 94
~ mûre **382** 44
~ mûre du cotonnier **163** 1
~ ouverte **375** 27
~ poricide **370** 96
~ spatiale **234** 65
~ spatiale Apollo **6** 9
~ surrénale **20** 29
~ témoin **161** 2
capsuleuse de bouteilles **76** 46
captage d'une source **269** 24-39
capteur **10** 22
~ de mesure **234** 42
~ plan **155** 19, 28
~ plan à surface absorbante noire **155** 29
~ solaire **155** 19, 32
capuche *Cost.* **30** 69
~ *Alpin.* **300** 19
capuchon *Mil.* **258** 21
~ *Eglise* **331** 56
~ amovible **31** 21
~ avec indication d'épaisseur de trait **151** 40
~ de l'anorak **300** 19
~ de valve **187** 32
~ de ventilateur **223** 41
capucine **53** 4
car de reportage **239** 1-15
~ de voyage **194** 17
~ long-courrier **194** 17
carabidé **358** 39
carabine *Chasse* **86** 4
~ *Sports* **305** 26
~, petite **86** 30
~ à air **305** 34, 40
~ à répétition automatique **87** 2
~ à un coup **87** 1
~ courte **305** 35
~ de compétition **305** 40-49
~ de petit calibre **305** 48
~ superposée à trois canons **87** 23
caractère *Compos.* **174** 7; **175** 38
~ *Bureau* **249** 29
~ *Ecriture* **342** 1-15
~, œil du **174** 31
~ de machine à écrire **247** 7
~ gras **175** 9
~ gras étroit **175** 10
~ italique **175** 7
~ machine **342** 9
~ maigre **175** 8
~ mi-gras **175** 3
~ trois-quarts gras **175** 2
caractéristique **345** 6
carafon à liqueur **45** 48
~ de vin **266** 32
carambolage **277** 7
carambole **277** 12
caramels **98** 77
carapace **364** 29
caravane *Camping* **278** 52
~ *Cirque* **307** 34
~ de chameaux **354** 1
~ pliante **278** 3
caravelle [«Santa Maria» 1492] **218** 27-43
~ «Santa Maria» **220** 37
carbone **242** 63
~, fibres de **235** 20, 32
carborundum, disque en **24** 35
carburant *Pétr.* **145** 54
~ *Ch. de f.* **209** 20
~ *Mar.* **221** 71
~ *Astron.* **234** 58
~, réservoir de **6** 7, 29, 37
~ diesel **145** 56
carburateur *Motocycl.* **189** 4
~ *Autom.* **192** 1-15
~ horizontal **190** 79
~ inversé **192** 1-15
carbure métallique **149** 46
carburéacteur **145** 57
carcasse de bois recouverte de peaux **353** 13
~ d'os recouverte de peaux **353** 13
~ du kayak pliant **283** 67
cardamine des prés **375** 11
cardan *Mach. agric.* **64** 40, 48
~ *Agric.* **67** 28
~ *Ch. de f.* **211** 51; **212** 29, 83
~ *Navig.* **224** 50
~ du propulseur **6** 36
carde **163** 34, 51
~ à chapeaux **163** 34
cardia **20** 41
cardinal **363** 5
~, nombre **344** 5
Carena **3** 46
carénage *Opt.* **113** 13
~ *Astron.* **235** 20
~ arrière **235** 63
~ des propulseurs **234** 6
~ intégral **189** 44
Carène **3** 46
carène d'hélice **227** 21
car-ferry **216** 10
cargaison **223** 77
~ inflammable **253** 38
cargo **221** 23, 57
~ à manutention horizontale *Mar.* **221** 54
~ à manutention horizontale *Ports* **226** 17
~ de transport roll-on roll-off **226** 17
~ mixte **221** 96
~ mixte passagers - marchandises **223** 1-71
~ porte-conteneurs *Mar.* **221** 89
~ porte-conteneurs *Ports* **225** 45; **226** 5
~ roll-on - roll-off **221** 54
cargue-bouline **218** 36
cargue-fond **219** 71
cariste **205** 30
carlin **70** 9
carlingue **283** 50; **288** 19
~ centrale **222** 53
~ latérale **222** 52
carnassier *Chasse* **86** 22
~ *Zool.* **367** 11-22; **368** 1-11
carnassière **86** 3

carnaval **306**
~, cortège de **306** 57-70
~, prince **306** 58
~, princesse **306** 61
carneau à gaz **152** 12
~ d'air **148** 2
carnivore **367** 11-22; **368** 1-11
carotide **18** 1
carotte longue **57** 17
~ ronde **57** 18
caroubier **384** 41
carpe *Anat.* **17** 15
~ *Zool.* **364** 4
~ miroir **364** 4
carpelle **59** 13; **374** 2, 26
carpocapse *Bot.* **58** 62
~ *Agric.* **80** 9
carpophore **381** 2
carquois **352** 27
carre **302** 21; **303** 11
~ d'acier **301** 4, 50
~ supérieure en aluminium **301** 51
carré *Méc.* **143** 9
~ *Ch. de f.* **203** 1-6
~ *Mar.* **228** 25
~ *Math.* **346** 33; **347** 31
~ de service **293** 12
carreau *Maison* **49** 19
~ *Jeux* **276** 41
~ de fenêtre **124** 16
~ de poêle en faïence **266** 35
carrelet **89** 29
carrier **158** 5
carrière *Cartogr.* **15** 87
~ *Carr.* **158** 1
~ *Equitation* **289** 1
~ d'argile **159** 1
carrossage **195** 17
carrosse **186** 1-3, 26-39, 45, 51-54
carrosserie autoporteuse **191** 1
carrosserie en plastique **193** 14
carrousel **114** 77
cartable **260** 9
carte **15** 1-114
~ à jouer **276** 36
~ allemande **276** 42-45
~ astronomique **3** 1-35
~ climatique **9** 40-58
~ d'électeur **263** 19
~ d'entrée au casino **275** 14
~ des vins **266** 31
~ du jour **266** 21
~ du monde **14** 10-45
~ géographique **14; 15**
~ météorologique *Météor.* **9** 1-39
~ météorologique *Ecriture* **342** 66
~ murale **260** 44
~ perforée *Poste* **237** 64
~ perforée *Informat.* **244** 13
carter **143** 79
~ de chaîne étanche **188** 46
~ de la poulie de tension de la bande **133** 32
~ de protection *Forge* **138** 9
~ de protection *Serr.* **140** 20
~ de protection *Imprim.* **180** 58
~ de protection *Ch. de f.* **202** 35
~ des cônes **163** 30
~ des deux tambours perforés **163** 21
~ d'huile *Mach. agric.* **65** 45
~ d'huile *Autom.* **192** 17
~ du train de roues amovibles **149** 7
~ du vilebrequin **242** 51
~ en tôle **187** 37
~ inférieur d'huile **190** 41
~ latéral amovible **188** 48
~ protecteur **157** 65
~ supérieur d'huile **190** 40
carter-cylindres *Moteur* **190** 19
~ *Autom.* **192** 21, 27
cartésiennes, coordonnées **347** 1
cartilage costal **17** 11
~ thyroïde **20** 3
cartomancienne **308** 36
carton **184** 12
~ à chapeaux **205** 11
~ apprêté **338** 22
~ bitumé **122** 62
~ d'avertissement **291** 63
~ de lait **76** 22
~ de table **45** 13
~ de transport **76** 30
~ d'expulsion **291** 63
~ feutre bitumé **122** 62
~ jaune **291** 63
~ rouge **291** 63
carton-cible **305** 30-33
carton-pierre **122** 62
cartouche *Chasse* **87** 54
~ *Dess.* **151** 31
~ *Carr.* **158** 27
~ *Arts* **336** 7
~ à percussion annulaire **305** 35
~ à plombs **87** 49
~ calibre 222 **305** 39
~ calibre 22 **305** 38
~ de papier à cigarettes **107** 17
~ de pellicule petit format 135 **114** 7
~ de ruban encreur **249** 16
~ d'encre de Chine **151** 36
~ en matière plastique **83** 25
~ filtrante **190** 29
~ fusible rechargeable **127** 36
caryatide **334** 36
caryophyllacée **60** 6; **69** 12
caryopse *Agric.* **68** 13, 25, 37
~ *Bot.* **375** 43
casaque de course **289** 26
cascade **272** 9
~ artificielle à gradins **272** 9
case blanche **276** 2
~ d'affichage de la destination **205** 22
~ d'affichage de l'heure de départ **205** 23
~ d'affichage du retard du train **205** 24
~ de l'échiquier **276** 6
~ de réception de cartes **195** 14
~ des équipements **234** 53
~ noire **276** 3
caserne des sapeurs-pompiers **270** 2
casier *Maison* **42** 2, **46** 4
~ *Bureau* **245** 4
~ à aliments **207** 83
~ à bagages **207** 71
~ à bouteilles **79** 11
~ à bouteilles de la contre-porte **39** 6
~ à clichés **245** 10
~ à correspondance **245** 30
~ à couverts **266** 48
~ à journaux *Univ.* **262** 16
~ à journaux *Café* **265** 8
~ à marchandise **47** 36
~ à médicaments **24** 7
~ à œufs **74** 32
~ à revues **262** 15
~ de boîtes postales **236** 13
~ de lit **46** 19
~ de peinture portatif **315** 34
~ du courrier avec les cases **267** 2
casino **274** 8
casoar **359** 1
casque *Electr. gd public* **241** 66
~ *Hérald.* **254** 4, 7-9
~ *Police* **264** 35
~ *Equitation* **289** 18
~ *Sports* **292** 24
~ *Alpin.* **300** 53
~ *Chevalerie* **329** 39-42
~ (à écouteurs) **309** 24
~ antifeu avec couvre-nuque **270** 38
~ de joute **329** 77
~ de protection *Sylvic.* **84** 23
~ de protection *Serr.* **140** 22
~ de protection *Police* **264** 21
~ (de protection) *Sports* **290** 3
~ de protection en plastique antichoc **127** 48
~ de scaphandre **6** 22
~ de ski **301** 13
~ d'écoute *Bureau* **249** 63
~ d'écoute *Ecole* **261** 38
~ d'écoute sans fil à récepteur infrarouge **242** 30
~ protecteur *Carr.* **158** 10
~ protecteur *Sports hiver* **303** 14
~ sèche-cheveux **105** 25
casquette **35** 40
~ (à bandes réfléchissantes) **199** 8
~ à visière avec cocarde **264** 8
~ blanche **268** 32
~ de chasse **86** 5
~ de cuir **35** 32
~ de dame **35** 1-21
~ de marin avec visière **35** 29
~ de service **264** 8
~ de ski **301** 18
~ de toile **35** 8
~ de velours **35** 25
~ de vison **35** 17
~ d'homme **35** 22-40
~ rouge **205** 43
casse *Compos.* **174** 3
~ *Bot.* **380** 16
casse-fil **165** 19, 37
Cassegrain, télescope de **5** 4
casse-lunettes **61** 1
casse-noix **45** 49
casserole **40** 16
~ d'hélice **230** 33
cassette de film **242** 18
~ de film 8 mm **117** 39
~ de film super 8 sonore **117** 29
~ de film universelle **242** 44
~ de pellicule format 126 **114** 15
~ de son **242** 17
~ Instamatic **114** 15
~ pour urographie **27** 14
~ stéréo **241** 33
~ très petit format 110 **114** 17
~ vidéo **243** 5
cassettes X **27** 2
Cassiopée **3** 33
Cassiopeia **3** 33
cassolette **332** 41
castagnettes **324** 46
castor **366** 14
Castor et Pollux **3** 28
catacombe **331** 59
catalogue de mode **104** 6
~ principal **262** 21
catamaran **284** 64
cataphote **187** 45
catapulte de lancement double **259** 14
cataracte **11** 45
catégorie d'abeilles **77** 1, 4, 5
caténaire *Tramw.* **197** 41
~ *Ch. de f.* **211** 41, 44-54
cathédrale **335** 1-13
cathétère cardiaque droit **25** 53
~ sous emballage stérile **26** 31
cathétérisme cardiaque **27** 30
cathode **178** 6
~ à chauffage direct **240** 25
catogan **34** 6
cautère **24** 43
cavalier *Constr.* **121** 14
~ *Jeux* **276** 11
~ de fichier **248** 4
~ de rodéo **319** 39
cave à vin **79** 1-22
~ à viscose **169** 11
~ de fermentation **93** 7
~ de stockage **93** 12
caveau de famille **331** 27
caverne *Géogr.* **13** 76
~ *Cartogr.* **15** 85
caviste **79** 12
cavité de l'ovaire **370** 62
~ de nidification **359** 29
~ de segmentation **74** 67
~ pour roue **195** 28
~ utérine **20** 80
cayeu **54** 29
cécidomyie destructive **80** 40
cédant **250** 27
cédille **342** 33
cèdre **372** 65
ceinture **29** 55; **30** 11; **31** 10, 12, 41; **32** 39; **33** 23, 59
~ coulissante **29** 67
~ coulissée **31** 66
~ de calme **9** 46-47
~ de cheveux **352** 38
~ de couleur indiquant le grade **299** 15
~ de natation en liège **282** 19
~ de plomp **279** 14
~ de plongée alourdie par des tares en plomb **279** 14
~ de protection de l'arbre **118** 80
~ élastique **31** 63
~ en soie **319** 23
~ nouée **31** 19
~ scapulaire **17** 6-7
ceinturon à mousquetons **270** 44
céleri **57** 27
célesta **325** 1

cella **334** 51
cellier **79** 1-22
cellule *Apicult.* **77** 26-30
~ *Photo* **114** 63
~ contenant l'œuf **77** 27
~ de la reine **77** 37
~ de lecture magnétique **241** 26
~ de mesure **116** 55
~ photo-électrique *Opt.* **112** 50
~ photo-électrique *Photo* **115** 37
~ photo-électrique dans l'axe creux **312** 49
~ rétinienne **77** 22
~ solaire **155** 34
cellulose, alcali- **169** 9
~, feuille de **169** 1, 2, 4, 6
~, plaque de **169** 1
~, xanthate de **169** 9
~ de hêtre **169** 1
~ de pin **169** 1
cément **19** 29
cendres de la résurrection **327** 10
cendrier *Maison* **42** 29
~ *Cout.* **104** 5
~ *Centr.* **152** 8
~ *Bureau* **246** 33
~ d'accoudoir **207** 46
~ pivotant **208** 29
~ sphérique **266** 5
~ ventilé **210** 6
cent **252** 19, 33
Centaure *Astr.* **3** 39
centaure *Best. fabul.* **327** 52
centaurée **61** 1
~, petite **380** 10
~ jacée **376** 12
Centaurus **3** 39
centavo **252** 23
centesimi **252** 20
centime **252** 15, 16
centimètre **103** 2
céntimo **252** 22
centrage du module de balayage **240** 23
central privé relié au réseau public **237** 17
~ téléphonique **237** 27-41
~ téléphonique privé **245** 13
centrale à béton **201** 19
~ atomique **154** 19
~ de concentration de données **242** 20
~ d'enrobage bitumineux **200** 48
~ électrique *Min.* **144** 13
~ électrique *Centr.* **152** 1-28; **153**
~ hydraulique **217** 39-46
~ inertielle **6** 43
~ nucléaire **154** 19
~ thermique **152** 1-28
centre *Hérald.* **254** 17
~ *Sports* **292** 42
~ *Math.* **346** 43
~, angle au **346** 55
~ d'accueil **204** 45
~ de calcul **244**
~ de courbure **346** 23
~ de gravité **346** 26
~ de la cible **288** 56
~ de loisirs **281**
~ de symétrie **351** 3
~ de transmission de données **248** 43
~ dépressionnaire **9** 5
~ du cristal **351** 3
~ d'usinage **150** 41
centre-ville **268**
centrifugeuse **23** 59
~ à caillebotte **76** 41
~ réunissant les filaments **169** 17
cep **78** 6
cèpe **381** 16
~ bai **381** 15
~ comestible **381** 16
~ de Bordeaux **381** 16
céphalopode *Zool.* **357** 37
~ *Faune abyss.* **369** 4
céramique cordée **328** 10
~ d'oxyde **149** 46
~ incisée **328** 35
~ rubanée **328** 13
Cerbère **327** 29
cerceau *Tonell.* **130** 8
~ *Cirque* **307** 58
~ de gymnastique **297** 46
cerclage **163** 5
cercle *Tonell.* **130** 8
~ *Math.* **346** 42; **347** 39
~, arc de **346** 53
~ annuel **84** 24
~ avec deux massues **297** 37
~ central **291** 2
~ circonscrit **346** 29
~ concentrique **346** 58
~ de charge **288** 67
~ d'envoi **292** 16
~ en fer **163** 5
~ extérieur de la cible **288** 59
~ gradué **113** 27
~ inscrit **346** 31
~ intérieur de la cible **288** 57
~ limite des étoiles circumpolaires **3** 5
~ médian de la cible **288** 58
~ méridien **113** 26
~ métallique **130** 3
~ polaire **14** 11
~ tendeur **324** 56
~ transversal au cheval d'arçon **296** 54
cercueil **331** 35
céréale **68** 1-37
cerf **88** 4
~ au brame **86** 12
~ bramant **86** 12
~ wapiti **367** 2
cerf-volant *Ecole* **260** 71
~ *Jeux enf.* **273** 42
~ *Math.* **346** 38
~ *Zool.* **358** 24
cerise **59** 5, 6-8; **370** 99
cerisier **59** 1-18
cerne **84** 24
cerveau **17** 42; **18** 22
cervelet **17** 45; **18** 23
cervidé à bois palmés **88** 40
C.E.S. **261** 1-45
cessionnaire **250** 26
cestode **81** 35
cétacé **367** 23-29
Cetus **3** 11
chabotte **139** 17, 31, 40
chacal **367** 11
chadburn **224** 25
chaînage **120** 34
chaîne *Agric.* **75** 15
~ *Comm.* **99** 95
~ *Tiss.* **165** 43; **166** 39
~ *Text.* **167** 24
chaîne *Text.* **171** 2
chaîne *Bicycl.* **187** 36
~ *Motocycl.* **188** 17; **189** 22
~, deuxième **239** 5
~, maillon de **36** 39
~, première **239** 4
~ à godets *Cours d'eau* **216** 57
~ à godets *Ports* **226** 42
~ à mortaiser sans fin **132** 50
chaîne à picots **168** 24
~ à pinces **168** 24
~ à rouleaux **187** 36
chaîne à rouleaux de commande de la pompe à huile **190** 25
~ à scier **85** 14
~ antidérapante **304** 10
chaîne articulée sans fin **132** 50
chaîne avec pièces **36** 36
~ compacte **241** 52
~ d'alimentation **74** 14
~ d'amenage *Papet.* **172** 67
chaîne d'amenage *Papet.* **172** 69
chaîne d'ancre **222** 77; **223** 50
~ d'arrêt **152** 38
~ d'attelage **65** 13
~ d'avancement **157** 17
~ de chapeaux **163** 45
~ de flèche **71** 20
~ de la scie **120** 16
~ de l'encensoir **332** 39
~ de montagnes **12** 39
~ de mouillage *Mar.* **222** 77
~ de mouillage *Navig.* **224** 72
~ de palan **139** 44
~ de sûreté **126** 3
~ de traction **65** 17
chaîne dentée sans fin **132** 50
chaîne double à rouleaux **190** 10
~ du dérailleur **290** 20
~ haute-fidélité *Maison* **42** 9
~ haute-fidélité *Discoth.* **317** 22-23
~ modèle **167** 19
~ rivée double **190** 49
~ stéréo modulaire **241** 13-48
chaîne-guide **65** 13
chaînette **71** 27
~ de sûreté **118** 30
chair à saucisse **96** 41
chaire *Ecole* **260** 22
~ *Univ.* **262** 4
~ à prêcher *Eglise* **330** 19
~ à prêcher *Arts* **337** 15
chaise **42** 34; **44** 10
~ à porteur **21** 21
~ bain de soleil **278** 59
~ biplace **214** 17
~ de camping **278** 43
~ de cuisine **39** 43
~ de jardin **37** 49
~ de laminoir **148** 61
~ (de poste) **186** 54
~ du juge-arbitre **293** 20
~ en tube métallique **41** 21
~ haute **28** 33
~ longue *Maison* **37** 47
~ longue *Jard.* **51** 2
~ longue *Thermal.* **274** 13
~ monoplace **214** 16
~ pliante *Puéricult.* **28** 33
~ pliante *Camping* **278** 43
~ tournante **248** 25
chaland **216** 25
~ de débarquement **258** 89
~ de transport **226** 46
chalaze **74** 63
chalcographie **340** 14-24
châle **31** 71
~ de couleur **355** 10
~ triangulaire **31** 71
chalet **278** 7
chaleur, échangeur de **259** 66
~, résistant à la **235** 34
chaloupe **258** 12, 45, 61
chalumeau *Orfèvre* **108** 14
~ *Soud.* **141** 19
~ *Rest.* **266** 46
~ *Mus.* **322** 10, 14
~ à gaz inerte **142** 33
~ à propane **125** 5-7
~ à souder **350** 9
~ de soudage à l'arc en atmosphère protégée **142** 33
~ oxyacétylénique **130** 14
~ soudeur **141** 11, 28
chalutier *Pêche* **90** 11
~ *Mar.* **221** 46, 86
chalvar **306** 42
chaman **353** 24
chamane **353** 24
chambranle **41** 26
chambre *Atome* **1** 66
~ *Mil.* **255** 10
~, robe de **32** 35
~ à air *Agric.* **74** 61
~ à air *Bicycl.* **187** 30
~ à bulles **1** 58
~ à condensation **2** 24
~ à coucher **43**
~ à deux lits avec salle de bains **267** 27-38
~ à vide *Atome* **2** 52
~ à vide *Lutte pestic.* **83** 12
~ à vide *Briq.* **159** 12
~ d'accrochage **144** 26
~ de captage d'une source **269** 24
~ de chauffage de l'air **147** 30
~ de chauffage du gaz **147** 28
~ de chauffe **259** 93
~ de combustion *Centr.* **152** 6
~ de combustion *Aéron.* **232** 37
~ de déflection d'air **199** 45
~ de détente de Wilson **2** 24
~ de fermentation **97** 72
~ de la reine **333** 3
~ de l'amiral **218** 27
~ de lancement de 4 roquette-s de faible portée **259** 26
~ de levage de la pâte **97** 72
~ de mélange **83** 62
~ de mesure **112** 43
~ de mise en charge **217** 40
~ de navigation **223** 14; **228** 22
~ de ponte **77** 46
~ de prise de vue **14** 63
~ de réverbération **311** 31
~ de séchage *Briq.* **159** 17
~ de séchage *Text.* **168** 28; **170** 49
~ de stockage **154** 71, 76
~ d'eau **242** 54
~ d'enfant **47**
~ des machines **221** 10
~ des machines auxiliaires *Mar.* **223** 70
~ des machines auxiliaires *Mil.* **259** 56

~ des moteurs électriques **223** 68
~ d'explosion **153** 55
~ d'extinction **153** 55
~ d'hôtel **267** 27-38
~ d'ionisation **2** 2, 17
~ du capitaine **218** 45; **223** 13
~ du moteur principal **223** 72
~ du roi **333** 2
~ d'un officier **223** 21
~ froide *Abatt.* **94** 21-24
~ froide *Mar.* **223** 56
~ froide de stockage **225** 50
~ funéraire **333** 5
~ grand format à soufflet **114** 49
~ métrique universelle de photogrammétrie **112** 67
~ photographique **112** 20; **113** 40
chambre-laboratoire compacte **177** 32
~ universelle **177** 24
chambrière **307** 53
chameau *Ethnol.* **354** 1
~ *Zool.* **366** 29
chamois **367** 3
champ **63** 4, 17
~, joueur de **292** 2, 41
~ de bataille **15** 93
~ de céréales **63** 32
~ de foire **308** 1
~ de lave **11** 14
~ d'inondation **216** 42, 48
~ du viseur **115** 51
~ en chaume **63** 33
~ stérile **26** 38
champagne, bouchon de **267** 58
~, seau à **267** 59
~, verre à **45** 85-86
champignon **381** 3, 10, 11
~ à lamelles **379** 10
~ comestible **381**
~ de couche **381** 1
~ de Paris **381** 1
~ du rail **202** 2
~ vénéneux **379** 10-13
championnat d'échecs **276** 16
chancelière *Puéricult.* **28** 38
~ *Hiver* **304** 27
chandelier de table **45** 16
~ pascal **330** 45
chandelle *Constr.* **119** 13; **121** 81
~ *Gymnast.* **295** 29
~ à crémaillère **119** 86
~ avant droite **282** 13
~ avec tonneau déclenché **288** 6
~ de cire **77** 66
chanfrein *Cheval* **72** 6
~ *Méc.* **143** 62
~ *Chevalerie* **329** 84
change *Aéroport* **233** 51
~ *Banque* **250** 10
~, agent de **251** 4
~, lettre de **250** 12
changement de carre **302** 12
~ de face au cheval **297** 30
~ de marche **210** 18, 56
~ de route **285** 27
~ de vitesse **211** 50
~ de vitesse de la prise de force **65** 23, 40
changeur de monnaie *Tramw.* **197** 33
~ de monnaie *Ch. de f.* **204** 22
~ de prise **211** 10, 13
~ de prises haute tension **153** 13
chanlatte **122** 43
chanterelle **323** 9
~ comestible **381** 14
chanteur **315** 22
chantier **120** 1-59
~ de construction **118; 119**
~ de construction navale **222** 1-43
~ de triage **206** 42
~ naval **222** 1-43
chanvre **383** 9
chape *Opt.* **113** 13
~ *Mus.* **326** 15
~ *Hist. cost.* **355** 26
~ de finition lissée **123** 40
~ de mortier **123** 27
~ d'égalisation **123** 39
~ lissée **123** 14
chapeau **381** 4
~ à brides **306** 23
~ à plumes **35** 12
~ à plumes en mohair **35** 6
~ d'artiste **35** 38
~ de chasse **86** 5
~ de dame *Coiffures* **35** 1-21
~ de dame *Maison* **41** 11
~ de feutre **35** 22
~ de feutre de poil **35** 15
~ de feutre de poil rêche **35** 24
~ de nettoyage **164** 22
~ de paille **35** 35
~ de palier du vilebrequin **190** 22
~ de plage **280** 20
~ de soleil *Cost.* **29** 16
~ de soleil *Plage* **280** 20
~ de vison **35** 18
~ des aiguilles à crochet **167** 56
~ d'étaiement **119** 61
~ d'été en tissu **35** 37
~ d'homme **35** 13, 14, 22-40
~ du battant **166** 6
~ florentin **35** 21
~ galvanisé **122** 102
~ haut de forme *Coiffures* **35** 36
~ haut de forme *Voit. chev.* **186** 25
~ loden **35** 23
~ mou à larges bords **35** 38
~ mou de cow-boy **319** 37
~ orné d'un bouquet **35** 7
~ rond de picador **319** 20
~ rond et noir du torero **319** 29
~ thessalien **355** 4
chapelet *Cours d'eau* **216** 57
~ *Ports* **226** 42
~ *Eglise* **332** 30
~ de chapeaux **163** 45
chapelle *Cartogr.* **15** 61
~ *Aéroport* **233** 49
~ castrale **329** 29
~ commémorative **331** 12
~ du château **329** 29
~ du cimetière **331** 28
~ mortuaire **331** 21
~ votive **331** 12
chapellerie **268** 38
chaperon du faucon **86** 44
chapiteau **334** 20-25
~ à palmette-s **333** 25
~ à protomes de taureau **333** 28
~ à quatre mâts de corniche **307** 1
~ arabe **337** 18
~ campaniforme **333** 16
~ cubique **335** 21
~ du cirque **307** 1
~ lotiforme **333** 14
chapon **73** 21
char à bancs **186** 33
~ de carnaval **306** 57
~ de combat **255** 80
~ de lutte antichar **255** 88
charançon **80** 49
~ du blé **81** 16
~ du maïs **81** 26
~ du pin **82** 41
charbon *Orfèvre* **108** 37
~ *Text.* **170** 1
~, parc à **225** 19
~, pelle à **38** 43
~ à coke **156** 1
~ actif **270** 58
~ de bois **278** 48
~ de carbonisation **156** 1
~ négatif **312** 41
~ positif **312** 40
charbonnage **144** 1-51
charcuterie *Bouch.* **96** 6-11
~ *Epic.* **98** 4
~ en tranches **96** 14
chardon **61** 32
~ argenté **61** 32
~ des champs **61** 32
chardonneret **360** 1
charge **73** 5
~ complète **206** 52
~ de plombs **87** 51
~ de poudre **87** 57
~ immobilisée **299** 5
~ unitaire **226** 21
~ unitaire emballée **225** 42; **226** 9
~ unitaire emballée de marchandises diverses **226** 11
chargement du coke **156** 15
~ en pontée **221** 90
chargeur *Mach. agric.* **64** 72
~ *Chasse* **87** 15
~ *Constr.* **118** 35
~ *Imprim.* **181** 7
~ *Mil.* **255** 7, 15, 21
~ à barillet avec changement des cannettes **166** 5
~ à lumière du jour **177** 50
~ de cassette **249** 72
~ de film **311** 7
~ des batteries du stimulateur du patient **25** 51
~ hydraulique de balles **63** 37
chargeuse **163** 9
~ à alimentation automatique **163** 33
chariot *Mach.-out.* **150** 13
~ *Text.* **167** 39
~ à bagages **205** 32
~ à bec pivotant **222** 21
~ à benne basculante **147** 64
~ à bouteilles **141** 23
~ à bras **120** 6
~ à commande par chaîne **133** 38
~ à fourche **226** 8
~ à laitier **147** 10
~ à provisions **50** 87
~ à ridelles **309** 86
~ auxiliaire **157** 11
~ cultuel **328** 36
~ cultuel miniature **328** 36
~ de chargement *Min.* **144** 8
~ de chargement *Cokerie* **156** 6
~ de David **3** 29
~ de déchets de bois **157** 16
~ de golf **293** 85
~ de la chambre de fermentation **97** 73
~ de la table d'opération **26** 36
~ de métal portant les casiers à œufs **74** 31
~ de pantographe **175** 53
~ de peinture **315** 36
~ de rectification **150** 3
~ de roulement **152** 41
~ de scie **132** 71
~ de serrage **157** 12
~ de soudage autogène **138** 35
~ de transport *Agric.* **74** 39
~ de transport *Sports* **283** 66
~ déposeur **159** 18
~ d'extinction avec locomotive **156** 10
~ d'extinction du coke **144** 11
~ d'outillage **195** 42
~ électrique **205** 29; **206** 34
~ élévateur *Brass.* **93** 23
~ élévateur *Briq.* **159** 18
~ élévateur à fourche *Ch. de f.* **206** 16
~ élévateur à fourche *Ports* **225** 44
~ extincteur avec locomotive **156** 10
~ guide-coke **156** 9
~ longitudinal **149** 42
~ porte-aiguilles **185** 24
~ porte-bobines **164** 30
~ récepteur à bord **226** 15
~ répartiteur de béton **201** 5
~ roulant *Métall.* **147** 3
~ roulant *Mar.* **222** 14, 28
~ supérieur **149** 22
~ transporteur *Scierie* **157** 52
~ transporteur *Ports* **226** 4
~ transporteur de terre à foulon **199** 38
~ transversal **149** 23, 39
chariotage, barre de **149** 33
chariot-cuve **147** 10
chariot-treuil **222** 14
charlatan **308** 12
charme **371** 63
charmeur de serpents **353** 45
charnière **111** 14
~ en X **151** 50
charpente *Constr.* **120**
~ *Vann.* **136** 25
~ *Arts* **334** 52; **337** 9
~ de comble **120** 7
~ de la grue **226** 53
~ du navire **222** 44-61
~ longitudinale **222** 44-56
~ métallique **5** 18
charpentes de combles **121** 27-83
charpentier **120** 12
charretée de fumier **63** 15
charriage **12** 7
charrue **63** 6
~ à avant-train **65** 1
~ à quatre socs **63** 40
~ monosoc **65** 1

~ de la noctuelle **80** 44
~ de la piéride du chou **80** 48
~ processionnaire **82** 16
~ squelettisant la feuille **80** 8
chénopode **61** 25
chermès **82** 38
cheval *Zool.* **71; 73** 2
~ *Cheval* **72**
~ *Gymnast.* **296** 1; **297** 1
~, corps de **327** 27, 45, 54
~, crins de **323** 15
~, culotte de **289** 5
~, en fer à **260** 1
~, patte de **327** 42
~, queue de *Barbes, coiffures* **34** 27
~, queue de *Taurom.* **319** 26
~ ailé **327** 26
~ au dressage **289** 3
~ caparaçonné **319** 18
~ d'arçon **296** 5
~ d'attelage **186** 28
~ de bois **308** 2
~ de cirque cabré **307** 30
~ de côté **186** 47
~ de front **186** 46
~ de poste **186** 43
~ de relais **186** 43
~ de voiture **186** 28
~ des steppes **352** 4
~ du poète **327** 26
~ en peluche **47** 15
~ entier **73** 2
~ marin **364** 18
~ pie **289** 29
cheval-arçons **296** 5
chevalement **144** 1
~ de pompage **145** 22
chevalerie **329**
chevalet *Cartogr.* **14** 50
~ *Vann.* **136** 10
~ *Mus.* **322** 17; **323** 5; **325** 32
~ *Peintre* **338** 3
~ de dessinateur **338** 34
~ de pointage **255** 42
~ d'échafaudage **122** 66
Chevalet du Peintre **3** 47
chevalet freineur **304** 6
~ portatif **338** 26
~ portatif du vitrier **124** 9
~ pour tirer au cordeau **118** 69
chevalier **329** 38-65, 67
chevalière **36** 20
~ à monogramme **36** 40
cheval-sautoir **296** 1
chevauchement *Géogr.* **12** 7
~ *Constr.* **122** 100
chevêche **362** 19
chevelure **16** 3
~ de l'ennemi **352** 15
chevet, lampe de **43** 15
chevêtre **120** 41; **121** 71
cheveux, brosse à **28** 7
~, épingle à **301** 69
~ en brosse **34** 11
~ longs **34** 1
~ postiches **105** 38
chevillard **94** 1
cheville *Orfèvre* **108** 22
~ *Mus.* **323** 18; **324** 11
~ d'accord **324** 23; **325** 17
~ d'assemblage d'escalier **123** 46
~ de bois **121** 92
~ percutante **94** 4
chevillère **291** 33
chevillier **323** 19, 22; **324** 10, 19
chevillure **88** 8
chèvre **73** 14
~, tête de **327** 18
chevreau **73** 14
chèvrefeuille **374** 13
chevrette *Zool.* **73** 14
~ *Chasse* **88** 34
~ adulte **88** 34
~ vierge **88** 34
chevreuil **86** 17; **88** 28-39
chevrillard **88** 39
chevron *Constr.* **121** 28, 36; **122** 19
~ *Arts* **335** 16
~ d'arête **121** 62
~ intermédiaire **121** 56
chianti **98** 61
chibouk **107** 32
chibouque **107** 32
chicane Allais **301** 72
~ antiballottante **234** 13
chicorée **57** 40
~ frisée **57** 40
~ sauvage **376** 25
chicot retaillé **24** 27
chien **73** 16
~, biscuit de **99** 37
~ attaché **99** 7
~ courant **70** 24
~ d'arrêt **70** 41, 43
~ de berger **73** 16
~ de chasse **86** 7
~ de fusil **255** 4
~ de garde **62** 32
~ de garde et de compagnie **70** 25
~ de meute *Chasse* **86** 33
~ de meute *Equitation* **289** 47
~ de police **264** 6
~ de traîneau **353** 2
~ d'Esquimau **353** 2
~ d'étoffe **47** 7
~ dressé à la chasse du sanglier **86** 33
~ d'utilité **70** 25
~ esquimau **70** 22
~ gardien de l'enfer païen **327** 29
~ policier **264** 6
chiendent **61** 30
chienne **73** 16
chiens, traîneau à **353** 3
chiffre arabe **344** 2
~ des centaines **344** 3
~ des centièmes **344** 20
~ des dixièmes **344** 20
~ des dizaines **344** 3
~ des millièmes **344** 20
~ des milliers **344** 3
~ des unités **344** 3
~ romain **344** 1
~ 1 **253** 33
~ 0 **253** 34
chifonie **322** 25
chignole **140** 13
chignon **34** 29
chimère **327** 16
chimpanzé **368** 14
chinoise **341** 5
chiot 73 16
~ à laitier **147** 9
chiourme **218** 48
chips **45** 41
chique **107** 19
chiroptère **366** 9
chirurgien dentiste **24** 1
chistera **305** 69
chitarrone **324** 1
chiton **355** 5
chitonactis **369** 20
chloration du benzène **170** 8
chlore **170** 7
chlorobenzène **170** 9, 11
chlorure **1** 10
~ de calcium **350** 43
~ de sodium *Atome* **1** 9
~ de sodium *Text.* **170** 13
chocolat **98** 80
~, tablette de **98** 78
~, truffes au **98** 86
chocolats, boîte de **98** 79
chœur *Théât.* **315** 21
~ *Eglise* **330** 32
~ *Arts* **335** 4
~, enfant de **330** 40; **331** 45
cholecystographie **27** 4
chope *Rest.* **266** 3
~ *Marché puces* **309** 53
chopper **188** 56
chou **57** 32
~ à la crème **97** 27
~ cabus **57** 32
~ de Bruxelles **57** 30
~ de Milan **57** 33
~ frisé **57** 34
~ pommé **57** 32
~ rouge **57** 32
choucas **361** 2
chouette **252** 2
~ chevêche **362** 19
~ effraie **362** 17
chou-fleur *Agric.* **57** 31
~ *Comm.* **99** 84
chou-rave **57** 26
chow-chow **70** 21
chrisme **332** 67
Christ, tableau représentant le **330** 50
chromolithographie **340** 28
chronocomparateur **109** 27
chronomètre *Méd.* **27** 35
~ *Radiodiff.* **238** 62
~ électronique **238** 31
chronométreur **282** 24; **299** 47
chronomicromètre **23** 40
chrysalide *Apicult.* **77** 30
~ *Zool.* **365** 11
chrysanthème *Jard.* **51** 29
~ *Bot.* **61** 7
chute de la grand-voile **284** 45
~ de neige **8** 18
~ de papier d'apprêt **128** 8
~ de pluie **8** 18
~ de tissu **103** 16
~ d'eau **11** 45
~ libre **288** 60-62
cible **305** 66
~ cruciforme **288** 52, 56
~ de tir **305** 30-33
~ mobile **305** 33
~ pour le tir à 50 mètres *Sports* **305** 30
~ pour le tir à 100 mètres *Sports* **305** 32
~ tracée au sol **288** 52-54
~ vivante **307** 39
ciboire avec les petites hosties **332** 48
ciboulette **57** 22
cicatricule **74** 66
cicéro **175** 28
cierge de Notre-Dame **376** 9
~ du maître-autel **330** 34
~ pascal **330** 44
~ votif **330** 53
cigare *Ust. fumeurs* **107** 2
~ *Hôtel* **267** 49
cigarette *Ust. fumeurs* **107** 12
~ *Hôtel* **267** 49
~ *Cité* **268** 69
~ à bouquin **107** 14
cigarette-filtre **107** 12
cigarillo **107** 3
çikkara **337** 26
cil **19** 41
~ vibratile **357** 10
cimaise **128** 29
cime *Géogr.* **11** 6; **12** 40
~ *Bot.* **370** 4
ciment **118** 43
~, sac de **118** 43
~, silo à *Constr.* **119** 30
~, silo à *Constr. rout.* **201** 22
cimenterie **160**
cimetière *Cartogr.* **15** 106
~ *Eglise* **331** 21-41
cimier *Chasse* **88** 18, 35
~ *Hérald.* **254** 1, 1,11,30-36
~ de bœuf **95** 35
cinéma **310; 311; 312** 1; **313**
~ ambulant **312** 52
~ d'amateur **117**
Cinémascope, caméra **310** 47
cinq-mâts barque **220** 32-34
~ carré «Preussen» **220** 35
cinquième octave **321** 48
~ porte **193** 16
~ position **314** 6
~ position ouverte **314** 5
cintre **126** 83
~, arc en plein **336** 27
~ à vêtements **41** 3
cintres **316** 1-60
cintreuse de tubes **126** 82
cirage, boîte de **50** 39
~, brosse à **50** 42
~, tube de **50** 43
circonférence **346** 44
circuit de vapeur d'eau **154** 51
~ d'eau de refroidissement **154** 10
~ eau - vapeur **154** 45
~ électronique **110** 8
~ en éléments modulaires **242** 68-72
~ intégré *Horlog.* **110** 16
~ intégré *Enseign.* **242** 68
~ primaire *Nucl.* **154** 42
~ primaire *Mil.* **259** 65
~ primaire de refroidissement **154** 2
~ primaire de sodium **154** 2
~ secondaire *Nucl.* **154** 45
~ secondaire *Mil.* **259** 63
~ secondaire de refroidissement **154** 7
~ secondaire de sodium **154** 7
circuits **110** 16
circulaire d'évacuation des gaz du four **147** 53
circulation atmosphérique générale **9** 46-52
~ d'air **199** 45
~ sanguine **18** 1-21
circumduction costale **297** 39
cire **339** 26
~, bougie de **260** 76
ciré **228** 4
cirque *Ch. de f.* **206** 20
~ *Cirque* **307**
~ ambulant **307** 1-63
cirro-cumulus **8** 14

cirro-stratus **8** 7
cirrus **8** 6
cisaille *Orfèvre* **108** 23
~ *Ferbl.* **125** 1
~ à blooms **148** 52
~ à carton **183** 16
~ à chantourner **125** 2
~ à gazon **56** 48
~ à haies **56** 49
~ à main **119** 22, 87
~ américaine **119** 87
~ articulée **100** 39
~ circulaire à carton **184** 20
~ coupe-boulons **119** 87
~ pour bracelets métalliques **109** 19
cisaille-guillotine **125** 26
ciseau *Gymnast.* **295** 39
~ *Arts graph.* **340** 7
~ à bois *Constr.* **120** 71
~ à bois *Bricol.* **134** 30
~ à bords biseautés **132** 11
~ à os **24** 49
~ biseauté **132** 7
~ biseauté à brides **132** 11
~ de menuisier **132** 7
~ de tourneur **135** 24
~ plat **339** 14, 19
~ pointu **140** 25
ciseaux **260** 49
~ à désépaissir **105** 8; **106** 33
~ à effiler **105** 8; **106** 33
~ courbes **22** 51; **26** 42
~ de coiffeur **105** 7; **106** 34
~ de coupe *Cout.* **103** 3
~ de coupe *Coiff.* **105** 7
~ de lingère **100** 43
~ de tailleur **103** 3; **104** 11
~ de tapissier **128** 34
~ «sculpteurs» **106** 34
~ simples **298** 21
cistre **322** 21
citerne *Tonell.* **130** 17
~ *Autom.* **194** 30
~ remorquée **194** 30-33
cithare **322** 15; **324** 21
citron *Zool.* **365** 4
~ *Bot.* **384** 23
~ confit **98** 10
citronnat **98** 10
citrouille **57** 23
city-bike **188** 20
civadière **218** 43
civière *Pompiers* **270** 23
~ *Eglise* **331** 41
civil, en **264** 33
civilisation des gobelets campaniformes **328** 14
~ des gobelets en entonnoir **328** 12
~ mégalithique **328** 11
clafoutis **97** 22
~ de la Forêt-Noire **97** 24
claie *Jard.* **55** 6
~ *Constr.* **118** 85
~ circulaire à lamelles en bois et à ferrures **130** 2
clair **9** 21
clairière **15** 2
clameau à deux pointes **121** 97
clap **310** 35
clapet d'aération *Maison* **38** 52
~ d'aération *Mil.* **259** 92
~ de pied **269** 6, 14, 43
~ de surpression d'huile **190** 67
~ d'épandage **200** 42
~ d'évacuation des gaz d'échappement **259** 92
clapman **310** 34
claque **100** 60
claquebois **324** 61
claquement de main de synchronisation **117** 69
claquette *Carnaval* **306** 40
~ *Ciné* **310** 35
clarinette *Boîte nuit* **318** 4
~ *Mus.* **323** 34
~ basse **323** 34
clarinettiste **318** 5
classe de voilier **284** 49-65
classeur *Papet.* **172** 57
~ *Bureau* **245** 4, 6; **248** 5
~ à anneaux **260** 15
~ à levier **247** 37
~ à timbres **236** 20
~ de microfilms **237** 37
~ de relevés **247** 40
~ rotatif **172** 23
clavaire dorée **381** 32
claveau **336** 22
clavecin **322** 45
~ à marteaux **325** 1
clavette **143** 73-74
~ à talon **143** 74
~ normale **143** 73
~ noyée **143** 73
~ ordinaire **143** 73
clavicorde **322** 36
~ libre **322** 36
~ lié **322** 36
clavicule **17** 6
clavier *Photocomp.* **176** 2
~ *Poste* **236** 44; **237** 70
~ *Bureau* **249** 2-6
~ *Mus.* **322** 28; **324** 40; **325** 4-5, 48
~, téléphone à **237** 20
~ à boutons poussoirs **245** 14
~ à touches **245** 14; **246** 14
~ de l'installation téléphonique de service **238** 14
~ de machine à écrire **245** 27
~ de sélection **25** 50
~ de service **261** 45
~ d'élève **242** 4
~ d'introduction de données **238** 13
~ inférieur **322** 47
~ manuel I du positif dorsal **326** 42
~ manuel II du grand orgue **326** 43
~ manuel III de récit **326** 44
~ manuel IV de bombarde **326** 45
~ Monotype **174** 32
~ supérieur **322** 46
claviste **176** 4
clayette **39** 3
~ de comptage des œufs **89** 19
clayonnage **216** 54
clé *Serr.* **140** 33-35
~ *Autom.* **195** 44
~ *Mus.* **320** 8-11
~ à crémaillère **126** 68
~ à molette **126** 66
~ anglaise **126** 67
~ d'accordeur **325** 20
~ d'antivol **187** 50
~ d'arc **215** 31
~ de bras avec levier de jambe **299** 10
~ de fa **320** 9
~ de jambe, double **299** 11
~ de sol **320** 8
~ de sûreté **140** 48
~ de voûte **335** 32; **336** 23
~ d'ut quatrième **320** 11
~ d'ut troisième **320** 10
~ dynamométrique **195** 45
~ en fer **328** 32
~ pendante **121** 68
~ plate **140** 48
~ serre-tubes **126** 59
~ tricoise **270** 27
clef **140** 33-35
~ d'accord **323** 59
~ de clarinette **323** 35
~ de flûte **323** 32
~ de la chambre **267** 9
cliché *Imprim.* **178** 38
~ *Bureau* **245** 8, 9, 10
~ *Arts graph.* **340** 59
~ cylindrique **178** 13
~ cylindrique pour rotative **178** 21
~ de cuivre **340** 53
~ de la chambre de Wilson **2** 26
~ de similigravure **178** 38
~ de trait **178** 42
~ de zinc **340** 52
~ latéral **27** 3
~ panoramique **24** 21
~ simili **178** 38
~ tramé **178** 38
client *Comm.* **99** 2
~ *Opt.* **111** 2
~ *Bureau* **248** 18
~ *Rest.* **266** 25
~ *Magasin* **271** 55
~ de l'hôtel **267** 14
~ du bar **267** 55
~ du café **265** 22-24
cliente *Epic.* **98** 43
~ *Comm.* **99** 18
~ *Rest.* **266** 25
~ *Magasin* **271** 16
~ de la banque **250** 6
clignotant *Motocycl.* **189** 37
~ *Tramw.* **197** 22
~ arrière **189** 42
~ intégré **189** 45
clignoteur avant **191** 19
-climat, zone de **9** 53-58
climat boréal **9** 56
~ équatorial **9** 53
~ polaire **9** 57-58
climatiseur **239** 15
climatologie **9**
clinch **299** 31
clin-foc **219** 12, 23
clinopinacoïde **351** 24
clinoprisme **351** 24
clip **2** 18
clipper anglais «Spindrift» **220** 36
clips obturant le trou de graissage **187** 62
cliquet de remontage **110** 34
clitellum **357** 26
clitocybe géotrope **381** 25
clitoris **20** 88
clivie **53** 8
cloche *Plomb.* **126** 16
~ *Ch. de f.* **212** 49
~ *Navig.* **224** 75
~ *Sports* **288** 5
~ à fonctionnement électrique **331** 9
~ à fromages **40** 7
~ de haut fourneau **147** 6
clocher **331** 2
~, coq du **331** 3
~, flèche du **331** 6
clochette de la sacristie **330** 46
~ liturgique **332** 52
cloison acoustique **248** 20
~ de bois **38** 19
~ de décrochage **231** 8
~ de planches **119** 25; **120** 9
~ de séparation de la couche limite **257** 13
~ de séparation des réservoirs **234** 16
~ d'insonorisation **248** 20
~ en charpente **120** 48
~ étanche de pressurisation **231** 32
~ interventriculaire **20** 52
~ maçonnée **120** 59
~ pare-feu **305** 91
~ séparatrice **248** 1
~ vitrée **317** 28
cloisonnette **248** 1, 39
cloître **331** 52
~, arc de **336** 41
cloporte de cave **81** 6
clôture *Maison* **37** 53
~ *Sylvic.* **84** 7
~ *Vann.* **136** 18
~ à claire-voie *Maison* **37** 53
~ à claire-voie *Jard.* **52** 10
~ de fond **136** 20
~ de protection pour le gibier **199** 13
~ du chantier **118** 44
~ électrique **62** 46
~ en fil de fer **15** 39
~ en lattis **52** 10
clou **143** 51
~ à ardoise **122** 74
~ à tête large **122** 96
~ de girofle *Agric.* **80** 11
~ de girofle *Bot.* **382** 28
~ décoratif **253** 8
clous **268** 24
cloutage **253** 8
clown **307** 24
~ musical **307** 23
clowns, entrée des **307** 25
club **283** 23
~, fauteuil **267** 26
~ en bois **293** 91
~ en fer **293** 92
club-house **283** 23
cobaye **366** 12
cocarde *Zool.* **71** 16
~ *Police* **264** 8
coccinelle **358** 37
coccinellidé **358** 37
coccyx **17** 5; **20** 60
coche **186** 1-3, 26-39, 45, 51-54
cochenille **80** 35
Cocher *Astr.* **3** 27
cocher *Voit. chev.* **186** 32
~ de la diligence **186** 40
cochevis huppé **361** 19
cochon *Agric.* **62** 10
~ *Zool.* **73** 9; **366** 12
~ *Chasse* **86** 32
~ de boucherie **94** 11
~ de lait **73** 9
~ d'Inde **366** 12
cochonnet **305** 23
cocker spaniel **70** 38
cockpit **283** 8; **285** 38; **288** 10
cocktail **317** 33
~, verre à **267** 56

coco, noix de **383** 53
cocon *Agric.* **80** 7
~ *Zool.* **358** 51
cocotier **383** 48
cocotte *Ust. cuis.* **40** 14
~ *Carnaval* **306** 37
~ minute **278** 35
codage des images **242** 8-10
~ du son **242** 11-14
code **191** 20
~ des pavillons **253** 29
Code international des signaux **253** 29
code postal **236** 43
coefficient **345** 4
cœlentéré **357** 14
cœlenthéré **369** 5, 9, 14, 20
cœur *Anat.* **18** 14; **20** 8, 24-25, 45-57
~ *Hérald.* **254** 17
~ *Jeux* **276** 40
~, ligne de **19** 74
~ d'aiguille **202** 24
~ de Jeannette **60** 5
~ de Marie **60** 5
~ du bois *Constr.* **120** 84
~ du bois *Bot.* **370** 13
~ du réacteur **259** 68
coffrage de fourche **188** 50
~ de la poutre maîtresse **119** 12
~ du poteau **119** 11, 73
~ et ferraillage du béton **119** 54-76
coffre *Horlog.* **110** 26
~ *Autom.* **193** 17, 23
~ *Mil.* **259** 19
~ à bagages **191** 24; **194** 13
~ à linge **50** 21
~ (à tiroirs) avec trappe abattante **246** 5
~ à tiroirs du bureau-ministre **248** 37
~ à vêtements **212** 63
~ de la corniche **122** 42
~ de pierre **328** 17
~ d'horloge **309** 57
coffre-bloc **246** 22
coffre-fort **246** 22
coffret à bijoux **36** 31
~ de commande **179** 33
~ de commande électrique **168** 25
~ de compteur **127** 31
~ de coupe-circuit fusible **166** 23
~ de jeux **47** 18
~ de phonographe **309** 35
~ de raccordement **237** 67
~ de télévision **240** 2
~ électrique **41** 19
~ électrique de commande **168** 58
cognac **98** 59
cognassier **58** 46
~ du Japon **373** 17
cognée à équarrir **120** 73
coiffe **235** 20
~ de cuir **354** 26
~ de la racine **19** 28
~ de soudeur **142** 3
coiffeur *Coiff.* **106** 1
~ *Aéroport* **233** 53
~ *Ciné* **310** 36
~ pour dames **105**
~ pour hommes **106**
coiffeuse *Maison* **43** 25
~ *Coiff.* **105** 19, 35
coiffure *Barbes, coiffures* **34**
~ *Coiffures* **35**
~ *Coiff.* **106** 3
~ *Ethnol.* **354** 9
~ à chignon **34** 28
~ à frange **34** 35
~ à la garçonne **34** 34
~ à macarons **34** 37
~ afro **34** 26
~ bouclée **34** 18, 33
~ de dame **34** 27-38
~ de style Louis **355** 81
~ en diadème **34** 31
~ masculine **34** 1-25
coin *Sylvic.* **85** 4
~ *Constr.* **119** 15
~ *Menuis.* **132** 19
~ *Carr.* **158** 7
~ *Argent* **252** 40-41
~ *Jeux* **276** 27
~ *Sports* **292** 18
~ de bois dur **121** 96
~ de fixation **85** 9
~ de la rue **198** 12
~ de serrage **181** 39
~ du feu **267** 22
~ fenêtre **207** 58
~ freineur **304** 2
~ inférieur **252** 41
~ neutre **299** 38
~ optique **176** 22
~ repas **42** 33-34; **44** 1-11
~ supérieur **252** 40
coing poire **58** 50
~ pomme **58** 49
coke **147** 2
~, menu **156** 14
~ fin **156** 14
~ grossier **156** 14
cokerie *Min.* **144** 7-11
~ *Cokerie* **156** 1-15
~ pour la distillation sèche du charbon **170** 2
col *Géogr.* **12** 47
~ *Cost.* **31** 23; **33** 58
~ *Eglise* **332** 6
~ à parement **186** 22
~ à volants **31** 46
~ de cygne **175** 50
~ de cygne, bâti en **27** 17
~ de fourrure **30** 63
~ de la crosse **87** 7
~ de l'utérus **20** 85
~ de papier **106** 5
~ en tricot **33** 31
~ long **350** 38
~ marin **30** 5
~ officier **30** 43
~ rabattu **31** 69
~ roulé **30** 2
col-boule **30** 3
colchique **379** 3
coléoptère **82** 26, 42
~ lamellicorné **82** 1
~ ravisseur **358** 39
~ stercoraire **358** 39
coléoptères **358** 24-39
coli de détail **206** 4
colibri **363** 4
colis, guichet des **236** 1
~ de détail **206** 31
~ express **204** 1
collage **260** 50-52
collant **29** 42; **32** 12
~ pied nu **32** 11
collatéral **335** 2
colle **48** 4
~, pot à **260** 57
~, tube de **260** 51
~ à dispersion **128** 28
~ à tapisser **128** 23
~ blanche **134** 36
~ pour film **312** 22
~ (pour machine à encoller) **128** 26
~ pour papiers peints **128** 4
~ spéciale **128** 24
~ universelle **260** 51
collecteur **10** 40, 45
~ de boues *Nett.* **199** 47
~ de boues *Ch. de f.* **210** 28
~ de condensat **172** 17
~ de fuites **190** 53
~ de gaz **156** 17
~ de poussière **133** 20
~ de poussières *Métall.* **147** 14
~ de poussières *Papet.* **172** 6
~ de vapeur **210** 21
~ d'eau de retour **172** 26
~ d'échappement **190** 36
~ du fluide frigorigène **92** 7
collecteur-pulsateur **75** 32
collection de crânes **261** 15
collège d'enseignement secondaire **261** 1-45
collerette **306** 20
collet *Méc.* **143** 64
~ *Inst. fluv.* **217** 67
~ *Hist. cost.* **355** 39, 56
~ avec le carré découvert **95** 6
~ de betterave **68** 46
colleuse **117** 89
collier *Joaill.* **36** 2
~ *Zool.* **71** 15
~ *Viande* **95** 20
~ *Constr.* **122** 31
~ à contrepartie et embase plate **126** 53
~ à contrepartie et embase taraudée **126** 54
~ d'amulettes et d'os **354** 40
~ de chien **70** 13
~ de corail véritable **36** 34
~ de fleurs **306** 17
~ de griffes d'ours **352** 14
~ de perles **36** 32
~ d'ivoire **36** 28
~ en perles de culture **36** 12
~ folklore **31** 28
~ simple **126** 56
collimateur *Mil.* **255** 36
~ *Cristallogr.* **351** 30
colline **13** 66
~ contournée **13** 12
~ du cyclorama **310** 13
colombelle **342** 47
colombin de pâte **161** 8
Colombine **306** 27
côlon ascendant **20** 19
~ descendant **20** 21
~ transverse **20** 20
colonie **369** 8, 9
~ de pucerons **80** 34
colonnade **274** 9
colonne *Reliure* **185** 65
~ *Ecriture* **342** 45
~, fût de la **334** 26
~ à chapiteau campaniforme **333** 15
~ à chapiteau floral évasé **333** 15
~ à chapiteau floral fermé **333** 13
~ à chapiteau lotiforme **333** 13
~ à chapiteau palmiforme **333** 17
~ ascendante **287** 21
~ centrale *Photo* **114** 46
~ centrale *Constr.* **123** 78
~ corinthienne **334** 10
~ de concrétion calcaire **13** 82
~ de direction **192** 56
~ de distillation à plateaux **145** 37
~ de guidage **139** 42
~ de mercure **10** 2
~ de perceuse **150** 21
~ de production **145** 25
~ de refroidissement **170** 43
~ dorique **334** 8
~ engagée **335** 35
~ historiée **333** 18
~ inclinée **116** 28
~ ionique **334** 9
~ montante **126** 7
~ montante d'alimentation **62** 12
~ montante de refoulement **145** 24
~ montante d'injection de boue **145** 13
~ Morris **268** 70
~ portante **2** 29
~ profilée **116** 42
~ taurine **333** 23
~ vertébrale **17** 2-5
colonnes, galerie à **334** 67
~ jumelées **336** 6
colophane **323** 11
colposcope **23** 5
coltin **142** 5
columbidé **359** 23
colza **383** 1
combat **319** 24
~ au sol **299** 8
~ de boxe **299** 20-50
~ debout **299** 6
~ pour le titre **299** 35-50
combinaison chauffante **279** 9
~ de compétition **301** 31
~ de fond **301** 17
~ de mécanicien **31** 53
~ de plongée en néoprène **279** 9
~ de ski *Cost.* **29** 38
~ de ski *Sports hiver* **301** 9
~ de ski de fond **301** 43
~ en cuir **290** 26
~ en jersey **29** 17
~ fixe **326** 46
~ libre **326** 40, 46
~ matelassée **29** 38
~ spatiale **6** 18-27
combinaison-short **29** 22
combinateur **197** 27
~ arrière **197** 8
combiné *Poste* **237** 7
~ *Bureau* **245** 15; **246** 16
~ d'instrumentation **191** 38
comble **38** 12
~ à entrait retroussé et à poinçons latéraux **121** 37
~ à panne et à poinçon unique **121** 42
~ à plancher suspendu **121** 65
~ à poinçons latéraux et à jambettes **121** 46
~ mansardé **121** 18
~ polygonal **121** 52
~ sur chandelles **121** 72
comburant **234** 10
combustible nucléaire **154** 4

~ de cour **355** 79
~ de danse **354** 36
~ de marin **309** 62
~ de plage *Cost.* **33** 24
~ de plage *Plage* **280** 19
~ de théâtre **315** 51
~ de week-end **33** 17
~ espagnol **355** 27
~ jeans **33** 20
~ pantalon **30** 57
~ tailleur **31** 1
cotangente **346** 32
cote **289** 37
~ de la Bourse **251** 8
~ des cours **250** 8
~ du gagnant **289** 39
côte **17** 9
~ anglaise **171** 48
~ basse **13** 35-44
~ couverte à la noix **95** 18
~ élevée **13** 25-31
~ flottante **17** 10
~ première **95** 18
côté **346** 26
~ chant **324** 39
~ cuir **131** 13, 18
~ d'accompagnement **324** 43
~ de l'angle droit **346** 32
~ feutre **173** 31
~ pignon **37** 15
~ poil **131** 12, 17
~ toile **173** 34
coteaux **78** 1-21
côtelette de porc **95** 46
côtés de l'angle **346** 7, 3
cotillon **309** 85
coton *Filat. coton* **163** 1-13
~ *Bot.* **383** 19
~ à démaquiller **99** 30
cotonnier **383** 16
cotons mélangés **163** 7
cotre **220** 8
cotte **355** 37
~ de mailles **329** 51, 63
cotylédon **370** 87
cou *Anat.* **16** 19-21; **19** 1-13
~ *Cheval* **72** 15
~ *Chasse* **88** 3
~, tour de **36** 16
couard **86** 35
couchage simple **54** 10
couche, champignon de **381** 1
~ annuelle **84** 24
~ antigel *Rue (coupe)* **198** 1
~ antigel *Constr. rout.* **200** 60
~ atomique **7** 32
~ calorifuge **155** 36
~ chaude **55** 16
~ D **7** 20
~ d'argile damée **269** 39
~ de base bitumineuse **198** 2
~ de ciment lissé **123** 14
~ de circulation **198** 5
~ de drainage **199** 25
~ de fondation **200** 59
~ de la chaussée **198** 1-5
~ de matières végétales décomposées **13** 15
~ de neige sur le toit **304** 20
~ de profilage inférieure **198** 3
~ de profilage supérieure **198** 4
~ de protection contre le gel **198** 1
~ de ralentissement **1** 54
~ de séparation **7** 10
~ de sphaignes anciennes **13** 22
~ de sphaignes récentes **13** 20
~ de surface **7** 7
~ de tubes **381** 17
~ d'ozone **7** 13, 19
~ du battant **166** 42
~ d'usure **123** 41
~ E **7** 27
~ F_1 **7** 28
~ F_2 **7** 29
~ filtrante de gravier **199** 23
~ filtrante morainique **199** 24
~ imperméable *Géogr.* **12** 28
~ imperméable *Serv. eaux* **269** 36
~ intermédiaire **11** 4
~ isolante horizontale **123** 4
~ limite **256** 6; **257** 13
~ perméable **269** 2, 38
~ poreuse formant roche-magasin **12** 29
~ protectrice de vernis **340** 56
~ rocheuse imperméable **13** 78
couché abdominal **295** 45
~ costal **295** 46
~ dorsal **295** 44
couche-culotte jetable **28** 22
couchette pliante **259** 84
coucheur **173** 49
coucheuse à râcles **173** 29-35
~ du côté feutre **173** 31
~ du côté toile **173** 34
couchis **123** 8
coucou *Horlog.* **109** 31
~ *Bot.* **376** 8
~ gris **359** 30
coude *Anat.* **16** 45
~ *Maison* **37** 12
~ *Cheval* **72** 20
~ à cardan **67** 6
~ de raccordement de pompe **67** 8
~ de tuyau de poêle **309** 6
~ grand rayon 90° **126** 46
~ 90° **126** 52
~ 90° femelle-mâle à visser **126** 51
~ réducteur 90° **126** 49
coudière **303** 16
coudrier **59** 44-51
coulé **277** 3
coulée continue **148** 24-29
~ de lave **11** 18
coulemelle **381** 30
couleur *Métall.* **148** 8
~ *Jeux* **276** 38-45
~ *Couleurs* **343**
~ de l'arc-en-ciel **343** 14
~ d'incandescence **343** 16
couleurs, boîte de **338** 10
~ de l'arc-en-ciel **343** 14
couleuvre à collier **364** 38
coulisse, trombone à **323** 46
~ (de trombone) **323** 47
~ et arrière-plan **310** 33
coulisseau **87** 69
~ du diaphragme d'ouverture **112** 16
~ porte-outil **149** 22; **150** 13
~ transversal *Mach.-out.* **149** 23, 39
~ transversal *Compos.* **174** 48
couloir *Géogr.* **12** 44
~ *Maison* **41** 1-29
~ *Tramw.* **197** 18
~ *Sports* **282** 31
~ *Sports hiver* **301** 71
~ central **208** 23
~ de circulation **75** 3
~ de lancer franc **292** 37
~ de service **75** 24
~ du film **312** 31
~ latéral **207** 11
coup avec effet à droite **277** 5
~ avec effet à gauche **277** 6
~ bas **299** 34
~ de billard **277** 2-6
~ de figure à droite **294** 23
~ de pied de coin **291** 41
~ de pied de réparation **291** 40
~ de pied latéral **299** 19
~ de pied retourné **291** 45
~ de pointe **294** 27
~ droit *Sports* **293** 40
~ droit *Escrime* **294** 7
~ franc **291** 43
~ interdit **299** 34
coupe *Ust. table* **45** 86
~ *Parc* **272** 23
~ *Bot.* **370** 60; **374** 15; **378** 28; **381** 6, 11
~ à blanc-étoc **84** 13
~ à compote **45** 29
~ à fruits **45** 40
~ à hosties **332** 50
~ A-B **151** 28
~ consistométrique pour mesurer la viscosité **129** 38
~ de barbe **34** 1-25
~ de cheveux **106** 3
~ de communion **330** 10
~ de tissu **104** 2
~ du câble à la longueur habituelle des fibres **170** 60
~ du reps en chaine irrégulier **171** 25
~ du reps en trame **171** 14
~ d'un pont **215** 1
~ d'une rue **198**
~ en brosse **34** 11
~ en exploitation **84** 15-37
~ fine **107** 25
~ glacée **266** 76
~ longitudinale **371** 45, 62; **372** 10, 48, 57; **373** 5, 14, 22; **374** 19, 24; **375** 6, 16, 19, 46; **381** 3; **382** 5, 18, 20, 32, 39; **383** 3, 24, 44, 47, 51, 52; **384** 13, 18, 20, 25, 60, 65
~ marine **107** 25
~ médiane du sous-marin **259** 55-74
~ montrant les asques **381** 12
~ suivant A - B **151** 28
~ suivant la trame **171** 14
~ transversale **370** 7; **372** 31, 53; **382** 35; **384** 21, 27, 46, 57, 59
~ transversale du bassin **281** 36
coupé *Voit. chev.* **186** 3
~ *Autom.* **193** 25
coupe-ardoises **122** 84
coupe-asperges **56** 10
coupe-carbone **107** 45
coupe-cigares **107** 9
coupe-circuit à fusible **127** 36
~ avec fil fusible **127** 68
~ de sécurité **168** 19
coupée, échelle de **221** 98
coupe-frites **40** 43
coupe-joint **201** 16
couperet **94** 18
coupe-tubes **126** 84
coupe-tuiles **122** 33
coupeur **159** 15
coupeuse *Briq.* **159** 15
~ *Papet.* **173** 42
~ à bois avec dépoussiéreur **172** 1
coupe-verre **124** 25-26
~ à diamant **124** 25
~ à molettes en acier **124** 26
~ circulaire **124** 22
couplage au réseau électrique **154** 16
~ delta **153** 21
~ du transformateur **153** 19
~ en étoile **153** 20
~ en triangle **153** 21
~ Y **153** 20
couple *Mar.* **222** 58
~ *Aéron.* **230** 55
~ *Sports* **285** 51
~ annulaire intégralement renforcé **235** 47
~ comprimé avant **235** 19
~ d'amoureux **272** 72
~ de construction **222** 29
~ de courbure **258** 8
~ de danseurs *Hôtel* **267** 46
~ de danseurs *Discoth.* **317** 17-18
~ d'extrêmité hémisphérique **235** 48
~ principal **235** 10
coupleur de remorque **278** 55
coupole **334** 58
~ bulbeuse **121** 25
~ centrale **334** 72
~ de projection **5** 21
~ pivotante **5** 12
coupon **251** 17
~ du dividende **251** 18
couque lourde **375** 5
cour de débord **206** 8
~ de ferme **62** 31
~ d'équarrissage **319** 13
~ des chevaux **319** 15
~ intérieure **329** 2
courant *Cartogr.* **14** 30-45
~ *Bot.* **58** 20
~ *Cours d'eau* **216** 9
~, prise de **261** 12
~ ascendant de front **287** 25
~ ascendant de pente **287** 28
~ atmosphérique **9** 25-29
~ austral occidental **14** 45
~ austral oriental **14** 38
~ d'air chaud **9** 28
~ d'air froid **9** 29
~ de Benguela **14** 43
~ de Californie **14** 39
~ de Humboldt **14** 42
~ de la Somalie **14** 36
~ d'eau souterraine **269** 3
~ des Agulhas **14** 37
~ des Canaries **14** 41
~ du Brésil **14** 35
~ du Labrador **14** 40
~ équatorial nord **14** 32
~ équatorial sud **14** 34
~ marin chaud **14** 28
~ marin froid **14** 27
~ triphasé **153** 42
courant-jet **7** 5
courbe *Sports* **305** 19
~ *Math.* **346** 21; **347** 13
~ balistique **87** 79

~ de la tige **89** 81
~ de niveau **15** 62
~ de profondeur **15** 11
~ des températures **7** 37
~ du second degré **347** 14
~ du troisième degré **347** 18
~ hypsométrique de la surface de la Terre **11** 6-12
~ inverse **305** 20
~ plane **347** 11
courbette **71** 6
courbure, centre de **346** 23
~, rayon de **346** 22
coureur *Sports* **290** 25
~ *Athl.* **298** 5
~ cycliste **290** 8
~ cycliste sur routes **290** 8
~ de demi-fond **298** 5
~ de fond *Sports* **290** 14
~ de fond *Athl.* **298** 5
~ de six jours **290** 2
~ sur piste **290** 2
couronne *Anat.* **19** 37
~ *Méd.* **24** 28, 33
~ *Argent* **252** 24, 25, 26, 27
~ *Hérald.* **254** 37,38,42-46
~ à pivot **24** 31
~ antipoussière **187** 57, 82
Couronne boréale **3** 31
couronne circulaire **346** 57
~ de baron **254** 44
~ de comte **254** 45
~ de démarreur **192** 31
~ de feuilles *Hérald.* **254** 12
~ de feuilles *Arts* **334** 25
~ de feuilles *Bot.* **384** 62
~ de fleurs d'oranger **332** 19
~ de forage **145** 21
~ de Francfort **97** 42
~ de l'arbre **370** 3
~ de noble non titré **254** 43
~ de pivotement **215** 64
~ de remontoir **110** 42
~ de rotation de la lame **200** 22
~ dentée *Méc.* **143** 90
~ dentée *Bicycl.* **187** 74
~ ducale **254** 39
~ en or **24** 28
~ héraldique **254** 43-45
~ impériale **254** 38
~ mobile **217** 52
~ murale **254** 46
~ royale anglaise **254** 42
~ solaire **4** 39
couronnement crénelé **329** 6
~ de la digue **216** 39
~ du barrage **217** 59
courre, chasse à **289** 41-49
courrier **236** 55
~, corbeille à **245** 30; **248** 41
~, court et moyen **231** 4, 11, 17
~, distribution du **236** 50-55
~, long **231** 13, 14
~, moyen *Aéron.* **231** 12
~, moyen *Mil.* **256** 14
~, tri du **236** 31-44
courroie *Chasse* **86** 45
~ *Ecole* **260** 11
~ *Sports* **290** 22
~ abrasive sans fin **133** 15
~ cloutée en caoutchouc **64** 79
~ de guidage **303** 4
~ de sécurité **301** 3
~ de transmission **103** 10
~ transporteuse **144** 40
~ trapézoïdale **180** 58
cours *Banque* **250** 8
~ *Univ.* **262** 1
~ de biologie **261** 14-34
~ de chimie **261** 1-13
~ de l'eau **216** 9
~ d'eau *Géogr.* **13** 61
~ d'eau *Cartogr.* **15** 76
~ d'eau *Parc* **272** 45
~ d'eau navigable **15** 45
~ élémentaire **260**
~ moyen **260** 1-85
course **298** 1-8
~, position de **295** 2
~ à l'aviron **283** 1-18
~ à voile sur patins **302** 27-28
~ au galop **289** 50
~ au trot attelé **289** 23-40
~ cycliste **290** 1-23
~ cycliste sur route **290** 8-10
~ de fond **290** 11-15
~ de haies **298** 7-8
~ de motocyclettes **290** 24-28
~ de six jours **290** 2-7
~ de slalom **301** 64
~ de taureaux **319** 1-33
~ de tout-terrain **290** 33
~ de véhicules à moteur **290** 24-38
~ en montagne **290** 24-28
~ motonautique **286** 21-44
~ sur gazon **290** 24-28
~ sur glace **290** 24-28
~ sur routes **290** 16, 24-28
coursie **218** 46
coursier **236** 17
court de tennis **293** 1
~ et moyen courrier **231** 4, 11, 17
courtier **251** 4
~ assermenté **251** 4
~ libre **251** 5
courtine **329** 19
couseuse à fil **185** 16
cousin **358** 16
cousoir **183** 9
coussin *Joaill.* **36** 56
~ *Maison* **42** 27; **46** 17
~ à or *Peint.* **129** 50
~ à or *Reliure* **183** 6
~ d'air *Audiovis.* **243** 27
~ d'air *Sports* **286** 63, 66
~ d'appui-tête **207** 68
~ de belle-mère **53** 14
~ de siège **42** 23
~ d'orfèvre **108** 29
coussinet *Méd.* **21** 13
~ *Mil.* **255** 47
~ amortisseur **100** 16
~ de câble porteur **214** 33
~ de glissement **202** 22
~ de volute **334** 24
~ élastique **192** 82
~ en caoutchouc **192** 67, 82
coussinet-peigne de filière **140** 61
couteau *Ust. table* **45** 50
~ *Reliure* **185** 8, 29
~ à araser **128** 43
~ à beurre **45** 73
~ à caviar **45** 81
~ à contours **340** 10
~ à découper *Piscic.* **89** 38
~ à découper *Bouch.* **96** 31
~ à dépecer **96** 35
~ à dépouiller **94** 13
~ à désosser **96** 36
~ à deux manches **120** 79
~ à écailler **89** 39
~ à écorcher **94** 13
~ à émarger **128** 38
~ à fromage **45** 72
~ à fruits **45** 71
~ à maroufler **128** 42
~ à mastiquer *Vitr.* **124** 27
~ à mastiquer *Peint.* **129** 24
~ à or *Peint.* **129** 51
~ à or *Reliure* **183** 7
~ à palette **338** 14
~ à plomb **124** 12
~ à pointe relevée **96** 37
~ à poisson **45** 64
~ à saigner **94** 14
~ à servir **45** 69
~ à viande **96** 35
~ de boucher à pointe relevée **94** 15
~ de bronze à manche de bronze **328** 31
~ de chasse **87** 42
~ de cordonnier **100** 50
~ de décolletage **64** 87
~ de peintre **338** 15
~ de plis croisés **185** 12
~ de plongeur **279** 8
~ de relieur **183** 13
~ décolleur de papier peint **128** 15
~ d'électricien **127** 63
~ étendeur **129** 23
~ frappeur **84** 33
~ pour couper les joints **201** 17
~ universel **134** 28
couteau-fendoir **94** 17
couteau-pochoir **129** 43
couteaux de boucher **96** 31-37
coutelas **87** 41
coutil **43** 10
coutre **65** 10
~ circulaire **64** 66; **65** 69
~ en disque **64** 66; **65** 69
~ rayonneux **65** 76
couture **183** 8, 34
couturier **18** 45
couturière **131** 8
couvée d'œufs d'autruche **359** 3
couvent *Cartogr.* **15** 63
~ *Eglise* **331** 52-58
couvercle *Ust. cuis.* **40** 13
~ *Lutte pestic.* **83** 40
~ *Orfèvre* **108** 9
~ *Tonell.* **130** 10
~ *Mus.* **322** 27
~ *Chim.* **350** 31
~ à robinet **350** 52
~ à succion **177** 35
~ à tige **130** 19
~ avec filtre **2** 14
~ coulissant **179** 2
~ de carter **143** 80
~ de cuve **178** 37
~ de la boule **249** 30
~ de la sphère **249** 30
~ de la tête d'impression **249** 30
~ de l'encensoir **332** 40
~ de l'essoreuse **168** 18
~ de pipe **107** 37
~ du battant **166** 6
~ du dôme **38** 48
~ du lecteur **243** 47
~ du puits **38** 46
~ vitré **269** 56
~ vitré du châssis **179** 15
couvert *Météor.* **9** 24
~ *Maison* **44** 5
~ *Ust. table* **45** 3-12, 7
~ *Ch. de f.* **207** 85
~ *Rest.* **266** 27
~ *Marché puces* **309** 47
~ à café **265** 18
~ à poisson **45** 8
~ à salade **45** 24
~ à servir **45** 69-70
couverture *Maison* **38** 1; **43** 8
~ *Constr.* **122**
~ *Reliure* **184** 6; **185** 40
~ d'ardoises **122** 78
~ de feutre **353** 20
~ de protection **185** 37
~ de selle **71** 44
~ de tuiles à recouvrement **122** 2
~ de tuiles plates chevauchantes **122** 2
~ en carton **184** 7
~ en coupoles **334** 72-73
~ en tuiles **122** 45-60
~ piquée **43** 8
couvre-chaîne **187** 37
couvre-cordes **324** 17
couvre-culbuteur **190** 48
couvre-cuvette **187** 55
couvre-joint **119** 65
couvre-lame **66** 18
couvre-nuque **270** 38
couvre-oreilles **304** 28
~ de fourrure **35** 32
couvre-radiateur **304** 11
couvre-roue **197** 11
couvreur **122**
~ en ardoise **122** 71
cow-boy *Carnaval* **306** 31
~ *Taurom.* **319** 36
cowper **147** 15
Cowper, glande de **20** 75
coyau extérieur **121** 31
crabe *Zool.* **358** 1
~ *Faune abyss.* **369** 16
cracheur de feu **308** 25
crachoir **23** 25; **24** 12
craie *Maison* **48** 15
~ *Peintre* **338** 5
~ *Arts graph.* **340** 26
~ (blanche) **260** 32
~ lithographique **340** 26
craie-tailleur *Cout.* **104** 24
~ *Magasin* **271** 39
crampon *Constr.* **119** 58
~ *Alpin.* **300** 48
~ *Bot.* **370** 80
~ d'acier **303** 24
~ vissé **291** 28
cran de marche **211** 36
~ de mire *Chasse* **87** 66
~ de mire *Mil.* **255** 22
~ de sureté **255** 14
~ du caractère **175** 47
crâne *Anat.* **16** 1; **17** 1, 30-41
~ *Ecole* **261** 15
~ de l'australopithèque **261** 20
~ de l'Homme de Néanderthal **261** 19
~ de l'Homo sapiens **261** 21
~ de l'Homo steinheimensis **261** 17
~ d'hominidé **261** 19
crantage pour distribution **174** 30
crapaud *Ch. de f.* **202** 9
~ *Zool.* **364** 23
crapaudine **91** 10
crassier **144** 19

cratère **11** 16
~ de météorite **6** 16
~ d'effondrement **11** 49; **13** 71
~ du charbon **312** 44
~ d'un volcan éteint **11** 25
cravache **289** 22
cravate *Cost.* **32** 41
~ *Drapeaux* **253** 9
~, épingle de **36** 22
crawl **282** 37
crayon **47** 26
~ à bille **47** 26
~ à dessin **260** 5
~ de charpentier **120** 77
~ de couleur **47** 26; **48** 11
~ de maçon **118** 51
~ gras *Maison* **48** 11
~ gras *Ecole* **260** 6
~ gras *Arts graph.* **340** 26
~ lithographique **340** 26
~ pastel **338** 19
crayon-feutre *Maison* **47** 26
~ *Ecole* **260** 19
crayon-gomme **151** 41
création de programmes **242** 7
crécelle **306** 47
crèche **62** 9
crémaillère *Opt.* **112** 39
~ *Ch. de f.* **214** 4, 4-5, 5, 7-11, 9
~ *Inst. fluv.* **217** 69
~ circulaire **143** 93
~ horizontale double **214** 11
crème **99** 46
~ aigre **76** 42
~ Chantilly **97** 28
~ de jour **99** 27
~ fouettée *Boul.-pâtiss.* **97** 28
~ fouettée *Café* **265** 5
~ hydratante **99** 27
~ pour les mains **99** 27
crémier *Maison* **44** 31
~ *Café* **265** 21
crémoir **148** 17
créneau *Chasse* **86** 52
~ *Chevalerie* **329** 7
crénelée **370** 46
crépi **123** 6
crépine *Autom.* **192** 18
~ *Serv. eaux* **269** 14, 32
~ à clapet de pied **269** 6, 43
~ d'aspiration **67** 12
crépuscule **4** 21
crescendo **321** 31
cresson de fontaine **378** 30
cressonnette **375** 11
crête *Géogr.* **12** 36
~ *Zool.* **73** 22
~ de la digue **216** 39
~ de l'épaulière **329** 44
~ dorsale **364** 21
~ du barrage **217** 59
creuset **174** 25
~, pince à **350** 32
~ de terre réfractaire **350** 31
~ en graphite **108** 10
creux, gravure en **340** 14-24
~ d'attaque **340** 55
~ poplité **16** 51
crevasse *Géogr.* **11** 52
~ *Alpin.* **300** 23
~ de glacier **12** 50
crevette abyssale **369** 12
criblage du coke grossier et du coke fin **156** 14
crible à béquille **55** 13
~ à grenure **340** 24
~ à terreau **55** 13
~ de menues pailles **64** 17
~ élévateur **64** 69
~ plus fin **64** 19
~ rond **91** 26
~ vibrant **158** 21
cricket **292** 70-76
cri-cri **81** 7
criée au poisson **225** 58
crieur **308** 64
crinière *Cheval* **72** 13
~ *Zool.* **368** 3
crinoline **355** 72
crins de cheval **323** 15
criquet **358** 8
criss **353** 44
cristal **351** 29
~ de chlorure de sodium **1** 9
~ de cristobalite **1** 12
cristallin **19** 48
~, édifice **351** 1-26
cristalline, association **351** 1-26
~, forme **351** 1-26
~, structure **351** 1-26
cristallographie **351**
cristallométrie **351** 27-33
cristobalite **1** 12
croc *Apicult.* **77** 55
~ *Abatt.* **94** 21
~ à fumier **66** 8
~ à incendie **270** 15
~ à pommes de terre **66** 6
~ à viande **96** 55
~ de remorquage **227** 27
croche **320** 16
~, double **320** 17
~, quadruple **320** 19
~, triple **320** 18
crochet *Coord.* **100** 62
~ *Constr.* **122** 32, 51
~ *Sports* **305** 18
~ *Mus.* **320** 5; **324** 67
~ *Arts* **335** 38
~ à ardillon **89** 80
~ à barbillon **89** 80
~ à grumes **85** 7, 9
~ à la face **299** 33
~ d'arrêt **122** 64
~ d'auget **122** 23
~ de broche **164** 49
~ de couvreur **38** 6
~ de faîtage **122** 65
~ de fixation **81** 38
~ de la corde à linge **38** 22
~ de levage **145** 9
~ de palan **139** 45
~ de service **122** 69
~ de suspension **94** 21
~ de traction *Mach. agric.* **65** 19
~ de traction *Pompiers* **270** 49
~ d'échelle **122** 15
~ du cordon d'alimentation **50** 65
~ du pare-neige **122** 16
crochets **342** 25
crocodile du Nil **356** 13
croisé *Ballet* **314** 16
~ *Chevalerie* **329** 72
croisée de fond **136** 21
~ d'ogives **336** 43
croisement du fil **165** 11
croiseur lance-missiles **259** 21, 41
~ lance-missiles à propulsion nucléaire **259** 41
croisillon *Constr.* **118** 88
~ *Mach.-out.* **149** 43
croissant *Boul.-pâtiss.* **97** 32
~ *Comm.* **99** 13
~ *Drapeaux* **253** 19
~ de Lune **4** 3, 7
croissante, Lune **4** 3
croix *Plomb.* **126** 50
~ *Ecole* **260** 28
~, chemin de **330** 54
~ à deux barres **224** 98
~ ancrée **332** 69
~ ansée **332** 63
~ cardinalice **332** 65
~ chrétienne **332** 55-72
~ constantinienne **332** 67
~ d'avertissement **202** 41
~ de faîte **331** 10
~ de fer aux anneaux **296** 50
~ de Lorraine **332** 62
~ de Malte **312** 38
~ de procession **330** 47; **331** 42
~ de Saint-André *Ch. de f.* **202** 41
~ de Saint-André *Gymnast.* **295** 35
~ de Saint-André *Eglise* **332** 60
~ de Saint-Antoine **332** 59
~ de Saint-Lazare **332** 71
~ de Saint-Pierre **332** 58
~ des larrons **332** 61
~ d'infamie **332** 61
~ du Saint-Sépulcre **332** 72
Croix du Sud **3** 44
croix en tau **332** 59
~ fourchue **332** 61
~ grecque **332** 56
~ latine **332** 55
~ papale **332** 66
~ pastorale double **332** 64
~ potencée **332** 70
~ recroisettée **332** 68
~ russe **332** 57
~ sur sphère **224** 90
~ tombale **331** 25
~ tréflée **332** 71
cromorne **322** 6
croque-mort **331** 40
croquet **292** 77-82
croquis **315** 40
~ au tableau **260** 33
cross, parcours de **289** 17
crosse *Chasse* **87** 3
~ *Viande* **95** 28
~ *Constr.* **119** 71
~ *Mil.* **255** 6, 38
~ *Ciné* **313** 37
~ à trou **305** 47
~ d'appui de l'épaule **255** 9, 39
~ de fusil **255** 24
~ de hockey **292** 13
~ de hockey sur glace **302** 30
~ de l'aorte **18** 10
crotte de chocolat **98** 80
croupe *Cheval* **72** 31
~ *Constr.* **121** 11; **122** 10
~ faîtière **121** 17
croupier **275** 4
~ de tête **275** 6
croupière **71** 34
croûte **97** 4
croûton **97** 5
cruche à anse **328** 35
~ en terre cuite **260** 78
crucifix **332** 33
~ de la table de communion **330** 12
~ du maître-autel **330** 35
crustacé *Zool.* **81** 6; **358** 1, 1-2
~ *Faune abyss.* **369** 1, 12, 15, 16
Crux **3** 44
cryothérapie **22** 63
cube *Math.* **347** 30
~ *Cristallogr.* **351** 2
~ à facettes octaédriques **351** 16
~ de boulier **48** 17
~ de glace **266** 44
~ de mosaïque **338** 39
~ en bois **302** 40
cubilot **148** 1
cubital postérieur **18** 58
cubitière **329** 48
cubitus **17** 14
cueille-essaim **77** 54
cueille-fruits **56** 22
cuiller **89** 73
~ à encens **332** 43
~ à entremets **45** 66
~ à légumes **45** 74
~ à pommes de terre **45** 75
~ à salade **45** 67
~ à sauce **45** 18
~ à servir **45** 74
~ à soupe **45** 61
~ avec écailles **89** 74
~ écaillée **89** 75
~ tachetée **89** 74
cuillère en bois **40** 3
cuilleron **45** 63
cuir *Chasse* **88** 56
~ *Reliure* **184** 12
~ à semelle **100** 31
~ de chasse actionnant le sabre **166** 22
cuirasse **329** 62
cuisine *Maison* **39**
~ *Ch. de f.* **207** 29, 33, 80
~ *Mar.* **223** 42
~ de la charcuterie **96** 31-59
cuisinière à gaz **39** 12
~ électrique **39** 12; **46** 32
~ électrique à 8 plaques **207** 30
cuissard **329** 52
cuisse *Anat.* **16** 49
~ *Cheval* **72** 35
~ avec la jambe de derrière **95** 14
~ avec le jarret de derrière **95** 14
~ avec le trumeau de derrière **95** 14
~ de dinde **99** 59
~ emplumée **362** 3
cuisseau avec le jarret de derrière **95** 1
cuisson dans la salle de brassage **92** 42-53
cuissot **88** 21, 37
cuivre, cliché de **340** 53
~, plaque de **340** 53
~ gris **351** 1
cuivres **323** 39-48
cul brun **80** 28
~ doré **80** 28
culasse *Chasse* **87** 9
~ *Centr.* **153** 14
~ *Moteur* **190** 45
~ *Enseign.* **242** 47
~ *Mil.* **255** 54
~ mobile **87** 20
culbute **308** 43
culbuteur *Métall.* **147** 44, 59
~ *Moteur* **190** 33
culée *Ponts* **215** 29, 45
~ *Arts* **335** 27

culot **87** 58
~ à vis **127** 59
culotte *Viande* **95** 35
~ *Sports* **291** 57
~ *Oiseaux* **362** 3
~ à jambes **32** 10
~ courte **29** 25
~ de cheval **289** 5
~ de peau **29** 32
~ d'escalade **300** 7
~ ouvrante **29** 10
~ pantin **28** 24
~ sur les pattes arrière **77** 3
cultivateur *Agric.* **62** 6
~ *Mach. agric.* **65** 55
~ à main **55** 21
culture **84** 9
~ bactériologique **261** 29
~ de plein champ **68**
~ du houblon **83** 27
~ maraîchère **55**
cumulo-nimbus *Météor.* **8** 17
~ *Sports* **287** 26
cumulus *Météor.* **8** 1
~ *Sports* **287** 22
~ congestus **8** 2
cunéiforme, écriture **341** 8
cupule **371** 5
curculionidé **80** 49
cure de repos **274** 12-14
~ d'inhalation **274** 6-7
curé **330** 39
cure-dents **266** 23
cure-pipe **107** 47
curetage **26** 52
curette **22** 50
~ pour le curetage **26** 52
curiste en train de boire l'eau **274** 18
curling **302** 41-43
~ allemand **302** 38-40
curseur *Chasse* **87** 69
~ *Filat. coton* **164** 55
~ *Chim.* **349** 33
~ d'arrêt du compteur horaire **249** 75
~ de balance **22** 68
~ de blocage **247** 43
~ de réglage du format **249** 34
~ de sélection du format **249** 34
~ du diaphragme d'ouverture **112** 16
cusson **81** 19
custode **330** 8; **332** 53
cuve *Météor.* **10** 46
~ *Moulins* **91** 20
~ *Tonell.* **130** 1
~ *Papet.* **173** 47
~ à babeurre **76** 18
~ à chargement en plein jour **116** 5
~ à coloration **23** 50
~ à crème **76** 19
~ à déchets d'épuration **172** 59
~ à développement multiple **116** 3
~ à eau **261** 33
~ à fumier **221** 72
~ à lait cru **76** 5
~ à lait écrémé **76** 17
~ à lait frais **76** 15
~ à lait stérilisé **76** 16
~ à mazout **38** 44
~ à moût **92** 52
~ à niveau constant **192** 14
~ à poussière **50** 86
~ à purin **62** 13
~ à vin **79** 3
~ baptismale **332** 11
~ contenant le tambour rotatif **168** 17
~ d'affinage de crème **76** 31
~ de clarification **92** 50
~ de dégraissage **178** 1
~ de développement *Photo* **116** 1
~ de développement *Imprim.* **182** 11
~ de fermentation **93** 8
~ de gravure **178** 24, 31; **182** 16
~ de haut fourneau **147** 7
~ de malaxage **96** 40
~ de présure **76** 48
~ de transport des poissons **89** 4
~ d'électrolyse **178** 4
~ d'épaississement **172** 62
~ du réacteur *Nucl.* **154** 22
~ du réacteur *Mil.* **259** 67
~ du silo **225** 69
~ du transformateur **152** 40
~ en acier spécial **79** 4
~ en béton **79** 3
~ en matière plastique **79** 4
~ remplie de verre fondu **162** 50
cuvelage **145** 20
cuve-matière pour la cuisson de la trempe **92** 44
cuvette **309** 65
~ contenant l'agent de décoloration **105** 1
~ de cabinet **49** 13
~ de développement **116** 25
~ de développement semi-automatique à thermostat **116** 56
~ de frein **187** 67
~ de lavabo **105** 29; **106** 12
~ de rinçage **116** 15
~ du compas **224** 49
~ galvanisée **122** 102
~ lave-cheveux **105** 29; **106** 12
cuvier *Papet.* **172** 25
~ *Marché puces* **309** 69
~ à pâte épurée **172** 85
~ de machine **172** 86
~ de mélange **173** 1
~ de tête **172** 86; **173** 13
~ de vidange **172** 81
cyclamen **53** 5
cycloergomètre **23** 26
cyclohexanol **170** 16
~ pur **170** 18
cyclohexanone **170** 20
~, oxime de la **170** 22
cyclomoteur **188** 6
~ (de randonnée) **188** 24
cyclone **9** 5
cyclorama *Ciné* **310** 12
~ *Théât.* **316** 9
cyclotron **2** 49
Cygne *Astr.* **3** 23
cygne *Parc* **272** 54
~ *Oiseaux* **359** 16
~ tuberculé **359** 16
Cygnus **3** 23
cylindre *Tonell.* **130** 27
~ *Serr.* **140** 45
~ *Constr. rout.* **200** 37
~ *Inst. fluv.* **217** 65
~ *Bureau* **249** 18
~ *Math.* **347** 38
~ à aiguilles **167** 8, 11
~ à picots débiteur **312** 26
~ à picots récepteur **312** 27
~ à vapeur **210** 32
~ basse pression **153** 25
~ cannelé *Tonell.* **130** 30
~ cannelé *Tiss.* **165** 10; **166** 47
~ compresseur *Mach. agric.* **64** 64
~ compresseur *Menuis.* **133** 46
~ d'acier **180** 54
~ d'acier cannelé **164** 10
~ d'alimentation **163** 27, 52
~ d'arrachage **163** 71
~ d'avancement **85** 19, 24
~ de blanchet **180** 24, 37, 54, 63, 79
~ de coupe **56** 35
~ de cuivre poli **182** 7
~ de fonture **167** 25
~ de frein **212** 7
~ de marteau **139** 30
~ de pression **340** 40
~ de roue **192** 54
~ de sortie **164** 59
~ décatisseur **168** 50
~ développé **182** 13
~ d'exploration **177** 45
~ d'impression *Photogr.* **177** 67
~ d'impression *Imprim.* **180** 35, 64; **181** 2, 59
~ distributeur **62** 23
~ droit **347** 38
~ enregistreur **10** 5, 16, 20
~ entraîneur **165** 32
~ entraîneur inférieur **168** 6
~ entraîneur supérieur **168** 3
~ étireur **164** 13
~ exprimeur **165** 46
~ gravé **182** 12
~ guide-tissu **168** 5
~ haute pression **153** 23
~ hélio copié **182** 17
~ hélio recouvert de papier charbon **182** 10
~ héliogravé **182** 22
~ imprimant **181** 44
~ inférieur *Métall.* **148** 55
~ inférieur *Filat. coton* **164** 10
~ moyenne pression **153** 24
~ plongeur **165** 45
~ porte-aiguilles **185** 21
~ porte-clichés **181** 51, 60
~ porte-masque **177** 48
~ porte-modèle **177** 64
~ porte-plaque **180** 25, 38, 53, 62
~ porte-recouvrement **184** 10
~ presseur chauffé **168** 41
~ refroidisseur *Text.* **170** 27
~ refroidisseur *Papet.* **173** 25
~ rotatif **273** 45
~ sécheur **173** 22, 26
~ sécheur chauffé **173** 33
~ secteur **167** 25
~ submersible immergé **217** 68
~ supérieur **148** 54
~ supérieur garni de matière plastique **164** 11
~ sur sphère **224** 89
~ tondeur **168** 44
~ tournant **275** 28
~ tournant avec les numéros de 0 à 36 **275** 31
cylindrée, grosse **189** 31-58
cymaise **128** 29
cymbale **323** 50
~ double à coulisse **324** 50
~ fixe **324** 51
cymbalum **322** 32
cyme bipare **370** 70
~ unipare hélicoïde **370** 77
~ unipare scorpioïde **370** 76
cynips **82** 35
~ du chêne **82** 33
cynorrhodon **373** 27
cypéracée **53** 17
cypérus **53** 17
cyprès **372** 58
cyprinidé **364** 4
cypripède **376** 27
cytise **374** 32
czimbalum **322** 32

D

dactyle pelotonné **69** 25
dactylo(graphe) **248** 21
dactyloscopie **264** 28
dagoba **337** 28
dahlia *Jard.* **51** 20
~ *Bot.* **60** 23
~ pompon **60** 23
daim **88** 40-41, 40
~, veste en **30** 58
daine **88** 40
dais **331** 49
~, porteur du **331** 46
dallage **123** 26
dalle armée **123** 28
~ béton **123** 13
~ commémorative **331** 14
~ de compression **123** 38
~ de pierre **331** 61
~ de recouvrement **198** 17
~ de structure **123** 38
~ de verre cristal **179** 24
~ du livreur **292** 49
~ en béton armé **123** 28
~ lumineuse **177** 20
~ orthotrope de tablier **215** 2
~ rocheuse **300** 2
daman d'Afrique du Sud **366** 24
dame *Constr. rout.* **200** 33
~ *Café* **265** 23
~ *Jeux* **276** 9
~ *Hist. cost.* **355** 59, 64, 68, 70
~ à béton **119** 83
~ à moteur **200** 26
~ de nage **283** 29, 41
~ du bar *Discoth.* **317** 2
~ du bar *Boîte nuit* **318** 14
~ du comptoir **265** 7
~ du vestiaire **315** 6
~ en costume de cour **355** 79
~ française **355** 51
~ patricienne d'Augsbourg **355** 48
dames, jeu de **276** 17-19
dameur à explosion **200** 26
damier *Jeux* **276** 17
~ *Arts* **335** 14
~ pour le jeu de halma **276** 26
~ pour le jeu de trictrac **276** 22

~ de bande magnétique *Enseign.* **242** 32
~ de bande magnétique *Informat.* **244** 9
dérouleuse **173** 39
~ à placage **133** 1
derrick *Géogr.* **12** 33
~ *Pétr.* **145** 1; **146** 12
~ *Mar.* **221** 67
dés **276** 29
~, cornet à *Maison* **47** 42
~, cornet à *Jeux* **276** 30
désacidification **169** 19
descenseur hélicoïdal **144** 28
descente *Mar.* **223** 24
~ *Mil.* **258** 24
~ *Sports hiver* **301** 32
~ avec freinage du pied **300** 29
~ centrale **259** 86
~ d'alimentation en tissu **168** 47
~ de lit **43** 22
~ en rappel **300** 28-30
désembuage de la lunette arrière **191** 80, 82
déséquilibre avant **299** 13
désert **9** 54
déshydrogénation **170** 19
désinfection à sec des semences **83** 52
~ cutanée **22** 60
désintégrateur conique **172** 82
désintégration spontanée d'une matière radioactive **1** 28
dessert, assiette à **45** 6
desserte **105** 31
~ ferroviaire **15** 90
~ roulante **45** 32
dessicateur **350** 51
dessin humoristique **342** 53
~ industriel **151** 16
~ jacquard **30** 37
~ réalisé par ordinateur **248** 19
dessinateur de costumes **315** 38
dessous **316** 1-60
~ de toit **121** 3
~ de toit en voliges **122** 27
dessus de lit **43** 7
dessus-de-cou **71** 30
destination **205** 22
destroyer de combat **258** 1, 38
désulfuration **169** 20
~ du gaz comprimé **156** 28
détecteur **309** 23
~ de tension **127** 55
~ d'orientation **10** 69
~ solaire **10** 69
détection sous-marine **259** 40
détective privé **275** 16
détendeur *Soud.* **141** 5
~ *Energ.* **155** 7
~ des bouteilles d'air comprimé **279** 22
détente *Chasse* **87** 12
~ *Abatt.* **94** 6
~ *Mil.* **255** 5
détrempe **338** 17
détritus **268** 22
détroit de Gilbraltar **14** 24
~ maritime **14** 24
deutéropyramide **351** 20
deutschemark **252** 7
deux coques **284** 65
~ sans barreur **283** 15
~ temps **305** 92
deuxième arbitre **293** 68
~ assise **118** 68
~ balcon **315** 17
~ base **292** 43
~ bille blanche **277** 13
~ chaîne **239** 5
~ étage S-II **234** 18
~ flux **232** 41, 44, 50
~ louvoyage **285** 20
~ octave **321** 45
~ orteil **19** 53
~ position **314** 2
deux-pièces *Cost.* **31** 11
~ *Plage* **280** 26
~ fillette **29** 50
~ jeans **31** 58
~ pour bébé **29** 12
~ tricot **30** 33
~ tunique **30** 45
deux-points **342** 17
deux-roues **188**
dévanâgari **341** 9
devanture **268** 42
développement **182** 11
développeuse automatique à rouleaux **116** 60
déversoir *Moulins* **91** 43
~ *Inst. fluv.* **217** 60
~ *Ports* **226** 45
dévidoir *Agric.* **62** 30
~ *Coord.* **100** 29
~ *Papet.* **173** 39
~ à fil **185** 17
~ à mousseline **185** 19
~ de fil métallique **184** 18
~ de table de ruban adhésif **247** 28
~ mobile pour tuyaux souples **270** 28
devon en deux parties **89** 70
~ en une partie **89** 69
~ sphérique **89** 71
dextre **254** 18, 20, 22
diabétique **22** 26
diable *Ch. de f.* **206** 14
~ *Carnaval* **306** 14
diablotin **219** 28
diabolo **305** 34
diadème *Barbes,coiffures* **34** 32
~ *Hist. cost.* **355** 21
~ de perles **355** 16
diagnostic **195** 7
~ auto **195** 1-23
~ automatique **195** 33
diagonale **346** 33
diagramme de courbes **151** 11
~ de statistiques **248** 36
~ figuratif des voies **203** 66
diamant *Compos.* **175** 20
~ *Cristallogr.* **351** 10, 13
~ conique ou elliptique **241** 26
~ de vitrier **124** 25
diamètre **346** 45
~ du cylindre à aiguilles **167** 16
diapason **110** 9
diaphragme *Astr.* **5** 22
~ *Anat.* **20** 9, 26
~ *Enseign.* **242** 82
~ à lamelles **2** 33
~ à secteurs **313** 8
diapositif de perfusion **25** 11
diapositive de formulaire **242** 42
~ (publicitaire) **312** 23
diapositives, projecteur de *Marché puces* **309** 42
~, projecteur de *Ciné* **312** 23
diathermie **23** 22, 23
diaule **322** 3
diazo, plaque **179** 32, 34
dicentra **60** 5
dictaphone **22** 27
dictionnaire **262** 17
~ médical **22** 22
didelphidé **366** 2
Didot **342** 6
dièse **320** 50
Diesel, groupe **259** 94
diesel-oil **145** 56
différence **344** 24
~ des ensembles **348** 7, 8
différent de **345** 18
différentiation, signe de **345** 13
différentiel *Mach. agric.* **65** 32
~ *Moteur* **190** 75
différentielle **345** 13, 14
diffuseur *Papet.* **172** 11
~ *Ciné* **310** 38
~ circulaire **83** 23
~ d'oxygène gazeux **234** 15
digitale pourprée **379** 2
digitée **370** 39
dignitaire chinois **306** 29
digue de clôture du champ d'inondation **216** 48
~ de défense contre les crues **216** 32
~ de retenue **155** 38
~ de rivière **216** 49
~ d'été submersible **216** 48
~ d'hiver insubmersible **216** 32
~ longitudinale d'écrêtement **216** 32
diligence **186** 1-3, 26-39, 39, 45, 51-54
~ anglaise **186** 53
diminuende **344** 24
diminuteur **344** 24
dinar **252** 28
dinde **73** 28
dindon **73** 28
dindonneau **73** 28
dinghy pneumatique à hors-bord **286** 1
dioptre **305** 41
~ de visée avec guidon à lame **305** 51
~ de visée avec guidon à trou **305** 50
Dior, pli **30** 52
diplôme de maître-coiffeur **106** 42
diprotodonte d'Australasie **366** 3
diptère **358** 16-20
~ gallicole **80** 40
dipyramide tétragonale **351** 18
direct **299** 28
directeur **248** 29
~ de cirque **307** 17
~ de l'hôtel **267** 19
~ de post-synchronisation **311** 38
~ de production *Radiodiff.* **238** 22
~ de production *Ciné* **310** 26
~ des émissions **238** 22
~ général **251** 16
direction *Autom.* **192** 56-59
~ *Tramw.* **197** 20
~ *Ch. de f.* **205** 21
~ à vis globique **192** 56-59
~ à vis sans fin **192** 56-59
~ de déplacement de la tête vidéo **243** 30
~ de la course **290** 4
~ des rayons solaires **4** 9
~ du déroulement de la bande **243** 29
~ du vent *Météor.* **9** 9; **10** 31
~ du vent *Sports* **285** 1-13, 6
~ hydraulique avec transmission réversible **65** 41
~ par châssis articulé **85** 31, 37
~ pivotante **85** 31, 37
~ structurale **12** 2
disamare **371** 57
discipline sportive **305**
discjockey **317** 25
discothèque **317**
diseuse de bonne aventure **308** 36
disjoncteur *Maison* **41** 20
~ *Centr.* **152** 34
~ à visser **127** 19
~ (de protection) du moteur **269** 46
~ instantané à air comprimé **152** 34; **153** 51-62
~ miniature **127** 19, 33
~ ultra-rapide **152** 34
~ ultra-rapide à air comprimé **153** 51-62
dislocation avant aux anneaux **296** 55
~ du terrain **11** 50
dispositif antiballottement **235** 53
~ antidérailleur **214** 75
~ antirecul **255** 44
~ anti-skating **241** 25
~ d'accord **326** 30
~ d'accrochage **65** 61
~ d'ajustage **133** 36
~ d'ajustage de la meule **157** 45
~ d'alimentation en papier **245** 11
~ d'amenée **64** 6
~ d'appel d'alarme **237** 4
~ d'arrêt *Tiss.* **166** 43
~ d'arrêt *Chim.* **349** 37
~ d'arrosage **316** 6
~ d'arrosage mobile **67** 3
~ d'aspiration de la poussière de meulage **133** 28
~ d'aspiration d'eau **281** 39
~ d'aspiration des germes **92** 38
~ d'assemblage **133** 5
~ d'attelage **65** 30
~ d'attelage à l'avant **65** 50
~ d'attelage rapide **65** 86
~ de basculement des poubelles **199** 2
~ de blocage **2** 43
~ de circulation du gaz **83** 16
~ de collage de la bobine vierge **180** 3
~ de collage des surfaces jointives **133** 29
~ de commutation électronique **237** 42
~ de coupe *Dess.* **151** 15
~ de coupe *Verr.* **162** 19
~ de coupe du câble à une longueur déterminée **169** 30

~ de déchargement **62** 42
~ de démarrage et freinage automatiques **168** 20
~ de dépose alternée du tissu **168** 35
~ de détente **255** 20
~ de fermeture **90** 27
~ de fixation **150** 15
~ de fixation des panneaux **132** 70
~ de graissage des boudins **211** 52
~ de levage *Ch. de f.* **206** 56
~ de levage *Inst. fluv.* **217** 34
~ de levage de la porte **139** 55
~ de macrophotographie **115** 81-98
~ de marquage à la mousse **83** 9
~ de mesure **112** 51
~ de mesure nivométrique **10** 48
~ de microphotographie **115** 89
~ de nettoyage **92** 36
~ de perforation du film **242** 10
~ de perfusion pour médicaments hydrosolubles **25** 14
~ de pesage **92** 32
~ de pinces à chaînes **180** 56
~ de pliage **249** 46
~ de production de vide **145** 51
~ de protection **290** 13
~ de pulvérisation **83** 58
~ de ramassage replié **62** 41
~ de réception des clichés **245** 9
~ de réglage de la hauteur de coupe **157** 49
~ de réglage de la largeur **100** 19
~ de réglage de la longueur **100** 20
~ de réglage de la table en profondeur **133** 21
~ de réglage de la tension du fil **100** 22
~ de réglage de tension de l'élévateur de betteraves **64** 94
~ de repérage **177** 12
~ de secousses **64** 70, 77
~ de serrage *Atome* **2** 43
~ de serrage *Bricol.* **134** 42
~ de serrage *Métall.* **148** 61-65
~ de serrage *Mach.-out.* **150** 15
~ de serrage amovible **133** 48
~ de serrage de la lame de scie **157** 47
~ de signalisation **268** 54
~ de soulèvement du bras **241** 28
~ de synchronisation **117** 77
~ de troisième pli **185** 14
~ de vidage étanche **199** 2
~ de vidange **89** 9
~ d'éjection **236** 49
~ d'élimination de cailloux **64** 9
~ d'encollage **184** 4
~ d'ensachage **92** 39
~ d'entraînement **238** 57
~ d'épandage **62** 22
~ d'évacuation **185** 35
~ d'homme mort **211** 21, 25; **212** 13
~ d'intercalage **181** 11
~ d'introduction **236** 48
~ électronique d'arbitrage **294** 32
~ margeur-sortie **181** 14
~ Norton **149** 8
~ pendulaire **2** 35
~ pivotant d'éclairage sans ombre portée **26** 10
~ tendeur **168** 13
disposition des ailes **229** 1-14
~ des disques en X **65** 83
~ des fruits **371** 44, 69, 72; **373** 8; **374** 18
~ des microphones **310** 30
~ des quilles **305** 1-11, 14
~ des sièges en 2ème classe **211** 58
~ du fruit **371** 22
~ d'un blessé inanimé **21** 24-27
disque *Maison* **46** 15
~ *Sports hiver* **301** 8
~ *Marché puces* **309** 32
~ *Discoth.* **317** 24
~, frein à **191** 17-18; **192** 48-55
~ à calcul **182** 19
~ à polir **134** 23
~ crénelé **65** 85
~ d'argent **10** 24
~ de cadran **237** 11
~ de fonture **167** 26
~ de frein *Méc.* **143** 98
~ de frein *Autom.* **191** 17; **192** 48
~ de papier abrasif **134** 25
~ de polissage en toile de coton **100** 10
~ de ponçage **100** 7
~ de tension du fil **165** 21
~ du frein **166** 60
~ en carborundum **24** 35
~ en porcelaine **350** 54
~ facial **362** 18
~ germinatif **74** 66
~ métallique **309** 15
~ perforé **309** 15
~ plein **65** 84
~ porte-matrices **176** 20
~ solaire **4** 36
~ solaire ailé **333** 12
~ souple **244** 8
~ vidéo **243** 44
~ vidéo longue durée **243** 51
disquette **244** 8
dissipation de chaleur **1** 55
dissolution **340** 49
~ du xanthate dans la soude caustique **169** 10
dissolveur **172** 37
distance de freinage **203** 14
~ des droites **346** 5
~ entre tireurs **294** 10
distillation **170** 17
~ discontinue du goudron **170** 4
~ sèche du charbon **170** 2
distiller **350** 46, 50
distributeur *Agric.* **62** 42
~ *Briq.* **159** 7
~ *Compos.* **174** 20
~ *Bureau* **249** 51
~ à trois voies **92** 34
~ automatique de billets **268** 28
~ automatique de cigarettes **268** 69
~ de bière **266** 68
~ de billets avec changeur de monnaie **197** 33
~ de blé empoisonné **83** 31
~ de boîtes **74** 53
~ de composition **162** 13
~ de copies **249** 43
~ de coton **22** 36
~ de fumier **62** 21
~ de monnaie **236** 28
~ de papier hygiénique **49** 10
~ de papier ménage **40** 1
~ de ruban adhésif **247** 27
~ de serviettes en papier **196** 10
~ de sparadrap et de petites pièces **22** 64
~ de timbres **236** 19
~ de tracts **263** 9
~ d'eau **274** 17
~ linéaire **159** 7
distribution *Compos.* **174** 30
~ *Serv. eaux* **269** 22
~, conduite de **235** 56
~ d'eau potable **269** 1-66
~ des matrices **174** 22
~ du courrier **236** 50-55
divergent **90** 13
dividende *Bourse* **251** 18
~ *Math.* **344** 26
divinité de la mer **327** 23, 40
~ hindoue **337** 19
diviseur **344** 26
~ de chaumes **64** 1
~ optique **240** 35
division **344** 26
~ de fréquence **110** 16
~ de la voûte céleste **3** 1-8
~ optique **240** 35
dizaine de chapelet **332** 32
DM **252** 7
doberman **70** 27
dock flottant *Mar.* **222** 34-43, 36-43
~ flottant *Ports* **225** 16
~ flottant, structure du **222** 37-38
~ flottant immergé **222** 41
~ flottant remonté **222** 43
document confidentiel **246** 25
dodécaèdre **351** 22
~ pentagonal **351** 8
~ rhomboïdal **351** 7
dog-cart **186** 18
dogue danois **70** 14
doigt, bout du **19** 79
~ de guidage **243** 21
~ d'entraînement **157** 44
~ levé **260** 20
doline **13** 71
dollar **252** 33
dolly **310** 49
dolmen **328** 16
~ à couloir **328** 16
domaine d'exploration par fusée **7** 24
~ d'exploration par satellite **7** 33
dôme à bulbe **121** 25
~ de la cuve **92** 45
~ de vapeur **210** 12
~ montagneux **12** 35
domiciliation **250** 22
domino *Jeux* **276** 34
~ *Carnaval* **306** 15
~ basculant **326** 39
dominos **276** 33
dompteur **307** 52
donjon **329** 4
donnée technique **151** 32
données géologiques d'une mine de sel **154** 57-68
~ traitées par calculateur **238** 13
doreur **183** 2
dormant **120** 51
dorsal **18** 59
dorure **129** 40
~ du dos d'un livre **183** 1
doryphore **80** 52
dos *Anat.* **16** 22-25
~ *Ust. table* **45** 56
~ *Cheval* **72** 29
~ *Reliure* **185** 41
~, encollage du **183** 14
~ d'âne **206** 46
~ de la chambre **114** 54
~ de la main **19** 83
~ de l'appareil **115** 23
~ du pied **19** 61
~ d'un livre **183** 1
~ spécial pour enregistrement des données **115** 67
dosage du kieselguhr **93** 3
doseur de durcisseur **130** 33
~ de pâte **172** 3
dosifilm **2** 8
dosimètre **2** 8-23
dossard **301** 37
dosse **120** 96
dosseret de pied **43** 4
~ de tête **43** 6
dossier **42** 25
~ confidentiel **246** 25
~ de siège **207** 66
~ inclinable **191** 35
~ suspendu **248** 2, 3
dossier-classeur **245** 6
dossière **71** 17
douane **217** 24
doublage **311** 37-41
~ des rubans de carde **164** 5
double *Jeux* **276** 35
~ *Sports* **293** 2 *à* 3
~ bémol **320** 53
~ bollard d'amarrage **217** 11
~ ciseau **298** 40
~ clé de jambe **299** 11
~ contre-octave **321** 42
~ croche **320** 17
~ dames **293** 2 *à* 3
~ dièse **320** 51
~ flux **232** 46
~ fond cellulaire **222** 60
~ jersey **171** 47
~ messieurs **293** 2 *à* 3
~ mixte **293** 2 *à* 3, 49
~ pause **320** 20
~ porte **267** 27
~ porte à vantaux pliants et pivotants **208** 7
~ porte verticale décalée **301** 70
~ rideau **44** 13
~ ronde **320** 12
~ saut périlleux arrière groupé **282** 42
~ toit **278** 22
~ trois **302** 14
doubleau **335** 18
doublier **168** 56
doublure de braguette **32** 24
~ de toile **355** 57
~ en peluche **101** 3
~ en tricot **101** 17

doucette **57** 38
douche *Maison* **49** 39, 40, 42, 44
~ *Mar.* **228** 30
~ *Aéroport* **233** 46
~ *Sports* **282** 2
~ à main **105** 30; **106** 13
~ tiède **281** 29
douchette *Plomb.* **126** 30
~ *Imprim.* **179** 7
~ réglable **49** 41
douille **305** 36
~ à baïonnette **127** 65
~ en carton **87** 50
~ pour lampe à incandescence **127** 60
~ pour lampe fluorescente **127** 62
douve *Tonell.* **130** 9
~ *Chevalerie* **329** 37
~ *Zool.* **356** 3
douzaine, dernière **275** 27
~, première **275** 25
~ intermédiaire **275** 26
douze **175** 28
~ derniers **275** 27
~ du milieu **275** 26
~ premiers **275** 25
drachme **252** 39
drag **289** 48
dragage, godet de **226** 44
Drago **3** 32
Dragon *Astr.* **3** 32
~ *Sports* **284** 57
dragon *Best. fabul.* **327** 1
~, corps de **327** 19
dragonne *Alpin.* **300** 32
~ *Sports hiver* **301** 7
drague **258** 87
~ à chaîne à godets **216** 56
~ à godets **226** 41
~ aspiratrice **216** 59
~ flottante **216** 56
~ suceuse **216** 59
dragueur de mines rapide **258** 84
draille de clin-foc **219** 12
~ de foc *Mar.* **219** 14
~ de foc *Sports* **284** 15
drain **26** 47
~ de ciment **200** 62
~ d'évacuation **216** 36
drainage **200** 61
draisine **213** 32
drakkar viking **218** 13-17
drap **43** 9
~ de lin **43** 9
~ de lit **50** 5
drapé **338** 33
drapeau *Drapeaux* **253** 7-11
~ *Sports* **293** 88
~ à damier **273** 34
~ de coin **291** 8
~ de départ **273** 34
~ de gymnastique **297** 49
~ de ligne médiane **291** 64
~ de l'ONU **253** 1-3
~ des Jeux olympiques **253** 5
~ du Conseil de l'Europe **253** 4
~ du juge de touche **291** 60
~ en berne **253** 6
~ européen **253** 4
~ national **253** 15-21
~ olympique **253** 5
~ tricolore **253** 16
drêche **92** 50
dressage **289** 1-7, 3
~ en liberté **307** 30-31
dresseur **307** 31, 52
dressoir *Ust. table* **45** 44
~ *Rest.* **266** 41
dribble **291** 52
drifter **90** 1
drille *Orfèvre* **108** 4
~ *Tourn.* **135** 22
~ *Serr.* **140** 13
drilling **87** 23
drink, long **317** 32
drisse **253** 2
~ de pavillons **223** 10
~ de pic **219** 49
drive **293** 83
driver **293** 91
~ en casaque de course **289** 26
droit **252** 8
~ de vote **263** 24
droite **347** 12
~, pente de la **347** 12
~, segment de **346** 16
~ du faisceau **346** 20
~ gg2 **346** 2, 3
dromie **358** 1
droséra **377** 14
drupe **59** 1-36; **370** 99; **382** 51
~ déhiscente **59** 41, 43
dryade **51** 7
duc d'albe *Mar.* **222** 35
~ d'albe *Ports* **225** 12
duffle-coat **271** 21
dundee **90** 1
dune **13** 39
~ en croissant **13** 40
~ mouvante **13** 39
dunette *Mar.* **223** 33
~ *Mil.* **258** 22
duodénum **20** 14, 43
duolet **321** 23
duramen **120** 84
durillon **72** 27
duvet *Text.* **168** 43
~ *Camping* **278** 30
dynamo **190** 76
~ de vélo **187** 8
dynamomètre **308** 11
dynastart **212** 30

E

eau, château d' *Cartogr.* **15** 81
~, château d' *Serv. eaux* **269** 18
~, conduite d' **334** 54
~, jet d' **272** 22, 62
~, jeux d' **272** 8
~, ligne d' **282** 31
~, niveau d' **349** 16
~, pièce d' **272** 50
~, vache à **278** 32
~ ammoniacale **156** 39
~ brute **269** 4
~ de pâte **172** 55
~ de refroidissement *Nucl.* **154** 18
~ de refroidissement *Moteur* **190** 62
~ de refroidissement *Ch. de f.* **212** 21, 65, 78
~ de retour **172** 26
~ de table **98** 87
~ de toilette **106** 9
~ dentifrice **49** 36
~ douce **221** 70
~ du baptême **332** 12
~ filtrée **269** 12, 13
~ gazeuse **98** 87
~ minérale *Epic.* **98** 87
~ minérale *Rest.* **266** 61
~ potable **269** 1-66
~ résiduaire **156** 38
~ salée **274** 4
~ sous-jacente **12** 32
~ souterraine **12** 21
~ usée **199** 20
eau-forte **340** 14-24
eaux d'infiltration **216** 37
~ résiduaires **172** 63
ébarbage et le parachèvement des pièces moulées **148** 38-45
ébarbeur *Mach. agric.* **64** 10
~ *Métall.* **148** 43
ébarboir **340** 17
ébauche **162** 40, 47
~ gravée **338** 41
ébauchoir **339** 10
ébène, touche en **325** 5
ébéniste **132** 38
éboueuse **199** 41
éboulement **11** 46
~ de la berge **216** 5
éboulis **11** 47
ébrasement de fenêtre **118** 11
ébrasure de fenêtre **118** 11
écaille *Arts* **335** 15
~ *Zool.* **364** 11
~ *Bot.* **372** 5, 38, 42
~ avec sacs polliniques **372** 45, 50
~ chinée **365** 8
~ de cire **77** 25
~ du cône **372** 8, 14, 27
~ du cône femelle **372** 34
~ du fruit **372** 67
~ martée **365** 7
écart, grand **314** 20
~ maximal des jambes **298** 25
écarté **314** 15
écarteur **119** 81
~ en fil **26** 50
E.C.G. de longue durée **25** 45
échafaudage *Constr.* **118** 86-89; **122** 34, 66
~ *Ponts* **215** 62
~ *Mar.* **222** 18
~ de cale **222** 19
~ en tubes d'acier **119** 46
échalas **78** 7
échancrure **324** 74
échangeur auxiliaire de chaleur de l'huile **212** 43
~ de chaleur *Nucl.* **154** 6, 44
~ de chaleur *Cokerie* **156** 27
~ de chaleur *Ciment.* **160** 4, 6, 7
~ de chaleur *Papet.* **172** 19
~ de chaleur *Autom.* **192** 61
~ de chaleur *Ch. de f.* **207** 6; **209** 15
~ de chaleur *Mil.* **259** 66
~ de chaleur à cyclone **160** 6
~ de chaleur de l'huile **212** 55
~ de chaleur de l'huile de transmission **212** 36
~ de chaleur pour gaz d'échappement **155** 9
~ de température **192** 61
échanson **329** 69
échantillon médical **22** 41
échappement **195** 51
~, lumière d' **242** 58
~, silencieux d' **305** 93
~, soupape d' **242** 53
~ des turbines **146** 5
écharpe **121** 30
~ nouée en cravate **253** 9
~ utilisée pour soutenir le bras **21** 2
échasse *Constr.* **118** 23; **119** 47
~ *Parc attr.* **308** 49
~ blanche **359** 19
échassier **359** 18
échauguette **329** 28
échéance **250** 16
échec et mat **276** 15
échecs **276** 1-16
~, joueur d' **265** 17
~, partie d' **265** 17
échelle *Cartogr.* **14** 29
~ *Méd.* **21** 32
~ *Maison* **38** 15; **47** 5
~ *Constr.* **118** 42, 86
~ *Ch. de f.* **211** 43
~ *Inst. fluv.* **217** 8
~, grande **270** 10
~ à crochets **270** 16
~ à poissons **89** 93
~ avec aiguille de mesure **114** 58
~ coudée rotative **5** 20
~ coulissante **270** 14
~ d'accès **6** 35
~ d'accès au niveau inférieur **235** 28
~ d'avance de coupe **157** 61
~ de corde *Jeux enf.* **273** 49
~ de corde *Cirque* **307** 8
~ de coupée **221** 91, 98
~ de couvreur **38** 4
~ de descente **221** 123
~ de hauteur de coupe **157** 10
~ de hauteur de trait **157** 60
~ de jardin **52** 8
~ de marée **225** 37
~ de mesure **242** 75
~ de mise au point **115** 4
~ de réduction triangulaire **151** 34
~ de rondins **273** 22
~ de temps **10** 17
~ de tirants d'eau **222** 73
~ d'écluses **217** 17-25
~ d'enregistrement **224** 66
~ d'épaisseur de débit **157** 58
~ des altitudes **7** 35
~ des diaphragmes **115** 56
~ des gris **343** 15
~ des températures **7** 36
~ d'étiage **15** 29
~ double **128** 52
~ en acier **270** 10
~ graduée *Mach.-out.* **149** 63
~ graduée *Bureau* **249** 12
~ mécanique **270** 10
~ musicale **321** 42-50
~ orientable automobile **270** 9
~ plate de couvreur **122** 63
~ pliante **129** 5
~ verticale **296** 21
échelon *Maison* **38** 17
~ *Serv. eaux* **269** 28
échenilloir élagueur **56** 11
échiffre **123** 15
échine **334** 21
~ de porc **95** 47

F

feutre *Papet.* **173** 51
~ *Ecole* **260** 19
~ *Arts graph.* **340** 42
~, botte de **353** 30
~, couverture de **353** 20
~ à larges bords **355** 55
~ coucheur **173** 17, 18
~ de verre **162** 58
~ du marteau **325** 24
feux **224** 68-108
~ antibrouillard **191** 63
~ antibrouillard avant et arrière **191** 64
~ de croisement **191** 59
~ de détresse **191** 68
~ de position **257** 36
~ de route *Autom.* **191** 69
~ de route *Navig.* **224** 29
~ piétons **268** 55
fève **69** 15
~ de cacao **382** 19
FF **323** 6
F.I. **240** 4
fiacre **186** 26
fibre chimique **169; 170**
~ de polyamide **170** 1-62, 61, 62
~ de verre **151** 48
~ de viscose **169** 34
~ discontinue **169** 28-34
~ du nerf optique **77** 23
~ en nappes multiples **169** 31
~ végétale **352** 18
fibres de carbone **235** 20, 32
fibroscope urinaire **23** 20
fibule **328** 27
~ à deux pièces à spirales **328** 30
~ à plaques rondes **328** 30
~ en arbalète **328** 28
~ en archet **328** 27
~ en barque **328** 28
~ serpentiforme **328** 28
ficaire **375** 36
ficelage **206** 12
ficelle *Compos.* **174** 16
~ *Reliure* **183** 10
~ du cerf-volant **273** 44
fiche d'arrivée **267** 12
~ de caisse **98** 44
~ de caisse acquittée **271** 7
~ de dossier **248** 8
~ de travail **261** 27
~ femelle de prolongateur **127** 12
~ mâle à contact de terre **127** 9
~ mâle à 3 broches **127** 67
~ mâle de prolongateur **127** 11
~ mâle de sécurité **127** 9
~ mâle pour triphasé **127** 14
~ médicale **22** 8
~ médicale périmée **22** 7
~ multibroche normalisée **241** 70
fichier *Maison* **46** 10
~ *Bureau* **245** 23
~ *Univ.* **262** 23
~ central **248** 43
~ d'archivage **248** 2
~ de cartes programme **195** 10
~ (de la) clientèle **248** 24
~ des diabétiques **22** 26
~ des patients **22** 6
~ électoral **263** 18
fichu **355** 39
fidèle **330** 29, 61; **331** 17
fidélité, haute **241** 13-48
figue **384** 13
~ d'hévéa **383** 35
figuier **384** 11
figurant *Ciné* **310** 29
~ *Théât.* **316** 39
figuration des blasons **254** 17-23
figure de proue à tête de dragon **218** 16
~ de terre glaise **339** 7
~ de voltige **288** 50-51
~ d'école **289** 7
~ du portail **333** 36
~ en mosaïque **338** 38
~ imposée **302** 11-19
~ mythologique **327** 1-61
~ symbolique **327** 20
~ symétrique **346** 24
figurine de cire **308** 69
~ de terre cuite **328** 20
~ en cire **339** 26
fil *Piscic.* **89** 63
~ *Orfèvre* **108** 3
~ *Filat. coton* **164** 53
~ *Text.* **167** 17, 36
~ *Cirque* **307** 41
~ *Théât.* **316** 8
~ à coudre **103** 12
~ à filet **102** 24
~ à plomb **118** 50, 71
~ croisé **165** 8
~ d'argent **108** 3
~ de chaîne *Tiss.* **166** 39
~ de chaîne *Text.* **171** 2, 17, 18
~ de chaîne baissé **171** 8
~ de chaîne levé **171** 7
~ de commande de vol **288** 90
~ de contact **205** 58; **211** 28
~ de fer **143** 12
~ de rayonne viscose **169** 13-27
~ de réserve **89** 21
~ de silionne **162** 56
~ de soudure d'étain **134** 20
~ de trame **171** 3
~ de trame baissé **171** 15
~ de trame levé **171** 16
~ de verre **162** 54
~ de viscose **169** 13-27
~ de viscose sur cône pour mise en œuvre textile **169** 27
~ déroulé **89** 21
~ d'étendage **50** 33
~ d'or **108** 3
~ du cerf-volant **273** 44
~ du marteau **298** 44
~ du rasoir **106** 40
~ hygroscopique **10** 9
~ renvidé **164** 56
~ retors **164** 60
~ sur enrouleur **294** 31
~ tramé **171** 43
filage **169** 25
filament à double boudinage **127** 58
~ bispiralé **127** 58
~ de cellulose plastique **169** 15
~ de polyamide **170** 43, 46
~ primaire de verre **162** 52
filature de coton **163; 164**
fil-de-fériste **307** 40
filé de verre **162** 54
filer de l'huile à la surface de l'eau **228** 11
filet *Zool.* **71** 7-13
~ *Pêche* **90** 8
~ *Trav. fém.* **102** 22
~ *Text.* **167** 29
~ *Sports* **293** 13, 53
~ *Mus.* **323** 26
~ à bagages **207** 51; **208** 27
~ à chapeaux et petits bagages **208** 28
~ à encadrement **183** 3
~ au-dessus du trou de sortie **86** 27
~ cernant **90** 25
~ de bœuf **95** 24
~ de grimper **273** 50
~ de pêche **89** 31
~ de ping-pong **273** 3
~ de porc **95** 44
~ de protection **307** 14
~ de sécurité **259** 17
~ de tennis **293** 13
~ de veau **95** 7
~ dérivant **90** 2-10
~ tournant **90** 25
~ vertical **90** 8
filetage *App. mén.* **50** 50
~ *Agric.* **67** 38
~ *Méc.* **143** 16, 68
~, pas de **149** 9
~ à pas rapide **149** 4
~ pour bois **143** 47
filière *Orfèvre* **108** 15
~ *Briq.* **159** 13
~ *Text.* **169** 14; **170** 41, 42
~ à main **126** 85
~ brisée **140** 32
~ électrique **125** 12
filigrane *Trav. fém.* **102** 30
~ *Argent* **252** 31
filin d'amarrage **288** 66
~ de retenue **288** 66
filler **200** 51, 52
film *Atome* **2** 10, 13
~ *Photocomp.* **176** 25
~, cassette de **242** 18
~, projecteur de **311** 22
~ de format réduit **313** 31
~ (de format) standard **313** 1
~ de scanner **177** 72
~ de 35 mm **313** 1
~ exposé **117** 42
~ magnétique **311** 2
~ non exposé **117** 41
~ pornographique **318** 20
~ rétractable *Laiterie* **76** 25
~ rétractable *Ports* **226** 12
~ sonore pisté avec piste magnétique latérale **117** 82
~ vierge **117** 41
filmdosimètre **2** 8
~ personnel **2** 11
filmothèque **310** 5
filoir d'écoute **284** 29
filon **11** 31
filtration rapide **269** 9
filtre *Atome* **2** 9, 12
~ *Piscic.* **89** 10
~ *Text.* **170** 32
~ *Papet.* **172** 20
~ *Chim.* **349** 12
~ à air **191** 55
~ à air à bain d'huile *Mach. agric.* **65** 54
~ à air à bain d'huile *Ch. de f.* **212** 79
~ à bière **93** 15
~ à huile *Moteur* **190** 43
~ à huile *Autom.* **192** 20
~ à kieselguhr **93** 4
~ à lessive noire **172** 28
~ à manche **83** 54
~ à poussière **270** 59
~ à sédiments en acier **79** 8
~ coloré **316** 49
~ correcteur **311** 19
~ d'aiguillage **241** 14
~ de synchronisation **311** 27
~ du masque à gaz **270** 57
~ en papier plissé **350** 41
~ escamotable **116** 46
~ sécheur **173** 23
~ solaire **6** 22
filtre-presse *Porcel.* **161** 12
~ *Text.* **169** 12
fin d'alinéa **175** 15
fincelle **90** 7
finesse du filé **164** 40
finisseur **201** 1
~ de revêtements noirs **200** 43
Finn **284** 51
fiole d'Erlenmeyer *Papet.* **173** 2
~ d'Erlenmeyer *Chim.* **350** 39
~ jaugée *Papet.* **173** 3
~ jaugée *Chim.* **350** 28
~ pour filtration sous vide **350** 40
fission **1** 43
~ nucléaire **1** 34, 46
fissure *Géogr.* **11** 52
~ *Alpin.* **300** 3
five o'clock **267** 44-46
fixatif **105** 24
fixation à câble *Alpin.* **300** 52
~ à câble *Sports hiver* **301** 40
~ à sandows **278** 51
~ de la bougie de préchauffage **190** 55
~ de plaque **178** 27
~ de sécurité **301** 2
~ du cube à éclairs **114** 13
~ du flash-cube **114** 13
~ du tissu par chaînes à picots **168** 24
~ du tissu par chaînes à pinces **168** 24
~ rottefella **301** 15
flache **120** 89
flacon à épices **39** 32
~ à produits chimiques **261** 23
~ à tare **349** 24
~ à trois tubulures **350** 57
~ à whisky **42** 31
~ de parfum *Maison* **43** 27
~ de parfum *Coiff.* **105** 36
~ de perfusion **25** 12
~ d'eau de toilette **105** 37
~ d'encre de Chine **151** 63
~ laveur **350** 58
~ pour premier révélateur **116** 10
~ souple pour révélateur **116** 9
flacon-laveur **261** 32
flamant **272** 53
flambée **267** 25
flamme *Poste* **236** 56
~ *Plage* **280** 11
~ «Aperçu» **253** 29
~ chiffrée **253** 33-34
~ de la résurrection **327** 10
~ du Code international des signaux **253** 29
~ numérique **253** 33-34

flan *Boul.-pâtiss.* **97** 22-24, 24
~ *Argent* **252** 43
flanc *Anat.* **16** 32
~ *Chasse* **88** 26
flanchet **95** 2, 15-16, 15
flancois **329** 86
flash **309** 38
~ à accumulateur séparé **114** 65
~ à cubes **114** 73
~ compact **114** 68
~ électronique **309** 40-41
~ sous-marin **279** 25
flashcube **114** 74
flasque **187** 59, 79
~ de mécanique **325** 16
~ de support du cylindre **130** 28
~ d'ensouple **165** 30
~ du banc **164** 26
~ plastique **289** 25
flat twin **189** 47
fléau **349** 29
flèche *Zool.* **71** 21
~ *Chasse* **87** 77
~ *Constr.* **119** 36
~ *Mar.* **221** 26, 59; **223** 36
~ *Ports* **226** 24
~ *Sports* **305** 60
~ *Best. fabul.* **327** 53
~ *Ethnol.* **352** 28
~, aile à double **229** 18
~, aile à faible **229** 20
~, aile à forte **229** 21
~, pointe de **352** 29
~ de cote **151** 26
~ de la grue *Ports* **226** 49
~ de la grue *Mil.* **255** 95
~ de la pelle **200** 4
~ de lard **96** 2
~ d'eau **378** 51
~ du clocher **331** 6
~ support de canon **255** 62
flèche-en-cul **219** 31
fleur *Bot.* **58** 4; **59** 9; **370** 23, 51; **373** 5, 11; **375** 6, 16, 20, 46; **376** 2, 5; **378** 16, 20, 28, 32, 37, 47, 53, 57; **382** 4, 18, 29, 34, 42, 55; **384** 56, 57
~ *Agric.* **68** 42
~ d'ananas **384** 64, 65
~ d'aristoloche **376** 23
~ de colza **383** 3
~ de coquelicot **61** 4
~ de grenadier **384** 18
~ de haricot **57** 9
~ de la bourse à pasteur **61** 10
~ de la grande consoude **69** 14
~ de la moutarde sauvage **61** 19
~ de la Passion **53** 2
~ de la ravenelle **61** 22
~ de la renouée **376** 11
~ de la véronique **375** 23
~ de l'abricotier **59** 34
~ de l'anthyllide **69** 7
~ de laurier-rose **373** 14
~ de l'érable **371** 55
~ de lis **254** 13
~ de l'orme **371** 52
~ de paturin annuel **375** 40
~ de peuplier **371** 17
~ de pois **57** 2
~ de saxifrage **375** 3
~ de sésame **383** 47
~ de spirée **374** 24
~ de sureau **374** 36
~ de troène **373** 7
~ des champs **375; 376**
~ des jardins **60**
~ des prés **375; 376**
~ d'hévéa **383** 36
~ d'hysope **374** 6, 7
~ d'olivier **383** 31
~ d'oranger **384** 25
~ du bananier **384** 34
~ du cerisier **59** 3
~ du chanvre **383** 12
~ du chèvrefeuille **374** 15
~ du cornouiller sanguin **373** 31
~ du cotonnier **383** 17
~ du framboisier **58** 26
~ du frêne **371** 40
~ du groseillier à maquereau **58** 6
~ du hêtre **371** 35
~ du jute **383** 27
~ du lierre terrestre **375** 19
~ du marronnier **371** 62
~ du palaquium **383** 39
~ du pêcher **59** 27
~ du poirier **58** 38
~ du pommier **58** 54
~ en tube **375** 32
~ épanouie de la vigne vierge **374** 17
~ fanée **58** 55
~ femelle **59** 38; **371** 6, 13; **372** 43; **373** 20; **378** 25, 53; **382** 32, 50; **383** 50; **384** 7, 14, 42, 43
~ forcée **55** 24
~ hermaphrodite **382** 12, 14
~ hermaphrodite du houx **374** 10
~ mâle **371** 14; **372** 43; **373** 21; **378** 23, 53; **382** 13; **383** 51, 55; **384** 5, 15, 44, 51
~ mâle avec les étamines **59** 39
~ mâle du houx **374** 11
~ précoce **55** 24
~ privée de ses pétales **374** 21
~ radiée **375** 31
fleuret **294** 11
~ électrique **294** 26
~ français **294** 37
~ italien **294** 39
fleuretiste tirant en assaut **294** 5-6
fleuriste **204** 48
fleuron **335** 37
fleuve *Géogr.* **13** 1, 61
~ *Cartogr.* **15** 76
~ régularisé **216** 31
flexible d'aspiration **50** 75, 84
flexion arrière du tronc **295** 34
~ avant du tronc **295** 33
~ et esquive latérale **299** 29
~ latérale du tronc **295** 32
flic-flac au sol **297** 24
flocons d'avoine **98** 37
floraison **382** 53
flore alpine **378** 1-13
~ aquatique **378** 14-57
~ des marais **378** 14-57
florin **252** 19
flots, ruban de **334** 39
flotte **90** 7
flotté **171** 40
flotteur *Piscic.* **89** 43-48
~ *Pêche* **90** 2
~ *Plomb.* **126** 15
~ *Autom.* **192** 15
~ *Cours d'eau* **216** 12
~ *Inst. fluv.* **217** 34
~ *Navig.* **224** 71
~ *Aéron.* **232** 6
~ *Mil.* **258** 87
~ *Sports* **286** 44
~ avec plume **89** 45
~ de harpon **353** 11
~ de natation en liège **281** 7
~ en bois **90** 6
~ en liège fusiforme **89** 43
~ en polystyrène **89** 46
~ plastique **89** 44
flotteur-glisseur plombé **89** 48
fluide caloporteur **155** 31
fluorine **351** 16
fluothane **26** 26
flûte *Ust. table* **45** 85
~ *Boul.-pâtiss.* **97** 12
~ *Mus.* **322** 4
~ *Ethnol.* **353** 47
~ à bec **322** 7
~ de Pan **322** 2
~ double **322** 3
~ traversière **323** 31
flûteau **378** 44
flux, deuxième **232** 41, 44, 50
~, double **232** 46
~ de soudage **141** 18
Flying Dutchman **284** 49
FM **255** 16
foc *Mar.* **220** 2
~ *Sports* **284** 16; **285** 3
~, draille de *Mar.* **219** 14
~, draille de *Sports* **284** 15
~, écoute de **284** 23
~, grand **219** 22
~, petit **219** 20
~, second **219** 21
~ d'artimon **219** 27
focomètre universel **111** 21
foie **20** 10, 34-35
foin **75** 13
~ épandu **63** 25
foire **308** 1-69
~, champ de **308** 1
folio **185** 63
follicule **370** 91; **378** 42
~ et ovule **20** 84
fonceuse à râcles **173** 29-35
fonction respiratoire **23** 31
~ trigonométrique **346** 32
fond **144** 21-51
~, coureur de *Sports* **290** 14
~, coureur de *Athl.* **298** 5
~, course de **290** 11-15
~, épreuve de **289** 16
-fond, exploitation au **144** 21-51
fond, ski de **301** 14, 14-20, 42
~ à tuyères **147** 69
~ de cale avant **259** 80
~ de coffrage **119** 54
~ de convertisseur **147** 47
~ de dent **143** 84
~ de la coque **286** 32, 35, 39
~ de la vallée *Géogr.* **13** 67
~ de la vallée *Ponts* **215** 60
~ de tarte **97** 47
~ de tulle **102** 16
~ du tonneau **130** 10
~ en forme d'étoile **136** 19
~ océanique **11** 10
~ racleur amovible **62** 24
fondant *Orfèvre* **108** 36
~ *Métall.* **147** 2
fondation **118** 75
~ des pylônes **214** 81
~ sur pieux **216** 8
~ sur pilotis **216** 8
~ sur semelle **123** 2
fonderie de fer **148** 1-45
fondeur **148** 7
fondeuse à clichés cylindriques **178** 13
~ à stéréos cylindriques **178** 13
~ Monotype **174** 39
fondoir de goudron et de bitume **200** 46
fonds, brosse à **338** 9
fontaine **272** 21
~ à eau potable **205** 33
~ jaillissante **12** 26
~ murale **272** 15
fontange **355** 65
fonte liquide **148** 11
fonts baptismaux **332** 10
fonture **167** 55
~ en cours de tricotage **167** 51
foot **291** 1-16
football *Jeux enf.* **273** 10
~ *Sports* **291**
~, ballon de **291** 17
~, chaussure de **291** 21
~, terrain de **291** 1-16
~ américain **292** 22
forage, plate-forme de **221** 66
~ en mer **221** 32
~ off-shore **146**
~ offshore **221** 32
~ pétrolier **145** 1-21
forain **308** 25-28
forçat **218** 48
force de corps **175** 18, 46
~ d'impression **249** 10
~ du papier **173** 9
~ du vent **9** 10
forceps **26** 53
forcerie **55** 4
Forces armées **255; 256; 257**
foret **134** 49
~ américain **140** 59
forêt **84** 1-34
~ de conifères **9** 56
~ de protection **304** 7
~ mixte **15** 14
~ tropicale **352** 25
foreur **158** 9
foreuse électrique **120** 21
forficule **81** 11
forge **137** 1-8, 1
~ avec le feu de forge **138** 34
forgeage libre **139**
forgeron *Forge* **137; 138**
~ *Zool.* **358** 38
formaldéhyde **242** 64
formation de la cyclohexanone **170** 20
~ de la lactame **170** 25
~ de l'oxime de la cyclohexanone **170** 22
~ du coussin d'air **243** 27
~ d'une maille **167** 65
~ karstique **13** 71-83
forme *Coiffures* **35** 2
~ *Coord.* **100** 32
~ *Arts graph.* **340** 32
~ à main **173** 48
~ cristalline **351** 1-26
~ d'aile **229** 15-22
~ de croix chrétienne **332** 55-72
~ de feuille **370** 31-38; **378** 52

goujonneuse **133** 6
goulotte d'alimentation *Agric.* **74** 15
~ d'alimentation *Scierie* **157** 55
~ d'évacuation **147** 39
goupille **140** 47
~ à encoches **143** 40
~ conique **143** 37
~ cylindrique **143** 40
~ fendue **143** 19, 78
goupillon **332** 54
gourmette **71** 12
gousse *Agric.* **57** 6
~ *Bot.* **69** 8, 16; **370** 92; **384** 46
~ de vanille **382** 48
~ verte **374** 22
gousset **119** 6
~ de latte **284** 43
goutte à briolet **36** 86
~ à goutte, perfusion **25** 13
~ lisse **36** 85
gouttière *Géogr.* **12** 18
~ *Méd.* **21** 12
~ *Maison* **37** 6
~ *Constr.* **121** 4; **122** 28, 92
gouvernail *Mar.* **221** 43; **222** 69-70; **223** 63; **228** 26
~ *Sports* **283** 26, 51-53; **285** 34; **286** 65
~, mèche du **222** 68
~ de direction *Mil.* **257** 23
~ de direction *Sports* **288** 22
~ de direction arrière **259** 95
~ de profondeur *Mil.* **257** 21
~ de profondeur *Sports* **288** 24
~ d'étambot **218** 24
~ d'étrave **224** 23
~ latéral **218** 6
gouverne de direction **229** 25; **230** 60; **231** 6; **232** 7
~ de profondeur **229** 27; **230** 63
gradateur d'éclairage de la salle **312** 17
gradin *Cirque* **307** 15
~ *Taurom.* **319** 8
~ de repos **281** 20
gradine **158** 37
~ grain d'orge **339** 13
gradins, toit à **337** 2
~, tour à **333** 32
graduation *Chasse* **87** 68
~ *Bureau* **247** 36
~ *Chim.* **349** 36
~, bâtiment de **274** 1
~ angulaire **313** 14
~ en degrés **260** 39
~ en millibars **10** 3
~ mobile **349** 23
grain **68** 15
~, gros **332** 31
~, petit **332** 32
~ de blé **68** 25
~ de café **382** 6
~ de maïs **68** 37
~ de poivre **382** 39
~ de pollen **370** 65
~ de riz **68** 30
~ desséché **80** 21
~ germé **68** 14
~ parasité par un champignon **68** 4
~ vert pour potage **68** 25
graine *Plantes* **54** 3
~ *Bot.* **58** 23, 37, 60; **59** 8; **370** 83; **371** 20, 65; **372** 10, 15, 28, 37, 54, 60, 71; **375** 25, 28; **378** 33, 34; **382** 5, 20, 35, 39, 45; **383** 15, 23, 24; **384** 10, 20, 21, 47, 58
~ ailée **372** 9
~ avec les pores germinatifs **383** 57
~ de cacao **382** 19
~ de marronnier **371** 60
~ oléagineuse **383** 5
graissage sous pression **192** 16-27
graisse végétale **98** 23
graisseur *Méc.* **143** 81
~ *Bicycl.* **187** 65
~ à chapeau **187** 65
graminée *Bot.* **69** 27
~ *Vann.* **136** 26
gramophone **309** 31
grand axe **347** 23
~ bassin **282** 23
~ cacatois **219** 66
Grand Chien **3** 14
grand compartiment **207** 59, 61; **208** 9
~ coq de bruyère **88** 72
~ cormoran **359** 10
~ dentelé **18** 42
Grand d'Espagne **306** 26
grand droit de l'abdomen **18** 44
~ duc **86** 48
~ écart **314** 20
~ écart antéro-postérieur **295** 14
~ écart facial **295** 15
~ étirage **164** 14
~ fessier **18** 60
~ foc **219** 22
~ galop **72** 43-44
~ gibier **88** 1-27
~ heaume **254** 7
~ huit **308** 39
~ hunier **219** 25
~ hunier fixe **219** 39, 62
~ hunier volant **219** 40, 63
~ largue **285** 12
~ magasin *Cité* **268** 41
~ magasin *Magasin* **271**
~ mât **218** 40; **219** 5-7, 5
~ mât à voiles longitudinales **220** 15
~ mât arrière **220** 30
~ mât de hune **219** 6
~ mât de perroquet **219** 7
~ miroir **224** 6
~ oblique **18** 43
~ orgue **326** 1, 43
~ pavois **221** 85
~ pectoral **18** 36
~ perroquet **218** 53; **219** 26, 53
~ perroquet fixe **219** 41, 64
~ perroquet volant **219** 42, 65
~ porte-queue **358** 52
~ rond **18** 55
~ spitz **70** 20
~ tambour **163** 43
~ tétras **88** 72
~ titre **185** 46
~ voilier *Mar.* **219; 220**
~ voilier *Oiseaux* **359** 24
grand-duc **362** 15
grande capitale **175** 11
~ ciguë **379** 4
~ consoude **69** 13; **375** 45
~ échelle **270** 10
~ écoute **284** 28
~ église à deux tours **15** 53
~ fourchette **45** 70
~ hostie **332** 35
~ marguerite **376** 4
Grande Ourse **3** 29
grande radiaire **376** 7
~ roue **308** 37
~ routière à carénage intégral **189** 43
Grande-Bretagne **253** 15
grandes lignes **207** 1-21
grand-hune **219** 52
grand-mât **220** 22
~ arrière **220** 34
~ central **220** 33
grands ciseaux pour couper les empeignes **100** 42
grand-vergue **218** 37; **219** 38
grand-voile *Mar.* **219** 61; **220** 11
~ *Sports* **284** 46; **285** 2
~ carrée **218** 33
~ d'étai **219** 24
granulation **340** 47
granulométrie **119** 26
graphique de statistiques **248** 36
~ statistique des ventes **248** 46
graphite **1** 54
grappe **370** 68
~ à fleurs du groseillier **58** 15
~ de fleurs **374** 33
~ de fruits **58** 11
~ de raisin **78** 5
grappin **157** 29
~ à bois **85** 29
~ d'abordage **218** 11
grasset **72** 33
grassette **377** 13
grattoir *Orfèvre* **108** 51
~ *Serr.* **140** 63
~ *Dess.* **151** 43
~ à fibres de verre **151** 47
~ avec brunissoir **340** 17
~ de plâtrier **128** 10
~ en métal **301** 24
~ triangulaire **140** 63
grave **241** 17
graveur de poinçons **175** 32
~ sur cuivre **340** 44
gravier *Constr.* **118** 36; **119** 26
~ *Parc* **272** 18
~ de concassage **158** 23
~ filtrant **269** 10
gravillonneuse automotrice **200** 41
gravité **257** 32
~, centre de **346** 26
gravure *Joaill.* **36** 41
~ *Arts graph.* **340**
~, correction de **182** 21
~ à la manière noire **340** 14-24
~ à la roulette **340** 14-24
~ à teintes **340** 1
~ au burin **340** 14-24
~ au grain de résine **340** 14-24
~ au lavis **340** 14-24
~ de chape **326** 14
~ de sommier **326** 13
~ décorative **87** 28
~ en manière de crayon **340** 14-24
~ en relief **340** 3
~ en taille d'épargne **340** 2
~ en taille-douce **340** 14-24
~ sur bois *Ecole* **260** 83
~ sur bois *Arts graph.* **340** 1-13
~ sur cuivre **340** 14-24
~ sur pierre **340** 25-26
Grec **355** 3
Grèce **252** 39
gréco-romaine, lutte **299** 6-9
grecque **341** 15
grecques, ruban de **334** 43
gréement courant **219** 67-71
~ dormant **219** 10-19
~ et voilure d'un trois-mâts barque **219** 1-72
~ inférieur **219** 16
~ intermédiaire **219** 17
~ supérieur **219** 18
green **293** 82
Greenwich, méridien de **14** 5
greffe **54** 30-39
~ à l'anglaise **54** 39
~ en écusson par œil levé **54** 30
~ en fente **54** 36
greffoir **54** 31
greffon **54** 37
~ mis en place **54** 34
grêle **9** 36
grelin **217** 23
grelot *Jeux* **276** 45
~ *Hiver* **304** 26
~ des Halles **57** 18
grenade **384** 19
~ sous-marine **258** 34
grenadier **384** 16
grenaille d'acier **148** 38
grenat **351** 7
greneur **340** 45
grenier **37** 4; **38** 1-29, 18
grenoir **340** 19
grenouille à moteur **200** 26
~ verte **364** 24
grenouillère **29** 11
~ pour enfants **273** 28
grenure **340** 24, 47
grésil **9** 35
greyhound **70** 24
griffe *Scierie* **157** 13
~ *Best. fabul.* **327** 3, 13
~ *Oiseaux* **362** 7
~ à accessoires **115** 20
~ à couder **119** 77
~ à pommes de terre **66** 20
~ à trois dents **56** 13
~ d'acier **303** 24
~ de fixation d'accessoires **114** 4
~ de serrage **133** 10
~ d'entraînement de pellicule **115** 25
~ d'établi **132** 36
~ d'oiseau **327** 61
~ double **77** 8
~ d'ours **352** 14
griffon **327** 11
gril **316** 4
~ pour saucisses grillées **308** 33
grillage *Constr.* **123** 71
~ *Parc* **272** 33
~ *Sculpteur* **339** 35
grille *Ust. cuis.* **40** 40
~ *Serv. eaux* **269** 11
~ *Parc* **272** 31
~ à barreaux **163** 26
~ à flammèches **210** 24
~ à reine **77** 47
~ acoustique **309** 19
~ avec couteau hacheur **96** 54

~ basculante **210** 5
~ d'aération **194** 16
~ d'aspiration **100** 13
~ de coupage **141** 14
~ de déblaiement **264** 17
~ de la cage aux fauves **307** 50
~ de la rigole d'écoulement **89** 5
~ de microphone **241** 50
~ de microprismes **115** 54
~ de protection *Constr.* **118** 90
~ de protection *Motocycl.* **188** 16
~ de protection des feuilles margées **181** 24
~ de retenue **89** 10
~ de ventilation **258** 43
~ de vitesses **192** 47
~ d'égout **268** 8
~ du briseur **163** 54
~ du grand tambour **163** 55
~ en fer forgé **272** 31
~ essoreuse **129** 12
~ mobile **199** 34
~ protectrice **168** 45
grille-pain **40** 30
grille-panier **64** 11
grillon domestique **81** 7
grimpereau **361** 11
griotte **59** 5
gris, échelle des **343** 15
grive musicienne **361** 16
groin *Zool.* 73 10
~ *Chasse* **88** 53
groom *Ch. de f.* **204** 17
~ *Hôtel* **267** 18
gros bétail **73** 1-2
~ fer **91** 12
~ gibier **88** 1-27
~ grain **332** 31
~ lot de la tombola **306** 11
~ œuvre **118** 1-49
~ orteil **18** 49; **19** 52
~ peigne **105** 15
~ pied **381** 16
~ porteur **231** 14, 17
~ romain **175** 30
groschen **252** 13
groseille **58** 12
~ à maquereau **58** 9
groseillier **52** 19
~ à grappe **58** 10
~ à maquereau *Jard.* **52** 19
~ à maquereau *Bot.* **58** 1
grosse caisse **323** 55; **324** 47
~ cylindrée **189** 31-58
grosses tenailles **100** 41
gros-texte **175** 29
grotte **272** 1
~ à concrétion calcaire **13** 79
~ à stalactites **13** 79
groupage **206** 4
groupe à retiration du cyan **180** 8-9
~ à retiration du jaune **180** 6-7
~ à retiration du magenta **180** 10-11
~ à retiration du noir **180** 12-13
~ auxiliaire **231** 33
~ de joueurs *Maison* **48** 20
~ de joueurs *Sports* **305** 25
~ de miroirs **176** 21
~ de pavillons **15** 28
~ de retiration **181** 52
~ de touristes **272** 28
~ Diesel **259** 94
~ imprimant **180** 6,8,10,12, 7,9,11,13, 41, 80
~ imprimant le recto **181** 48
~ imprimant le verso **181** 49
~ imprimant réversible **182** 26
~ moteur **145** 12
~ turbo-alternateur **154** 33
~ turbo-alternateur à vapeur **153** 23-30
Grue *Astr.* **3** 42
grue *Maison* **47** 39
~ *Mar.* **221** 5
~ *Mil.* **258** 88
~ à chevalet **222** 20
~ à flèche **225** 24
~ à portique *Scierie* **157** 27
~ à portique *Mar.* **222** 25, 34
~ à portique fixe **206** 55
~ à tour pivotante **119** 31
~ américaine **310** 49
~ automobile **270** 47
~ de bord **259** 10
~ de cale **222** 23
~ de chantier **119** 31
~ de chargement **85** 28, 44
~ de dépannage **270** 48
~ de dock **222** 34
~ de pont **221** 61
~ flottante **226** 48
~ marteau **222** 7
~ pivotante à volée variable **222** 23
~ tournante **146** 3
~ tripode **222** 6
~ volante **232** 16
grue-portique **222** 25
grume *Sylvic.* **85** 23
~ *Constr.* **120** 83
~ *Scierie* **157** 30
~ soulevée **85** 41
gruppetto **321** 21
Grus **3** 42
grutier **119** 35
~, cabine du **226** 52
guanaco **366** 30
guépard **368** 7
guêpe, taille de **355** 53
guêpier d'Europe **360** 2
guéridon à fleurs **267** 36
guerre, hache de **352** 16
~, peintures de **352** 13
~, trophée de **352** 15, 30
guerrier Masaï **354** 8
guet, tour de **329** 35
guêtre **289** 32
~ de montagne **300** 55
~ de protection **142** 12
guetteur **329** 9
gueule *Zool.* **70** 3
~ *Chasse* **88** 13, 45
~ à langue bifide **327** 5
gueule-de-loup **51** 32
gueules **254** 27
gueuse **147** 40
gui, balancine de **219** 48
~ d'artimon **219** 44
~ de brigantine **219** 44
guichet **236** 30
~ de change **250** 10
~ de cricket avec la barre horizontale **292** 70
~ de l'agence des spectacles **271** 26
~ de renseignements **250** 9
~ de vente des timbres **236** 15
~ des affranchissements **236** 15
~ des billets **204** 35
~ des colis **236** 1
~ des opérations financières **236** 25
guichetier **236** 16
guidage **303** 24
~ de la masse mobile **139** 8
~ de la remorque **227** 9
~ du câble **201** 7
guide **71** 25, 33
~ à onglets **133** 19
~ à roulettes **141** 19
~ d'enfilage automatique **165** 18
~ d'entrée **184** 23
~ d'onglet **132** 65
~ du rouleau de nappe **163** 48
guideau **89** 94
guide-bande **243** 22
guide-chaîne **85** 16
guide-champ **166** 13
guide-fil *Piscic.* **89** 60
~ *Coord.* **100** 30
~ *Text.* **167** 3, 54
~ de filage **169** 16
~ plaçant le fil sur l'aiguille **167** 64
guide-fils **167** 2
guide-ligne transparent **249** 19
guide-papier mobiles **249** 17
guiderope **288** 69
guide-tuyau **67** 25
guidon *Chasse* **87** 71
~ *Bicycl.* **187** 2
~ *Drapeaux* **253** 22
~ *Mil.* **255** 3
~ *Sports* **305** 42
~ à lame **305** 51
~ à trou **305** 50
~ de départ **205** 42
~ de randonnée **187** 2
~ (du vélo) de course **290** 18
~ réglable en hauteur **188** 3
~ relevé **188** 11
~ séparé en deux **188** 57
~ sport **188** 45
guigne **59** 5
guignette **86** 52
guignol de l'aileron de profondeur **257** 39
guillaume **132** 25
guillemets **342** 26
~ à la française **342** 27
guillemot de troïl **359** 13
guillochis *Argent* **252** 38
~ *Arts graph.* **340** 54
guimauve **380** 12
guimbarde **132** 26
guindant de la grand-voile **284** 42
guindeau *Mar.* **223** 49
~ *Mil.* **258** 6, 23
~ de remorque **258** 86
guirlande *Carnaval* **306** 5
~ *Arts* **335** 54
guiro **324** 60
guitare *Boîte nuit* **318** 8
~ *Mus.* **324** 12
~ de jazz **324** 73
guitariste **318** 9
Gulf stream **14** 30
gutta-percha **383** 37
gymkhana **290** 32
gymnastique, pas de **295** 41
~ aux agrès **296**; **297**
~ avec les engins manuels **297** 33-50
~ de club **296** 12-21; **297** 7-14
~ féminine **297**
~ scolaire **296** 12-21; **297** 7-14
gynécée **329** 10
gynérium **51** 8
gypse **351** 24, 25
gyro directionnel **230** 13
gyrocompas **224** 31, 51-53
gyrodyne **232** 29
gyrophare **264** 11

H

habit **33** 13
~ à basques **355** 76
~ du valet **186** 21
~ monacal **331** 55
habitacle *Atterr. Lune* **6** 41
~ *Astron.* **235** 16
~ *Sports* **288** 10, 19
habitation **37**
~ du gardien **224** 108
~ flottante **353** 31
~ individuelle **37** 1-53
~ seigneuriale **329** 30
habits, brosse à *App. mén.* **50** 44
~, brosse à *Cout.* **104** 31
habitué **266** 40
hache *Sylvic.* **85** 1
~ *Constr.* **120** 73
~ à douille **328** 23
~ de bronze emmanchée **328** 23
~ de combat en pierre **328** 19
~ de guerre **352** 16
~ de sapeur-pompier **270** 43
hache-marteau **328** 19
hachette de charpentier **120** 70
hache-viande **96** 53
hachis **96** 16, 41
hachoir **96** 53
~ à viande **40** 39
haie *Cartogr.* **15** 98
~ *Equitation* **289** 8
~ *Athl.* **298** 8
~ de clôture **62** 35
~ taillée **272** 37
~ vive *Maison* **37** 59
~ vive *Jard.* **51** 9; **52** 32
haies, course de **298** 7-8
halage **216** 27
hale-bas de bôme **284** 21
haléři **252** 27
hall central **271** 11
~ d'accueil **267** 1-26
~ d'attente **233** 28
~ de gare **204**
~ de l'hôtel **267** 18-26
~ du vestiaire **315** 5-11
halle à (aux) marchandises **206** 7, 26-39
~ de construction **222** 3-4
~ de montage **222** 4
halma, jeu de **276** 26-28
halothane **26** 26
halte *Cartogr.* **15** 27
~ *Tramw.* **197** 35
haltérophile **299** 2
haltérophilie **299** 1-5
hamac **278** 4
hameçon **89** 79-87
~, triple **89** 85
~ à anguille **89** 87

~ à carpe **89** 86
~ à cran **89** 86
~ à trois crochets **89** 85
~ anglais droit **89** 84
~ double **89** 83
~ droit **89** 87
~ simple **89** 79
hampe **253** 7
hamster **366** 16
hanche *Anat.* **16** 33
~ *Cheval* **72** 32
hand-ball **292** 1
~ en salle **292** 1
hangar **62** 15
~ à bateaux **283** 24
~ d'aérodrome **287** 14
~ d'hélicoptères **259** 38
hanneton **82** 1
hansom **186** 29
harde à portée de tir **86** 15
hardtop **193** 27
harem **306** 41
hareng **364** 14
harenguier **90** 1
haricot *Méd.* **23** 45
~ *Agric.* **57** 8, 11
~ à rames *Jard.* **52** 28
~ à rames *Agric.* **57** 8
~ d'Espagne **57** 8
~ nain **57** 8
~ vert **57** 8
harle bièvre **359** 15
harmonica **324** 35
harmonie, cor d' **323** 41
~, table d' **323** 24; **324** 3
harmonium **325** 43
harnachement **71** 7-25
~ de poitrail **71** 26-36
~ de tête **71** 7-11
harnais *Zool.* **71** 7-25
~ *Sports* **288** 43
~ pelvien **300** 57
harpaille à portée de tir **86** 15
harpaye **362** 13
harpe **323** 60
~ à pédales **323** 60
harpie *Hérald.* **254** 35
~ *Best. fabul.* **327** 55
harpon *Préhist.* **328** 3
~ *Ethnol.* **353** 10
~ manuel **280** 40
hasard, jeu de **275** 1-33
hase **88** 59
hauban *Ponts* **215** 47
~ *Aéron.* **229** 12; **232** 4
~ *Sports* **284** 18
~ *Cirque* **307** 13
~ d'artimon **219** 16
~ de grand mât **219** 16
~ de grand mât de hune **219** 17
~ de grand mât de perroquet **219** 18
~ de mât de perroquet de fougue **219** 17
~ de mât de perruche **219** 18
~ de misaine **219** 16
~ de petit mât de hune **219** 17
~ de petit mât de perroquet **219** 18
~ de ring **299** 37
~ du cadre **187** 20
haubanage *Energ.* **155** 44
~ *Gymnast.* **296** 10; **297** 5
haubert **329** 63
hausse *Inst. fluv.* **217** 77
~ *Sports* **305** 56
~ d'archet **323** 13
~ de tir **255** 22, 28, 36
haussière *Pêche* **90** 4
~ *Inst. fluv.* **217** 23
haut de forme *Voit. chev.* **186** 25
~ de forme *Equitation* **289** 6
~ de pyjama **32** 18
~ de tige rembourré **101** 20
~ du cylindre **217** 66
~ fourneau **147** 1
~ fût **84** 12
~ plateau **352** 23
~ vol **282** 5
hautbois **323** 38
~ baryton **323** 38
~ d'amour **323** 38
~ de chasse **323** 38
~ ténor **323** 38
haut-de-chausses bouffant **355** 34
~ rembourré **355** 31
haute école **71** 1-6
~ fidélité **241** 13-48
~ fréquence **7** 26
~ futaie **84** 4
~ mer **227** 4
hauteur *Géogr.* **13** 66
~ *Math.* **346** 27; **347** 44
~ de moule **175** 45
~ en papier **175** 44
haut-fond isolé **224** 87
haut-parleur *Electr. gd public* **241** 14
~ *Police* **264** 12
~ *Ciné* **311** 46
~ d'aigus **241** 15
~ de commande **238** 52
~ de contrôle *Radiodiff.* **238** 15
~ de contrôle *Télév.* **239** 9
~ de contrôle *Ciné* **311** 13
~ de graves **241** 17
~ de la chambre de réverbération **311** 32
~ de préécoute **238** 50
~ de quai **205** 27
~ de sonorisation **238** 37
~ d'écoute *Radiodiff.* **238** 15
~ d'écoute *Télév.* **239** 9
~ d'ordres **238** 8, 52
~ incorporé **249** 70
~ médium **241** 16
haut-talon **101** 27
Havane **107** 2
Hawaiienne **306** 16
hayon *Agric.* **62** 26
~ *Autom.* **193** 16, 20
heaume **254** 4, 7-9
~, grand **254** 7
hébraïque **341** 7
hélianthe **51** 35; **52** 7
hélianthème **377** 20
hélice *Vitic.* **79** 6
~ *Inst. fluv.* **217** 52
~ *Mar.* **221** 44; **222** 72
~ *Aéron.* **230** 32; **231** 1-6
~ *Sports* **286** 64; **288** 36
~ à pales orientables **155** 39
~ à pas variable **224** 19
~ à trois pales **223** 62
~ bipale **155** 45
~ carénée **227** 20
~ de direction **256** 20
~ de propulsion **256** 19
~ de queue **264** 4
~ de queue anticouple **232** 28
~ d'étrave **228** 33
~ du loch **224** 55
~ et le gouvernail **228** 26
hélicon **323** 44
hélicoptère *Mar.* **221** 20
~ *Aéron.* **232** 11-25
~ *Mil.* **259** 38, 39, 53
~ de sauvetage **228** 16
~ de surveillance de la circulation **264** 1
~ de transport **232** 21
~ léger **232** 11
~ léger de transport et de secours **256** 18
héliograveur **182** 18
héliostat **5** 29
héliotrope **69** 20
héliozoaire **357** 7
hélisurface **259** 39, 53
hélium **1** 5
heller **252** 27
hémipyramide **351** 24
hémisphère boréal **3** 1-35
~ céleste austral **3** 36-48
heptolet **321** 23
héraldique **254** 1-36
héraut **329** 75
herbe, mauvaise *Bot.* **61**
~, mauvaise *Sylvic.* **84** 32
~ à coton **377** 18
~ à la coupure **377** 9
~ au charpentier **376** 15
~ aux chantres **61** 16
~ aux chats **380** 5
~ aux chevaux **379** 6
~ aux écus **375** 26
~ des pampas **51** 8
Hercule **3** 21
hercule forain **308** 27
Hercules **3** 21
Herero **354** 25
hérisonne **365** 7
hérisson **366** 5
~ avec le boulet **38** 32
herminette **120** 70
héron **359** 18
~ cendré **359** 18
héros **310** 28
~ de cinéma **310** 28
herse **329** 24
~ à trois sections **65** 88
~ cloisonnée **316** 13
hétéroptère **81** 39
hêtre **371** 33
~, fruit du **371** 37
heure de départ **205** 23
heurtoir *Scierie* **157** 18
~ *Ch. de f.* **206** 51
hévéa **383** 33
héxaèdre **351** 2
hexagone **351** 15
~ à angles vifs **36** 64
~ à facettes croisées **36** 65
hexoctaèdre **351** 13
hibernie défeuillante **80** 16
hibou grand-duc **362** 15
~ moyen-duc **362** 14
hiéroglyphe de l'Egypte ancienne **341** 1
hi-fi *Maison* **42** 9
~ *Electr. gd public* **241** 13-48
high hat **324** 50
hile du foie **20** 34
hiloire *Mar.* **222** 64
~ *Sports* **283** 43, 59
himation **355** 6
hippocampe *Best. fabul.* **327** 44
~ *Zool.* **364** 18
hippodrome **308** 59
hippopotame **366** 31
hirondelle **361** 20
~, queue d' **351** 25
~ de cheminée **361** 20
~ de fenêtre **361** 20
~ de mer **359** 11
histrion **308** 25-28
hochet **28** 44
~ de rumba **324** 59
hockey **292** 6
~ sur glace **302** 29-37
hockeyeur *Sports* **292** 15
~ *Sports hiver* **302** 29
Hollande, fromage de **99** 42
holoèdre **351** 2
holothurie **369** 18
home base **292** 51
hominidé **261** 19
homme, trou d' *Astron.* **234** 30
~, trou d' *Serv. eaux* **269** 51
~ d'affaires en voyage **209** 29
~ de barre *Mar.* **218** 2
~ de barre *Navig.* **224** 16
~ de base *Sports* **292** 44
~ de base *Cirque* **307** 29
Homme de Néanderthal **261** 19
homme d'équipe **206** 33
~ mort **211** 21, 25; **212** 13
hommes, rayon **271** 12
homme-sandwich monté sur des échasses **308** 49
Homo sapiens **261** 21
~ steinheimensis **261** 17
homogénéisateur **76** 12
hongre **73** 2
honneur, demoiselle d' **332** 24
hôpital **25**; **26**; **27**
~ du port **225** 26
horizon **4** 12
~ artificiel **230** 3
horizontale de l'ouverture **87** 74
horloge *Horlog.* **110** 24
~ *Marché puces* **309** 56
~ à coucou de la Forêt-Noire **109** 31
~ de gare **204** 30
~ de l'église **331** 7
~ de paroi **109** 32
~ mére **245** 18
~ synchrone **245** 18
horloger **109** 1
horlogerie **110**
hors-bord **283** 7
~ à coque de catamaran **286** 21
hors-jeu **291** 42
horst **12** 10
hortensia **51** 11
horticulteur **55** 20
horticulture **55**
hostie **332** 28
~, grande **332** 35
~, petite **332** 48
hôtel **267**
hôtesse **272** 27
hotte *Maison* **39** 17; **46** 31
~ *Vitic.* **78** 15
~ *Forge* **137** 7
~ *Papet.* **173** 27
~ d'aspiration des poussières **163** 10
~ d'évacuation de la chaleur **182** 5
houblonnière **15** 114
houe **66** 24
houillère **144** 1-51
houle artificielle **281** 1

I

J

jambier antérieur **18** 47
jambière *Sports* **292** 9
~ *Chevalerie* **329** 54
~ avec sa chevillère **291** 33
~ de daim **352** 17
~ en fer **319** 19
jambon **95** 38
~, noix de **95** 52
~ à l'os **96** 1
~ de manche **95** 51
~ de pays **99** 52
~ démangé **95** 54
jambonneau *Viande* **95** 38, 42, 49
~ *Bouch.* **96** 17
jamboree **278** 8-11
jante *Bicycl.* **187** 28
~ *Motocycl.* **189** 25
~ *Autom.* **191** 16; **192** 77
Japon **253** 20
japonaise **341** 6
jaquette *Méd.* **24** 28
~ *Reliure* **185** 37
~ courte **355** 45
~ publicitaire **185** 37
jardin, banc de **272** 16, 42
~, fauteuil de **272** 48
~ à la française **272** 1-40
~ anglais **272** 41-72
~ d'agrément **51** 1-35
~ d'appartement **248** 13
~ d'enfants **48**
~ du cloître **331** 53
~ particulier **37** 57
~ potager **52**
~ potager et fruitier **52** 1-32
~ zoologique **356**
jardinet *Maison* **37** 58
~ *Jard.* **52** 1-32
jardinier *Jard.* **55** 20
~ *Parc* **272** 66
~ amateur **52** 24
~ du dimanche **52** 24
jardinière *Maison* **37** 20
~ *Bureau* **248** 13
~ d'enfants **48** 1
jarret **72** 37
~ de derrière **95** 1, 10
~ de devant **95** 5, 8, 28
jarretelle *Cost.* **32** 6
~ *Boîte nuit* **318** 28
jars **73** 34
jasmin jaune **373** 4
jauge *Agric.* **75** 31
~ *Carr.* **158** 26
~ de poussière **50** 61, 73
~ de profondeur **149** 68
~ d'écartement **122** 18
~ d'épaisseur **140** 53
~ d'essence **191** 38, 65
~ d'huile **190** 47
~ droite **230** 17
~ gauche **230** 16
Jauge Internationale, 5,50 m **284** 58
~ Internationale, 6 m **284** 59
jaune *Hérald.* **254** 24
~ *Couleurs* **343** 2
~ de l'œuf **74** 68
javeline **352** 40
javelot *Athl.* **298** 51-53
~ *Ethnol.* **353** 9
jazz, batterie de **324** 47-54
~, guitare de **324** 73
~, instrument de **324** 47-78
~, trompette de **324** 65
jeannette *App. mén.* **50** 20
~ *Cout.* **104** 28
~ blanche **60** 4
jeans **31** 60; **33** 22
~, costume **33** 20
~, deux-pièces **31** 58
~, veste **31** 59; **33** 21
jeep de 0,25 t **255** 96
jéjunum **20** 15
jerrycan **196** 25
jersey, double **171** 47
~, tricot **171** 44
jet *Plantes* **54** 16
~ *Centr.* **153** 29
~, poignard de **354** 15
~ d'eau **272** 22, 62
~ d'eau et de vapeur **11** 22
~ diffusé en brouillard **83** 8
~ franc **292** 5
jetée *Inst. fluv.* **217** 15
~ *Ports* **225** 30, 66
~ *Aéroport* **233** 13
~ en pierre **15** 48
jeton **275** 12
jet-stream **7** 5
jette-feu **210** 5
jeu, terrain de **291** 1
~ à anche **326** 41
~ de balle **291; 292; 293**
~ de balle au poing **293** 72-78
~ de ballon **291; 292; 293**
~ de billard **277** 1-19
~ de boules **305** 21
~ de cartes françaises **276** 37
~ de casseroles **40** 12-16
~ de clés plates **134** 2
~ de construction **28** 41
~ de constructions en bois **48** 27
~ de constructions mobiles **48** 22
~ de cubes **48** 21
~ de cylindres **148** 54-55
~ de dames **276** 17-19
~ de dés **276** 29
~ de domino **276** 33
~ de fraise **56** 21
~ de halma **276** 26-28
~ de hasard **275** 1-33
~ de meules **111** 28
~ de meules pour façonner le verre **111** 35
~ de pavillons **253** 22-34
~ de pédale **326** 3
~ de quilles **305** 1-13
~ de récit **326** 2
~ de reconnaissance des formes **48** 19
~ de salta **276** 20
~ de société **276**
~ de stylos à encre de Chine **151** 38
~ de tournevis **109** 6
~ d'échecs **276** 1-16
~ des petits chevaux **47** 19
~ d'orgue **316** 2
~ du clavier principal **326** 1
~ d'ustensiles en bois **40** 2
jeune Apache **306** 9
~ biche **88** 1
~ cochon **75** 39
~ larve **80** 54
~ plant repiqué **55** 23
~ porc **75** 39
~ taureau **319** 35
jeux d'eau **272** 8
Jeux olympiques **253** 5
jiu-jitsu **299** 13-17
joint **122** 94
~ à cardan **67** 28
~ de couvercle **40** 26
~ de rail **202** 11
~ universel **284** 6
jonc **136** 28
~ fleuri **378** 39
~ odorant **377** 22
jonque **353** 32
jonquille **60** 3
joubarbe **51** 7
joue *Anat.* **16** 9
~ *Chasse* **87** 4
~ *Menuis.* **132** 23
~ de coffrage d'une poutre de rive **119** 55
jouet **48** 21-32
~ de bois **260** 80
~ d'enfant *Jeux enf.* **273** 30, 62, 65
~ d'enfant *Parc attr.* **308** 13
~ flottant **28** 10
joueur **305** 25
~ central **293** 76
~ de billard **277** 8
~ de boules **305** 22
~ de champ **292** 2, 41
~ de champ effectuant un tir en suspension **292** 3
~ de croquet **292** 80
~ de curling **302** 41
~ de football **292** 23
~ de golf exécutant un drive **293** 83
~ de hand-ball **292** 2
~ de hockey **292** 15
~ de mini-golf **272** 69
~ de pelote basque **305** 68
~ de roulette **275** 15
~ de tennis **293** 16
~ de tennis de table **293** 49
~ d'échecs **265** 17
~ marquant un panier **292** 35
joug **65** 14
journal *Maison* **46** 20
~ *Ch. de f.* **205** 51
~ *Café* **265** 25
~ *Ecriture* **342** 37-70
~ de bord **244** 15
~ de mode **104** 4
~ de modes **271** 36
~ plié **181** 56
journaliste sportif **299** 50
journaux, casier à **262** 16
~, marchand de **268** 75
~, sortie de **182** 29
jours **102** 14
joute, casque de **329** 77
~, équipement de **329** 76
~, lance de **329** 81
~, targe de **329** 79
judas **41** 29
judo **299** 13-17
judoka **299** 14
juge **299** 43
~ à l'arrivée **282** 25; **290** 5
~ de classement **282** 25
~ de filet **293** 23
~ de ligne **291** 59; **293** 69
~ de ligne de côté **293** 24
~ de ligne de fond **293** 26
~ de ligne de service **293** 27
~ de ligne médiane **293** 25
~ de touche **291** 60
~ de virage **282** 26
juge-arbitre **293** 19
~ en chef **292** 55
jugulaire **329** 42
Jumbo-Jet **231** 14
jumeau *Anat.* **18** 62
~ *Viande* **95** 32
jumelles *Opt.* **111** 17
~ *Mar.* **221** 128
~ de campagne **86** 6
~ de théâtre **315** 9
jument **73** 2
jumper **29** 41
jumping **289** 8-14
jupe *Cost.* **29** 46, 52; **31** 24
~ *Sports* **283** 56
~ arrière *Autom.* **193** 21
~ arrière *Astron.* **235** 63
~ de cocktail **30** 56
~ de raphia **306** 18
~ de tailleur **31** 3
~ en loden **30** 67
~ enfermant le coussin d'air **286** 66
~ fendue sur le côté **30** 51
~ plissée **30** 32
~ portefeuille **31** 13
jupe-culotte **29** 59; **31** 48
Jupiter **4** 48
jupon *Cost.* **32** 14
~ *Marché puces* **309** 85
~ de danse **314** 31
jus de fruit **266** 58
~ de fruits **98** 18
~ de fruits en boîte **99** 75
jusquiame noire **379** 6
justaucorps de gymnastique **297** 51
jute *Filat. coton* **163** 4
~ *Bot.* **383** 25

K

kangourou roux **366** 3
kapokier **383** 20
karaté **299** 18-19
karateka **299** 18
kart *Jeux enf.* **273** 33
~ *Sports* **305** 83
karting **305** 82
kayac **353** 12
kayak *Sports* **283**
~ *Ethnol.* **353** 12
~ biplace **283** 5
~ de promenade **283** 61, 70
~ de sport et de course **283** 69
~ lapon **283** 68
~ monoplace **283** 4, 54
~ pliant **283** 54-66
~ pliant biplace **283** 61
kermesse **308** 1-69
kerrie **373** 28
ketch **220** 9
ketchup **45** 43
keuper inférieur **154** 57
kick **188** 43; **189** 38
kieselguhr, dosage du **93** 3
~, filtre à **93** 4
kimono **353** 40
kiosque **258** 67; **259** 71
~ à musique **274** 19
~ roulant **205** 16
Kipp, appareil de **350** 59
Kirghiz **353** 22
kirri **354** 33
klaxon **188** 53
knock-out **299** 40
K.O. **299** 40
Kocher, pince **22** 49

~, jeune *Apicult.* **77** 28
~, jeune *Agric.* **80** 54
~ dans son nid **82** 36
~ du taupin **80** 38
~ prête à la nymphose **80** 53
larynx **20** 2-3
laser **242** 81
~ à l'hélium - néon **243** 57
~ d'enseignement **242** 81
lasioderme de la cigarette **81** 25
~ du tabac **81** 25
lasso *Taurom.* **319** 40
~ *Ethnol.* **352** 5
~ de jet et de capture **352** 31
latine **342** 12
latitude **14** 6
latrines de chantier **118** 49
latte **284** 44
~ de garde *Constr.* **118** 29
~ de garde *Tiss.* **165** 31
~ de protection **165** 31
~ de recouvrement **123** 57
~ double **122** 43
lattis **122** 17; **123** 70
laurier-rose **373** 13
lavabo *Méd.* **24** 15
~ *Maison* **49** 24
~ *Ch. de f.* **207** 40
~ *Camping* **278** 6
~ *Arts* **334** 68
~ double **267** 32
~ pour le lavage des cheveux **105** 28; **106** 11
lavage **169** 19; **170** 56
~ des bobines **170** 48
lavande vraie **380** 7
lave, champ de **11** 14
~, coulée de **11** 18
~, nappe de **11** 14
lave-linge **50** 23
laveur **157** 21
~ d'acide sulfhydrique **156** 22
~ d'ammoniac **156** 23
~ de benzène **156** 24
lave-vaisselle **39** 40
laye **326** 12
layette *Puéricult.* **28**
~ *Cost.* **29** 1-12
~ de rangement des pièces de rechange **109** 22
lé **122** 91
~ de papier peint **128** 19
~ vertical de la bande de carton **122** 95
leçon de natation **282** 16-20
lecteur **262** 3, 24
~ de bande **176** 13, 15, 30
~ de journaux **265** 24
~ de microfilms **237** 36
~ de ruban **176** 13, 15, 30
~ de son magnétique **312** 28
~ de son magnétique à quatre pistes **312** 50
~ de son optique **312** 45
lecteur-perforateur de cartes **244** 12
lecture, livre de **260** 16
~, règle de **349** 35
~, salle de **262** 13
~, tête de **309** 33
~ de voyage **205** 18
lédon des marais **377** 21
legato **321** 33
légende *Cartogr.* **14** 27-29
~ *Cité* **268** 4
~ *Ecriture* **342** 59
legging **352** 17
légume **57**
~ en conserve **98** 17
légume-feuille **57** 28-34
légumes surgelés **99** 61
légumier **45** 25, 31
légumineuse **57** 1-11
lentille **242** 83
~ corrective **115** 72
~ de champ **115** 40
~ de Fresnel avec anneau dépoli et stigmomètre **115** 64
~ de l'objectif **113** 36
~ d'eau **378** 35
~ frontale **115** 7
~ macro **117** 55
lentilles d'éclairage **112** 7
Leo **3** 17; **4** 57
léopard **368** 6
lépidoptère *Bot.* **58** 62
~ *Zool.* **365**
lépiote élevée **381** 30
lépisme saccharin **81** 14
lepta **252** 39
lepton **252** 39
Lerne, Hydre de **327** 32
lés à joints vifs **128** 20
~ posés bord à bord **128** 20
lésène **335** 11
lessive de cuisson **172** 46
~ épaisse **172** 34
~ épuisée **172** 45
~ noire **172** 28, 29
~ verte **172** 43
~ verte non clarifiée **172** 41
lessiveur **172** 7
lest **285** 33; **288** 65
~ d'eau **223** 78
~ en plomb **285** 36
lettre «A» **253** 22
~ bas-de-casse **175** 12
~ commerciale **245** 33; **246** 7; **248** 30
~ de change **250** 12
~ de voiture **206** 30
~ haut-de-casse **175** 11
~ lumineuse **268** 45
lettres, boîte à **236** 50-55, 50
~, papier à **245** 12
~ et chiffres pour la désignation des cases de l'échiquier **276** 6
~ liées **175** 6
lettrine **175** 1
leucanthème vulgaire **376** 4
leucite **351** 12
leurre **89** 65-76
levade *Zool.* **71** 4
~ *Cirque* **307** 30
levain **97** 53
levé **171** 17
levée des boîtes à lettres **236** 50-55
lève-ligne **174** 14
levier *Serr.* **140** 5
~ *Carr.* **158** 32
~ à main *Menuis.* **132** 55
~ à main *Reliure* **183** 31
~ à pédale **163** 28
~ à plusieurs bras en étoile **340** 39
~ classeur **247** 42
~ correcteur de mélange **288** 16
~ d'aiguille **203** 55
~ d'aiguille et de signal **203** 62
~ d'armement *Chasse* **87** 22
~ d'armement *Mil.* **255** 12
~ d'armement du déclencheur à retardement **115** 15
~ d'arrêt **163** 40
~ d'arrêt de la machine **164** 6
~ d'arrêt du banc **164** 32
~ d'arrêt du frein **56** 38
~ d'avancement de la pellicule **115** 16
~ de blocage **188** 2
~ de changement de vitesse **150** 35
~ de changement de vitesse au plancher **191** 91
~ de changement du couple moteur **65** 34
~ de commande *Mach. agric.* **64** 59
~ de commande *Ciné* **117** 63
~ de commande *Mach.-out.* **149** 11
~ de commande *Text.* **167** 22
~ de commande *Constr. rout.* **201** 8
~ de commande *Navig.* **224** 19
~ de commande *Mil.* **257** 8
~ de commande *Magasin* **271** 48
~ de commande *Sports* **288** 14
~ de commande *Ciné* **313** 11
~ de commande *Théât.* **316** 58
~ de commande à main **202** 17
~ de commande de direction **192** 58
~ de commande du réducteur **149** 3
~ de commutation **50** 59
~ de débrayage **132** 56
~ de débrayage de l'arbre porte-meule **157** 46
~ de dégagement **10** 15
~ de dégagement de la bobine croisée **165** 13
~ de dégagement du papier **249** 20
~ de démarrage **163** 17
~ de filetage normal **149** 4
~ de frappe **249** 21
~ de frein à main **191** 93
~ de jambe **299** 10
~ de la chasse d'eau **49** 17
~ de la pompe à piston **83** 45
~ de l'écrou embrayable de vis mère **149** 19
~ de libération du cylindre **249** 24
~ de manœuvre *Plomb.* **126** 19
~ de manœuvre *Constr. rout.* **201** 12
~ de manœuvre du réducteur **149** 3
~ de marche arrière **249** 21
~ de marche-arrêt **181** 32
~ de mise en marche **178** 20
~ de mouvement longitudinal ou transversal **149** 17
~ de parcours **203** 58
~ de pas d'avance et de filetage **149** 9
~ de pression *Filat. coton* **163** 16
~ de pression *Arts graph.* **340** 61
~ de rappel **249** 21
~ de recul **249** 21
~ de réglage de la force d'impression **249** 10
~ de réglage d'excentrique **166** 58
~ de réglage du zoom **117** 54
~ de relevage et de descente du cylindre **181** 3
~ de renversement de marche de la vis mère **149** 6
~ de retour du chariot **249** 21
~ de serrage **132** 67
~ de serrage de la bande **133** 16
~ de signal **203** 56
~ de sûreté **2** 40
~ de touche **322** 38, 49
~ de variation de la focale **313** 22, 36
~ de verrouillage **87** 25
~ de verrouillage d'aiguille **203** 55
~ de vitesse **65** 35
~ de vitesses **191** 91; **192** 46
~ de zoom **313** 22, 36
~ d'échappement **325** 30
~ d'embrayage *Tiss.* **165** 17; **166** 8
~ d'embrayage *Text.* **167** 44
~ d'embrayage *Motocycl.* **188** 32; **189** 28
~ d'embrayage à deux vitesses **188** 12
~ d'embrayage-débrayage du groupe imprimant **180** 80
~ d'encrage des plaques offset **249** 50
~ d'itinéraire **203** 58
~ du frein **166** 62
~ du mécanisme d'avance **149** 10
~ du renversement de marche du dispositif d'avance **149** 14
~ du sifflet **211** 40
~ flottant **65** 43
~ oscillant **67** 34
~ régulateur d'alimentation **163** 28
~ régulateur d'aspiration **50** 74
~ régulateur de mélange **288** 16
lèvre **19** 25
~, plateau de **354** 23
~ inférieure *Anat.* **19** 26
~ inférieure *Cheval* **72** 10
~ inférieure *Mus.* **326** 26, 31
~ supérieure *Anat.* **19** 14
~ supérieure *Cheval* **72** 8
~ supérieure *Mus.* **326** 27
lèvres **20** 87
~, commissure des **16** 14; **19** 19
lévrier afghan **70** 23
levure de boulanger **97** 53
lexique **262** 17
lézard **364** 27
~ sans pattes **364** 37
liaison **321** 24
~ des modules **242** 70
~ intérieure **224** 27
~ téléphonique **242** 20
liant **200** 53
liasse de feuilles **249** 56, 57
libellule **358** 3

liber **370** 9
libero **291** 11
Libra **3** 19; **4** 59
librairie **268** 37
~ de la gare **204** 26
lice **329** 31
licorne *Hérald.* **254** 16
~ *Best. fabul.* **327** 7
lien d'angle **121** 57
lierre terrestre **375** 18
lieu de paiement **250** 15
~ d'émission **250** 13
~ théâtral **315** 14-27
lièvre **86** 35
~ de plaine **88** 59
ligature **175** 6
~ de raphia **54** 35
ligne *Piscic.* **89** 63
~ *Compos.* **175** 4
~ *Sports* **291** 59
~ *Mus.* **320** 43
~ *Math.* **346** 1-23
~ à haute tension **15** 113
~ à voie étroite **15** 25
~ aérienne double **194** 43
~ centrale **293** 54
~ d'amarrage **221** 119
~ d'arbres **223** 60
~ d'attaque **293** 65
~ de base **122** 81
~ de bout **292** 36
~ de but **291** 7; **292** 71
~ de cœur **19** 74
~ de côté **292** 17; **293** 55
~ de côté pour le double **293** 2 *à* 3
~ de côté pour le simple **293** 4 *à* 5
~ de crête **13** 60
~ de départ et d'arrivée **286** 30
~ de distribution à haute tension **152** 32
~ de faille **12** 5
~ de faîtage **121** 2
~ de flottaison *Mil.* **258** 27
~ de flottaison *Sports* **285** 31
~ de flotteurs **282** 32
~ de foi **224** 48
~ de fond **293** 3 *à* 10
~ de jet franc **292** 5
~ de lancer franc **292** 38
~ de lettre **175** 43
~ de mise en garde **294** 3
~ de pénalité **292** 48
~ de pureau **122** 89
~ de raccordement téléphonique d'immeuble **198** 20
~ de recouvrement **122** 89
~ de sauvetage **228** 3
~ de service **293** 6 *à* 7, 72
~ de sonde **224** 60
~ de tête **19** 73
~ de texte **174** 15
~ de touche **291** 9
~ de vie **19** 72
~ d'eau **282** 31
~ d'envoi **292** 72
~ des pôles **4** 10
~ du fond **224** 67
~ médiane *Sports* **291** 3; **293** 8 *à* 9
~ médiane *Escrime* **294** 4
~ photoréceptrice pour la mesure du carrossage **195** 21
~ photoréceptrice pour la mesure du pincement **195** 22
~ principale de chemin de fer **15** 21
~ réseau **237** 18, 24
~ secondaire **15** 23
~ téléphonique de transit **198** 16
~ tube **31** 14
ligne-bloc **174** 27
ligule *Agric.* **68** 22
~ *Bot.* **370** 84
liliacée *Plantes* **53** 13
~ *Bot.* **60** 12
limaçon *Anat.* **17** 63
~ *Zool.* **357** 27
limbe *Agric.* **68** 20
~ *Navig.* **224** 2
~ *Bot.* **370** 28, 85
~, bord du **370** 43-50
~ gradué **351** 32
~ vertical de calage **113** 27
lime **140** 8
~ à bande **140** 16
~ à bois **132** 2
~ à dégrossir **134** 9
~ bâtarde **140** 8
~ demi-ronde **140** 29
~ douce **140** 8
~ mi-douce **140** 8
~ plate *Orfèvre* **108** 49
~ plate *Serr.* **140** 27
~ queue de rat **108** 47
~ ronde **140** 29
limeuse **140** 15
limicole **359** 19-21
limitation de vitesse **203** 41, 44
limite d'arrondissement **15** 103
~ de clôture **292** 40
~ de la marée **13** 35
~ de vitesse codée **203** 37
~ entre couches **13** 21
limiteur **238** 44
limon **38** 26
~ apparent **123** 44
~ recourbé **123** 49
limonade **265** 15
limonière **186** 30
lin *Hist. cost.* **355** 5
~ *Bot.* **383** 6
linaigrette **377** 18
linéaire **370** 31
linge **32**
~ sale **50** 22
lingère **267** 31
lingerie **32** 1-15
~, rayon **271** 56
lingot **181** 40
~ d'acier **147** 33
~ d'acier brut moulé **148** 48
~ en cours de solidification **148** 25
~ méplat **148** 48
lingotière **147** 32, 37
link **293** 79-82
Linotype **174** 19
~, matrice de **174** 29
linteau *Maison* **37** 25
~ *Constr.* **120** 57
~ *Hôtel* **267** 24
~ de béton armé **118** 13
~ de fenêtre **118** 9
Lion *Astr.* **3** 17; **4** 57
lion *Cirque* **307** 56
~ *Zool.* **356** 5; **368** 2
~, corps de **327** 14, 22
~, tête de **327** 17
liqueur **98** 58
liquide correcteur **247** 13
~ de dégraissage **111** 32
~ du bain en excès **169** 23
~ gommeux **358** 46
lire **252** 20
lis, fleur de **254** 13
~ blanc **60** 12
~ martagon **377** 4
liseron des champs **61** 26
lisière **171** 20
~, lame de **171** 22
~ du champ **63** 3
~ du tissu **166** 11
~ en armure «toile» **171** 24
lissage **119** 9
lisse *Tiss.* **166** 36
~ *Sports* **283** 43; **285** 55
~ arrière **287** 37
~ avant **287** 34
~ d'appui **120** 56
~ métallique **166** 27
lissoir **128** 11
liste des prix de promotion **96** 19
~ informatique **248** 47
listel *Vitr.* **124** 3
~ *Arts* **334** 19
lit **43** 4-6
~, bois de **43** 5
~, descente de **43** 22
~ à la française **43** 4-13
~ de ballast **205** 61
~ de crue **216** 41
~ de hautes eaux **13** 62
~ de sable **123** 8
~ d'enfant **47** 1
~ d'enfant à roulettes **28** 1
~ deux personnes **43** 4-13
~ du fleuve **13** 68
~ du malade **25** 10
~ encastrable **46** 16
~ majeur **216** 41
lithochromie **340** 28
lithodes **369** 16
lithographie **340** 25-26
lithosphère **11** 1
litière **74** 8; **75** 6
lits jumeaux **267** 38
~ superposés **47** 1
livre *Maison* **46** 8
~ *Reliure* **185** 36
~ ancien **309** 55
~ de classe *Maison* **47** 25
~ de classe *Ecole* **260** 23
~ de lecture **260** 16
~ de rendez-vous **22** 11
~ d'enfant **47** 17
~ des cantiques **330** 30
~ d'image **48** 23
~ d'orthographe **260** 17
~ du maître **261** 28
~ ouvert **185** 52
~ sterling **252** 37
livrée **186** 21
livres, réserve de **262** 11
livret-horaire **210** 52
livreur **292** 50
LM **234** 54, 55
lobe *Anat.* **17** 57
~ *Aéron.* **229** 30
~ du foie **20** 35
~ supérieur du poumon **20** 7
lobée **370** 48
local de service **207** 41
localisateur lumineux **2** 34
loch à hélice **224** 54
~ remorqué **224** 54
locomotive à accumulateur de vapeur **210** 68
~ à condensation **210** 69
~ à tender séparé pour train rapide **210** 38
~ à vapeur **210** 1-69
~ articulée **210** 64
~ de (grande) vitesse **205** 35
~ de manœuvre **206** 43
~ de traction sur rails **216** 29
~ Diesel **212** 1-84, 5
~ Diesel à voie étroite **200** 24
~ Diesel de route **212** 1
~ Diesel hydraulique **212** 1, 24, 47; **213** 1
~ Diesel monomoteur **208** 1
~ électrique **205** 35; **211** 1
~ électrique à crémaillère **214** 4
~ Garratt **210** 64
~ sans foyer **210** 68
locomotive-tender **210** 65
locotracteur **200** 24
~ Diesel pour le service des manœuvres **212** 68
locuste **358** 8
loden **29** 31; **30** 64
~, jupe en **30** 67
lof **285** 9
logarithme **345** 6
~, symbole du **345** 6
loge **319** 7
~ à porcelets **75** 36
~ avec les pépins **58** 36, 59
~ d'artiste **315** 43-52
~ de cirque **307** 16
~ de mise bas **75** 40
~ des animaux **356** 10
~ du manager **292** 56
logement de cassette *Electr. gd public* **241** 6, 34
~ de cassette *Audiovis.* **243** 8
~ de pile **115** 10
~ des animaux **356** 10
~ des cames d'aiguille **167** 13
~ du filtre **112** 57
~ du sac à poussière **50** 62
loggia **37** 18
lombe **16** 24
lombric **357** 24
lombricoïde **81** 31
long bois **84** 19
~ courrier **231** 13, 14
~ drink **317** 32
~ extenseur du pouce **18** 56
~ péronier **18** 64
long rifle **305** 38
long supinateur **18** 39
longe *Chasse* **86** 45
~ *Viande* **95** 40
~ avec les côtes de veau **95** 3
longeron *Ponts* **215** 44
~ *Aéron.* **230** 45, 47, 57
~ *Sports hiver* **303** 5
~, faux **287** 33
~ central du fuselage **235** 9
~ du train de galets **214** 67
~ latéral **235** 3
~ principal **287** 30
~ secondaire **287** 33
longeron-caisson **287** 30
longicorne **358** 16, 38
longitude **14** 7
longrine **119** 64; **120** 2
longue taille **144** 33-37
longueur oblique de flotté **171** 38
~ verticale de flotté **171** 41
longue-vue *Maison* **42** 15
~ *Opt.* **111** 18
looping **288** 1
lophobranchie **364** 19

M

~ d'oblitération des bulletins d'expédition **236** 7
~ d'oxycoupage **141** 34
~ d'oxycoupage universelle **141** 36
~ «IS» **162** 21
~ offset **180** 46
~ offset à plat **180** 75
~ offset de bureau **180** 70
~ offset une couleur **180** 46, 59
~ principale **221** 81
~ sectionnelle **162** 21
machine-outil **149; 150**
machinerie **316** 1-60
machinisme agricole **138**
machiniste **315** 28; **316** 46
mâchoire *Anat.* **16** 17
~ *Menuis.* **132** 31
~ *Serr.* **140** 3
~ *Zool.* **358** 26
~ d'acceptation **149** 60
~ de frein *Forge* **138** 12
~ de frein *Méc.* **143** 100
~ de frein *Autom.* **192** 51
~ de refus **149** 61
~ fixe **132** 33
~ supérieure **19** 27
macis **382** 34
mâcle en queue d'hirondelle **351** 25
maçon **118** 18
macramé **102** 21
macreuse **95** 29
macronucléus **357** 11
Macropharynx longicaudatus **369** 2
macroséismologie **11** 45-54
madère, verre à **45** 84
madrépore **357** 17
madrier *Constr.* **119** 16
~ *Scierie* **157** 34
~ de faîtage **121** 48
magasin *Ciné* **117** 45
~ *Ch. de f.* **206** 53
~ à bobine **249** 33
~ à miel avec les rayons **77** 45
~ à trames **177** 9
~ à tubes **146** 4
~ contenant les matrices **174** 21
~ d'alimentation **98** 1-87
~ d'alimentation libre service **99** 1-95
~ de cartouches **87** 17
~ de couronnes de feuillard **148** 73
~ de couvertures en carton **184** 7
~ de détail **98** 1-87
~ de diapositives **176** 27
~ de film **311** 7
~ de margeur **185** 26
~ de matériaux **146** 6
~ de mode **268** 9
~ de station-service **196** 24
~ de vente **111** 1-19
~ du chargeur **255** 7
~ du film photographique **112** 65
~ du pistolet **264** 25
~ petit format **112** 35
~ pour 10 m de film **115** 80
~ vertical à clichés **245** 8
magma des profondeurs **11** 29-31
magnétophone *Electr. gd public* **241** 56
~ *Discoth.* **317** 21
~ *Boîte nuit* **318** 17
~ à bande **309** 37
~ à bande magnétique d'un quart de pouce **238** 4
~ à deux pistes **242** 12
~ à mini-cassette **117** 76
~ à quatre pistes **242** 13
~ portatif piloté par quartz **310** 24
magnétoscope **243** 7
magnolia **373** 15
maharadjah **306** 28
mail-coach **186** 53
maille *Trav. fém.* **102** 23
~ *Text.* **167** 62; **171** 30
~ fermée **171** 36
~ ouverte **171** 30
mailles, cotte de **329** 51
maillet *Constr.* **120** 67
~ *Ferbl.* **125** 18
~ *Camping* **278** 25
~ *Sculpteur* **339** 21
~ à tête rectangulaire **132** 5
~ de croquet **292** 81
~ plat **132** 5
mailloche **323** 56; **324** 64
maillon de chaîne **36** 39
maillot **291** 56; **299** 25
~ de bain **280** 42
~ de corps **32** 25
~ de corps filet **32** 22
~ de gymnastique **296** 61
~ du coureur **290** 9
~ rembourré **292** 26
main **16** 47; **17** 15-17; **19** 64-83
~, dos de la **19** 83
~, lignes de la **19** 72-74
~ courante *Maison* **38** 28
~ courante *Constr.* **123** 53, 79
main-courante **41** 23
maïs **68** 31
~ d'eau **378** 17
maison à chauffage solaire **155** 17
~ à deux logements **37** 64-68
~ à quatre logements **37** 69-71
~ de lotissement **37** 54
~ d'habitation **62** 1
~ du garde-barrière **202** 43
~ du gardien de digue **216** 45
~ du passeur **216** 45
~ en bandes **37** 58-63
~ en bois **37** 84-86
~ forestière **15** 3
~ individuelle **37** 1-53
~ miniature à éléments de construction interchangeables **273** 56
~ sur pilotis **328** 15
maître boucher **96** 38
~ d'armes **294** 1
~ de chai **79** 17
~ de manège **307** 31
~ d'équipage *Mar.* **221** 114
~ d'équipage *Equitation* **289** 45
~ verrier **124** 8
maître-à-danser **135** 23
maître-andouiller **88** 6
maître-brasseur **92** 49
maître-coiffeur **106** 1
maître-couple **235** 10
maître-nageur *Natation* **281** 4
~ *Sports* **282** 15
maître-tourneur **135** 20
majeur **19** 66
majuscule **175** 11
Malacosteus indicus **369** 10
malade à la cure d'inhalation **274** 7
malaxeur **97** 59
~ à mélange forcé **201** 23
mâle *Apicult.* **77** 5
~ *Zool.* **81** 34
malle **191** 24
~ d'osier **204** 3
malléole externe **19** 59
~ interne **19** 60
malle-poste **186** 39, 53
mallette à biberons **28** 21
~ pour nécessaire de bébé **28** 18
malt, élévateur de **92** 35
~, préparation du **92** 1-41
~, séchoir de **92** 16-18
~, silo à **92** 37
~ vert **92** 23
maltage **92** 1-41
Malte, croix de **312** 38
malterie **92**
mamelon **16** 28
~ mâle-mâle à visser **126** 38
mammifère **366; 367; 368**
~ écailleux **366** 10
~ ovipare **366** 1
~ volant **366** 9
man **82** 12
manager **292** 57; **299** 45
manche *Ust. table* **45** 51, 59, 62
~ *App. mén.* **50** 64
~ *Sylvic.* **85** 3
~ *Coiff.* **106** 39
~ *Menuis.* **132** 10
~ *Forge* **137** 30
~ *Sports* **283** 37
~ *Mus.* **324** 7, 18
~ à air **287** 11
~ à balai *Maison* **38** 37
~ à balai *Aéron.* **230** 24
~ à balai *Mil.* **257** 8
~ à balai *Sports* **288** 14
~ à gigot **355** 49
~ à parement **186** 24
~ à revers **30** 6
~ ballon **31** 27
~ bouillonnée **355** 60
~ chauve-souris **31** 16
~ de faux **66** 16
~ de gonflement **288** 70, 81
~ de la crosse **302** 31
~ de la scie à guichet **132** 4
~ de lime **108** 50
~ de raquette **293** 30, 46
~ de ratissoire **66** 2
~ du balai **50** 49
~ du couteau **96** 34
~ du marteau **325** 25
~ du violon **323** 2
~ en entonnoir **355** 46
~ galonnée **186** 24
~ kimono **30** 36
~ longue **30** 15
~ pagode plissée **30** 54
~ retroussée **31** 62
~ volantée **29** 14
mancheron **65** 3
manchette *Cost.* **30** 14; **32** 45
~ *Ecriture* **342** 44
~ blanche **268** 31
~ en cuir **191** 92
manchon **126** 43
~ antipoussière **2** 48
~ d'écubier **222** 76
~ d'entrée **153** 40
~ du câble lest **214** 74
~ du câble tracteur **214** 73
manchon-guêtre **300** 55
manchot **359** 4
mandarin **306** 29
mandarine **384** 23
mandat **236** 27
mandibule **358** 25, 41
~ inférieure **359** 8
mandoline **324** 16
mandrin **134** 48
~ à deux mors **135** 10
~ à main **109** 16
~ à quatre mors **149** 35
~ à serrage rapide **132** 54
~ à trois mors **149** 37
~ creux **135** 6
manège *Equitation* **289** 1
~ *Cirque* **307** 21
~ d'avions **308** 4
~ de chevaux de bois **308** 2
manette *Menuis.* **132** 55
~ *Ch. de f.* **203** 57
~ d'avancement **100** 28
~ de blocage du fourreau **149** 28
~ de chauffage **191** 84
~ de commande **83** 21
~ de gaz **288** 15
~ de guidage **240** 29
~ de serrage **260** 48
~ de ventilation **191** 83
~ des gaz **257** 9
~ du curseur **349** 32
mangeoire **62** 9; **74** 4, 21; **75** 37
~ automatique **74** 13
manifestation **264** 15
manille de tendeur **208** 17
~ pendante **208** 19
manipulateur *Atome* **2** 38
~ *Forge* **139** 32
~ *Ch. de f.* **211** 20; **212** 12
~ à joints sphériques **2** 38
~ jumelé **2** 47
~ master-slave **2** 47
manipulatrice **27** 11
manique *Maison* **39** 18
~ *Gymnast.* **296** 47
manivelle *Mach. agric.* **64** 43
~ *Ciné* **117** 50
~ *Text.* **168** 52
~ d'armement **114** 32
~ d'avancement du film **114** 32
~ de commande **309** 81
~ de la grille basculante **210** 40
~ de pédalier **187** 41
~ de pointage **255** 48
~ de réglage de la hauteur **64** 57
~ de rembobinage *Photo* **114** 6; **115** 12
~ de rembobinage *Ciné* **117** 93
~ de tirage **340** 33
~ de translation **201** 18
~ du jette-feu **210** 40
manne **89** 66
mannequin **271** 34
~ articulé **338** 31
~ de tailleur **103** 6
manœuvre *Constr.* **118** 19
~ *Ch. de f.* **206** 43
~ spatiale **235** 44
manomètre *Agric.* **67** 10

~ *Lutte pestic.* **83** 42
~ *Forge* **138** 15
~ *Imprim.* **178** 8; **180** 74
~ *Autom.* **195** 29; **196** 20
~ à air comprimé **211** 24
~ à contact **316** 56
~ à mercure **25** 18
~ à minimum et à maximum de pression **349** 19
~ à vide **349** 20
~ basse pression **141** 6
~ de chaudière **210** 47
~ de contrôle de pression **279** 13
~ de distribution d'oxygène **25** 22
~ de frein **210** 50
~ de la conduite blanche **212** 6
~ de pression d'admission **230** 7
~ de pression d'huile **157** 7
~ du cathétère cardiaque droit **25** 53
~ du chauffage **210** 44
~ du cylindre de frein **212** 7
~ du réchauffeur **210** 43
~ du réservoir d'air principal **212** 8
~ haute pression **141** 4
Manque **275** 22
mansarde **38** 20
mante de dentelle **355** 66
manteau *Géogr.* **11** 3
~ *Hérald.* **254** 14
~ de bec **350** 10
~ de ciré **228** 7
~ de drap **30** 61; **33** 66
~ de fourrure **30** 60
~ de pourpre **355** 18
~ de vison **131** 24
~ d'été **31** 20
~ d'hiver **30** 61
~ d'ocelot **131** 25
~ en popeline **33** 60
~ fillette **29** 54
~ modèle **103** 7
~ trois-quarts **271** 21
~ vague **271** 41
manteau-cape **30** 68
mantelet **71** 19, 31
mantisse **345** 6
manuel *Ecole* **261** 28
~ *Univ.* **262** 17
~ *Mus.* **325** 48
~ I du positif dorsal **326** 42
~ II du grand orgue **326** 43
~ III de récit **326** 44
~ IV de bombarde **326** 45
~ inférieur **322** 47
~ supérieur **322** 46
manuscrit *Compos.* **174** 6
~ *Photocomp.* **176** 3
~ *Univ.* **262** 5
~ *Théât.* **316** 41
manutention horizontale des conteneurs **226** 7
manutentionnaire **206** 33
mappemonde **42** 13
maquette de décors **315** 42
~ de scène **315** 41
maquilleur *Ciné* **310** 36
~ *Théât.* **315** 48
marabout **278** 8
maracas **324** 59
maraîcher **55** 20
marais *Géogr.* **13** 24
~ *Cartogr.* **15** 20
marbre *Imprim.* **180** 78; **181** 17
~ *Arts graph.* **340** 41, 64
~ à dresser **125** 3
marcassin **88** 51
marchand ambulant **308** 12, 51
~ de cigarettes **308** 51
~ de glaces **308** 30
~ de journaux **268** 75
~ forain **308** 10, 12
marchande **308** 65
marchandise **271** 10
~ de détail **206** 4, 27
~ de groupage **206** 4
~ encombrante **206** 18
marchandises diverses **225** 9, 14; **226** 11, 13
marche *Maison* **38** 27; **41** 24
~ *App. mén.* **50** 38
~ *Aéron.* **230** 42
~ *Alpin.* **300** 17
~, chaussure de **101** 18
~ à droite ou à gauche **149** 11, 34
~ arrière **192** 44
~ d'accès **281** 32, 37
~ d'accès à la table de communion **330** 5
~ de chaque pièce **276** 14
~ de départ **123** 18, 42
~ de la terrasse **37** 39
~ des rayons lumineux **1** 62
~ d'escabeau **50** 38
~ d'escalier **123** 32, 47
~ du maître-autel **330** 31
~ du train **211** 7, 38; **212** 14, 38
~ palière **123** 19
~ pleine **123** 17
~ taillée dans la glace **300** 17
marché au poisson **225** 57
~ aux puces *Parc attr.* **308** 60
~ aux puces *Marché puces* **309**
~ des valeurs **251** 2
~ libre **251** 5
marchepied *Voit. chev.* **186** 13
~ *Tramw.* **197** 15
~ *Mar.* **219** 46
~ d'embrayage **168** 48
~ métallique **50** 35
marcottage en archet **54** 10
~ en pot **54** 18
~ par stolons **54** 14
marcotte **54** 11
~ enracinée **54** 12
mare de tourbière **13** 23
marée **13** 35
~, échelle de **225** 37
marées, tableau des **280** 7
marelle **276** 24
~, tableau de **276** 23
~ assise **276** 18, 23-25
~ double **276** 25
margarine *Epic.* **98** 21
~ *Comm.* **99** 48
marge *Imprim.* **181** 21
~ *Reliure* **185** 55-58
~, table de **180** 32, 49
~, tambour de **180** 33, 34
~ de grand fond **185** 57
~ de petit fond **185** 55
~ de pied **185** 58
~ de tête **185** 56
~ extérieure **185** 57
~ inférieure **185** 58
~ intérieure **185** 55
~ supérieure **185** 56
margelle **272** 25
margeur *Photo* **116** 35
~ *Imprim.* **180** 31; **181** 6, 22
~ *Bureau* **249** 49
~ à feuilles **180** 48
~ à succion **180** 72
~ automatique **180** 48
~ automatique de feuilles **181** 5
~ de feuilles *Imprim.* **180** 68
~ de feuilles *Reliure* **184** 16; **185** 25
~ de pliage **184** 17
~ droit **249** 14
~ gauche **249** 13
marguerite **51** 24
~ dorée **61** 7
mariage religieux **332** 14
marié **332** 16
mariée **332** 15
~, bouquet de la **332** 18
~, voile de la **332** 20
mariés **332** 15-16
marie-salope **226** 46
marimba **324** 61
marinier **216** 26
marinière *Cost.* **29** 48
~ *Sports* **282** 36
~ de tricot **30** 4
marionnette **260** 74
marlotte **355** 50
marmelade **98** 52
marmite à pression *Ust. cuis.* **40** 21
~ à pression *Camping* **278** 35
marmotte **366** 18
marotte **306** 59
marquage **129** 40
~ à la craie **104** 21
~ de la balle **163** 6
marque **293** 38
~ à laisser d'un côté **285** 18
~ à virer **285** 17; **286** 31
~ centrale **293** 11
~ d'aile **74** 55
~ de bâbord **224** 95
~ de balisage **224** 68-83
~ de bifurcation **224** 89
~ de cheminée **223** 2
~ de départ et d'arrivée **285** 14
~ de jonction **224** 90
~ de parcours **289** 19
~ de soudeur **142** 39
~ de transition **224** 98
~ de tribord **224** 96
~ d'éditeur *Reliure* **185** 48
~ du tireur **305** 65
marqueur *Maison* **48** 18
~ *Sports* **293** 71
~ de buts **273** 13
marquise *Ch. de f.* **205** 5
~ *Thermal.* **274** 14
~ *Carnaval* **306** 67
marraine **332** 13
marron **371** 60; **384** 52
marronnier **371** 58
Mars **4** 46
marsault **371** 24
marsouin **367** 24
marsupiaux **366** 2-3
marte **367** 14-17
marteau *Anat.* **17** 61
~ *Bricol.* **134** 7
~ *Athl.* **298** 42
~ *Mus.* **325** 3
~ à battre les faux **66** 9
~ à bigorner **125** 14
~ à ciseler **108** 41
~ à emboutir **340** 14
~ à façonner **108** 40
~ à frapper devant **137** 22
~ à main *Plomb.* **126** 78
~ à main *Forge* **137** 23
~ à piquer **141** 25; **142** 17
~ à planer *Forge* **137** 35
~ à planer *Autom.* **195** 46
~ à plomb **124** 11
~ à poinçon **137** 36
~ à pointes **125** 15
~ à réflexes **22** 73
~ d'ardoisier **122** 73
~ de battage **226** 38
~ de charpentier **120** 74
~ de cordonnier **100** 37
~ de couvreur **122** 20
~ de forgeron **137** 23
~ de maçon **118** 53
~ de pilon **139** 12
~ de sondage des bandages **205** 40
~ de tympanon appenzellois **322** 35
~ de vitrier **124** 18
~ feutré **325** 3
~ numéroteur rotatif **85** 12
~ pneumatique **158** 11
~ rivoir **134** 40
marteau-pilon à contre-frappe **139** 5
~ autocompresseur **139** 24
~ pneumatique **137** 9
marteau-piolet **300** 37
marteau-rivoir **140** 23
martinet noir **359** 24
martingale de beaupré **219** 15
martin-pêcheur **360** 8
martre *Chasse* **86** 22
~ *Zool.* **365** 7; **367** 14-17
Masaï **354** 8
mascarade **306** 1-48
masque *Méd.* **27** 48
~ *Sculpteur* **339** 37
~ à compensateur **279** 10
~ à gaz **270** 40
~ compensé **240** 22
~ d'argile **260** 75
~ de bois **354** 16
~ de carnaval **306** 7
~ de plongée *Sports* **279** 10
~ de plongée *Plage* **280** 38
~ (de sabre) **294** 22
~ (d'escrime) **294** 13
~ facial **279** 10
~ perforé **240** 17
~ protecteur *Sports* **292** 11, 25
~ protecteur *Sports hiver* **302** 34
~ respiratoire **279** 10
masse **339** 16
~ à pans **137** 33
~ d'air homogène **8** 1-4
~ d'argile **161** 10
~ de carrier **158** 6
~ de pilon **139** 12, 26
~ du mobile **11** 43
~ inférieure **139** 7
~ meuble du volcan **11** 19
~ oscillante de remontoir automatique **110** 32
~ supérieure **139** 6
~ tombante **137** 10
masséter **19** 7
massette *Constr.* **118** 54
~ *Plomb.* **126** 77
~ *Carr.* **158** 35

~ *Mus.* **321** 17
~ *Arts graph.* **340** 51
~ inférieur **321** 20
morelle noire **379** 5
morène **378** 29
morille conique **381** 27
~ jaune comestible **381** 26
morio **365** 5
morion **329** 60
morphologie du cheval **72** 1-38
morpion **81** 40
Morris, colonne **268** 70
mors **71** 13, 52
~ de force **71** 53
~ de serrage **149** 36
~ d'étau **140** 3
~ fixe **132** 33
~ mobile **132** 31
morse **367** 20
mortadelle **96** 7
mortaiseuse **120** 17
~ à chaîne **132** 49
mortier *Constr.* **118** 39
~ *Chim.* **349** 9
~ *Ethnol.* **354** 24
~ AM 50 de 120 mm **255** 40
morts-terrains **144** 48
mosaïque **338** 37
~ de verre **260** 69
mosquée **337** 12
moteur *Sylvic.* **84** 34
~ *Métall.* **148** 64
~ *Tiss.* **165** 34
~ *Text.* **168** 55
~ *Imprim.* **178** 14
~ *Serv. eaux* **269** 45
~ *Sports* **288** 35
~ à combustion interne **190**
~ à courant continu à vitesse réglable **150** 9
~ à deux cylindres à plat **189** 47
~ à deux temps *Jard.* **56** 30
~ à deux temps *Enseign.* **242** 55
~ à deux temps *Sports* **305** 92
~ à deux temps refroidi par air **188** 7
~ à explosion **190** 2
~ à explosion à 8 cylindres en V et injection **190** 1
~ à explosion monocylindre à deux temps **190** 6
~ à gaz naturel **155** 5
~ à quatre temps **242** 45
~ à refroidissement par eau **189** 39
~ actionnant un arbre porte-mèche creux **133** 7
~ arrière **195** 49
~ auxiliaire **211** 17
~ coulissant **132** 69
~ d'avance **177** 43
~ d'avancement démontable **115** 78
~ de grue **157** 28
~ de levage **150** 22
~ de pilotage **6** 5
~ de sélecteur **237** 48
~ de traction **211** 6, 15
~ d'entraînement *Agric.* **74** 37
~ d'entraînement *Cout.* **103** 9
~ d'entraînement *Forge* **139** 25
~ d'entraînement *Pétr.* **145** 12
~ d'entraînement *Mach.-out.* **150** 9
~ d'entraînement *Filat. coton* **163** 12, 23
~ d'entraînement *Compos.* **175** 61
~ d'entraînement *Imprim.* **178** 12, 28; **179** 11
~ d'entraînement *Inst. fluv.* **217** 47
~ d'entraînement à courroie plate **163** 49
~ Diesel *Energ.* **155** 5
~ Diesel *Moteur* **190** 4
~ Diesel *Ch. de f.* **211** 47; **212** 25
~ Diesel *Mar.* **223** 73
~ Diesel à 5 cylindres en ligne **190** 3
~ Diesel à turbocompresseur **212** 51
~ Diesel auxiliaire **209** 19
~ Diesel de traction **209** 4
~ Diesel 4 cylindres **65** 44
~ Diesel 6 cylindres **64** 28
~ Diesel 6 cylindres sous plancher **209** 23
~ Diesel 8 cylindres **212** 73
~ du ventilateur **74** 33
~ électrique *Maison* **38** 59
~ électrique *Forge* **138** 2
~ électrique *Tiss.* **166** 18
~ électrique *Mar.* **223** 69
~ hors-bord *Camping* **278** 15
~ hors bord *Sports* **283** 6, 7; **286** 1
~ hors-bord de course **286** 23
~ latéral **228** 29
~ monocylindrique à deux temps **188** 26
~ monocylindrique à quatre temps refroidi par air **189** 3
~ multi-usage **109** 13
~ pas-à-pas **110** 17
~ principal *Mar.* **223** 73
~ principal *Navig.* **224** 21
~ quatre cylindres à plat **230** 34
~ quatre temps à quatre cylindres **189** 50
~ refroidi par eau **189** 31
~ rotatif **190** 68
~ rotatif à deux rotors **190** 5
~ synchrone **176** 19
~ triphasé à collecteur **164** 35
~ vernier **6** 5
~ Wankel **190** 5
moteur-fusée *Atterr. Lune* **6** 30
~ *Astron.* **234** 8, 37
~ d'accélération **234** 22, 48
~ de commande d'orientation **234** 38
~ de pilotage **234** 63
~ de séparation arrière **235** 62
~ de séparation avant **235** 60
~ principal de manœuvre spatiale **235** 44
moto à quatre cylindres en ligne **189** 49
~ de course **290** 27
~ de course à carénage intégral **290** 31
~ grande routière **189** 31
motobineuse **56** 18
motocross **290** 24-28
motocyclette *Motocycl.* **189**
~ *Sports* **290** 27
~ à side car **189** 53
~ (de l'entraîneur) **290** 12
motocycliste *Cité* **268** 34
~ *Sports* **290** 11, 25
~ exécutant le numéro du mur de la mort **308** 54
motocyclette **268** 35
~ tout-terrain **189** 16
motonautisme **286**
motopompe **270** 8
~ à essence **83** 41
~ portative **270** 52
motopropulseur d'avion **232** 33-60
motrice *Tramw.* **197** 5, 7
~ *Ch. de f.* **209** 2
~ à turbine à gaz **209** 8
motte **63** 7
mouche *Barbes, coiffures* **34** 17
~ *Piscic.* **89** 65
~ *Escrime* **294** 45
~ *Carnaval* **306** 24
~ à asticot **81** 15
~ à fruits **80** 18
~ à miel **77** 1-25
~ à viande **358** 18
~ bleue **358** 18
~ caniculaire **81** 1
~ commune **81** 2
~ de Hesse **80** 40
~ des cerises **80** 18
~ domestique **81** 2
~ piophile **81** 15
~ piqueuse **81** 4
~ tsé-tsé **81** 43
moucheron **358** 16
mouette **359** 14
~ rieuse **359** 14
moufle *Forge* **137** 20
~ *Pétr.* **145** 8
~ de repassage **104** 30
~ de soudeur **142** 8
mouflon **367** 6
mouillage *Tiss.* **165** 44
~ *Imprim.* **180** 40, 52
~ *Cours d'eau* **216** 13
~ *Mar.* **223** 49-51
~ *Navig.* **224** 73
~, chaîne de **224** 72
~, écubier de **258** 54
~ avec ses rouleaux **180** 61
mouilleur de bureau avec éponge **247** 31
~ de mines **258** 94
moulage **148** 30-37
~ de crânes **261** 15
~ et emballage du beurre **76** 32
~ par soufflage **162** 38-47
~ sous vide **162** 28
moule *Coiffures* **35** 3
~ *Coord.* **100** 15
~ *Trav. fém.* **102** 25
~ *Métall.* **148** 34
~ à cake **40** 28
~ à kouglof **40** 29
~ de chauffe **161** 4
~ démontable **40** 27
~ ébaucheur **162** 26, 34
~ finisseur **162** 26, 34
~ fixe **178** 22
~ pour éprouvette cubique **119** 84
~ pour la barbotine **161** 15
~ pour soufflage **162** 47
mouleur **148** 30
mouleuse *Laiterie* **76** 35
~ *Briq.* **159** 11
moulin à café électrique *Maison* **39** 24
~ à café électrique *Epic.* **98** 69
~ à eau *Cartogr.* **15** 77
~ à eau *Moulins* **91** 35-44
~ à prières **353** 29
~ à vent *Cartogr.* **15** 31
~ à vent *Moulins* **91** 1-34
~ hollandais **91** 29
~ hydraulique **91** 35-44
~ sur pile **91** 31
moulinet *Piscic.* **89** 59-64
~ *Roulette* **275** 32
~ *Parc attr.* **308** 15
~ à multiplication **89** 59
~ à tambour fixe **89** 61
moulure **124** 3
~ du capot d'hélice **258** 74
mouron des champs **61** 27
mousqueton *Pompiers* **270** 44
~ *Alpin.* **300** 46
mousse *Brass.* **93** 31
~ *Mar.* **221** 112
~ *Bot.* **377** 17
~ anti-incendie **228** 28
~ d'air et d'eau **270** 64
~ de la bière **266** 4
mousseline **183** 33; **185** 20
mousseux **98** 63
mousson d'été **9** 52
moustache *Barbes, coiffures* **34** 8
~ *Zool.* **367** 21
~ en brosse **34** 19
moustique **358** 16
moût **92** 50; **93** 10
moutarde **98** 28
~ sauvage **61** 18
mouton *Zool.* **73** 13
~ *Gymnast.* **296** 17
~, peau de **353** 23
mouvement apparent du Soleil **4** 10-21
~ de l'avion **230** 67-72
~ de rotation de l'axe de la Terre **4** 22-28
~ d'horlogerie *Météor.* **10** 14
~ d'horlogerie *Horlog.* **110** 36
~ orogénique **12** 4-20
moyen courrier *Aéron.* **231** 12
~ courrier *Mil.* **256** 14
moyen-duc **362** 14
moyenne montagne **12** 34
moyeu **187** 26
~ à roue libre **187** 63
~ anticollision du volant **191** 57
~ de la roue avant **187** 52
mufle **70** 4
muflier des jardins **51** 32
muguet **377** 2
~ de mai **377** 2
~ des bois **377** 2
mule **101** 25
~ de bain **101** 22
mulet **73** 8
muleta **319** 33
mulette perlière **357** 33
multimètre *Electr.* **127** 41
~ *Enseign.* **242** 73
multiplicande **344** 25
multiplicateur **344** 25
multiplication **344** 25
~ des plantes **54**
~ par caïeux **54** 27

~ d'échafaudage **118** 30
~ du catogan **355** 78
~ du treillis **215** 37
~ papillon **32** 47; **33** 11
~ papillon blanc **33** 16
noir *Hérald.* **254** 26
Noir *Roulette* **275** 21
noir *Couleurs* **343** 13
Noir *Ethnol.* **354** 13
noire **320** 15
noirs **276** 5
noisetier **59** 44-51
noisette **59** 49
noix *Bot.* **59** 41, 43
~ *Filat. coton* **164** 48
~ *Bot.* **370** 98; **384** 60
~ d'Amérique **384** 53, 59
~ d'arec **380** 20
~ de coco **383** 53
~ de galle **82** 34
~ de jambon **95** 52
~ de muscade **382** 35
~ de réglage arrière **114** 55
~ de réglage frontale **114** 51
~ d'entraînement de la broche **164** 50
~ du Brésil **384** 53, 59
~ pâtissière **95** 12
nom de rue **268** 7
~ d'étoiles **3** 9-48
~ du bateau **286** 7
~ du club **286** 8
~ du joueur **293** 36
~ du malade **25** 5
nomade **353** 19
nombre **344** 1-22
~ à quatre chiffres **344** 3
~ abstrait **344** 3
~ cardinal **344** 5
~ complexe **344** 14
~ concret **344** 4
~ de sets joués **293** 37
~ entier **344** 10
~ fractionnaire **344** 10, 16
~ fractionnaire égal à l'inverse **344** 16
~ impair **344** 12
~ négatif **344** 8
~ ordinal **344** 6
~ pair **344** 11
~ positif **344** 7
~ premier **344** 13
nombril **16** 34
nomenclature **151** 32
~ des pièces de rechange **195** 32
nonne **82** 17
nonpareille **175** 23
non-tissé repassé **103** 27
nord **4** 16
Norvège **252** 26
notation du plain-chant **320** 1
~ médiévale **320** 1-2
~ mesurée **320** 2
~ musicale **320; 321**
~ sténographique **342** 13
note **185** 62
~ de musique **320** 3-7
~ en bas de page **185** 62
~ filée **321** 29
~ marginale **185** 68
~ tenue **321** 30
noue **121** 15, 64; **122** 11, 82
nougat **98** 81
nougatine **98** 85
nouilles **98** 34
noulet **121** 64; **122** 11
nourrisseur **62** 9
nourrisson **28** 5
nouveautés, rayon de **271** 63
nouvelle brève **342** 50
~ Lune **4** 2
~ sportive **342** 61
novillero **319** 2
novillo **319** 35
noyau *Bot.* **59** 7, 23
~ *Constr.* **123** 78
~ *Métall.* **148** 36
~ *Centr.* **153** 17
~ *Sports hiver* **301** 47
~ atomique **1** 2, 16, 29, 51
~ atomique lourd **1** 35
~ avant la fission **1** 43
~ avec la graine **384** 40
~ de coulée **178** 18
~ de la datte **384** 10
~ de plomb **326** 20
~ découvert **374** 12
~ d'hélium **1** 30-31
~ terrestre **11** 5
noyé **21** 34-38, 35
noyer **59** 37-43
nuage **8** 1-19
~, sans **9** 20
~ à développement vertical **8** 1
~ cumuliforme **8** 2
~ de beau temps **8** 1
~ de cristaux de glace **8** 6
~ de cristaux de glace en voile **8** 7
~ de front chaud **8** 5-12
~ de front froid **8** 13-17
~ de pluie **8** 10
~ de rotor **287** 18
~ déchiqueté **8** 11, 12
~ des masses d'air homogènes **8** 1-4
~ en banc **8** 3
~ en boule **8** 1
~ en nappe **8** 3, 4, 8, 9, 10
~ lumineux **7** 22
~ orageux **7** 2
nuageux **9** 23
nucléus **357** 2
nucule **59** 49
nudisme, camp de **281** 15
nudiste **281** 16
nuit, boîte de **318** 1-33
~, chemise de **32** 16
numérateur **344** 15
numéro **289** 33
~ d'appel **237** 38
~ de chaque partant **289** 36
~ de cirque **307** 25
~ de fabrication de la bicyclette **187** 51
~ de la prise **310** 35
~ de ligne **197** 20, 21
~ de mains-à-mains **307** 43
~ de page *Reliure* **185** 63
~ de page *Bourse* **251** 14
~ de plan **310** 35
~ de quai **205** 4
~ de réparation **195** 48
~ de série **252** 36
~ de strip-tease **318** 27-32
~ d'électeur **263** 19
~ d'emplacement **278** 42
~ d'immatriculation **286** 7
~ d'ordre **251** 13
~ du concurrent **290** 28
~ 1 **283** 12
nu-pied *Chauss.* **101** 48
~ *Plage* **280** 23
nuque *Anat.* **16** 21
~ *Cheval* **72** 12
Nurembergeoise **355** 38
nutation **4** 24
Nydam, barque de **218** 1-6
nylon **101** 4
nymphe *Apicult.* **77** 30
~ *Agric.* **80** 4, 25, 43
~ *Zool.* **81** 3, 21, 24; **82** 13, 21, 32
~ *Piscic.* **89** 66
~ *Parc* **272** 2
~ *Best. fabul.* **327** 23
~ *Zool.* **358** 20; **365** 11
~ de la mer **327** 23

O

oasis **354** 4
obélisque **333** 10
obi **353** 41
objectif *Photo* **115** 3-8, 32; **116** 32
~ *Photocomp.* **176** 23
~ *Audiovis.* **243** 2, 52
~ *Ciné* **313** 2
-objectif, barillet d' **115** 3
objectif à focale continûment variable **313** 23
~ à focale variable **112** 41
~ à miroir **115** 50
~ de caméra **313** 19
~ de focale moyenne **115** 47
~ de grande ouverture **115** 62
~ de prise de vue **114** 26
~ de projection **312** 35
~ de très grande focale **115** 49
~ de visée **114** 25
~ d'ouverture à partir de 1/3,5 **115** 63
~ en position inversée **115** 84
~ fish-eye **115** 44
~ grand angle *Photo* **115** 45
~ grand angle *Ciné* **117** 48
~ interchangeable *Opt.* **112** 62
~ interchangeable *Photo* **115** 43
~ macro-zoom **117** 53
~ normal *Photo* **115** 3-8, 46
~ normal *Ciné* **117** 49
~ primaire **5** 11
~ rentrant **114** 5
~ secondaire **5** 11
~ zoom interchangeable **117** 2
objet de céramique **308** 66
~ de fouilles préhistoriques **328** 1-40
~ en laque sculptée **337** 6
~ fabriqué par l'élève **260** 67-80
~ liturgique **332** 34-54
~ tourné **135** 19
obligation communale **251** 11-19
~ convertible **251** 11-19
~ hypothécaire **251** 11-19
~ industrielle **251** 11-19
oblitération par rouleau à main **236** 60
obsèques **331** 33-41
observateur **257** 7
observatoire **5** 1-16
~ austral européen **5** 1-16
~ solaire **5** 29-33
~ surélevé **86** 14
obstacle fixe **289** 20
~ semi-fixe **289** 8
obturateur **130** 21
~ de gaz brûlés **255** 34
obturation **24** 30
obusier M 109 G de 155 mm **255** 57
ocarina **324** 32
occipital **17** 32; **18** 50
occiput **16** 2
occlusion **9** 25
océan Antarctique **14** 22
~ Arctique **14** 21
~ Atlantique **14** 20
~ glacial Antarctique **14** 22
~ glacial Arctique **14** 21
~ Indien **14** 23
~ mondial **14** 19-26
~ Pacifique **14** 19
océanide **327** 23
ocelle *Zool.* **73** 32
~ *Apicult.* **77** 2
occlot, manteau d' **131** 25
octaèdre **351** 6
~ à facettes cubiques **351** 14
Octans **3** 43
Octant **3** 43
octave **321** 13, 42-50
~, engagement en **294** 50
octogone **351** 17
oculaire *Opt.* **113** 20
~ *Photo* **115** 42
~ avec œilleton **117** 14
~ du microscope **14** 53
~ du viseur **313** 6
~ du viseur avec lentille correctrice **115** 22
~ pour contrôle visuel de l'enregistrement **311** 9
~ réglable **115** 74
oculus **335** 12
~ zénithal **334** 75
odalisque **306** 41
œil *Anat.* **16** 7; **19** 38-51
~ *Cheval* **72** 4
~ *Chasse* **88** 15, 33, 60
~ *Forge* **137** 29
~ à facettes *Apicult.* **77** 20-24
~ à facettes *Zool.* **358** 7
~ composé **77** 20-24
~ du caractère **174** 31; **175** 42
~ magique *Electr. gd public* **241** 39
~ magique *Marché puces* **309** 18
œil-de-bœuf **336** 2
œillard de meule **91** 19
œillère **71** 26
œillet *Piscic.* **89** 82
~ *Coord.* **100** 63
~ d'accrochage pour le transport **152** 48
~ de fixation de la courroie **115** 9
~ de lisse **166** 28
~ de navette **166** 29
~ des fleuristes **60** 7
~ des poètes **60** 6
~ d'Inde **60** 20
~ giroflée **60** 7
œilleton *Mil.* **255** 22
~ *Alpin.* **300** 35
~ *Sports* **305** 41
~ de l'oculaire **115** 73
~ d'oculaire **313** 34
œillette **380** 15
œnothéracée **53** 3
œsophage *Anat.* **17** 49; **20** 23, 40
~ *Apicult.* **77** 19
œuf *Apicult.* **77** 26
~ *Agric.* **80** 15, 55

ouïe *Marché puces* **309** 19
~ *Mus.* **323** 6
~ *Eglise* **331** 8
~ de dégivrage **191** 42, **192** 64
ouragan tropical **8** 17
ourdissoir **165** 22, 27
ours à bascule **48** 30
~ blanc **368** 11
~ brun **368** 10
~ en peluche *Puéricult.* **28** 46
~ en peluche *Jeux enf.* **273** 26
~ en peluche *Marché puces* **309** 12
~ polaire **368** 11
oursin *Zool.* **357** 39
~ *Faune abyss.* **369** 19
outil **195** 43
~ à dresser les fonds **149** 51
~ à emboîture **126** 63
~ à plaquette à jeter **149** 45
~ à plaquette rapportée en carbure **149** 48
~ à poser et enlever les barrettes à ressorts **109** 9
~ à saigner **149** 53
~ agricole **66**
~ barrette à ressorts **109** 9
~ coudé **149** 52
~ de forgeron **137** 22-39
~ de jardin **66**
~ de menuisier **132** 1-28
~ de tournage **149** 45-53
~ de tourneur **135** 14, 15, 24
~ de tranchage des pointes **85** 22
~ du maçon **118** 50-57
~ du tailleur de pierres **158** 35-38
~ presto pour enlever les aiguilles **109** 10
outillage **119** 77-89
~ à creuser **132** 7-11
~ à façonner **132** 15-28
~ de plombier **126** 58-86
~ du charpentier **120** 60-82
outils, boîte à **134** 35
~, caisse à **212** 45
outre **322** 9
outrigger à huit rameurs avec barreur **283** 10
~ à quatre rameurs sans barreur **283** 9
~ à un rameur avec barreur **283** 18
~ de course **283** 9-16
~ de course á plusieurs équipiers **283** 9-15
outsider **289** 53
ouverture de chargement *Forge* **139** 49
~ de chargement *Métall.* **147** 51
~ de contrôle **64** 27
~ de fenêtre **120** 30
~ de la trappe **38** 14
~ de l'arc **215** 26
~ de rideau **315** 1-4
~ d'entrée **278** 39
~ du pont **215** 14
~ du toit **213** 23
~ pour observation de la cuisson **161** 2
ouvrage de dame **102**
~ de jeux en plein air **273** 21
~ de référence **262** 17
~ de vannerie **136** 4, 16
~ tressé **136** 4
ouvre-bouche **22** 48
ouvre-bouteille **45** 47
ouvre-porte du foyer **210** 63
ouvreur **315** 12
~ de loge **315** 12
ouvreuse *Ciné* **312** 4
~ *Théât.* **315** 12
ouvrier agricole **63** 5
~ forestier **84** 18
ouvrière *Apicult.* **77** 1
~ *Zool.* **358** 22
ovaire *Anat.* **20** 83
~ *Bot.* **58** 40; **370** 54, 60; **373** 2, 5; **375** 34
~ infère **58** 7
overarm stroke **282** 37
oves, ruban d' **334** 42
oviducte **20** 81
ovoïde **370** 36
ovule *Anat.* **20** 84
~ *Bot.* **58** 39; **370** 63
~ à placentation centrale **59** 14
oxer **289** 8
oxime de la cyclohexanone **170** 22
oxyde de chrome **241** 55
~ de fer **241** 55
oxygène *Atome* **1** 13
~ *Astron.* **234** 61
~ *Enseign.* **242** 65
~ *Chim.* **350** 11, 13
~, inhalateur d' **270** 20
~ gazeux **234** 15
~ liquide **234** 10, 12, 24, 39, 51; **235** 51, 56
~ liquide à haute pression **235** 42
oxymètre **27** 13
oxyure **81** 31
oyat **15** 7
ozone, couche d' **7** 13

P

P1 **255** 1
pacage **62** 44
Pacifique **14** 19
pack de bière *Brass.* **93** 28
~ de bière *Comm.* **99** 72
pagaie *Mar.* **218** 8
~ *Sports* **283** 34
~ *Ethnol.* **353** 14
~ double **283** 39
page **185** 53
~, première **342** 38
~ de calendrier **247** 33
~ de faux titre **185** 43
~ de garde **185** 49
~ de journal **342** 37
~ de notes **247** 34
~ de titre **185** 45
~ intérieure **342** 52
~ sur deux colonnes **185** 64
pagne **354** 31
pagode **337** 1
paillasse *Carnaval* **306** 69
~ *Cirque* **307** 24
paillasson *Jard.* **55** 6
~ *Constr.* **123** 25
paille **136** 30
~ pour boire **266** 46
pain **97** 2
~, corbeille à **45** 20
~ aux germes de blé **97** 48
~ bis **97** 6
~ blanc **97** 9
~ blanc français **97** 12
~ boulot **97** 6
~ complet **97** 10, 48
~ croustillant **97** 50
~ de campagne *Boul.-pâtiss.* **97** 6
~ de campagne *Comm.* **99** 14
~ de mie **97** 40
~ de munition **97** 10
~ de seigle **97** 8
~ de sucre **99** 64
~ d'épice(s) **97** 51
~ long **97** 8
~ moulé **97** 10
~ noir de Westphalie **97** 49
~ rond **97** 6
pains préemballés **97** 48-50
Pair **275** 20
pair, nombre **344** 11
paire de jumelles **111** 17
~ de meules **91** 21
pair-oar **283** 15
paisseau **78** 7
paix, calumet de **352** 6
Palaeopneustes niasicus **369** 19
palais **19** 20
~ de Sargon **333** 29
~ Renaissance **335** 47
~ royal **333** 29
palan **221** 27, 104
~ à câble **118** 91
~ auxiliaire du pont roulant **147** 61
~ de garde **219** 70
~ d'étarquage **284** 17
~ mobile **145** 8
palancre **90** 28
palangre **90** 28
palanque **289** 8
palaquium **383** 37
palastre **140** 36
palâtre **140** 36
pale **217** 52
~ de la crosse **302** 32
palée **222** 12
palefrenier **186** 27
paléolithique **328** 1-9
paleron **95** 19, 30
palet **302** 39
~ de hockey **302** 35
~ pour le trictrac **276** 18
paletot **29** 3
palette *Viande* **95** 50
~ *Ch. de f.* **206** 32
~ *Ports* **225** 43
~ *Peintre* **338** 28
~ de cartons de bière **93** 24
~ d'instruments de mesure **235** 69
~ normalisée **226** 10
palier *Moulins* **91** 10
~ *Photogr.* **177** 61
~ avant de stabilisation de la broche **150** 40
~ d'arbre à cames *Moteur* **190** 11
~ d'arbre à cames *Autom.* **192** 24
~ de butée **259** 60
~ de déclinaison **113** 6
~ de décompression **279** 17
~ de la molette d'aiguisage **163** 41
~ de laminoir **148** 60
~ de pédalier **187** 42
~ de repos **123** 34-41, 52-62
~ de tête de bielle **192** 25
~ de vilebrequin **192** 23
~ d'entrée **123** 23
~ d'escalier **123** 34-41
~ fixe **215** 11
~ intermédiaire **123** 52-62
~ mobile **215** 12
palier-guide **113** 14
palissade *Constr.* **119** 25
~ *Chevalerie* **329** 36
~ de planches **118** 44
palla **355** 10
palma-Christi **380** 14
palmaire **18** 40
palmature **88** 41
palme *Sports* **279** 18
~ *Bot.* **384** 3
~ de plongée **280** 41
palmer **149** 62
palmeraie **354** 5
palmette **334** 41
~ candélabre **52** 1
palmettes, chapiteau à **333** 25
palmier **97** 30
~ à huile **383** 54
~ dattier **384** 1
~ en fruits **384** 2
palmure *Zool.* **73** 36
~ *Oiseaux* **359** 7
palonnier *Mar.* **222** 15
~ *Mil.* **257** 10
palpe **358** 27
palpeur **175** 57
palplanche **119** 17
~ en acier **217** 6
pampille **36** 82-86
~ à facettes **36** 84
~ lisse **36** 83
pamplemousse **384** 23
pampre **78** 2
Pan, flûte de **322** 2
pan bombé **336** 48
~ de maçonnerie **120** 59
panache *Chevalerie* **329** 78
~ *Hist. cost.* **355** 82
panama **35** 16
pancarte de limitation de vitesse **203** 18, 19
~ électorale **263** 13
~ publicitaire **308** 50
pancréas **20** 44
pandore **322** 21
pangolin **366** 10
panicule **370** 69
panier **292** 32
~ à bois **309** 10
~ à bouteilles **79** 13
~ à clichés **245** 10
~ à courrier empilé **236** 32
~ à couvercle **204** 2
~ à papier **46** 25
~ à plants **66** 21
~ à récolte **66** 25
~ à vaisselle **39** 41
~ de la friteuse **40** 42
~ de pêche **89** 25
~ de séchage **50** 29
~ en copeaux **136** 11
~ en fil métallique *Jard.* **55** 50
~ en fil métallique *Motocycl.* **188** 23
panne *Constr.* **121** 39, 76; **122** 54
~ *Forge* **137** 27
~ *Alpin.* **300** 34
~ de marteau **66** 10
~ de porc **95** 45
~ en béton **119** 4
~ faîtière **121** 43
~ inférieure **121** 44; **122** 40
~ intermédiaire **121** 51
panneau *Pêche* **90** 13

~ de palplanches **217** 5
~ de protection contre les radiations **154** 74
~ du canon **87** 35
~ glaciaire **300** 14
~ intérieure du canon **87** 39
~ latérale à claire-voie **213** 29
~ latérale de la trémie de stockage **200** 35
~ portante **121** 77
~ rabattue du caisson insonore **313** 18
~ raide **12** 43
~ rocheuse *Carr.* **158** 15
~ rocheuse *Alpin.* **300** 2
~ transparente **25** 8
paroissien **330** 38
parpaing en béton de ponce **119** 24
parquet **123** 62
~ à lames à rainures et languettes **123** 74
parrain **332** 13
partant **289** 36
partenaire **293** 18
parterre **272** 39
~ de fleurs en bordure **52** 18
Parthénon **334** 1
parti **263** 20
particule alpha **1** 30-31; **2** 27
~ béta **1** 32
partie arrière **193** 35
~ centrale du tube **113** 9
~ de l'involucre **378** 12
~ d'échecs **265** 17
~ des basses **324** 43
~ des dessus **324** 39
~ 2ème classe d'une voiture mixte **207** 10; **208** 22
~ du toit **121** 1-26
~ femelle de l'épi **378** 24
~ imaginaire **344** 14
~ inférieure du caisson insonore **313** 17
~ mâle de l'épi **378** 22
~ non imprimante **178** 43
~ 1ère classe d'une voiture mixte **207** 17
~ réelle **344** 14
~ supérieure du caisson insonore **313** 16
parties du marteau **137** 26
partition **254** 17-23
parure *Coiffures* **35** 4
~ *Joaill.* **36** 1
~ à frange **353** 25
~ de plumes *Ethnol.* **352** 12
~ de plumes *Hist. cost.* **355** 82
~ de tête **352** 12
~ florale **266** 78
pas *Zool.* **71** 2
~ *Cheval* **72** 39
~ *Navig.* **224** 20
~ alternatif **301** 26
~ couru **295** 41
~ d'âne *Maison* **37** 45
~ d'âne *Bot.* **380** 8
~ d'avance **149** 9
~ de chaîne **166** 40
~ de filetage **149** 9
~ de gymnastique **295** 41
~ de montée **301** 26
~ de rivetage **143** 60
~ de trois **314** 27-28
~ espagnol **71** 3
Paschen, série de **1** 22
pas-de-géant **273** 8
pasiphæa **369** 12
passage *Zool.* **71** 3
~ *Arts* **337** 4
~ à demi-barrière **202** 45
~ à l'air **165** 48
~ à niveau *Cartogr.* **15** 26
~ à niveau *Ch. de f.* **202** 39-50
~ à niveau de quai **205** 15
~ à niveau gardé **202** 39
~ avant droit **305** 5
~ avant gauche **305** 3
~ clouté *Rue (coupe)* **198** 11
~ clouté *Cité* **268** 24
~ de canards sauvages **86** 41
~ de l'aiguille dans la maille **167** 63
~ d'entrée **272** 32
~ du fil dans le peigne **171** 6
~ du fil dans le ros **171** 6
~ du fil dans les lames *Text.* **171** 5
~ du fil dans les lames de lisière *Text.* **171** 20
~ du gibier **86** 16
~ inférieur **15** 22
~ inférieur du sentier **15** 44
~ non gardé **202** 49
~ piétons **268** 24, 51
~ pour piétons **198** 11
~ souterrain d'accès aux voies **204** 23
~ supérieur **15** 40
~ supérieur d'accès aux quais **205** 3
~ supérieur du chemin de fer **15** 42
~ supérieur pour piétons **268** 48
~ vers l'espace interstellaire **7** 34
~ zébré *Rue (coupe)* **198** 11
~ zébré *Cité* **268** 24
passager *Mar.* **221** 109
~ *Aéron.* **230** 38
passagère **268** 36
passagers en transit **233** 27
passant **268** 18
passavant **221** 3
passe *Géogr.* **12** 42
Passe *Roulette* **275** 19
passe *Sports* **291** 47
~ *Taurom.* **319** 24
~ courte **291** 49
~ de corrida **319** 1
~ redoublée **291** 49
passé de jambe au cheval d'arçon **296** 51
passe-documents **236** 30
passée de gibier **86** 16
passe-monnaie **265** 3
passe-plats **266** 66
passepoil **30** 13; **31** 7
passeport **267** 13
passereau **360** 1; **361**
passerelle *Cartogr.* **15** 78
~ *Maison* **38** 3
~ *Jard.* **55** 22
~ *Métall.* **147** 38
~ *Mar.* **221** 6, 12, 39; **223** 12-18
~ *Mil.* **258** 14; **259** 3, 28
~ *Parc* **272** 46
~ *Théât.* **315** 29
~ arrière d'accès à l'Orbiter **235** 49
~ de manœuvre **217** 72
~ de navigation *Mar.* **223** 4-11
~ de navigation *Navig.* **224** 10-13, 14-38
~ de navigation *Mar.* **227** 24
~ de projecteurs **310** 53
~ de service *Inst. fluv.* **217** 72
~ de service *Théât.* **316** 5
~ des treuils **217** 73
~ inférieure **228** 24
~ supérieure **228** 23
~ télescopique **233** 14
~ tressée **215** 18
passeur **216** 17
passe-vues **309** 43
passiflore **53** 2
Passion, fleur de la **53** 2
passoire **96** 45
pastel, crayon **338** 19
pasteur, robe de **332** 4
~ en surplis **330** 22
~ protestant **332** 3
pasteurisateur **76** 13
pât **86** 43
pataugeoire **37** 44
~ pour enfants **273** 28
pâte, eau de **172** 55
~ à modeler *Maison* **48** 12
~ à modeler *Sculpteur* **339** 8
~ à papier **173** 1
~ au sulfate **172** 1-52
~ chimique **172** 77, 78, 79, 80
~ d'amandes **98** 82
~ décapante **141** 18
~ dentifrice **99** 31
~ épurée **172** 85
~ mécanique **172** 53-65, 77, 78, 79
pâté **96** 15
~ de sable **273** 66
patène **330** 9; **332** 51
patère *Maison* **41** 2
~ *Ch. de f.* **207** 50
~ à chapeaux **266** 13
~ à vêtements **266** 14
pater-noster **170** 36
pâtes alimentaires **98** 32-34
patient **22** 2; **24** 2
~ ayant pris rendez-vous **22** 3
patin *Forge* **137** 15
~ *Sports hiver* **302** 20-25
~ amortisseur **100** 16
~ d'atterrissage *Atterr. Lune* **6** 33
~ d'atterrissage *Aéron.* **232** 15
~ d'atterrissage *Mil.* **256** 21
~ de bois **355** 43
~ de hockey **302** 23
~ de piston **133** 47
~ de ponçage amovible **133** 34
~ de vitesse avec bottine **302** 20
~ de yacht **302** 45
~ d'échafaudage **119** 50
~ du rail **202** 4
~ mobile **303** 10
patinage par couples **302** 4
~ sur glace **302** 1-26
patin-bascule **47** 16
patineur **302** 1
~ à voile **302** 27
~ de vitesse **302** 26
~ solo **302** 1
patineuse **302** 1
pâtisserie **97** 17-47
patron **228** 31
patrouille **264** 9
patte *Barbes, coiffures* **34** 24
~ *Chasse* **88** 46, 50, 81
~ *Constr.* **122** 32
~ *Zool.* **368** 4
~ à vis **126** 55
~ antérieure **82** 6
~ arrière **70** 7
~ avant **70** 5
~ de cheval **327** 42
~ de derrière **88** 63
~ de devant **88** 64
~ de lièvre **202** 25
~ d'oie prolongeant le filet **288** 74
~ d'oiseau **327** 61
~ médiane **82** 7
~ postérieure **82** 8
~ postérieure gauche d'une ouvrière **77** 6-9
~ préhensile **358** 5
~ sauteuse **358** 11
patte-mâchoire **358** 41
pattemouille **104** 32
pattes **82** 6-8
pâturage **62** 44
paturin annuel **375** 39
paturon **72** 25
Pauli, principe de **1** 7
paume **19** 71
paumelle à équerre **140** 50
~ double **140** 49
paumure **88** 41
paupière inférieure **19** 40
~ supérieure **19** 39
pause *Bureau* **249** 73
~ *Mus.* **320** 21
~, demi- **320** 22
~, double **320** 20
pavage **198** 8
~ en brique **123** 7
pavillon *Anat.* **17** 56
~ *Drapeaux* **253**
~ *Marché puces* **309** 34
~ *Mus.* **323** 37, 42, 48; **324** 70; **326** 22
~ à deux pointes **253** 22
~ à lettre **253** 22-28
~ à signal **253** 22-34
~ de club **286** 6
~ de douane **253** 35-38
~ de la source **274** 15
~ de quarantaine **225** 27
~ de transport de poudre **253** 38
~ d'étrave **223** 54
~ «douane» des navires du service des douanes **253** 35
~ du club **283** 25
~ du club dans la barre de flèche tribord **286** 9
~ national **253** 15-21
~ pilote **253** 23
~ rectangulaire **253** 28
~ signalant que le navire a été inspecté **253** 36
~ signalétique **223** 9
Pavo **3** 41
pavois **221** 120; **222** 67
~, grand **221** 85
pavot somnifère **380** 15
paysage de rivière **13** 1-13
~ d'hiver **304**
~ tropical **356** 21
paysan **62** 6
Pays-Bas **252** 19
peau *Chasse* **88** 56
~ *Orfèvre* **108** 21
~ *Fourr.* **131** 13, 18
~ *Mus.* **323** 52; **324** 31
~, culotte de **29** 32
~ de batterie **323** 52
~ de bœuf peinte **354** 11
~ de la pomme **58** 57

~ de l'épaule **88** 55
~ de mouton *Bricol.* **134** 21
~ de mouton *Ethnol.* **353** 23
~ de tambour **323** 52
~ de timbale **323** 58
~ tannée **352** 18
peaucier du cou **19** 12
pêche *Bot.* **59** 31
~ *Piscic.* **89** 20-94
~, canne à **89** 49-58
~ à la carpe en barque **89** 26
~ à la ligne **89** 20-94
~ à la ligne de fond **89** 20-31
~ à la palancre **90** 28-29
~ à la palangre **90** 28-29
~ au chalut **90** 11-23
~ au filet dérivant **90** 1-10
~ côtière **90** 24-29
~ hauturière **90** 1-23
~ maritime **90**
pêcher **59** 26-32
pédale *Cout.* **103** 11; **104** 13
~ *Bicycl.* **187** 40, 78
~ *Motocycl.* **188** 25
~ *Sports* **305** 85
~ *Mus.* **323** 62; **324** 54
~ commandant la pression d'électrode **142** 31
~ d'accélérateur **191** 46, 94
~ d'aspiration **103** 26
~ de commande **139** 27
~ de commande de direction **230** 27
~ de commande de direction du second pilote **230** 28
~ de commande électrique **50** 2
~ de direction **257** 10
~ de frein *Imprim.* **179** 12, 30
~ de frein *Motocycl.* **188** 52
~ de frein *Autom.* **191** 45, 95
~ de levage des galets transporteurs **132** 72
~ de marche-arrêt de la presse **181** 12
~ de piano **325** 8-9
~ de tirasse **326** 48
~ de vélo **187** 78
~ de vitesses **190** 77
~ d'embrayage *Tiss.* **165** 35
~ d'embrayage *Autom.* **191** 44, 96; **192** 28
~ d'expression **326** 50
~ d'introduction des tutti **326** 49
~ douce **325** 9
~ droite **325** 8
~ du piano à queue **325** 41
~ du soufflet **325** 46
~ forte **325** 8
~ gauche **325** 9
~ réflectorisée **187** 78
pédalier *Bicycl.* **187** 35-39
~ *Mus.* **325** 46
pédalo **280** 12
pédicelle **370** 52
pédoncule **58** 13, 34, 61; **370** 52
Pégase *Astr.* **3** 10
~ *Best. fabul.* **327** 26
Pegasus **3** 10
peigne *Puéricult.* **28** 8
~ *Tiss.* **166** 10
~ à chignon **105** 6
~ à fileter le bois **135** 14
~ à jet d'air chaud **106** 29
~ chauffant **105** 22
~ circulaire **163** 68
~ d'abattage **167** 52
~ de coiffeur **106** 28
~ de parure **105** 6
~ détacheur **163** 39
~ extensible **165** 26, 36
~ fin **106** 28
~ nacteur **163** 67
~ sèche-cheveux **105** 22; **106** 29
~ soufflant **105** 22; **106** 29
peigneur **163** 42
peigneuse **163** 56, 63
peignoir *Cost.* **32** 20
~ *Coiff.* **105** 34; **106** 4
~ *Plage* **280** 25
~ de bain **29** 24
peintre *Peint.* **129** 2
~ *Peintre* **338** 2
~, couteau de **338** 15
~ de décors **315** 35
~ décorateur **315** 35
~ sur porcelaine **161** 17
peinture **129** 1
~ à dispersion **129** 4
~ à l'huile **338** 11
~ au pistolet **129** 28
~ au trait **129** 46
~ d'apprêt **128** 6
~ de guerre **352** 13
~ murale **338** 40
~ pariétale **328** 9
~ rupestre **328** 9
pékinois **70** 19
pélargonium **53** 1
pèlerine *Cost.* **30** 65
~ *Autom.* **196** 26
péliade **364** 40
pélican **359** 5
~ blanc **359** 5
pelle *Sports* **283** 38
~ *Eglise* **331** 36
~ à asperges **45** 77
~ à charbon **38** 43
~ à feu **137** 2
~ à neige **304** 23
~ à poussière *App. mén.* **50** 52
~ à poussière *Ecole* **260** 60
~ à terreau **55** 14
~ de déblaiement **255** 77
~ de prélèvement **98** 72
~ en bois **91** 24
~ équipée pour travail en butte **200** 1
~ mécanique *Constr.* **118** 81
~ mécanique *Jeux enf.* **273** 65
pelleterie **131**
pelletier **131** 1
pelletière **131** 8, 23
pellicule avec l'amorce de chargement **114** 9
~ en rouleau 120 **114** 19
pelote à épingles **104** 20
~ adhésive **77** 9
~ basque **305** 67
~ de ficelle **183** 11
~ de pollen sur les pattes arrière **77** 3
pelouse *Maison* **37** 46
~ *Parc* **272** 36
~ de jeux **272** 44
~ de repos **274** 12
peluche **47** 41
~, ours en **28** 46
pelure d'oignon **57** 25
pénalité **292** 48
penalty **291** 6, 40
pendage **12** 3
pendant d'oreille **36** 11
pendentif *Arts* **334** 74
~ *Hist. cost.* **355** 17
~ en pierres fines **36** 14
penderie **267** 30
pendoir **94** 21
pendule *Géogr.* **11** 41, 42
~ *Horlog.* **110** 27
~ *Marché puces* **309** 87
~ à gril **109** 33
~ compensateur **109** 33
~ de billard **277** 17
~ de cheminée **42** 16
~ de cuisine *Maison* **39** 20
~ de cuisine *Horlog.* **109** 34
~ de Harrison **109** 33
~ de parquet *Horlog.* **110** 24
~ de parquet *Marché puces* **309** 56
~ de quai **205** 46
~ d'échecs **276** 16
~ d'horloge **309** 58
~ murale **109** 32
pêne demi-tour **140** 37
~ dormant **140** 39
péniche *Cours d'eau* **216** 22
~ *Ports* **225** 8
~ de débarquement **258** 89
~ remorquée **216** 25
pennatule **369** 14
penne rectrice **88** 68
~ rémige **88** 76
penny **252** 37
pénombre **4** 34
pensée **60** 2
pentacrinus **369** 3
pentagone **351** 9
pentagonododécaèdre **351** 8
pentaprisme en toit **115** 41, 70
pente **12** 3; **13** 65
~ continentale **11** 8
~ de la droite **347** 12
~ transversale **200** 57
penture droite **140** 51
pépin **58** 37, 60; **384** 20
pépinière *Cartogr.* **15** 111
~ *Jard.* **55** 3
~ *Sylvic.* **84** 6
péplos **355** 2
péplum **355** 2
perçage **162** 24
perce-neige **60** 1
perce-oreille **81** 11
perceuse *Constr.* **120** 21
~ *Forge* **138** 22
~ à dénoder **132** 52
~ à main **56** 19
~ à percussion **134** 43
~ à table **150** 25
~ électrique *Orfèvre* **108** 6
~ électrique *Bricol.* **134** 16
~ radiale **150** 18
perche *Mach. agric.* **65** 9, 71
~ *Chasse* **88** 11
~ *Piscic.* **89** 30
~ *Cours d'eau* **216** 16
~ *Athl.* **298** 28
~, saut à la **298** 28-36
~ aérienne **307** 46
~ anémométrique **256** 11; **257** 1
~ de bâbord **224** 100
~ de bambou **307** 46
~ de distance **117** 59
~ de microphone télescopique **117** 23
~ de tribord **224** 99
~ pivotante du trolley **194** 41
perchman **310** 22
perchoir **86** 49
percolateur *Maison* **39** 38
~ *Café* **265** 2
percussion **323** 51-59
percuteur *Chasse* **87** 21
~ *Abatt.* **94** 4
perdrix **88** 70
perforateur **247** 3
~ de bande **176** 5
~ (de bureau) **22** 28
~ de papiers peints **128** 12
~ de ruban **176** 5
perforation de manipulation **247** 39
perforatrice de roche **158** 11
perfusion, flacon de **25** 12
pergola *Maison* **37** 80
~ *Jard.* **51** 1
~ *Parc* **272** 17
périnée **20** 64
période **344** 22
~ de suspension **72** 44
~ propre du pendule **11** 41
périscope d'attaque **259** 88
périssodactyle **366** 25-27
péristyle **334** 2
péritoine **20** 58
perle *Joaill.* **36** 8, 32
~ *Compos.* **175** 21
~ *Zool.* **357** 35
~ de culture **36** 9, 12
perles, ruban de **334** 38
péroné **17** 24
péronier, long **18** 64
perpendiculaire **346** 6
perré *Cours d'eau* **216** 55
~ *Inst. fluv.* **217** 2
perron **37** 66
perroquet *Agric.* **63** 29
~ *Oiseaux* **363** 1
~, barres de grand **219** 53
~, barres de petit **219** 51
~, grand **219** 26
~, grand mât de **219** 7
~, petit **219** 58
~, petit mât de **219** 4
~ fixe, grand **219** 41, 64
~ fixe, petit **219** 35
~ volant, grand **219** 42, 65
~ volant, petit **219** 36
perruche **218** 54
~, étai de **219** 29
perruque *Coiff.* **105** 38
~ *Théât.* **315** 49
~ à bourse **34** 4
~ à la Cadogan *Barbes, coiffures* **34** 5
~ à la Cadogan *Hist. cost.* **355** 77
~ longue bouclée **34** 2
~ Louis XIV **34** 2
perruquier **315** 48
persienne *Maison* **37** 30
~ *Ch. de f.* **212** 84
persil **57** 19
personnage de conte de fée **306** 65
personne inanimée **21** 25
~ tombée à l'eau à travers la glace **21** 28
~ venue assister à l'enterrement **331** 33
personnel de salle **266** 18
perturbation **9** 5
~ radioélectrique **237** 27
pervibrateur **119** 88
pervibration **119** 89
pesade **71** 4
pesage, trémie de **225** 22
pèse-bébé **22** 42
pesée **74** 43
pèse-lettres **236** 24
pèse-personne **49** 47

pistolet-pulvérisateur **83** 18
piston *Moteur* **190** 37
~ *Enseign.* **242** 46
~ *Mus.* **323** 40; **324** 66
~ à déflecteur **242** 56
~ de la presse **133** 52
~ hydraulique *Forge* **139** 41
~ hydraulique *Théât.* **316** 60
pit **243** 60
Pithecanthropus erectus **261** 16
piton à anneau **300** 39
~ de fixation en caoutchouc **187** 84
~ de rappel **300** 39
~ universel **300** 38
Pitot, tube de **256** 11; **257** 1
pivot *Méd.* **24** 34
~ *Coiff.* **106** 36
~ *Ponts* **215** 69
~ central **91** 34
~ de fusée **192** 79
~ de l'essieu avant **65** 48
pivotement **215** 64, 65
placage **133** 2
placard *Ch. de f.* **207** 35
~ *Ecole* **260** 43
~ à portes glissantes **248** 38
~ publicitaire **204** 10
place assise **319** 8
~ assise individuelle **197** 17
~ de départ **298** 3
~ de théâtre **315** 20
~ debout **197** 18
~ du marché **15** 52
placement du dos jambes tendues au sol **296** 52
plafond **123**
~ à entrevous **120** 43; **123** 68
~ du ballast **222** 54
~ en béton armé **119** 8
plafonnier **24** 20
plage *Géogr.* **13** 35-44
~ *Plage* **280**
~ *Natation* **281** 2
~, chaussure de **280** 23
~, pantalon de **280** 22
~, sac de **280** 24
~, veste de **280** 21
~ arrière **223** 32
~ avant **259** 12
~ en terrasse **11** 54
plain-chant **320** 1
plaine de lave **11** 14
plan *Dess.* **151** 16
~ *Ch. de f.* **207** 10-21, 26-32, 38-42, 61-72, 76
~ carré **336** 50
~ de gauchissement **288** 28
~ de la locomotive **211** 10-18
~ de la ville *Ch. de f.* **204** 15
~ de la ville *Cité* **268** 2
~ de préparation des aliments **39** 11
~ de projection **261** 9
~ de repassage inclinable **103** 23
~ de sustentation **287** 29
~ de symétrie **351** 5
~ de travail **50** 31
~ de travail bureau **246** 3
~ de travail carrelé **261** 5
~ de travail principal **39** 11
~ directeur **268** 2
~ du pont **259** 12-20
~ du réseau ferroviaire **204** 33
~ fixe *Astron.* **234** 7
~ fixe *Mil.* **256** 22
~ fixe de direction **230** 59
~ fixe horizontal *Aéron.* **229** 26; **230** 62
~ fixe horizontal *Mil.* **256** 31
~ fixe horizontal *Sports* **288** 23
~ fixe vertical *Mil.* **256** 32
~ fixe vertical *Sports* **288** 21
~ fixe vertical à deux longerons **235** 1
~ horizontal de l'empennage **230** 61
~ vertical de l'empennage **230** 58
~ vertical longitudinal **259** 2-11
planche *Constr.* **120** 91
~ *Scierie* **157** 35
~ à arêtes vives **120** 95
~ à dessin **151** 1
~ à laver **309** 70
~ à modeler **48** 14
~ à roulettes **273** 51
~ à voile **284** 1-9, 5
~ avivée **120** 95
~ costale **295** 31
~ d'appel **298** 38
~ d'aquaplane **280** 15
~ d'asperges **52** 25
~ d'assemblage **273** 57
~ de balançoire **273** 40
~ de bois de bout **340** 1
~ de bois de fil **340** 2
~ de cœur **120** 93
~ de coffrage **118** 41; **119** 18, 76
~ de coffrage latéral **123** 10
~ de contre-marche **123** 56
~ de fleurs **55** 37
~ de garde **118** 29
~ de garde du banc d'étirage **164** 7
~ de hausse **87** 67
~ de légumes **52** 26; **55** 39
~ de moelle **120** 93
~ de plantes vivaces **52** 22
~ de recouvrement **55** 9
~ de revêtement **123** 56
~ de sortie **168** 7
~ de surf vue de dessus **279** 1
~ de surf vue en coupe **279** 2
~ de timbres **236** 21
~ de travail **136** 7
~ de vol **77** 49
~ en grume **120** 94
~ équarrie **120** 95
~ faciale dissymétrique **295** 30
~ mobile guide-nappe **163** 19
~ non équarrie **120** 94
planchéiage **120** 36; **121** 75
plancher **123**
~ avec poutre armée **119** 56
~ de filtre **269** 11
~ de forage **145** 3
~ de travail **120** 36
~ d'échafaudage **122** 70
~ du parc **28** 40
~ en dur **123** 28
~ massif **118** 16
~ nervuré en béton armé **123** 35
planchette de tête **284** 47
~ pour formage du pied de verre **162** 42
planchiste **284** 1
plane **120** 79
planétarium **5** 17-28
planète **4** 42-52
planeur à dispositif d'envol incorporé **287** 8
~ de haute performance **287** 9
~ remorqué **287** 3
planigraphe stéréoscopique **14** 66
planisphère **14** 10-45
~ céleste **3** 1-35
planning mural **151** 12
plant *Plantes* **54** 6
~ *Agric.* **68** 39
~, jeune repiqué **55** 23
~ de bouture **54** 24
~ de pépinière **83** 15
~ de tomates **55** 44
~ de vigne **83** 15
~ d'oranger **55** 49
plantain d'eau **378** 44
~ lancéolé **380** 11
plantation **84** 6
~ après repiquage **84** 10
plante **370** 15
~ à la floraison **382** 53
~ anémophile **59** 44-51
~ carnivore **377** 13
~ d'appartement *Maison* **42** 36
~ d'appartement *Plantes* **53**
~ d'appartement *Bureau* **248** 14
~ de rocaille **51** 7
~ des bois **377**
~ des landes **377**
~ des tourbières **377**
~ d'intérieur **248** 14
~ du pied **19** 62
~ en baquet **55** 47
~ en fleurs **378** 36
~ en fleurs et en fruits **58** 17
~ en pot *Maison* **39** 37; **44** 25
~ en pot *Jard.* **55** 25
~ femelle en fruits **383** 10
~ fourragère **69**
~ fourragère de culture **69** 1-28
~ grimpante *Jard.* **51** 5
~ grimpante *Agric.* **57** 8
~ industrielle **383**
~ médicinale **380**
~ mère **54** 15
~ ornementale **373**; **374**
~ sarclée **68** 38-45
~ vénéneuse **379**
~ verte **39** 37
~ volubile **52** 5
plantoir **54** 7
~ à crosse **56** 1
plantule *Jard.* **52** 9
~ *Bot.* **382** 21
~ enracinée **54** 17
plaquage du battant **166** 42
plaque *Roulette* **275** 12
~ *Zool.* **364** 11
~ à colle-émail **179** 32
~ à dresser **125** 3
~ à planer **125** 4
~ arrière **85** 40
~ avec le numéro de départ **305** 84
~ chauffante **50** 4
~ cirière **77** 25
~ commémorative **331** 14
~ d'aluminium bitumée **155** 29
~ d'amiante **350** 19
~ d'assise *Métall.* **148** 56
~ d'assise *Filat. coton* **164** 36
~ d'assise *Text.* **167** 34
~ de base du moteur **164** 36
~ de butée **157** 18
~ de ceinture **328** 24
~ de cellulose **169** 1
~ de charbon de bois **108** 37
~ de compétition **290** 28
~ de couche **87** 14
~ de cuisson **39** 15
~ de cuivre *Imprim.* **179** 9
~ de cuivre *Arts graph.* **340** 53
~ de fixation sur la caisse **192** 72
~ de fond à trou **96** 54
~ de foulage **340** 31
~ de garde **123** 21
~ de glissement **202** 22
~ de magnésium **179** 9
~ de marbre **265** 12
~ de nom de rue **268** 7
~ (de numéro) **189** 18
~ de pierre **331** 61
~ de séparation **164** 43
~ de serrage **202** 9
~ de verre **54** 9
~ de zinc *Imprim.* **179** 9; **180** 53
~ de zinc *Arts graph.* **340** 52
~ de zinc gravée **178** 32, 40
~ d'entreprise **118** 47
~ des sonneries **267** 28
~ diazo **179** 32, 34
~ d'immatriculation *Motocycl.* **189** 8
~ d'immatriculation *Sports* **285** 46
~ d'impression **340** 59
~ d'itinéraire **205** 38
~ frontale **85** 35
~ numérotée avec le numéro de la chambre **267** 10
~ offset *Imprim.* **179** 1
~ offset *plaque offset* **249** 50
~ offset couchée **179** 16
~ ondulée **122** 98
~ optique droite **195** 18
~ photographique **309** 50
~ polie **116** 58
~ présensibilisée **179** 31
~ tournante *Autom.* **194** 31
~ tournante *Ports* **226** 56
plaquette *Opt.* **111** 12
~ *Sculpteur* **339** 38
~ à jeter **149** 45, 46
~ d'arrivée **123** 19
~ de coupe en carbure fixée par brasage **149** 50
plastron **329** 46
~ plissé **32** 44
plat *Méc.* **143** 10
~ *Rest.* **266** 17
~, gravure à **340** 25-26
~ à compartiments **40** 8
~ à gâteau **97** 25
~ à hors d'œuvre **40** 8
~ à rôti **45** 26
~ chaud **266** 67
~ cuisiné surgelé **96** 23
~ de côtes **95** 31
~ de côtes découvert **95** 21
~ de légumes **45** 33
~ de poisson **266** 53
~ de viande garni **266** 55
~ froid **266** 49
~ préparé surgelé **96** 23
platane **371** 67
plat-bord **283** 30
plateau *Géogr.* **13** 46
~ *Ust. cuis.* **40** 37
~ *Maison* **42** 30
~ *Constr.* **122** 70
~ *Electr. gd public* **241** 20
~ *Rest.* **266** 19, 63

porte-pot de carde **163** 36
porte-revues **265** 8
porte-rouleaux de papier **151** 13
porte-savon **49** 21
porte-scie à métaux **126** 71
porte-serviettes **49** 8
porte-têtes **311** 25
~ magnétiques **311** 3
porte-toner **249** 41
porte-tubes **22** 46
porteur *Ch. de f.* **205** 31
~ *Cirque* **307** 29, 45
~, action au **251** 11
~, gros **231** 14, 17
~ de croix **331** 43
~ de hotte **78** 14
~ du ballon **292** 23
~ du dais **331** 46
porte-vent **326** 11
porte-voix **283** 21
portier *Hôtel* **267** 1
~ *Magasin* **271** 44
portière *Voit. chev.* **186** 11
~ *Tramw.* **197** 14
portillon d'entrée **99** 4
portique *Mar.* **221** 87; **222** 26
~ *Ports* **225** 40
~ *Jeux enf.* **273** 47
~ *Arts* **334** 7, 50, 56; **335** 43; **337** 3, 11, 24
~ à 2 balançoires **273** 39
~ de cale **222** 11
~ de chargement **225** 20
~ de guidage du fer à repasser **103** 24
~ de suspension **177** 13
~ des isolateurs **152** 31
~ d'extrémité **215** 38
~ roulant **222** 25
~ support **214** 24
portoir à pipettes pour la photométrie **23** 52
~ de tubes capillaires **23** 42
Portugal **252** 23
pose du papier peint **128** 18-53
~ d'un garrot à la cuisse **21** 15
posemètre **114** 56
~ d'agrandissement **116** 53
~ d'agrandissement à minuterie **116** 24
poser des antérieurs **72** 43
positif dorsal **326** 5, 42
position *Navig.* **224** 45
~ *Ballet* **314** 1-6, 1, 2, 3, 4, 5, 6
~, feu de **258** 56
~, feu de latéral **258** 15
~, feux de **257** 36
~ à genoux avec appui facial **295** 20
~ accroupie **295** 6
~ assise en tailleur **295** 11
~ basse des bras **295** 47
~ correcte des mains **293** 56-57
~ de chargement en chaux **147** 56
~ de chargement en fonte liquide **147** 55
~ de chasse **305** 72
~ de coulée **147** 58
~ de course **295** 2
~ de départ **276** 1
~ de frappe **292** 63
~ de la remorque en l'absence de retenue **227** 15
~ de préparation **305** 72
~ de recherche de vitesse **301** 33
~ de salut avant l'assaut **294** 18
~ de soufflage **147** 57
~ de tir **305** 27-29
~ de tir «à genoux» **305** 28
~ de tir «couché» **305** 29
~ de tir «debout» **305** 27
~ d'essais et de mesures **237** 29
~ en chute libre **288** 60-62
~ en garde **294** 33
~ en grenouille **288** 61
~ en T **288** 62
~ en X **288** 60
~ face à l'engin **296** 22-39
~ horizontale des bras **295** 48
~ initiale **89** 33
~ latérale de sécurité **21** 24
~ latérale des bras **295** 48
~ «saut de haies» **295** 12
~ verticale des bras **295** 49
poste *Chasse* **86** 9
~ *Verr.* **162** 40
~ *Poste* **236; 237**
~ avant **227** 18
~ central **237** 23
~ d'abonné privé **245** 17
~ (d'aiguillage) électrique **203** 61
~ d'aiguillage mécanique **203** 53
~ d'alimentation manuelle **184** 2
~ de bosse **206** 44
~ de butte **206** 44
~ de cantonnement **15** 24
~ de chargement de vrac **226** 29
~ de chargement par chariots **225** 41
~ de chargement roll-on roll-off **225** 39
~ de codage **236** 35
~ de codage vidéo **236** 39
~ de commande *Photogr.* **177** 5
~ de commande *Ch. de f.* **214** 65
~ de commande *Théât.* **316** 1
~ de commande à tableau de contrôle optique **203** 65
~ de commande avec tableau synoptique **92** 25
~ de commandement **224** 14
~ de conduite *Mach. agric.* **64** 33
~ de conduite *Tramw.* **197** 25
~ de conduite *Ch. de f.* **209** 6; **210** 39-63
~ de contrôle **146** 32
~ de cuisson **39** 12-17
~ de découpage autogène **148** 67
~ de diagnostic auto **195** 1-23
~ de douane **225** 4
~ de mesure de la consommation de COg2 **27** 49
~ de mesure pour cathétérisme cardiaque **27** 30
~ de pilotage *Aéron.* **231** 19
~ de pilotage *Astron.* **235** 16
~ de pilotage *Sports* **288** 10
~ de radio **309** 16
~ de renseignements **237** 34
~ de rognage **184** 3
~ de secours *Plage* **280** 46
~ de secours *Parc attr.* **308** 61
~ de soudage en atmosphère inerte **138** 29
~ de télévision **242** 28
~ de télévision domestique **243** 6
~ de tir **305** 78
~ de transformateurs **92** 21
~ de transformation **217** 46
~ de T.S.F. **309** 16
~ d'éclairage **226** 27
~ d'équipage **6** 41
~ d'incendie **270** 1-3
~ d'indexation **236** 35
~ d'intercommunication **246** 13
~ dirigeur **237** 23
~ du conducteur **214** 65
~ extérieur de commutation **152** 29-35
~ permanent de feu *Aéroport* **233** 8
~ permanent de feu *Pompiers* **270** 1-3
~ principal **237** 22
~ principal d'un central privé relié au réseau public **237** 17
~ radiotélégraphique **223** 12
~ supplémentaire **237** 19, 21, 26
~ téléphonique **237** 6-26
~ téléphonique privé avec touche d'appel **127** 3
~ télex **237** 65
~ transformateur **23** 56
postes, ruban de **334** 39
postiche **105** 38
postillon **186** 40
post-synchronisation **311** 37-41
postsynchronisation télévision **238** 27-53
pot **28** 47
~ à anse **129** 8
~ à colle *Reliure* **183** 15
~ à colle *Ecole* **260** 57
~ à fleurs **54** 8
~ à lait **40** 15
~ à poignée fixe **129** 7
~ à ruban **164** 3
~ à semis **54** 8
~ au noir **9** 46
~ de colle **236** 5
~ de colle forte **132** 13
~ de crème **99** 27
~ de fer **329** 59
~ de fluorure **128** 7
~ de fromage blanc **76** 45
~ de miel en verre **77** 63
~ de peinture **129** 7-8
~ de réception du ruban de carde **163** 35
~ d'échappement *Mach. agric.* **64** 38
~ d'échappement *Autom.* **191** 29
~ d'échappement *Ch. de f.* **212** 69
~ d'échappement quatre dans un **189** 51
~ d'échappement relevé **188** 15; **189** 15
~ d'étirage **164** 20
~ fermé **162** 46
~ lance-fumigène **255** 83
potage en cubes **98** 26
~ en tablettes **98** 26
poteau *Constr.* **120** 25; **121** 40
~ *Sports* **291** 37
~ «abaissement du soc» **203** 35
~ avertisseur de signal **203** 26-29
~ cornier **120** 52
~ d'angle **120** 52
~ de but **291** 37
~ de fenêtre **120** 51
~ de refend **120** 53
~ de support **293** 15
~ des feux de signalisation **268** 53
~ indicateur **15** 110
~ indicateur de chasse-neige **203** 34-35
~ principal **120** 53
~ «relèvement du soc» **203** 34
potence *Opt.* **112** 2
~ *Menuis.* **132** 63
~ *Sculpteur* **339** 24
~ à colonne réglable **112** 32
~ à ouvrir et fermer les boîtes de montre **109** 11
~ de pose des verres à bague de tension **109** 29
~ de pose des verres armés **109** 29
~ du pylône **214** 80
~ porte-câbles **195** 15
potentiomètre à curseur *Radiodiff.* **238** 47
~ à curseur *Ciné* **311** 18
~ de réglage de l'éclairage intérieur **191** 77
~ rectiligne **238** 47
poterie **308** 66
pou **81** 41
~ de San-José **80** 35
~ du pubis **81** 40
poubelle *Bouch.* **96** 46
~ *Nett.* **199** 3
~ *Jeux enf.* **273** 25
pouce **19** 64
poucier **323** 45
poudre à émailler **260** 65
~ de cacao **382** 19
~ noire **87** 53
~ sans fumée **87** 53
poudrier **43** 28; **49** 35
pouf *Maison* **47** 8
~ *Hist. cost.* **355** 69
poulailler *Agric.* **74** 11
~ *Théât.* **315** 16
~ d'élevage **74** 5
poulain **73** 2
poulaine **355** 42
poularde *Epic.* **98** 7
~ *Comm.* **99** 58
poule *Agric.* **62** 36
~ *Zool.* **73** 19
~ *Comm.* **99** 60
~ d'eau **359** 20
~ des bois **88** 69
~ des coudriers **88** 69
~ faisane **88** 77
~ naine **74** 56
~ pondeuse **74** 57
poulet *Zool.* **73** 19-26
~ *Agric.* **74** 9, 12
~ *Bouch.* **96** 24
~ à rôtir **98** 6
poulette **74** 12
pouliche **73** 2
poulie **221** 28, 105
~ à corde **135** 9
~ à gorge et toc d'entraînement **135** 9

Q

R

racle **168** 61
râcle **173** 29-35
raclette **38** 33
racloir **96** 42
racloir-brunissoir **340** 17
radar **259** 29
~, antenne *Mar.* **221** 7; **223** 8
~, antenne *Navig.* **224** 104
~, antenne *Mil.* **259** 8, 29, 48, 91
~, antenne de **258** 36
~, installation du **224** 10-13
~, mât **224** 10
~ de conduite de tir **258** 51
~ de rendez-vous **6** 42
~ de télépointage **258** 35
~ météorologique **231** 18
radeau de sauvetage *Mar.* **228** 19
~ de sauvetage *Sports* **286** 19
radiateur *Maison* **38** 76
~ *Mach. agric.* **65** 51
~ *Plomb.* **126** 20
~ *Energ.* **155** 15
~ *Autom.* **191** 9
~ *Ch. de f.* **212** 54
~ à gaz **126** 25
~ de diathermie **23** 23
radiation solaire **10** 36
radical, signe **345** 2
radicelle *Agric.* **68** 18
~ *Bot.* **370** 18
~ galeuse **80** 27
radicule **370** 88
radier de la cale **222** 31
~ de la cale de construction **222** 17
~ du barrage **217** 79
~ du bassin **222** 31
~ du canal **217** 30
radio *Radiodiff.* **238**
~ *Télév.* **239**
~ *Marché puces* **309** 16
~ dans les triages **212** 50
radio-cassette **241** 1
radiocommunication **237** 50
~ intercontinentale **237** 54-55
radiocompas **230** 5
radiodiffusion *Radiodiff.* **238**
~ *Télév.* **239; 240**
radiogoniomètre **258** 17
radiolaire **357** 8
radiologie **27** 1-35
radiomètre **10** 71
radionavigation, appareil de **288** 13
radiosonde **10** 55
radiotéléphone **22** 14
~ du train **212** 23
radiotéléphonie **224** 28
radis **57** 15
~ noir **57** 16
~ sauvage **61** 21
radius **17** 13
radome **256** 10; **258** 52, 77; **259** 49
~ de l'antenne du radar météorologique **231** 18
raffinage du pétrole brut **145** 36-64
raffinerie de pétrole **145** 65-74
raffineur **172** 84
~, lame du **172** 74
~ conique **172** 27, 60, 73, 83
rahat loukoum **308** 18
rai de roue **143** 88
raidisseur profilé **130** 16
~ transversal **215** 53
raie de côté **34** 14
~ de milieu **34** 9
~ des fesses **16** 41
raifort **57** 20
rail **202** 1; **205** 59; **214** 10
~ compensateur **202** 26
~ de guidage *Ports* **226** 39
~ de guidage *Magasin* **271** 54
~ de guidage de la vanne **217** 75
~ de réglage **49** 43
~ de retour **214** 22
~ de roulement **201** 15
~ du curseur **349** 31
rail-frein **206** 48
rails de tramway **268** 23
rainette **364** 24
rainure *Géogr.* **13** 30
~ *Moulins* **91** 17
~ *Sports* **291** 29
~ à craies **260** 31
~ d'aiguille **167** 15
~ dans le tambour de la tête **243** 27
~ de clavetage **143** 66, 85
~ de guidage *Photocomp.* **176** 18
~ de guidage *Inst. fluv.* **217** 75
~ de guidage *Sports hiver* **301** 39
~ du tâteur de navette **166** 32
~ s'engageant sur le coulisseau transversal **174** 48
rainure-guide **217** 75
raisin **99** 89
~ d'ours **377** 15
raisins de Corinthe **98** 9
~ secs **98** 8
ralenti *Moteur* **190** 51
~ *Autom.* **192** 1
~ *Audiovis.* **243** 49
~, air de **192** 2
~, vitesse au **192** 11
ralentissement permanent **203** 41, 42
~ provisoire **203** 39, 40
ralingue de fermeture du filet **90** 26
~ de pied **90** 9
rallonge **151** 57
~ du crible **64** 18
ramassage du fil **89** 64
ramasseur de balles **293** 22
ramasseuse-chargeuse **63** 27
rambarde **221** 122; **222** 66
rambate **218** 49
rame *Mar.* **218** 5
~ *Camping* **278** 19
~ *Sports* **283** 35-38
~ automotrice **205** 25; **209** 1
~ automotrice à turbine à gaz **209** 1
~ automotrice Diesel **209** 1
~ automotrice électrique rapide **211** 60
~ automotrice expérimentale **209** 23
~ de haricots **52** 28
~ de tramway **268** 46
~ élargisseuse **165** 54
~ sécheuse **168** 21
rameau **370** 6
~ à fleurs femelles **384** 42
~ avec de jeunes fruits **371** 59
~ avec des fleurs mâles et des fleurs femelles **372** 43
~ avec fleurs et fruits **382** 17; **383** 46
~ avec ses chatons **371** 10
~ avec un cône **372** 36
~ de dattes **384** 8
~ en boutons **371** 25
~ en fleur **378** 27
~ et fruits composés **384** 12
~ feuillu **371** 27; **383** 61
~ florifère **371** 2, 10, 16, 32, 34, 39, 51, 54, 66, 71; **372** 33; **378** 2; **382** 3, 8, 12, 23, 27, 31, 41, 47; **383** 22, 26, 30, 34, 38, 42; **384** 17, 24, 37, 49, 54
~ florifère avec fleurs femelles **382** 50
~ florifère de l'abricotier **59** 33
~ florifère du cerisier **59** 1
~ florifère du groseillier **58** 14
~ florifère du groseillier à maquereau **58** 2
~ florifère du noisetier **59** 44
~ florifère du noyer **59** 37
~ florifère du pêcher **59** 26
~ florifère du poirier **58** 32
~ florifère du pommier **58** 52
~ fructifère **59** 48; **371** 3, 11, 18, 31, 36, 41, 47, 50, 56, 64; **372** 40, 51, 59, 63, 66, 70; **382** 2, 37; **384** 38
~ fructifère du pêcher **59** 30
~ fructifère du prunier **59** 19
rameur *Mar.* **218** 3
~ *Sports* **283** 12
~ de pointe **283** 13
ramoneur **38** 31
rampant **334** 11
rampe *Maison* **38** 25
~ *Théât.* **316** 26
~ *Boîte nuit* **318** 25
~ à bestiaux **206** 1
~ arrière **221** 88
~ d'accès *Cartogr.* **15** 16
~ d'accès *Constr.* **119** 41
~ d'accès *Nett.* **199** 15
~ d'accès *Ch. de f.* **206** 1; **213** 36
~ d'accès *Mar.* **221** 55
~ d'accès de la digue **216** 47
~ d'arrosage oscillante **67** 1
~ d'aspersion **83** 3
~ de chargement **206** 9
~ de culbuteur **190** 34
~ de défournement du coke **156** 12
~ de lancement **255** 66
~ de lancement de missiles Tartar mer-air **258** 49
~ de lancement des missiles **258** 71
~ de triage **206** 46
~ d'éclairage de quai **205** 48
~ d'escalier **123** 50
~ d'escalier à barreaux de fer **123** 22
ramure **88** 5-11
rancher **85** 30, 47
~ articulé en acier **213** 6
randonnée de haute montagne **300** 1-57
rang de composition **174** 2
~ de faîtage **122** 47
~ de gouttière **122** 49
~ de rames **218** 12
rangée d'aiguilles **167** 27
~ d'arbres **199** 11
~ de fauteuils **312** 9
~ de livres **42** 4
~ de mailles **171** 42
~ de sièges doubles **207** 63
~ de sièges individuels **207** 62
~ de tuiles débordeuses **122** 49
~ de tuiles faîtières **122** 47
~ de vigne **83** 51
~ de vitres pour l'éclairage par la toiture **121** 21
~ inférieure d'aiguilles **167** 47
~ supérieure d'aiguilles **167** 46
rangement des disques **241** 48
rapace **362**
~ diurne **362** 1-13
~ nocturne **362** 14-19
râpe à bois *Menuis.* **132** 1
~ à bois *Bricol.* **134** 8
~ à bois *Ecole* **260** 55
~ de cordonnier **100** 49
râpe-scie **134** 6
raphia *Plantes* **54** 35
~ *Vann.* **136** 29
rappel **300** 28-30
~ en Dulfer **300** 30
rapport **345** 7
~ d'agrandissement **116** 34
~ d'armure **171** 12
~ du gibier **86** 36
rapporteur **260** 38
raquette de badminton **293** 43
~ de ping-pong *Jeux enf.* **273** 4
~ de ping-pong *Sports* **293** 45
~ de tennis *Maison* **41** 13
~ de tennis *Sports* **293** 29
rasette *Mach. agric.* **65** 11
~ *Mus.* **326** 21
rasoir à désépaissir **105** 9; **106** 41
~ à main **106** 38
~ effileur **105** 9; **106** 41
~ électrique **49** 37
rat de cave **77** 65
~ d'eau **366** 17
rate **20** 12, 27
râteau *Jard.* **51** 4; **56** 4
~ *Mach. agric.* **64** 44
~ *Agric.* **66** 23
~ *Roulette* **275** 5
ratelier à bobines **164** 28
~ à bobines chargé **164** 41
~ à fourrage **86** 28
râtelier *Menuis.* **132** 35
~ *Hiver* **304** 6
~ à foin **75** 12
~ à pipes **42** 11
~ à queues **277** 19
ratissoire à tirer **66** 1
raton laveur **368** 9
ravenelle **61** 21
ravinement de la berge **216** 5
ravitaillement en vol **256** 7
ravitailleur **258** 92
~ de forage offshore **221** 32
ray-grass **69** 26
rayon *Bicycl.* **187** 27
~ *Motocycl.* **189** 24
~ *Univ.* **262** 12
~ *Math.* **346** 47
~ à couvain **77** 46
~ artificiel **77** 42
~ bonneterie **271** 17

S

T

U

W

X

Y

Z

Index

Ordering

In this index the entries are ordered as follows:

1. Entries consisting of single words, e.g.: 'hair'.
2. Entries consisting of noun + adjective. Within this category the adjectives are entered alphabetically, e.g. 'hair, bobbed' is followed by 'hair, closely-cropped'.
   Where adjective and noun are regarded as elements of a single lexical item, they are not inverted, e.g.: 'blue spruce', not 'spruce, blue'.
3. Entries consisting of other phrases, e.g. 'hair curler', 'ham on the bone', are alphabetized as headwords.

Where a whole phrase makes the meaning or use of a headword highly specific, the whole phrase is entered alphabetically. For example 'ham on the bone' follows 'hammock'.

References

The numbers in bold type refer to the sections in which the word may be found, and those in normal type refer to the items named in the pictures. Homonyms, and in some cases uses of the same word in different fields, are distinguished by section headings (in italics), some of which are abbreviated, to help to identify at a glance the field required. In most cases the full form referred to by the abbreviations will be obvious. Those which are not are explained in the following list:

Agr.	Agriculture/Agricultural
Alp. Plants	Alpine Plants
Art. Studio	Artist's Studio
Bldg.	Building
Carp.	Carpenter
Cement Wks.	Cement Works
Cost.	Costumes
Cyc.	Cycle
Decid.	Deciduous
D.I.Y.	Do-it-yourself
Dom. Anim.	Domestic Animals
Equest.	Equestrian Sport
Gdn.	Garden
Hydr. Eng.	Hydraulic Engineering
Impl.	Implements
Inf. Tech.	Information Technology
Intern. Combust. Eng.	Internal Combustion Engine
Moon L.	Moon Landing
Music Not.	Musical Notation
Overh. Irrign.	Overhead Irrigation
Platem.	Platemaking
Plant Propagn.	Propagation of Plants
Rm.	Room
Sp.	Sports
Text.	Textile[s]
Veg.	Vegetable[s]

A

B

C

chipping hammer *Gas Weld.* **141** 25
chipping hammer *Arc Weld.* **142** 17
chip remover **157** 50
chiropter **366** 9
chiropteran **366** 9
chisel **120** 71
chisel, bevelled-edge ~ **132** 7; **339** 19
chisel, blacksmith's ~ **137** 38
chisel, broad ~ **158** 37
chisel, flat ~ **140** 26; **339** 14
chisel, hollow ~ **339** 17
chisel, pneumatic ~ **148** 45
chisel, toothed ~ **339** 13
chisels **132** 7-11
chitarrone **324** 1
chiton **355** 5
Chitonactis **369** 20
chivalry **329**
chive **57** 22
chlorine **170** 7
chlorine ion **1** 10
chlorobenzene **170** 9, 11
chock *Bldg. Site* **119** 40
chock *Iron Foundry etc.* **148** 61
chocolate **98** 80
chocolate, bar of ~ **98** 78
chocolate box **98** 79
chocolate liqueur **98** 83
choir **330** 32; **335** 4
choir organ **326** 5, 42
choke cymbals **324** 50
choke flap **192** 6
choker **36** 16
choker collar **355** 74
cholecystography **27** 4
Chopper **188** 56
chopper drum **64** 34
chopping board **96** 57
chord *Aircraft* **230** 56
chord *Music. Not.* **321** 1-5, 5
chord *Maths.* **346** 51
chord, lower ~ **121** 73, 79
chord, upper ~ **121** 74, 80
chorus **315** 21
chow **70** 21
christening **332** 1
christening dress **332** 8
christening robe **332** 8
christening shawl **332** 9
Christian **330** 61
chromatic scale **320** 49
chromolithograph **340** 28
chronometer **230** 11
chrysalis **77** 30, 32; **80** 4, 25, 43; **81** 3, 21, 24; **82** 13, 21, 32; **358** 20; **365** 11
chrysanthemum **51** 29; **61** 7
chuck *Meat* **95** 19
chuck *D.I.Y.* **134** 48
chuck *Turner* **135** 6
chuck, four-jaw ~ **149** 35
chuck, independent ~ **149** 35
chuck, quick-action ~ **132** 54
chuck, self-centring ~ **149** 37
chuck, three-jaw ~ **149** 37
chuck, two-jaw ~ **135** 10
church **15** 53, 61, 107; **330**; **331** 1; **332**
church, Baroque ~ **336** 1
church, Gothic ~ **335** 22
church, Protestant ~ **330** 1-30
church, Renaissance ~ **335** 42
church, Roman Catholic ~ **330** 31-62
church, Romanesque ~ **335** 1-13
church banner **331** 44
church clock **331** 7
church door *Church* **331** 16
church door *Art* **335** 24
churchgoer **330** 29; **331** 17
church landmark **15** 64
church organ **326** 1-52
church owl **362** 17
church roof **331** 11
church spire **331** 6
church wedding **332** 14
church window **330** 14
churchyard **331** 21-41
churchyard gate **331** 19
churchyard wall **331** 18
chute *Docks* **226** 45
chute *Fair* **308** 40
chute, spiral ~ **144** 28
chute, three-way ~ **92** 34
ciborium **332** 48
cigar, Brazilian ~ **107** 2
cigar and cigarette boy **267** 49
cigar box **107** 1
cigar case **107** 8
cigar cutter **107** 9
cigarette, filter-tipped ~ **107** 12
cigarette, Russian ~ **107** 14
cigarette beetle **81** 25
cigarette case **107** 10
cigarette holder **107** 16
cigarette lighter **107** 27, 30
cigarette machine **268** 69
cigarette packet **107** 11
cigarette paper **107** 17
cigarette roller **107** 15
cigarettes and tobacco kiosk **204** 47
cigarette seller **308** 51
cigarette tip **107** 13
cigarette tray **267** 50
cigarillo **107** 3
cigar lighter **191** 88
ciliate **370** 49
ciliate infusorian **357** 9
cilium *Man* **19** 41
cilium *Invertebr.* **357** 10
cilium *Bot.* **370** 50
cinchona **380** 17
cincinnus **370** 77
cine camera **117** 1
cine film **117**
cinema **312** 1
cinema, mobile ~ **312** 52
cinema advertisement **268** 57
cinema audience **312** 5
cinema box office **312** 2
cinemagoer **312** 5
cinema projector **312** 24
cinema projector, narrow-gauge ~ **312** 52
cinemascope camera **310** 47
cinema ticket **312** 3
cine projector **117** 78; **318** 20
cinnamon **382** 25
cinnamon bark **382** 25
cinnamon tree **382** 22
cinquefoil **335** 40
circle *Sports* **305** 31
circle *Maths.* **346** 42
circle, circumscribed ~ **346** 29
circle, divided ~ *Optic. Instr.* **113** 27
circle, divided ~ *Crystals* **351** 32
circle, graduated ~ *Optic. Instr.* **113** 27
circle, graduated ~ *Crystals* **351** 32
circle, inner ~ **288** 57
circle, inscribed ~ **346** 31
circle, middle ~ **288** 58
circle, outer ~ **288** 59
circle, upper ~ **315** 17
circles, concentric ~ **346** 58
circles, polar ~ **14** 11
circle template **151** 70
circling engagement **294** 49
circuit, integrated ~ *Clocks* **110** 16
circuit, integrated ~ *Inf. Tech.* **242** 68
circuit, primary ~ **154** 2, 42
circuit, secondary ~ **154** 7, 45
circuit breaker **127** 19, 33, 36; **152** 34; **153** 51-62
circuit breaker, miniature ~ **41** 20
circuit breaker consumer unit **127** 33
circular broom **199** 40
circular saw attachment **84** 33; **134** 52
circular saw blade **132** 59
circulation, atmospheric ~ **9** 46-52
circulation pump **154** 43, 54
circulatory system **18** 1-21
circumcircle **346** 29
circumference *Cooper* **130** 23
circumference *Maths.* **346** 44
circumference, staved ~ **130** 2
circumflex **342** 32
circus **307**
circus, travelling ~ **307** 1-63
circus act **307** 25
circus attendant **307** 27
circus band **307** 10
circus box **307** 16
circus caravan **206** 20; **307** 34
circus horse **307** 30
circus manager **307** 17
circus marksman **307** 38
circus rider **307** 26
circus tent **307** 1
circus trailer **307** 34
cirrocumulus **8** 14
cirrostratus **8** 7
cirrus **8** 6
cist, long ~ **328** 16
cist, stone ~ **328** 17
cistern **49** 16
cithara **322** 15
cittern **322** 21
city **15** 51
city banner **218** 22
city wall **333** 30
Claisen flask **350** 50
clamp *Atom* **2** 43
clamp *Overh. Irrign.* **67** 30
clamp *Goldsm. etc.* **108** 34
clamp *Joiner* **132** 51; **133** 9
clamp *Bookbind.* **183** 18; **185** 3
clamp *Chem.* **350** 33
clamp, horizontal ~ **14** 57
clamp, vertical ~ **14** 55
clamp handle **133** 8
clamping device *Atom* **2** 43
clamping device *Mach. Tools* **150** 15
clamping plate, hinged ~ **117** 90
clamping screw **133** 23
clamping shoe **133** 10
clamp lever **132** 67
clamp tip **149** 46
clamp tip tool **149** 45
clapper *Carnival* **306** 47
clapper *Films* **310** 35
clapper board **310** 35
clapper boy **310** 34
clappers **162** 42
clarinet **318** 4; **323** 34
clarinettist **318** 5
clasp, white gold ~ **36** 10
clasp nut **149** 19
classes, social ~of bees **77** 1,4,5
classification siding **206** 47
classification track **206** 47
classification yard **206** 42
classification yard switch tower **206** 44
classifier **172** 50
classroom **260** 1-45
classroom cupboard **260** 43
clavicembalo **322** 45
clavichord **322** 36
clavichord mechanism **322** 37
clavicle **17** 6
clavilux **317** 13
claw **327** 3; **362** 7
claw, bird's ~ **327** 61
claw, double ~ **77** 8
claw chisel **339** 13
claw head **120** 75
claws, griffin's ~ **327** 13
clay **160** 1; **260** 79; **339** 8, 31
clay, impure ~ **159** 2
clay, raw ~ **159** 2
clay box **339** 30
clay column *Brickwks.* **159** 14
clay column *Porcelain Manuf.* **161** 8
clay pigeon shooting **305** 70-78
clay pit *Map* **15** 88
clay pit *Brickwks.* **159** 1
cleaner, centrifugal ~ **173** 11
cleaner, ultrasonic ~ **109** 23
cleaning brush *Hunt.* **87** 62
cleaning brush *Office* **247** 10
cleaning fluid **111** 32
cleaning machine *Brew.* **92** 36
cleaning machine *Watchm.* **109** 30
cleaning plant **144** 20
cleaning rag **50** 55
cleaning rod **87** 61
cleaning shop **148** 38-45
cleaning tank **178** 1
cleaning tow **87** 63
cleanout door **38** 39
cleansing pond **89** 6
clear-felling system **84** 4-14
clearing *Map* **15** 2
clearing *Forestry* **84** 13
clearstory **334** 70
cleat *Carp.* **120** 45
cleat *Floor etc. Constr.* **123** 67
cleaver, butcher's ~ **94** 18
cleaving hammer **85** 5
clefs **320** 8-11
cleft, anal ~ **16** 41
clench planking **285** 50-52
clerestory **334** 70
clergyman **330** 22; **331** 37; **332** 22
clergyman, Protestant ~ **332** 3
clerical assistant **248** 7
clerk **263** 26, 27
clew **284** 41
click **110** 34
click beetle **80** 37, 38
click wheel **110** 35
cliff **13** 28
cliff face **13** 28
cliffline **13** 25-31
cliffs **13** 25-31
climate, artificially maintained ~ **356** 21
climate, boreal ~ **9** 56
climate, equatorial ~ **9** 53
climates **9** 53-58
climates, polar ~ **9** 57-58
climatic map **9** 40-58
climatology **9**
climber *Flower Gdn.* **51** 5
climber *Fruit & Veg. Gdn.* **52** 5

D

G

I

J

K

M

N

O

P

S

T

U

V

W

X

Y